THE CAMBRIDGE HISTORY

EARLY MEDIEVAL C

c. 600–c.

The key focus of this book is the vitality and dynamism of all aspects of Christian experience from Late Antiquity to the First Crusade. By putting the institutional and doctrinal history firmly in the context of Christianity's many cultural manifestations and lived experiences everywhere from Afghanistan to Iceland, this volume of *The Cambridge History of Christianity* emphasizes the ever-changing, varied expressions of Christianity at both local and world level. The insights of many disciplines, including gender studies, codicology, archaeology, and anthropology, are deployed to offer fresh interpretations which challenge the conventional truths concerning this formative period.

Addressing eastern, Byzantine and western Christianity, it explores encounters between Christians and others, notably Jews, Muslims, and pagans; the institutional life of the church including law, reform, and monasticism; the pastoral and sacramental contexts of worship, belief, and morality; and finally its cultural and theological meanings, including heresy, saints' cults, and the afterlife.

THOMAS F. X. NOBLE is Robert M. Conway Director of the Medieval Institute and Professor of History, University of Notre Dame. He previously held positions at Texas Tech University and at the University of Virginia, as well as several prestigious fellowships in both the United States and Europe. He has written or edited six books and over thirty book chapters or journal articles.

JULIA M. H. SMITH is Edwards Professor of Medieval History, University of Glasgow. She is a Fellow of the Royal Historical Society and has previously taught at Trinity College, Hartford, CT, and at the University of St. Andrews. Professor Smith has written numerous journal articles and is the author or editor of four books including, most recently, *Europe after Rome: A New Cultural History 500–1000* (2005).

THE CAMBRIDGE HISTORY OF

CHRISTIANITY

The Cambridge History of Christianity offers a comprehensive chronological account of the development of Christianity in all its aspects – theological, intellectual, social, political, regional, global – from its beginnings to the present day. Each volume makes a substantial contribution in its own right to the scholarship of its period and the complete *History* constitutes a major work of academic reference. Far from being merely a history of western European Christianity and its offshoots, the *History* aims to provide a global perspective. Eastern and Coptic Christianity are given full consideration from the early period onwards, and later, African, Far Eastern, New World, South Asian, and other non-European developments in Christianity receive proper coverage. The volumes cover popular piety and non-formal expressions of Christian faith and treat the sociology of Christian formation, worship, and devotion in a broad cultural context. The question of relations between Christianity and other major faiths is also kept in sight throughout. The *History* will provide an invaluable resource for scholars and students alike.

List of volumes:

Origins to Constantine
EDITED BY MARGARET M. MITCHELL AND FRANCES M. YOUNG

Constantine to c. 600
EDITED BY AUGUSTINE CASIDAY AND FREDERICK W. NORRIS

Early Medieval Christianities c. 600–c. 1100
EDITED BY THOMAS F. X. NOBLE AND JULIA M. H. SMITH

Christianity in Western Europe c. 1100–c. 1500
EDITED BY MIRI RUBIN AND WALTER SIMON

Eastern Christianity
EDITED BY MICHAEL ANGOLD

Reform and Expansion 1500–1660
EDITED BY RONNIE PO-CHIA HSIA

Enlightenment, Reawakening and Revolution 1660–1815
EDITED BY STEWART J. BROWN AND TIMOTHY TACKETT

World Christianities c. 1815–c. 1914
EDITED BY BRIAN STANLEY AND SHERIDAN GILLEY

World Christianities c. 1914–c. 2000
EDITED BY HUGH McLEOD

THE CAMBRIDGE HISTORY OF CHRISTIANITY

*

VOLUME 3
Early Medieval Christianities, c. 600–c. 1100

*

Edited by

THOMAS F. X. NOBLE

and

JULIA M. H. SMITH

*

Assistant editor

ROBERTA A. BARANOWSKI

CAMBRIDGE
UNIVERSITY PRESS

CAMBRIDGE
UNIVERSITY PRESS

32 Avenue of the Americas, New York NY 10013-2473, USA

Cambridge University Press is part of the University of Cambridge.

It furthers the University's mission by disseminating knowledge in the pursuit of education, learning and research at the highest international levels of excellence.

www.cambridge.org
Information on this title: www.cambridge.org/9781107423640

First published 2008
3rd printing 2012
First paperback edition 2014

A catalogue record for this publication is available from the British Library

Library of Congress Cataloguing in Publication data
Early medieval Christianities, c. 600–c. 1100 / editors, Thomas F. X. Noble, Julia M. H. Smith; assistant editor, Roberta A. Baranowski.
p. cm. – (The Cambridge history of christianity; v. 3)
Includes bibliographical references and index.
ISBN 978-0-521-81775-2 (hardback)
1. Church history – Middle Ages, 600–1500. I. Noble, Thomas F. X. II. Smith, Julia M. H. III. Baranowski, Roberta A.
BR252.E27 2008
270.2 – dc22 2007050262

ISBN 978-0-521-81775-2 Hardback
ISBN 978-1-107-42364-0 Paperback

Contents

Illustrations

Maps

Contributors

LESLEY ABRAMS, Fellow of Balliol College and Lecturer in the Faculty of History, University of Oxford

BAT-SHEVA ALBERT, Professor of Medieval History, Department of General History, Bar Ilan University

ARNOLD ANGENENDT, Emeritus Professor, Westfälische Wilhelms-Universität Münster

JULIA BARROW, Reader in Medieval Church History, School of History, University of Nottingham

JANE BAUN, Greyfriars Hall and Faculty of Theology, University of Oxford

ALAIN BOUREAU, Centre de recherches historiques, École des hautes études en sciences sociales, Paris

PETER BROWN, Rollins Professor of History, History Department, Princeton University

LESLIE BRUBAKER, Professor of Byzantine Art History; Director, Centre for Byzantine, Ottoman, and Modern Greek Studies; Associate Director, Institute of Archaeology and Antiquity, University of Birmingham

THOMAS M. CHARLES-EDWARDS, Jesus Professor of Celtic, University of Oxford

LYNDA L. COON, Associate Professor, Department of History, University of Arkansas

MARY B. CUNNINGHAM, Lecturer, Department of Theology, University of Nottingham; Honorary Fellow, Institute of Advanced Research in Humanities and Social Sciences, University of Birmingham

IGOR DORFMANN-LAZAREV, Lecturer in Greek and Oriental Patristics, Department of Theology and Religion, Durham University

SIDNEY H. GRIFFITH, Ordinary Professor, Department of Semitic and Egyptian Languages and Literatures, The Catholic University of America, Washington, DC

ANNE-MARIE HELVÉTIUS, Professor of Medieval History, Centre de recherches historiques, Université Paris VIII (Vincennes-Saint-Denis)

PEREGRINE HORDEN, Professor of Medieval History, Department of History, Royal Holloway University of London

DOMINIQUE IOGNA-PRAT, Centre nationale de la recherche scientifique, Paris

MICHEL KAPLAN, Professeur d'histoire Byzantine, Unité de formation et de recherche d'histoire, Université Paris I (Panthéon-Sorbonne)

HUGH KENNEDY, Professor of Arabic, School of Oriental and African Studies, London

TIA M. KOLBABA, Assistant Professor, Department of Religion, Rutgers University

GUY LOBRICHON, Professeur d'histoire du Moyen Âge, Université d'Avignon

ANDREW LOUTH, Professor of Patristic and Byzantine Studies, Department of Theology and Religion, Durham University

E. ANN MATTER, William R. Kenan, Jr. Professor, Department of Religious Studies, University of Pennsylvania

ROB MEENS, Universitair docent, Instituut Geschiedenis, Universiteit Utrecht

ROSEMARY MORRIS, Visiting Fellow, Department of History, University of York

JANET L. NELSON, Professor Emerita, Department of History, King's College London

THOMAS F. X. NOBLE, Professor of History, Robert M. Conway Director of the Medieval Institute, University of Notre Dame

ÉRIC PALAZZO, Professeur d'histoire de l'art du Moyen Âge, Directeur du Centre d'études supérieures de civilisation médiévale, Université de Poitiers

FREDERICK S. PAXTON, Brigida Pacchiani Ardenghi Professor of History, Department of History, Connecticut College

PHILIP ROUSSEAU, Andrew W. Mellon Professor of Early Christian Studies; Director, Center for the Study of Early Christianity, The Catholic University of America, Washington, DC.

JONATHAN SHEPARD, Formerly University Lecturer in History, University of Cambridge

JULIA M. H. SMITH, Edwards Professor of Medieval History, Department of History, University of Glasgow

JOHN H. VAN ENGEN, Andrew V. Tackes Chair of Medieval History, Department of History, University of Notre Dame

IAN N. WOOD, Professor of Early Medieval History, School of History, University of Leeds

Preface

Christianity arose, spread, and strengthened its claims on people's lives in the ancient world in the period covered by volumes 1 and 2 of the *Cambridge History of Christianity*. Volume 3 treats the history of Christianity during the centuries usually labeled "early medieval" that stretch from about 600 to about 1100. This long, dynamic, and creative era saw both the consolidation of ancient Christianity's achievements and dramatic new developments.

One way to grasp the changes and continuities that marked the early medieval period is to read the first and last chapters in this volume. The opening one presents a panoramic view of Christianity in about 600 with occasional looks into the past and glimpses of the future. The closing chapter takes a similarly panoramic view in about 1100. In 600 Christianity was still fundamentally a Mediterranean phenomenon. Almost all its creative centers hugged the shores of the inland sea, as did its key administrative sites. The vast majority of all Christians then alive lived within two hundred miles of the sea. Christianity's most impressive territorial expansion beyond the Mediterranean basin lay in the east and in Africa. Western Europe was just then becoming visible as a potential site of growth and development. By 1100 Christianity's creative core was located squarely in western Europe. The rapid and continuous expansion of Islam had diminished Christianity's presence in Mediterranean Europe and Africa, as well as in central and western Asia. Islam also constituted a persistent challenge for Byzantium and thus for Orthodox Christianity. Indeed, Byzantium's reach shortened not only in the eastern Mediterranean but also in the north where Avar, Bulgar, and Slav peoples and states challenged historic Byzantine claims. Christianity had meanwhile spread to every corner of Europe itself, with the exception of some areas lying along the eastern Baltic. If places such as Antioch and Alexandria had been the intellectual powerhouses of ancient Christianity, sites such as Winchester, Cologne, Paris, and Chartres were the dominant influences in the centuries on either side of the turn of the millennium.

In the dawning twenty-first century Christianity is very much a world religion, increasingly marginalized in Europe but vigorous on other continents. The early medieval centuries inaugurated a long period when Christianity seemed to be an essentially European phenomenon that in due course was exported, eventually in both Catholic and Protestant versions, to much of the rest of the globe. Today's congeries of Christianities artfully blend peoples, localities, languages, cultures, and historical experiences. That is what the Christianities of 600 also looked like, and it is still what they looked like in 1100, albeit the center of gravity had shifted to the north and west and the forces of homogeneity were becoming evident.

This volume is entitled *Early Medieval Christianities*. The use of the plural is not meant to deny that all Christians could trace their roots to the Mediterranean world of Antiquity, or that they took inspiration from versions of the same scriptures, or that they worshiped in tolerably similar ways, or that their churches shared many legal and institutional features. Instead, the plural signals the futility of speaking in overly generalized terms about an ever-changing religion that extended from Ireland to Afghanistan, from Norway to Nubia. Christianity transformed every people and culture with which it came into contact but it was itself transformed by peoples, cultures, antecedent histories, and even by landscapes. The plural, in short, denotes not chaos, confusion, or disunity, but richness, creativity, and complexity.

What is more, Christianity must be understood in a variety of complementary ways that, taken together, again urge the descriptive plural. Christianity is an ecclesial phenomenon everywhere, but it evolved very different kinds of churches and of ecclesiological conceptions to sustain and explain those churches. Christianity is also a body of teachings to which people grant varying assents of mind and heart and body. Those positions had to be defined, articulated, and transmitted. In Antiquity they were frequently the occasion of bitter strife. In the early Middle Ages there were fewer doctrinal quarrels, but there were also large bodies of Christians who did not believe all the same things and who had relatively little to do with each other. Christianity also attends the major moments of life from birth to death; it is lived experience as much as or more than a set of doctrinal formulations. Ancient Christianity was a fundamentally urban phenomenon. Cities were not a conspicuous feature of early medieval Europe. Curiously, however, Christianity retained structures, practices, and outlooks that were essentially urban even as it took root in what were essentially rural and agrarian societies. Adaptation and local particularity are equally evident in that respect. No matter what place, time, or topic engages our attention, we cannot usefully reduce Christianity to a *singular* phenomenon.

An awareness of these basic guiding principles will help the reader to grasp the arrangement of this volume and to see the connective tissue that holds the organizational skeleton together. The volume's first part constitutes a geographical and historical tour of the major, identifiable regions within which Christianity either extended its ancient achievements or else began anew. The first chapter in this part surveys the late Roman scene and the following ones explore the Byzantine world, the many forms of eastern Christianity, and then Christianity in Slavic, Germanic, and Celtic lands. The volume's next part addresses explicitly encounters between Christianity and Judaism; Christianity's confrontation with Islam, both along its expanding frontiers and within the caliphate; meetings between Greek and Latin Christians; and, finally, Christianity's lengthy engagement with Germanic and Slav paganism. These two sections emphasize the broader political, cultural, and religious milieux which helped to shape early medieval Christianities.

The next set of chapters deals with what might be broadly characterized as institutional issues: ecclesiastical organization, monasticism and asceticism, the making and implementing of law, property and material concerns, ideas of reform, and locations of cult. Unlike the chapters in the first two parts which tend to focus on specific regions or incidences of cultural contact, the chapters in part 3 range widely across all the Christianities included in this volume. They balance a high level of generalization with enough concrete examples and case studies to make key issues both clear and vivid.

The volume's fourth part takes up critical themes in the history and practice of Christianity as a lived experience with particular attention to the sacramental life of the church and its Christian communities. Its premise is that modes of worship, ritual, and prayer tell us a good deal about what people believed, or about what they were expected to believe. Rites that attended birth and death open the discussion. Penance, both the practice of penance and ideas of sin and redemption, follows the discussion of baptism and final anointing. There follows a treatment of sickness and healing that combines reflections on both medical and spiritual remedies. The ensuing chapter explores gender, sexuality, and the body. This chapter permits insights into how writers talked about the people, both lay and clerical, who actually were the Christians of the early medieval period. The part concludes with a two-fold discussion of worship: the theology behind the celebration of the Eucharistic liturgy, everywhere the church's central act of worship, and the performance of the liturgy itself, including some discussion of the books needed for that performance.

The fifth and last part in the volume treats intellectual and cultural issues that pertain to both formal learning and to Christianity's imaginary. The lead chapter discusses some of the myriad ways in which early medieval people thought and wrote about God. The next addresses "God-talk," theology, directly by inquiring into doctrinal quarrels. These were fewer in number and intensity than those in Antiquity and perhaps less deeply rooted in the ordinary experience of most early medieval Christianities. The Bible, always and everywhere *the* crucial Christian book, or collection of books, is treated in its textual and interpretive frameworks. Books as objects, with particular attention to the books of the eastern Christian tradition, come in for a thorough discussion. Saints, the holy men and women who were thought to have lived exemplary lives, are analyzed for what they can teach us about the aspirations and expectations of ecclesiastical elites and ordinary believers. Finally, appropriately, the "Last Things" conclude the volume: How did Christians imagine the other world, the world beyond the grave?

Taken overall, this volume presents the reader with the main ways in which twenty-first-century scholars imagine the other world of early medieval Christianities. The interpretations offered here can never be definitive: much in the pages which follow challenges and refreshes debates or assumptions that have long been deeply embedded in the history of Christianity. In reappraising them, the book dislodges some issues from the center of attention and substitutes other, more timely ones for the rapidly changing world of the third Christian millennium. It is hoped that it will challenge and refresh those who read it, as preparing it has its editors and contributors.

Thomas F. X. Noble
Julia M. H. Smith

Acknowledgments

Editing this volume has been much more of a collaborative effort than the presence of the editors' names on the title page might imply: we acknowledge wholeheartedly the role of all the contributors in helping bring it into being. All have responded graciously to our suggestions about the content and presentation of their chapters, and many have provided us with expert advice and guidance on a wide range of specific details. They have also borne unforeseen and unavoidable delays in the editorial process with good grace and patience, for which both editors are deeply grateful.

This undertaking could not have been realized without the extremely generous financial and practical support of the University of Notre Dame. At Notre Dame, the Medieval Institute and Institute for Scholarship in the Liberal Arts jointly defrayed the costs of bringing contributors together from three continents, whilst the McKenna Center provided an ideal environment in which colleagues exchanged vigorous and stimulating critiques of each other's draft chapters. This colloquium enabled the volume to acquire a coherence which editorial guidance alone could not have achieved, and the pages which follow are an expression of participants' appreciation of the intellectual stimulus and geniality of those three days. At all stages of the preparation of the book from conference to impeccable typescript in paper and electronic formats, Roberta Baranowski, the Medieval Institute's Assistant Director, has provided invaluable administrative support and sub-editorial energy: it is a pleasure to acknowledge publicly our profound debt to her.

Two translators applied their linguistic sensitivity and subject area knowledge to original German and French texts from our chapter authors and produced English versions. Dr. Rona Johnston Gordon, University of St. Andrews, provided the translation, from the German, for Professor Angenendt's chapter. Andrew Irving, University of Notre Dame, translated the chapters by Professors Boureau, Helvétius and Kaplan, Iogna-Prat, Lobrichon, and Palazzo from the French.

We are equally indebted to all those at Cambridge University Press who have been involved with this volume: Kevin Taylor for the invitation to undertake it; his successor in charge of the Religion desk, Kate Brett, and her assistant, Gillian Dadd, for their generous supply of moral support, practical help and patient forebearance at all times; and Liz Davey for overseeing production with great efficiency. The Press kindly took on responsibility for the index.

In the final stages of production, Christopher Riches, of Riches Editorial Services, meticulously coordinated the correction of the proofs and improved the book in many other significant ways. We are immensely grateful for his exceptional professionalism.

TFXN & JMHS

Abbreviations

AASS	*Acta sanctorum quotquot toto orbe coluntur*. Ed. J. Bollandus et al. Antwerp and Brussels, 1634–.
Bede, *HE*	Bede. *Historia ecclesiastica gentis Anglorum*. Ed. and trans. B. Colgrave and R. A. B. Mynors. *Bede's Ecclesiastical History of the English People*. Oxford Medieval Texts. Oxford: Oxford University Press, 1969.
BMFD	*Byzantine Monastic Foundation Documents: A Complete Translation of the Surviving Founders' Typika and Testaments*. Ed. J. Thomas and A. C. Hero, with G. Constable. 5 vols. Washington, DC: Dumbarton Oaks, 2000.
CC	*Corpus christianorum*
CCCM	*Corpus christianorum continuatio mediaevalis*
CCSG	*Corpus christianorum series graeca*
CCSL	*Corpus christianorum series latina*
CSCO	*Corpus scriptorum christianorum orientalium*
CSEL	*Corpus scriptorum ecclesiasticorum latinorum*
DOP	*Dumbarton Oaks Papers*
EME	*Early Medieval Europe*
Haddan and Stubbs	A. W. Haddan and W. Stubbs, eds. *Councils and Ecclesiastical Documents Relating to Great Britain and Ireland*. 3 vols. Oxford: Clarendon Press, 1869–78.
Histoire du christianisme 3	*Les églises d'orient et d'occident*. Ed. L. Pietri, J.-M. Mayeur, and B. Beaujard. Vol. 3 in *Histoire du christianisme des origines à nos jours*. Paris: Desclée, 1998.
Histoire du christianisme 4	*Évêques, moines et empereurs (610–1054)*. Ed. G. Dagron, P. Riché, and A. Vauchez. Vol. 4 in *Histoire du christianisme des origines à nos jours*. Paris: Desclée, 1993.

Histoire du christianisme 5	*Apogée de la papauté et expansion de la chrétienté* (1054–1274). Ed. A. Vauchez and J. Kłoczowski. Vol. 5 in *Histoire du christianisme des origines à nos jours*. Paris: Desclée, 1993.
Mansi	Mansi, G. D., ed., *Sacrorum conciliorum nova et amplissima collectio*. 31 vols. Florence, 1759–98; rev. ed. J.-B. Martin and L. Petit. 53 vols. in 60. Paris, 1899–27.
MGH	*Monumenta Germaniae Historica*
MGH SRG	*MGH scriptores rerum germanicarum*
MGH SRM	*MGH scriptores rerum merovingicarum*
NCMH 2	*The New Cambridge Medieval History*. Vol. 2: *c. 700–900*. Ed. R. McKitterick. Cambridge: Cambridge University Press, 1995.
ODB	*Oxford Dictionary of Byzantium*. Ed. A. Kazhdan. 3 vols. Oxford: Oxford University Press, 1991.
PO	*Patrologia orientalis*
PG	*Patrologia graeca* = *Patrologiae cursus completus. Series graeca*. Comp. by J.-P. Migne. 161 vols. Paris, 1857–66.
PL	*Patrologia latina* = *Patrologiae cursus completus. Series secunda in qua prodeunt patres . . . ecclesiae latinae*. Comp. by J.-P. Migne. 221 in 222 vols. Paris, 1844–64.
SC	*Sources chrétiennes*
SCH	Studies in Church History

Note regarding footnote citations

In general, the footnote citation system used in this volume punctuates chapter, page, and volume references as follows: author, *title of work* volume number if any, chapter, section within the work, page number from specific edition. E.g., Anonymous, *Historia* 2, II.ii.3, 346–47. Thus, chapter 2, section 2, part 3 on pages 346–47 in the edition cited in the bibliography of volume 2 of the work entitled *Historia* by an anonymous author. Unless necessary for clarity, edition editor / translator names are omitted in the footnotes and provided only in the bibliography. E.g., Anonymous, *Historia* 2, 25–37 (ed. Smith, 399–401) means sections 25 to 37 (or, if these are numbered individually, documents 25 to 37) in volume 2 of *Historia* by Anonymous are found on pages 399 to 401 in the edition by Smith.

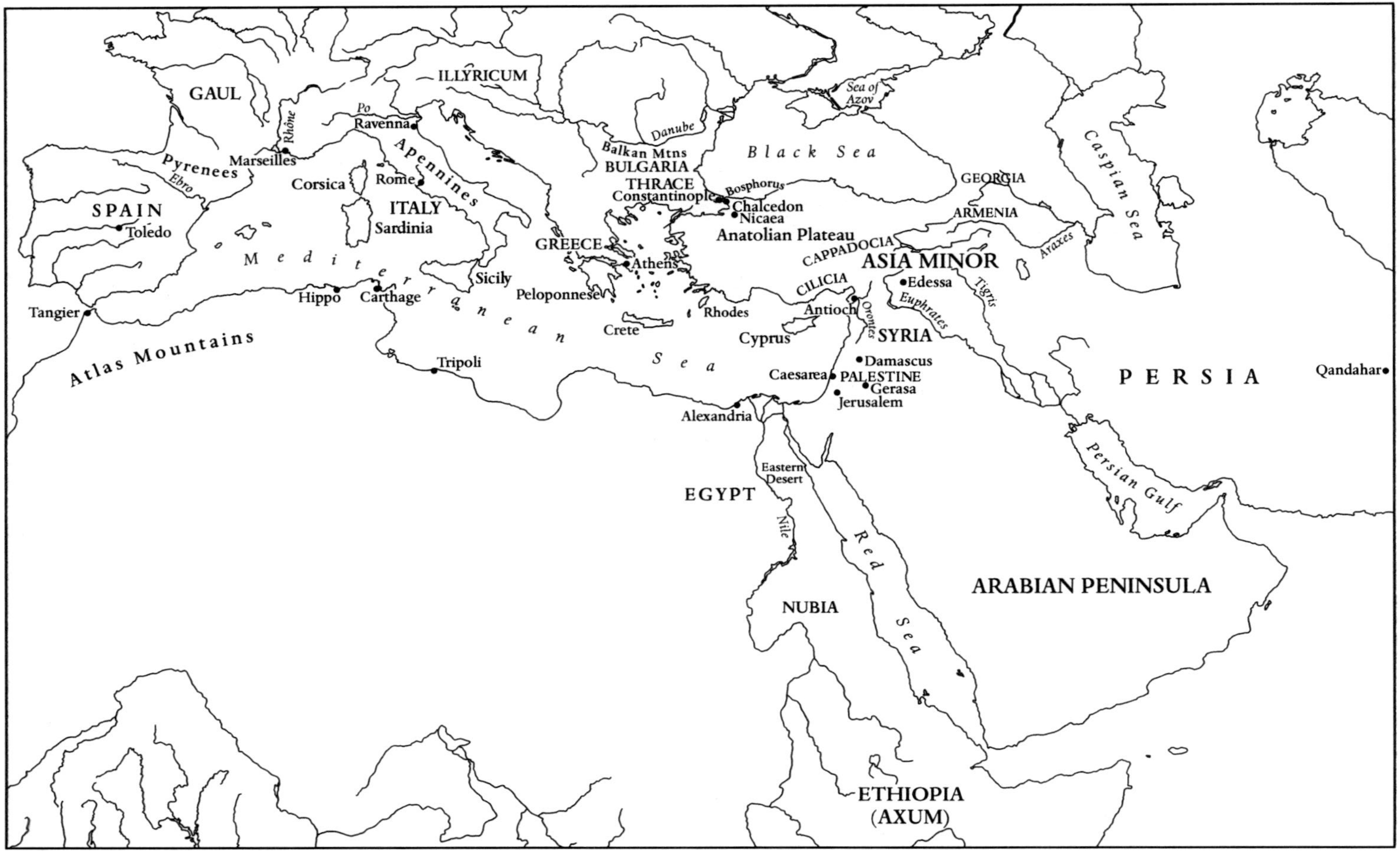

Map 1. The Christian Mediterranean

Map 2. The Christian East

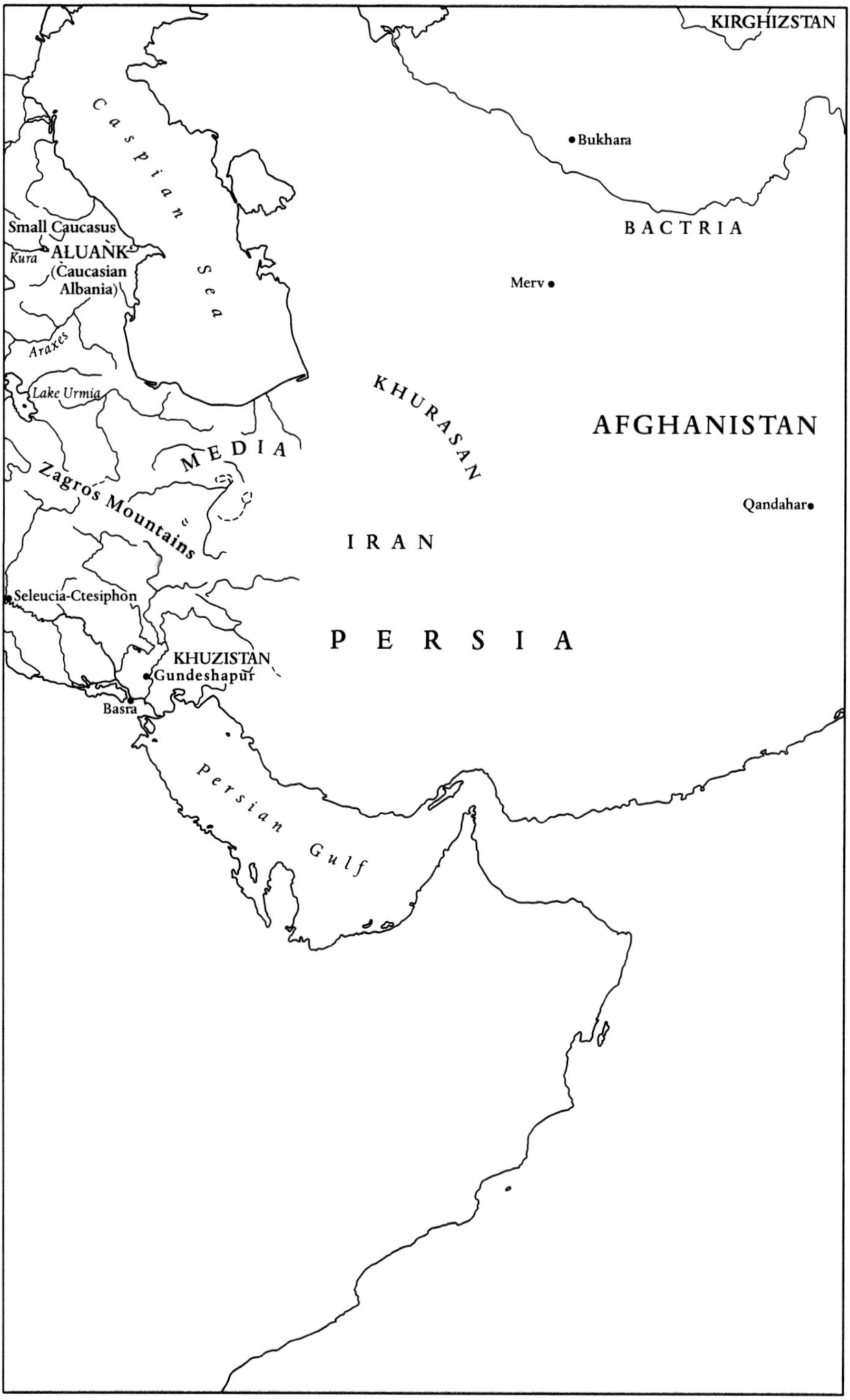

Map 2. The Christian East (*continued*)

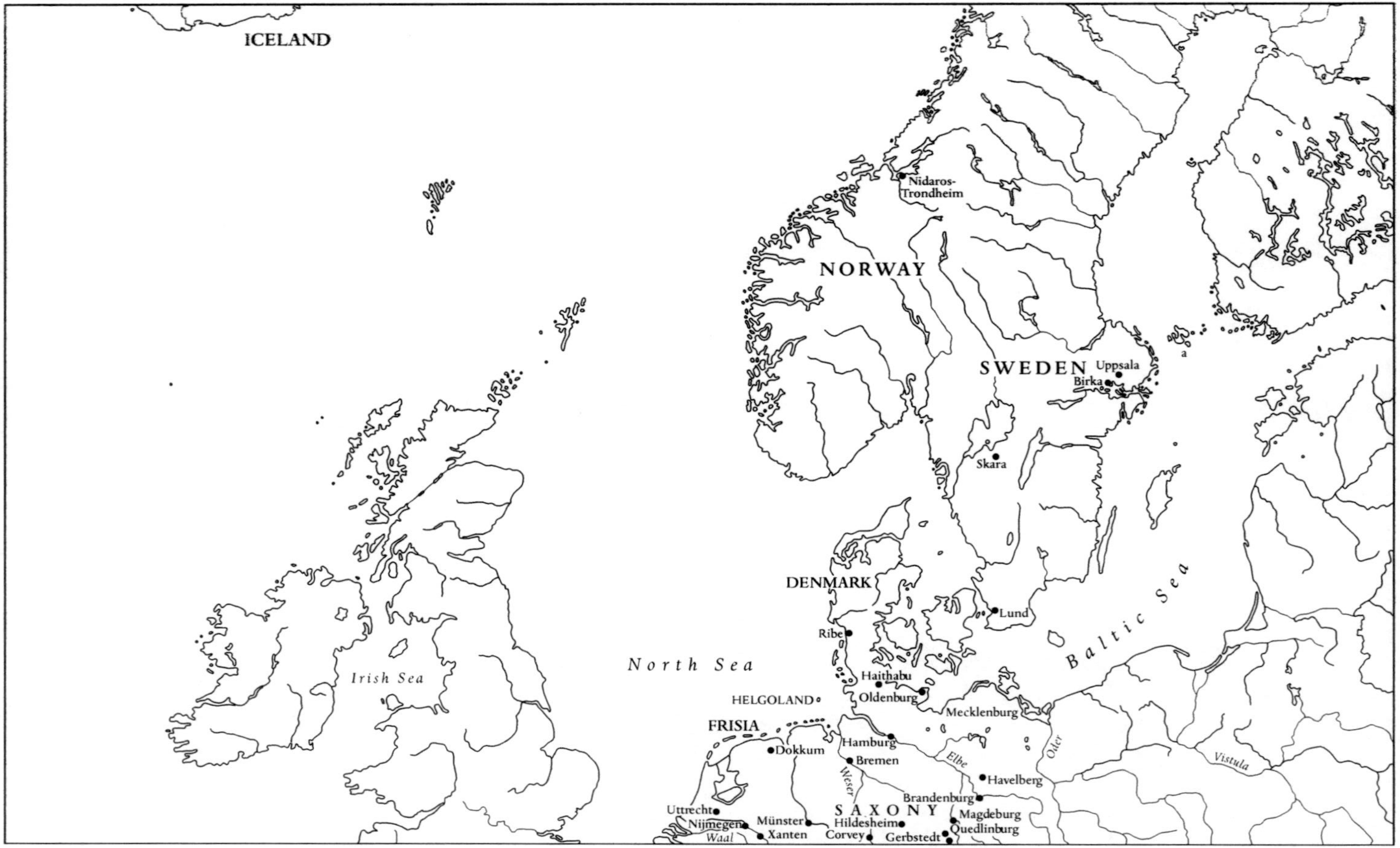
ICELAND
NORWAY
Nidaros-Trondheim
SWEDEN
Uppsala
Birka
Skara
a
DENMARK
Lund
Ribe
Haithabu
Oldenburg
Mecklenburg
Baltic Sea
North Sea
Irish Sea
HELGOLAND
FRISIA
Dokkum
Hamburg
Bremen
Weser
Elbe
Oder
Vistula
Havelberg
Brandenburg
Magdeburg
Quedlinburg
Gerbstedt
SAXONY
Hildesheim
Corvey
Münster
Xanten
Uttrecht
Nijmegen
Waal

Map 3. Western Europe

Map 4. The Slavic World

Map 5. The British Isles

Introduction: Christendom, c. 600

PETER BROWN

The Kingdom and the kingdoms

A little after 680 CE, Julian, bishop of Toledo, the capital of the Visigothic kingdom of Spain, was challenged to answer a constant objection made by the Jews against Christianity. Christians were misguided to think that, in the person of Jesus of Nazareth, the Messiah – the "Christ," the Anointed One – had come. The Messiah had not come. The world was only five thousand years old. The sixth age in which the Messiah would arrive had not yet even begun. The recent centuries lacked meaning. They were a blank space, a time of waiting for the arrival of the true Christ – the Anointed One of God.

To the bishop of Toledo, his imagined Jewish interlocutors could not have been more wrong. History was already tinged with excitement. The Messiah had come. Christ had been born in Bethlehem in the days of the Emperor Augustus. His coming to earth had left a palpable trace. For it had coincided with a moment of almost supernatural quiet, throughout the Mediterranean world, associated with the foundation of the Roman Empire. Civil wars ceased. Peace returned to the cities. Relieved of military emergencies, the civilian population returned to the fields: "and the business of war was delegated to the Roman legions alone, to be conducted against barbarian nations."[1] For Julian, the peace of the Roman world in the age of Augustus, now over six centuries in the past, had been nothing less than the footprint on time of the incarnate God. The peace of Rome itself had not lasted. For Julian, the present age was an age of war. But that distant and momentary lull in the laws of history proved to Julian that the Jews were wrong. The Messiah had come. His arrival had been marked, in time, by a thin fleck of peace. From that time on, the world had entered its last, sixth age. And this sixth age was to be lived out under the shadow of a vast, invisible empire. The entire world now belonged to the Kingdom of Christ: "The Lord has made bare His holy arm in

1 Julian of Toledo, *De comprobatione sextae aetatis*, 1.13, 160.

the sight of all the nations; and all the ends of the earth shall see the salvation of our God."[2]

What we moderns call (with deliberate vagueness) the "spread of Christianity" was, for Julian of Toledo, the proclamation, through the Catholic Church (and through no other body admitted by him), of the fact that the Kingdom of Christ had happened, and could be seen to have happened, "in the sight of all the nations . . . and [to] all the ends of the earth."[3]

It was not a claim calculated to convince a contemporary with any degree of geographical knowledge. The Jews raised the fact that many "barbarian" nations had plainly not become Christian. Julian's answer to such skeptics is revealing. He divided the world into two zones. The first was fully Christian; and it was fully Christian because it was ruled by Christian rulers. "For although there are still unbelieving peoples in some regions, they are nonetheless unable to escape the Lordship of Christ. For they are suppressed by rulers in whom it is known that Christ already dwells through their faith in Him."[4]

The second zone formed a less well-defined penumbra of the first: "For nor do I think [Julian continues] that there is any population left which does not know of the name of Christ. And although it may not have a preacher [of the Gospel present among them] it cannot but know of Christ from what it has heard from other nations."[5]

It is with this notion of a double zone within the single, overarching territory of the world-wide Kingdom of Christ that we must begin our account of what we now call "Christendom" in 600 CE.

Julian was already out of date when he wrote. One could not guess from his pages that, by 680, Muslim armies had already entered North Africa and would soon pass into Spain. But he was a scholarly bishop whose eyes in the year 680 looked at the world through the lens of books. For such a person, Christianity still lived in the shadow of empire. It was at its most confident and populous within the structures of two great empires who had (until recently) controlled most of the agrarian land of the western hemisphere from the Atlantic coast of Julian's Spain to the edge of Central Asia and Afghanistan – the Roman Empire and the Sasanian, Persian Empire. It was of these empires that contemporaries first thought when they contrasted the grandiose Kingdom of Christ with the "kingdoms of the world."

2 Isa. 52:10.
3 Julian of Toledo, *De comprobatione sextae aetatis*, 1.13, 160.
4 Ibid.
5 Ibid., 1.14, 161.

The sixth century had shown that the age of empires was far from over. Under the Emperor Justinian (527–65) the Roman Empire, ruled from Constantinople, reasserted its rights to large areas of the western Mediterranean – to much of Italy, to North Africa, and even to parts of Spain. Even outside the frontiers of the newly reconquered imperial territories, in Visigothic Spain and in the Frankish kingdoms, strong kingship still wore a recognizably "Roman" face. And a "Roman" face was a face borrowed from Constantinople. With a population of over half a million, Constantinople had become overwhelmingly the largest city in the Mediterranean and the Middle East. In Gaul and Spain, the Roman Empire, as it continued at Constantinople, had remained the preeminent model for earthly power at its most ebullient, formidable, and God-fearing.[6]

In western Asia, the Sasanian Empire (which embraced Iraq, Iran, and parts of Central Asia) showed that it was the equal of the Roman Empire. Under Chosroes I Anoshirwan (530–79) and again under Chosroes II Aparwez, "the Victorious" (590–628), the Sasanian Empire entered into a period of military and diplomatic confrontation with Constantinople which stretched throughout the Middle East from the northern Caucasus to Yemen. It was a colossal confrontation. It reached so deep into Central Asia and Inner Asia that it stirred the interest of the Chinese court in the affairs of the distant West for the first time since the days of Marcus Aurelius (121–80).[7]

The vast horizons still embraced by these "kingdoms of the world" imparted a sense of immensity to the Christian conviction that a yet wider Kingdom of Christ stood, as it were, as the invisible backdrop to the history of western Eurasia. How the various "kingdoms of the world" related to the Kingdom of Christ was a matter of concern to contemporaries. In around 550, at the far end of the Mediterranean, over two thousand miles from Toledo, a merchant and amateur theologian from Antioch engaged the same questions as did Bishop Julian. Cosmas (later called Cosmas the India-Merchant) was an experienced traveler. He had lived in Alexandria. He had traveled as far as Axum (Ethiopia) at the southern end of the Red Sea. He had even sailed on the Indian Ocean. For a subject of the Roman Empire, his religious loyalties were somewhat eccentric. Cosmas favored the views of the Christians of Persia, and spoke with admiration of the teaching of a converted Iranian, Mar Aba, who had traveled all the way from Mesopotamia to Alexandria and Constantinople in

6 Ward-Perkins, "Constantinople."
7 Mikawaya and Kollautz, "Ein Dokument zum Fernhandel."

the 520s before returning to Ctesiphon, near modern Baghdad, to become the head of the Church of the East.[8]

Cosmas's views on the Kingdom of Christ were conventional. The Kingdom of Christ alone was the truly "eternal" Kingdom spoken of by the prophet Daniel: "His dominion is an everlasting dominion, which shall not pass away."[9]

Cosmas took for granted that, in some way, a shadow of that eternity had fallen on the Roman Empire. Because Christ had been born within its territories, this kingdom had received special "privileges" from God. Though frequently damaged, for its sins, by barbarian invasion, it would last until the end of time. The world-wide acclaim of the rulers of Constantinople was known to Cosmas from his experience of the trade routes of Asia. He reported with pride that, as far away as Ceylon, the golden *solidus* of the Roman emperors was regarded as the best currency in the world.

This did not mean that Cosmas viewed the Roman Empire of his days as a "universal" empire: the Kingdom of Christ was alone in that. But it was unbeatable. Its unshakeable prestige among the nations ensured that the Christian faith would never be "narrowed down" to one region alone.[10]

Faced with the Persian empire, Cosmas propounded a more "de-centered" view of the world than that which reigned in Constantinople. He found a place for Persia, also, in the Kingdom of Christ. Persia was not simply the traditional barbarian antithesis to the Christian empire. Though not a Christian state, the Sasanian Empire had a role in God's providence. For the Magi had come to Christ from the East. By bringing gifts to the newborn Christ in Bethlehem, they had paid homage to him as the true Emperor of the world on behalf of all Persia. This act of homage had given the Sasanian Empire certain "privileges."[11] The Christian church within its boundaries could be treated as the equal, in prestige and even in numbers, of the churches of the West.[12]

In this "de-centered" view of the world, Cosmas was in touch with the realities of his time. The Roman Empire, though privileged, was one state among many. Its universal claims had been tacitly refused by the western kingdoms of the Franks and the Visigoths. In the East, the Sasanian Empire had shown itself to be on a par with Rome. The "Church of the East" was so called precisely because it was the Christian church within the territories of the Persian Empire, the "Empire of the Sublime Region of the

8 Wolska-Conus, *La topographie chrétienne*.
9 Dan. 7:14.
10 Cosmas Indicopleustes, *Topographie chrétienne*, 2.74–77, 389–93.
11 Monneret de Villard, *Le leggende orientali sui Magi evangelici*.
12 Cosmas Indicopleustes, *Topographie chrétienne*, 2.76, 391.

East." The Kingdom of Christ now towered above a world made up of many kingdoms.

We need only look eastward, to the Christian communities within the Sasanian Empire to which Mar Aba returned after his tour of the West, in order to appreciate how much the Christians of this time, in all places, still thought of themselves as living in the shadow of empire. The King of Kings and his aristocracy were loyal to their traditional Zoroastrian religion. But they had long extended a tolerance to the religious beliefs of their non-Iranian subjects which was far greater than any extended in Constantinople to religious dissidents.[13] As a result, the Sasanian Empire stretched above the Christianity of the East as distant, but as much taken for granted as the sky. When Mar Aba summoned a council in 544 to impose order on the Church of the East, the council met at the imperial capital of Ctesiphon and at the direct behest of Chosroes I: "In the Year of the Victory of the sweet, the merciful, the beneficent Khusro [Chosroes], the King of Kings . . . by the care of this new Cyrus, who is greater than all kings . . . to whom Christ has suggested to constantly lavish gifts upon His church."[14]

Though largely concentrated at this time in the towns and villages of northern Iraq, in the foothills of the Zagros, and in the trading posts of the Persian Gulf, the Church of the East partook in the vast horizons of the Sasanian Empire.[15] Mar Aba's spiritual empire stretched as far as Zerang and Qandahar, in modern Afghanistan – over a thousand miles to the east of Iraq – where he was helped in his negotiations with the local bishops by the good graces of "Suren of Beth Garmai [northern Iraq] the Keeper of the Queen's Camels." There was a Christian bishop at Merv, the great oasis city on the far eastern frontier of the Sasanian Empire.

Thus, it was as a religion protected by the structures of the Persian Empire "of the Sublime Region of the East," that the "Church of the East" (which has come to be known to us as the Nestorian Church) entered the world of Central Asia. A generation after 600, at a time when the pattern of world-empire itself changed, with the dramatic rise of Islam and the consequent reconfiguration of the lands between Merv and China, the "Nestorian" church moved yet further east, to establish itself in China. It did so in the train of upper-class refugees from Persia, diplomats, and career generals. Christian monks and clergymen entered Hsian-fu in 635 less as "missionaries" than as part of the shattered remnants

13 Brock, "Christians in the Sasanian Empire."
14 Council of Ctesiphon (544), *Synodicon orientale*, 315.
15 Fiey, *Communautés syriaques*.

of the Sasanian Empire within whose framework a vigorous Christian church had grown up and expanded far into Asia in the fifth and sixth centuries.[16]

"Rulers in whom it is known that Christ already dwells"[17]

What emerges from this brief tour of the horizons of Christianity in around the year 600 is the crucial importance of what were seen as the imperial "heartlands" within which Christianity had grown to prominence. Whether it was in the post-Roman kingdoms of the West, in the surviving Roman Empire of Constantinople, or in the Sasanian territories of the "Empire of the East," the majority of Christians still moved in a world where grandiose imperial structures seemed the norm. They were a fitting foreground for the invisible Kingdom of Christ.

It is easy to forget how long-established Christianity felt itself to be in such a world. Antiquity was now on the side of Christianity. By 600, the conversion of Constantine (in 312) lay three centuries in the past. The Roman Empire had already been a Christian empire for almost as long as it had been pagan. In Rome, the most splendid basilicas of all (Saint Peter's and the Lateran) had been built in the reign of Constantine. Their income was assured by complexes of estates in the Roman countryside and elsewhere, whose title deeds, preserved in the archives for the clergy of this time to read, reached back almost three hundred years. In a very ancient Italy, the boundaries of these estates themselves had not changed since the days of the Roman Republic.

But it was not only around the Mediterranean that Christianity had aged gracefully. In Trier, near the Rhine frontier, the awesome dimensions of the city's first cathedral (probably built by Constantine's pious son), its naves supported on gigantic columns of black Rhineland granite, was a standing reminder, in an age of smaller and less stable states, of what the concentrated power and wealth of a united Christian empire had been like. It was repaired at the end of the sixth century by an aristocrat bishop, Nicetius.

Nicetius himself represented a class with a long past. He came from a group of Christian aristocratic families, some of whom were proud to trace their descent back four hundred years, to a senator who had been martyred at Lyons in 177. As the writings of Gregory, bishop of Tours (d. 594), made plain, the clerical aristocracy of Gaul associated themselves with a "deep"

16 Pelliot and Forte, *L'inscription nestorienne*; Brown, *Rise of Western Christendom*, 279–85.
17 Julian of Toledo, *De comprobatione sextae aetatis*, 1.13, 160.

past, associated with the tombs of martyrs and saints (many of them in elegant classical marble) which lay in ancient crypts and in family mausolea scattered in Roman cemeteries outside the cities. Many such saints were the ancestors of living bishops. Their history led back into the long past of Christian Gaul. This continuity meant more to a man such as Gregory than did the conventional turning points of Roman history. Gregory, for instance, seemed oblivious to the end of the Roman Empire.[18]

For Gregory and his contemporaries the great mutation had already occurred. They lived in a world of Christian cities, under Christian rulers. His works contain a Latin translation of a legend of the Seven Sleepers of Ephesus. The Seven Sleepers retired to a cave at the time of the persecution of Christians in the third century. They woke up again in the fifth century. There was one sign of the times which instantly drew their attention. The Sign of the Cross was carved above the gates of every city. They saw what any sixth-century Christian of the Mediterranean and much of the Middle East could have seen every day.[19]

Christianity as a whole was far from being exclusively an urban religion in the year 600. But it had remained a religion whose "nerve centers" had remained urban bishoprics, many of which dated back for half a millennium. Cities still stood for solidity. In Roman Britain, where urban life had always been tenuous, Christianity had mutated in such a way as to become almost invisible to outsiders by the year 600 – as we shall see. Once one crossed the Channel, the cities with their walls began, growing ever more dense as one reached the Mediterranean. Frankish Gaul had 116 bishoprics, Visigothic Spain had 66. With 237, for its relatively small size, Italy positively buzzed with bishops, as did North Africa, with 242, increasingly clustered along the eastern coastal regions. With over 680 bishops, the territories of the Roman Empire of Justinian and his successors remained the true center of gravity of the Christian world, especially as many of its cities were considerably larger than those of the West. Across the Roman frontier, the very different cities and large villages of the Sasanian Empire supported over 50 bishops. The church of Armenia could rally some 20 bishops, distributed, rather unevenly, according to the holdings of the noble families of the region.

With the exception of Lombard adventurers in northern and central Italy and the "stateless" chieftaincies of the Slavs who had moved into the Balkans under the hegemony of the nomadic pagan Avars, from the Euphrates to the

18 Mitchell, "Marking the Bounds."
19 Gregory of Tours, *Passio sanctorum martyrum septem dormientium apud Ephysum*, 401.

Channel coast, and even in western England and Wales, all organized society was headed by Christian rulers. The power and ideological pretensions of these states varied. But all thought of themselves as existing through the protection of Christ. All thought that the duty of a ruler was, at the very least, to secure the observance of Sunday and respect for other Christian festivals, to suppress pagan sacrifices, and to make sure that the Jewish communities in their midst did not get above themselves. The empire of Justinian was a model for them all because it appeared to do this more effectively than did any other kingdom.

Subjects of Justinian were left in little doubt that they lived in a Christian state. A mosaic on the floor of the tax office of Caesarea Maritima (on the coast of modern Israel) cites a blunt passage from St. Paul's *Letter to the Romans*: "If you would not fear the authority, do good."[20]

Christian preaching upheld the authority of the ruler. Christian prayers, publicly offered at every liturgy, secured the safety of the empire. The divinely ordained "harmony" of Church and State, which Justinian had proclaimed in his legislation, was more than a rhetorical flourish. It grew from the ground up in 680 cities. Ecclesiastical and secular were intextricably mixed through the collaboration of the bishop and clergy with the local elites in order to handle the day-to-day business of government. The bishop was now a principal agent in the communication between the capital and the provinces.[21] Imperial edicts on matters as thoroughly secular as the control of banditry would be received by the bishop and read out to the local council in the bishop's audience hall adjoining the Christian basilica. They would be posted on the walls of the church.[22] In Gerasa (Jerash, Jordan), it was the bishop who built and ran the local jail: "to the advantage of the city."[23] As Severus, the patriarch of Antioch, told a local bishop in no uncertain terms in around 515: bishops were there to keep the cities going. "It is the duty of bishops to cut short and to restrain the unregulated movements of the mob . . . and to set themselves to maintain good order in the cities and to watch over the peaceful manner of those who are fed by their hand."[24]

It is important to remember that the crushing load of administrative duties which Gregory the Great took over when he became pope in Rome (between 590 and 604) was in no ways unusual. It did not reflect any sudden crisis by which the pope was forced to rescue ancient Rome, by subjecting the city to

20 Rom. 13.3 quoted in Holum, "Inscription in the Imperial Revenue Office."
21 Liebeschuetz, *Decline and Fall*, 104–68.
22 Feissel and Kaygusuz, "Un mandement impérial."
23 Gatier, "Nouvelles inscriptions de Gérasa."
24 Severus of Antioch, *Select Letters*, 1.8, 43.

the spiritual power. Still less did Gregory's care for Rome reflect a wish to become independent of the empire. It was simply "business as usual" for a bishop in the empire of Justinian and his successors.[25]

It was with a sense of representing a stable social order, with a long past behind it, that the inhabitants of a "heartland" of Christian kingdoms turned to the outside world.

"Although it may not have a preacher . . . it cannot but know of Christ from what it has heard from other nations."[26]

In 578, the monks of a monastery perched in the Pharaonic ruins of Thebes in Upper Egypt wrote up a prayer for the empire sent to them, from Alexandria, by their patriarch, Damianus. They should pray "for the prosperous life of the kings . . . and that every barbarian nation, unto the ends of the earth, may be in subjection under their hands, and that the whole world may become one body."[27]

It is revealing that the patriarch to whom the monks owed obedience was not even the patriarch recognized by the emperors for whom the monks prayed – Damianus was the miaphysite patriarch of Alexandria. Deemed a "heretic," his patriarchate was, technically, illegal. But the public language he adopted was identical to that of any other bishop within the empire.

It was taken for granted, in official circles, that Christianity would come to the barbarians when God wished it; and that, when it came, it would come through the magnetic attraction of the Christian empire. Often this ideology appeared to come true. Resident in Constantinople, John of Biclaro, a Spanish predecessor of Julian of Toledo, witnessed such ceremonies of integration. In 569, the Garamantes (a tribal confederation on the Saharan frontier of North Africa) "asked through their envoys that they be incorporated into the peace of the Roman state and into the Christian faith."[28]

So did the Maccuritae, from the Dongola region of the northern Sudan. In 573, their ambassadors arrived. Bringing elephant tusks and a giraffe, "they placed themselves on friendly terms with the Romans."[29] The gifts were a reminder that, through the prestige of the Christian empire, the Kingdom

25 Delogu, "Solium imperii-urbs ecclesiae."
26 Julian of Toledo, *De comprobatione sextae aetatis*, 1.14, 161.
27 Crum and Evelyn-White, *Monastery of Epiphanius at Thebes* 2, 148–52.
28 John of Biclaro, *Chronicon*, ch. 7, 63.
29 Ibid., 9, 64; 28, 67.

of Christ had become known far south of the rainless zone of Egypt, in the savannah lands that edged the northern tip of Equatorial Africa. Even there, empire left its mark. The churches of Dongola are faithful copies of Byzantine models. As late as the eleventh century, the tomb inscriptions of the region used Constantinopolitan Greek prayers for the passing of the soul.[30]

What this "ideology of attraction" failed to recognize was that, by the year 600, Christianity had spread, in less formal ways, less easily condensed into the triumphant "sound bites" of contemporary narratives. The heartlands of Christianity were already ringed by an extensive "penumbra." In the words of Julian of Toledo, no "preacher" had come to many nations: that is, no "preacher" such as would have been recognized in official circles – no royal or imperial embassy had reached them; no bishop and clergy commissioned for the purpose had set up churches among them. Nonetheless, Christ was known to them, "from what it has heard from other nations."[31]

The ideology of the Christian heartlands tended to censor this slow trickle of knowledge of Christianity into Asia, Africa, and northern Europe. The "Kingdom of Christ" might be universal, but it only worked through clearly visible representatives: through a clergy supported, to varying degrees, by the prestige of a Christian state. What this view failed to recognize was that, for outsiders accustomed to a diversity of spiritual powers, sixth-century Christianity, in and of itself, was an exciting source of potential blessing and protection. Its symbols and rituals were known to be powerful. They were frequently grafted on to other systems.

Religious *bricolage* of this kind occurred all over Europe and Asia. The Cross appears frequently on ceramics in Iraq and even on coins in Sasanian Merv.[32] In 591, even a party of Turks from Kirghizstan, on the frontier of China, appeared in Constantinople with the Sign of the Cross on their foreheads: "They declared that they had been assigned this by their mothers: for when a fierce plague was endemic among them, some Christians advised them that the foreheads of their young should be marked with this sign."[33]

It was the same in Saharan Africa. The spread of knowledge of Christianity, and the adoption of selected elements of its rituals, cannot be reduced to the few moments of contact between the imperial authorities and the Berber and Tuareg confederacies which stretched far to the south of the frontiers of Roman North Africa. In the Tuareg language of the western Sahara, the

30 Godlewski, "New Approach."
31 Julian of Toledo, *De comprobatione sextae aetatis*, 1.14, 161.
32 Simpson, "Mesopotamia," 65; Hermann et al., "International Merv Project," 64.
33 Theophylact Simocatta, *History*, 5.10.15, 146–47.

word for "sacrifice," *afaske*, echoes the Christian term for "Pascha" / "Easter" – the high festival of the Christian world. Other words of clerical Latin, such as *abbekad*, from *peccatum* (sin), also entered the language. It is an echo from a world far to the south of the coastal plains of Mediterranean North Africa.[34]

It is easy to forget that the territories of Christianity itself were subject to constant flux. "De-Christianization" was just as much a feature of the Christian world in 600 as was "Christianization." Barbarian invasion, deportation, or sheer neglect by distant authorities could produce entire "unchurched" populations, for whom Christianity remained a residual religion, but without ecclesiastical structures. When, in around 520, Symeon the Mountain-Dweller, a Syrian hermit, came to an upland valley in northern Iraq, he found a community of scattered pastoralists, living in well-built houses. But their churches were empty. They had never heard a reading of the Scriptures. They did not know what the Eucharist was. "There are men on these mountains [they told him] who, unless they have heard from their fathers, who carried them to church and had them baptized, do not know what a church is."[35]

Even a self-confidently "Christian" society, such as the empire of Justinian and his successors, lived with large swaths of gray – of unchurched and even pagan communities – in its midst.

Other former Christian communities suffered yet more drastic dislocation. An Armenian population, forcibly deported by the Persians to the edge of Central Asia, lost everything: "They had forgotten their own language, lost the use of writing, and lacked the priestly order."[36]

Only generations later were they "re-churched" through the intervention of an Armenian general in Persian service: "They were confirmed in the faith and learned to write and speak their language. A certain presbyter among them called Abel [whose family evidently had maintained some form of priestly status] was appointed to priestly rank in that territory."[37]

This process of alternating "churched" and "unchurched" Christianities can be seen most clearly on the northern shores of the Black Sea. The Crimea and the Sea of Azov, where the Don opens up a route into the steppes of southern Russia, was an immemorial corridor of populations. The Black Sea was vital for Roman strategy. In the Crimea, a Roman presence was maintained along the shoreline, beneath the mountain ridges. Yet Christianity spread sporadically

34 Camps, "Rex gentium Maurorum et Romanorum."
35 John of Ephesus, *Lives of the Eastern Saints*, 16, 235.
36 Sebeos, *Armenian History*, 24.97, 44.
37 Sebeos, *Armenian History*, 24.97, 44.

in this crucial area, in ways which revealed the weaknesses of the official "ideology of attraction."[38]

Ever since the fourth century, bishops "of the Goths" (from the northern Black Sea area) appeared occasionally at Constantinople.[39] But these were a passive presence. The major moments of official Christianization coincided with diplomatic offensives against the nomads in the Russian steppes and against Sasanian penetration in the Caucasus. The language of the official sources speaks of these as brisk triumphs. Under imperial guidance, coastal and mountain tribes of the Black Sea and the Caucasus stepped from darkness into light, and from "the beast-like life" of barbarians into that of civilized persons and Christians.[40] What they do not tell is how far Christianity had already penetrated these areas in less formal ways. This penetration is revealed only by fleeting signs, such as the appearance of the Sign of the Cross on belt buckles in Crimean mountain settlements at some distance from the "Roman," Christian coast.[41]

Nor do these accounts betray the fact that many of the groups who were swept up into the diplomacy of Constantinople had lived for long periods as largely "unchurched" Christians. An incident recorded by Procopius (mid-sixth century) throws some light on this gray zone. The Goths of the Bay of Azov had long been Christians. But they had forgotten what sort of Christians they were. "Now as to whether these Goths were once of the Arian belief, as the other Gothic nations are . . . I am unable to say, for they themselves are entirely ignorant on this subject."[42]

Modern archaeological studies of many areas of the Balkans, of the Danube, and of northern Europe confirm the impression of a Christendom ringed by a penumbra of de-Christianized, "unchurched" regions, mixed with regions in which Christianity was present, if only as one religious system among others.

The most tantalizing example of all, of course, is the Britain to which Gregory I sent his famous delegation headed by the monk Augustine (d. c. 604) to Æthelberht (d. 616), the pagan king of Kent, in 597. The conventional ideology of Christianization which Gregory took for granted when he embarked on this mission had little place for the Christianity which had developed in this strangely silent island.[43]

38 Ivanov, *Vizantiiskoe missionerstvo*, 82–88.
39 Mathisen, "Barbarian Bishops and Churches."
40 Maas, "Delivered from their Ancient Customs."
41 Kazanski and Soupault, *Les sites archéologiques*, 72.
42 Procopius, *Wars*, 8.4.9, 84.
43 Markus, *Gregory the Great*, 83–96, 177–87.

It appears that the British church had retained many features that linked it still to the Continent. Visitors from Gaul, in the middle of the sixth century, would have found, in sites like Verulamium (St. Albans), basilicas of the saints such as Gregory of Tours would have recognized. Some members of the clergy had remained learned. They drew on a severely restricted fund of books. Many of these were out of date. Some were written by ardent followers of the arch-heretic, Pelagius (a fellow Briton of the late-fourth/early-fifth century). Yet a Briton such as Gildas had succeeded in creating a vivid literary culture from this meager store. His book *On the Ruin of Britain* (written around 530) places him in a tradition of lamentation on the state of the church which had recognizable parallels in Gaul. This Latin learning had passed across the Irish Sea, to the communities founded in Ireland by Patricius (Patrick) – who may have died in 493 – and to the more shadowy settlements associated with Bishop Palladius, who had been sent to "the Irish who believe in Christ" on a rare papal initiative as early as 431. These were impressive achievements, of which Gregory appears to have known nothing.[44]

Even in the areas settled by the Saxons, a "heathen darkness" had not descended on the land. On arriving in Kent, Augustine was puzzled to learn that the shrine of a certain martyr, Sixtus, was still an object of veneration by the local Britons. The shrine must have dated from Roman times. The locals knew little about the martyr. They possessed no text of his martyrdom (a *sine qua non* for a successful cult in most regions of the Continent). Yet they had continued tenaciously to worship at his grave.[45]

Altogether, in the course of the sixth century, Christianity had survived and mutated in Britain and in the "barbarian" island of Ireland. Yet we learn nothing of this from Continental sources. Even the name of Patricius first appears in a European text in 658 – almost two hundred years after his death. In the words of an alert modern scholar, "the silence of the age" had descended on a region whose low profile and truly post-imperial Christianity had no place in a map of the world still dominated by an ideology generated by great empires.[46]

The mission of Gregory the Great to the Anglo-Saxons, in 597, has conventionally been regarded as a starting point in the history of western Christianity. Yet it is perhaps helpful to see it, also, as the last gesture of an "apostolic" leader in a century where Christianity had spread, almost unwittingly, far beyond the limits of its own mental maps, with dramatic and unforeseen results. In order

44 Sharpe, "Martyrs and Local Saints"; Herren and Brown, *Christ in Celtic Christianity*; Charles-Edwards, *Early Christian Ireland*.

45 Stancliffe, "British Church."

46 Ivanov, *Vizantiiskoe missionerstvo*, 80.

to appreciate this, let us end by turning three thousand miles to the southeast of Rome – to Ethiopia, to the Arabian peninsula, and to the Persian Gulf.

Lying within range of the rainfall of Equatorial Africa, both the kingdom of Axum, in the foothills of modern Ethiopia, looking down upon the western side of the Red Sea, and the kingdom of Himyar (the Hadramawt in modern Yemen), facing the Indian Ocean at the southern end of the Arabian peninsula, were long-settled civilizations. Their religious history had moved to a rhythm of its own. While the pagans of the north could be dismissed as "living like animals . . . who worship sticks and stones" (to use the choice words of Gregory the Great on the unabsorbed highlanders of Sardinia), and the Zoroastrians could be spoken of as mere "murmurers," mindless adherents of a largely oral religious tradition, without the dignity of books, the inhabitants of the kingdom of Axum and of Himyar / Saba had long been literate and even monotheist. As a result, Christians and Jews competed to put their own stamp on a strong surge of loyalty to one High God, known as al-Raḥmānān, "the Merciful." We know of al-Raḥmānān through victory inscriptions. He was the High God of aggressive, warrior kings, whose campaigns ranged as far as the Blue Nile from Axum and from Himyar (through an alliance of dependent Arab tribes) up to the very edge of Iraq.[47]

Both kingdoms guarded the gate through which the trade of the Indian Ocean reached the Mediterranean and the Middle East. As a result, they were distinctive, but never isolated. Cosmas the India-Merchant, to take only one example, had visited Axum and was well informed about the affairs of Himyar. A Jewish woman from Himyar was buried in Palestine with an inscription in Sabaean, Hebrew, and Aramaic.[48] Both kingdoms had opted, as early as the fourth century, to replace the cult of the High God by a more radical and up-to-date form of monotheism. The kings of Axum had become Christian around 340.[49]

From around 380, by contrast, the kings of Himyar were Jewish. Thus, two monotheisms faced each other across the Red Sea. Both claimed biblical authority for their rule. The inscriptions of the Axumite king, Ella Atsbeha (c. 519–c. 531), were heavy with warlike passages of the Psalms: "The Lord strong and brave, the Lord mighty in battle . . . in Whom I Believe, who has given me a strong kingdom. . . . I trust myself to Christ so that all my enterprises may succeed."[50]

47 Robin, *L'Arabie antique*.
48 Nebe and Sima, "Die aramäisch / hebräisch-sabäische Grabinschrift der Lea."
49 Munro-Hay, *Aksum*; Brakmann, *Die Einwürzelung der Kirche*.
50 Axum inscription of Ella Atsbeha in Munro-Hay, *Aksum*, 230.

The inscriptions of his Jewish rival in Himyar, Yūsuf As'ar Yath'ar (522–30), known as Dhū Nūwas, "He of the Forelock," were equally fierce. "By the Lord of Heaven and Earth and by the power of my warriors," Dhū Nūwas ousted a Christian king set up in Zafar by Ethiopian troops. He turned the great Christian church in Zafar into a synagogue. In 523 he closed in on the Arab trading city of Najran (placed on the routes between Zafar and the Hijaz) massacring the Christian clergy and aristocracy when they refused to adopt Judaism.[51]

Dhū Nūwas told them that it was not as if he were asking them to become polytheists and to worship the Sun. They could worship God, "the Merciful." All they had to admit was that Jesus of Nazareth had been a mere man: "All countries understand that he was a man and not God. Even the land of the Romans, who first erred concerning Him [by considering him divine]," he added, was slowly coming to its senses.[52]

Yûsuf was defeated and killed by the Ethiopian army of Ella Atsbeha. Sharing no language with their fierce liberators from across the Red Sea, the local Christians protected themselves from the Ethiopian warriors by showing the Cross tattooed on their hands. Up to 570, the kingdom of Himyar was in the hands of Christian rulers, supported by military manpower drawn from the highlands of Ethiopia. A large church was built in San'â by the Christian king, Abraha. Known as Al-Qalîs, (from the Greek *ekklesia*, the church) its Byzantine plan, with high naves and shimmering mosaics, was long remembered in the Arab world.[53] On one of his routine expeditions to show his power to the Arab tribes of the north, Abraha was believed to have brought with him a war elephant. The grandiose gesture was remembered, five hundred miles away, in Mecca, in the Hijaz. "The Year of the Elephant" was the year in which the Prophet Muḥammad (c. 570–632) was believed to have been born.

What these dramatic incidents reveal is the fact that areas of the world which seemed very far removed from the Christians of the heartland were held together by a web of communications which escaped conventional narratives of the spread of Christianity. Far from being an isolated region, opaque to outside influence, the Arabian peninsula, caught between Persia and Rome, had become, in the sixth century, a veritable "echo chamber" of religious conflict. From Iraq and Syria to the Hadramawt, "the gloves were off" between Judaism and Christianity. The remarkably articulate argument between Christianity and Judaism which runs throughout the Qur'ān of Muḥammad (the

51 Beaucamp, Briquel-Chatonnet, and Robin, "La persécution des chrétiens."
52 *Book of the Himyarites*, 13, cix.
53 Finster and Schmidt, *Die Kirche des Abraha in San'â*.

recital of the visions which began to be revealed to him in 610 – only six years after the death of Gregory the Great) echoes a stormy century, where just these issues had been hotly contested along the whole length of the Arabian peninsula.

There were two reasons for this development. First, it is a reminder that empire mattered. For reasons of prestige and strategy, both Rome and Persia were prepared to reach down to the Indian Ocean. The Ethiopian "protectorate" of the coast of southern Arabia received the full blessing of the emperors of Constantinople. But Ethiopian, Christian hegemony was held in check. Persia offered persistent support for a Jewish kingdom that would keep the Ethiopians out of the Himyar, thereby blocking Roman penetration, through Christian allies, along the Hadramawt to the mouth of the Persian Gulf. After 570, Persian intervention secured just that. With Persian help, a local leader drove the Ethiopians back again across the Red Sea.[54]

All that remained of a Christian hegemony, apart from memories of the great church of Abraha at San'â and of his war elephant, was a vivid reference, in Muḥammad's Qur'ān to the martyrs of Najran. They had died

> For no other reason than
> That they believed in God,
> Exalted in Power,
> Worthy of All Praise![55]

But second, and equally remarkable, were the religious personnel who became involved in this Arabia-wide confrontation. Few of them were members of the established church of the empire. Rather, they were miaphysite Christians, bitterly opposed to the emperor's determination to uphold the Council of Chalcedon of 451. As the sixth century progressed, the opponents of Chalcedon found themselves forced to set up a rival hierarchy within the empire itself. And, in so doing, they created a new map of the Christian world. For they saw themselves, increasingly, as the defenders of a universal Christian truth. And this was not a universal truth which had, somehow, come to rest at the center of a single empire. It was a "de-centered" truth that was wider than the kingdoms of this world.[56]

Across the Middle East, they entered with truly "missionary" zeal into a competition for souls. This "zeal" reached out with particular attention to communities, such as the Nubians on the southern frontier of Egypt, who

54 Bowersock, *Hadramawt*.
55 *Sura* 85:8.
56 Fowden, *Empire to Commonwealth*, 100–37.

had already had long contact with Christianity. The miaphysite leaders had to make sure that, if the Nubians were to be "churched," this church should come from themselves, and not from the imperial upholders of the "Great Prevarication" of Chalcedon. By so doing, they introduced a fracture into the previous "ideology of attraction," by which all roads to Christianity had led, through correct diplomatic channels, to Constantinople.[57]

Miaphysite clergy crossed with ease the frontier between Romans and "barbarians," and even between Rome and Persia. They gathered support from the Arab tribes along the frontier. The most notable of these were the Banu Ghassan. The Banu Ghassan met regularly with other Arab tribes at the shrine of Saint Sergios at Rusafa, placed at the northern edge of the Arabian desert in "the Barbarian Plain" that flanked the Euphrates. After 550, miaphysite monks and clergymen penetrated the Arab tribes of the Persian frontier, centered around Hira, so as to compete there also with the Nestorianism of the "Church of the East."[58] To reach down to the southern end of the Red Sea, to Axum, and to the southern end of the Arabian peninsula, to Himyar, was a logical extension of a network without frontiers, equally dedicated to holding in check Chalcedonians on the edge of the Roman territories and Nestorians on the edges of Persia.

Behind these activities lies a cultural change whose full significance has not yet been fully appreciated. This was the "globalization" of culture which occurred throughout the Middle East in the course of the sixth century. As the journey of the Iranian Mar Aba to the West made plain, cultural frontiers no longer coincided with political boundaries. It was possible to read in Iraq, in Syriac, and even in Pahlavi translations, works of Greek philosophy and theology produced in Alexandria and Antioch. A world had opened across the Middle East, bound together by shared intellectual concerns and by shared religious confrontations. People in distant lands (largely irrespective of language) felt touched by identical issues and drew on identical skills.[59] It was a wider world than even the diplomats had dreamed of. The clear outlines of an orthodox map of the world determined by the frontiers of Christian kingdoms had begun to dissolve.

Altogether, it was a time for "apostolic" action. In the triumphant letters which reported to the patriarch of Alexandria the success of the mission of Augustine to the Saxons of Kent, Gregory the Great dwelt on this "apostolic"

57 Kirwan, *Studies*.
58 Fowden, *Barbarian Plain*.
59 Walker, "Limits of Late Antiquity."

theme: "Both he and those who were sent with him shine with such miracles that the miracles of the Apostles seem to live again."[60]

Gregory the Great may well have sensed the spirit of an age whose horizons had fallen open. But, of course, he had written to the wrong patriarch. It was the miaphysite patriarch of Egypt, and not his "official" Chalcedonian rival, who would emerge as the unchallenged patron of the Christianity of Ethiopia and of the valley of the Nile as far south as Khartoum. And not every "Apostle" had to be a Christian. It was the preaching of Muḥammad, as the "Apostle of God," to Arabs who had been sensitized by the experiences of the past century to the possibilities of a militant and conflictual monotheism which would prove as important, on the stage of world history, as would be Gregory's preaching of the gospel to the Anglo-Saxons.

60 Gregory the Great, *Epistolae*, 8.29, 551.

PART I

★

FOUNDATIONS: PEOPLES, PLACES, AND TRADITIONS

I

Late Roman Christianities

PHILIP ROUSSEAU

Theological identities, regional differences

Under the heading "identities," we must ask what gave late Roman Christian communities their specific characters. We are dealing with a plural: "Christianities." The late Roman period was, in religion as in much else, a fractured age. What lay at the root of the resulting variety? Leaders of government and church pleaded for universal loyalty – to empire and orthodoxy above all. By 600 CE, Christians found themselves nevertheless divided geographically into four main blocs. The Latin West was extensively settled by "barbarians" and strained in its relations with the East. The "Chalcedonian" church, centered on Constantinople, retained a more nuanced attachment to the Council of 451. Disaffected Christians in Egypt and western Syria, opposed to the Council, subscribed more explicitly to a "one-nature" or "miaphysite" theology. The church of East Syria distanced itself increasingly from all such preoccupations, deeply affected by its proximity to Persia and the Arabs.

It is tempting to describe and therefore explain those divisions in terms of theological dispute. Dispute there certainly was, and it was not a mere front for other principles or prejudices: the issues at stake affected the core of Christian belief and must be paid respect.[1] The disorder and acrimony of the fifth and sixth centuries had roots reaching back at least to the Council of Nicaea (325). Arius, condemned at that council, appeared to qualify the divinity ascribable to Jesus. Forceful opponents of his position – notably Apollinarius of Laodicea (d. c. 390) – downplayed the permanence of God the Son's humanity in the name of divine unity. Fifth-century churchmen, therefore, strove to discover a formula that would defuse the exaggerations of both parties. The humanity of Jesus had to be safeguarded, for otherwise his fellow humans could not share in the transformation of their nature that he promised them; the divinity of Jesus had to be safeguarded, for otherwise his offer lacked both authority and the

1 Jones, "Were Ancient Heresies National or Social Movements."

possibility of fulfillment. Yet, how could one describe Jesus as at once human and divine without prejudice to one nature or the other, and without dividing his very person?

Unfortunately, antagonisms were exacerbated before compromises could be achieved. Especially intense was the rivalry between the bishops of Alexandria (heirs of Athanasius, the Arians' greatest foe, and guardians of a long theological tradition) and of Constantinople (upstart capital of the new Christian empire); a rivalry that had already led to the downfall of John Chrysostom (originally from Antioch) in 404.[2] Now, Nestorius (also bishop of Constantinople and another Antiochene) was condemned at the Council of Ephesus (431) for overemphasizing the humanity of Jesus. The council's acclamation of Mary, the mother of Jesus, as *Theotokos* or "God-bearer," crowned with temporary success a long struggle for ascendancy by Cyril (bishop of Alexandria since 412); a success that reinforced an emphasis on the transcendent nature of the divine Logos (whence the term "miaphysite"). Cyril's supporting documentation reflected convictions developed over many years and colored much of the subsequent debate.[3] Although opposed by John, bishop of Antioch, Cyril had also (at the expense of some honest clarity) gained the support of Pope Celestine I (422–32) in Rome. So, already at Ephesus, a metropolitan quartet was set in place, destined for dissonance more than harmony.

A degree of arrogant intransigence edged out more moderate opinion. Such was the fate of the Antiochene exegete Theodore, later bishop of Mopsuestia (d. 428). Theodore had taught Nestorius and was unfairly identified with his pupil, even though his theology was at once clearer and more moderate. Cyril's successor Dioscorus (bishop 444–54) inflamed suspicion of Theodore and attacked two of his Syrian supporters – Theodoret, bishop of Cyrrhus, and Ibas, bishop of Edessa. The ploy affected debate for well over a century. Theodore's most ardent admirers emerged in the East Syrian church, where he was seen as "illustrious and eminent among the teachers of the true faith."[4] That East Syrian religious culture, described in more detail in a later chapter, had its immediate roots in Ibas's see, Edessa.[5] The scholar Barsauma (subsequently bishop of Nisibis) and his colleague Narsai were active in the city from the 430s. After the Council of Chalcedon, opposition to its "two natures"

2 See Dagron, *Naissance d'une capitale* and *La romanité chrétienne*; Haas, *Alexandria in Late Antiquity*; Baynes, "Alexandria and Constantinople."

3 *Acta conciliorum oecumenicorum*, 1.1.1, 23–42. See Cyril of Alexandria, *Select Letters*; Wessel, *Cyril of Alexandria*.

4 Synod of Bet Lapat (484 CE) quoted by Gero, *Barsauma of Nisibis*, 45, and see 29–31.

5 See Segal, *Edessa*, 110–91; Baum and Winkler, *Die apostolische Kirche des Ostens*; Gillman and Klimkeit, *Christians in Asia*.

formula (in both Antioch and Alexandria) encouraged further antagonism towards Theodore (not least because Chalcedon had affirmed his orthodoxy). Those Syrians sympathetic to Theodore's cause were forced to leave Edessa, with Narsai in the lead; and Barsauma's see further east seemed a natural place of refuge. There, the two set up the so-called "School of Nisibis" – traditionally in 489, although events are "shrouded in impenetrable darkness."[6] Barsauma proceeded to make the city an intellectual center, partly as a competitive gesture towards the *catholicos* of Seleucia-Ctesiphon, who claimed virtually patriarchal status over all the churches within the Persian sphere. Soon, study at Nisibis became a *sine qua non* for anyone aspiring to clerical eminence in the East Syrian church. Internal disputes were often stormy, especially in the later decades of the sixth and the opening decades of the seventh centuries. What matters here is that the continuing rise and fall of Theodore's reputation (as of Theodoret and Ibas), coupled with the East Syrian Christians' involvement with Persia, inevitably contributed to not only the theological but also the strategic crises of the following hundred or more years.

But this is to anticipate. Theodore's temporary restoration to favor reflects the more general importance of the Council of Chalcedon.[7] The theological developments of the following century or so were a prolonged attempt to escape from its unforgiving precision. Authorities in Constantinople, both civil and religious, strove always, by dint of compromise, to entice opponents into a semblance of unity; but they were never able to cede enough. The council had created, moreover, a new arena within which Constantinople had to contend with the bishops of Rome. Pope Leo the Great (440–61) was more formidable than his immediate predecessors, and precisely in relation to Chalcedon defended an interpretation of its decrees that made concessions further east even harder to confirm.

In that respect, the antecedents of the council were as important as its results. A Constantinopolitan monk and court favorite, Eutyches, had put himself forward as a forceful opponent of Nestorius, questioning the distinct humanity of Jesus.[8] He gained the support of the emperor, and of Dioscorus, but was opposed at Antioch. Thus, Leo was brought into the fray, since Eutyches sought his backing. He gained little comfort from the pope's response – his so-called *Tome*, addressed to Flavian of Constantinople in 449.[9] Dioscorus tried

6 Vööbus, *History*, 33.
7 See Grillmeier and Bacht, *Das Konzil von Chalkedon*.
8 Eutyches linked with Apollinarius: *Corpus iuris civilis: Codex Justinianus*, 1.5.8 (455 CE), 52; see also 1.1.5–7 (527–33 CE).
9 Eutyches' appeal: *Acta conciliorum oecumenicorum*, 2.2.1, 33–35; preceded by Leo's letter to Flavian, 24–33.

to vindicate Eutyches at what Leo later called the "Robber Council," which affirmed the orthodoxy of Cyril and the errors of Theodoret and Ibas.[10] But a die had been cast: Leo's pronouncements commanded the greater respect, and his *Tome* was accepted at Chalcedon itself as the clearest expression of the council's theological position. Unfortunately, Leo's Latin articulation of the "two natures" argument encouraged the western church and its allies in the East to resist every subsequent attempt to modify the council's decrees in the interests of reconciliation. The *Tome* ceased to summarize existing belief and enshrined a relentless exercise in the control of the future.

The search for universal agreement is described in detail in the previous volume of this *History*. My task here is to identify its later effects. They fall under three headings: the exercise of religious authority by the emperor (an issue now restricted to the East), the imperial government's difficulty in controlling the religious loyalties and customs of Syria and Egypt (later to fall under the dominance of Islam), and that government's eagerness (often humiliating but never wholly successful) to enlist papal support in both endeavors. In that last respect, the period between the accession of Leo and the death of Pope Gregory the Great (590–604) moves from independent self-assurance through enforced subservience under Justinian I (527–65) to a painful restoration of papal status and influence. The restoration was precarious, as the fortunes of Pope Martin I (649–55) were to show; but Gregory was able to create a sense of the papacy's role in the West, and to initiate pastoral and administrative policies that would last for centuries.

Imperial policy and papal response were intertwined throughout the post-Chalcedonian era. The first major attempt to defuse contention was the *Henotikon* issued by the emperor Zeno in 482. His plea that "limbs be attached to limbs," that the church was "the incorruptible and never-ending mother of our scepters," that he was acting "not in order to make innovations in the faith but so as to reassure you," set a tone that would persist.[11] Acacius, bishop of Constantinople and the document's doctrinal architect, saw Zeno's move as an opportunity to enhance his own status. The *Henotikon*, however, while affirming traditional orthodoxy in general terms, was not sufficiently anti-Chalcedonian for eastern extremists – another portent. Nor were western churchmen delighted by Zeno's apparent concessions. Pope Felix III

10 Leo to the Empress Pulcheria: *in illo Ephesino non judicio sed latrocinio*, see his *Epistola*, 95.2 in *PL* 54.943B.

11 Evagrius Scholasticus, *Ecclesiastical History*, 3.14, ed. Bidez and Parmentier, 111.15–16, 112.5, 113.21–2 or trans. Whitby, 147–49. See Allen, *Evagrius Scholasticus*.

(483–92) excommunicated Acacius in 484, and the resulting "Acacian Schism" lasted for more than thirty years.[12]

In spite of tensions within the Roman see itself, the tenure of two subsequent popes, Gelasius I (492–6) and Symmachus (498–514) reinforced western suspicion of eastern doctrine and vaunted authority. The two men were aided by the indecisive policies of the emperor Anastasius I (491–518) and the opportunist tolerance displayed by the Arian Ostrogoth Theoderic (master of Italy 493–526). Those rulers created a space for papal independence: the legacy of Leo could be protected and the religious influence of secular rulers called into question.

Anastasius's even-handedness was his own undoing: as Evagrius put it, "each of the prelates conducted himself according to his beliefs," and "the situation became more absurd."[13] In Constantinople, dangerous riots (511–12) combined religious outrage with political disaffection. Theological debate focused increasingly on the question whether God could be said to have suffered in the Incarnation (subsequently described as the "theopaschite" position), which seemed an inevitable consequence of miaphysite doctrine; one that Nestorius had striven to avoid, but at the cost of undermining divine agency in Jesus' redemptive sacrifice. The army supported the greater cautions of Chalcedon, hoping that Anastasius would make concessions to the more rigorous westerners. A new pope, Hormisdas (514–23), as intransigent as his predecessors, insisted on a humiliating bargain. Eventually, he forced John of Constantinople to accept Chalcedon on Leo's terms. John was effusive in recognizing Roman authority: "the Catholic religion has always been kept inviolable by the Apostolic See."[14] As for the miaphysites, Anastasius's ambiguity encouraged a new generation of leaders with formidable talent, Philoxenus of Mabbug (bishop 485–523) and Severus of Antioch (bishop 512–18).[15] They interpreted Zeno's *Henotikon* as an explicit attack on Chalcedon, which they happily anathematized, along with Leo's *Tome*. John of Ephesus later described the Council as "anathematized not only by us [the miaphysites], but also by the angels of heaven" – a spirit rooted in the belief that only a pagan could have persecuted Christians.[16]

12 See *Publizistische Sammlungen*.
13 Evagrius Scholasticus, *Ecclesiastical History* 3.30, ed. Bidez and Parmentier, 126 or trans. Whitby, 166–67.
14 *Collectio Avellana, Epistola* 159, 608.
15 See Chesnut, *Three Monophysite Christologies*; De Halleux, *Philoxène de Mabbog*; Torrance, *Christology*; Allen and Hayward, *Severus of Antioch*.
16 John of Ephesus, *Lives of the Eastern Saints* 2, vol. 17: 24 and his *Historia ecclesiastica*, 3.2.39. See Grillmeier, *Jesus der Christus im Glauben der Kirche*, trans. Bowden 2.1, 273 and following.

The accession of Justin I (518), more loyal to Chalcedon, did not meet all western expectations. Justinian I, his nephew and successor (527), was even less helpful. Bishops of Rome quickly learned that their role was to support the emperor – an emperor more opinionated and interventionist than Zeno and Anastasius. They were also caught up in his forceful overthrow of the Ostrogothic regime. Justinian quickly hit his mark. He condemned both Nestorius and Eutyches, and launched a broad attack on Manichees, Montanists, Samaritans, pagans, and eventually Jews.[17] Later difficulties were heralded, however, in his frequently modified but obstinate belief that the second person of the Trinity had taken upon himself "both the wonders and the sufferings" of the flesh, which at once appealed to and affronted the Cyrillian view.[18] Julian of Halicarnassus (d. after 518) had already carried the "theopaschite" debate in the other direction, stressing the unity preserved in the Incarnation to the extent of suggesting that Jesus had only *appeared* to suffer corruption – a view dubbed "aphthartodocetism" by its critics. In practical matters, Justinian was more resolute. He controlled tightly the selection and training of clergy, having a clear notion of his ideal churchman; and he virtually monopolized the erection and funding of churches and other religious institutions by ensuring that no one would be allowed to endow church building on a grander scale than he did.[19]

The Nika riots of 532 gave pause to that initial confidence, inducing a sense of political insecurity. Justinian decided that anti-Chalcedonian fears had to be assuaged by debate rather than coercion. He held a conference, therefore, between Anthimus of Constantinople (Chalcedonian), Theodosius of Alexandria (miaphysite), and the exiled Severus (who had continued to keep in the forefront of debate the theological stance he epitomized as bishop).[20] The situation looked as hopeful as it ever became; but more rigorous supporters of Chalcedon complained to Rome. There followed a brief moment of papal assertiveness. With his campaigns in Italy at a crucial stage, Justinian was willing to recognize Rome as "more ancient" than Constantinople, the *summi pontificatus apex*.[21] But his attempts to translate dialogue into law had ignored Leo's *Tome*. Pope Agapetus I (535–36) succeeded in getting the

17 *Corpus iuris civilis: Codex Justinianus* 1.1.5 (527 CE), 1.5.18 (529 CE); *Novellae* 45 (537 CE), 146 (553 CE).

18 *Corpus iuris civilis: Codex Justinianus* 1.1.5 (527 CE).

19 *Corpus iuris civilis: Codex Justinianus* 1.2.19, 1.3.41 (both 528 CE); *Novellae* 6 (535 CE).

20 Evagrius Scholasticus, *Ecclesiastical History*, 4.10; John of Ephesus, *Lives of the Eastern Saints* 48.

21 *Corpus iuris civilis: Codex Justinianus* 1.1.7 (533 CE), 8; *Novellae* 9 (535 CE), 91.

emperor's orders reversed.[22] The pope was fearlessly unambiguous: he praised Justinian's "painstaking faith," but undercut any layman's claim to "preaching authority."[23]

Such a rebuff could not go unavenged. Justinian was prepared at first to accept his wife's intervention in support of a new papal candidate, Vigilius (pope 537–55),[24] and even urged him to ratify the judgments of Agapetus. Vigilius obliged. The emperor may have feared that Theodora was becoming too independent in her religious loyalties.[25] John of Ephesus always called her "the believing queen," "appointed by God to be a support for the persecuted against the cruelty of the times," and described how the empress sheltered anti-Chalcedonian monks in the palace of Hormisdas in Constantinople.[26] It may have seemed unwise, especially given the military situation in Italy, to leave a bishop of Rome exposed to such ambiguities. By the time Theodora died in 548, however, Justinian's ecclesiastical diplomacy had entered a new phase, destined to leave Vigilius the victim of much greater threats. The emperor succumbed to the notion of a renewed attack on at least portions of the work of Theodore, Theodoret, and Ibas (the so-called "Three Chapters"). These, it was argued, could be made to look anti-Cyril and pro-Nestorius, and their condemnation would assuage the eastern opponents of Chalcedon. Justinian first employed the ruse in an edict of 544, now lost. Churchmen in Italy and Africa were immediately disturbed (and we can sense why from Justinian's later pamphlet *On Right Faith*, issued in 551, likely to provide the gist of the earlier decree, and explicit in subscribing to a Cyrillian view).[27] Justinian reacted promptly: in 548, imperial officials virtually kidnapped Vigilius, forcing him to ratify the edict of 544 in a *iudicatum*. Stirred by commendable scruple, the pope boycotted the second Council of Constantinople (553), but then buckled in a *constitutum* the following year.[28]

Humiliated and broken, Vigilius died on his way back to Rome; but he had long become a marked man among his western colleagues. He was condemned at a council in Carthage in 550, even though recalcitrant Africans, only shortly before, had been exiled or arrested. Their strong feelings were inspired in part by the adamant rejection of imperial pretensions by the deacon Ferrandus. Facundus of Hermiane (another humiliated victim of the council's

22 *Corpus iuris civilis: Novellae* 42 (536 CE).
23 *Collectio Avellana, Epistola* 82.3, 229.
24 See Procopius on his changeable predecessor, Silverius: *Wars*, 5.11.26, 5.14.4, 5.25.13.
25 Procopius, *Secret History*, 10.13; Evagrius Scholasticus, *Ecclesiastical History*, 4.10.
26 John of Ephesus, *Lives of the Eastern Saints* 25 and 47, vol. 18: 529 and 676–84.
27 *Drei dogmatische Schriften*, 73–111.
28 See *Vigiliusbriefe*.

aftermath) also rallied later to the defense of the condemned trio, vigorously and at length,[29] as did the *quaestor* Junillus.[30] Since Belisarius's swift defeat of the Vandals in the 530s, Africa had faced more than a decade of cultural ignorance and military and financial ineptitude, and the time had come to express embitterment.[31] Later writers gradually wove that resentment into a fuller account of Justinian's failure. Corippus, "the last African to write a secular poem in the classical manner," had tried (in 549) to persuade his compatriots that they had gained something from fifteen years of war. With the accession of Justin II in 565, he obligingly supplied a less rosy view in a panegyric at Justinian's expense. Agathias achieved something of the same effect, in contrast to Procopius earlier, who had been unwilling to spoil the image of African "liberation."[32]

The "Three Chapters" controversy marked a vital hiatus, not only in relations between the western church and the imperial authorities, but also in relations within the western church itself. It brought home to the bishops of Italy and Africa the extent to which an undermining of Chalcedon had been inseparable from "reconquest": the subjection of the West had served an eastern agenda. But that subjection had been only partially achieved – thanks not least to western defense of the legacy of Leo the Great. Justinian's final settlement for post-Ostrogothic Italy, the "Pragmatic Sanction" of 554, strengthened the local authority of bishops in civic affairs, but demonstrated also the emperor's failure to impose any direct control over the old western provinces or to gain the allies essential to that control.[33] Meanwhile, bishops of Rome from Pelagius I onward (after 555) were left with the task of redeeming their city's reputation, even among the bishops of northern Italy, not to mention the West more broadly. The task was not made easier by the almost immediate intrusion of the Lombards. In the thirty years before his accession, an agenda was thus marked out that would govern the episcopate of Gregory the Great. It explains that pontiff's meticulous attention to church government in Italy, Africa, and eventually in Gaul, so fully documented in his *Letters*, and his readiness to articulate the needs and hopes of the West independently of the emperor in Constantinople.

29 Facundus of Hermiane, *Pro defensione trium capitularum*. See Cameron, *Procopius*, 27.

30 Junillus, *De partibus divinae legis*. He was successor to the lawyer Tribonian, acquainted with Syrian churchmen, and later praised by Cassiodorus: Jones, Martindale, and Morris, *Prospography*, IIIA, 742; Cassiodorus, *Institutiones*, 10. Negative portrait: Procopius, *Secret History*, 20.17–19, with Cameron, *Procopius*, 28, 63, 231.

31 Frend, *Rise of the Monophysite Movement*, 281.

32 Jones, Martindale, and Morris, *Prosopography*, III, 354–55; Cameron, *Procopius*, 21, 62, and 127 (but note 184–86); Cameron, *Agathias*, 124 and following.

33 *Corpus iuris civilis: Novellae* appendix 7; see *Codex Justinianus* 1.27 (534 CE).

Developments in the East were no less ominous. The council of 553 had achieved little reconciliation, partly because opponents of Chalcedon could not agree among themselves. Already in the early 540s, Theodosius of Alexandria – frustrated at the failure of religious diplomacy, and encouraged by Ghassanid Arabs (allies of Rome but sympathetic to the anti-Chalcedonian cause) – had consecrated two new bishops, Jacob Baradaeus in Edessa and Theodore in Bostra; the latter as bishop of all Arabia. The move represented a crucial shift in the center of gravity of Syrian anti-Chalcedonianism. Jacob in particular represented a growing fault line, carelessly accepted by Paul of Antioch (bishop 557–81) and never wholly bridged. As a freelance missionary, he spread monastic ideals, fostered strong theological loyalties, and gave church government a looser structure. John of Ephesus describes his bewildering speed and bedraggled disguises as he traversed the East, leaving his Chalcedonian pursuers "beating the air."[34] Geopolitics were also involved. Not only were West Syrians venturing more deeply into Ghassanid territory, they were also adding fuel to resentment among the neighboring Lakhmids, closer allies of Persia and sympathetic towards the East Syrian Church. Many of those adverse to Justinian's religious hopes were thus becoming essential players in an all-important buffer zone between two great polities: they would affect not only relations with Persia in the shorter term but also with Islamic Arabs later.

Imperial reaction was no more successful than it had been a hundred years before. Justin II at first rested content with the vague assertion of ancient orthodoxies – a timeworn strategy. His efforts were stymied by anti-Chalcedonian extremists. He then tried to condemn the Three Chapters afresh and honor the memory of Severus – an unacceptable outrage in the eyes of many. In 571, he formulated a miniature *Henotikon* of his own, emphasizing the need for peace (and showing some theological inventiveness).[35] "Pathetic rather than vicious," he finally resorted to persecution until his death in 578.[36] His successor Tiberius II – for John of Ephesus, the "God-loving emperor" – was more preoccupied with Slavic encroachment in the Balkans than with religious coercion. As he put it, "barbarian wars are enough for me: I do not want to take upon myself a war with my own people."[37] Maurice displayed the same attitude after him;

34 John of Ephesus, *Lives of the Eastern Saints* 49, vol. 18: 694.

35 Evagrius Scholasticus, *Ecclesiastical History*, 5.4, foreshadowing seventh-century "monothelite" debate.

36 John of Ephesus: early ignorance, *Historia ecclesiastica*, 3.1.16; later oppression, 3.3.1 and following. Cameron, *Procopius*, 65.

37 John of Ephesus, *Historia ecclesiastica*, 3.3.12, repeating 3.1.37.

but even he became harshly exasperated.[38] The whole period was remarkable for its bitter confusions, which remained essentially disputes between the four great cities involved in the prelude to Ephesus: the development of their theological identities was still governed by their rivalry with one another.

Fractured church, fractured empire

So much for the "theological narrative." As soon as we construct it, however, we stumble upon other developments that had an equally deep effect on Christian self-understanding. Our concern has to be, therefore, not with what lay *behind* religious controversy but with what *accompanied* it. Everything said so far draws us into a web of other developments – barbarian settlement in the West, for example, and associated challenges and opportunities (not least for bishops of Rome); the spectacular growth of Coptic and Syriac cultures in provinces soon to be subject to Islam; the enduring threat of Persia; and changes in the status of emperors and the understanding of empire (illustrated vividly by the high hopes and catastrophic failures of Justinian). The church was, in other words, fractured within a fractured empire. By 500, the old Roman hegemony – single in form, easily traversed, its frontiers merely the boundaries of current aspiration – had gone for ever. With its departure, a different dynamic began to affect the Roman world. Twofold in character, it created for Christianity a new arena within which to define itself and fulfill its purposes.

First, what Romans had previously considered "outside" or beyond themselves was now embedded within their world. Roman culture acquired as a result a richer tone. In the East, Copts and Syrians acclaimed new cultural heroes – Ephraim (d. c. 373) and Shenoute (d. c. 450). Egypt and Syria could no longer be regarded as backwaters or fringes, the haunts of peasant ignorance: an increasing level of literary and theoretical sophistication displayed and invigorated a confident self-identity. In the West, the settler kingdoms seemed to represent a greater inversion of tradition. The Vandal acquisition of North Africa (definitive by 439), the Frankish engulfing of Gaul (widespread by 511), the earlier establishment of a Visigothic kingdom in the same province (by 418, extending eventually into Spain), and of an Ostrogothic kingdom in Italy (by 493) have often been taken as emblems of destruction and discontinuity. Yet, the "kings" concerned – Gaiseric, Clovis, Alaric, and Theoderic – were Roman in their tastes and ambitions, eager to accept Romans as their colleagues: in

38 John of Ephesus, *Historia ecclesiastica*, 3.3.15, and following.

the words of Theoderic, "Every Goth with aspirations plays the Roman."[39] Their novelty, therefore, needs to be carefully defined.

Second, the arrival of those adventurers at once followed and provoked a bewildering series of migrations, which transformed in turn the way in which imperial space was conceived. Modern examples of dismantled empires have accustomed us to the notion that old peripheries occupy traditional centers. The resulting mobility allows new and multiple assertions of identity, carried over long distances. Not surprisingly, the barbarian disturbance of the Roman Empire prompted fresh movement within it. Earlier imperial power had centered equally on a mobile emperor, and authority attached as much to persons as to places; but now, both Romans and barbarians were faced with more numerous epicenters of power. Travel between them accelerated. An eastern embassy to the Huns in the 440s encountered Roman traders and agents on the same road.[40] In the Ostrogothic period, numerous Greek speakers traveled west to Italy and beyond, and numerous Latin speakers tasted "exile" in Constantinople: Dionysius Exiguus and Cassiodorus illustrate a broader trend.[41] Churchmen were prominent as ambassadors, answering the *basilikē keleusis*, the imperial summons to that service.[42] Others were forced into exile by religious controversy, often accompanied by their followers. Pilgrimage, a prominent feature of late Roman devotion, not only peopled existing routes, but also transformed both the points of departure and return and the goals of religious fervor, whether close or distant.[43] Along the same routes, saints' relics were increasingly transported, to bring objects of devotion closer to home and to enhance the religious standing of the churches and churchmen who sought them out.[44]

That constant movement, by both the intrusive and the itinerant, betokened instability. The new kingdoms, for example, were liable to collapses of their

39 "Romanus miser imitatur Gothum et utilis Gothus imitatur Romanum," in Anonymus Valesianus, pars posterior, 12 (61), 546.

40 Priscus, *Fragmentum Historicorum Graecorum*, 11.2.144–48, 313–55, 407–35; Blockley, *Fragmentary Classicizing Historians*, 252, 262–64, 266–68.

41 See Burns, *History of the Ostrogoths*; O'Donnell, *Cassiodorus*. Examples of later easterners in the West: Gregory of Tours, *History of the Franks*, 10.26; Gregory the Great, *Dialogues*, 3.14.

42 Justinian, *Corpus iuris civilis: Novellae* 6.2 (535 CE), 40. See Lee, *Information and Frontiers*.

43 See Hunt, *Holy Land Pilgrimage*; Walker, *Holy City, Holy Places*; Wilken, *Land Called Holy*; Frankfurter, *Pilgrimage and Holy Space*.

44 Vignette: *Life of Eugendus* in *Vies des pères du Jura*, 3.16 (155–56), ed. Martine 404–406, trans. Vivian 172–73. Other examples: Gregory of Tours, *History of the Franks*, 10.31; Épaone (517 CE), canon 25, *Concilia Galliae*, 30. See Grabar, *Martyrium*; Brown, *Cult of the Saints*; Heinzelmann, *Translationsberichte*; Hayward and Howard-Johnston, *Cult of the Saints*. More generally: Burns and Edie, *Urban Centers and Rural Contexts*; Mills and Grafton, *Conversion*.

own, barbarian supplanting barbarian. Visigoths and Burgundians in Gaul were battered by both Huns in the fifth century and Franks in the early sixth; Vandals and Ostrogoths, finally destabilized by the armies of Justinian in the 530s and 550s respectively, had already antagonized one another and, in the case of the Ostrogoths, had faced strong pressure from the Franks. Lombards in the 560s simply filled a vacuum left by Justinian's limited victories. Relations with Persia were analogously labile, governed to some extent by events within Persia itself. An "endless peace" was declared in 532, but disrupted by two decades of intermittent warfare after 540. A "fifty-years peace," sealed in 562, was similarly annulled by a new phase of aggression at the end of the century, which resulted in the Persian occupation of much of the East, only brought to a close by the emperor Heraclius in 632.[45] Over the same period, ominous new intrusions in the Balkans preoccupied Tiberius, Maurice, and Phocas (602–10), and adjustments of loyalty developed, as already mentioned, among Byzantium's Arab allies, not to the empire's advantage.

The Christianity of the future

The correlation between the two processes – doctrinal estrangement and geopolitical instability – remains problematic. The course of Christian history in the seventh century and beyond is certainly unintelligible without attention to both, and each provides a context, if not an explanation, for the other. It remains to describe the characteristics of Christian life that were at once the product of that disruption and the legacy of a more distant past. The disruption undoubtedly affected the legacy. The "Byzantine" or "Syrian" or "early medieval" churches were not radically removed from their ancestry, any more than was the empire itself; but they now faced questions inevitably recast by new circumstance. How was one to define and maintain a Christian community, and how was one to defend its ideals persuasively and with effect?

Defining the community

Christian communities were defined, as had long been the case, by their cult: by baptism and the Eucharist, by bishops and priests, and by the buildings within which those cultic leaders acted out their roles.[46] Definition was essentially a local achievement. We have already seen with what difficulty the great cities of the empire had, in religious affairs, acquired and maintained their

45 Menander Protector, *History*, 6.1, 54–75.
46 See Elm, *Die Macht der Weisheit*; Sterk, *Renouncing the World*.

influence. They did not exercise unchallenged control over large blocs of territory: their immediate influence may have been strong, but it became less marked with distance – Constantinople's over Armenia or the western Balkans; Alexandria's over the upper Nile; Antioch's over the Persian borderlands; and Rome's over Italy, Africa, and Gaul. The same limitations affected proportionately the more humble centers of religious life. John of Ephesus provides a vivid example in his portrait of Symeon (the "mountaineer," as he calls him), who knocked discipline into wild villagers of the hills, ordered their liturgies, schooled their children, and dragooned as many as possible into the ascetic life (a telling list of priorities).[47] Bishops in both East and West would have been at once grateful for the extension of their influence and fearful of its potential independence.[48]

In the West, a wealth of anecdote makes it paradoxically difficult to build up a precise picture of how bishops functioned. Gregory of Tours (d. 594) appears a rich source; but one must beware his governing program, especially his view of the proper relationship between a bishop and a king: he wished upon his peers the status he aspired to himself.[49] Occasionally, however, we gain a less guarded glimpse, as in the tale of Parthenius the tax collector. Pursued by a crowd swearing vengeance against his harsh methods, Parthenius seeks the aid of no less than two bishops, asking them "to quell the riot of the enraged citizens by their sermons." His expectation is as revealing as their subsequent failure. The story ends with a skirmish between people and church officials, resulting in the discovery of the doomed Parthenius hiding in a chest of church vestments. So many components of religious power are brought together in this anecdote: relations between secular and religious leaders, the implied force of a bishop's words, the independence of the people, and the supposition (disappointed) that church buildings, church guile, and church property will remain protected.[50]

The story reminds us also that the influence of churchmen could be impeded not only in rural or remote areas but also in the very towns over which they presided. Their wish to affect rural populations depended upon recasting in Christian terms the traditional nexus between *municipium* and *territorium*. Hence their care in transporting beyond the city's walls the rituals of the urban church – processions, for example, or ceremonies of veneration at the tombs

47 John of Ephesus, *Lives of the Eastern Saints* 16, vol. 17: 229–47.

48 Western examples: Orange (511 CE), canon 25, *Concilia Galliae*, 11; Clermont (535 CE), canon 15, *Concilia Galliae*, 109; Orange (541 CE), canon 7, *Concilia Galliae*, 133–34.

49 Heinzelmann, *Gregory of Tours*, trans. Carroll, especially 36–93.

50 Gregory of Tours, *History of the Franks*, 3.36.

of martyrs.[51] And the bishop, no less than the distinguished aristocrat, was a potential country dweller. We know from the will of Caesarius of Arles (d. 542) that a bishop might command substantial property beyond a city's walls.[52] Quintianus, bishop of Rodez, fleeing from Arian opponents, sought refuge with his colleague Eufrasius of Clermont-Ferrand, whereat his host gave him "accommodation with fields around and vineyards," which he described as "resources of this diocese . . . sufficient to support us both."[53] Religious leaders thus followed the same path as their secular counterparts. In the fourth century, provincial elites had given their loyalty to regimes that honored them on the broader stage of imperial office. By the fifth century, they had begun to focus their energies, bishops included, on local settings better calculated to enhance their status.[54]

In the East, a bishop's world was more built about, even outside the major cities. There was a greater density of urban and village settlement, and correspondingly a larger number of episcopal sees. The interstices of open country were smaller in extent, and only higher and less fertile land was distinctly remote. Other factors made the East different from the West. In the Balkans, destructive encroachment and vigorous campaigning, from the late sixth century onward, disrupted the rhythms of settled life and penned it within narrower confines – to an extent from which the West was now beginning to recover. In Egypt, the centralized authority that Alexandria had long enjoyed continued to make control of the south problematic. In Syria, the world represented by Jacob Baradaeus created among churchmen closer to Antioch and the coast a sense of having lost their grip on the wilder border country to the east. But, for all those differences, localism was as prevalent in Syria as it was in Gaul. The independence and, in some cases, self-interest of bishops under Persian threat in the sixth century was as marked a century later under the threat of Islam.[55]

The bishop, as definer of a community, came most into his own during the celebration of the Christian liturgy. The setting for that drama was as important as the drama itself. A bishop would see a new or refurbished basilica as

51 Rogations: Avitus of Vienne, *Homilia de rogationibus*; Orange (511 CE), canon 27, *Concilia Galliae*, 11–12; Lyons (567–70 CE), canon 6, *Concilia Galliae*, 202; Gregory of Tours, *History of the Franks*, 4.5, 9.21.

52 Caesarius of Arles, *Testament* (especially 9), 67–76.

53 Gregory of Tours, *History of the Franks*, 2.36. See Épaone (517 CE), canon 12, *Concilia Galliae*, 27.

54 See Clark and Bowes in Burns and Edie, *Urban Centers*; for the broader context: Magdalino, *New Constantines*.

55 Procopius, *Wars*, 2.6.15–2.7.37, 2.13.8–15, 2.20.1–7; Al-Balâdhuri, *Kitâb*, 172–74, 200, trans. Hitti, 269–73, 314–15.

an act of generosity towards his *civitas*, as well as an investment calculated to enhance his influence and safeguard his memory. Such motives had long inspired the grand architectural gesture, the stylistic embellishment of cities. They provided a space – a temple, perhaps, but also a bath or a hippodrome – in which the citizen could find an identity at once elevated and shared. In later centuries, we can expect to find a shift in the perceived purpose and intended audience of such enterprises. Christian buildings at once symbolized and reinforced the new communities that bishops were willing to preside over – a "people of God." Sturdy brickwork, opaque windows, and unpretentious tiling were almost exercises in understatement. Exteriors were more massive than inspiring, hinting at capital, rank, and the command of a long-term workforce – characteristic resources of their (often lay) patrons. Inside, however, the reassuring structures were overlaid with vibrant mosaics and frescoes, worn like a richly encrusted garment over a plain body. Surrounded by such texture and movement, the worshiper felt less rooted to the ground, at once enfolded and uplifted.

Ancient forms were thus carried into new settings: a rich body of scholarship continues to explore the survival in the Christian empire of artistic themes and motifs traditional to classical culture.[56] But artistic endeavor can never be divorced from context. The raw material, the patronage, and the skill may have been expensive, dependent on leisure and an informed sense of antecedent, reflecting the wealth and sensibility of the elite. As times changed, however, the bishop was the impresario. The décor presented images of virtue, scenes from sacred writings, emblems of a universal salvation, and a fulfillment beyond death and time. The implications were entirely theological. Gregory of Tours presents a telling vignette: the wife of Namatius, bishop of Clermont-Ferrand, "used to hold in her lap a book from which she would read stories of events which happened long ago, and tell the workmen what she wanted painted on the walls." The anecdote reinforces several points: the church being decorated with "colored frescoes" was outside the city; and a passing "poor man," who had popped in to pray, mistook the bishop's wife for "one of the needy" and promptly gave her a piece of bread. Within the embellished fabric, a scene of reminiscence and artistic skill, a new type of social drama was played out: mercy was bestowed, rank rendered ambiguous.[57]

Those Christian buildings did not stand lifeless, but were put to use – indeed, took on their full form only when they *were* in use. The interdependence of

56 See Elsner, *Art and the Roman Viewer*; Krautheimer, *Early Christian and Byzantine Architecture*; Mathews, *Art and Architecture* and *Clash of Gods*.

57 Gregory of Tours, *History of the Franks*, 2.17.

sacred space and sacred action is most obvious in the startling inventiveness of eastern church building in the sixth century. Unimpeded movement and vision were increasingly made possible – in contrast to a lingering conservatism in the West, where the old basilica style, elongated and colonnaded, lasted longer. For accounts of what happened in the eastern buildings, we have to rely on evidence from the seventh century and later. The shape, décor, and atmosphere of the church, all skillfully conceived, were designed to bring out the theological meaning of the liturgy conducted within it.[58] The liturgy provided the indispensable setting within which to make lessons clear – not only in homilies, but also in singing, processions, the images of earthly hierarchies (emperors, bishops, courtiers, and soldiers) and their heavenly counterparts (God or Jesus enthroned as judge or teacher and the surrounding company of saints and martyrs), and even in the simple depiction of scriptural event. The religious portraiture of the period used to be thought of as static and hieratic; but, when figures are multiplied within a single space, they contribute to a lively and mobile scene with dramatic or narrative force.

Defending the ideal

Few bishops were faced, on their accession, with a clean sheet: one inherited one's diocese, with its habits of mind and webs of patronage. The career of Hilary of Arles (d. 449) illustrates brilliantly how cautious and subtle one might have to be.[59] Bishops, especially in the East, were also exposed to the force of government displeasure: deposition, exile, and destitution permanently outstripped, in their case, negotiation as tools of enforcement.[60] But the greatest challenge was the very Christianity of the people one was appointed to govern. One could never take for granted the quality of their devotion. As with an emperor's aspirations, the impact of homilies or conciliar decrees was neither predictable nor assured. The ostensibly Christian populace still needed awakening to the full implications of their adhesion, still needed to be taught how much of their religious legacy they should reject and how much they might tolerate and retain.[61] Gregory the Great, a generation later, recounts many instances of persistent appeal to alternative sources of healing and exorcism.[62] "Christianization" was not a matter merely of defeating "paganism": it

58 See opening chapters of Mathews, *Art and Architecture* and throughout *Early Churches*; Mango, *Byzantine Architecture*, especially 97–160; Mainstone, *Hagia Sophia*.
59 See Honoratus's *Life of Hilary of Arles*, with Mathisen, *Ecclesiastical Factionalism*.
60 *Corpus iuris civilis: Codex Justinianus* 1.5.8 (455 CE); 1.5.18 (529 CE).
61 See Flint, *Rise of Magic*; Mills and Grafton, *Conversion*. More negative: MacMullen, *Christianity and Paganism*.
62 Example: Gregory the Great, *Dialogues*, 1.10.

meant implanting more securely the system of belief that the population had already in theory embraced – converting the converted. Nor could a bishop rest content with the force of law or secular authority, no matter how friendly he might be with those who wielded it. He was faced with more than criminal intransigence, and had to deploy other traditional forms of role and status – those of the orator, the scholar, the man of virtue – in order to bring to bear in this new cause the established techniques of instruction and persuasion.

The chief instrument of episcopal power, therefore, was the homily. We must be cautious in the face of selective editing (not always sanctioned by the preacher himself); but in homilies – where they were personal or spontaneous – we see close up the bonds between priest and people. In the late Roman West, there was a striking proliferation of sermon collections, which attached the authority of an eminent figure to material that any churchman might make use of. (Where a bishop or priest was absent, a deacon might read a sermon from the writings of the fathers.[63]) Augustine proved a mother lode; but a collection like the *Eusebius Gallicanus* shows how much eastern material could also infiltrate the West. Caesarius of Arles presents us with another model – indeed, he seems to have been ready to countenance such a collection under his name, designed to spread his own message and to bolster the impact of his colleagues.[64] He himself had drawn in similar ways on those who had come before him.

What was the effect of this material? There is at times a hectoring tone, and evidence of decreasing exegetical sophistication; but the chief aim seems to have been to forge agreement, to impress upon hearers that they were defined by their membership of the church more than by their personal ambitions or failures.[65] Selfishness and willful isolation were the features most deplored by priests and most frequently identified as causes for regret. "If we refuse," said Caesarius, "to do what we have promised to God [in baptism], I do not know whether we will be able to preserve fidelity to men." On the other hand, "Then there will be true and perfect peace, when we are at peace, not only with others, but also with ourselves." And he described brilliantly a new species of interplay between "public" and "private" virtue, between the civic and the personal: "One who gives alms out of the desire to be praised by men gives them publicly, even if he bestows them in secret, since he seeks praise from men. However, one who gives alms solely out of love for God, in order that other men may imitate him in this good work and that God, not himself, may

63 Vaison (529 CE), canon 2, *Concilia Galliae*, 79.

64 Flint, *Rise of Magic*, 42–45, 88. See Klingshirn, *Caesarius of Arles*.

65 See Bailey, "Building Urban Christian Communities."

be praised, gives them in secret even if he does so in public."[66] Faith in oratory persisted in the work of Gregory the Great, for whom the "true preacher . . . stretches out his arms at the end of his address and calms the troubled spirits of the assembled people, calling them back to one way of thinking." The pope's *Pastoral Care* was designed in part to facilitate that effect: "He, then, who strives to speak wisely, should greatly fear lest by his words the unity of the hearers [*audientium unitas*] be confounded."[67]

In the East, there was a comparable dependence on patristic antecedents – John Chrysostom especially.[68] It is hard to judge whether insistence on regular preaching was an indication of neglect. The Trullan or "Quinisext" synod of 692 summed up expectations operative since the time of Justinian: sermons were to be preached on Sundays and festivals throughout the empire, strictly in accord with the teaching of the fathers.[69] A sixth-century collection of sermons, preserved under the name of the Constantinopolitan presbyter Leontius, has a special interest. Freed from the responsibilities of episcopal address, he seems to have established an easier rapport with his audience. He was also surprisingly original.[70] In other respects, the setting and splendor of the liturgy may have compensated for a lack of explicit exhortation. One should not underestimate the homiletic effect – indeed, intention – of extended chant, such as the *kontakia* composed by Romanos (fl. c. 540), which had some antecedent in the *madrashe* and *memre* of Ephraim (d. 373).[71]

The thought-world revealed in sermons seems at times vitiated by superstition and vulgarity – emblematic of the degree to which "Christianization" had failed. Yet, we face here simply another example of how the formerly extraneous was incorporated into a changing culture. To preach was still to exercise an elite skill, and to reach beyond the elite was always difficult; but it was usually attempted, and those speaking and listening, writing and reading at the cultural hub had been captured by a new sensibility and interest. Similar considerations should govern our understanding of hagiography, which was also the product of elite industry and probably designed (more than

66 Caesarius of Arles, *Sermones*, 12.3, ed. Morin, vol. 103: 60, and trans. Mueller vol. 1: 70; 166.4, ed. vol. 104: 680, trans. vol. 2: 400; 146.1, ed. vol. 104: 600, trans. vol. 1: 309.

67 Gregory the Great, *Dialogues*, 4.4, trans. Zimmerman, 193; *Cura pastoralis*, 2.4.67–9, ed. Rommel 192, trans. Davis 54; see also 1.7, 3.39. Compare with John Chrysostom, *De sacerdotio*, 5.1–3.

68 See Krumbacher, *Geschichte*, 160–76.

69 Mansi 11, 952.

70 See Leontius, *Fourteen Homilies*.

71 Romanos: Grosdidier de Matons, *Romanos le Mélode*, and Schork, *Sacred Song*; Ephraim: Brock, *Luminous Eye*, and Griffith, "Ephraem, the Deacon of Edessa" and "Images of Ephraem." See also Petersen, *Diatessaron*.

sermons) for an elite audience. Secure in their privilege and comfort, the refined could live dangerously and invite into their villas or town houses the strange but impressive heroes of a world that they would never visit and that even their informants might not have known at first hand.[72] There was no simple lapse or decline, therefore, in any of this material, whether oral or written. It remained firmly in educated hands, and many who deployed it retained a capacity for skepticism.[73] When we witness in hagiography, for example, the persistence of visions, we detect a readiness not only to control and legitimate such experiences, but also to incorporate the popular into stable and orthodox communities.[74] Writers acknowledged an old and rich tradition of dreams and visions, even as they admitted that the frontier between the explicable and the wondrous was never stable.[75] In that sense, they made available to a broader audience what had hitherto been a sophisticated indulgence – exactly the reverse of what is often imagined.

Alongside this rhetoric, we overhear a jangle of anxiety and effort in a sudden abundance of conciliar documents. In the East, the ebb and flow of Christological debate, dominating most of the gatherings, was complicated by imperial pressure. Equally in the sixth-century West (during a golden age of conciliar industry), the *consensus* of barbarian kings was deemed essential to the enforcement of episcopal *sententia*.[76] Even so, bishops were able to attend independently to disciplinary needs. The "Quinisext" synod, with its desire for *taxis* or "order" (its opening word), provides an inherited compendium of odd behavior: giving communion to the dead, singing in church without restraint, observing in traditional ways the appearance of the new moon, using accounts of martyrdom to validate pagan error, and (naturally) telling fortunes.[77] In Gaul, the majority of canons (as at Chalcedon) were concerned with relations among the clergy themselves, and then with marriage and sexual conduct.[78] Repetitive exasperation reveals in another register the bishops' failure to secure an orthodox approach to either doctrine or devotion. If the

72 See Patlagean, "Ancienne hagiographie byzantine"; Rousseau in Hayward and Howard-Johnston, *Cult of Saints*.

73 Dagron, "L'ombre d'un doute"; Gregory the Great, *Dialogues*, 3.37.

74 Flint, *Rise of Magic*, echoed by Moreira, *Dreams, Visions and Spiritual Authority*. De Nie, *Views*, attributes more control to the clergy.

75 Miller, *Dreams*. Sulpicius Severus, *Vie de saint Martin*, see commentary by J. Fontaine, ep. 2.2–3, vol. 135: 1188–96.

76 Clovis as precedent: Orange (511 CE), introduction, *Concilia Galliae*, 4.

77 Canons 61, 63, 65, 75, 83 in Mansi 11, 969–80. On communion and the dead, see Auxerre (561/605 CE), canon 12, *Concilia Galliae*, 267.

78 Clerical relations: Chalcedon, canons 9, 13, 19, *Acta conciliorum oecumenicorum*, 2.1, 160–61; Épaone (517 CE), canon 5, *Concilia Galliae*, 25; Clermont (535 CE), canon 11, *Concilia Galliae*, 107; Orange (538 CE), canon 16, *Concilia Galliae*, 120–21.

Christians of Gaul were indulging in what councils forbade – swearing on the heads of animals, visiting sacred trees and fountains, forgetting the new meaning attached to old festivals, consulting *incantatores* and *divinatores* – their full conversion lay very much in the future.[79] Virtue and miraculous power could be dangerously confused with wizardry and hysteria.[80] In such an atmosphere, few bishops could settle quietly and map out their plans for their own communities. Episcopal letters, whether surviving accidentally or deliberately collected, testify to the chaotic involvements such men might face. Even in calmer instances, the story of daily commitment is swamped by complaint, inquiry, flattery, and defense – a trajectory of increasing distraction in both East and West.[81] Even the epistolary influence of "holy men" – Isidore of Pelusium (d. c. 440), for example, Nilus of Ancyra (d. c. 430), or Barsanuphius (d. 540) and his correspondent John – was achieved at the cost of interruption and compromise.

A particular difficulty afflicted the western church: the weaning of Christian barbarian settlers from their Arian loyalties (the accidental result of their original conversion under Arian emperors). The problem had arisen within the Roman frontiers, and alliances between the empire and its northern intruders were always threatened by the settlers' abiding heresy. Hence, long after the definitive condemnation of Arius and his later admirers at the Council of Constantinople in 381, churchmen remained fearful of Arian influence. Their faithful allusions to Nicaea and their conservative litanies against Marcionites and Paulinianists were quickly injected with alarm when they considered the contemporary errors that pressed upon them. They were naturally disturbed by extreme examples of persecution, such as that inflicted by the Vandals, especially under Huneric (477–84) and to a lesser degree by the Visigoth Euric (466–84) in southern Gaul. Even the milder Theoderic induced tension in Italy and exacerbated relations with both Constantinople and the Franks.

When it came to the doctrinal integrity of a local community, a nearby Arian bishop could seem as dangerous as an Arian king.[82] Gregory of Tours prepared his readers for what they might expect of Arians anywhere, with a vivid tale of martyrdom inflicted by the Vandals even before they had left Spain for Africa. But then he presented an equally circumstantial account of

79 See *Concilia Galliae* for Orange (541 CE), canon 16, 136; Council of Bishop Aspasius (551 CE), canon 3, 163–64; Auxerre (561/605 CE), canon 3, 265; Tours (567 CE), canon 23, 191; Narbonne (589 CE), canon 14, 256.

80 Gregory of Tours, *History of the Franks*, 9.6, 10.25, 29. See Rousselle, *Croire et guérir*.

81 Succinct vignette: Sidonius, *Poems and Letters*, *Epistola* 4.9.5, vol. 2: 106. The whole letter is a brilliant portrait, together with *Epistola* 4.25 and 7.9.5–25, vol. 2: 164–68 and 338–58.

82 Gregory the Great, *Dialogues*, 3.28–9.

later rivalry among African bishops (this under Huneric), pitting a vain and powerless Arian against Eugenius of Carthage (later exiled to Gaul). Truth was at stake in their contest, but so also was the standing of a bishop in the eyes of his people.[83] It might be thought that the (ultimately) Catholic loyalty of the Franks countered real danger. As Gregory's Clovis puts it, "I find it hard to go on seeing these Arians occupy a part of Gaul. With God's help let us invade them."[84] Yet, the Franks were at first ambiguous in their inclinations, having strong ties with Arian settlers elsewhere.[85] Gregory, some ninety years later, still felt a need to present a potted history of "that evil sect." He rounded off his account of the early days with a careful declaration of his own orthodoxy; and he voiced a hesitant assurance: "the true believers may well lose many things . . . the heretics on the other hand have not much advantage to show."[86] All that, in spite of the fact that, by his own time, matters had improved. In Visigothic Spain, a natural stronghold of the Arian cause, the ill-fated king Hermenegild converted to orthodox Christianity in 582, partly persuaded by his Frankish wife Ingund. (He had also colluded hopefully with the emperor Tiberius, but then fell victim to his own father's deceit.) The Catholicism of the kingdom as a whole was confirmed under his brother Reccared at the Council of Toledo in 589.

Transcending space and time

Christians in this liminal age displayed a striking ability to stretch their imaginations beyond the limits not only of their late Roman world, but also of their individual lives and the temporal order. Their classical forebears had shown an interest, either scornful or intrigued, in the religions of other peoples, and had some sense of an afterlife and an immaterial realm. Christianity, in its earliest centuries, developed more precise notions: of salvation as a divine gift for the whole of humanity, and of judgment, fulfillment, eternal bliss; in some ways immediate upon individual death, in others a postponed achievement for the community of believers. What sets apart the sixth and seventh centuries is an intensification of both processes, particularly in the West. The universal character of the Christian economy reinforced the obligation to establish it as widely as possible – a belief that had been surprisingly slow in taking root.

83 Gregory of Tours, *History of the Franks*, 2.2–3.
84 Gregory of Tours, *History of the Franks*, 2.37.
85 *Pace* Gregory of Tours, *History of the Franks*, 2.30–31. See Wood, *Merovingian Kingdoms*.
86 Gregory of Tours, *History of the Franks*, 3, preface. An Arian bishop's depression: 9.15.

Meanwhile, eternal life pressed more closely upon the living,[87] less frequently symbolized in a martyr's dramatic sacrifice, and more often enlivened by the heightened expectation of whole communities. The radical disturbance of the western provinces made such intensification more understandable: in the East, where the structures of the Christian empire were, for a time, apparently more secure, the urgency was less evident. The West was thus better prepared, paradoxically, for a future it believed might never materialize, while the East awaited the more spectacular shock of further invasion and enclosure, which would test severely its Christian self-confidence.

Reaching beyond the familiar: the development of a "missionary life"

In the East, the "missionary" image only gradually acquired a form that future periods could make use of. Wanderers like Jacob Baradaeus operated at first within the Roman orbit and sought allies among exiles rather than among genuine strangers. Only the passage of time would make them seem exotic in a more literal sense. Indeed, all the peripheral polities to the east and south upon which Byzantium relied for defense against Persia – Armenia and Ethiopia, for example – were firmly established centers of Christianity. We discover, therefore, in "missionary" sources a postponement of implication: both the manner and the motive of movement beyond the empire were later creations.

The same was true of the West. Sulpicius Severus (d. c. 430?) pitted Martin of Tours against rustic unbelievers, and his biography encouraged later and more adventurous explorers;[88] but in his own day Gaul was visibly Christian. Noricum, evangelized by Severinus in the late fifth century, would scarcely have seemed pagan or remote to readers of Eugippius's *Life of St. Severin* in Italy a generation later (c. 511). In the case of Patrick – often thought of as an emissary to an alien world – it is difficult to judge from contemporary evidence (the *Confessio* and the *Letter to Coroticus*) what his role in Ireland might have been; but he clearly faced a society already familiar with Christian beliefs and institutions. Only later narratives (notably the seventh-century *Life* by Tírechán) picture him venturing into pagan country; and they were constructed for different audiences to serve different purposes.[89] Jonas of Bobbio wrote his biography of Columbanus soon after his hero's death (c. 615). He portrays a wanderer, but one without clear and immediate purpose. Columbanus subsequently

87 Gregory the Great, *Dialogues*, 4.43.
88 Sulpicius, *Vie de St. Martin*, 12.1–14.7; Stancliffe, *Saint Martin*.
89 See Wood, *Missionary Life*, 26–28; De Paor, *Patrick*; Thompson, *Who Was Saint Patrick?*

turned reformer, placed by Jonas for his Italian audience at the head of a tradition that still had fresh and local relevance. Only later could he be cast as a convincing missionary.[90] Gregory of Tours, always ready to present his own career as a blueprint for other churchmen, sometimes made his bishops look like missionaries; but they are tellingly tied to specific places and cast in traditional roles.[91] The Anglo-Saxons seem, like Patrick, a special case; but Augustine journeyed to Kent to strengthen a Christian presence long familiar within the old Roman province. The apostle recalled by Bede depended on Frankish allies, and was anxious (like Gregory himself) to extend the influence of the Roman church in Gaul.[92]

The heavenly future

Images of the future always represent a reordering of the present. The sixth-century church continued to use eternal destiny as a judgment upon presumptuous industry and material success. But the fractured nature of the old *oikoumenē* induced a greater sense of impermanence, a more urgent demand for adapted expectations – already a prominent feature of Augustine's *City of God*. The social models, the reconfiguration of cities, the invitations extended to new audiences, the skillful redeployment of traditional images, literary and artistic, all contributed to a new and dramatic disengagement from the world. As suggested above, art and ceremony reflected the inclination. The heavenly setting of the Eucharistic celebration dissolved the apparent solidity of the building in which it took place. In the words of John Chrysostom, "Do you think [faced with the sight of a priest at his sacrificial task] that you are still among men and standing on the earth? Are you not rather transported to the heavens?" Worshipers were thus brought into the presence of a God elsewhere – the hallmark of Christian achievement in a post-pagan world.[93]

That made for unexpected contrasts on the eve of the seventh century. The *Dialogues* and *Letters* of Gregory the Great and the vivid narratives of Gregory of Tours display both material ebullience and institutional practicality; but that should not distract us from both men's eschatological convictions. Outlining

90 See Wood, *Missionary Life*, 35–39; Clarke and Brennan, *Columbanus*; Lapidge, *Columbanus*.
91 See Wood, *Missionary Life*, 29.
92 See Mayr-Harting, *Coming of Christianity*. Organization of new territory: Gregory the Great, *Registrum epistularum*, 11.39 (601 CE). Gregory to Brunhild and Theuderic, 8.4.20 ff. (597 CE); 11.47.23 ff. and 11.48.6 ff. (both 601 CE); to other figures in Gaul, 11.34.22 ff., 11.38.38 ff., 11.40.32 ff. Bede includes versions of this correspondence, making the preoccupation clear to later generations: *HE*, 1.23 ff., with particular emphasis on Arles, 1.24, 27 (7), 28.
93 John Chrysostom, *De sacerdotio*, 3.4.21–23, 144; see also 3.4.1–3.

the woes of Italy in his day, Gregory the Great could conclude, "I do not know what is happening elsewhere, but in this land of ours the world is not merely announcing its end, it is pointing directly to it."[94] Italy and Gaul had already been transported into another economy, a system of selflessness and wonder that constantly undercut the expectations of false ambition and rooted interest. Yet, an ordered church supplied the social element, the *societas Christiana*, within which the spiritual growth of individuals could be fostered and preserved.[95]

This may be the best context within which to place what was possibly Christianity's greatest contribution to the centuries that followed; greater than its impact on governance and law, its channelling of violence and repudiation of feud, its enduring attachment to the legacy of the ancient world – namely, the exaltation of virginity and the development of the monastic life. The wealth of literature that illustrates the early phases of that development – *Rules* and *Lives* especially – was essentially a literature of nostalgia. Cassian's *Conferences*, the *Lives* of Martin or Daniel the Stylite, the anecdotal histories of Palladius, Theodoret, John of Ephesus, Cyril of Scythopolis, or John Moschus, the *Sayings of the Fathers*, the *Rule* of Benedict: all were designed to recall and preserve a discipline deeply admired and in danger of disappearing. They exaggerated the value of submission and detachment, which readers then attempted to put more literally into practice. Above all, they presented an image of virtue and suggested the circumstances in which it could best be fostered and perfected.

Christianity had never been the only religious system to encourage such an emphasis, and its expression of the ideal owed much to pagan antecedents. The nature of the inner life, the capacity of human freedom, the tendencies of history and the plans of God: all were the staples of ancient thought. What Christianity emphasized was anticipation over realization: the virtuous did not simply bring to the surface their innate capacities, but waited upon the reward of their otherwise unpromising efforts. The virtuous Christian was *homo eschatologicus*; Christian fulfillment was essentially delayed. Yet, the resulting suspense was rarely allowed to be passive or indifferent. The chief characteristic of the period may have been its manner of organizing the unfulfilled. Believers who placed their bets on an eternal destiny were nevertheless remarkably industrious. In the words of Gregory the Great, "our predestination to heaven has been so ordained that we must exert ourselves to attain it."[96] Such Christians reinforced their sense of God's presence in glorious (and

94 Gregory the Great, *Dialogues*, 3.38, trans. Zimmerman, 187.
95 Heinzelmann, *Gregory of Tours*, trans. Carroll, 172–81.
96 Gregory the Great, *Dialogues*, 1.8, trans. Zimmerman, 32.

expensive) churches, inventive in both structure and decoration. They pursued their transcendent virtue in monasteries of growing complexity and wealth – magnets of admiration (and therefore centers of power), springboards of political influence, and serious-minded exploiters of agricultural wealth. They fortified their commitment to an enduring community by impelling the powerful to a sense of service and by caring in ordered ways for the vagrant, the sick, and the poor.[97]

The sense of what the future might hold was different in different areas of the ancient world – there were still "Christianities." The East may have been more complacent about the ultimate fortunes of the Christian empire; the West may have been more fearful in the face of ethnic change, economic decline, and royal government. Nevertheless, to walk abroad in the towns and cities of this increasingly Christianized domain was to walk along streets and among buildings whose very permanence, grandeur, authority, and sheer usefulness were solid symbols of a *civitas* yet to come.

97 See Patlagean, *Pauvreté économique et pauvreté sociale*; Brown, *Poverty and Leadership*, and in Brown, Cracco Ruggini, and Mazza, *Governanti e intellettuali*. Gallic bishops were *obliged* to provide such services: Orange (511 CE), canon 16, *Concilia Galliae*, 9. For Italy: Gregory the Great, *Dialogues*, 3.34, 4.23.

2

The emergence of Byzantine Orthodoxy, 600–1095

ANDREW LOUTH

Introduction

The period from 600 to 1095 CE was a period of enormous change for the Byzantine Empire, the most significant cause of this change being the rise of Islam in the first part of the seventh century and the continuing presence in the east thereafter of an Arab empire. Islam administered a massive shock to the Byzantine world, from which it took the empire almost two centuries to recover. This recovery was nevertheless partly due to changes in the Arab empire itself, which, with the shift of its capital from Damascus to Baghdad in 750, became a much more eastward-facing society, thus relieving the pressure on Byzantium. For this initial period, 600 to 850, traditional historical sources are sparse, leaving us in ignorance about many issues. From the ninth century onwards, the Byzantine Empire began to recover, and in the tenth and early eleventh centuries, under the Macedonian dynasty, expanded and regained something of its former glory. The church shared in this new mood of expansion and prosperity, in which it found the opportunity to build on the sense of orthodoxy that had emerged with the repudiation of iconoclasm and the "Triumph of Orthodoxy" in 843. This sense of emergent Orthodoxy manifested itself in the realms of art and scholarship, in monastic revival and missionary expansion. Sources for this later period are more abundant, enabling much greater insight into the various facets of Christianity, as well as other aspects of the empire. For these reasons, the first part of this chapter, dealing with 600 to 850, will be primarily chronological, whereas the second part, dealing with the later period, will take a more thematic approach.

A historical survey, 600–850

At the beginning of our period, the Byzantine Empire was still recognizably the restored Christian Roman Empire of Justinian I (527–65). It could still make some claim to be a Mediterranean empire, embracing almost everywhere that touched on the Mediterranean coast, though its hold on Spain was quite fragile. Already by 600, however, this vision of the Christian Roman Empire was being fragmented. Slavs had begun to cross the Danube and settle throughout the Balkan peninsula in regions called by the Byzantines *Sklavinias*. Under the leadership of the more warlike Avars, the Slavs were beginning to threaten the Byzantine presence, laying siege to Thessaloniki and, in 626, to Constantinople. Their presence in the Balkans drove a wedge between the two capitals of the Byzantine Empire, Rome and Constantinople, impeding communication between West and East. To the east, Persia, the traditional enemy of the Mediterranean empire in its various historical forms, was poised to strike. Taking as an excuse the overthrow of the Emperor Maurice (582–602) by Phocas (602–10) in 602, the Persian Empire embarked on an invasion of the Byzantine Empire, taking Jerusalem in 614, and annexing its eastern provinces from Syria to Egypt. In these provinces seized from the Byzantine Empire, the Shah of Persia discovered divisions among the Christians that he sought to exploit.

Christological controversy[1]

These divisions went back to the Council of Chalcedon (451) that had attempted to achieve agreement on the Incarnation of Christ among Christians by affirming that, while in Christ there were two perfect natures, human and divine, there was only one *hypostasis*. For most Christians of the East, it was to Cyril, patriarch of Alexandria (410–44), that they looked for guidance in their understanding of Christ. The bishops at Chalcedon thought that their Christological definition expressed Cyril's understanding of the matter, but many disagreed and rejected Chalcedon. These anti-Chalcedonians, called by their opponents "monophysites," had not only survived in the decades after Chalcedon, but had prospered, especially in Syria and Egypt, despite periodic persecution by the Byzantine authorities. Shortly after the fall of Jerusalem to the Persians, the shah, Chosroes II (590–628), decided to exploit this situation by supporting the anti-Chalcedonians in Syria, Armenian and western Mesopotamia, and Egypt, after it fell to the Persians in 618. The anti-Chalcedonian patriarch of Antioch, Athanasius the Camel-Driver (595–631), welcomed this passing of the "Chalcedonian night."

This provoked a counter-move from the Byzantine Emperor Heraclius (610–41), and Sergius, patriarch of Constantinople (610–38), who, in consultation

1 See Dorfmann-Lazarev in this volume.

with bishops in Sinai and Egypt, came up with a compromise formula (monenergism), by which they hoped to reconcile the supporters and opponents of Chalcedon. This compromise maintained with Chalcedon that in Christ there were two natures and one person, with the refinement that there was only one activity (Greek: *energeia*), that Dionysius the Areopagite (fl. early sixth century) had called divine-human or "theandric." In 628 Heraclius successfully invaded Persia, provoking a court rebellion in which the shah was overthrown, and recovering from Ctesiphon the relic of the True Cross that had been taken there from Jerusalem. With this relic, Heraclius began a triumphal procession through the recovered provinces, proposing reunion with the anti-Chalcedonians on the basis of monenergism, and achieving, it appears, some success. But monenergism found its greatest success in Egypt. In 633, Cyrus, originally from Phasi in Georgia, whom Heraclius had appointed both patriarch of Alexandria and augustal prefect of Egypt (631–42), reached a major reconciliation with the Theodosians, as the Egyptian anti-Chalcedonians were called, set out in a Pact of Union, in nine chapters. Cyrus reported his success to Sergius of Constantinople, who in return reported it to Pope Honorius I (625–38). This achievement was, however, marred by the opposition of a distinguished scholar and monk, Sophronius (c. 560–638), for whom the Nine Chapters were simply heretical. Sophronius traveled to Constantinople, and then to Rome, with his grievance, but achieved nothing more than a decision from Sergius, in his *Psephos* of 634, to forbid any discussion of the number of activities in Christ. By this time Sophronius was Patriarch of Jerusalem. A further refinement of monenergism was proposed in 638, in the *Ekthesis*, composed by Sergius and promulgated by Heraclius, which affirmed that Christ, one person in two natures, had yet a single, divine will: a doctrine called monothelitism. This provoked opposition led by one of Sophronius's disciples, Maximus the Confessor (c. 580–662), then resident in North Africa (Sophronius now being dead), which culminated in the Lateran Synod of 649, masterminded, it would seem, by Maximus and called by Pope Martin (649–55), that condemned monenergism and monothelitism, and those churchmen who had endorsed these heresies.

By this time, however, the Byzantine Empire had fallen to a much more serious opponent than the Persians, namely the Arab tribes, united under Islam, that, within barely fifteen years of the death of the prophet Muḥammad (632), had crushed the Persian Empire and seized the eastern provinces of the Byzantine Empire, this time for good. Jerusalem fell in 638, surrendered to the caliph, Umar I (634–44), by Sophronius. The controversy over monothelitism, taking place against the background of Byzantine defeat, undermined the possibility it offered of union with the anti-Chalcedonians, now subject to Islam, and with it any Byzantine retaliation based on such a union. The sense that Maximus's theological stubbornness was tantamount to sedition is palpable in the accounts of his trial at the Byzantine court, which led to his condemnation for heresy, mutilation, and death in exile in 662.[2] By the time the Byzantine Empire formally renounced monenergism and monothelitism at the Sixth Ecumenical Council in 680–81, the Umayyad Empire was firmly established, with its capital in Damascus.

The definition of Orthodoxy

Despite the desperate political conditions of the seventh century, this was, paradoxically, one of the greatest periods of Byzantine theology. Maximus the Confessor based his opposition to the imperial Christological nostrums on a theological vision, drawing together the several strands of Greek theology – doctrinal, philosophical, ascetic, and liturgical – that has never been matched. He came to exercise a profound influence on all later Byzantine theology. Maximus's influence was immediately felt, however, not in Constantinople, which had no reason to look on him with any favor, but in the lands that had fallen to Islam, especially Palestine. There the effect of Islam was to remove political support for any brand of Christianity, creating a situation in which the different Christian groups were forced to define and defend their own position against the other Christian positions, and other religious options, not least of all Islam.[3] The most famous such statement of the Chalcedonian position is found in the works of John of Damascus (c. 675–c. 749), then a monk of Palestine, especially in his three-part work, *The Fountain of Knowledge*, the last part of which contains an epitome of Christian doctrine in a hundred chapters. John was also a notable defender of the traditional veneration of icons (see below) and a distinguished composer of the new style of liturgical poetry (especially the canon) that came to grace the monastic office of the Chalcedonian or "Melkite" monks (that is, those who supported the Byzantine emperor or *malka*). His fame as a defender of icons had reached Constantinople by the mid-eighth century, when he was roundly condemned at the Synod of Hiereia (754), but any detailed knowledge of his works seems not to have reached the capital until the restoration of Orthodoxy in the mid-ninth century, at about the same time the poetical enrichment of the monastic office, in which John had participated, reached Constantinople. It is an irony that "Byzantine

2 See Maximus the Confessor, *Maximus the Confessor and his Companions*.
3 See Griffith in this volume.

Orthodoxy" found its definitive expression not in the capital, and indeed not in the empire at all.

The end of the seventh and beginning of the eighth centuries saw several attempts on the part of the Byzantines to recover their nerve: emperors took names such as Constantine and Justinian, indicative of fresh beginnings. In 691–92, Justinian II (685–95, 705–11) called a council in the domed chamber (Latin: *trullus*) of the imperial palace, that sought to complete the work of the two earlier councils held in Constantinople in 553 and 680–81, which had issued only doctrinal decrees. This council, which seems to have regarded itself as a continuation of the Sixth Council, though it came later to be called the Fifth-Sixth (Quinisext) or the Trullan Council, drew up 102 canons that constituted a recapitulation of the entire canonical tradition of the Byzantine Church. Its attitude is conservative and defensive, affirming the traditions of Constantinople against those of Rome (on clerical celibacy, especially) and Armenia, forbidding contact with Jews, and outlawing various remnants of pagan practices. Military pressure from the Arabs continued, Constantinople being blockaded by the Arabs from 674 to 678 and facing another siege in 718. The relatively short imperial reigns at the end of the seventh and beginning of the eighth centuries are a further sign of instability. The accession of Leo III (717–41) in 717 marked the beginning of a long period of political stability, continued under his son Constantine V (741–75) – their combined reigns covering nearly sixty years – during which the Byzantine Empire began to recover its strength. It was also the period of the first stage of iconoclasm, during which religious imagery was destroyed and forbidden at the imperial command.

Iconoclasm

The origins of iconoclasm are much disputed, as is the initial sequence of events. Both our historical sources – Nicephorus's *Short History* and Theophanes' *Chronicle* – attribute the introduction of iconoclasm to the emperor's reaction to an earthquake in the Cyclades in 726 which threw up another island close to Thera and Therasia, themselves the result of earlier volcanic activity. Fearful of divine wrath, Leo caused the icon of Christ at the bronze gate of the palace to be removed. It is, however, far from clear that there was an icon of Christ there at that time, and it was only in 730 that Germanus, the patriarch, resigned over the imperial policy. It seems beyond doubt, however, that Byzantine iconoclasm was a matter of imperial edict, rather than a response to any sort of popular movement. By the beginning of the eighth century, religious art occupied a prominent place in Byzantine society, both in public and in private. The removal of all religious pictorial art must have had a profound impact. The visual field would have been rudely altered: secular depictions and images of the emperor would remain, but instead of depictions of Christ, the Mother of God, and the saints – in mosaics, frescoes, on boards, and woven in fabric (maybe in statues, though there is little evidence of this) – the only religious depiction allowed was the Sign of the Cross, itself one of the imperial symbols. This suggests that one motive behind iconoclasm may have been the unambiguous assertion of imperial authority, free from the competing claims of various forms of holiness. There is little evidence as to the course of imperial iconoclasm in Leo III's reign; indeed, our sources make rather more of the extensive damage caused by an earthquake in Constantinople in 740.

Our picture of the theological reaction to Leo's iconoclast edict is limited to various letters and treatises of Germanus and the three treatises against the iconoclasts by John of Damascus, writing from the safety of Umayyad Palestine. These treatises, especially John's replete with patristic proof-texts, drew on the Christian response in the seventh century to Jewish objections to Christian veneration of icons, part of the religious dispute that flourished under the political ascendancy of Islam. The Jews had argued that the second commandment proscribed the veneration of icons (Leo seems to have made the same objection in his now-lost edict). Christians had replied that the second commandment forbade idolatry, in the sense of worshiping the creature as God, but not veneration of pictures of holy men and women, whose holiness expressed their closeness to God. A distinction was drawn between prostration (*proskynesis*) expressing worship (*latreia*), due to God alone, and that expressing honour (*timé*), which could be rendered to the saints, or even to holy objects. St. Basil's remark that "the honor offered to the image passes to the original" was also frequently cited. The eighth-century defenders of the veneration of icons, especially John of Damascus, added to these arguments a fundamental appeal to the Incarnation; whereas God in himself is beyond circumscription, in becoming incarnate as a man he made himself circumscribable, and now as incarnate can be depicted – indeed, as incarnate, he must be capable of depiction.

On his death in 741, Leo was succeeded by his son Constantine V, after a brief attempt to gain the throne by his son-in-law Artabasdus. Constantine is presented in our sources as a sacrilegious villain. However, for the better part of ten years, he made no further move in promoting iconoclasm, being occupied with the defeat of Artabasdus, taking advantage of the burgeoning civil war among the Arabs (which led to the foundation of the Abbasid dynasty in 750), and coping with plague and earthquake in the empire. In 754, however, he called a synod in the palace at Hiereia, on the Asian shore opposite Constantinople, to endorse iconoclasm. Prior to that, he had circulated to his bishops a collection of "inquiries" (*peuseis*), raising various questions about icons. The synod itself issued a long "definition" (*horos*), preserved because it was subject to detailed refutation at the council, now regarded as the Seventh Ecumenical Council, held in 787. This definition took the argument against icons on to a thoroughly theological level. Instead of arguing that icons were idols, it argued that an icon of Christ was impossible: either it depicted the humanity of Christ, separate from his divinity, which entailed Nestorianism, or it depicted his humanity fused with his divinity, which entailed monophysitism. Depiction of Christ was therefore tantamount to heresy. A further argument urged that the real image of Christ was the Eucharist, in which bread and wine received priestly blessing and became an image or type of the body and blood of Christ.

After the decision of the self-styled "seventh ecumenical" council of Hiereia, Constantine V seems to have intensified the persecution of those who opposed iconoclasm. He also took action against the monastic state, forcing monks and nuns into marriage and the abandonment of their vows. There is, however, no evidence, even in the iconodule sources, that Constantine's persecution of iconodules and of monks were related, and it has been plausibly argued that the most prominent of the iconodule martyrs, St. Stephen the Younger (c. 713–64), was put to death on suspicion of being involved in seditious intrigue, rather than for his defense of icons as such.[4]

Constantine V died in 775 and was succeeded by his son, Leo IV (775–80), whose wife, Irene, was an Athenian noblewoman. Leo died in 780, and Irene became regent for their young son, Constantine VI (780–97). After the death of Paul IV (780–84), Irene appointed a bureaucrat, Tarasius, patriarch (784–806), and in 787 veneration of icons was reaffirmed at the Seventh Ecumenical Council, held in Nicaea. Clergy who renounced their former iconoclasm were readily reinstated by Tarasius, who was anxious for reconciliation, though this laid him open to charges of laxity from the more vehement iconodules, especially the monks associated with Theodore, later known as the Studite (d. 826). It was the same group of monks who loudly opposed Constantine's divorce of his wife Maria in 795 in order to marry a lady of court, Theodote, ironically Theodore's cousin. Theodore was also favored by Irene, who invited him and his monks from the Sakkoudion monastery in Bithynia to Constantinople to revive the Studios monastery, just within the Golden Gate.

Irene herself, having secured the blinding and deposition of her son, acceded to the throne in 797 in her own person (the only woman ever to do so), but

4 See *La vie d'Étienne le Jeune* and Auzépy, *L'hagiographie et l'iconoclasme byzantin*.

after only five years, she was deposed and succeeded by Nicephorus I (802–11). His reign ended ingloriously in defeat at the hands of the Bulgarians, whose khan, Krum, had his skull turned into a silver-inlaid drinking goblet. Nicephorus's son, wounded in the same campaign as his father, was succeeded by the unsatisfactory Michael I Rhangabe (811–13), who was deposed in 813 by Leo V (813–20). In little over a year, Leo had reintroduced iconoclasm at a synod held in Constantinople that reasserted the synodal authority of Hiereia. The patriarch, Nicephorus (806–15), was forced to resign, and Theodore and the monks of the Studios Monastery were scattered and sent into exile. Although Leo had the decisions of Hiereia reinstated, the nature of iconoclasm and the issues had changed. The question was no longer one of the very existence of icons, rather it was a matter of their veneration; some icons high up on walls, beyond reach of veneration, were permitted to remain. Theodore the Studite's defense of icons comes to turn on the question of the legitimacy of the veneration of the *hypostasis* (the technical theological term for "person") depicted on the icon, which is identical in the icon and the original. One reason for this change of perspective may well have been the desire on Leo's part to secure the support of the Franks who at their synod at Frankfurt in 794 rejected the veneration of icons, without endorsing thoroughgoing iconoclasm.

With Leo's death in 820, iconoclasm was less strictly enforced and exiles recalled, though Michael II (820–29) refused to sanction the veneration of icons, at least within Constantinople itself. Under his successor Theophilus (829–42), persecution of iconodules seems to have intensified, notable among such iconodules being the two brothers Theodore and Theophanes, monks from Palestine, whose faces were branded with (poor quality!) iconoclast verses. With Theophilus's death in 842, the veneration of icons was again reintroduced, again by a widowed empress acting as regent for her son, in this case Theodora and her son, Michael III (842–67). As in 815, this was done by the home synod of Constantinople reaffirming the decrees of an eighth-century council, in this case the second council of Nicaea, the Seventh Ecumenical. The decision of this home synod, held under the chairmanship of the new patriarch, Methodius I (843–47), was proclaimed by the *Synodikon of Orthodoxy* – a formal acclamation of Orthodoxy and its defenders and anathematization of heresy and heretics – before the Divine Liturgy in the Great Church of Hagia Sophia on the first Sunday of Lent, 843. This ceremony was to be repeated yearly, first in Constantinople, and eventually throughout the Byzantine world, each first Sunday of Lent, which came to be known as the Sunday of Orthodoxy. Although some resistance to icons within the Byzantine world remained, the veneration of icons was henceforth to remain Byzantine policy.

Aspects of Byzantine Orthodoxy, 850–1095

The patriarchate

One might have expected that the ease with which, in the period 600 to 850, emperors found compliant patriarchs of Constantinople to support religious policies eventually declared to be heretical – monothelitism and then iconoclasm – would have damaged the standing of the institution of the patriarchate itself. On the contrary, however, the patriarchate emerged in the ninth century as much more powerful than two and a half centuries earlier.

There seem to be several reasons for this. In various ways the jurisdiction of the patriarchate was both clearer and greater in 850 than in 600. Originally, the archbishop of Constantinople had been granted no very clear jurisdiction, despite being granted "privileges of honor" (*ta presbeia tês timês*) after the bishop of Rome by the Ecumenical Councils of Constantinople I (381; canon 3) and Chalcedon (451; canon 28), the latter further specifying that these privileges were "equal" to those of Rome, with Constantinople taking "second place." Having no clear territory, the archbishop had no bishops to summon to a regular synod as envisaged by the Council of Nicaea I (325; canon 5). His synodal authority therefore came to be exercised through the so-called "home synod" (*endêmousa synodos*), consisting of any bishops who happened to be in Constantinople at the time – a fluctuating constituency, but dependable, given the presence of the court. This synod gradually gained authority, so that, in the ninth century, the reintroduction of both iconoclasm in 815 and the veneration of icons in 843 could be authorized by a session of the home synod. By this time the home synod was a much more permanent body, reinforced, as it was, by bishops (and even patriarchs) who had taken refuge in Constantinople because their dioceses had either fallen to Islam or suffered regular harassment by Arab troops or Slav occupation.

The Arab conquest of the eastern provinces had also clarified the question of the extent of Constantinople's jurisdiction. Chalcedon had granted Constantinople the right to consecrate metropolitans in the nearby provinces of Pontos, Asia, and Thrace, though since the time of St. John Chrysostom in the early fifth century, Constantinople had claimed the right to consecrate (and therefore ultimately supervise) the metropolitans of Asia Minor, a claim disputed by the patriarchate of Antioch. But with the fall of the east to Islam, the Melkite patriarch of Antioch was either subject to the Arabs or in exile in Constantinople, in neither case in any position to dispute Constantinople's jurisdiction throughout Asia Minor. The patriarch's jurisdiction was further extended by Leo III who, in retaliation against Rome's refusal to implement iconoclasm, transferred the jurisdiction Rome had traditionally exercised over Illyricum, that is, the western Balkans south of the Danube, to Constantinople. With the loss of Ravenna to the Lombards in 751, the jurisdiction of the patriarch of Constantinople became virtually co-extensive with the territory ruled by the Byzantine emperor. The patriarch, together with the clergy of the Church of Hagia Sophia, thus became the hub of ecclesiastical authority throughout the Byzantine Empire.

The taint of heresy was skillfully removed, or obscured, by propaganda taking the form of hagiography, issuing from the patriarchal court. The *Vitae* of St. Stephen the Younger, St. Ioannicius (c. 754–846), and of the patriarchs Tarasius and Nicephorus – all emanating from the patriarchal court – presented a picture of resistance to iconoclasm in which the patriarch had played a noble role.[5] The patriarchal office thus emerged from iconoclasm greatly strengthened, both in power and esteem. Patriarch Methodius, appointed by the Empress Theodora to reintroduce the veneration of icons in 843, was able to pursue his own policy, despite the prestige of the Studite monks, who claimed victory, though this was partly achieved by exploiting the divisions that had emerged within the monastic party during the second phase of iconoclasm between the supporters of St. Theodore the Studite and of St. Ioannicius.

The power and prestige of the patriarchate continued to develop in the centuries that followed. It became an element in the growing estrangement between the Latin West and the Byzantine East. Both with Patriarch Photius (858–67, 878–86) and Pope Nicholas I (858–67), and with Patriarch Michael I Cerularius (1043–58) and Pope Leo IX (1049–54), part of the clash must be put down to an encounter between notions of patriarchal and papal power, both of which had developed in independence in the seventh and eighth centuries, and continued to develop in now independent political regimes, both focusing on the person of the patriarch or pope.[6]

The patriarch also came to gain in authority from the expansion of the Byzantine Empire during the Macedonian dynasty, and in particular from the spread of Byzantine influence through the creation, from the ninth century onwards, of what Dimitri Obolensky called the "Byzantine Commonwealth."[7] Byzantium's expansion east brought it into relationship with Armenia, which

5 All now available in new editions and / or translations: *La vie d'Étienne le Jeune*, ed. Auzépy; *The Life of Patriarch Tarasios*, ed. Efthymiadis; and translations of the *Vitae* of St. Ioannicius and Nicephorus, in *Byzantine Defenders of Images*, 243–351, 25–142.

6 See Kolbaba in this volume.

7 Obolensky, *Byzantine Commonwealth*.

had been unrepresented at the Council of Chalcedon and subsequently found itself drawn into the anti-Chalcedonian camp. Relationships with Armenia – and any attempt to incorporate it into the Byzantine Empire – therefore involved issues of theology, and also religious customs, analogous to those raised with the Latin West.[8] Patriarchs from Photius onwards were inevitably involved. The case of the spread of Byzantine Christianity among the Slavs gave the patriarch a peculiar preeminence, for whereas the Slav nations, beginning with Bulgaria, accepted Byzantine Christianity, they were not incorporated into the Byzantine Empire, but rather entered into the loose alliance of the Byzantine Commonwealth. Within that "commonwealth," the authority of the patriarch was clearer than that of the Byzantine emperor, for the patriarch appointed the archbishop in Bulgaria (save for about a century, when Bulgaria had an independent patriarch) and the metropolitan of Kiev and all Russia.[9]

Learning – from Photius to Psellus

The ninth century saw the beginnings of what has been called the "Macedonian Renaissance," or "le premier humanisme byzantin."[10] The epithet "Macedonian" is misleading, not least because the renaissance of learning was already well under way decades before the accession to (or usurpation of) the imperial throne by the founder of the Macedonian dynasty, Basil I, in 867. Like the roughly contemporaneous Carolingian renaissance, it was marked by a technical innovation – the use of the cursive minuscule hand for literary manuscripts – and also by a revival of classical learning, though such classical learning had never suffered such a decline in the East as the West had known. The earliest witness to the use of the minuscule hand for a literary manuscript – the so-called Uspensky Gospel Book of 835 – comes from the Studios Monastery, but although it is likely that St. Theodore the Studite's monastic reform involved the setting up of something like a scriptorium for the copying of biblical, liturgical, and patristic texts, this isolated witness is not sufficient to establish that the introduction of the minuscule hand for literary purposes was a Studite innovation, though the Studios Monastery must have been one of the first places to adopt it.

This renaissance had several elements. I have already mentioned the religious aspect, involving rediscovering and making available the writings of the fathers. The origins of this can be traced back several centuries, to the

8 See Dorfmann-Lazarev in this volume.

9 See Shepard in this volume.

10 See Lemerle, *Le premier humanisme byzantin*. See also Treadgold, "The Macedonian Renaissance," in *Renaissances before the Renaissance*, 75–98.

controversies of the seventh century over Christology and those of the eighth and ninth over iconoclasm. In both cases appeal to the fathers of the church entailed serious scholarship to ensure that the authorities being cited were authentic – to such an extent that Adolf Von Harnack called the Sixth Ecumenical Council (Constantinople III; 680–81) a "Council of antiquaries and paleographers."[11] The florilegia of citations from the fathers presented at all these synodal gatherings demonstrate the extensive learning on hand; it is an awesome thought that the fathers of Constantinople III spent a whole session listening to readings from the fathers interpreting Christ's agony in the garden. Theodore's monastic reform also revived interest in the Great Asceticon of St. Basil the Great (c. 330–79), as well as other ascetical works, such as those associated with the sixth-century monks of the Gaza desert (Barsanuphius, John, and Dorotheus) and the *Ladder* of St. John of Sinai (John Climacus: fl. probably early seventh century). On the literary side, the other aspect is the recovery of (Greek) classical learning. The single great monument to the extent of this renaissance is the *Myrobiblion* or *Bibliotheca* of Photius, patriarch of Constantinople. This is a collection of what have been called "book reviews," sometimes including extensive citation of the books in question, some 280 in total. Photius says that it was written in a hurry, before he set out on an embassy to the Arabs; the work bears many signs of haste. There is no structure; secular and religious books intermingle. Photius discusses more religious books than secular ones, but tends to give greater attention to the secular works, with the result that the sections dealing with religious books amount to less than half the whole. Nor is it clear what the principle of selection was: Are these all the books Photius could lay his hands on? Or do they represent what interested him? Photius certainly knew more than he included, as is clear from his other works, and a good deal can be gleaned from the *Myrobiblion* about writers whose books are not included, for example Plato. Poetical works constitute a striking omission. Photius's other works include a *Lexicon*, which is itself evidence that enough people were reading ancient literature to need such an aid, and his letters and "Amphilochia," these last being discussions of problems in Scripture and the fathers, allegedly put to him by a certain Amphilochius, metropolitan of Cyzicus; they represent a genre of theological reflection first used extensively by St. Maximus the Confessor (in his *Ambigua*, "Difficulties" – many also addressed to a bishop of Cyzicus – and various "questions"), which became popular in Byzantium (Michael Psellus (1018–81) being a contributor to the genre).

11 Von Harnack, *History of Dogma* 4, 261.

What structures of education supported this learning is obscure. Claims that there were patriarchal or monastic schools, on the analogy of such in the West, have been questioned.[12] It is also clear that the traditional educational system collapsed sometime in the wake of the Arab conquests. And yet education must have been available, even if not of a very high standard (on the evidence we have, command of literary Greek in the eighth century, at least in Constantinople, seems to have been poor).

Most of the manifestations of the Macedonian renaissance in the tenth century are outside our compass: compilations of political and administrative material under Constantine VII Porphyrogenitus (913–59), the *Suda*, and the Palatine Anthology, though theological and religious material can be gleaned from these. The next century saw the ascendancy of Michael Psellus and his disciples, who drew on philosophical, especially Neoplatonic, sources. This active interest in learning, that was sometimes quite openly pagan, exposed the rift that had developed between what the Byzantines had come to call "outer learning" (*hê thurathen paideia*) and "inner learning," that is, Christian doctrinal and ascetic theology. Psellus escaped outright condemnation, but not his pupil, John Italus (c. 1025–after 1082), who was tried and condemned for heresy and paganism in 1082, under Emperor Alexius I Comnenus (1081–1118). The additions to the *Synodikon of Orthodoxy*, promulgated by Alexius as part of his drive to establish himself as a guardian of Orthodoxy, include a condemnation of "those who pursue Hellenic learning and are formed by it not simply as an educational discipline, but follow their empty opinions, and believe them to be true."[13]

Monasticism

Monasticism had been a prominent feature of Byzantine society from the beginning – the fourth century seeing the dramatic rise of monasticism – firstly in Egypt, and then in other parts of the Roman Empire, both in the East and the West. Fourth-century monasticism of the Egyptian desert came to be looked upon by later ages as a kind of golden age of monasticism. In the fifth-century collections of stories and sayings of the fathers of the Egyptian desert, known as the *Gerontikon* in Greek and the *Apophthegmata Patrum* in Latin, were put together, probably in Palestine, and these collections became the core of monastic wisdom passed on down the ages. From the beginning these collections of sayings were complemented by other material: *Vitae* of saints,

12 Lemerle, *Le premier humanisme byzantin*, 95–96, 103–4.
13 *Le Synodikon d'Orthodoxie*, 59.

such as St. Antony the Great, the monastic rules associated with Pachomius and Basil of Caesarea, and other accounts of the Egyptian monks, such as the *Lausiac History* and the *History of the Monks of Egypt*.[14] Later on further additions were made to this body of literature, such as the account of the beginnings of Palestinian monasticism in various *Vitae* by Cyril of Scythopolis (c. 525–after 559); the letters of the great ascetics of Gaza, Barsanuphius and John (both d. c. 540), and their disciple Dorotheus (fl. mid-sixth century); the account of a journey to various monastic sites made by John Moschus (c. 550–634) and Sophronius of Jerusalem, the *Spiritual Meadow*; and finally the great *Ladder of Divine Ascent*, by John (before 579–after 650), abbot of the Monastery of the Burning Bush at Sinai (known after his work as Climacus), probably belonging to the seventh century.

From the beginning there emerged three forms of monasticism that continued to be characteristic of Byzantium. There were hermits or solitaries, who lived remote from human society, either deep in the desert, like St. Antony (251?–356) or on the top of a pillar or *stylos*, like St. Symeon the Stylite (c. 390–459) (monks who lived in remote caves in mountains were also called stylites); there were monks who lived in communities, called cenobites (after the Greek, *koinos bios*, "common life"), who lived either remote from human society, as in the monastery founded by Pachomius (c. 290–346) at Tabennisi, or in cities, as in Basil's foundation at Caesarea; there were also monks who pursued the solitary life, but accepted the guidance of a superior and met each weekend for fellowship and to receive Holy Communion – such groups were called lavras or (later) sketes. Given that the solitary life normally required preparation in a community, it was not uncommon to find a cenobitic monastery acting as a mother community to hermits and groups of lavras; famous examples are the Monastery of Sinai, and the Great Lavra of Mar Saba in the Judean Desert, both of which flourished throughout the Byzantine period, and still continue.

The seventh and eighth centuries are a dark period for Byzantine monasticism. This is mainly for lack of information. Apart from John's *Ladder* and what can be gleaned from the ascetic and theological writings of Maximus the Confessor and Anastasius of Sinai (all from the seventh century), there is little to go on, and anyway all this material comes from regions that had either been lost or were soon to be lost to Islam. Within what remained of the empire itself, it is likely that monasticism suffered considerable disruption. When the Persian armies marched across Asia Minor in the 620s, many monks fled (Maximus among them). The harassment of much of Asia Minor by the

14 See Louth, "Literature of the Monastic Movement."

Arabs later in the seventh century is likely to have hindered any resettlement, but there is evidence that monasteries survived in the eighth century on and around the holy mountains of Mount Auxentius and Mount Olympus, both south of the Sea of Marmara, not too remote from the capital. The monasteries in Constantinople are likely to have suffered from the severe depopulation experienced by the city in the seventh and eighth centuries, the result of endemic plague and recurrent earthquakes. Constantine V's drive against monasticism must further have depleted the monastic ranks, though to what extent it is impossible to judge. On the other hand, the impression given of monastic decline at the end of the eighth century by the *Vitae* of monastic reformers such as Theodore the Studite should probably not be taken too seriously, as it is a *topos* in the *vita* of a monastic founder.

There is no doubt, however, that the ninth century saw the beginning of a period of monastic reform, in which Theodore and his restoration of the city monastery of St. John the Forerunner of Studios played a central role.[15] This is evident from the way in which the arrangements for that monastery (detailed in its *typikon*, that is, its foundation document) became a pattern for later Byzantine monasticism, not least the monasteries founded on Mount Athos from the tenth century onwards. Theodore's reform, focused on the Studios Monastery, which he was invited to take over by the Empress Irene in 798, is often seen as an attempt to restore the traditions of monasticism established by St. Basil the Great in the fourth century. There is no doubt that this was an inspiration – like Basil, Theodore valued cenobitic monasticism and discouraged the solitary life, and the Studios Monastery is responsible for one of the recensions of Basil's *Asceticon* – but Theodore found inspiration elsewhere, too. In contrast to Basil, he lays great emphasis on the abbot, elected by his monks, who was to be their spiritual father. This points to the influence of Pachomius (though it reminds one, too, of St. Benedict). The abbot is to exercise his spiritual fatherhood through regular catechesis of his monks (very many of Theodore's survive), and also through *exagoreusis*, in which each monk opened his heart to the abbot, confessed his thoughts (not just sins), and received counseling and absolution. Other influences on Theodore's monastic ideals were the ascetics of the Gaza Desert (Barsanuphius, John, Dorotheus) and John of Sinai. Further principles of Studite monasticism as introduced by Theodore include the prohibition of slaves in the monastery (they must be freed), the forbidding of any female domestic animals, a realistic emphasis

15 See Morris, *Monks and Laymen*. For the Studite reform, see, most conveniently, Leroy, "Le monachisme studite." See also *BMFD*.

on poverty and manual labor, and promotion of learning and the copying of manuscripts of the fathers and liturgical texts. The pattern of liturgical prayer followed in the Studite monasteries is that already established by the sixth century: the midnight office, orthros, and lauds during the night leading up to dawn; services at the first, third, sixth, and ninth hours during the day; vespers at sunset; and compline. Probably during Theodore's lifetime, however, the Studite office adopted the complementation of the monastic office with liturgical verses, especially the canon (a collection of verses composed to be sung with the Old Testament canticles at orthros), that had been used in Palestine from the late seventh century onward.

Particularly in the tenth century, monastic foundations attracted the support of the emperors, especially Nicephorus II Phocas (963–69) and John I Tzimiskes (969–76). This was particularly true of the new foundations on the peninsula north of Thessaloniki that reaches down into the Aegean, known by synecdoche as "Mount Athos," the first of which was the Great Lavra, founded by St. Athanasius the Athonite, with the support of the Emperor Nicephorus Phocas, in 964. Gradually the monastic communities on Mount Athos acquired a unique spiritual authority, which continues to the present day.

The tenth and eleventh centuries saw a host of monastic foundations throughout the Byzantine world. The influence of the Studite reform was great, but not exclusive. Monastic founders who drew in their own way on the wealth of the Byzantine monastic tradition include John of Rila (c. 876–946) and Nikon the Preacher of Repentance (c. 930–c. 1000),[16] Lazarus of Mount Galesius (c. 981–1053)[17] and Christodulus of Patmos (d. 1093). The career of St. Symeon the New Theologian (c. 949–1022) across the turn of the millennium, with his profound ascetic and mystical theology and his clashes with patriarchal authority, illustrates the potential tension that existed between institutional authority and the charismatic appeal of the monk. It also illustrates one of the ways in which monks related to contemporary society: through the provision of spiritual counseling.

Liturgy, art, devotion

The proclamation of the triumph of Orthodoxy in 843, which marked the defeat of iconoclasm, was ultimately to have a profound effect on the place of religious art in Byzantium, and beyond that in the Slav countries that were soon to embrace Byzantine Christianity. Initially the impact was slow, doubtless

16 See *Life of Saint Nikon*.
17 See *Life of Lazaros*.

because of the fear of provoking an iconoclast backlash. Eventually, however, the crosses that had replaced icons in Byzantine churches were removed and icons erected instead. On the dedication of the icon of the Mother of God, replacing the iconoclast cross in the apse of the Church of the Holy Wisdom, on Holy Saturday 867, Patriarch Photius declared:

> having mingled the bloom of colors with religious truth, and by means of both having in holy manner fashioned unto herself a holy beauty, and bearing, so to speak, a complete and perfect image of piety, she is seen not only to be fair in beauty surpassing the sons of men, but elevated to an inexpressible fairness of dignity beyond any comparison beside.[18]

The use of art in Byzantine churches now became an imperative, not just an optional decoration. Gradually, a fairly fixed pattern of artistic decoration developed. The ground for this had already been prepared, however, in the interpretations of the liturgical ceremonies, especially the Divine Liturgy of the Eucharist, and of the ecclesial space in which this took place, which go back to the fourth century. Such interpretation received further development in the works ascribed to Dionysius the Areopagite, whose whole theology has a liturgical context, but particularly influential for the whole Byzantine period were the *Mystagogia* of Maximus the Confessor[19] and the oddly entitled "Ecclesiastical History and Mystical Contemplation" by Patriarch Germanus of Constantinople (715–30), which could perhaps be rendered: "What Happens in Church and its Hidden Meaning."[20] Fundamental to these interpretations was the division of the church into two parts, the sanctuary and the nave, separated by a templon consisting of a low barrier and a gate with, later, columns and an architrave (the solid iconostasis, characteristic of modern Orthodox churches, is a later medieval development). The church thus divided symbolized heaven and earth, so the church building itself symbolized the whole cosmos: the church was a microcosm, as, too, was the human being. In the period after iconoclasm, the decoration of the church building, generally cruciform with a dome over the nave, was determined by this fundamental perception. In the dome was depicted Christ the Pantocrator, ruling over the cosmos, and illuminated by light entering through the small windows at the base of the dome and reflected upwards. The rest of the church came to be decorated with icons (frescoes or mosaics) of the saints, of both the Old and the New Testaments, angels, and scenes from saving history, especially the life

18 Photius, Homily 17.4, *Homilies of Photius*, 292.
19 *I Mystagogia*; English translation by Berthold in Maximus, *Selected Writings*, 183–225.
20 Germanus of Constantinople, *On the Divine Liturgy*.

of Christ and the Virgin. It was then a peopled cosmos, or rather a cosmos consisting of people, following an already well-established Christian tradition that saw the cosmos in terms of living beings, rather than the celestial bodies of pagan antiquity.[21] Icons were also used in private devotion, thus carrying into the private sphere the cosmic dimension expressed in the church decoration.

Heresies[22]

Byzantine Orthodoxy, as defined by the Ecumenical Councils, represented a middle way between various heresies about the nature of God and the Incarnation. After the defeat of iconoclasm, such heresies ceased, for the most part, to trouble the Byzantines. In their stead, there emerged various heresies that have been characterized as dualistic, that is, holding that the cosmos is not the creation of a single good God, but is the product of a conflict between powers of good and evil, that are equally ultimate. These heretics were called Paulicians and Bogomils. The Paulicians were traced back to the late seventh century to a certain Constantine of Mananalis, an Armenian, though they probably owe their name to a certain Paul, who refounded the Paulicians in Armenia in the early eighth century. The Bogomils came later, named after a priest called Bogomil (Slavonic for Theophilus), who lived in Bulgaria in the tenth century. For their beliefs we are dependent on refutations of them by Orthodox opponents, especially the ninth-century Peter of Sicily, who wrote against the Paulicians; a tenth-century sermon on the Bogomils by one Cosmas; and the early twelfth-century *Dogmatic Panoply* by Euthymius Zigabenus. This is very unsatisfactory, as all these Orthodox writers regard them as some kind of Manichee, and present their beliefs accordingly. For it is quite certain that there is no historical link between these Byzantine heretics and the Manichees, who, after their persecution by Justinian, turned their attentions eastward. Like the Cathars (dualist heretics who emerge in the West in the mid-twelfth century), who were probably inspired by the Bogomils, the root of these "heresies" probably lies in a reaction against the institutional church and a search for the purity of the Gospel. At the heart of the beliefs of the Paulicians was faith in Jesus Christ, as a spiritual being; they rejected the Old Testament, and based themselves on the New Testament (or most of it). They rejected the sacraments, veneration of the cross, the cult of the saints, and icons; instead they were devoted to a spiritual Christ. It is easy to see how such a rejection of matter smacked of Manichean dualism to an

21 See Mathews, *Clash of Gods*, 150–61.
22 For this see *Christian Dualist Heresies*.

Orthodox opponent. That they were led by a supreme teacher, a *didaskalos*, who was regarded, we are told, as an apostle, would only have reinforced their identification as Manichees. The Bogomils may have had a more developed dualistic teaching. Their principal threat seems to have lain in the attraction of the apostolic simplicity of their lives, which led others to seek them out as a source of spiritual counseling.

Conclusion

The "Byzantine Orthodoxy" that emerged in this period, with roots that went a long way back, is highly ambivalent. For such Orthodoxy became, and was established as, imperial policy, and the Byzantine state was, in aspiration at least, absolutist. It had little time for those who questioned that Orthodoxy; indeed, Christian heretics had fewer rights than the Jews, who had some small protection as a "standing witness" to the truth of the faith they rejected. However, in the first part of our period, the emperor and his advisers adopted as Orthodoxy theological positions – monenergism, monothelitism, and finally iconoclasm – that were eventually to be rejected as heresies. The proclamation of the "triumph of Orthodoxy" in 843 was intended to draw a veil over that period, and to set out clearly the nature of "Byzantine Orthodoxy." The *Synodikon of Orthodoxy*, which made that proclamation a yearly liturgical event, was later to become a political manifesto of the Orthodoxy claimed by the Comneni and Palaeologan emperors. What came to be known as "Byzantine Orthodoxy" was forged, however, not at the capital, but on the periphery – in regions on the edge, or beyond the edge – of the Byzantine Empire. Nevertheless, it was only as received in the Byzantine tradition that these theologians – Maximus, Anastasius, John, and others – made their mark, and the Byzantine tradition was increasingly to be defined by what went on in Constantinople. This suppression of diversity was part of a whole outlook, and doubtless represents an impoverishment: the voices of those in the country and in cities outside the capital were drowned out, as were the voices of those who questioned Byzantine Orthodoxy. But its establishment as tradition enabled the exploration of the abundant resources of the riches of Christian reflection as it had developed in the Greek East, leaving a legacy that still commands attention.

3

Beyond empire I: Eastern Christianities from the Persian to the Turkish conquest, 604–1071

IGOR DORFMANN-LAZAREV

This chapter traces the history of the churches of the eastern and southeastern coasts of the Mediterranean sea, northeastern Africa, the Arabian peninsula, Persia, Transcaucasia, and eastern Asia Minor, as well as the development of their theological thought. Particular attention will be dedicated to the Christian cultures of Syriac and Armenian traditions.

We must begin by recalling that, towards the end of the sixth century, two chief kinds of ecclesiastical communities could be distinguished in the Byzantine East, each with its own clergy.[1] On the one hand, there were the churches centered on the hellenophone cities, which were characterized by their special bond to the ongoing theological elaborations of Byzantium which perpetuated classical Greek philosophical categories. On the other, there were the churches attached above all to the ascetic traditions moulded in the two cradles of Christian monasticism, Egypt and Syria. Their followers were particularly receptive to the non-Chalcedonian Christology which viewed Christ's humanity primarily as the instrument of divine activity in the world. Those who had rejected the *Definition* of the Council of Chalcedon (451 CE) were later called by their opponents "monophysites" (i.e., those who believe in "one only nature," *monê physis*). To avoid this pejorative name, it is preferable to call them "miaphysites" recalling the formula *mia physis tou Theou Logou sesarkômenê*, "One incarnate nature of God the Word,"[2] which had originally been proposed by Apollinarius of Laodicaea (d. c. 390), then adopted and reinterpreted by Cyril of Alexandria (d. 444), and inherited from him by the non-Chalcedonians. Thus we shall distinguish them from the "dyophysites" who professed Christ "in two natures" (*en dyo physeis*): the Church of the East, which had rejected the Council of Ephesus (431) and was consequently

1 See Rousseau in this volume and also Maraval, "L'échec en Orient."
2 Cyril of Alexandria, *Contra Nestorium*, *Epistula* 40, *Epistula* 45, and *Epistula* 46.

called by its opponents "Nestorian" (hereafter, Eastern dyophysites), and from the Byzantine Church.

Non-Chalcedonians and Chalcedonians on the eve of the Persian conquest

By the end of the sixth century, in spite of the imperial persecutions, the miaphysites constituted the majority in the Syriac-speaking regions of the Anatolike diocese, which lay to the east of the river Labotes and the Amanus mountains: in Euphratensis, Osrhoene, Mesopotamia, in the countryside of Antioch and Apamea, as well as in Arabia. In these areas the Syriac monasteries functioned as intellectual and spiritual epicenters. The influence exercised by the Syriac divines also proved decisive for the determination of the Armenian Church's Christological position during the course of the sixth century. The hellenophone Chalcedonian communities, by contrast, represented the majority in western Syria and Palestine and especially in the coastal cities. Their intellectual centers were situated in Jerusalem and in the monastic enclaves of the Judean desert, where Greek literary and theological traditions were especially cultivated.

The situation in Egypt was comparable to Syria: the Chalcedonian faith had been accepted or enforced mainly in the cities, which were culturally and linguistically Greek. In them the Chalcedonian patriarchs – the only prelates recognized by the emperor – enjoyed unrivaled sway. The Coptic monks, however, supported by the rural population, were largely opposed to the innovative Christological language introduced by the Council of Chalcedon. The recusant miaphysite prelates thus found refuge in the Coptic monasteries situated far from the administrative centers of the empire. The most important of these were located in the Wadi Natrun, in the oasis of Fayum, in the Western desert, in Upper Egypt, to the north of the Asyut, and in the Eastern desert. The rural areas of Upper Egypt were all miaphysite strongholds. During the second half of the sixth century, Coptic missionaries advanced up the Nile, allowing the miaphysite faith to become the prevalent form of Christianity in Nubia, Eritrea, and Ethiopia.

The Syro-Mesopotamian desert, through which ran the frontier between Byzantium and the Persian Empire, was inhabited by Arab tribes.[3] The Ghassanid confederation – the dominant group of Byzantine Arab *foederati* – owed their miaphysitism to Empress Theodora (d. 548) and Jacob Baradaeus (Bishop

3 Shahid, *Byzantium and the Arabs*, 922–48.

of Edessa in exile, fl. 542–78), and took an active part in spreading Christianity in the Arabian peninsula. The Ghassanids constituted a buffer kingdom between Byzantium and the Lakhmid Arab confederation (of East Syrian allegiance) which was based on the western bank of the lower Euphrates, where it served as the Sasanians' frontier guard. The relationship between Byzantium and the Ghassanids deteriorated after the empire embraced the Chalcedonian doctrine. When, in 584–85, the Emperor Maurice cut subsidies to the Ghassanids, their confederation fell apart. The Byzantines' weakening support of the *foederati* was later to strengthen Islam's attraction as the Arab national religion.

The bishops ordained by Jacob Baradaeus for Asia Minor, Syria (where they constituted the church later known as "Jacobite"), and Egypt were almost exclusively of monastic origin, and in the following centuries the miaphysite hierarchies were to maintain a decidedly monastic character. The monastic background of the miaphysite churches facilitated their survival under Islamic domination: the persecutions of non-Muslims were particularly devastating in the urban areas where the caliphate's governors resided, whereas the Christian communities of the remoter districts often succeeded in escaping direct control. In the following centuries the miaphysite monasteries were able to cultivate learning and to develop new literary and spiritual traditions both in Syriac and Coptic.

Non-Chalcedonian churches and the Church of the East: two Christologies in synopsis

Divergent conceptions of the Incarnation, which were articulated in opposition to the theology adopted by the empire, stood at the core of the distinctive doctrinal and cultural identities of the churches of Syria, Egypt, Persia, and Armenia and were to play a decisive role in their history during the seventh century.

Christology of the Church of the East

The Christology of the Church of the East derived from the Antiochene exegetical tradition. It had as its supporting structure the historical dimension of revelation. In the light of Heb. 10.5–7, stress was laid on Christ's integral humanity as the culminating point of God's salvific activity. In the light of Luke 2.40, 52, it accentuated the gradual character of divine revelation in the world and, following the exegesis of Theodore of Mopsuestia (d. 428), suggested a progressive unification of the two natures, divine and human, in the course of

Christ's life. For this reason the Church of the East's theological discourses insisted upon duality in reference to the divinity and humanity of Christ.

At the beginning of the seventh century, the language of two *qnome* was promoted by Babai the Great (d. 628) and subsequently adopted by the Church of the East as its official teaching. The term *qnoma* had an ancient history, but in the texts of the period under discussion it may be interpreted as "concrete existence," that is, the individual instance of a particular nature. The *Definition* of the assembly of bishops of 612 (presumably held at Seleucia-Ctesiphon) contained the phrase "Christ is two natures and two *qnome*" and expressed two main concerns. Its theological concern, by distinguishing between divinity and humanity, intended to maintain the perfect transcendence of the former and avoid any idea of its suffering. The other concern was soteriological. By designating Christ's humanity, side by side with his divinity, as *qnoma*, the Church of the East intended to affirm its integral character, for Christ was the new Adam, the stem of new humankind (1 Cor. 15.45–49). Viewed from this perspective, humankind may acquire the hope of resurrection from the dead because, in Christ, it was the human being who is in him, the new Adam, who died and rose, but it was the God who is in him who raised him up. To affirm "one incarnate nature of God the Word"[4] was to declare that those who are not consubstantial with God cannot be saved. This concern clearly emerges from the writings of Narsai (399–502) and Catholicos George (c. 680) as well as from the Oriental Synodicon edited by Catholicos Timothy I (780–823).[5] Moreover, according to Timothy I, to affirm that Christ's humanity is the common nature of humankind allows us to attribute to it the individual human names found in the Prophets, such as "slave" or "servant," and thus to affirm its mortality, but God the Son, who had united it to himself, gradually subjected it to his will and rendered it immortal.[6]

The high degree of autonomy reserved for Christ's humanity in East Syrian Christology permitted this church to inscribe the Son of Man in various religious traditions: Christianity thus was presented to different Asian cultures with wide flexibility. For example, the inscription composed by the eastern dyophysite monk Adam in Chinese and Syriac in 781 near Chang'an, the capital of the Chinese Tang dynasty, borrowed numerous Taoist, Confucian, Buddhist, and Manichean expressions in order to explain the Christian doctrine.[7]

4 See above, note 2.
5 Brock, "Christology of the Church," 165–76.
6 Timothy I, *Epistula de incarnatione*, 186, l.13–23.
7 Pelliot, *L'inscription nestorienne*, 95–146.

Christology of the non-Chalcedonian churches

At the opposite pole stood the miaphysite Christology whose origins went back to the exegetical tradition of Alexandria.[8] Beginning with Origen, the Alexandrians interpreted Scripture in the framework of the Platonic distinction between two levels of reality, the sensible and the intelligible, of which the former was the latter's image. This distinction also provided the key for a sacramental interpretation of the universe and of man. Christ's humanity was conceived of merely as a channel of God's revelation in the finite world. In the light of several biblical theophanies (Isa. 29.5; Mal. 3.1; Luke 2.13; Acts 9.3; 22.6), this tradition insisted upon the atemporal and immediate character of divine revelation as "Heavens torn apart" (Mark 1.10). In the light of John 1.14, the miaphysites were above all concerned to affirm the uninterrupted unity of the divine subject in Christ, sole actor of salvation, thus speaking of two births of the only Son of God. The above-quoted miaphysite formula expressed the union of divinity and humanity in Christ "asymmetrically": it allowed the understanding of the events of Christ's earthly life and his deeds as the "incarnate" extension of God's salvific activity in the world.

The controversy concerning the incorruptibility of Christ's body before the Resurrection, which had been opened by Julian of Halicarnassus and Severus of Antioch around 520, continued to divide the miaphysites for several centuries. The Council of Mantzikert, convoked in 726 at the joint initiative of the Armenian Catholicos John of Ōjun (717–28) and the West Syrian Patriarch Athanasius III (724–40), formulated an intermediate position: by assuming "decayed and corruptible" humanity, the Son of God rendered it "incorruptible." Incorruptibility did not mean, however, that Christ was exempt from the weaknesses of the human condition including the sufferings of the Passion. Yet Christ suffered not by inevitability but by sovereign divine decision. The acts of Mantzikert are one of the most important inter-ecclesial agreements achieved in the history of theological ideas, especially in view of the fact that the search for harmony was not promoted by any overarching authority seeking political cohesion. In Egypt, the quarrels between the various miaphysite groups persisted longer than elsewhere. Patriarchs Jacob (819–30) and Shenuda I (859–80) succeeded in dissolving the last groups that professed aphthartodocetism (the doctrine that rejected the reality of Christ's human sufferings) only at the beginning of the ninth century.

8 Grillmeier, *Jesus der Christus*, 7–35, 53–59.

The exclusion of aphthartodocetism allowed the Armenian Church to stabilize its Christological position.[9] According to John of Ōjun, the affirmations of oneness and duality in Christ formed an antinomic pair of which each member was equally important and served to balance the other.[10] Following Cyril of Alexandria,[11] the miaphysites refused to attribute the same ontological status to the spheres of *theologia* (concerned with God's eternal being, including the begetting before all ages) and of *oikonomia* (concerned with God's action within the created order, including the birth at Bethlehem). To the mind of Xosrovik the Translator (d. c. 730), it was one thing to consider Christ's humanity in its own right and another to examine it in its union with the Creator's hypostasis: "The Lord's body is human by nature, but divine by union."[12] The humanity assumed by God, although integral, no longer belonged to a man, hence this humanity is *Divine*. According to Isaac Mrut (c. 820–c. 890), "Christ has manifested to the world his *paternal* nature united to his *maternal* nature," that is, the "nature" whose subject is God the Father united to the "nature" whose subject is the *Theotokos*. In this way the Armenian divines linked their Christological language to the creedal theology of Nicaea I, which first defined Christ as "begotten of the Father" and only later spoke of him as "incarnate of the Virgin." Thus the miaphysites maintained the ancient kerygmatic character of Christological discourse, placing the Incarnation in the soteriological perspective and considering it as a sovereign act of the Trinity.

The miaphysites rejected the conceptualization proposed by the Council of Chalcedon which had conceived of Christ's divinity and humanity as *two* comparable entities belonging to one and the same category of *nature*, and which later were also construed as active principles discernible in the Savior. As a consequence, in the domain of ethics and social organization, the miaphysites have always remained extraneous to the distinction, later developed in Byzantine and Roman churches, between the spheres of spiritual and profane activities.

Christian communities during the last Sasanian conquest (604–24)

Following the deposition and murder of Emperor Maurice in 602, King of Kings Chosroes II (590–628) soon succeeded in regaining Persian territories lost to the Byzantines.[13] Between 604 and 611, the Sasanian army directed successful

9 Dorfmann-Lazarev, *Arméniens et Byzantins*, 96–129.
10 John of Ōjun, *Sermon*, 57.
11 Cyril of Alexandria, *Commentarii in Iohannem* 2, 10.15, 232.
12 Xosrovik T'argmanič', "Chapter I," 50, 54.
13 Dagron, "L'église," 13–24.

campaigns in Armenia (thence proceeding to Georgia), Upper Mesopotamia, Syria, and Cappadocia. Antioch and Apamea were occupied in 610, Emesa in 611, Damascus and Tarsus in 613. Thus Syria was cut off from the empire. In 614 Jerusalem was sacked, the Chalcedonian population slaughtered, the Church of the Holy Sepulcher burned, and the relic of the True Cross carried off to Seleucia-Ctesiphon, the Persian capital. This last had a particularly demoralizing effect on Byzantium and was interpreted by many as an apocalyptic event. Shortly afterwards Tarsus and Cilicia were occupied. Alexandria fell in 619, and by 620 Africa was conquered as far as Ethiopia to the south and Libya to the west.

The Chalcedonian clergy, whom the invaders associated with their enemy, were expelled from Mesopotamia and Syria. Those Christians who had been at variance with the imperial church became, in the eyes of the Persians, potential allies.[14] The miaphysites, who had been driven underground by the imperial regime, did not oppose the invaders and occasionally welcomed them, seeing in the Persians liberation from the emperor's persecution. Since Jacob Baradaeus's time the miaphysites had expanded into the Persian lands and now represented the dominant Christian group in the territories controlled by the King of Kings. Consequently, Chosroes chose to rely on them in order to consolidate his conquests. He allowed them to establish church structures in the conquered territories, to recover their goods confiscated by the imperial administration, to take over the abandoned sacred buildings of the Chalcedonians, and to build new churches.

The Persian reconquest facilitated the formal condemnation of the Chalcedonian doctrine in Armenia in 607. Thereafter the Church of Ałuankʿ (Caucasian Albania) succumbed progressively to confessional and cultural dependence on the Armenian Church.[15] In Georgia, by contrast, where Persian control was looser, the local church was able to affirm its pro-Byzantine religious affiliation in an effort to escape Armenian tutelage. Thus in the years 608–10, the schism between the Armenian and Georgian churches was consummated. In southern Mesopotamia Chosroes II seems to have supported the dominance of the Church of the East.[16] Chosroes' benevolence toward his Christian subjects did not endure, however, and when, in 625, the Persian army began losing battles to the Byzantines, the king turned against both eastern dyophysites and miaphysites.

14 Flusin, "Église," 667–705.
15 Mahé, "L'eglise arménienne," 462–74, 507–509.
16 Winkler, "Zeitalter der Sassaniden," 38–42.

The advent of Heraclius and monenergism (616–38)

When the Emperor Heraclius (610–41)[17] undertook to recover the lands lost to the Persians, the support of the Christians of this area appeared to him – as to Chosroes several years before – of the utmost strategic importance. That assistance, however, could be obtained only as the result of doctrinal reconciliation. As in the age of Justinian, Heraclius's eastern politics therefore depended on a Christological settlement. Of all the opponents of imperial orthodoxy living in Persia, the theological effort of the emperor – who was of Armenian descent and presumably bilingual – was directed above all to the miaphysites. They were more numerous than the "Nestorians" in the lands lost to the Persians, and their theology was closer to imperial orthodoxy, especially after the Fifth Ecumenical Council which had proposed a rereading of the Chalcedonian *Definition* in the light of the Christology of Cyril of Alexandria.

Towards 616 Patriarch Sergius of Constantinople (610–38) – who was of Syrian miaphysite descent and a close friend of Heraclius – proposed a definition of the unity of the concrete activity (*energeia*) of the incarnate Logos in the hopes of persuading the miaphysites to accept the *Definition* of Chalcedon. If the activity were attributed not to the nature but rather to the hypostasis, the doctrine of one single activity could serve as a point of convergence of the two opposing sides, for there was no dissension between the miaphysites and the Chalcedonians concerning Christ's single hypostasis. It would allow the viewing of Christ's two natures not in the perspective of their divergent potentialities, but rather of their coming together into one single hypostasis, of which the single activity was the manifestation. To sustain his view, Sergius could notably draw on Cyril of Alexandria and Dionysius the Areopagite (end of the fifth century) who were respected both by miaphysites and Chalcedonians.[18] In Cyril's view, on account of the hypostatic union, which implied the definition of Christ's humanity as the Word's own, the Word's divine action took the form of human acts. The doctrine of one single activity was consequently accepted by numerous bishops and abbots in the eastern provinces, and by 622 Sergius had won Heraclius over to what came later to be known as monenergism.

Heraclius began his major counteroffensive against Persia in 624, and by 629 succeeded in restoring the Emperor Maurice's frontier. Thus the miaphysites, who had enjoyed relative freedom under Persian rule, found themselves once again subjected to a hostile emperor. In 630 Heraclius personally reinstated in

17 Kaegi, *Heraclius*, 100–299.

18 Cyril of Alexandria, *Scholia de incarnatione Unigeniti* 2, p. 221; Pseudo-Dionysius Areopagita, *Epistola* 4, p. 161, l. 9.

Jerusalem the True Cross, which had been rescued from Persian possession by Heraclius's four Armenian generals. After this event, which was deeply felt by all of the Christian communities, the Byzantine ruler conceived a new project for reuniting Christendom. The empire urgently needed to secure confessional unity in order to consolidate the reconquest of the East.

Military success encouraged Heraclius to envisage negotiations not only with the miaphysites but also with the Church of the East, which was the best established and most influential Christian community of Persia. At the time, this church was enjoying a phase of rapid expansion and was incorporating large numbers of converts from Zoroastrianism and from various polytheistic religions of Arabia, Asia, and China. On the eve of the Muslim conquest the missions of the Church of the East were by far the widest spread amongst all Christian churches. In 630 Heraclius met Catholicos Išoʿyahḇ II at Berrhoea (Aleppo). The catholicos celebrated a liturgy in the presence of the emperor and a group of Byzantine bishops, and the sovereign himself received communion from his hands. The division, however, between the Byzantine Church and the Church of the East was to prove too great, and the precipitate reunion was immediately contested amongst the East Syrians and soon broke down.

Heraclius next turned to the miaphysites and succeeded in winning numerous bishops and hegumens to the cause of monenergism. The Syro-Byzantine council of 631 at Mabbug (Hierapolis), the Armeno-Byzantine council of 632–33 at Karin (Theodosiopolis), and the council of 633 at Alexandria achieved reunion with the Byzantine church of the three miaphysite churches on the bases of monenergist formulae. Nevertheless, following the negotiations of the agreements, many in Syria, Palestine, and especially in Egypt refused to accept Chalcedon in spite of their acceptance of monenergism. Heraclius then attempted to impose imperial orthodoxy by force and inaugurated violent persecution against the intransigent miaphysites. However, the newly elected Chalcedonian patriarch of Jerusalem, Sophronius (634–38), organized opposition to monenergism, and the emperor, now contested by both miaphysites and Chalcedonians, found himself obliged to terminate his initiative in 638.

The Arab conquest (630–56) and monothelitism

In the same year that Heraclius triumphantly restored the True Cross to Jerusalem, Muslim troops conquered Mecca and, advancing up the Arab peninsula, confronted the troops of the Byzantine and Sasanian Arab client tribes. In several instances they succeeded in gaining the support of the miaphysite and eastern dyophysite Arab populations and in converting them to the new religion. In late 633 Muslim troops began to penetrate into southern Palestine and Nabatea, where the imperial forces, weakened by the recent wars against the Persians, were unable to resist. After years of Persian occupation, the region's institutional, economic, and ideological links with Byzantium had been weakened, and its populations were not inclined to resist the new conquerors. Damascus was captured in 635, Antioch in 637, and Jerusalem in 638. Caesarea, the last Byzantine coastal stronghold in Palestine, fell in 640–41.

As the Arabs rapidly advanced, Heraclius made a last, unsuccessful attempt at Christian reunion in the hopes of gaining the loyalty and support of the miaphysites. At the end of 638 he published the *Ekthesis* composed by Patriarch Sergius and drafted by Pyrrhus of Chrysopolis, which forbade the affirmation of either "one" or "two" activities, but nevertheless reaffirmed that all activity proceeds from the divine Logos. In this way it attempted to maintain the logic of monenergism whilst avoiding the expression that had scandalized Sophronius's party. To emphasize the unity of the incarnate Logos, the "one single will" in Christ was also affirmed, thus introducing a new term into the Christological discourse. Yet the *Ekthesis* was rejected by the larger part of the miaphysite East. The Armenian divine Stephen of Siwnik' (c. 680–735) was later to epitomize the discussion: "Christ accomplished his Father's deed by means of his body . . . [and] because of the divinity of his nature he reveals through his activity that his body is equal in power [to his divinity]."[19]

After the invasion of Palestine and Syria, the Arabs vigorously engaged the Persians. By 640 the conquest of Mesopotamia was completed, and in 641 central Armenia was invaded and its capital, Duin, was pillaged and its population massacred. The army then marched on to Georgia which was subdued within a few years. Advances into Egypt resulted in Byzantine withdrawal from Alexandria in September 642 and the opening of routes for further Arab advances, southward along the Nile Valley and westward along the African coast. Soon after, the Muslim army penetrated beyond Aswān and made its first incursions into Nubia. In 642, and again in 652, the Nubian kingdoms succeeded in resisting the Islamic forces, and the treaty which was later signed between the caliphate and the Nubians recognized the sovereignty of the latter.

By 642 the Arabs completed their takeover of the Christian East, thus nullifying the ecclesiastical politics of Heraclius. As a result of less than ten years of warfare, the ancient Roman provinces of Palestine, Syria, and Egypt, together with their predominantly miaphysite populations, were cut off from the political body of Christendom. Byzantium lost the Holy Land, three patriarchal

19 Stephen of Siwnik', *Response*, 441–42.

sees, and the intellectual centers which, for three and a half centuries, had generated reflection on the person of the Savior, and witnessed violent conflicts between Christologically opposed thinkers, factions, and populations. The Sixth Ecumenical Council, held at Constantinople in 680–81, at which the "monophysite" communities were not even considered, was to end the long era of Christological debates within the empire.

"Monothelitism," however, the doctrine of a single will in Christ, found enduring support in central Syria, especially at Edessa, Hierapolis, Berrhoea, and Emesa, and the later reversal of the imperial doctrine was not to be accepted by all of the Antiochene Chalcedonians. In 727, the Syriac monastery of Saint Marun near Apamea, unwilling to recognize the teaching of the Sixth Council, seceded from the Antiochene Patriarchate, together with the adjacent parishes over which it exercised influence. In 742, when the Chalcedonians of Syria were authorized by the caliph to elect a patriarch, the church was split into two, the monothelite "Maronite" Church and the church professing the imperial doctrine and thus called "Melkite," that is, "royal."

The rise of Islam and the status of Christians in Islamic society

As in the case of the Sasanian conquest a quarter of a century before, the persecutions of dissenters on the part of imperial authorities facilitated the swift Islamic takeover of the Byzantine East. In 634 the miaphysites were not inclined to resist the monotheist Arabs any more than the "pagan," "fire-worshiping" Persians. In the earliest stage of Islam the affiliation of the new religious teaching to the texts of the Bible and Apocrypha was manifest to Christians, and some even placed their hope of eschatological liberation in the army of the Prophet of Islam.

The conquerors shaped a radically new system of social relations, which, in its fundamental characteristics, was to last until the end of the Ottoman sultanate in 1922, and, in the case of certain Christian communities, until the present day. It conferred specific features on the Christians' relationships with the rulers and influenced the formation of distinctive identities among them, with respect to individual ethos and spirituality. Its origins lay in the self-understanding of the nascent religion in the social and religious environment of the Near East and particularly in the way it envisaged its relations with the Christianity present in the Arabian peninsula from ancient times. Muḥammad viewed his teaching as the "rediscovered" primordial monotheistic religion proper to humankind. The Qur'ān (7.157; 61.6; 6.92) states in fact that before sending the Arabs the definitive message of submission (*Islām*), God had sent analogous, although less complete, "Books" to the Jews and to Christians, in which Muḥammad's coming had also been predicted.[20] On this ground the Qur'ān, and the Muslim law developed from it, distinguished two categories among the conquered populations. The "polytheists" were subject to obligatory conversion or enslavement, whereas the "Detainers of the Book," *Ahl al-kitāb*, were formally tolerated. The term "Book" was used to designate the Pentateuch, the Psalter, and the Gospels, perceived above all as legal texts, and their "Detainers" were Jews and Christians. The Qur'ān (62.27; 5.82–84) presents the Christians in a more favorable light than the Jews and even affirms that the people most friendly toward Muslims are to be found among Christians, whose devotional attitudes and moral virtues are also praised.

Muḥammad's failure to engage Christians in his "Community of Believers," followed by the military resistance which the Muslim troops encountered from the Arab Christian tribes, conditioned, however, the Qur'ān's ultimately negative attitude toward Christianity. In many places (3.78; 5.13; 2.59,75) the Qur'ān condemns the doctrines of Jews and Christians as falsifications of the authentic instructions in the true universal monotheistic religion, which had been given to them in the past. According to the Qur'ān (18.4–5; 5.17; 4.171), the Jewish and Christian Scriptures are not identical with the portions of the heavenly "Book" transmitted to Moses and Jesus, but reflect the erroneous imagination of Jews and Christians, which ultimately makes them disobedient to God and blasphemous. Yet the Qur'ān shows no direct acquaintance with the canonical books of the Bible. In the following centuries, the doctrinal contrasts between "Nestorians," various miaphysite factions, Maronites, and Melkites, as well as the Christians' general tendency to doctrinal controversies and sectarianism, which were familiar to the Muslims, sometimes provided grounds to suspect them of worshiping different gods.

In several instances (4.169; 5.76–77; 9.31; 17.111; 19.36; 23.93; 25.2) the Qur'ān applies to Christians the term *mushrikūn*, "associators," which elsewhere in the Qur'ān is the normal term for polytheists – those committing the worst of sins by worshiping "associates" along with God. It is against this background that we should consider the Qur'ān's direct injunction "to fight against those to whom the Scriptures have been given . . . until they pay tribute [*jizya*] out of hand and are utterly humiliated" (9.29–35). This precept is dated to the end of Muḥammad's prophetic activity, that is, following the conquest of Mecca in 630, after Muslim troops had already confronted the Christian populations of

20 Thomas, "Early Muslim Responses."

Yemen, northwestern Arabia, and Nabatea, and shortly before his death in 632. It probably reflects the conditions of the truce offered by the Muslims to the inhabitants of the conquered cities. The later pacts of submission, which the defeated cities were forced to sign with their Islamic conquerors, followed the pattern set by Muḥammad.

The Christian communities of the Near East under caliphal rule

The general principles of the treatment of the non-Muslims, on which the Islamic state's legislation later drew, were thus shaped in the course of the first *Djihad*. The legal convention that regulated relationships between the Islamic power and the subdued "Detainers of the Book," *dhimma*, defined the latter's obligations and the former's guarantee of security. Thus it conferred on the "Detainers of the Book" who recognized the Islamic domination and were disposed to pay the *jizya* (a progressive *tributum capitis*) the status of "Conventional Population," *dhimmī*.[21] The conventions knew a variety of formulations: to the extent that divergent attitudes among the different ethno-confessional groups inhabiting the conquered regions persisted, the new masters treated each community differently.[22] The Arab Christians, whom the Muslims at first recognized as kin, were granted certain privileges in paying tribute. The eastern dyophysite polemics against the Theopaschite language (i.e., language that attributed Christ's sufferings and death to God the Son) used by the miaphysites seemed to the Muslims to point in the same direction as their own rejection of Jesus's divinity. Consequently, the eastern dyophysite version of Christianity, in Muslim eyes, stood closer to the true religion, hence the Syriac Church of the East was also granted a privileged place amongst the Christian communities. At any time, however, all Christian subjects of the caliphs might be associated with the rival empire, and announcements of Byzantine victories on the distant Anatolian frontier were often accompanied by massacres of Christians in the caliphate, especially in northern Syria and Egypt.

Since non-Muslims were tolerated in the land of Islam as "Detainers of the Book," it was their patriarchs or catholicoi who were recognized as the legal chiefs responsible to the Islamic authority. Religious structures were thus the only form of autonomy left to *dhimmī*, while they were deprived of the capacity to give their religions political dimension. The caliphate supported the

21 Rubin, *Dhimmis and Others*, 116–24; on Arabic Christianities, see Griffith in this volume.
22 Troupeau, "Églises et chrétiens," 375–456, 407–11.

jurisdiction of the churches, seeing in them institutions able to assure civil control over the conquered populations. The accumulation of civil responsibilities in the hands of the prelates transformed them into political figures unparalleled elsewhere. Within their communities, the patriarchs also acquired the moral authority of protectors against the exactions of a hostile state and the authority of national leaders. In the case of the miaphysite Syrians, Copts, and Armenians, the triple role of their leaders stimulated a transformation of the anti-Chalcedonian confession into an integral element of ethnic identity. This transformation was not inconsistent with the miaphysites' doctrinal views: the confluence of religious, civil, and national prerogatives in the figures of the miaphysite patriarchs was rather in harmony with the monenergist Christology generally adopted by these churches.

However, the prelates enjoyed only limited immunities, and the caliphs exercised absolute power over their lives. From the eighth century on, the caliphs also exercised increasing influence in the nominations of the prelates of the Syrians and Copts. The "Conventional Populations" found all external manifestations of their cult prohibited, including the construction of new sacred buildings, as well as the reconstruction of ruined ones. In reality, the last injunction was often interpreted as a proscription of any kind of church repair. Prohibiting every kind of missionary activity in the land of Islam further strengthened the association between confessional and ethnic identities and encouraged conservative attitudes among Christians. Moreover, any innovation in the *dhimmī*'s way of life was considered as a further deviation from the originally revealed laws by which the "Detainers of the Book" were expected to abide.

The destruction caused by the war of conquest and the control maintained by the caliphate over communications between different churches contributed to the reciprocal isolation of the various Christian cultures. However, while in certain regions this caused the extinction of Christianity, in others it created conditions for the original development of local traditions based on native languages. On the southern borders of the caliphate, for example, the autonomous Nubian and Ethiopian kings assumed important ecclesiastical responsibilities which accentuated the link between religious and national identity and also conditioned the survival of Christianity in their countries. By the end of the seventh century the Nubian kings recognized the authority of the Alexandrian patriarch, and in Nubia in the following decades the miaphysite faith was to prevail over the Chalcedonian, owing to the proximity of Alexandria and to the absence of contacts with the empire. Moreover, the Nubian kings on various occasions were able to exercise pressure upon the caliphate in order to protect their Coptic coreligionists from the caliphs' exactions. However, the obstacles placed by the caliphate on communication between the Alexandrian patriarchate and the Nubian kingdoms, as well as the Muslim colonization of the Red Sea coasts of Africa (as, later, of the Ethiopian plateau) contributed, from the ninth century, to the weakening of Christianity in Nubia and, a century later, to a long period of decay in the ancient Christian kingdom of Axum in the Eritrean highlands.[23]

Another example may be drawn from the northern borders of the caliphate, where the Georgian Church acquired in the middle of the seventh century an effective autocephaly which a century later was officially recognized by the Melkite patriarch of Antioch. Thereafter, the existence of an ancient literary tradition in the national language rendered possible the development of a distinct culture in Georgia.[24] In Armenia, literary activity in the national language had continued practically uninterrupted ever since the invention of the Armenian alphabet in 406. The Melkite communities, concentrated in the urban areas of the patriarchates of Antioch and Jerusalem and deprived of easy communication with the hellenophone empire, were the first amongst the Christian communities to adopt, already in the course of the eighth century, the conquerors' language in their writing. Although in the course of the ninth century the Arabic language was also introduced into the writing of the East Syrians and, later, of the West Syrians and Maronites, Syriac has always remained the liturgical language of these communities. As for Egypt, in the course of the ninth century the monastery of St. Macarius in the Wadi Natrun adopted the Bohairic Coptic dialect of Lower Egypt, which thus supplanted the ancient Sahidic dialect of Upper Egypt. Although from the middle of the tenth century on Arabic was progressively introduced into Coptic Church writing, Bohairic has ever since remained the liturgical language of the Coptic Church.

The Muslim conquerors mainly aspired to convert Arabs, and during the greater part of the Umayyad period (661–749) the idea of Arab ethnic identity prevailed over the universalistic trend dominant in the Qur'ān (4.79; 7.158; 34.28). Conversion to Islam of non-Arabs was often obstructed, particularly during the age of the early Umayyads, because it would reduce the income of the caliphate's treasury.[25] The Arab tribes experienced the heaviest pressure to convert and most of the bishoprics of the Arabian peninsula and the Persian Gulf were extinguished toward the last quarter of the seventh century. Although most of them abandoned Christianity by the end of the eighth

23 Cuoq, *Islamisation*, 9–63.
24 Martin-Hisard, "Christianisme et église," 554 ff., 576–84.
25 Waardenburg, *Muslims and Others*, 97–98.

century, a portion of the Lakhmids, who shared the confession of the Church of the East favored by the caliphate, remained Christian at least until the beginning of the eleventh century. Also a small section of the miaphysite Taghlibids, a nomadic Arab tribe of Upper Mesopotamia, remained Christian throughout the Abbasid period.

During most of the Umayyad period, high capitation was a major cause of defection from the Christian faith. The Caliph ʿUmar II (717–20) significantly augmented the *jizya*, began to oust the *dhimmī* from administrative positions, and prohibited them from testifying in court. He also seems to have been the first caliph to prescribe external discriminatory signs for the *dhimmī*. These were meant to express their humiliated position and to induce their conversion to Islam. In the later centuries the payment of *jizya* was usually accomplished as a public rite, meant to express, according to Muslim jurists, the humiliation of the *dhimmī*.[26] Under these conditions, social pressure became as important a reason for Christian defections as the burden of tribute, especially under the caliphs who reinforced the discriminatory signs and vexatious rites. By the second half of the eighth century the conversions to Islam reached significant proportions. Nevertheless, in Egypt, Palestine, Syria, and Mesopotamia, Christian populations remained in the majority at least until that time and in some rural and mountainous areas for much longer. Furthermore, for more than two centuries following the Arab conquest, the administrative and medical professions in the caliphate were still dominated by non-Muslims.

The gradual augmentation of the *jizya* (towards 868 it was double that of the previous period) provoked several revolts, the fiercest in Egypt and Armenia. In Egypt, the drastic impoverishment of the Coptic Church caused the introduction of simony. The worst persecutions befell Christians under the Umayyad ʿUmar II, the Abbasid al-Mutawakkil (847–61), and the Fatimid al-Ḥākim (996–1021). The hardening exactions during the Abbasid period (750–1258) increased the hostility of Christians toward the religion of Muḥammad. No longer did they associate him with the biblical patriarchs and prophets as they had done in the early period. The deteriorating conditions of the *dhimmī* under the Abbasids, particularly during Byzantine advances in Asia Minor, provoked their emigration from Armenia and Syria to Byzantium and Georgia, and from Arabia and Egypt to Nubia and Ethiopia. Many communities took refuge in mountainous regions.[27]

The progressive installation of Muslim populations, first on the periphery of Christian cities and then at their centers, intensified the contacts between

26 Fattal, *Le statut légal*, 264–91.
27 Morony, "Age of Conversions," 135–50.

Muslims and Christians and created more occasions for conversions to Islam. It also resulted in the abandonment by Christians of numerous inhabited centers and in the Islamicization of vast regions. The steadiest decline in numbers occurred among the Melkites, and especially among those who resided outside Palestine, for linguistically they represented the most Arabicized group. By the time of the Byzantine reconquest, Christians had become a minority in most of the cities of the eastern Mediterranean region. In certain places, the Christian communities were completely extinguished either as a result of conversion to Islam (especially in the cities) or of emigration (especially in areas adjacent to frontiers). Nevertheless, in spite of the efforts of the Umayyads to integrate Jerusalem into Islam by the construction of two important mosques in 691 and in 705–15, the city remained the focal point of pilgrimage for Christians of all confessions. In 1009, Caliph al-Ḥākim ordered the demolition of the complex of the Holy Sepulcher. Three years later, however, in 1012, the new governor of Syria allowed its reconstruction. The complex was entirely restored with Byzantine help between 1027 and 1048.

In the caliphate and beyond: two cases

The Church of the East and its missions

The Church of the East was chiefly established in Upper and Middle Mesopotamia, and it was there that it was also able to offer the most effective resistance to Islam.[28] The East Syrians were upholders of the ancient medical tradition of Gundeshapur and served numerous caliphs as physicians. This essential role played by the East Syrians at the courts of the caliphs was one of the reasons for the privileged position enjoyed by their catholicoi. Under the first Umayyads, the East Syrians were able to found several new monasteries, an exceptional accomplishment for other Christian communities. The size of the East Syrian population in the Baghdad region, where the Abbasids established their new capital, as well as their importance in the social life of the city, conferred on them an influential position in the new administration and enabled Catholicos Timothy I to transfer the seat of the catholicosate to the capital. As a result the East Syrian catholicoi, the only Christian prelates allowed to reside in Baghdad, often functioned as general representatives at the court of the caliphs for all the Christian communities.[29]

28 Baum, "Zeitalter der Araber," 43–74.
29 Fiey, *Chrétiens syriaques*.

For several centuries following the Arab conquest, Gundeshapur, Nisibis, and Merv continued as intellectual centers of the Church of the East, where a notable and varied literature was produced. Inheritors of the exegetical school of Antioch, the East Syrians bequeathed to posterity important exegetical works, among which a particular place is occupied by the biblical commentary of Išuʿdad of Merv. The writings of Isaac of Nineveh (second half of the seventh century), a hermit in the Khuzistan mountains, were to cross the confessional frontiers and to be translated into Greek, Georgian, Geʾez, and Slavonic. The works of John of Dalyatha (mid-eighth century), a monk of the Qardu mountains, were popular not only among East Syrians, but also among the Syriac, Coptic, and Ethiopian miaphysites despite their author having been accused of Sabellianism and Messalianism.

Three features of the Church of the East conditioned the dynamism of its missions: its internal life was not bound to any state structure and its members were used to living among non-Christians, while its theology was the least formulaic and the most flexible of the Christian confessions. Between the fourth and seventh centuries, the East Syrians spread Christianity southeastward, to Arabia, Socotra, the Maldive Islands, India, Ceylon, and Malaysia, and northeastward, to Bactria, Sogdia, Choresmia, and Turkestan, by the eighth century reaching as far as Tibet, Lake Balkash, and, by the eleventh century, Lake Baikal. This missionary activity was supported by the translation of numerous texts into Pahlavi, Sogdian, and Turkic languages. In 635 the missionaries of Catholicos Išoʿyahḇ II reached China where two metropolitan sees were established. Catholicos Ṣaliba (714–28) appointed metropolitans for Media, Sīstān, and Sogdiana, and Catholicos Timothy I for the southern Caspian provinces, Makran, Tibet, China, and eastern Turkestan. In China, the Imperial Edict of 638 allowed the preaching of the "Persian religion," that is, Christianity.[30] By the turn of the millennium more than five hundred writings had been translated from Syriac and Sogdian into Chinese. Nevertheless, Christianity was never able to achieve in the Far East the success of Manicheism or Zoroastrianism. Chinese persecutions against monks of all foreign religions began in 843–45. Without exterior support, foreign religions in China and Tibet were bound to decline, yet the eastern dyophysite communities survived in the steppes of western China under Tibetan domination, reemerging in the late tenth century under the Liao dynasty.

30 Riboud, "Tang."

The churches of Transcaucasia

Although the first Arab invasions into Armenia began in 640, and in 693 direct control over Transcaucasia was established, the countries of this region maintained considerable autonomy until c. 699–701, when the province of Armīniya was created, incorporating Armenia, eastern Georgia, and Ałuankʿ into the caliphate. Thereafter the Arabs attempted several times to suppress the traditional Armenian aristocracy, yet they never succeeded in creating a coordinated administrative system in the area. Georgia, on account of its remote position, was generally spared the repression that was to befall Armenia. The caliphate failed to achieve firm control beyond the Kura, and this allowed Georgia to continue the Christianization of the isolated mountainous regions of the Great Caucasus where Christianity had been unknown until the seventh century.[31]

The Armenian and Georgian princes had never completely lost their political importance, and in the first half of the ninth century, when the power of Baghdad began to weaken, they were able to restore the semi-autonomous principalities which, in the course of several decades, acquired ever greater independence. In 885 the caliphate recognized the royal title of the Armenian Bagratide Prince Ašot and in 888, of the Georgian Bagratide Prince Adarnarseh. The Transcaucasian princes promoted cenobitic monastic foundations on their estates by offering them protection and generous gifts.[32] The Armenian and Georgian monasteries attracted the population of the surrounding regions, becoming nuclei for the repopulation of deserted territories, and for economic development and learning. The erudite Anania of Narek (tenth century) worked in the monastic school of Narek close to the southern shore of Lake Van, as did his disciple, the poet Gregory of Narek (c. 945–1010), whose *Book of Lamentations* has left a particularly profound stamp on Armenian spirituality.

From the Byzantine reconquests to the battle of Mantzikert (926–1071)

The Byzantine army crossed the Euphrates between 873 and 883, and early in the tenth century the political influence of the empire was extended over the greater part of Armenia. Between the years 926 and 944, under the command of General John Courcouas (Armenian Gurgēn), the Byzantine army, which included an important number of Armenians, seized Melitene (934) and advanced northward beyond Lake Van and southward to Syria. In 949 it

31 Martin-Hisard, "Christianisme et église," 561.
32 Mahé, "L'église arménienne," 513–17; Martin-Hisard, "Christianisme et église," 567–71.

occupied Karin and in 966 annexed the Armenian principality of Tarōn. Advancing through Cilicia, the Byzantines next occupied northern Syria and in 967–69 conquered Antioch. In 974 they entered Mesopotamia and in 975 moved into northern Palestine.

The conquest of Armenia and Syria was accompanied by the implantation of imperial orthodoxy and by the creation of Chalcedonian bishoprics. Together with the Melkite hierarchy, Greek and Bulgarian governors renewed persecutions of the predominantly miaphysite population. After the reconquest of Antioch, close imperial control over the Melkite Church was established. As earlier in Jerusalem, so now also at Antioch, Byzantine canonical practices and the Greek rite were imposed. In the course of the tenth century, the Byzantine rite celebrated in Greek prevailed also in Alexandria.

The occupied Armenian principalities were incorporated into the imperial provincial system. The new administration and its mercenary troops supplanted the hereditary rulers who had been the traditional defenders against the successive invasions of the country. The annexation of the Armenian territories by the empire was accompanied by forced extradition of the Armenian population to Cappadocia, a region decimated by Arab–Byzantine warfare. Thus Armenia was gradually deprived of its traditional administrative structure, of its confessional cohesion, and of a significant part of its population. Previously Armenia had often acted as a buffer state: its capacity for any resistance to future invasions was now drastically reduced. The politics adopted by the empire in Armenia thus facilitated the rapid Seljuk conquest of Asia Minor a century later.

Between the years 1011 and 1064, the Byzantine army gradually extended its hold over the larger part of Armenia, stopping just short of Duin. As the Seljuk Turks multiplied their incursions into the region, the Armenians and Syrians, unwilling to convert to the Chalcedonian faith, were regularly persecuted, particularly by Constantine IX Monomachus (1042–55) and Constantine X Ducas (1059–67). As a result, many Armenians deserted from the Byzantine army. In 1045, the Armenian king, Gagik II, was forced by the emperor to surrender his capital of Ani and to choose honorable exile. The next year, Catholicos Peter I was imprisoned by the Byzantines and subsequently brought to Constantinople. But it was easier for the Byzantines to take Ani from the Armenians than to defend it from the Turks: the former Armenian capital fell to the Seljuks in 1064. In 1071 the unprepared Byzantine army lost the battle at Mantzikert, and two years later the Turks began their systematic occupation of central Anatolia. This opened a new era of political and religious change in the Near East.

Conclusion

At no moment after the Council of Chalcedon was the Christian church able to achieve its vision of unity. In this contested environment, the Persian and then Arab conquests perpetuated the extant divisions of doctrine and allegiance. Moreover the spread of Islam exercised lasting influence upon the character of the Christian cultures of the Near East. Throughout the eastern Mediterranean and Near East, conquest, conflict, and persecution gave the churches of this area the impulse to anchor their identities upon the figures of their first fathers and upon the teachings handed down by them. Attachment to their autochthonous origins allowed these churches to overcome the disruptions of their history, and can thus be recognized as one of their distinguishing features. Under hostile regimes, the religious concerns of Christians were above all dedicated to the maintenance of the ancient traditions of their communities, to justifications of the points of their Creed which were contested by Muslims (such as the authenticity of the Scriptures and the divinity of Christ), and to the preservation of the memory of their martyrs. The formation of national churches made possible the survival of Christianity in the caliphate, and anticipated similar developments among the churches of Byzantine tradition under Ottoman rule. The Islamic conquest thus contributed to the maintenance of specific characteristics of each of the various Christian cultures of the Near East, while the Byzantine Church, as later also the Roman Church, tended to ever greater uniformity.[33]

33 The author wishes to express his gratitude to Professors Bernadette Martin-Hisard, John Lindsay-Opie, and Andrew Louth, and to Father Timothy Gorham, for their suggestions made for this chapter.

4

Beyond empire II: Christianities of the Celtic peoples

THOMAS M. CHARLES-EDWARDS

The inheritance

For this chapter, the Celtic peoples are those which still, in 600 CE, spoke a Celtic language. The continental Celts of antiquity are thus excluded, leaving only the Britons, who inherited their Christianity from Roman Britain, the Irish, who received theirs mainly from the Britons in the fifth and early sixth centuries, and the Picts. By 600 the initial constructive phase of Irish Christianity was over. It was three years since Columba died on Iona; Columbanus had already left Bangor for Burgundy. The great churches of the Irish were nearly all founded in the sixth century. There remained, however, many traces of that earlier period when, because of Irish settlements in Britain and British missionaries in Ireland, the church of the smaller island had been formed in the image of the church of the Britons. The insular scripts, shared by Britons and Irish, are only one especially obvious sign of the connection. The years about 600 were also, however, the time at which the younger Irish Church began to overshadow its British foster-parent. On the one hand, the British Church was suffering territorial loss and impoverishment from the English advance.[1] On the other hand, Columbanus's letters to the papacy betray a pride in the flourishing Christianity of his homeland.

Not only had the British Church suffered from English advance, it was also threatened by the implications of the Gregorian mission to the English. Moreover, its Breton offshoot had, by 600, been instrumental in driving a wedge between the Christianity of "the Romans" of Gaul, those whom we call Gallo-Romans, and the Christianity of the Britons. In principle, Brittany was only part of the province of Lugdunensis Tertia and should therefore have been subject to the metropolitan bishop of Tours. Yet, as the works of one such metropolitan bishop, Gregory of Tours (d. 594), make evident, Brittany was as unruly a member of the Gallic Church as it was of the dominion of the

1 Pryce, "Ecclesiastical Wealth," 22–25.

Franks.[2] There were slowly evolving cultural changes driving the Britons and the Gallo-Romans apart. By 600 Gallo-Romans were speakers of a Latin on the road to Romance; and, whereas in 400 there were many Britons whose first language was Latin, their numbers decreased in the period 400 to 700, and by the end of that period British Romance was probably extinct. Since the native Celtic language of the Britons established itself so strongly in the western half of Brittany, the politically and culturally dominant element among the settlers from across the Channel must have been British-speaking. This explains the paradox of the Britons: for the English and initially also for the Franks, they were *Walas* (*Wealas*), namely "foreigners who had been part of the Roman Empire";[3] and yet, for Venantius Fortunatus (c. 530–c. 610), priest and poet, and later bishop of Poitiers, they were barbarians, non-Roman foreigners, as were Saxons, Franks, and Alamans.[4] The cultural community bequeathed by the Latin-speaking west of the Roman Empire had gradually extruded those unassimilated elements, Britons and Basques, and now considered them as foreign as "the tribes from across the Rhine" and thus to be feared by all right-thinking Gallo-Romans.[5] The Britons themselves, however, still thought of themselves in 600 as fellow-citizens of the Romans.[6]

In Britain, as in Brittany, post-Roman epigraphy long continued, largely in the Roman manner, with letter-forms descended from Roman capitals. But, in the seventh century, the distinction between epigraphic letter-forms and those appropriate for book scripts collapsed. In the late-seventh century, on the other hand, the English adopted epigraphy in the Roman tradition, as illustrated by the dedication inscription of Bede's monastery, Jarrow, put up by Ceolfrith in 685.[7] As one culture abandoned Roman traditions, so the neighboring culture adopted them. For the Britons, the seventh century was a watershed between a post-Roman world and one in which the Roman Empire and all its works had receded into the past. For the English, it was a period in which they reconnected with the Roman past of the island which they had made their home. After the Synod of Whitby in 664, the contrast acquired a new sharpness.

2 Gregory of Tours, *Libri historiarum X*, IV.4; IX.18, 20.

3 *Pactus Legis Salicae*, Title xli or see *Laws of the Salian and Ripuarian Franks*, 86–87. The best witness to the Malberg glosses, Eckhardt's *A 2*, is defective for xli. 8, but its exemplar may well have had *uualaleodi* as in xli. 9–10.

4 Venantius Fortunatus, *Opera Poetica*, Appendix 2. *Ad Iustinum et Sophiam Augustos*, ll.31–32, 83–84.

5 *Epistolae Austrasicae* no. 9 (Germanus of Paris, "Letter to Queen Brunhild"); Gregory of Tours, *Libri historiarum X*, IV.49.

6 *Canones Wallici*, Version A, § 61 in *Irish Penitentials*, 148–49.

7 Higgitt, "Dedication Inscription."

The watershed of the seventh century was, however, crossed by many paths. One reason why it has been possible to assert (falsely) that British Christianity was not an inheritance from the Christianity of late Roman Britain is that later Welsh and Breton writers were concerned to recall sixth-century churchmen but only fourth-century emperors.[8] Most saints who came to be the vehicles of remembrance for their churches were dated to the sixth century: thus St. David, patron saint of the premier church of Wales, was believed to have died either in 589 or 601.[9] They all tended to be made into contemporaries, because what mattered later was the relationship between their churches, and that relationship was expressed as a relationship between the patron saints, who therefore had to be portrayed as living at the same time. The occasional exceptions, such as Patrick, were unusual and were linked with the main "Age of the Saints" by other means, mainly by prophecy.

Division and reconciliation

The Gregorian mission to the English made a huge difference to the position of the British Church. The latter had been successful in maintaining a Christian tradition across the violent centuries following the end of direct central Roman authority in Britain. Although the British Church was later condemned by Bede because it had failed to preach to the English, its role in the conversion of the Irish demonstrates that it was not a church unconcerned with the salvation of neighboring peoples; and there is reason to believe that, even for the English, Bede's verdict was unduly harsh.[10] That the British Church was not, as is often claimed, cut off from continental Christianity is apparent from the history of Brittany – Brittany was certainly not cut off either from Britain or from the rest of Gaul.[11] It is easy to forget that, even in Burgundy, when Columbanus sought the aid of a neighboring abbot in the early days of his foundations, that abbot bore a British name, Carantocus;[12] and even Gregory of Tours, who had little good to say about the Bretons, once thought that he had found for his city of Tours a truly saintly ascetic in the shape of Winnoch, a Breton.[13] In the seventh century, the Breton King Iudicail refused to eat with King Dagobert, but he was quite prepared to enjoy the hospitality of a great monastic patron, Dado, whose morals were more to his taste than were those of the Frankish

8 Sharpe, "Martyrs and Local Saints," 145.
9 *Annales Cambriae*, *s.a.* 601; *Chronicle of Ireland*, *s.a.* 589.
10 Sims-Williams, *Religion and Literature*, 75–86.
11 Chédeville and Guillotel, *La Bretagne*, 113–51.
12 Jonas, *Vita S. Columbani*, chap. 7, 165.
13 Gregory of Tours, *Libri historiarum X*, V.21, VIII.34.

king.[14] In Ireland, a major role for the British Church in the conversion period was entirely consistent with a continuing remembrance of the role of Rome itself in the first beginnings of Irish Christianity.[15]

Rome, however, came to establish its principal British bridgehead in Canterbury, a former Romano-British *civitas* capital in the far southeast of the island, now laid out as a new reflection of Rome in the northwest.[16] Moreover, although Gregory was concerned with the conversion of the English, he prescribed two metropolitan bishoprics for the whole of Britain, including the Britons; both metropolitan bishops were to have sees in eastern England. Those he picked, London and York, were probably chosen because of their role in Roman Britain; yet, when Canterbury replaced London, that only accentuated the eastward tilt of Gregory's new framework for a Christian Britain. It was also important for the position of the British Church in the new order that communication between England and Rome went via Francia: it is apparent from the letter of Laurence, archbishop of Canterbury, to the Irish Church that Canterbury's opinions of its neighboring churches were strongly influenced by Frankish opinion – and, moreover, by a party in the Frankish Church hostile to Columbanus, a party which saw a connection between Columbanus and the Britons. British as well as Irish monks within Columbanus's communities were to be expelled from Burgundy in 610, while Franks and others could remain.[17] In this way, the uncomfortable relations between the Church of Gaul and the Britons of Armorica were transferred to Britain and soured relations between the new English Church and its British neighbor. As the Church of Brittany stood to the Church of Gaul, until the Carolingian conquest in the reign of Louis the Pious, so, until the twelfth century, the British Church stood to the new Gregorian order established among the English.

Relations between the first Gregorian missionary bishop of Canterbury, Augustine, and the Britons reveal differences in organization between the British and English Churches, and also the Church of Gaul.[18] The Council of Nicaea partly assumed, partly promulgated a rule that each city should have its bishop, and each province its synod of bishops, presided over by a metropolitan bishop. In northern Gaul the *civitates*, and thus the territories attached to each episcopal see, were large. In Roman Britain *civitates* were also large. In accordance with this rule, there should, therefore, have been

14 Fredegar, *Chronica*, IV.78.
15 Columbanus, *Epistola*, V.3 (see *Opera*, 38–39).
16 Brooks, "Canterbury, Rome."
17 Bede, *HE*, II.4; Jonas, *Vita S. Columbani*, I.20, 196.
18 Stancliffe, "British Church."

few bishops in Britain because there were few *civitates*. But in the British Church there appear to have been many more bishops than one would, on this basis, expect. When Augustine of Canterbury made his first approach to the British Church, it took the form of a meeting with representatives from "the neighboring British kingdom," arranged through the influence of King Æthelberht of Kent on what was, in Bede's day, the border between the Hwicce and the West Saxons.[19] From this single kingdom came a plurality of "bishops and teachers." Aldhelm's letter to Geraint, king of Dumnonia, probably to be dated to the 670s, was addressed also to the bishops of Geraint's kingdom; moreover it also mentioned the bishops, in the plural, of Dyfed.[20] Yet both Dumnonia and Dyfed were former Romano-British *civitates*, and both should, therefore, have had a single bishop. If we assume that the church of fourth-century Britain was evolving a structure following the ruling at the Council of Nicaea, we must also posit a change to a different structure in the post-Roman period. And, since this multiplicity of bishops was also characteristic of the early Irish Church, it is probably safe to assume that the change came in the fifth century, with the completion of the conversion of Roman Britain and thus much greater numbers of Christians requiring the pastoral care of bishops.

Another difference is indicated by Bede's account of Augustine's dealings with the Britons and confirmed by the organization of the Irish Church. Abbots and *doctores* attended synods, alongside bishops, apparently as full members. In contemporary Gaul, as elsewhere in the church, synods were conceived as meetings of bishops; if other clergy attended they did so in a subordinate role. Decisions of a synod were, in Gaul, made on episcopal authority; but in the British and Irish Churches they might rest as much on the authority of ecclesiastical scholars as on that of bishops.[21] Again, this is likely to have been a development of the fifth century, since it was as characteristic of the Irish as of the British Church.

This shared authority attributed to scholars is probably connected with another feature. As we have seen already, British Latin, on its way to Romance, was in decline from the fifth to the seventh century; the dominant language was now the native British Celtic. Moreover, before the Gregorian mission the center of gravity of the church in the British Isles as a whole had been shifting westward, because of English settlements in the east and the conversion of

19 Bede, *HE*, II.2.

20 Aldhelm, *Letter IV*, *Aldhelmi opera omnia*, 481, 484 or in English translation, *Prose Works*, 155, 158.

21 *Canones Hibernenses*, III and VI in *Irish Penitentials*, 166–68, 174, are ascribed to synods of *sapientes*.

the Irish in the west. It was shifting away from those parts of Britain which, in the fourth century, had been most Romanized and thus, one may assume, most prone to use Latin as a first language. The linguistic and cultural position of the British Church – increasingly – and of the Irish Church from the start was the polar opposite of the situation of the Gallic Church, apart from the northeast of Francia. As the Gallo-Romans abandoned Gaulish and came to regard themselves quite simply as Romans, speaking Latin, the language of Rome, they made the position of the Church apparently much easier: both priests and their congregations shared the one language, and that language was the language of their liturgy and their Bible. True, it was a regional dialect of Late Latin, well-removed from the standard language taught by Donatus and other grammarians; but, even so, the liturgical and intellectual life of the Gallic Church did not rest upon an education in a foreign language. In Britain it increasingly did, and in Ireland it did from the start. Schools in which one might learn Latin and subsequently all the intellectual equipment that a priest or bishop needed were an essential part of the British and Irish Churches.[22]

One should not suppose that such schools provided a free education. Admittedly, Bede expressly says that they did so for the English who went to Ireland for their education in the seventh century;[23] but that was a special situation, the outcome of an Irish mission to the English. What is more likely, to judge by the situation implied by Gildas and revealed in the richer Irish sources of the seventh and early eighth centuries, was that education and high status were closely linked. As it had been appropriate for an aristocrat in the Late Roman Empire to have a refined literary education, so, in the British and Irish Churches, learning in the Latin-based culture of the western church conferred a qualification for high rank. This must have been more than merely an unconscious outcome of cultural change, since it involved a major change to the organization of the church: leading scholars were now admitted as full members of synods.

The British and Irish churches, therefore, had much in common – unsurprisingly so, since the British Church had played the major role in the conversion of the Irish. In some ways, also, the British and Irish churches were diverging from their Gallic neighbor. That does not justify any talk of "a Celtic Church" or even of "the Celtic churches" or "Celtic Christianity."[24] First, "Celt" and

22 Charles-Edwards, "Language and Society," 715–26, and "Context and Uses of Literacy," 64–68.

23 Bede, *HE*, III.27.

24 Hughes, "Celtic Church"; W. Davies, "Myth of the Celtic Church"; Meek, *Quest for Celtic Christianity*.

"Celtic" were not part of their conceptual world. Secondly, the fact (unrecognized at the time) that the Britons and the Irish spoke related languages had a merely accidental relationship with any shared characteristics in their Christianity. The Britons did not play a major role in the conversion of the Irish because they spoke related languages, but because the two peoples were neighbors who had become yet more closely involved with each other after the Irish had settled extensively along the western coasts of Britain.

In 664 the Synod of Whitby ended the authority of Iona over the church in Northumbria and, via Northumbria, in much of southern England. Subsequent bishops among the Northumbrians were English and owed no allegiance to Iona. Moreover, the Synod of Whitby was only one episode in a long-running controversy in which the prestige of Iona was also threatened in Ireland and among the Picts. From 664 to 716, when Iona adopted the Roman Easter, the dominant opinion in England and in southern Ireland was that Iona and those churches which agreed with it, were heretical and schismatic.[25] Eventually, in the work of Bede, another opinion was to triumph, namely that Columba and his successors were wrong but orthodox.[26] Modern scholars have sometimes found it difficult to appreciate that one reason why Bede made much of the paschal controversy was that he proposed to rescue the reputation of Aidan and Columba from the harsh condemnations of such men as Theodore, archbishop of Britain, and Wilfrid, bishop of York, condemnations already foreshadowed in a letter sent c. 632 by Cummian to Ségéne, the abbot of Iona who sent Aidan and Fínán to Northumbria.[27] From then until c. 685 the Irish Church was split into two camps, the "Romans," *Romani*, and the "Hibernians," *Hibernenses*. As the titles show, there was more to the controversy than a dispute over how astronomy and exegesis should be used to determine the Christian calendar. The Irish Romans wished to align themselves with the papacy and with the Universal Church: so much is evident from the arguments used by Cummian.[28] The Hibernians upheld the traditions they had received from the sixth-century founders of the great Irish monastic churches, such as Columba.[29] A tradition in which the status of a church was bound up with the status of its founder was bound to find major change difficult.

25 Cummian, *De controversia Paschali*, 94, lines 294–96; Theodore, *Penitential*, II.ix.1–3, 323–24 or in trans. McNeill and Gamer, 206–207; Stephen, *Vita S. Wilfridi*, chaps. 5, 47 or trans. Colgrave, 12, 98.

26 Bede, *HE*, III.17; *Anonymous Life of St. Cuthbert*, i.5 or in trans. Colgrave, 68–71.

27 Cummian, *De controversia Paschali*, 56–97.

28 Ibid., especially lines 86–149, 277–85.

29 Bede, *HE*, III.25.

The achievement of Adomnán, abbot of Iona from 679 to 704 or 705, was to transcend the paschal controversy by his scholarship and diplomacy. His *Life of Columba*, written between 697 and his death, celebrated a saint whose reputation was to be independent of the issue of Easter.[30] Although Adomnán's conversion to the Roman Easter, in the course of a diplomatic mission to Northumbria, failed to carry the community of Iona, it did bring over many churches in the northern half of Ireland as well as the Britons of what is now southern Scotland.[31] His success in securing the promulgation of "The Law of Adomnán" in 697 showed how a legal innovation could be made to embrace the whole of Ireland and also the Picts.[32] The Law of Adomnán is preserved in Old Irish and is thus aligned with native Irish law, whereas normal early Irish canon law was in Latin. The two major law-books, the *Senchas Már* and the *Collectio Canonum Hibernensis*, one for native Irish law, the other for canon law, date from the generation after Adomnán; but the texts from which they were compiled were in active production during his lifetime.[33] Both legal traditions were common to the whole island and were constituents of a culture rather than instruments of a state (there was no single Irish state, although the kings of Tara enjoyed an island-wide primacy). Alongside these forms of law was a third, the *rechtge* or *cáin*, of which the normal form was promulgated by a king in conjunction with an assembly of his people. The authority of an edict of this kind was naturally confined to a particular kingdom within Ireland.

The Law of Adomnán was such a *cáin* but was promulgated at a major assembly at the monastery of Birr, close to the frontier between Munster and Mide (Meath) and thus between the southern and northern halves of the island. It embraced rulers or their representatives from all provinces of the island and most kingdoms of any significance. The old text (preserved in a later edition, prefaced by hagiographical material about Adomnán himself) includes a list of guarantors, of which the clerical half is headed by the bishop of Armagh and the lay half by Adomnán's cousin, Loingsech mac Óengusso, king of Tara. The intention of the Law was to secure immunity from violence for non-combatants – clerics, women, and children. Once a boy had reached the age at which he took arms, he was no longer a non-combatant, whether or not he had actively participated in conflict. The mechanism by which this immunity was to be safeguarded was, for a period of years, to increase the

30 Adomnán, *Vita Sancti Columbae*, I. 3 (Columba simply prophesies the divisions caused by the controversy).
31 Bede, *HE*, V.15.
32 *Cáin Adamnáin* or trans. Ní Dhonnchadha, "Law of Adomnán."
33 Kelly, *Guide to Early Irish Law*, 242–46.

normal compensation for killing and, from this increased sum, to give a share to all authorities, whether king or ordinary lord or church, who enforced the Law. The intent was to mobilize all social power, not just that of the king. The mechanism was temporary but the effect was to be permanent; and since the mechanism was temporary the Law of Adomnán could be re-promulgated, as it was thirty years later, in 727.

The Law of Adomnán bridged several gaps: as a mechanism it was an offshoot from ordinary edicts promulgated by king and people for a single kingdom, and yet this Law embraced all Ireland. The assembly which promulgated it was not the normal "gathering" of a people, *óenach*, but a mixture of royal meeting on the frontier, *rígdál*, and synod. Normal native Irish law was in Irish because it was ancient tradition, *senchas*, for the Irish; and yet this Law of Adomnán, although it was in Irish, also extended to the Picts. Whereas native Irish law presented the relationship between the church and the laity as a contract, in which the church had obligations as well as privileges, the *Collectio Canonum Hibernensis* avoided such a contractual approach and was more concerned to limit the obligations of individual churches; the Law of Adomnán, however, embraced lay and clerical authority, and likewise lay and clerical non-combatant, on an equal footing.

An approach, which was ready to employ the devices of Irish culture in an enterprise which went beyond the island of Ireland and beyond, also, the Irish people, is exemplified in the art found within what we may call the domain and former domain of Iona. The art of the insular Gospel Books – such as the Book of Durrow; the Lindisfarne, Durham, Echternach, and Lichfield Gospels; and the Book of Kells – employed a range of devices some of which were of Irish origin, others came from Pictland, and yet others from English territory. It was an art by which the British Isles as a whole might revere "the Good News" of Christ's human birth, passion, resurrection, and ascension.

Religion and literature

The Law of Adomnán was, as we have seen, in Irish, and thus exemplifies the extent to which a literacy which came to Ireland with Latin now embraced the native language of the Irish. Similarly among the Britons, although there is much less surviving evidence, the same transition from Latin to the vernacular occurred by the seventh century. Vernacular written literature first flourished in the British Isles for the understandable reason that Latin was, except vestigially among the Britons, a language learnt at school. By the time that Aidan preached Christianity to the Northumbrians in a land of which many inhabitants would still have been speakers of a Brittonic dialect, both Irish and the Brittonic dialects had made the transition: it is most unlikely that on the part of the Irish missionaries there was any resistance to the use of the vernacular among the English.

The imprint of Christianity on Irish and Welsh literature is perhaps at its most profound when a text betrays no trace of Christianity or, indeed, any other religion. Two general principles lie behind both early Irish and early Welsh literature: the first is that narrative was in prose not verse; the second is that, within the broad category of narrative, hagiography and saga were two genres which did not, at this period, explicitly interact. Thus the early British poem, *Y Gododdin*, was occasioned by an event, but does not narrate it; instead it is a series of laments for warriors who were recruited by the ruler of the British people called the Gododdin (Votadini) to his fortress at Edinburgh – warriors who then died in battle against the Deirans at Catraeth. These two principles were not universal and absolute: a significant exception to the first is that verse was sometimes used to tell stories derived from the Bible or the Apocrypha, as in the work of the late eighth-century Irish poet Blathmac.[34] As for the second principle, explicit interaction is already seen in a particular genre, that of the *Immram* or "voyage" tale, as in the ninth-century *Immram Curaig Maíle Dúin*.[35] It would become widespread in the tenth century, especially in texts probably associated with Clonmacnois. Until then, however, the two genres of saga and hagiography normally formed separate spheres.

This separation of spheres stems from early British and Irish attitudes to violence. A feature which distinguishes much early Irish hagiography is the open hostility to a lay life characterized by violence.[36] For the Briton Gildas in the sixth century or the Irishman Adomnán at the end of the seventh, for someone who has taken vows of non-combatancy as a cleric to return to the violent world of the layman was a spiritual catastrophe.[37] The deaths of kings were divided between natural death and death by violence; the former was a special blessing, the latter the common fate of kings. But death by violence was not just a misfortune but also an indication of the bad spiritual state of the slain. The Iona annals lying behind the existing Irish annals for the period from 590 up to 650 gave the title of king of Tara to those who died in their beds, but not to those who died in battle or, even worse, by an individual killing.[38]

34 *Poems of Blathmac*.
35 *Immram Curaig Maíle Dúin*.
36 Sharpe, "Hiberno-Latin *Laicus*."
37 Gildas, *Ruin of Britain*, § 34, on Maelgwn; Adomnán, *Vita Sancti Columbae*, I.36, on Áed Dub.
38 Charles-Edwards, *Early Christian Ireland*, 503–5.

This standpoint appears behind the early British and Irish penitentials. If a cleric committed a particularly grave sin, he was degraded and lost the status he held as a cleric; but if a layman committed grave sin and underwent penance, he had to live like a cleric, abjuring violence and abstaining from sex.[39] Part of his penance also involved fasting and abstaining from meat and alcoholic drink. Meat-eating was believed to make the passions of anger and sexual desire stronger, while alcoholic drink made such grave sins more likely.[40] Violence and unregulated sex characterized a this-worldly manner of life, dominated by death and reproduction; the life of the penitent should remain apart, looking toward heaven.

When early Irish and British literature kept Christianity and saga apart, this was not because its Christianity was purely for clerics but because it maintained a radical critique of the life of a lay aristocrat. When Adomnán's *Life of Columba* included a passage in which the dead saint appeared in a dream to King Oswald and promised him his protection in battle against the British king Cadwallon, that was exceptional and, in the terms of early Irish hagiography, startling.[41] Much early Irish literature placed its characters in a remote pre-Patrician past (by the eighth century, Irish Christianity was held to begin with Patrick) and there was thus no difficulty in portraying heroes whose values were utterly remote from those espoused by the penitentials. But even a saga about a Christian king of Leinster of the seventh century, *Fingal Rónáin*, kept Christianity and, indeed, all religion out of the narrative.[42] When the characters make verse-speeches, and so reveal their motivations, the same rule of separation continued to apply: the nearest *Fingal Rónán* came to admitting Christianity was a reference to burial in a shroud and a coffin. The chasm between the values of the aristocratic lay world and those of the pre-Viking church was only rarely bridgeable. Irish clerics may have enjoyed listening to stories about Cú Chulainn, the Achilles of early Irish saga, but they long kept him at arm's length.

This separation of spheres did not mean that the laity were abandoned to the Devil. The vernacular laws betray considerable evidence of the moral demands made by the church, even in the sexual domain, where the behavior of most kings appears to have been, at best, one of serial monogamy.[43] On the other side, the laity made demands on churches – that they should pray for

39 Penitential of Finnian, §§ 8, 12 (clergy), 35–37 (laity), in *Irish Penitentials*, 76, 86.
40 *Monastery of Tallaght*, §§ 6, 11, 60.
41 Adomnán, *Vita Sancti Columbae*, I.1.
42 *Fingal Rónáin*, 3–11, or translation Ní Dhonnchadha, *Celtic Heroic Age*, 274–82.
43 For example *Críth Gablach*, §§ 15 (lines 199–202), 24 (lines 341–47); *Uraicecht na Ríar*, § 6, 104.

the dead, that mass should be offered, that people should be baptized.[44] The converse is that by the tenth century the gap between lay aristocratic values and those of the Irish Church was much less acute than it had been. That was what explained the extensive cultivation of saga and the interpenetration of saga and hagiography in such a leading monastery as Clonmacnois.

Some early Irish and Welsh narrative texts introduce the former pagan gods as characters, but they normally keep them in the pre-Christian past. The Welsh *Four Branches of the Mabinogi* is later than our period but had a long prehistory.[45] If it is fair to see the early Welsh sense of their past as divided into three eras – pre-Roman (and also pre-Christian), Roman, and post-Roman – the former gods of *The Four Branches* were firmly placed in the first era. Similarly, the gods of one of the principal tales of the Irish "Mythological Cycle," *The Battle of Mag Tuired*, fought their great battle against the Fomorians centuries before Christ, even though this late ninth-century saga was told in such a way as to make the Fomorians evident forerunners of the Vikings, while the gods represented the Irish.[46] It is arguable that early Irish narrative came to be written in such profusion because it could be taken for history.[47] The pagan gods were thus safely placed in an early period of the history of Ireland, a history which would culminate in conversion: that the whole history of Ireland would end in a Christian present took the sting from that remote pagan past.

Monasteries, bishops, and scholars

Most of the great monastic churches of the Britons and the Irish were already founded before 600. The age of monastic foundation was not entirely over, however: Lismore in Munster was founded in 636, after the founder, Mo Chutu, had been expelled from his previous church at Rahan in Co. Meath.[48] It would become a notably distinguished center of theological studies almost immediately after its foundation: the anonymous *De Mirabilibus Sacrae Scripturae* was written there in 655.[49] During the seventh century the major Irish monastic churches were extending their influence and increasing their wealth. Lesser churches became subject to them; and they also acquired numerous *manaig*, "monks" in the secondary sense of lay and usually married tenants of a church

44 *Corpus Iuris Hibernici*, 529.20–22; 2211.27–28 = First Third of *Bretha Nemed Toísech*, § 6, 10. See also *Monastery of Tallaght*, § 18.
45 As shown by the poem *Echrys ynys*; see also Carey, "British Myth of Origins?"
46 *Cath Maige Tuired*, esp. §§ 50–51; Mac Cana, "Influence of the Vikings," 94–95.
47 Toner, "Ulster Cycle."
48 *Annals of Ulster*, *s.a.* 636.
49 Grosjean, "Sur quelques exégètes irlandais"; Kenney, *Sources for the Early History*, no. 104.

who were considered to be members of the monastic community. As such, they were subject to the rule of the abbot and were, unlike the majority of the laity, expected to be buried in the monastic cemetery.

Scholars are still not agreed on the relationship between the leading monasteries and an ecclesiastical organization in which, according to such sources as the *Collectio Canonum Hibernensis* and the vernacular laws, bishops retained a central role. In the central decades of the twentieth century, the standard view (still supported by some historians) maintained that an episcopally governed church was only characteristic of the fifth and early-sixth centuries, even though this organization left a lasting imprint on prescriptive sources.[50] In the late-sixth and seventh centuries, it was largely replaced by the power of the abbots of the major monasteries. As we have seen already, Ireland inherited from Britain a situation in which there might be several bishops in a major kingdom (roughly equivalent to a Gallo-Roman or Romano-British *civitas*). Such a major kingdom was, however, divided into smaller kingdoms, often called *tuatha* (sg. *tuath*); and it was considered proper that a *tuath* should have a bishop as well as a king.[51] According to the traditional argument, the head of a major monastery enjoyed a power extended into several *tuatha* and thus came to overshadow the bishop of a single *tuath*. The latter retained his sacramental functions, but in the government of the church he was of little account beside the abbot of an important monastery. To take one example, Clonmacnois, founded by Ciarán mac int Shaír, was among the most powerful of Irish monasteries. It was situated in a minor kingdom, Delbnae Bethra, on the east bank of the River Shannon. Already by the late seventh century, however, it had dependent churches in Connaught, the province on the west side of the Shannon, and by 900 it was the leading church of the entire province, even though Delbnae Bethra was not merely a minor kingdom, but was part of the province of Mide, to the east of the Shannon.[52] The power of Clonmacnois transcended, therefore, the boundaries of Delbnae Bethra (a *tuath*), and also the boundaries of the province of Mide; it came to predominate in a province, Connaught, to which it did not itself belong. "The heir of Ciarán mac int Shaír" was a far more considerable figure in the Irish Church than any mere bishop of Delbnae Bethra (just as the abbot of Cluny in the eleventh century was a more imposing figure than the bishop of Mâcon). While the annals regularly

50 Kenney, *Sources for the Early History*, 291–93; Hughes, *Church in Early Irish Society*, 57–90; Ó Corráin, "Early Irish Churches"; Ó Cróinín, *Early Medieval Ireland*, 147–68.
51 *Corpus Iuris Hibernici*, 1123.32–33.
52 Tírechán, *Collectanea*, § 25.

record the obits of abbots of Clonmacnois, they never mention a bishop of Delbnae Bethra.

It has not been denied that such extensive monastic overlordships grew up by the end of the seventh century.[53] What has been questioned is, first, whether the term *parochia* (sometimes spelt *paruchia* by Irish writers), as used by Tírechán for Armagh, by Cogitosus for Kildare, and by the annals for Clonard, normally meant a federation of monasteries of the kind described by Bede for Iona, or rather "a sphere of jurisdiction" including an episcopal diocese in the modern sense and also a larger territory. Tírechán and Cogitosus used it for the island-wide authority claimed by Armagh and Kildare.[54] Secondly, it has rightly been observed that some bishops were not confined to a single *tuath*: there were higher levels of bishop approximately corresponding to the metropolitan bishop and even the archbishop found elsewhere in the western church by the end of the seventh century. The contrast between the mere bishop of a *tuath* and the abbot of a great monastery is unfair. A more appropriate comparison would be between a bishop of a *tuath* and the abbot of a minor local monastery, or between a bishop of such a church as Kildare, a "bishop of bishops," and the abbot of Clonmacnois or Glendalough.

It has also been noted that the authority of a leading abbot over a distant church might be more akin to late-medieval "appropriation of churches," namely, essentially economic lordship. If its function was to ensure that some of the revenue of the subordinate church passed to the major monastery, it could leave the pastoral authority of the bishop intact. Moreover, the forms of ecclesiastical overlordship were every bit as varied as their lay counterparts. Some references to the overlordship enjoyed by the great monastic churches do indeed indicate an overriding interest in revenue. On the other hand, when a church had dependent ecclesiastical tenants, *manaig*, its subordination to another church might entail the consequence that its *manaig* became dependent on the abbot of the leading monastery; and for the spiritual welfare of a monastery's *manaig*, the abbot of that monastery was indeed responsible. Ecclesiastical lordship and pastoral responsibility were not entirely separate issues.

The *Collectio Canonum Hibernensis* opens with a book devoted to the office of bishop. It is, so it declares in words taken from Isidore of Seville, an *onus* not an *honor*, a burdensome job not a rank; and yet it is plain from other parts

53 For the new view: Sharpe, "Some Problems"; Etchingham, *Church Organization in Ireland*.
54 Tírechán, *Collectanea*, § 18; Cogitosus, *Vita S. Brigitae*, Prologue, 135.

of the laws, both canon and native Irish, that the episcopal office was indeed a rank in seventh-century Ireland. As the king was the head of the ordinary lay hierarchy, so the bishop headed the ordinary hierarchy of the church, the *ollam* the hierarchy of poets, and the *suí litre*, "scholar of the written word," the hierarchy of Latin learning. Ireland was a thoroughly hierarchical society, and the church had to be given its place. One can see this necessity encompassing the most unlikely figures: the *peregrinus pro amore Dei*, "exile for the love of God," might abandon his native land, following the lead of Abraham, in order to separate himself from those entanglements of social obligation and privilege that were inescapable as long as he remained at home; yet the *deorad Dé*, "exile of God," had a status equivalent to that of a bishop.[55]

Another figure who had to be included was the abbot of a major monastery. To take one example, Columba was a priest, not a bishop, and thus, as we learn from Bede, his successors were also priests. As priests they were inferior in rank to any local bishop. The difficulty was solved by a two-way relationship between the rank of the person and the rank of a church. A church was of higher rank if it was episcopal, understood as meaning that it either currently had or had had in the past a bishop and was thus fit to have one in the future. This was on the analogy of the branch of a kindred, which was of higher rank if a king or kings were members. On the other hand, an eighth-century legal tract declared that the head of a great church was of a rank equivalent to that of a "noble bishop," namely, to judge by the context, the chief bishop of Munster: he was "the supreme head of a great church," *ollam mórchathrach*, and the tract cites the abbots of Emly and Cork, major Munster monasteries, as examples.[56] Some heads of great churches were themselves bishops: as Patrick was a bishop so his heirs were bishops of Armagh until the Viking period. Yet it is striking that, when the guarantor-list of *Cáin Adamnáin* (697) is examined, the ecclesiastical section is dominated by the abbots of great monasteries. When Cummian (c. 632) consulted some major figures of the contemporary Irish Church, he specified the abbots of Emly (episcopal), Clonmacnois, Mungret, Clonfertmulloe, and either Birr or Clonfert.[57] The highest rank in ecclesiastical society indeed had its episcopal members, but it would have been outnumbered by those who owed their standing to that of their churches. This mattered, since they would all have attended the synods which governed the different provinces of the Irish Church.[58] Yet, if this allows us to perceive the early Irish

55 Charles-Edwards, "Social Background," 54, 57–58.
56 *Corpus Iuris Hibernici*, 1618.7–8; 2282.27.
57 Cummian, *De controversia Paschali*, 90.
58 For provinces, see *Annals of Ulster*, *s.aa.* 851.5, 859.3.

Church as unusually monastic, it should also allow us to see it as unusually respectful toward the authority of scholars. They, too, were numbered among the guarantors of the Law of Adomnán, and they, too, were normal members of synods. It seems that all those whose rank was at least equivalent to that of an ordinary king – ordinary bishop, leading scholar, and abbot – were entitled to attend a synod; and it was the synod which we can see exercising power over laymen by taking pledges from representatives of their kindreds.[59] The composition of the synod appears to be directly related to the unusually hierarchical nature of early Irish society: the synod was a meeting among the heads of different ecclesiastical hierarchies.

This poses a problem in understanding the British Church. As we have seen, its synods were also attended by scholars and abbots as well as bishops. Yet we have no good evidence that this accorded with the nature of British society in the way we have seen it fitted the different hierarchies of Irish society. Admittedly, this is partly because nothing survives on the scale of the early Irish evidence, and even the few scraps are often later than 900. The archbishops of St. Davids and of Gwynedd mentioned by Asser and the *Annales Cambriae* probably correspond to the "noble bishop" of the Irish law-tract *Uraicecht Becc*, who was the chief bishop of Munster.[60] The territory over which St. Davids had primacy is likely to have included all of southwest Wales; if so, it would have included Llandeilo Fawr in Carmarthenshire, which undoubtedly had a bishop at one point in the ninth century.[61] The area to which Llandeilo Fawr belonged, Ystrad Tywi, "The Vale of the Tywi," is likely to have belonged to the Romano-British *civitas* of the Demetae, if we are right in taking Carmarthen (Moridunum) to have been its capital. This may still have been true when Aldhelm referred to the bishops of Dyfed. Even the narrower limits of what was called Dyfed in the post-Viking period may still have had more than one bishop. The short text entitled "The Seven Bishop-Houses of Dyfed," preserved in the Welsh laws, has been dated to the ninth or tenth century.[62] It seems to have one "bishop-house" for each of what became the seven *cantrefi* of Dyfed. As in Ireland, these were probably not always sees of bishops, but rather churches where previous bishops lay buried and might have living bishops again. They were churches of episcopal standing. More than one church in Cornwall had, in this sense, episcopal status.[63] At roughly the same period,

59 *Críth Gablach*, § 20.

60 *Annales Cambriae*, *s.a.* 809; *Asser's Life of King Alfred*, chap. 79; see above note 53.

61 *Text of the Book of Llan Dâv*, xlvi.

62 Charles-Edwards, "Seven Bishop Houses."

63 Olson, *Early Monasteries*, 51–56, 62–63, 70, 73–74.

Glamorgan had three principal monastic churches: the abbots of Llantwit Major, Llancarfan, and Llandough were of a higher rank than other heads of monastic communities.[64] Now that the continuing importance of bishops in the early Irish Church has been established, the contrast between the Welsh and Irish churches, which used to be drawn, no longer stands.[65]

The ninth century saw Brittany first incorporated into the Carolingian Empire under Louis the Pious and then attain a political unity within it. The Breton Church was brought into closer relation with the Frankish Church, especially in its higher institutions – bishoprics and monasteries.[66] The Carolingian reforms therefore affected Brittany as they did not affect the other Celtic countries, other than in offering numerous opportunities for insular scholars in the schools of Francia. But in other ways the broad development of the Churches of Ireland, Scotland, and Wales was similar to those of western Europe as a whole.

After the Vikings

The impact of the Vikings on the church was highly variable in both time and space. In Ireland and in Wales, the church survived remarkably well. The important monastery of Lusk, within the territory which came to be ruled by the Dublin Vikings, appears to have survived largely untouched. On the other hand, Finglas, an important monastery in the eighth and early-ninth centuries, and even closer to Dublin, is not mentioned in the main annals after 867, although it did survive to become a parish church in the later Middle Ages. For most churches the Viking impact was only spasmodically severe; and, by the tenth century, churches within the Viking domain sometimes suffered disastrously from the Irish.[67]

On the other hand, the effect on the wider Gaelic and Pictish world was more profound: the Northern Isles were transformed into outposts of Scandinavia, but further south the impact became more patchy. A vivid portrait of the change is given by the Irish scholar Dícuil, writing a geographical treatise for Emperor Louis the Pious in 825.[68] He recalled the year 795, when he himself was in the Hebrides, a year of Viking raids which soon transformed the northern seas. Instead of Irish monks seeking "a desert in the ocean," an enterprise

64 *The Text of the Book of Llan Dâv*, nos. 175, 176b (charters are cited by the page on which they occur, using a, b, etc. if there is more than one).
65 An example of such a contrast is W. Davies, *Early Welsh Microcosm*, 146–47.
66 Smith, *Province and Empire*.
67 Etchingham, *Viking Raids*.
68 *Dicuili Liber de Mensura Orbis Terrae*, vii.11–15.

still recorded by inscribed crosses all the way to Iceland, the sea-routes from Orkney through the Hebrides and the North Channel, and so into the Irish Sea, became a Scandinavian domain.[69] The kingdom of the Picts and its successor, the kingdom of Alba, came under more sustained pressure than Ireland was ever to suffer. The northern British kingdom centered on Dumbarton became, after the sack of the fortress in 870 by Olaf and Ivar from Dublin, a kingdom of Strathclyde under strong Viking influence. After the Vikings were expelled from Dublin from 902 to 917, their settlements were scattered all round the Irish Sea – in Cumbria, in the Wirral, on Anglesey, on the Isle of Man, and perhaps also in Galloway. Yet Strathclyde was no less Christian for being under Viking influence, and the pagan phase on the Isle of Man appears to have lasted only about thirty years, up to c. 930.[70] Although the leading churches in the Columban federation were now Kells and Dunkeld, Iona survived several raids to become the chief church of Innsi Gall, "the Islands of the Foreigners." It was to Iona that Olaf Cuarán, king of Dublin, went in pilgrimage after his great defeat at Tara in 980 at the hands of Máel Sechnaill, king of Mide and now king of Tara. Yet the subsequent attack on Dublin itself, yielding a liberation of its Irish slaves, was portrayed by the Clonmacnois chronicler as "the harrying of the Babylon of Ireland, to be compared with the Harrowing of Hell."[71] Scandinavian settlement around the Irish Sea would spread the cults of Irish saints into what is now northwestern England and southern Scotland.

Welsh links with Ireland survived through the Viking period: Kells, founded in the early ninth century as a new center of the Columban federation, contained the "House of the Britons." The cult of Coemgen (Kevin) of Glendalough took root in North Wales, where the church of Diserth Cwyfien both carries the name of the patron saint of Glendalough and uses a vernacular version of Latin *desertum*, something that came into fashion in Ireland in the ninth century.[72]

A major change in the Celtic countries, as elsewhere, was the shift to burial in a churchyard. In the early eighth-century *Collectio Canonum Hibernensis*, it is assumed that monks and monastic tenants will be buried in the monastic cemetery; but ordinary laymen were likely to be buried in "paternal cemeteries" not attached to a church. Even at that date, some kings were granted burial in a church cemetery, and the *Hibernensis* appears to be favorable to a spread of

69 Fisher, *Early Medieval Sculpture*; Ahronson, "Further Evidence."
70 Graham-Campbell, "Early Viking Age," 116–20.
71 *Chronicum Scotorum*, *s.a.* 978 = 980.
72 *Martyrology of Óengus*, Notes, 26 October, 228; Mac Shamhráin, *Church and Polity*, 124–25; *Bonedd y Saint*, ed. Bartrum, § 50; Edwards, "Early Medieval Inscribed Stones," 36.

this practice. Later annals reveal the spread of church burial when they claim that it happened to early kings, who were most unlikely to have been buried in an ecclesiastical cemetery. Thus the tenth-century Clonmacnois chronicle claimed that the mid-sixth-century king of Tara, Diarmait mac Cerbaill was killed and decapitated in Ulster, that his body rested in the church of Connor in that province, but that the head had been taken to Clonmacnois. The reason for the claim is apparent from the statement in the *Hibernensis* that someone would rise again at the Last Judgment where his head lay and from Diarmait's position as ancestor of the rulers of the midlands.[73]

In Wales the shift to burial in a churchyard may be associated with the spread of the word *llan* as the normal word for a church settlement. It is occasionally found in the names of churches in Ireland, alongside older words such as *domnach* (from Latin *dominicum*) and newer terms, especially *cell*. In Wales and Ireland, an earlier variety in the fifth and sixth centuries gave way to domination by one word, *cell* in Ireland and *llan* in Wales, both of them being used for the church complex rather than being restricted to what we would call a church. The documents in the Book of Llandaff show that by the eleventh century it was the norm for a church to lie within a cemetery, and also within a sanctuary, *noddfa*.[74] The same source also shows that in some parts of Wales, at least, the density of churches was high, as it was in parts of Brittany, Cornwall, and Ireland.[75] Sculptural evidence from the Gwaun valley in southwest Wales (Dyfed) suggests that in that area this density goes back to the seventh century and that there was an earlier link between church and cemetery there than in North Wales.[76]

At a local level, then, there were important similarities between developments in Ireland, Brittany, and Wales, but there was one major difference. Among the Celtic countries, only Brittany participated in the Benedictine reform sponsored by Charlemagne and Louis the Pious, a reform which spread to parts of England in the tenth century. Carolingian policy introduced a clear contrast between monks and canons and sharpened the contrast between monks and secular clergy. In the tenth and eleventh centuries, however, this contrast was growing less sharp in Ireland, Scotland, and Wales. For the larger churches, those that sustained a community rather than an individual priest, the norm was something akin to the Anglo-Saxon minster rather than the

73 O'Brien, *Post-Roman Britain*, 54.

74 On churchyard burial in Wales, see Pryce, "Pastoral Care," 43–46.

75 *Text of the Book of Llan Dâv*, 275–78 (Ergyng); O'Brien, "Churches of South-East County Dublin"; Olson and Padel, "Tenth-Century List"; W. Davies, "Priests and Rural Communities."

76 Edwards, "Early Medieval Inscribed Stones," 30–31.

Carolingian monastery.[77] In the ninth century the documents written into the Lichfield Gospels when they were at Llandeilo Fawr in South Wales exemplify such a church. In one witness-list there is a bishop of St. Teilo, a *sacerdos* of St. Teilo, and a *scholasticus*, who wrote the text in good insular minuscule.[78] The *sacerdos* appears to have been the priest in charge of the sacramental life of the church, while the *scholasticus* was the teacher. With the bishop they were the principal figures in the *familia Teliaui*, the community of St. Teilo. The obits of Armagh clergy in the *Annals of Ulster* in the tenth and eleventh century reveal a more elaborate range of officers: because the abbot of Armagh was often on circuit, there was a *fosairchinnech*, "resident superior," as well as a *secnap*, "second abbot," a bishop, a teacher, a "head of the poor" (an almoner), and, in earlier obits, a steward. Many of these offices became the perquisites of particular powerful kindreds or became the spoils of competition by two or more kindreds. The hold of *Clann Sínaig*, "the kindred of Sínach," on the abbacy of Armagh in the eleventh and early twelfth centuries was notorious.[79] Some clerical families were learned as well as pious: an outstanding example is the family of Sulien, bishop of St. Davids.[80] Yet, it was easy for reformers from the late eleventh and twelfth centuries to tar them all with the same brush.

That is not to say that there was no movement of monastic reform in Ireland, Scotland, and Wales. The so-called "clients of God," the *céli Dé* or "culdees," emerged as a group in Ireland in the eighth century and spread to Scotland, and, probably, to Wales between 800 and 1100.[81] The principal ninth-century texts associated with one of their leading churches, Tallaght (southwest of Dublin), reveal them as looking to the sources of monasticism in Egypt, Palestine, and Syria, and to the heroic age of Irish and Welsh monasticism in the sixth century, rather than to Carolingian Benedictinism. Yet, by the twelfth century, the *céli Dé* normally formed a community within the broader clerical community of a particular church – a community with particular property interests and sometimes particular kinship connections. They were not, by 1100, demonstrably different from other clerical communities.

This chapter has been about the forms of Christianity found in countries speaking a Celtic language between 600 and 1100. As events turned out, this scope matches real similarities – which, even in 1100, still remained among

77 Pryce, "Pastoral Care," 51–55.
78 *Text of the Book of Llan Dâv*, xlvi.
79 Ó Fiaich, "Church of Armagh."
80 Lapidge, "Welsh-Latin Poetry."
81 O'Dwyer, *Céli Dé*; Reeves, *Culdees*.

the churches of Ireland, Scotland, and Wales (and to a lesser extent Cornwall and Brittany). They stemmed from the conversion of Ireland in the fifth century and from the close and enduring links between Ireland, Scotland, and Wales throughout the period. In the eleventh century they were sustained by continuing links across the Irish Sea, between Ireland and Scotland, where a shared vernacular, Gaelic, was important, between Ireland and Wales, where there was no medieval knowledge of any linguistic connection, and between Cumbria and Wales, where shared language was of diminishing significance. They do not, however, justify talk of a Celtic Church – these were separate churches – nor, even, Celtic churches or Celtic Christianity, since the Celticity of the languages spoken by the Irish, the Scots, the Welsh, the Cornish, and the Bretons was unknown at the time and had no intrinsic relationship with ecclesiastical contacts. The latter were primarily in Latin, the universal language of the western church: the Christianity of Iona was not debarred from spreading among English-speaking Northumbrians in the middle of the seventh century. In 1100 it was possible for Cumbria to pride itself both on its native saints and on its capacity to include people of different languages, English, Scandinavian, and Gaelic as well as Cumbrians. It is also characteristic of most of these churches that, from the ninth to the late-eleventh century, they experienced no great Benedictine reform of monasticism, such as prevailed in the Carolingian Empire and in southern and eastern England. Events elsewhere could make Celtic-speaking countries look more alike; and yet Brittany was an exception in participating in the reform, while, on the other hand, much of England was, like Wales, Ireland, and Scotland, beyond the reach of the reformers.

Although the origins of the connection lay in the deep influence of post-Roman British Christianity on its neighboring island, Ireland soon became and remained the main center. Her many rich churches were influential on the Continent as well as in the lands around the Irish Sea, in countries where a Celtic language was spoken, and in countries where it was not. What is illuminating is to think, not of Celtic Christianity, but of a Christianity centered around the Irish Sea in a period when Ireland was the richest country and home to the most vigorous culture in the region.

5
Germanic Christianities

LESLEY ABRAMS

A rich combination of ingredients – biblical, Roman, and Irish – contributed to the character of Christian life in the Germanic world of the early Middle Ages, blending with the legacy of the pre-Christian Germanic past. To apply a linguistic category to religion and religious practice and talk of a typical Christianity practiced by speakers of Germanic languages would be misleading, especially across such a vast area and such an eventful half-millennium. "Germanic Christianities," interpreted geographically not ethnically, will be taken here to relate to the churches and Christian communities that developed in the Germanic-speaking world, first in the context of the barbarian successor-states within the old Roman Empire, and then, thanks to political and economic forces, as well as missionary activity, in new lands well beyond the old frontier.

There was nevertheless an ethnic dimension to the earliest Germanic conversions. The first converts, the Goths, subscribed to the teachings that came to be condemned as the Arian heresy, and, after their conversion in the fourth century, Arianism became identified with Germanic Christianity. While it lingered in Italy among the Lombards through the seventh century, in Spain by 589 CE the last major Arian ruler, the Visigoth Reccared, had accepted Catholicism. It has been suggested that upon entering the Roman world the Germanic peoples chose, and subsequently remained committed to, this increasingly unorthodox form of Christianity as a means of asserting their social identity and cultural independence.[1] The circumstance that the Roman emperors who presided over the initial Gothic conversion were Arians had led the first converts in a direction that the mainstream church soon abandoned. But barbarian commitment to Arianism persisted. Inherent (and distinctive) qualities of its theology and organization can, to some extent, account for its popularity, as can its use – like other Greek-inspired missions – of the vernacular. The Goths' successes after their conversion likewise must have contributed to Arianism's spread

1 Thompson, *Visigoths*.

among other Germanic peoples. But while the imperial church condemned Arianism as heretical, Visigoths, Ostrogoths, Vandals, and Lombards remained committed, some to the point of persecuting Catholic opponents. Arian Christians in Germanic successor-kingdoms may have seen an exclusively barbarian form of Christianity as a way of preventing cultural absorption by their host societies (although retaining their traditional religion would have done so more forcefully). Certainly it allowed the manifestation of separatism through an alternative geography of spiritual power and institutional authority.

The continuing success of Arianism demonstrates a potential role for a church which, if not ethnically conceived, at least had ethnic overtones. However, although Bede in his *Ecclesiastical History of the English People* wrote of a (notional) *gens anglorum*, ethnic definitions do not seem to have significantly marked those churches which succeeded the Arian in Germanic kingdoms. Instead, if a common culture was aspired to, the template was Roman, not Germanic. Though "Rome" meant different things to different early medieval regimes, its inclusive aspirational resonances – of military glory, cultural leadership, spiritual authority (past and / or present) – proved more useful to ecclesiastical and political authorities than more narrowly defined identities.

After the conversion to Catholic Christianity of the Frankish king, Clovis (d. 511), Arianism in the continental successor-kingdoms lost out to the orthodox Christianity of the native population. From then on, Christianity progressed through the efforts of native and foreign churchmen and churchwomen. In the increasingly dominant kingdom of the Franks, Gallo-Roman, Frankish, and Irish bishops and missionary monks carried the work of Christian teaching from the towns – where Christianity had first been established in imperial times – to the countryside, a much more pagan place,[2] where Gallo-Roman cults probably mingled with traditional Germanic practices. In the seventh century, churchmen with connections to the Merovingian kings and the monastery of Luxeuil (established by the Irishman, Columbanus) extended the authority of the church to those regions in northeastern Gaul that were still pagan. The former frontier region was re-Christianized, missions were sent to the Frisians, and the monastic movement helped to expand Frankish power among the Alemanni and Bavarians as well. The several kingdoms of Anglo-Saxon England – evangelized from 597 by Italians, Franks, and Irish – in their turn exported missionaries who, from the late seventh century, worked both within and without the bounds of the old empire. From the late eighth

2 While the term "pagan" may smack of Christian distaste (in both medieval and modern writers), no obvious judgment-free alternative suggests itself. On the meeting of Christianity and paganism in the North, see further Wood in this volume.

century, Anglo-Saxons, Frisians, and Franks extended Christianity into Saxony. At times this process was ethnically conceived: Bede alluded to the desire of Anglo-Saxon churchmen to carry the word of God to their ancestral homelands on the Continent;[3] a similar feeling of kinship with the Scandinavian peoples may have inspired Anglo-Scandinavian missionaries in the tenth and eleventh centuries.

The influences brought by these churchmen and churchwomen were hardly homogeneous. Furthermore, each new church developed its own aspect, as barbarian kings converted to Christianity one by one, and churches organized themselves around the political authorities of their kingdoms. The national churches that developed in these centuries consequently displayed distinctive regionality. The campaign for "correct" Christianity waged on the Continent by the Englishman Boniface in the eighth century, and the Carolingians' subsequent preoccupation with conformity and consistent religious practice, were natural reactions to this heterogeneous past. Rome was the symbolic, if not always real, archetype. Thanks to the heritage of its Gregorian mission, the early Anglo-Saxon Church particularly prized Rome as an exemplar, as did the Carolingian state, which in the late eighth and ninth centuries urged religious conformity on its subjects. In the tenth century, Anglo-Saxon and Ottonian reform vigorously targeted diversity, building on the conception that religious unity was a matter of imperial principle. Despite this impulse towards standardization across western Europe, the English Church that Norman ecclesiastics encountered in 1066 – unreformed, teeming with native saints, practiced in vernacular as well as Latin religious expression – struck them as rustic and alien. Not until the Gregorian movement of the mid- to late-eleventh century were the mechanisms in place to enforce consistency, now defined by the pope, before twelfth-century movements gave rise to a more universal western European clerical culture.

Given the nature of religious conversion, it is as misleading as it is traditional to chart the progress of Christianity among the Germanic peoples by presenting a catalog of royal baptisms or a list of diocesan and monastic foundations. However, the king's role in conversion entrenched a crucial and enduring connection between secular power and Christian authority; and although the establishment of bishoprics need not indicate that conversion of the population had been achieved, the formation of an institutional church did mark a significant step in the progress of the new religion, as it redrew the map of territorial power, both physically and symbolically. Diocesan centers,

3 Bede, *HE*, v.9.

like monasteries, provided bases for the training and support of missionaries. In England, bishoprics covered large areas, and while their centers and borders shifted at politically strategic times, total numbers remained much the same in 1100 as in 750. On the Continent, smaller (ancient) urban bishoprics reflected different patterns of power and population. New foundations moved outward from the Frankish center. From the 690s, a bishopric was established for the Frisians; in the 730s and 740s Boniface refounded sees in Bavaria, Hesse, and Thuringia which had been established earlier in the century. Episcopal foundations accompanied Carolingian military expansion: eight Saxon dioceses were established from 805 after Charlemagne's conquest and forced conversion of the Saxons. In 948 Otto I founded a string of bishoprics along the frontiers of his empire. Monastic foundations kept pace with this extension of episcopal activity eastward and northward.

The tide was checked when it reached Scandinavia, however. No monasteries are known to have been founded to play a role in conversion in Denmark, Norway, or Sweden; only in the twelfth century, with the arrival of the new religious orders, did monasticism become an important force. Despite early missionary efforts from Hamburg-Bremen in the mid-ninth century, Denmark's dioceses were not created until 948; even then, they could not have been activated until after the conversion of the Danish king, Harald Bluetooth, probably in the 960s. Sweden, also evangelized in the ninth century by Hamburg-Bremen, resisted conversion until the eleventh century, when a number of dioceses were established under the aegis of Christian kings. Norway's sees were arguably carved out by King Olaf Tryggvason (c. 995–1000) on the basis of existing administrative divisions and with English help. Iceland, a uniquely kingless society converted by popular decision in 999, acquired its first territorial bishop in 1056 and its second diocese fifty years later. In 1103/4 a metropolitan see for the North was established at Lund (then in Denmark).

Can this range of peoples be said to have shared a common experience of conversion or a distinctive form of Christianity? Efforts to identify a "Germanic" Christianity have generally focused not so much on particularities of doctrine but on the invasive influence of secular culture. The premise of a specifically "Germanic" Christianity has run into methodological problems from the start, however. Leaving aside unsavory efforts in earlier centuries, driven by nationalism and ideology, to identify a primeval pan-*Germanitas*, recent attempts to establish a Germanic Christianity "brand" have produced a score-sheet of attributes, with "pagan" characteristics on one side and "authentic" Christian traits on the other. According to this view, Christianity became "Germanized" when missionaries allowed converts to retain the former at the expense of the latter.[4] Apart from the question of what conversion could be expected to entail, to which we shall return, establishing what is "authentically" Christian and what is purely Germanic – the exercise that underpins this approach – is deeply problematic. Changing circumstances make their impact on living religions as a matter of course; Christianity had already undergone major transformations thanks to its legalization and subsequent incorporation into the Roman Empire, and by 600 it had behind it a substantial experience of accommodation to non-Christian environments. As for the Germanic peoples, long before their conversion they had been in contact with the Celtic and Roman worlds. Identification of exactly what aspects of their societies predated this contact and originated in a pristine Germanic past is impeded by the absence of sources. Nor would conversion have been the only factor provoking change at this stage. The Germanic peoples experienced considerable development as they assumed secular leadership of western Europe and much of Britain, and the multiplicity of influences before, during, and after their conversion to Christianity makes it difficult to distinguish the effect of a change in religion from the more general effects of social upheaval, migration, economic development, and transformation of political authority. The institutional church itself was as influenced by these developments as by the absorption of new peoples with different cultural backgrounds.

Missionary policy has a profound impact on the nature of the religion adopted by converts, but not all Germanic peoples experienced conversion in the same way. Some conversions (in what had been Gaul, for example, or in the English west midlands), appear to have occurred organically, as non-Christians settled among Christians and integrated through normal social processes such as marriage. More notoriously, most other conversions in the Germanic world are described as taking place in a top-down direction, with rulers accepting baptism (often in consultation with their secular advisers), followed by the conversion of their people. Although politically driven, these could be peaceful processes. Occasionally, they were violent, sometimes extremely so. Top-down, "national," conversion of this sort was apparently imposed by mass baptism, and, because of its collective quality, it may have carried few expectations of immediate and wholesale change. Millennial thinking may have been relevant. Mass baptism had an eschatological logic, which had a particular urgency at various times between 600 and 1100. In some contexts, while the converts' grasp of doctrine may have been weak and their moral lives less than perfect, the missionary could perhaps console himself with the thought

4 Russell, *Germanization*; Cusack, *Conversion*.

that many thousands of newly baptized souls would at least have a chance of salvation at the great reckoning that the end of the world was about to bring. On the other hand, even for those who converted on orders from the king, religious issues could be sensitive and contested. Verses addressed to the Norwegian king, Olaf Tryggvason, by his court poet Hallfreðr vandræðaskáld express conflict and regret despite affirming belief in Christ.[5]

Hagiographies, histories, and missionary correspondence paint a picture of early evangelizing, including a detailed record of instructions sent by the pope, Gregory the Great, who had conceived of the conversion of the English. In one letter written in 601, Gregory urged the English king Æthelberht to suppress the worship of idols and overthrow pagan buildings and shrines.[6] In another, he instructed the missionary Mellitus to destroy the idols, but not the structures; "take holy water and sprinkle it in these shrines, build altars and place relics in them." Animals, previously sacrificed to the Devil, should be slaughtered there for food in praise of God; "with changed hearts, [the people] were to put away one part of the sacrifice and retain the other. . . Since the people were offering them to the true God and not to idols, they were not the same sacrifices."[7] This kind of accommodation has been seen as particularly characteristic of the conversion of Germanic peoples, and to have extended beyond the treatment of shrines to all aspects of pagan culture, creating a Christianity which was either "nominal" or "a broadly syncretistic fusion of pre-Christian and Christian."[8] But this policy of substitution was not unique to Germanic pagan sites, having been practiced, for example, on classical temples in the eastern (and, less commonly, the western) Mediterranean.[9]

There is no doubt that establishing common ground (literally and metaphorically) between pagan and Christian would have eased the transition from one to the other. How far the church would have accepted long-term accommodation or syncretism, however, is less clear. Syncretism – properly defined as an attempt to reconcile diverse beliefs or practices, but often used to mean a "pick-and-mix" attitude to religious life – doubtless existed. So too did pragmatic inclusivity: the Danes before the tenth century are only one example of converts who were said to have accepted Christ and continued to worship their

5 "Reluctantly, since the rule of [Óðin] suited the poet well, I bestow hatred upon [him], because we serve Christ. . . . Last year I forsook the delusion of Njörðr. I will beseech Christ and God for all love. I am compelled away from the children of Njörðr to pray to Christ"; translation from Poole, '"Conversion Verses,"' 16–18.

6 Bede, *HE*, i.32.

7 Bede, *HE*, i.30.

8 Quotations from Russell, *Germanization*, 152; Cusack, *Conversion*, 178–79.

9 Ward-Perkins, "Reconfiguring Sacred Space."

gods as before.[10] However, syncretism and inclusivity, although consistent with polytheism, ran counter to the monotheism of Christianity. Despite a well-developed rhetoric of prohibition, it is unlikely that there was immediate and widespread recognition that some aspects of Christianity were nonnegotiable; but to discourage deviant practice the church could instead frame the Christian message in order to respond to pagan concerns and sensibilities, without losing doctrinal integrity or liturgical coherence in the process. Pagans understood the supernatural to play a utilitarian role in the life of the group and expected their gods to intervene and create success in this world, for example. The Christian God could match and raise the stakes by offering salvation in the next as well. The extent to which accommodating pagan thinking in this way would have been seen to dilute the authenticity of Christianity (if such a concept has any virtue) and threaten the essential message of Christ and his redemption of humankind must have varied in specific circumstances and in individual minds.

Sermons and letters give some indication of how churchmen believed laypeople should live as Christians. Æthelberht, king of Kent (560–616), was urged by Pope Gregory to "strengthen the morals of your subjects by outstanding purity of life, by exhorting them, terrifying, enticing, and correcting them, and by showing them an example of good works."[11] The pope's missionary, Augustine, wrote from England with questions about personal behavior. (How soon after the birth of a child may a man have sex with his wife? Can a menstruating woman receive communion?)[12] Though some historians (perhaps like the original audience) have chosen not to take them seriously, missionaries' texts insisted that Christian living had profound implications for every individual. Converts (and, later, all who had been baptized) were required to know the Creed (what to believe) and the Lord's Prayer (what to ask for from God).[13] These encapsulated the fundamentals of the faith and were taught in the vernacular. Sophisticated Christian thinking was undoubtedly restricted to a tiny elite, but if the surviving evidence represents reality and practice, rather than wishful thinking, all converts were expected to live their lives in a new way and to understand the core Christian message.

We will never really grasp what churchmen would have expected the process of conversion to involve. As far as we can determine from our fragmentary evidence, paganism and Christianity should not be conceived of as two cards

10 Widukind, *Die Sachsengeschichte*, iii.65, 140.
11 Bede, *HE*, i.32.
12 Bede, *HE*, i.27.
13 Lynch, *Christianizing Kinship*, 171.

from the same pack, different versions of a definable entity called "religion." In pagan societies, sacral activity which brought the supernatural and human worlds together suffused public and private acts, aiming to interpret and control the forces that acted on the community. Customary culture and traditional religion may have been inseparable in Germanic societies in their pristine state, but by the time of their conversion, contact with Christians was likely to have provoked perception among pagans of a line between the secular and religious – and a confusion about where to draw it. It would therefore be anachronistic to isolate strands labeled "religion" and "other" in pagan society, but an extension of this argument – that cultural continuities necessarily indicate that Christianity in the Germanic lands was soft on paganism – does not necessarily follow, as much of what has been identified as "pagan" in Germanic culture would not now come within most definitions of religion. Disentangling what was "religious" in traditional practice from what was not must have been one of the missionaries' more difficult tasks. Clearly, conversion to Christianity could not entail a complete overhaul of all aspects of life which until then had had a supernatural connection. The boundary between what was "Christian" and what was "pagan" inevitably varied and was set by the limits of clerical tolerance. Although in the period 600 to 1100 the definition of "right" Christian living became increasingly explicit, there was still room for regional flexibility. While some cultural habits earned censure from clerical critics – putting your daughter on the roof to cure a fever, as condemned in seventh-century England by Theodore's Penitential, for example – others, such as infanticide in Iceland in 999, were allowed.[14] To some (Alcuin, for example, writing in 797 to a Northumbrian abbot), traditional songs would have been unchristian ("what has Ingeld to do with Christ?").[15] To others (such as Charlemagne, who ordered their preservation in writing),[16] they were not.

Attempting to understand the interaction between pagan and Christian in the early Middle Ages is to face a series of complicating oppositions: real versus ideal, popular versus professional, countryside versus court. We are, of course, at the mercy of our sources. Pagan voices come through a Christian filter, and prescriptive pronouncements and scholarly texts are more likely to survive than representative descriptions. There was, furthermore, a significant social distance between top and bottom. The rural working population must have made its break with paganism in a different way from those on the mead

14 Haddan and Stubbs 3, 190. Trans. in *Medieval Handbooks*,198; *Íslendingabók* (trans. Hermannsson, 53, 66–67).

15 *Epistolae karolini aevi* (no. 124), 183; Alcuin, *Alcuin of York* (no. 160), 154–56.

16 Einhard, *Vita Karoli*, ch. 29, 33 or see trans. Dutton, 34.

bench. A monastic church would have offered a different Christian experience from the local holy well. The various environments of the Germanic world raised different challenges on the church's road to dispelling what it saw as pagan darkness. But whether at court or in the country, at least one aspect of the process was the same: the old familiar forms could be retained and filled with Christian meaning, as Gregory had proposed.

Naturally, when conversion radiated outward from royal courts and aristocratic circles, Christianization lower down the social scale was achieved more slowly. Traditional Germanic paganism was animistic. Spirits activated the great natural processes that ruled the agricultural year and ensured society's survival, and the landscape, charged with metaphysical energy, embodied mythical forces. To counteract this cosmology, Christian clergy had to create a new popular understanding of the natural and supernatural forces that invigorated the world. Saints' cults took up some of these functions, from the seventh-century Northumbrian *rex christianissimus*, Oswald (whose venerated head may have mirrored earlier cult practices), to the eleventh-century Norwegian St. Olaf (whose image, red-bearded and armed with an axe, like Oðin, was paraded around the fields to ensure fertility). Although Christianity concentrated most of its metaphysical energy in built structures, saints could also appropriate the local landscape in the same way as gods, spirits, and ancestors had done.

Christianity came to agrarian societies of long standing which had rituals associated with agricultural fertility and domestic life deeply ingrained in the different domains of male and female. The pressing concerns of survival were of course perennial, and after conversion they continued to manifest themselves in folklore (the countryside's collective memory of its pre-Christian past) and in magic.[17] Although the church repeatedly condemned folk rituals and those who conducted them, the number of so-called pagan survivals prohibited in ecclesiastical regulation, even centuries after the formal conversion of a region, suggests that it was a losing battle. The church did not always have the ability, especially in the countryside, to deliver sufficient pastoral instruction and supervision to impose its prohibitions. It would be optimistic to see these rituals as preserving an ancient paganism independent of Christianity, however. Repeated condemnations of "superstition" probably refer less to surviving pagan practice than to popular, unlicensed, practitioners and practices proscribed as "incorrect" for Christians. Canonical literature even hints at unsanctioned clerical participation. From the beginning to the end of

17 Flint, *Rise of Magic*.

the period 600 to 1100, the church struggled unsuccessfully to eradicate such behavior and establish itself as the exclusive orchestrator of society's relationship with the supernatural. However, as clerical provision in the countryside increased, popular belief and folk culture could be given an increasingly Christian framework.[18] In conservative rural societies, rites such as baking loaves with holy water and burying them in the fields, or charms that incorporated Christian liturgy, pagan gods, and herbs, probably preserved fragments of pre-Christian custom. But they are less significant as pagan "survivals" than as demonstrations of the potency of Gregory's instructions: the transfer of credit to God for the power of charms made them Christian, whatever their source. This absorption of folk ritual, performed by local priests embedded in vernacular communities, indicates the success of Christianity across the social spectrum, not simply among the learned. Nevertheless it was the learned who preserved the rituals in written form.

At the top of the social scale, assimilation of the new religion by a warrior nobility offered different opportunities. The Anglo-Saxon aristocracy, for example, "had no intention of abandoning its culture"; it was, instead, "willing to throw its traditions, customs, tastes, and loyalties into the articulation of the new faith."[19] As we shall see below, Christianity enthusiastically took on the trappings of heroic society, recasting culture in a vernacular and secular idiom which gave color to the expression of the Christian story. God could be described as "Rome's king" who had conquered heathen lands,[20] or the apostles as thegns of God, "twelve mighty heroes honored under heaven in days of old."[21] Like folk custom, elite culture was converted to express Christian identity. The court poetry of Cnut, king of England and Denmark in the early eleventh century, displays what has been called "cultural paganism," for example.[22] Although Cnut himself was a benefactor of churches and a visitor to Rome, his poets applied traditional pagan idiom in a Christian context to create an identity for the new Danish conquerors of England. "Secular" should not be equated with "pagan," nor should a heroic literary style disguise the prevailing consistency of content with existing Christian writing.

Rather like the church in early Christian Ireland, Scandinavian and Icelandic Christianity showed a particularly high tolerance of and an exceptional interest in pre-Christian beliefs. Much of what we think we know about Germanic

18 Jolly, *Popular Religion*; see also Flint, *Rise of Magic*.
19 Wormald, "Bede," 57; see also his "Anglo-Saxon Society."
20 By Eilífr Goðrúnarson in late tenth-century Norway; quoted in D. Edwards, "Christian and Pagan References," 35.
21 In the Old English poem *Andreas*; see *Early English Christian Poetry*, 122.
22 Jesch, "Scandinavians," esp. 63.

paganism, in fact, has been transmitted through these channels.[23] Elaborate mythological poems and prose pieces, legendary history, and historical fiction in the form of short narratives and sagas set in the preconversion age were committed to parchment, occasionally in Latin, as in the work of the Dane, Saxo Grammaticus (in the early thirteenth century),[24] but mainly in Old Norse, most famously by the Icelander Snorri Sturluson (1179–1241). Snorri justified the mythological lore in his *Edda*, a treatise on poetry, with the barest of excuses – that after the Flood had wiped out knowledge of God, real wisdom was replaced by such "earthly understanding."[25] His account of gods and goddesses was motivated by pragmatic antiquarianism: young poets needed to know the mythological narratives in order to practice their craft.[26] On the other hand, many of the sagas, also from the thirteenth century, present ordinary pre-Christian people up close and personal, conducting sacrifices, negotiating with gods, and causing posthumous trouble from their burial mounds. Stories set on the cusp of the conversion include "noble heathens," portrayed as precursors of right Christian living in a process which romanticized paganism and harmonized it with Christianity. There is striking pagan color in historical narratives as well, such as the law attributed to the tenth-century settler Ulfljótr in *Landnámabók*, the thirteenth-century history of Icelandic settlement. Ulfljótr's Law specified how pagan priests should conduct legal cases (bearing on their arms rings of silver weighing at least two ounces, bathed with the blood of sacrificed cattle), spelled out at length the wording of oaths sworn to the gods, and advised people how to behave towards land-spirits.[27] Whether these pictures of paganism represent authentic practice or imagined recreation, they are by and large morally neutral. This sympathetic cultivation of the pagan past, as exemplified by the "pre-Christian setting and knowledge" and the "un-Christian interests and values" of the sagas,[28] has been used to argue that Iceland in the thirteenth century had yet to assimilate Christianity to a significant degree. But this late and literary display of paganism was thoroughly grounded in Christian thinking and shaped by Christian learning. The relative proportions of authentic pagan survival and antiquarian reinvention in this Christian literature will continue to be a matter for debate.

Although Anglo-Saxon poetry also gave literary life to "good" pagans like Beowulf, Germanic paganism made little impression on written culture

23 Clunies Ross, *Prolonged Echoes*; Davidson, *Gods and Myths*.
24 Saxo Grammaticus, *History*.
25 Snorri Sturluson, *Edda*, 1–2.
26 Ibid., 64–65.
27 *Íslendingabók* (ed. Benediktsson), ch. H268, 6–7 and 313–15; Page, *Chronicles*, 174.
28 Foote, "Observations," 99.

outside Iceland and Denmark, being elsewhere almost entirely restricted to the purposes of prohibition. Bede, for example, limited himself to a brief discussion of Old English gods in his treatment of time and a few dogmatic set-pieces, such as the story of Coifi, in his *Ecclesiastical History*.[29] Attitudes to the classical past in the early medieval West may provide more of a parallel to Iceland's tolerance of native paganism. The Franks, after all, appropriated Rome's Trojan origin for themselves. Of course there were always some who disapproved of the study of classical culture. In the late seventh or early eighth century, the English churchman Aldhelm criticized the Irish for their interest in gods, goddesses, and "the troublesome meanderings of the (worldly) philosophers."[30] In the late eighth and ninth centuries, however, despite an uneasy recognition of its dangers, Carolingian scholars built on what had been preserved by their Christian predecessors and used classical learning to enhance the *romanitas* of the new empire. As Hrabanus Maurus, a ninth-century Frankish scholar, put it,

> when we read the pagan poets and have books of secular wisdom in our hands, we ought, if we find something in them of use, to convert it to our authorized learning (*dogma*); if, however, we find superfluous things about idols, and love, and secular business, . . . we cut them away.[31]

Whereas these scholars of the Carolingian *renovatio* appropriated ancient pagan base metal to turn it into Christian gold, however,[32] medieval Icelanders liberated ancient native myths from their pagan setting largely by secularizing, not Christianizing, them.

Although the pagan identity of their pre-Christian past does not appear to have preoccupied other societies with Germanic roots, we may wonder whether Iceland's cultivation of pagan tradition might reflect a pattern which ran its course elsewhere in earlier times, but with the odds more stacked against survival of the evidence. Conditions specific to medieval Iceland help to explain why the pagan past could live on there in such detail and with such allusive force, however. The relatively recent demise of paganism has sometimes been cited in explanation, but more than two hundred years separated Snorri from the official conversion, and (judging only on the basis of what survives) historical writing in England at a similar remove showed no such comfort with the old ways. Like England, Iceland had been settled before the conversion.

29 Bede, *De temporum ratione*, ch. 15, in *Bedae opera* 2, 329–32; Bede, *Reckoning of Time*, 53–54; Bede, *HE*, ii.13.

30 Aldhelm, *Aldhelmi opera*, 479; *Aldhelm, Prose Works*, 154.

31 Hrabanus Maurus, *De institutione clericorum*, iii.18, 470.

32 Brown, "Introduction," 38.

The origins of Anglo-Saxon identity lay firmly in the Christian period, however, while the separate identities of the continental successor-kingdoms had emerged out of the coalescence of Roman and barbarian before, during, and after the Germanic conversions. In Iceland, on the other hand, national identity was formed in the time of paganism. In the absence of kingship, family networks provided Iceland with its social, legal, and cultural infrastructure, and the status of the bishops, priests, chieftains, and ordinary farmers who were authors and audience in the twelfth and thirteenth centuries, when the literate habit really took hold, had been established in the pre-Christian past. National and local identities therefore depended on declaring links with ancestors whose paganism was undeniable, especially given the public character of the vote to accept conversion at the assembly of chieftains in 999. The contemporary European vogue for romances and aristocratic patronage of vernacular literature doubtless also played its part, encouraging literature independent of clerical culture.[33] Furthermore, the Icelandic Church as an institution was deeply embedded in secular society, and its written culture may therefore have reflected, more than any other church in the Germanic world, the uninhibited interests and attitudes of native, non-clerical, life.

Some reference points of ancestral culture and religion survived in all Germanic societies, however – in the days of the week and royal genealogies, for example. Genealogies extant from Gothic, Lombard, Anglo-Saxon, Scandinavian, and Icelandic contexts show that, as in the Celtic world, the habit of tracing one's lineage back to gods and heroes was widely shared.[34] The prefix "Os-," which occurs in many early Northumbrian royal names, originally signified "god" or "divinity" (cf. ON sg. *ás*, pl. *aesir*, the family of gods). Gold bracteates (coin-like disks bearing animal and human figures, manufactured c. 450–550 and found in England, Scandinavia, and other parts of northern Europe) have been interpreted as advertisements for royal dynasties and, in particular, badges of attachment to Woden / Oðin, manifesting the link between the gods and earthly authority.[35] In the prologue to his *Edda*, Snorri Sturluson recounted how Oðin led his people from Thrace to Saxony, Westphalia, France, Jutland, Sweden, and Norway, establishing a son as king in each land.[36] Stories such as these provided a logic for the existence of kingship and may have lain behind the Anglo-Saxon genealogies tracing descent to Woden

33 Tulinius, *Matter of the North*, esp. 59–65.

34 Fredegar referred to the Merovingians' descent from a quinotaur, but no Frankish genealogies survive from the period. See his *Chronicon* iii.9 in *Fredegarii et aliorum chronica*, 95; extant Carolingian genealogies lack divine ancestors.

35 Behr, "Origins of Kingship," 33–52; Hedeager, "Myth and Art."

36 Snorri Sturluson, *Edda*, 3–5.

or Seaxnot, for which there is written evidence from the early eighth century. Among Germanic peoples in the pre-Christian period – as in many other cultures – this descent from the gods apparently gave a dynasty its special power and its authority to rule. Abandoning the old gods ran the risk of severing these divine roots, but a genealogical Woden/Oðin, euhemerized and drained of divinity, was made safe for Christian use.[37] It would be naive, however, to see the presence of gods in histories or the early layers of genealogies (to which a cast of ancestral heroes of continental stock came to be added) as simply a tenacious survival of tradition from the pagan period. Genealogies gave royal houses ancestral weight, and names were added to or subtracted from these instruments of validation as fashion and political need dictated. Literary models – both classical and biblical – played their part. In late Anglo-Saxon England and in Iceland (from the twelfth century), antiquarian genealogical exercises extended ever backwards in the constant search for authority, happily incorporating Jesus, the Trojans, Noah, and Adam.[38]

What little we know of traditional Germanic religions suggests that kings had a special relationship with the gods. The late tenth-century jarl Hákon, for example, was pictured in verse as possessing the land of Norway (seen as a goddess, the deserted wife of Oðin) in a kind of marriage.[39] The ruler's medial position between the gods and his people, which gave him responsibility for ensuring survival and success, was not exclusive to Germanic paganism, however. A fourth-century medallion showing the hand of God placing a crown on Constantine's head exemplifies the starting-point for this theme in the Christian West.[40] One school of thought has it that the positioning of the king between the divine and the mortal in Germanic societies before their conversion had a profound impact on Christian rulership as it developed in the medieval West.[41] However, the early medieval conception of the king as mediator of the divine and guardian of cult was evidently habitual thinking, deriving intellectual support from a variety of traditions. The rhetoric of royal power shows clearly that any influences transmitted from a Germanic past were accompanied by Roman, Old Testament, New Testament, and Irish ideas of royal charisma bestowed by divine grace, all with the same message: the king represented divine authority in the world and had the responsibility of preparing his subjects for the kingdom of heaven.

37 Dumville, "Kingship," 77–80; Quinn, "From Orality to Literacy."

38 Sisam, "Anglo-Saxon Royal Genealogies"; Faulkes, "Descent from the Gods."

39 Snorri Sturluson, *Edda*, 67, 130.

40 Markus, "From Rome," 70–71.

41 Chaney, *Cult of Kingship*; but see also Cormack, "Murder and Martyrs," and Nelson, "Royal Saints" and "Kingship and Empire," esp. 77.

The king's status as channel to the supernatural meant that the religious allegiance of his people was within his gift. He was therefore the natural target for missionaries and the top-down conversions discussed above. His conversion may have severed links with the old gods, but it allowed a new form of spiritual and secular leadership to develop, defined in Christian terms. Various strategies ensured that kings did not lose the "inherent tendency towards sacrality" of pre-Christian times;[42] in fact, the church was careful to institutionalize it. From the second half of the eighth century the church used the ceremony of anointing, for example, to claim and control the special quality of kings. Subsequently, periodic reforms articulated an exalted spiritual identity for the king, providing ideological support for his position as head of the church. Legislation stated and manifested the secular and spiritual reach of his powers: a law of Æthelred (978–1016), king of an England much influenced by the Carolingian and Ottonian worlds, reflected conventional thinking with the declaration that "a Christian king is Christ's deputy among Christian people, and he must avenge with the utmost diligence offences against Christ."[43] At a time of extreme crisis during the Viking wars, Æthelred ordered a national program of alms-giving, fasting, and prayer; he also issued a series of pennies bearing an image of the lamb of God on one side and a dove, symbol of the Holy Spirit, on the other.[44] On the Continent, the Holy Lance, martial and divine in its associations, became the symbol of Ottonian kingship in the tenth century. In the succession struggle of 1002 after the death of Otto III, one of the candidates, Henry of Bavaria, briefly imprisoned the archbishop who had tried to keep this crucial piece of regalia out of his grasp.[45] The remarkable extensions of secular power and moral force achieved by kings in this period were validated, sustained, and displayed by Christian ideology, ritual, and symbol.

The possession of relics helped to demonstrate royal links with the source of supernatural power, as did the creation of royal saints' cults. Anglo-Saxon England (and later, Scandinavia) particularly promoted royal saints. Royal cults claimed sanctity for the ruling family and could also provide a "solution of honor" in cases where kings died unavengeable deaths at the hands of rival claimants within the kin.[46] The seventh-century murdered kings culted in Northumbria were of no perceptible sanctity in life, and the power of their decapitated bodies, disembodied heads, and spilt royal blood may have drawn

42 Yorke, "Adaptation," 252.
43 VIII Æthelred 2.1 in *Laws of the Kings*, 118–19.
44 VII Æthelred in ibid., 108–17; Keynes, "Vikings," 80–81.
45 Thietmar of Merseburg, *Chronicon*, iv.50, 188–91, or trans. Warner, 59.
46 Cormack, "Murder and Martyrs," 63–67.

upon pre-Christian traditions of royal sacrality.[47] More conventionally, from the Christian point of view, several early Anglo-Saxon kings also abdicated to enter monasteries or go to Rome. But monastic retirement was incompatible with the martial side of kingship (as contemporary Frankish attitudes make clear), and there was, therefore, an opening for women to become the "religious specialists" of royal houses.[48] Merovingian and Anglo-Saxon queens and aristocratic women played major roles in conversion narratives, and many became saints. Communities of religious women under royal leadership proliferated, allowing women to participate in ecclesiastical culture as well as carry on dynastic politics with new tools. These powers, especially among Franks and Anglo-Saxons in the seventh century and Ottonians in the tenth and early eleventh, were deployed through important religious houses.[49]

Naturally, men of royal families likewise found frequent employment among the ecclesiastical elite. The highest social levels continued to provide society with its bishops, as in the Roman world, while monastic life and the promise of salvation also caught the aristocratic imagination. Investment by secular aristocracies created a surge of foundations, thanks to strategies of landholding and lordship which accommodated their vested interests. If ecclesiastical endowments were treated as personal property, subject to the rights of kin, the diversion of resources from estates could be avoided, and assets could be kept in the family. Lay or hereditary abbacies allowed family members to continue in charge of religious houses, and episcopal intrusion was thereby kept to a minimum. While monastic communities founded with prevailing royal or aristocratic interests could undoubtedly develop into centers of piety and scholarship, they could also – through liturgical, artistic, and architectural display – manifest the glory of God and of their founders in equal measure.

Monastic communities, whether episcopal or secular in origin, had some chance of leaving records of foundation, but the genesis of local churches is much more obscure. The proprietary church – a private possession in lay hands, rather than property subject to centralized and / or communal lordship – reflected ingrained thinking about property and patronage and was the norm in western Europe for much of this period. Proprietary churches could be bought and sold, though whether they were in fact perceived as "belonging" to their owners in the same way as other seigneurial possessions is uncertain.[50] Wills, such as that of the mid-ninth-century Frankish woman

47 Thacker, "*Membra disjecta.*"
48 Yorke, "Adaptation," 254.
49 Foot, *Veiled Women*; Leyser, *Rule and Conflict*, 63–73.
50 Reynolds, *Fiefs and Vassals*, 418.

Erkenfrida who gave property to Trier and Prüm, record the inheritance, acquisition through gift, and disposal of churches.[51] Over time such churches metamorphosed to become cult buildings for their local communities and, by the twelfth century, centers of parishes. Although evidence for the origins of private churches is difficult to come by, the jurisdictional problems they raised early on are attested by Continental records of tension between bishops and the lords (both lay and ecclesiastical) of churches within their dioceses. Boniface roundly denounced laymen who, "*per violentiam*," wrested churches from their bishops, abbots, and abbesses and held "property bought by the blood of Christ."[52] In England, however, religious communities appear to have had little competition from such private churches until the tenth century,[53] though source survival may distort the picture. In Scandinavia, rapid proliferation of private churches in the eleventh century is implied by an enthusiastic comment by Adam of Bremen,[54] potentially credible because of the general lack of centralized institutions and the strength of local lordship. Private churches could be served by hereditary priests: a late tenth- or early eleventh-century Norfolk woman's will states that "my church is to be free and Wulfmær my priest is to sing at it, and his issue, so long as they are in holy orders."[55] That clerical families of this sort are only sparsely documented is unsurprising in the light of the church's consistent condemnations of clerical marriage, which remained ineffective in many areas until late in the period. Seigneurial church building took place in urban as well as rural settlements, as attested by the London churches of St. Nicholas Acon (i.e., Hakon) and St. Mary Woolnoth (Wulfnoth), whose names appear to preserve those of lay proprietors, probably of the tenth or eleventh century.[56] A list from c. 1100 names churches in London given by individuals – including Brihtmær, *senator* (probably ealdorman) – when they joined the religious community at Christ Church, Canterbury.[57]

Under the circumstances, tensions between lay and religious interests were inevitable. Secular aristocracies had extensive religious responsibilities, imposed by their ownership and patronage of churches. Churchmen, on the other hand, exercised secular power like laymen, because of their vast lands. They also created kings. Regular cycles of reform drew and redrew the lines

51 Nelson, "Wary Widow," esp. 96–102.
52 Haddan and Stubbs 3, 381, or *Anglo-Saxon Missionaries*, 133.
53 Blair, *Anglo-Saxon Church*, esp. 368–425.
54 Adam of Bremen, *Gesta*, iv.7, 234–35 or trans. Tschan, 191.
55 *Anglo-Saxon Wills*, 92–93.
56 Brooke and Keir, *London*, 138–39.
57 Kissan, "Early List," 57–60; also in *English Historical Documents, 1042–1189* (no. 280), 1022–24.

between the secular and ecclesiastical, precisely because they overlapped and were not easy to separate. From the eighth century the church introduced legislation aiming to uncouple the hereditary principle from abbatial appointments and fight the retention of income as private property. Canon law increasingly overturned family rights, limited aristocratic power, and extended centralized authority, whether episcopal or royal. It came to be understood that one remedy for the problem of lay authority over God's domain could be to place the church directly under the king's protection. However, by 1100, reform had established the idea that churches were the property of God, not kings. Secular control of appointments was vigorously (though not always successfully) condemned. Royal and aristocratic wealth, manifested in the sponsorship of prayer and the patronage of artists and scholars, nevertheless still flooded into churches, which acted as centers of burial and remembrance.

Latin was the primary language through which Christian culture was transmitted. Only those Germanic languages spoken in northern and western Europe have left any written evidence from after 600. Before their conversion to Christianity, most Germanic peoples had used a runic alphabet – primarily designed to be cut into wood – to write vernacular texts. After conversion, runic writing fell out of use in Francia but continued on all kinds of objects in England, including coins, Christian memorials, and devotional sculpture, such as the Ruthwell Cross, as well as in occasional literary contexts. In Scandinavia, several thousand runestones attest to the continued popularity of the runic vernacular after conversion.[58] In England the non-runic vernacular played a particularly vigorous role. Irish missionaries, who helped to evangelize the English, had had a rich vernacular tradition to draw on; and the influential archbishop of Canterbury, Theodore (668–90), who was a Greek, probably brought with him to England the Eastern Church's accommodating attitude to indigenous languages. There seem to have been two attitudes toward the vernacular in the West. One was contempt (or at best ambivalence). Vernacular culture – *rustica* and *barbara* – was redolent of secular values and, of course, initially oral. Translation of religious material from Latin did not just risk secular contamination, it brought with it the possibility of introducing error and leading people dangerously astray, as Ælfric (c. 950–1010), a prolific writer of vernacular prose, observed.[59] On the other hand, the spread of Christianity into the Germanic world offered new opportunities for the use of the vernacular. It was, after all, a necessity of conversion that missionaries preach, teach,

58 Page, *Runes*.
59 Ælfric, *Prefaces*, 127.

and communicate with royal and aristocratic patrons, and to perform these functions the Roman churchmen in England, for example, though supported by Frankish interpreters, required a knowledge of English. Soon after their arrival in 597, English made the momentous transition from a spoken to a written language. Missionaries on the Continent and in Scandinavia (many of them English) faced the same problem of instructing both laypeople and clerics in an unwritten language; vernaculars there were also turned to Christian use, though not always in writing.[60] Bede, for example, emphasized how important it was for people to be able to say the Creed and the Lord's Prayer in their own languages;[61] written texts of these, however, appear only later in the period. The first vernacular texts to survive in writing in England are four legal tracts from seventh-century Kent and Wessex, perhaps reflecting the church's desire to flatter kings with imperial associations.

The fear of misunderstanding as well as misrepresentation may have discouraged full translation of the Bible. Although Bede was said to have been translating the Gospel of St. John into English on his deathbed in 735, in the late tenth century Ælfric worried that translations of the Old Testament could give "foolish men" the wrong idea about how to live in the present day.[62] Only the Gospels, the first seven books of the Old Testament, and the Psalms are extant in Old English translations. A vernacular Gospel of St. Matthew is preserved in a Rhenish Franconian manuscript of the late eighth century. Religious poetry, vernacular in both language and idiom, is attested from the early eighth century in England. Bede tells us of the "godly and religious songs" of Caedmon, an illiterate herdsman living in the monastery of Whitby: "Whatever he learned of holy Scriptures by means of interpreters, he quickly turned into extremely delightful and moving poetry in English, which was his own tongue."[63] English missionary foundations (such as Fulda) presumably channeled influence to the continent. From the beginning of the ninth century several poetic reworkings of the Gospels – "not word for word, but in accordance with the sense"[64] – were produced: the *Heliand* and *Genesis*, in Old Saxon, and, in the mid-ninth century, Otfrid of Weissenberg's *Liber evangeliorum* ("Why should the Franks . . . not sing God's praise in Frankish?").[65] Both

60 Green, *Language and History*.

61 Haddan and Stubbs 3, 316. Trans. in *English Historical Documents, c. 500–1042* (no. 170), 801–802; cf. Wallace-Hadrill, *Frankish Church*, 377.

62 *Old English Version*, 76–77.

63 Bede, *HE*, iv.24.

64 Ælfric, *Prefaces*, 127 (quoting Jerome).

65 Bostock, *Handbook*, 168–212; C. Edwards, "German Vernacular Literature," 154, for quotation.

patronage of and audience for these religious poems remain controversial and difficult to determine. Possibly connected to the royal court, and certainly suitable for an illiterate lay audience, the verses also could conceivably have been read out during the Divine Office or in the refectory.[66] Renditions of Christian doctrine in vernacular poetic form demonstrate how Christian ideas – concerning baptism, for example – could be translated into story, thereby making the liturgy "something compelling, close at hand."[67]

The earliest surviving texts in Old High German, however, are glossaries. Continental use of the written vernacular, in contrast to England, may have at first been limited to translation exercises, moving on in the ninth century to more varied written reflections of the oral culture that continued to flourish (although the vagaries of survival may skew this picture). In addition, vernacular baptismal vows, creeds, pater nosters, confessions, oaths, boundary clauses, and magico-medical material all survive from the Continent. Many of these types of texts are also found in ninth-century England, but vernacular charters, royal writs, aristocratic wills, leases, and other practical documents also abounded there. By the late Anglo-Saxon period, English was the "ordinary language of much written business."[68] Although documentary records were essentially secular, associated with the functioning of government and local lordship, they all had had an ecclesiastical origin of some kind, as religious houses blazed a trail in the articulation (literal and conceptual) of property transactions, and churchmen's literate expertise made possible increasingly sophisticated administration of power at local and national levels.

Some vernacular texts, such as translations of the Benedictine Rule, were clearly written for a professional ecclesiastical audience. Some of (perhaps much of) the audience for vernacular hagiography – particularly popular in Anglo-Saxon England and medieval Iceland – would have been clerical. Other works had a wider dissemination. Although the Carolingian *renovatio* focused primarily on Latin learning, Charlemagne's "grammar of his native language,"[69] unfortunately now lost, was part and parcel of an ambitious program of education and social engineering inspired by ideals of Christian rulership. Church synods insisted that the laity was to be routinely instructed through vernacular sermons detailing heavenly rewards for those who performed good deeds on earth. These pastoral aims can also be seen in vernacular verses such as *Muspilli*, a ninth-century poem on the Last Judgment

66 C. Edwards, "German Vernacular Literature," 152–53.
67 Cramer, *Baptism and Change*, 202, on *Andreas*.
68 Campbell, "Observations," 158.
69 Einhard, *Vita Karoli*, ch. 29, 33 or trans. Dutton, 34.

which encouraged Christians to repentance and good works.[70] In England King Alfred's celebrated literacy and translation program of the 890s, also anchored on Christian values, was explicitly vernacular, encouraging lay people to learn to read their native language.[71] English versions of selected texts, some by the king himself, were intended to make Christian wisdom more accessible to a population – including some clerics – for whom Latin learning had become too esoteric, and whose consequently sinful state was jeopardizing the fate of the kingdom. The *Anglo-Saxon Chronicle*, a major work of history begun in 892, demonstrates how significant an alternative to Latin English had become. In the second half of the tenth century a reform of religion encouraged a more vigorous vernacular literature in England. Four major codices written between c. 970 and 1025, mostly adapting and versifying biblical stories, represent a much larger and more accomplished body of vernacular poetry than survives on the Continent.[72] At the same time, sermons and saints' lives in rhythmical prose by Ælfric and his contemporary Wulfstan (archbishop of York 1002–23) took the vernacular to new heights of elegance and eloquence in the service of religious instruction. After 1066, when English was replaced as the language of culture and government by Latin and French, vernacular writing did not disappear from the ecclesiastical context. The Anglo-Saxon Chronicle, homilies, and other didactic pieces continued to be produced in English in Anglo-Norman religious houses.[73]

At some stage after the acquisition of literacy, works of sheer entertainment were also committed to writing. Some had probably circulated for a long time in a variety of oral forms before being captured in script by ecclesiastical scribes – the controversy over the context and date of *Beowulf* illustrates the obscurity of the process.[74] Although the past they portrayed was an imaginary one, tales tapping a pool of Germanic legend which centered on historical figures of the fourth, fifth, and sixth centuries, such as Theodoric and Ermanaric, surfaced in England, Francia, and Scandinavia (especially after the Carolingian Empire made inclusive *Germanitas* politically more interesting).[75] Alfred had a book, now lost, of such "Saxon songs" (and learned them by heart),[76] and five poems surviving in the Old English poetic collections prominently feature Germanic legends. Of this heroic genre, epitomized by *Beowulf*, only one poem,

70 Bostock, *Handbook*, 135–54.
71 Asser, *Life of Alfred* (trans. Keynes and Lapidge), 126.
72 For translations, see *Anglo-Saxon Poetry*.
73 Treharne and Swan, *Rewriting Old English*.
74 Chase, *Dating of Beowulf*.
75 Frank, "Germanic Legend"; Innes, "Teutons or Trojans?"
76 Asser, *Life of King Alfred*, ch. 76 (ed. Stevenson, 59), (trans. Keynes and Lapidge, 91).

the *Hildebrandslied*, survives from the Continent, probably because use of the written vernacular was much more restricted there; having flowered in the ninth century, it seems to have withered in the tenth.[77] In England, by contrast, some have seen in the success of English in the tenth and eleventh centuries not just a vernacularization of church culture, but also a crucial step towards the creation of a political nation, as "ordinary people" had access through the vernacular to the machinery of central government and local administration.

In Denmark, Norway, and Sweden, non-runic literacy and traditional Latin learning are assumed to have arrived with foreign churchmen, but the vernacular retained a place, especially in practices involving devotion and the working of institutions. Religious, legal, and historical texts were written down in alphabetic vernaculars, starting in the late twelfth century, while memorializing, declarations of ownership, and magic were still written in runes. Scandinavia mimicked but never matched England's use of the written vernacular. In Iceland, on the other hand, the native language broke out in new directions, as we have seen. In addition to the thirteenth-century poems and prose discussed above, surviving law-collections, histories, saints' lives, and grammatical treatises from the twelfth century attest to the stature of the vernacular. The first missionaries in the field, who struggled to create Christian vocabularies for the Goths, Franks, English, Saxons, and Northmen, would probably have found this late medieval literary exuberance – and the political and social impact of secular literacy – unimaginable. Vernacular writing had come a long way since churchmen first faced the problem of communicating Christian concepts to potential converts in a language which they could understand.

The peoples speaking a Germanic language in the period 600 to 1100 were diverse and widespread. They inhabited the dominant kingdoms of western Europe and small marginal polities on the fringes of the political world. Some, nearest the influence of the Roman Empire, had become Christian before 600. Others, at a greater distance, were still in the process of abandoning their traditional religion in the twelfth century. By 1100 the distinctive Christianities of the early medieval church were increasingly giving way to a more universal Christendom. Any search for a "Germanic" experience in these centuries must acknowledge the range of external influences at play, the amount of change experienced over the period, and the variety of lived experience within it. Christianities were stratified socially as well as separated temporally and spatially, and different rhythms of Christianization distinguished the experience

77 C. Edwards, "German Vernacular Literature," 169.

in different regions and at opposite ends of the social scale. Furthermore, the church constantly moved the goalposts when defining a Christian life. Nor did it live up to its stated standards, not always having had the resources to help realize the goals articulated by church councils, penitentials, and sermons. Christians and their churches in the Germanic world were, in consequence, a variegated lot, but what they did have in common was the experience of conversion. From 600 to 1100, foreign churchmen travelled to one part or another of the Germanic world to face the heathen. At any one time, somewhere, from Rheims to Rochester to Reykholt, missionaries were coming to terms with the business of introducing a foreign religion and reinterpreting traditional societies in Christian terms. This process of transforming traditional culture was played and replayed, each time with new factors in action, as contexts changed and Christianity moved toward its second millennium.

6

Slav Christianities, 800–1100

JONATHAN SHEPARD

The coming of Christianity to the Slavs and Bulgars

To the inhabitants of the Balkans, whether members of Greek-speaking communities or newcomers, the phenomenon of the Roman Empire was virtually inescapable. In the provinces south of the Danube overrun by the Slavs in the seventh and eighth centuries, imperial authority of the traditional stamp had dissolved. The emperor's writ was restricted to fertile coastal plains, whose inhabitants sought protection in fortresses and towns. The townsfolk, in turn, looked to their patron saints: St. Demetrius repeatedly had to intervene to stop Avars and Slavs from capturing Thessalonica[1] and Patras almost fell to the Slavs at the beginning of the ninth century. A later tale claimed that, awe-struck by the sight of St. Andrew leading the charge against them, these Slavs sought sanctuary in his church; they and their properties were subsequently assigned to maintaining the church.[2] Uncertain as events might be, both assailants and assailed could reckon upon the eventual return of regions of significance to imperial rule. Constantinople's governors would never permit otherwise, as their ceaseless rounds of palace ceremonial broadcast: with God's help "the Christians" would always prevail over "the nations" around them. This message, and its trappings, reached remote recesses of the Balkans and beyond. The Rus *Primary Chronicle* tells of a certain Kii's visit to "Tsargrad" where the emperor received him with "great honor." The legend is designed to show that Kii, eponymous founder of Kiev, enjoyed high status among his people.[3] But it suggests what an honorific association with the emperor could do for aspiring chieftains – all the more so for those within range of Byzantine strike-forces. To the leaders of groupings in the "Slavic regions" (*Sklaviniai*), reaching as far as Thessalonica, hospitality and gifts were on more or less standing offer.

1 *Les plus anciens recueils*, 120–89, 198–241.
2 Constantine VII, *De administrando imperio*, 228–31; Turlej, "Legendary Motif," 374–99.
3 *Povest' Vremennykh Let*, 9.

Traces of certain leaders' affinities come from their seals. Judging by the Greek inscriptions, their owners could hold court titles and honor the cross, while retaining their Slav names.[4]

The metamorphosis of Slav community leaders into wholehearted "subjects" of the emperor was tortuous, varying between areas. Ambitious individuals were apt to head for the imperial city and the emperor's service: Constantinople was worth a Christian name.[5] The standing of those staying behind rested on their capacity for coping with the "Greeks." Only gradually did Slavs influential in their locality take on Byzantine ways and foist them on their fellows. One instance may be that of Danelis in the mid-ninth century. This wealthy widow, probably a leading figure in a *Sklavinia*, was eager to forge influential connections for her son at Constantinople. Her estates near Patras contained large-scale workshops, manufacturing deluxe textiles that were valued in Constantinople itself.[6] Danelis's workmen stood to prosper and were thus better disposed toward Greek ways, religion, and ultimately, authority. Their outlook probably owed as much to the Byzantine economy's upswing as it did to pastoral efforts of the Patras clergy. Around 806, soon after withstanding the Slavs' assault, the see of Patras was raised to metropolitan status, a showpiece of imperial solicitousness for outlying areas. Monks were prominent in imperial missionary endeavors, and it may be no coincidence that a monk was "spiritual father" to the widow Danelis.[7]

The priorities of emperors furthering mission work emerge from Leo VI's (886–912) account of his father's efforts. Basil I (867–86) "persuaded" the Slavs "to change their old ways and, having Grecized (*graikōsas*) them and subjected them to rulers on the Roman pattern, and having honored them with baptism, he . . . schooled them in fighting against the peoples hostile to the Romans . . . on account of this he freed the Romans from care about the rebellions that had often been mounted by Slavs."[8] This sums up imperial policy towards the Slavs in Greece. Chief among the "hostile peoples" were the Bulgars, and, although in 870 Basil reached a church settlement with Khan Boris, he saw the need to tighten supervision of the *Sklaviniai* straddling ill-defined borderlands. Similar considerations, the desire to ring-fence the newly Christian Bulgaria,

4 Nystazopoulou-Pelekidou, "Sceaux byzantins," 16–17; Seibt, "Siegel," 28–33; Seibt, "Weitere Beobachtungen," 459–66.

5 See Ditten, "Prominente Slawen."

6 Theophanes Continuatus, *Chronographia*, 226–28, 317–19; Ševčenko, "Re-reading Constantine," 192 and note 68; *Prosopographie*, #1215.

7 Theophanes Continuatus, *Chronographia*, 227; Turlej, *Chronicle*, 66–70.

8 Leo VI, *Tactica*, XVIII.101, col. 969.

probably lay behind Basil's readiness to send "an imperial agent and priests" to baptize Serbs and other Slav groupings of the southwest Balkans. Constantine VII (945–59), relating the episode, treats it as the reimposition of "Roman" rights.[9] Further south, mountainous areas of little strategic significance such as the Taygetus were, in practice, left alone; their inhabitants long remained Slav-speaking and loosely provided for. The church of Patras, charged with restoring ecclesiastical organization and imperial surveillance in the western Peloponnese, only had three suffragan sees at first. Their number rose to five in the tenth century, all on or near the coast.[10]

If material well-being, imperial power, and Christianity were interwoven in the southern Balkans, this was also the case further north, in *Sklaviniai* coming under Bulgar sway and among the Bulgars themselves. The challenge for khans was how to hold their own with the "Greeks" in material splendor and signs of divine favor. The Bulgars had brought from the steppes concepts of monarchy and a supreme sky-god, and the ruler presided over collective worship. They contrived to uphold these ways while semi-sedentary, living partly off tribute raised from Slav and other communities in the mountains stretching far to the southwest. No Bulgar structure, material or political, could match the Greeks for indestructibility, and St. Demetrius had Slav admirers around Thessalonica well before their formal conversion. Military success was a precondition, and after Nicephorus I's death in battle in 811, Khan Krum (802–14) made sure that the chiefs of *Sklaviniai* under his sway drank from the emperor's gilded skull.[11] The conquests of Krum in Thrace brought Christian townsfolk and churchmen beneath his rule, and his successor's attempt to make them abjure their religion created hundreds of martyrs, commemorated in Byzantine service books. Avowed regard for law and order, military discipline, and service obligations engraved on inscriptions at the khan's residence gave him title to rule. But when it came to articulating monarchical authority, the empire next door had the best tunes, and Greek inscriptions terming him "the ruler from God," preceded by *kanasybigi*, drew on imperial formulae. Interpreting the latter, presumably Turkic, term is controversial, but its essence probably echoes the Greek: the khan's authority was heaven-given.[12] Omurtag (814/5–31) also issued gold medallions portraying himself in imperial garb,

9 Constantine VII, *De administrando imperio*, 124–27.
10 Turlej, *Chronicle*, 110, 114–16, 124, and map on 164.
11 Theophanes, *Chronographia*, 491 (trans. Mango and Scott, 673–74).
12 Beshevliev, *P'rvob'lgarski nadpisi*, 77–79, 136, 216, 225; Stepanov, "Bulgar Title," 4–7, 13–19.

holding a cross; the legend gives only his name and *kanasybigi*.[13] Omurtag was using Byzantine media to demonstrate near-parity, declaring his status in terms at once comparable with those of the *basileus* and distinctively Bulgar: appropriating a Greek formula to encapsulate existing notions of his authority. Omurtag probably also hoped to tap into the fortune lavished by the supreme God on the Greeks.

There is no firm evidence that the khans' authority was progressively eroded by the presence within their realm of Christian Greek communities or by the outward stream of ambitious Bulgars seeking hospitality, honors, and employment on the Bosporus. Returnees were not necessarily subversive of the Bulgar political order, and shortly before Boris's (852–89) baptism, monks and Christian laypersons were not uncommon in high places. One anecdote has the still-pagan Boris commissioning a monk to paint scenes on his hunting-lodge walls.[14] The foundations of Boris's power at the time of his baptism in (probably) 865 are laid out in the questions addressed to Pope Nicholas I (858–67) in the following year. It was a matter of reinforcing the existing functions of the khan, rather than drastic transformation. Boris sought all the advantages of a well-regulated cult without impairing his military organization's combat-readiness. But equally, he did not want to stymie prospects for victory by infringing Christian rules. Thus he asked about campaigning on Sundays and in Lent and sought guidance on divination before battle.[15] Basing godly order on the written word seems to have appealed greatly. Boris's foremost request was for "the Christian law," seemingly in book form.[16] A written code of beliefs and exemplary conduct offered opportunities for self-reliance and this, too, signaled Boris's priorities. His request to Nicholas for a patriarch[17] was less a mark of ignorance than a bid for an ecclesiastical organization coterminous with his realm. Papal reluctance to endorse Boris's choice as high-priest was one reason why he switched back to the Byzantines, whose priests had baptized him. Through the settlement of 870, he gained a discrete church organization, headed by an archbishop but under the ultimate oversight of the patriarch of Constantinople.

A massive church-building program, begun with western Christian assistance, continued, and Boris drew heavily on Byzantine technical skills.

13 Beshevliev, *P'rvob'lgarski nadpisi*, 249; Iurukova and Penchev, *B'lgarski srednovekovni pechati i moneti*, 21–23, plate 1:3; Stepanov, "Bulgar Title," 6–7.
14 Theophanes Continuatus, *Chronographia*, 163–64.
15 Nicholas I [pope], *Epistolae*, 580, 581, 585.
16 Ibid., 568–69.
17 Ibid., 592–93.

Conversely, erecting stone inscriptions, already less in fashion in the mid-ninth century, ceased to be an attribute of rulership. Virtually the only inscription associated with Boris records that, changing his name to Michael – the emperor's – he was baptized "together with the people given to him by God."[18] The inscription stood in the southwestern periphery of Boris's dominions, and this may be no accident. His episcopal sees "girdled" the realm, according to Theophylact of Ochrid (c. 1050–after 1126), who credits him with the building of seven cathedral churches.[19] The imagery may not be fiction, for several sees were in peripheral zones, looking toward Byzantine lands or power points. He also promoted the cult of the relics of the Fifteen Martyrs of Tiberiopolis, recalling the early Christian past of borderland towns.[20] Further to the southwest, in the later 880s, Boris assigned the Slavic churchman and scholar Clement (c. 840–916). Clement, with a few fellow-pupils of Cyril (826–69) and Methodius (c. 815–85), had found sanctuary at his court after Methodius's death in 885 and the disintegration of his Middle Danube mission. Boris does not seem to have followed up the opportunities presented by the religious works now translated from Greek into Slavonic through the labors of Cyril, Methodius, and their pupils. According to the *Life of Constantine-Cyril*, sufficient texts for celebration of the liturgy had been translated into the new literary language Cyril had created, by the time of his arrival in Rome in 867.[21] Yet Boris did not impose Slavonic as the language of worship, and Greek – probably still the mother-tongue of his most senior clergy – remained the principal liturgical language of worship among the Bulgarians until, seemingly, the late twelfth century.[22] The uses of Slavonic for evangelizing, and training indigenous clergy, were, however, appreciated by Boris, and Clement showed versatility upon being assigned to the southwestern borderlands. His journeying between communities, preaching "in a loud voice," bore fruit, not least in the form of teachers and clergymen – 3,500 according to his *Life*.[23] Clement's output included hymns, panegyrics of saints, and also sermons written in straightforward Slavonic, readily understandable when read out by priests before their congregations. Clement seems to have been aiming, with Boris's backing, for the grassroots, in areas peopled by Vlachs and Albanians, as well as Slavs. The lakeside town

18 Beshevliev, *P'rvob'lgarski nadpisi*, 151–52 and fig. 78.

19 Iliev, "Long Life," 101.

20 Obolensky, *Six Byzantine Portraits*, 73–75.

21 *Life of Constantine-Cyril*, 105, 108. See also *Life of Methodius*, 191. On the brothers' mission to Rastislav of Moravia, see Shepard, "Slavs and Bulgars," 241–42; Tachiaos, *Cyril and Methodius*, 77–78, 84–86.

22 Hannick, "Les nouvelles chrétientés," 931–33.

23 Iliev, "Long Life," 98–99; Obolensky, *Six Byzantine Portraits*, 25–26.

of Ochrid became the focal point of his earlier mission work, although subsequently he was appointed to a see further east. Clement's church-building and translation work acted, in part, as a culturo-political counterforce to the attractions of Byzantine-held Dyrrachium and Thessalonica.

Clement's mission work received enthusiastic patronage from Boris's son, Symeon (893–927), after he became ruler in 893. Symeon had been groomed for the monastic life – and probably headship of the church in Bulgaria. He was whisked from a monastery onto the throne to substitute for his elder brother, Vladimir. Boris had abdicated and himself withdrawn to a monastery, but emerged to depose Vladimir after he launched a pagan reaction. Symeon's achievements were praised in the *Life of Clement*: a Solomon to his father's David, completing his Temple. This imagery is borne out even by critical contemporaries: Patriarch Nicholas Mysticus (901–907, 912–25) recognized his wisdom and seriousness of character.[24] Symeon provoked imperial loathing through his ready recourse to arms in vindication of what he considered rightful dignity. To the Byzantines' bemusement, Symeon saw no contradiction between self-determination, piety, and the furtherance of Christian worship and normative values among his people. At least as much as his father, Symeon saw Christianity as a means toward consolidating his realm, earning divine protection, and salvation. Reportedly, he compared himself with Moses.[25] Presumably he was drawing attention to his leadership of this New Israel out of captivity, whether that portended by the Byzantines or by relapse into paganism.

Symeon's sense of mission took literary forms. The treatise on imperial duties and good practice composed for Justinian by Agapetus was translated into Slavonic at the turn of the ninth and tenth centuries, almost certainly at Symeon's behest.[26] This mirror for princes laid down principles by which the Christian ruler should guide and instruct his people, while making plain that he was answerable only to God for his actions. Symeon himself scarcely needed a translation: able to write as well as read Greek, he directed some of the translation projects, choosing which sermons of St. John Chrysostom should be rendered into Slavonic. His mirror for princes was presumably intended for members of his elite and others equal to written Slavonic, but defeated by Greek. Symeon's self-image was burnished by a eulogy composed at his court: he is likened to a "labor-loving bee," gathering nectar from

24 Nicholas I [patriarch], *Letters*, 26–27, 34–35, 68–71, 90–91, 114–15, 132–35, 150–51.
25 Ibid., 176–77.
26 Nikolov, "Tsariat–bogopodrazhatel," 115–17.

sacred writings and feeding it to his boyars.[27] The translated treatise set out his ideology for their benefit. Some resisted the high moral tone, and John the Exarch berated their irreverence during church services. But piety bound up with devotion to Symeon and an alternative to Byzantine overlordship enthused his numerous office holders. The gravestone of Mostich records that he gave up all his property and the senior post he had held for eighteen years under "Tsar Symeon," and then his son "Tsar Peter," to become a monk.[28] A warrior named Clement was also of high status. His narrow escape from Hungarian marauders (c. 895) is recorded in a miracle collection containing some Bulgarian-derived tales that was translated into Slavonic: "the Hungarians were chasing us, my horse began to weaken and tire." Thanks to St. George's intervention, Clement's horse recovered and he got away, dodging "many an arrow"; his comrades were mostly "captured and killed."[29]

Spiritual salvation was also of keen concern, and Mostich was probably not the only man of action to end his days in a monastery near the capital, Preslav. Symeon himself lived austerely, "stinting his belly like a hermit on the mountains, tasting no wine."[30] Monasteries proliferated across the realm, for example near the house founded by Clement at Ochrid, and Bulgarians visited holy men living in the Byzantine empire. John (876/80–946), seeking solitude in a cave and for a while in an oak tree, chose a starker degree of monasticism than that common in well-heeled cenobitic houses. He gained a reputation as a wonder-worker: through "the power of the holy father's prayer" a deadly serpent was turned to marble, pieces of it being taken by local people for purposes of healing.[31] John living out his days in the "wilderness" of the Rila mountains did not escape the attention of Tsar Peter (927–69), himself an avid letter writer to St. Paul of Latros. Peter saw to the composition of a *Life* and recognition of John as a saint soon after his death in 941. Peter was of a godly disposition and his motivation was predominantly other-worldly. Yet through patronizing the hermit, Peter brought him within the fold. The large monastic complex cut out of the rock at Murfatlar seems to have performed more direct services for Bulgarian security. Located beside the dyke topped by a stone wall that obstructed incursions from the north, it probably provided for the spiritual needs of the nearby garrison forts, one of whose commanders, Demetrius, is

27 *Simeonov Sbornik*, 202.
28 Stanchev, "Nadgrobniiat nadpis," 61–76; Beshevliev, *P'rvob'lgarski nadpisi*, 240–42 and fig. 166.
29 Angelov, *Iz starata b'lgarska literatura*, 85; Turilov, "Vizantiiskii i slavianskii plasty," 81–84, 92–94.
30 Nicholas I [patriarch], *Letters*, 94–95.
31 Ivanov, *Zhitiia*, 31.

known from an inscription of 942/3.[32] The monks' liturgies and prayers may also have served as a kind of supernatural shield, supplicating the saints to fend off the nomads, as St. George had done c. 895. It may be no coincidence that the cult of John as a saint was initiated in what amounted to a border zone. Thus saints could also serve the princely order.

As the withdrawal of John of Rila shows, holy men were far from being state stooges, and the sheer number of monasteries in tenth-century Bulgaria implies support from a broad social base. In fact the tendency of Bulgarians to abandon families and possessions as jeopardizing their spiritual salvation and to become monks was condemned by a churchman, Cosmas (fl. later tenth century), writing in, probably, the 960s. It is no accident that his principal targets were those shunning the pollution of this world and seeking self-effacement in the spirit through radical – and to his mind heretical – methods: the Dualists who followed the priest Bogomil's teaching believed that all matter was the Devil's work and the good God of the New Testament was pure spirit. The followers of Bogomil, shunning the flesh and all worldly goods, provided living enactment of Christ's teaching. Cosmas denounces their "false humility" and fasting as, Gospels in hand, they win over ordinary people to unwitting perdition.[33]

The Bogomils would not have been readily distinguishable from holy men such as John of Rila, save perhaps in their proselytizing fervor, traveling around rural communities. Only gradually was their radicalism divulged: rejection of the established church and authorities – the emperors and their officials, the rich and powerful. Cosmas blames slack pastoral care for the Bogomils' inroads and criticizes the bishops for failing to supervise their local clergy.[34] Our evidence is too scant for such criticism to be easily assessed. Tracts such as Peter the Monk's *Salvation of the Soul* attest to some orthodox efforts to care for laypersons' needs and church attendance, whether or not this Peter is identifiable with Peter the tsar.[35] The level of pastoral care available may have been no worse than that which Byzantine clergy across the border provided. But lay expectations may not have been wholly met by a predominantly Greek-language liturgy, despite the repertory of hymns and other liturgical texts composed or translated by Clement and his brilliant contemporaries, Naum

32 Curta, "Cave and Dyke," 130–31 and 144–49.

33 Cosmas the Priest, *Kozma presviter v slavianskikh literaturakh*, 330; trans. Puech and Vaillant, *Le traité contre les Bogomiles*, 76.

34 Cosmas the Priest, *Kozma presviter v slavianskikh literaturakh*, 313–18, 387–91; trans. Puech and Vaillant, *Le traité contre les Bogomiles*, 64–67, 123–27.

35 Pavlova, *Pet'r chernorizets*, 20–45 (introduction) and 313–28 (text); Turilov and Floria, "Khristianskaia literatura," 413.

and Constantine.[36] At the same time, access to the Scriptures in Slavonic probably whetted readers' and hearers' appetites for further explanation of the paradoxes of Bible stories. The Bogomils' success may well be due to a spirit of questioning, anxiety about salvation and need for reassurance, which the church services and monasteries had aroused, but could not fully satisfy. The style of itinerant preaching set by Clement could scarcely be sustained with the same intensity by later generations of prelates or priests. Equally, the charges and exactions imposed on the population were probably no less heavy than they had been in the days of the ninth-century khans, and Bulgarian military organization remained formidable. As we have seen, the ruling elite of Bulgaria took pains to adopt exemplary Christian lifestyles, and many were swept along in their wake. But to those seeking answers to questions or disenchanted with the established church, the Bogomils offered guidelines to personal salvation.

The picture painted and personified by Cosmas the Priest is one of cultural vitality and self-criticism, rather than of terminal malaise, and a glance at subsequent Bulgarian history suggests that competing strands of spirituality persevered, flourishing even in adverse or alien circumstances. The new "royal family" – probably of Armenian stock – that constituted itself in reaction to the Byzantines' dissolution of Bulgaria as a state made orthodoxy a rallying point of loyalties. One of the first actions of Samuel (987/8–1014), the self-styled tsar, was to seize the relics of St. Achilleus from Byzantine Larissa, as a way of legitimizing his new center of authority in Prespa.[37] After Samuel's son and heir Gabriel (1014–15) was assassinated, his cousin, murderer, and successor John Vladislav (1015–18) sought to bolster his regime by a combination of military measures and pronounced piety. A stone inscription records his restoration of the fortress of Bitola, helped by "the holy Mother of God"; it was to be a "refuge and salvation for the Bulgarians."[38] Vladislav's efforts did not prevent eventual Byzantine victory in 1018, but Basil II (976–1025) took care to privilege the Bulgarian church as a separate "autocephalous" church, with a Bulgarian archbishop in charge.[39] Not all Basil's successors shared his deftness in accommodating Bulgarian sensibilities, and from 1037 the senior churchmen were Greeks, including Theophylact, who in high-style letters to friends could dismiss the Bulgarians as bumpkins. Yet it is to Theophylact that we owe much information about Christian Bulgaria in the generation following its conversion. Theophylact's Greek version of the *Life of Clement*, his precursor

36 Turilov and Floria, "Khristianskaia literatura," 402–3, 409–10, 417–21.
37 John Scylitzes, *Synopsis Istoriōn*, 330.
38 Zaimov and Zaimova, *Bitolski nadpis*, 33–34; Stephenson, *Legend of Basil*, 28–30.
39 Stephenson, *Byzantium's Balkan Frontier*, 74–75.

at Ochrid, draws on a much earlier Slavonic *Life*, and he also wrote on the Fifteen Martyrs of Tiberiopolis. Theophylact endorsed Clement's use of Slavonic and wrote approvingly of his literary output: the Bulgarians were a "holy nation" thanks to their conversion. Theophylact and his fellow members of the imperial establishment were acknowledging the strength of feeling among the Bulgarians, not contriving it. Without positively sponsoring the copying of Slavonic texts, they let this go on, at least in remoter western areas.[40] The works were mostly service books of undemanding intellectual caliber. The use of such texts could nurture piety at the grassroots level, and Byzantine authorities had little choice but to come to terms with this. They also failed to suppress the Bogomils' robust spirituality which drew inspiration from the Gospels and a burgeoning assortment of tales and prescriptions. The Bogomils' pastoral care remained active, as did their proselytizing zeal among the rural population. By the mid-eleventh century, they were gaining sympathizers, even believers, in Byzantium itself. Around 1100 Basil, a fashionable preacher wearing a monk's habit, even aspired to win over Alexius I Comnenus (1081–1118) himself in Constantinople. The faith which had sustained the empire for so long against "barbarian" neighbors was now, in mutant form, coming back from the Bulgarians to haunt it.

West Slavs: priestcraft and statecraft

To generalize about the encounters of the Western Slavs with Christianity is hazardous in the extreme, in view of the many differences in stance and prospects between, say, the masters of Moravian hill-forts, inhabitants of emporia on the Baltic coast such as Wolin and Szczecin, and populations living further inland along the fertile valleys of rivers such as the Vistula. Much as their societies varied, so did rites, assumptions, and beliefs, and very few gods or customs commanded respect or veneration throughout the Slav lands. One phenomenon known to most of them, though, was the material wealth, military prowess, and uniformity of cult observance of the Christians to their west and south. Christian political leaders did not present an unvaryingly united political front, and the more astute Slav potentates took advantage of this to extend and consolidate their own regimes. But they were all reacting, to a greater or lesser degree, to the corporate faith and *force majeure* looming over them. No full fathoming of their reactions can be attempted here. Instead, we shall consider contrasting yet related instances: the situation of

40 Floria et al., *Sud'by*, 120–35.

Slavs who found themselves facing resurgent *imperium*, once the Saxons had fended off the Hungarian raids of the earlier tenth century and themselves impinged on the populations east of the Elbe. Several Slav groupings in the border lands perforce came to terms and some chiefs adopted Christianity and sought privileged treatment on the strength of this. Further east, however, taking advantage of a remoter geographical location, trade routes, and political ties with the already-Christian Czechs, a Slav potentate gained dominance over many surrounding populations, using the Christian religion not only as an agent of dominion, but also to fend off the Christian Goliath to his west. Polish Christianity, one must stress, was *sui generis*, and ideally it should be compared closely with that of the Czechs: the Czech-born Vojtech-Adalbert (d. 997) was the object of competitive veneration from Czechs and Poles alike. But the Polish experience is no less significant for being distinctive: it bears comparison with that of the Bulgarians who likewise had to contend with an overmighty neighbor.

The pre-Christian western Slavs have left no more literary materials of their own than their counterparts to the south and east, and, as with the latter, our information about their sacral places and customs is filtered through unsympathetic churchmen's lenses. Writers such as Thietmar of Merseburg and Adam of Bremen were dismissive of practices which they dubbed demonic and the product of ignorance. They sometimes imputed to pagan Slavs greater coherence of thought and cult organization than was in fact the case, fitting them into stereotypes derived from Scripture and from their own preconceptions as to what any religion worth combating comprised.[41] Nonetheless, Slavs facing submission to stern Christian overlords clearly drew a connection between force, devotion to potent gods, and victory, as is suggested by the vigor with which they wrecked churches and altars during their rebellions. According to Thietmar, the rebellious Slavs' switch to "demonic" cults instead of Christ and St. Peter in 983 "was hailed not only by the pagans but also by the Christians." He describes the Liutizi parading behind idols of their gods as they joined forces with the Saxon army to fight the Christian Poles in 1005.[42] Some chiefs sought a role as intermediaries, forming marriage ties with German-speaking marcher lords and almost certainly being baptized, for example, Pribislav of the Stodorane in the late tenth century. Others, such as Henry Borivoj of the Abodrites, had Christian names. They presumably hoped thereby to forge peaceful relationships and tap the benefits that the Christian God brought

41 Rosik, *Interpretacja*, 36–42, 210–34; Zaroff, "Polabian Slavs," 81–96.
42 Thietmar of Merseburg, *Chronicon*, III.17, 104–5 and VI.22–23, 266–69.

their neighbors. They did not, however, try to impose Christianity on their fellows and probably lacked the means to do so. Certain communities seem to have developed cults and rites of collective worship as alternative fulcrums of power, material and supernatural, to those of the Christian realm next door. They devised hierarchies of priests replete with sanctuaries and rituals, most notoriously on the island of Rügen. It seems likely that these drew inspiration from the Christian church, although their origins are controversial.[43] The cult of Sventovit at Arkona attests the advantages – above all, protection – which well-ordered worship was thought to earn for communities. In that sense, Christian writers' insistence that their religion was setting the agenda for all humankind was not empty bluster.

One potentate who early spotted the trend and sought to turn it to his advantage was Mieszko (d. 992), lord of important strongholds in what became known as Greater Poland. Mieszko's ancestry is traced back to a simple farmer, named Piast, by the chronicler Gallus Anonymous, and excavations have revealed fairly ancient origins for such strongholds as Giecz and Ostrów Lednicki.[44] Nonetheless, dendrochronological evidence points to the destruction of many earth-and-wood structures during the mid-tenth century, and this should almost certainly be ascribed to the activities of Mieszko and perhaps his immediate predecessor. Some places over which the Piast dynasty (as it became known) gained dominion already had important shrines, notably Gniezno.[45] Mieszko, however, did not rest on the aura of such sanctuaries. Around 966 he was baptized, at the same time as marrying Dobrava (d. 1014) and forming an alliance with her father, the Christian Bohemian prince Boleslav (d. 977). Besides further enhancement of his status, Mieszko probably also hoped to render his new-found power acceptable to Otto of Saxony (936–73) – or at least not casually dissoluble. Otto's victories over the Hungarians and then over Slav groupings led by the Abodrites in 955 showed his potential for subjugating the Slavs further east. The missionary archbishopric instituted in 968 at Magdeburg encompassed "all the people of the Slavs beyond the Elbe and the Saale, lately converted and to be converted to God."[46] Mieszko's alignment with the Christian religion and church hierarchy is best understood against this background. Mieszko laid himself open to Christian priestcraft but seemingly maneuvered to have bishops assigned on his own terms: Jordan and later

43 Rosik, *Interpretacja*, 238–48, 258–76, 303–11; Zaroff, "Perception," 83; Zaroff, "Origins" 9–18.
44 Kurnatowska, "Ostrów Lednicki," 167–68, 182; Kurnatowska, "Stronghold in Giecz," 207–11.
45 Kurnatowska, "Elementy sacrum," 112–17; Urbańczyk and Rosile, "Poland," 267, 271.
46 *Diplomata Ottonis*, 502–3.

Unger were missionary bishops directly answerable to the papacy, rather than associates of the bishop of Prague or subordinate to mighty German sees. Thus Mieszko could hope for, literally, the blessings of Christianity without institutional absorption within Christian *imperium*. Mieszko's priorities are encapsulated in the *Dagome Iudex*, a brief eleventh-century note on a deed making over his main stronghold and all his possessions to St. Peter. This territorialized Mieszko's aspirations, delineating areas he had yet to dominate; only children by his second wife, the *senatrix* Oda, feature as fellow donors of the family concern.[47] In other words, a polity defined on Mieszko's terms was placed under the protection of St. Peter and his vicar on earth.

Not even this device could guarantee the succession of the younger sons against the sense of blood-right of Mieszko's first-born, Boleslav I (992–1025). And the standing of the polity remained contentious. An unforgivable act of Otto III (983–1002) was, in Thietmar's eyes, to make a lord of Boleslav, who had been a tributary. Yet the episode which drew Thietmar's ire was in many ways a vindication of the Piasts' harnessing of Christianity to "nation-building." Otto III placed his own crown on Boleslav's head before a gathering of nobles at Gniezno in 1000, declaring him "brother and partner in the empire."[48] At the same time he confirmed that Boleslav's realm should have five sees, all but one within 150 miles of Gniezno, headed by an archbishop at Gniezno. Otto joined Boleslav in venerating the relics of his own former mentor, Adalbert, beheaded by Prussians barely three years earlier. The missionary saint's half-brother, Gaudentius-Radim (d. 1006/12/22), became the first archbishop, a living link between Boleslav's church organization and sacred time. Otto III's appreciation of Piast aspirations to self-determination died with him, but Adalbert's relics, working "a thousand miracles," attracted pilgrims to Gniezno. *Palatia*, halls with adjoining circular chapels, displayed the interlinking of prayer and rightful authority at several strongholds: Poznań, Przemyśl, Giecz, and on a massive scale, the island of Ostrów Lednicki.[49] Gniezno's and Cracow's churches seem to have been planned to form a cross, invoking Christ's protection for entire towns. Besides the early stone churches built in Boleslav's core lands between Gniezno and Poznań, other known churches and monasteries of the earlier eleventh century mostly studded the outer reaches of Piast dominion, for example, the monastery in honor of five missionary-martyrs at Międzyrzecz. Boleslav himself became a lay member of this monastery, where miracles were

47 Kürbis, "Dagome iudex," 394–95.
48 Gallus Anonymus, *Chronica*, I.6, 20.
49 Urbańczyk and Rosile, "Poland," 292–3, 296.

reported. His priorities recall those of Boris, whose sees reportedly "girdled" his realm.

Under Boleslav's auspices, *Lives* of missionaries such as Adalbert and the five missionary-martyrs were written or revised, and soon after Boleslav's death in 1025 his son and heir, Mieszko, received a copy of the Roman liturgy from his cousin, Mathilda of Swabia, together with a letter of exhortation: his father had used "iron" to make "barbarous and most ferocious peoples" heed the Lord's Word; now the highly educated Mieszko could bring them spiritual enlightenment.[50] Mieszko was not, however, destined to play Symeon to his father's Boris. Challenged by his brothers and menaced by Rus and Germans, he fled, ousted by his elder brother Bezprym, who seems to have tapped currents of hostility to the church and to government exactions. Bezprym himself fell victim to them in 1032, and a pagan reaction ensued, assailing the new political culture. According to Gallus Anonymous, the people turned on "the bishops and priests of God, and some they treated to death by the sword, but others were deemed worthy of a viler death, by stoning."[51] The bishop of Wrocław had to flee. The ramparts of the town's royal stronghold were dismantled: a temple housing an idol took its place, a horse's skull beneath the foundations. This construction, datable to around 1033, marks a determined attempt to impose unchristian order, involving craftsmen.[52] Concerted though these attempts to throw off the Christian yoke were, too many powerful outsiders had an interest in maintaining it, and Mieszko's son Casimir restored Christian worship, with the aid of German soldiers, soon after a Czech expedition had abducted the relics of Adalbert and the five missionary-martyrs. For some time wild beasts made their homes in the cathedral ruins of Gniezno and Poznań, according to Gallus Anonymous,[53] and the missionary drive by which earlier rulers had made their names faltered. But material aid came from the west, especially the Rhineland, and monasteries were built for the Benedictines at Mogilno, Lubiń, and Tyniec. Tyniec's church stood over a wooden predecessor.[54] The sculpted planks of Wrocław's temple were sawn off near the base, and by 1051 Bishop Hieronimus was the incumbent at Wrocław, although probably not yet resident.

How far these foundations affected peasant society is very difficult to gauge. In the early twelfth century, the missionary bishop Otto came upon an

50 *Kodeks Matyldy*, 139–40.
51 Gallus Anonymus, *Chronica*, I.19, 42–43.
52 Moździoch, "Archeologiczne ślady," 176–85; Moździoch, "Wrocław-Ostrów Tumski," 330–32, 334–35, and 333 (fig. 13).
53 Gallus Anonymus, *Chronica*, I.19, 43.
54 Urbańczyk and Rosile, "Poland," 286, 296.

open-air sanctuary at Wolin, and in Szczecin he saw several temples, one of which housed the god Triglav's statue. With the support of Boleslav III, the Wry-mouth (1102–38), Otto staged mass baptisms and built churches.[55] That outlying peoples such as the Pomeranians persisted with organized pagan rites is not so surprising. Latin churchmen frowned effectively upon the pre-Christian practice of heaping earthen barrows over graves and the custom persisted only in eastern areas such as Przemyśl, where the Orthodox churchmen conducting worship were less disposed or able to banish barrows.[56] Supervision of ritual carried out underground was harder, and cremation ashes continued to be buried in the same cemeteries as inhumations near Białystok and elsewhere in the eastern regions, besides Pomerania.[57] Cremation was in flagrant contravention of church rules. Other deviations are less clear-cut, for example the so-called "anti-vampire burials." Starting around the time of the conversion in the late tenth century and increasing through the eleventh, these occurred mainly away from churchyards, and priestly eyes. The bodies lay face-down or on their sides, heads cut off, with stakes or knives driven through them. The aim seems to have been to prevent the dead from rising. It has plausibly been suggested that fears were fanned by enforced abandonment of cremation, and rather literal interpretations of doctrine on the resurrection of the dead.[58] The number of such burials is no more than thirty, and they at least suggest awareness of what the new religion taught.

The church organization in the later eleventh century had still to recover fully from pagan and Czech depredations. Gniezno had lost its prize relics, and the seat of princely power at Cracow lacked metropolitan status. Gregory VII (1073–85) expressed his concern over the disarray in a letter to Boleslav II (1058–1081/2) in 1075: the bishops were not acting by the canons and more bishops were needed to provide for "such a multitude of men."[59] Gregory's injunctions do not seem to have been heeded, stone churches were still built mostly in or around *castra*, and there was no equivalent of the Rus cult of Sts. Boris and Gleb to fuse popular faith, princely authority, and miracles of healing. In fact, Bishop Stanislav of Cracow perished at Boleslav's behest in 1079 and would eventually be venerated as a martyr. Still, a yearning for sacred apparatus at the grassroots level is evident from the medley of amulets placed in graves or the foundations of houses. These include the colored clay

55 *S. Ottonis*, 42–45; Ebo, *Vita S. Ottonis*, 73–77.
56 Zoll-Adamikowa, "Postępy," 103–109.
57 Urbańczyk and Rosile, "Poland," 279–81.
58 Żydok, "Wczesnośredniowieczne," 43, 50–52, 54–63.
59 *Registrum Gregorii VII*, 234.

egg rattles (*pisanki*) found throughout Polish lands from the early eleventh century onward, often in adult women's graves, and seemingly symbolizing fertility and resurrection, as they did among the Rus.[60]

Christianity was inseparable from princely order, and rulers such as Boleslav were addressed by popes in respectful, if condescending, terms. To that extent, Mieszko's bid to vest his political "clout" in sacral, more-or-less territorialized form, had paid off, and the idea of monarchy had churchmen's blessings. But whether these initiatives would jell into a single, lasting polity was still an open question.

Along the "East Way"

A third sphere of Christianity overlapped the other two, but included quite different forms of culture, society, and landscape. Few inhabitants of the expanses between the Black Sea steppes, the Baltic, and the White Sea had direct experience with Roman monuments, Christian communities, or intimidation by rulers zealous for the Christian God. The Slavs, Balts, and further north, Finns were not, for the most part, disposed in such a pattern as to generate elites or to throw up "big men" who might try to associate their predominance with particular gods. The more sophisticated sections of the population practising agriculture lived fairly static lives, remaining within reach of the burial grounds of ancestors and the spirits of woods, rivers, and lakes. They were not, however, entirely cut off from other cults and cultures. The furs which were the "drivers" of local exchanges were highly valued in distant markets, and from the second half of the eighth century an elaborate exchange nexus developed. This involved traders from Scandinavian-dominated parts of the Baltic bringing beads and other wares made further west, Finns living as far north as the Arctic hunting and trapping furry animals, Slavs likewise hunting and able to deliver furs to emporia, and dealers bearing silver coins from the Muslim world. By the mid-ninth century, northern-based traders known as "Rus" were taking their pelts across the Caspian to the markets of Baghdad. They tried to pass themselves off as Christians, to qualify for the reduced rate of tax payable by "peoples of the Book."[61] The Rus' claim gained plausibility from the fact that their journeys passed through Khazaria. Christians lived in the Khazars' main city, Itil, and Greek-speaking towns in the Crimea and the Straits of Kerch housed churches. Thus long-distance traders brushed with Christian communities at either end of the nexus bartering silver for furs. At Birka, in Central

60 Urbańczyk and Rosile, "Poland," 281.
61 Ibn Khurradadhbih, *Kitab al-Masalik* (ed. Lewicki), 76–77; (trans. Hadj-Sadok), 22–23.

Sweden, there were Christian households and, more spasmodically, priests.[62] The encounters of trading bands from the northern forests with Christians, Jews, or Muslims did not necessarily induce monotheism. But some traders may have drawn a connection between wealth and the southerners' cults and craftsmanship.

From the late ninth century, the towns at major communication hubs on the riverways expanded greatly, providing numerous markets and workshops, notably Staraia Ladoga, Gorodishche (Novgorod), and Gnezdovo (Smolensk). Insights into the mobile society that coalesced there are provided by chamber graves.[63] The seventy or more chamber graves excavated east of the Baltic mostly follow the axis from Staraia Ladoga, Pskov, and Gorodishche in the north to Kiev and Shestovitsa in the Middle Dnieper zone. Beside swords, bows and arrows, and riding-gear, everyday provisions were usually supplied, as were weights and balances. They betoken business as eternal, if not usual, and the corpses' kaftans and horses' bridle ornaments register oriental luxuries and proximity to the steppes. Located near the trading nodes, chamber graves act as "tracers" of the political structure encompassing these regions. Their occupants were probably associates or retainers of the Rus princes, who were themselves of Scandinavian stock.

Silver dirhams continued to stream into the Rus emporia, their actual numbers increasing through the first half of the tenth century, but from the beginning of that century the Rus were trading directly with Byzantium and, by the 930s, the locus of political power shifted south to the Middle Dnieper region. Now the Rus were engaging with an established, insistently Christian state. The emissaries sent to negotiate the first full trade treaty between the Rus leadership and Byzantium were reportedly taken round the churches and shown relics of Christ's Passion.[64] A hint of the Rus' response is the fact that the number of Christian Rus warranted special procedures in the Russo-Byzantine treaty of the mid-940s: emissaries who were Christian made their sworn undertakings separately, in a palace church. Some years later Olga (d. 969), their honorary ruler and widow of Prince Igor (d. 945/6), was herself baptized in the palace. She was renamed after Empress Helena, while Constantine VII became her godfather. Olga and her entourage were received at court, Olga herself being excused from the full obeisance to the emperor required of her fellow Rus. She made only "a slight nod of the head."[65]

62 Rimbert, *Vita Anskarii*, 42, 54–64, 90–92.
63 Mikhailov, "Drevnerusskie."
64 *Povest' Vremennykh Let*, 20.
65 Constantine VII, *De cerimoniis aulae byzantinae*, II.15, 597.

Olga's months on the Bosporus appear to epitomize the advantages enjoyed by the Rus rulers compared to leaders in the two spheres discussed earlier. The Rus had leeway to choose what suited them best, in as eclectic a fashion as the styles of ornament favored by their retainers. Not long after being baptized at Constantinople, Olga turned to Otto of Saxony requesting a mission, clearly with the intention of bringing the Rus under formal pastoral care. But Olga's initiative also illustrates the dilemmas facing leaders who sought to change their people's ways. The Germans soon gave up and the specially consecrated bishop, Adalbert, reported that he had only narrowly escaped death.[66] Olga's son, Sviatoslav (d. 972), rebuffed her attempts to convert him, allegedly exclaiming "My retainers will laugh at this!"[67] About that time a prince or notable was buried in a huge barrow at Chernigov and among his grave goods was a statuette of Thor. Thor had devotees among the wealthier echelons of the Rus, judging by the finds of his pendant hammerlets at emporia. The use of these amulets seems to have peaked around the mid-tenth century. Yet the elite also included believers in the powers of the Cross, notably those interred with small crosses round their necks in the Middle Dnieper region and at Gnezdovo. The suggestion that Thor's pendant hammerlets were worn in reaction to the spread of Christian rites and symbols may apply as well to Rus, as to the Baltic centers that were even more exposed to western Christian practices.[68] One should not, however, assume hostility between adherents of Christ, Thor, and other gods. Some individuals (or those responsible for their burial), hedged their bets by being buried with both crosses and hammerlets or other symbols of non-Christian forces. The coexistence of Christians and non-Christians is implied by the large burial-ground on the Starokievskaia hill at Kiev: Christian burials were interspersed with what seem to have been sacrificial shrines. It is possible that the chamber graves themselves were designed to outdo Christian coffins, seeing that they appear in the Scandinavian world at peripheral points of Christendom such as Hedeby, and spread to other emporia and then to Staraia Ladoga at the end of the ninth century.[69] The Christians had rites yielding palpable material benefits, but theirs was not the only fruit-bearing seed.

Thus Olga's leeway had its drawbacks, in the sense that belief and ritual were largely a matter of individual preference. It is likely that scores, if not hundreds, of Christians frequented the population centers straddling "the way

66 Adalbert, *Continuatio*, 218–19.
67 *Povest' Vremennykh Let*, 30.
68 Staecker, "Cross Goes North," 467–70.
69 Mikhailov, "Drevnerusskie," 164, 170–71.

from the Varangians (Scandinavians) to the Greeks." Until her death in 969, Olga retained at least one priest, and she gave instructions as to her funeral: no feast over her tomb in pagan fashion, and burial in a place that remained accessible to "all people."[70] Her son, Sviatoslav, "wept for her" and took part in the funeral, presumably in a church. Sviatoslav's legitimacy did not depend on a comprehensive public cult: his string of victories heightened the mystique already accruing from his princely blood. When Sviatoslav's occupation of the Balkans ended and he had to pledge to withdraw and keep the peace with Byzantium, he and his fellow leaders swore by Perun and another god widely venerated among the Slavs, "Volos, god of cattle."[71] This implies a hierarchy among the gods as well as assimilation of Slav gods into the Rus' own thought-world, but beliefs were still a matter for arms-bearing individuals. It is no accident that the sanction invoked to deter transgressors of the Russo-Byzantine treaties was death by their own weapons.

A cocktail of cults and rites presided over by a sacral ruler was volatile, yet not unsustainable. This was, after all, characteristic of the Khazars' realm even after their elite adopted Judaism in the mid-ninth century. But crosscurrents probably intensified in the late tenth century, as forms or adaptations of the Christian cult proliferated in Rus population centers and several counterparts of the Rus prince were baptized: Mieszko of the Poles, Géza (c. 972–97) of the Hungarians, and Harald Bluetooth (c. 958–87) of the Danes. Viewed against this background, the initiatives and drastic policy reversals of Prince Vladimir (c. 978–1015) make sense. Soon after wresting the throne from his half-brother, Iaropolk, who was murdered, he instituted a cult in which the citizens of Kiev were expected to acquiesce, if not participate. The "pantheon" of wooden idols set up outside his hall was headed by Perun but included gods worshiped mainly in the Middle Dnieper region and the steppes. Sacrifices were offered up to the idols, including boys and girls chosen by lot. The theme of victory and thanksgiving for victory appears to have been prominent in Vladimir's new ensemble, as it was in the public worship of the Ottonian and Byzantine emperors.

In fact, it may have been cessation of a run of victories that caused Vladimir to look elsewhere for a winner. Seemingly soon after failing to subjugate the most sophisticated power nearby, the Volga Bulgars, Vladimir began his "Investigation of the Faiths" which covered, besides Islam (the Volga Bulgars' faith), Judaism, and the western and Byzantine variants of Christianity. Much of the

70 *Povest' Vremennykh Let*, 32–33.
71 *Povest' Vremennykh Let*, 34.

Primary Chronicle's account of Vladimir's enquiries derives from doctrinal texts, originally without any relevance to Rus, and the narrative of his dispatch of emissaries to the Muslims, Germans, and "Greeks" to observe their forms of worship is thin on substance. But the shortcomings of the material do not detract from its indication that, in the mid-980s, Vladimir compared the merits of the monotheistic religions, seemingly together with other members of his elite. An eleventh-century Persian writer refers to a Rus ruler who sent envoys to Khorezm and received an instructor to teach "the religious laws of Islam."[72] As the *Chronicle* itself implies, Vladimir's choice of Byzantine Christianity was not foreordained. Rather, a turn of events momentarily aligned Vladimir's interests with those of the Byzantine emperor, Basil II. The details are irredeemably obscure, with only the outlines clear: Basil, beleaguered in Constantinople by rebels, came to terms with Vladimir, sending his sister in exchange for military aid; Vladimir's baptism was a foreseeable precondition of the marriage tie.[73] The warriors sent by Vladimir played a key role in quashing the rebellion, and by around 990 Anna Porphyrogenita was installed in Kiev with her spouse, who took the Christian name of Basil after his brother-in-law. A full-blown religious mission accompanied her. A near-contemporary, Yahyah of Antioch, regards the whole people of Rus as baptized at the hands of Vladimir's "metropolitans and bishops."[74] Around this time a metropolitanate of "Rhōsia" was added to the list of sees under the jurisdiction of the patriarch of Constantinople.

Vladimir's choice can be viewed as essentially a means of consolidating his regime, a maneuver to unify the disparate populations under his sway and impose a new cultural order. Support for this interpretation comes from Rus writers zealous to praise Vladimir as a "new Constantine," who led his people to enlightenment. In his sermon reviewing the Rus' progress, following other Christian peoples to grace and redemption, the mid-eleventh century churchman Ilarion (1051–54) extolled Vladimir's temporal power and his readiness to enforce baptism so that "not one single person" resisted his "command."[75] For Ilarion, as for the slightly later *Primary Chronicle*, violence against false gods accompanied mass baptism. Pagan sanctuaries were extirpated and Vladimir ordered "wood to be cut and churches put up on the sites where idols had

72 Sharaf al-Zamān Tahār Marvāzi, *On China*, 36; *Povest' Vremennykh Let*, 48–49.

73 Summary of alternative reconstructions of events in Franklin and Shepard, *Emergence of Rus*, 162–63.

74 Yahyah of Antioch, *Histoire*, 423.

75 Ilarion, *Sermon on Law and Grace*, 44–45, trans. in *Sermons and Rhetoric*, 19.

stood."[76] Archaeological evidence bears out these claims, for example, the destruction of the idol of Perun at Perynia, near Novgorod. Vladimir's Church of the Mother of God was built partly over the pagan burial ground on the Starokievskaia Hill. This was the church of Vladimir's palace complex, built of brick and stone by "masters" from Byzantium, and adorned with wall paintings and marble furnishings. The church's layout and design, like its dedication, apparently evoked the main church in Constantinople's Great Palace, the Mother of God of the Pharos. The church was entrusted to priests from Cherson, relics of St. Clement brought from Cherson were installed, and looted antique statuary put on display. Thus symbols of supreme craftsmanship, victory, and ancient piety were, literally, superimposed on an assortment of shrines and graves. Vladimir's sponsorship was expressed by the name which the church acquired from an early date, the "Tithe-Church," after the tenth of his property which, with Old Testament overtones, Vladimir dedicated to it. Building upon existing military and political advantages, Vladimir turned the throne city he had seized into a sacral center, sending out regular intercession which might bring the forces of God to earth.

From the ruler's point of view, then, standardized Christian worship could set new bonds around the teeming settlements along the major riverways of Rus. The ritual conducted by Christian priests in churches built at his expense was alone legitimate, at once protected by and enhancing princely authority. The urban network continued to accommodate a motley population. Thietmar of Merseburg in 1018 remarked on the size of Kiev: the town "like all this land, is populated by runaway slaves rushing hither and thither and especially by fast Danes."[77] These persons were well-provided-for spiritually, if Thietmar's figure of 400 churches for Kiev means anything, and Yahyah's account of the conversion highlights church building.[78] The modest number of stone churches known to have been built during the eleventh century understates the total since wooden churches are seldom identifiable from archaeological excavations, and most churches were of wood. Vladimir himself commissioned one at Vasilev, in thanksgiving for a close escape from marauding Pechenegs. Vasilev lay south of Kiev, in land reclaimed from these nomads. Strongholds and adjoining settlements were built along the main tributaries of the Dnieper and lines of earthworks, the "Snake Ramparts," were put up to obstruct the raiders. Vladimir populated his settlements with "the best men" picked from

76 *Povest' Vremennykh Let*, 53; Ilarion, *Sermon on Law and Grace*, 44–45, trans. in *Sermons and Rhetoric*, 19.

77 Thietmar of Merseburg, *Chronicon*, VIII.32, 474–75.

78 Yahyah of Antioch, *Histoire*, 423.

the northern forests, Finns as well as Slavs.[79] Removed from familiar haunts and intermingled, they were more amenable to the new cult, as well as to learning techniques to work the fertile but heavy Black Earth. It is no accident that towns in the steppe frontier zone comprise most of the earliest firmly attested episcopal sees in Rus: Belgorod, Iur'ev, Pereiaslavl' and, further north, Chernigov.[80] The *Life of St. Theodosius* depicts an orderly way of life in the towns of Vasilev and Kursk towards the mid-eleventh century: churchgoing and banquets on feast days at the governor's hall were routines of polite society.[81] These idealized scenes match the archaeological evidence, judging by the finds of bronze book clasps and styluses for writing on boards covered with wax or on birch bark. Customs and beliefs in the unfortified settlements around the towns are harder to gauge. But the burial grounds within a 250-kilometer radius of Kiev suggest that Christian norms were observed above ground as well as below. The dead were mostly nailed down in coffins, some wearing amulets (pendants symbolizing the sun, or miniature axes, for example), while others wore pectoral or necklace crosses. There was little sense of contradiction among these cult objects, which were sometimes placed in the same grave. Religious sentiments were no less intense for being loosely regulated by the authorities. Already in the 1030s or 1040s "wandering folk" were on the move seeking out holy places, a kind of collective disengagement from the world that recurs through Russian history.

More prosaically, Christ's cross and cheap medallions of his saints accompanied those earning their bread from frequent dealings between urban centers. Their appeal was much as it had been in the tenth century for long-distance risk takers who preferred a cross to Thor's hammer. But now they moved in wider circles. The birch-bark letters found in Novgorod and other towns demonstrate this, besides attesting that many traders and craftsmen could read and write in Slavonic. The letters are mainly to do with business, but their calendar is governed by saints' feast days and they presuppose that an oath sworn on the cross is binding. The earliest letter to allude to the kissing of the cross for this purpose dates from the eleventh century.[82] Christianity could be an asset to the mobile, hard-bargaining society of the riverways of Rus, invoking shared normative values, and saints as potential guarantors of agreements. The settlement pattern known as "compact nests" had emerged

79 *Povest' Vremennykh Let*, 54.

80 See Podskalsky, *Khristianstvo*, appendix (by A. Poppe), 443–44.

81 *Life of Theodosius* (ed. Likhachev), 359–62; (trans. Heppell), 29–31.

82 Artsikhovsky and Borkovsky, *Novgorodskie gramoty*, 67–68; Franklin and Shepard, *Emergence of Rus*, 285.

in the northern forests: large interconnected groups of villages, often far-flung from other such "nests," but involved in one way or another with the fur trade. Furs were bartered not only for beads and other semi-luxuries, but also for metalware. Dealings, direct or indirect, with outsiders were a matter of course, and a common ethical code was at least useful. The interrelationship between "compact nests" and cities on the riverways helps explain indications that country folk were familiar with Christian symbols. Few icons, crosses, or pendant crosses have been found in rural burial grounds, but recent excavations of the settlements themselves have unearthed quantities of crosses and pendants, notably at Lake Kubenskoe.[83] The cross was widely venerated as a Christian symbol and personal talisman, but did not usually accompany its owner to the grave in these burial grounds. The dead wore their finest clothes, equipped with pendants in the form of everyday objects, animals, and their fangs. Barrows were usually heaped over graves, against the preference of churchmen. The pattern of finds near Lake Kubenskoe, as also north of Novgorod, suggests that villagers adapted Christian rites to their personal needs, a kind of "do-it-yourself" system governed by communal norms and pressures,[84] rather than by priests or princely coercion.

Parishes had yet to form in the eleventh and earlier twelfth centuries. Thus, when around 1071 shamans exploiting a famine traveled from the Volga basin to Lake Beloe Ozero – not far from Lake Kubenskoe – they do not seem to have encountered a priest until a tribute collector, Ian, intercepted them. The priest in Ian's retinue was killed when Ian tried to halt their activities; the locals were sympathetic towards the shamans, who produced food from women's bodies. This episode suggests that priests traveling with princely agents were the sole providers of pastoral care, perhaps periodically carrying out mass baptisms or performing the liturgy. At the same time, the shamans' statements suggest that ideas as well as goods could circulate far. They claimed that man's body had been made by the Evil God, while his soul was installed by the Good God.[85] This is a variant of Bogomil Dualism. The Bogomils proselytized throughout the Byzantine Empire and it would not be surprising if some followed trade routes to Rus.

The church in Rus remained a missionary church throughout the eleventh century. John II – Greek-born like most metropolitans in Rus – provided for the non-physical correction of wizardry in his answers to clergymen's questions

83 Makarov, "Kresty-tel'niki," 263–65, 269, 271–72, and map on 270.
84 On the role of the kin-group and other social groupings as enforcers, see Dewey and Kleimola, "Russian Collective Consciousness," 180–91.
85 *Povest' Vremennykh Let*, 76.

in the 1080s.[86] Shamans could suddenly amass supporters in cities, as one did in Novgorod. The bishop of Novgorod was threatened with death and was saved only by the presence of mind of the prince, who made a mockery of the shaman's predictions before a large crowd and then hacked him to pieces. It is not surprising that sees were all located at or near the throne towns of princes. The number of throne towns – though not of sees – proliferated greatly from the late eleventh century onward, a mark of the partible inheritance among the princely family. Christianity did not induce veneration for monarchy in Rus; churchmen concentrated on urging rival princes to keep the peace and acknowledge the eldest in each generation as their notional father. Byzantine-born church leaders gave their approval to the veneration of two of Vladimir's sons who had been murdered in cold blood in the power struggle following his death in 1015. The texts acclaiming Boris and Gleb (d. 1015) as saints had a somewhat ambivalent ideology: lesser princes, like Boris and Gleb, should heed and respect the senior prince, but execration was heaped upon Prince Sviatopolk, who had sought "sole rule" over his brothers' dead bodies. The cult tended to uphold partible inheritance and power sharing among princes, while further enhancing the dynasty's status, in that Vladimir's descendants partook of the blood of Boris and Gleb. Unlike Vladimir, whom some churchmen exalted as a new apostle and worthy of veneration, Boris and Gleb soon worked miracles, and by the time of their translation to a new stone church in Vyshgorod in 1115, the saints' reputations went before them: for three days "the rich and the humble, the healthy and the sick" thronged past, so as to be allowed to touch the "noble coffins."[87] Senior princes and pious monks of Kiev's Cave Monastery promoted the formal cult, acclaiming the brothers as "martyrs," models of nonresistance for ordinary Christians. But besides helping and healing individuals, they were depicted on icons as warrior-saints, protecting all the land of Rus. Literary claims that Boris and Gleb were revered across a broad social spectrum gain corroboration from finds of cheap icons of the twelfth century and later. The find of an unfinished stone icon depicting Gleb in Beloozero indicates that local craftsmen were providing for the cult in a region not well-stocked with priests or princely agents.

The cult of Boris and Gleb has a somewhat "roller-coaster" quality, conveying something of the distinctiveness of Christianity in Rus. The metamorphosis from two princes murdered during dynastic strife into widely venerated martyrs for the faith has few parallels in those polities whose religious establishments were vetted fairly closely by external arbiters. The closest analogies

86 [John II], "Otvety," 110–11.
87 *Tale of the Passion* (ed. Abramovich), 65; trans. Hollingsworth, 133.

are the Bohemian prince, Wenceslas (d. 929/35), slain by his brother, and Vladimir of Duklja, one of John Vladislav's victims in the struggle for mastery after the death of Samuel of Bulgaria, who was recognized as a saint by some local churchmen.[88] The cult of the "home grown" saints Boris and Gleb seems to have unfolded at least partly thanks to widespread demand for princes as sacrificial martyrs, healers, and protectors, and by the early twelfth century, a corpus of hagiographical texts provided guidelines for keeping the formal cult within the bounds of orthodox tradition. If piety in Rus was one of the least regulated variants in Christian Europe, it possessed sacral spaces and centripetal forces of its own. Some were princely confections, such as the palace complex of Vladimir at Kiev, but grassroots feelings became entangled with the cult of Boris and Gleb.

Thus, in many ways Rus provides a classic case of "top-down" Christianity, imposed by the prince for his own self-legitimization or self-aggrandizement. And yet local populations – even those in the far northeast of Rus, which were only loosely supervised – seem to have adopted the new cult: it met their everyday needs for welfare and fertility, as well as offering the hope of personal, physical protection and consolation for bereavement. It was therefore possible for Christianity of a sort to flourish without parish organization. The same could be said of Christian rites at the grassroots in Poland, judging by the finds of clay egg rattles and other evidence of burial rituals discussed above. The way in which Christian rites seem to have spread rapidly across northern Rus reflects the unique dynamics of intensive exchanges among the "compact nests," even when widely scattered. Religious beliefs and practices there most probably accommodated many idiosyncracies and outright deviations from orthodoxy, but they were seldom concerted or orchestrated sufficiently to give rise to sustained dissent, and any such outbreaks were likely to attract the attention of princely agents such as Ian. In other societies such as Bulgaria, pastoral care was more tightly meshed, and there are indications of a significant stratum of literate, inquiring, lay piety. While this helps explain the vitality of monasticism in many parts of Bulgaria, it could also provide a breeding ground for organized dissent, in the form of the Bogomils. Perhaps the most important reasons for the distinctive and sophisticated features of Christian life in Bulgaria are the most obvious: many members of the Bulgar elite and some members of their agrarian subject populations were directly exposed to Byzantine Christian political power, or to a substratum of Greek-speaking

88 Ingham, "Martyrdom," 210–14.

communities, from the time of their arrival in the Balkans in the late seventh century onwards. And their polity bordered on the Byzantine Empire. That they should have absorbed heavier doses of Christian rites, beliefs, and outlook is hardly surprising. The Poles and the Rus were comparative latecomers to the Christian sphere, and their leaders' adoption of Christianity came more than a century after that of the Bulgars. They had, in more than one sense, farther to go.

PART II

★

CHRISTIANITY IN CONFRONTATION

7

Christians and Jews

BAT-SHEVA ALBERT

In the long history of Jewish–Christian relations, the early Middle Ages stands as a period in which the anti-Jewish attitudes of the church fathers and councils, and the legislation of the Christian Roman Empire regarding Jews integrated into Theodosius II's Code (438 CE), were both adopted and perpetuated. The Code recognized the legitimacy of Judaism and offered protection to Jews and their property, while at the same time subjecting them to various kinds of discrimination.

While it is true that the barbarian kings and their churches did ratify these fourth- and fifth-century laws and conciliar canons, they were often incapable of enforcing them. What is more, this period witnessed the advent of something entirely new: namely, the introduction of forced conversions by royal (Visigothic Spain) or imperial (Byzantium) decree. However, while it is certainly the case that the barbarian conquest of the West did affect the circumstances of western Jewry, Islamic victories had still greater repercussions. Around the year 600 Jews were living under Byzantine control in Greece, central Italy, Asia Minor, Syria, Palestine, North Africa, and Egypt, and those in northern Italy, Gaul, and Spain were subject to the rule of both orthodox and Arian barbarian kings. By 1100 Jews in the Near East, North Africa, Egypt, and in part of Spain were all living in lands that had been conquered by Muslims.

In addition, Byzantine repression and the conquest of northern and central Italy (after 950) by German emperors (followed by commercial expansion in the Rhine valley and toward the Slavic east) spurred on the migrations that had begun under Charlemagne. Thus, alongside the older communities at Lyons, Mâcon, Chalon-sur-Saône, and Arles, by the beginning of the ninth century there were Jewish merchants at Verdun. By the end of the tenth century, eminent Jews had emigrated from Lucca to Mainz, and there is evidence of a Jewish presence in the Mosan region as in Aachen, Metz, Trier, Xanten, and Neuss. Downstream, we find communities at Cologne, Bonn, Mainz,

Worms, and Speyer, to which Bamberg on the river Main, Heilbronn on the Neckar, Merseburg on the Saale, and Regensburg on the Danube may be added. Further east, communities sprang up in Magdeburg on the Elbe, and in Prague.[1] In France, a Jewish presence can be traced in Limoges, particularly in Champagne (Rheims, Troyes, Sens, Auxerre, and Châlons-en-Champagne), later an important center for Jewish studies, and in Rouen from which Norman Jews emigrated to London after 1066. In the German Empire, these new communities enjoyed privileges which occasionally replaced or came to be attached to late antique Roman legislation. This new political stance toward Jews, which was to be maintained for successive centuries, did not, however, generally work in the Jews' favor. All in all, the early Middle Ages witnessed the foundation of numerous new Jewish communities in western and central Europe.

As for the evolution of Christian attitudes to Judaism, the early Middle Ages was a period of transition, and of a fluctuation between two different anti-Jewish attitudes. The first faithfully upheld the stance of the church and of Christian Roman law; the second likewise claimed a patristic heritage, but drew from it rather more hostile and repressive tendencies which perhaps allowed it to go beyond the limits of the anti-Jewish discrimination dictated by Christian Roman legislation. It is unfortunate that, with the exception of Byzantium and Byzantine Italy, the dearth of Jewish sources[2] prevents a direct encounter with these "others"[3] and with their reaction to these two stances which were represented, in the West, by the last of the church fathers, Pope Gregory the Great (590–604) and Isidore of Seville (d. 636).

As a man who respected tradition, Gregory scrupulously observed the Theodosian Code. He adopted Augustine's view which assigned to Jews the role of guardians of the very Scriptures that proved both the advent of Christ and the voluntary conversion of Jews at the end of time. Gregory recommended obtaining conversions by dint of preaching, which he

1 On the importance of these migrations, see Schwarzfuchs, *Les juifs*, 12–16.

2 Only one Jewish (vehemently) polemical anti-Christian work survives, written around the middle of the ninth century, in a Muslim-controlled territory. Purporting to be the work of a certain priest, Nestor, who had converted to Judaism, it attacks Jesus' origins, and shows knowledge of the New Testament. The *Book of Nestor the Priest* had much success among later Jewish polemicists. See *Polemic of Nestor the Priest* for the text. Seventh-century Jewish apocalyptic writings (see footnote 62 below) worked a veiled polemic into their anticipation of the imminent coming of the Jewish Messiah.

3 *The Chronicle of Ahimaaz*, written in Hebrew by Ahimaaz of Oria (Byzantine Apulia) around 1054 describes Jews' lack of security in Apulia during the conversions enforced by Basil I, and curses the latter's memory. Ahimaaz of Oria, *Megillat Ahimaaz*, 18, 20.

considered more efficacious than coercion in effecting sincere conversions.[4] Further, he ordered the provision of judicial or financial assistance to converts as a way of encouraging conversions.[5] He protected the Jews of Terracina, whom the local bishop had expelled from their synagogue, and allowed them to start another despite the intrigues of the bishop; he made the same response to the situation in Palermo, where the bishop had confiscated the synagogue and all the buildings belonging to it, and to that in Cagliari.[6] Gregory did not, however, hesitate to prohibit severely the possession or sale of Christian slaves to Jews,[7] and did occasionally make rather malicious remarks regarding Jews.[8]

The pontiff was, nonetheless, impartial. He was responsible for drafting the famous letter *Sicut Iudaeis* which, with some highly significant variants, would guide papal policy toward Jews for several centuries. Gregory affirmed that "Just as the Jews (*Sicut Iudaeis*) shall not dare to exercise a liberty in their synagogues which exceeds that permitted to them by law, neither shall they suffer any loss of what has been granted them."[9] The tone of his letters is more sympathetic to the Jews when he reprimands those who, like the bishop of Terracina, had wronged them unjustly. For their part, Jews knew perfectly well that the pope would do them justice: they did not hesitate to lodge complaints against their clerical prosecutors. In principle (and this principle was certainly

4 Compare this with Gregory's correspondence (591) with Peter, bishop of Terracina, in *Jews in Legal Sources* [702] 1:34, 417–18 and with Virgilius, archbishop of Arles, and Bishop Theodore of Marseilles (594): "in illis partibus Iudeorum vi magis ad fontem baptismatis quam praedicatione perductos" (ibid. [703] 1:45, 418–19). See also the letter of Pope Alexander II to Prince Landulf of Benevento (1065), in which the pope recommends gentleness to obtain conversions (in Schreckenberg, *Die christlichen Adversus-Judaeos Texte*, 554–55).

5 See Gregory's letter to the subdeacon Peter, rector of the Sicilian Patrimony, regarding a certain Jewish woman who had been prosecuted because she had converted after having received betrothal gifts. According to Jewish law, she ought to have obtained a divorce; despite this, she had in fact married a Christian. The pope ordered the cessation of the legal proceedings against her. *Jews in Legal Sources* [705] 1:69, 420–21.

6 For the synagogue at Terracina (591), see *Jews in Legal Sources* [702] 1:34, 417–18 and [706] 2:6, 421–22; for Palermo (591), see ibid. [706] 2:6, 421–22; for the order to restore books and ornaments to the confiscated synagogue at Palermo (598), see ibid. [717] 9:38, 434–35: "eis contra iustitiam et aequitatis ordinem nec praeiudicium nec aliquod debet inferri dispendium;" for Cagliari, see ibid. [719] 9:196, 438–39.

7 See his letter (599) to Fortunatus, bishop of Naples, in ibid. [718] 9:105, 436; and to Brunhild, the queen of the Franks, in ibid. [720] 9:214, 440.

8 See his letter (593) to Libertinus in ibid. [708] 3:37, 424: "Nasas, quidem sceleratissimus iudaeorum."

9 Letter (598) to Victor of Palermo in ibid. [716] 8:25, 433: "Sicut Iudaeis non debet esse licentia quicquam in synagogia ultra quam permissum est lege praesumere, ita in his quae eis concessa sunt, nullum debent praeiudicium sustinere."

subject to some notorious exceptions[10]), it was Gregory the Great's opposition to the use of coercion to obtain conversions leading to the salvation of Jews and of Christendom that was adopted by the papacy that followed him.

While he declared his great admiration for the pope, Isidore of Seville did not, in fact, follow in the Roman pontiff's footsteps in this regard. He closes the patristic era on a note of declared hostility toward the Jews, considered as the last people impervious to the call of conversion.[11] These two church fathers' different temperaments doubtless informed their reactions to Judaism; however, it remains that attentive clerical readers of Gregory and Isidore found in their writings two contradictory stances. Both would guide and dictate future attitudes which would frequently swing alternately from one patristic authority to the other.

In this chapter, we shall trace the evolution of Jewish–Christian relations in this period in three parts, illustrating the desultory seesawing of these ecclesiopolitical stances and measures. The first part will describe the use of repressive measures and the introduction of forced conversions in Visigothic Spain and in the Byzantine Empire. The second will outline the rather more benign stance of the Merovingian kings (c. 500–751), their Carolingian successors (768 to 911 in eastern Francia and until 987 in the west Frankish kingdom), and the German emperors from Otto I (936–73) to Henry IV (1056–1106). The third and final section will treat the important *Contra Iudaeos* literature. The heir to a significant tradition of anti-Jewish writings and exegeses, *Contra Iudaeos* literature continued to inspire writing of this kind throughout the early Middle Ages. The second and third sections will afford glimpses of both the beginnings of changes in the status of Jews at the dawn of the Crusades, and the evolution of the debate against Judaism at the beginning of the twelfth-century renaissance.

Repression and forced conversion

After the conversion of the Visigothic King Reccared to orthodox Christianity in 587, which was followed by that of the Lombards in the seventh century, the Jews – that "stiff-necked people" – were, for a long time, the only religious dissidents of the West, for, since Arianism disappeared, western Christianity did not experience any significant heretical movements until the

10 In a letter (937) responding to a query of Archbishop Frederick of Mainz regarding the forced conversion of the Jews of the city, Pope Leo VII allowed the archbishop to expel the Jews if they refused the conversion preached to them. Ibid. [728] No. 79, 447–49: "hoc vobis praeceptum mandamus [. . .] cum reverentia illis praedicare non desistatis. [. . .] Si autem credere noluerint, de civitatibus vestris cum nostra auctoritate illos expellite."

11 For Isidore of Seville and the Jews, see my analysis elsewhere in this chapter.

eleventh century. Spanish Adoptionism in the late eighth/early ninth century vanished rapidly. As the only resisters remaining and thereby delaying the last coming of Christ by their recalcitrance, Jews had reason to fear the increasing efforts at their conversion. It is true that the Byzantine Empire continued to confront religious dissidents (especially those who promoted or opposed iconoclasm), but even though according to Roman law Judaism was licit, in Visigothic Spain and in Byzantium alike, all religious dissidents, including Jews, were perceived as a threat to the body politic. From this time on, Jews would often have to choose between baptism and voluntary exile or expulsion.

Visigothic Spain

Visigothic Spain was the scene of the most fanatical and cruel repression of Jews in the early Middle Ages. Historians are still striving to identify the motives for this fierce persecution which qualified as nothing short of anti-Semitism.[12] The last Visigothic kings, Ervig and Egica, however, did furnish their reasons for intervening against Jews.

Ervig, who ascended the throne in suspicious circumstances in 680, intended to win the support of the powerful Visigothic church and indeed made no secret of this fact. At the Twelfth Council of Toledo (681) he implored clerics to "purge the realm" of the sins that were impeding it, "and, above all these," to hound Jews and to ratify the anti-Jewish laws he had recently promulgated.[13] Following the conversion of the Visigoths to orthodox Christianity in 587, the legal status of Jews had progressively deteriorated. It is unclear to what extent the day-to-day existence of Jews was affected by these measures; certainly, the repetition and the increasing severity of the laws gives some cause to doubt their efficacy. After the Third Council of Toledo following Reccared's conversion to orthodoxy (589), Gregory the Great congratulated the king on the anti-Jewish legislation enacted there.[14] In 616, King Sisebut, motivated by genuine faith, ordered forced conversions. Preferring persuasion to coercion, his friend Isidore of Seville criticized him, but nonetheless decided that conversion by whatever means could not be revoked.[15] After Isidore of Seville, conciliar canons and royal legislation were distinguished both by their severity and by the hateful language in which they were formulated: the codes of kings Recceswinth (654) and Ervig (680) proved merciless toward Jews.

12 Saitta, *L'antisemitismo*, "Prefazione," 1–3.

13 Council of Toledo XII (*Jews in Legal Sources* [857], 514–17); canon 9 of the same council contains an abbreviated version of the anti-Jewish legislation (ibid. [858], 517–21).

14 Ibid. [722] 9:229, 441–42.

15 Council of Toledo IV (633), c. LVII, *Concilios visigóticos*, 210–11.

The question of the influence of the church on this anti-Jewish attitude has long been debated.[16] The conversion enforced by Sisebut and Isidore of Seville's reaction has already been mentioned. Further, canon 60 of the Fourth Council of Toledo (633), presided over by Isidore, ordered the separation of Jewish children from their parents and their education by Christians. The same council forbade not only Jews, but even converts, from holding public office.[17] Was this a measure designed to eliminate Spanish Judaism by encouraging Jews, frightened that their children would be taken from them, to convert? The exclusion of converts and of the Christian descendants of Jews clearly gives the appearance of hereditary ethnic discrimination. In any case, conciliar and royal legislation became more and more oppressive: on the eve of the Sixth Council of Toledo (638), Jewish converts of that city had to swear a profession of faith (*professio*). They renounced Judaism and its laws, promised not to keep company with their former coreligionists and no longer to observe their teachings, and to give assurances that transgressors would be executed.[18] A public oath (*placitum*) was required of Jews in Toledo in 654.[19] There were many judgments, and those of Toledo XII (681), XVI (693), and XVII (694) and the legislation of kings Ervig and Egica were particularly ferocious. Having sought the assistance of the church, Ervig presented his anti-Jewish laws to the Twelfth Council for their ratification. Jews and their children were to be baptized; furthermore, they were no longer able to practice Judaism since they were forbidden to observe Jewish laws and festivals.[20] The king alone had the power to exercise clemency toward converts.[21] The church perhaps had shrunk away from the king's legislative measures, and Ervig warned it that any cleric found negligent in the execution of these laws would be excommunicated and would pay a fine of one gold pound.[22] The last councils of Toledo, Toledo XVI (693) and XVII (694), were convoked by King Egica. The realm was slipping into a serious social and economic crisis: famines,

16 Bachrach, "Reassessment" and Albert, "Un nouvel examen."

17 Council of Toledo IV (633): for the measures regarding Jewish children, canon 60 (*Jews in Legal Sources* [843], 488); for the holding of public office, canon 65 (ibid. [848], 490–91).

18 *Confessio vel professio Judaeorum civitatis Toletanae* (638) in ibid. [851], 494–500).

19 *Leges Visigothorum* (hereafter *LV*), 12:2:17, Recceswinth, Ervig et. al. (ibid. [541], 278–81): converts were obliged to marry Christians and committed to burning or stoning their own who broke this oath.

20 Prohibition of the observance of the Sabbath and of Jewish festivals: *LV*, 12:3:5 Erv. (ibid. [547], 293–94); prohibition of the circumcision of Jews: *LV*, 12:3:4; prohibition of the observance of dietary laws; *LV* 12.7 (ibid. [549], 296–97); Jews must meet with the bishop on appointed days: *LV* 12:3:21 (ibid. [563], 323–25).

21 Clemency, that is, if the Jews "should happen to be snatched from the Devil's snares and laudably believe in the Holy Trinity" (*LV* 12:3:27; ibid. [547], 330).

22 *LV* 12:32:24 Erv. (ibid. [566], 326–28).

epidemics, and the flight of slaves followed one after the other. The king broke off the persecution of converts. He firmly believed that the salvation of the realm lay in faith, and that it was his obligation to cure society of its ills with salutary remedies: baptism, even if coerced, brought the baptized into a state of grace. Therefore, he sought the church's support to cure the realm: idolatry was to be rooted out, but above all "the accursed perfidy of the Jews must be crushed."[23] Lastly, the king argued before Toledo XVII (694) that he had tried everything to convert Jews by persuasion, but that they had not kept their promises. Therefore, he relied on the church to promote the cause of justice. Bespattered with Christ's blood, the Jews were plotting the ruin of the land. For this reason, their property was to be seized, and they were to be dispersed throughout Spain and reduced to slavery in perpetuity.[24]

The near total symbiosis of church and crown, and the constitutional weakness of the monarchy – the Visigothic kings were unsuccessful in establishing a hereditary monarchy – do not, however, satisfactorily explain the extremism of Visigothic anti-Judaism. Nevertheless, these measures, which were exceptional among the barbarian kingdoms, did remain an isolated phenomenon. Their significance lies in their partial integration into the important canon collections of Burchard of Worms and Ivo of Chartres (c. 1040–1115),[25] later retained by Gratian (d. c. 1159). Canonists, however, did not approve these later Toledan canons, the prohibitions against the practice of Judaism, and the enslavement of Jews in flagrant contradiction with Christian tradition. Canon law only adopted the canons of Toledo IV (633), which increased the discrimination of previous conciliar legislation but nonetheless preserved the legal status conferred by Isidore, the sainted bishop who had presided over that council.

Byzantium

Although Emperor Justinian I (527–65) had promulgated very severe anti-Jewish laws in the famous Code that bears his name, it was the emperor Heraclius (610–41) who ordered the forced conversion of Jews in 634 as a means of achieving religious uniformity. At that time, Byzantium was confronting Islam and receiving a significant number of Persian Christian refugees, and apocalyptic

23 Council of Toledo XVI (693), (ibid. [859], 522–27; [860], 527–29).
24 Council of Toledo XVII (694), (ibid. [861], 529–32); canon 8 (ibid. [862], 535–38).
25 Burchard of Worms, *Decretum* (c. 1008–12) 4:83 (ibid. [1150], 635) = Toledo IV, canon 57; Burchard, *Decretum* 4:84 (ibid. [1151], 635) = Toledo IV, canon 62. Burchard likewise retained canon 9 of Toledo XII containing the list of all of Ervig's anti-Jewish laws. See also: Ivo of Chartres, *Panormia*, 1:74 (ibid. [1233], 677–78) = Toledo IV, canon 60 = Burchard's *Decretum* 4:83 = Ivo of Chartres' *Decretum* 1:277.

aspirations,[26] fueled by the victories of the Persians and later those of Islam, were aggravating Christian hostility toward Jews.[27] It would seem, however, that this measure was only implemented in North Africa:[28] in 691 the Trullan or Quinisext Council was still criticizing Jewish–Christian relations as too friendly for the liking of the council fathers.[29]

The matter would arise again under the iconoclast emperor Leo III (717–41). Like Heraclius, Leo intended to eliminate all religious dissidence, reasoning that political stability would be guaranteed by religious uniformity. When the Second Council of Nicaea reestablished the cult of icons (787), it also indirectly condemned the anti-Jewish stance of Leo III on the grounds that those who had been converted by force were continuing to practice Judaism secretly in any case; only a sincere conversion was considered effective.[30] The iconoclast emperors of the eighth century hounded their orthodox adversaries and vice versa. Later, the emperors persecuted syncretistic and other sects in Asia Minor, intending to eliminate utterly all dissidents, including Jews. The campaigns of Basil I (874–86) against the Paulicians, who had established a state on the Byzantine–Arab border and had allied themselves with the Arabs, sharpened his antagonism toward heretics. Adding to the mix, there arose at Amorium a sect professing a kind of Judeo-Christian puritanical monotheism. As a self-proclaimed adversary of dissidents,[31] Basil I sought the help of the church to smudge over his humble roots and the crimes he had committed to ascend the throne. By his own account, he had attempted persuasion by convoking debates with renowned rabbis, but the failure of this method led to forced baptisms (c. 874). Nevertheless, the code drafted by Basil I, the *Basilica* (886), which was destined to replace Justinian's Code, adopted from the latter the anti-Jewish legislation which legitimized the existence of Judaism, with certain severe restrictions. Basil's son, Leo IV (886–912), later abandoned the anti-Jewish policy of his father. However, under the usurper emperor Romanus I Lecapenus, persecution resumed. In 932, Romanus ordered forced conversions and gave his order the force of law. A number of Jews took refuge in the Jewish kingdom of the Khazars in Central Asia; the Jews of Byzantine

26 See a further discussion later in this chapter.
27 Kaegi, *Heraclius*, 217.
28 Olster, *Roman Defeat*, 161.
29 Council in Trullo, canon 11 (*Jews in Legal Sources* [803], 460).
30 Council of Nicaea II (787), canon 8 (ibid. [804], 461–62).
31 *Basilica* (shortly before 886) A 1:1:42 (ibid. [197], 102): "It is clear that anything that dissents from the religion of the Christians opposes the Christians." This law was directed against the *celicoli*, the "believers in heaven," a sect having Jewish traits. Despite provision for forced baptisms, the *Basilica* did retain the permission of Jews to observe the Sabbath: *Basilica*, A 1:1:43 = B 1:1:39 (ibid. [198], 102–103).

Italy were persecuted. It was the intervention of the Jewish minister at the court of the caliphate of Cordoba, Hasdaï ibn Shaprut, that finally put an end to this episode.

Thereafter, until the First Crusade, Jews lived in peace, and the empire even welcomed Jews who had fled the persecutions of the Fatimid Egyptian al-Ḥākim (996–1021). At the beginning of the eleventh century, the empire entered a series of crises: thirteen emperors ascended the throne in the fifty-three years between 1028 and 1081. The Turkish Seljuks inflicted a resounding defeat on the Byzantines in 1071, and Byzantium lost vast territories in Asia Minor, Armenia, and in Cappadocia. Compared with these crises, the Jewish question rather lost its urgency.

It would seem then that these various attempts at the conversion of Jews met with only partial and temporary success, and that they were not definitively ratified by legislation. Despite grave difficulties, the imperial throne held firm and Byzantium remained a great power into the eleventh century. Byzantine caesaropapism ensured that the emperor continued to impose anti-Jewish policies. The contradiction between Judaism's permanent legal status (which though discriminatory was nonetheless licit) and conversions enforced by imperial decree would explain why all the conversions were temporary and ended in failure.

A more benign approach: the Merovingians, the Carolingians, and the German Empire

Jews were troubled little in Merovingian Francia.[32] Frankish conciliar legislation[33] ratified a prohibition of the Council of Elvira (300–6) against Christians' taking their meals with Jews, but this is a measure implying that precisely these sorts of encounters were taking place. Jews were also forbidden to assume public office, and to sell, possess, and circumcise Christian slaves,[34] these measures being drawn from late antique conciliar precedent, and from the Theodosian Code. There followed a short lull in anti-Jewish legislation under Charlemagne (768–814) and especially under Louis the Pious (814–40), who was even accused by Archbishop Agobard of Lyons (d. 840) of exhibiting too much favor toward

32 Local forced conversions in the Frankish realms date from the sixth century.

33 Council of Mâcon (581–83), canon 15 (ibid. [824], 474–75); Council of Clichy (626–27), canon 13 (ibid. [832], 479–80).

34 For the prohibition against holding public office: Council of Paris (614) canon 17 (15), and Edict 10 of Clothar II (ibid. [830] and [831], 478–79). For the treatment of Christian slaves, see: Clichy, canon 13 (ibid. [832], 479–80); Rheims (627–30), canon 11 (ibid. [833], 480–81); Châlon (647–53), canon 9 (ibid. [834], 481–82).

Jews.[35] Between 822 and 827, Louis granted the *Praeceptum Iudaeorum* to the rabbi Donatus and his nephew Samuel. This privilege protected their persons and their property, exempted them from tax payable on transported merchandise, and from the ordeal. Furthermore, in an unprecedented measure, it forbade Christians to convince the slaves of Jews to convert to Christianity.[36] Another "precept," intended to benefit Jewish merchants, promised protection and exemption from military service, and a high-ranking court official, the *Magister Iudaeorum*, was to be charged with meting out justice to Jews.[37] Under Charles the Bald (843–77), the climate was somewhat less propitious. The Council of Paris-Meaux (845–46) did ratify the Visigothic canons against Jews,[38] but there was hardly any physical persecution of Jews under Carolingians, nor under the German emperors Otto I (936–73), Otto II (973–83), and Henry IV (1056–1106).[39]

Henry IV confirmed in 1090 (with some alterations) the important privilege granted by Bishop Rudiger Huozman to the Jewish community in Speyer in 1084 – a move which foreshadowed the evolution in social status for Jews at the beginning of the twelfth century. In order to encourage Jewish merchants to settle, Huozman reserved for their use a quarter (surrounded by a wall to protect them), a plot of land to bury their dead, and allowed their provost, the *archisynagogus*, to arbitrate in disputes between or against Jews. Moreover, he bestowed on them freedom of commerce in the city, the right to employ Christian servants of both sexes (except on holy days), and the right to participate in the defense and fortification of their quarter.[40] The bishop granted them, as it were, most-favored-nation status, and, in the case that another city in the empire should draft a comparable document, he undertook to bestow on them a yet more favorable privilege.

Both church and royal legislation, however, already forbade Jews to have Christian servants and to serve in the military. Moreover, this apparent amelioration in the condition of Jews proved precarious. In practice, privileges were prone to revocation, and had to be reconfirmed by the donor's successors. Later, the very threat of revoking the freedoms bestowed, or refusing to reconfirm them, opened the way for financial extortion that would weigh

35 For Agobard, see later in this chapter.

36 *Praeceptum Iudaeorum* (822–27), canon 30 (ibid. [572] 333–35); see also the prohibition of the baptism of slaves bought abroad: *Praeceptum Iudaeorum*, canon 31 (ibid. [573], 336–38).

37 *Praeceptum negotiatorum*, 52 (ibid., [576] 341–43).

38 For the Paris-Meaux Council, see below.

39 Henry II confirmed privilege for the Jews of Merseburg, but expelled the Jews of Mainz in 1012. Henry IV included Jews in the Peace of Mainz (1103), which was intended to reestablish order in an empire shaken by civil war.

40 Schreckenberg, *Die christlichen Adversus-Judaeos Texte*, 557–58.

heavily on Jewish communities in the following centuries. Perhaps an even graver consequence was the fact that the privileges underlined the alterity of Jews. While it is true that the separation and fortification (no doubt at their own request) of their living quarters did proffer them daily protection, on the other hand, it also led to Jews becoming a more visible target during riots. This was certainly the case when, at the end of the eleventh century, urban economic competition became more and more fierce, and church reforms (in the second half of the eleventh century) together with the First Crusade (1096–99) ignited a popular religiosity that was at once more fervent and, henceforth, more anti-Jewish. As far as anti-Jewish sentiment was concerned, instead of being hounded for their sins against the Savior, deicidal Jews had been favored by the authorities, and what is more, were actually enjoying economic advantages. Protected from then on solely by these privileges, Jews were at the mercy of their protectors – protectors who were sometimes recalcitrant or powerless in the face of hostile forces and anti-Jewish rioting. While the massacres committed, especially in Germany, by crusaders and by one sector of the urban populace in the summer of 1096 were not repeated, in the centuries that followed Jews remained subject to violent persecutions, extortions, and, later, expulsions.

The *Contra Iudaeos* literature

Contra Iudaeos literature including polemical treatises, disputations (usually fictional), biblical commentaries, and even hagiographical writings, was written throughout the period. These works continued in the tradition of the patristic *Contra Iudaeos* literature and retrieved from it principally exegetical material found in Jerome, Augustine, Gregory the Great, and Isidore of Seville. Indeed, until the twelfth century, virtually all anti-Jewish arguments were based on allegorical commentaries on the Old Testament. It is worth noting that polemical works properly speaking, entitled *Contra* or *Adversus Iudaeos*, were rare in Latin Christendom between the seventh and the beginning of the eleventh centuries.[41] In contrast, they were numerous in the Byzantine Empire, and the Greek and Syriac examples are rather more original than those of

41 The *Altercatio aecclesie contra synagogam*, a treatise written perhaps in England between 938 and 966, above all reproduces pseudo-Augustinian works in particular: see the *Sermo contra Judaeos, paganos et Arianos* (probably written by Quodvultdeus, Augustine's successor at Hippo), and the *Altercatio ecclesiae et synagogae* (before 476); see also Dahan, *La polémique chrétienne*, 85. The *Altercatio* is a later example of this kind of imitative summary.

Latin Christendom – their line of argument being adapted to historical and theological crises.

What was the influence of this literature on the evolution of Jewish–Christian relations? Clearly, the reading of these works was liable to fuel the antipathy of their readers (predominantly clerics), and served, on occasion, to justify anti-Jewish measures that were strictly speaking illegal. Inevitably, the rehearsal of numerous anti-Jewish passages drawn from patristic sources did contribute to keeping the Jewish question on the agenda, even though the Jewish population was of negligible proportions and posed no real threat of "Judaization" or faith-based conversions to Judaism:[42] the only known proselytes are Bodo, the arch-chaplain of the Carolingian court (839), and a German cleric named Wecelin (1106).

Another question is whether anti-Judaism took a turn toward anti-Semitism in the early Middle Ages. This is a thorny problem, as the transition from one to the other occurs imperceptibly.[43] The rehearsal ad nauseam of the sins of the Jews enumerated in the Old Testament and the innumerable accusations of deicide (which were also repeated in the Good Friday liturgy) served to blacken the Jewish people's image. The love that God had shown toward them was now over, and his election transferred to Christians, the True Israel (*Verus Israel*). Certain readings from the Gospels and from the Pauline epistles leant themselves readily to anti-Jewish commentary[44] and aroused irrational sentiments: considered despised by God, Jews were inevitably despised by his truly faithful people.

Isidore of Seville's treatise, *On the Catholic Faith against the Jews* (*De fide catholica ex veteri et novo testamento contra Judaeos ad Florentiam sororem suam*[45]) stands, in the seventh century, at the head of Western polemical literature. This lengthy treatise picks up patristic polemics (especially Jerome and Augustine) in its choice of subject matter, line of argument, and tone. It is divided into two parts: the first undertakes to demonstrate that the virgin birth of Christ and the narrative of his life until his resurrection were announced in the Old Testament, and that the criminal and unbelieving Jews had been punished by

42 The problem of circumcision or of the conversion of slaves by their Jewish masters was of a different order, as Jewish law commanded their conversion. Moreover, it was in the slaves' interest to convert since according to Jewish law a Jewish slave had to be freed after serving six years. Likewise, Jews converted their non-Jewish spouses. It is impossible to estimate the number of these conversions at a time when they had been forbidden for centuries.

43 Langmuir, "Anti-Judaism," 383–89.

44 See Heil, *Kompilation oder Konstruktion?*

45 Isadore of Seville, *De fide*.

the Destruction of the Temple, the loss of their political independence, and exile. The second part sets about proving that after Christ's coming the laws of the Old Testament had passed away. Isidore's work was enormously successful: twenty-one manuscripts produced before the eleventh century are extant, and the work was translated into Old High German in the ninth century.[46] Its short chapters contain biblical verses followed by a brief exegesis inspired by or citing the works of Jerome, Augustine, and Gregory the Great. The treatise is completely unoriginal since Isidore sets out solely to arm his clerical readers against the Jews with polemical exegesis.[47] Jews figure in other exegetical works by Isidore, and are always presented pejoratively.[48] Isidore's anti-Jewish polemic had its heirs in Visigothic Spain, notably in the writings of Julian of Toledo (b. 644), who was himself of Jewish descent, and who attacked Jews more violently than had Isidore for the reason that they stubbornly refused to accept that the Messiah had already come.[49]

In Byzantium, anti-Jewish polemic was exacerbated by three crippling crises that beset the empire between the seventh and ninth centuries: Heraclius's campaigns against the Persians (627–29); Muslim victories in the Middle East, Egypt, North Africa, and Spain (622–711); and, lastly, the iconoclast crisis (c. 725–87 and 814–43). Byzantine treatises blamed the Jews for all these woes: for having aided the Persians, for having been among the earliest followers of Islam, for having incited the Muslims against the Christians – what was more, it was argued that it was two Jews who concocted Islam in the first place[50] – and lastly for having provoked iconoclasm. Christian defeats fueled this explosion of anti-Jewish writing,[51] which proceeded to put Jews in the same category as Muslims. Greek and Syriac polemical writers argued that the defeat of the Jews by the Romans after the Passion of Christ promised victory against Islam for the latter's Byzantine heirs (after penance). From the seventh century, Eastern Christians used anti-Jewish rhetoric as a way of making veiled attacks on Islam: in so doing they attempted to rouse the morale of the faithful, while

46 Weinhold, *Die altdeutschen Bruchstücke*; Eggers, *Der althochdeutsche Isidor*; and Ostberg, "Aspects."

47 Isidore of Seville, *De fide*, 449–50. See also the detailed discussion in Drews, *Juden und Judentum*. Schreckenberg, *Die christlichen Adversus-Judaeos Texte*, 441 argues that Isidore's attitude toward Jews was generally amicable and practical.

48 See Isidore of Seville, *Allegoriae* and *Quaestiones*.

49 Julian of Toledo, *De comprobatione*.

50 Griffith, "Jews and Muslims," 80–81.

51 Maximus the Confessor (c. 580–662), Heraclius's secretary, attributed the Arab victory to the Jews, "the most impious people on earth." See *PG* 91, 540–41 cited by Schreckenberg, *Die christlichen Adversus-Judaeos Texte*, 447.

minimizing Christian military defeats.[52] The Syriac treatises, *The Trophies of Damas* and the *Dialogue of the Jews Papiscus and Philo with a Monk*, were inspired by the influential *Dialexis kata Ioudaioon* (second half of seventh century) by Anastasius of Sinai, the abbot of St. Catherine's Abbey at Mt. Sinai. Destined quickly to become widely popular, this work discusses traditional themes: the Trinity and the coming of Jesus as proclaimed by the prophets. It also broaches the question of the worship of images and cult objects by Jews.[53] If we take into account the work's date before iconoclasm, what we have here is a work designed to justify images against Judaism and Islam. The most important of these polemical writers, Theodore Abū-Qurra (c. 755–c. 830), a Melkite bishop in Mesopotamia, attacked Jews as "the most detestable people among all the nations."[54]

Under the Abbasids, *majlis* were inaugurated, comprised of scholarly colloquia or of disputations between the representatives of the three religions invited to participate by the caliph or important Muslims. Although the disputants were supposed to uphold the rules of courtesy, Jews, whom the Muslims occasionally charged with the responsibility of controlling the accuracy of the Christians' biblical quotations,[55] complained that they were being denigrated by both Christians and Muslims. One Coptic patriarch compared them unfavorably with oxen and asses; the monk Abraham of Tiberias, citing the Qur'ān, reminded them that Jesus had transformed some Jews into "monkeys and pigs," and the Fatimid vizier, Ibn Killis (after 977), a convert from Judaism, treated them with absolute disdain.[56]

The Byzantine iconoclasts, in the early stages of the controversy, argued that images were idols, condemned by the Old Testament. For this reason, the Second Council of Nicaea (787), which reestablished the use of images, put iconoclasts in the same category as Jews and Samaritans.[57] In the Byzantine *Contra Judaeos* literature of the seventh and eighth centuries, apologetics for the cult of the True Cross, relics, and icons came to be added to the traditional anti-Jewish subject matters: namely, Messianism and the divinity of Jesus, deicide, the punishment of the Jews, and so on.[58] The key argument proposed that Jews had made themselves guilty of idolatry by worshiping the golden calf,

52 Olster, *Roman Defeat*, 116–37.
53 Külzer, *Disputationes Graecae*, 152–53.
54 Griffith, "Jews and Muslims," 71.
55 Griffith, "Monk in the Emir's *Majlis*," 27–29 regarding the intention of the emir in a *majlis* in Jerusalem between 815 and 820.
56 Ibid., 22–37; for Ibn Killis, see Cohen and Somekh, "Interreligious *Majaālis*," 128–36.
57 Council of Nicaea II, Mansi 13, 167C-D.
58 Leontius of Neapolis (Cyprus, first half of seventh century): see Külzer, *Disputationes Graecae*, 147–50.

the tablets of the Law, and the cult objects of the Tabernacle.[59] Inspired by Leontius of Neapolis, Theodore Abū-Qurra recalled that Moses, David, and Solomon had used images; in so doing, he attempted to discredit iconoclasm by evoking anti-Jewish prejudices that animated both Eastern Christians and Muslims,[60] despite the fact that the latter were, like the Jews, fierce opponents of images and of the cross as an object of veneration.

The conflict between Byzantium and Islam stirred Messianic expectations among both Christians and Jews. For the author of the *Apocalypse of Pseudo-Methodius* (Syriac; Greek redaction c. 675), both Jews and Arabs were the instruments of divine punishment, but Byzantium would emerge victorious; in the Greek version of the text, the invincibility of the Roman Empire remained restricted to its victory over the Jews.[61] As for Jewish writers, they expected the final defeat of the Byzantines, and made their rebuttal with their own apocalypses written in Hebrew:[62] Heraclius was given the name Armilus (the name of the Enemy of the Messiah) and his defeat was interpreted as announcing the advent of the Age of the Jewish Messiah.

The Carolingian renaissance likewise produced a number of original works, though authors in this period did not pride themselves on originality. The *Contra Judaeos* polemic mostly appeared in their biblical exegesis as the writing of biblical commentaries was very highly esteemed in the Carolingian period. The exegesis of Jerome, which bristles with condemnations of Judaism, and Augustine's *City of God*, containing his essential statement regarding the fate of Jews in a Christian world, nourished the anti-Judaism of Carolingian exegesis.

However, interest in both the Hebrew text of the Bible and Jewish exegesis underwent a revival. This reawakening of an appetite for Jewish knowledge of the Scriptures, after the nearly four hundred years that had passed since the death of Jerome, was not confined to knowledge of the Hebrew language, as it was in the case of the latter. In Lyons, a circle of scholars comprising Archbishop Agobard and the Visigoths Florus and Amolo were interested in the contents of Jewish books with which Jerome had not been familiar. For the first time, the *Contra Judaeos* made use of post-biblical Jewish sources to serve polemical ends; it was an interesting initiative, but one that was not picked up again until the twelfth century.

59 Anastasius of Sinai, *Dialexis*; *The Trophies of Damas*; *The Dialogue of the Jews Papiscus and Philo*: see Külzer, *Disputationes Graecae*, 151.
60 Griffith, "Jews and Muslims," 77; Külzer, *Disputationes Graecae*, 170–72.
61 Alexander, *Byzantine Apocalyptic Tradition*, 54.
62 For the Jewish works, see: *The Book of Zerubabel* (*Sefer Zerubavel*) and *The Signs of the Messiah* (*Otot Ha Mashiah*) as referenced by Sharf, *Byzantine Jewry*, 102 and footnote 44.

Theodulf of Orleans (d. 821), the eminent Carolingian master, undertook to produce a Latin Bible more faithful to the "Hebrew truth" (*hebraica veritas*) of the biblical text than the Hieronymian translation known as the Vulgate. He enlisted the services of a Jew, probably a convert to Christianity, known by the name of "Pseudo-Jerome" and the author of the *Quaestiones* on the books of Kings and Chronicles. His works contain numerous Jewish traditions, and medieval readers attributed them to Jerome because they thought that he alone possessed sufficient knowledge of Hebrew to write them.[63] Theodulf must have learned that Jerome's Latin translation did not always render the exact meaning of the Hebrew text of the Bible; he turned then to a *hebraeus* to annotate Jerome's translation. This "Hebrew," none other than our Pseudo-Jerome, marked with *h.[ebraeum] non habet* ("the Hebrew [text] does not have [this]") all those passages where the textual elaborations of the Hieronymian translation were not present in the original Hebrew. Theodulf's Bible did not, however, meet with the success it warranted as a quasi-scientific undertaking: only five manuscripts survive.

Other Carolingian men of letters showed interest in the Hebrew text of the Bible, notably Claudius of Turin (d. after 827), Agobard of Lyons,[64] and Florus of Lyons. It is worth noting that three of these "Hebraists" – Theodulf, Claudius, and Florus – were Visigoths, as was perhaps Agobard also. It might then be asked where their interest in the Hebrew Bible sprang from, and what was its motive. Indeed, many questions await satisfactory answers. The Carolingian appetite for the study of the Old Testament was, no doubt, anchored in a political ideology which thought of Charlemagne as a new David, and of Louis the Pious as Solomon; space limitations do not allow me to treat here the origin or the meaning of this biblical identification. Note, however, that it is precisely in the *Quaestiones* of Pseudo-Jerome, in those of Claudius of Turin, Hrabanus Maurus (c. 780–856) – who also made use of Pseudo-Jerome – and Angelomus of Luxeuil (c. 850) on the books of Samuel and Kings[65] that we find these borrowings from Jewish exegesis.[66] This interest reflected, perhaps, the

63 Saltman, *Pseudo–Jerome*.

64 Agobard employs the Hebrew word *araboth*, the name of the second heaven in the Jewish mystical tradition (which he evidently knew), which is translated in the Vulgate as *occasum* in the singular, whereas, in the Hebrew, the word "evening" is in the plural.

65 Claudius of Turin, *Quaestiones XXX* (c. 822); Hrabanus Maurus, *Commentaria in Libros IV Regum*, 11–124; Angelomus of Luxeuil, *Enarrationes in Libros Regum*, 245 ff. For Hrabanus's and Angelomus's borrowings from Pseudo-Jerome's *Quaestiones*, see Saltman, *Pseudo-Jerome*, 23–29.

66 Theodulph showed some notable interest in the books of Kings: see Gorman, "Theodulf of Orléans," 286.

less hostile atmosphere surrounding Jewish–Christian relations under Charlemagne and Louis the Pious, expressed elsewhere in the privileges granted to Jewish merchants. However, we must caution against drawing overly hasty conclusions regarding Jewish influence at court on the basis of privileges granted to particular Jews, or on the basis of Agobard and Amolo's anti-Jewish vituperations. The former were restricted to just a few Jewish merchants, and the latter constituted thinly veiled acts of propaganda.

The interest of these exegetes in Jewish sources notwithstanding, their writings do nonetheless bristle with anti-Jewish commentaries (Jews often being presented as cruel, perfidious, envious, and ungrateful, etc.) – commentaries which sometimes reek of something awfully like anti-Semitism.[67] While Hrabanus Maurus's anti-Judaism was literary, Agobard and Amolo of Lyons (archbishop 840–50) undertook a social segregation of Jews and Christians in the diocese of Lyons and in the wider Midi. Jews were simply too influential and Jewish–Christian relations too amicable for their liking, and it was their intention to convince Louis the Pious to withdraw his protection from Jews. Between 826 and 850 they collected together those Jewish traditions which seemed to them most risible, such as the mystical calculation of God's measurements,[68] or offensive, such as those in the *Toledot Jeshu*.[69] Agobard wanted, above all, to besmirch the standing of Jews who were converting their slaves and attracting Christians to Judaism. He did not hold back, however, from attacking their powerful protectors at court, including in his sights even Wala, abbot of Corbie, and cousin to Charlemagne.[70]

This attack would not have been too serious in itself, as Louis the Pious despised Agobard, who was happy to return the feeling.[71] In 839 however, the scandalous conversion of the court arch-chaplain Bodo to Judaism served to justify Agobard's position. It suddenly became imperative to introduce the anti-Jewish legislation of the Visigothic councils into the Carolingian empire. Amolo took charge of the move; he claimed to have daily discussions with Jews, and he knew the *Toledot Jeshu* and Jewish traditions regarding a Jewish Messiah imprisoned in underground cells in Rome, traditions which, he

67 E.g., Hrabanus Maurus, *Expositio super Jeremiam*, 1249B; Hrabanus Maurus, *Commentaria in Libros IV Regum*, II, XVIII, 110A-C.

68 Agobard of Lyons, *De iudaicis superstitionibus*.

69 Amolo of Lyons, *Epistola seu liber contra Judaeos*, XL, 169S. The *Toledot Jeshu* (*The Story of Jesus*) is an ancient and offensive Jewish satire on the birth and life of Jesus.

70 Agobard of Lyons, *Contra praeceptum* (addressed to Abbot Hilduin of St. Denis and to Wala).

71 See Heil, "Agobard, Amolo."

argued, obviously contradicted the gospel and Christ's Messianism.[72] Amolo succeeded where Agobard had failed. Employed as a specialist in Judaism at the Council of Paris-Meaux (845–46), he caused two decisions of Toledo IV to be adopted there which forbade showing favor to Jews (canon 74) and ordered the separation of Jewish children from their families in order that they might be raised by Christians.[73] Moreover, the council retained the original phrasing of canon 60 of Toledo IV which ordered the separation of Jewish children (and not of the baptized children of Jews)[74] from their parents – a decision which would have led to the disappearance of Judaism (but for the fact that the Frankish aristocracy refused to ratify the majority of the canons of Paris-Meaux). The originality of the Carolingian *Contra Iudaeos* would find no successors until the twelfth century.

It was at the beginning of the eleventh century that disputation reappeared in the form of discussions, usually fictional, between a Jew and a Christian regarding the truth of Christianity in the face of Judaism's lies. The earliest disputation was an exchange of letters between Henry, a cleric at the imperial court of Henry II, and the cleric Wecelin who had converted to Judaism (c. 1006). The themes of this correspondence return to the traditional questions of Jewish–Christian polemics: the validity of the Jewish Law after the coming of Christ, the Messianism of Jesus, the Incarnation, the Trinity, and the divine election of Christians replacing that of the Jews. The proselyte's tone is aggressive: Christian faith is accursed, and his Christian opponent an imbecile. It is worth noting, however, that Wecelin's letter is very short, whereas his opponent replies at length, thereby giving priority to Christianity.[75] In 1093, shortly before the First Crusade was radically to upset Jewish–Christian relations, Gilbert Crispin, abbot of Westminster, wrote the remarkably successful *Disputatio Iudei et Christiani*. It is not an original work, but within it, its disputants mutually promise to remain calm, and, for once, the discussion proceeds peaceably. In the treatment of the Incarnation, Gilbert puts forward the

72 Amolo of Lyons, *Epistola seu liber contra Judaeos*, XII, 148A, following the Babylonian Talmud, Sukka 52A. For other Jewish traditions reported by Amolo, see Albert, "*Adversus Iudaeos*."

73 Paris-Meaux (845–46), canon 74 (*Jews in Legal Sources* [847], 546–47) = Toledo IV, canon 58; Paris-Meaux, canon 75 (ibid. [868], 547–48) = Toledo IV, canon 60.

74 For the discussion regarding versions of this decision, see Albert, "Isidore of Seville," 216, footnote 37. Gratian retained the original version and did not add "[*filios*] *baptizatos*" (baptized children) as the canonists Burchard of Worms (d. 1025) and Ivo of Chartres (1090–1116) had done.

75 See Sapir Abulafia, "Eleventh-Century Exchange"; also Lotter, "Die Vertreibung," 53–64. Lotter situates Wecelin's proselytism within the context of the heresies of the beginning of the eleventh century.

possibility that God became man by distinguishing between divine nature and divine person, echoing Anselm of Canterbury's argument in his *Cur deus homo* (1095–98). Gilbert was helped in the philosophical aspects of the disputation by Anselm. These philosophical arguments opened new intellectual horizons in the Jewish–Christian dialogue. Though traditional biblical exegesis would remain the recognized weapon in disputations, it would henceforth be accompanied by a new tool: reason (*ratio*). The question then may be asked whether recourse to *ratio* could lead to a rapprochement between Jews and Christians: this is the question with which the twelfth century would be concerned.

8

The Mediterranean frontier: Christianity face to face with Islam, 600–1050

HUGH KENNEDY

Islam came face to face with Christianity from its beginnings. Christians and Jews were regarded as "People of the Book" because they had a revealed monotheistic religion. Even though they had corrupted this religion and turned away from the true path, they deserved a measure of respect and tolerance, unlike pagans with whom no coexistence was possible. Nevertheless, the new religion developed an ideology of confrontation with non-Muslims which almost inevitably led to conflict. The idea of holy war or *jihād* is developed in a number of suras of the Qur'ān but, as often in the Qur'ān, the message is not a simple and unequivocal one. The sacred text presents apparently conflicting advice to the faithful as to how they should confront the enemies of the new religion. There are a significant number of passages which advise nonviolent argument and preaching when dealing with the "People of the Book."[1] In contrast there are other passages in which the Muslims are exhorted to go and fight in the path of God, and those who do not are castigated for failing in their religious duties.[2] These culminate in 9.5:

> When the sacred months are past, kill the idolators wherever you find them and seize them, besiege them and lie in wait for them in every place of ambush: but if they repent, pray regularly and give the alms tax, then let them go their way, for God is forgiving, merciful.

Traditionally, Muslim scholars have reconciled the apparent contradiction by arguing that the quasi-pacifist exhortations are early revelation, from the time when the Muslims were few and they had to avoid confrontation to survive, while the more militant passages date from later when the Muslims were in a more powerful position and could challenge their enemies openly. The later, more militant passages abrogate the earlier ones and represent the definitive Muslim position. Recently it has been argued that a pacifist and a

1 Collected in Firestone, *Jihad*, 69–73.
2 Ibid., 84–91.

bellicose tradition in early Islam coexisted for some years, but that by the death of the Prophet in 632, it was the warlike tradition that was in the ascendant.[3]

The word *jihād* itself does not necessarily imply warfare. It means "striving," and Muslim writers – both ancient and modern – have contended that there is a form of *jihād* which is spiritual struggle to resist temptation and become a better Muslim. However, the Qur'ān and other early Islamic accounts often use phrases about fighting and killing in the cause of Islam which make it clear that real warfare was involved. At the time of the first Muslim conquests (632–41) it is clear that many of the faithful believed that it was right to fight the unbelievers in the name of Allah and that those who were killed in this endeavor would be martyrs and transported to the joys of paradise. In short, the obligation of *jihād* in its militant, holy war sense was not clearly and unequivocally incumbent on all Muslims at all times. It was rather a latent idea which could be activated, either by rulers seeking to use it to establish their religious credentials or by popular religious movements, impatient with the apparent laxity and inaction of their leaders.

The Muslim conquests of the Christian lands of the Mediterranean began in the years immediately following the death of the Prophet Muḥammad in 632. The exact chronology of the earliest phases of this conquest is uncertain, but we can be fairly sure that Damascus and much of Syria and Palestine were under Muslim rule by the end of 636, and that the fall of Jerusalem followed soon after. Caesarea, the last major city of the eastern shore of the Mediterranean to fall to the Muslim armies, was taken by 641.[4] The conquest of Egypt followed in the same year.

The Muslim conquest of North Africa followed a couple of generations later. In 693–94 Muslim armies took Carthage and began establishing the province of Ifriqiya (modern Tunisia). In 703 Tangier was taken and Muslim forces reached the Atlantic Ocean. The conquest of much of the Iberian peninsula followed from 711 to 716, and armies continued to raid further north, up the Rhône valley and more widely in southern France, until 732. The final phase of Muslim expansion in the Mediterranean came with the conquest of Crete in 827 and Sicily from 827 onward. The fall of Taormina in 902 signals the completion of this process.

At both ends of the Mediterranean Sea, and in the islands and peninsulas between, the boundaries between the Christian and Muslim worlds had been established by the middle of the ninth century.

3 For these different views, see ibid., especially 67–91.
4 For a full account, see Donner, *Early Islamic Conquests*.

In the lands of the eastern Mediterranean, the position of the frontier was largely decided by geography. The furthest expansion of Muslim political control followed the 1,000-meter contour line through what is now southern Turkey. Despite repeated and very damaging raids, the Muslims were never able to establish a permanent presence north of the Taurus mountains and, indeed, they only made very sporadic attempts to do so.

The Christian–Muslim border lands in the East went through several phases of evolution.[5] From the time of the Muslim conquest of Syria until the failure of the great expedition against Constantinople in 717–20 it seems as if the frontier itself was vague and largely undemarcated. Byzantines and Arabs were separated by areas of what was essentially no-man's land, only sparsely populated and rarely fortified. The failure to take Constantinople seems to have resulted in a significant change in policy. The late Umayyad caliphs and their early Abbasid successors made a conscious decision to fortify the frontier and establish garrisons and key points in the valleys and plains to the south of the main Taurus range. In the Cilician plain, the main bases were at Tarsus, Adana, and Massissa (Mopsuestia). All these were cities which had flourished in antiquity, but evidence suggests that the sites had largely been abandoned in fighting during the seventh century and that these settlements were essentially Islamic new towns. The old ecclesiastical organization had disappeared along with the Christian population. Further to the east, where the landscapes are wilder and more open, lay Marash (Germaniceia), Hadath, and Malatya (Melitene).

These frontier districts (*thughur*) came to assume an important role in the ideology and imagination of the Muslim community. At first these frontier strongholds were garrisoned by members of the regular army of the caliphate, mostly Syrians under the Umayyads and Khurasanis after 750 under the Abbasids. From the late eighth century, the frontier provinces were granted a unique fiscal status, which meant that revenues collected in the area could be devoted to their defense rather than being forwarded to the central treasury at Baghdad. They also began to attract large numbers of volunteers (*ghāzīs*) who would come to serve in the armies of Islam, sometimes just for a year or two, sometimes for longer. They never formed an organized order like the Templars or Hospitalers of the later Christian West, but they were a constant presence, supplementing the regular troops of the Muslim state. In Tarsus in the ninth century, there were lodgings for men from all over the Muslim

5 For the geography of the frontier, see Honigmann, *Die Ostgrenze*; also Haldon and Kennedy, "Arab–Byzantine Frontier."

world who wished to devote at least some of their lives to the pursuit of the *jihād*. These areas on the limits of the Muslim world were also the areas where militant piety was most fully developed and where the ideology of the *jihād* was worked out.[6]

The Byzantines were, and always remained, the enemy par excellence. They were the only outside enemies against whom ruling caliphs took up arms in person. Caliphs like Hārūn al-Rashīd (786–809) consciously used the command of the *jihād* as a way of establishing their legitimacy and prestige among their Muslim subjects. Along with the leadership of the *hajj*, the annual pilgrimage to Mecca, the command of Muslim armies against the ancient foe was one of the ways in which caliphal rulership was most clearly demonstrated and performed.

Raids into Byzantine territory were almost annual occasions. They were certainly damaging to the frontier lands. The Christian inhabitants of these areas must have lived in fear and apprehension, gathering in fortified castle sites or even carving out underground cities in which to take refuge. At the same time, the Muslims made little effort to conquer new territories, and Muslim troops rarely wintered north of the mountain passes. In many years the coming of the Muslim armies was a sort of military transhumance, in which army commanders led their men and animals to enjoy the summer grazing in the cooler mountain uplands.

If Christian emperors and Muslim caliphs saw their opposite numbers as enemies with whom there could never be lasting peace, they also saw them as worthy foes who could be dealt with almost on a basis of equality. The Byzantine emperors played an important role in early Muslim tradition; Muḥammad himself was widely (but almost certainly wrongly) believed to have written to the Emperor Heraclius, and the emperor is portrayed in the early Muslim tradition with some respect and admiration.[7] When the Umayyad caliph al-Walīd I (705–15) sought to beautify his great new mosque in Damascus, he looked to Byzantine mosaicists to provide suitable imperial decorations.[8] By the ninth century, Byzantine emperors like Theophilus were prepared to accept that they could learn from the developed and elaborate court culture of the Abbasids.

In the East, by the mid-ninth century, if not before, the Christian–Muslim frontier had reached a kind of stasis: hostility combined with a sort of mutual respect provided a sort of stability.

6 Bonner, *Aristocratic Violence*.
7 El Cheikh, *Byzantium*, 39–54.
8 Creswell, *Early Muslim Architecture* 1, 154–65; El Cheikh, *Byzantium*, 54–60.

In the Iberian peninsula the confrontation between Christian and Islamic forces showed parallels with the East but was in many ways different.[9] Here, too, the initial conquest of 711–16 was followed by a period of fluidity: Muslim raids continued in France until 732. This was the period of the *"jihadist"* state when the revenues and rewards of the ruling elite were largely dependent on booty from their conquests. The period of consolidation of the frontier can be fixed in the reign of ʿAbd al-Raḥmān II (822–52) when the borderlands were divided into *thughur* (sing. *thaghr*). There were three of these districts based on Zaragoza (Saragossa), Toledo, and Merida. The term *thaghr* was based on eastern administrative practice, and it is likely that the districts in al-Andalus enjoyed a measure of fiscal independence comparable with the *thughur* of Syria and al-Jazira. However, in contrast to the East, where the governance of the *thughur* remained in the hands of officials appointed by the caliphs, control in al-Andalus in some cases passed into the hands of families which might be described as "marcher lords," notably the Tujibis of Zaragoza, who effectively established a dynasty which was to last until the eleventh century.

In geographical terms, the land frontier fell into two distinct zones. To the east, in the Ebro valley and the foothills of the Pyrenees, the 1,000-meter rule, already observed in the East, largely held true in Spain. The Muslims occupied the plains and the Christians the mountains, and their interactions were as much the interactions of plains dwellers and mountain peoples as they were of Christians and Muslims. Christian and Muslim settlements were separated by short distances, and communications on an everyday basis must have been close. Further west, permanent Muslim settlement effectively halted at the foothills of the Cordillera Central. To the north of these mountains there seems to have been an area of no-man's land, somewhat similar to the Cilician plain, in the Duero river basin, or at least an area without major permanent settlements.[10] As in the East, this "no-man's land" was eventually filled by advancing settlement, but in the case of Spain and Portugal this settlement was achieved not by Muslims going over the Cordillera Central, but by Christians pushing south from bases like Leon and Burgos.

Frontier warfare, raids, and local disputes were a natural consequence of this division of territory, though it is by no means clear that Christian–Muslim conflict was more widespread or continuous than conflicts between different Christian or Muslim polities. It does not seem to have been until the tenth century that a state-sponsored *jihād* tried to bring Muslims together on the

9 On the Muslim frontier lands in the Iberian peninsula, see Manzano Moreno, *La frontera*.
10 Sanchez-Albornoz, *Despoblacion y Repoblacion*.

basis of their religion to face a common enemy. ʿAbd al-Raḥmān III (912–61) proclaimed himself caliph in 929 with the title of al-Nasir, the victorious. Not surprisingly, he looked to the East for a model of caliphal behavior and, while be could not lead the *hajj* to Mecca as the Abbasids had done, he could lead the Muslims in holy warfare. Until his defeat at the battle of Alhandega / Simancas in 937, ʿAbd al-Raḥmān conducted a series of campaigns in which he led the army of Cordoba and the military followings of the various lords of the *thughur* against the Christians of the north. As in the East, there seems to have been little or no attempt to gain new territory, nor can the material booty offered by the small and simple settlements of the Christian north have been a major motivating force for a sovereign who had the riches of the Muslim south at his disposal. It was rather a public display of his role as leader – a role which enabled him to command the frontier lords who would otherwise jealously maintain their independence.

After the defeat of 937, caused at least in part by the defection of the Tujibis, the leading frontier lords, al-Nasir never again took the field against the Christians, and this pacific tradition was maintained by his son and successor al-Ḥakam II (961–76). It was not until power was assumed (or usurped) by the military dictator Ibn Abī ʿĀmir, called al-Mansur (the Victorious), that the Muslims once again brought the *jihād* to the heart of Christian territory.

It is interesting, in this context, to compare the use of *jihad* by the Abbasid caliph Muʿtaṣim (833–42) and Ibn Abī ʿĀmir. Muʿtaṣim came to the throne by coup d'état and was able to impose his authority because of the strength of his new Turkish army. For many Muslims, however, the legitimacy of both the army and the caliph himself were dubious. One important way in which the caliph sought to establish his political credibility was by leading his new army in person against the Byzantines. He also chose a high-profile objective, or at least one he could portray as such. Constantinople itself was now far beyond the reach of Muslim armies, but in 838 he launched an attack on the city of Amorion, birthplace of the Byzantine emperor Theophilus. The city was duly taken, and while no effort was made to hold or settle the site, it could be portrayed as a famous victory. A detailed account of the achievement of caliphal arms was written and poems were composed to celebrate the event. The military importance of the conquest can be debated, but it was certainly a public relations triumph. Immediately after the sack of Amorion, the caliph took advantage of his strengthened position to embark on a ferocious purge of his political opponents.

Ibn Abī ʿĀmir, beginning in 976, was in a not-dissimilar position. While he did not usurp the title of caliph (unlike Muʿtaṣim he was not a member of the ruling family), he had taken control out of the hands of the young caliph Hishām II (976–1009) and introduced a new body of elite troops, in this case Berbers from North Africa. He launched a series of devastating raids against the kingdoms of the Christian north culminating in the sack of a high-profile target, the city and cathedral of Santiago de Compostella in 999. Once again, though, no attempt was made to retain control or advance Muslim settlement in the area. Accounts of his triumphs were read out in the mosque in Cordoba, and a plentiful supply of new slaves must have helped the populace to accept his rule. In both these cases we can see how the *jihād* had become a political device used to legitimize a ruler, rather than an expression of popular militant piety.

As in the East, there were cultural and diplomatic contacts between Christians and Muslims.[11] Often these involved the sending of emissaries from the Christian kingdoms and counties to Cordoba and, on occasion, Christians taking refuge from their rivals with the Muslims. A distinctive feature of the frontier of relations in Spain was intermarriage between the Umayyad rulers and princesses from Christian ruling families, especially the kings of Pamplona (Navarre). There is no parallel to this in the East: many of the Abbasid caliphs were in fact sons of Greek slave concubines and there was no tradition of marriage alliances between the ruling families. Needless to say, these relations were in all cases the marriage of Christian girls to Muslim men; there is no record of high-status Muslim women having relations with Christians until the possible marriage of Zaida to Alfonso VI (1072–1109) in the last quarter of the eleventh century. It is not clear whether these princesses of Christian origin converted to Islam or maintained female Christian households in the court in Cordoba.

At both ends of the Mediterranean, the initial Muslim conquests were followed by a period when the frontier with the Christians was vague and fluid, expansionist *jihād* was still a realistic proposition, and the revenues of the new elite were derived from the booty of war. By the end of the eighth century, the frontiers had stabilized, fortified strongholds had been established on both sides, and *jihād* was undertaken sporadically for reasons of prestige and to legitimate new sovereigns or regimes.

In the East, the balance of power and initiative began to shift in favor of the Christians during the second half of the tenth century. The main reason for this was the disintegration of the Abbasid caliphate from the 860s onward. This led to power in the frontier provinces being taken over by local lords.

11 See El-Hajji, *Andalucian Diplomatic Relations*.

They could no longer rely on the fiscal and military support of the rulers of the Muslim world, and their own puny resources were completely inadequate for opposing the resurgent power of the Byzantine armies under the Macedonian dynasty.

The first important step in the Byzantine advance was the conquest of Malatya in 934. Not only did this eradicate the main Muslim base in the strategic Upper Euphrates valley, but it demonstrated beyond all doubt the inability of the enfeebled government in Baghdad to defend the frontiers of the Muslim world. A generation later, Byzantine armies advanced again, and the Hamdanid ruler of Aleppo, Sayf al-Dawla (945–67), celebrated by the great poet al-Mutanabbī as a hero of Islam, was quite unable to defend the cities of the Cilician plain. The loss of Tarsus in 965 meant that Cilicia (Muslim and Arabic-speaking since the eighth century) passed into Byzantine hands; Arabic has never been spoken there since. The Byzantine capture of Antioch in 969 opened the gate for taking most of the mountain areas of northeast Syria in the next decades and establishing Byzantine administration. These were areas which the Muslims conquered in the 630s during the first wave of expansionist warfare, and it was the first time any of these areas had been lost to Islam. The conquests did not result in a large Muslim population under Christian rule. The new districts were purged of their Muslim inhabitants – a sort of religious cleansing – and when the Byzantine emperor stabled his horses in the ancient mosque in Tarsus, it was a clear signal of the radical nature of the change which had taken place.

The newly reconquered areas around the cities of Melitene (Malatya), Germaniceia (Marash), and Samosata (Samsat) were repopulated by Christians.[12] This seems to have been a pragmatic response by the Byzantine authorities to the problems of consolidating the frontier. There was no expressed ideology or rhetoric of Christian solidarity. Despite that, the fact that these immigrants were encouraged because of their religious beliefs rather than, say, their military or agricultural skills, suggests that religious solidarity was seen as important. Many of these immigrants were drawn from areas under Muslim rule (Egypt and Syria) and were attracted by the Byzantine authorities to settle in areas close to the Arab frontier where Greeks were afraid to live. It has been calculated that between 936 and 1072 around thirty episcopal sees are mentioned in this area for the first time.[13] In the same period, 56 of the 156 monasteries known to have existed in the area are recorded for the first

12 For this movement see Dagron, "Minorités ethniques et religieuses," 177–216.
13 Ibid., 188.

time. Most of them were not Greek-speaking and, more importantly, they belonged to the Syrian miaphysite church which was normally considered to be heretical by the authorities in Constantinople. There was a clear perception by the Byzantine authorities at this stage that Christians, even heretics, were preferable to Muslims as subjects, but they were confined to frontier areas, well away from the center of Greek Christianity and Byzantine government at Antioch. This acceptance was to be strained in the next century. By the 1030s there are clear indications that many miaphysites saw the Byzantine government as oppressive, while the authorities viewed their non-Chalcedonian populations as potential traitors.[14]

Muslim governments were ineffectual at stemming the Byzantine advance, at least until the Fatimids began to assert their power in Syria after 969, but there was considerable popular indignation in the Muslim world at the loss of these territories. In 966 a large group of volunteers from Khurasan attempted to march to the Byzantine frontier but were prevented and dispersed by the Buyid ruler of Rayy, who feared that they might threaten his rule.[15] In 972 there were demonstrations and riots in Baghdad as the Muslim population demanded that the caliph and his Buyid protector lead them against the infidel.[16] The enthusiasms of the pious were not translated into action, and there is no indication that any of these volunteers reached the front line or participated in campaigns against the Byzantines. Popular enthusiasm for the *jihād*, without state support, could not achieve meaningful success.

In the Iberian peninsula, the Muslims retained the initiative for longer. Throughout the tenth century the Muslims were able to maintain their frontier outposts and raid into Christian territory. As in the East, it was Muslim disunity that allowed the balance of power to change. The breakup of the caliphate of Cordoba after 1012 allowed the Christians to take advantage of Muslim rivalries. They first appeared as valued mercenaries and allies in disputes for the control of the capital. Soon they began to make financial demands. Rather than occupying new territory, the Christians strove to take advantage of Muslim weakness by forcing the Taifa kings[17] to pay *parias* (regular cash tribute payments).

14 Ibid., 205–16.

15 Miskawayh, *Eclipse* 1, 234–42.

16 Ibid., 326–28.

17 The Taifa kings were the rulers of the small realms, sometimes no bigger than a single town, into which al-Andalus was divided after the break-up of the caliphate of Cordoba at the beginning of the eleventh century. After 1086 the Taifas lost their independence and were incorporated into the Almoravid Empire.

The advance of the Christian frontier in the Iberian peninsula was a story of advancing settlement rather than conquest. Christian kings and counts settled such ancient sites as Leon and Burgos in the ninth century. As in the East, the tenth century saw the development of frontier monasticism as a major force in the Christianization of the land. Another similarity with the East was that some of these communities were immigrants from areas under Muslim rule to the south, who were encouraged by the kings of Leon to settle in their territory. The evidence for this movement can still be seen in churches like San Miguel de Escalada, south of Leon, founded in 913, where the surviving church shows how the Mozarab monastic community brought with them the distinctive architectural forms of al-Andalus, in addition to the Mozarab liturgy and distinctively Arabized personal names.[18] The importance of monasteries in settling and Christianizing frontier areas is often associated with the Cistercians and other new orders of the twelfth century but, in fact, we can clearly see its antecedents in southeastern Anatolia and northern Spain two centuries before.

While the Muslim caliphates in the East and Iberia evolved from conquest societies, where raiding and booty were the rewards of the military classes, into settled polities, where they lived off the proceeds of regular taxation, there were other areas where the raiding bands lasted much longer and in which government structures were effectively nonexistent.

It was probably Muslim adventurers from al-Andalus who set up a base for piracy and raiding at Fraxinetum (Fréjus) on the coast of Provence in 891. Like their near-contemporaries on the Garigliano in southern Italy, these marauders did not acknowledge the authority of any Muslim ruler and certainly made no attempt to set up a Muslim state in the areas in which they operated. From their coastal stronghold they were able to raid far into the hinterland. Despite repeated attempts by local rulers and the intervention of the Byzantine navy in 944–45, the Muslims were able to resist all attempts to dislodge them until 973.[19]

The history of Christian–Muslim confrontation in southern Italy and Sicily follows many of the same trends as in the East and the Iberian peninsula, but the position is complicated by the many divisions and rivalries on both Christian and Muslim sides of the religious divide.

The Muslim conquest of Sicily took three-quarters of a century from the arrival of Asad ibn al-Furāt in 827 until the final fall of Taormina in 902. The

18 De Palol and Hirmer, *Early Medieval Art*, 48–54; Bishko "Salvus of Albelda," 559–68.
19 Eickhoff, *Seekrieg und Seepolitik*, 279–80, 315–18, 358–59.

slowness of the Muslim advance, compared with other areas taken in the great conquests of the seventh and early eighth centuries, was partly a consequence of the small size of the Muslim armies and the strength of resistance in such hilltop fortresses as Enna (Castrogiovanni). Another important factor was the constant strife between the Muslims settled in Sicily and the Aghlabid amirs of Qayrawan, whose attempts to impose political control and taxation on the Muslims on the islands provoked vigorous resistance. Muslim Sicily remained a *jihad* state with a very underdeveloped administration until well into the tenth century.

The Muslims also confronted the Christians on the mainland of southern Italy. Here they were aided by rivalries among Byzantines, the papacy, and Lombard dynasts. Muslim naval power was often instrumental in affecting the outcome of disputes between Christian powers. As early as 835–37, we find Arab allies supporting the dukes of Naples in their struggle to remain independent of the Lombard dukes of Benevento. In return, Duke Andrew helped the Muslims in the conquest of Messina from the Byzantines in 842–43. Despite the condemnation of the papacy, the Neapolitans returned to the policy of alliance with the Muslims on several occasions.

In 902 the position changed significantly. As already mentioned, Taormina fell to the Muslims, and in the same year the Aghlabid amir Ibrahim, who had retired to dedicate himself to the *jihad*, was killed in an unsuccessful attempt to take Cosenza in Calabria. This defeat marked the end of any serious Muslim attempt to conquer southern Italy.

It did not mark, however, the end of raids or of Christian–Muslim confrontation in the area. The most famous center of conflict was the Muslim base established in about 881 at the mouth of the Garigliano river. Here, as at Fréjus, a *ghāzī* community maintained itself by raiding far into the interior and was able to sack the monastery at Monte Cassino in 881–83. Attempts to unite the Christian powers of the area against the marauders were undermined by the policies of Gaeta and Amalfi. Both cities were determined to maintain their independence from the Lombard dukes of Benevento and the Amaliftans likewise were equally concerned to maintain their trading with Muslim Tunisia. It was not until 915, when the papacy was able to put together an alliance of Lombard and Byzantine forces and secure the neutrality of Gaeta and Amalfi, that the Muslim base was finally destroyed. Thereafter, there were occasional Muslim raids on southern Italy, such as the one which sacked Taranto in 928, but Muslim pressure became sporadic.

The political position in Sicily changed again after 969 when the Fatimids abandoned North Africa to establish their power in Egypt. They allowed a prominent local family descended from the Arab tribe of Kalb to become, in effect, hereditary rulers of the island. The Kalbis in turn sought to consolidate their position by renewing the *jihād* in southern Italy under state auspices. Like their Andalusi contemporary Ibn Abī ʿĀmir al-Mansur, the Kalbi rulers tried to use the *jihād* as a way of asserting their legitimacy and their authority over their Muslim subjects. The amir Abū'l-Qāsim (970–82) began this process by leading repeated attacks on Cosenza, Taranto, and Otranto and extracting tribute from them all. In 982 a Muslim army defeated the forces of the Emperor Otto II at Capo Controne, but the amir died as a martyr in the conflict.

The death of Abū'l-Qāsim did not spell the end of Muslim raids, but none of his successors pursued the *jihād* with the same vigor. Under Jaʿfar ibn Yūsuf (998–1019) there was increasing unrest culminating in an army mutiny in 1015 and a rebellion against over-taxation in 1019 when the amir was forced into exile. His successor Ahmad (1019–36) tried to safeguard his position by making an alliance with the Byzantine emperors and, like contemporary Muslim rulers in Aleppo and elsewhere in the East, he was given the Byzantine honorific title of *magistros* in 1035. This Christian alliance provoked considerable popular hostility and enabled his opponents in Sicily to rise in rebellion and kill him. This simply led to further feuds and divisions in the Kalbid amirate. As in Muslim Spain at exactly the same time, divisions and disputes among the Muslims laid their lands open to penetration and eventual conquest by Christian aggressors.

Another *ghāzī* polity was established in Crete which was taken from the Byzantines in 827 by a group of Muslim outlaws who had been expelled from al-Andalus and then from Alexandria, where they had taken refuge. The Muslim emirate of Crete never developed into a fully fledged state but remained a pirate base, continuously threatening the sea-lanes of the Aegean.[20]

Not all contacts between Christians and Muslims happened at the level of political conflict and the expansion and contraction of territories. There were peaceful contacts between individual Christian travelers and merchants throughout the period, though the numbers involved were certainly much smaller than those who traveled across the Mediterranean in Late Antiquity. Recent research has identified some 105 western Europeans who visited Jerusalem (then, of course, under Muslim rule) between c. 700 and c. 900 and seven who went to Baghdad.[21] Virtually all of these went for religious reasons or as ambassadors. The number of western merchants recorded as active in the lands of the caliphate in the same period is very small indeed – certainly no

20 McCormick, *Origins*.
21 Ibid., 171.

more than ten – and it is indicative that the fullest account we have of western commercial activity comes from the narrative of the theft of St. Mark's body from Alexandria by Venetian merchants in c. 828.

Pilgrimage, diplomacy, and trade were the motives which encouraged Christians to visit the lands of Islam. Of the individuals responding to these motives, pilgrims were almost certainly the most numerous group and certainly the best publicized.

The best-documented of the pilgrims who visited Palestine was St. Willibald.[22] Willibald was an Anglo-Saxon who, with several companions, left his home in Hampshire in the spring of 721. They traveled overland to Italy, staying in a monastery in Rome for a year and a half, and then moving on to the south Italian port of Gaeta where they found a ship from Egypt. This took them around the Peloponnese to Asia Minor, and they spent another winter in Patara on the Lycian coast. In the spring they set out again and eventually reached the Syrian coast at Tartus. From here they walked to Homs where they were arrested as spies. Fortunately for them, they were interrogated by a Spaniard whose brother was a eunuch in the entourage of the caliph: presumably both brothers had been taken as prisoners of war at the time of the Muslim conquest, barely thirty years before. As a result of this intervention, the caliph, who happened to be in Homs at the time, granted them permission to continue their journey and even excused them from the tax. They set off south, via Damascus, for the holy places. Over the next two years, Willibald made a comprehensive tour of Palestine as far south as Gaza and Lebanon and back again to Homs, where he secured written permission to take ship from Tyre to Constantinople. He may also have been financing his travels with a bit of trading on the side. He related with some glee how he managed to smuggle some very valuable balsam, which he had bought in Jerusalem, out of the country. The rest of his travels to Constantinople, Rome, and Germany (where he finished a long and distinguished career as Bishop of Eichstatt) do not concern us here. His account makes it clear that there was passenger shipping between Christendom and the Muslim world and it was possible for private citizens, which is effectively what he was, to make use of it. Both arriving and leaving he had to acquire the necessary paperwork, but while he was there he seems to have been able to circulate freely, and there is no suggestion of popular hostility to these wandering tourists. The main hazards were disease, possibly including bubonic plague, and shortage of food – both problems which affected the local people as well as visitors. We cannot

22 See *Vita Sancti Willibaldi*.

know how far Willibald's experience was shared by others but it does give us some insight into the possibilities of travel.

While it is difficult to produce exact data, it seems clear that the tempo of pilgrimage to Palestine increased greatly in the eleventh century. Prior to this, pilgrims had been like Willibald and his companions, small groups who negotiated their passage and subsistence with the local people. From the year 1000 onward, westerners began to come in much larger numbers. Rodulfus Glaber speaks of "an innumerable multitude from the whole world, greater than any man could have hoped to see" who began to travel to Jerusalem and goes on to note a new phenomenon, "numerous women, noble and poor, undertook the journey."[23] We also find very prominent figures going on pilgrimage: Bishop Conrad of Constance (d. 975) went three times as did Fulk Nerra, Count of Anjou, and the great German pilgrimage of 1064 is said to have numbered 7,000 or even 12,000. All these pilgrims, would, of course, have passed through Islamic lands and come into contact with Muslim society. Even allowing for exaggeration and over-enthusiasm on the part of our sources, it is clear that the eleventh century saw a vastly greater interaction between Christians from western Europe and the Muslim world than in the earlier Middle Ages.

The reasons for this growth are not entirely clear. It may well be that increasing commercial contacts made the East more familiar and accessible. It may be, too, that there was an increased emphasis on visiting the lands where Christ had lived and died and been raised from the dead as distinct from visiting the relics of martyrs. The Holy Land could offer very few relics, but it could offer the one, essential site of Christ's resurrection from the dead, even if all you could see there was an empty tomb.

Diplomatic contacts between the Byzantines and the Muslims had begun in the aftermath of the initial conquests of Syria and Egypt.[24] While there was no formal peace agreement, it suited both Christian and Muslim rulers to arrange truces from time to time, especially when they were preoccupied with enemies closer to home. It seems to have begun in 650–51 when Constans II made an agreement with the governor of Syria, Mu'āwiya ibn Abī Sufyān, to prevent Arab naval attacks while he was preoccupied by trouble in the Balkans. In the ninth century the focus of diplomacy changed. In this period of comparative stability and parity of esteem, the purpose of diplomatic missions was usually to arrange for the exchange of prisoners: we are told of twelve official

23 Rodulfus Glaber, "History of his Own Time," in Wilkinson, *Jerusalem Pilgrims*, 272–73 or for Latin original, see *PL* 142, 272–73.

24 Kennedy, "Byzantine–Arab Diplomacy."

meetings between 805 and 946 at which between 2,000 and 6,000 prisoners were exchanged, usually on the River Lamys in Cilicia. In order to arrange these meetings, Muslim ambassadors were sent to Constantinople and Christian ones to Baghdad. In 917 two Christian envoys were given an extremely lavish and elaborate reception by the caliph al-Muqtadir (908–32) to demonstrate to his subjects how the weakened and impoverished caliphate could still command the respect of representatives from the other great power.[25]

With the collapse of the caliphate and the Byzantine advances in northern Syria from the mid-tenth century, the focus of Byzantine diplomacy shifted to making client relationships with local Muslim powers. Muslim rulers of Aleppo were given Byzantine administrative titles like *magistros* and *patrikios*. Constantine IX in the mid-eleventh century provided funds for the reconstruction of the Church of the Holy Sepulcher in Jerusalem, perhaps asserting some sort of right to protect Christian communities under Muslim rule.

Not surprisingly, diplomatic links between western Christendom and the caliphate were slower to develop and more sporadic. The most famous episode was Charlemagne's embassy to Hārūn al-Rashīd in about 797. The point at issue was the emperor's desire to set up a monastery and hospice in Jerusalem. There is no evidence for these contacts in the Arabic sources, but it seems that the response was favorable, that permission was given, and that the caliph sent a number of gifts including the celebrated elephant, which made a big impression at the emperor's court. The monastery and hospice certainly flourished and when Bernard the Monk visited Jerusalem in 867, he was able to stay "in the hostel of the most glorious Emperor Charles."[26]

The emperor sent another embassy in 802 and a delegation from Baghdad bearing gifts returned the favor in 806, but this imperial diplomacy did not pave the way for continuous contacts. In 906 the Margravine Bertha of Tuscany sent a mission to the caliph al-Muktafi in Baghdad bearing gifts which included male and females slaves from the Slav lands and swords.

It is clear that there were commercial contacts across the religious divide, but it is difficult to assess the extent and scale of these. Ever since Pirenne argued that the coming of the Muslims caused an almost complete break in commercial links across the Mediterranean, the question of trade or lack of it has been caught up in more general controversy about the origins of the medieval western economy.

We can, however, make certain generalizations with some confidence. In comparison with the commercial links that were to grow up from the eleventh

25 Miskawayh, *Eclipse* 1, 56–60.
26 *Itinerarium Bernardi Monachi Franci.*

century onward, contacts in the early Middle Ages were very sporadic. There are no surviving commercial treaties between Christian and Muslim powers and no sign of any permanent trading colonies. This does not seem to have been the result of any distaste among Muslims for doing business with the Christians but more simply because the Christian world produced very little that the Muslims wanted. The poverty-stricken West was hardly a market for the fine textiles and spices which were the stock-in-trade of long-distance commerce. Only the demand for northern European slaves was consistent and buoyant, and these were acquired by violence and capture as much as by commercial relations.

After a low point around the year 700, demand for goods (either produced in the Muslim world or transported through it) revived. Silks were coveted luxury items and some still survive today in ecclesiastical treasuries.[27] Popes in the late eighth and early ninth centuries were particularly lavish givers of silks as rewards and diplomatic gifts. While some of these silks were no doubt of Byzantine origin, others certainly came from Muslim lands. A piece preserved at Huy in Belgium bears a Soghdian inscription suggesting that it was manufactured near Bukhara in the eighth or ninth centuries.

Spices like pepper and cinnamon were highly valued, not just to flavor food, but as ingredients in medicines and potions, and some of the recipes for these potions were themselves of Muslim origin.[28] Perhaps the most distinctive import was incense. Incense was very important in the rituals of both Carolingian and Byzantine churches and clearly large quantities were consumed.[29] True incense, however, comes from a very restricted geographical area in south Arabia and the horn of Africa. It can only have been brought to the Mediterranean and thence to Christian lands by Muslim merchants, yet the process is virtually invisible in the historical record. The use of incense on such a large scale must have implied continuous and harmonious dealings on the frontiers of Christendom, but who conducted them and where is by no means clear.

These extensive imports did not seem to result in a balance of trade crisis. The presence of very considerable numbers of Muslim dirhams and dinars in western Europe, and the almost complete absence of Christian coins in the Middle East, suggests that Europe may actually have been running a surplus.

Christendom certainly exported furs and timber to the Islamic world, but the most important, and the most fraught, interactions were in the slave trade.

27 McCormick, *Origins*, 715–26.
28 Ibid., 708–16.
29 Ibid., 716–19.

From the mid-eighth century onward, there was an apparently inexhaustible demand for European slaves in the countries of the Islamic East. The trade may have had a kick start from the decline in population caused by the last spasm of the early medieval plague which afflicted the Near East after the year 747, but the slave trade continued to develop after the demographic emergency had passed.

Since the early days of the Muslim conquest, Byzantine prisoners of war had been an important source of slaves in the Muslim world. Some of them at least had been manumitted becoming *mawali* or freedmen, and some came to play an important role in politics and administration. They were important supporters of the Umayyad family, and it was *mawali*, either ex-slaves themselves or sons of ex-slaves, who formed the core support of the first of the Umayyad rulers of Cordoba, Abd al-Rahman I, in 756 when he first entered al-Andalus. Byzantine slave girls were highly prized in the harems of the Abbasid caliphs of the ninth and early tenth centuries. At least one of them, al-Mu'tadid (892–902), spoke Greek as well as Arabic, for it was, literally, his mother tongue.

From the late eighth century, slaves were purchased from further afield. Western and northern European slaves commanded high prices in Byzantium and even higher ones in the lands of Islam. Christian and Muslim merchants alike could make massive profits buying on the northern shores of the Mediterranean and selling in the south. The main entrepôt was Venice where Muslim merchants would come to purchase slaves from eastern Europe, but there was also more informal trading in other Italian ports like Naples and more simply on the beaches where people captured in local raids would be brought for sale. When Bernard the Monk from Champagne and his two companions went on pilgrimage to the Holy Land in 867 they went to Bari, then in Muslim hands, to find a ship to take them to Alexandria. They received guarantees of safe-conduct from the Arab Amir Sawdan and were sent on to Taranto to take ship. Here they found 9,000 unfortunate Christian captives, recently taken on Muslim raids on Venafro and Monte Cassino who were on board six ships, ready to set out for the slave markets of Tunisia and Egypt. Amazingly, Bernard and his companions were taken on as fare-paying passengers and, protected by the documents Sawdan had given them, made the month-long, direct journey to Alexandria, apparently in the same vessel as their wretched coreligionists. When they left the vessel, the sailors demanded two gold pieces from each of them as a fare and they continued their pilgrimage unmolested.[30] We hear nothing more of the prisoners' fate.

30 *Itinerarium Bernardi Monachi Franci*, 309 or trans. Wilkinson, 261–62.

The slaves Bernard saw were Italian townspeople and villagers, but many of the slaves who passed through Venice were Slavs from eastern Europe, captured or purchased there, and then sold in Venice. Throughout the Carolingian period, the church made repeated and no doubt genuine attempts to prevent the sale of Christians into Muslim hands. Many of the Slavs were pagan and so could be bought and sold with an easy conscience. However, the demand was so high and the potential profits so tempting that the Venetians and other Italian merchants persistently infringed these ecclesiastic prohibitions.

As with pilgrimage traffic, the eleventh century saw a qualitative and quantitative expansion of trade with the Muslim world. By the year 1000 there were Italian merchants in Alexandria and Fustat (Old Cairo). In the eleventh century, the Geniza documents are full of references to "Franks," their importance for the market in spices and odoriferous woods, and their willingness to accept inferior goods.[31] The cities of Egypt were not the only points of contact: when Nasir-i Khusraw was travelling from Iran to Egypt in the mid-eleventh century, he found that Tripoli in Lebanon was frequented by western European ships.[32] Meanwhile, the fleets of Genoa and Pisa were increasingly active in Tunisia and along the coasts of Muslim Spain.

In the early Middle Ages, relations between Christians and Muslims were intermittent. In the East and in Spain there were areas in which localized, unrecorded contacts must have been common. The best-recorded contacts were military. In the earliest phase, the Muslim *jihād* state was based on a policy of continuous raid and expansion, in which booty, both goods and slaves, provided the income and reward of the military elite. This phase ended in the East by 720, in the Iberian peninsula by 750, and in Sicily and southern Italy by 900, though it survived in outposts like Fréjus and the Garigliano River until well into the tenth century. The *jihād* states were replaced by polities in which the professional army was paid salaries out of taxation raised from both Muslim and Christian populations. The *jihād* became institutionalized and used by rulers to assert their prestige and legitimacy. The third phase is the gradual Christian expansion at the expense of the Muslims, from the mid-tenth century in the east and the mid-eleventh in Spain and Portugal.

Pilgrims, merchants, and ambassadors also forged links. In the case of merchants and pilgrims, the numbers involved were small, and there seem to have been no organized institutions except for Charlemagne's hostel in Jerusalem. In the eleventh century, the picture changed with increasing rapidity as both

31 Goitein, *Mediterranean Society* 1, 42–46.
32 Nasir-i Khusraw, *Book of Travels*, 17.

the scale and frequency of contacts increased. Ships from western European ports were to be found in ever-increasing numbers in the harbors of the Levant and Egypt. In the Iberian peninsula, the Christians of the north were making military gains at the expense of the divided Taifa kingdoms, and the Normans were embarking on the conquest of Sicily from its Muslim overlords. There can be little doubt that the frontiers of Christendom were being expanded significantly in the half-century before the First Crusade.

9
Christians under Muslim rule

SIDNEY H. GRIFFITH

By the year 732 CE, just one hundred years after the death of the prophet Muḥammad, Arab military forces, in the name of Islam, consolidated their hegemony over a large stretch of territory outside of Arabia. This expanse of territory, embracing major portions of the Roman and Persian empires of Late Antiquity, included many indigenous Christian communities, in several denominations. They all came under Muslim rule, but demographically they made up the religious majority in many places until well into the eleventh century. There were strong Christian communities in Spain (al-Andalus) and in the territories of the former eastern patriarchates of the Roman Empire, as well as in Persian Mesopotamia.[1] During the first four centuries of the *hegira* (i.e., the Islamic era) most of these Christian subjects of the Muslim caliph gradually adopted the Arabic language, while retaining to a greater or lesser extent, depending on local circumstances, their traditional, patristic, and liturgical languages for church purposes.

Christians in the Qur'ān and in early Islam

Arabic-speaking Christians were in the audience to whom the Qur'ān first addressed the word of God, as it claimed, in "a clear Arabic tongue" (Qur'ān 16.103 and 26.105). Indeed the Qur'ān presumes the priority of the Torah and the Gospel in the consciousness of its hearers, and insists that in reference to the earlier divine revelations it is itself "a corroborating scripture in the Arabic language to warn wrong doers and to announce good news to those who do well" (Qur'ān 46.12). In the Qur'ān, God advises the Muslims, "If you are in doubt about what we have sent down to you, ask those who were reading scripture before you" (Qur'ān 10.94).

1 Bulliet, *Conversion to Islam*.

The Qur'ān presumes in its readers a ready familiarity with the stories of the principal narrative figures of the Old and New Testaments, as well as with an impressive array of Jewish and Christian lore, faith, and practice. The Qur'ān also warns Christians not to go to excess in their religion and not to "follow the fancies of a people who went astray in the past and led others astray and themselves strayed from the right path" (Qur'ān 5.77). It offers a critique of Christian faith and practice. The most comprehensive verse addressed directly to Christians in this vein says:

> O People of the Book, do not exaggerate in your religion, and do not say about God anything but the truth. The Messiah, Jesus, Mary's son, is only God's messenger, and his word he imparted to Mary, and a spirit from him. Believe in God and in his messengers, and do not say, "Three." Stop it! It is better for you. God is but a single God; he is too exalted for anything to become a son to him, anything in the heavens or anything on the earth. God suffices as a guardian. (Qur'ān 4.171)

Given this level of knowledgeable critique of Christian doctrine, and taking cognizance of the Qur'ān's presumption of a Christian presence in its immediate audience, the question arises about the identity of the Christians in Arabia in Muḥammad's day. But the text itself does not offer much help to answer the question. Once it mentions the "People of the Gospel" (Qur'ān 5.47), and some fourteen times it refers to "the Nazarenes," in which context it obviously means Christians. But the fact is that the Qur'ān never uses the term "Christians," preferring for the most part to include Christians, along with the Jews, among those it calls "People of the Book" or "Scripture People" (Qur'ān 54x).

Presumably, the Christians whom the Arabic Qur'ān had in mind when speaking of "those who say, 'We are Nazarenes'" (Qur'ān 5.14, 82), were Arabic-speaking Christians. Probably the Qur'ān's Arabic term here, *al-Naṣārā*, reflects the cognate Syriac term *Naṣrāyê* in the sense of "Nazoreans" or "Nazarenes," a term widely used to designate Christians in Syriac works by east Syrian writers living in the Persian Empire, particularly when reporting the references of non-Christian speakers to Christians. It is reasonable to suppose that the Arabic / Qur'ānic usage followed suit. While Christians in Egypt and Ethiopia were also present to the early Muslims, the larger, Arabic-speaking Christian communities in the immediate geographical milieu in which Islam was first preached all had connections with church communities in the Sinai, Palestine, Trans-Jordan, Syria, lower Mesopotamia, or even southern Arabia. They all belonged to communities whose liturgies, doctrines, and ecclesiastical associations were originally Aramaic.

In the case of Christians living in Sinai, Palestine, or Trans-Jordan, where Byzantine-style Orthodoxy officially held sway from the mid-fifth century onward (and where Greek was the dominant ecclesiastical language in the numerous international monastic communities), the Aramaic dialect of the local churches was Christian Palestinian Aramaic.[2] In Syria and Mesopotamia, where the local Christian communities straddled the frontiers of the Roman and Persian empires (and where Byzantine, imperial Orthodoxy was widely rejected) Syriac was the Aramaic dialect that served as the dominant ecclesiastical language.

Most Syriac-speaking Christians in Muḥammad's day accepted Christological formulae echoing the earlier theology of St. Cyril of Alexandria (d. 444) and best articulated in the Greek texts of Severus of Antioch (c. 465–538) and in the Syriac writings of Philoxenus of Mabbug (c. 440–523). They also favored the Syriac works of Narsai (d. 503) and Babai the Great (551/2–628) (who reflected the positions of Theodore of Mopsuestia (c. 350–428) composed originally in Greek a hundred years earlier).[3] The three mainline, Christian denominations to be found in the Aramaic- or Syriac-speaking popular communities (whose Arabic-speaking coreligionists were most likely the "Nazarenes" in the Qur'ān's audience) were the very ones whom later Christian and Muslim writers alike would refer to as "Melkites," "Jacobites," and "Nestorians."[4]

Until the very last years of the seventh century, the only notice taken of Christians in the Islamic sources are the references to churches, churchmen, and their public rites that sometimes appear in the texts of treaties and the stipulated conditions that allowed for the continuance of daily life after the conquest. These stipulations would later be collected, edited, and enfranchised as the *Covenant of 'Umar*. This legal document came to be considered by Muslim jurists as giving some authoritative specification to the Qur'ān's general dictum regarding the People of the Book, namely, that Muslims should fight them "till they pay the poll-tax *(al-jizya)* out of hand and submissively *(ṣāghirūna)*" (Qur'ān 9.29).[5]

One symbolic, public phenomenon in the Muslim–Christian confrontation signaled the inauguration of serious interreligious discussions by noticeably declaring the Islamic bid for social hegemony in the now securely occupied lands. It was the campaign of the caliph 'Abd al-Malik (685–707) and his sons and successors, roughly in the first third of the eighth century, to display Islam

2 Griffith, "From Aramaic to Arabic."
3 Trimingham, *Christianity among the Arabs*.
4 *Pace* De Blois, "*Naṣrānī* and *Ḥanīf*."
5 Tritton, *Caliphs and their Non-Muslim Subjects*.

culturally and politically, and thereby symbolically appropriate Arab-occupied territory for the new political allegiance. From the religious perspective, the program for the display of Islam had two principal features. Positively, there were the efforts in stone, mortar, and coinage to broadcast declaratively the Islamic *shahāda* (testimony) throughout the land; negatively, there was the correlative campaign to erase the public symbols of Christianity, especially the ubiquitous sign of the cross. Positively, the most dramatic enactment was the building in Jerusalem of the caliph ʿAbd al-Malik's monument to Islam, the Dome of the Rock, with its explicitly anti-Christian inscriptions, taken substantially from the Qur'ān.[6] But perhaps the policy with the most far-reaching subsequent effects was the caliph ʿUmar II's (715–20) program for promoting the equality of all Muslims, be they Arab conquerors or new converts to Islam.[7] This policy became a plank in the political platform of the movement that brought about the Abbasid revolution by the middle of the eighth century and ushered in an era of growth and development for classical Islamic culture. Socially speaking these developments had their effects among the Christians living under the caliphs' rule. They may well have made conversion to Islam a more attractive social option than heretofore, especially among the more upwardly mobile Christian families. By the time of the Abbasid revolution, historical circumstances began to favor the efforts of Christian communities in occupied territories outside of Arabia both to accommodate themselves to Islamic culture and to resist its religious challenge in the very idiom of the new polity.

Christianity in Arabic

The first step of inculturation was the adoption of the Arabic language in the churches. For a number of reasons, this step seems to have been taken first in Melkite communities, whose ecclesiastical and cultural center was Jerusalem, with its attendant monastic establishment.[8] But it was not long before the other churches followed suit. By the mid-ninth century the Melkites, Jacobites, and Nestorians would all be fluent in Arabic, and by the mid-tenth century the Copts in Egypt had joined them, and were poised to become the major producers of Arab Christian texts by the thirteenth century.[9] By far the greatest numbers of texts produced in Arabic by the Christian communities

6 Griffith, "Images, Islam and Christian Icons."
7 Dennett, *Conversion and the Poll Tax.*
8 Griffith, *Arabic Christianity.*
9 Griffith, *Beginnings of Christian Theology.*

in the Islamic world in the eighth and ninth centuries were translations of the Scriptures and the patristic and liturgical classics of the churches. These translations were for the most part done from Greek and Syriac originals. Arguably, this translation activity enhanced the identity of Christian communities in the Islamic world as much as the comparable contemporary translation movement among Muslim scholars in Baghdad defined cultural life among the Abbasid elite during the same period of formation for classical Arab Islamic culture.[10]

It was within this context, in the eighth century, that the literary awakening of Christian communities to the religious challenge of Islam first appeared. The earliest texts emanate from Syria / Palestine, and they are in Greek, Syriac, and Arabic. At first, Syriac-speaking writers reacted to the establishment of Islam in apocalyptic terms. They interpreted the new sociopolitical arrangements in reference to the prophetic passages in the biblical book of Daniel.[11] In general, they proposed that the Islamic conquest was a punishment for the sins of Christians, which would run its course and eventually end with the restoration of the Messiah's rule. The most well-known text in this genre is the *Apocalypse of Pseudo Methodius of Patara*, written originally in Syriac, in the early years of the eighth century.[12] It was soon translated into Greek and Latin, and from these versions it came quickly into early modern, European languages, where it exerted a tremendous literary influence on the formation of western Christian attitudes toward Islam in the Middle Ages. But it was not long before Christians in the conquered territories began responding to the call to Islam in apologetic and even polemical tracts, written in Greek, Syriac, and Arabic largely for a Christian audience.

The tract most familiar to westerners is contained in chapter 100 of the *De Haeresibus* section of John of Damascus's (d. c. 749) landmark Greek work written in Palestine, *The Fount of Knowledge*.[13] While there has been much scholarly discussion about the authenticity of this chapter on the "Heresy of the Ishmaelites," it clearly comes from the Melkite milieu of the eighth century, and most likely from the pen of John himself. Its importance is in the fact that, while the author is certainly hostile to Islam (and not above presenting caricatures of Islamic doctrines and practices), nevertheless he is clearly well informed, not least about Islam's view of Christian faith and works. In fact, the topics he discusses are those that will be the standard ones in Muslim / Christian apologetics and polemics for centuries to come. But his work is also the only

10 Gutas, *Greek Thought, Arabic Culture*.
11 Martínez, "La literatura apocalíptica."
12 Reinink, *Die syrische Apokalypse*.
13 Le Coz, *Jean Damascène*.

one of its kind in Greek to appear in the world of Islam. Thereafter, from the ninth century onwards, Greek Christian texts on Islam are produced in Byzantium; they are overwhelmingly polemical in character, a feature which obscures their apologetic dimension.[14] Their primary purpose is to demean, even to ridicule Muḥammad, the Qur'ān, and Islam. It is otherwise with the works written in Syriac and Arabic by Christians from the 750s onward. Here, apology is the dominant concern. It is an apology that seeks to commend the veracity of Christianity – or of a particular Christological formula – to both Christians and Muslims, often in the very religious idiom of Islam. While these works frequently include a polemical component (for example, they argue that Islam is not the true religion), the apology's primary goal is the reasoned defense of the Christian religion, or of a particular Christian creedal formula.

The challenge of Islam elicited a range of apologetic and theological strategies from Syriac- and Arabic-speaking Christians not previously in evidence in Christian thought. In this context the dynamics of the interpretation of the Bible and of the Qur'ān – of traditional Christian theologies and Islamic traditions – interacted to give birth to Christian theologies of a new and unfamiliar profile. They made no small contribution to the evolving estrangement between the Greek- and Latin-speaking Christians of western Christendom, and the mostly Syriac-, Coptic-, and Arabic-speaking Christians of the Islamic commonwealth, which would become a notable feature of their mutual antagonism in the high Middle Ages.

It was only in the time of the Muslims that the several ecclesial communities in the Orient, those whom both Arabic-speaking Christians and Muslims called Melkites, Jacobites, and Nestorians, came to the final defining terms of their separate, denominational identities. It was largely in response to questions posed by Muslims in Arabic, as well as by their own Christian adversaries about their doctrinal differences, that required the spokesmen for the denominations to articulate their differing Christologies in Arabic as clearly as possible. The new phenomenon for the Christians was not just that their conversations with the Muslims were conducted now in Arabic, but so were their conversations and controversies with one another.

The Nestorians and Jacobites were already socially identifiable communities before the rise of Islam; their popular names were widely used by both Greek and Syriac writers. But those who would be called Melkites by their adversaries

14 Khoury, *Les théologiens byzantins*; idem, *Polémique byzantine*; idem, "Apologétique byzantine."

after the Council of Constantinople III (680/681) became a sociologically and doctrinally distinct Christian community only in Islamic times. In modern times, the name "Melkites" is used only for the "Greek Catholic Melkites" (*Rūm Catholiques*). The original Melkites were for the most part Aramaic- and Arabic-speaking upholders of the orthodoxy of the first six ecumenical councils, from Nicaea I (325) to Constantinople III. They lived in the world of Islam and the see of Jerusalem and the monasteries of the Holy Land became their ecclesiastical point of reference, although their members could be found throughout the caliphate. Their patristic and liturgical heritage was principally Greek, and their chief theologian was John of Damascus, whose teachings were soon widely popularized in Arabic, initially in the works of Theodore Abū-Qurra (c. 755–c. 830).[15]

Unlike the situation in pre-Islamic times, once the caliphate drew new cultural and geopolitical lines on the map of the Middle East, the Nestorians and Jacobites (including the Copts, Ethiopians, and Armenians) were the Christian majority, contrasted against the now much smaller, nascent community of Melkites, whose coreligionists in Byzantium were beyond the borders of the Islamic world. By the ninth Christian century, when all these ecclesial communities had found their voices in Arabic, they made their translations and composed theological, apologetic, and polemical tracts in response not only to the religious challenge of Islam, but often also in reaction to one another.[16]

Christian Arabic writers of the ninth century from the three denominations, such as Theodore Abū-Qurra for the Melkites, Ḥabīb ibn Khidma Abū-Rā'iṭa (d. c. 851) for the Jacobites, and 'Ammār al-Baṣrī (fl. c. 850) for the Nestorians, not only wrote to show that Christianity was the true religion (as opposed to Islam), but that the theological and Christological formulae of their own denominations represented the true Christianity. The writers of later generations in these communities, such as the Jacobite Yaḥyā ibn-'Adī (893–974), the Nestorian Elias of Nisibis (975–1046), and the Melkite Eutychius of Alexandria (877–940) all followed suit. Meanwhile Muslim scholars and writers were taking note of this development. Some of them, such as Abū-'Īsā al-Warrāq (d. c. 860) and the Mu'tazilī *mutakallim* 'Abd al-Jabbār al-Hamadānī (d. 1025), not to mention the Andalusian polemicist Ibn-Ḥazm (994–1064), set out to take account of the three denominations of Christians in their midst. Since by this time, in fact, all the Jacobites and Nestorians lived within the world of Islam, while only the Melkites, and latterly the Maronites, had coreligionists outside

15 Griffith, "Melkites, Jacobites."
16 Khoury, *Matériaux*; Millet-Gérard, *Chrétiens mozarabes*; Burman, *Religious Polemic*.

of the caliphate, it came about that the standard denominational definitions of the three traditional Christian communities in the Middle East (when viewed from the community-building perspective as opposed to just their theological or Christological profiles) were all in Syriac or Arabic. One finds these definitions most clearly articulated in the chronicles and histories composed by writers in the several denominations, as they strove to give voice to their communities' experiences under Muslim rule. They belonged to the cultural world of Islam, isolated from and in large part estranged from western Christians, both Latin- and Greek-speaking. Tellingly, when the latter did come into the world of Islam, as they did increasingly after the time of the Crusades, they lived apart from and often in tension with the local Christians.

The culture of Christians under Muslim rule

The communal life of Christians from Baghdad to Cordoba lost its erstwhile dominant public presence as the Christians were gradually absorbed into what had become the readily recognizable "Islamic world" so aptly described by Albert Hourani:

> By the third and fourth Islamic centuries (the ninth or tenth century A.D.) something which was recognizably an "Islamic world" had emerged. A traveler around the world would have been able to tell, by what he saw and heard, whether a land was ruled and peopled by Muslims. . . . By the tenth century, then, men and women in the Near East and the Maghrib lived in a universe which was defined in terms of Islam. . . . Time was marked by the five daily prayers, the weekly sermon in the mosque, the annual fast in the month of Ramadan and the pilgrimage to Mecca, and the Muslim calendar.[17]

After Christians in the world of Islam adopted the Arabic language, theological writers of the first Abbasid century, like Abū Qurra, Abū-Rā'iṭa, and 'Ammār al-Baṣrī, together crafted a distinctive theological response in Arabic to the challenge of Islam. Composed in equal measures of polemic and apologetic elements, it addressed both their Muslim challengers and, at the same time, their theological adversaries in the other Christian communities of the Islamic world. As a result, their discourse presents a readily recognizable, literary and conceptual profile that cannot easily be mistaken for Christian theology in any other community of discourse. Their approach to the reasoned articulation in Arabic of Trinitarian doctrines, and the Incarnation in particular, involved

17 Hourani, *History*, 54–57.

the effort to express the former in terms of contemporary Islamic discussion on the ontological status of the divine attributes (the Qur'ān's "beautiful names of God") and to voice the latter in the distinctive language of the Qur'ān's prophetology, supplemented by defenses of each community's traditional Christological formulae. This theological development became traditional in Arabic-language Christian theological discourse in the Islamic world; it was improved over the centuries by many subsequent writers, but scarcely ever abandoned until modern times. It makes sense and carries intelligibility and conviction only in the Arabic-speaking, Islamic milieu; it is not easily translated into the theological idioms of the West. And it underpins a very different expression of a Christian estimation of Muḥammad, the Qur'ān, and Islam than almost anything one can find in Greek, Latin, or other languages of the Christian West in the same time period.[18] There is in it a willingness to recognize not only a challenge, but also an opportunity to put forward Christianity's claims to veracity in a new key using the categories of the religiously *other*.

The first moment of the Christian adjustment to life in the world of Islam thus inaugurated not only a new ecclesiastical language, but also a new development in theology. In the second moment, comprising a period extending roughly from 850 to 1050, Christian scholarship in the caliphate, and particularly in Baghdad, made major contributions to intellectual life in the Islamic world at large. Unlike the earlier, theological development, which is hardly recognized beyond the boundaries of the Islamic world itself even by Christians, the indigenous Christian contribution to the Greco-Arabic translation movement in Baghdad is well known and often discussed by western scholars.[19] Even today, historians in the West are likely to recognize the names of "Arab Christians" such as Ḥunayn ibn Isḥāq (808–73), Yaḥyā ibn 'Adī (893–974), or Abū-'Alī 'Īsā ibn Isḥāq ibn Zur'a (943–1008), to name only three of them, who played active roles in the enterprise to provide Arabic translations of the philosophical, scientific, and medical texts of the Greco-Roman world, most often on the basis of earlier Syriac versions of the originally Greek works. Many of the works of Aristotle were of particular importance. In their Arabic versions they played an important role in developing the thoughts of world-class, Arabic-speaking philosophers, such as al-Fārābī (870–950), Ibn Sīnā / Avicenna (980–1037), or Ibn Rushd / Averroes (1126–98), not to mention polymath, non-Muslim, Arabic-speaking scholars such as the Jew Moses Maimonides

18 Samir, "Prophet Muḥammad."
19 Gutas, *Greek Thought, Arabic Culture*.

(1135–1204) or the Christian Barhebraeus (1226–86).[20] Of course, most of these names were to become familiar to western scholars of the high Middle Ages due to yet another translation movement, the one associated with centers such as Cordoba, Toledo, or Barcelona in the eleventh and twelfth centuries. There the Arabic versions of Greek-speaking philosophers' and scientists' works came into Latin translations and sparked yet another intellectual renaissance.[21]

What is not to be missed in the story of Christians living under Muslim rule between the conquest and the beginning of the twelfth century (that is, basically until the eruption of the Crusaders from the West into the Islamic world) is the demographic strength of the Christian presence in that world, even in quintessentially Islamic locations like Baghdad, founded in 763 to be the Islamic city par excellence. Baghdad came to have a significant number of churches and monasteries, and even a Christian quarter.[22] Christian physicians, scientists, civil servants, court officials, and intellectuals were everywhere in the Abbasid society of the period, many of them from prominent Nestorian families.[23]

The figure of the Aristotelian philosopher and logician the Jacobite Yaḥyā ibn ʿAdī (d. 974) might well be taken as a model of how high a degree of *convivencia* was possible, at least in some places in the heart of the Islamic world, such as tenth-century Baghdad. No account of intellectual life at that time would be complete without at least a mention of this Christian philosopher. For a generation he was the leading figure in the Baghdad circle of Aristotelians. He was himself the student of the Nestorian Christian logician Abū Bishr Mattā ibn Yūnus (d. 940) and the Muslim philosopher al-Fārābī. In his own turn, Yaḥyā was the master of a whole group of students, Muslims and Christians, Jacobites and Nestorians, whose names historians still recognize readily as major players in the humanistic "renaissance of Islam" in the Buyid age.[24] We know from Yaḥyā's own works that he envisioned a society in which Muslims and Christians devoted to knowledge and science could work together in pursuit of philosophy. They would be concerned, he said, with attendance at churches and mosques, and have it as their purpose to "give people an interest in eternal life."[25] One cannot help but recognize the interreligious vocabulary he chose to voice his ideals. But many in Islamic society, both Christian and Muslim,

20 Peeters, *Aristotle and the Arabs*.
21 Makdisi, *Rise of Humanism*; Butterworth et al., *Introduction of Arabic Philosophy*; Roisse, "La circulation du savoir."
22 Allard, "Les chrétiens à Baghdad"; Fiey, *Chrétiens syriaques*.
23 Massignon, "La politique islamo-chrétienne."
24 Kraemer, *Humanism in the Renaissance*.
25 Yaḥyā Ibn ʿAdī, *Reformation of Morals*, 3.45, 62–63.

in fact were unhappy with the easy relationships between the communities in certain highly privileged places. Many Christians complained of persecution and ill-treatment; many Muslims chafed at the freedom of speech enjoyed by non-Muslims.

In this connection, one may cite an interesting passage from the biographical dictionary of Spanish Arabs by the eleventh-century CE author Abū ʿAbdallāh ibn Muḥammad al-Ḥumaydī (d. 1095). He tells the story of a certain Abū ʿUmar Aḥmad ibn Muḥammad ibn Saʿdī, who visited Baghdad at the end of the tenth century, not long after the death of Yaḥyā ibn ʿAdī. While he was there, Abū ʿUmar twice visited the sessions of some famous Muslim scholars of the city, but he vowed he would never attend them again. He was shocked at what he found in them. He is reported to have given the following account of his experience:

> At the first session I attended I witnessed a meeting which included every kind of group: *Sunnī* Muslims and heretics, and all kinds of infidels: Majūs, materialists, atheists, Jews and Christians.
>
> Each group had a leader who would speak on its doctrine and debate about it. Whenever a leader arrived, from whichever of the groups he was, the assembly rose up for him, standing on their feet until he would sit down, then they would take their seats when he sat. When the meeting was jammed with its participants, and they saw that no one else was expected, one of the infidels said, "You have all agreed to the debate, so the Muslims should not argue against us on the basis of their scripture, nor on the basis of the sayings of their prophet, since we put not credence in it, and we do not acknowledge him. Let us dispute with one another only on the basis of arguments from reason, and what observation and deduction will support." Then they would all say, "Agreed." Abū ʿUmar said, "When I heard that, I did not return to that meeting. Later someone told me there was to be another meeting for discussion, so I went to it and I found them involved in the same practice as their colleagues. So I stopped going to the meetings of the discussants, and I never went back."[26]

Clearly, Abū ʿUmar can be taken as a spokesman for the Muslim traditionalists in the later Abbasid era, who may well have been in the majority in Yaḥyā ibn ʿAdī's day. He clearly disapproved of the very easy exchanges between the intellectuals of the several religious communities in the Islamic commonwealth that Yaḥyā himself was so fond of promoting.

In the twelfth and thirteenth centuries, the center of gravity in Arab Christian cultural evolution shifted from Baghdad and the East, westward into Egypt. The Copts had begun to write theology in Arabic and to translate their

26 Abū ʿAbd Allāh al-Ḥumaydī, *Jadhwat al-Muqtabis*, 101–102.

church books into the language of the dominant culture only in the tenth century. The earliest Copt regularly to write in Arabic, whose name we know, is Severus ibn al-Muqaffa' (c. 905–87). In the Arabic-speaking world Severus's apologetic works have been among the most frequently copied and the most widely disseminated of Christian texts in Arabic.[27] After the time of Severus ibn al-Muqaffa', Arabic quickly became the principal language of the Copts, and they went on to produce more texts in Arabic than all the other Christian communities in the caliphate put together.

In the thirteenth century CE in Egypt there dawned what many have called a golden age in Arab Christian literature.[28] It is symbolized by the activities of a remarkable family of Christian scribes and writers who are altogether called the Awlād al-'Assāl, who flourished during the middle years of the century (1230–60). Three principals emerged, aṣ-Rafī, Hibatallāh, and al-Mu'taman, who undertook impressive programs of manuscript discovery: copying, translating, and composing original works of Christian theology in Arabic.[29] One of the notable features of their work is the obviously ecumenical character it assumed; they relentlessly sought out the best Christian tracts in Arabic wherever they could find them, whether their authors were Nestorians, Jacobites, or Melkites. One of them, al-Mu'taman (probably taking his cue from an earlier writer named Abū 'Alī Narīf ibn Yumn (d. after 983), a Melkite in the circle of the Jacobite Yaḥyā Ibn 'Adī in Baghdad) in his magisterial *Summary of the Principles of Religion* spoke of how all Christian communities and denominations professed the same faith in Christ, albeit differing in their theologies.[30]

Finally among the Copts there was Shams al-Ri'āsa Abū l-Barakāt, often known under the name Ibn Kabar (d. after 1321). He wrote a virtual encyclopedia of Christian theology in Arabic, into which he subsumed texts of many earlier writers from the several communities. His work is almost a reference book for Christian theology and ecclesiastical practice in Arabic, from its beginnings to the thirteenth century.[31] He called it *A Lamp in the Darkness*. The title evokes a sense of the many difficulties and disabilities that Christians under Muslim rule increasingly came to experience, especially in the wake of the Crusades, and during the long years of Mamluk rule (1254–1517) in Egypt and in the Arabic-speaking world of Islam more generally when Christian populations began their long decline.

27 Griffith, "*Kitāb miṣbāḥ al-'aql.*"
28 Rubenson, "Translating the Tradition."
29 Graf, *Geschichte* 2, 387–414.
30 Samir, "Un traité."
31 Graf, *Geschichte* 2, 438–45.

The sorrows of "dhimmitude"

Christians under Muslim rule during the first half-millennium of the Islamic commonwealth no doubt opened a new chapter in Christian history, one which western historians have been slow to read in detail. Internally, there were remarkable developments in Christian life and thought, evident in the texts written in Arabic in all three of the principal Christian denominations in the Middle East. Externally, in terms of the contributions Christians made to the growth and development of classical Islamic culture, the record is in many instances extraordinary. But in spite of these accomplishments, the Christian experience in the caliphate up to the time of the Crusades, albeit one of a mighty and faithful religious witness, was not in fact an entirely happy one. From the very beginning of the Islamic conquest, Christians consistently testified to the multiple hardships they suffered at the hands of Muslims. In chronicles and other literary genres there is a continuous record of persistent deprivation and even intermittent persecution.

The history of Christians under Muslim rule is a history of continuous, if gradual, diminishment. Over the centuries the numbers decreased from a substantial majority of the population in many places in the conquered territories before the Crusades to significant minorities in most of the Islamic world by Ottoman times. The history of the consolidation of Muslim rule, therefore, is also the history of the decline of the public presence of Christianity in the Islamic commonwealth. It is hard to pinpoint the proximate causes of this gradual Christian diminishment, beyond the natural attrition that the attractiveness of a new religious allegiance would have held for upwardly, socially mobile individuals in the subject, Christian communities. But there is one factor in the process that has not received as much scholarly attention as it should. It is the social condition of Christians, theoretically mandated in Islamic law, which one might most handily identify by the neologism "dhimmitude."

The Qur'ān speaks of the special poll-tax *(jizya)* that is to be demanded of the People of the Book who live in the world of Islam, and of the appropriately submissive, low, social profile that they should assume in paying it (Qur'ān 9.29), later to be regulated by the stipulations of the *Covenant of 'Umar*. Historically, the tax has been interpreted as the price for the special "protection" *(al-dhimma)* or responsibility which the Islamic government would then assume for the People of the Book in Islamic society – a kind of answerability for dependent persons (not without a note of dispraise in the verbal root of the Arabic word). Persons of this condition are then described by the Arabic adjective *dhimmī*, meaning someone under the protection and responsibility of the Islamic government, hence the neologism, "dhimmitude."[32] The Christian populations under Muslim rule were considered to be *dhimmī* populations; they were often governed through the offices of their own leaders, in a so-called millet system, to give the arrangement the name it had in late Ottoman times. "Millet" is the Turkish form of the Arabic word *milla* (pl. *milal*), used in the present context in the sense of "religious denomination or creedal community" implying as well a certain political or "national" distinctiveness.[33] Under the Abbasids, theoretically the official Christian leader was the catholicos/patriarch of the Nestorians and resident in Baghdad.

There is no doubt that up to Crusader times, the *dhimmī* populations in the Islamic world were "second-class citizens." The legal disabilities which governed their lives required subservience, often accompanied by prescriptions to wear distinctive clothing and to cease public display of their religion, and, of course, to refrain from inviting converts from among the Muslims. What is more, Christian wealth, buildings, institutions, and properties were often subject to seizure.[34] As a consequence, over the course of time, the number of bishoprics, churches, monasteries, and schools gradually decreased, having fallen victim to the conditions inherent in the official establishment of Islam as the public religion of the polity. These circumstances necessarily put *dhimmī* groups such as the Christian communities at risk; in spite of their numbers they became sociological minorities, subaltern populations subject to discrimination, disability, and at times even persecution. In response, their disadvantaged situation in life inevitably elicited from these Christians both a discourse of accommodation and a discourse of resistance; attempted philosophical or religious rapprochement, along with a literature of ideological subversion and martyrdom.

Martyrologies were popular among Christians under Muslim rule. The few which tell the stories of martyrs in Islamic times, the so-called "new martyrs," were for the most part narratives whose tales of their sufferings, and especially of their speeches, consciously evoked memories of the old martyrs from the early Christian era under the persecuting Roman emperors before Constantine (r. 324–37). The new martyrologies in Greek, Syriac, Coptic, Arabic, or even in Latin in Islamic Spain, which recount the stories of fatal confrontations between Christian martyrs and Muslim authorities, are rich in details that almost by the way contain accounts of the vicissitudes of Christian life under the

32 Ye'or, *Decline of Eastern Christianity*; see rather Y. Friedman's *Tolerance and Coercion*.
33 Ursinus, "Millet."
34 Fattal, *Le statut légal*.

Muslims.[35] In the literary repartee between the martyrs and their persecutors, the martyr always trumps his interrogator. The not-so-subtle or hidden subtext here for the *dhimmī* Christian reader was the message that, in spite of all appearances to the contrary, he should rest confident that Christianity really is the true religion. There is also the clear suggestion that Christians actually do have the scriptural and reasonable arguments available to prove their moral superiority, if only the oppressive power of established Islam would allow listeners to accept the inescapable conclusions of persuasive demonstrations. But martyr narratives from the Christian communities under Muslim rule were in fact relatively few. The participation of Christians in the cultural life of the world of Islam, albeit in dhimmitude, meant that the customary messages of martyrologies had to be communicated in other genres as well.

A prevalent genre of popular apologetics and polemics among Arabic-speaking Christians in the caliphate regularly featured a monk or other Christian notable being interrogated in a caliph's or an emir's court.[36] These literary dialogues, written by Christians for Christians, sometimes had a basis in well-known, historical encounters; often they were simply true-to-life fiction as history. As in the martyrologies, in these works the monk always trumps his interrogators. What is not to be missed in them is the fact that in the context of a fetching story, full of witty repartee, the narratives do supply ready answers to the questions and challenges which Muslims customarily posed to Christians about their religion. Perhaps this feature explains the enduring popularity of these compositions among Christians living under Muslim rule.

On the Muslim side there was also a steady supply of polemical tracts written against Christians and Christianity.[37] From the ninth century until the time of the Crusades, and increasingly after the Mongol invasions of the thirteenth century and the destruction of Baghdad in 1258, one can detect a distinctive hardening of approach in Islamic writings on the subject of interreligious relations. A harbinger of the attitude to come can be seen in Ibn Taymiyya's (1263–1328) *al-Jawāb al-Ṣaḥīḥ*, a text that established a distinctly and widely influential hardline approach to the *dhimmī* populations which would become enormously influential in later, more traditionalist Muslim circles.[38]

After the golden age of Christian Arabic literature in the thirteenth century in Egypt, Christians of course continued to write in Arabic and often to

35 Griffith, "Christians, Muslims and Neo-martyrs"; Wolf, *Christian Martyrs*; Coope, *Martyrs of Córdoba*; Zaborowski, *Neo-Martyr*.

36 Griffith, "Monk in the Emir's *Majlis*."

37 Bouamama, *Littérature polémique musulmane*; Waardenburg, *Muslim Perceptions*, esp. 18–69, 312–26.

38 Michel, *Muslim Theologian's Response*.

take prominent positions in Islamic society. But by this time the distinctive profile of their culture had already been determined, and the vicissitudes of the struggle to survive absorbed more and more energy from the churches. In Ottoman times, and later under colonial rule, many Christians under Muslim rule formed protective relationships with Christians outside the world of Islam. In practice, this step often meant further divisions among them, a circumstance that has hastened their demographic decline in modern times, as many eastern Christians have emigrated to the West.

10

Latin and Greek Christians

TIA M. KOLBABA

At the end of Late Antiquity, when this chapter begins, the Alps were a Great Divide between Mediterranean cultures and transalpine ones; Rome and Constantinople had more in common with one another than either did with Germanic groups in the north. The emperors in Constantinople still wielded enough authority in Rome to arrest popes who resisted their policies, and the papal *apokrisiarios* at the imperial court was an important figure in Rome. But by 1100 the popes themselves often came from north of the Alps, few in the West knew Greek, and imperial authority, when acknowledged in Rome, came from Germany. The Latin world, developing with, assimilated to, and combined with the Germanic world of northwestern Europe, had lost sympathy for imperial and Byzantine ways of ruling while developing its own hierarchies. The role and prestige of the popes in the western church was beyond the ken of Byzantines, while the role of the emperor in the eastern church puzzled and appalled Latin Christians. Theological and ritual differences added to a general sense of estrangement, reflected most famously in chronicles of the crusades. To describe relations between Greek and Latin Christians between the seventh century and the eleventh is, then, to write the history of the schism between the Roman Catholic and Greek Orthodox churches. Yet overabundant hindsight lurks in such a statement. A narrative which begins at the end – with schism – tends to overemphasize disagreements in earlier eras and to overlook charity and cooperation. It tends to rely on sources that "explain" the origins of the schism and to overlook sources that assume or explicitly say that there was no schism at all. And it therefore tends to flatten and obscure what should be a textured and clear portrait of two societies and their churches, connected by a common past yet increasingly alienated by different experiences in the early Middle Ages.

600–751: three invasions

In the seventh century Muslims began to build an empire that changed the structure of the Christian world. By the early eighth century they controlled the eastern and southern shores of the Mediterranean and the Iberian peninsula. Ironically, one problem that had plagued relations between Rome and Constantinople in the sixth and seventh centuries was thus solved: the empire no longer needed to balance the anti-Chalcedonian populations of the East, now mostly under Muslim rule, against the Chalcedonian leadership of Rome.[1] Instead of easing relations between Rome and Constantinople, however, this new situation made them more contentious. Already before the Arab invasions, the patriarchs of Constantinople had sought recognition of their see's equality with Rome, including a universal jurisdiction in the East to match Rome's jurisdiction in the West.[2] But when, in the sixth century, the patriarch of Constantinople used the title of "ecumenical (*oikoumenikos*) patriarch," Rome protested.[3] Constantinople, the popes maintained, had no legitimate claim to authority beyond its own see, while Rome's primacy throughout the Christian world was based on the apostle Peter's status.[4] After the Arab invasions, Constantinople was the only eastern patriarchate not under Muslim rule, its claims to eastern primacy were therefore more convincing, and papal objections to those claims were more strenuous.

The Arab invasions contributed to the separation of Constantinople from the western provinces in other ways as well. The eastern empire's fight for its own life left few resources to send westward, while Lombard invasions made Rome and Ravenna islands in a Lombard sea. The popes led the response of northern Italy to this invasion. Gregory I (590–604) was not the only pope to organize the defense and supply of Rome during sieges and to negotiate with "barbarian" attackers, although he is the most famous. The result of such vigor was another increase in papal autonomy and prestige.

The third invasion of the period further disrupted communications between Latin and Greek Christians. From the middle of the sixth century to the middle of the seventh, Slavic groups settled in the Balkan provinces and the Peloponnese. Thessaloniki became the last Greek, Christian outpost in territory otherwise belonging to polytheistic Slavs. The imperial land routes across the region, connecting Constantinople to Thessaloniki and then to ports on the Adriatic

1 See Dorfmann-Lazarev and Louth in this volume.
2 Dvornik, *Byzantium and Roman Primacy*, 80.
3 Pelagius II, *Epistola VI*; Gregory I, *Registrum epistolarum* I, v.37, 39, 41.
4 Dvornik, *Byzantium and Roman Primacy*, 40–59.

Sea, were severed, significantly reducing the everyday flow of people and information. Slavic pirates also disrupted communication by sea. In the fifth and sixth centuries some art forms, theological ideas, institutional forms, and literary trends had shared common features throughout the Mediterranean world; in the seventh century such commonality was much diminished. Moreover, Latin speakers and Latin churches in the Balkans, not uncommon through the sixth century, disappeared in the wake of the Slavic invasions – the loss of some of the bilingual, bicultural intermediaries who had formed a kind of permeable membrane between the Latin and Greek ends of the Mediterranean.

As their worlds shrank, the worldviews of westerners and easterners narrowed. In Italy, the empire and its Hellenic culture became less and less relevant to the day-to-day concerns of popes, aristocrats, and people. Meanwhile, the eastern empire had survived the seventh century by retreating to a limited heartland with a broad frontier of defense-in-depth. The old Mediterranean-wide empire and church had encompassed many different *ethnoi*, many different cultures, many different rituals. The new, contracted empire was largely Greek-speaking with less variation in religious practice. Its people consoled themselves with the belief that their troubles had been God's way of purifying his Chosen People, but if the favor of God and the survival of their empire depended upon their purity, any deviance had to be eliminated. The opponents of Chalcedon had their just desserts, sentenced to be ruled by infidels. Those "deviants" who remained in the empire had to be corrected as well. Jews, for example, had to be baptized – by force, if necessary; to tolerate deviance was to risk God's wrath and the survival of the *oikoumene*.[5]

Still, Rome was not deviant. St. Peter was in Rome, as were his successors, the premier defenders of orthodoxy. In 680–81, bishops gathered in Constantinople to condemn the monothelitism of Heraclius (610–41) and his heirs. Pope Agatho (678–81) sent doctrinal letters from Rome to this Sixth Ecumenical Council, explicating orthodox teaching on the two natures, wills, and operations in Jesus Christ. His teaching was praised and endorsed by the assembly in its official proceedings and in letters to the emperor and the pope.[6] Such papal prestige had been made possible by papal autonomy; the popes had led the resistance to monothelitism because the emperors could not control them. Nevertheless, widespread admiration of the pope was outweighed by diminished contact between East and West. The same council that praised Agatho included so few representatives of western sees that eastern bishops

5 Haldon, *Byzantium*, 38–40, 324–75, 436–58.
6 Mansi 11, 665, 684; cited and translated by Dvornik, *Byzantium and Roman Primacy*, 92.

might have thought that the western church was shrinking to a small minority population.[7] That was a dangerous illusion. Overlooking the Christians of northwestern Europe, the Byzantines failed to understand how those northerners were revitalizing the western church. The pope's flock grew by looking northward for new sheep, and those sheep, with little knowledge of eastern Christians and little respect for eastern emperors, heeded the voice of the shepherd in Rome in ways no Constantinopolitan understood.[8]

Moreover, if it was easy to praise the pope from a distance and on a matter of doctrine which had been settled before the council met, disciplinary canons were different. The Fifth and Sixth Ecumenical Councils had provided no such canons, the world had changed a great deal between the Fourth Ecumenical Council and the end of the seventh century, and churchmen in the empire needed rules responding to those changes. Emperor Justinian II (685–95, 705–11) therefore convened a council, known as the Council in Trullo or the Quinisext Council, in Constantinople in 692.[9] Although there were officially representatives of all five patriarchates at the council, of the 220 bishops who signed the final collection of canons, 183 represented sees within the patriarchate of Constantinople. Only ten – all from Illyricum – were under the jurisdiction of Rome. The pope would normally have sent a legate invested with authority to act for the Holy See. Instead, the *Acta* of Trullo were signed only by the *apokrisiarios*, the pope's semipermanent representative in Constantinople who was not empowered to act for the pope at an ecumenical council.[10]

The Quinisext Council comprised, in short, bishops from the eastern empire. It concentrated on two issues important to the imperial church: the reorganization and preservation of the ecclesiastical hierarchy of the empire within its diminished territory and the uniformity of liturgy and practice within the empire. The former had little relevance for Latins and they paid it scant attention. The latter, however, raised hackles in Rome. Obsessed with uniformity and convinced that Constantinople's practices ought to be the norm, the eastern bishops condemned various Roman customs that differed from their own. In addition, the first canon of the council included Pope Honorius I (625–38) in the catalogue of heretical monothelites, while the thirty-sixth confirmed the twenty-eighth canon of the Council of Chalcedon, which had stated that the Patriarch of Constantinople "is to enjoy privileges equal to those of

7 Mansi 11, 583–88; Murphy and Sherwood, *Constantinople II et Constantinople III*.

8 See Abrams in this volume; Noble, "Tradition and Learning," 244–46.

9 Mansi 11, 929–88; Laurent, "L'œuvre canonique"; Nedungatt and Featherstone, *Council in Trullo*.

10 Laurent, "L'œuvre canonique," 13–15; Dagron, "L'église . . . entre les invasions et l'iconoclasme," in *Histoire du Christianisme* 4, 60–61.

the see of the older Rome and to be magnified as it is in ecclesiastical affairs, coming second after it" – a canon that Rome had never accepted.[11] When Pope Sergius I (687–701) refused to sign the *Acta*, Justinian II sent an imperial official to arrest him. The people of Rome, backed by troops from Ravenna and the Pentapolis, defended the pope. Instead of seizing the pope, the official found himself in mortal danger and escaped only because the pope protected him. The difference between the eastern church, in which imperial power was omnipresent and dominant, and the western church, in which no unified secular power challenged the papacy, was obvious. So, too, the popes had another occasion to celebrate themselves and their predecessors as the defenders of orthodoxy against the tyranny of the emperor.[12]

Not only defenders of orthodoxy, the popes were also defenders of the orthodox flock. When Islamic invasions drove large numbers of eastern Chalcedonian Christians into exile, many settled in Rome, southern Italy, and Sicily. When iconoclasm became imperial policy in the eighth century, still more Greek-speaking, Greek-rite people settled within the Roman patriarchate. Their influence was substantial; between 678 and 752, eleven of the thirteen popes were Greek speakers from Syria, Sicily, or Constantinople. Although this seems to have meant little in terms of their attitudes toward the emperor – they defended their see's prerogatives as vigorously as any Roman-born pope – they exemplify a period in which Roman awareness of the eastern churches and the empire was very high. Numerous Greek monasteries in Rome added to the relatively high level of Hellenic influence in this period.[13]

751–843: popes and Franks

For the Byzantine Empire, the seventh century had been traumatic, while the eighth century saw progress toward a new equilibrium. Muslim and Avar armies had been turned back at the walls of Constantinople, and the thematic system of provincial military and civil administration provided a stable defense. This was a much diminished empire, but it had some leisure to consider its altered position in the world. Although the eighth century is known as the period of iconoclasm, and iconoclasm as a period of great strife, recent interpretations have challenged that view, coming to see the era not as "a crisis that lasted 120 years," but rather as "a period of stability and consolidation

11 Mansi 6, 182–87; Nedungatt and Featherstone, *Council in Trullo*, 114.
12 Noble, *Republic*, 18–19.
13 Noble, *Republic*, 185; Sansterre, *Les moines grecs et orientaux*, passim.

after a crisis."[14] The Latin church, in contrast, was not yet through with crises; stability and consolidation had not yet come to Italy. Seeking greater security, the popes made a move that changed the world.

In 749, faced with a revival of the Lombard threat, the popes turned northward for protection. In 753 Pope Stephen III (752–57) became the first Roman bishop to cross the Alps into the Kingdom of the Franks. There he contracted an alliance with Pippin III (751–68), crowning and anointing Pippin and his sons while they undertook to defend St. Peter's patrimony.[15] Pippin's heirs, the Carolingian kings, deferred to the popes and took Roman liturgy, theology, and canon law as models, while Frankish military might enabled the papacy to consolidate its independence from Constantinople without becoming subject to the Lombards. When, on Christmas Day 800, Pope Leo III (795–816) crowned Charlemagne Emperor of the Romans, he threw his see's authority and prestige behind "the Emperor of the Romans" who hailed from Francia. The long-term implications of these moves were enormous.

But was it clear at the time that the popes had, once and for all, chosen this western emperor over the Emperor of the Romans in Constantinople? Romans and Constantinopolitans still shared a certain condescension toward the Franks. Although both recognized that the Franks had become too important to ignore, nobody expected them to *think*. To western *Romani* and eastern *Romaioi* alike the Franks were the pope's devoted-but-barbarous servants. In this belief, they were wrong. Some men who worked for the Frankish king were not illiterate warriors, but scholars who could think, read, and argue theology – even to the point of disagreeing with the pope. The Seventh Ecumenical Council (787), the second held in Nicaea, provided the occasion for such disagreement. In 785 the Empress Irene (780–802), her son Constantine VI (780–97), and the Patriarch Tarasius (784–806) sought Rome's support for a council to restore the veneration of icons. Pope Hadrian I (772–95) sent representatives to Nicaea, but nobody consulted the Franks. When the council refuted the arguments of the iconoclasts and promulgated its own doctrine of icon veneration, the pope's representatives signed, and the pope rejoiced. Still, it seems, he did not send the *Acta* of 787 to the Frankish king. Instead, the Franks acquired a copy of a Latin translation of the *Acta* in such a way that they thought the document was an official record of the council.[16] Charlemagne's scholars were appalled. Perhaps, given the lack of Frankish representation at

14 Dagron, "L'iconoclasme et l'établissement de l'Orthodoxie," in *Histoire du Christianisme* 4, 93.
15 Noble, *Republic*, 80–88, 277–91.
16 Freeman, "Carolingian Orthodoxy," 76–80; Noble, "Tradition and Learning," 230–31.

the council, they would have rejected the Nicene decisions even if they had had an accurate translation; as it was, they had a woefully inaccurate one.[17] They compiled a list of the faults they found in the document and sent it to Rome.[18] Theodulf of Orleans composed a more-complete and organized refutation of the Acts of 787, the *Opus Caroli Regis contra Synodum (Libri Carolini)*. Although Hadrian rejected their arguments and praised the council, the Frankish hierarchy did not forget the issue; it arose again during the second period of iconoclasm in the East. At a synod in 825, Louis the Pious (814–40) and his clergy revealed a continuing conviction that the Greeks had gone too far at the Seventh Ecumenical Council. They reaffirmed the didactic purpose of images, quoting Pope Gregory I: "What Scripture is to those who read, images are to the ignorant, for in those images the ignorant see what they must do."[19] But they also continued to claim that *veneration* of icons was idolatry.

Charlemagne's and Louis's theologians were erudite and confident of their own abilities, but they were hampered by a bad translation and by a lack of sympathy for eastern traditions. In all these ways they foreshadowed their descendants, the northern churchmen who were to play a large role in the separation between Rome and Constantinople in the eleventh century.

Nor was the reaction to the Seventh Ecumenical Council the only time that the Franks differed with the popes in the ninth century, for at the very heart of the Christian creed there was a difference between Francia and Rome. In the late sixth or early seventh century the Frankish church had accepted an addition to the Nicene-Constantinopolitan creed: where that creed originally read, "I believe in the Holy Spirit . . . who proceeds from the Father," the phrase "and from the Son" (in Latin, *Filioque*) was added. This addition, which was never accepted in the East, was not accepted in Rome yet, either. Although Pope Leo III (795–816) explicitly agreed with the theological statement that the Spirit proceeds from the Father and the Son, he ordered the Franks to stop reciting the *Filioque* in the creed and had the creed in its "correct" form, without the *Filioque*, inscribed on plaques and erected in St Peter's.[20] In other words, on the form of the creed at least, Rome and Constantinople agreed against Aachen. The two-way interchange between Rome and Constantinople that

17 Noble, "Tradition and Learning," 243–44.

18 Freeman, "Carolingian Orthodoxy," 105–106; Noble, "Tradition and Learning," 231–32.

19 Freeman, "Carolingian Orthodoxy," 101–106; Herrin, *Formation*, 469–72; Gregory I, *Registrum epistolarum* 2, xi.10.

20 On the nature of this ninth-century conflict, it is especially important to understand certain problems with sources that record an East–West conflict over the *Filioque* in the early ninth century. See Sode, *Jerusalem–Konstantinopel–Rom*; Callahan, "Problem of the 'Filioque'."

had characterized the seventh and eighth centuries was yielding to a three-way relationship among popes, Byzantines, and Franks.

843–996: the triangle: popes, Byzantines, and Franks

Throughout the ninth and tenth centuries, the rivalry of the great sees of Rome and Constantinople continued, for the pope continued to assert his right to judge the other patriarchs, and the patriarchs continued to disagree. Some of the resulting quarrels are rightly famous, crucial as they are for the history of relations between Roman popes and Constantinopolitan patriarchs. The so-called "Photian Schism" of the ninth century saw much papal assertion of jurisdiction, even over other patriarchs, countered by equally vehement patriarchal denial of such claims. The tetragamy crisis – in which a patriarch excommunicated the emperor because of his fourth marriage, but the pope granted a dispensation – raised the same issues. So, too, the popes continued to object to the eastern patriarch's use of the title *oikoumenikos* – only the pope had "ecumenical" authority, in the western view. Important for many reasons, these conflicts mostly reprise longstanding issues of papal versus patriarchal authority.[21]

The new feature of this period was the relationship among popes, Byzantines, and Franks. By their consistent opposition to iconoclasm, their welcome for iconophile refugees from the empire, and their role in the Seventh Ecumenical Council, the popes of the eighth and early ninth centuries had added to their treasury of esteem in Constantinople. Such esteem was clearly one factor behind the willingness of Byzantine missionaries in Slavic lands to acknowledge papal jurisdiction in central Europe. Moreover, papal support for the Byzantine mission in Pannonia was part of a struggle between the popes and the East Frankish rulers for control of the churches in that region.[22] Meanwhile, Byzantines and Franks were in direct contact in Bulgaria, as well. Here again debates did not always feature the pope and Frankish missionaries on one side and Byzantines on the other. Although the popes supported and sometimes controlled the Latin mission, the Franks were teaching the *Filioque*, which Rome had still not accepted, to the Slavs. Differences between Rome and the Franks regarding the *Filioque*, the role of lay rulers in the church, and the use of icons remained. Meanwhile, Photius (patriarch of Constantinople

21 Photian schism: Hussey, *Orthodox Church*, 72–86. Tetragamy: ibid., 103–108. Photius and the meaning of "ecumenical patriarch": Dagron, "L'église et l'état," in *Histoire du Christianisme* 4, 206–207.

22 Dvornik, "Significance of the Missions," 206–209.

858–67, 877–86) produced a statement regarding the erroneous teachings of the Frankish missionaries in Bulgaria, headed by the *Filioque*. He knew, however, that the popes in Rome had not accepted the addition to the creed.[23] It would have been impossible at this point to predict the alliances and schisms of the centuries to come.

On the other hand, powerful forces were moving the papacy and the Franks closer to one another. The most important factor remained the protection that Frankish rulers could provide. Although the breakup of Charlemagne's empire after the treaty of Verdun (843) diminished Frankish influence in Rome in the ninth and tenth centuries, the alternative was not attractive: a papacy dominated by contests among Roman noble families who treated the papal throne as one of the spoils of victory. The prestige of the papacy suffered as a result. It was going to take a dramatic change to restore the pope's reputation throughout Europe.

996–1100: the transformation of the western church

The change came from north of the Alps through a motivated group of men dedicated to papal independence, supported by a new line of rulers, the Ottonians, who intervened effectively in papal elections. This intervention consolidated the alliance of popes and northerners and broke most of the bonds which still connected Rome to Constantinople. Ottonian involvement in Italy differed in two fundamental ways from earlier Carolingian efforts. First, the Ottonian emperors, with their ambitions to control southern Italy, were enemies of the Byzantines in a way that the Carolingians had never been. The resulting political and military enmity contributed to other kinds of hostility, as the infamous invective of Liutprand of Cremona shows. In Liutprand's account of his embassy to Constantinople for Otto I (king 936, emperor 962–73), the contempt of Germans for *Greci* and of *Romaioi* for Germans is never far from the surface. Second, the Ottonians differed from the Carolingians in their handling of contested papal elections and a corrupted papacy. They moved to install reformers from their own lands – "reformers" whose ideas about the role of laity in the church were really quite radical – on the papal throne and thereby began a transformation of western Christian institutions which would divide the churches for centuries to come. In spite of some fits and starts, the general movement of the late tenth and eleventh centuries was toward greater involvement for both German rulers and German clergy in the papacy. No

23 Photius, "Encyclica."

matter who eventually triumphed in the struggle between the German emperors and the popes, the substantial German influences in Rome drove a still larger wedge between the old Rome and the new. In 1014, at the coronation of Henry II (king 1002–24) as emperor, the *Filioque* was introduced into the creed chanted in Rome. This was important in its own right and symbolic of a larger movement, for as the eleventh century progressed, German church reformers went beyond influencing the papacy to controlling it. Meanwhile, Byzantines saw German influence as a kind of usurpation of the ancient see. Small "histories of the schism between Rome and Constantinople" appear in this period, beginning with an account of this Germanic takeover:

> After the adjournment of the seventh council . . . [Pope] Leo summoned a certain Charles from the interior of Francia, and he crowned him as emperor. . . . Some of those who accompanied Charles were heretics . . . and when they entered Rome, they began to corrupt the people of God by saying that the all-holy Spirit proceeded *not* from the Father alone but also from the Son, and by teaching them to offer unleavened bread. And they spoke other nonsense foreign to the Church's tradition.[24]

If this account and others like it are not historically accurate, they nonetheless reflect a common Byzantine perception of what had happened to Rome: a previously civilized and respectable civilization had been swamped by an influx of barbarians.

The early days of papal reform also coincided with the Norman conquest of Byzantine and Lombard lands in southern Italy. Together, papal reform and Norman conquest form the context of the most famous encounter between representatives of the Greek and Latin churches. In 1053 and 1054 one of the German reformer-popes, Leo IX (1049–54), was fighting for his throne in Italy. He sought Constantinople's help against both those who resisted the reform movement and the Normans in southern Italy, who threatened the hard-won independence of the republic of St. Peter. Constantinople's emperor, also fighting the Normans, was willing to form such an alliance. Leo chose Humbert, Cardinal of Silva Candida, to lead a mission to Constantinople to discuss an alliance. Humbert epitomized the reform movement – a northern European, he had come to Rome in the entourage of a German pope and had written an impressive body of polemic on behalf of the reform movement's goals. He was, moreover, already suspicious of the Greek church, for he knew that Greeks criticized the Latin use of unleavened bread (azymes) in the Eucharist.[25] Incensed

24 See "Opuscula de origine schismatis," in *Monumenta graeca*, 155–56.
25 See Leo of Ohrid, *Epistola ad Ioannem*, 835–43.

at any criticism of Roman practice, he especially despised Michael Cerularius, patriarch of Constantinople (1043–58), a known opponent of azymes who was in no way inclined to acknowledge the reformers' version of papal primacy. Humbert went to Constantinople prepared to deal with the patriarch's intransigence.

Seen from Constantinople, however, the *Filioque* was an innovation, the pope's claims to jurisdiction outside his own patriarchate were arrogant, the use of unleavened bread in the Eucharist was illicit, and Germans were barbarians. Cerularius opposed any alliance with the papacy. Humbert talked peace and alliance with the emperor while treating the patriarch as an intransigent suffragan. The results were disastrous. After months of mutual snubbing, wrangling over protocol, and hurling accusations at one another about azymes and other issues, Humbert strode into the Church of Hagia Sophia and deposited a bull of excommunication on the altar; Cerularius responded by convening the standing synod of Constantinople and condemning the papal legates.

These events in 1054 did not mark the final moment of schism, but they do highlight several issues that remained contentious for the rest of the Middle Ages: differences in ritual and theology (azymes, the *Filioque*); differences in ecclesiology (papal *plenitudo potestatis* versus the authority of an ecumenical council in which representatives of Rome, Constantinople, Alexandria, Antioch, and Jerusalem participated); and a lack of charity and mutual respect. The last is most important. Humbert knew some Greek, but he knew little of the eastern church's history, lacked respect for Hellenic culture, and exhibited no desire to understand Hellenic traditions. If Greek practices or doctrine differed from Roman ones, then the Greeks must be wrong. Cerularius was equally contemptuous of Latin rituals and culture. In a letter to the eastern patriarchs he set an unfortunate precedent by including such complaints as the clean-shaven faces of Latin priests in a list of "the obviously lawless, forbidden, and abominable" customs of the Roman church.[26] The goal of Humbert's legation was not achieved. In 1059, the popes accepted Norman rule in southern Italy and contributed to the centuries-long process by which the last of the bilingual, bicultural bridges between Greek and Latin Christians was eroded away.

Yet in the eleventh century, lack of charity and respect was still limited to a few men. None of the breaks between Rome and Constantinople discussed so far involved many people. The contempt that Humbert and Cerularius had

26 Michael Cerularius, *Epistola ad Petrum*, 789–92 or Eng. trans. Kolbaba, *Byzantine Lists*, 23–24.

for one another was not shared even by all of their fellow hierarchs,[27] and it would be some time before it penetrated more deeply into their flocks. The conflicts between the hierarchs of Rome and Constantinople were certainly important, but the centuries before the Crusades were also characterized by positive contact between Greek-speaking, Greek-rite Christians and Latin-speaking, Latin-rite ones. Stories of this contact reveal awareness of differences, but conflict is rare, while cooperation and mutual admiration are common. What follows are a few brief examples of such amity, drawn from the world of monasticism.

In the late tenth century, cenobitic monasticism began to flourish on Mt. Athos.[28] Among the monasteries established during that period was the Great Lavra (963),[29] whose founder, Athanasius the Athonite (c. 925–c. 1001), was a proponent of communal living. Although most of his monastery's rules were based on the *Typikon* of the Studite monastery in Constantinople, Athanasius also had a Greek translation of the Rule of St. Benedict. Monastic traditions varied considerably from a Latin to a Greek monastery, but Athanasius's use of Benedict's Rule is one of many examples of texts common to both cultures. After all, many of the ideals of monks, East and West, came from a common foundation in Scripture and early monastic classics.[30]

The translator of the Athonite's copy of St. Benedict's Rule was probably a Greek from southern Italy.[31] There were houses of Italo-Greek monks from Sicily and Calabria on Athos; the Sicilians were there by 986.[32] Such southern Italian monks were often translators in more than one sense. They could move text from one language to another, manuscripts from one region to another. A few of them were not only bilingual but also bicultural, literally occupying a space between the two worlds.

Meanwhile, Latin monks had also settled on Athos shortly after the Great Laura was founded.[33] St. Athanasius first welcomed the Latin monks into his house and then helped them build their own monastery. The Latin monastery

27 Peter III, Patriarch of Antioch (1052–56), rebuked Cerularius for his intemperate list of Latin "errors" (Peter III, *Dissertatio [ad Michaelem Cerularium]*); Kolbaba, *Byzantine Lists*, 93–98. Later in the century Theophylact of Ohrid found such complaints risible and lacking in charity: Theophylact of Ohrid, *Proslalia*.

28 See Louth in this volume.

29 See Talbot and Kazhdan, "Athos, Mount"; Morris, *Monks and Laymen*, 43–47.

30 See Louth in this volume.

31 Leroy, "S. Athanase l'Athonite," 121.

32 Pertusi, "Monasteri e monaci italiani"; Morris, *Monks and Laymen*, 51.

33 Pertusi, "Monasteri e monaci italiani," 220–24, 230–31; Rousseau, "L'ancien monastère bénédictin"; Lemerle, "Les archives du monastère des Amalfitains"; Pertusi, "Nuovi documenti"; Balard, "Amalfi et Byzance"; von Falkenhausen and Kinney, "Amalfi."

followed the Benedictine rule, and its way of life was admired by its Greek neighbors. For more than a century these Latin monks prospered in the heartland of Greek monasticism. Like the Greek monks of southern and central Italy, they became interpreters and translators. Eventually their brothers in an Amalfitan monastery in Constantinople served in the same way.[34]

Still more interaction between Greek and Latin monks was happening in western monastic centers. In southern Italy, holy men such as Nilus of Rossano continued a renaissance of Greek monasticism that had begun a century earlier. A contemporary of St. Athanasius the Athonite, Greek by birth, education, and rite, Nilus also admired St. Benedict and St. Gregory the Great and advised western emperors and popes.[35] Born in Rossano, Calabria around 910, educated in the traditions of the Greek church, he became a renowned interpreter of the Greek fathers and composer of hymns. Between c. 957 and 980, he founded more than one monastery in northern Calabria. Then, around 980, he left Calabria and went north – first to Capua, then to a house donated by the monastery of Monte Cassino. Living only a few kilometers north of Cassino, Nilus and his brothers spent fifteen years (980–95) in close and friendly relations with Latin monks. The Calabrian composed hymns in honor of St. Benedict, which he and his monks chanted at an all-night service in Monte Cassino's church. The hymns reveal Nilus's knowledge of Gregory the Great's life of Benedict in the original Latin.[36] When the rule of a new abbot at Monte Cassino led to a deterioration of relations between Nilus and the Cassinese house, he and his followers went to Serperi, near Gaeta.[37] Around 1001, he moved for the last time, to found the monastery at Grottaferrata, southeast of Rome, where he died in 1004. Grottaferrata remained an island of Greek monasticism near Rome long after the other Greek monasteries of Rome had either been abandoned or relinquished to Latin monks. Later abbots of Grottaferrata often served as intermediaries between the papacy and the empire. As Greek-speaking, Greek-rite monks who accepted papal authority and lived in Italy, they were the perfect go-betweens.

Although he chose not to settle in Rome, Nilus knew and admired other Greek monks there, especially those who inhabited the monastery of

34 Balard, "Amalfi et Byzance," 87–88; Pertusi, "Monasteri e monaci italiani," 234–37.

35 Other examples of friendly contact between Greek and Latin monks: McNulty and Hamilton, "Orientale Lumen et Magistra Latinitas."

36 On the hymns, see Rousseau, "La visite," 1116–28. On Gregory the Great's *Dialogues* and Nilus's Latin, see Rousseau, "La visite," 1125.

37 The house at Valleluce remained Greek after Nilus's departure, down to 1014: McNulty and Hamilton, "Orientale Lumen et Magistra Latinitas," 186.

St. Alexius, which was at its peak in the 990s.[38] The monastery's history began in 977 when Pope Benedict VII (974–83) and Sergius, the Chalcedonian archbishop of Damascus who had been forced to flee from Syria, revived a diaconia dedicated to St. Boniface of Tarsus. There were not enough Greek monks in Rome to fill the new monastery, so the pope made a radical decision: it would house both Greek and Latin monks and be headed by a Greek abbot. Under its second abbot, Leo (981–99), the primary dedication of the house shifted from St. Boniface to St. Alexius. The monks of this house achieved "a full synthesis of Greek and Latin spirituality," unparalleled by any other monastery, medieval or modern.[39] Several members of the house became powerful figures in the Latin church. Two became saints. One of them, Gregory of Cassano, was a Greek-speaking monastic leader from southern Italy who traveled to Rome with some of his disciples around 987 and later became an abbot in Germany. The other was Adalbert of Prague. A Latin-speaking Slav, Adalbert was bishop of Prague until he fled from a conflict with the secular powers in 989. He set off on a pilgrimage to Jerusalem, but went first to Rome and Monte Cassino. At the latter stop he met Nilus of Rossano, who persuaded him to abandon his pilgrimage and enter a monastery. But when Adalbert wanted to join Nilus's house, the Calabrian refused. As a Latin, he said, Adalbert did not belong in a Greek monastery. Instead, Nilus sent him off to St. Alexius with a letter of reference for the abbot, who was a friend of Nilus's, and a Greek. Adalbert did as he was told and spent a few years there before he was forced to return to his diocese of Prague in 992. His legacy lived on at St. Alexius, which became a training center for priests preparing to go to lands where Byzantino-Slavic traditions mixed with Latin ones. The monastery's mixture of Greek and Latin customs and languages made it the ideal place for such men.

Although such friendly and fruitful interaction was important, neither the monastery of St. Alexius nor individuals like Nilus of Rossano were typical. Most of the Greek monks in Rome moved in a Greek world, neither knowing nor particularly wanting to know Latin. On the other side, few Latins knew Greek.[40] The uniqueness of St. Alexius is signaled for us by St. Nilus's insistence that Adalbert, a learned Latin from Germany, does not belong in Nilus's Greek community. Further south, Greek-speaking, Greek-rite monks had even less contact with Latins and most lived in a world of Greek language

38 The decline of the Greek monasteries in Rome: Hamilton, "City of Rome and the Eastern Churches," 7–8, 24; Sansterre, *Les moines grecs et orientaux*, 206–12. St. Alexius: Hamilton, "City of Rome and the Eastern Churches"; Hamilton, "Monastery of S. Alessio"; Sansterre, *Les moines grecs et orientaux*, map III.

39 Hamilton, "City of Rome and the Eastern Churches," 15–16.

40 Sansterre, *Les moines grecs et orientaux*, 62–76.

and ritual. When Italo-Greek holy men were tempted by worldly glory, it came in the form of Byzantine emissaries inviting them to the imperial court. Faced with such an offer, Nilus of Rossano refused for fear that he would be revered in the capital.[41] According to his hagiographer, St. Gregory of Cassano left the Byzantine lands of southern Italy for a similar reason; the imperial governor of Bari wanted to take him to Constantinople to meet the emperors.[42] For the authors of the *Vitae* of Nilus and Gregory, in the stories of the imperial invitations and elsewhere, the emperor in Constantinople is the highest earthly authority.[43] In short, Italo-Greek monasticism was intimately linked both to Greek monasticism further east and to the empire.

Nor was all interaction between Greek and Latin Christians as friendly as Nilus's relations with Monte Cassino. Any Greek who came into sustained contact with Latins became aware of differences in ritual and discipline. The most famous instance of such awareness in the middle Byzantine period resulted from competition between Frankish and Byzantine missionaries in Bulgaria in the second half of the ninth century – the Franks seeking to establish western customs, rites, and doctrine among the Bulgarians, while various Byzantine missionaries sought to establish eastern ones. In the course of this competition, the Byzantine missionaries became aware of a number of doctrinal and disciplinary errors, as they saw it, in the Frankish church. This conflict, however, ended quickly, never involved the whole western church, and had few echoes in the following centuries.[44]

In a less competitive context, Nilus of Rossano and the abbot and monks of Monte Cassino were also aware of differences. According to Nilus's hagiographer, when the abbot invited Nilus and his monks to visit, he quoted Scripture about the lion and the ox lying down together. Nilus replied with the Babylonian lament, "How shall we sing the Lord's song in a strange land?" But he then granted the Latin abbot's request. Having written hymns in honor of St. Benedict, he and his monks visited the church of Monte Cassino, where they chanted the office all night.[45] Impressed by the beauty of Nilus's hymns and the Greek service, the Benedictine monks gathered around to ask him some questions. Two of their questions stemmed from differences between Greek and Latin practice which, in later centuries, would be part of the vast arsenal of complaints compiled by anti-Latin easterners. A Cassinese monk asked Nilus

41 *Bios kai politeia*, para. 64–66, 72 (pp. 104–107, 112) or trans. Giovanelli, para. 64–66, 73 (pp. 80–83, 89). Rousseau, "La visite," 1114.

42 Hamilton, "Monastery of S. Alessio," 283.

43 Sansterre, "Les coryphées," 521–22.

44 Dvornik, *Photian Schism*, especially Part II, chs. 5–6.

45 Rousseau, "La visite," 1116–28.

what could be wrong with eating meat once a year, so long as he disciplined his body and fasted the rest of the year. Nilus's answer was sharp and sarcastic: What could be wrong with breaking your leg one day, so long as the rest of the time you are healthy?[46] Another monk asked him about fasting on the Sabbath: the Latin church fasts on Saturday; the Greek church does not.[47] Is this a serious problem? This time Nilus's answer was imbued with an enduring strain of Christian thought that considers matters of fasting and meat-eating secondary to charity. As Nilus put it, "Let him who eats not despise him who does not, and let him who does not eat not judge him who eats, for God has accepted both of them." Fasting or not fasting is not the question: the question is what one intends by fasting or eating.[48]

Perhaps this is not primarily the moderation of Nilus himself. Our account, written by a monk of Grottaferrata sometime within the first two decades after Nilus's death, was intended for the edification of the monks of Grottaferrata.[49] What were they to learn from this incident? Their sainted founder was admired by Latins and admired them in return. The differences between Latins and Greeks were not important. For the monks of Grottaferrata, living between the Greek and Latin worlds, subject to the pope but Greek in their customs and rituals, such a lesson was crucial. Without its leaders cultivating the kind of tolerance and respect for Latin customs advocated by Nilus's hagiographer, Grottaferrata could not have survived.

The history of the separation of the churches of Rome and Constantinople has traditionally been told thus: in the early Middle Ages, when there was little contact between Byzantines and westerners, the churches subject to Rome and the churches subject to Constantinople diverged in their rituals and customs. Byzantium, for example, emerged from the iconoclast controversy with icons as a central feature of Byzantine piety, while the West never revered images in the same way. The western church, meanwhile, was influenced by "Germanic ideals"[50] and much more centered around the papacy. In the eleventh century, when Greeks and Latins again came into regular contact with one another, they could not help noticing these differences. Since very few medieval people could see such differences with anything like cultural relativism, each side also tended to condemn the differences. As contact increased, so did knowledge and

46 Greek and Latin monastic meat-eating: Kolbaba, *Byzantine Lists*, 46–47.

47 Kolbaba, *Byzantine Lists*, 34–35.

48 *Bios kai politeia*, para. 72–78 (pp. 112–17) or trans. Giovanelli, 89–95.

49 Giovanelli in *Bios kai politeia tou*, 12–24, dates it more precisely and attributes it to Bartholomew of Grottaferrata; others have questioned this attribution. See Sansterre, "Les coryphées," 517–18, n. 6.

50 A problematic concept in itself; see Abrams's chapter in this volume.

condemnation. Combined with the kinds of ethnic hatred that the crusades and other contacts engendered, this awareness of differences between the churches resulted in a "schism" which has yet to be mended.

While many details of this story cannot be gainsaid, the story itself is flawed by its teleology of "the schism." Sources that report friendly interaction between Latins and Greeks in the early Middle Ages are as numerous as sources that report conflict. If we seek always the origins and causes of "the schism," we look to the sources that tell us what caused "the schism." But those sources reveal only causes which existed for centuries before "the schism" was "complete." What changed between c. 1050 and c. 1300? Not the "causes," such as differences in the Eucharistic bread or the addition of the *Filioque* to the creed, but the willingness to consider these differences matters of indifference. The loss of that willingness resulted from historical developments on each side, including hostility engendered by increased contact and altered opinions about what constituted an acceptable difference in ritual or theology – changes that await the twelfth century, with its crusades and its revolutionary developments in canon law and theology.

11

The northern frontier: Christianity face to face with paganism

IAN N. WOOD

Christianity, deviance, and paganism

Officially the Roman Empire had been Christianized by the end of the fourth century. Although the barbarians who crossed its frontiers in the fourth and fifth centuries were pagan, the majority of them soon accepted Christianity. By the sixth century the religion had even spread beyond the borders of what had been the empire. Christians were to be found in the Celtic west, notably Ireland, and also in the heartlands of Germany in the land of the Thuringians. On the other hand Christianity was by no means a monolithic religion, even in its old heartlands. The leaders of the church might have wanted it to be, but the bishops of Rome, Constantinople, and Alexandria, to name but three, frequently differed in their own definitions of their religion. Moreover different regions and groups adopted different doctrines and different patterns of organization, not least because of preexisting social patterns. This is most obvious in a region as distinctive as Ireland, but every part of Christendom had its own practices: its own liturgy as well as its own attachment to different saints and cults. The depth of Christianization was also a matter of concern. Many pre-Christian practices intended to ensure good harvests or safe childbirth, to predict the weather, or to ward off evil had not been abandoned, and indeed in some cases would not be abandoned until well into the modern period. Leading bishops, whose own religious commitment was radically more impressive than that of the majority of the population, understood their religion, and the demands it made, very differently from most of the laity. In the far west of Spain, Martin of Braga (c. 520–80) inveighed against superstitious practices in a work drawn on by generations of future ecclesiastics faced with congregations whose beliefs were far from pure. But even in as urbanized a center as the city of Arles, Caesarius (d. 542) was less than impressed by the Christian standards of his fellow citizens. The fact that later writers, up to the eleventh-century Burchard of Worms (d. 1025) and beyond, excerpted the strictures of Caesarius and Martin means that a somewhat homogenized picture of deviant practice existed.[1] In reality deviance must have been as varied as orthodoxy. Moreover, the image of Christian deviance to be found in the sources is such that historians have sometimes regarded it as defining paganism rather than Christianity. The eighth-century *Indiculus Superstitionum et Paganiarum*, for instance, in dealing with practices such as *nodfyr* (creating fire by rubbing two sticks together, presumably on particular occasions), was addressing activities performed by Christians, although in origin the rites were pagan.[2] Christianity was neither monolithic nor pure. Any discussion of its interface with paganism needs to recognize this.

While the majority of the Germanic migrants who entered what was or what had been Roman territory quickly converted, some did not. Those who traveled to Britain, settling in what would become the Anglo-Saxon kingdoms, were unusual in remaining pagan. This may not have meant that their religion was traditional: what little is known of early Germanic religion does not suggest a coherent body of beliefs. There would appear to have been considerable regionalism in the attachment to particular gods, and it is by no means clear when a notion of a pantheon, such as can be found in the writings of the thirteenth-century Icelander Snorri Sturluson (1179–1241), emerged. Deities, such as Woden, Thor, and Frey (and their regional variants), which are well known to modern scholars, are no more significant in the sources of the early Middle Ages than Fosite, culted probably on Helgoland, about whom practically nothing is known, or Eostre, who gave her name to Easter.[3] Classical and early medieval sources put at least as much emphasis on the importance of cult sites, especially groves or objects, notably the Irminsul of the continental Saxons (though exactly what this column of Irmin was is less than clear). If place was as central to Germanic paganism as our sources imply, migration must have disrupted previous belief systems. The Anglo-Saxons could not take their groves with them from Germany to Britain. At the same time, once in Britain they came across an established religion, Christianity, which revolved around priests and churches. What little Bede (d. 735) has to say about Anglo-Saxon paganism suggests that there were temples and priests (though possibly not many of them). Since there is scarcely any indication of either in sources relating to the paganism of the continental Germans before the eleventh century, except in those areas, like the western parts of Frisia, which had once been Roman, or were heavily influenced by Roman or Christian neighbors,

1 Boudriot, *Die altgermanische Religion*.
2 Dierkens, "Superstitions."
3 Helm, *Altgermanische Religionsgeschichte 2*.

one may wonder to what extent Anglo-Saxon paganism was created after the Angles and Saxons settled in Britain.[4]

Bede's *History*

The history of the Christianization of the English has often been told, not least because an incomparable narrative is provided by Bede. No historian before him had focused so directly on the history of the mission, but his account was to influence writers from the eighth century onward.[5] In factual terms the basic outline he provides is unlikely ever to be challenged.[6] The major phase of mission to England began in 596 when Gregory the Great (590–604) sent Augustine and his companions from Rome. From the moment of his arrival in Kent in 597 Augustine achieved remarkable success, and more missionaries had to be sent. Thousands were baptized on the first Christmas after Augustine's landing, though it is not clear whether the king was included: it is possible that he had already accepted baptism. Moreover, because of Æthelberht's political dominance in southern England, Christianity quickly spread beyond the borders of his kingdom. This initial period of success, however, was checked when the king died in 616, and for almost two decades missionary expansion alternated with apostasy. Apart from the events in Kent, the most notable example of this was in Northumbria. King Edwin (616–33), who married a granddaughter of Æthelberht, was converted in the mid 620s, but his death in battle led directly to a resurgence of paganism. From the 630s onward, however, a new source of missionary activity opened up. Missionaries set out from the Irish monastery founded in 563 by Columba on the Scottish island of Iona. From here Aidan (d. 651) evangelized Northumbria in the days of King Oswald (634–42). Since Oswald, and later his brother Oswiu (642–70), like Æthelberht, held some sort of overlordship among the English, they too helped spread Christianity beyond the borders of their kingdom.

It has become clear that Bede's narrative underplays various aspects of the Christianization of the English.[7] He effectively presents the missionaries as either Roman or Irish. He provides some slight indication that the Franks played a part, and this observation can be strengthened by recourse to other sources, notably the *Lives* of Frankish saints. On the other hand Bede allows no British input into the process of Christianization: indeed he explicitly blames

4 Wood, "Some Historical Re-identifications," 28–31.
5 Wood, *Missionary Life*, 44–45.
6 Mayr-Harting, *Coming of Christianity*.
7 Campbell, "First Century," and his "Observations."

the Britons for not evangelizing the earliest generations of Anglo-Saxons. There is, however, evidence for some survival of British Christianity in eastern Britain,[8] which may have influenced the incomers. That the Britons of the southwest influenced their English neighbors is certain.[9]

It is not just in his concentration on Romans and Irish that Bede has determined how the Christianization of the Anglo-Saxons is understood.[10] His presentation of the Roman mission is radically different from that of the Irish, largely because of his own source material. The Roman mission is seen largely through the letters of Gregory the Great. The picture is somewhat formal, almost legalistic. By contrast the image given of Aidan's mission is essentially hagiographical, being dominated by the image of the saint, which Bede may well have derived from traditions current in Aidan's monastery of Lindisfarne, or indeed more generally in Northumbria. One result is that historians have sometimes contrasted the Roman mission, which is seen as ill-attuned to what it must have regarded as the very alien world of Kent, with the Irish mission, which is thought to have been thoroughly at home in the tribal world of Northumbria. There may well be an element of truth in this contrast. At the same time, the distinction is one at least in part caused by the sources. Roman bureaucracy versus Irish charisma is to some extent an image determined by the contrast between the two types of source material on which Bede depended. Nowhere is this more significant than in the portrayal of Augustine himself, who is known from his epitaph to have been regarded as a wonder worker, but whose miracles are not recorded, perhaps because, as we know, Gregory gave him strict instructions not to talk about them. At times the history of mission can very usefully be categorized in terms of charisma and of organization: it is not clear that the categories are useful in understanding the Christianization of the Anglo-Saxons.

Mission and the institution of the church

One period of missionary history where these two types of approach are significant is that of the late-seventh, eighth, and early-ninth centuries, when large areas of Germany east of the Rhine and what is now eastern Austria and its borders were Christianized. The history of the Carolingian missions in these areas can easily be portrayed from the point of view of the institution of the church. The Christianization of Saxony can be told as a series of wars between

8 Wood, "Some Historical Re-identifications," 31–34.
9 Sims-Williams, *Religion and Literature*, 54–86.
10 Wood, "Augustine and Aidan."

Charlemagne (768–814) and the pagan Saxons, with almost every major Frankish victory followed by baptism and church foundation, but also, the moment that Charlemagne's attention was directed to problems elsewhere, by military retaliation and apostasy on the part of the Saxons.[11] The extent to which Charlemagne misjudged the situation is most clearly revealed in a poem, *De Conversione Saxonum*, written about the year 777, which describes the king's successes in taming and Christianizing the Saxons in what was to prove a most premature panegyric.[12] Further, Charlemagne's victories were on two occasions backed up with legislation relating to Saxony, the first of which, possibly issued in 782, heavy handedly enforced baptism and imposed tithe. Both these actions exacerbated the situation, leading to further Saxon resistance. Equally, they prompted criticism from within the Carolingian Empire, not least by Alcuin, who argued that baptism should only take place after sufficient instruction had been given, and that tithe should be first exacted at a much later date.[13] It was only after 785, when the most successful of the Saxon leaders, Widukind, submitted and accepted baptism that a relatively uninterrupted history of diocesan foundation could follow.

Despite the setbacks in Saxony, similar mistakes were made in the course of Christianizing the Avars, a Hunnic people who had established themselves in the region of Hungary in the fifth century. In the course of what was to prove to be the destruction of the Avar kingdom in 796, a council was held to deal with the administration of baptism. As in the case of the Saxons, tithe was imposed shortly after conquest, leading once more to pagan reaction. The subsequent history of the Christianization of the region is presented by our sources in terms of the sending of priests and the establishment of churches by the bishops of Salzburg. The fullest version of this tale is recorded in remarkable detail in a text known as the *Conversio Bagoariorum et Carantanorum*, written in c. 870.[14]

Missionaries and their *Lives*

Military action, church legislation, baptism, the imposition of tithe, and the foundation of churches and dioceses fill the official narrative of the Christianization of both the Saxons and the Avars. There is at the same time a parallel

11 Büttner, "Mission."
12 Rabe, *Faith, Art and Politics*, 54–74.
13 Alcuin, *Epistola* 110 or trans. in *Reign of Charlemagne*, 120–23.
14 Wolfram, *Conversio Bagoariorum et Carantanorum.*

charismatic history told in the saints' *Lives*.[15] This begins nearly a century before the reign of Charlemagne, with the Frisian missions of the Anglo-Saxons Wilfrid in 678 and Willibrord from 690 to 739. These in turn were continued by another Englishman, Boniface, who, after an abortive journey in 716, arrived on the Continent in 718 and who met his death while preaching to the people of Dokkum in northern Frisia in 754. This work would be continued, and would be extended into Saxony, by Boniface's disciples, Sturm, Lull, and Gregory of Utrecht, and yet more importantly by Lebuin, Liudger, and Willehad. Lull as bishop of Mainz (754–86), Sturm as abbot of Fulda (747–79), and Liudger (804–809) and Willehad (787–89) as respectively the first bishops of Münster and Bremen, can be tied in with the institutional history of ecclesiastical organization.

At the same time, there are certain respects in which the hagiographical accounts of these figures present a picture of mission that does not fit neatly alongside the official history of Charlemagne's missionary policies. Already in the seventh century Willibrord had determined to embark on his missionary work from outside the Frankish world: his decision was taken in Ireland. So, too, Boniface made up his mind to evangelize the continental relatives of the Anglo-Saxons while he was still in Wessex. This tradition was continued by Willehad, who was sent to work in Frisia by a council of the Northumbrian Church, held in c. 770. He would seem to have attracted the attention of Charlemagne only rather late in his career. In other words, missionaries were active before the Frankish king developed a missionary strategy. At least one seems to have carried out his mission partly in order to forestall Charlemagne's actions. According to his *vita*, Lebuin (d. c. 773) preached to the Saxons, urging them to convert before their Frankish neighbors invaded and forced Christianity on them.[16]

The hagiographical record provides a very useful addition to the evidence of the laws, letters, and chronicles. It adds a good deal of immediacy to the picture we have. It is, at the same time, problematic as a quarry for fact, though not in the way that much hagiography is thought to be difficult: the saints' *Lives* of the missionary saints of the eighth and ninth centuries are not stuffed full of miracles, indeed for the most part they provide remarkably sober narratives. They are, however, texts designed to put across particular messages.[17] The *Lives* of Boniface, for instance, present a series of different interpretations of the saint, influenced by Frankish politics and by the requirements of individual

15 Wood, *Missionary Life*.
16 *Vita Lebuini antiqua*, 4–6 or trans. Talbot, 232.
17 Wood, *Missionary Life*.

Christian centers: among them his diocesan center of Mainz, the Frisian city of Utrecht, and his monastic foundation of Fulda, which was also his place of burial. Although Boniface always wished to work among the Saxons as a missionary, he never achieved his goal. Despite being killed while evangelizing the Frisians, most of his continental career was spent organizing and reforming the church in large areas of east Francia, Bavaria, Hesse, and Thuringia. All these regions were already Christianized, yet Boniface's Carolingian masters wished to portray them for political reasons as semi-pagan. The mid-eighth-century rulers of Bavaria, Hesse, and Thuringia had opposed Carolingian rule; one way of casting aspersions on their legitimacy was to portray them as inadequate supporters of the church. As a result, the *Lives* of Boniface exaggerate his missionary achievements. The second *Life*, in particular, written from the viewpoint of Utrecht, radically overstates the extent to which he was active in mission.

Other works of hagiography are *parti pris* in different respects. Alcuin (d. 804), for instance, seems to have used the *Vita Willibrordi* to set out a model for missionary activity.[18] In Alcuin's account force is never used by the protagonist, who relies entirely on preaching. Although the missionaries themselves are sometimes the victims of violence, vengeance is left to God. Such ideas are also expressed by Alcuin in letters written at the same time, notably those addressed to Arn of Salzburg (785–821), one of the leaders of the Avar mission. Although the factual content of the *Life of Willibrord* is of little use, despite the presence of important chapters on attempts to convert the Danish king, and confrontations with the guardians of the shrine of Fosite and of that on Walcheren, the text nevertheless provides considerable insight into Alcuin's ideology. In certain respects, even more interesting is the ideology of later writers of missionary hagiography, who in the course of the ninth, tenth, and early eleventh centuries were frequently missionaries themselves. Thus, in the case of Liudger's *Life of Gregory of Utrecht*, Rimbert's *Life of Anskar*, or Bruno of Querfurt's *Life of Adalbert of Prague*, we find missionaries exploring their own views of mission through the medium of a revered model's biography. In the cases of Rimbert and Bruno, the probability is that their narratives are reasonably well founded. In the case of Liudger this is questionable. The text, however, remains important for what it reveals of the author's attitude towards missionary work: in this instance the standpoint is very similar to that of Alcuin.

18 Ibid., 80–86.

Women and mission

Hagiography also provides much of the evidence for an understanding of the role that women could play in mission.[19] They did not, of course, preach, and most certainly not in front of pagans. Indeed they were rarely in the real vanguard of mission. Boniface's letters, however, reveal his dependence on female correspondents for support in terms of prayers, and also in the provision of books. Most famously he commissioned a copy of the Epistles of Peter in gold letters (to impress the pagan) from Abbess Eadburg of Thanet.[20] Nunneries, although rarely if ever actually in missionary territory, could play an important role, not just in the production of books and vestments, but also in deepening the Christianization of the surrounding countryside.

On the other hand there is evidence for women promoting Christianity in pagan society in the historical and hagiographical narratives. Christian princesses married to pagan kings could play a valuable role in opening up the opportunities for evangelization. This is most apparent in England, where the pagan Æthelberht was married to the Christian Frankish princess Bertha, while their granddaughter married the pagan ruler of Northumbria, Edwin. But women lower down the social scale could also be influential. According to the *Life of Lebuin*, the saint, who certainly did not have official Frankish backing, relied on support from noble Saxon families, and in particular from the matron Avaerhilda.[21] The *Life of Liudger*, written by the saint's nephew Altfrid, provides a history of the Christianization of Frisia that is essentially conceived of as family history.[22] Liudger's great-grandmother on his mother's side was resolutely pagan, and tried to have her granddaughter exposed to ritual drowning. His paternal grandmother, by contrast, was a staunch Christian, and had the distinction of handing over her brothers to Willibrord to be trained for the priesthood. Yet further into pagan territory, Rimbert's *Life of Anskar* tells of two (probably Frisian) Christian women, Frideburg and her daughter Catla, heroically continuing in their faith, even after the mission to the Swedish trading station of Birka had collapsed.[23] Such figures do not appear in the chronicles, and certainly not in the legislative material. The hagiography provides at least a fleeting view of the role that women could play in the interface between paganism and Christianity.

19 Nelson, "Les femmes et l'évangélisation."
20 Boniface, *Epistola* 35 or trans. Emerton, 42–43.
21 *Vita Lebuini antiqua*, 3 or trans. Talbot, 230.
22 Altfrid, *Vita Liudgeri*, I.1–5.
23 Lebecq, "Religiosa femina."

The evidence of language

There is one other vital source of information that sheds light on missionary activity: linguistics.[24] Words can reveal something of the origins of ideas. Intriguingly the Christian vocabulary of the lands to the east of the Rhine suggests that the religion was not introduced to or established in that region by Anglo-Saxons, as the hagiography might imply, or indeed by Irishmen, as some scholars have argued, but rather by Franks. There are, in fact, some few indications of missionary work carried out by Frankish bishops east of the Rhine, notably by Amandus of Maastricht and by Wulfram of Sens.[25] The philological evidence, on the other hand, suggests a much more sustained influence on the part of Frankish clerics, probably exerted by relatively minor figures over a long period of time.

Various strands of evidence thus come together to produce a remarkably complex, and not always consistent, picture of missionary activity up to and including the early years of the reign of Louis the Pious (814–40). Although it is possible to debate the relative importance of the input of Franks, Anglo-Saxons, and Irish, and equally of the official policy of Charlemagne and his episcopate, as opposed to the influence of charismatic individuals, and although the picture is not one of consistent success, the evidence suggests a picture in which Christianity was expanding further and further to the east of the Rhine and into the regions of the middle Danube. Essentially the impression is an optimistic one.

Scandinavia, the edge of the known world

In the 820s Louis the Pious went further than his father had ever done and supported missions to the Danes.[26] Initially these were led by Ebbo (archbishop of Rheims, 816–34; bishop of Hildesheim, 846–51), though his involvement was to be interrupted as a result of his support for Louis's rebellious sons. Before this, however, he had already seen his missionary work taken over by the monk Anskar, who himself looked back positively on Ebbo's achievements in a letter written to Louis the German in 864. Anskar initially achieved a remarkable amount in both Denmark and, after 829, among the Swear of Lake Mälaren. The archaeology of the island of Birka provides striking support for the development of a Christian community in the early ninth century.[27] Yet

24 Green, *Language and History*, 273–391.
25 Lebecq, "Vulfran."
26 Palmer, "Rimbert's *Vita Anskarii*."
27 Nilsson, "Early Christian Burials."

when his hagiographer Rimbert came to record Anskar's life shortly after 865, he presented a very different picture.[28] For him, the mission to the Danes was an uncomfortable voyage into danger. In part, Rimbert's views were colored by a generation of upsets, caused largely by Viking aggression. Not only had Anskar's missions to the Danes and the Swear encountered opposition, equally discouraging, Hamburg, his missionary base after his elevation to the episcopate in 831, had been sacked in 845. Bremen, which had been added to his diocese as a result of the devastation, was also subjected to an attack in c. 860.

There is, however, another aspect to Rimbert's sensitivity toward missionary work. His account of Anskar's life is dominated by dreams and visions, which had originally been set down by the saint himself. On occasion the tone of these is eschatological: there is a sense that the saint was working at the edge of the world. Since Matthew's Gospel had linked the preaching of the gospel to the furthest corners of the earth with the end of the world, it is not surprising to find that Rimbert was genuinely fearful. This fear, however, was combined with personal experience of the northern mission field. Like his master Anskar, he had worked among the Danes and Swear. This, however, had not made the world any less exotic for him. Although scholars have tended to assume that in the medieval imagination monsters were never really close at hand, Rimbert fully expected to meet them. He wrote to Ratramnus, the abbot of Corbie, asking whether, when he met dogheaded men *(cynocephali)*, he should kill them as animals, or convert them as humans. In a long and remarkable reply Ratramnus concluded that, since they were social beings with a sense of reason, they should be regarded as human and baptized.[29]

Rimbert's sense of working on the edge of the unknown marks a remarkable shift in missionary history. Hitherto, those missions that we know about were directed largely at peoples about whom the missionaries had some good knowledge. Admittedly Augustine of Canterbury and his followers were overcome with fear as they traveled to Kent in 596. But for the most part missionaries worked among pagan peoples who shared a border with established Christian states. To move into the land of the Swear was to move to a country that was not well known to the Christians (though it is clear that merchants were already trading with the region). It is in this context that the debate over the *cynocephali* makes sense. Certainly there may have been good reasons for linking dogheaded peoples with the Scandinavian world: surprisingly realistic

28 Rimbert, *Vita Anskarii*.
29 Ratramnus, *Epistolae variorum* 12 or trans. Dutton.

animal masks were found in the excavations of the harbor at Haithabu.[30] Nevertheless, classical ethnography had usually placed the *cynocephali* in the East, between Mesopotamia and India. From the mid-ninth century onward, mission in the North meant something more than contact with pagans, for the northern world, like the lands on the eastern shores of the Baltic, came to be seen as distinctly Other.

When in the late eleventh century Adam of Bremen came to write up the history of the church of Hamburg, and particularly its missionary activity, and the jurisdiction derived therefrom, he found that his sources ran out after the death of Rimbert in 888. It would seem that Viking activity led to a near-collapse of missionary activity in the last decades of the ninth century and the first of the tenth. Archbishop Unni (913–36) did revive something of the missionary activities of the diocese. The major successes in spreading Christianity in Scandinavia during the tenth century, however, were not the work of the Church of Hamburg-Bremen. The irreversible Christianization of Denmark began in this period, with the conversion of Harald Bluetooth by the priest Poppo, possibly around 960.[31] Since, however, Poppo was not an agent of the Church of Hamburg, Adam passed over his achievements as quickly as possible, just as he ignored the contribution made by Anglo-Saxon missionaries to the Christianization of Denmark and Sweden in the later tenth and eleventh centuries. What can be reconstructed of this story of Christian expansion depends on fragments of information preserved in England and in Scandinavia, which do not amount to a coherent narrative.[32] Equally fragmentary is the evidence for the spread of Christianity to Norway, although it would seem that Norse contact with England led to the Vikings taking the religion back to their homeland. Harald Finehair's son, Hakon, was brought up at Athelstan's court, and missionaries would seem to have followed him back home. Political rivalries, however, ensured that the Christianization of Norway did not proceed smoothly, but was rather interrupted by warfare and bloodshed, which could be construed as martyrdom. Despite this problematic history, it would seem that the Norse king Olaf Tryggvason did play a role in the Christianization of Iceland. The inhabitants of this independent island found it convenient to agree to accept Christianity on their own terms at a meeting of the Althing, held according to tradition in the year 1000, rather than face constant harassment at the hands of Olaf.[33]

30 Wood, *Missionary Life*, 219.
31 Thietmar of Merseburg, *Chronicon*, 2.14 or trans. Warner, 101–102.
32 Sawyer, "Process of Scandinavian Christianization" and Abrams, "Anglo-Saxons."
33 Strömbäck, *Conversion of Iceland*.

Adam of Bremen's account of the Christianization of Scandinavia largely reflects the point of view of the institution of his own church.[34] He leaves out information on the achievements of missionaries originating elsewhere, which he regarded as an infringement on the jurisdiction of Hamburg-Bremen. In Adam's day Hamburg's authority was a particularly sensitive issue, because his own archbishop, Adalbert (1043–72), was keen to establish a patriarchate in the North, which would have given the diocese jurisdiction throughout Scandinavia and in the northern Slav lands. Adalbert's successor, Liemar (1072–1101), who was the dedicatee of Adam's history, was in addition a leading critic of Gregory VII and his reforms. Given Adam's biases, it is not always easy to be sure how to understand his information. The most famous part of his description of Scandinavia is an account of a temple at Uppsala, dedicated to Thor, Woden, and Fricco.[35] Extensive archaeological investigation has so far failed to identify anything remotely like the building described by Adam, and it may well be that the description is an attempt to discredit those in the region, by presenting them in as extreme and exotic a light as possible.

Rethinking mission in the southern Baltic

Adam's silences seem often to have been deliberate, but he is not the only author to have failed to pass on information for reasons of personal bias or commitment. Thietmar of Merseburg (d. 1018), writing at the start of the eleventh century, was rarely well disposed toward the Piast ruler of Poland in his day, Boleslav Chrobry (992–1025), doubtless because he presented a threat to the eastern frontier of the Ottonian empire, and thus to his own diocese. Thietmar did, however, recount the marriage of Boleslav's father, Mieszko, to the Christian Dobrava, daughter of the ruler of Bohemia, in c. 964.[36] Thietmar commented on the woman's name, which meant good, and saw it as an omen of the resulting conversion of the Piast ruler. Details of the establishment of Christianity in Poland largely elude us.[37] Nevertheless, by Boleslav's reign the church was well established, and the ruler was indeed a champion of Christianity within and beyond the borders of his realm.

Boleslav was to support two missionaries whose experiences in working within alien societies are reminiscent in certain respects of those of Anskar

34 See comments by ed. Reuter in Adam of Bremen, *History of the Archbishops*, xiii–xix.
35 Adam of Bremen, *Gesta Hammaburgensis ecclesiae pontificum*, IV.26–7 or trans. Tschan, 207–208.
36 Thietmar of Merseburg, *Chronicon*, IV.55 or trans. Warner, 191.
37 See Shepard in this volume.

and Rimbert. The first, Adalbert of Prague, was a member of one of the leading Bohemian families, the Slavniks.[38] Having been educated at Magdeburg, in 983 he was appointed bishop of Prague. Appalled by the Christian standards of the city, he abandoned his post after five years, retiring to Italy. He was forced to return in 992 but left again two years later. The massacre of his relatives by the duke in 995 made further return impossible. Adalbert had already shown some interest in missionary activity and would seem to have worked for a while among the Hungarians. In 996, therefore, he set off to work in the Baltic region, passing through the Piast state, where he founded a monastery, Meseritz. He traveled up to the territory near Gdańsk, but made little impact. Before he could return, however, he was martyred in 997. Boleslav secured his body and had it enshrined at Gniezno.

Adalbert's career immediately attracted attention. There is some debate over the dates and authorship of the various texts that followed, but it would seem that a verse life was written very soon after the martyrdom. This apparently provided the model almost immediately for a work now seen as coming from the Aachen–Liège region, but once ascribed to John Canaparius, abbot of the monastery of SS. Boniface and Alexius, where Adalbert had resided in Rome. This second *Life* seems in turn to have inspired a further hagiographer, Bruno of Querfurt, who wrote an account of Adalbert in c. 1004, revising it four years later. Yet another, much shorter account was written, perhaps at Meseritz, soon afterwards.

Quite why Adalbert attracted such attention is unclear, though by all accounts he was an extraordinary figure who inspired intense devotion. That Boleslav Chrobry was keen to cultivate his memory for political as well as personal reasons is also clear enough: for much of the first decades of the eleventh century Boleslav was in conflict with Emperor Henry II (1002–24), and any opportunity to enhance his own Christian credentials must have been welcome. Easiest to understand is Bruno's interest. He too was a remarkable figure.[39] A relative of Thietmar of Merseburg, he spent a while at Otto III's court in Italy before entering the monastery of SS. Boniface and Alexius in Rome. There he must have become fully acquainted with the work of Adalbert. He had already shown some interest in mission and had witnessed the departure of two of his friends for the Slav mission field, promising to secure a papal license for their missionary activities. As it so happened, they were murdered before he acted. When he himself set out to work as a missionary he was in

38 Wood, *Missionary Life*, 207–25.
39 Ibid., 226–44.

part driven by guilt at not having provided his friends with their license. This is apparent in the account that he wrote of their murder. His *Life of Adalbert*, on the other hand, is effectively an exploration of missionary practice: on the need not to stand out from the people one is trying to evangelize, but rather to "go native." He envisages one reason for the rejection of Adalbert as being the fact that he was too easily identified as coming from another society, and he puts into Adalbert's mouth a remarkable speech in which he proposes that he and his companions should attempt to live like those they were trying to convert.[40] Nevertheless, there were certain things one could not give up: notably correct performance of the liturgy – and this not just because of the canons, but also because the liturgy and liturgical objects provided an element of reassurance to missionaries in the field, or so it would seem. Interestingly, despite his meticulous analysis of the society that he intended to evangelize, Bruno, like Rimbert, envisaged being surrounded by *cynocephali*. Thus prepared, and having already worked as a missionary among the Rus and the Pechenegs, he set off to the area of Adalbert's last mission, where he, too, was martyred in 1008.

Anskar, Rimbert, Adalbert, and Bruno all emerge as men working in alien worlds. Notably, at least three, and perhaps all, of them wrote up their own ideas of mission and did so by writing about saints they wished to imitate.[41] To some extent, these works, exploring as they do the attitudes and practices of the authors themselves, are autobiographical. They allow us to understand something of the experience and expectation of a missionary in the ninth, tenth, and eleventh centuries. They also make plain just how alien the mission fields of the period were. This was not the same as working among people who had officially been converted, but whose standards were lax; nor was it the same as working among tribes who had for generations been neighbors of Christians, and who, for all their paganism, were not unknown quantities. It is important not to underestimate the extent to which missionaries from the ninth century onward were confronted with an alien world.

Nor was the world in which they were working alien simply because it was geographically removed from ancient centers of Christianity. Adalbert and Bruno were both active among the Slavs and Balts. Slav paganism would seem to have been very different from that of the Germanic peoples. While in the Germanic world there is little evidence for temples and priests,[42] the Slavs boasted an array of awesome, if local, gods who were associated with large

40 Wood, "Pagans and Holy Men," 358–59.
41 Wood, *Missionary Life*, 264–65.
42 Wood, "Pagan Religion and Superstitions."

temple complexes and an established priesthood.[43] The only equivalents in the Germanic world come in regions where Roman temples or Christian churches may have served as models. If one accepts at face value Adam of Bremen's description of Uppsala, this may be compared with the temple complexes of Slavonic paganism, which may indeed have influenced it. Contact between Scandinavia and the Slav lands of the southern Baltic is well attested.

Extraordinary descriptions of Slav cult sites survive in the sources: notably there is Thietmar of Merseburg's account of Rethra[44] and Saxo Grammaticus's of Arcona, the center of the cult of Swantovit, on Rügen.[45] At Rethra there was supposedly a triangular-shaped enclosure in the middle of the forest, and within it a large number of idols. There the priests took charge of the casting of lots. This and similar descriptions of other temples and rituals, for instance provided by Helmold of Bosau (d. c. 1180),[46] can plausibly be linked with the evidence of archaeology, which tends to confirm that Slavonic paganism was radically different from that of the Germanic peoples. It is, therefore, scarcely surprising that the world of the pagan Slavs was regarded as so alien by clergy of the German Reich, or indeed by a man like Adalbert of Prague, himself a Slav, but brought up in a supposedly Christian state and educated in Merseburg. Scandinavia may, of course, have been rather less alien than the Slav lands, but lying on the very edge of the known world it brought its own terrors to Anskar and Rimbert.

Pagan and Christian in the time of Adam of Bremen

Adalbert and Bruno had not set out simply to work among the Slavs, but to penetrate far into their territory, and indeed into the lands of the non-Slavonic speaking Balts. They could have found Slavonic pagans a good deal nearer to home. By 1000 the continental Germanic world had been Christianized, as had much of Scandinavia. Among the Slavs, the Bulgarians (Slavonic except at the highest levels of society), Bohemians, Poles, and Russians had been Christianized, as had the Magyars. The Baltic Slavs, however, remained largely pagan. For much of the eleventh century even the Wagrians and Abodrites, Slav tribes based in the Oldenburg and Mecklenburg regions, presented problems to the church of Hamburg, their near neighbor. The history of mission among the Abodrites is best known to us through the career of their prince Gottschalk

43 Slupecki, *Slavonic Pagan Sanctuaries*.
44 Thietmar of Merseburg, *Chronicon*, VI.23–4 or trans. Warner, 252–53.
45 Saxo Grammaticus, *Gesta Danorum*, XIV.39, 493–511.
46 Helmold of Bosau, *Cronica*, I.84 or trans. Tschan, 218–25.

(d. 1066). He was sent by his father to be educated at the monastery of Lüneburg, but on hearing of his father's murder by a Saxon, rejected his faith and set out to exact vengeance. Subsequently, however, he regained his faith, married the daughter of the Danish king, Svein Estrithson, and became a friend of Archbishop Adalbert, for whom he worked to spread Christianity among the Abodrites, until his martyrdom at Lenzen.[47]

The death of Gottschalk was one event in the long history of alternating Christianization and apostasy among the northern Slavs. It is a history that has as much to do with politics, that is, the relations of individual Slav leaders with the kings of Germany and Denmark, as well as the duke of Saxony, as it has to do with religion. The conflicts occupy much of Book Three of Adam's *History*, and the whole of the chronicle of Helmold by Bosau, who was effectively Adam's continuator. Both of them record the attempts of the archbishops of Hamburg to Christianize the south coast of the Baltic, and while their histories provide ample evidence of the jurisdictional ambition, they are also studded with vignettes like that of Gottschalk's career. Helmold, who was himself active as a Christian priest among the Slavs, provides eyewitness accounts of paganism, and the power of its priests, alongside his narrative of the problems in restoring dioceses destroyed in the course of the political and religious conflicts of his day. The see of Oldenburg, for instance, was vacant between 1066 and 1159. Helmold also refers in passing to the last of the great missionary bishops to be active before the establishment of the German Orders, and the resulting Baltic Crusades: Otto of Bamberg (1102–39).

With the Baltic Crusades the history of mission in the North changes. Although one can see in Charlemagne's dealings with the pagan Saxons a germ of a crusade notion, there is nothing in the eighth or ninth centuries to equal the monastic or military orders of the twelfth century. Hitherto, mission had certainly had its bureaucratic aspects, but these had been balanced by the personal charisma of individual missionaries. The mission field itself, however, had changed. Whereas the missionaries of the seventh and eighth centuries had dealt with peoples in Britain or across the Rhine who had strong and often longstanding contacts with the Christian world, those of the ninth and tenth centuries worked in areas which, initially at least, were much less known. Moreover, religion in the Slav lands, and indeed the social structures of southern Baltic peoples, were very different from those of the Carolingian or Ottonian Reich. Add to this the fact that, momentarily at least, Christendom met its physical match in the Vikings and the Magyars, and it is easy to see why

47 Ibid., I.19–22 or trans., 90–98.

the missionaries of the ninth and tenth centuries seem in the sources to lack the optimism of their seventh- and eighth-century predecessors. What may once have seemed a relatively straightforward task, the Christianization of the peoples east of the Rhine, had turned into something much more complex and unexpected. It is perhaps not surprising that the Christianization of the northern Slavs and their Baltic neighbors needed a new approach.

PART III

★

CHRISTIANITY IN THE SOCIAL AND POLITICAL ORDER

12

The Christian church as an institution

THOMAS F. X. NOBLE

We live in a post-ecclesiastical world. Popular and scholarly surveys repeatedly confirm that fewer and fewer people possess strong feelings of identity with specific ecclesial bodies. As the majority of studies in this volume demonstrates, medievalists have in recent decades exchanged an almost exclusive focus on institutions and high theology for new foci on ordinary people and lived experience.[1] Nevertheless, in the Middle Ages, Christianity was inseparable from the institutional frameworks through which Christianity spread and functioned.

This chapter, which stretches in summary fashion from Ireland to Mesopotamia, will pursue three lines of inquiry in an attempt to form a sense of the church as an institutional reality. First, we shall look at the ebb and flow of institutional existence itself as new ecclesiastical hierarchies were created while others were disrupted or even disappeared. Second, we shall explore, by means of some illustrative examples, how the institutional church actually functioned. Third, we shall ask how the church thought about itself as an institution by taking some soundings in the complementary fields of ecclesiology and institutional identity. In other words, we shall see how common understandings of structure, office, law, and ideas transcended time and place.

In the year 600 an ecclesiastical hierarchy was functioning in most of the lands that Rome had once ruled with faint beginnings visible beyond Rome's former frontiers. By 1100 conditions had changed dramatically through processes of contraction and expansion. Let us survey the scene, beginning in the eastern Mediterranean world and moving clockwise across North Africa to western Europe and then eastern Europe. Often the church was buffeted by forces over which it had no control and little influence: the rise and spread of Islam is a prime example. In some places local or regional politics played decisive roles: Frankish, Scandinavian, and Slavic rulers will provide examples

1 Van Engen, "Christian Middle Ages" and "Future."

of this dynamic. Occasionally, large-scale diplomacy was critical: German and Byzantine rivalries in eastern Europe typify this problem.

Ecclesiastical hierarchies

The Orthodox Church of the Byzantine Empire, centered on Constantinople, emerged amidst conciliar decrees, especially those of Constantinople I (381) and Chalcedon (451), which accorded Constantinople second place after Rome in the ecclesiastical order; the effect of the legislation having been to elevate Constantinople above the older sees of Antioch and Alexandria, and over Jerusalem, too, whose "patriarchal" (see below) status only really emerged at Chalcedon. Constantinople's initial problem was that the bishops of the city did not have a clearly defined territory within which their authority was both acknowledged and effective. The bishops, or patriarchs, of Constantinople possessed in principle metropolitan rights (see below) over the regions of Pontos, Thrace, and Asia Minor. As a direct consequence of imperial authority, the bishops of Constantinople also exercised some influence in the patriarchates of Alexandria and Antioch. By 642, however, Arab conquests diminished, sometimes severed, Constantinople's connections with Syria, Palestine, and Egypt. In the ninth and tenth centuries, the Byzantine patriarchate extended its influence into Bulgaria, Serbia, and Rus.[2] Contraction on one flank was compensated by expansion on another. On the Arab frontier, moreover, conditions could change dramatically. For example, between 949 and 975 Byzantine reconquests in Anatolia and northern Syria spurred the reestablishment of some thirty bishoprics.[3] There were also changes in the western Mediterranean. Signaling his displeasure with papal opposition to his religious and political enactments, Emperor Leo III (717–41) transferred the bishoprics of Dalmatia and Illyricum, along with those of southern Italy and Sicily, from the authority of the bishops of Rome to that of the bishops of Constantinople. We will return below to the fate of the Balkan bishoprics. Those in Italy, however, suffered under the Muslim conquest of Sicily (827–44), Muslim raiding in the peninsula, and the growing power of various Christian potentates in southern Italy. The Byzantine Empire simply could not maintain its authority in Italy. By the middle of the eleventh century, the Norman conquest of southern Italy and Sicily, coupled with their alliance with the papacy, left southern Italy under papal authority. It is not easy to say at any given moment how many bishops were

2 Dagron, "L'église"; Hussey, *Orthodox Church*; also Louth and Dorfmann-Lazarev in this volume.

3 See Kennedy in this volume.

under Constantinople's authority, but the number of bishops in attendance at councils provides some sense of the extent of the church's reach, as well as a gauge of the degree of disruption exerted by military and diplomatic issues:

Council Year	680	692	754	787	869/70
Signatories	174	211	338	319	110(?)[4]

The lands and peoples lying to the east of Constantinople found themselves in an extremely complicated ecclesiastical and political situation. The fundamental dynamics in a broad zone running from Armenia to Egypt were two: the bitter legacy of the Christological quarrels of Late Antiquity and Byzantium's struggles, first with Persia and then with the Arabs and Islam. The two dynamics fused when Jacobite and Nestorian Christians willingly acquiesced to the Muslim authorities, who demanded submission and taxes but did not intrude into religious struggles among Christians. Melkite (from *malka*, emperor) Christians, those who looked to Constantinople politically and theologically, became a dwindling and powerless minority throughout vast eastern provinces where they had once held sway.[5]

The largest of the eastern Christian communities was the Jacobite Church centered in Syria and focused on the patriarchs of Antioch. This church began its rise when Antiochene theologians rejected the decrees of Chalcedon, developed its teaching under Jacob[6] Baradaeus (c. 500–78) who gave his name to the whole movement, and secured its liberation from Constantinople during the Arab conquests. The Councils of Nicaea I and Constantinople I assigned Antioch authority over Syria, Palestine, Cyprus, Arabia, Mesopotamia, Persia, and India. Down to the seventh century there were some eleven metropolitan provinces. The Arab conquests reduced the number of bishops dependent on Antioch from about 158 to perhaps 60. Virtually all bishoprics in the Arabian peninsula and the Persian Gulf region were extinguished. After 750 the Abbasid caliphs exercised occasional influence on the appointment of Antioch's patriarchs and their subordinate bishops throughout the East. The *dhimmī* status of Christians made it difficult for the church to function openly and effectively.[7]

The Nestorian Christian community of the East comprised those who embraced the teachings of Nestorius (d. after 451) and his followers after their

4 That many signed the *acta*, although attendance lists for the various sessions reveal fewer names.

5 See Dorfmann-Lazarev and Griffith in this volume.

6 See Dorfmann-Lazarev in this volume.

7 Troupeau, "Églises et chrétiens," 411–38 (with bibliography) and Atiya, *History*, 167–235. See also n. 5 above and "Syrian Orthodox Church," in *Oxford Dictionary of the Christian Church*, 1582–83 (with further bibliography).

condemnation at the Council of Ephesus in 430. For a time the Nestorians contested Syria with the miaphysites, but when they lost their stronghold of Edessa in 449, their sphere of free activity moved to Mesopotamia. In that region they gained considerable freedom of action under the Persians, who mistrusted the Jacobite bishops who were loyal to Antioch. By 498 the Nestorian catholicos at Seleucia-Ctesiphon claimed equality with the other eastern patriarchs, but they never recognized his claim. The catholicos himself had at least four suffragan bishops, and the eight metropolitan sees in existence at the time of the Arab conquest grew to approximately twenty by 1000. In 1200 there may have been as many as 200 to 250 Nestorian bishops spread from China to Arabia. In the 770s the catholicosate moved to Baghdad. Succession was frequently disrupted by the caliphs.[8]

In Armenia the church emerged in the interstices between Roman–Persian and then Byzantine–Arab rivalries. At one time or another Antioch, Constantinople, and Rome each claimed authority over the Armenian church. All the while, the Armenian catholicos insisted that he was the equal of all other patriarchs. The catholicosate was centered in Etschmiadzin and had four or five subordinate patriarchates; Armenian terminology is unusual in this regard. It is difficult to say how many bishoprics there were. The Catholicos Imbat struck a bargain with the caliph in 703 that made him the guarantor of his people's good behavior in return for virtual liberation from Constantinople. As the caliphate declined in power, Armenia became a virtually independent state between the ninth and early eleventh centuries. The church functioned as the only "national" institution, a fact not lost on the Seljuk Turks, who reduced the church to impotence when they conquered the region in the mid-eleventh century.[9]

There was also an important Christian community in Jerusalem. The bishops of Jerusalem were only recognized as patriarchs by Chalcedon in 451. The Persian and Muslim conquests were devastating, and the bishops lost much ground to Jacobite churches and even to Nestorian ones. Alone among the eastern patriarchates, however, Jerusalem's official church remained Melkite and also maintained sporadic relations with Rome. It is a sign of the impact of the Arab conquests that the patriarchal throne was vacant from 638 to 691. The

8 Troupeau, "Églises et chrétiens," 438–54; Atiya, *History*, 239–90; and further references in the bibliography to Dorfmann-Lazarev in this volume.

9 Mahé, "L'église arménienne"; Atiya, *History*, 307–47; further references in the bibliography to Dorfmann-Lazarev in this volume.

caliph 'Umar I (634–44) agreed to respect churches and clerics, and conditions were generally tolerable except under the brutal al-Ḥākim (996–1021).[10]

As long as the emperors controlled Alexandria, the religious situation in Egypt was tense. A majority of the population and the clergy was miaphysite whereas the official church was Melkite, that is to say, Chalcedonian. The distinctive strain of Christianity that evolved in Egypt is usually labeled "Coptic," the word coming from the Egyptian dialect used for worship. When the Persians captured Alexandria, a Coptic patriarch was elected, but he fled on Byzantium's reconquest of the city, only to return in 641 when the Arabs expelled the Byzantine secular and religious authorities. The patriarchate was located at Alexandria until it was moved to Damrū and then to Cairo in 1046. The patriarchs, who always regarded themselves as the equals of the patriarchs of Rome, Antioch, and Constantinople, seem to have had authority over around fifty to sixty bishops. One key achievement of the Coptic Church was the extension of Christianity into Nubia. The Coptic Church prospered except under the reign of al-Ḥākim.[11]

The Arab conquest of North Africa from the borders of Egypt to the Atlantic seems to have wiped out the flourishing Christian culture of Late Antiquity. An almost complete absence of sources may make the situation seem darker than it really was, but it appears that one of the greatest contractions of the Christian church in the early Middle Ages took place in North Africa. Pockets of Christians certainly survived – in the eleventh century Pope Gregory VII (1073–85) corresponded with one of them – but an organized church vanished.[12]

Western Europe presents a multifaceted spectacle. The surviving sources are unevenly distributed and are sometimes difficult to interpret. Primarily the story is one of expansion. But Viking incursions in the ninth and tenth centuries were occasionally disruptive. For example, Hamburg, erected as a bishopric in 832/3, was burned in 845 and the bishopric soon shifted to Bremen. A pagan Slavic uprising in 983 temporarily shut down the sees of Brandenburg and Havelburg. The best evidence for contraction comes from the Iberian peninsula after its conquest by Muslims in 711 to 716, although in many cases interruptions of episcopal succession occurred well after the initial conquest. A few representative examples of gaps in succession will illustrate the situation:

10 Gil, *History*, 432–57, 478–82, 769–78, and passim.
11 Atiya, *History*, 11–145; "Coptic Church," in *Oxford Dictionary of the Christian Church*, 419–20; further references in the bibliography to Dorfmann-Lazarev in this volume.
12 Baus, "North African Christianity"; Dell'arche, *Scomparsa del cristianesimo*.

Avila	802–1087
Barcelona	689–858
Calaborra	871–1020
Cartagena	638–1241
Cordoba	988–1237
Coria	688–876
Cuenca	693–849
Gerona	693–778
Ivia	683–800
Saragossa	693–849.[13]

Some Iberian sees disappeared completely.

Following the development of the church in Ireland is complicated by contradictory sources and historiographical battles. The latter turn around the relationships between episcopal authority, secular rulership, and monastic power.[14] Throughout the early Middle Ages Armagh and Kildare regularly, and Iona occasionally, claimed archiepiscopal/metropolitan status and authority, but there is little evidence that these claims were effective. Concepts of hierarchy and province were always in evidence, however, even if we cannot see how things worked on the ground. The former issue can be exemplified by narrative sources that show twenty-three bishops in the seventh century, twenty-five in the eighth, fifty in the ninth, and forty-eight in the tenth.[15] It is simply unsafe to draw conclusions from this kind of evidence. That there was a growing and continuously functioning Irish church under territorial bishops seems indisputable. How that church worked in practice is very much open to question.

The overall situation in England is much clearer owing to a deeper fund of evidence. The plot of the story here is steady expansion. Roman Britain had a rudimentary ecclesiastical organization. The settlement of the pagan Anglo-Saxons between about 450 and 600 seems to have obliterated Christian structures from the areas that would become England, while leaving scattered remnants in the more heavily Celtic west. In the years around 600 Britain experienced two waves of Christianizing efforts. From the monastery of Iona, founded in 563 by Columba (d. 597), Irish missionaries spread their customs in Scotland and Northumbria, establishing the bishopric of Lindisfarne in about 635. In 597 missionaries sent by Pope Gregory I (590–604) landed in Kent. Basing himself on Roman imperial documents, Gregory planned to create metropolitan sees at London and York, and to furnish each see with

13 Information compiled from Gams, *Series episcoporum*.

14 See Charles-Edwards in this volume and, more fully, his *Early Christian Ireland*. See also Etchingham, *Church Organisation*, 12–46, for a detailed discussion of the historiography. The key statement of older views is Hughes, *Church*.

15 Etchingham, *Church Organisation*, 158–70, 478–82.

twelve suffragans. The plan proved unrealistic. Canterbury, the seat of the kings of Kent, was established as a metropolitan see, and other sees were soon established at Rochester and London. By 625 York had been elevated to episcopal status, too. Rivalries between followers of Roman and Celtic usages led to the Synod of Whitby (664), where the assembled clerics and laymen decided in favor of Roman usages. In 668 Rome sent Theodore as Archbishop of Canterbury (668–90). He arrived to find a scandalous bishop in London, an irregular one in York, and another without a fixed see. Through patient labor Theodore erected a functioning hierarchy of two metropolitan sees and twelve further bishoprics. Complications arose from England's small-scale political geography, the Viking invasions, and a lack of urban nuclei upon which to base a well-articulated church structure. There were adjustments to Theodore's scheme in later times. These examples typify the process: the small sees of Norfolk and Suffolk were united at Norwich in 957; in 909 the large see of Sherborne was divided, and new sees were created at Crediton and Wells. Then in 1046, Crediton and Sherborne were united at Exeter, while the see of Wells was moved to Bath in 1088/91.[16]

The European continent presents regions of quite different ecclesiastical development. The lands lying west of the Rhine and south of the Danube, in other words, lands that had once been part of the Roman Empire, experienced overall continuity with some adjustments. The German lands to the east of the Rhine that were part of the Frankish kingdoms and empire saw dramatic growth. Scandinavia and the Slavic lands were wholly new entrants into the Christian world.

In the former Roman lands, the empire left behind a far-flung network of *civitates* (Roman provincial capitals), most of which had possessed bishops since the fourth century or earlier. In southern and central Gaul, the network was thicker, ecclesiastical territories smaller, and bishops often formidable local figures. As one moved further north, there were fewer towns and bishops, larger territories under the authority of single bishops, and, for good or ill, closer contact between ecclesiastical structures and the government of the Frankish kings. Political turmoil, always and everywhere a threat to the smooth functioning of ecclesiastical structures, disrupted the church in the Frankish realms in the second half of the seventh century, although conditions never got as bad as contemporary, or later, critics alleged.[17] The eighth century inaugurated almost two centuries of steady growth.

16 Blair, *Church*, with rich bibliography. Price, "Christianization."

17 Riché, "De Grégoire le Grand," 607–82; I. Wood, *Merovingian Kingdoms*, 71–87; Wallace-Hadrill, *Frankish Church*, 1–123.

In 716 the Duke of Bavaria approached the pope about the creation of an ecclesiastical hierarchy in his lands. In the next decades bishoprics were created at Salzburg, Freising, Passau, Säben, and Regensburg. Not until 798, and then under Charlemagne's aegis, was Salzburg elevated to metropolitan status. In northern and central German lands the efforts of the Anglo-Saxon missionaries Willibrord (c. 658–739) and Boniface (c. 675–754) were critical in four respects. First, new bishoprics were created at such places as Utrecht, Würzburg, Eichstätt, Buraburg, and Erfurt, although the latter two did not survive. Second, both missionaries effected strong, if not always easy, working relations with the key Frankish rulers, the Carolingian mayors of the palace Charles Martel (714–41), Carloman (741–47), and Pippin (741–51). The Franks were prompted to undertake structural reforms of the church in the Frankish realms. Third, both missionaries visited Rome, established close relations with the papacy, and worked as agents of papal influence north of the Alps. Fourth, in 732 Boniface was accorded a *pallium* – a white wool liturgical vestment sent by popes to metropolitan bishops to signify their close ties to Rome – and shortly thereafter made archbishop (at first without a see and then at Mainz). Boniface struggled mightily to erect a metropolitan hierarchy but had only limited success in Germany and none at all in western Francia, where he tried to elevate Rheims and Rouen. Boniface's work bore ripe fruit in the next generations. When Charlemagne (d. 814) drew up his will, he made donations to twenty-one metropolitan sees. By the ninth century every metropolitan, or archbishop as they were usually called in Francia (see below), was required to seek a *pallium* from Rome. Saxony, conquered by Charlemagne in a long series of wars, is a spectacular case of growth, going from zero to eight bishoprics.[18]

The tenth and eleventh centuries witnessed little structural change in the West Frankish kingdom but continued growth in the east. To the Carolingian archiepiscopal sees of Mainz, Cologne, Trier, and Salzburg were added Hamburg-Bremen, with four new suffragan sees, and Magdeburg, with five. Evidence for French archbishops' seeking *pallia* in Rome is thin, but German archbishops regularly did so. What is more, German rulers and bishops kept a watchful eye on their Scandinavian and Slavic neighbors.[19]

Carolingian missionaries made efforts to introduce the faith into Scandinavia but without durable success. It was many years between the baptisms of the Danish kings Harald Klak in 826 and Harald Gormsson ("Bluetooth")

18 Riché, "Le christianisme"; Wallace-Hadrill, *Frankish Church*, 124–419.
19 Martin and Parisse, "La chrétienté occidentale"; Hauck, *Kirchengeschichte*, vols. 2 and 3.

in 965. In each of the Scandinavian realms sources attribute key roles to kings. We can also discern important roles played by German rulers and bishops, English kings and missionaries, and some contributions by the papacy. Before Harold (961–85) became king there was certainly a bishopric at Haithabu and possibly others at Aarhus and Ribe founded by Archbishop Adaltag of Hamburg-Bremen (937–88). By 1060 there were nine bishoprics in Danish territory. Adalbert of Hamburg-Bremen (1043–72) was made papal legate and vicar for the North by Pope Leo IX in 1053. He seems to have wished to become a sort of patriarch of the North. Hamburg-Bremen's ambitions were checked when Lund was elevated to archiepiscopal status for Denmark in 1104. Since the middle of the eleventh century Denmark's kings had been trying to gain ecclesiastical independence for their kingdom, partly to escape the influence of the German crown and church. In Norway, Christianization began with King Hakon the Good (921 or 935–60), who was raised at the court of King Æthelstan (924/5–39) in England and who may have brought an English bishop with him to Norway. Later traditions assign central roles to kings Olaf Tryggvason (995–1000) and Olaf Haraldsson – St. Olaf (1015–30). Legends that surely contain grains of truth give Olaf Tryggvason credit for persuading the Icelanders to accept Christianity in 999/1000. King Cnut, who ruled both England (1016–35) and Denmark (1018–35) while holding sway over much of Norway, seems to have begun regularizing church structures, perhaps based on what he saw in England. It was not until 1152, however, that Nidaros-Trondheim became a metropolitan see. The situation in Sweden is considerably less clear. Olof Sköttkonung (c. 994–1020/1) was the first king to be baptized, traditionally in 1008, and the first bishopric was established at Skara in 1014. Much of Sweden remained pagan well into the twelfth century, and the realm's organization dates from that period, as does the creation of its metropolitan see at Uppsala in 1164. The growth of the church in Scandinavia was an impressive accomplishment.[20]

The Slavic world is a complicated region historically, ethnically, linguistically, and hence, ecclesiastically. Two powerful dynamics helped and hindered Christianization: local political pressures and German–Byzantine rivalries. Although the ninth century witnessed promising beginnings in areas such as Croatia, Moravia, and Bohemia, the Magyar invasions of the late ninth century proved massively disruptive. Solid work with a future was the product of

20 Sawyer and Sawyer, "Scandinavia Enters"; Sawyer et al., *Christianization*; Kempf, "Spread"; Sawyer and Sawyer, *Medieval Scandinavia*, 100–21; Kaufhold, *Europas Norden*, 57–98.

the tenth century. We will look first at a band of territories stretching between the Balkans and the Baltic and then turn to Kiev and the land of Rus.[21]

Christianization in Croatia began in antiquity, but earlier achievements were severely damaged by the Avar invasions in the sixth century. After the defeat of the Avars, the bishop of Salzburg and the patriarch of Aquileia divided the mission field in south-central Europe at the Drava River. Thus Croatia fell to Aquileia with, always, important papal influences. A metropolitan see was re-created at Split, and the first known bishop, Grgur of Nin, was consecrated by Pope Nicholas I in 860. A few years later the Croatians and the papacy quarreled with Louis the German (806–76), who wished to erect a metropolitan see at Sirmium (Sremska Mitrovica) which lay just inside Bulgaria's territory. In Bohemia and Moravia the brothers Constantine-Cyril (826–69) and Methodius (c. 815–85), missionaries requested from Byzantium by the Moravian leader, labored long and hard to convert people, but had little success in erecting firm ecclesiastical structures, mainly owing to strong objections by East German kings and Bavarian bishops. The Magyar invasions were disruptive, but some Christian communities survived under the nominal authority of the bishops of Regensburg. In the tenth century the Přemislide dynasty organized the region. Generally, they were allied with Germany's Ottonian kings, and out of that partnership emerged two bishoprics, at Prague (973) and Olomuc, or Olmütz, (1063). Both submitted to the archbishops of Mainz.[22]

The church in Poland came into being rather rapidly. In c. 964 King Mieszko married Dobrava, the daughter of Boleslav I of Prague, and received baptism in 966. In 968 sources report on a Bishop Jordan (968–82), seemingly in Poznań, who was subject to Magdeburg. The archbishops of Magdeburg always had an interest in extending their authority to the east, and this may have occasioned Mieszko's approach to Rome in 992 when he offered Poland to St. Peter. He may have been seeking ecclesiastical independence from Germany or confirmation of Poland's independence. In 999 Otto III and Boleslav Chrobry erected an archiepiscopal see at Gniezno and immediately subordinated to it new bishoprics in Cracow, Wrocław, and Kolberg. Within a few years Poznań was detached from Magdeburg and placed under Gniezno. Poland's dioceses persisted through times of severe political uncertainty in the high Middle Ages.[23]

21 Gieysztor, "L'Europe chrétienne."

22 Tomljenović, "Wann begegneten"; Polek, "Great Moravian State"; Steinhübel, "Kirchliche Organisation"; Čaplovič, "Archaeology"; Kłoczowski, "La nouvelle chrétienté"; Kempf, "Evangelization"; Vlasto, *Entry of Slavs*, 86–154.

23 Barford, *Early Slavs*, 200–23; Vlasto, *Entry of Slavs*, 113–41; see also Kłoczowski and Kempf as in footnote 22.

Returning to the south, we encounter the two important cases of Bulgaria and Hungary. The Bulgarian state began emerging in the 680s as an amalgamation of proto-Bulgars and Slavs, all of whom were pagan. It is possible that there were some Christian, Hellenized Slavs nearby, but the records are vague. The creation of a church dates from the time of Khan Boris (844/5–88), who was baptized in 864 and immediately entered into correspondence with Pope Nicholas I (858–67) who sent replies to 106 questions but no assurances of an archiepiscopal see. Boris then turned to Byzantium and received Greek bishops. In the time of Khan Symeon (893–927) the Bulgarian church became an autonomous member of the "Byzantine Commonwealth," with an archbishopric that alternated between Preslav and Dristra. The archbishops and bishops were usually Greek and appointed in Constantinople. Emperor Basil II (958–1025) launched a major war against the Bulgarians which devastated the western portions of the region and tightly subjected the eastern regions to Constantinople. The seat of the archbishopric was transferred to Ochrid, and Bulgaria's claims to a patriarchate were extinguished. At least four bishoprics survived Basil's onslaught.[24]

The pagan Magyars wreaked havoc on central Europe (and on other regions, too) until they were defeated in 955 and 970 and began to settle on the Pannonian plain and to commingle with resident Slavs. In 972/3 King Geza (d. 997) turned to Otto I for an alliance after the German emperor made peace with Byzantium in 971. Hungary had hostile Byzantines on one side, abetted by their new Bulgarian allies, and ambitious Germans on the other side. Latin missionary work, mainly directed from Bavaria, flowed into Hungary. The complexity of the situation can be seen from the fact that Geza's wife Sarolt was a daughter of the eastern frontier prince Gyula who was a Greek Christian. It seems that Geza and his son Vajk were baptized in 973. The key work of creating a church dates from Vajk (997–1038), known more commonly by his baptismal name, Stephen. He succeeded in obtaining an archiepiscopal see at Esztergom (or Gran) in 1000/1 with five suffragans and then, in 1008, a second archiepiscopal see in the east at Kolocsa, with three initial suffragans. Although Hungary wound up as a Latin-rite country, Kolocsa was always open to Greek influences.[25]

There were certainly some Christians in the lands of the Rus before Princess Olga went to Constantinople in 954/5 (or possibly 946). Arab geographers say that there was a church in Kiev as early as 944. She was unsuccessful in obtaining

24 Wasilewski, "L'église"; Vlasto, *Entry of Slavs*, 155–87.
25 Sághy, "Aspects"; Kempf, "Evangelization," 240–45.

a bishop and turned to Otto I in 961/2 who sent St. Adalbert (d. 981), later the first bishop of Prague, who returned after a short time, having been unable to accomplish anything. Olga may have been motivated by an awareness of developments in Bulgaria. Prince Vladimir of Kiev (980–1015) was baptized in 988/9, as a consequence of his alliance with Byzantium, and began the serious Christianization of his lands. It is not clear when Rus got its first bishop (the first secure mention of one coming in 1037), but a date as early as 967 is possible. Kiev's cathedral of St. Sophia was probably dedicated in 1046, but this does not preclude an earlier date for the see. New bishoprics were founded in the eleventh and twelfth centuries to an eventual number of seventeen. Most early Kievan bishops were Greeks appointed by Constantinople, but the archbishops usually appointed their suffragans with occasional interference by Rus's rulers.[26]

Ecclesiastical structures

Having noted in summary fashion the creation of ecclesiastical hierarchies spreading outward from the former Roman Empire, it is time now to look at some examples of how those hierarchies were organized and how they worked. There is better evidence for western Europe than for anywhere else, but numerous hints suggest that the same basic principles applied everywhere. The hierarchies created in Roman times were bequeathed to later centuries. Typically these involved a metropolitan see in the *civitas*, the capital of a Roman province, surrounded by varying numbers of subordinates, or suffragans. In most of the West, from the Carolingian period, metropolitans were normally called archbishops, whereas the metropolitan title persisted in most other areas, with the catholicos/catholicosate title common in parts of the East. Nevertheless, one can find archbishops all over the Christian world, and in the West the archiepiscopal title was sometimes conferred as a personal honor without jurisdictional implications.

The basic structure of the church consisted of patriarchates, including the Roman papacy which usually did not use the patriarchal title, metropolitans (or archbishops), bishops, and priests. There were lower orders of clergy, too, typically deacons, subdeacons, lectors, exorcists, and doorkeepers. In the East, one regularly encounters cantors, and Constantinople had deaconesses, who assisted in the baptism of adult women, until the twelfth century. The two largest churches were in Rome and Constantinople.

26 Fennell, *History*, 6–58; Vlasto, *Entry of Slavs*, 236–95; see also Shepard in this volume.

Rome's bishops, like others, were elected by "clergy and people." It is difficult to observe the electoral process at any moment or to determine the composition and interests of contending parties. Until the election of Zachary I in 741, the newly elected pope had to obtain confirmation of his election from the emperor at Constantinople before he could be consecrated. Under Louis the Pious (814–40), the Carolingians insisted that the newly elected pope renew the pact of *amicitia, pax et caritas* ("friendship, peace, and love") with the Carolingian emperor before consecration could take place but did not demand the former Byzantine right of confirmation, requiring only that elections be completed canonically. What canonical meant before 769 is hard to say. In that year a Roman Synod, which included twelve Frankish bishops, attempted to limit the electors to Rome's cardinal clergy (see below). By 816 the "people" were again participating in elections. Until the middle of the eleventh century "people" meant essentially the Roman nobility, and the gradual decline of Carolingian influence in Rome made the requirement for canonical elections a dead letter. In 1059 a Roman Synod under Nicholas II issued an electoral decree giving the prime role to the cardinal bishops, while reserving vague rights to the German emperors. By the early twelfth century, Rome's cardinal priests and deacons gained rights as electors making an electoral body of fifty-two (or fifty-three) cardinals which, with some later procedural modifications, remains the electoral body to this day. Only rarely (963, 964, 1046) did German emperors depose reigning popes and impose their own candidates. Carolingian rulers never did so, but in the tenth century the Roman nobility routinely intruded themselves into the process of naming popes.[27]

Liturgical administration radiated from the altars of Rome's cathedral church, St. John Lateran, and the other "patriarchal" basilicas – churches where the official, albeit not the daily, celebrant was the pope. In the pope's place, the suburbicarian bishops – bishops in such suburban towns as Ostia, Velletri, Porto, etc. – celebrated at Rome's major altars according to an intricate rotation. The suburbicarian bishops, usually seven in number, were the cardinal bishops of the Roman Church. Closely annexed to the cathedral and patriarchal basilicas were the title churches, around twenty in number as our period opens and twenty-eight by its end. Each *titulus* had a staff of several priests, one presiding as the title priest. The title priests were the cardinal priests of the Roman Church. Key papal advisers, they were often elected as popes. Over the centuries, the pope himself gave visible form to the supervision of

27 Baumgartner, *Behind Locked Doors*.

"his" urban church by celebrating stational masses, up to 180 through the year, at the *tituli*, again according to a regular rotation.[28]

The administrative system, headquartered in the Lateran Palace, consisted of a few great officers and a troop of deacons. The Primicerius, for example, led the notaries and archives. The Nomenculator was the chief ceremonial officer. The Arcarius and Saccelarius oversaw the collection and disbursement of revenues. Other officers managed the church's vast patrimonies, maintained Rome's churches, and presided in courts of law after the disappearance of secular authority. The deacons served in numerous ad hoc capacities, frequently as ambassadors, but had chief responsibility for charitable services of all kinds. Seven "regionary" deacons administered districts of Rome and were the cardinal deacons of the Roman Church.[29]

The pope's practical authority was confined to Rome and the suburbicarian bishoprics, although the popes regularly tried to extend their power over Ravenna, Milan, and other sees in northern Italy. Over the years the popes gradually built their Roman synods into a more effective tool of governance in Italy, as can be seen in the spectacular increase in their numbers:

By century	7th	8th	9th	10th	11th
No. of synods	9	8	17	16	42

The pope's authority over western metropolitans / archbishops grew as a result of the conferral of the *pallium*. The crucial precedent was Boniface's swearing of the same oath of allegiance as that sworn by the suburbicarian bishops. Beginning around 800, metropolitan bishops regularly sought and received a *pallium* from Rome after their elections. In principle they could not exercise their metropolitan office or sit on their thrones until they had received their *pallium*. This emerging system symbolized the yoking of all episcopal authority to that of the bishop of Rome, but actual papal authority was limited by the pope's inability to control the naming of archbishops and his relative inability to coerce those who had been named.

Papal authority over the western church as a whole was limited. Since antiquity popes demanded that "major cases" be submitted to Rome for arbitration. In reality, popes could rarely draw cases under their purview. The Pseudo-Isidorean Decretals – a remarkable set of forgeries produced in ninth-century Francia – gave a powerful boost to papal juridical authority, but the underlying force of the documents was an attempt by suffragan bishops

28 Baldovin, *Urban Character*; Noble, *Republic*, 212–30, and "Papacy."
29 Noble, *Republic*, 212–55.

in the Carolingian world to limit the power of their metropolitans, not to enhance papal power.[30] Gregory's mission to England is well known, but the actual papal role in early medieval missionary activity was secondary.[31] The earliest papal canonizations of saints occurred right around the turn of the millennium, but the papal role in canonizations was not regularized until the thirteenth century.[32] Popes had always sent envoys to rulers and churchmen to address particular concerns, but the formal system of legation was only beginning to take shape in the eleventh century.[33] The popes possessed two coercive disciplinary tools: excommunication, the separation of an individual from the sacraments of the church and from interaction with other Christians, and interdict, the suspension of most sacramental services in a defined region in an attempt to bring pressure to bear on a specific person. The former was used often, but not spectacularly, in major cases before the breach with Constantinople in 1054 and the multiple excommunications of King Henry IV of Germany by Gregory VII. Interdicts are occasionally heard of in the early Middle Ages but first achieved real prominence when Alexander III laid Scotland under interdict in 1163.[34] The Carolingians turned to Rome for authoritative guidance on canon law[35] and liturgy[36] long before the popes began to assume a leading role in these areas. On topics such as holy images and the procession of the Holy Spirit, the Carolingians and the popes agreed to disagree. The multitudes of pilgrims who went to Rome enhanced papal eminence, but they went there to worship at the tombs of the apostles and martyrs.[37] Sending *pallia* to archbishops strengthened their ties to Rome even though the papacy had little say in who became archbishops in the first place. The "Papal Monarchy" of the high Middle Ages is only dimly visible in the earlier medieval centuries.

The "Great Church," the Church of Hagia Sophia in Constantinople, was also large, complex, and influential in both direct and indirect ways.[38] The patriarchs of Constantinople were chosen as follows: the metropolitans in the "Standing Synod" (see below) sent the names of three candidates to the

30 See Nelson in this volume.
31 Sullivan, "Papacy."
32 Kemp, *Canonization*.
33 "Legate, Papal," in *Oxford Dictionary of the Christian Church*, 969, with references.
34 Vodola, *Excommunication*; "Interdict," in *Oxford Dictionary of the Christian Church*, 845.
35 See Nelson in this volume.
36 Vogel, "Les échanges liturgiques."
37 Birch, *Pilgrimage to Rome*.
38 For what follows: Hussey, *Orthodox Church*, 297–318; Kazhdan, "Constantinople"; Potz, *Patriarch und Synode*, 17–24; Darrouzès, *Recherches*, 1–50.

emperor; he could choose one or propose a fourth. The emperor then announced and invested the patriarch in the Magnaura Palace, and on the following Sunday the newly elected patriarch was consecrated in Hagia Sophia. This prominent imperial role was absent in the West. The patriarch's duties comprised maintaining orthodoxy and suppressing heresy, pastoral and disciplinary management, direction of ecclesiastical courts, oversight of liturgy, control of church property, supervision of monasteries depending directly on the patriarchate, and dealing with the emperor.

The Great Church had perhaps 600 officials in the seventh century and not many fewer in later times. Like Rome, Constantinople had both liturgical and administrative sides, but whereas individual bureaux were highly articulated, the whole system was less compartmentalized, leading to anomalies such as deacons being in charge of priests. Officials were called *archons*. The main departments, *offikia*, were initially under deacons but in later times were led by other clerics or even laymen. The five great branches of the government were led by deacons, the *pentas*, who bear some similarities to Rome's cardinal deacons. The Great Oeconomos had charge of finances and properties. The Skeuophylax was the liturgical and ceremonial officer and had responsibility for vestments and vessels. The Great Saccelarius controlled monasteries in and around the capital. The Protecdicus had charge of discipline, marriage certificates, sanctuary, repentant apostates, and foreign converts. The Great Chartophylax led the chancery and archives.

An unusual feature of the Orthodox Church was the "Standing Synod" (*endemousa synodos*). This synod consisted of the metropolitans and bishops who happened to be present in Constantinople at any moment. It met three times per week under the patriarch or, if he were absent, under the Chartophylax. The cathedral archons prepared its agenda and assisted in its deliberations. The synod, in existence by the fifth century, became prominent by the tenth.

The authority of the patriarchs was complicated by several factors. The rise of Islam was the greatest challenge. Byzantium's introduction of the Theme System of government between the late sixth century and the early eighth tended to separate secular from ecclesiastical geography. Iconoclasm compromised patriarchal relations with some metropolitans.[39] The extension of authority into new areas such as Bulgaria and Rus was impeded by local sensitivities as well as by the actions of local and imperial officials.

39 See Louth in this volume.

The hundreds of bishoprics into which Christianity was organized were all smaller than those of the great patriarchates. At different times, particularly in the West, certain bishops, usually but not always metropolitans, were treated as vicars.[40] That is, they were inserted, typically by kings but sometimes on the insistence of a local church, into the hierarchy between the pope and other bishops. At different times Metz, Sens, Rheims, Hamburg-Bremen, Mainz, Trier, Magdeburg, Milan, and Ravenna played this role. The Jacobite church had its own version of this intermediate jurisdiction. From the seventh century, the Maphrian of the East, usually in Tikrit, served as a sort of subpatriarch for the eastern regions that looked to Antioch.[41] But patriarchs, popes, vicars, and metropolitans were all bishops. So we should ask: What did ordinary bishops do?

From at least the third century the bishop was the key official everywhere in the Christian church. Naturally the roles and duties of bishops evolved over time. By the early Middle Ages, the principal functions of a bishop were: governing in councils or synods; ordaining members of the clergy; supervising the intellectual and moral instruction of their clergy; preaching and teaching; combating pagans and heretics; consecrating churches and altars; organizing and presiding over the liturgy; caring for the poor, widows, and orphans; administering the landed wealth of their churches; presiding, directly or through subordinates, in ecclesiastical courts; blessing holy oils used for the sacraments in local churches; and conducting annual, sometimes semi-annual, visitations of their dioceses.

Bishops were supposed to be elected by the clergy and people of their diocese, but several factors militated against local and clerical control of the process. Bishops were too important and influential for rulers to be unconcerned with them, and the political, social, and economic interests of local aristocratic elites were imbricated in episcopal governance. Emperors took an active role everywhere in the Byzantine Empire, as did rulers in newly emerging Christian regions. Muslim authorities carefully watched episcopal elections in their lands. Frankish (and then German) kings and emperors were especially interested in episcopal appointments because bishops were critical agents in the exercise of royal power. When a bishop died, the cathedral clergy (see below) requested from the ruler permission to proceed to an election. Rulers usually appointed a visitor to supervise the see (from *sedes*, or "seat") until a new bishop was elected. The newly elected was presented to

40 Kempf, "Metropolitans," 290; Reynolds, "Organisation," 596–600.
41 Atiya, *History*, 220–21.

the king, who could refuse to accept him. This right of refusal was tantamount to a right of designation. In 921 Pope John X told the archbishop of Cologne that "ancient custom" permitted kings to name bishops.[42] By the middle of the eleventh century papal rejection of that custom helped to launch the Investiture Controversy.[43] Many bishops, particularly in tenth- and eleventh-century Germany, had served in the royal chapel and were trusted associates of the ruler. In Germany, bishops tended to come from a small number of families. The Roman nobility dominated the papacy between 900 and 1046, and urban elites tended to control appointments elsewhere in Italy and in southern France.[44]

Bishops had many *ministri* to help them accomplish their manifold tasks. A *primicerius* or *cantor* supervised the liturgy. A *scholasticus* directed the school. A *custos*, usually aided by a *sacrista* and a *saccarius* oversaw the moveable wealth of the cathedral, ranging from money to liturgical books, vessels, and insignia. A *praepositus*, assisted by a *camerarius* and a *cancellarius*, constituted the primary administrative and financial officers. Often an archdeacon served as a sort of *locum tenens* for the bishop.[45] Perhaps under ascetic and monastic influence, cathedral clergy from at least the fourth century sometimes organized themselves into chapters, from the *capitula* of a rule which they devised or adopted. In sixth-century Gaul one begins to hear of *clerici canonici*. Not every cathedral had a body of canons and not every community of canons belonged to a cathedral. Chrodegang of Metz initiated the process of regularizing the canonical life, and the legislation (816–19) of Louis the Pious began to systematize the canonical order within the context of the church as a whole.[46] On average, churches had perhaps thirty to forty canons although Chartres had seventy-two, Nevers sixty, and Auxerre fifty.[47]

The regular organs of episcopal governance were two. First, metropolitans were expected to gather their suffragan bishops in synod at least once per year, while diocesan bishops were to meet annually with their priests, if possible on Holy Thursday when the priests came to the cathedral to collect holy oils. The surviving evidence for councils is patchy but nevertheless testifies to an effective system. In the Frankish world there exists some documentation for at

42 John X, *Epistola* 10, in *Papsturkunden*, 81.

43 See Barrow in this volume. On the controversy generally, Blumenthal, *Investiture Controversy*.

44 Imbart de la Tour, *Les élections épiscopales*; Lot and Fawtier, *Histoire*, 43–48; Kempf, "Metropolitans," 294–95; Reuter, "'Imperial Church System'"; Santifaller, *Zur Geschichte*; and Schieffer, "Der Ottonische Reichsepiskopat."

45 Kempf, "Diocesan Organization," 258–61.

46 Claussen, *Reform*.

47 Lot and Fawtier, *Histoire*, 13–14.

least 169 councils between the time of Boniface and the late ninth century.[48] The English church met regularly right through the period covered by this volume in meetings that sometimes had "national" but more often local import.[49] Segments of the French church gathered nearly 160 times between 900 and 1100. Most of these meetings were small and local compared to their Carolingian predecessors and German contemporaries. Almost sixty councils of varying size met in Germany in the same two centuries. In both lands, the eleventh century saw a dramatic increase in numbers over the tenth. Beginning in 972 the once vigorous conciliar life of the Iberian church came back to life. More than two dozen meetings took place, many of them quite local. We know of a single council in Hungary, Armenia, Baghdad (Nestorian), and Egypt. The Jacobite church assembled at least three times. The conciliar tradition in Constantinople has left unimpressive traces after major meetings in 869–70 and 901.[50] The growing prominence of the poorly documented standing synod may make the surviving records illusory. Bishops did meet with their priests and treat with them on a wide array of moral, spiritual, and disciplinary issues. From the Carolingian period 54 episcopal "statutes" survive, generally reflecting the work of bishops' diocesan synods.[51] One suspects that many of the French and some of the German synods were also diocesan. More research is needed on the poorly published records.

The second aspect of episcopal governance involved episcopal visitations of their territories. One visitation per year was the rule, although legislation sometimes called for two. The bishop, or occasionally his representative, met in local communities with *testes synodales*, usually seven in number. These "witnesses," assumed to be persons of probity, might be laymen or clerics. They were asked to give testimony on such issues as murder, perjury, adultery, incest, prostitution, theft, superstition, and the observance of fasts and feastdays. Individuals might also be checked on their understanding of the Pater Noster and the Creed. There is insufficient evidence to say what happened to persons denounced by the *testes*.[52]

48 Hartmann, *Die Synoden*. For the documents: *Concilia aevi Karolini* and *Die Konzilien der karolingische Teilreiche*. The conciliar material from the later ninth century must still be consulted in Mansi, vols. 17–20.

49 Cubitt, *Anglo-Saxon Church Councils*; Vollrath, *Die Synoden Englands*. Documents accessible in Haddan and Stubbs, *Councils and Ecclesiastical Documents*.

50 See Mansi, vols. 17–20 for the documents. *Die Konzilien Deutschlands* provides a critical edition, so far published up to 960.

51 *Capitula episcoporum*.

52 Angenendt, *Das Frühmittelalter*, 393–94; Imbert, *Les temps carolingiens*, 138–39. Key sources are Hincmar, *Capitula quibus* and *Collectio de ecclesiis et capellis*, which expands on the former. Also, Regino of Prüm, *Libri duo de synodalibus causis*.

How did bishops and priests effect routine administration over the lands subjected to their authority? For the East and for the newly Christianized lands of the West the sources are either absent or silent. The lands that fell under Frankish and Anglo-Saxon authority are substantially, if confusingly, documented. One of the most complex and obscure questions in early medieval church history turns around the nature of the local church and the structural relationships between bishops and local churches. Local churches (baptismal churches or simple oratories) were in principle established by bishops in the territories outside their cities. Initially, these churches were served by clerics from the cathedral. Gradually, local churches gained resident priests and became the regular sites where local people heard mass, received baptism, and were buried. In seventh-century Gaul most people lived within seven miles of a church, and a little later in England minsters were within five to six miles of the majority of the population.[53] Royal and conciliar legislation attempted to protect the integrity of these churches. Two other kinds of churches dotted the countryside: "proprietary churches" created by laymen on their estates and rural churches founded by the many monasteries that assumed responsibility for the "care of souls" in their districts.[54] For varying reasons, the possessors of these latter kinds of churches were reluctant to permit bishops too much authority over them. Pastoral care by monasteries declined over the early Middle Ages, and one of the more effective achievements of the Investiture Controversy was the restriction of lay control over local churches. What sorts of numbers can be imagined? England had hundreds of minsters; Denmark, one thousand parishes in the twelfth century, many of them doubtless earlier; Kiev and its region had, perhaps, four hundred churches; a medium-sized town like Metz had nine churches in the city, eleven outside, and six in monastic villages.[55] To put all of this into slightly different terms, the early Middle Ages witnessed the steady growth of the parish system in many areas. That growth was partly the application of royal and papal policy and partly the elimination of obstacles by resolute bishops.

How, then, did bishops exercise authority and influence over their rural churches, regardless of what kinds of churches they were? Councils and visitations were important. More important, however, were various intermediate levels of administration. In the Frankish world, especially in the north where the dioceses tended to be very large, chorbishops were sometimes appointed

53 Stancliffe, "From Town to Country"; Blair, *Church*, 149–52.

54 Stutz, *Geschichte*, remains the classic study; Constable, "Monasteries."

55 Blair, *Church*, 149–52, 368–83, 426–63; Brink, "Formation," 19–44; Nicholas, *Growth*, 91–92.

to represent episcopal authority in rural districts (*chora*).[56] In the ninth century the chorepiscopate became increasingly controversial, and eventually the office was suppressed. Rural authority began to radiate more directly from the cathedral. Archdeacons came to govern the clerics in the cathedral and gradually came to have territorial jurisdiction in the countryside. Large rural churches, sometimes called by scholars "mother parishes," and usually headed by an archpriest, tended to assume responsibility for smaller churches. As more and more rural churches became free standing, territories were divided up under deans. These deans regularly visited their parishes in a compact version of the visitation system used by bishops. Nowhere in Europe in the early Middle Ages was the parish system or the structure of archdeacons, archpriests, deans, and deaneries completely in place. In England, indeed, there was no intermediate level of administration between the bishop and the parish in 1100. The system was most fully developed in France.[57]

Many forces, therefore, contributed to creating a system that was both hierarchical and densely articulated. But there were also countervailing forces and some that were ambiguous in impact. Among the former, mention might be made of the deleterious effects for ecclesiastical geography of high politics. The Carolingian civil wars of the mid-ninth century carved up large dioceses such as Cologne, Rheims, and Trier, leaving archbishops struggling to control suffragans who found themselves under the authority of different kings. Many councils were called by kings or emperors who lent their power to the church's work but also, at times, dominated the church. Royal or aristocratic appointment of bishops quite often brought forward eminent men, but just as often put men with modest spiritual, moral, or intellectual gifts at the head of key nodes in the ecclesiastical system. Proprietary churches were a major stumbling block to the extension of uniform episcopal control, but the church could not function without the acquiescence of the very elites who controlled those churches. Old and entrenched monastic rights were almost everywhere an obstacle to episcopal authority, and some monasteries (such as Bobbio, Benevento, Cluny, Farfa, Fulda, Monte Cassino, and Saint-Denis) enjoyed papal exemption from episcopal control.[58] Many bishops divided the clerical allotment of their revenues between themselves and their canons (a *mensa episcopalis* and a *mensa canonicorum*). As canons, particularly in Germany, declined to live the common life and took prebends (individual allotments)

56 Gottlob, *Der abendländlischen Chorepiskopat.*

57 Blair, *Church*; Imbart de la Tour, *La paroisses rurales*; Aubrun, *La paroisse*, 12–131; Boyd, *Tithes and Parishes.*

58 Anton, *Studien.*

they tended to divide the church's properties and revenues.[59] The Carolingians developed a three-pronged strategy for tying the bishops closer to the ruling regime. The prongs were immunity, royal protection, and advocacy. The immunity denied ordinary secular officials rights of *introitus*, *exactio*, and *districtio* (entry, collection, and jurisdiction). Immunized territories accorded considerable power to the immunist, frequently a bishop. Royal protection drew bishops under the legal and moral authority of the rulers and insulated them, to a degree, from the travails of local politics. Advocacy, uniformly demanded by 802, mitigated the losses to state interests of the prohibition of *exactio*. There was a certain quid pro quo. Bishops themselves and their territories were subjected to various forms of royal service. Bishops might exercise "regalian" rights such as minting or toll collecting, and some bishops were appointed as counts. This blurring of the lines between bishops' ecclesiastical and secular responsibilities surely led to an enhancement of the bishops' power and influence but could dangerously compromise their religious authority. "Reformers" regularly fought against both secular control of bishops and secular roles allocated to bishops.[60]

Conceptual foundations

In conclusion, we may turn from institutions proper to ecclesiology: the doctrinal and ideological conceptions on which church government rested. We have already noticed that the eastern patriarchates, as they emerged, claimed equality with the elder peers. That equality was never achieved in practice, but throughout the early Middle Ages Christian leaders in the eastern Mediterranean world spoke in terms of a "Pentarchy," a five-headed church led by Rome, Constantinople, Antioch, Alexandria, and Jerusalem, and given visible expression in ecumenical councils (351, 381, 451, 553, 680, 787).[61] The last three patriarchates were absorbed into the Islamic world and rarely participated with their colleagues between the seventh century and the crusades. That left Rome and Constantinople in an uneasy tension. The patriarchs of Constantinople were prepared to accord Rome a kind of precedence of honor but no specific jurisdictional or theological rights.[62] Where the Orthodox world was concerned, Constantinople thought in terms of a "Byzantine Commonwealth,"

59 See in general Morris in this volume.
60 See Barrow in this volume.
61 Peri, "La pentarchia," 209–311.
62 Dvornik, *Byzantium and Roman Primacy*.

a collaborative union of churches under the guidance, if not the jurisdiction, of the patriarch.[63] Rome, on the other hand, made grand claims from time to time that were hard to translate into concrete rights and powers.

On what principles did the popes act? Leo I (440–61) spoke of his *plenitudo potestas*, but he did so in specific quarrels that make it difficult to discern how widely Leo imagined his "fullness of power" to extend, and it is clear that virtually no one submitted to his claims. Gelasius I (492–96) famously claimed that the world is governed by the "authority" of priests and the "power" of kings. *Auctoritas* and *potestas* are words with rich connotations in Roman thought so the force of Gelasius's words is clear enough. But neither he nor his successors down to the eleventh century were able to give practical effect to them.[64] In 829, Carolingian bishops gathered in council in Paris reinterpreted Gelasius's words so as to give the episcopal order precedence over Carolingian kings.[65] They did this as one element in an ecclesiology that harkened back to ancient ideas of episcopal collegiality and that articulated a collaborative, not a directive, role for the pope. Nicholas I (858–67) spoke more forcefully about papal prerogatives than any of his predecessors. In a letter to Michael III of Byzantium he said:

> It is immediately clear that the judgments of the apostolic see, than which there is no greater authority, cannot be handled by any other tribunal, nor is it possible for any to sit in judgment upon its decision. Appeals are to be made to this see from any part of the world. Such is the meaning of the canons. And no appeal is allowed from that see.[66]

Nicholas's bold claim may be read against the cry of some Frankish clerics in 864 who lamented that "the lord Pope Nicholas makes himself master of the whole world."[67] The Franks remonstrated against the pope's lack of fatherly kindness and brotherly love along with his violation of justice, reason, and canon law. They were willing to work with him, they said, but not to be commanded by him. A little later Regino of Prüm said of Nicholas that he "commanded kings and tyrants and surpassed them in authority as if he were the king of the world."[68] If it looks as though one can draw a line from Leo

63 Obolensky, *Byzantine Commonwealth*, put the term into wide circulation.
64 Although still controversial, Ullmann, *Growth of Papal Government*, remains fundamental. See, too, Morrison, *Tradition and Authority*.
65 Ullmann, *Carolingian Renaissance*, and Morrison, *Two Kingdoms*.
66 Nicholas I, *Epistola* 88, 480.
67 *Annales Bertiniani*, anno 864, 107.
68 Regino of Prüm, *Chronicon*, anno 868, 218.

I through Nicholas I to Gregory VII's breathtaking *Dictatus Papae*,[69] then it must be remembered that one can draw another line joining the Carolingian complaints with the fiery letter of Gregory VII to Archbishop Hermann of Metz answering the charge of the German bishops that he had seriously overstepped his bounds.[70] Western ecclesiology was a work-in-progress in the early Middle Ages.

Books, ideas, and offices

Several kinds of books, finally, attest to some of the ways in which prominent authors and churchmen thought about the church in institutional terms. The law books of the early medieval church constitute impressive evidence of a deep-seated interest in rule and order as well as a powerful sense of institutional memory. The collections that appeared in the high Carolingian period are instructive. The so-called *Dionysio-Hadriana*, received by Charlemagne from Hadrian I in about 774, survives in ninety-one manuscripts with a very wide geographical distribution. The *Collectio Dacheriana*, dating from around 800, survives in fifty-one manuscripts, and Ansegis's *Collectio capitularium*, from the 820s, exists in fifty-four. The main recension of Pseudo-Isidore can be found in one hundred and eight manuscripts, and a further forty-five contain substantial extracts. There are forty-nine more collections that were of local importance.[71] This constant attempt to learn and apply the rules of proper ecclesiastical governance is important, as is the mantra-like openings of so many of the texts which routinely insist that only the ancient rules universally transmitted may be, and indeed must be, applied.[72] The tenth century saw an impressive canonist in Burchard of Worms (d. 1025), and in the second half of the eleventh century legal studies and treatises proliferated.

History was written in such a way as to formulate and transmit institutional awareness and memory. The most famous such history is the *Liber Pontificalis*, written in Rome from the early sixth century to the late ninth and then begun again from time to time. This book combines personal and institutional details through a stately succession of pontificates.[73] Rome's *Liber Pontificalis* was

69 A set of chapter headings included in Gregory's *Register*. The document may represent chapter headings for a treatise that was never written.

70 Gregory VII to Hermann of Metz in Jaffé, *Regesta Pontificum Romanorum*, 5201 or (Eng. trans.) Gregory VIII, *Correspondence of Gregory VII*, 166–75.

71 Kéry, *Canonical Collections*, for the data here; but see further Nelson in this volume.

72 Somerville and Brasington, *Prefaces*.

73 *Liber Pontificalis*.

emulated in Naples and Ravenna.[74] Local pride and perhaps the Roman model led to episcopal histories such as those of Flodoard of Rheims[75] and Adam of Bremen (c. 1000–72).[76]

Finally, mention might be made of liturgical commentaries. These commentaries, beginning with Isidore of Seville's *De ecclesiasticis officiis*[77] and continuing down through Amalarius of Metz's (c. 780–c. 850) *Liber Officialis*,[78] Hrabanus's (c. 780–856) *De institutione clericorum*,[79] Walafrid Strabo's (c. 808–49) *Libellus de exordiis et incrementis*,[80] and continuing through various tenth-century texts[81] to John of Avranches's (d. 1079) *De officiis ecclesiasticis*,[82] have certain things in common. They all tend to explicate language and terminology; to describe and explain the ranks and offices in the ecclesiastical hierarchy; to discuss vestments, vessels, and books; to analyze the parts of the mass and the canonical hours; to detail the rules and times for fasting; and to describe the major feasts of the liturgical year. The remarkable similarities among these signals an ecclesiastical mentality that pushed for order and uniformity. Where the texts differ is interesting, too. Walafrid Strabo produced the West's first history of the liturgy. Once again we encounter the idea that the past is the only sure guide to the present and the future. Hrabanus laid particular stress on the formation of the clergy, producing a kind of handbook for priests, the key figures in the church's encounter with the world.[83] There were manuals of a different kind for bishops. The last sections of the fourth book and the whole of the fifth book of Rather of Verona's *Praeloquiorum* constitute a sort of *speculum episcopi*, full of sage advice about the duties of bishops as well as about the moral and political challenges they are most likely to encounter.[84] Hincmar wrote a little treatise, *Capitula quibus*, which he later expanded into his *De ecclesiis et capellis*, as a handbook for his subordinates when they undertook rural visitations on his behalf.[85] The book is at once a treasure trove of information and a window into the way a great bishop conceived of his task. A generation

74 *Gesta episcoporum Neapolitanorum*; Agnellus of Ravenna, *Liber Pontificalis ecclesiae Ravennatis*.
75 Flodoard of Rheims, *Annales*.
76 Adam of Bremen, *Storia*.
77 Ed. Lawson.
78 Ed. Hanssens.
79 Ed. Zimpel.
80 Ed. and trans. Harting-Correa.
81 Reynolds, "Marginalia."
82 This is the familiar title from the superceded *PL* edition, vol. 147: 27–62. See now the edition of Delamare, *Ordo servicii*.
83 Picker, *Pastor Doctus*.
84 Ed. Dolbeau; Eng. trans. Reid.
85 Hincmar, *Capitula quibus* (*PL* edition) and *Collectio de ecclesiis et capellis* (ed. Stratmann).

after Hincmar, Regino of Prüm wrote his *Libri duo de synodalibus causis*.[86] This book generalizes and universalizes the points made by Hincmar. It provided episcopal clergy with a valuable, usable handbook for conducting one of their major duties, the visitation of their dioceses. But it also shows us churchmen thinking *sub specie aeternitatis*, that is, institutionally.

86 Ed. Hartmann.

13

Asceticism and its institutions

ANNE-MARIE HELVÉTIUS *and* MICHEL KAPLAN

Between 600 and 1100, asceticism met with extraordinary success in the East and West. While some scholars attempt a global treatment of the history of late antique asceticism in both West and East,[1] traditional historiography generally outlines separate histories for the early medieval period in the two zones.[2] With this in mind, this chapter emphasizes points of comparison between the two, outlines shared traits and divergences, and seeks to explain them.

In their origins, the two traditions emerged from what was, in effect, a shared mould. The Roman world and its peripheries (the world of the fourth to sixth centuries in which various peoples, ideals, and texts circulated and interpenetrated) would furnish the shared bases for all later definitions of asceticism. For the authors of the seventh to the ninth centuries, in addition to the Scriptures (including numerous apocryphal writings), this corpus of literature generally included the acts of plenary and local councils, together with the writings of the church fathers, and hagiography and ascetic treatises ranging from the *Life of Anthony* to John Climacus's *Ladder of Divine Ascent*. For these writers, there was a necessary equivalence between the terms "ascetic" and "monk"; we shall return to this equivalence in the first part of this chapter, which will examine the shared basis and the ensuing forms of monasticism.

The earliest Christian ascetics appeared long before the Peace of the Church was established by the Edict of Milan in 313; however, the phenomenon experienced considerable growth after Constantine's death in 337.[3] As the church became an essential cog in the wheels of state, and began to develop an institutional character, the question arose as to how much room it would afford to ascetics. The latter were predominantly lay people whose sole vocation was the quest for perfection: to this end, at first they recognized only the

1 Most recently, see Caner, *Wandering, Begging Monks*.
2 Two recent colloquia use a comparative approach: Dierkens, Misonne, and Sansterre, *Le monachisme à Byzance*; and Lemaître, Dmitriev, and Gonneau, *Moines et monastères*.
3 Markus, *End of Ancient Christianity*, 199–211; C. Leyser, *Authority and Asceticism*.

evangelical ideal as their guide, and quickly came to represent a disrupting force in the social order. Through the influence they exercised on Christian communities, they came into direct competition with members of the clergy. As early as the Council of Chalcedon (451), both the emperor and the ecclesiastical hierarchy reacted to their unsettling presence; the one abiding concern of this council was to confine monks within monasteries under the control of the local bishop.[4]

Chalcedon by no means dealt with all the problems that ascetics were posing. Moreover, it was constrained on two fronts: first, by the limitations of a Roman world in which conciliar acts were obliged to be enforced by imperial authority, a state of affairs which excluded, for example, Ireland or the Christianities of the Sassanid Empire from consideration; and secondly, the council was restricted by the degree to which it was itself accepted – miaphysite and Nestorian Christians utterly rejected Chalcedon. Monasticism was, nonetheless, beginning to take shape in a process that was to continue during the centuries that followed. The second part of the present chapter will be concerned with these developments, and with reforms and their limits.

When monks led ascetic lives in deserted places, distant from towns and villages, indeed, in rural areas, they upset little; it was, however, quite another matter when they wanted to play an active role in civic society. While the Council of Chalcedon aimed to get monks into line, it was first and foremost in order to put an end to the civil unrest they had brought to Constantinople,[5] disorder which neither the emperor nor bishop could tolerate. The council passed over another issue in silence: monks needed the physical wherewithal to survive, which is to say, they needed some share in the division of wealth and in the allotment of land. The status of monks in society and in the economy will be the subject of the third section.

The shared basis and ensuing forms of monasticism

The primary motivation for the earliest Christians who set out on the path of ascesis was to obtain evangelical perfection as defined in Matt. 19.21: "If you would be perfect, go, sell what you possess and give to the poor, and you will have treasure in heaven; and come, follow me." In the East as in the West, this was at first interpreted radically, in accordance with the example of the apostles and, notably, following the apocryphal Acts of Thomas.[6] One

4 Council of Chalcedon, canons 4, 8, 18, 23, and 24.
5 Dagron, "Les moines et la ville."
6 "Acts of Thomas"; Caner, *Wandering, Begging Monks*, 57–65.

of the most widespread forms of ascesis in the early centuries was based on a life of peregrination, radical poverty, preaching, prayer, and begging. The earliest ascetics defined themselves as monks in the spiritual sense of the term: they were now *one* (Greek: *monos*) with God, who alone guided their steps and provided them with what they needed to live. Working or planning for tomorrow was out of the question. The Lord had said, "Look at the birds of the air: they neither sow nor reap nor gather into barns . . ." (Matt. 6.25–34). Having thus cut all ties, the ascetic became a stranger everywhere, a *peregrinus* or *xénos*, practicing *peregrinatio* or *xeniteia*. Detractors would style him a gyrovague.[7]

In fact, this radical form of ascesis quickly came to take on the appearance of a threat to social order. Wandering monks found their way into even the largest cities, begging their measly livings, and seeking out the patronage of aristocratic families in exchange for their spiritual services. They caused trouble for bishops, draining them of their nascent authority and threatening the resources of the official church.

Hence, the numerous reactions aimed at proposing viable alternatives, mainly based on the imposition of manual labor (as opposed to begging), and *stabilitas loci* (instead of peregrination). Athanasius, bishop of Alexandria (d. 373), presented Anthony disappearing into the Egyptian desert (*eremos*), where he died in 356, as one making a city of a desert. His *Life of Anthony* asserted the superiority of *anachoresis* (retreat from the world) in the desert over all other forms of ascesis and was the major reference work for later hagiographical writing.[8] It introduced manual labor as a necessity for ascetics, citing 2 Thess. 3.10, "If any one will not work, let him not eat." Confronted with a veritable proliferation of lawless ascetics in the Cappadocian city of which he was made bishop in 370, Basil of Caesarea[9] issued a series of laws which would influence monastic reformers in both East and West. While he considered eremitism the ideal of spiritual perfection, in practice he attempted to impose the primacy of the common life in a monastery, cenobitism, which had already been practiced by the Egyptian monk Pachomius (d. 346). Shortly thereafter, Jerome (d. c. 420) and John Cassian (d. 435) advocated models of monasticism based on manual labor and cenobitism.[10] On the eve of the Council of Chalcedon, apostolic peregrination remained the dominant model, but the corpus of literature in favor of regularization was already in place.

7 von Campenhausen, "Ascetic Ideal"; Guillaumont, "Le dépaysement."
8 Athanasius of Alexandria, *Vie d'Antoine*; Chitty, *Desert a City*; Brown, *Making of Late Antiquity*; C. Leyser, *Authority and Asceticism*, 9–24.
9 Gribomont, *Saint Basile*.
10 O. Chadwick, *John Cassian*; de Vogüé, *Histoire littéraire*; Rebenich, *Hieronymus und sein Kreis*; C. Leyser, *Authority and Asceticism*.

One hundred and fifty years later, around 600, institutionalization already seems to have been quite advanced in the East, thanks, no doubt, to imperial continuity and a constant collaboration between political power and the ecclesiastical hierarchy. Synthesis between eremitism and cenobitism prevailed, and the church managed one way or another to integrate the extreme forms of ascesis which threatened this equilibrium. On the other hand, the division between Chalcedonians and miaphysites allowed a large degree of independence to those monks in predominantly miaphysite regions in Egypt and Syria.[11]

Besides these two centers, aspiring ascetics converged on Palestine, attracted by a visit to Jerusalem.[12] From the beginning of the fifth century, on the initiative of the Cappadocian monk Euthymius, and later in the sixth century on that of his disciple Sabas, the system of lavras was set up in the desert separating the Holy City from the Dead Sea. Each monk in the lavra lived the entire week in his *kellion*, a small building containing a place to sleep and a workroom where he would do basket weaving; *kellia* were isolated by at least an hour from the center of the lavra where the monks would gather on Saturdays and bring in what they had made to share both a meal and prayers. On Sunday mornings, after the divine office, each monk would leave again, taking with him the materials he needed for his work. Cognizant that this kind of work was difficult, Euthymius and Sabas surrounded their lavras with a series of cenobia, in which a stay lasting several years was obligatory preparation for gaining admittance to the lavra. The Arab invasions did not disrupt life in Sabas's lavra, which, indeed, continues in operation to this day. Thus the Sabaite system ordered both cenobitism and eremitism, but it was an eremitism tempered by the common life.

The term "lavra" was subsequently used in Byzantium for any monastery that was not fully cenobitic, though experienced ascetics lived there, more often than not in small groups, rather than on their own. This evolution was doubtless inspired by that major work on the shelves of the monastery libraries, John Climacus's *Ladder of Divine Ascent*, written at the monastery of St. Catherine of Sinai in the first half of the seventh century. In the work, John divided monks into three categories: "either the retreat and solitude of the spiritual athlete; or a life of *hesycheia* [angelic life of renunciation] with one or two companions; or living in a cenobitic monastery." He gave preference to

11 Flusin, "L'essor du monachisme oriental."

12 Cyril of Scythopolis, *Vita Euthymii* and *Vita Sabae* (Eng. trans. Price); Chitty, *Desert a City*; Hirschfeld, *Judean Desert Monasteries*; Patrich, *Sabas*; Flusin, *Miracle et histoire*.

the second of these modes of life.[13] In continuity with ancient tradition, his work presented the stages that would lead the monk to perfection as having thirty separate steps.

The established church managed without any apparent difficulty to isolate, minimize, and eventually to rehabilitate in hagiographical form certain extremist ascetics such as the "grazers" (*boskoi*) and the "fools of God" (*saloi*), who seem to have disappeared by the beginning of the seventh century. With Symeon Stylites (d. 459), however, the scale of the question was immediately transformed, even as compromise proved easy. Initially a cenobite at the foot of Mount Coryphaeus in northern Syria, Symeon climbed to the summit of this mountain where he set himself up on a pillar, from which he would not descend. Even though he was visible to everyone from some distance, Symeon thereby combined isolation and stability into extreme ascesis, allowing the ecclesiastical hierarchy, which he nonetheless despised, to sacralize him even while he was still alive.[14] His numerous successors in Syria, but also in the region of Constantinople itself, allowed themselves, without too much resistance, to be constrained to live surrounded by a cenobium. Stylitism continued into the eleventh century, when Lazarus of Mt. Galesion (d. 1054) understood the three successive pillars upon which he established himself in the vicinity of Ephesus as the center of a cenobium. The virulent controversy that put him into conflict with the metropolitan of Ephesus had nothing to do with his mode of life, but with control over the monastery's property.[15]

The fortunes of the term "lavra" notwithstanding, the Byzantine East saw the coexistence of a great variety of forms for monastic life. Cenobia tended to predominate in cities and for women, but they were also found in rural areas. Cities were the preferred sites for female monasteries, but not exclusively so; the same applies for double monasteries.[16] Moreover, the propensity of some prosperous land-owning farmers to become monks with a few of their fellow laborers on their own land led to the creation of numerous rural sites of ascesis. This multiplicity of monastic forms never managed to squeeze out two phenomena which persisted throughout the period: the practice of complete solitude set apart from inhabited places and peregrination in both cities and in the countryside.

A similar diversity characterized monastic life in the West around 600, geopolitical and regional peculiarities aside. The sixth century witnessed the

13 John Climacus, *Ladder of Divine Ascent.*
14 *Lives of Symeon Stylites*; Kaplan, "Forme di ascesi"; Sansterre, "Les saints stylites."
15 *Vita S. Lazari*; Kaplan, "Evergetis Typikon."
16 Talbot, "Comparison."

flourishing nearly everywhere of monastic initiatives which would become actual models in the centuries that followed, not without, however, considerable debate and discussion.[17] Thus, the Burgundian monarchy promoted a monastic ideal founded on perpetual prayer at the expense of manual labor at Saint-Maurice d'Agaune.[18] Caesarius, bishop of Arles (d. 542), inspired a strictly cenobitic urban monasticism for both men and women,[19] which, at the instigation of Queen Radegund, was extended to Poitiers.[20] The monks at Lérins were the first to put into writing the earliest Gallican monastic rules, a fact which attests to the existence at that time of cenobites *stricto sensu*, as well as monasteries comparable with the lavras of the East.[21] Whereas monks in Ireland continued to be afforded considerable liberty, and the ideal of *peregrinatio* flourished there,[22] Visigothic Spain for its part undertook in the seventh century a policy of regulating asceticism that did not, however, exclude the existence of a number of important double monasteries.[23] In Gaul, the writings of Gregory of Tours (d. 594) witness to the existence of numerous wandering ascetics, who were more or less tolerated, and of efforts undertaken by the church hierarchy to stifle more extreme manifestations of asceticism such as stylitism.[24] In Italy, Gregory the Great's *Dialogues* also took into account the extreme diversity in forms of asceticism and represent one of the most important attempts to put them into some order. The work aimed to impose as its dominant model the monasticism typified by Benedict of Nursia, presenting him as an ideal monk rather than a real person.[25] This papal attempt at standardizing the monastic world was accompanied by the progressive

17 For a somewhat dated overview, see *Il monachesimo nell'Alto Medioevo*. For a general but controversial overview of the Frankish world, see Prinz, *Frühes Mönchtum*, 19–117.

18 Theurillat, *L'abbaye de Saint-Maurice d'Agaune*; Moyse, "Les origines du monachisme"; Wood, "Prelude to Columbanus"; Rosenwein, "Perennial Prayer" and "One Site."

19 Klingshirn, *Caesarius of Arles*.

20 For the *status quaestionis* and bibliography, see Van Dam, *Saints*, 30–41. See also Rosenwein, *Negotiating Space*, 52–58; Van Rossem, "De poort in de muur"; Diem, *Das monastische Experiment*.

21 *Les Règles des saints Pères*. The origins of the Lérins community remain controversial. See especially Pricoco, *L'isola dei Santi*; Kasper, *Theologie und Askese*; Carrias, "Vie monastique"; de Vogüé, "Les débuts"; C. Leyser, "This Sainted Isle."

22 Ryan, *Irish Monasticism*; Hughes, *Church in Early Irish Society* and *Early Christian Ireland*; Sharpe, "Some Problems"; Herity, "Layout"; Dumville, "Origins"; Charles-Edwards, *Early Christian Ireland*.

23 Mundò, "Il monachesimo"; Orlandis, *Estudios*; Bishko, *Spanish and Portuguese Monastic History*; Díaz, *Formas económicas y sociales*, "El monacato," and "Monasticism and Liturgy."

24 Gregory of Tours, *Decem libri historiarum*, VIII.15–16, IX.6 and his *Vitae patrum*, passim. See Helvétius, "Ermites ou moines," 12–13; for the repression of peregrination in the West, see Sansterre, "Attitudes."

25 Gregory the Great, *Dialogues*. See the recent work of Fried, "Le passé."

circulation of the rule bearing Benedict's name,[26] and may be observed in connection with the mission sent by Gregory to evangelize the Anglo-Saxons, in which, for the first time, the task of preaching was entrusted to monks.[27]

Gregory the Great's character and reputation ought not to conceal the existence of numerous tensions within the Christian West from 600 to 1100. Contrary to the East, there did not exist in the West any centralizing power capable of unifying the Christian churches of the various kingdoms. Numerous debates regarding the interpretation of key texts for asceticism regularly pitted monks against the church hierarchy and against secular clergy as a whole.[28] Furthermore, what precisely distinguished a monk from a cleric remained fluid. Thus, monasticism's prodigious success led the church to attempt to impose part of its ascetic models on the members of its clergy. Augustine had already attempted to constrain his clergy to lead celibate lives in a community.[29] The ideal, peculiar to the West, according to which sacerdotal purity was linked to celibacy, was born in this context, even though it did not come to predominate until the thirteenth century.[30]

It is to be noted that around 600, monasticism in the East and West remained profoundly open both to influences from each other and to new influences from elsewhere: while it is true that westerners were less frequent among the pilgrims to Jerusalem, the Irish did travel to the continent, and Syrians traveled throughout the West. Gregory the Great spent six years in Constantinople as the pope's representative and could not have failed to frequent the numerous monasteries that were flourishing there at the time.

Monks and the authorities: reforms and innovations

By the beginning of the seventh century, all the defining elements of monastic spirituality were already in place. Later innovations arose rather from the ordering and organization of monasticism, in other words, from relations among monks and political and church hierarchies. The notion of reform, which has stirred up some debate, merits clarification.[31] In the context of a defined establishment, reform can signify a return to the purity of the original mode of life. More generally, it may also designate the introduction of a rule judged to be closer to an idealized vision of the "monasticism of the earliest

26 *La Règle de saint Benoît.*
27 H. Chadwick, "Gregory the Great"; Wood, "Mission."
28 Helvétius, "Comment écrire."
29 Possidius, *Vita Augustini.*
30 For the *status quaestionis*, see Bertram, *Chrodegang Rules.*
31 See the chapter by Barrow in this volume.

centuries" and applied to any current establishment, whether founded in the distant or recent past. Lastly, some scholars understand the word in the more modern sense of reorganizing a whole group of monasteries according to criteria common to all. In this last sense, the term is only applicable in our period to the West at certain particular moments.[32]

In fact, the situation in the East and that in the West differed considerably. In the East there existed a single political power, which was legally responsible for the application of canonical decisions, incontestable in its authority if not in its actual decisions, and possessed of a strong hold over the church hierarchy. In the West, secular power structures were more fragmented: the need to organize a true reform of the church, including monasteries, was invoked at two particular moments – each time in circumstances in which a new centralizing political power was asserting itself. This was the case when the Carolingian rise to power, accompanied by massive territorial expansion, culminated in Charlemagne's imperial coronation and *Renovatio imperii* (the renewal of the Roman Empire). The evangelization of newly subdued peoples necessitated agreement on the message to be conveyed to them. It was also the case when, in the late eleventh century, the bishop of Rome sought recognition as the sole leader of the western church (to the detriment of princes and bishops), and sought to impose on ecclesiastical institutions a far more rigid and hierarchical organization than hitherto existed.

These organizational differences between East and West did not obviate shared problems. The first of these was the status of monks relative to clerics and lay people, which was far from clearly defined around 600. The Council of Chalcedon limited itself to affirming the authority of bishops over monasteries in general terms, without, however, defining the status of monks. In the East, the Council in Trullo (692) reaffirmed this authority and insisted on a clear distinction among clerics, monks, and laity. It aimed first and foremost to reform the morals of the clergy and to distinguish them from the rest of society. As for monks, it imposed tonsure on them (clerics retained long hair) and obliged them to enter a monastery, unless they confined themselves to deserted places.[33]

Iconoclasm radically altered the situation by precipitating spasms of conflict between bishops and monks. In attacking icons and later relics, which assured a significant portion of monasteries' income through offerings (especially during the pilgrimages which they attracted), the iconoclast movement

32 For the East, see the debates in Mullet and Kirby, *Theotokos Evergetis*; for the West, see Kottje and Maurer, *Monastische Reformen*.

33 Council in Trullo, canons 40–49.

of the eighth to the ninth centuries roused the opposition of a group of monks against a church hierarchy, either instructed or constrained to obey the iconoclastic policies initiated by the Isaurian emperors. Already present at the Council of Hiereia (754), which defined iconoclast doctrine, monks played an even more important role at the Second Council of Nicaea (787), which reestablished images for the first time. Though present, they nonetheless were not actually part of the council itself, which remained exclusively a meeting of bishops. Rather, the monks played a dual role at the council. First, they supplied supporting theological literature, some of which was only available in their libraries; and to this they added hagiographical polemics, a genre from an entirely monastic perspective. Secondly, they loudly intervened to oppose the restoration of erstwhile iconoclast bishops. In so doing, they posed as judges of the church hierarchy. Well aware of its own unity, the monastic *tagma* (military contingent), thereby entered conciliar history, previously the exclusive domain of the clergy.[34]

Monks did not succeed in remaining at the forefront of theological debate, however. Theodore the Studite, the most illustrious of the monks, was certainly present during the debates prior to the reestablishment of iconoclasm in 815, but it was the patriarch of Constantinople, Nicephorus, and a number of metropolitans who actually intervened.[35] In 843, during the final reestablishment of the cult of images, the monks once again attempted to lay down the law to bishops accused of heresy or relapse. The resultant fierce battle dragged on for half a century, but the monks were forced, in the end, to toe the line. It was up to the patriarch, and, in theory, his synod (in practice, the emperor), to choose bishops, and this principle preserved the patriarch's authority over most monasteries, from which bishops often came.

The most blatant conflict between a patriarch and a monastery – the conflict that in 843 set the patriarchate of Constantinople in opposition to the Studios, the most important monastery in the capital city – seems to have been resolved by the end of the tenth century, as indicated by the imperial choice of two Studite monks as patriarchs in less than fifty years.[36] Conflicts did nonetheless remain alive: throughout the first half of the eleventh century, as soon as he had left the cenobium where he had settled in order to be close to the nearby mountain, Lazarus of Mt. Galesion was in constant conflict with the metropolitan of Ephesus, to such an extent that the monks were afraid that their monastery would disappear in the absence of its holy founder.

34 Auzépy, "La place des moines."
35 Kaplan, "L'évêque."
36 Darrouzès, "Le patriarche Méthode."

The problem of the respective standing of clerics and monks occurred in the same terms in the West. In a number of realms, ever since Chalcedon, bishops in council had endeavored to take measures to constrain monks within their monasteries and to define the roles of clerics and of monks. However, lively tensions remained. The vast number of conciliar canons on this matter shows that monks were, at the very least, reticent about accepting their application.[37] In the Frankish realms, the need to ease these tensions led kings to propose compromises. In fact, for the Franks the image of the obedient monk constrained within his monastery and under the authority of the bishop was scarcely compatible with that of the missionary preachers promised by Gregory the Great, or with that of the great charismatic Irish abbots, such as Columbanus or Fursey, celebrated in hagiography.[38] In this context, seventh-century Frankish kings adopted the custom of granting privileges to a few "model" monasteries, which agreed to be put at the service of the realm. Luxeuil was destined to be widely influential. Following its lead, certain monasteries were placed under the direct authority of the sovereign, and thereby eluded the control of their diocesan bishop. In exchange, they were expected to adopt a certain way of life which was then defined as "the rule of Benedict and Columbanus." Although it was limited to a few communities, this Merovingian initiative may be considered as a first foray into monastic reform, a move that would be furthered, albeit in a slightly different guise, during the reign of Queen Balthild (d. c. 680).[39]

In the following century, in the milieu of the Carolingians' rise to power and of new missionary ventures which supported their policies of conquest, a more sweeping reorganization was deemed necessary. The endless competition between monks and clerics had fostered some muddling of their respective roles. On one hand, monks were undertaking preaching journeys through lands in need of conversion; on the other hand, bishops were imposing celibacy and common life on their clergy. There are even examples of abbot-bishops leading monasteries populated by monks, many of whom were ordained clerics.[40]

37 For a good overview, see Häussling, *Mönchskonvent und Eucharistiefeier*, 114–75.

38 Jonas of Bobbio, *Vita Columbani*; *Vita Fursei*. For a basic bibliography, see Dierkens, "Prolégomènes," 373–82 (for Columbanus) and 385–88 (for Fursey). For a more general treatment, see Wood, *Missionary Life*.

39 In addition to the works of Ewig, collected in *Spätantikes und fränkisches Gallien*, see Dierkens, "Prolégomènes," 388–93; Rosenwein, *Negotiating Space*, 59–96; Diem, "Was bedeutet *regula Columbani*?"

40 Frank, *Die Klosterbischöfe*; Felten, *Äbte und Laienäbte*; Dierkens, *Abbayes et chapitres*; de Jong, "Carolingian Monasticism," 627–29.

Given this environment, those in power found it useful to define, once and for all, two separate *ordines*, namely the *ordo clericorum* and the *ordo monachorum*. From Pippin III's reign, Carolingian capitularies and Frankish conciliar canons required each community to align itself with one of the two orders.[41] The influence of Anglo-Saxon missionaries, disciples of Gregory the Great, combined with the alliance between the Pippinids and the papacy to promote a single model of a "Roman" monasticism centered on the Rule of Benedict of Nursia.[42] The *ordo monachorum* would henceforth be defined by adherence to this Rule, and all those who rejected it would find themselves forced to accept clerical ordination and direct episcopal control. The confusion that this reform caused in communities that were as much clerical as they were monastic led the church hierarchy to make a number of specific clarifications in order to render it practicable. Thanks largely to the assistance of his adviser, Benedict of Aniane (the author of the *concordia regularum*), Louis the Pious was in a position to propose a complete program for the reform of religious communities to the church councils gathered in Aachen in 816, 817, and from 818 to 819.[43]

The details of this reform may be summarized as follows: each monastery would henceforth be centered on a Benedictine cenobium. Monks would each receive the same initiation, based on obedience to the abbot, and a balanced division of their daily life into prayer, study, and manual labor. They would be obliged to observe the Rule of Benedict of Nursia, to which would be added a series of *consuetudines* (customs) which the abbot could adapt according to his wishes, but drawing inspiration from the pattern established by Benedict of Aniane.[44] It being understood that the Rule of Saint Benedict, by the author's own admission, was only addressed to beginners,[45] seasoned monks could consider leaving the cenobium in order to lead a more spiritual life, but could only do so within the monastic enclosure and always under the control of the abbot.[46] This more perfect life would be founded on the Scriptures and

41 See Semmler's numerous articles, notably: "Karl der Grosse"; "Pippin III"; "Mönche und Kanoniker"; "Die Kanoniker und ihre Regel."

42 De Jong, "Carolingian Monasticism," 629–34.

43 *Capitularia monastica concilii Aquisgranensis* (816–817), 453–68 (816) and 471–82 (817); *Capitulare ecclesiasticum* (818–819) in *Capitularia regum francorum* 1, 273–91; Benedict of Aniane, *Concordia regularum*.

44 Semmler, "Benedictus II," "Benediktinische Reform," and "Le monachisme occidental"; see also Bonnerue's introduction to his edition of Benedict of Aniane, *Concordia regularum*.

45 *La règle de saint Benoît*, 73.8: "hanc minimam inchoationis regulam descriptam" ("this little rule written for beginners"). Compare a passage from the Life of St. Benedict in Gregory the Great, *Dialogues*, II.2.4, (*SC* 260) 138–40.

46 Helvétius, "Ermites ou moines," 9–10.

the teachings of the fathers, among whom St. Basil was accorded particular esteem, being the only father mentioned by name in Benedict's Rule,[47] and therefore the reference model for both western and eastern monasticism.

The alternative was, of course, ordination, which authorized the recipient to retain his property and to lead an active life in the world in the service of a public church and under the authority of the diocesan bishop. In practice, some communities (such as of the basilica of Saint-Denis[48]) preferred to renounce their monastic status rather than accept the constraints of Benedictine cenobitism: their members all became *clerici canonici*, that is, canons, placed under the authority of the bishop, and obliged to conform to the *Institutio canonicorum*, likewise promulgated during the Aachen councils.[49] As for women's communities, the authorities did indeed attach less importance to them as there was less at stake. From the beginning, it had been understood that an active life in the world was forbidden them, just as was priestly ordination.[50] The Carolingian reform, nonetheless, did put forward a rule specifically for them, the *Institutio sanctimonialium*. It was recommended for all women who did not wish to follow the Benedictine Rule, and was stricter in its requirement to renounce all personal property.[51]

The success of this Carolingian reorganization was restricted. Apart from a few large and famous monasteries which were to serve as examples, the communities that accepted the Benedictine Rule without any reservation were few and far between. On the other hand, large numbers of communities chose to make the move into the *ordo clericorum* or continued to vacillate between the two models.[52] Nevertheless, the idea of the superiority of the Benedictine cenobitic model came to predominate throughout the West, albeit interpreted in diverse ways by various "reformers."[53]

Thus the tenth and eleventh centuries saw so-called reforming initiatives blossom, especially in Lotharingia (Brogne, Gorze, Verdun), in western France (Cluny, Fleury, Saint-Victor in Marseilles, and elsewhere), and southern England (Winchester, Abingdon, Ely, Worcester, and elsewhere). All replicated the Carolingian ethos in very different political contexts. For the most part, these reforms were promoted by princes desirous of having model monasteries at

47 *La règle de saint Benoît*, 73.5: "regula sancti Patris nostri Basilii" ("the rule of our holy father Basil").
48 Semmler, "Saint-Denis."
49 *Institutio canonicorum concilii Aquisgranensis* (816).
50 Muschiol, *Famula Dei*.
51 *Institutio sanctimonialium concilii Aquisgranensis* (816–817); Schilp, *Norm und Wirklichkeit*.
52 For examples, see Helvétius, *Abbayes, évêques et laïques*, 204–208.
53 Semmler, "Das Erbe der Karolingische Klosterreform."

their disposal to augment their own power and prestige.[54] For example, the initiative of Gerard, the monk of Saint-Denis who founded a monastery at Brogne in 919, was in accord with the interests of King Rudolf (western Francia) and Gilbert, Duke of Lotharingia, before it attracted the attention of Arnulf, the Count of Flanders. From 941, the latter entrusted Gerard with the restoration of strict Benedictine monasticism in all the monasteries under his control in his principality (Saint-Pierre at Mont-Blandin, Saint-Bavon, Saint-Bertin, Saint-Wandrille, and Saint-Amand), all of which were ancient and illustrious foundations. Gerard's influence was felt as far afield as England, where his customs were cited together with those of Fleury-sur-Loire in the *regularis concordia*, and promulgated in the kingdom of Edgar (959–75) at the Synod of Winchester led by Dunstan, Archbishop of Canterbury, in 970.[55]

From the ninth century, certain powerful lay founders of monasteries, such as William of Aquitaine at Cluny (909), placed their foundations under the protection of the papacy with the aim of avoiding the control either of the diocesan bishop or of potential rivals within the aristocracy.[56] By this date, when Carolingian centralization was nothing more than a dim memory, this protection had the advantage of being both distant and purely symbolic; nevertheless, it facilitated a rise in papal power from the beginning of the eleventh century. The expansion of Cluny began in earnest from the abbacy of Odilo (994–1049), and consisted of the circulation of Cluniac customs in a large number of other monasteries, which thereby themselves became staging posts for the dissemination of papal propaganda. Going back, in part, to Benedict of Aniane's customs, those of Cluny substituted liturgy for manual labor, which in turn led to an increase in the number of ordained priests. The latter enjoyed a freedom that was all the greater, as the privilege of exemption removed them from the control of their diocesan bishop.[57]

For the period that concerns us, the "Gregorian reform" represents the final stage in the institutionalization of the monasteries in the West. Using the logic of exemption styled as *libertas romana*, the papacy attempted at once to attach to itself the greatest possible number of powerful monasteries, and to group together other monasteries around these strongholds throughout the

54 For a starting point in the vast bibliography on this subject, see Kottje and Maurer, *Monastische Reformen*.

55 For Gerard of Brogne's reform, see Dierkens, *Abbayes et chapitres*, 229–47; Misonne, "La restauration monastique." For the Benedictine reform in England, see Cubitt, "Review Article."

56 For the origins of this process, see Falkenstein, "Monachisme," 389–403; for Cluny's foundation, see most recently Méhu, *Paix et communautés*.

57 See among many other works: Constable, *Cluniac Studies* and *Religious Life and Thought*; Wollasch, *Cluny*; Iogna-Prat, *Agni immaculati* and *Ordonner et exclure*.

West. In the last analysis, this would lead to the birth of the idea of a religious order.[58] The tendency to insist upon the cenobitic life grew even stronger and attacked the forms of eremitism that were subsisting or attempting a revival. The latter were integrated into new orders possessed of an eremitic ideal, but a cenobitic structure, such as the Camaldolese and the Vallumbrosans. These strictly enclosed communities were permitted to lead a form of life comparable to that of the Byzantine lavras, but under the authority of the Benedictine rule (augmented by certain particular customs). These few novel instances aside, other experiments in eremitism were subjected to a process of cenobitic institutionalization. They became, in turn, the primary seedbed for new forms of monasticism, such as, notably, the Cistercian movement at the very end of the eleventh century.[59]

The situation in the East was not radically different.[60] Though the East did not experience such an organized reform, the tendency towards "cenobitization" asserted itself there as well, albeit rather more gradually. The iconoclast crisis and the difficulties encountered at that time by the monasteries exposed their relative weakness. At the end of the eighth century, Theodore the Studite (d. 826) deemed it necessary to promote the cenobitic model. Installed in 797 by the Empress Irene in one of the greatest monasteries in Constantinople, Saint John the Baptist of Studios, founded at the end of the fifth century, Theodore established there a strictly codified form of cenobitism.[61] Even more than moral precepts (such as the insistence on stability and the personal poverty of the monks which went so far as to require them to swap their habits every week without regard for the condition or size of the garment) he emphasized strict organization. Drawing on the writings of Basil of Caesarea,[62] he insisted on the importance of carefully regulated work. Each monk was given a diaconal ministry of either service (in the garden, bakery, laundry, or elsewhere) or production (such as copying, or stone-, leather-, and iron-work). This work was not only seen as a remedy for *accidie* (spiritual weariness), but as an indicator of fervor: it was the monk's equivalent of the mass, for a Studite monk was not usually a priest. Every monk labored like the poor, no matter what his former social status, which, in this aristocratic monastic world, was usually high.

58 Neiske, "Papsttum und Klosterverband."
59 H. Leyser, *Hermits*; Caby, "*Finis eremitarum?*."
60 For a differing view, see Oexle, "Les moines d'Occident."
61 Dagron, "Économie et société chrétiennes"; Leroy, "La réforme studite"; Pratsch, *Theodoros Studites*.
62 Leroy, "L'influence de S. Basile."

Theodore exercised considerable influence on later Byzantine monasticism, as the large number of extant manuscripts of his works amply testifies. On the other hand, for want of any real support from emperors or patriarchs, he failed to create a lasting organization. Through family connections, he gathered around Studios a group of five monasteries, but this association of communities did not extend any further than that, and indeed scarcely survived him. Moreover, the rigorous cenobitism that he preached did not really establish any dominance in the face of persistent tendencies towards eremitism or to loose groups of lavras[63] – tendencies irresistibly drawn to one of the most marked features of Byzantine monasticism, the holy mountain.

From the eighth to the tenth century, the most important of these mountains was Olympus in Bithynia, south of Bursa.[64] When a community's success began to threaten its founder's tranquility, the holy mountain allowed the founder to go further up the slopes in the quest for *hesycheia*, following the example of Anthony. The founder's reputation would in turn attract disciples, and a new establishment would then be created. Furthermore, Olympus served as a refuge for those who rejected iconoclasm since it was too far from the capital for repressive measures to have any real effect. Olympus was thus surrounded and covered halfway up its slopes with lavras and *kellia*, which grouped together two or three hermits. Through reciprocal visiting, the ascetics maintained simple connections among themselves. This relative overpopulation eventually drove those whose vocation to the eremitic life was particularly strong to seek other foundations.

From the beginning of the ninth century, Mount Athos provided just such a place for retreat. Completely devoid of inhabitants, it was used by farmers as a place through which to herd their flocks. From the beginning of the tenth century, the hermits organized themselves in order to defend against the intrusion of farmers and against neighboring monasteries' ambitions. They appointed a leader, the *protos*, who was installed at Karyes at the center of the peninsula, which was soon known for its lavras.[65] At the end of the 950s, Athanasius (c. 925–c. 1001), a confirmed ascetic, came and established himself on the peninsula. He had received the monastic habit at another holy mountain, Mount Kyminas, where he had made the acquaintance of Nicephorus Phocas (912–69), a prestigious general who aspired to the ascetic life.[66] When the latter departed to reconquer Crete in 961, he took Athanasius with him – the

63 Papachryssanthou, "La vie monastique."
64 Talbot, "Les saintes montagnes."
65 *Actes du Prôtaton*, 1–69.
66 *Sancti Athanasii Athonitae vita prima*; Lemerle, "La vie ancienne."

primary mission of the monk was, after all, to pray for the empire. After his victory, Nicephorus gave to Athanasius the means to build what was to become the most famous Byzantine monastery, the Great Lavra on the point of the peninsula.[67]

Though he made ample use of the writings of Theodore the Studite, notably with respect to the organization of labor, Athanasius introduced some important modifications.[68] Each monk lived in a cell, the cells together comprising the monastery enclosure. Anthanasius did, however, make provision for five senior monks to be installed in a *kellion* at some distance from the monastery, either on their own, or with a companion, but under the control of the superior, the *higumenos* (or abbot). In addition, endowed by successive emperors, Athanasius made a number of investments that enraged the hermits. The confrontation was, however, short-lived. Thanks to imperial support, Athanasius managed to get the Lavra integrated into the Athonite hermits' general organization. Foundations based on the same model as his multiplied, and by the end of the tenth century there were already around fifty lavra on the peninsula. Mount Athos had become the most prestigious holy mountain. The new model of the lavra, in Athanasius's loosely cenobitic sense, had triumphed.

For all that, the strictly cenobitic model did not disappear, since it was successfully adapted to urban areas, starting with Constantinople and its suburbs. Another tradition came from the city's suburbs, where the monastery of Christ Evergetis was founded in 1054, and endowed with a *typikon* (a charter describing the monastery's foundation and organization) by his successor.[69] This *typikon*, which drew extensively from the writings of Basil of Caesarea and Theodore the Studite, was in turn frequently copied word for word in numerous later foundations. Can this, however, be considered a "reform"? Apart from the fact that it was not imposed on any existing house, use of the Evergetis *typikon* did not prevent each monastic founder from acting independently, and from planning the sort of organization he wished. These monasteries' only commonality was the autonomy bestowed by their founders.[70]

Monasticism in the economy and in society

The social role of ascetics is inextricably associated with their means of subsistence. The question of the distinction between clerics and monks recurs, as

67 *Actes de Lavra* 1, 13–48.
68 Athanasius the Athonite, *Typikon du monastère de Lavra*.
69 *Typikon of Theotokos Evergetis*; also see Mullet and Kirby, *Theotokos Evergetis*.
70 Lemerle, *Cinq études*, 103–105, 184–86; Kaplan, *Les hommes et la terre*, 295–97.

also between their respective tasks. From a purely theoretical point of view, clerics alone enjoyed the privileges corresponding to an active life, which they were assumed to lead in the service of society in general; the *cura animarum* (care of souls) justified their support at public expense. Monks, on the other hand, were supposed to be content to lead a contemplative life apart from the world and to provide for their own needs. In practice, however, monks were often convinced of their social role, and were confirmed in this view by their success among the faithful masses. From the start, the question of their means of subsistence was cause for debate.[71]

Monks were far from being cut off from the world. The Christian population flocked to them, hoping to benefit from their prayers, reputed healing powers, and spiritual guidance. In addition to the fruits of their own labors, monks thus benefited from offerings made by their visitors, to the detriment of the income of bishops and clergy. This kind of monastic *cura animarum* led to the increased presence of priests in monasteries.

Increasingly, monks became implicated in wider social life. A consensus rapidly developed regarding the role of monastic prayer: sovereigns did not neglect to remind them that their primary task was to pray for the peace of the realm or of the empire, for the sovereign's person, for his family, and for the success of the army. The holiness recognized in monks rendered them privileged intercessors before God in the eyes of the Christian faithful. In the course of time, this mission of prayer grew to include the prayer for the salvation of the souls of the living, and especially those of the dead. The intercession of monks was deemed to atone for the sins of those for whom they prayed, justification enough for the foundation and endowment of monasteries by the wealthy and the powerful. Further, they offered the wealthy a convenient means of atoning, by acts of charity, both for their sins and for their wealth, which, in theory, the Kingdom of Heaven forbade them.[72]

Monks also became associated with a whole series of support activities. Social and welfare services, which in Late Antiquity had been the responsibility of towns and cities, had naturally devolved upon bishops and their clergy. However, a number of monasteries participated in the provision of these services, whether by choice or by necessity. Justinian (527–65) attempted to organize this state of affairs by distinguishing centers of assistance from

71 For the relations between the monks and society in general, see Wollasch, *Mönchtum*; Milis, *Angelic Monks and Earthly Men*.

72 For the East, cf. Michael Attaleiates, *Diataxis*; Lemerle, *Cinq études*, 101, 109–10. For a synthesis of the situation in the West, see de Jong, "Carolingian Monasticism," 645–51; on the Carolingian understanding of liturgical *memoria*, see the overview in Borgolte, "*Memoria*"; on charity, see Ganz, "Ideology of Sharing."

both churches and monasteries, the former being clearly independent, but attached to the bishop, and therefore no doubt served by diocesan clergy.[73] Nevertheless, these measures were powerless to prevent the growing hold of monks on social aid.

In the East, this evolution was retarded by the massive intervention of imperial power, for which euergetism (benefit exchange) was an important major obligation. Centers of imperial aid, being a part of the imperial fisc and being managed as such by court officials, multiplied or simply continued to exist until the tenth century, when the emperor transformed them into monasteries.[74] This situation was unparalleled in the West, where aid centers were nearly always attached to a church or a monastery.[75]

The role of monks in the *cura animarum* likewise took various forms. If, in the towns and their environs, bishops and their clergy retained control over preaching and the administration of the sacraments, even if that meant allowing a few monasteries to participate, the situation in rural areas was far less clear-cut. Many monasteries played an active role in the pastoral care of rural populations in both East and West.[76] The precise circumstances frequently remain obscure due to the lack of documentation. It is as difficult to evaluate the relationship between monasteries and bishops in Ireland, for example,[77] as it is to define precisely the status of Anglo-Saxon minsters.[78] Rural monasteries, founded either on the property of lay landowners or by simple villagers, mostly eluded control, but doubtless constituted an important part of the religious structure for the faithful. In the West, when monks were officially associated with missionary work beyond the Rhine, they clearly exercised a prerogative originally assigned to clergy. The precedent set by Gregory the Great (590–604) in the evangelization of the Anglo-Saxons would even lead later bishops in these regions to surround themselves with monks.[79]

It was, however, in the area of the transmission of knowledge that monks occupied an incomparable place in both the East and West. Numerous monasteries had a *scriptorium* and a library of greater or lesser importance. It was in these *scriptoria* that the shift to minuscule took place simultaneously in both

73 Kaplan, *Les propriétés*, 17–21.
74 Kaplan, "Maisons impériales et fondations pieuses."
75 For an overview, see Angenendt, *Geschichte der Religiosität*, 591–92.
76 For the West, see Berlière, "L'exercice du ministère paroissial."
77 See Picard's "Pour une réévaluation."
78 For the *status quaestionis*, see Cambridge and Rollason, "Debate: Pastoral Organization"; Blair, "Debate: Ecclesiastical Organization."
79 After Angenendt, *Monachi peregrini*, see Wood, *Missionary Life* for a general perspective, and Mostert, "Les moines" for Utrecht.

the East and the West from the beginning of the eighth century,[80] which in turn engendered a "script revolution" and with it a much wider circulation of books. Far from confining themselves to Christian works, monks undertook to copy the works of pagan antiquity, many of which are known today only through the work of these copyists.[81]

The role played by monks in the different levels of instruction given both to lay people and to future monks would merit further research. There is, however, one readily perceptible difference between the West and the East in this regard: contrary to the West, most male monasteries in the East refused to accept adolescents before the age of sixteen or seventeen, rejecting the system of oblation.[82] Moreover, there were private schools for lay people in the East, which supplied elementary education throughout the empire, and in Constantinople provided secondary instruction.[83] In the West, on the other hand, monasteries once again entered into competition with secular clergy for the education of young people, and, as was the case in the East, held a virtual monopoly over the education of young girls.[84]

Another aspect of the social use of the monastery was confinement. Monasteries tightly controlled by political powers were ideal places to relegate conquered enemies when the conqueror did not wish to mete out a more definitive solution. They likewise provided places to which to remove members of the ruling family, members of the most conspicuous families of the aristocracy who had proven a nuisance, youngest sons, and unmarried daughters. In the case of political opponents, relegation to a monastery was justified by the idea of penitence and moral correction. This practice, however, met with only limited success since the person thus confined ended up by leaving the monastery and once again taking up his political activity without "correcting" his conduct. Thus Ebroin, mayor of the palace of Neustria, having been confined to a monastery in Luxeuil in 673, left it in 675, and, after new intrigues which proved in the end unsuccessful, was finally executed in 680.[85]

All of these social tasks being conferred on monasteries presumed that they had the requisite means at their disposal in order to perform the tasks.[86] The

80 For the East, see Lemerle, *Le premier humanisme byzantin*, and in this volume the chapter by Brubaker and Cunningham; for the West, see Ganz, "Book Production."

81 See the numerous works of McKitterick, especially *Carolingians and the Written Word* and "Le rôle culturel des monastères."

82 For the West, see de Jong, *In Samuel's Image*.

83 Lemerle, *Le premier humanisme byzantin*, 242–66.

84 For the West, see Contreni, "Carolingian Renaissance" for an overview of scholarship and bibliography.

85 de Jong, "Monastic Prisoners or Opting Out?" A comparable study for the East is awaited.

86 See further in the chapter by Morris in this volume.

original opposition between those intent on living from begging and those who lived from manual (usually artisanal) labor was soon a thing of the past. From the sixth century, some monasteries became truly powerful landowners. Justinian was forced to legislate on monastic property, which was carefully distinguished from church property and from that of episcopal charities.[87] In the same period, the Rule of the Master directed that landed property be entrusted to a secular administrator in order to remove this crushing responsibility from the monks.[88] Even the Rule of St. Benedict presumed that the bulk of the farm work would not be carried out by the monks.[89]

This property could have diverse sources, which would lead to the traditional classification of monasteries into three groups: royal or imperial, episcopal or patriarchal, and private. In the West, the enthusiasm of aristocratic families for the monastic movement showed itself very early. In the Frankish world, particularly from the beginning of the seventh century, monastic foundations multiplied and were very generously endowed.[90] These endowments allowed families simultaneously to mark out a territory, to shelter a portion of their property from confiscations by placing it under the inalienable protection of monastic property, and to augment their prestige by divine sanction. This tendency is particularly noticeable in connection with women's monasteries, indeed even in double monasteries, such as Nivelles, Saint-Jean at Laon, and Faremoutiers.[91]

In the East, there is little evidence for this enthusiasm before the second half of the eighth century.[92] Until that time, important monasteries could be founded by persons of relatively modest means following the example of Sabas in Palestine. If, after the 750s, some monasteries continued to be founded by modest villagers, the interest of powerful families of important officials, such as that of Theophanes the Chronicler or of Theodore the Studite, evinced this new tendency, which again was perhaps more noticeable in connection with women's houses. As in the West, with respect to a family's wealth in property, there was no longer any distinction between the monastery and the aristocratic "house" (*oikos*).[93] This model subsequently spread throughout the aristocratic pyramid from top to bottom.

87 Justinian, *Corpus Juris Civilis: Codex Justinianus*, I.3, I.22 and *Novellae* 5 (535), 7 (535), 46 (537), 76 (538), 120 (544), 123 (546).
88 *La règle du Maître*, 86.1–2.
89 *La règle de saint Benoît*, 48.7.
90 For examples, see Dierkens, *Abbayes et chapitres*; Helvétius, *Abbayes, évêques et laïques*; see also Lebecq, "Role of Monasteries."
91 Le Jan, "Convents."
92 Kaplan, "Les moines."
93 Magdalino, "Byzantine Aristocratic *Oikos*."

The fact of landed wealth ought not to obscure other monastic sources of revenue, starting with those linked to the cult and commemoration of the dead. In both West and East, many monasteries held relics which they promoted in order to attract visitors and pilgrims with their offerings. These relics also attracted competing desires for control and eventually became the object of other power struggles, or of a veritable business.[94] In certain cases, they spawned whole networks between monasteries sharing the same patron saints or the same pilgrims. One might cite, for instance, the translations of relics to Saxony in the ninth century,[95] or the connections between Mont-Saint-Michel in Normandy and Monte Gargano in southern Italy, also dedicated to the archangel Michael.[96] In the West, in addition to spontaneous offerings from the faithful, from the eighth century there were also considerable revenues from the tithe for all churches including monasteries, which was made obligatory at the beginning of Charlemagne's reign (768–814).[97]

The growth of monastic wealth placed monasteries at the center of economic expansion, notably the development of trade, in both West and East. In Neustria, from the seventh-century monasteries such as Saint-Denis, Saint-Germain-des-Prés, Ferrières-en-Gâtinais, Saint-Wandrille, and many others, came the engines driving the growth of cross-Channel trade from the port of Quentovic.[98] From the end of the tenth century, the monasteries of Athos obtained for their boats an exemption from trade tax (*kommerkion*) for a tonnage much higher than the selling of their produce necessitated.[99] In the *typika* of the monasteries founded by Byzantine aristocrats in the eleventh century, these foundations were supposed to provide a surplus, the distribution of which among the family of the founder, the monastery itself, charitable works, and even on occasion the peasant farmers, was meticulously ordered by the charter.[100] From this time on, the administration of property formed a major part of daily monastic undertakings.

This involvement had been present in monasticism since its beginnings: in theory, monks held everything in common, but this common property and the fruits of their own labor had to be administered well. Hence the great theorists of monasticism such as Pachomius, Basil of Caesarea, Jerome, and Cassian all defined a role for a monk in charge of the monastery's administration (called

94 Bozóky and Helvétius, *Les reliques*.
95 Röckelein, *Reliquientranslationen*.
96 Bouet, Otranto, and Vauchez, *Culte et pèlerinages*.
97 *Capitulare Haristallense* (779); see Semmler, "Zehngebot und Pfarrtermination."
98 Lebecq, "La Neustrie et la mer."
99 *Actes d'Iviron*, n. 6 (984); *Actes de Lavra* n. 55 (1102).
100 Michael Attaleiates, *Diataxis* (1077), 53–55; *Typikon of Gregory Pakourianos*.

a bursar or cellarer) to whom was given responsibility, under the abbot, for the monastery's property and its uses. In the West, the Rule of St. Benedict defined the qualities required of this cellarer, who, as a result, was to be found in all Benedictine monasteries.[101] In the East, it would take until the eleventh canon of the Second Council of Nicaea (787) for ecclesiastical legislation to make a monastic bursar obligatory.[102]

The growth in wealth led, however, to the growing involvement of lay people in property administration in analogous ways in East and West. This evolution took place earlier in the West, where the power stakes in monasteries for the aristocracy and rulers had been clear early on. By the eighth century, the richest monasteries had adopted the custom of granting to lay people a portion of the landed property as a benefice; furthermore, in the royal monasteries, the sovereign would similarly allocate a portion of the property to support his subjects.[103] Moreover, Charlemagne implemented the widespread adoption of the *advocatus* system, consisting in the nomination of a lay representative of the crown within the royal monasteries. In particular, this *advocatus* was charged with protecting the monastery, and with representing it in legal matters. From the ninth century, the abbacy itself could be granted as a benefice to a powerful lay person, who would from that time on be charged with the administration of the monastery's property as a whole.[104] In order to avoid possible abuses of this system, a levy reserved for the community was instituted, with the aim of preserving at least a minimum of the monastery's revenues for the living needs of the monks. In the course of the tenth and eleventh centuries, this dual system of lay abbacies and of *advocati* allowed many landed princes to use monasteries to establish their power in their principalities. The Gregorian reform would endeavor to put an end to lay abbacy, without, however, suppressing the *advocatus* system.[105]

In a parallel movement, some foundations, in the cause of reform, obtained complete autonomy in order to avoid any lay administrative involvement. Placed under the direct protection of the sovereign or of the church of Rome, they thereby become model monasteries, administering their own property. A few large monasteries thus found themselves in charge of a group of priories, which in turn contributed to their influence and their enrichment. Cluny is one of the most fully developed examples of this.[106]

101 *La règle de saint Benoît*, 31.
102 Council of Nicaea II, canon 11.
103 For an overview, see Devroey, *Économie rurale*, 278–85.
104 Felten, *Äbte und Laienäbte*, 280–88.
105 For examples and bibliography, see Helvétius, *Abbayes, évêques et laïques*, 298–303.
106 See especially Poeck, *Cluniacensis ecclesia*; Iogna-Prat, *Ordonner et exclure*, 35–99.

In the East, Theodore the Studite devoted a number of his works (including a poem![107]) to diaconal ministries which, in Byzantine monasteries, were devoted to the administration of property. The bursar played such an essential role that he soon appeared as the prospective successor of the *higumenos*; for this reason the latter tended to choose him on the basis of criteria other than the qualities of an administrator.[108] At the end of the tenth century, the poor administration of monastic wealth was patent: in 964, Emperor Nicephorus Phocas devoted his *novella* to precisely this problem.[109] At the same time, a new institution was established, namely the practice of *charistike* (which we might translate as "gift in benefice"). When all is said and done, this practice was of the same order as lay abbacies, and was destined to cause monasteries to be administered by powerful lay people. A layman would receive a monastery for one, two, or three generations; he had to provide for the upkeep of the monks and for the charitable obligations envisaged by the founder, in consideration for which he received the surplus in its entirety.[110] Even if some prominent church figures eventually rose up against abuses of this system,[111] such as the appropriation of property or the installation of lay people in monasteries, at the outset these were the very monasteries which sought *charistikaroi*.

The trend toward lax administration was not, however, the rule everywhere. The monasteries of Athos, in particular, beginning with the Lavra, proved themselves exceptional in this regard, judiciously making interest-bearing investments and purchases of land in addition to the donations they received. Further, a system that parallels *charistike* arose. Monasteries having some financial difficulties were entrusted to a prosperous monastery as an *epidosis*, a benefice identical to *charistike*, but with no time constraints. In reality, these monasteries soon lost any independence, becoming *metochoi* (associates) comparable to priories in the West. Monastic wealth was, therefore, concentrated and *epidosis* thus replaced *charistike*, which quietly disappeared.[112] A good number of the new aristocratic foundations of the second half of the eleventh century were granted self rule, which was an explicit recognition of the quality of their administration. Thereafter, these monasteries were in their own possession, even when they managed to preserve for the founder the useful status of protector.

107 Theodore the Studite, *Jamben*, 107, n. 7.
108 Kaplan, "Evergetis *Typikon*."
109 Svoronos, *Les novelles*, 150–61.
110 Morris, "Byzantine Aristocracy," "Monasteries and their Patrons," and *Monks and Laymen*; Kaplan, "Les monastères."
111 John of Antioch, *Treatise against Charistikè*.
112 Kaplan, "Evergetis *Typikon*," 118–23.

The period from 600 to 1100 corresponds in both West and East to a long process of institutionalization of asceticism, which was progressively constrained within monasteries that were themselves more and more organized. If this was theoretically more rigorous in the West than in the East, in practice monasteries confronted similar problems and found solutions comparable in their diversity. Such similarities ought not to surprise us: they rest upon the shared tradition of the origins of asceticism, which constituted the very foundation of medieval monastic thought. It is this shared tradition that explains the tremendous success with which monasticism was met during the period: for the majority of the faithful in both East and West, the saint was first and foremost the monk.

14

Law and its applications

JANET L. NELSON

The term "law" has a deceptive consistency. It may be said to result from "a particular political ideology or even cosmology."[1] Yet even within a given tradition, geographical setting, or institutional context, its applications and meanings are far from consistent. To study law in history is to study change. The subject of this chapter, the law of the early medieval Church, or canon law, turns out to be a disparate and lumpy mix, resistant to categorization in terms of later-medieval legal assumptions and modern ones alike. A canon in Greek is literally a yardstick, hence, a rule. The term stuck, in West as well as East. By 600, the canons issued by the great councils of the fourth and fifth centuries were widely regarded as authoritative. Thereafter, in the various provinces and kingdoms of the early medieval West, no single authority issued or taught or interpreted the rules of canon law. Bishops assembled in councils made law from time to time, legal collections continued to be made and circulated on private and local initiatives, and law was applied by bishops acting as judges. The situation was not so different in the East, and scholars nowadays are alive to the prevalence there, despite the concentration of evidence emanating from Constantinople, of provincial activity and diversity. In both East and West, canon law and secular law were associated in practice, and secular and ecclesiastical concerns overlapped in imperial legislation. For the church, as for secular rulers in the West, the Theodosian Code (438) remained an occasional reference point for much of the period covered in this chapter, while in the East, the Justinianic Code (534) remained the basis of canon and secular law throughout.[2] Such codifications, though, not least because they were massively unwieldy, never constituted all that passed for law. In both East and West, abbreviations and anthologies multiplied.

1 Ullmann, *Law and Politics*, 25.
2 van der Wal and Lokin, *Historiae iuris graeco-romani delineatio*, passim.

As soon as churches acquired permanent possessions, churchmen became concerned to gain protection for property rights from secular law.[3] In the East, officially at least, the persistence of the Roman state and Roman law tradition maintained the rights of individuals to alienate property, and the rights of churches, as corporate holders, to own in perpetuity. In the West, where the imperial state had been replaced by multiple smaller and more personalized powers, those in charge of churches, which in practice meant, above all, bishops and abbots, had to devise new survival strategies. They had to recognize more extensive and enduring family claims, and devise more flexible terms (*precariae, beneficia*, for instance) to accommodate them.[4] Proprietary churches have often been seen by modern historians of church law as unfortunate side effects of declining ecclesiastical standards and secular rapacity and violence. An alternative, more sympathetic interpretation sees here another adaptive strategy: a mesh of legal arrangements (rather than a "system") was devised to engage lay Christians in support for churches and to stabilize the provision, and meet the costs, of religious services.[5] Arrangements created by mutual agreement functioned effectively in terms of contemporary interests, needs, and assumptions. In other words, law worked with the grain of social relations in a world of relatively weak states but endowed aristocracies and peasant communities with a certain negotiating power. Far from being specifically Germanic, this adaptive strategy was used right across the early medieval West, from southern Italy to Ireland.

Similar adaptation to early medieval conditions is visible in the West in multiple tendencies for hierarchical relations between churchmen to be conceptualized, and then legally formulated, as dyadic pairs, bound by mutual service and protection. Two good examples, again from the eighth century onward, are the vernacular oath of loyalty increasingly often demanded, in German-speaking lands, of a priest to his bishop, and the profession of faith but also of obedience made by a new bishop to his archbishop, as a condition of consecration.[6] The early medieval church's hierarchy could not be maintained by institutional or appointive, still less bureaucratic, structures of office offered by the canon law inherited from the late Roman Empire. Particularly evident in northern Europe, the fidelity of man to man was an alternative and workable model in a world of social relations held together by lordship. The

3 Tellenbach, *Church in Western Europe*, 75–76.
4 See the chapter by Morris in this volume.
5 Tellenbach, *Church in Western Europe*, ch. 3; S. Wood, *Proprietary Church*; cf. Blair, *Church in Anglo-Saxon Society*.
6 Esders and Mierau, *Die althochdeutsche Klerikereid*; *Canterbury Professions*.

model worked from the bottom up to affect, and inflect, relations at every level of the church's structure in the West.

The church universal at the beginning of this period had a model of its own: a pentarchy of patriarchates.[7] In the fourth and fifth centuries, there were varying traditions of the rank order among these: bishops of Rome consistently affirmed their see's primacy of honor, and this formulation was generally acknowledged by the other patriarchates (Constantinople, Antioch, Jerusalem, and Alexandria).[8] Augustine, reflecting everyday speech, distinguished a "western church" coterminous with the Roman patriarchate from an "eastern" one comprising the other four patriarchates.[9] The Arab conquests of the 630s and 640s took political control of Antioch, Jerusalem, and Alexandria out of Christian hands. Constantinople's claims to "equal precedence" with Rome[10] were considered reconcilable with Rome's being first in honor. Papal primacy, then, was not interpreted as implying practical legal authority to hear appeals from subordinates of other patriarchs or to override their decisions. Within the West, too, popes in the century or so after Gregory the Great generally imitated him by operating in a conciliar style and writing fraternally to bishops, tactics that fitted well with actual conditions that limited popes' will or capacity to lay down the law. In the eighth century these conditions began to change because popes now pursued more and wider contacts with the various parts of western Christendom, and because western churchmen and rulers more often sought popes' advice and support in their own uses and applications of law. It was a function of Latin Christendom's increasingly effective operations internally (in maintaining a territorial order based on dioceses, and in achieving lay funding) and externally (missions) that competition between different churches, between bishops and monasteries, between different levels of the hierarchy, between rival Christian rulers, propelled ever more visitors to Rome in search of justice and judgment.[11] At various times between the eighth century and the eleventh, the papacy as a legal institution moved from passive to active mode. Mostly, however, popes spoke when spoken to. Only toward the close of the period covered in this chapter did demand for papal judgment exert a steady enough pressure to evoke an institutionalized response, with agents and agencies to match; and a new period in church history then began.

7 Herrin, "Pentarchy," especially 591–96.
8 Nicaea c. 6; and for its fifth-century alteration and interpretation, Chadwick, *East and West*, 16, 51.
9 Ibid., 31.
10 Ibid., 226–27.
11 Smith, *Europe after Rome*, 279–82.

Last but not least in the list of adaptive strategies peculiar to, because peculiarly necessary for, the early medieval West, was the church's use of its law to create a new model of protective political power in the shape of consecrated kingship.[12] In this context, law was twinned with the church's specialty, liturgical performance of personal consecration. To this was added an ecclesiastically reshaped conception of mutual fidelity as occurring between (faithful) men and their king. At the heart of the rite of royal coronation was a sworn commitment to justice given by the king-elect and then his anointing by bishops in the presence, and with the declared assent, of leading laity. This rite has a continuous history in both Anglo-Saxon England and Francia from the eighth century onward, with further refinements in the ninth and tenth.[13] It is, among other things, a remarkable application of law by early medieval churchmen in the West, to which the East offers no parallel.

Yet there were plenty of similarities between the models of Christian monarchy in East and West. In the East, emperors summoned the councils that legislated for the church. In the West, kings performed comparable roles, though it was not only churchmen but often lay assemblies who shared in the making of ecclesiastical law, committed themselves to uphold it, and sometimes backed their ordinances by secular sanctions. In East and West, especially in and after the eighth century, "New Davids," legislators who saw themselves as representing a new Chosen People, borrowed liberally, and sometimes literally, from the Old Testament. In the East, law evoked, for subjects and emperors, "a symbolic universe";[14] in the West's many smaller universes, a kingdom's or region's law, comprising ecclesiastical along with secular elements, functioned as "a potential rallying-cry" to express and reproduce political and social identity.[15] Funding for local churches was organized in characteristically different ways: in the East, the state's fiscal arrangements seem to have been adapted to provide for churches, whereas in the West, from the eighth century, laypeople were required to pay their local churches' tithes, conceived as a return for pastoral care.[16]

In modern scholarship, medieval canon law in the West (the East is not covered in this historiography) has often been thought to characterize the

12 Semmler, *Der Dynastiewechsel*, especially 87–110; Becher and Jarnut, *Der Dynastiewechsel*.

13 Nelson, *Politics and Ritual*, especially 239–307.

14 Haldon, "Byzantine State," 6.

15 Innes, "Danelaw Identities," 83.

16 Kottje, *Studien*, 11–43, 62–66; S. Wood, *Proprietary Church*, 478–518; Tinti, "'Costs' of Pastoral Care."

firm and consistent powers of a church-state.[17] This was Richard Southern's view of the central Middle Ages, "the age of growth." Law was absent from his account of the church of the "primitive" early medieval period, with its "limited . . . powers of organization," addiction to ordeals and "gorgeous ceremonies," and such government as there was "especially subject to the curse of meaningless flux": "as a science, canon law had barely begun before 1050."[18] Compare James Brundage's now-classic account of medieval canon law: the early medieval period's "isolationism and particularism" were mirrored in the "inward-looking character" of its canon law, while "the problem [was] . . . there was too much of it . . . numerous rules that were contradictory, obsolete or unworkable . . . a maze of conflicts and inconsistencies."[19] Though one of these two distinguished historians saw no canon law of the right sort and the other saw too much of the wrong sort, they both condemned early medieval canon law for not being properly medieval, meaning later medieval, but also for not being modern: that is, for not being state-sponsored, systematized, professionalized, and university-taught. The argument of this chapter is that some early medieval churchmen, between c. 600 and c. 1100, knew their way around the maze: that is, they produced and applied canon law that was workable in, hence distinctive to, their own world, thus enabling the church to sustain itself politically as an institution, and to wield social authority in collaboration with, rather than by asserting dominance over, the laity, who after all, from another perspective, *were* the church.[20]

The Council in Trullo 691–92: contexts and meanings

By the late seventh century, after much furor, theological debate had quietened down in both East and West. On the legal front, it was time for concerted action. The Council summoned in 691 by the Eastern emperor, Justinian II (685–95, 705–11), to meet *in Trullo*, that is, in the domed hall-church of the imperial palace, was thoroughly traditionalist in intent: the legislative tradition of the empire's glory days was to be resumed.[21] No new disciplinary canons had been issued since Chalcedon. Now the decisions of Justinian I's 553 Fifth

17 Ullmann, *Law and Politics*, 29, 47, 119–20; see also R. Davies, "Medieval State," 291; cf. Gierke, *Political Theories*, 11–15.
18 Southern, *Western Society and the Church*, 17–22, 27–33.
19 Brundage, *Medieval Canon Law*, 22–24.
20 See further the chapter by Iogna-Prat in this volume.
21 Nedungatt and Featherstone, *Council in Trullo*, 43–186.

Ecumenical Council and the Sixth Council of 680–81 were to be confirmed and universally promulgated.[22] Of the 102 canons, few dealt with theology and none of those was contentious. The point was to make law about Christianity as it was lived. The canons were more or less equally divided between those for clergy and those for laity. The new Justinian was determined to restore formal unity to Christendom.[23] Many of the canons were equally acceptable to easterners and westerners, and not new: the prohibition of simony, for instance, or of charging fees for ministering the sacrament (cc. 22, 23), or the condemnation of abortion as murder (c. 91). Lay cross-dressing at the rites of spring was condemned (c. 62), as it had been by the sixth-century Bishop Martin of Braga in northwest Iberia (though sophisticated clergy tolerated similar behavior in Rome until the twelfth century).[24] By contrast, what sound like urban, even metropolitan, offenses forbidden in 691–92 are not paralleled in western canons: priests keeping taverns, or worse, pimping (cc. 9, 86); clergy attending horse races or theaters; clergy or monks visiting the baths when women were washing (cc. 24, 51, 77); law students practicing pagan rites (cc. 71, 76); and seductive hairstyles (c. 96). Divergence between eastern and western customary practices had perhaps become more obvious, but obvious, too, were the reasons for these differences. There was nowhere in the West like Constantinople. A major aim of these canons clearly was to differentiate the priest's lifestyle more sharply from the layman's; and this coincided with the stress on the correct performance of the Eucharist and the purity of sacred space (cc. 69, 76, 81), and the regulation of the practice of celebrating the liturgy in private chapels and homes, apparently in the capital (cc. 31 and 59). The reaffirmation of Constantinople's possession of privileges equal to Rome's, though Rome was first in honor (c. 36), raked over old arguments, but caused few practical problems. Neither, apparently, did the setting out of alternative rules for the deacons' and priests' ordinations, with the eastern tolerance for married men in these offices juxtaposed to the western requirement of celibacy, insisted on in principle since the fourth century though widely flouted in practice (c. 13). This needs to be read in conjunction with c. 3, forbidding second marriages for priests, and presenting this as a middle way of "kindness and consideration," and c. 12, forbidding bishops to be married.[25] To my mind, these canons invite a view of the cluster of issues as differences

22 Hence the alternative name of this council, the Quinisext, "Fifth-and-Sixth."

23 See Herrin, *Formation of Christendom*, 284–90; Dură, "Ecumenicity"; Chadwick, *East and West*, 64–70; Magdalino, "Making of Byzantine Orthodoxy," 5–7.

24 Martin of Braga, *Capitula*, cc. 72, 73; Markus, *End of Ancient Christianity*, 103–106.

25 Pitsakis, "Clergé marié et célibat."

of custom and hence tolerable, like different fast-days, or beards versus shaven chins.

The Trullan canons were issued only in Greek.[26] But any temptation to construe this linguistic change as symptomatic of wider lack of understanding between East and West should be resisted. The Trullan texts were readily understood at Rome itself where the pope and plenty of other clergy knew Greek. Pope Sergius (687–701) refused to endorse Trullan "erroneous novelties," perhaps referring to the urban eastern "house-churches" dealt with in cc. 31 and 59 (see above).[27] But the Trullan canons were accepted by Pope Constantine (708–15) when he visited the East in 710 in a spectacular gesture of unity that reflected the spirit of the Council in Trullo itself.[28] Since no one then could have suspected that this was to be the last such papal visit until the late twentieth century, it takes a certain willfulness to read the Council in Trullo as a parting of the ways.

When, c. 500, Dionysius Exiguus had organized his great canon law collection "systematically," rather than chronologically, into conciliar decrees and papal decretals, the distinction denoted not contradictory but complementary forms of church legislation. The Council in Trullo cited conciliar authority but sought papal confirmation. There were divergent customs. "Sexy" icons,[29] for example, were forbidden in 691–92 (c. 100), as were icons representing Christ as a lamb rather than a man (c. 82). These concerns had no parallels in the West, not just because there were fewer icon painters, but because icons were less central to personal devotion. The celebrations of the liturgy in private chapels or homes, banned in cc. 31 and 59, seem to refer to city houses. In the West, and without any reference to the papacy, c. 14 of the Council of Chalon (647/653) condemned a long-standing practice whereby *potentes* (powerful people) built *oratoria* on their country estates, appointed clergy, and amassed material resources (*facultates*) there, flouting bishops' attempts to oversee or control.[30] When c. 3 of the Council of Clichy (626/7) prohibited sworn associations of priests against their bishop or plots to ambush him, "something forbidden even by secular laws," they were actually quoting Chalcedon c. 18;[31] but this was not one of the Chalcedonian canons cited at the

26 Landau, "Überlieferung und Bedeutung," 225–26, for the eighth-century Latin translation.

27 *Liber Pontificalis (Life of Sergius)*, 373 (trans. Davis, vol. 1, 84).

28 *Liber Pontificalis (Life of Constantine)*, 390–91 (trans. Davis, vol. 1, 91).

29 For the adjective, see Chadwick, *East and West*, 66.

30 Sixth-century partial precedents: Clermont, c. 15, in *Canons des conciles mérovingiens*, 218–19; IV Orleans, c. 7, ibid., 270–71.

31 Clichy, cc. 3 and 14, ibid., 530, 536–38.

Council in Trullo, when episcopal security was hardly perceptible as an issue. Absences have their stories. So, too, do new presences. There is hard-edged actuality in c. 1 of the Council of Bordeaux (673/5): "Clerics must scrupulously wear the permitted habit, and they must not have or carry lances or other weapons or wear lay clothing."[32] This is no mere repetition of any conventional regulation on clerical dress but a new voicing of concern that would resonate in western canons from the seventh century to the tenth and beyond.[33] In the East, with its state-organized army to protect the church's personnel, there was no conciliar censure of warrior-clerics.

What eastern and western churches shared in the seventh and eighth centuries, and also what divided them, becomes clear from comparing receptions of Old Testament law. The Council in Trullo c. 65 forbade a number of practices that modern scholars have seen as of pagan or folkloric origin; but "jumping over fires," wizardry, and idols recall the wickedness of King Manasseh.[34] It was these "abominations" that King Josiah "purged" from Judah and Jerusalem, thereafter ruling his people "according to the whole law of Moses."[35] But this echo was faint in 691; and Byzantine canon law continued to consist largely of the decrees of the ecumenical councils. If the most precious relic in the imperial chapel in Constantinople was the rod of Moses, this was not a reminder that the emperor's law was Mosaic, but a symbol of earthly rule mirroring God's cosmic rule.[36] By contrast, the early eighth-century Irish *Senchas Már* treated old Irish law as quite literally complementing Old Testament law, and Irish canons are replete with "biblical tendencies" on such matters as Sunday observance, food prohibitions, and sexual impurity.[37] In part thanks to Irish influence, eighth-century Franks, and Bavarians as well, developed strong biblical tendencies of their own. Old Testament law became something to be literally followed by the New Israel, and tithes adopted from the Bible, hitherto patchily prescribed by churchmen, were reinforced by Bavarian and Frankish rulers at about the same point in the mid-eighth century.[38] In the coronation

32 Ibid., 568; for the date, Rouche, *L'Aquitaine*, 104.

33 Prinz, *Klerus und Krieg*, 6–7, and passim.

34 2 Kgs. 21.6–7; cf. 2 Chr. 33.6–7.

35 2 Kgs. 23.25; cf. 2 Chr. 35.

36 Dagron, *Emperor and Priest*, 84–85.

37 Fournier, "Le *Liber ex Lege Moysi*"; Meens, "Uses of the Old Testament," 67–78.

38 Lev. 27.30, 32; Num. 18.20–28. Constable, *Monastic Tithes*, 9–56, especially 19–28. Bavarian legislation backed by Tassilo is extant in Council of Aschheim, c. 6 (see *Concilia aevi Karolini 742–842*, 57), dated "before 757," by Wolfram, *Die Geburt Mitteleuropas*, 102. Cf. Pippin I to Archbishop Lull of Mainz (probably 765), *Capitula episcoporum* I, no. 17, 42, a particular demand, and Charlemagne, Capitulary of Herstal (779), ibid., no. 20, c. 7, 48, a generalized and legally enforceable one.

rites of Byzantine emperors were prayers invoking the models of anointed Old Testament kings, yet no one thought of literally anointing emperors.[39] In the eighth- and ninth-century West, churchmen reinvented royal anointing through direct borrowing from the Old Testament, then enshrined this consecration rite in canon law, and drew legal inferences from it about royal duties and, in the case of the ninth-century Franks, the authority of priestly consecrators.[40]

Christian apologists before the fourth century had managed with vague and very unspecific appeals to biblical law for authoritative guidance on questions of ethics and social responsibility. Thereafter, churchmen had to state explicitly the norms from which more precise, practical, and timely rulings could be deduced, and lay down clear procedures for pursuing claims, settling disputes, and bringing appeals. This entailed first, the elaboration of rules governing the functions and conduct of the clergy, and the forms and limits of episcopal jurisdiction; second, clarification of the terms on which the church would negotiate its lodging within the world. Crucially involved in the first was the provision of greater institutional structure and coherence to the clerical hierarchy; and in the second, the legal definition of the church's material resources and of ecclesiastical authority vis-à-vis the laity. Again, conflicting interpretations of the law on these subjects inevitably arose – so often, in fact, as to provide threads leading through the entire period covered by this chapter, at least in the West. But the church's negotiating position should not be seen as weak, nor was its "ductility," as a "frail aqueduct across which the cultural reservoirs of the Classical world now passed to the new universe of feudal Europe," a risky achievement against the odds.[41] The church was well-embedded in solid Roman and post-Roman foundations. In its capacity to enlist law in the dogged maintenance of its property, "the patrimony of the poor," against the avarice of the powerful, the church proved itself anything but frail.[42]

In the West, bishops had to assume new responsibilities. Heavier pastoral loads that in practice involved administrative functions were imposed by circumstances, offering bishops legal business which may not have been unwelcome. Frankish rulers in the seventh century, and Bavarians in the eighth, issued secular, so-called "barbarian" laws and/or edicts (capitularies) demonstrably

39 Nelson, *Politics and Ritual*, 259–81.
40 Semmler, *Der Dynastiewechsel*, 87–110.
41 Anderson, *Passages*, 131–32.
42 Ganz, "Ideology of Sharing," 17–30, especially 24, 26. Cf. Claussen, *Reform*, 184–203, especially 191–93.

influenced by the Theodosian Code; bishops advised on such legislation, and often specifically in relation to clerics and their dependents. Some people thought that the church itself was subject to Roman Law. The inhabitants of the southern part of Gaul used versions of the Code, calling themselves *Romani* to signal that fact; and a bishop of Clermont in 675 cited the Code in defense of his refusal to appear in the king's court on Easter Saturday.[43] By the time of Charlemagne and Louis the Pious, churchmen were more heavily involved than ever in royal legislation. Some, though, were fiercely critical of the savagery of the "old law," whether Roman or barbarian. In 799, Theodulf, shortly to become bishop of Orleans, urged that judges' courtrooms would be fit for Christ's presence only if mercy as well as probity was to be found there.[44]

The author of a legal formula c. 600 exclaimed in apparent happy surprise when he found "what Roman law teaches" coinciding with "the custom of the locality [*pagus*]."[45] It was in such "customary" contexts that arbitration was so frequently used as an alternative to a court case, with family and friends (*amici*) using their good offices to reach out-of-court solutions that were both legal in terms of customary law, and socially effective. This is the new Christian law in action: informal, consensual, and a form of patronage. The law's workings, enmeshed in social relations, hence performative and symbolic, involved the negotiation of power. What we might label the private sphere had grown at the expense of what classical Romans would have called the public. Yet this did not make canon law redundant: on the contrary.

Bishops in councils were the main legislators for the provincial and regnal (in the sense of kingdom-wide) churches of the early Middle Ages. Substantial collections of post-600 conciliar canons survive from Spain (until the Muslim conquest in 711 ended the series) and from Gaul, with a break from c. 680 until 743 (Boniface exaggerated a little when he wrote in 742 of an eighty-year gap), but thereafter in increasing volume and frequency through the later eighth and ninth centuries, with additional records from councils held east of the Rhine; and from the Anglo-Saxon kingdom some sixty references to Southumbrian

43 I. Wood, "Code in Merovingian Gaul," 161–77, especially 161, 167 (referring to Codex Theodosianus 2.8.19), 169, 171, 175–76. For Anglo-Saxon bishops' involvement in royal legislation from the early seventh century onward, see Wormald, *Making of English Law*, chs. 5 and 6.

44 Theodulf, *Contra iudices*, 515; Hincmar of Rheims was acquainted with this poem: Nees, *Tainted Mantle*, 53–55, 210; cf. Agobard of Lyons, *Adversus legem Gundobadi*; *Carmen de Timone Comite* in Brown, *Unjust Seizure*, 1–5.

45 *Formulae Andegavenses*, no. 54.

councils before c. 850, but only a handful of detailed records of conciliar decisions, and eleven references to Northumbrian ones (none after 800).[46] From east and west Francia in the tenth and eleventh centuries, there are, as with England, some references to councils' decisions, and many more to episcopal judgments, but few extant decrees, hence little evidence for the normative texts on which decisions were based.[47] Still, the total tally is impressively large. We need to revisit, in a more positive frame of mind, Brundage's claim that there was too much early medieval canon law. Why did early medieval churchmen produce so many canon law collections? The answers are that churchmen had many uses for legal texts, not least as aids to memory, and that the authority they ascribed to them was totemic and inspirational as well as practical. Did the compilers, given the collections' deficiencies in ordering and indexing, expect their work to be used for reference, and applied? The very fact that so many collections, from the eighth century on, were systematically organized (that is, rather than listing texts chronologically, they broke them up thematically, in numbered titles listed in a table of contents) suggests utilitarian uses among others.

Early canon law collections

Three of the canon law collections made in the West between 600 and 800 hold particular interest, both in themselves and because of their influence.[48] The so-called *Collectio Vetus Gallica*, plausibly credited to Bishop Etherius of Lyons in the late sixth/early seventh century, was "systematic."[49] Eleven manuscripts are from places within the Carolingian Empire and date from the reigns of Charlemagne and his ninth-century successors. These statistics constitute evidence of use, in the Carolingian period at any rate, and imply a strong connection between the Carolingian period and the Merovingian, analogous to

46 *La colección canónica Hispana*, vols. 4, 5; *Les canons des conciles mérovingiens*; *Concilia aevi Karolini 742–842*; Cubitt, *Anglo-Saxon Church Councils*, 247–92. See further Reynolds, "Rites and Signs"; and *Die Konzilsordines*.

47 Schröder, *Die westfränkische Synoden*; Hartmann, "Probleme des geistlichen Gerichts"; cf. Wormald, *Making of English Law*, 100, 106, ch. 6 passim, especially 430–49.

48 Kéry, *Canonical Collections*, lists some fifty separate collections made between the fifth century and the eighth, of which some twenty belong to the 600 to 800 period. See also Fransen, *Les collections canoniques*.

49 Mordek, *Kirchenrecht und Reform*, 79–82; Kéry, *Canonical Collections*, 50–53; for the term "systematic" in the case of Cresconius's sixth-century *Concord of Canons*, see Zechiel-Eckes's discussion in Cresconius, *Concordia canonum*, 1, 62. Brundage, *Medieval Canon Law*, 10 understandably terms Dionysius's chronological collection "more systematic than its predecessors," using the term non-technically.

that demonstrable in the case of liturgy.[50] The *Hispana*, consisting of decrees of early councils through to Chalcedon and continuing with African, Gallican, and Spanish councils, with a final section of papal texts from Damasus to Gregory I, was a chronological collection made in seventh-century Spain, and much redeployed thereafter in the Frankish world.[51] The "systematic" *Collectio Canonum Hibernensis*, produced in early eighth-century Ireland, became quite widely known on the Continent, especially in excerpted form.[52] Its sixty-seven numbered titles assembled texts culled not just from the Bible but from the Fathers, as well as from conciliar decrees and papal letters, and, distinctively, with some Irish material: penitentials, proverbial sayings, and synodal canons. It began with an engagingly frank preface, declaring itself "most pleasing," and promising to "edify readers." "If something therein seems discordant, the text that is judged to be of greater authority should be chosen." No criteria were given on how to assess authority. "Considering the immense number of synodal texts," the author continued,

> and seeing the almost useless obscurity in most of those clumsy products and a discordant diversity more destructive than constructive in the rest, I assembled into one volume from an enormous forest of writings a brief, full, and harmonious exposition. I added many things, abbreviated many things, preserved many things just as they were, liberated many things, disregarding the sequence of words, from one sense to another, and strove in all for this alone, that what appeared as recommended in these texts should not be ascribed to my judgement. I have placed the name of each author in front of each testimony. But the reader should not neglect, when having recourse to the general titles which, out of necessity, we placed at the beginning, to pay careful attention to the numbers; and those having been observed, he will find without any delay the subject which he wants.[53]

It is not clear how exactly this collection was used in an Irish context. The author envisaged a readership, but edification is not the same thing as judgment. Penitentials straddle liturgy and law, and perhaps some of the "testimonies" included here were for monastic reflection. One, at least, may have arisen from a dispute over the conduct of nuns: according to Title 45, c. 14, "The *Romani* say: . . . virgins adorned with the clothing of virgins are to be

50 Hen, *Royal Patronage*, 21–64.
51 Kéry, *Canonical Collections*, 61–67, 71–72, for manuscripts of a systematic version, apparently made in the ninth century.
52 Kéry, *Canonical Collections*, 73–80.
53 Somerville and Brasington, *Prefaces*, 58; cf. Sheehy, "*Collectio Canonum Hibernensis*," and "Bible and the *Collectio Canonum Hibernensis*"; and Reynolds, "Unity and Diversity."

segregated from the view of men, and to live thus until death." This "exhortation to claustration" is unparalleled in Ireland before the eleventh century, and jars with Irish evidence for nuns "working side by side with men of the Church" and also for Irish women going on pilgrimage.[54] Other Irish canons clearly do represent Irish ecclesiastical law, for instance, on the status of the ruler of a monastery as *princeps*.[55] Yet others were presumably intended for use in dispute settlement. Title 32, c. 17 cited the Old Testament women Axa and Dinah to authorize women's rights over property which they could then give to the church. The utility of Title 46, on marriage, comprising thirty separate canons is indicated, at least once transferred to Continental contexts, by its separate existence as the *Collectio XXX capitulorum*, which survives in no fewer than twenty-two manuscripts dating from between the ninth and twelfth centuries.[56]

The Carolingian period

The production of legal texts was one thing; knowledge and application of them another. An exemplary study of early medieval canon law manuscripts shows few such texts surviving from anywhere before the eighth century, and then a concentration of the evidence in "the Frankish kingdoms."[57] The currency of some canon law collections seems to have been confined to a single region; the influence of others was supraregional; sometimes a church council was the spur to diffusion, more often the explanation for both production and diffusion seems to have lain in the efforts of a single bishop. What the Carolingians supplied was the contacts, the sense of urgency, the political impetus, to make the breakthrough into widespread diffusion of canon law texts.

In March 774, Charlemagne left subordinates to continue the Franks' siege of the Lombard capital and headed, unexpectedly, south to Rome. Pope Hadrian presented him with a copy of the Dionysian collection, with additions, and prefaced by an acrostic dedicatory poem apparently written in haste, hailing the king as protector of the church and calling on him "always to love divine law."[58] It was some years before Charlemagne seriously addressed Hadrian's gift. The Dionysio-Hadriana was never given "official" status: manuscripts of

54 Harrington, *Women in a Celtic Church*, 95, 187.

55 W. Davies, "Clerics as Rulers."

56 Kéry, *Canonical Collections*, 81–82.

57 McKitterick, "Knowledge of Canon Law," noting, 115–17, that the absence of Anglo-Saxon manuscripts may well be misleading, since "ghosts" of Anglo-Saxon influence remain.

58 Hadrian I, *Domino excell. filio carulo magno regi*, line 11.

other collections continued to be copied in the ninth century.[59] Yet in drawing heavily on Dionysius's collection, Alcuin, the probable compiler of the *Admonitio generalis*, a set of decrees issued by a council held at Aachen in 789, was following the longstanding practice of deriving church law from late antique councils. The *Admonitio*'s first fifty-nine chapters selected "what seem to us the more necessary *capitula* of the canonical decrees," which bishops, above all, were to practice and preach, and enforce with the help of royal officers (*missi*). "So that God, who has conferred so many *honores* on our kingdom, may deign to preserve us and our kingdom by his protection forever," Charlemagne would "strive like the Old Testament king Josiah to recall the kingdom which God had given him to the worship of the true God." The "more necessary *capitula*" began with rules of order, urging episcopal solidarity (no bishop should receive in communion anyone excommunicated by another bishop, c. 1, cf. c. 56), metropolitan authority over suffragans, and bishops' authority over their rural auxiliaries (*corepiscopi*, cc. 8 and 9), insisting on the distinctiveness of the clerical and monastic ways of life (cc. 26, 27, cf. 52), and affirming the authority of bishops (no monks or clerics to conspire or plot against their pastor, c. 29); then asserted the legal separateness of churchmen from laity (clerics must be judged by bishops or churchmen, not laymen, cc. 28, 38) but with qualifications (only laymen of proven reputation could bring accusations against clerics; only people of proven reputation could accuse bishops or men of high birth, cc. 30, 35; and people of lowly status could not accuse at all, c. 45); and ended with miscellaneous injunctions against embezzling "offerings that belong to the poor" (c. 47), against sodomy (c. 49), and against ignorant or disobedient priests (cc. 55, 58).

The remaining *capitula* (cc. 60–82), termed "useful," consisted of a string of injunctions taken from the law books of the Old Testament and their echoes in the New, a biblical stamp that was to be a hallmark of Charlemagne's legislation for the church.[60] There were rules on maintaining peace and concord (c. 62); judging justly and eschewing bribes (c. 63); not swearing falsely (c. 64); not practicing magic (c. 65), or being covetous (c. 66), or killing "within the fatherland (*infra patriam*) except according to law" (c. 67); keeping churches clean and correcting books properly to allow proper prayer (cc. 71, 72). Various forms of correct conduct and correct belief were specified (cc. 78–82), among them

59 Kottje, "Einheit und Vielfalt"; Mordek, "Dionysio-Hadriana und Vetus Gallica" and "Zur Kirchenrechtsreform," 134–36, citing manuscript evidence for glossing of the Dionysio-Hadriana in Old High German.

60 Kottje, *Studien zum Einfluß des Alten Testament*, 52–56; Cubitt, *Anglo-Saxon Church Councils*, 160–90.

(c. 81) rules for Sunday observance which excepted the work involved in cartage and provisioning for the host (*ostilia carra vel victualia*), or the burial of the dead. Organization in *capitula* is abandoned as the final section morphs into a little sermon, drawing on St. Paul, where canon law is embraced in Christian ethics, yet the author never loses sight of the practical requirements either of the church, for distinguishing clergy from laity and maintaining order within the hierarchy (notably through episcopal and metropolitan authority), or of the state, for securing its military needs and claiming overall responsibility for law (notably in the legislation against feud, c. 67). The program of the *Admonitio*, amplified in further conciliar statements at Frankfurt (794), set the compass for later Carolingian canon law.[61] The competing interests of bishops, of bishops and clergy, of clergy and laity, and of laymen of higher and lower status were explicitly acknowledged, but contained and controlled by a clearly defined hierarchy. The decrees of the great councils of the fourth and fifth centuries, and the decretal letters of early medieval popes, often more narrowly focused yet equally of universal application, set out structures and procedures for judging and resolving the disputes that arose when lines of authority were blurred or contested.

Just here, along the borderlines and faultlines, in local cases, other types of canon law evidence throw less direct light, fitful yet intense, on everyday struggles over church order and competing interpretations of what it meant to live in Christian fashion. Following "a report that has reached our ears," Charlemagne was deeply worried in 802 about "filthiness in monasteries . . . and especially a sodomite monk [whose activities] threaten ruin for all Christians."[62] A few clauses on is the only direct mention of case law in Charlemagne's capitularies: bishops are responsible for bringing to judgment those guilty of incest, "but if someone refuses to agree to the bishop's judgement concerning his atonement, then he is to be brought into our presence, mindful of the example which was made of the incest which Fricco perpetrated upon God's nun."[63] A few years later, Charlemagne bestowed on the monastery of Prüm lands lawfully confiscated from a man guilty of "incest and other misdeeds."[64] The treatment of highborn and propertied widows raised other difficult questions. *Admonitio* c. 59 decreed "that no bishop should presume to veil widows."[65] A Council in 818 enjoined widows, before deciding to become

61 Mordek, "Aachen, Frankfurt, Reims."

62 *Capitularia regum Francorum* 1, 94–95, for Charlemagne's capitulary, *Missorum generale*, no. 33 (802), c. 17.

63 *Capitularia regum Francorum* 1, 97, for c. 33 of the same capitulary.

64 *Caroli Magni Diplomata*, no. 205 (28 April 807), 274.

65 This was widely diffused in Ansegis, *Collectio capitularium*, 1.57, 460.

veiled, to seek the advice of the bishop, but also of their "kin and friends" (*parentes et amici*).[66] Churchmen, noble almost to a man, understood the concerns of *parentes*, threatened with the prospect of lands seeping away from the family through widows' donations to churches in which these women remained stakeholders as (the bishops reached for feminine forms of normally masculine functions) "women-guardians and women-administrators" (*excubatrices et administratices*). This was "noxious liberty." The Council of Paris (829) decreed that widows must not be permitted to continue living in their own homes with opportunities for "moving about in various places, endangering their own souls," but instead were to enter convents and live enclosed under episcopal surveillance. Aristocratic women tended to have minds of their own. The Council of Mainz (888) left veiled widows the option of remaining at home. Whether there or in convents, propertied widows were themselves hot property, liable to be abducted by would-be suitors. Bishops inveighed repeatedly against such *raptores*, but were often willing to declare lawful a widow's subsequent marriage to her abductor provided her *parentes* consented, and the man did penance.

Archbishop Hincmar of Rheims (845–82), expert canonist, wrote a treatise against such *raptores*, and gave legal opinions on other slippery cases involving women and sex.[67] The alleged sodomite incest of Queen Theutberga elicited a particularly lengthy and detailed treatment, which concluded that the lady was innocent and her husband, King Lothar II, therefore unable to divorce and remarry.[68] In the case of Count Stephen, anxious to break off an engagement that politics had made inconvenient and hoping that concern about incest would give him legal grounds for doing so, Hincmar, noting that the kingdom had been shaken by the scandal, judiciously concluded that Stephen and his fiancée should be parted, but that the dower Stephen had proffered should remain in the hands of the young woman's father. In this application of the law, there was undoubtedly some manipulation, attributable less to cynicism than to a genuine concern for social peace.[69] Marriage was a subject in which churchmen had a strong professional interest; and the Carolingian period saw a marked increase in ecclesiastical involvement. Some cases, though, risked being too hot for churchmen to handle. When the noblewoman Northild

66 Nelson, "Wary Widow," 91, with further references to the conciliar legislation cited below.

67 Hincmar of Rheims, *De coercendo et exstirpando raptu viduarum, puellarum et sanctimonialium*. See Stone, "Invention."

68 Hincmar of Rheims, *De divortio Lotharii*; see Airlie, "Private Bodies."

69 Hincmar of Rheims, *Epistola* 136, 89–106.

complained to the Emperor Louis the Pious at the Council of Attigny (822) about the *inhonesta*, the dishonorable treatment, her husband had been inflicting on her, the emperor handed the case over to the bishops – who promptly pleaded lack of expertise in such matters, and batted the case to the "judgement of laymen and married men," who, Hincmar wrote, were gratified to have their rights over their wives thus acknowledged.[70] In 834, in the dying days of the rebellion of Louis the Pious's son Lothar, a noble nun, Gerberga, sister of Louis's erstwhile chamberlain, was seized by Lothar's men at Chalon, accused of witchcraft, tried by a court composed of the wives of Lothar's counselors, put in a wine barrel, and hurled into the Saône.[71] No churchmen are recorded as having claimed an interest here: they chose their legal battlegrounds with prudence when great ones and high politics were involved. It is worth noting that, while Charlemagne's ecclesiastical legislation forbade divorce, formulae for divorce proceedings were copied in a number of eighth- and ninth-century Frankish formularies. Does this imply lay practice persisting, with the collusion of clerical notaries, in defiance of canon law?[72]

Opportunities for bishops, and the pope himself, to apply legal punishment in a socially crucial area cropped up in the case of the "vagabond" wife, Engeltrude daughter of Matfrid, who had quit her husband for one of his vassals, and whom Nicholas I excommunicated.[73] On the other hand, Nicholas gained prestige by offering protection to Queen Theutberga, whom he judged to have been shamed and wronged by a brutal husband, and Hadrian II amnestied a repentant churchman caught on the husband's side in Theutberga's case, Archbishop Gunther of Cologne. To the unique, late ninth-century copy of what seems to be Hadrian's synodal speech on these matters was attached the earliest papal collection of forged papal decretals on the theme of papal jurisdictional power.[74] These came from the so-called collection of Pseudo-Isidore.[75]

70 Hincmar of Rheims, *De divortio Lotharii*, Responsio 5, 141–42; see Nelson, "England and the Continent," 20–21.

71 Thegan, *Gesta Hludowici imperatoris*, ch. 52, 244.

72 *Concilia aevi Karolini, 742–842*, no. 21 (Concilium Foroiuliense, 796), c. 10, 192–93; *Capitularia regum Francorum*, 103, for Charlemagne's *Capitulare missorum item speciale*, no. 35 (802?), c. 22. See Wemple, *Women in Frankish Society*, 77–78 and note 17, and on formularies in general, see Rio, "Early Medieval Frankish Formularies."

73 *Concilia aevi Karolini, 860–874*, no. 16 (Rom Oktober 863), c. IV, 154–55, in which Nicholas I in council at Rome in October 863 excommunicated Engeltrude; see *Annales Bertiniani* (862, 863), 95, 101–103 (Nelson trans., 103, 106–109).

74 *Concilia aevi Karolini, 860–874*, no. 32 (Montecassino oder Rom 869), speech on 366–71, decretals on 371–79; Kéry, *Canonical Collections*, 189–90.

75 Marital law, like many other topics, did not interest the Pseudo-Isidorean compilers, whose specific aims are discussed below.

Pseudo-Isidore was by far the largest collection of the period, and the one which has elicited most comment from modern scholars. Over the past generation, large advances have been made in understanding what is now recognized as not one but several different collections. Their authors were driven by a variety of concerns, and wrote over a period of time (mid-830s to c. 850), but they demonstrably worked at a single site with a well-stocked library, and the context of their efforts was the time of intradynastic conflict, with the attendant woes of internal divisions within the elite and external exploitation by neighbors on-the-make, that racked the Carolingian Empire recurrently between c. 830 and 847.[76] One shared purpose of the Pseudo-Isidorean authors was to give bishops legal protection, whether from high-level political attack (at worst, deposition), from local economic attack (filching of church property by lay claimants or by clerical subordinates exploiting episcopal vacancies), from institutional subversion (the insubordination of priests, or of monastic communities) or institutional oppression (the new claims of metropolitans), or from combinations of these threats.

Explicable in terms of this agenda were four features of the authors' work methods. First, they were keen to establish bishops' own legal authority within the church. At the collection's beginning was placed the liturgical service (*ordo*) for celebrating a church council:

> When a crown [i.e., a circle] has been made of the bishops' seats, there then sit behind the bishops' backs those priests whom the metropolitan has selected to sit so that they can give their judgement with him on any point and settle a case. . . and then the laymen enter, those who have been thought worthy to take part by a parallel selection. . . . [Then the bishops pray together]: "We are here, Lord, Holy Spirit, we are here, hampered as we are by the immanence of sin, but assembled together for a special purpose in thy name. Come to us! . . . Teach us what we must do! . . . Be the safeguard, the suggester, and the carrier-into-effect, of our judgements. Do not allow us to be disturbers of justice . . .[77]

Liturgy reinforced law: the council's authority came from the Holy Spirit.

A second priority was the identifying of correct criminal procedure in ecclesiastical cases. No layman could accuse a cleric, nor could any inferior accuse his ecclesiastical superior; and for a bishop's condemnation, seventy-two episcopal

76 For details, see Pseudo-Isidore, *Decretals*. Schon and Zechiel-Eckes, through their ongoing Projekt Pseudoisidor website, have already transformed the study of the subject. See also Zechiel-Eckes, "Auf Pseudoisidors Spur."

77 Projekt Pseudoisidor website, Part I, *Konzilsordo*, V630, f.3rb; cf. *Die Konzilsordines*, pp. 128, 138–41.

witnesses were required.[78] On the other hand, bishops had jurisdiction over laymen in any case involving church rights.[79]

The third feature was the insistent emphasis, in certain parts of the collection, on papal authority, for instance on the right of any accused bishop to appeal to the pope, and on the principle that "the Holy Roman Church holds the primacy of all churches, to whom the highest affairs of bishops and judgments and disputes involving them and also more important questions involving churches must always be referred as to the head."[80] Qualifying the first point above, implicit in the conciliar liturgy, about the Holy Spirit as the source of a council's authority, was the repeated assertion that the legality of a church council was derived from the fact that a pope had convoked or approved it.[81]

Fourth and inseparable from the preceding point is the fact that the texts emphasizing papal legal authority are forged or falsified: they are decretal letters attributed to a series of early popes (including some martyr-popes). Given that genuine texts did not exist to support the claims in question, was it a case of necessity knowing no law? These learned fabricators were nothing if not practical – indeed their efforts were devoted to tackling urgent contemporary issues. One or two of the forged texts were taken up at Rome by the early 850s; some were used by Hincmar of Rheims himself, who bitterly denounced forgery perpetrated by others.[82] But perhaps the earliest users were the bishops of Soissons and Laon, two of Hincmar's suffragans, who had their own bones to pick with the metropolitan.

How do we explain the mentality of the pious fraudsters of the mid-ninth century? Though not the first to forge canon law, these men forged on a heroic scale.[83] Forgery was part of the expert canonist's intellectual tool kit, allowing him to insert original links in ancient citation-chains. Once such improvement had been effected, it was the very force and conviction carried

78 Projekt Pseudoisidor website, Part III, V630 f.185ra. In practice, so many bishops would have been hard to assemble, even from the entire Frankish kingdom: Schon, ibid., "Überblick über die Fälschungen," p. 2. Cf. also ibid., Part I, *praefatio* iv, v, vi, V630, f.2ra.

79 Ibid., Part I, Anacletus-Brief I, Bcan4. XVI, V630 f.21rb. For a full discussion, see Fuhrmann, *Einfluß und Verbreitung der pseudoisidorischen Fälschungen* 1, 41–44; 134.

80 Projekt Pseudoisidor website, Part III, Papst Vigilius an Bischof Euterus, vii, V630 f.280va.

81 Ibid. Part I, *praefatio* viii, V 630, f.2va; Marcellus-Brief 1,2; 11, 10, V630, ff. 66rb, 67va; Part III, Julius I an die orientalischen Bischöfe, V630, ff. 185vb–186r; Pelagius II an das Konzil in Konstantinopel, V630, f.283rb. See Robinson, "Church and Papacy," 267, 269, 285.

82 Fuhrmann, "Fälscher unter sich."

83 For the Symmachean forgeries c. 500, see Epp, "499–799"; Chadwick, *East and West*, 97. For heroic forging, see Weidemann, *Geschichte des Bistums Le Mans* 2, 361–402; Schieffer, *Die Streitschriften Hinkmars von Reims und Hinkmars von Laon*, 104; cf. Landau, "Gefälschte Recht."

by legal texts themselves, texts that looked right, and traveled in the best of canonical company, that made them so appealing to certain members of the ecclesiastical elite for whom the law as lore constituted a code. Battles of wits and of principles were fought with these glittering rhetorical weapons. But what was the real-life significance of Pseudo-Isidore in the ninth century? Were these "perhaps the most welcome gifts the papacy ever received?"[84] Historians need to be particularly wary of hindsight here, for too much interpretation has been bathed in the anachronistic light of the eleventh century. It is true that some two hundred years after the forgers' workshop closed down, Pseudo-Isidore's papal-monarchic passages attracted much attention in Rome. In the ninth century, however, attitudes at the papal court ranged from cautiously positive to indifferent.

Hincmar of Rheims (806–82, archbishop of Rheims 845–82)

No fighter in legal combat with ecclesiastical colleagues or subordinates was more skilled than Archbishop Hincmar of Rheims. Because he wrote so profusely on canon law, descriptively as well as prescriptively, and because he was so closely involved with the main canonistic trends of the ninth century, it is worth spending some time on him. For Hincmar, metropolitan rights were tactics for keeping suffragans well under control, in principle and in practice.[85] Hincmar excommunicated Bishop Rothad of Soissons for maladministration of his see – then for disobedience to himself as metropolitan – and was correspondingly outraged when Rothad, Pseudo-Isidorean weapons in hand, appealed to Pope Nicholas I.[86] When King Charles the Bald stood aside, the pope was able to reinstate Rothad, as Hincmar bitterly grumbled, *non regulariter* (according to the legal rules) *sed potentialiter* (by power).[87] A second case of episcopal insubordination was that of the archbishop's own nephew and namesake, the bishop of Laon. This time Hincmar senior was able to stage-manage a legal triumph, because Hincmar junior was suspected of conniving with King Charles's rebellious son in 870, and so his fate was

84 Ullmann, *Growth of Papal Government*, 178; cf. Ullmann, *Law and Politics*, 129: "the real winner was the papacy" – undoubtedly true in the long run, but not in the short run.

85 Hincmar of Rheims, *Epistola* 30 *(De iure metropolitanorum)*, 189–210 (though in 876, when this was written, Charles the Bald, now emperor, was Hincmar's target).

86 *Annales Bertiniani* (862), 91–92 (trans. Nelson, 101–102); Fuhrmann, *Einfluß und Verbreitung der pseudoisidorischen Fälschungen* 2, 254–63, 266–70.

87 *Annales Bertiniani* (865), 118–19 (trans. Nelson, 123: "an arbitrary and overbearing decision"); cf. Nelson, "'Not Bishops' Bailiffs,'" 24 (reprint, 134).

sealed, *potentialiter*, by the king. It was settled *regulariter* by the proceedings at the Council of Douzy, August–September 871, presided over by Archbishop Hincmar, with eight archbishops and fourteen bishops participating in the judgment.[88]

Dealing with wayward priests was easier, since high politics were less salient, but even priests' wrongdoings could be tricky in legal terms. Of eight cases recorded in the extensive writings of Hincmar of Rheims, one priest accused of crime turned to the *iudicium civile*, though such cases were supposed to be dealt with "by judgment not of the *mallus* [the local court] or by civil judges but by bishops and synods."[89] Another priest, condemned by the archbishop and his colleagues, appealed to the pope.[90] The consequences of such appeals for transalpine bishops, Hincmar wrote, were very serious: however lawful the bishops' judgment, they might be unable to find envoys to send to Rome, nor to find suitable witnesses to make the journey to rebut the priest's false defense.[91] Where details are known, the ninth-century criminous priests' offenses always involved sex. A generation later, bishops assembled at Tribur (895) complained bitterly that in such cases, when bishops received papal letters full of priests' lies, the papal yoke was *vix ferendum*, "hardly to be borne"![92] Tensions arising from appeals to Rome were now a permanent feature of clerical life. It was not so much that they foreshadowed the big issues of the Gregorian Reform, rather that they revealed underlying, and hitherto latent, features of ecclesiastical life that long predated the eleventh century, and in fact became permanent from the Carolingian period onward, once communication between Rome and other western churches became more frequent. From now on, clergy at all levels were aware of the potential benefits of having friends at the papal court. On the other hand, no new system was yet in place, nor dreamed of in any clerical philosophy. The volume of appeals was still small enough for canon law to work in familiar ways. Something resembling the old homeostatic balance between Rome and the provinces was maintained through the later ninth and tenth centuries.

On legal procedure in the cases of criminous priests, Hincmar was confident that he could rely on the impeccable authority of papal practice, namely the use of oaths and oath-helpers. He began his treatise, *De presbiteris criminosis*, with

88 Council of Douzy in *Concilia aevi Karolini, 860–874*, 411–572 (the entire dossier), with the archbishop's charges, 420–87.

89 Flodoard, *Historia remensis ecclesiae*, III.26, 335.

90 Hincmar responded to Hadrian II's request for a written report, see his *Opuscula et Epistolae*, 646–48. See van Rhijn, *Shepherds of the Lord*, 231–34.

91 *De iudiciis et appellationibus* (Epistola 32) in Hincmar, *Epistolae*, 240.

92 Council of Tribur, c. 30, in *Capitularia regum Francorum* 2, 231.

the model case of Pope Leo III, accused of crimes (apparently including sexual ones) in the late 790s, who, according to "the first book of the Emperor Charles's Capitulary Collection, c. 34," had cleared himself by an oath of purgation supported by twelve episcopal oath-helpers.[93] "Following this example," the capitulary went on, a priest under suspicion should clear himself by his own oath and the oaths of "three or five or seven good and neighboring priests." Hincmar was here citing the collection of Benedict the Levite, now known to have been a rampant forger. This particular "capitulary" was forged, and Hincmar's modern editor, rubbing salt into the wounds, notes that Hincmar, "characteristically," got the number wrong – it should have been c. 35.[94] Did Hincmar know his text to be a forgery? Was his follow-up of this citation with a flood of genuine canon law texts, including one from the Theodosian Code, mere showing off? When he said, finally, that the Frankish church had followed these procedural rules for seventy years and more, was Hincmar knowingly making false claims about customary legal practice? When he insisted, with further invocation of authorities, that "It is permitted to no one to be ignorant of the laws,"[95] was it humbug?

Hincmar's knowledge of canon law may have been more limited, and hazier, than that of the legal historians who have criticized him so sharply. Hincmar used, as and when he could, texts that swam within his ken. Yet his notion of what the *mos consuetudinarius* (customary tradition) actually was may have been truer to his own experience than his modern critics recognize. Oaths and oath-helpers were just one aspect of cisalpine catholic procedure that bore the hallmarks of authentic borrowing from, and adaptation to, provincial, Frankish, secular practice. Not seven but six oath-helpers were employed in particularly doubtful cases, to allow for the seventh man to take an ordeal to test the truth of the oath.[96] It was easy to believe, given the procedure in Leo III's case, that there had been oath-helpers, too, in 800, and that Charlemagne had joined this up with customary procedure for clergy lower down the hierarchy. Hincmar often quoted from memory – and sometimes got details a shade wrong. If he himself sometimes forged, he shared contemporaries' assumptions about the necessity, sometimes, and hence the rightness, of reconstructing the rules that governed legal action *regulariter*.[97]

93 Hincmar of Rheims, *De presbiteris criminosis*, 65–69 and commentary by Schmitz, 18–32.
94 Ibid., 65, note 3.
95 Ibid., 96, cf. commentary at 36.
96 As Schmitz observes, ibid., 25–26; cf. also ibid., 18, for a sympathetic word on Hincmar's way of thinking about good law as old.
97 For an emphatic judgment on Hincmar as forger, see Fuhrmann, "Fälscher unter sich."

In the Carolingian period, threefold promises (*professiones*, *proposita*) of stability, of obedience, and of keeping to the law, were being made by priests and deacons to the bishop at ordination, analogous to the threefold promises of monks to abbots at their profession. The practice may not have depended on any royal command, though Charlemagne evidently wished to standardize it (*Admonitio generalis*, c. 26). Benedictus Levita provided a forged capitulary to this effect.[98] But the origins of such commitments lay deep in "customary tradition." The bonds that held the ecclesiastical hierarchy together in real life were not just (or not mainly) legal concepts of office and obligation, but personal ties of protection / favor and loyalty between patron (or lord) and dependent. This was the context in which, in early ninth-century Bavaria, there appeared a vernacular oath of fidelity for the priest to make to the bishop. Legal historians have remarked on a shift from a commitment to perform a specific legal action to a more fundamental "disposition to loyalty."[99] Perhaps this "fundamental distinction" was less clear-cut in contemporary minds, just as when a man swore *fidelitas* to Charlemagne, he saw the obligations he undertook as both very specific and extremely wide-ranging: legal and supra-legal. The Carolingian state's 60 *solidi* sanction on breaches of fidelity must have been applied variably in practice (if only because such monetary payments were beyond the reach of nearly all), but carried huge symbolic weight. The priest bound in a similar way to be true to his bishop knew his own economic and political dependence, as *pauper* to *potens*.[100] He was indeed obliged. By the tenth century, the obligation was translated into liturgical form, and into Latin, in the *Romano-German Pontifical*; and it became widespread.[101] But from at least the time of Charlemagne it was associated with a conception of the priest's church as church property conferred by the bishop.[102]

Hincmar was determined to apply law in cases when rights in churches competed. When a powerful family claimed the estate of Neuilly, Hincmar counterclaimed for Rheims partly through political action, partly by rehearsing the estate's history over the past century, and partly by assembling a dossier of forty-two capitula from secular and ecclesiastical law.[103] More diffuse were the problems that arose when the church of Rheims had founder's rights in

98 Benedictus Levita, *Capitularium collectio*, III, 466 (ed. Pertz, *MGH LL* 2,2, S. 132) cited in Esders and Mierau, *Der althochdeutsche Klerikereid*, 46–47.

99 Esders and Mierau, *Der althochdeutsche Klerikereid*, 56–68.

100 Nelson, "Making Ends Meet."

101 Esders and Mierau, *Der althochdeutsche Klerikereid*, 14–21, 191–92, 244–45.

102 Ibid., 194–204.

103 Hincmar of Rheims, *De villa Noviliaco*, 295–300, with Hincmar's own key part in the story at ch. V, 297–98.

a number of churches in the dioceses of suffragans or in other provinces. It was, strikingly, at Soissons, Troyes, and Laon, all politically hot *sedes*, that such disputes were fiercest. Actual disputes, documented in Hincmar's letters, had caused Charles the Bald to be besieged by many *clamores*, hence to seek the best legal opinion on hand.[104] Hincmar's response was that canon law clearly distinguished the diocesan's normal authority to ordain and manage (*potestas, dispositio*) from the right of a holder of *dominium*, that is, lordship. Lay lords too ("men and women") had rights of *senioratus* over churches they had founded (including the relics in them), notably to give churches away, and to present clerics for ordination to churches (by implication possessed by women, too).[105] While the priest had rights in his church (tithes, and the renders of the manse), he owed his *senior(es)* spiritual services (*obsequia spiritalia*; *spiritalia ministeria*).[106] So far, so clear. The problem was that *potestas* could in practical understandings slip easily into *senioratus*; and at one point Hincmar's own terminology slid that way.[107] Everything could work only if everyone involved were actuated by fear of shame.[108] And perhaps, with a bishop like Hincmar, they often were. It was as a canon lawyer, though, not just as Pangloss or a deep-dyed conservative, that Hincmar found good arguments, especially Frankish canons, old (canons of Orange, 441, and Orleans, 511), and quite new (Worms, 829), to legitimate lordship's place in the economy of the church. His "rational and in the long run constructive" refusal to make episcopal authority depend on proprietary right offered the basis for the kind of legal compromise that emerged from the convulsions of the eleventh century in the shape of the *ius patronatus*.[109]

On the frontiers

Law's applications lead deep, vertically as it were, into the church's everyday existence in rural life and material culture. Other mid-ninth-century applications lead horizontally, toward Christendom's neighbors and potential recruits.

104 Hincmar of Rheims, *Collectio de ecclesiis et capellis*, ed. Stratmann, 63, and cf. 8–10, 18–20. I have relied on this exemplary edition, including the editor's comments, along with the discussion by S. Wood, *Proprietary Church*, 804–12.

105 Hincmar of Rheims, *Collectio de ecclesiis et capellis*, 86–87, 95.

106 Ibid., 92.

107 Ibid., 1.1, 77 (as noted by S. Wood, *Proprietary Church*, 806); and cf. Wood, 811: "'*potestas*' was genuinely ambiguous or elastic."

108 Hincmar of Rheims, *Collectio de ecclesiis et capellis*, 82–83; see S. Wood, *Proprietary Church*, 487, 514–15.

109 The citation is from S. Wood, *Proprietary Church*, 811. Hincmar, as noted, gives just a glimpse of the implications of lordship for women as patrons, a subject on which later medieval canon lawyers were reticent.

On the frontiers, the Moravians and Bulgars found themselves courted by East and West. Their rulers applied for missionaries, respectively, to the emperor in Constantinople and the East Frankish king in and around Bavaria and Franconia. Where mission fields met and were competed for, and where missionaries encountered customs strange to them, the patriarch of Constantinople on the one hand and the pope on the other were asked for rulings on what Christian conversion meant. To the Bulgars, the Patriarch Photius (858–67, 877–86)[110] responded with a lengthy letter on doctrine. Pope Nicholas I responded with law or advice on customs, in the form of 106 canons, of which 8 were about the observance of Lent (was hunting permissible then?) and 10 about marriage (could a man show his betrothed, before the marriage, the cattle and horses he would offer as bride-gift?). That Nicholas's *responsa* did literally respond to a Bulgar questionnaire shows that the Bulgars must have known quite a lot about the pope's legal expertise and his capacity to make it stretch. It was indeed a notable application of law to a society of pastoralists, in which women as well as men wore trousers (c. 59, customs which the pope, when asked, did not condemn). The pope seized the chance to highlight points on which "Greek" custom allegedly differed from the practice of the Roman church, and this found an echo in his letter to the Frankish bishops in 867 denouncing the Greeks' accusations against the "Latins."[111] The later ninth century, though, saw deep changes in East–West relations. After Photius's death in or soon after 893, the Emperor Leo VI sought and got conciliation. The canon law difficulties resulting from Leo's four successive marriages had little resonance in the West. At the turn of the ninth into the tenth century, popes beset by enemies in their own backyard had little alternative to low-key stances: detente with the East, traditional consensus with bishops, and collaboration with whoever wielded secular power in Italy. In Byzantium, where Photius had challenged the papacy, engaged in the grubbier forms of Constantinopolitan politics, extracted oaths of loyalty from bishops and clergy, and modeled himself on the high priests of Israel, "perhaps dreaming of a sacerdotal kingship," the Emperor Leo VI (886–912) reasserted imperial authority in a series of Novels – new laws – in which he "mounted the pulpit" and "ruled on problems of canon law" in Justinianic style.[112] Both East and West, it seemed, had resumed normal play.

110 The disruption to Photius's tenure of the patriarchate reflects a turbulent career; and he spent his last seven or eight years removed from office.

111 Nicholas I, *Epistolae*, no. 100, 600–609; *Annales Bertiniani* (867), 139 (trans. Nelson, 141–42). Note also especially c. 13, on law, where Nicholas suggested various gentile models for the Bulgars.

112 Dagron, *Emperor and Priest*, 226–35, with citations at 234, 235, and a brisk dismissal of Photius's contributions to Basil I's legal manual the *Eisagoge* (or *Epanagoge*) as a *pièce*

A new world for old law

Penance was the area that attracted Brundage's disparaging comment about early medieval canon law's "inward-looking character."[113] True enough, penance necessarily involves introspection, but recent historiography has reassessed the stereotype of radical contrast between the eighth/ninth centuries and the twelfth in the specific case of penitential practice.[114] Penance, it turns out, was central to canon law's application between the Carolingian period and the Gregorian Reform. Together with liturgy[115] and saints' *Lives*, penitential regulations offer historians an escape from the impasse of prescriptive evidence alone. Regino of Prüm (d. 915) wrote his canon law collection in c. 906 at the behest of the archbishop of Trier, and also sent a copy to the archbishop of Mainz.[116] Part 1 begins with Hincmar's episcopal statutes, and continues with canons detailing how episcopal visitations must be conducted, and how priests must be supervised. Much of the collection of almost a thousand canons, organized in two parts on a broadly thematic basis, is devoted to penitential rules.[117] Relevant extracts from capitularies are cited from Ansegis's collection.[118] Though Regino's world produced no new capitularies, it had uses for old ones.

Burchard of Worms (d. 1025) was not, any more than was Regino, a Gregorian *avant la lettre*, but a legal traditionalist addressing diocesan concerns.[119] His *Decretum*, c. 1015, contains over 1,700 canons, in twenty books which can truly be termed systematic (though they are uneven in length). Like Regino's, Burchard's collection is largely structured around penance: Book 6, for instance, on varieties of manslaughter, with relevant penances; Book 10

d'occasion without lasting significance, save in its replacement of the idea of pentarchy by a straight partition between Constantinople and Rome, "an ecclesiastical Yalta." Cf. Fögen, "Reanimation of Roman Law," 17–22.

113 See footnote 19 above.

114 See Meens in this volume; also Meens, "Penitential Questions."

115 For the importance of the tenth-century *Pontificale Romano-Germanicum*, see Hamilton, *Practice of Penance*, ch. 5.

116 Prefatory letter in Regino of Prüm, *Libri duo de synodalibus causis*, 1–2: "New kinds of wickedness, unprovided for in earlier times, had been condemned by modern episcopal rules," and "just as various peoples differ . . . in type, customs, language and laws, so the holy universal Church spread through the whole world . . . differs from one place to another in ecclesiastical customs." (Cf. trans. Somerville and Brasington, *Prefaces*, 92–94.) For the manuscripts, see Kéry, *Canonical Collections*, 128–31.

117 Regino of Prüm, *Libri duo de synodalibus causis* I, chs. 288–331 (penitential discipline for clergy), and II, passim (for laity).

118 Schmitz, "Ansegis und Regino."

119 Reuter, "Ein Europa der Bischöfe"; Müller, "Die Kirchenrechtssammlung"; Austin, "Jurisprudence."

on varieties of magic, with appropriate penances.[120] But whereas Regino, a scholar and abbot-in-exile, calmly observed, as it were from a great height, the diversity of ecclesiastical customs, Burchard's worm's-eye view was of "confused, diverse and disordered laws and penances"[121] as a problem to be tackled. Burchard was a bishop painfully aware of local disorderliness, as is clear from the Ordinances (*lex*) for his episcopal *familia* (his household and dependents in and around Worms) which he wrote just a few years after he completed the *Decretum*, "so that no advocate or agent or official or any other person among them may impose on them [the *familia*] anything new; rather, let it be known before everyone that there is one and the same law, common to rich and poor alike."[122] The *Decretum* was designed to ease the difficulties of priests. Regino had offered the interrogating priest 40 questions: Burchard offered a nicely differentiated 190, and embedded them in the liturgical context of the rite of penance. His book was at once didactic and practical. Where he found the canons' censure excessive, he offered means-tested commutation, *secundum misericordiam*.[123] Where he found discrepancies or contradictions, he "reconciled" them by improving his texts.[124] This, too, was in line with Carolingian tradition. Burchard drew on Pseudo-Isidore, but sparingly. His concerns were pastoral, hence local to the diocese.

Many others shared similar concerns: thus the presence of the *Decretum* before 1100 in libraries at Trier, Eichstätt, Cologne, Constance, Parma, Milan, Nonantula, Lucca, Besançon, Rheims, Tours, and Angers.[125] Penitential procedures were recorded in a variety of books.[126] Charismatic German bishops are reported as giving judgment through invocations and applications of supernatural power via ordeals.[127] New canon law collections in the second half of the eleventh century borrowed heavily from Pseudo-Isidore's papal decretals, which had by then acquired the legitimacy of age. Pope Gregory VII's (1073–85) famous *Dictatus papae*, more aide-mémoire than manifesto, was similarly

120 Körntgen, "Canon Law and the Practice of Penance."
121 Prefatory letter to Burchard of Worms, *Decretorum libri XX*, 537 (trans. Somerville and Brasington, *Prefaces*, 99–104).
122 See trans. S. Lane online in the Internet Medieval Source Book (http://www.fordham.edu/halsall/sbook.html); and see K. Schulz, "Das Wormser Hofrecht Bischof Burchards," 251–78.
123 Hamilton, *Practice of Penance*, 42–43, and note 90.
124 Hoffmann and Pokorny, *Das Dekret des Bischofs Burchard*, 158–59; for Burchard's use, and "improvement" of Pseudo-Isidore, see *Capitula Angilramni, Enleitung*, Projekt Pseudoisidor website. For Burchard's forgeries as responses to "dissonance" between canons, see Austin, "Jurisprudence," 937–38, 942–43, 953–54.
125 Kéry, *Canonical Collections*, 133–48; Hamilton, *Practice of Penance*, 33, note 40.
126 Meens, "Penitentials and the Practice of Penance."
127 Hartmann, "Probleme des geistlichen Gerichts," especially 649–65.

derivative.[128] But if the law was as old as the ninth century, the contexts in which it was now being applied were new. The schism of 1054, brusquely disturbing a venerable status quo, signaled a new papal assertiveness toward the East.[129] Scholarly heresy and popular heresy, too, had elicited papal jurisdiction on new fronts.[130] With Gregory VII, law's remit extended not just in Pseudo-Isidorean terms to the clerical and monastic orders, but to the laity, high and low. New networks were created, new agents and agencies were summoned into action; law was on the verge of becoming professionalized in both canon and civil guises; and last, but not least, the papacy's law-powered voice sounded forth to new audiences promising new applications of justice.[131] The delivery of spiritual services, increasingly manifested as legal services, came under more central direction, just as "the examination of all government, secular and ecclesiastical, was to become the *ex-officio* province of the papacy."[132] Burchard's "Europe of bishops" would have a long future; but over it watched an increasingly centralized and proactive church government, reconnecting "Rome" with "canon law" in the minds of western Christians.

128 Gilchrist, "Canon Law Aspects," "Gregory VII," and *Collection in Seventy-Four Titles* (trans. of *Diversorum patrum sententiae sive Collectio in LXXIV titulos digesta)*; Fuhrmann, "Papst Gregor VII. und das Kirchenrecht"; Cushing, *Papacy and Law*, 64–102, 127 with note 17, contrasting Burchard with Anselm of Lucca on coercion.

129 See the chapter by Kolbaba in this volume.

130 Fichtenau, *Heretics and Scholars*, 48–49, 287–89.

131 Robinson, "Gregory VII and the Soldiers of Christ."

132 Leyser, "Polemics," 153.

15

The problems of property

ROSEMARY MORRIS

The great bronze doors of the main basilica of the Benedictine monastery of Monte Cassino still bear extraordinary witness to its early medieval landed wealth. Inscribed on thirty-six panels are the names of the estates the monastery held or claimed by the early twelfth century. The first four panels list the forty-one possessions of the *Terra S. Benedicti*, the core properties of the house, claimed around 1105–15; most of the following panels can be associated with the abbacy of Oderisius II (1123–26). These claims were not exaggerated; of the 620 Cassinese charters contained in the *Register of Paul the Deacon* (compiled 1131–33), some 300 deal with estates mentioned on the doors.[1] The monks were concerned to parade their landed wealth because for them, as for all other early medieval landowners, property represented not only an economic, but also a social resource. Nothing that the church wished to achieve – prayer and the performance of the liturgy, preaching and conversion, or charitable work – could be done without property. Ownership of land also defined status for institutions as much as for individuals; it was the means by which power was both created and expressed.[2] The means by which religious institutions acquired, maintained, and protected their property in a dangerous world and the uses to which they put their possessions were issues with profound implications for their survival. So, too, was their degree of success in negotiating the web of human relationships which centered on the ownership of land. Much depended on churches and monasteries balancing their own needs and asserting their own rights against the claims both of the surrounding lay communities, which provided the bedrock of their spiritual and financial support, and of more distant secular powers, which sought to

1 Bloch, *Monte Cassino* 1, 167–465 and vol. 2. Plan of the doors and concordance with written documents: Vol. 1, 168, fig. D. Cowdrey, *Age of Abbot Desiderius*, xi–xx discusses the major written sources.

2 Innes, *State and Society*, 68, 93. For a wide survey of all aspects of ecclesiastical land holding in Francia, see Lesne, *Histoire*.

regulate both the monastic and secular churches for their own ends. Many challenges faced ecclesiastical property owners in this period; it is with these challenges and the strategies evolved to cope with them that this chapter is chiefly concerned.

The problems of the sources

Not many early medieval ecclesiastical institutions gloried in their property in quite such an ostentatious way as did Monte Cassino, but all of them were concerned to record what they considered to be rightfully theirs. One of the difficulties of studying property in this period, however, is that these claims were often unwritten. While the progression "from memory to the written word" took slow hold in the lands farther removed from the written Roman cultures of the Mediterranean, oral procedures were still to be found even in that far more literate world. The power of individual and group memory remained strong.[3] When, in 943, after a series of bitter exchanges, the boundary between the Byzantine monastic community on Mount Athos and its lay neighbors was finally established, an important part of the process was the walking of the boundary and the agreement (drawing on the memories of local men as well as on the claims of the monks and the official boundary markers placed by imperial land surveyors) as to where it should be. In many documents concerning disputes over property, the part played by oral witnesses to the extent of lands and to their present and past ownership was of crucial significance.[4]

Nonetheless, much of what we know of the property holdings of the early medieval church comes from documentary sources, in particular the charters and privileges which recorded their acquisition, disposition, and protection. Through charters we can understand both title deeds and written accounts of gifts, leases, sales, and the records of dispute resolutions. But the charter was never the instrument by which action was taken over land; it was a "stylized record" or memorandum concerning what had already been done. A charter represents, therefore, the culmination of a whole process of oral negotiation between concerned parties, which might well gloss over major difficulties that surrounded the property concerned. It could be drawn up some days or even years after the events described, and the legal support of the signatures or marks of valued witnesses to it was often sought for years to come. The Anglo-Saxon Council of Chelsea (816) emphasized the inviolability of documents

3 Clanchy, *From Memory*.
4 Morris, "Dispute Settlement."

"strengthened by the sign of the Holy Cross."[5] So while charters and other formal documents associated with land remain a prime source for the study of property holding, they must always be seen as the product of artifice. The same is true of collections of charters, especially the aptly named "narrative cartularies," such as the twelfth-century *Chronicon Vulturnense* by the monk John, which contained versions of some two hundred documents concerning the lands of the central Italian monastery of San Vincenzo al Volturno. A similar enterprise for Farfa, the *Chronicon Farfense* by Gregory of Catino (b.1060), included some three thousand documents concerning its landed estates.[6]

The care taken in preserving, copying, and, indeed, falsifying charters testifies to their importance. Many charters, wills, and leases were copied into preciously guarded Gospel Books.[7] In the West, the earliest known cartulary is that of the German Monastery of Lorsch (ninth century), into which hundreds of property transactions dating from the previous century were copied. The monks of St.Gall in Switzerland kept their documents in drawers marked with Roman numerals. The documents in the Athonite archives were often kept in bags which preserved the geographical unity of the properties concerned. Byzantine documents also listed and summarized property and rights in the way that western *pancartes* or "mega-charters" did. The *Typikon* (foundation charter) of the late eleventh-century general Gregory Pacurianus for his foundation at Bačkovo in southern Bulgaria listed all the chrysobulls (imperial privileges) concerning the lands with which he intended to endow his monastery and declared that copies of them should be held for safekeeping not only in the house itself, but also in Hagia Sophia in Constantinople.[8]

The purpose of establishing and preserving written documents about land was very clear. As the Burgundian *Cartulary of Marcigny* (1045–1144) put it, it was done in order "to commit to writing those things we do in the present so that indisciplined posterity will not violate things done by their predecessors."[9] Property came to be seen as being subject to perpetual ownership, to which

5 Cubitt, *Anglo-Saxon Church*, 95.

6 *Chronicon Vulturnense*; *Chronicon Farfense*; and see Stroll, *Medieval Abbey*, 7–12; Bouchard, *Sword*, 37–9; Wickham, "Monastic Lands," 139.

7 Cubitt, *Anglo-Saxon Church*, 82. Constable, "Forgery and Plagiarism," 3 points out that they served "to justify profound social and political needs." In the case of the "Le Mans forgeries" of the ninth century, the "need" was to assert the exclusive ownership of the Bishop of Le Mans in western France over all church lands in Maine, see Goffart, *Le Mans Forgeries*, ch. 5.

8 Bouchard, *Sword*, 40–41 (Lorsch Cartulary); Rosenwein, *To Be the Neighbor*, 62 (on *pancartes*); *Chartae Latinae Antiquiores* 1, viii and vol. 2, xii-xiii (St. Gall documents); Morris, "Mount Athos" (Athos documents); and Gregory Pakourianos, *Typikon* (Gautier, ed.), 35–45, 125–31 or *BMFD* 2, 523–27, 555–57.

9 Cited in Bouchard, *Sword*, 39.

preserved written deeds (or their summaries) could testify. Public oral rituals and ceremonies of witnessing were all very well for possession limited to the span of the longest memory of those involved; what written documents did was to extend this span indefinitely into the future. In addition, as well as – hopefully – guaranteeing secure possession, charters gave their holders the right to alienate land, a matter of extreme concern both to them and to others who might legitimately lay claim to it.[10]

Charter evidence, then, though unsatisfactory in that it often tells us mainly about land, rather than the wealth derived from it, and about boundaries rather than resources, remains the bedrock of any discussion of early medieval ecclesiastical landholding. Where charters are lacking, as in early medieval Ireland, there is extreme difficulty in establishing how Christian institutions were established and supported.[11] However, the earnest concern of early medieval hagiographers to name, and indeed locate, foundations made by their heroes provides a different perspective on those for which no charter evidence remains and which often enjoyed an extremely ephemeral existence. Were it not, for instance, for the long and extremely detailed *Life of St. Lazaros of Mount Galesion*, the series of mid-eleventh-century monastic foundations made by the saint in western Asia Minor, which soon gained imperial patronage and considerable property, would have remained completely unknown. Similarly, it is only from the hagiography of the eleventh-century Italian wandering saint, Dominic of Sora (c. 951–1031), that we learn of a series of small foundations made in the mountains of the Abruzzi – none of which lasted for very long. In some cases nothing is known of what were clearly very powerful houses. The Monastery of San Salvatore Maggiore near Rieti may have rivaled its great neighbors of Subiaco and Farfa, but a lack of documentation means that its history remains obscure.[12]

Stability and sufficiency

The local dramas of land acquisition and exploitation were played out in this period against a background of violence and warfare. Indeed, it is often difficult to see where the violent norms of aristocratic behavior prevalent in many parts of Europe ended and warfare began. The Viking attacks on northwest Europe in the eighth and ninth centuries, the Persian and Muslim conquests in the Near

10 Wormald, *Bede*, 22–23 for the implications of charters.

11 Hughes, *Church* and Charles-Edwards, "Pastoral Role," where evidence on land holding is drawn from hagiography, canonical collections, and secular law.

12 *Vita S. Lazari*; Howe, *Church Reform*; Toubert, *Les structures* 2, 900.

East and Asia Minor and subsequent Muslim raids in the Mediterranean and the Aegean in the seventh to eleventh centuries, and Magyar, Slav, and Bulgar attacks in the Balkans, central Europe, and Italy from the sixth to the tenth centuries provided an almost incessant experience of widespread, extreme, and unfamiliar fear both for lives and for properties. Ecclesiastical chronicles from Britain to Armenia told tales of terror, destruction, and bloodshed. The evidence of actual damage, however, is often contradictory and, in the Viking context, what has been termed the "discourse of disruption" is still a matter of lively debate.[13] Indeed, while Bláthmac, Abbot of Iona, was reportedly killed by Vikings in 825 for refusing to reveal the whereabouts of the rich tomb of St. Columba, there is no *archaeological* evidence of destruction on the island and its Celtic crosses (unlike those at the Pictish site of Tarbat in Easter Ross) were left standing. Alcuin of York (d. 804) could write that the church of St. Cuthbert was "sprinkled with the blood of the priests of God," yet the monks of Lindisfarne preserved their famous Gospel Book and the relics of St. Cuthbert. Indeed, their apparently directionless wanderings through northeastern England before they settled at Durham may, in fact, have been a progress through their own estates. But the excavation of the monastic sites at San Vincenzo al Volturno (sacked by Muslims on October 10, 881) revealed a scene not only of wanton destruction – the abbey church of San Vincenzo Maggiore was so devastated that it lay in ruins until the eleventh century and a veneer of charcoal in the crypt church and fragments of imploded glass in the guest refectory told their own story of widespread fire – but also of energetic pillaging. Fragments of metal, enamel, and smashed glass testified to the looting of its workshops and their produce. In 897, hearing of an imminent Muslim attack, the monks of Farfa hurriedly dispersed their books and liturgical treasures to Rome and elsewhere. At the height of Viking attacks on western and central Francia, many relics and precious books were removed to safety; that they were not returned was, however, often due to the wish of powerful lay and ecclesiastical interests to retain in their new locations the spiritual power that they represented.[14]

The damage to property was twofold. Buildings and their decoration and furnishings were either severely damaged or lost altogether. The northern

13 Hirschfeld, *Judean Desert Monasteries*; Redgate, *Armenians*, 170–72. For the "bloodthirsty Vikings" and their historiography, see Nelson, "England and Continent in Ninth Century, II" and Lifshitz, "Migration."

14 Hodges, *Light*, 146–49, 154; McKitterick, *Frankish Kingdoms*, 230; but see also Lifshitz, "Migration." For debate on the impact of the Vikings on the church in Britain, see Abrams, "Conversion and Assimilation"; Barrow, "Survival and Mutation"; Crawford, "Vikings," 44–45, 52–53; and Hadley, "Conquest," 117.

English monasteries of Wearmouth, Jarrow, and Whitby vanished in the ninth century and were only refounded after the Norman Conquest.[15] Potentially serious in the long term, clerical and monastic communities were dispersed and the ownership and control of their territories put in jeopardy. The monks of San Vincenzo fled to Capua, where they remained in exile for thirty-three years. In Francia, the monks of the monasteries of Saint-Wandrille and Jumièges fled in the mid-eighth century, and there were no bishops in Lisieux, Bayeux, or Evreux in "Normandy" from the second half of the ninth century until the end of the tenth. The monks of St.-Maximin, Trier, fled inside the city to escape Viking attack in 882; their abbey and its archives were destroyed. In the Aegean, Crete was finally recaptured from the Muslims in 961 and Cyprus in 965. Reestablishing the Christian faith, restoring churches, repairing material depredations, and recreating the territorial base to support their institutions was thus a major preoccupation of Christian monks and priests throughout Europe and the Near East from the tenth century onward. Those lucky enough to avoid direct threats to their lives and property were burdened with taxation to pay off the raiders. In 853, an evaluation of church property ordered by the Frankish king, Charles the Bald (840–77), was almost certainly aimed at assessing future contributions toward paying off the Vikings; it has been estimated that, between 845 and 926, 40,000 lbs of silver was paid out to them, much of it raised from the church.[16]

However, most of the difficulties faced by those responsible for lands dedicated to the church, whether they were bishops, priests, canons, monks, nuns, or hermits, came not from the "heathen," but from their fellow Christians. Attacks exacerbated existing situations; they did not create new ones.[17] These difficulties arose from the geographical, social, and political worlds in which churchmen and laymen coexisted and, indeed, from the fact that there was often no clear difference between the activities of either group, though a distinction between their orders was certainly emerging.[18] One of the most fundamental challenges was the assurance of enough property to support the ecclesiastical institution to which it had been dedicated. The distinction between churches and monasteries was often blurred in western Europe. The small baptismal churches of Lombard Italy, manned by communal groups of clergy, were frequently referred to as *monasteria* (monasteries) and *abbatia*

15 Pryce, "Christianization," 158.

16 Hodges, *Light*, 35; McKitterick, *Frankish Kingdoms*, 190, 233, 236–37; and Nightingale, *Monasteries and Patrons*, 169. See *Life of St. Nikon* for the tenth-century reevangelization of Crete.

17 A point graphically illustrated in the Breton context in Davies, *Small Worlds*, see 22–24.

18 Tellenbach, *Church*.

(abbeys). Irish bishops were sometimes described as "abbots" and Martin of Braga (c. 520–80) held his episcopal seat in Spain in a monastery. The key issue in terms of adequate property was the size of the unit concerned. Large monastic communities had to be well supported, but the bishops of the secular church also needed enough land (and the produce and revenues from it) to support the foundation of churches, the preaching, and the parochial administration that lay within their particular remit. Even the humblest rural priest had to be assured of enough property to maintain the fabric of his church and feed himself and – certainly in the Byzantine world and often in the West – his family.[19]

Monasteries differed dramatically in size at their foundation and over time. They could be extremely small: Byzantine legislation of the late tenth century envisaged monasteries of less than ten monks, and the ninth-century history of the monastic communities on Mount Athos is one of tiny hermitages and solitaries eking out a meager existence from the crops that could be coaxed from their rocky surroundings. This kind of marginal monasticism was also found in other demanding geographical contexts, notably the mountains of Italy and the Celtic West.[20] The problems faced by such men and their small groups of followers were those of sheer survival. Elsewhere the problem was the need to cater for increasing numbers entering the communal life. An extreme example is that of the Great Lavra on Mount Athos which was founded on inhospitable territory in the mid-tenth century and for which its founder St. Athanasius (c. 925–c. 1001) surprisingly envisaged a monastic complement of 80 monks (and later allowed for 40 more). By 1030, however, the house apparently contained some 700 monks, and an act of 1102 referred to "a great increase in monks." On his death in 1054, the monastic houses founded by St. Lazarus on Mount Galesion contained some 12 to 40 monks respectively. In a completely different agrarian context, it has been estimated that the Ottonian nunnery of Gerbstedt, founded in 985, had a population of 24 in c. 1075 and 120 by the twelfth century. Some Carolingian houses were even larger: Fulda and its dependencies housed some 600 monks under the abbacy of Hrabanus Maurus (822–29). These figures probably do not include the lay servants of the houses concerned; at Ely in the early twelfth century, to a community of some 50 monks should probably be added an equal number of servants.[21]

19 Pryce, "Pastoral Care," 52, 55; Hughes, *Church*, 69; Nelson, "Making Ends Meet," 25–35; and Kaplan, *Les hommes*, 227–31.

20 Basil II, *Novel* (996); Morris, *Monks and Laymen*, 201–202. Hughes, *Church*, ch. 16, for hermits.

21 Morris, *Monks and Laymen*, 181–82; K. Leyser, *Rule and Conflict*, 71; Berlière, "Le nombre"; Miller, *Abbey*, 36.

Property was thus a necessary prerequisite for the survival of any new monastic foundation or the continuation of the work of any bishopric. In order to contribute to the prosperity of the institution, it needed to be in places which could provide foodstuffs and raw materials for clothing, manufacturing, and building. Liturgical needs also needed to be supplied: supplies of oil and beeswax for lighting and wine for the Mass were essential. But where the quest for solitude had been literally interpreted, the geographical setting of houses was often extremely inconvenient. The expansion of the estates of the Athonite houses beyond the Holy Mountain into the rich agrarian plains of Thrace and Macedonia in the late tenth and eleventh centuries unavoidably compromised the ideals of the early founders, but it was driven by the impossibility of feeding such enormous numbers from the unproductive terrain of the mountain itself.[22] But "inconvenient geography" could also arise from the unimpeachable motives of donors. The original *terra* of San Vincenzo al Volturno comprised a gift of some 300 square kilometers of unproductive mountain land in the upper Volturno valley from Dukes Gisulf I (689–706) and Arichis II (758–60) of Benevento, which soon became inadequate to support the monastery's needs. But by the beginning of the ninth century, it had managed to accumulate estates on the coastlands around Capua, near Benevento, and on the plain of Apulia. Such estates not only produced useful agrarian surpluses, but also provided access to salt and fish and brought the house into contact with the burgeoning trade between Benevento and North Africa.[23]

In England, the unprepossessing marshland surrounding the Isle of Ely, the original focus of Ely Abbey's lands at its foundation in the seventh century, had, after its refoundation by Bishop Æthelwold in 970, been supplemented by the time of *Domesday Book* (1086) by the possession of demesne (directly exploited) lands in 116 villages in six counties and by some 1,200 dependent tenures. They were well organized to fulfill the needs of the house, for Abbot Leofsige, during the reign of King Cnut (1016–35), apparently "assigned *feorms* (food renders) for the provision of the church throughout the year . . . and chose for the purpose . . . villages . . . known by their more abundant fertility and fruitful fields."[24] Each of the manors concerned provided a week's supply of food; the manors of the Isle of Ely itself were kept in reserve in case there should be a shortfall in supply. It was a system well suited to the stable and

22 Morris, *Monks and Laymen*, ch. 8. There may have been more than 3,000 monks on Mt. Athos by the end of the tenth century.

23 Hodges, *Light*, 199–213; Wickham, "Monastic Lands," 138–45 and the map on 141.

24 From *Historia Eliensis*, II.84, trans. in Miller, *Abbey*, 38. See Raftis, *Estates*, for a similar case from the Fens.

regular requirements of a monastic community. Some estates seem to have specialized in stock farming: Doddington in the Isle of Ely had more than 100 cattle and 24 mares in 1086; the monastery also possessed 2,000 pigs and 9,000 sheep on its demesne manors. In addition, the monastery's estates paid rents in kind over and above the *feorms*: in salt, in timber, in honey, and in the 95,000 eels reported by the Domesday commissioners.[25] Much of this was surplus to the monastery's requirements and could be sold for profit on the open market.

The possession of a viable landed base was just as important for bishoprics. While the extraordinary extent of the estates of Bertram, bishop of Le Mans (some 300,000 hectares in the Seine Valley, the Bordelais, the Saintonge, the Auvergne, Lorraine, Burgundy, Provence, and the Pyrenees), revealed in his will of 616, may have had much to do with the reparations attempted by King Clothar II (583–629) for the loss of the bishopric's lands in the north, it nonetheless emphasizes the point that bishops could be landholders of major significance with an eye to the diversification of productive assets.[26] On a far more local scale, the English bishopric of Worcester, founded in 680, held by the time of *Domesday Book* about a quarter of the land of Worcestershire and had substantial holdings in the neighboring shires of Gloucestershire and Warwickshire. Its main acquisitions in the period 680 to 880 were in areas of high-quality soils in the river valleys of the Avon and Severn. But it also owned woodland in the north and west of Worcestershire which provided building material and fuel for its lucrative salt works at Droitwich, as well as game. In the ninth and tenth centuries it gained properties outside the diocese as far away as Oxford and London. Such widely dispersed landholdings could, however, also pose practical problems. They demanded a large-scale infrastructure of suitable exploitation, tenurial arrangements, management, and transportation, requiring considerable financial investment, attention, and expertise from the institution concerned.[27]

How, though, was produce to be best assigned to supply the needs of religious communities? Byzantine *typika* frequently specified food and clothing allowances for clergy and monks and for the poor and pilgrims whom they served. Provision was also made for liturgical expenditure, particularly the provision of holy vessels and lighting.[28] In the West, however, a great deal of

25 Miller, *Abbey*, 38–43.

26 Wood, *Merovingian Kingdoms*, 207.

27 Dyer, *Lords and Peasants*, 7–9, 19–27; Verhulst, *Carolingian Economy*, especially ch. 3; Devroey, *Études*; Renard, "La gestion"; and Lebecq, "Role of Monasteries."

28 For *typika*, Talbot, "Typikon, Monastic"; Morris, *Monks and Laymen*, 208–12 and table 5; and Dembinska, "Diet," 431–62.

strife arose over the mechanisms by which abbots and monks or bishops and cathedral clergy should divide their assets. Episcopal property was sometimes disposed of almost as a personal matter. Toward the end of his life, St. Wilfrid (d. 709) divided the treasury of his cathedral at Ripon (north Yorkshire) into four parts: one for the Church of SS. Mary and Paul in Rome, a second for the poor, a third for those who had accompanied him in exile, and a fourth to the Abbots of Hexham and Ripon "to purchase the friendship of kings and bishops."[29] The canons serving cathedrals and great churches often held individual prebends, shares in the ecclesiastical property which supported them individually and could not be sold, though they could be passed on. Thus Albuin, a canon of the cathedral of Autun (d. 1109), could leave some of "his" property to the other canons, with the consent of his nephew Falco (also a canon) who was to succeed him in his prebend "by hereditary law."[30]

Matters were rather more complex in monasteries where the Rule of St. Benedict demanded individual poverty, but where large communal needs clearly had to be met. The *Supplex libellus* (812–17), a series of anguished complaints submitted to Charlemagne and Louis the Pious by the monks of Fulda about the behavior of their megalomaniac abbot Ratger (abbot 802–17), obsessed with the building of an "immense and unnecessary" new church, included accusations that he had cut their food and clothing allowances and had leased to laymen monastic property meant to supply their wants, in order to gain ready cash for this grandiose enterprise. The monks of Moyenmoutier approached Charlemagne via his *missi* (royal officials) Frotharius, bishop of Toul (813–837), and Smaragdus, abbot of Saint-Mihiel at Mosen (d. c. 840), declaring that they would rather starve and be forced to leave their house than continue to trust the false promises of their abbot, Ismundus, to provide enough property to support them. This problem was sometimes solved by the appearance of clauses in charters making specific provision for the *mensa* (table) of the monks, that is estates designated to support the community rather than the abbot. In 806, Hererich, in a donation to the Monastery of Prüm, specified land for the support solely of the brethren, declaring that they should also get extra rations on his memorial day once a year. Like him, many lay donors specified that if this land was usurped by the abbot, then it would revert to their heirs. In other houses, agreement was reached internally. A late eleventh-century document from Ely reveals what share of the produce entering the monastery was to be enjoyed by the brethren: it included at least

29 Eddius Stephanus, *Life*, ch. 63.
30 Lesne, "Les origins"; Bouchard, *Sword*, 47–52, 79.

200 pigs per year, butter and cheese from designated estates, 700 quarters of wheat, 1,000 quarters of malt and £70 for their clothing.[31]

A more wide-reaching issue was that of tithes. These generalized taxes of a tenth on all produce were originally instituted to support churches whose priests performed the services of baptism and burial but later also provided funds for bishops to promote preaching and charitable work. Their payment does not seem to have been uniform even after they were made compulsory in the Carolingian West by the *Capitulary of Herstal* (779). There were no such dues in Byzantium, although there is some evidence of customary payments in kind to churchmen (*kaniskia*). Whether tithes should be collected and administered by bishops, by monasteries who held titheable lands, by the owners of private churches, or by the leaseholders of church properties was an issue which was never satisfactorily resolved. But it was an important one as it could concern a large proportion of the profits of property. In the mountainous valley of Garfagnana in tenth-century Tuscany, for example, the tithes from some thirty villages granted away by the Bishop of Lucca could exceed annual rents from all but the largest estates.[32]

At the root both of the origin and of the maintenance of ecclesiastical fortunes, therefore, lay land and what it could provide in terms of produce and revenue. But there were always some voices which criticized the apparently insatiable acquisition of land by monastic houses, and others which worried either about the possible incompatibility of the spiritual life with the holding and management of ecclesiastical property or about the way in which such land should best be managed. These concerns all had practical implications. Bede complained in his *Letter to Ecgberht* (734) that wealth which could have been donated to establish bishoprics (and thus forward the preaching of the faith) had been given to monasteries. In tenth-century Byzantium, the Emperor Nicephorus II Phocas (963–69) criticized monastic houses for accumulating land which they could not cultivate efficiently. A recurrent theme of the tenth-century "reformers" in England was their dislike of the "corruption" of individual prebends in monasteries and cathedrals and a wish to see a norm for communal ownership of property imposed. Houses which followed the Benedictine Rule were nervous about allowing the direct participation of the abbot and brethren in the management of estates and so created large numbers

31 Bernhardt, *Itinerant Kingship*, 2 and 93–98; passages from *Supplex libellus* trans. in Nelson, "Medieval Monasticism," 588–91; and Miller, *Abbey*, 39.

32 Boyd, *Tithes and Parishes*; Constable, *Monastic Tithes*; Toubert, *Les structures* 2, 879 warns that ecclesiastical (as opposed to secular) tithes were not general in Latium even in the twelfth century; Wickham, *Mountains and the City*, 95 and 108; and for the *kaniskion*, see Papadakis, "Kaniskion."

of leases. By 1066, for instance, over half of Glastonbury Abbey's lands were leaseholds, the cause of major losses to their holdings when their Anglo-Saxon tenants were displaced after the Norman Conquest.[33]

Ownership and tenure

Land held by churches and monasteries did not, however, exist in some kind of parallel universe. Most of it had, at some time or other, belonged to the laity, and all of it continued to be intertwined in complex ways with other, neighboring properties which were not dedicated to God's service. One of the most intractable issues was that donors of land to the church, though often individuals, did not stand in isolation. They all had families; in the non-Roman world they also had kin, and thus the act of donation had widespread implications. In Byzantium, the rights of individuals to donate or bequeath their personal property and the rules of inheritance specifying what shares should be received by heirs in a predominantly vertical scheme had long been established in Roman Law. The customary law of large parts of the Germanic West gave much more prevalence to the rights of far more extended horizontal groups. Byzantine canon law, fully supported by secular legislation, emphasized the duty of heirs to complete the work of building churches and monasteries begun by defunct founders, even to the extent of renting or selling their own property to do so. There was certainly no provision for them to challenge the donor's intentions, even if he had not left a will.[34] This relative simplicity stands in stark contrast to the situation obtaining in Salian Germany. The complex history of the foundation of the Monastery of Zwiefalten in Swabia may stand as a salutary example. At some point before 1089, Counts Cuno and Liutold, having outlived all their brothers, decided to found a monastery. Cuno had three illegitimate sons, who thus could not inherit; Liutold was childless. They had gained the agreement of their sister Withberger's son by granting him compensation. In 1092, Liutold was still alive, but was beset by claims on the land he had donated from the two sons of another sister, Matilda, from the sons of his five other dead brothers and from two other relatives – brothers – claiming through their grandmother who had been kin to Liutold and Cuno's father, Count Rudolf. Thus the tentacles of

33 Bede, *Epistola ad Ecgbertum*; Nicephorus II Phocas, *Novel* (963/4); Yorke, *Bishop Æthelwold*, 1–12; Thacker, "Æthelwold and Abingdon," 47; and Abrams, *Anglo-Saxon Glastonbury*, 267–69, 281.

34 *Syntagma canonum*, 564; Noailles and Dain, *Les novelles*, Novel XIV, 55; Van der Wal and Lokin, *Historiae*, 87–89.

claims on this particular monastic property stretched backward and forward through both agnates and cognates over a number of generations.[35]

Such claims could prove very damaging. The nuns of Borghorst in the diocese of Münster lost their case at the court of Otto III in 989 when Bertheida, the daughter by her first husband of their foundress Bertha, claimed that she had been deprived of her inheritance. Some time later, c. 1035, Duke Robert I of Burgundy "gave" the property of Veuvey to the Monastery of St.-Bénigne, Dijon. This property had *already* been granted to the house some thirty years previously by Count Otto-William of Burgundy, but Duke Robert maintained that *he* had inherited it from his great-uncle, Henry of Burgundy, Otto-William's stepfather, so only now was the property being rightfully disposed. Documents from the first two hundred years of the monastery of Cluny reveal the same properties apparently being granted to the house more than once; a state of affairs that, along with the large number of quitclaims (the formal abandonment of claims to land) must reflect an often long drawn-out process by which dissatisfied kin attempted either to overturn the gifts of their relations or to find ways of gaining the credit for making the gift themselves or for renouncing claims to the land involved. Indeed, by the eleventh century, it had become common in western France for the *laudatio parentum* (approval of relatives) to be invoked when land was given to the church in order to prevent later challenges (*calumniae*).[36]

Families and kin thus often found it difficult to accept that land granted to the church might be lost to them forever. The high incidence of precarial grants (grants of the usufruct, or simple use) of monastic land for the lifetime of the recipient – and sometimes his children – in return for a nominal rent among the charters of Cluny and Gorze, for example, shows that monks were well aware of this. Many such grants concerned land which had once belonged to the relatives of the recipient and thus not only made possible continuing family control over it, but also, by sugaring the pill of final donation, cemented friendships and alliances between the monastery and its lay neighbors. Although *precaria* were much criticized by some ecclesiastical opinion – Charles Martel (d. 741) was castigated (perhaps wrongly!) for his activity in this regard and Abbot Teutsind of Saint-Wandrille (c. 840) was attacked for alienating a third of the house's land in grants of this kind – this was perhaps more because the grants had been made to people who were not deemed to be "friends" of the monastery than

35 K. Leyser, "German Aristocracy," 173, 185–86.

36 K. Leyser, *Rule and Conflict*, 66; Bouchard, *Sword*, 213–14; Rosenwein, *To Be the Neighbor*, 134 and 52–53 for quitclaims (*werpetitiones*) concerning the estate of Fontana; and White, *Custom* and "Inheritances" for the *laudatio parentum*.

because the nature of the grant was inherently damaging.[37] In Byzantium, the involvement of lay "protectors" (*charistikarioi*) in the management of monastic estates was virulently attacked in the eleventh century by the Patriarch John of Antioch, though there is some evidence to suggest that, for many houses, this was a beneficial arrangement.[38]

But many monasteries and churches, both in Byzantium and the West, remained to all intents and purposes the possessions of their founders who thus made such arrangements for them as they thought fit. A glimpse into the "small world" of Garfagnana can illustrate what the concept of the "proprietary church" involved and what problems it raised. Eight charters concerning the affairs of the Church of S. Maria di Campori cover the period from its foundation in 761 by the cleric (later priest) Gundualdo and his brothers, to c. 850. By 776, Gundualdo was issuing leases to tenants of the church; by 780 he had given it and most of his personal property to the Bishop of Lucca, while keeping, with his two nephews, the usufruct of the land in return for a rent of one *solidus* per year. The foundation then passed into the hands of his nephews. Meanwhile, the family had flourished, and of the twenty-odd houses in Campori, some two-thirds were in the hands of Gundualdo's family or their church by 850. The last appearance of the family in the charters was in 848–49, when Rachiprando and Andrea di Gundi illegally occupied land that another relative, Ratchis, had given to the church, claiming it was part of their inheritance. A few weeks later, Rachiprando, Andrea, and some cousins sold all the property they possessed to the bishop, but this was leased back to them in 849 along with half that which had been donated by Ratchis. Thus, after a series of claims and compromises, it can hardly be said that the Gundi still "owned" S. Maria di Campori in the same way they had when it was founded. But their foundation had given considerable status to the family; they still retained a stake in its fortunes. They never exercised a damaging level of control over it and they seem to have accepted that their foundation should be under the control of the bishop as canon law decreed.[39]

Another sounding, among the grand *Eigenklöster* (proprietary churches) of the Ottonian state, provides a rather different perspective. The problems here were twofold. Firstly, it was difficult to maintain that the status of such churches and monasteries could be reconciled to conciliar teaching that all religious institutions should come under the oversight of diocesan bishops. Secondly,

37 Bouchard, *Sword*, 98; Nightingale, *Monasteries and Patrons*, 7–8; 51–58; Rosenwein, *To Be the Neighbor*, 41, 81, and 114; Fouracre, *Age*, 134–37; Wood, "Teutsind."

38 Gautier, "Réquisitoire"; and Morris, *Monks and Laymen*, 160–61, 263–65.

39 Wickham, *Mountains and the City*, 41–47.

the houses found themselves in a difficult position when it came to responding to the claims made upon them by their powerful owners. The most extreme cases were to be found in the houses founded by monarchs. Although private and royal foundations were, of course, to be found in many parts of the West and, indeed, Byzantium, in Ottonian Germany the proportion was extremely high. There were both advantages and disadvantages attached to this position. Royal monasteries might enjoy the right to elect their own abbots (subject to royal approval); they could not (supposedly) be alienated, and they enjoyed royal protection. They were thus completely free from episcopal oversight and control.[40]

The effects of royal patronage on the landed endowments of these favored monasteries and sees were dramatic. The convent at Quedlinburg, founded in 936 at the burial site of King Henry I (d. 936) in Saxony, was soon granted possession of the settlement and land surrounding it; a ninth of all agrarian produce and revenues from Quedlinburg and thirteen other named places and the total produce from five others; a tenth of the game trapped in two royal reserves; rights to establish a market, mint, and toll station; and the supply of ten wagon loads of wine and forty large bushels of honey each year from the royal manor of Ingelheim in the Rhineland. Before it became an archbishopric in 968, the monastery of St. Maurice at Magdeburg gained over forty charters from Otto I (936–73) by which extensive grants of a tenth on sales and taxes (especially in the newly conquered Slav and Bohemian regions) were granted, as well as pasture and forest rights.[41]

But a high price was paid for royal favor. The *servitium regis* (royal services) consisted not only of prayers for the king, attendance by abbots and bishops at court, and the provision of diplomatic agents for the crown, but also in the supply of huge amounts of food and materials for the itinerant monarch and his court and of soldiers for his army. A land register from the monastery of Werden in Westphalia indicates that the following were required each year for royal hospitality: 8 cows, 43 pigs, 10 piglets, 30 sucking pigs, 195 chickens, 95 cheeses, 870 eggs, bread, oats, 172 *amphorae* of beer, as well as bowls and drinking vessels. The *Indiculus loricatorum*, a mobilization order issued in 981/2 after the defeat of the Emperor Otto II (973–83) at Cotrone in southern Italy, summoned 2,000 armed cavalrymen, of whom bishops and abbots were to provide three-quarters. The Archbishop of Trier was to provide 70 of them; the

40 Thomas, *Private Religious Foundations*; Morris, *Monks and Laymen*, 148–53. Stutz, *Geschichte*; Bernhardt, *Itinerant Kingship*, 71–74.

41 K. Leyser, "Ottonian Government," 83–85, 88–89; Bernhardt, *Itinerant Kingship*, 139–41, 162–68.

Abbot of Reichenau, 60. While monasteries such as Corvey and Magdeburg might enjoy the *Burgbann*, the right to enforce work on fortifications and extract the profits of justice over local dependent peasants, they also had to garrison exposed royal defenses. In 997, Giselher, archbishop of Magdeburg, personally led the garrison in the Arneberg fortress for a month.[42]

It is not, of course, the case that royal food rents and the provision of both soldiers and supplies for armies were unknown elsewhere. Other peripatetic kings, such as those of Anglo-Saxon England, certainly received hospitality from religious houses as a right. A fiscal document dating to the reign of the Byzantine Emperor Romanus I Lecapenus (920–44) dealt with the requisitioning of horses for the army from the monasteries of the Peloponnese, and Byzantine monasteries were extremely eager to obtain exemptions from the duty of providing supplies of fodder and food as well as billets for imperial armies. The monastery at Ely was providing forty knights for the king's service as early as 1072, but the Ottonian example demonstrates what could happen when the demands became extreme. The principle, enunciated by the Council of Estinnes in 744, that churches and monasteries should only hold a "necessary" amount of land could not be sustained. The royal monasteries and bishoprics of the Ottonian Reich needed far more property than subsistence demanded in order also to fulfill their duties to their rulers.[43]

Property and politics

These royal demands ultimately derived from the belief that, since it was the ruler's duty to protect the church and its institutions for the good of his people, then it was the duty of churchmen, in return, to contribute to the well-being of the kingdom. This idea of reciprocity percolated all the way down through society. No gift was made without a counter-gift, and this applied to land as much as anything else. Moreover, if the demands of the secular world required that royal property should be alienated or granted away, then even that held by proprietary churches and monasteries could not be immune from seizure.[44]

42 Fleckenstein, *Early Medieval Germany*, 128; Bernhardt, *Itinerant Kingship*, 30, 57, 75, 118, 181; K. Leyser, "Ottonian Government," 83.

43 Constantinus Porphyrogenitus, *De administrando imperio* 1, ch. 52, 257 and vol. 2, 204; Miller, *Abbey*, 68; Wallace-Hadrill, *Frankish Church*, 138; Bernhardt, *Itinerant Kingship*, 85.

44 See, for example, the Coronation Oath of King Odo of Francia (888–98): "I will provide defense against the predators and oppressors of your churches and of church property . . . I will grant the property of your churches . . . to remain [together] in integrity and immunity without any dishonor," trans. in Rosenwein, *Rhinoceros*, 62; and Geary, *Living*, chap. 4.

Ecclesiastical opinion, however, both in East and West, not only saw all lands donated to the church as sacrosanct, but also as subject to strict controls about who might enter or receive profits from them.

It is this inherent paradox about the nature of church property and the uses to which it could legitimately be put that helps to explain the otherwise apparently contradictory behavior of many monarchs, particularly the kings of the Franks. Charles Martel confiscated the lands of Ainmar, Bishop of Auxerre, even though the bishop had supported him in his campaign in Aquitaine (732), and distributed them to his followers. He granted his nephew, Hugh, immense ecclesiastical properties. His successor Carloman declared at the Council of Estinnes that wholesale restitution of church lands could not be made, "because of war and attacks of other peoples." Louis the Pious and Charles the Bald, keen church reformers both, confiscated church property to reward their followers. Half a world away, in the eleventh century, the Emperor Alexius I Comnenus (1081–1119), the self-styled "Thirteenth Apostle," caused a furor within the church by ordering the melting down of church treasures to finance his defensive wars against the Normans in the Balkans.[45] Property, its produce, and its revenues were needed by kings and lay aristocrats to express and enhance their own power and reputation, to reward faithful followers, and simply to deploy in times of emergency. Ecclesiastical property was never immune to being used in this way. This kind of behavior was emulated by their relatives in the episcopate, who articulated their power not only by controlling the secular priesthood of their dioceses and the lands which supported them, but also by emphasizing their rights of jurisdiction over monasteries.

The vulnerability of church property to attack, encroachment, and confiscation was, however, a matter which greatly exercised the minds of abbots and bishops.[46] The most successful mode of defense against all but the most determined pillagers was to create ties of family and friendship, so that a monastery or church would not stand alone. This could be achieved by replicating family relationships in an ecclesiastical context: many bishops such as the two Carolingian Hincmars, of Rheims and Laon, were closely related to one another. So, too, were the *hegoumenoi* (abbots) of Iviron in the first forty-odd years of its existence, following a pattern of family monasticism well established in their Georgian homeland. Spiritual relationships and those predicated on friendship were important as well, especially in Byzantium. At Cluny, those who gave

45 Wallace-Hadrill, *Frankish Church*, 135, 138–39; Morris, *Monks and Laymen*, 86–87, 270–71.
46 Rosenwein, Head, and Farmer, "Monks."

lands to the monastery or who entered into tenurial relations with it were made to feel that St. Peter himself had become their neighbor.[47]

But another more lasting means of protecting monasteries and churches from the grasping hands of lay and ecclesiastical predators – claimants of jurisdiction, taxes, resources, manpower, and land – was to obtain a charter of exemption or immunity. These, usually granted by monarchs but sometimes by the papacy, aimed to create "clear space" around the institution concerned and both forbade the entry of hostile or, more often, merely royal or episcopal agents onto its property. They often "recycled" the payments and dues concerned back into the hands of the holders. It is perfectly true that immunities and exemptions were sometimes ignored, especially when, in the case of papal immunities, their holders dwelt far away from Rome, but their prevalence in this period must suggest that they served some practical use.[48] Here the important role of the written word in the establishment of ecclesiastical rights can be seen again. By such documents, general principles about the status of church property were made geographically specific, as individual churches and monasteries strove to establish their inviolable and perpetual territorial rights. In the process, the principle was slowly established that the laity, though always tied to the church by bonds of spirituality, worship, family, friendship, and tenure, could no longer be proprietors but must now see themselves as patrons.

The strategies used by churches and monasteries to acquire and protect the property essential to their survival thus frequently led to compromise and accommodation both with neighboring lay communities and with more distant secular powers. But by 1100, another long-standing moral problem was again coming to the fore. The solitary, eremitic life had always formed part of the monastic heritage in both East and West. In Byzantium, hermits were slowly being incorporated into monastic structures; in the eleventh-century West, however, a new eremitic movement, centered in Italy and southern France, began to pose with new urgency the question of whether true spirituality was compatible with property holding. Poverty, rather than property became a new rallying cry for the church.[49]

47 McKitterick, *Frankish Kingdoms*, 189; Morris, *Monks and Laymen*, 81–82; Talbot "Byzantine Family"; Mullett, "Byzantium"; and Rosenwein, *To Be the Neighbor*.

48 See Nelson, "England and Continent in Ninth Century, I," 20; Rosenwein, *Negotiating Space*; Morris, "Monastic Exemptions"; Oikonomidès, *Fiscalité*, 153–260.

49 Morris, *Monks and Laymen*, 293–94; Magdalino, "Byzantine Holy Man"; Little, *Religious Poverty*; H. Leyser, *Hermits*.

16

Ideas and applications of reform

JULIA BARROW

> The Gregorian reform is perhaps the greatest achievement in the religious history of the Middle Ages.[1]

Students of ecclesiastical history of this period or, more particularly, of the Carolingian period and of the tenth and eleventh centuries, cannot avoid encountering references to "reform" in modern works on the subject: indeed, the pontificate of Gregory VII (1073–85) has been inextricably linked with the term since the nineteenth century. At the same time, however, it is hard to find any analysis of the term or discussion as to the appropriateness of its use. There is a noticeable contrast between the quantity of debate aroused by the word "renaissance" and the word "reform" for the earlier and high Middle Ages.[2] The history of the western church is narrated with "reform" as the storyteller's framework, but within our period the term itself rarely becomes a theme for discussion. The word "reform" has been used by historians of the Byzantine church for well over a century,[3] but has become a prominent theme in Byzantine church history only fairly recently, and its applicability has only occasionally been discussed.[4] Gerd Tellenbach in his *Die westliche Kirche vom 10. bis zum frühen 12. Jahrhundert* is almost the only historian of modern times to have complained about the lack of discussion of "reform" in writings on the Gregorian period; listing the many types of composite constructions in which "reform" occurs (reform aims, reform papacy, and many more), he complained, with justification, of a lack of substance: "What church reform in the eleventh century really was is usually defined so inadequately that one can only describe it as an empty formula."[5] As Tellenbach remarked, historians

1 Fliche, *La réforme grégorienne*, v.
2 Burdach, "Sinn und Ursprung"; Patzelt, *Die karolingische Renaissance*; Benson and Constable, *Renaissance and Renewal*.
3 Le Barbier, *Saint-Christodule*, 20, 57; Leroy, "La réforme studite."
4 Magdalino, *Empire of Manuel I*, 271.
5 Tellenbach, *Church*, 158.

of this period, with few exceptions, notably Gerhart Ladner (1905–93),[6] use the term completely unreflectively, unaware that they are influenced by ideas about the Protestant reformation or the Counter Reformation, and they also tend to see "reform" as a Good Thing (or, as Tellenbach put it, "Reform is generally taken to be self-evidently progressive and positive"), without pausing to think about alternative views.[7] A brief account of the history of the term is essential, and, before turning to the language and the programs of the people trying to effect change in the church between 600 and 1100, I shall consider how the Latin terms *reformare* and *reformatio* and their derivatives in European languages have become anchored in our thinking processes.[8]

Reformare emerges in Latin in Ovid's *Metamorphoses* as a translation of Greek *metamorphoun* between 2 and 8 CE, and *reformatio* first occurs in the writings of Seneca a few decades later.[9] More influential for medieval Latin Christian writers were the Vetus Latina and Vulgate translations of the Epistles of St. Paul, in which *metamorphoun* was rendered as *reformare*. (In the Vetus Latina, see 2 Cor. 3.18, "Nos itaque omnes revelata facie gloriam domini speculantes ad eandem imaginem reformamur a gloria in gloriam, sicut a domini spiritu." "Therefore we all, observing the glory of the Lord with face revealed, are **reformed** into the same image from glory to glory, as by the Spirit of the Lord." And see Rom. 12.2, "Et nolite conformari huic saeculo, sed reformamini in novitate sensus vestri." "And do not be conformed to this world, but be **reformed** in the newness of your mind," and Phil. 3.21, "Qui reformabit corpus humilitatis nostrae." "Who [Christ] **will reform** the body of our humility," in the Vulgate.[10]) All these references deal with the same concept, the transformation of the individual into the likeness of God. Reform here is, as later medieval authors would say, *reformatio in melius*, reform for the better or reform as improvement. *Reformatio ad pristinum statum*, reform as a return to the former state, with the connotation of a return to the Good Old Days, emerged in the patristic period.[11] Fuller development of the idea of "reform" as the transformation of the human individual into the likeness of God came particularly in the writings of Ambrose and Augustine.[12] Even so, the verb *reformare* does not occur with great frequency in patristic writings, and does not occur in church councils

6 Van Engen, "Images and Ideas"; Benson, Constable, and Van Engen, "Gerhart Burian Ladner."

7 Tellenbach, *Church*, 157, 158, note 78.

8 For helpful, though all too brief, surveys of the evolution of the term, see Ladner, *Idea of Reform*, 1–5; Wolgast, "Reform"; Innes, "'Reform'"; Miethke, "Reform."

9 Ladner, *Idea of Reform*, 39–42.

10 Ibid., 41.

11 ibid., 142–43.

12 For surveys of their views and those of other patristic authors, see ibid., 142–43, 194.

until late.[13] A recent study of how church councils of the period before c. 500 coped with change has noted the reluctance of bishops to appear to be changing anything: "The words for requiring change – *corrigere, emendare, meliorare, recreare, regenerare, renovare, reparare, restaurare* – are astonishingly rare in episcopal writings and conciliar texts."[14] Churchmen were mindful of the ruling of Pope Stephen I (254–57): "Nihil innovetur nisi quod traditum est" ("let nothing be renewed save what has been handed down"). Change could only be justified if it could be presented as the removal of a perceived abuse; by contrast, the upholding of tradition was all-important.[15] Appeals to tradition, coupled with official reluctance to effect changes, remained more deeply entrenched in the Greek East than in the Latin West.[16]

The verb *reformare* did not become really widespread until the fourteenth century, though significant growth in its use can be observed from the twelfth century onward. Where it does occur, it is often in a monastic context. Monasticism allowed a significant development in the use of the word to occur, a shift noticed by Ladner when he compared Gregory the Great's use of *reformare* with Gregory VII's. Whereas the former had used the verb for personal and internalized contexts, the latter used it on four occasions in his letters to demand the transformation of entire churches.[17] The claim that Gregory VII was the originator of the concept of "reform" for the universal church has been voiced enthusiastically in recent works.[18] But, as Tellenbach commented in 1988, four occasions over the corpus of Gregory VII's letters are relatively few, and each one deals with the internal reform of an individual church, the archbishoprics of Dol and Ravenna and the monasteries of Montmajour and Sainte-Marie-de-Grasse, and not with the universal Church, the Church with a capital C.[19] This small move to a more comprehensive use of *reformare* was not begun by Gregory VII, and had probably evolved in a monastic context in which one might easily jump from the idea of transforming or improving an individual monk to improving an entire monastic community. In his early career Gregory VII is likely to have been either a monk[20] or a regular canon,[21] and in either case this language would have been familiar to him. From slow origins in the tenth and eleventh centuries the monastic uses of *reformare* and

13 The earliest occurrence I have found is in IV Toledo (633), ch. 3; see Mansi 10, 617.
14 Sotinel, "Church."
15 E.g., Morrison, *Tradition and Authority*, 77.
16 See footnote 49 below.
17 Ladner, "Gregory," 1–26.
18 Robinson, "Reform and the Church"; Robinson, *Papal Reform*.
19 Tellenbach, *Church*, 160 cites Gregory VII, *Das Register*, 303 (IV.5), 532 (VIII.12), 582 (IX.6).
20 Cowdrey, *Pope Gregory VII*, 28–29.
21 Blumenthal, *Gregor VII.*, 38–40.

related words burgeoned, especially in the twelfth century with the arrival of the new monastic orders: "The new orders of monks and canons used the imagery of renewal not only to legitimize their reforms but also, beginning in the 1130s, to celebrate the creation of new forms of religious life."[22] The concept of reform was used by twelfth-century Benedictines also, notably Wibald of Stavelot (d. 1158), who used the terms *reformare* and *reformatio* in diplomas which he drafted for Conrad III (1138–52) and for Frederick Barbarossa (1152–90).[23] Wibald's example was followed by other clerks drafting Frederick's diplomas.[24]

Monastic use of reform terminology perhaps also influenced Innocent III (1198–1216), who in canon 12 of the Fourth Lateran Council (November 1215) demanded that Benedictine abbots hold regular chapters-general for the *reformatio* of their order. A letter he wrote a couple of months earlier to the abbey of Monte Cassino contains the same term.[25] More significantly, in the letters to archbishops and their provinces inviting attendance at Lateran IV, he said it was for the reform of the universal church as a whole (*ad . . . reformationem universalis ecclesiae*),[26] thus giving "reform" a broad connotation for the first time. The idea of reforming the church as a whole thus entered the mainstream of Catholic thought and was picked up in the thirteenth century by Jacques de Vitry (d. 1240) and Alexander of Roes (d. after 1288). It was further developed by William Durandus the Younger (d. 1330), who initiated the concept of "reform in head and members."[27] By the early fifteenth century with the Council of Constance (1414–18) it had become a popular catchword. From the sixteenth century *reformatio* and its vernacular derivatives were hard to separate from the Protestant Reformation; indeed, as late as the middle of the twentieth century, the *Dictionnaire de théologie catholique* showed some distaste for the term *réforme*,[28] even though the word had a Catholic pedigree and had throughout the post-Reformation period continued to be used in monastic contexts.[29]

In the post-Reformation period it must have been possible for historians of monasticism, especially Catholic ones, to continue to conceptualize "reform" in an unbroken monastic tradition spanning the period from the fathers to the

22 Constable, "Renewal and Reform," 42.

23 *Die Urkunden Konrads III.*, 395, 455 (nos. 222, 262); *Die Urkunden Friedrichs I.*, i, 5, 11 (nos. 2, 5).

24 Listed in indices, *Die Urkunden Friedrichs I.*, I, 541; ii, 738; iii, 557; iv, 751.

25 Mansi 22, 1002; letter to Monte Cassino, *PL* 217, 249.

26 Mansi 22, 960.

27 Jacques de Vitry, *Historia Occidentalis*, 107, ch. 11; Wolgast, "Reform," 320.

28 Cristiani, "Réforme," 2020–21.

29 E.g., Jean Mabillon, *Elogium S. Odonis*, *PL* 133, 20.

Enlightenment, without, perhaps, necessarily being influenced too much by the idea of the Reformation. But it was not the only available term: Baronius (Cesare Baronio, 1538–1607), the great Counter Reformation historian of the sixteenth century, preferred the concept of restoration in a monastic context where a more modern author might think of reform.[30] He uses the phrase *restitutor monasticae disciplinae* of both Abbot Odo of Cluny (927–42) and Bishop Adalbero of Metz (929–62).[31] When it came to the papacy, historians writing in the period before the end of the eighteenth century were reluctant to use "reform" terminology, probably in part because medieval sources – at least for the period before Innocent III – had not tried to define what popes did as "reform." The Lutheran Centuriators of Magdeburg, who between 1561 and 1574 compiled a thirteen-volume history of the church in its first thirteen centuries, used the term *reformatio* rarely, and only to describe actions of secular rulers.[32] They did, however, use the verb *deformare* to describe Gregory VII's behavior toward Henry IV, in what must have been a deliberate piece of irony.[33] Baronius, writing the Catholic counterattack to the *Centuries of Magdeburg*, uses the term *reformatio* equally sparingly, sometimes in index entries,[34] sometimes in headings,[35] and apparently not for the activities of eleventh-century popes. It is difficult to define the point at which historians living in the post-Reformation era began to talk of the "Gregorian Reform," but surely a crucial figure in the process must have been Johannes Voigt (1786–1863),[36] who in 1812 wrote a thesis on Gregory VII in which he compared him to Martin Luther. The comparison with Luther is fully worked out in the conclusion, in a passage full of *Sturm und Drang*.[37] Voigt's work, published in 1815, paved the way for a stream of German Protestant scholars, often Prussian, who were keen to work on the papacy in general and on Gregory VII and the Investiture Contest in particular.[38]

The Protestant conversion, so to speak, of Gregory VII was not only a feature of nineteenth- and twentieth-century German historical scholarship. It also filtered into French historical thinking. The French statesman François

30 E.g., Baronius, *Annales*, X, 831.

31 Baronius, *Annales*, X, 822, 830.

32 Vlachich et al., *Ecclesiastica Historia*, saec. x, entry "reformationis ecclesiarum aulicae exemplum" in unpaginated index referring to col. 427, line 54; saec. xi, col. 394, line 12; saec. xii, col. 1101, line 33.

33 Vlachich et al., *Ecclesiastica Historia*, saec. xi, col. 419.

34 E.g., Baronius, *Annales*, VII, 316 (see also 535, item 8); XI, entry "reformatio ecclesiae Hispanicae" in unpaginated index referring to the year 1050, item 6.

35 E.g., Baronius, *Annales*, IX, 811 (see also 817, item 8); XII, 390 (see also 1145, item 7).

36 Lohmeyer, "Voigt."

37 Voigt, *Hildebrand*, 641–43; the passage is tacitly omitted from Jager's French translation, *Histoire*.

38 Fuhrmann, "Papstgeschichtsschreibung," 141–91; cf. Hiestand, "100 Jahre," 11–44.

Guizot (1787–1874), a Protestant who had been educated in Geneva, associated "reform" and Gregory VII in his widely read work *Histoire générale de la civilisation en Europe* (1828): "Gregory VII was a reformer upon the plan of despotism, as were Charlemagne and Peter the Great . . . He wished to reform the church, and through the church to reform society, to introduce therein more morality, more justice, and more law."[39] By the early twentieth century it was possible for the devout Catholic Augustin Fliche (1884–1951) to view the eleventh century chiefly as an age of ecclesiastical reform, succeeding nearly two centuries of decadence.[40]

The earliest author to apply reform terminology to Carolingian ecclesiastical policy may well have been Baronius, who termed Louis the Pious's legislation at Aachen in 816–17 *reformatio*.[41] By the 1920s it had became normal to define the activities of Boniface as "reform";[42] at the same time the term "reform" began to be applied to the scribal and educational changes under Charlemagne.[43] Otherwise Carolingian ecclesiastical legislation is viewed as "reform" by Louis Halphen, who in 1947 referred to Charlemagne in 813 "returning one last time to the question of the reform of the church."[44] By the 1970s and 1980s the word could be used quite automatically in writing about the Frankish church.[45] Critique of the applicability of the term to Boniface's activities was voiced by Timothy Reuter in 1994, who noted that the terms *reformare* and *reformatio* occur only once each in Boniface's extensive correspondence.[46] Most recently, a case has been made for using the term preferred by the Carolingians themselves, *correctio*, in place of "reform" to describe innovations in the Frankish church.[47] A similar argument had been put forward by P. E. Schramm in 1964 for the term *correctio* in preference to "renaissance" to define the cultural changes presided over by Charlemagne.[48]

39 Guizot, in Eng. trans. *History*, 116.
40 Fliche, *La réforme grégorienne*, passim.
41 Baronius, *Annales*, IX, 811 (see also 817).
42 Patzelt, *Die karolingische Renaissance*, 116 (in 1924); cf., later, Dawson, *Making of Europe*, 167–68 and Levison, *England and the Continent*, ch. 4.
43 Patzelt, *Die karolingische Renaissance*, 88–9; Calmette, *Charlemagne*, 252, 279; Halphen, *Charlemagne*, 231; Fleckenstein, *Die Bildungsreform*.
44 Halphen, *Charlemagne*, 217.
45 McKitterick, *Frankish Church*, ch. 1: "Legislation for Reform," 1–44; Wallace-Hadrill, *Frankish Church*, ch. 14: "Reform and its Application," 258–303; cf. Staubach, "Cultus divinus," 546–81.
46 Reuter, "Kirchenreform," 39–42.
47 Smith, "Emending Evil Ways," 189–92, 214–15.
48 Schramm, "Karl der Grosse," (reprint) 336–39.

In what follows I shall give an overview of some of the principal figures proposing change in the church between 600 and 1100, with some analysis of the language which they used. Unsurprisingly, "reform" figures relatively little in the terminology, and therefore it is particularly desirable to look at the words actually used, their biblical resonances, and the visual imagery they convey. The material is divided into four sections: first, one on the Byzantine church, and then three roughly chronological sections on the western church dealing in turn with the period from Pope Gregory I, "the Great" (590–604), to Atto of Vercelli (bishop of Vercelli 924–61), the monastic reform movements of the tenth and early eleventh centuries, and the Gregorian "Reform."

The Byzantine church

Use of the term "reform" to describe changes in the Byzantine church in this period is problematic, since no term equivalent to "reform" was used by the Byzantines; there was no attempt in the Greek-speaking world to develop St. Paul's concept of *metamorphosis* into a system of institutional transformation. Very profound transformations did indeed occur in the East, but were justified in church councils by the need to uphold or return to apostolic and conciliar traditions. Faced with the task of restructuring the shrunken eastern church after the Arab conquests, the Council in Trullo of 691 or 692 constantly appealed to traditions. It makes fairly frequent use of the term "to renew" (*'ananeoomai*), mostly with approval in the context of renewing canons of earlier councils,[49] but with disapproval where it attacked the renewal of "Jewish" practices by Nestorius (d. after 451).[50] Little of the language used in the canons of the council reflects change: even the canon which banned the portrayal of Christ as a lamb and thus foreshadowed the emergence of iconoclasm simply says that this is an order (*anastēlousthai orizomen*, "we order . . . to be set up").[51] The opening address, however, mentions the casting out of the first serpent, bringing people "to a better and holier life," restoring the stray sheep to the fold, and pulling out tares, all of these concepts conveying a sense of change.[52]

Iconoclasm doubtless had an extensive justificatory vocabulary of its own, but apart from the use of biblical texts forbidding idol worship, it is difficult to form a clear impression of the views of the iconoclasts since these survive

49 Nedungatt and Featherstone, *Council in Trullo*, cc. 3 and 49, 73 and 131; see also Herrin, *Formation*, 286.

50 Nedungatt and Featherstone, *Council in Trullo*, c. 1, 59.

51 Ibid., c. 82, 163.

52 Ibid., 46, 52, 53.

only in excerpted form in polemic literature produced by iconodules such as Germanus, patriarch of Constantinople (715–30), and Theodore the Studite (d. 826) in support of their own side.[53] The iconodules based their stance staunchly on the maintenance of traditions. According to Theophanes (d. 817), Germanus in 730 refused to subscribe to Leo's pronouncement against icons because he would not innovate in matters of faith without an ecumenical council, while the iconophile Council of Nicaea in 787 "introduced no new doctrine, but maintained unshaken the doctrines of the holy and blessed Fathers."[54] According to Michael's *Life of Theodore the Studite*, Theodore begged Leo V the Armenian (813–20) to be moved by the daily veneration of images, which had been confirmed over long periods of time and supported by the fathers.[55]

Theodore the Studite, who was the first leader of a revival of cenobitic monasticism in the Byzantine Empire in the ninth century, stressed the need to conform to traditions within the monastic life, insisting on following the ascetic practices of Basil (d. 379).[56] This monastic movement has often been viewed as a reform.[57] But since little is known about Byzantine monasticism before Theodore the term is not necessarily applicable, and it might be better to use Theodore's own terminology of "restoration" and "return."[58] The theme of adherence to the laws of the fathers is also prominent in the *typika* or monastic foundation documents of several eleventh-century monasteries (at the start of a new era of monastic foundations seeking greater independence from lay patrons).[59]

Just after the very end of our period, as the Byzantine church was beginning to feel the influence of the Gregorian movement in the West, the Emperor Alexius I Comnenus (1091–1118) issued an edict in 1107 (usually referred to as the Reform Edict) to improve both the educational standards for clergy of the Great Church in Constantinople and the supply of teachers. Alexius stated that his aim was to correct uncanonical practice and to bring about renewal (*anakainisis*).[60] Overall, renewal emerges as the closest Byzantine equivalent to "reform" in the Latin Church; oddly enough, the Greeks made no attempt

53 Cf. Germanus, *Epistolae dogmaticae*, 155–62, 163–90; Theodore the Studite, *Adversus iconomachos*, 485–98; see also Herrin, *Formation*, 326; Anastos, "Argument," 178–87. See also Louth in this volume.

54 Theophanes Confessor, *Chronicle*, 565, 637, see also Annus Mundi 6221, 6280.

55 Michael the Monk, *Vita et conversatio Theodori*, 176.

56 Ibid., 246; Cholij, *Theodore the Stoudite*, 29–30.

57 Leroy, "La réforme studite"; Cholij, *Theodore the Stoudite*, 28–37.

58 Morris, *Monks and Laymen*, 15.

59 Morris, *Monks and Laymen*, 53; *BMFD* 2, 441–53.

60 Magdalino, "Reform Edict," 199–218, esp. 202, 205; Magdalino, *Empire of Manuel I*, 274–75.

to use St. Paul's vocabulary for transformation to help them justify theological or legal change.

The western church: Gregory the Great to Atto of Vercelli

Although Gregory I died only three and a quarter years into the seventh century (March 604), these few final years of his life were actively occupied with anxieties about perceived faults in Christendom and how these could be emended. As Ladner has shown, the words principally used by Gregory for the correction of ecclesiastical failings were the verbs *emendare* (to emend) and *corrigere* (to correct).[61] *Reformare* occurs in Gregory's letters, but entirely in personal, pastoral contexts, and not in wider, structural ones. That said, however, it should be noted that Gregory's whole approach, whether to individuals or institutions, was overwhelmingly an ethical and pastoral one. Faulty structures are approached as groups of erring individuals: for example (here from the late sixth century), certain laymen in Francia obtaining tonsure on the deaths of bishops so that they could be appointed in their places without having to spend any time in any of the grades of ordination.[62] Here the verb used is *emendentur*. Gregory uses *emendare* also in two letters to the Austrasian queen Brunhild (d. 613), both of 22 June 601: the first demanding the correction of the shameless (but otherwise undefined) behavior of certain priests and the second ordering the removal of the heresy of simony.[63] In a letter of about the same date (June 601) to Theudebert II of Austrasia (d. 612) demanding the amputation of simony from its roots, Gregory uses both *emendatio* and *corrigere*.[64] Yet it is clear that the process of "emendation" and "correction" envisaged in all three of these letters was not limited to moral persuasion. Brunhild and Theudebert were being expected to hold synods to extirpate simony,[65] and Brunhild was being told to expect an envoy from Gregory who would act together with "other" priests (presumably not those behaving "shamelessly") to hold an inquiry into the misbehavior.[66] Progression from moral persuasion to more institutionalized systems of correction is observable in the part of the *Libellus Responsionum* where Gregory committed the British bishops to

61 Ladner, "Gregory," 23.
62 Gregory I, *Registrum Epistolarum* (v.60 to Childebert, 15 August 595), 373–75.
63 Ibid., xi.46 and xi.49, 318–19 and 321–22.
64 Ibid., xi.50, 322–23.
65 Ibid., xi.49–50, 321–23.
66 Ibid., xi.46, 318–19.

the authority of Augustine, archbishop of Canterbury (597–604/9): "we commit to you, my brother, all the bishops of Britain that the unlearned may be instructed, the weak strengthened by your counsel, and the perverse corrected by your authority."[67] Evidently Augustine was expected to use moral persuasion before launching into a more formal stage, correction; an earlier passage in the letter, outlining how Augustine was to meet and act together with the bishop of Arles to correct the vices of bishops, shows that correction was to be done by bishops together.[68] For Gregory, institutional lapses were the failings of individuals – individuals in the plural, but individuals none the less. His choice of verbs for correcting abuses, *corrigere* and *emendare*, is fairly bland, though both convey the idea of corporal punishment, and *corrigere* also has the connotation of "making straight." But the verbs lack the transformative resonance of "reform."

Influential though the letters of Gregory I (and those of several of his successors) were, it was chiefly in the forum of regional church councils that ecclesiastical issues were raised and dealt with in the seventh century. Large numbers of these were held in Visigothic Spain and in Francia in this period,[69] and from 673 councils were also held in Anglo-Saxon England.[70] In the councils in the western church before 600, groups of bishops, doubtless mindful of Pope Stephen I's adjuration, were reluctant to appear to be doing anything new. Quite often, items would be introduced simply with the verb *"Placuit"* (literally "It has pleased," and by extension "It is agreed") rather than a word suggestive of change, renewal, or improvement.[71] Reluctance to change is also characteristic of church councils after 600, though with slightly more leeway. As an example of continuity, we may note that Theodore (archbishop of Canterbury 669–90) conservatively worded the opening of the synodal decrees of Hertford in 673 with the words "Beloved brethren, I beseech you, for the fear and love of your Redeemer, that we should all deliberate in common for the benefit of the faith; so that whatever has been decreed and defined by holy fathers of proved worth may be preserved incorrupt by us all."[72] Theodore then selected items from an existing canon collection which he thought especially needful to know, and these were accordingly promulgated. But terms suggestive of "renewal" and "reform" also creep in, though carefully:

67 Bede, *HE*, i.27, 88–89.

68 Ibid., 79–81; cf. also Gregory I, *Registrum Epistolarum*, xi.50, 322–23.

69 Orlandis and Ramos-Lisson, *Historia*, 509; Pontal, *Histoire*, 374.

70 Bede, *HE*, iv.5, 348–53; the synod of Whitby 664 was not really a synod in the strict sense of the term; Cubitt, *Anglo-Saxon Church Councils*, 6.

71 Sotinel, "Church."

72 Bede, *HE*, iv.5, 350–51.

the 615 Council of Paris met "for the renewing of the precepts of ancient canons (*pro renovandis antiquorum canonum statutis*),"[73] and the Fourth Council of Toledo of 633 ordered the holding of synods on a more frequent basis than hitherto in order to "reform" what was wrong and correct the customs (*mores*) of the church.[74] True to their claims, the bishops at these councils made few, and only minor, innovations.

The eighth century marked a shift in attitudes to ecclesiastical change. Change was, still, presented as a return to ancient norms, but writers were readier to create their own agendas. A good example is the letter by Bede (d. 735) to Ecgberht, bishop of York (c. 732–66), written between 732 and 735, almost certainly, to judge by its transmission, at the explicit behest of the dedicatee, for whom Bede proposed a wide-ranging program. A significant item in the list was the teaching of the Apostles Creed and the Lord's Prayer in the vernacular to the laity. Bede claimed a partial, ancient support for this in Ambrose's statement that people should say the Creed every morning to drive away the demons which had attacked them at night, but clearly he was innovating.[75] It is worth noting that a similar scheme for teaching the laity the basic elements of the Christian faith was also to be propagated by Charlemagne (ruled 768–814). Although Bede's letter did not circulate widely, it would have been well known to Alcuin (d. 804) long before his departure for Charlemagne's court perhaps in, or just after, 786.[76] Equally, Bede backed up a demand for the creation of new dioceses (so that each bishop would find it easier to ensure that his flock was taught) with a comment about how Gregory I had wished the archbishop of York to be a metropolitan over twelve sees.[77] Bede also made a rather abstract appeal to the past: "I am praying that you may strive zealously to recall to the right way of life (*ad rectam vitae normam revocare*) any whom you see acting so wickedly" coupled with a request for the future "that . . . you may together put the Church of our people into a better condition than it has been up to now (*Quapropter velim sollerter illum admoneas, ut in diebus vestris statum nostrae gentis ecclesiasticum in melius, quam hactenus fuerat, instaurare curetis*)."[78] *Ad rectam vitae normam revocare* and *statum ecclesiasticum in melius instaurare* are stock phrases in ecclesiastical exhortations to improvement. Bede then moved on to attack family monasteries for greed, sexual license, and lack of

73 Mansi 10, 539 (*praefatio*).
74 Mansi 10, 616–17 (ch. 3).
75 Bede, *Ad Ecgbertum episcopum*, 409 (transl. *HE*, 345–46).
76 Thacker, "Bede's Ideal," 153; for dating of Alcuin's arrival at Charlemagne's court, see Bullough, *Alcuin*, 337–41.
77 Bede, *Ad Ecgbertum episcopum*, 412–13 (transl. *HE*, 349).
78 Ibid., 412 (transl. *HE*, 348).

religion and says that Ecgberht should correct (*corrigantur*; *corrigere*) not only them, but also the kings who over the last thirty years had encouraged their foundation by issuing charters for them. He should drag the Northumbrians away from their old errors and should lead them to a surer and straighter way (*ad certiorem et directiorem vitae callem reducere*).[79] Finally, Ecgberht should take note of Matt. 15.13: "Every plant that my heavenly Father did not plant will be eradicated."[80] Writers urging ecclesiastical change frequently make use of biblical language about planting and uprooting.

Frankish churchmen of the Carolingian period, too, were self-confident and robust about change, while always expressing loyalty to the past. Chrodegang, bishop of Metz (d. 766), innovated by compiling a rule for his cathedral canons that gave clerics a near-monastic way of life and by introducing Roman chant at Metz, though both were also a means of establishing continuity with what Chrodegang would have seen as a deeper past, the Roman one.[81] Charlemagne, followed by Louis the Pious (814–40), went much further, launching into a program of improvements which included liturgical observances, the correction of texts, education, lay knowledge of the elements of Christian faith, uniformity of monastic life under the Benedictine Rule,[82] and a rule for cathedral clergy. These improvements were not presented as innovations, but rested on a firm basis of earlier traditions, above all the Dionysio-Hadriana canon compilation. The words most favored for change were, unsurprisingly, the general purpose *corrigere* and *emendare*, both used even more often in secular contexts.[83] Charlemagne's first major statement of ecclesiastical policy, the *Admonitio Generalis* (789), however, had a more fully developed statement in which he compared himself to Josiah, the Jewish king who energetically uprooted idolatry: "For we have read in the Books of Kings (2 Sam. [2 Kgdms.], 22–3) how the holy Josiah sought to recall the kingdom which God had given to him to the worship of the true God by going around it, correcting and admonishing" (*Nam legimus in regnorum libris, quomodo sanctus Iosias regnum sibi a Deo datum circumeundo, corrigendo, ammonendo ad cultum veri Dei studuit revocare*).[84] *Circumire* (to visit), *corrigere* (to correct), and *ammonere* (to admonish) – none of them words occurring in the part of the Vulgate where Josiah appears – were significant terms in Carolingian legislation; visiting churches,

79 Ibid., 413–17, 419 (transl. *HE*, 350–53, 354).
80 Ibid., 421 (transl. *HE*, 356); cf. *Property and Piety*, 80.
81 Chrodegang of Metz, *Regula Canonicorum*; Paul the Deacon, *Liber de episcopis*, 268; Claussen, *Reform*, 7, 58–63, 267–68.
82 For unity terminology, see Ardo, *Vita S. Benedicti*, 103, 377.
83 Cf. Schramm, "Karl der Grosse"; Smith, "'Emending Evil Ways,'" 214–15.
84 *Capitularia regum francorum*, i, 54 (no. 22 of 789); Bullough, *Alcuin*, 380 on authorship.

counties, cities, and estates was a duty frequently undertaken by Carolingian officials, and correcting and admonishing were what they did on such occasions.[85] *Reformare* occurs rarely, and can refer simply to the punishment of serfs, but in one striking instance in the *Epistola generalis* Charlemagne expresses his determination to "reform" (*in melius reformare*) the readings of service books.[86] The 794 Synod of Frankfurt lacks vocabulary suggestive of change or correction in those sections which deal with ecclesiastical organization. Subsequent Carolingian legislation, however, made use of a great variety of such terms. The 813 Capitulary of Mantua uses uprooting and casting out metaphors: "so that the vices which have emerged in God's holy church in our times may be uprooted and expelled." Louis the Pious uses "emendation (*emendatione*)" and "warning (*monendo*)" in the 816 Aachen Rule for canons. Charles the Bald (840–77), influenced by Archbishop Hincmar of Rheims (845–82), calls for common reparation through penance at Pîtres in 862.[87] Frankish legislation did not have a fixed or even a theologically developed vocabulary for justifying ecclesiastical change, in spite of the enthusiasm for institutional innovations displayed by Charlemagne and his successors.

Imperial legislation for the church was matched at a more local level by intensive synod-holding by bishops, notably Hincmar and his colleagues in the Carolingian heartlands.[88] Here, too, the same desire to build on long-established canon law is observable, but words suggestive of change, let alone innovation, are uncommon. Episcopal legislation was aimed especially at the behavior of diocesan clergy. It is into this Carolingian tradition, with its vocabulary of correction and admonition, that the writings on clerical behavior by Atto of Vercelli[89] (885–961) and Rather of Verona (d. 974)[90] can be fitted. Both were bishops of northern Italian sees in the earlier tenth century; both were irritated by the fact that many of the clergy in their dioceses were married; and both tried to urge celibacy on them. Both were shriller in their demands for clerical celibacy than previous episcopal legislators had been, and they were also much more vocal than their predecessors on the subject of simony: on this

85 For the frequency with which these terms occur in Carolingian capitularies, see *Capitularia regum francorum*, ii, 589, 608 (over 100 times) and 571–72 (over 60 times).

86 *Capitularia regum francorum*, i, 80–81 (no. 30 of 786 x 800).

87 *Capitularia regum francorum*, i, 73–78 (no. 28 of 794); ibid., 194–95 at 194 (no. 92); *Concilia aevi karolini*. ii, part i, 312 (no. 39 of 816); *Capitularia regum francorum*, ii, 304 (no. 272 of 862).

88 Stratmann, *Hinkmar von Reims*, esp. 35–38; Dierkens, "La christianisation," esp. 313–14.

89 *Emendare, emendation* in Atto of Vercelli, *Capitulare*, ch. 1 (*PL* 134, 27); *corripere* in Atto of Vercelli, *De pressuris ecclesiasticis* (*PL* 134, 54).

90 Rather of Verona, *Synodica*, 554, 555 *(moneo)*; 558 *(admonemus)*.

topic they point the way forward to Humbert of Silva Candida, Peter Damian, and Gregory VII in the eleventh century.

Monastic movements of the tenth and eleventh centuries and "reform"

Characteristic of tenth-century monasticism in the West is the spreading of liturgical customs and ideas about the correct observance of the Benedictine Rule from a few monasteries regarded as having a high reputation in these fields to a growing number of other ecclesiastical communities – some new, some already existing as monasteries, and others staffed by secular clergy who might be driven out and replaced by monks at the behest of their patrons, or else persuaded to become monks. Cluny, Brogne, and Gorze, joined by their own protégés Fleury, St. Peter's Ghent, and Winchester, were each influential, in each case sending out monks trained to teach monastic customs.[91] The process aroused considerable opposition, usually presented in the sources (overwhelmingly produced by Benedictines) as unjust, and sometimes, indeed, as diabolical, but clearly the legal position of the "reformers" was often insecure. The forcible monasticization of Winchester cathedral under Bishop Æthelwold of Winchester (963–84) in 964[92] was only one of several questionable undertakings. Moreover some monastic houses of repute felt threatened by new liturgical customs: Widukind of Corvey (d. after 973) referred to the process as "grave persecution."[93] Certain characteristics can be observed in the monasteries which underwent this training process. First, they were expected to observe strict chastity, and their leaders maintained that celibacy, and indeed complete sexual purity, was essential for priests, even those who had not taken monastic vows. Odo of Cluny and Æthelwold of Winchester both stressed this energetically.[94] Rather, with similar views, had been a monk at Lobbes before becoming bishop. Secondly, houses were expected to follow the Rule of Benedict, though there was no attempt (rather, the reverse) to strip away the liturgical accretions that had grown up since Benedict's time. Services were expected to be lengthy and elaborate. Third, to make elaborate worship possible, communities needed to be quite large and required substantial endowments. Some rethinking of the arrangements by which monasteries held

91 Among a large literature note Hallinger, *Gorze-Kluny*; Kottje and Maurer, *Monastische Reformen*; Rosenwein, *To Be the Neighbor*; Nightingale, *Monasteries and Patrons*; Wormald, "Æthelwold."

92 Wormald, "Æthelwold," esp. 37–38; Barrow, "English Cathedral Communities," 35, 37–38.

93 Widukind of Corvey, *Rerum Gestarum Saxonicarum*, II.37, 98.

94 Odo of Cluny, *Secundi Collationum*, 552–53; *Councils and Synods*, vol. 1, pt. 1, 136–41, 143–54.

property and leased it out to tenants is observable in this period,[95] though it did not prevent monasteries from continuing to enjoy close links with neighboring aristocratic families.[96] On the issue of the relationships between monasteries and their patrons and their diocesan bishops there were divergences: Cluny was the most independent, Fleury obtained exemption from its diocesan bishop, while monasteries in the empire, Flanders, and England were happy to enjoy the protection of rulers and had variable attitudes toward bishops.[97] Further diversity was also supplied by an interest in eremiticism which figures throughout these two centuries: the lives of Greek hermits in southern Italy were attracting the admiration of John of Gorze (d. 974) fairly early in the tenth century.[98] By the earlier eleventh century Romuald (d. 1027) and John Gualbert (d. 1073) were founding monastic communities in central Italy influenced by eremiticism. By the late eleventh century eremitic life had a wide appeal in Burgundy and parts of northern and western France, and was to be one of the main ingredients in Cistercian, Carthusian, and other new branches of monasticism.[99]

Significant though the changes in the tenth century were, they did not result in a large body of apologetic literature. Those of the late eleventh century, by contrast, did, but that literature was written essentially in the period after 1100. The relative lack of tenth-century monastic *apologiae* is curious because one of the most important consequences of the Benedictinizing process was to encourage an increase in writings, especially homilies, saints' lives, and histories, by the inmates of the newly founded or refounded houses.[100] Of course, homilies, saints' lives, and histories all contain apologetic elements, but they do not usually give the author the freedom to develop ideas at length. One monastic leader who did produce a coherent body of writings justifying the changes was Æthelwold, abbot of Abingdon and later bishop of Winchester, author of *Regularis Concordia* (the joint customary for all English Benedictine houses). Others include a narrative known as *Edgar's Establishment of Monasteries* and the (re)foundation charter issued by Edgar, king of England (959–75), for New Minster, Winchester in 966.[101] These texts are rich in theological imagery which allows us to explore Æthelwold's thinking on monasticism. In all three texts clergy are accused of being filthy; Æthelwold

95 Rosenwein, *To Be the Neighbor*, 199–200; see also Morris, this volume.
96 Nightingale, *Monasteries and Patrons*, 87–93, 249–60.
97 Wormald, "Æthelwold," 21, 24, 26, 33.
98 John, Abbot of St. Arnulf, *Vita Iohannis abbatis Gorziensis*, 344.
99 Lawrence, *Medieval Monasticism*, 149–73.
100 Wulfstan of Winchester, *Life of St. Æthelwold*, xcii-xcix.
101 *Councils and Synods*, vol. 1, pt. i, 119–54; *Property and Piety*, 65–97; on Æthelwold's authorship of these texts, see Lapidge, "Æthelwold," 184–97, 482 and literature there cited.

was accusing them of impurity because they tended to be married.[102] Their expulsion from minster churches so that they could be replaced by monks was, Æthelwold thought, not only justifiable but meritorious. (He compared Edgar with Christ because Edgar encouraged the removal of clerks.)[103] In the 966 charter, Æthelwold actually compares the New Minster clerks with Lucifer, cast down from heaven, and with Adam and Eve, cast out of Paradise. Beyond this, the installation of monks is seen as an attempt to supply virtuous worshipers to fill the vacant thrones in heaven.[104] Another image used by Æthelwold, this time in a letter to an unnamed *marchio* (marquis), probably Count Arnulf II of Flanders (965–88), is that of the decay of monasteries and their repair.[105] Some of these themes also occur in tenth-century continental *Lives*: for example, the removal of clerics;[106] the impurity of clerks (figuratively represented by dung in the church of Gorze before 933 in the *Life* of John of Gorze);[107] and especially the theme of repair and rebuilding;[108] but with the partial exception of the *Life* of John of Gorze, without Æthelwold's powerful use of metaphor. Reform as a term for what was being done is rare until the eleventh century; then suddenly it makes frequent appearances in a work by the Burgundian monk Rodulfus Glaber (d. 1047), the *Life of William*, abbot of Saint-Bénigne, Dijon. This was the Lombard nobleman, William of Volpiano, who founded the abbey of Fruttuaria in 1001, was given the task of installing monks at Fécamp in 1001, and was abbot of Saint-Bénigne from 990 to 1031. On one occasion Rodulfus uses "reform" simply to mean rebuilding,[109] but more often for the reform of a monastic house.[110] The verb "reform" also occurs as the very last word of Glaber's *Five Books of the Histories*, in a passage probably written at the very end of his life in which he praises the otherwise shadowy Pope Gregory VI (1045–46): *Cuius uidelicet bona fama quicquid prior fedaverat in melius reformavit*. ("His good fame reformed for the better what his predecessor had corrupted.")[111]

102 Wulfstan of Winchester, *Life of St. Æthelwold*, 30–31; *Councils and Synods*, vol. 1, pt. i, 136, 150; cf. *Property and Piety*, 81; Barrow, "English Cathedral Communities," 35.
103 *Property and Piety*, 79.
104 Ibid., 75–76.
105 *Epistola ad Arnulfum*, 362; on authorship, see Lapidge, "Æthelwold," 96–98.
106 John, Abbot of St. Arnulf, *Vita Iohannis abbatis Gorziensis*, 349; cf. also the largely fictitious *Vita Gerardi*, 662, 664–65; for the date of the latter, see De Smet, "Recherches critiques," 42–43.
107 John, Abbot of St. Arnulf, *Vita Iohannis abbatis Gorziensis*, 347.
108 Widric, *Vita S. Gerardi*, 494–95.
109 Rodulfus Glaber, *Opera*, 272.
110 Ibid., 268, 270, 296.
111 Ibid., 252.

The era of Gregory VII

It has long been recognized that the Gregorian movement represented no enormous break with the past in its aims or even in its ideology. Rather, the break with the past consisted in the ability of Gregory and his successors to put the program of change into effect, though, admittedly, this process was not complete until over a century later. Peter Damian (1007–72) and Humbert of Silva Candida (d. 1061), with their emphatic rejection of clerical marriage and simony, were building on centuries of canon law decrees as well as on the criticisms uttered by Atto and Rather.[112] Atto had already, in his attacks on simony, laid as much blame on laity controlling clerical appointments through sale as on clergy for buying their way in.[113] A bigger change came in the support of Nicholas II (1058–61), at the 1059 Lateran Council, for the apostolic life (*vita apostolica*) as the approved way of life for communities of clergy. This led to the encouragement of the enlarged Rule of St. Augustine in many clerical communities, especially in southern and northeastern France, northern Italy, and in the early twelfth century, in southern Germany, Normandy, and England.[114] An even more significant development was Gregory VII's attack on lay investiture,[115] though this was significant not for its effects on the appointment of bishops so much as for its consequences on relations between the papacy and secular rulers: the latter lost some of their sacrality. (Most kings, and even, eventually, emperors could be persuaded to relinquish their hold on ritual, provided that they retained control over the choice of personnel.)

The language employed in the attacks on clerical marriage, simony, and lay investiture rarely makes use of reform concepts.[116] As we have seen, Gregory VII himself only used the word *reformare* four times.[117] Gregory was, to quote a recent biographer, "not himself of a speculative turn of mind, nor did his grasp of Christian truth owe much to dogmatic inquiry or reflection."[118] His letters concentrate on practicalities and do not spend time on justifications. They also lack visual imagery: however, there is one recurring image of significance, that of the church as the Bride of Christ: free, chaste, and catholic.[119] Of the

112 Peter Damian, *Liber gratissimus*, *Contra intemperantes clericos*, and *Contra philargyriam*; Humbert of Silva Candida, *Libri III adversus simoniacos*.

113 Atto, *De pressuris ecclesiasticis*, c. 2, 71, cited by Fliche, *La réforme grégorienne*, 67.

114 Mansi 19, 898 (ch. 4); Dickinson, *Origins*, 32.

115 Schieffer, *Die Entstehung*, 153–76.

116 Cf. Robinson, "Reform and the Church," 307–309; for instances of reform and renewal terminology, see ibid., 268–72 and Robinson, *Papal Reform*, 1–3.

117 Tellenbach, *Church*, 160.

118 Cowdrey, *Pope Gregory VII*, 495.

119 Gregory VII, *Epistolae Vagantes*, no. 54, 130.

epithets used to describe the church here, "free" meant perhaps the most to Gregory. The freedom of the church was his goal,[120] though it should be noted that in claiming freedom for the church he was tacitly redefining "church" in this context to mean the clergy: the laity were, for this purpose, excluded. In general, historiography has been too keen to portray Gregory VII as a "reforming" pope. It might be better to view him as a disciplinarian one, making constant demands for obedience.

Conclusion

In conclusion it is necessary yet again to emphasize how important it is for us to understand how the word "reform" has been shaped by developments of the period after 1100, and more particularly after 1500, before we try to employ it to describe events in the pre-1100 period. There was a rich language in the pre-1100 period to define change, especially those changes which were perceived to (or were supposed to be perceived to) remove existing abuses and return to a better past: the words chiefly used in the West were *corrigere*, *emendare*, *meliorare*, and sometimes *renovare* and *innovare*, and in the East, *ananeoomai*. To some extent they overlap in meaning with *reformare*, but each has its own set of resonances which differ from those of *reformare*; in particular, they lack the Pauline imagery of transformation or even transfiguration. *Corrigere* has its own set of resonances from Roman Law. The idea of returning to a better past was a recurring theme of legislation in the Middle Ages: innovation for its own sake was usually viewed as an abuse, and supremely so in the eastern church. However, the past could be used selectively, especially in canon law, where there were few attempts to comment on discrepancies before Gratian. The final point which needs to be considered in assessing the development of the concept of reform in the Middle Ages is the way in which the personal and moral uses of the word *reformare* were easily adapted by monastic writers to apply to developments within monastic communities as well as within monastic individuals. This encouraged the word to take on an institutional role. The rapid growth in the use of the term "reform" in the twelfth century is a sign of the dominance of monastic thinking within the church as a whole.

120 Cowdrey, *Pope Gregory VII*, 536–39; Tellenbach, *Libertas*, 151–64; cf. also Cowdrey, *Cluniacs*, 51–57.

17

Churches in the landscape[1]

DOMINIQUE IOGNA-PRAT

The Cluniac monk Rodulfus Glaber (d. 1047) owes his renown as a historian to his near-obsessive interest in all of the remarkable events that occurred around the turn of the first millennium after the birth and passion of Christ. He recorded various signs of the unraveling of a decrepit world: comets; famines; blood falling from the sky; the apostasy of Christians converting to Judaism; Norman, Hungarian, and Saracen invasions; the destruction of the Church of the Holy Sepulcher in Jerusalem; waves of heretics. Conversely, Glaber also found signs announcing a new covenant between God and his faithful people – traces of a veritable renewal of the world. It is worth noting that the proofs of this rebirth all evinced a strong connection to this world: the finding of relics; peace councils and the creation of violence-free zones; the construction of a "white mantle of churches"; pilgrimages to holy sites; the expansion of Christendom to the East with the conversion of Stephen, king of the Hungarians, which in turn opened up a route to Jerusalem by land. As a symbol of a world casting off the "rags of its old age," the construction (or reconstruction) of churches throughout the world as the third year after the millennium approached heralded, in Glaber's view, a vast program of monastic reform. Indeed, after this general observation, Glaber provided examples of monastic buildings and builders, especially at Cluny. In order to highlight the world-sanctifying activity currently under way thanks to monastic reform, he then added an account of the discoveries everywhere of saints' relics, as though "the white mantle of churches" of the age of monasticism was offering to Christianity's ancient martyrs a reliquary by which they might at last "unveil themselves to the gaze of the faithful."[2]

Historians of medieval heresy have long noted that "the white mantle of churches" hailed by Glaber was not stitched together without

1 The chapter title follows Morris, *Churches in the Landscape*. This chapter distinguishes between church (building) and Church (institution and the community of believers it represents).
2 Rodulfus Glaber, *Historiarum libri quinque*, III.iv.13, 162–65.

controversy; discordant voices made themselves heard by calling into question the very need for cultic sites at all. Thus, the *Book of the Miracles of Ste. Foy* of Conques recounts the story of a peasant of Bazadais who denounced the "stupidity" of addressing prayers to what was, in his eyes, nothing more than a "fairground stall" (*attegia forensis*).[3] Further north, in the course of a synod held at Arras in 1025, Gerard of Cambrai, an influential bishop active on the borders of the Capetian kingdom and the Salian empire, set straight certain heretics, who, among other deviant beliefs, held that "the temple of God has nothing more noble to it . . . than does a bedroom."[4] Following the example of the clerics in Orleans condemned to the stake in 1022, these anonymous heretics denied that "the container can define the content."[5] By this radical position, they stood in direct continuity with the Latin church fathers whose praise of monuments was extremely reserved, and they forced their opponents to undertake an unprecedented level of doctrinal investigation of the matter. Before the intense theological reflection of the twelfth century (in the context of the great sacramental synthesis associated with the names of Hugh of Saint-Victor (d. 1142), Peter Lombard (c. 1100–60), and Thomas Aquinas (1225–74)), orthodox polemicists in the first half of the eleventh century took to recalling the antiquity of the architectural monumental tradition upon which the Church drew as the typological equivalent of Moses' Tabernacle and of the Temple in Jerusalem. Above all, these theologians applied themselves to the definition of what distinguished a building set aside for worship from other edifices made by human hands. It was within this context that the first doctrinal formulation emerged of what might be called an ecclesial "plus-factor," which defined a church as a "superlative site" where God is "more present" and where "his grace pours forth more abundantly."[6]

The cultic site in the medieval West: between sanctity and sacrality

How was this position reached? How did the term *ecclesia*, which originally designated the assembly of the faithful, equally come to designate, in the Latin-speaking world, the cultic site? Why adopt precisely this ambiguous term when numerous other descriptors were possible: *aula, basilica, domus Dei, dominicum, fabrica, locus, templum* . . . ? Why and when did the church

3 *Liber miraculorum sancte Fidis*, IV.23, 258.
4 *Acta synodi Atrebatensis*, 1284C.
5 Andrew of Fleury, *Vita Gauzlini*, 56, 98.
6 *Acta synodi Atrebatensis*, 1285B and 1286A.

building become an indispensable element in the social visibility of the ecclesial institution, the Church? The progressive and universal insertion of the church building into the social landscape represented, in fact, a prodigious reversal of the values which Christianity had long held. It is the purpose of this chapter firstly to present in broad outline the slow evolution of an ecclesiology which, with the aid of sacramental doctrine, allowed the confusion, peculiar to the medieval West, between the container (the church as monument) and the content (the Church as community) to be justified. Secondly, it evaluates the societal effects of this materialization of the divine in stone edifices.

The sanctity of human persons

The biblical tradition was thoroughly ambivalent with regard to the localization of the divine. On the one hand, Yahweh does not hesitate to announce that the site of theophanies can be "holy" (Exod. 3.4–5; Josh. 5.15), or even "terrible" (Gen. 28.10–20) since it is the "gate of heaven." On the other, there is no lack of assertions that maintain with Solomon, the builder of the Jerusalem Temple, that a house made by human hand will never be able to contain God (3 Kgs. 8.27, Vulgate). This in turn led Augustine to hold that God is "without place" or "outside of place" (*illocalis*).[7] Lastly, let us not forget Christ's own message proclaiming that his Kingdom and the Kingdom of his Father are not of "this world."

In addition, the Church inherited from the late antique Roman world certain legal categories whose significance is critical for understanding the relationship people had to the land, and, specifically, for grasping the meaning of such qualifiers as "holy," "sacred," and "religious" in this context. Whatever the long-term influence of these notions upon civil and canon law formulations may have been, it is important to underline the fact that early Christianity was characterized by a manifest desire to break with every sort of antique sacrality, whether of pagan temples or of the multifarious forms of pagan pantheism. The disciples of Christ were members of a "de-territorialized" religion which maintained a minimal connection to this world. If, from the earliest centuries of Christianity, certain sites did indeed come to acquire value, this occurred both in an unsolicited fashion, and through intermediaries. The unsolicited nature of this change stemmed from a particular quality recognized in churches by late antique civil authorities. From the reign of Constantine, a number of laws were decreed, and later integrated into the Theodosian Code in 438, which sought to determine the

7 Augustine of Hippo, *De civitate Dei*, I.29.

fate of those slaves or fugitives who were taking refuge in churches. In order to justify the attribution of what had formerly been the exceptional status of temples to Christian places of assembly, legislation defined churches as "temples of the Most High God," declared altars to be "sacrosanct," and punished any infraction of asylum as "sacrilege."[8] It was, therefore, in civil law that the sacrality of Christian sites was first recognized.

As for the aforementioned intermediaries, these were certain exceptional persons, namely the "very special dead" – the saints – whose remains were venerated here below precisely because they represented a point of contact to the hereafter above. By dint of an extraordinary lexical evolution, the term *locus* (or *loculus*) in Christian Latin came to designate, in addition to its earlier meanings, a saint's relics or even the shrine in which they were kept: the site built in honor of the saint was henceforth thought of as a great reliquary made of stone. At the conclusion of a slow development that culminated in the eighth century, the rule was laid down that there could be no cultic site without relics. Thus it was that a specifically "Christian" space came to be constituted that was delineated by various poles or centers of gravity arranged in a vast network, relics being distributed from source sites (the Holy Land, Rome) and from way-station sites (Aachen and numerous other sacred places such as Tours or Auxerre) and ending up in widely scattered local sites. This phenomenon, which was of the utmost importance in the development of a Christian notion of territoriality for the first time, also marked the birth of a new literary genre – accounts of the translation of relics (the first example of which was the translation of Sts. Peter and Marcellinus by Einhard in the early ninth century). This new Christian space was organized on two complementary levels that rendered the Church the point of articulation between the local and the universal. Firstly, at the microscopic level, we may distinguish the small *patria* of the saint, who delineated his particular physical environs from the surroundings at his arrival (*adventus*), when his relics were welcomed into the very center of the site in which he rested (*occursus*). Secondly, the macroscopic level was constituted by Christendom itself, organized into multiple saints' or apostles' *patriae* according to the logic of *divisio apostolorum* first employed in the apocryphal Acts of the Apostles, and given canonical form in Isidore of Seville's (560–636) *De ortu et obitu patrum*.[9] Whereas until this point the term "Christendom" was used to designate the community of Christ's disciples, it now acquired a specifically geographical meaning, the first attestation of which

8 *Theodosian Code*, 9.45.4[8].

9 Isidore of Seville, *De ortu et obitu patrum*, 215–17; Smith in this volume on cults of local and universal saints.

occurred at the very end of the eighth century in the writings of Angilbert (d. 814).[10]

The sacrality of the site

The saint's remains not only hallowed the cultic site, they sacralized it. It is not uncommon in saints' lives or miracle stories to see the term *corpus* develop within the semantic field of the adjective *sacer*. If the body of the saint and the space that it occupied were "sacred," it was because relics were involved in the ritual of the consecration of the church building and its environs. The history of this ritual's development is long and rather complex. In the first centuries of Christianity, no specific consecration of the site where the faithful assembled to commemorate the sacrifice of Christ existed: it was the first Eucharistic celebration that "consecrated" the building, together with the installation of holy relics in the altar, like those of Gervasius and Protasius in Milan, whom Ambrose identified with the souls of the martyrs evoked in the Apocalypse (Rev. 6.9).[11] In the sixth century at Rome, a new ritual appeared in the form of a two-fold rite consisting of an exorcism, intended to purify the building of any demonic presence, combined with the deposition of saints' relics. For its part, the Gallo-Frankish liturgy initially used two separate rituals: on the one hand, the consecration of the altar and of the church; on the other, the solemn deposition of relics. In time, the two Gallican rituals melded together, as is attested in the earliest known example, the *Ordo* of Saint-Amand (between 594 and 650), and on the foundation of this more or less successful harmonizing of the two rituals the dedication ceremony was later enriched by the blessing of liturgical objects (vessels, ornaments, vestments) and by the lighting of the building. The eighth and ninth centuries constituted a major turning point in the development of the rite. In the context of the liturgical unification desired by the Carolingian monarchs, Roman and Gallican rites grew closer together and amalgamated: *Ordo romanus* 42 realized this combination.[12] Subsequently, this combined rite became further enriched, the *Ordo ad benedicandam ecclesiam* (840s) being included in the mid-tenth century in the Romano-Germanic Pontifical (*Ordo* 40), which in turn was transported to Rome in the eleventh century, where it received a few further additions in the thirteenth century.[13] At the end of this long development, the dedication ritual, which originally

10 Angilbert, *De perfectione Centulensis ecclesiae libellus*, in Hariulf, *Chronique*, II.ix, 61.
11 Ambrose of Milan, *Epistola 22*.
12 Andrieu, *Les* ordines romani, ch. 3.
13 *Pontifical romano-germanique*, XL, 124–73.

simply consisted of the Eucharistic sacrifice, had become one of the most splendid rites of the Latin liturgy.

The 840s was a period of synthesis and of the implementation of this unified ritual of church consecration throughout the empire, which gradually spread throughout Latin Christendom. This decade also saw the emergence of a commentary on the ritual, the *Quid significent duodecim candelae*.[14] This commentary allows us to establish a connection between liturgy and ecclesiology and, in so doing, helps us to understand the underlying sociological issues, for within this discursive context the word *ecclesia* established itself as a *terminus technicus* to denote the church building. The choice of this term by Latin Christendom (the Christian East continued to distinguish with different terms the site where Christians gathered, *naos*, and the community of the faithful, *ecclesia*), had weighty consequences already suggested by the anonymous author of *Quid significent duodecim candelae*. The *Ecclesia* (the Church community) and the *ecclesia* (the church building) maintain a sort of metonymic relationship according to which the container signified the content and vice versa. This conceptual confusion was the object of numerous and subtle interpretations in subsequent centuries. This says a great deal about the visibility of an institution, the Church, that, by means of the building which signified it, established itself in the social landscape. It was within this dynamic that the allegorical female iconographic type of *Ecclesia* came, in the course of the eleventh century, to be identified with a building appropriate for the organization of the Christian people into two distinct groups, clergy and laity.[15]

The sacramentalization of the cultic site in the age of ecclesiastical reform

After the ninth century, the era of Church reform in the eleventh and twelfth centuries represents the second important period in the definition of a doctrine of the cultic site. The Gregorian clergy had as a collective plan the construction of a Christian society. For them, in order to be *of* the Church, it was fitting that one be *within* the church; in order to accede to the spiritual temple, one had first to pass through the building of stone.

However, to be *within* presupposes that one can also be *outside*. There are the Christians – living stones of the sacramental community that is the Church – and there are the others. Clear attestation of the rift between the members of

14 Ibid., XXXV, 90–121.
15 See the southern Italian *Exultet* roll in fig. 2, p. 484 in this volume.

the body of Christ and those who did not belong is furnished from the 1050s by commentaries on the canon of the mass, and particularly on the formula *ut nobis corpus et sanguis fiat dilectissimi tui domini nostri Jesu Christi*. Citing the saying of Augustine that "there is no site of the true sacrifice outside the Catholic Church," exegetes defined "us" (*nobis*) restrictively to the exclusion of "others" – all others, that is, heretics, Jews, and, pagans (and more often than not, Muslims).[16] In response, heterodox movements from the 1020s until the Cathars (appearing in the second half of the twelfth century) were opposed to any ecclesial mediation; thus they refused to confuse the container (the church) with the content (the Church), and maintained that it is impossible to localize God in a building made of walls and stone.

The first scholastic *summae* were formulated on the fertile ground of these debates. They treated Scripture as a great cathedral, and, following the three hermeneutical meanings, the biblical monuments – Noah's Ark, Moses' Tabernacle, Ezechiel's Temple, Solomon's and David's Temple, all antetypes of the Church – were understood not only as representable buildings (in the historical meaning), but also as necessary frames by which to conceive of Christian society (in the allegorical meaning), and even of the spiritual life of each of the faithful (in the tropological meaning). It was not, therefore, simply a matter of describing the whole of society as a cathedral, but also, and indeed especially, of the architectonic construction of the whole of creation, as was achieved in Hugh of Saint-Victor's *De sacramentis*, a work of the utmost importance in doctrinal thought from 1050 to 1150 on the question of the cultic site. This discourse was organized around three principal concerns.

The first related to the debate on the Eucharist provoked by Berengar of Tours (c. 1010–88) in the second half of the eleventh century. From the beginnings of the controversy on the subject, which dated back to the dispute between Paschasius Radbertus (c. 790–c. 860) and Ratramnus of Corbie (d. c. 870) in the ninth century, two positions could be distinguished schematically: on the one side, those who held to Eucharistic "realism," according to which the consecrated species (the bread and wine) were transformed *really* into the body and blood of Christ; on the other hand, the "symbolists" (including Berengar) who maintained that the purported transformation was only an *image*, the purpose of the Eucharist being only to recall Christ's sacrifice at the Church's foundation, without there being any need of *real* rehearsal of this act. The triumph of the realists (at least officially) had an indirect influence on the question of the cultic site. The *real* transformation of the species

16 See, for example, Odo of Cambrai, *Expositio in canonem missae*, 1061D.

(also described as "transmutation" and even, from 1140, "transubstantiation") had the consequence of magnifying not only the time of the sacrifice (the mass), but also its site (the church). Both were considered to be endowed with the "plus factor" mentioned above, being solely and uniquely revelatory of the divine.

Secondly, a parallel discourse reflected upon the notion of sacramental *cause*. Peter Lombard maintained that the sacraments effect that of which they are a figure: "they cause grace in signifying it." Hugh of Saint-Victor advanced the notion of "dispositive causality" according to which the sacrament established the conditions that dispose the recipient to receive grace, rather like a vase or any container that is necessary for the realization of the contents. Applied to the church as monument, the full significance of this notion of a vase-sacrament was duly assessed.

Thirdly, reflection on sacramental cause was accompanied by a classification of the sacraments. Seven major sacraments (*sacramenta*: baptism, confirmation, Eucharist, penitence, extreme unction, orders, marriage), and a series of minor sacraments (*sacramentalia*: including the blessing of holy water and the imposition of ashes) were distinguished. The definition of the number of sacraments as seven did not occur without some difficulty. For example, for a long while there was some question as to whether the dedication of a church ought to be counted as one of the major sacraments. After many hesitations, the rite of dedication was excluded from the list of the seven sacraments or, rather, it was partly integrated by dint of an interesting division of the first sacrament, baptism. Baptism of a building emblematic of the community was distinguished from baptism of the faithful. In an influential dedication sermon, Ivo of Chartres (c. 1040–1115) explained that the consecration of a church represents the first step in a process: it was fitting that the building be baptized so that the faithful might also be baptized in turn, and so that the other sacraments might be performed within its functional space.[17] In other words, the baptism of the church disposed it to effect the other sacraments. Without it, there could be no sacramental place, and, therefore, no Christian community.

The spatialization of the sacred

Baptized just as though it was a person, the church building was also sanctified as such. At the end of a long process of doctrinal development, early scholasticism thus consecrated the "personalization," so to speak, of

17 Ivo of Chartres, *Sermo IV de sacramentis dedicationis*, 528D–529A.

the church building. This outcome, which paradoxically leads us back to our starting point, the sanctification of persons and not of sites, tells us a great deal about the reversal of values which took place within Christianity between the patristic period and the 1150s. Originally considered as an unimportant material necessity in comparison with the ineffable dwellings of the heavenly city, the church building so imposed itself on the landscape that it became the essential site of the organization and control of humankind.

The gradual formation of a sacramental doctrine of the cultic site outlined here is not only a chapter of the Church's history. Insofar as Church and society were coextensive and since, in the medieval West, there were no lay criteria for affiliation, it is also a chapter in the history of society as a whole, and an essential chapter in the long-term definition of the idea of territory: hence the need to move from the discussion of ecclesiastical doctrine to that of social practices. One example shall suffice to illustrate the necessity of this change of focus. It was noted above that in order to define the "we" of the canon of the mass, from around 1050 exegetes had recourse to the Augustinian saying that "there is no site of the true sacrifice outside the Catholic Church." This idea of a "site of the true sacrifice" seems to have passed quickly from the realm of doctrine to that of practice and to writings of a juridical nature. Thus, between 1030 and 1070, in Provence, certain authors of church foundation or endowment deeds held that the "house" (*aula*) which is termed a church because it contains the Church was instituted by Christ, the apostles, and the fathers as the "site of the true sacrifice." These texts, which are, it must be said, rare, emphasize with astonishing insistence the connection that united the sacramental act and the site of its realization. If it was a worthy act to offer a sacrifice to God, it was then fitting to do so in a site set aside for this purpose.[18]

The church as a unit

The church site was considered "proper" to the divine at the conclusion of a gradual architectural evolution whose history liturgical exegetes, such as Walafrid Strabo (c. 808–49), started to write beginning in the 840s.[19] Two phases of this history are relevant here: the early Christian emergence of Christian edifices (in the plural); then the gathering in a single site of the functions formerly scattered among several buildings.

18 Among other examples, see the deed of the endowment of Sainte-Marie in the territory of Saint-Maximin (1062). (I wish to thank M.-J. Gasse for affording me access to this document.)

19 Walafrid Strabo, *Libellus de exordiis et incrementis*, 6, 62–70.

The early Christians had no reason to endow themselves with special places in which to assemble, pray, and share the common meal that lay at the origins of the Eucharistic rite. Like the apostles, they were content for a long time with houses in which small groups gathered, and which were structurally adapted as needs arose. The earliest *domus ecclesiae* attested by archaeology is at Dura Europus (Syria), and dates from the beginning of the third century. It is simply a house in which two rooms have been specially adapted to the needs of the community: one for assembly meetings and the other for the rite of baptism. In Rome, the *Titulus Byzantis* was at first, in the second century, a modest cell-like room in a shop, then a *domus ecclesiae* destined to absorb a group of adjoining houses in the same block to form, in the fifth century, the basilica placed under the patronage of Sts. John and Paul. In order to respond to the pressure of growing numbers, to the needs of worship, and to the necessity within the assembly to mark out both the clergy from the faithful as well as men from women, the *domus ecclesiae* underwent a morphological transformation which rendered it a building for specific purposes (*aula ecclesiae*), endowed with a large room for the assembly and, from the fourth century, often adopting the form most widespread in civil architecture, namely that of the basilica.

Certainly, at the time of the Edict of Milan (313), the *aula ecclesiae* was only one of the buildings belonging to the Christian community. Early Christian architecture, in fact, comprised three functionally separate structures, which could indeed be linked, as is the case in paleo-Christian clusters of episcopal buildings, but which were not worked together into a single architecturally unified whole: the cultic site properly speaking, defined by the presence of an altar; the martyrs' chapel, founded on relics; and the baptistery centered on the baptismal font or pool. The principal transformation of the structure of ecclesiastical buildings in the early Middle Ages consisted in grouping together, linking, and organizing into a hierarchy these diverse functional centers of gravity, in order to produce a single building, namely the church as the conjunction of the zones of baptism, martyrs (or saints), and the Eucharist. The policy implemented by Gregory the Great at St. Peter's in Rome at the end of the sixth century provides a good picture of the morphological changes which were accomplished with varying degrees of rapidity elsewhere. The pope chose to highlight the altar by elevating it up a few steps; importantly, he located it directly above the crypt in which the relics were enshrined, in such a way as to establish a vertical and hierarchical relationship between Christ and the saints. In a later stage, also of fundamental import, between the ninth and the eleventh centuries, the baptismal font was installed within the building that already housed the altar and the saints' crypt (*confessio*).

A similar conflation of different elements was also at the core of the ritual for the consecration of a church. Gaining acceptance throughout Latin Christendom from the 840s, the ceremony focused on a single spot, the altar, which drew Christ and the saints into intimate but hierarchical association. Everything radiated outward from this sacral center of gravity. On the one hand, by means of blessings and consecrations, the rituals in liturgical *libelli*, and later in pontificals, were extended outward to include numerous objects (walls, bells, altar cloths) that all came together into a unified whole: the cultic site. On the other hand, the consecrated collective space itself spread and reached into its immediate surroundings which were set aside for the Christian dead. From the 960s pontificals recorded an *ordo* for the consecration of cemeteries supplementing the church dedication rite itself.[20] This is the origin of a dynamic articulation of space, in which altar and church were the central point around which a whole collection of concentric zones formed – cemeteries, churchyards-cum-sanctuaries, parishes, ecclesiastical lordships – each contributing significantly to the way in which settlements were sited and their inhabitants configured into groups and controlled.

The siting of settlements and the configuration and control of their inhabitants in groups

The spatialization of the sacred in the medieval West is thus part of a wider history of society – a history whose paradigms have been profoundly altered in the last fifty years thanks to the contributions made by the archaeology of settlement. These discoveries have forced medievalists, whether willingly or not, to reexamine their reflections on "feudal society" and on the role of the Church within it.

This profound renewal of paradigms has consisted in historicizing the question of the contexts in which people lived by challenging both the presumed fixity of ancient settlements and the antiquity of church structures. The argument propounded in the nineteenth century for a direct line from the Roman *villa* to the medieval village has now been unanimously rejected. Nonetheless, a number of historians of Late Antiquity still maintain – incorrectly – that "the Church's organization of burial sites reserved to Christians was accomplished by the middle of the third century,"[21] and that the "parish" (or whatever else the grouping of the faithful around a cultic site might be called) is a phenomenon that, from the fourth century, was structurally connected with the construction of churches.

20 *Pontifical romano-germanique*, LIV, 192–93.
21 Rebillard, *Religion et sepulture*, 4.

However, since the 1970s and 1980s, the old argument among medievalists for the antiquity of church structures has collided with the lessons of rural archaeology, which reveal that, in fact, settlement displacement was a recurrent phenomenon throughout the early Middle Ages. Populations only became fixed, with varying degrees of rapidity according to region, between the eighth and the thirteenth centuries – a process that both archaeologists and historians, working on different scales, explain differently. As Élisabeth Zadora-Rio has expertly shown, the historian's village is not the same as that of the archaeologist. On the macroscopic scale of broad-ranging systems of explanation, historians link this permanent siting of settlements with a large-scale social transformation, namely, the emergence of feudal society (dated varyingly according to the individual analysis of each author, somewhere between the 850s and around the first millennium). According to Pierre Toubert's model of *incastellamento*, settlement transformation and the reorganization of lands affecting Sabina and Latium in the tenth and eleventh centuries were the result of lords' desire to group people together in fortified locations perched on hilltops the better to control them. This argument, which renders the castle the center of a new way of organizing society, was generalized by Robert Fossier into the notion of the widespread confinement of people into "cells" (*encellulement*) by firmly attaching the populace around the castle, the church, the cemetery, and the parish. According to Fossier, these "cells" grouped people together, controlled them, and ruled them. This model does not satisfy archaeologists, who struggle to unearth equivalent interconnected phenomena such as concentrated settlement sites, fortifications and settlement boundaries. At most, then, the *encellulement* model holds only for western Europe's "infancy." After the first millennium of itinerancy and of displacement within confined territories, the Nordic world presented what is, in effect, a different paradigm for the siting of settlements in the eleventh to twelfth centuries: clusters of houses-cum-cattlesheds that owed nothing to either castles or churches.

"Inecclesiamento"

In two recent studies, Michel Lauwers has further systematized the ecclesiastical contribution to the history of *encellulement*, by speaking of *inecclesiamento*. A calque on *incastellamento*, the term is intended to characterize the process by which the Church as an institution created social space.

In order to appreciate the full import of this insight, it is appropriate to emphasize that this process, whose inception dates to roughly 850–900, stands in absolute contradiction to early Christianity's original lack of interest in any entanglement in earthly living circumstances. The early Christian communities inherited Roman territorial structures – in particular, cities and dioceses – without bestowing on this legacy any other significance than the material necessities of a sojourn in this world that one wanted to be as brief as possible. In order to describe the nature of the changes at work between the ancient world and the medieval world, some historians have not hesitated to speak of a transition from spatial ties to social ties. These entailed the increasing abandonment of models of land organization from Roman antiquity that were "founded on an understanding of a bounded, orthonormal, and stable space – an understanding which owes much to the practice of centuriation."[22] From an early date, the Church contributed in its own way to this process of territorial detachment. For example, in the context of a dispute between bishops regarding the control of an oratory that had yet to be consecrated, Pope Gelasius I (492–96) held that "it is not fitting that a diocese be defined by limits or according to pre-determined sites."[23] According to this logic, it was not the territory that made the diocese, but the presence of the faithful and the personal ties established between the community and the bishop's uniting authority.

Though it is impossible to give a detailed account here of the exact circumstances in which the reversal of this understanding was worked out, we must note that, from the beginning of the 800s, the papacy established an entirely different understanding of the Christian relationship to the world, with the development of the territorial, proto-state framework of the "Republic of St. Peter," which was a public structure endowed with a precise border. The earliest form of medieval terrritoriality was, therefore, as much a contribution of the Roman pontiffs in their role as both spiritual and temporal lords, as that of the Carolingian, Ottonian and Salian kings and emperors. Their kingdoms and empires blithely confounded political and ecclesial structures, as the history of the foundation of dioceses in eastern Francia and central Europe between 800 and 1050 attests, for this was as much an affair of royal charters as of papal bulls. From this point of view, it is striking to note that it was a Lotharingian pope, Leo IX (1049–54), bred on the practice of imperial power, who started the trend which became so characteristic of the reforming papacy: the great papal journeys to consecrate altars, churches, and spaces such as cemeteries and ecclesiastical estates whose boundaries were marked by ritual perambulations. In so doing, he bestowed an element of territorial

22 Lauwers, "Représentation et gestion."

23 Violante, "Le strutture organizzative," cites the source as *Fragmentum* 19 in *Epistolae romanorum pontificum genuinae*. Ed. A. Thiel. Vol. 1. Braunsberg, 1868, 493–94.

actuality on the *libertas romana* of his day, turning the sites and spaces which he consecrated into virtual "clones" of Rome. In this sense, Leo IX was a pope of the land, like many of his immediate successors, such as Urban II (1086–99). It was on the land that the Church would henceforth make its presence felt.

Zones dependent on altar and church

The new model of territorial organization to which, among the other structures of control of land and people, the Church contributed was as follows. Radiating from the central points of altar and church, a series of ecclesial zones spread outwards in widening concentric circles.

The first of these zones was the cemetery. Between antiquity and the Middle Ages, the relationship between the living and the dead underwent a complete reversal which profoundly affected topography. After centuries of separating the living and the dead by means of burial grounds outside cities, the Middle Ages saw a slow integration of the dead into the world of the living. Settlement archaeology has brought a long process to light whose chronology varies from region to region, but which generally comprises at least three phases: from field cemeteries to the clustering of graves in consecrated zones around churches, by way of an intermediate period when interment within the settlement itself was practiced. Originally, the term *coemeterium* referred only to the tomb itself. It was not until the sixth century that, in the monastic world, the practice of communal burial of Christians separate from non-Christians first appeared. Much later, however, this burial ground was set apart for Christians by means of consecration – the practice from the fourth century of burial *ad sanctos* having nothing to do with interment in a ritually consecrated zone. As we noted above, the earliest consecration rituals for a cemetery appear in tenth-century pontificals, and, for all that, there is virtually no documented example of the practice before the mid-eleventh century. Indeed, not until the twelfth century did canon lawyers provide a definition of the Christian cemetery conceived as a place enriched by the ashes of the faithful departed. This restrictive definition of the space for the Christian dead must be situated within the context of the contemporary expulsion of heretics, Jews, and Muslims – three emblematic figures of the "persecuting society" highlighted by Robert Moore.

On the front of the fight against Islam in Catalonia and Septimania, the establishment (or reestablishment) of peasant communities in the ninth, tenth, and eleventh centuries was recorded in large numbers of documents called "deeds of consecration." These provide a precise idea of the way in which the community's space was being organized around the newly consecrated church. Thus, on 15 November 985, Oliba, Count of Cerdanya, and his wife

Ermengard invited Bishop Sala of Urgel to consecrate the church of Sant Cristófor de Vallfogona. The deed prepared for this occasion specifies that parish bounds (*termini parroquiae*) were fixed, and the cemetery and an area of sanctuary (*sacraria*) were established "within the ambit" of the church (*in circuitu ecclesie*).[24] These concentric zones centered on the church within a determined area, the *circuitus*, a term which evokes both the ancient Roman juridical practice of delimiting property by deambulation and the consecration of cemeteries by a ritualized walking around the site carrying relics. The first concentric zone around the church was reserved for the dead; next came the *sacraria*, a circle of thirty paces for the living who sought asylum and sacred protection. A parallel configuration sometimes appears to have formed the core of a village (the *sagrera* or *cellera*) that some settlement archaeologists have gone so far as to term the "ecclesial village."

The outer concentric zone was constituted by the parish. How are we to understand this term in the last third of the tenth century? The term "parish" (*parochia*) for a long time designated an entirely different topographical entity from that which we understand by the term today. Contrary to the long-held opinions of historians, there was no continuity between the Roman landed estate and the medieval parish. The delimitation of parishes represented a way of marking off space that had no antecedents; it was a medieval innovation, still developing in the ninth and tenth centuries, which did not come to mature fruition until the eleventh and twelfth centuries. Moreover, in the early period the term *parochia* was used to designate either a macro-unit, the diocese as a whole, or a micro-unit, the basilica or church. The word did not acquire a clear and distinct territorial meaning until the twelfth century. This coincided with the end of the complex history of the gravitation of the Christian faithful to the church, which was by this date conceived as the essential site of the sacramental definition of Christians in community – baptism and death, more or less regular participation in the Eucharistic sacrifice, and reconciliation and reintegration for penitents. There were two principal factors at work in the genesis of the medieval parish. The first stemmed from tithing, which was obligatory from the Carolingian era, and which had to be paid to the cultic site. In this sense, the parish was primarily a fiscal unit of land, understood as the resort within which the faithful contributed to the needs of the "fabric" of the church, that is, for the needs of the incumbents and the upkeep of the building itself. Hincmar of Rheims (c. 806–82) emphasized this aspect in what was without doubt the earliest systematic treatise devoted to church

24 Cebrià Baraut, "Les actes de consecgracions," 107–108, n. 41.

property, the *Collectio de ecclesiis et capellis*.[25] The second aspect of the parish was the cemetery. From the Carolingian era, the faithful were instructed to have themselves buried in the place where they were paying their tithes. For a considerable length of time, the "natural" parishioner was the one who paid tithes and was buried in the same parish in which the tithe was paid. Hence, the frequent confusion between cemetery and parish in medieval thinking.

Saints' land and monks' space

It is appropriate to end with a word about the territorial policy conducted by the Cluniac monks, great ecclesiastical lords who possessed relics of the Roman saints Peter and Paul and took their inspiration from the Roman model. This example is emblematic of a general phenomenon, the territorialization of *libertas ecclesiae*, the liberty of the church.

The five thousand or so deeds earlier than 1120 brought together in the charter collection and then the cartularies of Cluny bear witness to the aggressive policy of landed property acquisition which marked the first two centuries of the history of the monastery, founded in 910. From the second half of the eleventh century, it was on this landed base that the Cluniac monks organized "the sites and circles of their seigniorial control."[26] The first phase of this territorial policy amounted to the inclusion of property of various kinds (lands, churches, castles, mills) in a single, common ecclesial structure, together with the creation of a network of obediences or "deaneries" (*decania*) which were multifunctional sites serving simultaneously as agricultural centers, places of commerce and business, hermitages, and pilgrimage churches. Subsequently, this network of "sites," centered on the abbatial church and on the high altar where the relics of Sts. Peter and Paul lay, was arranged in a circle of influence within which Cluniac sanctity imposed absolute inviolability.[27] Firstly, the immunity enjoyed by the monastery had to be sited on the land. This was the object of two solemn acts performed on-site by representatives of Roman power: the legate Peter of Albano, in 1080, and Urban II (formerly the Grand Prior of Cluny) in 1095. They ritually defined the bounds of the Cluniac "Sacred Ban," that is, the zone under St. Peter's jurisdiction, a jurisdiction given physical shape by boundary markers and crosses connected by roads. Two further circles of influence were added soon afterwards: a bull of Pascal II (1099–1118) established in 1107 a toll-free and castle-free zone allowing pilgrims, guests,

25 Hincmar of Rheims, *De ecclesiis et capellis*.
26 Cf. Méhu, *Paix et communauté*, 87, 133.
27 Ibid., ch. 3.

and merchants to reach Cluny and return freely from it. Finally, the exemption granted by Callixtus II (1119–24) in 1120 made Cluny into a "mini-diocese" in charge of several parishes.

A few weeks after having instituted Cluny's "Sacred Ban," Urban II issued his famous call at Clermont-Ferrand for a crusade to free the Holy Land. Conquered by the crusaders in 1099, this land in which the Christian story began was literally reconsecrated as the liturgy of the liberation of Jerusalem attests, for the ceremony was largely drawn from the formulas for the dedication of a church.[28] In a return to symbolic roots, it was as though the "white mantle of churches" evoked by Rodulfus Glaber was now going to cloak the very sites of the earthly sojourn of Christ himself. Long engrained in the Latin Church's memory of the destruction of the Temple, the earthly Jerusalem recovered by the crusaders was likened to a new church. It was purified in the way that a cultic site that had long been abandoned would have been restored to Christian sanctity. The earliest center of Christianity was thereby treated as if it were a church, and the topography associated with Christ was reinstituted by the dedication ritual. Always understood as a figure of the heavenly Jerusalem, the church gave renewed life to the earthly Jerusalem in expectation of the Parousia to come.

28 Linder, "Liturgy."

PART IV

★

CHRISTIANITY AS LIVED EXPERIENCE

18

Birth and death

FREDERICK S. PAXTON

When responding to birth and death, early medieval Christians leaned heavily upon two fundamental features of their culture: the centrality of birth, death, and resurrection in their faith, and the importance of families in their mental horizons and social organization. Over the course of the early Middle Ages, most Christians came to regard the baptism of newborns as a necessary and normal initiation into church, kin, and Christian society. At the same time, liturgical specialists expanded the comparatively simple funeral and commemorative practices of Christian antiquity into a fully articulated rite of passage meant to facilitate each step of the transition from the community of the living to the community of the faithful departed: preparing body and soul for death itself, properly disposing of the corporeal remains, and overseeing the successful incorporation of the soul into the ranks of the blessed. The faithful, both new and old, also gave up a variety of more or less ancient burial practices for an almost universal pattern of simple interment in and around churches at the heart of settled areas. When they did, the living and the dead became members of a single community, united in space and time. Overall, the business of preparing Christians for death and seeing to their welfare in the afterlife, which began at baptism, gave rise to an extraordinary system of spiritual and temporal exchange – an economy of salvation, based on gift-giving and fueled by the circulation of people, prayers, and property – that is one of the most striking features of the age.[1]

In the Latin West, political and institutional decentralization led to the most variegated expression of the early medieval economy of salvation. The churches of the East, in part because they remained in closer touch with the traditions of late imperial Christianity and in part because they faced Islam directly, from within or without, remained more conservative. Eastern Christians never took up certain rituals that developed in the early medieval West,

1 Cf. Geary, "Exchange and Interaction."

like anointing the dying, for example. Nevertheless, all Christians shared the belief that the living could, and should, bring rest or refreshment to the dead, gaining forgiveness for their sins and lessening their pains in the afterlife by offering alms, psalms, and masses in their name. As a consequence, the living directed significant resources to the care of the dead, most commonly in the form of endowments to church institutions, especially monastic communities, whose "voluntary" poverty qualified them for alms and who oversaw the care of the truly indigent for the living and the dead.[2] The efficacy of these efforts was broadcast through visions of the afterlife, in which the sufferings of the dead were made manifest to the living, along with visions of the dead, in which they asked the living for help or thanked them for the prayers and alms offered in their name.[3] But what happened in this world was no less significant (and considerably more accessible to historians), for the early medieval economy of salvation also generated whole new categories of relationships among individuals, families, and church institutions. The course of a Christian biography ran from the metaphorical death and rebirth of baptism through the death of the body to the final resurrection. Along the way, early medieval Christians took every opportunity to construct a web of relationships that both reflected and shaped their responses to the promise of birth, the fear of death, and the hope of resurrection.

The evidence for all this comes mostly from records left by ecclesiastics – monks and clerics, and, to a lesser extent, nuns and canonesses – and a few of the aristocratic and royal lay men and women who helped them spread the faith. However limited in perspective, these records, especially when tested and augmented with archaeological data, give substantial evidence of how Christian theology, liturgy, law, and custom affected, or failed to affect, the experience of birth and death in early medieval Christendom. It is important to note, though, that the kind of social and religious history that investigates such questions is fairly new, and these topics have not been investigated everywhere to the same degree. Much more work has been done on Latin than on Greek Christianity, in particular, not to mention the other eastern and African churches of the early Middle Ages, and the most complete research is on Anglo-Saxon England, whose Christian history coincides almost exactly with the chronological scope of this volume. There is, thus, much to be done before a full account that includes all regional variants can be attempted. The notion of an "economy of salvation" is, moreover, not meant to define the totality of religious

2 Paxton, "*Oblationes defunctorum*."
3 Cf. Baun in this volume.

responses to birth and death in all of early medieval Christendom, but simply to point to certain characteristics of the period within a frame large enough to encompass the current state of knowledge and leave room for differences and commonalities as yet undiscovered. Another frame is provided by geography, chronology, and degree of Christianization, which correlate rather closely in this case. In the year 600, Christianity was still mostly contained within the old imperial borders. Over the course of the early Middle Ages, from Rome and Constantinople, but also from regional centers like Ireland, Saxony, and Kievan Rus, the faith spread to new populations. By 1100, it had reached the limits of Europe in the west, north, and east and was beginning to wash back into old Christian territories that had lived for centuries under Muslim rule. As early medieval Christianity came of age, so did its peculiar economy of salvation.

While the Christianization of Europe was one of the fundamental historical processes of the early Middle Ages, it did not leave Christianity unchanged. Late imperial Christianity was already a highly negotiated product, and the religious practices that developed from the seventh through to the eleventh centuries were often hybrids of traditional, local ways and official norms and notions. Nowhere was this truer than around birth and death, which, like marriage, held so many consequences for families. Birth and death had always been family matters because families, especially powerful ones, always sought to pass down their property and power along clear lines of descent. The same goes for religious communities of cloistered men or women, however, who constituted for all intents and purposes spiritual families, and were often both the most successful agents and most ubiquitous products of Christianization. Complicating things further was the fact that the participation of individual priests, monks, nuns, and canonesses in religious life had important implications for their blood relatives, who were often founders and always benefactors of the cloistered communities in which they spent their lives. Finally, given the large role women had always played in the dramas of birth and death, and the degree to which men controlled the religious life of early medieval Christians, Christianization inevitably produced tensions along gender lines.

As a result, the distinctive early medieval religious practices that came to mark and sanctify the beginning and end of life were not simply imposed, but often carefully negotiated, over centuries, by men and women both inside and outside of the church hierarchy. That give and take made the Christianization of birth and death a peculiarly dynamic process, one that mutually reinforced the status and influence of lay and religious *familiae*. Thus, even in their most Christianized forms, early medieval responses to birth and death are more than usually representative of the personal and social commitments of the people who experienced them. Infant baptism became the expected norm, for example, but not without also becoming embedded in structures of parental power and familial interest. Death, burial and the commemoration of the dead were fully Christianized, but not without granting families, especially wealthy and powerful ones, a significant amount of control over their place within the economy of salvation. Moreover, while male clerics and monks managed the early medieval economy of salvation, women nevertheless occupied key positions within it: as educators of children; as monastic founders, abbesses, nuns, and canonesses; and at certain times and places as the primary overseers of liturgical *memoriae*, the formal religious commemorations of the dead that formed the linchpin of the whole system.[4]

Birth, death, and spiritual affinity

While some of the medical writers from Greco-Roman antiquity discussed conception, pregnancy, and birth, ancient physicians generally left women, their midwives, and their female relatives alone during childbirth.[5] As Christianity developed, churchmen followed suit, a situation that never really changed, even in the later Middle Ages when male physicians first began to stake their claims for a place around the childbed.[6] The most significant marker of the Christianization of birth itself was the penetration of Christian saints and symbols into the common stock of charms, amulets, and invocations used to promote conception and protect mothers and children before, during, and after birth. Ancient birthing belts or girdles, for example, were Christianized by association with Mary, the mother of Jesus.[7] The importance of the birth of Jesus in Christianity and devotion to his mother could not, however, overcome the ambivalence of male clerics toward intimate contact with women, and the "masculinization" of the clergy left them with no easy entry into such a fundamentally female sphere. Thus, childbirth remained a domestic, female event, which Christian priests neither attended nor ritualized.

The distance priests kept from childbirth meant that women, along with their midwives and families, routinely made decisions about abortion and the

4 Schmid and Wollasch, *Memoria*.

5 Temkin, *Soranus' Gynecology*; Orme, *Medieval Children*, 17–19; Shahar, *Childhood*, 33; Blumenfeld-Kosinski, *Not of Woman Born*, 15–21.

6 Blumenfeld-Kosinski, *Not of Woman Born*, 91.

7 Shahar, *Childhood*, 36; Orme, *Medieval Children*, 16.

viability of newborns outside of the purview of the clergy.[8] Midwives could be called upon to decide whether or not a newborn was healthy and to put an end to its life if it was not. In the West at least, they were explicitly allowed to baptize babies in imminent danger of death. Mothers with healthy babies usually felt the impact of their Christian faith first in the form of prohibitions against participating in church services right after birth. In both East and West, women were reminded of the essential impurity that childbirth brought – its taint of blood and sin – by being kept away from church services for up to forty days.[9] Once mothers and their newborns had shed the ritual impurity brought on by birth, however, they could, and increasingly did, participate in baptismal rites. Originally a ritual of death and rebirth, baptism only slowly became associated with the beginning of life.[10] Even in the late fourth century, it was far more likely to be performed at a deathbed than after the birth of a healthy baby, since normally only those who had undergone a long process of preparation and study as catechumens were baptized. By the year 600, though, infant baptism had become an accepted norm across Christendom, and that expectation was passed on to newly Christianized peoples in the early Middle Ages.[11] It may not have been without complications. Evidence from Anglo-Saxon burials suggests that the practice of baptizing infants in danger of death may have fed old fears of the malignity of infant ghosts and even led some to avoid baptizing healthy infants, at least in the early stages of Christianization.[12] Even later, many children must have gone unbaptized for a length of time because of the distance to a baptismal church or lack of concern by their parents. Nevertheless, by the twelfth century, in England as elsewhere, it was generally customary to baptize infants as soon as possible after birth, whether in danger of death or not.[13]

Baptism, especially after confirmation and anointing with chrism, made the recipient a member of a Christian family in an increasingly Christian society. In the East, in fact, children did not receive their complete individual identity until baptism, an attitude that lives on in the rural Greek practice of referring to unbaptized children as simply that male or female child.[14] The power of the ritual to create personhood may have been less intensely felt

8 Riddle, *Contraception and Abortion*.
9 Baun, "Fate of Babies," 115–25.
10 Paxton, "Communities of the Living and the Dead," 52–53.
11 Kelly, *Devil at Baptism*; Cramer, *Baptism and Change*.
12 Crawford, "Children, Death and the Afterlife," 345–53.
13 Orme, *Medieval Children*, 23–24; Cramer, *Baptism and Change*.
14 Baun, "Fate of Babies," 123–24.

in the West, where families named their children after their ancestors, rather than Christian saints, throughout our period, but there is no question that, all over Christendom, baptism became the basis of both social and religious identity in the early Middle Ages.[15] The reform of baptismal practice carried out under Charlemagne in the early ninth century, for example, highlighted the notion that a newly baptized person was not just one of the church faithful but also a *fidelis* of the lords of early medieval society, who used the same word for "vassal."[16] The large body of surviving ninth-century documents designed to instruct parish clergy in the correct procedures for baptism and basic instruction in the faith give eloquent testimony to the seriousness of the Carolingian reformers in reaching as many ordinary Christians as they could.[17] Their success set the foundations for the final stage of Christianization in western Europe, and for the deep interpenetration of religious understanding and social practice at the core of the early medieval economy of salvation, which reached its fullest expression in the tenth and eleventh centuries.

Since infant children could not speak for themselves, it was necessary to have someone else speak for them. At first, a child's parents acted in this capacity, but from the sixth century on, such roles were played increasingly by other adults and, by the eighth century, parents were explicitly forbidden to sponsor infants at baptism in both the Latin and Greek churches.[18] In the process, sponsorship became godparenthood. The characteristic forms of this new social phenomenon arose between the sixth and the tenth centuries and had fully matured by the year 1100. Godparenthood created multiple relationships: between children and their godparents, children and the clerics who baptized them, godchildren and the children of their godparents, and parents and the godparents of their children. The complexities of these bonds allowed great scope for the sacralization of personal relations within overlapping networks of individuals and groups, and thus also for the possibilities of influencing relations among them, defining such things as who could and could not marry, whom one could trust, and who would oversee the development of new members of Christian families and Christian society. The benefits accrued to all parties. Children got potential advocates and protectors outside of their immediate families, parents and churchmen got each other's support in the control and subordination of children, families got to choose the men and

15 Nelson, "Parents, Children, and Church," 105.
16 Keefe, *Water and the Word* 1, 3.
17 Keefe, *Water and the Word* 2.
18 Lynch, *Godparents and Kinship*, 134.

women who would look after their children, and the church got more people to accept the absolute normalcy of baptism as a feature of individual, social, and religious identity.[19] The power of families in this matter is well attested by the church's failure to control the proliferation of sponsors, especially in the West. One was enough for the church, but not for families, a situation that led, for example, to the separation of confirmation from baptism in the Latin church, so that they would have another opportunity to augment the family's spiritual kin with new sponsors.[20]

Although early medieval churchmen legislated against infanticide, they accepted child abandonment as part and parcel of societies living close to subsistence level, especially if the children were left at the doors of churches and monasteries and not simply exposed.[21] Such children, who were usually raised as servants, played at most a small role in the economy of salvation, though. A much larger role was given to children formally granted to religious communities as child oblates. The practice of child oblation grew steadily between the sixth century and the eleventh century, when it peaked. Like baptismal sponsorship and godparenthood, the gift of a child to a church or monastery as an *oblatio* (offering) forged reciprocal relationships between families, in this case, natural and spiritual ones. Oblates were themselves gifts, for they brought with them the promise of a lifetime of service to their new families, but they also helped sustain them through the other gifts that accompanied their entrance into a particular house. At the same time, the cloister gave them the leisure to dedicate a lifetime of prayer to their natural families, living and dead.[22] Such relationships were so highly valued that the wealthiest families almost always endowed their own foundations (*Familienklöster*), where they could be buried, and where a community would be devoted to their spiritual welfare in this life and the next. Kings and emperors also appropriated older houses into their royal or imperial domains, thus increasing the number of men and women dedicated to the care of their souls. Others participated through the oblation of their own children and gifts to existing cloisters, whether aristocratic or royal in origin. Such communities were the clearinghouses of the economy of salvation. They kept the records of the gifts and obligations of the living, and they saw to the acts of faith in this world that brought refreshment to the dead.

19 Nelson, "Parents, Children, and Church," 97–105.
20 Lynch, *Godparents and Kinship*, 205–18; Lynch, *Christianizing Kinship*, 122–34.
21 Boswell, *Kindness of Strangers*, 198–227.
22 Ibid., 228–55; Nelson, "Parents, Children, and the Church," 107–12.

Dying a Christian death

In the world in which Christianity emerged, death, like childbirth, was a private, family affair, which neither physicians nor religious personnel attended. Physicians generally removed themselves when cases became hopeless, and priests and priestesses served their gods, not ordinary people. For a long time, Christian clergy acted no differently, leaving ordinary Christians to practice whatever patterns of behavior were easily carried over into the new faith. Thus, a relative might bestow a final kiss or attempt to catch a dying person's last breath. After death occurred, the living closed the eyes and mouth of the deceased. They then washed the corpse, anointed it with scented oil and herbs, and wrapped it in a shroud or dressed it in clothing befitting the social status of the deceased. A procession, singing psalms if clergy were present, accompanied the body to the burial site outside the city walls. There it was laid to rest, often in a family plot that contained a structure to house the dead. The bereaved commemorated the dead, just as their pre-Christian ancestors had, on the third, ninth, and fortieth days after death, and on anniversaries, often with feasting at their graves.[23]

Things began to change only in the late fourth and fifth centuries. Churchmen preached against displays of worldly wealth and power at the graveside through lavish feasting, urging Christians to direct offerings of food and drink for the dead to the poor instead.[24] They also preached against self-mutilating displays of grief and excessive lamentation: that "disease of females" in the words of the Greek father John Chrysostom.[25] Ambrose of Milan urged baptized Christians to look forward to death with joy, since it meant the end of sin, but some of his younger contemporaries, like Augustine of Hippo, took a different view. Baptism did not guarantee salvation; only God could do that. Thus, the proper response to death ought to be fear – of human sinfulness, and of God's judgment. Such attitudes demanded a pastoral response from the clergy, which came in the form of a final communion as *viaticum* (provisions for a journey), originally granted to penitents by the first ecumenical council at Nicaea (325), and extended to all Christians in the fifth and sixth centuries.[26]

The death rituals that had emerged by the year 600 have persisted in the Greek Orthodox tradition down to the present. They include a final communion and prayers spoken for the dying person that emphasize the shared

23 Freistedt, *Altchristliche Totengedächtnistage*.
24 Agapitos, "La mort à Byzance," 48–49; Brown, *Cult of the Saints*, 23–49.
25 Alexiou, *Ritual Lament*, 28.
26 Rebillard, *In hora mortis*.

mortality of all Christians and strike a balance between awareness of sin and the need for penitence and the celebratory spirit of the Eucharistic liturgy.[27] In the West, the multitude of Christian kingdoms and local churches that emerged in the early Middle Ages fostered the development of a number of innovations in ritual responses to death and dying. In the seventh century, the Spanish, Visigothic Church developed an elaborate rite of deathbed penance that transformed the body and soul so radically that anyone who subsequently recovered was required to retire to a monastery for life. In Ireland, where Mosaic traditions of ritual purity deeply influenced the clergy, priests transformed a Gallican ritual of anointing the sick into a rite of preparation for death, laying the groundwork for what would become, in the twelfth century, the sacrament of extreme unction. In Frankish Gaul and in Anglo-Saxon England, the popularity of Pope Gregory the Great's *Dialogues*, with its stories about the power of the mass to ease the suffering of the faithful departed, led to the invention and proliferation of votive masses for the dead.[28] In the seventh and eighth centuries, Irish and Anglo-Saxon missionaries began to contract with one another, and with their monastic communities at home, for specific numbers of prayers, psalms, and masses after death. Around the year 800, Carolingian ritual books start including a rite for the death agony that may have its origins in eastern monastic traditions of apotropaic psalm singing at the soul's most "dangerous hour."[29] To aid the dying through the final struggle and keep demonic forces at bay, the community chanted the names of the denizens of paradise. Rhythmically calling on the Trinity, Mary, the angels, the prophets and patriarchs, the martyrs and confessors, and all living holy men and women, they wove a web of sung prayer to aid the soul's passing.

The reform of church and society undertaken by the Carolingian kings and emperors in the later eighth and ninth centuries led to the synthesis of all these different developments.[30] The rhetoric of the reform favored Roman traditions, and the Carolingians succeeded in making the Mass and certain elements of clerical and monastic culture, like chant, conform to Roman practice (real or imagined). When it came to death and dying, though, Rome provided only one piece of the Carolingian ritual synthesis, albeit an important one: an old Roman death ritual whose origins lay in the triumphant Christianity of the late empire. The rite refers to deathbed communion not as *viaticum* but as

27 Fedwick, "Death and Dying," 153–57; Abrahamse, "Rituals of Death," 125–29.
28 Angenendt, "*Missa specialis*," 153–221.
29 Abrahamse, "Rituals of Death," 128–29.
30 Paxton, *Christianizing Death*.

"a defender and advocate at the resurrection of the just," and to the bread and wine not as provisions for the soul's journey to the other world, but as a sign of its membership in the community of the saved, to be rendered at the Last Judgment.[31] The history of this Roman ritual is obscure, but its long-term survival attests to the fact that the Augustinian position did not sweep away all traces of early Christian optimism about death and dying in the Latin West. Its triumphant psalmody and salvation theology must have struck a chord in a church supported by powerful and pious men who saw themselves as heirs to the kings of Israel and the Christian emperors of antiquity. Its incorporation into the Carolingian synthesis gave the Latin rites some of the same balance and complexity as their eastern counterparts, so that fear of judgment did not overwhelm hope of forgiveness.

The Carolingian reformers resisted the anointing of the dying (for which they saw no scriptural basis), but deathbed anointing came into general use anyway, often via Irish texts and traditions, in the course of the ninth and tenth centuries. They had hoped to create community through shared ritual, but communities shaped ritual as much as ritual shaped communities. The synthesis that resulted from their activities reflected not just their official stance, but also all the myriad traditions of the local churches that flowed into and out of their vast realm. By the end of the ninth century, a rite for the dying had emerged that blended the triumphant psalmody of imperial Christianity with the concern for penance and purification of the early medieval world in a common tradition that also included rites of penance, absolution, anointing, and communion – each of which helped cut the ties that bound the dying to this world, ritually preparing them for entry into paradise.

The community of the living and the dead

However difficult the contemplation (or moment) of death might have been, early medieval Christians continually invented new ways of establishing and maintaining community with the dead. The most important was the cult of the saints, the "very special dead," who acted as powerful, and powerfully present, patrons of individuals and families, both natural and spiritual. The integrity of their relics (their resistance to decomposition) and their power to cure the sick were both proof of the resurrection and a powerful antidote to the fear of disintegration in the face of death.[32] The rise of the cult of the

31 Ibid., 37–44.
32 Brown, *Cult of the Saints*; Bynum, *Resurrection of the Body*, 59–114.

saints, more than any other factor, is responsible for the initial dissolution of the ancient boundaries between the cities of the living and the tombs of the dead, which lay outside the walls. On the one hand, shrines in honor of the saints brought people to worship, and eventually to settle, in cemeteries. Such settlements often then became the core of new urban centers, a process that can clearly be seen at work in the city of Tours on the Loire river.[33] On the other hand, first in the form of saints' relics, and then in the bodies of those who wished to be buried near them, the dead began coming to rest inside the walls, a process whose origins can be traced to the decisions of men like the Emperor Constantius, who brought relics of the apostles Luke and Andrew to Constantinople in 357, and Bishop Ambrose of Milan, who brought relics of Bolognese martyrs into the city in 393–94, some of which he then sent on to Bishop Victricius of Rouen.[34] After the year 600, bishops were regularly buried in the cathedral churches that they served.[35] In the newly Christianized and predominantly rural lands of the north, the relics of the saints attracted the bodies of the dead to the churches and churchyard cemeteries of the emerging parish system. Essentially complete by the year 1100, this process caused a clean break with antiquity and reconfigured the landscape of Christendom.

The coming together of the living and the dead occurred less by design than by happenstance, since old laws prohibiting burial inside city walls remained on the books for centuries, and the process proceeded differently in different places. In Constantinople, for example, the cemeteries established outside the Constantinian walls ended up within the walls built a century later by Theodosius II. The dead were still kept out of the old Constantinian center, but they happily resided between the old and new walls to the west. Elsewhere in the East old patterns persisted, although the demographic contractions that followed the Justinianic plague and the coming of the Slavs in the period after 600 led cities like Corinth, Athens, and Sardis to bury their dead in the center of town.[36] In the West, the boundaries fell everywhere. The process is best documented in Anglo-Saxon England. The spectacular but enigmatic seventh-century burials at Sutton Hoo may have actually been a response to the spread of Christianity, as "pro-Scandinavian, anti-Christian" kings poured the wealth gained from increased taxation and control over trading into elaborate burial goods and funeral rites designed to counteract the influence of the new faith.[37]

33 Galinié, "Tours."
34 Paxton, "Communities of the Living and the Dead," 57–58.
35 Picard, *Les souvenirs des évêques*, 347–55.
36 Dagron, "Le christianisme," 11–19; Ivison, "Burial and Urbanism."
37 Carver, "Cemetery and Society."

In the eighth century, pagan burials ceased in England and the Christian dead began to cluster around churches in simple, unfurnished graves. The arrival of pagan Vikings in the ninth and later tenth centuries only brought a temporary and localized return of alternative practices, for the new populations were quickly absorbed into Christian society.[38] As elsewhere, the completion of the Christianization of England coincided almost exactly with the universal practice of burials in and around churches, both urban and rural.[39]

The space of Christian society, however, only encompassed the living and those who died in good standing with the community. In both East and West, burials were placed according to a moral scale, with the holiest of the dead at the center and others around them in proportion to their own claims to holiness: saints, bishops, abbots, monks, and pious (and wealthy) lay men and women.[40] The Carolingians tried to change things by prohibiting church burials and ostentatiously choosing humble locations for their own resting places, far from the altars and the relics of the saints, but without much success.[41] For the most part, the medieval economy of death reproduced the social hierarchies of the living. Those not in good standing, like suicides, murderers, the excommunicated, and heretics, were relegated to unconsecrated ground away from both living and dead Christians. Research on Anglo-Saxon cemeteries, for example, has revealed the widespread presence of execution sites and cemeteries along parish boundaries, often in conjunction with ancient barrows. The un-Christian dead were left to the demons and dragons who haunted the spaces of the pre-Christian dead.[42]

Remembering and forgetting the dead

Once the dead were buried, attention turned to rites of incorporation, especially those commemorative practices that were designed to usher the soul into the community of the blessed dead. The ancient practice of commemorating the dead on the third, ninth, and fortieth days after death has persisted in all the eastern churches right up to the present. Commemoration on the third day persisted as well in the West because of the symbolism of the resurrection. Latin clerics, however, associated the ninth day with a pre-Christian Roman practice and so replaced it with the seventh day in honor of the Sabbath.

38 Daniell and Thompson, "Pagans and Christians," 65–89.
39 Bullough, "Burial, Community and Belief."
40 Dagron, "Le christianisme," 17–19; McLaughlin, *Consorting with Saints*, 113–32.
41 Dierkens, "Autour de la tombe de Charlemagne."
42 Reynolds, "Definition and Ideology," 33–41.

Aristotle taught that male embryos were ensouled after forty days, and Greek traditions held that it took forty days for the flesh of a corpse to decompose. Thus, the Christian commemoration on the fortieth day after death is rooted in a conception of life that began in the womb and ended in the tomb.[43] Latin clerics, however, replaced the commemoration on the fortieth day with the thirtieth. This change first was recommended in Gregory the Great's *Dialogues*. He proposed offering masses on seven and thirty consecutive days after death, known as the *septinarius* and *tricenarius*, which became a characteristic feature of early medieval monastic commemorations.[44] The forty-day period did survive in the Latin church, however, in the forty days of the Lenten period, which correspond to the ancient period of formal preparation for baptism on Easter, and in the forty days that women who had given birth had to wait before they could return to church services, so even there the ties between the beginnings and ends of mortal life persisted.

Between 760 and 762, a group of churchmen at the Carolingian royal villa of Attigny officially committed themselves to mutual commemoration after death. Not long afterwards, monastic congregations began to make similar arrangements with other houses. They also began to allow lay men and women to take vows at the end of life, so as to die in the monastic infirmary and be buried in the community's cemetery, and to record the names of all the participants in books, which grew to include as many as 40,000 entries by the twelfth century.[45] When alms for the poor were added to the psalms and masses sung for the dead, the final piece was in place in the early medieval economy of salvation. Cloistered men and women, themselves "dead to this world," and linked to a web of living and dead benefactors, mediated these exchanges. They accepted gifts to the poor (among whom they included themselves) in exchange for prayers for the souls of the givers and their dead relatives, who had been spiritually accepted into the monastic or ecclesiastical *familia*. They may have acted as much out of anxiety as out of confidence in the face of death, but whatever their motivations, their actions, like the actions of the saints, helped bind together the community of the living and the dead.

The ultimate goal of Christian commemoration was, however, not remembering but actually forgetting the dead, laying them to rest so that the living could go on with life. All the elements of the early medieval economy of salvation were directed at this end: "to help the living separate from the dead, to shorten the latter's stay in purgatorial punishment . . . and finally to enable the

43 Freistedt, *Altchristliche Totengedächtnistage*, 179–97.
44 Ibid., 34–35; McLaughlin, *Consorting with Saints*, 50–54.
45 Huyghebaert and Lemaître, *Les documents necrologiques*.

living to forget the deceased."[46] In the process families formed and reformed around the memories of their dead, especially in the tenth and eleventh centuries, when rapid social change brought new families to the forefront of Latin Christendom, families whose *memoriae* represented their sense of their own history and future.[47] Furthermore, as often as not, women played important roles in maintaining family memorials. In Germany, in particular, control over who remembered and prayed for the dead, and even for whom and to whom they prayed, remained primarily a family, even a female, affair, right through the end of the period under consideration.[48]

Taken up by the monastic reform movements of the tenth and eleventh centuries, the early medieval economy of salvation reached its most developed form at the Burgundian monastery of Cluny, which was at the epicenter of what may have been the densest network of relations between the living and the dead ever produced in Christendom. Cluny took in the most oblates, and the greatest number of gifts from donors, and buried and commemorated the most monks and laity of any church in Christendom.[49] This was especially true under Abbot Odilo (994–1049), who also established the feast of All Souls, thereby extending the benefits of Cluny's prayers to all Christians everywhere, and oversaw the maturation of Cluny's own highly developed death rituals, burial practices, and forms of commemoration.[50] By the end of the eleventh century the monks were engaged almost continuously in services for the dead and fed, clothed, and cared for thousands upon thousands in their names.

As the early medieval economy of salvation peaked, however, opposition to some of its central features began to emerge. The first indications came from Bulgaria, where late tenth-century religious dissenters, who followed a priest called Bogomil, rejected, among other things, baptism, especially the baptism of children, the authority of priests, and the cult of relics.[51] In the West, after the year 1000, other voices were raised against infant baptism, tithes, relics, and the efficacy of both Christian burial and prayers for the dead.[52] In all cases, those who advocated such views were called heretics. Even from within the Benedictine monastic tradition, the tide was turning. While the Cistercians

46 Schmitt, *Ghosts*, 5–6.
47 Geary, *Phantoms of Remembrance*, 48–80.
48 Althoff, "Gandersheim und Quedlinburg"; Innes, "Keeping it in the Family."
49 Iogna-Prat, "Des morts très spéciaux aux morts ordinaires" and "Les morts"; Poeck, "Laienbegräbnisse."
50 Paxton, "Death by Customary."
51 Peters, *Heresy and Authority*, 108–17.
52 Wakefield and Evans, *Heresies*, 71–121.

did not reject all the features of the Cluniac model, their intent to escape the ties that bound the old Benedictines to the aristocracy and the long hours in commemorative services that precluded private prayer and contemplation proved a powerful draw and weakened the hold of the old system. In the early twelfth century, Abbot Peter the Venerable had to defend Cluniac ways not just against the Cistercians, but also against radical dissenters like Henry of Lausanne and Peter of Bruys, who rejected infant baptism and the whole structure of the economy of salvation, arguing that there was nothing the living could do for the dead.[53]

As much as the leaders of Christendom wanted all Christians to think of themselves as related through baptism, and to understand death, dying, and the dead in Christian terms, over the course of the five hundred years between the sixth and the twelfth centuries they had brought these most intimate of family matters under their influence only slowly, and only in so far as they met the needs of Christian families. As the gift economy of the early Middle Ages gave way to a profit economy, new specialists, like the friars, and new ways to contract for care of the dead emerged.[54] One of them, the granting of indulgences, eventually helped spark the dismantling of much of the economy of salvation in the Protestant Reformation. Nevertheless, the products of the early Middle Ages were significant and lasting. The degree to which the faithful thought of birth, death, and the dead in Christian terms must have ranged widely, but there were no serious alternatives. Without replacing midwives with clerics at the births of children, baptism had become essential not just to one's identity as a Christian, but also to one's social identity, in a culture that was thoroughly, if never quite completely, Christian. Godparenthood had taken its place as a fundamental social institution, one that established lifelong relationships between children and their godmothers and godfathers, and between the families to which each belonged. Other relationships – with men and women in cloistered communities, and the saints they served – remained central to the culture of Christendom, even as the practice of child oblation waned. By the twelfth century, most ordinary Christians, in any sense of the word, sought baptism for their newborn children, confession and other sacraments before death, burial in consecrated ground, and liturgical commemoration by religious specialists afterwards. The Christian dead everywhere shared the same space as the living and the living regarded the

53 Iogna-Prat, *Ordonner et exclure*, 113–23.
54 Schmitt, *Ghosts*, 123–38; Little, *Religious Poverty*.

dead as continuing members of their families and communities who expected to receive their attention and their help. Reformers questioned some features of this system and others rejected many of them outright, but the medieval Christian culture of birth and death was essentially in place. The best evidence of this is the fact that, by the year 1100, those who resisted any of its elements, from infant baptism to prayer for the dead, were considered both heretics and rebels against the prevailing social order.

19
Remedies for sins

ROB MEENS

Man is a sinful creature. Even in paradise man sinned by disobeying the command of his Lord. After the Fall, man not only sinned in thoughts, words, and deeds, but was also affected by original sin. Christian grace was able to dispense with original sin through the ritual of baptism, but although the average Christian may have wanted desperately to abide by divine rules, in practice he never succeeded completely in doing so. Only a handful of saints were able to avoid every kind of sin. Therefore, one had to decide how to deal with sin. In the period we are dealing with here – the period from the sixth to the twelfth century – we can discern important developments in the way Christians tried to handle this question.

When the Irish abbot Cummian (fl. c. 632), in the seventh century, wrote a preface to his collection of penitential decisions, he listed twelve remedies for sins, or "remedies of wounds," as he called them. He presented these with biblical citations bolstering their effectiveness. The list of remedies starts with baptism, and continues with the virtue of love (*caritas*), the fruit of alms, the shedding of tears, the confession of crimes, the affliction of the heart and body, the emendations of one's ways, the intercession of saints, the merits of mercy and faith, the conversion and salvation of others, pardoning others for their sins, and finally, the passion of martyrdom.[1] Cummian did not invent this list of remedies, but based it on an earlier work, the *Collationes* of John Cassian (c. 360–430), one of the founding fathers of western monasticism.[2] Since Cassian's work and Cummian's preface were widely read in the early medieval West, this list was fairly well known. Another list of remedies for sins circulating in the early Middle Ages was based on the Greek church father Origen (c. 185–c. 254), who listed seven remedies in his homily on the book of Leviticus. These were: baptism, martyrdom, the giving of alms, pardoning others, amending

1 *Irish Penitentials*, 108–10.
2 John Cassian, Conlatio XX.8 in his *Conlationes XXIIII*.

other people's lives through preaching or good works, the abundance of love, and finally, by doing penance (*per paenitentiam*). According to Origen, the last remedy was particularly hard and difficult (*dura et laboriosa*).[3] Origen's list was known in the East and the West. In the Latin West it was adopted by Theodulf (c. 750–821), the ninth century bishop of Orleans, in his episcopal statute (and by his successor as bishop of Orleans, Jonas (c. 760–c. 841), in his educational treatise for the laity, known as *De institutione laicali*) but it also circulated as an independent treatise.[4] The main difference between these two lists is the absence of the formal rite of penance in the longer list. Neither Cassian nor Cummian mention the formal ecclesiastical procedure whereby sins could be forgiven. The fact that Cassian does not mention the rite of penance can be explained by the fact that he wrote his *Collationes* for monks, who already would be living the lives of penitents and, therefore, for whom formal penance was not a necessity. The omission of formal penance by Cummian, who also wrote mainly for a monastic audience, may have a different reason; it may indicate that in seventh-century Ireland such a procedure was not well established.

The lists of Origen and Cassian refer to several means of receiving remission of sins, oscillating between feelings of love (i.e., the love of God or one's neighbor) or the shedding of tears and formal rites like those of baptism and penance. In the more formal ecclesiastical procedures, which will serve as the core for discussion in this essay, most of these elements will play particular roles. Yet, we have to keep in mind that informal means of remedying sins have always been of great importance and that formal ways of doing penance are not always easy to distinguish from informal ones.[5] In Merovingian monasteries abbesses and senior nuns seem to have taken part in the penitential process, hearing confessions and assigning penances to the nuns in the convent, and possibly also to men and women outside the monastery. One could call this a formal way of doing penance, yet Carolingian bishops would certainly object severely to such a practice.[6]

Baptism, martyrdom, and public penance

Let us begin with the rite mentioned by Cassian and Origen (and all the subsequent authors using their work) as the first and apparently the most

3 Origen, *Homélies sur le Lévitique*, II.4, in *SC* 286, 108–10.

4 Theodulf of Orleans, *Capitula Episcoporum* 1, 134–35; Jonas of Orleans, *De Institutione Laicali*, I.5, 130C–131B; for its independent circulation, see Brommer, "Die bischöfliche Gesetzgebung."

5 Price, "Informal Penance."

6 Muschiol, "Men, Women, and Liturgical Practice," 210–11.

important one: the rite of baptism. Baptism, of course, had many connotations, but the idea of conversion had always been at its center. The basic notion of turning away from one's evil ways to a life devoted to God is symbolized by images of death and rebirth, just as the symbolism of purification points at the forgiveness of all former sins.[7] There is no evidence, however, from the period after 600 that baptism was being postponed to profit from its sin-forgiving qualities. After the general acceptance of the practice of infant baptism and the development of separate rites for doing penance, the practice of "clinical baptism" seems to have declined and disappeared.[8] That the idea of baptism and the absolution of sins was important in the context of the Christianization process of the peoples of northwestern Europe is shown by the penitential of Archbishop Theodore of Canterbury (668–90), written in the second half of the seventh century; a text which proved its usefulness for the missions among the Germanic peoples on the European mainland. Theodore stressed that in baptism sins are remitted, but that baptism does not terminate existing marriages.[9] Another text, clearly in use in a missionary field, made the same point a bit differently when it stated that people who had contracted a sinful marriage before they were converted to Christianity were not to be separated because their sins had been forgiven by baptism.[10] In Carolingian times, however, baptism seems to have lost much of this meaning. In the wealth of texts emanating from the inquest of Charlemagne on baptism, the stress is much more on baptism as an instrument of instruction and education and on the ritual itself. Remission of sins does not seem to have been at the forefront of the authors' minds in these texts.[11]

The second way mentioned by Origen to gain absolution of one's sins was that of martyrdom. Such "baptism in blood" was regarded as the most perfect kind of baptism which forgave all sins and brought the martyr into immediate communion with God. After their deaths, martyrs were regarded as favored intercessors between God and ordinary believers. In Late Antiquity they could even act as intercessors before their execution and thus help people in relieving the burden of their penance.[12] In the early Middle Ages, martyrdom was no real option in the Latin West – which may be reflected in Cassian mentioning martyrdom as the last means to obtain remission of sins,

7 Cramer, *Baptism and Change*.
8 See Lynch, *Christianizing Kinship*; Angenendt, *Geschichte der Religiosität*, 463–71.
9 Theodore of Canterbury, *Penitential*, II.4.1, 316.
10 *Paenitentialie Oxoniense II*, ch. 3 in *Paenitentialia minora*, 191; cf. Meens, "Christentum und Heidentum," 426.
11 Keefe, *Water and the Word*.
12 Poschmann, *Penance*, 76–77; Angenendt, *Geschichte der Religiosität*, 629.

whereas Origen had mentioned it as the second way to do so – but bloodless martyrdom, in the form of choosing an ascetic religious life, was an option. Conversion to a religious life amounted to choosing a life filled with penitential exercises, and the terms *conversio* and penance could be used interchangeably. Probably for this reason the ritual of public penance was not applicable for clerics and monks. Their conversion was already their second baptism and there was, therefore, no need for another second baptism: the ritual of formal penance.

By the year 600 we find in most regions some evidence for the existence of a public ritual for the absolution of serious sins committed by Christians, although it is questionable whether there ever existed a uniform Christian system of public penance which can be reconstructed on the basis of sources such as decisions of church councils or the work of Augustine of Hippo (354–430). A ritual for public penance continued to exist in seventh-century Armenia, with two grades of penitents, but in contrast to the system as we know it from the Latin West, in the Armenian church the rites of penance were no episcopal prerogative and could be administered by a priest or a teacher (*vardapet*).[13] In the Byzantine world there are signs that at least knowledge of public penance was still in existence, although there is no proof that such rites were still put into practice.[14] In the Greek monasteries it had become part of the daily routine to open up one's conscience to a more experienced fellow soldier in Christ and receive spiritual direction.[15] In due course this monastic practice would spread to the lay world and monks would become the favored soulmates, acting as confessors to a lay audience.[16] In the West, in the countries of Gaul, Spain, and Italy, rites of public penance were apparently not a regular feature of religious life by the year 600. One may even ask whether they ever had been. By the year 600 in Gaul, the ritual seems to have functioned mainly as a preparation for death, the so-called deathbed penance.[17] We do encounter elements taken from such a ritual, however, in the historical and hagiographical works of Gregory of Tours (d. 594), where they were sometimes used in a highly politicized setting. Kings and bishops in Merovingian Gaul used the ritual vocabulary of penance for political purposes, as their Carolingian successors would continue to do.[18]

13 Carr, "Penance," 65–69.
14 Holl, *Enthusiasmus und Bußgewalt*, 279–88.
15 Stewart, "Desert Fathers"; Hausherr, *Spiritual Direction*.
16 Holl, *Enthusiasmus und Bußgewalt*.
17 Vogel, *La discipline pénitentielle en Gaule des origines à la fin du VIIe siècle*.
18 E.g., Gregory of Tours, *Historiae*, VIII.20; cf. Buc, *Dangers of Ritual*, 104–106.

Tariffs for sins

Whereas in the regions which had once belonged to the Roman Empire some form of public penance ritual seems to have left its mark, this does not seem to have been the case in Ireland, which had never been part of the *Imperium Romanum*. In Ireland the role of bishops was less dominant than in Gaul or Spain, and ecclesiastical life was much more focused on monasteries.[19] From the sixth century onward we find texts written in a monastic setting that were meant for hearing confessions from lay folk. Just as in the Byzantine world, their spiritual authority turned monks into favored confessors who attracted sinners from the world outside the monastery. The oldest texts, the *Paenitentiale Ambrosianum* and the penitential of Finnian (d. 549) – both of them known in Ireland at a very early stage, although not necessarily written there – show clear signs of their monastic background, but they are undoubtedly meant to be used for lay people as well. Finnian's penitential, for example, prescribes a half-year of fasting on bread and water for a cleric plotting to hurt or kill his fellow man, but only a week of penance for a layman doing such a thing, because "since he is a man of this world, his guilt is lighter in this world and his reward is less in the world to come."[20] These texts list many sins and their appropriate atonement as an aid to the confessor for deciding on the kind of penance to be imposed on a contrite sinner. They deal with violent acts like murder or maiming someone, but also, as in the case above, with the intention to hurt someone without acting upon this intention. Another central topic in these texts concerns human sexuality, which is regulated in a detailed sexual code.[21] How far such a practice of confessing one's sins penetrated into early Irish society is hard to establish. The Old Irish laws, for example, although showing some signs of ecclesiastical influence, allow divorce and remarriage, whereas the Irish penitential texts display very strict standards regarding marriage and divorce and did not allow any form of divorce.[22] This suggests that the influence of the monastic practice of regular confession remained rather limited.

Peter Brown has recently suggested that the carefully balanced way of dealing with sin and penance that we encounter in penitential texts of this kind reflected ideas of authority and power in the societies where such texts originated. Whereas in late Roman society imperial ideas associated with justice,

19 See Charles-Edwards in this volume.

20 *Paenitentiale Vinniani*, chs. 6–7, in *Irish Penitentials*; citation in ch. 7: "quia homo seculi huius est, culpa levior in hoc mundo et premium minus in futuro," 76.

21 Payer, *Sex and the Penitentials*; Lutterbach, *Sexualität im Mittelalter*.

22 Charles-Edwards, *Early Christian Ireland*, 111–12.

grace, and amnesty lay behind the grandiose rituals of public penance, in Ireland and the surrounding Celtic kingdoms social order was much less differentiated and hierarchical. Peace was maintained in a "horizontal way" through a constant process of mediation and negotiation, and this social process was reflected in conceptions of sin and redemption. And, as sins were regarded as an insult to God, in a society where honor and insult were basic notions around which social relations revolved, God could not forgive any sin, not even those committed unknowingly.[23] This is an attractive way of looking at the careful tariffing of sins which we encounter in penitential handbooks, a tariffing which has in the past been compared to the legal obligations in the so-called barbarian laws, in which the payment of a certain sum as compensation ought to prevent the offended party from starting a feud.

In the days when Pope Gregory the Great (590–604) was sketching the contours of the "au-delà" in which the minor sins (*parva minimaque peccata*), even when committed unknowingly, had to be erased by a purgatorial fire, the Irish monk Columbanus (d. 615) brought the *medicamenta paenitentiae*, as they had been developed in Ireland, to the Continent.[24] Following the typical Irish impulse to leave his home country for the sake of God – the ideal of the *peregrinatio per Dei* – Columbanus went to Gaul, where he made a grand impression on the Merovingian kings and nobles. His ascetic way of life, his rigorous stand in questions of morality, and the *medicamenta paenitentiae* attracted followers as well as material support, which enabled him to found a monastic *familia*. According to his biographer, Jonas of Bobbio (d. c. 659), he arrived in a penitential wasteland, an assertion that was certainly an overstatement. There had been efforts to renew ecclesiastical discipline and the moral life of the laity, particularly in Burgundy in the decades before Columbanus arrived there.[25] In Gaul forms of doing penance without undergoing the public ritual of formal penance before the bishop had already been introduced, at least since the days of Caesarius of Arles (d. 542), who had distinguished between *paenitentiam accipere* and *paenitentiam agere*, the former indicating a formal entry into the state of a penitent, the latter the informal ways to atone for one's sins, such as giving alms and fasting.[26] In some respects, Columbanus, therefore, connected with existing tendencies in Merovingian Gaul, and recently his impact on the

23 Brown, "Vers la naissance du purgatoire"; Angenendt, "Deus, qui nullum peccatum impunitum dimittit."

24 Gregory the Great, *Dialogi*, IV.41 (*SC* 265); see Le Goff, *La naissance du purgatoire*, 121–31; Carozzi, *Le voyage de l'âme*, 43–61.

25 Meens, "Reforming the Clergy," 160–64.

26 Caesarius of Arles, sermo 67.1; see Vogel, *La discipline pénitentielle en Gaule des origines à la fin du VIIe siècle*; Klingshirn, *Caesarius of Arles*, 155.

area and his role as a "penitential innovator" have been reassessed.[27] Yet the fact that Jonas of Bobbio, forty years after Columbanus's death, chose to highlight the penitential innovation of the Irish monk cannot be easily overlooked. Penance is not only a central theme in the work of Jonas, but also in the *Regula Coenobialis* of Columbanus himself. Moreover, Columbanus composed a penitential handbook for use outside the monastery, a text which we know only from two late copies made in the monastery of Bobbio, but which influenced a great many later works of this genre. We must therefore conclude that for Columbanus, monasticism and penance were closely linked. In his foundations and the many monasteries influenced by his example the practice of confessing one's sins was not confined to the monastery itself; people (clerics and lay) seem to have flocked to the monastery to confess their sins. The fact that two public penitents, Bishop Leudegar of Autun (c. 616–79) and the mayor of the palace Ebroin (d. 680/1), fulfilled a penitential exile in Columbanus's foundation of Luxeuil should therefore not really surprise us.[28] There must have been something new which attracted men and women to Columbanus's foundations. One of these innovations probably was the fact that the person hearing confession was well equipped to do so and that on the other hand the sinner could be reassured that, after confession and penance, his or her sins were indeed forgiven. Both of these aspects were enhanced by the purity of the Columbanian monks within their strict enclosure, which not only enhanced their reputation but also their status as intercessors.[29] The fact that the foundations of Columbanus and his Irish (and later Anglo-Saxon) fellow *peregrini* were mostly located in the countryside made them attractive instruments for the Christianization of the less-Romanized northern and eastern parts of the Frankish world.

Irish missionary activity also must have spread the practice of hearing confession in a more private setting into England from the seventh century onward. The Venerable Bede (d. 735) described in a somewhat idealized fashion how Cuthbert (c. 636–87), when prior of the monastery of Melrose, regularly rode out to visit neighboring villages to preach the proper way of life. He did so in such a convincing way that nobody in the audience "would presume to hide from him the secrets of their hearts, but they all made open confession of their sins because they realized that these things could certainly never be hidden from him; and they cleansed themselves from the sins they had confessed by

27 Dierkens, "Prolegomènes"; de Jong, "Transformations," 215–17.
28 Cf. de Jong, "Transformations," 215; cf. de Jong, "What Was Public," 877–80.
29 See Diem, *Das monastische Experiment*; Rosenwein, *Negotiating Space*.

fruits worthy of repentance, as he bade them to do."[30] This passage shows how monasteries could serve as centers for pastoral care in neighboring villages, and particularly how important the arts of preaching and hearing confession were for parish pastoral care.[31] In a *Life* of his former abbot Boniface (c. 675–754), Willibald (fl. 760s) describes how priests and clerics went out to preach in villages and homes in England.[32] In the Anglo-Saxon mission to the Continent, preaching and penance seem to have been closely linked as the sermons attributed to Boniface show.[33] Irish penitential texts must have circulated in England, but the only trace we can find of them is in the penitential handbook composed by Theodore of Canterbury, written in the second half of the seventh century, who used a *scottorum libellus*, an Irish booklet.[34] Theodore, who grew up in the Byzantine East, spent a considerable span of time in a Greek monastery in Rome before being sent to England to become archbishop of the English church.[35] Although he did not always agree with ecclesiastical customs in England derived from Irish practices, he had no problem with the Irish way of hearing confession, although he remarked on the absence of formal penance and public reconciliation of sinners: "in this province [England] there is no public ritual of reconciliation, because there exists no public penance."[36] He further objected to monks hearing confession since this was the privilege of secular clerics; an objection that underscores the role that monks in England played in the practice of hearing confessions.[37] But although Theodore observed the differences with ecclesiastical customs as he had come to know them in Rome and the Greek East, he had no fundamental objections to the custom of hearing confession as it had been introduced into England from Ireland. Although differing in points of detail, his penitential is written in the tradition of the older Irish texts. He also pays tribute to the eastern tradition as represented in the canonical *Letters* of Basil the Great (c. 330–79).[38]

This way of hearing confession, which had its origins in Ireland and its neighboring regions and was subsequently transported to Gaul and England, is often called "tariffed penance" after the tariffs to be found in penitential handbooks. Others speak of "private penance," which is somewhat misleading,

30 Bede, *HE*, IV.27, 433.
31 Blair and Sharpe, *Pastoral Care*.
32 Willibald, *Vita Bonifatii*, ch. 1, 460.
33 Pseudo-Bonifatius, *Sermones*.
34 Theodore of Canterbury, *Penitential*, preface, 287–88.
35 On Theodore's career, see Lapidge, *Archbishop Theodore*.
36 Theodore of Canterbury, *Penitential*, I.13.4, 306.
37 Ibid., II.6.15, 321: "Nec non libertas monasterii est penitentiam secularibus iudicandam quia proprie clericorum est.
38 Basil the Great, *Letters* 188, 199, and 217, vol. 2: 120–31, 154–64, 208–17.

since there often was a great deal of publicity involved, or of secret penance, as it is known in some sources.[39] We can follow the trail of the early medieval penitentials through their affiliations and manuscript tradition to see how this penitential tradition followed in the footsteps of Columbanus and his followers, then spread to the northern French and eastern Frankish regions in the Rhineland and southern Germany. Whether penitentials spread from Columbanus's foundation at Bobbio in northern Italy, or were introduced in Italy from Francia in the wake of the Carolingian domination of this region, remains uncertain. In Spain the latter was clearly the case.[40] In Rome and southern Italy penitentials were used only from the tenth century onward, to judge from the texts and manuscripts that have come down to us. In England penitentials seem to have been reintroduced from Francia in the wake of the recovery from the Viking invasions under King Alfred the Great (871–99) and his successors. All the penitentials in England from the tenth century show signs of Carolingian influence. The Carolingian penitential of Halitgar of Cambrai (817–31) was even translated into Old English.[41]

Bishops and monks

The manuscripts containing penitentials show a remarkable increase in numbers from the second half of the eighth century onward. It seems, therefore, that the attempts of the Carolingian kings to strengthen the role of Christianity in their kingdom (attempts which are known as the Carolingian Renaissance or Carolingian Reforms) had an impact on the production of pastoral manuscripts containing such works and, we may infer, on the impact of the process of penance. We have already seen how Carolingian reformers were discussing the proper form of baptism, and it may come as no surprise that they also argued about penance and confession. The introduction of new authoritative texts, which were attributed to Irish abbots such as Finnian or Cummian, or were transmitted anonymously, had been unproblematic. Penitentials had been appended to canon law collections, such as the *Collectio Vetus Gallica*, while canons from such collections had been incorporated into penitentials and the other way around. In the beginning of the ninth century Carolingian bishops started to question the authority of these texts. In particular, the fact that they were often anonymous and that the penances prescribed showed a certain variety seems to have been a cause of criticism. This is also the time

39 De Jong, "What Was Public."
40 Bezler, *Les pénitentiels espagnols*.
41 Frantzen, *Literature of Penance*; Delen et al., "*Paenitentiale Cantabrigiense*."

that bishops started to increase their grip on the local clergy by composing special works for their instruction: the so-called *Capitula episcoporum*.[42] Moreover, Carolingian bishops tried to reconstruct what they thought was the ancient Christian way of handling penitents: public penance. Their "invention of tradition" in this respect seems to have deluded historians in their perception of late antique Christian penance.[43] The Carolingian bishops introduced the distinction of public versus secret in the field of penance, arguing that sins that had remained secret could be atoned for in a secret way, while sins of a public nature needed correction under episcopal control through the ritual of public penance. Only at this point did it seem that people became aware of the difference from the ancient rite of public penance as it was described in canon law collections or sacramentaries, a difference which, for example, Boniface and Pope Zachary (741–52) had not been aware of, when discussing the possibility of reinstating a penitent priest.[44]

While in the ninth century Carolingian bishops strengthened their grip on formal ways of doing penance, in Byzantium things developed in a different direction. In the West bishops stressed traditions of authority as transmitted in texts, whereas in the East, for monks like Theodore the Studite (d. 826), authority was first of all embodied in living men. The exemplary life of hermits or leaders of monasteries was as authoritative as texts, since God's commandments were expressed in conduct as well as in texts.[45] Since monks were following the traditions and examples of the Holy Fathers, who imitated the life of Christ himself, they must be following God's commandments. In the West the emphasis on authority and texts led to a strengthening of the ecclesiastical hierarchy as embodied in bishops and priests, while in the East the hierarchy had been discredited by the iconoclast movement, in which monks like Theodore the Studite had exemplified the virtues of the monastic life. After the iconoclastic controversy monks in Byzantium seem to have dominated the practice of penance, in contrast to developments in the West, where Carolingian bishops tried to gain more control in this field. In the West rules regarding the handling of sin had been put into writing in penitentials, while in the East spiritual fathers trusted more in their own abilities to guide a sinner. Therefore, we have no early penitential handbooks from the East. The so-called "canonical letters" of Basil the Great, in which the Cappadocian father

42 Brommer, *"Capitula Episcoporum." Die bischöflichen Kapitularien*; van Rhijn, *Shepherds of the Lord*.
43 De Jong, "Transformations."
44 Boniface, letter 91 (to Egbert of York), 378, 380, in *Briefe des Bonifatius*; Zachary, *Letter*.
45 Cholij, *Theodore the Stoudite*, 98.

had laid down rules for handling sinners, were probably still being read and used in the East, but we do not know exactly where they were being used or how they were understood. The fact, however, that Theodore, the monk from Tarsus who became archbishop of Canterbury in the seventh century, used Basilian canons in his penitential shows that these were still in use in the Greek world. The earliest text from the East written in the period under discussion with the specific aim to aid a confessor in choosing the appropriate penance for specific sins is the so-called *kanonarion* or *protokanonarion*. Traditionally it was ascribed to Patriarch John the Faster (d. 595), but probably it was written not earlier than the middle of the ninth century.[46] Whereas the western texts are more interested in a short description of the sin and advice for suitable penance, the *kanonarion* shows greater interest in the careful definition of the sins, mostly of a sexual nature. Later works attributed to Theodore the Studite, which probably were not written by this staunch opponent of the iconoclasts, but originated in Studite monasteries in the ninth century, also deal with other sins, such as theft, graverobbing, or forms of magic.[47] As with the canonical letters of Basil the Great, it is difficult to assess the influence of these texts in Byzantine society, for we still lack knowledge of either their diffusion or actual use.

Penance and the Carolingians

In Carolingian society penance became an increasingly important element. When confronted with all kinds of disasters – in war and in nature – Charlemagne (768–814) personally ordered a penitential litany to be sung in all churches in the empire to atone for the sins of the Franks, which apparently had angered God. Visions depicted great men and small, even the emperor himself, being tormented in the afterlife for their sins.[48] The great reform councils of 813 lamented the disappearance of public penance and the lack of authority for existing penitential handbooks. Bishops like Halitgar of Cambrai and Hrabanus Maurus (c. 780–856) tried to remedy the latter by composing handbooks which were in line with ancient ecclesiastical canons promulgated at authoritative councils.[49] Other texts such as the *Collectio Dacheriana* (one of the most important canon law collections composed in this period which particularly stressed the importance of penance) and the *Capitula episcoporum*

46 Hermann, "Il più antico penitenziale greco," 84–85.
47 *Peri Exagoreuseos* (Περὶ Ἐξαγορεύσεως), 24–27, 1730.
48 Heito, *Visio Wettini*; cf. Dutton, *Politics of Dreaming*.
49 Kottje, *Die Bussbücher Halitgars*.

tried to replace penitentials in the old style, but were only partly successful. The traditional texts were still being copied in the ninth century and new texts were composed using the old, although with a greater emphasis on the sources from which they originated.

We have seen that it is questionable whether penitential handbooks had much effect in Irish society. On their influence in the Carolingian world we can be more confident. Not only did many an ecclesiastical center possess one or more penitential manuals, as bishops had required in their capitularies, but the contents of the particular manuscripts preserving such manuals clearly suggest that these were meant to be used in a pastoral setting.[50] This does not necessarily mean that we should envisage a kind of practice in which lay people frequently went to confession. Confession was generally seen as a preparation for communion, and people were expected to take communion one to three times a year on the great Christian festivals of Easter, Pentecost, and Christmas. Confession at these times probably then had some kind of communal character. It has been argued that it is unlikely that penance was maintained in a regular way because of its "policing qualities." Penance, it has been claimed, functioned more as a means for ecclesiastical control, than as a pastoral instrument.[51] Yet, this approach seems somewhat one-sided. Priests may have acted as mediators not only between lay people and God, but also between individuals and society. Penitential handbooks deal with a lot of sins of a very public nature, in the sense that they must have caused public disturbance, *scandalum*. They deal with acts of murder and violence, adultery, drunkenness, and the like. While such acts may have remained hidden, it does not seem likely that in small-scale communities this happened very often, and even if it did, suspicion may have quickly fallen on specific persons. The right of sanctuary may have provided a safe haven for the culprit, as we can observe in the basilica of St. Martin of Tours, where a cleric convicted of some unknown crime sought refuge.[52] In such a case the local priest acted as mediator between the refugee and the offended party, and penance probably played a role in the settling of such disputes. The Council of Clichy (626/7), for example, declared that a refugee should not leave the church before promising to do penance for his crime.[53] The *Lex Baiuvariorum* ruled that punishment for someone who had taken refuge in a church should be determined "*cum consilio sacerdotis*."[54]

50 Meens, "Frequency and Nature."
51 Kerff, "Libri paenitentiales"; Murray, "Confession before 1215."
52 Alcuin, *Epistolae*, 245–49.
53 Council of Clichy (626/7), c. 9, 293.
54 *Lex Baiuvariorum*, I.7, 276–77.

In the *Letters* of Einhard (c. 770–840) we can see this former courtier intervene on behalf of people who had sought refuge in the churches established by him.[55] The metaphor of priests as judges and as mediators, which we so often encounter in penitential handbooks, would fit such a context very well.

Of course, penitentials provide examples of sins which are less scandalous, and we may accept that people at times confessed their sins without such social constraints. People seeking remedies for physical ailments in a church or a monastery probably also confessed their sins before delivering themselves to a monk, a priest, or a shrine.[56] We can observe that in sermon literature, as in the ninth-century collection attributed to Boniface (the Blickling homilies) or the homilies of Aelfric (c. 955–c. 1020) or Wulfstan (d. 1023), penance was a central theme, often in combination with a detailed description of diabolical punishments which awaited the unrepentant sinners in Hell.[57] Wulfstan explicitly demanded that sinners atone for their sins "as the books teach," probably directly referring to penitentials.[58] It is hard to believe that such sermons were written or remained in use if they had no practical effects among the laity. On the other hand, we should not forget that in practice there probably existed a bewildering variety of dealings with sins and sinners of which the theoretical constructions of canon law and conciliar legislation are only an imperfect reflection.

The importance of penance in the Carolingian world is further demonstrated by the political uses of the rituals of penance. Emperor Louis the Pious (814–40) even atoned for his sins twice in a public fashion. In the year 822 he did penance in public in Attigny, and in 833 he was forced to do so in Soissons after his troops had deserted him on the battlefield in the civil strife with his sons.[59] Other high-ranking aristocrats were put under strong pressure to do penance for their crimes. Paulinus of Aquilea (c. 730–802) around the year 794 gave the Lombard nobleman Aistulf the choice between entering a monastery to atone for his sins or to submit himself to a severe regime of public penance.[60] In 852 a council gathering at Mainz condemned a certain Albgis to a harsh penitential regime for abducting someone else's wife and a certain Batto to a lifelong penance for killing five people.[61] Although we do not know whether these high-status culprits could be forced to perform their penance, such cases

55 Einhard, *Epistolae*, 37, 46–49, and possibly 55.
56 Cf. Horden in this volume.
57 Pseudo-Bonifatius, *Sermones*; Frantzen, *Literature of Penance*, 150–74.
58 Wulfstan of York, *Sermo Lupi ad Anglos*, 63.
59 de Jong, "Power and Humility."
60 Paulinus of Aquilea, *Epistola* 16.
61 Council of Mainz (852), *Die Konzilien*, c. 11, 248–49.

must have had a wide resonance among the ecclesiastical and secular elites. Elements from the liturgy for penance were, moreover, widely adopted in rituals of submission (*deditio*) in a more secular sphere. Particularly from the Carolingian period through to the eleventh century, we hear of noblemen who were forced to submit themselves to others through a ritual which adopted so many elements from the penitential liturgy that it is sometimes hard to establish whether we are dealing with a secular or an ecclesiastical ritual, as, for example, the humiliation of Emperor Henry IV (1056–1106) at Canossa.[62] Not all aristocrats, however, had to be forced into a penitential mood. The penance of Louis the Pious undertaken in 822 seems to have been fully of the emperor's own volition, while courtiers like Alcuin (d. 804) and Einhard were thinking about their identity in terms of sin. Einhard identifies himself as "Einhard *peccator*" (the sinner).[63]

Rituals of penance

The "liturgical elaboration" of dispute settlement went hand-in-hand with the development of an increasingly elaborate liturgy of ecclesiastical penance itself, a process to which the liturgical *ordines* that are found in penitential handbooks testify. The earliest Irish penitential books did not contain liturgical material regulating the way one had to hear confession and to absolve the sinner. From the eighth century onward we find more and more texts of this kind attached to penitential handbooks, and from the tenth century onward also as separate tracts in miscellaneous manuscripts. This greater visibility of the penitential process may have been one of the reasons for bishops to try and get a better grip on this process which, as has been stressed, proved so pervasive in Carolingian society. From the late ninth century onward, penitential texts seem to have been preserved more in the context of episcopal collections of ecclesiastical regulations rather than in the pastoral manuscripts in which they were often to be found in the earlier period. Penance proved to be an important aspect of the handbook Regino of Prüm (d. 915) wrote in the early tenth century for episcopal inquisitions. Around the year 1000 Burchard (d. 1025), bishop of Worms, compiled his huge canon law collection in which he gave penitential rulings pride of place next to conciliar legislation.[64] In later canon law collections room is often made for a specific penitential part until Ivo of Chartres (c. 1040–1115) and Gratian (d. 1160) chose to omit this kind of

62 Goez, "Canossa als *deditio*?"; Althoff, *Die Macht der Rituale*, 117–18.
63 Einhard, *Translatio SS. Marcellini et Petri*, praef., 239; cf. Smith, "Einhard," 60–61.
64 Körntgen, "Fortschreibung," 209–10.

material. It has been stated that the growing importance of secular rituals of submission partly resulted from influences coming from penitential liturgy, but the elaboration of a penitential liturgy in the ninth and tenth centuries suggests that in the secular, as well as in the religious sphere, we can observe growing importance for an elaborate ritual.

From the ninth century onward, therefore, in the West penance and confession seems to have been ever more closely monitored by priests and increasingly so by bishops. The elaborate liturgy for forms of public penance, which were quite dynamic, focused on the powerful position of the bishop (and even more emphatically so in Lotharingia in the tenth century).[65] Yet, there is evidence that monasteries continued to play a role in the penitential process, as, for example, the sacramentary of Fulda suggests.[66]

In Byzantium, however, the penitential process became more and more dominated by monks, a development which should be seen in relation to the changing role of monasticism in Byzantine society. Monasticism had become more and more an urban movement, and interaction between monks and lay people had grown significantly.[67] Symeon the New Theologian (949–1022)[68] claimed that: "Before the monks, bishops alone by succession from the apostles had the power to bind and to loose. But with time the bishops did not use or used badly their power. This redoubtable function . . . was then transferred to the elect people of God, that is, the monks."[69] The difference between East and West is nicely demonstrated by the acts of the anti-Photian council of 869, when the protospatharius Theodore affirmed, following inquiries from papal legates, that he had confessed his sins. The legates then asked to whom he had confessed and whether it was a priest, and the protospatharius replied that he did not know whether his confessor had been a priest, but he did know that he was tonsured and had spent forty years on a pillar.[70]

Conclusion

It has been argued that from the eleventh century the character of penance changed drastically. The descriptions of sins that are found in penitential texts,

65 Hamilton, *Practice of Penance*, 104–72, particularly 162.
66 Ibid., 81–94, 129–30, and 136–50.
67 Morris, *Monks and Laymen*.
68 For the differences of opinion concerning the biographical dates of Symeon, see Alfeyev, *St. Symeon*, 28–29.
69 Symeon the New Theologian, *Letter on Confession*, ch. 11, 120; transl. from Erickson, "Penitential Discipline," 32.
70 *Sancta synodus octava generalis*, 150–51.

as well as the forms of penance assigned for such acts, consisting mainly of periods of fasting, are mainly concerned with "outward behavior." Penance could be commuted into shorter, more severe forms of fasts, but also into prayers or payments. It has been claimed that this changed in the latter half of the eleventh century. The exteriority of penance would have made room for a greater stress on its "interiority." This would lead to a different conception of sin in which the inner motivation was of more importance than the act itself. It would also enhance the importance of genuine contrition, at the cost of the satisfaction offered by the periods of fasting or other penitential acts. Pope Gregory VII's (1073–85) preoccupation with genuine contrition would have foreshadowed developments in the twelfth century, in which inquisitive minds like those of Peter Abelard (1079–1142/3) probed the inner secrets of the human heart.[71] Yet, if we look at earlier texts, particularly the instructional and liturgical treatises accompanying the penitential tariffs, then it becomes immediately clear that there already existed a strong tendency to look at the inner motives of a sinner, to the circumstances in which he was led to sin, and also to the sincerity of his repentance. Such an "interiority" of conceptions of sin and penance was no invention of the eleventh and twelfth centuries, although scholastic texts explored the inner condition of the sinner certainly with much more acuity than before. The importance of the inner life had to a greater or lesser degree been part of the penitential tradition, although we can imagine that it had not always been given full sway in practice. The scholastic approach certainly had a much greater impact on the cure of souls, but the penitential treatise written by no less an academic scholar as Robert Grosseteste (c. 1170–1253) shows that the need for simple tariffs did not disappear with the appearance of such scholastic texts.[72] The history of penance seems much less univocal and progressive than we have thought, which makes an investigation of the different ways in which people acknowledged and atoned for their sins richer and more rewarding.[73]

If we look back on the development of penance in this period then we can discern a few major developments. First, we can observe that in East and West monks played an important role in the development of the practice of confessing one's sins. From the ninth century, however, their ways seem to have parted. Whereas in the Greek world the practice of penance was ever more dominated by monasticism, in the West the secular clergy, priests, and

71 Cowdrey, "Spirituality of Pope Gregory VII," 14.

72 Robert Grosseteste, *De modo confitendi et paenitentias iniungendi*. See the edition published in Goering and Mantello, "Early Penitential Writings," 80–111.

73 Mansfield, *Humiliation of Sinners*.

bishops were increasingly able to control this process. In the West the practice of penance seems to have been ever more "scripted" by texts. The variety of sins, as well as the penitential acts which would atone for them, were described in great detail. From the ninth century onward an elaborate ritual of penance was developed. At the same time more and more aspects of life came to be seen in terms of sin and repentance. This holds true not only for all kinds of sexual activities, in and outside of marriage, the consumption of food and drink, a great variety of violent acts, and various forms of "magic", but also for feelings of lust, jealousy, or rage. One can indeed conclude that the world had become increasingly "peccatized."[74] The development of a parish structure in most of western Europe by the end of our period, together with the proliferation of texts dealing with confession and penance, laid the foundation for a practice of regular confession, which surely had come into existence by the twelfth century. Although in the later medieval period varieties of penance continued to exist, the efforts to control and monitor processes of penance by the secular clergy led to a greater stress on the formal ways of doing penance.

74 Brown, "Vers la naissance."

20

Sickness and healing

PEREGRINE HORDEN

Saints and others

In early medieval Basra (Iraq), a story circulated about a handsome deacon with a speech impediment.[1] Sorcerers were blamed for his eight years' suffering:

> His mother took him round to a monastery to be healed, but he received no healing, either from the monastery, or from anyone else. So she went off to the doctors, followers of Plato, but she received no help from Plato or his followers. So she set off on a journey . . . to some sorcerers, she [got] nothing either from them or from the wicked whom the demons had deceived.

Finally, she heard about a visiting holy man, John of Dailam. The outcome can be guessed. Merely laying his cross on the deacon's tongue, the saint triumphed where others – monks, doctors, "witch doctors" – had failed. (The doctors, as purveyors of philosophical medicine, were supposedly followers of Plato; more realistically they were disciples of Galen.) The following Sunday, to universal astonishment, the deacon read the Epistles in church.

Such was the miracle story included in a panegyric of John. Composed well after his death in the early eighth century, it apparently incorporates material from his own time. In England, much later on, a similar tale was told of a girl who suffered for two years from an ulcer on each foot.[2] "She endured such great pain and swelling that . . . she could not touch the ground with either foot." Her father carried her about among "doctors and holy places" – living physicians and dead saints. Eventually she found miraculous relief at the shrine of Gilbert of Sempringham (c. 1083–1189, canonized 1202).

Hagiographical narratives like these open windows onto the therapeutic landscape of the early Middle Ages. True, they offer only a partial view of illness and handicap. They were recorded by those hoping to promote a saint's

1 Brock, "Syriac Life," 127, 166–67, 187–88. I am much indebted to Klaus-Dietrich Fischer for comments on a draft of this chapter.

2 *Book of St. Gilbert*, ch. 19, 324–25.

cult by extolling his or her miracles; almost every story thus has the same happy ending. Normally, too, the background detail of the pilgrim sufferer's previous, unsuccessful attempts at cure is set out in a predictable sequence that echoes the Gospel prototype of Christ's healing of the woman with an issue of blood.[3] The pilgrim has tried doctors, who are expensive and useless, then turns to saintly medicine, which is free and immediately effective.

Still, the incidental details of the run-up to the cure must have been plausible. That was essential for the miracle narrative to persuade its audience of the attractiveness of the shrine. The various healers to whom the pilgrims had reportedly first turned may have been caricatured, but they could not have been totally misrepresented. Their costly failures would not have been worth cataloging so heavy handedly if they did not offer a credible, popular alternative to a miracle at a shrine. The hagiographers are the first to admit that the sick tried secular therapy first and its heavenly counterpart second.

The two stories retold above, however, differ slightly in structure from the standard type of miracle narrative. The deacon of Basra is led to monks, then to physicians, then to sorcerers. The hagiographer does not rearrange his mother's preferences into a neat progression, from superstition (sorcery) to earthly medicine (doctors) to religious healing (first monks, then saint). The English girl with the painful feet is taken indiscriminately to both doctors and saints. Such departures from the biblical prototype may increase our confidence in the accounts' broad veracity.

The saint does not even have to be the end of the story. In Anatolia, Theodore of Sykeon (d. 613), a living holy man, sometimes avoided miracle working by referring his patients to others:[4]

> If any required medical treatment for certain illnesses or surgery or a purging draught or hot-springs, this God-inspired man would prescribe the best thing for each, for even in technical matters he had become an experienced doctor. He might recommend one to have recourse to surgery and he would always state clearly which doctor they should employ.

Similarly, in the early eighth century, John, bishop of Hexham (northern England), did not hesitate to call upon physicians and surgeons as supplements to his own miraculous cures.[5] And throughout our period, dead saints, appearing to pilgrims in dreams and visions, would continue to instruct sufferers to embrace the techniques of secular medicine.

3 Mark 8.25–28; Luke 8.43–44.

4 *Vie de Théodore de Sykéôn*, ch. 145, 114 or trans. Dawes and Baynes, 182.

5 Bede, *HE*, V.2, V.6; ed. Colgrave and Mynors, 458–59, 468–69.

Since the 1980s medical historians have used the metaphor of the marketplace to characterize this therapeutic pluralism. For some tastes, that is too redolent of modern economics: it implies that patients could exercise more freedom of choice than will often have been possible. One advantage of the metaphor is, however, that it brings out the simultaneous availability of many different types of healer and the competition among them. This competition is well attested from the ancient and late antique worlds, and we sense it, from the early Middle Ages, in snippets of hagiography. A further advantage is that the metaphor accentuates the role of the patient – or the immediate caregiver – in deciding his or her own "hierarchy of resort":[6] a hierarchy in which the positions of saints, doctors, and sorcerers are not predetermined.

Granted, then, that there was a marketplace for healing in the early medieval world, obvious questions suggest themselves. Who was selling what to whom? What were the relative proportions of the different "sectors," and how did these vary over time and space? How important were gender differences among healers? Above all, what was the role of Christianity?

None of these questions is readily answered. Hagiography provides our best evidence for the "everyday life" of the period, and thus for healing, but does not take us far enough. For medicine in the various learned traditions, we have a substantial number of texts, but in most cases we do not know how they were used or by whom. The daily practice of the average healer – who learned his craft orally, through apprenticeship – is even more obscure. We do not have the inscriptions and papyri that elucidate the lower reaches of the medical "profession" in the classical world, or the archives that reveal their later medieval successors. Sorcerers and other magical healers, of the kind whom the deacon of Basra visited, are yet more obscure.

Overall, the relative scale that we can attribute to each type or source of healing is in inverse proportion to the volume of evidence for it that survives. Saints, so well documented, were demanding in their prerequisites (the pilgrim must have demonstrated full repentance of sin to merit cure). They can have catered to only a minority of the sick. At the other end of the spectrum, the "informal" sector of self-help or reliance on family and neighbors for basic nursing was presumably the largest, even if, among the poorer members of society, such support networks were fragile. Yet this sector is seldom documented. A few texts survive that are explicitly for the self-medication of those without access to doctors. The possibly magical impedimenta – pieces of cloth, herbs, animal substances, rings – found in women's graves, in boxes that hung

6 Horden, "Saints and Doctors," 12–13.

from the waist, across barely Christianized northern Europe at the start of our period have been interpreted as signs of female domestic therapy.[7] But if aristocratic ladies dispensed remedies to their households in the seventh century, as we know that they would in the seventeenth,[8] there is no direct trace of such activity. Hagiography once again offers suggestive glimpses of domestic support in its narration of who helped whom on pilgrimage. For example, in Anskar's *Miracles of St. Willehad*, the first bishop of Bremen (northwestern Germany), written in the 860s, one poor woman is shown helping her neighbor, blind for seven years, to travel to the saint's shrine because she had no one else.[9] It is not much to go on, and for detailed and evocative material we have to wait for the thirteenth century and the *Miracles of St. Louis*.[10] Even then, the material is necessarily skewed toward showing informal support only at its moments of failure. And what it tells us is hardly more than could have been intuited – that coresident household members and neighbors were more help in sickness than distant kin.

This bias of the evidence is not the only challenge. Unavoidably, the medical historian is embroiled in debates about the relationships between magic, science, and religion that have been running inconclusively since the nineteenth century. To give just one illustration: in a ninth-century Carolingian manuscript from a French monastery, seventeen remedies derived from the body of a freshly killed vulture are inserted on a blank page in the middle of a Latin version of the *Materia Medica* of the great first-century pharmacologist Dioscorides. Before decapitating the vulture to make, for example, a remedy for migraine, one should say "Angel, Adonai, Abraham."[11] Such a ritual utterance, with its implied coercion of hidden powers, its air of mechanical efficacy, bears all the hallmarks of the magical. How then do we conceptualize this short text's relationship to the surrounding medicine of Dioscorides? And how do we interpret its biblical elements? Is this Christianized magic or "magic-ized" Christianity, some unorthodox outgrowth of proper observance? Or does more depend on the way the text would have been used rather than on the words on the page? The triple invocation can be enunciated in a prayerful way, as ideally was the liturgy, rather than in a mechanical way that paid no attention to the words. The only path through these difficulties is found in respecting local definitions and conceptions, so far as we can establish them.

7 Meaney, "Women, Witchcraft and Magic," 9–12, 29–30.
8 Pollock, *With Faith and Physic*.
9 Anskar, *Miracula Sancti Willehadi*, ch. 9, 849.
10 Guillaume de Saint-Pathus, *Les miracles*; Farmer, *Surviving Poverty*.
11 MacKinney, "Unpublished Treatise," 495; Möhler, *"Epistula de vulture."*

For early medieval sufferers, the real contrast was less between incompatible systems of ideas – theology, medicine, magic – than between different authorities. Few disputed that ritual words and gestures had power over invisible forces – but whose words, and which forces?[12]

In what follows, then, headings are given – medicine, magic, religion – but they should be taken only as indicating movement along a continuum, not clear transitions from one category to another.

Medicine

In the history of medical learning, our period falls between two peaks of impressive activity, each of which marks a major transformation in the way medicine was conceived. At the start, more or less complete by 600, had come the subjugation of medical learning, at least in the Byzantine world, by Galenism. The achievement of Galen of Pergamum (129–216/17) was so comprehensive, his solutions to almost all the big medical questions seemingly so complete, that most subsequent medical scholarship in the Greek East was devoted to distilling his vast output and harmonizing its contradictions – rendering it "user friendly."

At the end of our period, in the second half of the eleventh century in southern Italy, the first steps were taken in the great translation movement that made Greek medicine and philosophy, preserved in Arabic, fully accessible to western scholars in Latin. That translation movement, initially associated with the name of Constantine the African (d. before 1099), laid the basis for a philosophically robust medicine capable of being taught in schools such as the famous one at Salerno (southern Italy) and later in universities. It ensured that Galenic medicine would dominate European medical learning for another 800 years.

In between these two developments, what was medicine like? The first general observation to make is that, early on in our period, learned medicine was not only shorn of its earlier pagan associations, it was domesticated by Christianity. Hippocrates had said that the doctor's fate was to harvest sorrow of his own from others' miseries.[13] In some respects obviously applicable to Jesus, the complaint subtly changed, and by around 400 CE had become a description of the ideal physician. So broadly compatible were the ethics of ancient medicine with those of Christianity that an eleventh-century Greek manuscript (now,

12 Jolly, "Medieval Magic," 16.
13 [Hippocratic author], *On Breaths*, ch. 1, 91; Temkin, *Hippocrates*, 247.

appropriately, in the Vatican) includes a text of the Hippocratic Oath in the shape of a cross.[14]

The second, related observation to make is that this medicine was very often practiced by priests and monks. It is a cliché that the medicine of the early Middle Ages was exclusively monastic; this may underplay the role of secular priests, especially at the end of our period, and it certainly underplays the role of lay healers. It is also a cliché that there was, on the other hand, some deep antithesis between the religious life and medical practice. Yet in Christianized Russia of the eleventh century (according to some later redactions of the "Law of Vladimir") healers were among those over whom the church was given exclusive jurisdiction.[15] As we shall see, the largest and medically most impressive hospital of its age, that of the Pantocrator, was based within a monastery; and the whole medical history of the period would look very different were it not for the texts copied and preserved in monastic scriptoria and libraries. Moreover, when canon law on the matter began to solidify, just after the end of our period, it placed relatively few restrictions on the practice of medicine by monks and clerics.

The third generalization that can be hazarded about the medical literature of the period is that the theory has largely been drained out of it. Overall, not counting Galen and a handful of others, theorists and practitioners had slowly been parting company for some centuries in classical Mediterranean medicine. The medical literature of the early Middle Ages takes this to an extreme. In the East the characteristic major product, in vogue at the start of our period and again, to a lesser extent, in the tenth and eleventh centuries, is the encyclopedic collection – artfully arranged excerpts from Galen and from the other authors needed to fill in the gaps that he left. On a lesser level, perhaps closer to everyday practice, is the treatment list. From both, all genuine discussion of medical ideas has been eliminated, as, mostly, has consideration of symptoms. "Against headache and migraine," read one much copied Greek remedy, "crush cress in vinegar with oil of roses; make an ointment of it. Rub it thoroughly into the head."[16] Plain and simple, and no vultures required.

The literate medicine of early medieval western Europe is harder to sum up. In formal terms the written medicine is more various than that of Byzantine medicine – from a few extended translations of ancient treatises to very short miscellanies. The latter texts are highly unstable: hardly any two surviving manuscripts resemble one another closely. And their stated

14 Leven, "Attitudes," 76.
15 Kaiser, *Laws of Rus'*, ch. 16, 44; Franklin and Shepard, *Emergence*, 234.
16 Jeanselme, "Sur un aide-mémoire," 148; Bennett, "Xenonika," 409, no. 2.

authorship – Galen or Hippocrates in many cases – is frequently questionable. Some collections, such as the late eighth-century *Book of Medicine* (essentially a substantial recipe book) copied in the great Carolingian abbey of Lorsch (south-western Germany), with its defense of medicine and brief introductory sections on medical ethics, the humors, and so on, were intended to have an air of comprehensiveness and order.[17] Other, lesser texts, often degenerate into unintelligibility through repeated copying. They survive in, to us, unlikely ways – as did gynecological treatises in monastic libraries. And many texts were quite unsuited to medical training. Consider *The Book of Medicine from Urines*, a short treatise by "Hermogenes," an author probably of the ninth century dignified with a classical name. It is preserved uniquely in a late tenth-century manuscript at the Italian abbey of Monte Cassino.

> For there are many signs and kinds of illness associated with white urine. And white urine denotes dissolution of vigour. . . . And there is another white urine which denotes a weakness lasting many days, and the blockage of the body's veins; and this illness often happens because of excessive drinking of wine. Where you see urine which is thick and white, you should know that one of the four humours is being liquefied. . . . And if you see urine with a strong yellow colour it proclaims the body is sick because of red melancholy. . . .[18]

There are traces there of the ancient theory according to which ill health reflected an imbalance of humors. Yet the text is vague about what diseases result from the imbalances mentioned, and silent on what should be done about them. It is hard to imagine at whom the treatise was aimed or how it could, without a great deal of supplementary instruction, be turned to practical advantage.

We know more about the medicine of the period, for all its obscurities, than we do about doctors. We know, of course, the names (and sometimes the writings) of a modest number of physicians at court or in the great monasteries: for instance Theophanes Chrysobalantes, who addressed a medical handbook to a Byzantine emperor, probably Constantine Porphyrogenitus (905–59).[19] We also know about those whom we might call gentlemen amateurs, beginning with the Emperor Charlemagne himself, knowledgeable about medicine as a part of a wider liberal education and occasional dispensers of advice to friends, yet hardly doctors. But nothing survives that would enable us to address the big sociological questions that bear on the full spectrum of practice.

17 *Das "Lorscher Arzneibuch."*
18 Wallis, "Signs and Senses," 273.
19 Theophanes Chrysobalantes, *Theophanis Nonni epitome.*

The fundamental problem is one of definition: what was it to be a doctor? The attempted legal definitions of antiquity scarcely apply in our centuries. There were some medical guilds in the Greek East, especially in Constantinople.[20] Yet no evidence suggests that they were able to enforce professional standards at all widely. Elsewhere, the designation "doctor" had simply to be claimed, and then retained through successful practice. Often it will have been a part-time activity; and so a great number of practitioners will escape our notice because they are never labeled as such.

One consequence of that is our inability to say much about women's practice. In this period, as later, women were far more likely to be part-time caregivers, nurses, or healers. Like most other female workers, they had "weak occupational identity" as well as inferior status. Hence, on the rare occasions when they surface in the documentation, they are unlikely to be identified as medical practitioners. It is impossible even to sketch the history of midwifery, a category of much broader scope in the early Middle Ages than it would later become. The one exception to all this obscurity is the nascent medical school of eleventh- to twelfth-century Salerno, with its handful of known women healers, especially Trota (the famous "Trotula" is not her name but the collective title of the texts attributed to her).

We should not imagine that the majority of male practitioners are any better placed. To look only at western Europe: Ireland in this period comes across as a land almost without medicine. Of course, practitioners of various kinds, some of them female, are attested (bone-setters, blood-letters, etc.). But of literate medical practice, or even of basic herbalism, there is little trace.

Anglo-Saxon medicine was much inspired by Latin medical wisdom and some one thousand manuscript pages of it survive; yet in pre-conquest England, too, the prosopography of doctors is slender. Only for France is the record more full: some forty-five named medical men for the period 600 to 1000; eighty-seven for the eleventh century (showing how far the picture can be distorted by the increasing survival rate of documents and widening literacy). But the careers of individuals in question are for the moment mostly unknowable. Perhaps charter evidence will shed more light on the French, German, and Spanish "medical" scene, as it has already begun to do for southern Italy.

On these fragile foundations it would be rash to erect any grand conclusions. Healers in the West were probably overall fewer in number and lower in status than those of the more urbanized East, with its concentrations of wealthier

20 Constantine Porphyrogenitus, *Le livre des cérémonies* 1, 10.

sick people. It was demonstrably like this in antiquity. It probably remained so in the early Middle Ages.

What was the reach, socially and economically, of the medicine dispensed? Archival work done on later medieval societies suggests that there could be a surprisingly intense and widespread appetite for medical learning. It could be imitated by illiterate "empirics" – or even by parish priests. A manual produced by the Abbey of Lorsch c. 900, perhaps for parish priests being sent out into some of its estates, includes the "Egyptian days," on which one should not be bled or given any medicine. It also lists preventative regimes for each month of the year.[21]

Magic

Beyond the frontier of this parish medicine should we place sorcery – a distinct alternative to Galenism or its western equivalents, as in the Syriac tale of a search for cure with which we began? It would be convenient to hold up the sorcerer as the poor person's physician: more accessible because there were more sorcerers than physicians and cheaper, too. Likewise it would be convenient to accept that sufferers tried sorcerers or magicians when naturalistic medicine had failed and something more powerful was needed. Much of the hagiography (though not my two opening examples) suggests as much. But hagiography, as we saw, has a particular slant on the topic and cannot be taken at face value. Anyone can in principle pronounce a spell or charm or construct an amulet; but that does not make magic simply the pauper's medicine. Sorcerers demand fees, too; and magic is not disdained by the educated. Like the manuscript referred to earlier, in which incantatory vulture medicine is found in the middle of an ancient treatise on drugs, many of the most learned and expensive texts copied in our period include remedies that we might classify as magical.

We know little, however, about the circumstances in which the sick resorted to magical remedies. Byzantium provides tantalizing vignettes. The first comes from the threshold of our period. The learned Greek physician Alexander of Tralles (?525–?605) happily condoned the use of charms and amulets. He included in his medical encyclopedia a traditional remedy for epilepsy that required the blood of a dead gladiator. This had been rejected by Galen. Yet for Alexander, writing centuries after the death of the last gladiator, it remained an "excellent and well tried remedy."[22] As for colic:

21 Paxton, *"Bonus liber."*
22 *Alexander von Tralles* 1, 565.

> since many patients, and especially the wealthy ones, object . . . to treating their bowels with enemas, they force us to cure the pain with the help of magical amulets. That is why I have thought it worthwhile to give you an account of these also, both the ones which I know from my own experience and those whose effectiveness is vouched for by trusted friends.[23]

Thus magic was not restricted to cases where Galenic methods had failed, but could be used when patients found conventional methods unpleasant. The good doctor, Alexander says, should omit nothing from his arsenal that might contribute to healing. For him, magic is characterized by its material vectors and its aura of secrecy. But he crosses the boundary between it and medicine without fear of censure from any medical or ecclesiastical authority. We have heard much about "the rise of magic" in the early Middle Ages. But magic did not rise as if engulfing the supposed rationalism of ancient medicine. It had always been there. Only Galen and a few like-minded souls rejected all but naturalistic explanations of phenomena. Alexander was enough of a Galenist to pigeonhole his magical remedies – not enough of one to eliminate them altogether.

Moving forward to just after the end of our period, we can, highly unusually, hear from a magician in his own words. Michael Italicus, a teacher of many subjects, including medicine, before he became a high-ranking churchman around 1145, writes to one Tziknoglus.[24] This man's sister has developed some chronic condition (perhaps a tumor) that conventional medicine cannot cure. She and her brother have heard about a magician who offers to help, and they consult Italicus about the wisdom of accepting the offer. Italicus counsels against resort to magic, which is contrary to Christian law. Even so, he clearly knows a great deal about it, and has read many books on it:

> I have also extended my eagerness for such knowledge to the daft babbling of the old women at the crossroads, and anything else going round the common people. I am in possession of charms, binding-magic, and a good many useful symbols which contain unspoken commands, and cures for stinking viscera, and relief for swellings.

Then he starts to protest too much: "but I have never acquired any of these for my own benefit, nor have I ever had any faith in them." Anxious to avoid direct involvement in the cure of Tziknoglus's sister, he has asked another magician to do him "a favor." He now has in his possession some ancient remedy which

23 *Alexander von Tralles* 2, 375 or trans. Duffy, "Byzantine Medicine," 26.

24 Michael Italicus, *Lettres et discours*, Letter 31, 201–203 or trans. Maxwell-Stuart, *Occult*, 148–49.

he will describe when he and Tziknoglus next meet because it would, he says, take too much space to write down.

Between Alexander and Michael, magic has been more broadly defined and vigorously prohibited than it was around 600. Hence Italicus's prudent reluctance to put his spell in writing. In the West, also, magical healing of this kind had been outlawed. A substantial body of hagiography, secular as well as canon law, penitentials, sermons, and polemics repeats, stereotypically, a catalogue of prohibited practices – soothsaying, divining, lot casting, enchanting, witchcraft. Sometimes it provides memorable examples in specifying punishment. "If a woman places her daughter on the roof or in an oven as a cure for fever, let her do penance for seven years."[25] Yet how widespread were such practices? Evidence suggesting their ubiquity is of two kinds. First, there is the frequency and stridency with which the practices were condemned throughout our period. Second, there is the extent to which the church increasingly accommodated some of their more beneficent forms, notably astrology. In the West much of the reality of everyday magic is obscure to us because we see it only through inflamed clerical eyes. Yet the sheer pressure that it apparently exerted on the church can at least be taken as testimony to its prevalence.

That prevalence may, however, have been a "regional" phenomenon. The argument does not apply so readily to the Byzantine world. There, the prohibitions were perhaps more all-embracing and more effective, as we can infer from Italicus's anxiety. Quasi-pagan charms and amulets largely disappeared after the ninth or tenth century in Byzantium, to be replaced by small portable crosses and other such orthodox items. There was not quite the same accommodation that has been detected in the West, even though magical beliefs were obviously by no means extirpated. Perhaps in the West, as has been suggested, sorcerers really were more numerous than priests at the start of the period, especially in the frontier zones of Christianity.[26] Dare we then conclude that there was more magical healing in the West than in the East? We have no means of measuring.

Religion

After science (medicine), and after magic, where can the chapter turn next but to religion? How did religion and healing interrelate in our period? Christianity began, in the gospels, as a religion of healing. And although historians dispute

25 *Penitential of Theodore*, I.15.2 in Haddan and Stubbs, *Councils* 3, 190 or trans. McNeill and Gamer, *Medieval Handbooks*, 198, modified.
26 Flint, *Rise of Magic*, 79.

the relative importance of healing miracles in its early propagation, there is no doubting the subsequent centrality of the wonder working of holy persons and their relics to both the expansion of Christendom and its internal dynamics.

The miracles with which the chapter opened were, however, only one element in the array of therapies developed by the early medieval church – therapies directed primarily at the immortal soul, rather than the body, and dependent on prayer and the sacraments rather than drugs and ointments. Between medicine and theology there was thus enormous potential for tension. At the start of our period the "profession" of medicine was too imbued with paganism to be acceptable to many church rigorists. Later on, its implicit naturalism may, it has been argued, have rendered medical theory suspect in a different way. Our period ends before, in the West, the recovery of Aristotle established philosophical common ground for theology and university medicine.

Was resort to medicine therefore really permissible? For Pope Gregory the Great (590–604), composing c. 590 his enormously influential manual for bishops, the sick among Christian congregations should be told that they must endure suffering on this earth if they were ever to reach heaven. "The health of the heart" (or soul) is bodily affliction, a great gift in that it "cleanses sins." Illness should be endured as Christ endured the cross. It is a way of disciplining or educating the soul. It removes the sins that, by implication, might have caused it and hinders the committing of further sins.[27] This seems to leave no room for secular medicine.

And yet Gregory himself, martyr to chronic pain, ascribed one of his own illnesses to melancholy, not to moral failing, and had a physician from the great medical school of Alexandria in permanent attendance. Nor did he hesitate to recommend physicians and their remedies to friends or colleagues.[28] The connection between sin and disease was far less often to the fore in early medieval accounts of sickness than has usually been imagined. Since the Fall, the general "background" sinfulness of humanity had brought disease into creation, but by no means all illnesses were to be related to specific sins. In a seventh-century Greek collection of "questions and answers" attributed to Anastasius of Sinai (d. c. 700), it is asked why there are more maimed, arthritic, gouty, and leprous people among Christians than among infidels.[29] The answer is equivocal. Some say that God has sent these afflictions to test his devotees'

27 Gregory the Great, *Regula pastoralis*, III.12; ed. Judic, Rommel, and Morel, vol. 2, 326–32.
28 Richards, *Consul of God*, 46–47.
29 Anastasius Sinaita, *Interrogationes*, ch. 94, 732–33.

faith and love. Others, though, argue that it is a question of climate, habitat, and diet. No one mentions sin.

The tensions between religion and medicine should thus not be overstressed. When few forms of secular healing could accomplish much, illness almost always had to be endured to some extent, thus leaving considerable scope for meditation on its spiritual significance. Of the various types of therapy that we have been reviewing, there was none, from learned medicine to simple herbalism or the use of Christian charms, that was widely seen in principle as incompatible with the Christian life. (Even the forms of "magic" that the church tried to prohibit fell within the framework of theological explanation, because they were, by definition, demonic.) There was only one axiom: sufferers and healers alike should always recall that true healing ultimately comes from God. The message that earthly medicine would fail if the soul had not previously been tended did not have to wait to be proclaimed by the fathers assembled at the Fourth Lateran Council (1215).[30] It had been enunciated some 1,400 years earlier in the book of Ecclesiasticus (38.1–15). "Honor the physician," we are told in a proof text for the Christian reception of medicine. God created medicines from the earth and the prudent man will not disdain them. But then: "in sickness . . . pray to the Lord, and he will cure you. Turn away from sin . . . and then give place to the physician." The physician will succeed when he, too, prays. Even so, he is best avoided, by following the path of goodness: "he that sins before his maker, let him fall into the hands of the physician!"

The most forceful demonstration of this qualified compatibility between medicine and religion lies in the frequency with which theologians used the physician as a "role model." Christ is not described as a physician in the Gospels. But within only decades of his death he had become one. From the early first century to – decisively for the West – Augustine (354–430), a sequence of church fathers elaborated the idea of Christus *medicus* or *iatros*, originally perhaps as a riposte to the cult of the pagan healing god Asclepius. Our period is replete with literary imagery reflecting the assumption that the careful physician is an effective and powerful figure. This respect is a more positive counterpart to the obloquy heaped on doctors (as effective rivals) by custodians of shrines. Both derive from the perception that the physician's therapy must be taken seriously. It was not only Christ and his saints who were associated with physicians in this way. The priest as confessor was also thought to benefit by association with the healer who carefully weighed symptoms and circumstances so as

30 Canon 22 in Tanner, *Decrees* 1, 245–46.

to arrive at a medicine wholly suited to the individual patient. In the early 1000s, Burchard of Worms (d. 1025) tellingly gave the penitential included as Book 19 in his collection of canon law the heading *Corrector et medicus*. It listed "corrections" for bodies and "medicines" for souls, the converse of what we might have expected.[31]

This medicine for souls was no less medicine than it was soteriology. Any given individual in the period under discussion may have held one or more "lay" notions of what constituted health – a balance of humors, freedom from demons or (in the Anglo-Saxon case) the attacks of elves, ability to work or procreate sufficiently, mere longevity, and so on. But any properly catechized Christian will also have added "freedom from unatoned sin." The health of the soul was no mere metaphor. Attention to it was a form of preventative medicine. In the East, where the Galenic tradition of "hygiene" or diet in the broadest sense remained unbroken, one could commission from a doctor a regimen, showing what to do and eat month by month. In the West, with its lack of such a central tradition and its emphasis on simple remedies, there are few signs of any comparable approach. But, in West as well as East, protective amulets could be worn, and *loricas* (protective verbal shields) could be chanted. The Old English text known as the *Lorica of Gildas* calls, for example, on heaven's army for defense against a wide range of dangers, enumerating all body parts internal and external.[32]

Nor is this just a matter for individuals. The early medieval chapter in the history of public health belongs under the heading of religion rather than medicine. The period is mostly lacking in the usual ingredients of public health history. It falls between the famous markers of Roman public health concerns – aqueducts, baths, sewers – and the legislation of the Italian cities of the high Middle Ages for the regulation of noxious (and thus pestilential) smells. In the gap between the Romans and the "Italians" we see occasional signs of a materialist approach. In the early seventh century, for instance, a Frankish bishop, Desiderius of Cahors (c. 590–655), anticipated later medieval Italian measures. He set up checkpoints to stop pestiferous merchants from importing the plague. He also wrote to another bishop asking for the loan of specialist craftsmen who would make the wooden tubing needed for planned refurbishment of his city's water supply.[33] More often, though, we encounter what remained a principal ingredient in the public health of the later Middle

31 Burchard of Worms, *Corrector et medicus*, 949 or trans., McNeill and Gamer, *Medieval Handbooks*, 323.

32 *Anglo-Saxon Remedies* 1, 40–56.

33 Horden, "Ritual and Public Health," 31.

Ages, too: the collective response to impending or actual epidemic manifested in processions and litanies, and led by the bishop. Once more it is a question of seeing religion not as a substitute for "the real thing" (according to our modern definition) but as the real thing itself.

Far more common than the processions, and the miracles some saints wrought to ward off disease, was the administration of the sacraments. Indeed the church's one, great, truly essential means of promoting good health was baptism. Baptism was the equivalent of early inoculation: the means to forgiveness of original sin and an exorcism, a rebirth into health. It was not the only sacrament relevant here. We have already sampled the therapy of penance. In both eastern and western rites, the potentially therapeutic effects of the Eucharist were also recognized. From the earlier fathers on, the Eucharistic liturgy was a *pharmakon* (drug or medicine), and the prayers for the healing of the sick incorporated into its text were unambiguous.

Hospitals

In no therapeutic setting was the interpenetration of medicine of the soul and that of the body so clear as in the hospital. Today's hospital is characterized above all by technological intensity and concentration of medical expertise on the seriously ill. Such a definition would have embraced only some of the institutions that were called hospitals in the Christian world before around 1800. Still less can it apply before 1100. The medievalist must conceive the hospital more broadly, as an establishment for the overnight accommodation of the poor and/or sick – hospice as much as hospital, charitable first and therapeutic only second.

The hospital in that sense – the hospital before the great "medicalization" of the modern age – was by origin a Christian invention and in our period its history is overwhelmingly a Christian history. It was therapeutic by medieval medical standards as a beneficial regulator of the environment in which the needy poor lived and slept. But still more was it therapeutic by medieval theological standards in that it looked after the health of the soul: the founder's soul through the prayers of patients; the patients' souls through the spiritual and physical healing of the liturgy and the sacraments.

The majority of early medieval hospitals would not have passed the test of medicalization imposed by the historiography of their nineteenth- and twentieth-century successors. But the presence of physicians is, however, recorded in a long sequence of them, from that of St. Basil of Caesarea established in Anatolia around 370 to the great projected hospital of the Pantocrator monastery founded in Constantinople by John II (1087–1143) and his wife Irene in the 1120s. In the latter, if the imperial couple's plans were fully realized, a huge staff of some fifty eminent physicians and supporting personnel cared for no more than fifty patients in astonishingly modern-seeming specialized wards.[34]

This "medicalization" – the intended presence, in some hospitals, of figures labeled doctors – is above all a phenomenon of the East in our period. It is a phenomenon of Byzantium primarily, and then of the cultures to which the model of the Byzantine hospital was exported, especially Sasanian and then Islamic Iran and Iraq. In the West, the explicit involvement of doctors with hospitals is rarer and comes mostly from the earlier part of our period. We must look to Visigothic Spain for an example recorded in any detail. Bishop Masona (d. 605) of Mérida

> built a *xenodocium* ("house for strangers," hospital), enriching it with a large patrimony and appointing ministers and doctors to serve travellers and the sick, giving them this command: that the doctors should go through the entire city without ceasing and whosoever they found that was sick . . . they were to carry in their arms to the xenodocium, and having prepared there a well-made bed set the sick man on it and give him light and pleasant food until, with God's help, they returned the patient to his former health.[35]

Although its doctors were thought to offer nothing but rest and diet, this hospital at least was somewhat removed from the stereotype of the premodern hospital as no more than a gateway to death.

We should not overestimate the impact of such institutions on the aggregates of sickness and deprivation among the poor. Hospitals were few in number, generally small, and restricted in geography (mostly to the larger cities of Byzantium, and to parts of Italy and Francia). Our period falls between the first wave of hospital foundations of the eastern Mediterranean in the fourth to fifth centuries on the one hand and, on the other, the great vogue for hospital building evident in twelfth-century Europe.

Despite these caveats, great claims for the precocious modernity of early medieval hospitals have been made. According to one influential recent account,[36] the hospital was "born" in the Byzantine Empire – not just as a charitable institution, not just as a place where doctors functioned, but (by the late sixth century) as a center of medical excellence, medical scholarship, and medical education. The tiny portion of surviving Byzantine medical manuscripts

34 "Le typikon," 82–112 or trans. *BMFD* 2, no. 28, 757–66.

35 *Vitas sanctorum patrum Emeretensium*, V.3, 50–51 or trans. Fear, *Lives*, 74–75.

36 Miller, *Birth*.

that can in any way be associated with hospitals tell a different story. Hospital medicine in Byzantium was not evidently superior to non-hospital medicine; indeed the two were very similar, and mostly rather basic.

Conclusion

As the first millennium drew to a close, one of the most famous physicians in Europe was a monk of St. Gall (Switzerland) called Notker (d. 975). The Duke of Bavaria knew of his reputation for accurate prognosis and decided to consult him. First, though, he tested the monk's expertise. He sent him a urine sample – not his own, but that of a servant girl. Having examined it carefully, Notker fell to his knees proclaiming a miracle: in thirty days the duke would give birth to a son. The duke's emissaries returned to court where they found that the servant had in fact been delivered of a boy. They later came back to St. Gall with the duke's own urine.[37]

The monastery of St. Gall lay about 150 miles from the Bavarian court. This story can thus be taken to suggest the extreme scarcity of good doctors. Yet, then as now, the elite will travel (or send a specimen) any distance to secure the very best in treatment. All the signs are that the therapeutic landscape of Notker's age was in fact rather crowded. Notker was a monk-physician of a religious house the library of which contained several medical volumes, including a small portable manual that still survives. His house was the home of the St. Gall plan, a famous ninth-century blueprint for the ideal monastery, including a sizeable infirmary. It was also the home of what specialists now reckon an important manuscript of the sixth-century monastic Rule of St. Benedict, in which the abbot's pastoral role is likened to that of "a wise physician."[38] Notker's skill at prognostication, akin to prophesy, was one that, in less respectable hands, might have seemed more magical than medical. He and his monastery are emblematic of the complex interplay of medicine and religion, the orthodox and the deviant in therapy, the individual and the institutional, the literate and the oral (for his was more than bookish skill), all of which makes sickness and healing in the early Middle Ages such a rich if recalcitrant topic.

37 Ekkehard IV, *Casus Sancti Galli*, 240.
38 *Regula Benedicti*, chaps. 27–28, 79–81.

21

Gender and the body

LYNDA L. COON

In his famous treatise on the origins of ecclesiastical offices, Isidore, bishop of Seville (d. 636 CE), provides generations of Christian altar servants with explicit instructions as to the care and cultivation of the public persona of the priestly body. These directives include a section on the management of the masculine voice during the celebration of the liturgy. Here, Isidore counsels his priests to refrain from uttering obscene language, to be mindful of both gesture and gait, and to monitor the pitch and gravity of their elocutions when performing sacred rites. According to Isidore, the priestly voice should be clear and simple, and it should possess the full vigor of manhood; it should never make rustic or clownish noises, nor should it sound too servile or too lofty, too fractured or too delicate. The lector uses his voice as an instrument through which he penetrates the intellects of his hearers. Most importantly, the perfect liturgical voice should in no way sound effeminate. In order to avoid the risk of appearing *femineus* ("effeminate," "womanly"), the lector's movements must be infused with *gravitas* ("dignity," "power").[1]

Scholars of classical gender and sexuality would immediately recognize vestiges of Roman views on the elite male body in Isidore's treatise on the clergy.[2] In fact, the connection between Rome and Visigothic Spain is direct – the bishop of Seville summons the oratorical mastery of the first-century rhetorician Quintilian to revamp the image of the modern priest. Quintilian, in his *Institutio Oratoria* (c. 90), provides meticulous instructions to neophyte orators as to the girding of the body, the proper positioning of the fingers, and somber striding. He also focuses heavily on the voice as an instrument of power – the orator should know where to pause, when to take a breath, and when to speed up or slow down. Above all, the skilled lector's reading should be manly and solemn, and his voice should never lapse into sing-song

1 Isidore of Seville, *De ecclesiasticis officiis*, 2.2 and 2.11.
2 Fredrick, *Roman Gaze*; Bartsch, *Mirror of the Self*.

speech or effeminate affectation.[3] For Quintilian and other Roman writers the possession of a "public mouth," that is, the legal right to speak in select spaces (temples, law courts, the *Curia*, the forum), is a marker both of the masculinity of the speaker and his political authority. Those who lack this public mouth – women, children, actors, slaves – are *infames*, "without reputation," or, closer still to the original etymology of the word, "without a voice."[4] This chapter unearths vestiges of classical gender constructions embedded in the writings of early medieval churchmen, including Isidore, who served a new political and cultural context. The analysis centers on the body and its parts – mouth, vulva, and phallus – in order to reconstruct the medical and philosophical understanding of "sex" as well as the ideological use of "gender" in influential texts of the early medieval period. Although the focus here is clerical, priestly anxieties concerning bodily control and purity were transferred – often in highly competitive modes – to elite lay circles.[5]

Like their late antique predecessors, early medieval churchmen imbibe and promulgate ancient gender constructions. When Isidore, in his widely read and copied *Etymologies* (c. 636), referred to "excessive love" as "womanly love" (*femineus amor*), he communicated to his medieval audiences a classical Roman notion that any kind of excess was feminizing, including an immoderate love for the opposite sex.[6] Rather than playing the stereotypical roles of sexual hedonists assigned to them by outdated models of the history of sexuality, Roman upper-class men were in reality only to have "sex with their wives and even then not too often."[7] Strict public control of the male body, corporeal inviolability, and personal austerity all characterized the virility of an elite Roman male (*vir*), a masculine ethos easily absorbed, albeit in the service of a new, spiritual enterprise, by patristic authors and their early medieval successors. Manliness in a Roman context centered on protecting one's public reputation from accusations of softness (*mollitia*), passivity (*pathicus*), and seeming too womanly (*femineus*). Isidore's *Etymologies* echo these male anxieties concerning softness and excess: "A man is soft [*mollis*] when he has weakened the vigor of his sex so that he brings shame to the body . . . he also makes himself soft on account of his immoderate libido."[8] Byzantine authors looked to the figure of the court eunuch as the embodiment of the feminine libido. Eunuch flesh stereotypically was soft, white, and reeked of musk; eunuch voices were

3 Quintilian, *Institutio Oratoria*, 1.8.2.
4 Edwards, *Politics of Immorality*, 118.
5 Nelson, "Monks, Secular Men," 141–42.
6 Isidore of Seville, *Etymologies*, 11.2.24.
7 Edwards, *Politics of Immorality*, 92.
8 Isidore of Seville, *Etymologies*, 10.179–80.

high-pitched and shrill, and effeminate eunuch gullets consumed an excess of food and drink. Because eunuchs were like women, Byzantine texts often characterize them as sexually enslaved to women, a Greek counterpart to the Latin *femineus amor*.[9] For Roman, Byzantine, and western medieval writers, an inability to control the libido is the hallmark of the feminine.

Early medieval adoption of the classical Latin vocabulary for sexual demeanor, sexual activity, and erotic body parts also illuminates the continuity between the two epochs. Classical Latin has over 120 terms for the penis, many of which, including the word *penis* ("tail") itself, are circumlocutions.[10] Early medieval writers incorporate classical euphemisms for male and female members: *veretrum, lumbus, genitalia, libido, inhonesta, pars tegenda*, and *pudenda*, to name but a few. Not surprisingly, churchmen avoid the most obscene words in the corpus of Latin sexual vocabulary: *cunnus* (the female organ) and *mentula* (the male). The decision to do so does not necessarily stem from prudish reasons, however. Although Romans of all classes employed obscene language in a variety of venues, there were clear spaces – such as the forum – where an elite male would not say *cunnus*, for decorum and austerity demanded otherwise. While medieval writers shun Roman obscenities, their sexual style is quite explicit in its description of fornication in the rear (*in tergo*), between the thighs (*in femoribus*), or in the mouth (*in os*).

For example, the language of the penitentials graphically depicts a variety of sex-acts, some of which echo classical usage. One penitential employs *semen in os miserit* (the ejaculation of semen into the mouth) to describe the defilement of oral sex, a slightly less vulgar rendering of the classical *mentulam in os inserere* (the thrusting of the "cock" [*mentula*] into the mouth).[11] Roman women penetrate sexual partners with artificial phalluses (*fascina*), while their medieval counterparts insert unspecified "devices" (*machinae*). Germanic law codes repeat certain classical metonymies for the male member (*virga*, "rod"; *veretrum*, "shameful part"), but add new ones as well, such as *vectis* ("crowbar").[12] Exegetical texts display the full range of sexual metaphors for the phallus, including "tail" (*cauda*), "nose" (*nasus*), and "member of members" (*membrum membri*). Both *lumbus* and *femur* emerge in late antiquity as important synonyms for sex organs, undoubtedly under the influence of Hebrew scripture's substitution of "thigh" and "loins" for the *pudenda*.

9 Ringrose, *Perfect Servant*, 36.
10 Adams, *Latin Sexual Vocabulary*, 77.
11 *Poenitentiale Theodori*, 1.2.15; Adams, *Latin Sexual Vocabulary*, 126.
12 *Lex Thuringorum*, 18; Adams, *Latin Sexual Vocabulary*, 16.

Latin translations of Hebrew and Greek scriptures often intensify the erotic and gendered meanings of the original languages. For example, the ninth-century Carolingian reformer and abbot of Saint-Mihiel, Smaragdus (fl. 809–17), frequently quotes a phrase from the Latin translation of Prov. 18.9, *mollis et dissolutus* ("effeminate and licentious"), when attacking the moral laxity of monks, for inordinate desire unmans the monk.[13] The Latin idiom, *mollis et dissolutus*, is very classicizing and part of a rich vocabulary of sexual invective in the service of crushing political opposition.[14] For Romans, the choice of *mollis* conjures up the image of a "painted young man of ambiguous sexuality."[15] Byzantine churchmen drew upon a classical Greek vocabulary of effeminacy: *gynaikodoulos* ("a man enslaved to women"), *gynaikotraphes* ("a man rendered effeminate because he was raised by women"), and *gynaiazo* ("a man sexually addicted to women").[16] While such continuities in both Greek and Latin are somewhat predictable, the duration of the gendered language of male effeminacy in exegetical and monastic texts is unexpected. Real monks, according to Smaragdus, are vigorous (*vividus*), strong (*fortis*), and hard (*rigidus*); their false brothers are yielding (*mollis*), tender (*tener*), and delicate (*delicatus*).[17]

Smaragdus's musings on "soft" monks suggest that the abbot of Saint-Mihiel viewed bodily habits and accoutrements as markers of gender. But how would the abbot have understood "sex"? Scholars of the history of sexuality have argued that premodern thinkers privileged a one-sex model of the human anatomy: male and female exist on the opposite poles of a unified, corporeal structure.[18] According to this one-sex model, women's sexual organs were the same as men's, but inverted and hence inferior. Only in the eighteenth century did Europeans put forward a new model of biological divergence. Other experts in the field of medical history argue that classical medical writers were never so monolithic in their views of the body that they totally ignored a two-sex model based on anatomical difference. As medieval writers were eclectic in their use of classical medical models, it is not surprising that they freely evoke, as Isidore does in his *Etymologies*, both the one-sex and two-sex paradigms.[19] Of course, both ancient models still place men at the top of the sex/gender system – the one-sex model devalues women through its claim of female *inversion* and *defection* from a male norm, and the two-sex model

13 Smaragdus of Saint-Mihiel, *Expositio in regulam S. Benedicti*, Prologue 7; 1.11; and 4.37.
14 Corbeill, *Controlling Laughter*.
15 Laqueur, *Solitary Sex*, 143.
16 Herrin, Kazhdan, and Cutler, "Women," 2201.
17 Smaragdus of Saint-Mihiel, *Expositio in regulam S. Benedicti*, 4.12.
18 Laqueur, *Making Sex*.
19 Cadden, *Meanings of Sex Difference*, 52–53.

through its privileging of male difference.[20] In any case, one thing is clear – medieval writers were just as confused as to the difference between sex (biological distinction) and gender (the process of inscribing culture on the body and its habits) as are contemporary theorists. When early medieval men wrote about the body, they imposed hierarchical notions of male and female on its material surface, thereby rendering any discussion of biological truths into a discourse on gender ideologies.

For example, in his *Etymologies*, Isidore highlights the anatomical difference between male and female. Only men have a penis (*veretrum*), which emits semen (*virus*), and they alone possess *testes*, or "witnesses" to their virility. Women are unique because they have both a uterus and *vulva* (the door to the *uterus*), which receive semen.[21] A eunuch – a category in-between male and female – is distinguished by weak and unproductive semen.[22] The hermaphrodite, a grotesque mixture of female and male, is discussed in a section devoted to monsters and portents, thereby calling attention to an ancient Hebrew notion that any kind of mixing is an abomination.[23] These unnatural creatures have the right breast of a man and the left of a woman, and, intriguingly, they can both inseminate others and give birth themselves.[24] Unlike hermaphrodites, real men have beards and wide chests; women's bodies are characterized by narrow chests and wide hips.[25] Women have teats (*mammae*), whereas men have nipples (*mamillae*).[26] The thigh (*femur*) is the major site of sex distinction, and both Roman and medieval writers find the *femur* to be a sexually charged body part.[27]

Not surprisingly, the bishop's ideological use of gender consistently intrudes upon his anatomical descriptions. The *locus* of lust in men is in the loins (*lumbi*); women find their erotic zones in the umbilical region (*umbilicus*), a variation in location that intensifies the attributes of female receptivity and male activity.[28] Furthermore, the etymology for *vir* ("man") stems from *vis* ("strength," "vigor," "power"), for according to Isidore, there is greater vigor in men than in women.[29] *Mulier* ("woman"), however, derives from *mollier*

20 Richlin, "Towards a History," 29; Martin, *Corinthian Body*, 32.
21 Isidore of Seville, *Etymologies*, 11.1.103–104; 11.1.134 and 137.
22 Ibid., 10.93.
23 Douglas, *Purity and Danger*, 51–71; Daston and Park, *Wonders*, 50–52.
24 Isidore of Seville, *Etymologies*, 11.3.11.
25 Ibid., 11.1.147.
26 Isidore of Seville, *Liber differentiarum*, 1.372.
27 Isidore of Seville, *Etymologies*, 11.1.106; 11.2.24.
28 Ibid., 11.1.98.
29 Ibid., 11.2.17.

("softer"), and she is subject to a man because of his greater *vis*.[30] Isidore's defense of male superiority hinges on linguistic grounds and not on a polemic of women's flawed anatomy. The bishop's Christianity prevents him from stressing the inherent corruptibility and defective nature of the female body, for, as he emphasizes, God formed the first woman (Gen. 2.22).[31]

Isidore's discussion of body fluids best gauges his hierarchical treatment of the materiality of male and female. Incorporating a Greek medical paradigm for the bodily process of concocting male flux, the bishop describes semen as drops of the brain.[32] According to this ancient theory, semen originates in the brain, is stored in the spinal cord, and from there, is sweated out into the kidneys. Once in the kidneys, this "obscene humor" (*obscenus humor*) is cooked by the heat of lust and runs down to the genitals, where it spurts from the body.[33] In this philosophical/medical system, the heat of desire metamorphoses male bodies into "outlets of a human Espresso machine."[34] For female flux, Isidore turns to the misogynist corpus of the Roman naturalists, who liken menstrual blood to a contagion. Women's defiling blood, according to the bishop, is so perilous that it can kill crops, sour wine, rust iron, and blacken copper.[35] Menstruation is a "lethal danger" both on account of its power to transform substances and its uncontrolled breaking of the boundaries of the body.[36] Although his view on "womanlies" (*muliebria*) is intensely negative, Isidore undoubtedly holds this natural function of the female body in awe because of menstrual blood's potent transformative ability.

The study of the material nature of the body – its anatomical structures and their corresponding functions – fascinate the bishop, as evidenced by his scrupulous exploration of body parts in the *Etymologies*. After the Bible, Isidore's *Etymologies* was the most read and copied text throughout the medieval period.[37] Its impact can be found in a variety of genres, including penitentials, conciliar legislation, saints' lives, monastic commentaries, and exegeses. In this encyclopedic work, Isidore bequeaths to the medieval church a "grammar of the human body," which, if properly decoded, unveils the hidden

30 Ibid., 11.2.18–19; Smith, "Gender and Ideology," 56–57.
31 Isidore of Seville, *Etymologies*, 11.2.20.
32 Jacquart and Thomasset, *Sexuality and Medicine*, 53–54; Cadden, *Meanings of Sex Difference*, 15.
33 Isidore of Seville, *Etymologies*, 11.1.97; 11.1.139.
34 Brown, *Body and Society*, 17.
35 Isidore of Seville, *Etymologies*, 11.1.140–142; Pliny the Elder, *Historia naturalis*, 7.15; Angenendt, "Mit reinen Händen," 305.
36 Douglas, *Purity and Danger*, 150.
37 See Fontaine's comments (*Traité de la nature*, 19) to his edition of Isidore of Seville, *De natura rerum*.

truths of creation and the relationship between *corpus* and cosmos.[38] The body mirrors the political and gendered structures of early medieval society: certain parts rule (the head) and other parts are ruled (the feet), just as men govern women and masters dominate slaves.[39] The decoding of this hierarchical body was an elite process largely carried out by a small group of privileged churchmen.

Like contemporary gender theorists, Isidore and his successors recognize that other contingencies affect the process of making a body sexed with a penis into the cultural product known as "man."[40] A famous theorist once defined gender as "a repeated stylization of the body, a set of repeated acts."[41] Early medieval churchmen, who routinely equate masculinity with physical performance and corporeal style, would concur. Feminine gestures alter a virile countenance, loose belts emasculate monks, and lavish hairstyles transform men into beguiling creatures. Gender also is, according to its contemporary theorists, a lifelong negotiation, shaped by contingencies of age, class, sexual-orientation, nationality, imperialism, ethnicity, and even the physical location of the body in its environment. For medieval intellectuals, religious affiliation was the most important component in the gender mix, followed closely by ethnicity, age, class, kin-group, ritual purity, and the positioning of the body in space.

The institutional rhythms of Benedictine monasticism, as reconstructed through the Rule of St. Benedict and subsequent commentaries, are instructive for understanding how early medieval gender functions in a precise context. Age, class, ritual purity, bodily inviolability, and proximity to the altar emerge as key factors in this hierarchical system where anxiety over the feminine prevails and not all males are real men. According to the Rule, the monastery is a place of combat and spiritual danger – it is the frontline in the war against the Devil. Simultaneously, it is Moses' *tabernaculum* in the desert, a sacred container in the midst of worldly contagion. Male ascetics, who indulge their own desires by rejecting the purgative space of the *claustrum* and the rigors of a monastic Rule, are unmanned (*molliti*). Their cenobitic counterparts are the "strong breed" (*fortissimum genus*), who train in the art of spiritual warfare. Hence, the Rule sets up an ascetic arena fraught with gender trouble. Strong monks continually fight against "vices of body and mind" (*vitia carnis vel cogitationum*), allurements closely associated with the feminine: self-indulgence, desire,

38 Jacquart and Thomasset, *Sexuality and Medicine*, 9–11.
39 Martin, *Corinthian Body*, 30–34; Gowers, "Anatomy of Rome."
40 Cohen and Wheeler, *Becoming Male*, xix.
41 Butler, *Gender Trouble*, 43–44.

sluggishness, and loquaciousness. In so doing, they ensure that their own bodies display the masculine (and classicizing) virtues of gravity, dignity, self-control, and austerity. A meticulous process of surveillance normalizes Benedictine masculinity, for God, the angels, and the abbot (who himself is an earthly embodiment of Christ) monitor every movement of a monk, even during sleep: "Let him recall that he is always seen by God in heaven, that his actions everywhere are in God's sight and are reported by angels at every hour."[42] From the day a monk enters the monastery, he no longer has "his own body at his disposal," a phrase repeated twice in the Rule (33.4, 58.25), referencing Paul's famous explanation of how the married Christian lacks authority over her/his own body (1 Cor. 7.4). Monks are men married to the altar, and as such, they relinquish control over their own flesh to a vigilant celestial hierarchy.

The Benedictine body emerges as the site for inculcating this hierarchy. Rank in the monastery depends on a variety of factors – date of entry, age, class, bodily inviolability, purity, and seating arrangements. Monks perform their low status within this cosmic pecking order through rituals of prostration, bowing the head, and keeping the eyes focused on the ground. The bodies of junior monks are subject to frequent beatings, and their ability to speak is severely limited, especially in the most scrutinized spaces of the monastery – the oratory and the refectory, sites devoted to the mouth. Monks under the ban of excommunication are forbidden to intone the psalms in the oratory, for transgressors of the Rule are cut off from the most status-oriented activity of the monastery, the speaking of the *logos*.[43] The regulation of what goes into and out of the mouth of a monk is a carefully controlled activity in the Rule, for eating, speaking, and intoning psalms all provoke anxieties concerning ritual status. The mouth is a treacherous orifice: it is the instrument of monastic power (the intoning of the Word), but its ingestion of food ruptures the perilous boundary between the interior and exterior worlds. Eating food prepared outside the sacred precincts of the monastery is forbidden unless the abbot makes an exception (Rule of Benedict 51.1–2). Furthermore, the mouth is, according to various penitentials, a sexual orifice, a passive recipient of semen (*semen in os miserit*). The mouth's ability to engage simultaneously in sacred, profane, and obscene activities makes it the most problematic – and commanding – orifice. Even idle talk is defiling to the male ascetic, for the high-status monk empties his body of everything save the Word. Prayer, meditation, and rumination on

42 Benedict of Nursia, *Regula*, 7.13 (trans. Fry, 195).
43 Leyser, *Authority and Asceticism*, 120–22; Flint, "Space and Discipline."

biblical texts alone fill the mind of a potent monk and function as markers of his ascetic masculinity. The oratory itself is a trope for the body of a perfected monk, as the Rule commands: "Let the oratory be what it is called. Let nothing else be done or stored there."[44] The chief goal of the Rule is to convert the bodies of its practitioners into storehouses of the Word.

Age also plays into the making of a monastic corporate ladder – boys under fifteen are the most beatable members of the monastery. They make mistakes in the oratory for which they are "whipped" (Rule of Benedict 45.3) and engage in frivolous conversation at table (Rule of Benedict 63.18). They are "males" in the process of becoming "men"[45] within the disciplinary strictures of the Benedictine system, wherein control of the mouth, access to the oratory, and freedom from physical assault are key components. The liminal position of young monks speaks to their malleable, soft, and penetrable nature. And, as the Rule insinuates, and subsequent commentaries and penitentials clarify, boys are sexual objects, and their presence in the monastery both destabilizes and enforces its gendered hierarchy. Early medieval science validates the problematic gender of Benedictine boys. According to both classical and early medieval medical teachings, masculine bodies are hotter and drier, and thus they are more stable and less subject to leakage. Feminine bodies are colder and moister, and this wetness underscores female instability and mutability.[46] Young boys are closer to the feminine temperature register, and the Rule consistently treats them as loquacious, self-indulgent, penetrable, and lacking in discipline – all feminized attributes.

The Benedictine hierarchy parallels the social pyramid created by the classical Roman sex/gender system, wherein elite *viri* have authority based on the use of the mouth, both in oratory and political invective. On the one hand, the ability to use the mouth in ritually sanctioned places – and the power to silence others – is the hallmark of classical masculinity. On the other hand, scurrilous political and literary invectives focus on the *os impurum*, "the unclean mouth that supposedly results from oral intercourse."[47] Silencing a political opponent is a metaphorical oral rape (*irrumo*), a powerful symbol of domination in the phallus-centered, Roman political hierarchy. Any elite man who allowed his mouth to be penetrated "violated his sexual integrity, his impenetrability (*pudicitia*)."[48] Fellatio was a lower-class sex act, something a senator might ask

44 Benedict of Nursia, *Regula*, 52.1 (trans. Fry, 255).
45 Frantzen, "Where the Boys Are," 59.
46 Carson, "Putting her in her Place."
47 Richlin, *Garden of Priapus*, 26.
48 Williams, *Roman Homosexuality*, 198.

a prostitute to perform on him, but never his upper-class wife. Romans were obsessed by the purity of the mouth: "It was the organ of speech and, above all, of public oratory."[49] *Viri*, the men on top, successfully protect their own bodies from verbal, physical, or sexual assault, and they freely beat and/or sexually penetrate low-ranking "others."[50] Elite boys undermine this classical sex/gender system, because they are both objects of male lust and, in theory, off-limits for sex because of their highborn status. In this Roman system, therefore, sex/gender is based simultaneously on anatomy *and* social, economic, and political status.

Similarly, the Benedictine Rule produces a gendered hierarchy, with God and the angels at its celestial apex, the abbot-Christ as its mediator and earthly potentate, followed by subsequent ranks of monks, whose status is based on the ritual use of the mouth, access to the oratory, and bodily inviolability. As in classical Rome, the sexual use of the mouth is a major taboo in early medieval monastic culture, and, in certain penitentials, the penance for oral copulation is lifelong, making it a worse offense than anal intercourse, interfemoral sex, or incest.[51] At the bottom of the Benedictine gender pyramid are the boys under fifteen (Rule of Benedict 70.4), whose mouths lack full, ritual power, and whose bodies are open to penetration (by striking hand or thrusting penis).[52] Boyish mouths – because they belong to damp, boyish bodies – produce sounds that are "reedy" and "thin"; their chants lack the power to penetrate the intellects of their hearers. In contrast, adult men have fat, penetrating voices.[53] God, of course, is the most powerful orator in the Benedictine community, and those monks closest to him are the ones who take "a more active part in speaking, in giving commandments, and in bestowing blessings."[54] The strongest monks therefore are those who come closest to being like God: a disembodied voice.[55]

The Rule is a kind of handbook for making the mystical leap from body to voice within the context of a carefully delineated ascetic masculinity. It also offers other important lessons to the interpreter of the early medieval body. The Benedictine body has no meaning apart from its membership in the body of Christ; therefore, its "ontological status" is more "like that of a slave in Roman law."[56] The ritual purity of an individual monk is a community concern, for any

49 Clarke, "Look Who's Laughing at Sex," 161–62.
50 Walters, "Invading the Roman Body."
51 Frantzen, *Before the Closet*, 162–63.
52 Hildemar of Corbie, *Expositio regulae S. Benedicti*, 22, 25, 30.
53 Corbeill, *Controlling Laughter*, 145; Holsinger, *Music, Body, and Desire*, 297.
54 Wathen, *Silence*, 180, 194.
55 Scarry, *Body in Pain*, 191–98.
56 Martin, *Corinthian Body*, 178.

bodily debasement is an occasion for collective pollution. One seventh-century monastic rule details the punishment of a monk accused of seducing boys: the offender's head is shaven, and he is publicly flogged, chained, verbally reviled, and spat upon by the entire congregation. He is then segregated from his peers and placed under the strict supervision of senior brothers, who monitor his every movement.[57] Transgression of hierarchy is thus inscribed on the body of a fallen monk, who serves as a visual reminder of the dangers of infraction. In this system, a monk's body is analogous to the uncontaminated space of the cloister; hence the exits and entrances of his body, like those of the monastery, are subject to heavy surveillance. It is no coincidence that the Rule stresses the importance of a porter (Rule of Benedict 66), who is to be a "wise old man" (*senex sapiens*) and custodian of the monastery's most vulnerable point – its entryway, which is an architectural version of a bodily orifice. Penitentials and canon laws pay close attention to pathic orifices, or "orifices that receive and submit to the penis,"[58] of all Christians, but especially of priests, monks, and nuns. Priests who submit to anal penetration weaken the church and summon plagues and famine upon its people.[59] Nuns who engage in same-sex acts, some using artificial devices (*machinae*), subvert the God-given hierarchy of male–female.[60] One Anglo-Saxon penitential cites the desecration of the mouth by semen as the "worst of evils" (*hoc pessimum malum*).[61] Considering the role of the mouth in the monastic enterprise, it is understandable that its pollution would be severely condemned. Yet, it is equally the case that any breach of the sacred body's inner / outer boundaries represents a rupture of community.

In addition to being corporate in nature, early medieval bodies possess two genders: one based on the material body and another on somatic transcendence. Isidore of Seville defines medieval man "as a double creature – he is both interior and exterior. The interior man is the soul and the exterior man is the body."[62] The two natures of human beings are intimately linked. In fact, the inner man could at any moment erupt on the body's surface. Drawing on the medical corpus of their classical predecessors, early medieval writers fret over the porous nature of the body, for the body is made up of little breathing holes (*spiramenta*) through which defiling substances enter and precious stuff, such as semen, oozes out.[63] Gregory the Great cautions the readers of his influential

57 Fructuosus of Braga, *Regula monachorum complutensis*, 16.
58 Richlin, *Garden of Priapus*, 68.
59 Council of Paris (829), canons 34, 69. See *Concilium Parisiense*,634–35 and 669–71.
60 *Poenitentiale Baedae*, 3.24; Matter, "My Sister," 89–90.
61 *Poenitentiale Theodori*, 1.2.15.
62 Isidore of Seville, *Etymologies*, 11.1.6.
63 Ibid., 11.1.80.

Pastoral Care (c. 591) that even minor sins can explode on the skin's surface like pustules. Major depravities, the pope argues, cause the body's internal fluids to rush to the genitals, producing an irksome and shameful swelling, an exterior manifestation of interior desires.[64] In this figurative scheme, the exterior of the body serves as a litmus test for the spiritual status of the interior. An effeminate soul (*mollitia animae*) can move the outer man to sin. Resurrected flesh must be purged of effeminacy and remain stalwart in its virility.[65] Monastic commentators and biblical exegetes make much of this inner / outer paradigm, frequently addressing their writings to the inner man or the outer man or both.

In this double rendering of human anatomy, external organs have internal parallels. For example, the stomach is an interior phallus, a vexing, insatiable organ that fights against salvation. It is an organ to be conquered.[66] For medieval interpreters of the body, an individual organ, like the stomach, can be read on three different levels: medical (as a transmitter of food to the intestines), moral (as a metonymy for excessive lust), and allegorical (as a trope for the disobedience of fallen humanity). As such, reading the body is a mystical act similar to the medieval practice of reading scripture – a tripartite strategy wherein the experienced exegete moves beyond literal and moral content to the decoding of occult truths. Medieval thinkers approach the body as a microcosm of God's universe, stressing that the Creator yoked together *corpus* and *cosmos* by infusing them with the same substances: earth, water, fire, and air.[67] Reading the body, therefore, is an esoteric enterprise, one capable of unlocking the secrets of creation and exposing the dangers of the Anti-Christ.

Early medieval exegetes and medical writers comment on a surprising range of human body parts and offer, in some cases, shocking elucidations of their functions and meanings. Churchmen frequently inscribe issues of great concern to the church on body parts: heresy, orthodoxy, salvation, and damnation. Some body parts have strong connections to Christ, such as the head; others are allied with the Anti-Christ, such as the phallus. The *Etymologies* of Isidore of Seville provides the foundation for early medieval readings of the vulva and phallus, and his intellectual heirs take the bishop's succinct and moralizing examination of the body and its parts and recast it into the esoteric world of allegory. In so doing, they blend classical views on the sex organs with Christian and Hebrew interpretations of their moral and anagogic meanings.

64 Gregory the Great, *Regula pastoralis*, 3.33; 1.11.
65 Alcuin, *Liber de virtutibus et vitiis*, 29; Bede, *Commentarii in Pentateuchum*, Lev. 12.
66 Alcuin, *Liber de virtutibus et vitiis*, 28.
67 Isidore of Seville, *Etymologies*, 11.1.16.

In classical Latin, the word *vulva* can stand for womb, vagina, and external *pudenda* of the female.[68] While Roman poets avoid referring to the *vulva* and its internal / external parts in erotic verse, crafters of invective characterize it as "smelly, dirty, wet, loose, noisy, hairy."[69] The foulest obscenity in the classical Latin corpus is the word *cunnus* ("cunt"), a word so taboo that Cicero castigates elite men who utter it in the *Curia*. In fact, Cicero avoids directly referring to the *cunnus* by writing "*cum nos*" instead.[70] Classical authors apply the vocabulary of the external body to describe the internal nature of the vagina and uterus. The womb is a mouth, the *labiae* lips, the clitoris a nose or tongue, the cervix a neck; hence, each internal organ has a visible, external parallel. Isidore notes that the Latin speakers of his day use *labiae* for female lips, and *labra* for male – a distinction suggesting that *labiae* had become closely identified with women's *pudenda*.[71] In this symbolic reading of the body, veiling a woman's head is akin to covering her sex, and violations of the veil are metaphorical equivalents of rape.[72] Early medieval writers carry over this internal / external tradition of the female *pudenda*. Holy women, according to their hagiographers, manipulate bodily metaphors to express outrage in the face of imminent rape. As barbaric hoards descend upon Christian cloisters, nuns cut their lips and noses, clear metonymies for the mutilation of the *pudenda*.[73] Not surprisingly, the veil is the most obvious sign of female inviolability, and by the early medieval period it possesses miraculous powers and is capable of thwarting swords, obvious phallic tropes (for in Latin, "sword" (*gladius*) is slang for "penis").[74]

The vulva finds its standard early medieval medical definition in the *Etymologies* of Isidore: "The *vulva* is named by analogy to a folding door [*valva*], that is, the door to the belly, because it receives semen there, or because the fetus proceeds from it."[75] As a door, the vulva represents a perilous breach between the inner and outer body; the analogy with a folding door relates to the organ's inner / outer layering. The vulva is the site for uncontrollable flux (the *menses*), a cyclical oozing dictated by the rhythms of the moon.[76] The bishop finds this lunar substance to be potent and terrifying because, he writes, contact with this gore (*cruor*) provokes madness in dogs and dissolves

68 Adams, *Latin Sexual Vocabulary*, 103–109.

69 Richlin, *Garden of Priapus*, 68.

70 Cicero, *Epistulae ad familiares*, 9.22.2.

71 Isidore of Seville, *Etymologies*, 11.1.50 (trans. Sharpe, 41, note to section 11.1.50); Isidore of Seville, *Liber differentiarum*, 1.336.

72 Martin, *Corinthian Body*, 235–37; Myerowitz, "Gendered Grammar."

73 Schulenburg, *Forgetful of their Sex*, 145–51.

74 *Vita S. Glodesindae*, 10–11; Adams, *Latin Sexual Vocabulary*, 21.

75 Isidore of Seville, *Etymologies*, 11.1.137; Adams, *Latin Sexual Vocabulary*, 101–109.

76 Isidore of Seville, *Etymologies*, 11.1.140.

glue.[77] The inability of the female to control her bodily fluxes is a central feature of early medieval misogyny and marks the crucial distinction between the masculine and feminine. Feminine bodies are open, porous, and subject to "liquefying assaults."[78] In contrast, the ideal masculine body is stable, dry, hot, and bounded. In the allegorical realm, the opposition between dry / masculine and wet / feminine is cast in an eschatological light: fallen humanity is cold, numb, and earthbound (i.e., feminine); when set on fire with the erotic language of Scripture, the fallen soul sheds its cold, labile nature and becomes hot and airy (i.e., masculine), rising up to meet its Beloved.[79]

One of Isidore's intellectual votaries, the Carolingian abbot of Fulda, Hrabanus Maurus (d. 856), takes his mentor's medical (and moralizing) treatment of the vulva and its fluxes an interpretive step further in his monumental *De universo* (c. 840s).[80] For this abbot and biblical exegete, the earthly vulva is intensely carnal, yet it fulfils the divine command to "be fruitful and multiply." Its esoteric counterpart, however, personifies the secrets of the faith and the interior nature of the soul, which can be used for good or evil. The vulva's inner layering also symbolizes the most hallowed part of the church, a space where "depraved heretics attempt to rush in, but they are aborted from the mother." For Hrabanus, the uncontrollable flux of the womb is a perfect allegory for the unruly and defiling flux of words, which spill from the mouths of idolaters and heretics. Like menstrual blood, such heretics are vomited out of the inner sanctum of the church, which Hrabanus likens to a uterus. Hrabanus's contradictory treatment of female and male body fluids speaks to the hierarchical treatment of gender in the Carolingian church. Semen, the abbot argues, is the Word of God because of its propagating nature, and the abbot of Fulda's conception of male flux is an allegorical extension of Isidore's medical reading of male seed as "drops of the brain."[81] In contrast, Hrabanus equates menstrual fluid to "the obscenities of idolatry and the pollution of errors." This gore, he reasons, causes the entire earth to turn violently "in error and idolatry." Catholic men, the abbot warns, must not approach menstruating women nor have intercourse with them, for to do so is to seek carnal union with pagans and heretics. The mouths of heretics are like the lascivious mouth of the whore in Prov. 5.3: idolatrous lips drip honey, and their sweet words ensnare wretched men.[82] Hrabanus reads the female *pudenda*, an amazing

77 Ibid., 11.1.141.
78 Carson, "Putting her in her Place," 138.
79 Gregory the Great, *Expositio in canticis canticorum*, 1–4.
80 Hrabanus Maurus, *De universo*, 6.1.
81 Ibid.; Coon, "What is the Word if not Semen"?
82 Hrabanus Maurus, *Expositio in proverbia Salomonis*, 1.5.

activity for a celibate monk, both for metaphors of purity (the inner layers of the vulva) and depravity (an inability to control flux).

Whereas classical writers disdain the mucky nature of the *cunnus*, they look to the penis (or phallus, its metaphorical counterpart) as the ultimate marker of male political and sexual prowess. The organ's thrusting movement during intercourse (*futuo*) is, for Romans, akin to the beating or striking of a weapon, for sex is an assault on a social inferior.[83] The phallus itself formed a variety of apotropaic functions in the Roman world, including the warding off of the evil eye. It assumed a diversity of material forms: amulets (*fascina*), shop signs, lamps, doorbells, and paving stones.[84] One of its classical circumlocutions, *verenda*, translates as the "parts that inspire awe or respect," mirroring a Roman concept that phallic power personifies imperial rule. The penis's most obscene designation is *mentula* ("cock"), a word assiduously avoided by early medieval writers.[85] Romans also refer to the penis or testicle as *nervus* ("sinew," "tendon") because of its sinewy, potent nature, a designation picked up by early medieval exegetes.[86] Like the vulva, the penis possesses external parallels: it is a nose, neck, gullet, or even a tail (*cauda*). One eleventh-century writer likens the release of semen occasioned by masturbation to the blowing of mucus from the nose; a ninth-century exegete identifies the Anti-Christ by his "stiff tail."[87] Compilers of early medieval law codes express anxiety over the slicing and dicing of the penis and testicles by calculating wergild compensations for mutilated male parts.[88] For early medieval biblical exegetes, the phallus retains some of its classical connotations of awe and reverence as it metaphorically stands for the "sword [*gladius*] of the spirit" (Eph. 6.17), and its ability to ejaculate serves as a trope for preaching the Word (Luke 8.11). The phallic sword of the Word penetrates (*irrumpo*) into the guts of vice and into the hearts of men.[89]

Isidore of Seville uses the word *veretrum* ("shameful," "modest") for penis, a classical circumlocution originally applied to both male and female parts. The bishop provides an etymology: "The *veretrum* is so named, for only men have them [*viri est tantum*], or because semen is emitted from it; for *virus* ["slimy fluid"] is the liquid which flows from the sex organs of men." The testicles (*testiculi*), Isidore notes, are a diminution from "witness" (*testis*), and they serve as a storehouse for the semen, which finds its origin, according to Greek

83 Adams, *Latin Sexual Vocabulary*, 118.
84 Kellum, "Phallus as Signifier."
85 Adams, *Latin Sexual Vocabulary*, 9–12.
86 Ibid., 38.
87 Peter Damian, *Liber Gomorrhianus*, 21; Hrabanus Maurus, *De universo*, 6.3.
88 *Lex Thuringorum*, 16–18.
89 Hrabanus Maurus, *De universo*, 6.1.

medicine, in the brain.[90] Isidore's incorporation of *testes* into his anatomical vocabulary reflects the influence of Hebrew on late Latin, for in the Torah (Gen. 24.2–3; 47.29), the act of testifying requires the man under oath to hold his *testes* as witnesses of his truth-telling, a ritual use of the male body familiar to the bishop.[91] Unlike female *pudenda*, which contain both exterior and interior layers, male anatomical members are wholly external and, as such, early medieval exegetes find in their uncontrollable swellings and ejaculations exterior manifestations of internal vice.[92] According to the Carolingian writer Theodulf of Orleans (d. 821), even the vigilant man who discharges his seed at the sight, touch, or even recollection of a woman suffers an "effeminate defilement" (*immunditia mollities*), which causes him to spill his impurity between his thighs (*inter femora*) or even the thighs of another.[93] Such effeminate individuals, Theodulf cautions, will be barred from the kingdom of heaven (*neque molles regnum Dei possidebunt*, referencing 1 Cor. 6.9–10). Uncontrolled spilling of seed makes men like women, who are helpless in the face of "liquefying assaults," for the litmus test of masculinity is the possession of a bounded, stable body.

Monastic garb serves as a prophylactic against effeminate oozings and troublesome erections and emerges as a major theme in the writing of early medieval ascetics. "Gird your loins, like a man" (*Accinge sicut vir lumbos tuos*, Job 38.3; 40.2) is a text favored by monastic fashioners of prophylactic dress. So too is Jerome's description of John the Baptist and Elijah as tightly girded, hirsute men in whom there is nothing soft or effeminate, for every inch of them is hard and virile.[94] Intimidated by the hyper-masculine models of John and Elijah, Hrabanus worries about the virility of the "loosely belted" monastic figure of his own day: " . . . having been hindered from the course of manliness and polluted with the squalor of earthly desire, [the unbelted priest] becomes vile."[95] For Hrabanus, tight-fitting clothing was the symbolic marker of a virile soul. His anxieties over proper girding of the loins mirror classical invectives against men who fail to restrain their *pudenda*. The state of being "loosely belted" (*discinctus*), according to authors as diverse as Cicero, Horace, Plautus, Pliny the Elder, and Martial, is the "metaphorical equivalent of having an effeminate lifestyle."[96] The Roman poet Horace could make an offhanded remark about a certain man, who sported a "low-hanging tunic," and his audience would

90 Isidore of Seville, *Etymologies*, 11.1.103–104.
91 Ibid., 10.265.
92 Leyser, "Masculinity in Flux."
93 Theodulf of Orleans, *Capitulare ad eosdem*, 2.7.11; Laqueur, *Solitary Sex*, 142–44.
94 Jerome, *De exodo, in vigilia paschae*, 540.
95 Hrabanus Maurus, *De institutione clericorum*, 1.17.
96 Corbeill, "Dining Deviants," 118.

immediately know that the poet was hinting at the sexual deviance of its wearer. Monastic writers of the Carolingian era, including Hrabanus Maurus, who read and cited Horace in his poetic works, clearly had some familiarity with Roman ideologies of masculinity and the public demeanor of the virtuous man. They fuse Roman notions of masculinity with Hebrew teachings on the girding of the loins both as a proof text of ascetic virility (Elijah and John the Baptist) and as a preparation for prayer (Moses in the Talmud). Proper girding enables the holy man to cut off secular ambition, conquer lecherous itching (*prurigo*), and eradicate *luxuria* ("excess," "sexual pollution"), vices symbolized by the wandering penis.[97] The eleventh-century clerical reformer Peter Damian recommends girding of the loins as an antidote to sodomy.[98] Cincturing preserves virility as embodied by the self-discipline of continence: "Priests wear tight linen – not in an effeminate manner but zealously – because they preserve the resolution of chastity."[99] Real men, the abbot reasons, restrain the labile nature of the peripatetic penis with tight linen.

In contrast to the tightly bound loins of the vigilant monk, the Anti-Christ's phallus and testes are as unrestrained as feminine flux. Following in the footsteps of Gregory the Great's epic *Moralia in Iob* (c. 591), several early medieval monastic writers, including Hrabanus, project the worst qualities of the male *pudenda* onto the gruesome body of the Hebrew sea-monster Behemoth (Job 40), whom they equate with the Anti-Christ.[100] His "member of members" (*membrum membri*) is a stiff "tail" (*cauda*), an external manifestation of his interior apostasy. Behemoth, Gregory calculates, has many testicles, or preachers of his wanton doctrines, which gush forth with the virulent semen of error and corrupt the human heart. His testicles are a web of tangled sinews (*nervi*), exemplifying the confused doctrines of the Anti-Christ and their power to entrap the orthodox. His mouth is as unruly as his bodily flux, for his contagious locutions infect the human spirit. The Behemoth/Anti-Christ figure, like his heretical counterparts, is oddly feminized – loquacious, uncontrolled, excessive, and imbued with *luxuria*. Behemoth dominates both women and men by infusing their erotic zones with *luxuria* – women through the umbilical region and men via the loins. This exegetical rendering of Behemoth thus adds a new, darker meaning to the monastic act of girding the loins – it is an apotropaic ritual designed to ward off the contagion of the Anti-Christ.

97 Hrabanus Maurus, *De universo*, 21.15.
98 Peter Damian, *Liber Gomorrhianus*, 25.
99 Hrabanus Maurus, *De institutione clericorum*, 1.16.
100 Gregory the Great, *Moralia in Iob*, 32.14.20–32. 20–35; Hrabanus Maurus, *De universo*, 6.1.

As Hrabanus Maurus warns his monastic audience: "Certain body parts are ascribed to the Devil."[101]

The study of the body and its parts – the devilish phallus, the heretic-aborting *vulva*, and the Benedictine mouth – suggests that defense of the male body from the contamination of the feminine is the key to the early medieval sex/gender system. Such effeminacy assumes many forms: uncontrolled spurting of semen, unbridled heretical speech, low-hanging tunics, and even excessive interest in the opposite sex (*femineus amor/gynaiazo*). But how much of this fear of effeminacy represents a radical departure from post-Enlightenment views on sex and sexuality, which were supposedly based on the more objective sciences of biology, psychiatry, and sexology? Historians of homosexuality have pointed out that the word heterosexual first emerged as a sexual pathology in the writings of late nineteenth-century sexologists. Heterosexuality was, like its twin term homosexuality, a pathology characterized by an excessive interest in the opposite sex or a desire to seek pleasure for non-procreative purposes (and any medievalist would recognize in this "scientific" definition vestiges of Augustinian theology). As late as 1923, dictionaries still defined heterosexuality as a "morbid sexual passion for one of the opposite sex," echoing classical and early medieval notions of *femineus amor* ("excessive love/womanly love").[102] The dread of surrendering male dominance through effeminate passivity continued to inform theories of masculinity and sexual identity well into the "objective" medical and psychiatric discourses of the twentieth century.

Yet, at the same time, early medieval churchmen were deficient of a sophisticated taxonomy of sex that characterizes Victorian sexology. Edifying in this regard is the infamous trial of the ninth-century Carolingian queen, Theutberga. Churchmen accommodate women – like Theutberga, whose husband, King Lothar II (d. 869), accused her of sodomitic incest – within the Apostle Paul's invective against men who sleep with male concubines (*concubitores masculorum*, 1 Cor. 6.10; 1 Tim. 1.10). Apparently there was no separate place for a nonconformist woman within early medieval, male-centered sexual rhetoric. In the opening volley of the Theutberga trial, the queen's accusers claim that she had played the part of passive male-concubine to her brother's insertive role, that the siblings had engaged in sex *inter femora* (a sexual style favored by male monastics), and that they had conspired to destroy the monstrously conceived fetus by concocting an abortive potion.[103] The perverse nature of

101 Hrabanus Maurus, *De universo*, 6.3.
102 Moore, *God's Beauty Parlor*, 16.
103 Hincmar of Rheims, *De divortio Lotharii*, 114.

Theutberga's *stuprum* ("defilement," "dishonor") combines a variety of clerical and classical angst about sex and the body: the fetishistic nature of the *femur*, the excessive libido of the female, incest, sodomy, abortion, the misuse of orifices, and the breakdown of the body politic occasioned by that misuse.[104] Isidore's ruminations on the vulva make a brief appearance in the trial narrative, where its author, Hincmar of Rheims (d. 882), invokes the best medical advice on female anatomy available to dismiss the charge that the queen could conceive through anal intercourse.[105] And, Theutberga's behavior during the divorce proceedings underscores the theory that early medieval women – like their classical counterparts – lacked public mouths (i.e., they were *infames*). The queen remains "passive, reduced to silence . . . her trial stage-managed by male bishops; she asks for permission to retreat into a monastery, the veil and silence." In contrast, her husband, Lothar, is "male and active: he asks the bishops not for permission to enter a monastery, but to let him remarry."[106]

Lothar's reasons for seeking a new wife expose the deeper, political context behind clerical constructions of masculinity and effeminacy. As a secular man, Lothar burned with carnal desires and could not control his libido. Separated from his wife and prohibited by his ecclesiastical counselors from seeking pleasures from female concubines, Lothar complained to his bishops that he needed a legitimate outlet for his lust.[107] The weak, secular male body, unlike its tightly girded monastic counterpart, is intensely vulnerable to venereal assault and the demonic allures of *luxuria* ("excess"), which Gregory the Great claims hit men directly in the loins.[108] As Carolingian churchmen stress: Love of Christ is not found "in a bed of carnal pleasures" (*in lectulo carnalium voluptatum*).[109] Clerical anxieties concerning masculinity and bodily control transferred readily into elite lay circles, even to the point where hagiographers created novel – if not clumsy – portraits of hyper-abstemious warlords, who wash compulsively after noctural emissions, express horror at nuptial pleasures, and instruct their troops to blunt the edges of their swords before they go into battle. The strategy is brilliant: it invites an audience of lay potentates to internalize ascetic values of bodily discipline and pacifism. Simultaneously, since the primary role of aristocratic men was to produce heirs and to bear arms, it guarantees that the lay body will never measure up to the ascetic ideal.[110]

104 Airlie, "Private Bodies," 7–8.
105 Hincmar of Rheims, *De divortio Lotharii*, 102.
106 Airlie, "Private Bodies," 37.
107 Ibid., 24–25.
108 Gregory the Great, *Moralia in Iob*, 32.14.20–21; Jordan, *Invention of Sodomy*, 39.
109 Smaragdus of Saint-Mihiel, *Expositio in regulam S. Benedicti*, 8.3.
110 Nelson, "Monks, Secular Men"; Airlie, "Anxiety of Sanctity."

Smaragdus's commentary on the Rule of St. Benedict makes the distinction between the lay and monastic male body quite clear: "Soldiers of the world are addicted to passions and desires and hold on to them." These men have "weak and slippery weapons" (*infirma et lubrica arma*). In contrast, Christ's warriors "crucify the flesh along with its passions and desires."[111] They are God's "most perfect wrestlers" (*perfectissimi luctatores*), and their arsenal includes the shield of faith and the helmet of salvation (Eph. 6.16–17).[112] Monks are like Isaiah's eunuchs (Isa. 56.4–5) whose dutiful service to God confers upon them "a monument and a name better than sons and daughters . . . an everlasting name," a biblical passage favored by fashioners of monastic masculinity from Smaragdus to Peter Damian (1007–72).[113] Clearly, competition with the secular world is deeply embedded in these spiritual tracts even to the point where celibate men believe that they have surpassed the power of their procreating lay peers to achieve immortality. Through virile liturgical voices, restrained *pudenda*, and defense of the body's margins, holy men move away from the place of man which is "in the body," and into the realm of the divine which is "in the voice."[114] Somatic transcendence then is the real test of virility.[115] In this ascetic reworking of the masculine power of the Roman orator, perfected monks become like Christ, whom Hrabanus Maurus identifies as "the mouth of God, because he is his Word."[116]

111 Smaragdus of Saint-Mihiel, *Expositio in regulam S. Benedicti*, Prologue 3.
112 Ibid., 1.4.
113 Ibid., 4.64; Peter Damian, *Liber Gomorrhianus*, 24.
114 Scarry, *Body in Pain*, 192.
115 Fredrick, *Roman Gaze*, 258.
116 Hrabanus Maurus, *In honorem S. Crucis*, C 1 (line 50).

22

Sacrifice, gifts, and prayers in Latin Christianity

ARNOLD ANGENENDT

Sacrifice has a role in all religions. Sacrifices are made to God or to gods in the hope of obtaining something which is beyond the realm of human action – something which can be achieved only by a more powerful force: a good harvest, health, protection from misfortune, continued life, a better life, and finally, eternal life itself. Sacrifices are made to God, or to the gods, in the hope that in their omnipotence they will grant those things which are believed to be essential to life, but which cannot be achieved by humans. This adds greatly to the subtleties within the performance of cult and ritual, and also increases the value of the sacrificial object itself. In order to obtain from God that which is unobtainable by humanity, the most valuable of items are offered, even human life. As a result sacrifice always involves art and ceremony, the most precious of human things in their highest form.

The altar is the central physical location of all sacrificial cults, for it is a divine site in the human world. Any item placed on the altar has entered a divine sphere and no longer belongs to humankind. Some sacrificial objects are removed forever (in sacrifice they are rendered non-functional or consumed in fire) while other objects return to the human world transfigured and endowed with divine power. Examples of the latter include flesh sacrificed for the community of the cult or foodstuffs laid on the altar in the belief that they will acquire the power to fortify. Sacrifice of first fruits is also a common practice, applied in many religious traditions to both harvest and animals, as well as to humans. In each instance the first gift from God is to be returned to him.

Discussion of sacrifice must also address the issue of the "development of religion." Modern research into religion has sought to eliminate the evolutionary tendencies so loved in the nineteenth century, but it must also acknowledge that the rituals of sacrifice did not have identical meanings in every historical epoch. Examples of change can be found in the criticism of sacrifice made by both Old Testament prophets and Greek philosophers and in ideas voiced in India or recorded in Near Eastern wisdom literature. These all demonstrate a move toward a greater spiritualization of sacrifice: inner attitude and a good life are judged to be more important than the act of sacrifice and accompanying ceremony.

Christianity also gave spiritualized meaning to sacrifice, as *thysia logike*, a spiritual sacrifice. Two major influences informed this conception: according to its Greek roots, spiritual sacrifice was the unconditional fulfillment of the truth; according to its Israelite roots, sacrifice was about hearing the Word of God and care of the poor. For Christians the original sacrifice was the self-sacrifice of Jesus Christ as he gave himself to fulfill the Word of God and for the sake of humanity, the poor in particular, even to the point of surrendering his own life. The Christian sacrifice was seen as a spiritual act, made through love and completed on the altar of the heart. In the Christian sacrificial liturgy, the Eucharist, all these elements came together to create a cultic act of celebration: the Word of God was heard, the communicants participated (*communio*) in the sacrificial death of Jesus Christ, and aid was given to the poor. Christians believed that their salvation had been ensured by Christ's sacrifice and gave thanks for it. This was inherent in the use of the term "Eucharist" (thanksgiving), the true Christian sacrifice as a "sacrifice of praise" (*sacrificium laudis*).

The Eucharist was the most frequently performed liturgical act. The first part was a "service of the Word," whose form was both simple and clear: *lectio* and *oratio* (reading of Scripture and prayer); God spoke and humanity answered. This was integrated into the shape of the liturgy: the Word of God was read out; it was then inwardly received by the listeners who responded in prayer. The readings were taken from the Bible, both Old and New Testaments. The specific passage to be read on each occasion of the celebration of mass was quickly established, based on the annual cycle marked out by Christmas, Easter, and Pentecost and by each Sunday and saint's day. Books known as lectionaries were produced specifically for this purpose. The sermon, in the form of an exposition of the biblical text, was intended to enable the listener to understand the passage which had been read out and to receive it inwardly. This was the least rigid element of the liturgy, for while the sermon was certainly based entirely on the Word of God, there were no set words or actions. The sermon was always part of the festive liturgy, in particular when performed by bishops or popes, although Gregory the Great was to be the last great preaching pope in the period covered by this book. Little is known about sermons preached in cathedrals and monasteries in this period, let alone in village churches. Charlemagne's *Admonitio generalis* of 789 ordered that "priests must preach correctly and honestly, they must preach to the people nothing which is uncanonical or of new form, nor recount things which they have invented according to their own minds and have not been taken from the Holy Writings."[1] In his sermon the preacher should demonstrate his knowledge of the godly persons of the Trinity, that Christ became human, the redemption, the resurrection, and the Last Judgment, and in addition the most important virtues and sins. Probably in practice the sermon frequently comprised only the recitation and repetition of the confession of faith (the Creed) and the Lord's Prayer, the two prayers which every baptized person was supposed to know. Often the sermon would have been an introduction to religious practice, explaining, for example, that baptism would keep a child alive, that communion would strengthen one's health, that the anointing of the sick would keep death at bay, that touching reliquaries would bring about cure, that repentance would bring protection from hell. These explanations were calls for action rather than "dogmatic" statements. The final act was the general prayer, made in response to hearing and contemplating the Word of God. The supplications contained in this prayer were more public than personal, for the church and the authorities, for those in distress, and for the poor. The "service of the Word" with its liturgical readings from the Bible turned Christianity into a religion of the book, and this in turn was accompanied by a large number of civilizing processes and cultural demands including reading and writing, book production, and textual interpretation.

The second part of the Eucharist was the "sacrifice of the offering." Early Christians had celebrated the sacrifice as an act of thanksgiving for redemption and as participation in the life of Christ. It was understood to be a sacrifice filled with the spirit, a dedication of the self in mind and spirit: "to present your bodies (= yourself) as a living sacrifice, holy and acceptable to God, which is your reasonable worship" (Rom. 12.1). Material objects could only fulfill this self sacrifice if they were themselves an expression of the heart. The bread and wine brought to the celebration of the Eucharist originally had no religious significance, although this could be ascribed to gifts for the poor which served God's special friends. The concept of the "spiritual sacrifice" which denoted the Greek spiritualization of the sacrifice therefore could also cover the social activity required by the Old Testament prophets: care for widows and orphans (see Isa. 1.23; Ps. 145.9)

This spiritualized concept was altered in the early medieval period. By Late Antiquity the liturgy was firmly established: it was recorded in written form and was to be followed precisely in both word and action; there were now

1 *Admonitio generalis*, 82, 61: ". . . ut recte et honeste praedicent; et non sinatis nova vel non canonica aliquos ex suo sensu et non secundum scripturas sacras fingere et predicare populo."

lectionaries and sacramentaries for the celebration of the mass. The liturgy was, of course, still understood as a divine act of salvation, but its original transparent meaning was less distinct. New explanations were developed, in accordance with new methods. The allegorical explanation was first proposed by Amalarius of Metz (d. c. 850), based on the assumption of the existence of a God-given "hidden meaning" which would now be brought to the fore. The life and suffering of Jesus Christ were the central precepts. The stages of the mass mirrored the life of Christ from beginning to end: the introit represented the foretelling of Jesus by the prophets, the canon of the mass paralleled the Passion, and the final blessing reiterated the blessing of the Apostles at the Assumption. This allegorical method continued to hold sway throughout the medieval period.

By becoming the mass, the Eucharist was further altered, changing from an act of thanksgiving to an act of supplication. Increasingly the sacrifice of the mass was seen as a path to God's salvation, as a way to attain reconciliation, and as a means to request help in all forms. From this point on the Eucharist was understood primarily as a blessing, an idea which was also contained in the word "mass," taken from the final blessing of the Eucharist, the "*Ite missa est*." This strengthened the logic behind the sacrifice: he who asks for something must offer something in return. The mass was the greatest sacrifice possible, for bread and wine were consecrated, turned into the body and blood of Christ, and offered by the priest to God, the Father. The emphasis on the realistic nature of the "sacrificial flesh" and "sacrificial blood" led to the first medieval Eucharistic quarrel between two monks of the monastery of Corbie, Paschasius Radbertus (d. c. 860) and Ratramnus (d. c. 870).[2]

The most important motive behind the increased frequency of the sacrifice of the mass was probably concern for the dead. All those who died in an imperfect spiritual condition were believed to be in a place of purification awaiting final purgation (*in purgatorio*). Acts of atonement by those they had left behind could have an impact in the otherworld. Masses were believed to be particularly efficacious. This explains the appearance of confraternities of prayer, with their innumerable masses for the souls of the poor.

The dominance of this new interpretation of sacrifice has been summarized thus:

> Within the term 'sacrifice' . . . the elements of supplication and penance (*finis impetratorius, finis propitiatorius*) were now strengthened. . . . When . . . distinct groupings or individual believers now gave the priest an oblation and

2 Macy, *Theologies of the Eucharist*.

> requested that he make a sacrifice, the request, or plea, or supplication was prominent. The gratitude and adoration given to God were no longer the central concerns: their place had been taken by the blessing which was sought from God and which might descend on the participant.[3]

As the flesh and blood which were offered were from the Son of God, expectation that these supplications would be answered was great, and as a result all manner of requests were made.[4] The oldest manuscript of the Gelasian Sacramentary, from the middle of the eighth century, contains instructions for masses to be celebrated for travelers, to bring love and harmony, at times of death and animal epidemics, and also specifically for kings, against bad knights, against the rebellious, for the conversion of the non-believers, and so on. The mass was good for any occasion. The so-called "private mass" in which primarily "private," rather than "public," supplications were made, was now common.[5] If there was a need, a priest could now celebrate mass up to twenty times in one day.[6] Such figures serve to demonstrate that the mass could no longer be celebrated as an act of "self-sacrifice." The mass was now a holy ritual, carried out according to precise instructions, and each time it was celebrated – a result of the sacrifice it contained – the mass produced a measure of divine mercy.

The whole mass was celebrated on all possible occasions, but in addition, the course of the ritual contained especially holy moments for particular purposes. The canon of the mass was the most holy element, in particular the canon which followed the preface (*Praefatio*), and within this the most holy words of the Lord's Supper, the *sacratissima verba* of Christ. The privilege of speaking the canon belonged expressly to the priests who, in making the sacrifice, now prayed *for* rather than *with* the laity who stood around (*circumstantes*). The words of the Lord's Supper were held to be a "dangerous prayer" (*oratio periculosa*) and extensive penance would be required of anyone who spoke them incorrectly. Since Late Antiquity the "holy" high prayer had come to include supplications on behalf of church and clergy and for the living and dying, but these were all spoken quietly by the priest on his own. The sign of the cross made during the canon also changed to become a sign of blessing with the power to bestow mercy, performed, for example, at healings or when the possessed were exorcised.

3 Jungmann, "Von der 'Eucharistie,'" 37.
4 Angenendt, "Missa specialis," 111–90.
5 Nussbaum, *Klöster, Priestermönch und Privatmesse*, 251–55.
6 *Paenitentiale Merseburgense a* [Vienna, National Library, Cod. Lat. 2225], art. 49, 138.

The medieval mass was conceived as a central religious event. As the most important and most frequently performed ceremony of the religious cult, it had a social impact on the community. Mass was celebrated regularly, particularly on Sundays and holy days, and often even daily. It was also performed at significant events such as marriages and deaths, births and illness, war and peace. The parish community, its boundaries clearly defined by c. 1100, had to gather for the mass, and all were bound to attend. It was the celebration of mass which brought together all those within the parish and turned them into a parish community. Only those who had been baptized and were able to take communion could be full members of this community. Serious misconduct was grounds for exclusion of the perpetrator from this community of the "saints" and "the saintly." In other words, anyone who misbehaved publicly was excluded from communion and from the community; such people were also to be avoided in social interaction, and if they had not performed penance then they could not even be buried in the graveyard by the church. As the pinnacle of religious celebration attended by all, the mass also became a useful focal point to determine the timing of all kinds of other activities and occasions such as markets and trade, appointments and engagements, festivals and celebrations.

The role which the mass had adopted also gave added importance to the sacrificial bread and wine. In early Christianity these objects had simply been laid out; there was no inherent ritual act and no special liturgical form. Every participant was required, however, to bring offerings to the mass, in particular as gifts for the poor. Increasingly these gifts were interpreted as religious "sacrifices" and eventually the concept of sacrificial gifts was incorporated into the wider meaning of the Eucharist itself. Since the participants hoped to gain something for themselves from the mass, they should in turn offer a gift, for only on the basis of (material) sacrifices could they hope for a merciful gift from God in return. The original (self-) sacrifice, primarily non-material and spiritual, began to give way to material offerings. This is the starting point for our understanding of medieval mass practice: sacrifice was part of every mass, naturally in the first instance in the form of a spiritual offering, but in practice as a material gift. If no material offering were brought, then the mass could not be expected to bring mercy in return.

This new understanding of sacrifice was tied in with the concept of the "pure" hands, an idea which gained growing prominence. Religious history demanded that that which was holy could only be touched by clean hands and must not be made unclean by contact with anything sexual. Anyone who had sullied himself or herself was deemed "unclean" in cultic terms and was therefore unfit for the celebration of the mass.[7] This idea led directly to clerical celibacy. The Carolingian age saw a fundamental process of institutionalization which would determine developments for the remainder of the medieval period. The lifestyle of the clergy should ensure that they were unsullied, and the best guarantee of this appeared to be provided by the communal life of the monastery;[8] conversely, those who lived a monastic life were unsullied and therefore made the best servants at the altar. The result was the interweaving of monastery and clergy: the clericalization of the monasteries and the monasticization of the clergy. From the time of Chrodegang of Metz (d. 766) attempts were made to distinguish between an *ordo monasticus* and an *ordo canonicus*. This division was institutionalized by the 816–19 Aachen legislation of Louis the Pious, which placed monks under the Rule of St. Benedict and clerics under the Rule for Canons. The goal was the "overwhelming chastity" of the priests in order to ensure that the "spirit called to prepare the body of Christ be clean and free of all dirt."[9] The intention behind this development is clear: every cleric should lead a "pure" life, if possible he should be a monk, or at least live according to this ideal. The canonical movement of the eleventh and twelfth centuries continued to work toward this goal.

After 800 and as a result of this concern with cultic purity, the selection and preparation of sacrificial offerings chosen for consecration became rituals in their own right. There were immediate implications for the laity: no longer were they allowed to proffer with their own hands the offerings of bread and wine which were necessary for the Eucharist. They could now bring the offerings only as far as the roodscreen where they were handed over to the clerics who alone, thanks to their "clean hands," were competent to make the sacrifice. This brought to an end the sacrificial procession formerly carried out by the faithful. The requirement that the bread and wine must themselves be pure, an idea postulated by Alcuin (d. 804), had similar impact. Bread taken from household supplies was no longer adequate; from now on only unleavened bread was to be used, formed into coin-sized hosts and prepared with particular care.

As the laity no longer gave the bread and wine as offerings it might seem that their active involvement in the sacrifice was now at an end. Yet the opposite was true. With the range of Eucharistic offerings no longer limited to bread and wine, there was a very dramatic increase in the nature of sacrificial offerings. As only the bread and wine which were required for consecration were to be

7 Gross, *Menschenhand und Gotteshand*.
8 Angenendt, "Mit reinen Händen," 245–67.
9 *Concilium Aquisgranense*, IX, 325.

placed on the altar,[10] the faithful now began to bring other gifts as offerings, as the English liturgist John Beleth (d. c. 1183) attested:

> Following the confession of faith the offertory is sung and the sacrificing priest speaks the words of the offertory; then we make our offerings. It should be noted that the sacrifice which we make must be threefold: first of all we sacrifice ourselves, then that which is necessary for the holy sacrifice, that is the bread, wine and water, and (finally) other suitable items. . . . At high festivals in some churches precious items belonging to the church are placed upon the altar or given at suitable places. This is followed finally by the hand offerings (*manuales oblationes*) of the laity.[11]

It appears that any product of the peasant or artisan economy had become a suitable offering and could be presented as a gift, along with objects used in the church or in the household.

The concept of "pure hands" not only changed the process by which offerings were made, it also placed new limits on the reception of communion. No longer could the communicant use his or her own hands to take communion, for they were now deemed to be unclean; the host was instead placed directly on the recipient's tongue.[12] However, as even legitimate marital sexual relations made one unfit in the eyes of the church, one had to abstain either from sexual relations before communion or from communion itself. As a result communion was taken infrequently, usually only once a year. But a possible alternative did emerge: part of the bread given in sacrifice would be blessed in the course of the mass and distributed subsequently as "eulogia," as a substitute for communion. And finally, it was now deemed necessary for all liturgical implements to be particularly fine, the altar with a golden frontal and both paten and chalice made of pure gold.

The celebration of mass was the salvific event with the greatest need for its own premises in the form of church buildings and its own personnel in the form of parish clergy. Originally the Eucharist had not required either a holy space or a special altar. The *kyriake*, the "House of the Lord" had existed, however, since Late Antiquity and it was here alone that mass was to be celebrated and,

10 Regino of Prüm, *De synodalibus causis*, I.63, 54.

11 John Beleth, *Summa de ecclesiasticis officii*, 41a.c, lines 2–17, 75–76: "a) Dicto symbolo cantatur offertorium siue offerenda, et dicitur offertorium ab offerendo, quia tunc offerimus. Sed notandum, quod tria debemus offere: Primo nosmetipsos, postea que sunt necessaria sacrificio, scilicet panem et vinum et aquam et ceterea sacrificio apta. . . . c) In quibusdam ecclesiis in magnis sollempnitatibus offeruntur preciosa utensilia ecclesie et in altari ponuntur vel in locis conpetentibus. Tandem secuntur manuales oblationes laicorum."

12 Lutterbach, *Sexualität*, 80–96.

if possible, baptism administered. As Christianity spread from the cities into the provinces more churches had to be erected, always with an altar for the celebration of mass and a font for the administration of baptism. Above all a priest had to be present to celebrate mass regularly, to carry out immediate baptism in critical situations, and to support the dying, including burial. The clergy no longer lived with the bishop, but now formed their own communities in the countryside by the church. These were the so-called "minsters" who could be found throughout the period spanning Late Antiquity and the early Middle Ages. As the network of churches grew, often only one cleric would live by the church, the parish priest. These parish clergy had to be maintained. As God's Word and the sacraments had a decisive role in salvation they should not be purchasable; on the other hand preachers and liturgists were supposed to be able to live from the altar. Payment was therefore made for liturgical services in the form of a stipend drawn from the offerings. This arrangement was initially designed for the episcopal churches. The Council of Orleans of 511 called by King Clovis (486–511) ordered "from that which is brought to the altar in faith, one half is claimed by the bishop and the other half is received by the clergy according to his status."[13] A different solution was required for the more remote rural churches: here offerings made locally were divided up and one part was used for the maintenance of the clergy. At that same Council of Orleans in 511 it was stated for the rural clergy that "of that which was brought to the altar, one third was to go to the Bishop."[14] By implication, the other two-thirds were to remain with the parish clergy, used for the care of the poor and for the maintenance of church and clergy. These altar gifts, the *dona altaria*, were the priest's principal source of additional income, supplementing the parish holding for which he was directly responsible. He also received the "stole" (meaning both a liturgical vestment and a symbol of office), the tax due on each occasion the sacraments or sacramentals were given; although the "stole" was always controversial, it was also always claimed.

The items needed to furnish the church and perform the liturgy could in turn become sacrificial gifts; even the church itself could be given as an offering. Both ruler and nobility endowed churches and monasteries: medieval inventories of church treasure list numerous vessels, implements, pictures, and books.[15] The Carolingians were particularly prominent donors. After

13 *Concilium Aurelianense*, 14.107–109, 9: ". . . ut de his, quae in altario oblatione fidei conferentur, medietatem sibi episcopus uindicet et medietatem despensandam sibi secundum gradus clerus accipit. . . ."

14 *Concilium Aurelianense*, 15.114–15, 9: ". . . quae in altario accesserint, tertia fediliter episcopis deferatur."

15 Bischoff, *Mittelalterliche Schatzverzeichnisse*, nos. 117–51, 119–53.

his imperial coronation Charlemagne gave liturgical implements as gifts to St. Peter's and to other churches in Rome.[16] It was probably after his imperial coronation that Charles the Bald (d. 877) donated the throne which became the "cathedra petri," still in existence today in the encasement designed by Bernini.[17] The *Chronicle* of Thietmar of Merseburg (d. 1018) tells of many donations made by rulers; their gifts could include liturgical books as well as altars and their furnishing. A particularly useful example is provided by the canonical foundation of the Victorines in Paris, well known in the twelfth century for its new theology. The Bibles used in this theological work came largely from donations which were each recorded in the memorial book as recompense for the commemoration of their donors.

From Late Antiquity every altar contained relics. This practice was founded on the words of the Apocalypse (Rev. 6.9 *subtus altare*) that in heaven the souls of the martyrs remain at the foot of the heavenly altar. Correspondingly, on earth the bodies of the martyrs and the saints must lie at the foot of earthly altars. Because the souls in heaven would be united with their resurrected bodies at the end of time, they retained a bond with their relics on earth. These relics provided a link between heaven and earth, for as Stephen had discovered when he was stoned, the words "open to heaven" (Acts 7.56) stood above the grave of a saint. It was this point of access to heaven which made the saint's grave a holy site. Many individual churches possessed only *brandea*, pieces of fabric which had lain on the grave of a saint and were therefore deemed to possess holy powers of salvation. Every religion believes the altar to be sacred, but the Christian interpretation now also personified this sacrality: the altar was sacred and the church was a sacred space, but this was achieved through the relics of a holy person resting on or in the altar.

Each saint's grave quickly became a site for sacrifice, often augmented by the presence of an altar. Here "extramissal" (outside the mass) offerings could be made. As the power (*virtus*) of the saint was present in both grave and altar, it was transferred to any object placed on the latter. Supplications to the saints were always associated with offerings, often in the form of *ex-voto* gifts: if the saint granted the request, then the recipient would make an offering in return. An offering, at least in the form of a candle, at the time the request was heard was also deemed indispensable. Grave, altar, and offering were reported to be the sources of numerous miracles, and as a result saints' altars became the focus of a vast array of activities: gifts were placed there both in supplication

16 *Liber Pontificalis*, 98 (Leo III), 377.29–378.11 in *Le Liber Pontificalis* 2, 7–8.
17 Staubach, *Rex Christianus*, vol. 2, pt. 2, 283–334.

and as an act of thanksgiving, for blessing, and for sacral confirmation. One famous example will suffice here: according to the eighth-century *Donation of Constantine* (*Constitutum Constantini*), Emperor Constantine (d. 337) executed a gift to the pope of imperial sovereignty over the West by placing the document on the altar above the tomb of St. Peter.[18] This grave became a site of special sacrifice: here bishops took their oath of office and at the same time recorded a written confession of faith.

At times the number of offerings made at the grave or at the shrine of a saint could be overwhelming. The *Gesta Abbatum Trudonensium* of the twelfth century contains a description of the gifts brought to the grave of Saint Trudo which borders on the fabulous:

> What can I say about the offerings at the altar? Saying nothing more I can pass over the animals, horses, oxen, cows, bulls, rams, and sheep which were given as offerings there in unbelievable number, but there were also linens and wax, bread and cheese – whose weight, number and price can hardly be estimated, also silver thread . . . and heaps of coins, so many that the vergers were exhausted by lifting them up and carrying them off and during the day could do nothing else. The offerings made by the pilgrims who thronged to the altar were innumerable, indeed inestimable, and the reputation of Saint Trudo and his miracles made our monastery overflow with riches.[19]

Reliquaries were even taken out of the church in order to be used to raise money by begging. The holy shrine was carried from place to place, even over long distances, and offerings were received for interventions and miracles. In the high Middle Ages this flow of gifts was given a legal basis. All offerings made in the name of a saint, particularly when placed in the offertory box in front of the image of the saint, were to be used for the construction and furnishing of churches; only the offerings dedicated to a saint but given for a mass to be said were excluded from this regulation.

Without doubt the flourishing and voluminous sacrificial activity of the early medieval period must be understood within the context of both earlier and

18 *Constitutum Constantini*, 20.294–95, 97: "super venerandum corpus beati Petri . . . posuimus."

19 *Gesta abbatum Trudonensium*, I.10.17–28, 234: "De oblationibus altaris quid dicam? Taceam animalia, palefridos, boves et vaccas, verres, arietes, oves, quae incredibili multitudine offerebantur; sed et linum et caera, panes et casei nullo pondere, nullo numero, nullo existimabantur precio, fila argentea et vix iam clauso vespere Olympo exhaustus denariorum acervus quam plurimos in recipiendo et recondendo custodes fatigabant, et preter id nichil penitus cotidie agere sinebant. Erat igitur non tam incomputabilis quam revera inestimabilis peregrinorum semper venientium ad altare oblatio, et nomen beati Trudonis frequentissimis mirabilibusque miraculis coenobiumque nostrum exuberans divitiis."

contemporary non-Christian practices. We know of Germanic sacrificial sites which were in use for many centuries and which contained weapons, clothes, jewelry, foodstuffs, utensils, horse harnesses, boats, and carts and often also animals such as horses and dogs. Even humans were sacrificed. Sacrifice also played an important role in the process of conversion, and missionaries immediately made great efforts to bring an end to this. Under Charlemagne human sacrifice became a capital crime, and indeed it seems to have been quickly eliminated by Christianizing missions.[20] Progress with other forms of sacrifice offered in rural settings, in fields and woods, was admittedly not so rapid, as the mid-eighth-century *Indiculus Superstitionum* (*Inventory of Superstitions*) attests in its lists of offerings made at trees, at springs, and at crossroads.[21] The new religion viewed this as a particular challenge, but acknowledging the general desire to give offerings, it sought to channel or to sublimate the act of offering. It was easy to apply a Christian interpretation to material gifts for the poor. The most significant act of sacrifice, the mass, however, required only very limited offerings of bread and wine. This accounts for the great increase in the nature and number of other gifts made during mass in the early medieval period. A new form of child sacrifice was created: both boys and girls were now placed in monasteries at about age seven, given as sacrificial offerings for the gratification of God.[22]

The new practice of ecclesiastical endowment was of greatest significance, and here the monasteries had a particularly prominent role. Originally altar offerings had been made at the monasteries only very rarely, for the older monastic communities were lay foundations, had very few priests (if any at all), and did not celebrate mass daily. The monasteries were not in a position to celebrate masses frequently and, therefore, gained no benefit from the offerings which accompanied mass. This changed with the development of early medieval monasticism: the number of monastic priests grew and they were able to celebrate mass frequently and to receive offerings in return. The background for this was provided by the new Irish penitential system: although fasting was the most usual act of penance, those with possessions were encouraged to support the poor and to give land for the benefit of a church or monastery. Above all the Irish penitential system allowed for penance to be performed by a representative: in other words monks could say the psalms or bring the offering at mass in the name of a member of the laity in order to limit the time the latter spent in penitence. In exchange for this act of deputization

20 *Capitulatio de partibus Saxoniae*, 9.8–9, 69.
21 Homann, "Indiculus superstitionum et paganiarum," 373.
22 de Jong, *In Samuel's Image*.

the priests required a contribution to their maintenance, and again this might take the form of a gift of land. Offerings therefore provided the monasteries with endowments, including land; in exchange they were required to perform penance in the name of the donor by praying the psalms and celebrating mass. These donations were the most substantial offerings in the medieval period. The transfer of lands which began in the eighth century turned the monasteries into major landowners.

This also raises the issue of payment for masses, a practice which was based on calculations which had been carried out by bishops since Late Antiquity in order to determine the specific value of each spiritual and liturgical act. These fees were the basis for a new and highly successful practice which saw priests paid for "private" work, often the celebration of special masses, on days when they had no specified liturgical role. In return for a specific sum paid by the laity, clerics carried out spiritual offices on days with no liturgical requirements, such as saying the psalms or, more commonly, celebrating mass. The celebration of special masses provided the clergy with a "private" income which was not insubstantial and which supplemented their quasi-official income. The *Rheinau Sacramentary* (c. 800) contains the following rates of exchange for money and masses: 12 masses = 1 pound = 240 denarii = 1,800 psalms; 3 masses [sic; correctly: 6] = 6 ounces = 120 denarii = 900 psalms; 3 masses = 1 ounce = 20 denarii = 150 psalms; 3 masses [sic; correctly: 2] = 1 solidus = 12 denarii = 100 psalms. This proved to be only the first step.[23] To perpetuate such payments "for eternity," landed possessions were gifted, ensuring the generation of additional income each year and therefore the celebration of additional masses. This marked the creation of endowments "for eternity." The donor's return was spiritual: acts of penance in the form of psalms prayed, masses celebrated, or offerings given to the poor. One of the first clear formulations of this spiritual return can be found in a prayer in the *Bobbio Missal*, composed soon after 700.[24] This prayer was subsequently included in numerous sacramentaries and prayer confraternities. This was based on the new Irish penitential system, according to which confession was followed by an act of penitence by a representative, and priests received alms and possessions from donors in whose names they then celebrated mass.[25] Atonement was sought for the sins of both the living and the dead and their names entered in the memorial book. This created the requiem mass which was celebrated in vast numbers.

23 *Sacramentarium Rhenaugiense*, CCLXXIII.1370b, 281.
24 *Bobbio-Missal*, No. 438, 130.
25 See Meens in this volume.

It must be noted that originally each Christian had performed acts of penance in person in the form of sacrifices brought to the altar and gifts for the poor and imprisoned. Now penance was increasingly focused on spiritual communities. It was here that spiritual intercessions were made, psalms prayed, mass celebrated, and material offerings given to the poor. Indeed a large number of poor people were always supported directly by the early medieval monasteries and indirectly by the laity who apparently believed that gifts for the poor distributed by the monasteries did greater service to God. Even the release of slaves worked in the favor of the monasteries, for serfs were transferred into the *mundium* (protection) of the patron saint of the monastery.

Each transfer of land generated a new documentary record. In St. Gall, for example, of the 800 charters which are still extant for the period up to the tenth century, 600 contain gifts of landed possessions *pro remedio animae* (for the salvation of the soul). From the monastery of Lorsch there are as many as 3,600 records which for the most part document the transfer of land. All these monasteries were outdone, however, by Fulda with its long register of deeds. The landed possessions of the monasteries were accordingly extensive, giving the monasteries political weight and turning their abbots into powerful players. The result was the creation of the efficacious system of "gift and countergift" which would reach its zenith in the medieval period.

From the tenth century a legal and liturgical framework determined the nature of lay involvement in the spiritual deeds performed by the monasteries. Possessions were gifted to the monasteries and in return the donors were guaranteed that acts of spiritual penance would be performed, often for those who had already died. The most extreme example of this process could be found at Cluny, where spiritual activity each day encompassed two high masses performed by the convent, individual masses performed by the monastic priests,[26] and an horary prayer which could include up to 215 sung psalms in one day.[27] Strict procedures were laid down for those who wished to be beneficiaries of these spiritual returns: the donor entered the chapter house where he requested a share in the spiritual fruits of the monastic community; the abbot and chapter expressed their agreement orally, yet accompanied by a gift of land or landed possessions; a legally binding record was drawn up and presented as an "offering" at the high altar of the abbey church.[28]

26 Häussling, *Mönchskonvent und Eucharistiefeier*, 35–40.
27 Schmitz, "La liturgie de Cluny."
28 Angenendt, "Cartam offerre."

There can be no doubt that this was a straight exchange: a donation was made and spiritual gifts were received in return in the form of prayers, masses, and care of the poor. Here we see the great surplus in spiritual provision which the monasteries could offer, but performed only in return for donations already received.

Little attention has been given up to now to offerings made in the hope of ensuring victory in battle. The religious significance of the "eternal victory" is well known.[29] War had its own liturgy in the early medieval period: God was asked to grant victory, and if the plea was answered, then an act of thanksgiving was performed in return. Although there is no evidence of Christianized forms for declaring and concluding war under the Christian emperors of antiquity, these are found in abundance for the early medieval period. After every victory an act of thanksgiving was required. The first to be performed throughout the West was celebrated by Charlemagne and Hadrian I after the baptism of the Saxon Widukind in 785. The pope promised Charlemagne God's gratitude and heavenly reward in return for the Saxon's conversion, identified as an "offering" (*offerre munus*).[30] The Ottonians held military victory to be a sign of God's confirmation of their rule.

God was to be thanked for granting victory, but those who had beseeched God for this victory in their prayers were also to be acknowledged. In 828 Louis the Pious had instructed the abbey of Fulda to celebrate one thousand masses and recite an equal number of psalters for a campaign in Bulgaria;[31] this then had to be repaid. A well-known example of an act of thanksgiving – also significant in art history – is provided by the late Carolingian altar-ciborium in the Munich Residenz, supposedly donated by Arnulf of Carinthia to the monastery of St. Emmeram in Regensburg in gratitude for a successful campaign in the Balkans. The famous acclamation of Otto the Great as Emperor by his army, recounted by Widukind of Corvey, climaxes in an act of thanksgiving: "made glorious by the magnificent victory, the King was greeted by his army as father of the fatherland and as Emperor. At this he ordered that God the highest be extolled and that worthy hymns of praise be sung in all churches."[32] Victories, too, were recorded in memorial books.[33]

29 McCormick, *Eternal Victory*.

30 *Codex Carolinus*, 76.30, 607 and 76.6, 608.

31 *Epistulorum Fuldensium fragmenta*, 4.7–11, 518.

32 Widukind of Corvey, *Res gestae Saxonicae*, III.49, 158: "Triumpho celebri rex factus gloriosus ab exercitu pater patriae imperatorque appellatus est; decretis proinde honoribus et dignis laudibus summae divinitati per singulas ecclesias. . . ."

33 Althoff, *Adels- und Königsfamilien*, 170–71.

Victory brought with it spoils of war which the king and his followers had traditionally divided up among themselves. When victory was the work of God, then he, too, and his "spiritual warriors," the priests and monks, deserved a portion of this bounty. Charlemagne's victory over the Avars was achieved, it was believed, as a result of papal-Petrine support, and this role in the victory was acknowledged by an offering made to St. Peter.[34] After his victory over the Hungarians at the Unstrut, Henry I gave the tribute which he previously paid them to the monasteries as an act of thanksgiving instead:

> When he returned home victorious, the king gave thanks in all ways to the honor of God, as was fitting, for the victory over his enemies which God had granted him: he gave the tribute which he had been used to giving to the enemy into the service of God, designating it for gifts for the poor. The army, however, greeted him as father of the fatherland.[35]

Penitential offerings were also integral to the act of giving thanks for victory, to compensate in the next world for killings carried out in war and in revenge. Penitential rites were carried out after the battle of Fontenoy (841) in the devastating fraternal war.[36] We know of bishops in the Ottonian–Salian period who made penitential offerings by performing or endowing masses for those who had fallen in battle; this became increasingly common later in the Salian period.[37] The foundation of a monastery was the most substantial offering given in return for a victory granted, and could be both an act of thanksgiving and an act of penance for those who had died. William the Conqueror (d. 1087) founded Battle Abbey on the site of his victory, a location which was hardly suitable for the monastery but which marked the spot where his opponent Harold, the last Anglo-Saxon king, had fallen and where William had been granted victory by God.[38]

The system of "gift and counter-gift" which runs throughout this discussion played a central role in determining the nature of early medieval religiosity. Yet some contemporary voices were raised in criticism of this practice. Even in the Carolingian period concern was expressed that the laity could attend

34 *Annales Regni Francorum*, anno 796, 98.

35 Widukind of Corvey, *Res gestae Saxonicae*, I.39.25–30,76: "Rex vero victor reversus modis omnibus gratiarum actiones divino honori, ut dignum erat, solvebat pro victoria de hostibus sibi divinitus concessa, tributumque, quod hostibus dare consuevit, divino culti mancipavit et largitionibus pauperum deservire constituit. Deinde pater patriae . . . ab exercitu appellatus. . . ."

36 Nelson, "Violence," 98–101.

37 Schmid, "Salische Gedenkstiftungen."

38 Hallam, "Monasteries."

confession and receive their penance in the monasteries and that monks were celebrating many individual masses. The Paris Council of 829 was critical of the fact that both clergy and laity could reject the penance determined by the bishop or the responsible priest, and could go instead to a monastery to confess and receive their penance, even though monastic priests were forbidden to hear confession.[39]

It was the criticism voiced by the poverty movement in the twelfth century which really hit home. The servants of God, both male and female, should not live off the income generated by their possessions; they should live from the tithe and sacrificial offerings, ideally from voluntary donations alone. The ownership of land was seen as a warning sign; this marked the failure to abide by the first vow of poverty. This criticism brought a sudden halt to the great epoch of Benedictine monastic life, both at Cluny and at Gorze.[40] Stephen of Muret (d. 1124), founder of the Benedictine order of Grandmont, can be cited as an example of this protest. Point by point he rejected the Cluniac system: monks should not own land, nor seek to acquire lucrative tithes or sacrificial offerings, rather they should beg for alms; they should enter no prayer confraternities where in return for payment the psalms were said and the holy offices performed; no documents should record the receipt or transfer of goods; and finally, if any possessions were given to the monastery as a deathbed legacy, then the prayers which had been requested were indeed to be said, but if there was any dispute with the heirs then the legacy was to be returned immediately.[41] The approach of the new Cistercian order was very similar, although the conduct this produced was less severe. They continued to receive gifts of land, but they intended to work this land themselves, and they refused payment in return for masses, confession, or burial:

> We will not hear confession, give Holy Communion nor bury any from outside the monastery except guests and our workers if they should die in the monastery. We will not accept sacrificial offerings for masses to be said in the convent, other than at Candlemas.[42]

39 *Concilium Parisiense*, anno 829, 640: "Nec etiam illud videtur nobis congruum, ut clerici et laici, episcoporum et presbyterorum canonicorum iudicia declinantes, monasteria monachorum expetant, ut ibi monachis sacerdotibus confessionem peccatorum suorum faciant, praesertim cum eisdem sacerdotibus monachis id facere fas non sit, exceptis his dumtaxat, qui sub monastico ordine secum in monasteriisdegunt."

40 Van Engen, "Crisis," 269–304.

41 *Regula Stephani Muretensis*, 4–26, 71–82.

42 *Einmütig in der Liebe*, 136.

They had fewer spiritual duties, and indeed the Cistercians reduced the number of prayers said in Cluny from two hundred sung psalms daily to the Benedictine regulation thirty-seven.

The conclusions which can be drawn here are threefold. First, in the early medieval period the idea of the *sacrum commercium* (holy commerce) developed in several directions. This was evident in the liturgy and in particular in the mass. An offering was made every time mass was celebrated and endowments were intended to ensure that mass was said as often as possible. The result was the exchange of possessions, often landed, in return for spiritual acts of penance which would benefit sinners both on earth and in purgatory, the site of purification in the next world. This exchange initiated a process of large-scale transfer of possessions: goods, often land, were given in return for freedom from sins and deliverance to eternal life. These were gifts given *pro redemptione animae* (for the redemption of a soul). However, from 1100 the poverty movement spoke out against this exchange system and condemned it as simony. This genuine reforming protest appeared to mark the end for the whole culture of donation. However, payments were still made, although no longer in the form of land, but rather in money, thanks to the emergence of a new economy. The developing contemporary urban economy generated testamentary donations and rents, again as payment for masses or as sacral gifts for the performance of the liturgy. In the thirteenth century, the mendicant orders championed the renunciation of all possessions, including land and housing, but they accepted donations in their revised form and therefore the new urban economy provided them with new possibilities.

The second conclusion is that when early medieval endowment-based piety, with its material sacrifices and its expectations for the redemption of sins, was measured against the early Christian idea of the strictly spiritual offering, then the former was found to be wanting. Reforming ideas proposed by critics of the system were certainly taken up by individuals and also set new movements in motion, but they could not change the whole reality. The comprehensive theological, religious, and mental impetus for total reform was lacking. Scholasticism sought to counter the realism of the flesh and blood in the sacrifice with the help of the teaching of transubstantiation: this was the transfigured body of Jesus Christ and not real bleeding flesh. But scholasticism was unable to resolve whether mass celebrated for one person alone did not in fact bring that person greater mercy than a mass celebrated for two people.[43]

43 Iserloh, "Der Wert der Messe."

The third conclusion addresses the cultural issue. It must be recognized that payments and endowments were of fundamental importance for western culture. The society of the early medieval period was not urbanized and the possessions of the monasteries provided the economic power base on which their great cultural contributions were founded; this wealth would not have existed without the gift of land. The production of a Carolingian Bible required the skins of approximately two hundred animals. Almost all that we know of art and culture in the early medieval period is a product of the monasteries. Even intellectual endeavors were fed by such payments. Many of the gifts and endowments of the early medieval period and many of the products of the monasteries created a cultural legacy which has been passed on to the world today.

23

Performing the liturgy

ÉRIC PALAZZO

> In effecting, at the very highest level of existence, the connection and constant transactions between man and God, between the tangible universe and eternity, the liturgy illustrated this propensity [for sensory participation] in an exemplary way. Spectacular, even in its smallest aspects, it *signified* the truths of the faith by means of a complex play on the senses of hearing (through music, chants, reading), sight (through the grandeur of the edifices; by the actors, their dress, their gestures, their dance and by the setting) and even touch: the sacred wall was touched; the foot, the reliquary, the episcopal ring kissed; the fragrance of incense and of candlewax inhaled.[1]

Without doubt, the liturgy – the ritual of the Christian church in antiquity and in the Middle Ages – is one of the fields of medieval studies to benefit most in recent years from new developments in both research methods and the sorts of questions raised. Long considered the preserve of clerical researchers (especially in France) where complementary theological and textual approaches held sway, the study of the liturgy has in recent years enjoyed a resurgence in the field of medieval studies. Responding to the various historiographical traditions of each country, this phenomenon was to a large extent made possible by the influence of historical anthropology. The study of rites and, more generally speaking, of ritual phenomena is central to this approach. Applied to the study of medieval civilization, historical anthropology has made the pivotal role played by the liturgy in medieval society more and more apparent. Other currents, internal to the evolution of liturgical scholarship concerned with the "history of the liturgy," have also contributed to a widespread shift to a fully historicized reading of the liturgy. There is only room here to mention one trait which characterizes this evolution. For much of the twentieth century, historians of the liturgy (mostly clergy) applied themselves to editing the major western liturgical texts with

1 Zumthor, *La lettre et la voix*, 287–88.

the primary objective of studying and identifying their textual archetypes, and bringing to light the history of each of the major liturgical books. Today, historians of the liturgy and medievalists in general continue to make use of these erudite works. Indeed, they remain indispensable for any historian who, while interested in the history of the ritual of the church in the Middle Ages per se, nonetheless, now approaches these documents with questions in mind that are largely those of historical anthropology. Moreover, I would add that the idea of a "liturgical source" is now no longer limited to liturgical texts, but has been greatly enriched by taking into account diverse documents such as hagiographic material, chronicles, and charters, or even images and archaeological sources, to mention only a few.[2]

Continuing in the same vein of a new reading within medieval studies of the history of liturgy, I wish to highlight the importance of a number of works which in recent years have shown that the ritual of the church was a veritable crossroads at which the political, theological, and social dimensions of medieval culture met and interacted. In other words, far from being a realm set apart and outside the flux of "life" in medieval society, liturgy in the Middle Ages appears, on the contrary, as a fundamental element in the functioning of this society – right in the thick of the political, theological, and social stakes. Medieval society is fundamentally a society of ritual.[3] Thus, ritual behavior in the Middle Ages concerns not only the church, but all the structures of medieval society. Furthermore, the vitality of rites in the Middle Ages stems largely from the interaction of the various rituals practiced within diverse sectors of society (the ecclesiastical, political, and judicial institutions).

It is useful, nonetheless, to bear in mind that medieval theologians who commented on the liturgy of the church principally considered it an office in the service of God and reserved to clerics. This is the understanding proposed by the two greatest commentators on the liturgy in the Middle Ages, Amalarius of Metz (c. 780–c. 850) in the ninth century, and William Durandus (d. 1296) in the second half of the thirteenth century. Both men composed great treatises on the history of the liturgy in which stress is laid principally upon the "historical" continuity between the liturgy that they experienced (i.e., the medieval liturgy) and biblical history as a whole. Amalarius and Durandus, like many other liturgical exegetes in the Middle Ages, situate the liturgy within the tradition of biblical history and propose a reading of the ritual of the church essentially centered on biblical symbolism.[4]

2 Palazzo, *Liturgie et société*.
3 Althoff, "Variability." See also Post, "Ritual Studies."
4 Reynolds, "Liturgy, Treatises on."

I shall consider the liturgy of the church of the Middle Ages principally in terms of its fundamentally multidimensional character. In many ways, this approach comprises an important element in the development of the medievalist's understanding of the liturgy, necessarily leaving behind the notion of a history of the liturgy restricted to the knowledge of ritual texts and their theology. It is true that the "textual" dimension, that is, orality, or more generally speaking "the written word," occupies a central place in both the definition of the liturgy and in its actual performance. However, liturgy in no wise limits itself to words transcribed in books, chanted, read, or intoned.[5] The ritual of the medieval church is multidimensional and, alongside the importance it places on "words" in the extended sense, it also accords enormous significance to places, persons, and objects (books included!), to music, to aromas, and indeed to light and, in a general way, to images. In the context of this discussion which is concerned with the idea of liturgical "performance," it seems appropriate to present a comprehensive overview of the multidimensional character of medieval liturgy. In this connection and by way of introduction, let us turn to the words of Hrabanus Maurus (c. 780–856), abbot of Fulda and archbishop of Mainz in the ninth century and an important theologian of the early Middle Ages. On the occasion of a homily for the dedication of a church, Hrabanus put forward in his own way a sort of definition of medieval liturgy, which is considered here in its multifarious dimensions, the emphasis being on the various components of the "performance" of the liturgy:

> You are well met together today, dear brothers, that we may dedicate a house to God. . . . But we do this if we ourselves strive to become a temple of God, and do our best to match ourselves to the ritual that we cultivate in our hearts; so that just as with the decorated walls of this very church, with many lighted candles, with voices variously raised through litanies and prayers, through readings and songs we can more earnestly offer praise to God: so we should always decorate the recesses of our hearts with the essential ornaments of good works, always in us the flame of divine and communal charity should grow side by side, always in the interior of our breast the holy sweetness of heavenly sayings and of gospel praise should resonate in memory. These are the fruits of a good tree, this the treasury of a good heart, these the foundations of a wise master builder, which our reading of the holy Gospel has commended to us today.[6]

5 Palazzo, *Histoire*.

6 Hrabanus Maurus, *Homilia* 39, 73–74. Trans. by M. Carruthers in her *The Craft of Thought: Memory, Rhetoric and the Making of Images 400–1200*. New York: Cambridge University Press, 1998, 275.

This chapter principally will consider the liturgy of the medieval West. I am, however, cognizant of the considerable importance of eastern, or Byzantine, liturgy in developing an understanding of ritual phenomena as a whole. In order to treat the eastern rites, it would be necessary to devote an entire chapter to this subject; since I am unable to do so here, nonetheless, I wish to draw the reader's attention to a few points which seem to me to need to be underlined.

First, the history of the liturgies of the East follows virtually identical principles to those observed in the evolution of the liturgy of the Christian West. It is certainly true that the main milestones of this history of the "Byzantine Rite," to use Robert Taft's expression,[7] are relatively different to those marking the important moments in the chronology of the liturgical history of the West.[8] In the East, the rhythms of this chronology are determined above all by the succession of dynasties on the imperial throne of Constantinople.

Secondly, it is appropriate to emphasize the originality and specificity of certain rituals of the Byzantine East. To illustrate this point, I mention only in passing the truly particular character of the Byzantine entry rites into the church and, more generally, the Byzantine stational liturgy – a ritual practice also known in the West.[9] The important consequences of these ritual practices for church space and liturgical planning aside, it is appropriate to highlight the pronounced relationship between the liturgical entry rite and imperial ritual, attested by numerous passages from the *Book of Ceremonies*, compiled from earlier sources by Constantine VII Porphyrogenitus (913–20, 945–59), and which is regarded as, without doubt, the most important of the ceremonial books of the imperial Byzantine court.

Lastly, I cannot conclude this all-too-rapid allusion to eastern liturgies without recalling that they, too, were marked by a multidimensional character which called into play the various "sensory" aspects of ritual practice in ways just as rich as in the West. One must, however, guard against the idea, still too widely accepted, that the liturgies of the East were "perfect" and had been preserved thus for centuries. This understanding of eastern liturgies, largely constructed in the West in the nineteenth century, is found to be far from the truth if we linger even for a moment on a few commentaries, which, while they flow from the pens of the greatest of the eastern theologians of antiquity and of the early Middle Ages, are hardly laudatory with respect to the contemporaries of these theologians, who took advantage of various

7 Taft, *Le rite byzantin*.
8 Palazzo, "Jalons."
9 Taft, *Le rite byzantin*, 40ff.

occasions literally to disrupt the unfolding of the liturgical "performance." St. John Chrysostom writes:

> Here, in the church, the uproar and the confusion are tremendous! Our gatherings are no different from what happens in a tavern, so noisy are the guffaws, so great the commotion, like the baths or the market, with everyone shouting and kicking up a row . . . [at church] we behave with more impudence than dogs, and we show as much respect to God as to a courtesan . . . the church is no different from the forum . . . nor even, for that matter, from the theatre, if one considers the way in which the women who gather here deck themselves out even more shamelessly than those unchaste women we find down there. This is why we see so many debauched men seduced by them – even here!, and if one of these men tried or intended to corrupt a woman, my guess is that nowhere would be easier than in a church.[10]

Ritual sites and the physical arrangements for the liturgy

In both antiquity and in the Middle Ages, Christian rites were conducted in places specially fitted out to accommodate the performance of the liturgy. I wish to correct immediately the predominant impression that arises from reading numerous works or articles on "liturgical space" in antiquity and in the Middle Ages: in point of fact, the liturgical site in this period is *not* exclusively the particular space of a church, that is, of the building constructed to allow the performance of the liturgy. It is true that theologians and liturgists of antiquity and of the Middle Ages constantly made a point of recalling that the privileged site of the liturgical celebration, indeed, the only site truly authorized for holding such celebrations was the church building. It is important, however, to see beneath this insistence the desire markedly present among theologians and liturgists to associate the image of the church building with the powerful ecclesiological notion of the construction of the *Ecclesia* made from the faithful who are the stones of the edifice that is the church.[11] Accordingly, in antiquity and for a good portion of the Middle Ages there prevails the idea that the celebration of Christian rites must be held in the church, in that place, that is, where fixed altars containing the relics of saints have been installed.

Nonetheless, in defining liturgical sites one important fact must be underlined: from the beginnings of Christianity and throughout the Middle Ages, celebrations which took place outside the church building, and,

10 Cited in Taft, "L'apport," 106.
11 See the chapter by Iogna-Prat in this volume.

sometimes, out in the open air, were certainly known and integrated into liturgical practice.[12] Numerous specific circumstances, which it is unnecessary to describe in detail here, conditioned the performance of open-air liturgical celebrations in particular, requiring the use of portable altars, and, from time to time, special liturgical arrangements, such as the use of tents. Moreover, we find that time and again theologians and liturgists comment that these liturgical celebrations in the open air bring to life the idea that the church is present *throughout* the world, and that it is not bounded by the space of the church building.

Nonetheless, in general church authorities will come to adopt a conservative position with respect to these celebrations outside the church, one that is perfectly summarized in the following extract from one of the episcopal capitularies of Theodulf of Orleans (c. 760–821) from the first half of the ninth century:

> The solemnities of the mass must under no circumstances be celebrated anywhere other than in a church, and not just in any house, nor in a secular place, but in the place that the Lord has chosen, according to what is written: "Take care not to offer sacrifices in every place that you have seen, but in the place that the Lord has chosen to put his name." An exception is made for those who, continuing to celebrate in the army, have tents and altars for this purpose with which they carry out the solemnities of the mass.[13]

Thus, throughout antiquity and in the Middle Ages the church building remains the principal site for the performance of the liturgy. Through the centuries, the church space underwent numerous transformations which would be tiresome to describe in detail here. Let us simply recall that these transformations continually aimed at the pursuit of a greater approximation of the type of celebration (monastic, presbyteral, episcopal, papal . . .) and the architectural form. In other words, as many authors have shown, the religious architecture of antiquity and of the Middle Ages more often than not is shaped according to the types of liturgical celebrations, and according to the transformation of these types, both through the centuries and in accord with local and regional uses in the medieval West.

One more point seems to me to be important to underline with respect to the definition of the liturgical site constituting the church space, namely, the specialization of ritual spaces in the church interior itself. The way the liturgy unfolded in the church interior in antiquity and in the Middle Ages made

12 Palazzo, "L'espace et le sacré."
13 Theodulf of Orleans, *Erstes Kapitalar* XI, 110–11.

the emergence of specific liturgical spaces inevitable: a place, for example, for consecrating, a place for the proclamation of the Scriptures, a place for penance, a place for baptism, not to mention the ritual routes followed by processions inside the ecclesial space. All this leads us to postulate that the performance of liturgical celebrations within the church interior, in the end, comes to determine specific ritual zones, the visual demarcation of which is considerably enhanced by the presence in churches of permanent or temporary monumental decor.

These individual liturgical zones in the church truly are spatially demarcated by the physical arrangements for the liturgy. By way of example, let us cite the following passage from the life of St. Benedict of Aniane (c. 750–821) by Ardo in the ninth century, which concerns the physical arrangements for the liturgy that Benedict of Aniane desired for the construction of the monastery church and which had powerful symbolic connotations.

> The venerable father Benedict, driven by a pious consideration, did not wish to take saints as patrons, rather it is in honor of the divine Trinity . . . that he consecrated this church. That what I have just said might be more clearly understood: he had three altars placed in the altar that is like the first of all the others, so that these [three] might appear to represent the persons of the Trinity; and the way this is arranged is marvellous, revealing the undivided Trinity in the three altars, and the divinity in essence in the single altar.[14]

There follows a long and precise description of the liturgical arrangements envisaged by Benedict for the various altars and the symbolic significance he attached to them.

In many respects, these descriptions, drawn from a literary genre that is not strictly speaking liturgical, namely hagiography, are relatively similar to those of the monk Garsias in the first half of the eleventh century regarding the important architectural remodeling of the church of Saint-Michel de Cuxa, undertaken at the initiative of his abbot Oliba. In a poem praising the latter, Garsias describes with relative precision the architectural remodelings, along with their symbolism, and the physical arrangements for the liturgy envisaged in this "new" church of Cuxa. As at Aniane in the ninth century, a large part of the symbolism of the church of Cuxa in the middle of the eleventh century is based upon the "figure" of the Trinity. Besides this, however, Garsias does not fail to relate the architectural typology and, indeed, most of the liturgical arrangements, such as, for example, the baldachin installed above the high altar, to the symbolism of the church interpreted as a vision, or rather as

14 Ardo, *Vie de Benoît d'Aniane*, 70–71.

a representation of the heavenly Jerusalem, and above all, as the Temple of Solomon.[15]

Actors and objects

In the Middle Ages, as in antiquity, the liturgy put into play actors who more often than not use objects to carry out the ritual actions for which each person was responsible. Christian liturgy generally envisages two categories of actors: the members of the clergy and the lay faithful, who are more commonly designated by the generic term "the assembly." Within these two groups of actors, several categories may be distinguished, particularly in the group of those who have received ordination and who belong to the ecclesiastical hierarchy. Whatever the kind of liturgical celebration (monastic, presbyteral, episcopal, or papal), different members of the ecclesiastical hierarchy were involved in the ritual according to their role and following the course of the rite as envisaged in the liturgical texts. In the early Middle Ages, and more particularly in the Carolingian period, certain theologians developed a theology of ecclesiastical hierarchy at the core of which we find an expression of the ecclesiology of the liturgy in this period. This ecclesiology is inherently built around the idea of the division of labor in the church, and, in particular, within the ecclesiastical hierarchy. Thus, at ordination each member of the hierarchy receives from the hands of the bishop (who alone can administer the sacrament of orders) that which is the instrument of his liturgical responsibility, but is equally the veritable symbolic badge of this responsibility. For theologians, this act of the bestowal of the liturgical instrument to each member of the ecclesiastical hierarchy, whether he belongs to the major or to the minor orders, constituted the most important moment of this ritual from the point of view of the theology of ordination. In fact, this *traditio instrumentorum* "truly" makes the ordained minister, and causes him to move from the status of layman to that of an ordained cleric, a member of the ecclesiastical hierarchy to whom, hereafter, will be allotted a particular liturgical responsibility in the performance of the rites.

In order to illustrate these remarks, let us turn our attention to the full-page miniature taken from the Carolingian Sacramentary of Marmoutier, produced at the Tours scriptorium around 845 and now in the Bibliothèque municipale of Autun (ms. 19 bis, fol. 1r) (fig. 1).[16]

15 Durliat, "L'architecture du XIe siécle."
16 Reynolds, "Portrait."

Figure 1. The orders of clergy, from the Sacramentary of Marmoutier: Autun, Bibliothèque municipale, ms. 19 bis, fol. 1r. Reproduced by permission of the Centre nationale de la recherche scientifique.

Appearing on folio 1r of the manuscript, this miniature opens the text of the Gregorian sacramentary in the use of Marmoutier and adapted in the eleventh century for the use of Autun cathedral. The opening folios of the manuscript contain the series of prayers pronounced in the course of ordination rituals. Their presence in a sacramentary is exceptional since these prayers are usually, at least from the ninth century, in separate manuscripts, namely the *ordines*, one of which contains the ordination rituals. In the latter, the prayers are combined with the rubrics which describe the performance of the ordination liturgies, while in the opening folios of the Marmoutier sacramentary, these prayers appear without the description of this *ordo*. In certain ways, the miniature of folio 1r proposes an "ideal vision" of the ecclesiastical hierarchy corresponding to the ordination prayers transcribed immediately following in the manuscript. In the upper part of the image, we see the bishop, wearing his pallium, enthroned in the center, framed by the priest seated on his right and the deacon, robed in dalmatic, on his left. The three compose the category of major orders. The miniature's composition in two registers visually expresses the idea of the ecclesiastical hierarchy being composed of two categories. Similarly, within the upper register, the bishop who is depicted larger than the two other figures, is placed in the center upon a throne, while the priest, second in the category of the major orders, is seated on the bishop's right on a smaller throne than that of the head of the church. His position, slightly in profile, likewise expresses the notion of hierarchy at work here. The deacon is shown standing and holds in his left hand the book of the Gospels, the symbol of his role in the liturgy, since it is he who is designated to read the Gospel of the day during the mass. The book of the Gospels is handed over to the deacon by the bishop in the course of the celebration of his ordination. This gesture is interpreted by theologians as that which truly *makes* the deacon. In this way the book of the Gospels becomes the badge of the liturgical office of the deacon. Above the figures, a Latin inscription points out that the right to confer ecclesiastical rank is the privilege of the bishop.

In the lower register of the miniature there are depicted figures representing the five office holders of the minor orders. The pyramid-shaped composition and the arrangement of the figures contribute, as in the upper register, to the expression of the idea of hierarchy within the category of minor orders. At the head of these orders we find the subdeacon, here placed in the center on a dais. In addition to his office as lector of the Epistle in the mass, he also served at the altar. This is the reason why he is represented holding the chalice and the cruet. Next, to the left and right, we see the porter, the lector, the exorcist, and the acolyte. Each is provided with the object of his liturgical office: keys, book,

book containing the ritual of exorcism, and the torch, respectively. In the course of the ordination of each of these members of the ecclesiastical hierarchy, the bishop carries out the *traditio* of the liturgical instrument of their office. Again, the theologians of the Carolingian period interpreted this moment in the ordination ritual as that which *made* the subdeacon, the porter, the lector, the exorcist, and the acolyte. In other words, this act of the *traditio instrumentorum* was the fundamental moment of this ritual because it not only contained *in nuce* all of the theological significance of ordinations, but also provided for the transmission by the bishop of each member of the ecclesiastical hierarchy's badge of liturgical office, a badge that the cleric will be called upon to use in the course of liturgical celebrations.

Without proposing a realistic representation of the ritual of ordinations in the Carolingian period, nor even of a precise moment in this liturgical celebration, the Marmoutier sacramentary miniature displays a synthetic vision of the theology of ordinations by emphasizing what appears as the most significant moment in the ritual and in its theology: the bestowal of the liturgical instrument on each ordained person.

Books and their images

Just as images form part of the monumental decor of a church, the miniatures in liturgical manuscripts likewise contribute to the visual dimension of the medieval church. Images appear in liturgical books in the West in the seventh century, at the time when the various texts of the liturgy were being codified. Varying according to the type of liturgical book, these illustrations evoke the life of Christ, depict the figures of the saints, the portraits of the evangelists, or even ritual scenes. The images elude any idea of a straightforward functionality in the liturgy, but correspond rather to diverse concerns: to pay homage to God by the richness of their decoration and to give expression to various liturgical, political, social, and even theological stakes. On the other hand, we do not know whether the images contributed to the actual performance of the rites; rather it is usually held that they represented the visual dimension of the liturgy. However, in certain instances it is not impossible that they may have played a role as visual snapshots of moments in the liturgy.[17] Let us note that in the Middle Ages the decoration of the liturgical book was not limited to the miniatures that accompany the texts within the body of the manuscript. The sumptuousness and the iconography of bindings, adorned

17 Bonne, "Rituel de la couleur."

with ivory panels or with gold and silver, indeed with precious stones and other fine materials, equally underline the desire to render glory to God by celebrating the liturgy with beautiful objects – this despite the admonitions to the contrary of medieval theologians and, before them, of certain fathers of the church who advocated the use of modest books in the rites.[18]

By way of examples, let us mention the miniatures painted on the Exultet rolls, which were produced for the most part in southern Italy, or more precisely at Benevento, between the tenth and the twelfth centuries.[19] On these rolls the text of the Exultet (the chant performed by the deacon at the Easter vigil when the Paschal candle is blessed and lit) is transcribed, alternating with illustrations of passages from the texts or from the liturgical events of the paschal liturgy (fig. 2).

While the text's *laus apum*, the famous poetic and theological passage in praise of the bee, is illustrated with scenes of beekeeping, most of the images in the Exultet rolls depict a precise moment in the Easter vigil: the blessing of the Paschal candle, the lighting of the candle, the procession to the baptismal font, the blessing of the font with the candle, baptism scenes, or even the depiction of the roll's *mise en scène* showing the deacon at the top of the ambo, roll in hand, singing the Exultet with the lit Paschal candle at his side. Other images emphasize to a greater degree the theological dimension of some sections of the Exultet, such as the iconography of Christ casting down death placed on the roll immediately after the mention in the text of Christ's victory over death. The distinctive codicological feature of these manuscripts is the inverted orientation of text and images, suggesting a didactic use of the images, intended for the faithful gathered in the nave for the performance of the chant, and a liturgical function for the text, chanted only by the deacon and only at this specific moment in the liturgical year.

In actual fact, the deacon did not need the written text since he knew the Exultet chant by heart, as is the case with most of the liturgical repertory in this period; as for the faithful, they were too far away from the ambo (at the top of which the deacon stood with his roll) to be able to make out any image at all. These features which are peculiar to the Exultet rolls actually touch on the strong symbolic connotation of the written word and images in the performance of medieval liturgy. In the Exultet rolls, the text was not read by the officiating deacon, nor were the images (oriented in the opposite direction to the text) seen by those who were intended to see them. In other

18 Steenbock, *Der kirchliche Prachteinband*.
19 Kelly, *Exultet*.

Figure 2. Exultet roll: Rome, Biblioteca apostolica vaticana, ms. Barberini Lat. 592, fol. 1. Reproduced by permission of the Biblioteca apostolica vaticana.

words, the codicological layout of this particular liturgical book corresponded to liturgical roles of text and image which were never fulfilled. Nonetheless, at the time for the performance of the Exultet in the Easter vigil, the deacon had to have in his possession one of these rolls in which was symbolized the role of the liturgical text and of the images accompanying it. Moreover, the deacon was strictly obliged to be provided with an Exultet roll on this occasion since this object was also the symbol of his liturgical role in the Easter vigil.

This symbolic function of the Exultet roll, considered as the liturgical badge of the deacon in the context of his performance of the Easter vigil ritual, may be compared to that of another book, the *cantatorium*, prepared for the chant performed in the liturgy. "After the reading of the Epistle by the subdeacon, the cantor ascends the ambo with his cantatorium and performs the responsary."[20]

This text is taken from a liturgical *ordo* (i.e., a book containing the description of the ritual) that defines both the meaning and the function of the cantatorium. It is a soloist's book, containing only those chants inserted between the readings at the beginning of the mass (the gradual responsary and the alleluia) and sometimes including the offertory verses that the cantor would need to perform the solo chants. Far from exercising any ancient role appointed for books, in practice the cantatorium had an honorific more than a real function in the performance of the liturgical celebration, and, as such, its role may be compared to the symbolic function described above with respect to the Exultet roll. Regarding the honorific function of the cantatorium, Amalarius of Metz, the great theologian and liturgical commentator, writes at the middle of the ninth century: "The cantor, without any need to read [them], holds in his hands the [ivory] tablets [of the cantatorium]."[21] Oblong in format – a format generally reserved for books of liturgical chant – the cantatorium, like many other liturgical books in the Middle Ages, was not uncommonly adorned with ivory panels which formed its binding. Amalarius of Metz's commentary on the cantatorium and its liturgical use by the soloist evinces the powerful symbolic weight accorded liturgical books, together with, in certain instances such as the Exultet rolls, the images that adorn them. Amalarius's exegesis forcefully underlines the eminently honorific character of the book in medieval ritual action. Most of the time the book is not, in fact, indispensable, but its presence together with the presence of its images is imperative since it defines certain aspects of the ritual: its written part and its visual dimension.

20 Amalarius of Metz, *Liber officialis* , III. XVI, 330.
21 "Cantor, sine aliqua necessitate legendi, tenet tabulas in minibus," Amalarius of Metz, *Liber officialis*, 303.

Sound, light, fragrance, and "liturgical drama" in ritual performance

The medieval church's ritual evinces a strong multidimensional character. I drew attention to this important aspect of the definition of medieval liturgy above, using a passage from Hrabanus Maurus's homily for the dedication of a church. With respect to ritual, this text alludes to "the decorated walls of this very church," "many lighted candles," "voices variously raised through litanies and in prayers," and "readings and songs." It is indeed true that medieval liturgy consists of texts that are to be read, recitations in prayer mode, images painted or sculpted on the inside walls of the church, or miniatures in manuscripts. But it also is made of light and chant, and to all this we could add the olfactory dimension of the ritual rarely mentioned in medieval liturgical texts or in liturgical commentaries. Fragrances, generally produced by the abundant use of incense, were an integral part of liturgical performance in the Middle Ages. This olfactory dimension is extremely suggestive symbolically in its own right, particularly in relation to the sacred fragrances described in the rites of the Old Law, and used by the priests officiating in the Temple of Solomon.

The dimension of sound also constitutes a major sensory element in the definition of the medieval church's ritual and in its symbolic significance.[22] This aspect of the liturgy includes the performance of liturgical chants in the course of the mass and within the frame of the celebration of sacramental rites in general (baptism, confirmation, dedication of a church and consecration of an altar, ordination, etc.) or, indeed, at the numerous daily offices celebrated by monks in monasteries in the course of the various liturgical hours. We cannot give here a detailed historical description of medieval liturgical music; rather, I wish simply to underline the central role played by the dimension of sound in the definition of ritual performance in the medieval church. Generally speaking, the chants of the liturgy doubly adorn the ritual performance, both in respect to sound and in respect to theology, given the exegetical import of many of the texts chanted, such as, for example, mass tropes. Occasionally, the medieval liturgy's soundscape can take dark turns. An innovative contribution to the field has recently examined the various sorts of cries in the medieval church's ritual.[23] From various liturgical sources and other types of texts, the author has clearly demonstrated the existence of set, defined, and / or forbidden

22 For this "sonic" dimension of medieval culture, see Fritz's excellent *Paysages sonores du Moyen Âge*, especially 263–308 which discusses "la théologie sonore: le verbe et la voix."
23 Collomb, "Vox clamantis in ecclesia."

cries expressing complimentary aspects of medieval piety and forming an integral part of ritualized expressions of medieval society.

From the beginnings of Christianity, light has held pride of place in the performance of the liturgy, and, more broadly speaking, in all kinds of ritual.[24] A passage from the famous liturgico-canonical text of the third century styled the "Apostolic Tradition," whose Roman origin has been challenged in contemporary scholarship, attests the role and significance of light in Christian liturgy. In the ritual described, light is materially present, but it is at the same time endowed with symbolic and theological meaning connected with the light of Christ who is eternal light, and the conqueror of death. As is readily discernible by even a brief glance through the principal medieval liturgical texts, especially the prayers and the rubrics, the liturgy of the Middle Ages as a whole reflects this ritual and theological signification of light. Indeed, light was frequently used in the course of medieval liturgy: during the ritual it was present through the agency of both fixed and portable candles. At various moments in the celebration of the Eucharist, for example, acolytes responsible for carrying the candles placed on portable candle holders took up and changed their positions in such a way that candlelight was at the very center of the liturgical action. Quite apart from liturgical texts, numerous other medieval sources, such as hagiographic accounts and chronicles, furnish interesting information regarding the place of light in the performance of the liturgy. More often than not, the authors emphatically stress the mysterious efficacy of a saint's or a sovereign's prayer that causes a blazing light to shine. Finally, the Christian liturgy of antiquity and of the Middle Ages accorded such importance to light that some rites were, in a manner of speaking, wholly set aside for it. Such is the case, for example, with the Candlemas procession, which takes place on the 2nd of February, the feast of the Presentation of Christ in the Temple and of the Purification of the Blessed Virgin Mary. We may also point to the liturgy of the "new fire," which was performed during the Easter vigil mentioned above, and during the course of which the deacon proceeded to bless and light the Paschal candle, symbol of the resurrection of Christ and of the foundation of the *Ecclesia*.

I cannot draw this brief exploration of liturgical performance in the early Middle Ages to a close without drawing attention to the importance of "liturgical drama," or more generally, of "dramaturgy," and of its relationship to ritual practices in the medieval western church.[25] These "liturgical dramas"

24 Palazzo, "La lumière et la liturgie."

25 Young, *Drama*. See also the contributions regarding *"Le drame liturgique médiéval"* brought together in a special volume of *Revue de Musicologie*.

appear in the tenth/eleventh century primarily in monastic settings where they gave rise to new liturgical books. For many decades, historiography has tended to style these new ritual displays "liturgical dramas," an expression, which though doubtless convenient, seems to me to be ill-suited to designate what these productions of the life of Christ or of other biblical characters really were. For my part, I am convinced that these new kinds of rites are in no wise "dramatic" in the modern sense of the term, and that it would be out of place to dislocate them from monastic ritual in its entirety. In point of fact, these liturgical "dramas" or "plays" are fully part of the accentuation of the splendor of monastic liturgy around the turn of the millennium, an accentuation perfectly reflected in contemporary monastic customaries which codify, among other things, the liturgical practices of the abbeys. In other words, these "dramas" reveal that monastic ritual at the turn of the millennium was evolving, in the sense that its "staging" was developing; the performance of "liturgical dramas" contributed to this development. This process in some ways came to counterbalance the "textual" dimension of the rites in the recitation of prayers, the reading of sacred texts, and even the performance of pieces of chant.

PART V

★

CHRISTIANITY: BOOKS AND IDEAS

24
Visions of God

ALAIN BOUREAU

No one can see God. St. Paul, rehearsing the ancient warning of the book of Exodus (33.20), maintained that before final beatitude, human beings cannot know God except "through a glass, darkly" (1 Cor. 13.12). In the patristic period from Irenaeus (c. 130–c. 200) to Pseudo-Dionysius (c. 500), contemplation may have appeared to provide a way of accessing the divine, a means, as it were, of getting beyond the mirror – though the East, influenced by the condemnation of the heresy of Eunomius (d. 394) in the latter half of the fourth century, long maintained the fundamental unknowability of God against the West. However, although this contemplative tradition did indeed continue, in our period of 600 to 1100 CE, it was the quest (both speculative and practical) for sensible and intellectual mediations between the divine and the human that predominated. This basic orientation, which resulted in a massive transformation of the landscape of human life – a landscape henceforth graced with a multifaceted structure of signs and images of divinity – corresponds to the period of Christianity's political and social establishment. As a religion established upon (and housed within) the fragmentation of social and political powers, Christianity found it necessary to display visible markers of identity and legitimacy. If the divine essence, though infinite, had disclosed itself to the finite perception of human beings, its manifestation in the created world (and notably in the presence of the incarnate Christ) had left traces or tracks which could be both found and followed. For instance, Christ had explicitly commanded the commemoration of his sacrifice. Further, as the Word, he had preached and had used human language to persuade his listeners. In the course of these centuries marked by vast missionary opportunities (and of unrecorded resistance), language itself thus proffered another medium. It is around these three principal themes – *the veneration of the incarnate Christ* (redeeming humanity and proclaiming the coming of the Holy Spirit), *the representation of sacred traces*, and *the construction of a theological logic* – that I shall attempt to group visions of God in the early Middle Ages.

By way of introduction, it is appropriate to recall the persistence in this period of the Neoplatonic tradition of the contemplation of God which uses a metaphor likening the ascent of the soul to God (with the aid of God's grace) to a vision. In the same vein, divinity was thought to allow itself to be glimpsed in "theophanies," or visual revelations. The most important theologian of seventh-century Byzantium, Maximus the Confessor (d. 662), took up and completed the teachings of Pseudo-Dionysius on this point by insisting on the notion of *theosis*, that is, the divinization attained by divine indwelling. At the end of our period, in Byzantium at the end of the tenth century, Symeon the New Theologian constructed a spirituality of abandonment to the Spirit which bore fruit still later in the influential teachings of Gregory Palamas in the thirteenth century. In the West, John Scottus Eriugena (d. c. 877), a reader and translator of both Pseudo-Dionysius and Maximus the Confessor, rediscovered the theme of a return to the One at the end of a mystical process aided by theophanies.

Maximus the Confessor had clarified the meaning of a fundamental distinction between two different discourses regarding God: the first, "theology," concerned the divine nature; the second, the "economy," was associated with the intervention of God in the created world, and especially with the incarnation of the Logos.[1] "Theology" had primacy by reason of the loftiness of what it considered. According to its Greek meaning, it was principally "negative," or "apophatic," since the divine essence was inaccessible: it could only be evoked by rejecting applicability of the only attributes that could be ascribed to divinity, such as being, power, goodness, will, etc. It was rather an affirmative theology that in the patristic period had been vitally important in the great Trinitarian debates, as they were expressed in the series of ecumenical councils from Nicaea (325) to Chalcedon (451), precisely because of the contemporary need for dogmatic demonstration. Nonetheless, the stubborn persistence of opposition to the canons of Chalcedon continued to nourish Christological debate within the church itself. Patristic "theology" ceded to an "economy" of the incarnate Person, as the principal episode in the seventh-century controversy – the debate regarding the activity and will of the person of Christ – clearly showed. In the East, debates regarding the *nature* of Christ remained lively, whereas the West concerned itself rather more with the *work* of the incarnate Word prolonged in the sacraments. This important difference also stems from a difference in theological and ecclesiastical environment: less clericalized and more highly educated, the eastern church was also more interested

1 Pelikan, *Christian Tradition*, vols. 2 and 3.

in speculation. Further, the marked differences in political systems also serve to explain the divergence which gradually opened between the two Christian traditions.

Divine economy and devotion to Christ

The teaching of Chalcedon had laid down the existence of two natures in Christ, one human and the other divine, forming in the Incarnation a single person or hypostasis. The Nestorian opposition to this teaching, which maintained the presence of two natures and two hypostases, persisted and found its most accomplished theorist in Babai the Great (d. c. 628), though Nestorian churches already established their own hierarchy from the sixth century. The miaphysite opposition to Chalcedon, which maintained the existence of a single (divine) nature (*phusis*) in Christ, had a longer influence in the Byzantine church, due to the secure establishment of Jacobite churches in Syria, Armenia, and in Egypt. Miaphysitism's great theologian was James of Edessa (d. 708).

These three Christologies – Chalcedonian, Nestorian and miaphysite – all of which were for some time concurrent in the East, entailed markedly different visions of God. Whereas Nestorians venerated the humanity of Christ as the locus of access to the godhead, miaphysites absorbed Christ's person within the divine. The cultic mediations and liturgical images likewise differ forcibly: the cult of the Virgin Mother of God (the *Theotokos*) or of images of the suffering humanity of Christ were more or less categorically rejected among miaphysites. The Chalcedonians' *via media* was more connected with the theme of deification (*theosis*) as a gift principally worked by the Incarnation of Christ. It is true that this theme hailed from venerable patristic origins and that it is found in the tradition of the desert fathers, John Cassian (c. 360-after 430), and Evagrius Ponticus (346–99) and was transmitted in the seventh century by Maximus's contemporary John Climacus (c. 570–c. 649). However, Christological tensions no doubt played an important role in the development of this Byzantine nexus of themes which did not reach the West until much later. Nonetheless, a direct and univocal link between representations of Christ and doctrinal debates cannot be drawn. Choices of iconography and the density of iconic programs depended largely on traditions which kept neither to the same rhythm nor to the same scope as contemporary doctrinal debates. Even as regards doctrine, perennially recurring and universal trends are to be discerned. Thus, a certain iconophobia, or at least a reluctance to multiply images, was part of the very ancient heritage of monotheistic religions, and as such periodically returned to prominent concern.

Moreover, this definitive presentation of three Christologies is, in point of fact, deceptive since it does not take into account the gradual detachment of miaphysitism (the isolation of which was provoked in part by the rise of Islam from the seventh century). Further, it grants too great a significance to Nestorianism, which was of marginal importance in the contemporary debates. In point of fact, the Nestorian churches lay outside the Byzantine Empire, irrespective of the latter's contractions or reconquests. Nestorian theology was thus in some wise expelled beyond the bounds of Christian orthodoxy, as is suggested by those legends that ascribe to Nestorius or to one of his disciples the invention of Islam and Muḥammad's ascendancy.

In contrast, the miaphysites, even those in far-flung regions, continued to be permanent interlocutors with Christian orthodoxy. Numerous ambiguities in patristic thought were able to be used to justify or lend support to miaphysite theology. The miaphysite tendency to reduce the person of Christ retained a lasting vitality, independent of precise transmission, and stemming from the intrinsic difficulty of the problem of the Incarnation itself. Moreover, it is important to note that the various Christological debates also had cultural and political dimensions that are irreducible to pure doctrinal debate, and which were connected with the fragmentation of Christian ecclesio-political identities that is so characteristic of our period.

Dogmatic anathematizations notwithstanding, this proximity of miaphysitism clearly appears in the debate on "monoenergism" or "monothelitism,"[2] lasting throughout the seventh century. From 617 to 618, the Byzantine church set about examining the question of the unicity of the activity or *energeia* of the incarnate Christ, beyond his two natures. Could the redemptive action of Christ be divided into two distinct spheres of action? In the course of the debate, this line of enquiry shifted toward the question of the will (*thelos*) of Christ and whether it is single or double. In point of fact, the term *energeia* contained meanings that were too practical in nature and risked only including those actions that were too exclusively human. What was at stake politically is clear: the Byzantine Empire and church, in a time of terrible threats from Persia and later Islam, had to find a rapprochement with miaphysite communities. Already at the very beginning of the affair we find a letter from Patriarch Sergius (d. 638) opening a correspondence with George Arsas, a miaphysite of Alexandria, in order to request of him writings on the single *energeia*. At

2 Winkelmann, "Die Quellen." See also Louth in this volume.

the same time, negotiations with the miaphysite patriarchs of Syria and Egypt were taking place.

However, institutional questions aside, the theological debate was real. The triumph of the doctrine of the two wills of Christ was only achieved with difficulty, and was affirmed in the sixth ecumenical council (Constantinople III) in 680–81. Though monothelitism does not appear to have had any discernible following after the beginning of the eighth century, it had nonetheless profoundly altered the understanding of the divine and the modes of access to revealed truth. In fact, as the actors involved themselves said, these were waters uncharted by earlier church fathers, and for which Scripture provided scant direct guidance. It was necessary, therefore, to examine carefully in detail the words of Christ (taken no longer as a source of dogmatic truth so much as indications of the truth to be constructed). A case in point was the diverse interpretations of the words of Christ on the Mount of Olives and at the time of his passion. Moreover, Maximus the Confessor, a defender and martyr of the cause for the two wills, had recourse to philosophical arguments, borrowing from Aristotle the idea that action is more tied up with nature than with the individual person. The distinctions among monastic *praxis* (necessary for the individual's salvation), *theoria*, and *theologia* (for establishing universal truth) on the one hand, and between biblical exegesis and the logic of demonstration on the other laid the foundations of a theological discourse that seems to bestow its own coherency on our period. This episode led to the development of a biblical exegesis that was more heuristic than contemplative, and is best represented in the West by the vast undertaking of the *Glossa ordinaria*.

The western church had played an important role in this crisis. Before his successors took up a position radically opposed to monothelitism, Pope Innocent I (402–17) had at first upheld a position considered monothelite, or at least reluctantly so, by the Byzantines. This reversal was later cited by Byzantine churchmen as an instance of the fallibility of the pontifical see (whose doctrinal positions were judged impeccable until that point). However, what the real import was of these Christological decisions is a different matter. After the conversion of the Visigothic king Recared at the Council of Toledo (589), Arianism, like all the other deviations from Trinitarian orthodoxy, ceased to play any decisive role in western Christendom. Adoptionism alone, which portrayed Christ as the adoptive son of God, constituted a brief exception at the close of the eighth century, and one whose impact was limited, even if it was the occasion of a veritable blossoming of theological thought in the Carolingian period.

Adoptionism[3] ought not to be lumped incautiously with the great Christological disputes of the preceding century, the widespread opinions of numerous heresiologists notwithstanding. Adoptionist heterodoxies have on occasion been attributed to Jewish, Arab, or even Nestorian influences, by way of eastern Christians following the Arabian armies. The reality would appear to be both more universal – since questioning with respect to the Incarnation remained lively for a long time – and more local. Thus, at the end of the eighth century, the Archbishop of Toledo, Elipandus (717–802), was obliged to welcome the mission for the reform of the Spanish church sent by Pope Hadrian (772–95) and by the Frankish church. Bishop Agila, who was in charge of this mission, was accompanied by a cleric, Migetius, who professed a strange teaching: Jesus, the Son of David, was one of the three persons of the Trinity! At a council held at Seville, Elipandus responded by affirming that Jesus had been adopted from the very beginning of his existence. Despite its clumsiness (or provocativeness) the verb "to adopt" could well have been understood as a variant for the verb "to assume" used in Chalcedonian Christology. It could also be twisted in a Nestorian direction. However, Elipandus's opponents, the two monks Beatus of Liebana and Etherius, went even further, falsely accusing Elipandus of maintaining that Jesus had been adopted by the Father at his baptism. Elipandus was then supported by Felix, bishop of Urgel (d. 818), who was in turn denounced by Charlemagne (768–814), called to Regensburg, and later sent before the pope in Rome. Felix renounced his doctrinal formulation, but the Spanish church maintained its support of Elipandus's and Felix's theories. Indeed, it appealed to Charlemagne who again turned to the pope: the pontiff roundly condemned their teaching. Charlemagne then called the Synod of Frankfurt in 794. The debate persisted for a few more years yet, and was the occasion of a number of treatises written in refutation of "Adoptionism," notably by Alcuin (d. 804). The intellectual quality of these treatises was high, and they constitute the first elements of a western theology independent of the patristic and Byzantine tradition.

This Christocentrism of the early Middle Ages exercised a powerful influence on the way in which the Godhead was represented. The variety and intensity of the doctrinal debates caused an increase in the ways in which Christ was represented, whether negatively (representing that which had *not* been condemned – namely, familiar or everyday representations of the life of Christ that were *not* susceptible to veneration), or compensatively. At the beginning of the ninth century, in a Carolingian West that was at the very

3 See Rivera Recio, *El adopcionismo en España*, and Heil, "Der Adoptianismus."

least reticent when it came to the adoration of images, representations of the cross dramatically increased. The divine thus became more visible. Though the Father, since he is not incarnate, could not be represented, Christ in some wise absorbed some of the Father's attributes, particularly from the close of the sixth century in Byzantium when portrayed as *Pantocrator*, or universal sovereign. A strict conception of theology in the Greek sense, superbly expressed in John Scottus Eriugena's *Periphyseon*, located divine essence and God the Father beyond being and, in some wise, delegated creation to the Word, and thereby authorized the image of Christ as creator.

Making the Spirit manifest: the *filioque* clause

The prominence accorded to the divine economy, particularly in the West, would seem to be belied by the famous *filioque* controversy which long set the Latin and Byzantine churches in opposition.[4] In fact, this is far from the case. As the Byzantines themselves pointed out, it was precisely an extrapolation from the economy to Trinitarian theology which, in part, provoked this enormous misunderstanding. Indeed, the biblical texts describing the relationship between the Son and the Spirit (primarily from the Gospel according to John) all concern the temporal mission of the Spirit as Paraclete, as protector and advocate ("And I will ask the Father, and he will give you another Advocate, to be with you for ever." John 14.16).

Modern theologians have tended to minimize the significance of this doctrinal difference of opinion. For historians, however, this remains an important episode since the *filioque* very quickly took pride of place in the list of disagreements between the churches which resulted in the proclamation of the schism. From 867, the Byzantine patriarch Photius (c. 810–c. 895) condemned the position of the Latin church and explicitly defined the contrary teaching, namely the procession of the Spirit from the Father alone. In the process he hardened what were rather more supple patristic judgments which had been able to be aligned with both doctrinal formulations. These reproaches from the patriarch must, however, be understood within the context of an ecclesiological conflict which turned on the control of new Christian, ecclesio-political identities and on the primacy of the Roman see. As far as contemporaries were concerned, this entrenchment of ecclesiastical institutions and of their sense of identity (undertaken again in 1054 when the "schism" was overtly declared) never precluded, as far as medieval writers were concerned, the idea

4 One of the best works remains Congar, *I Believe in the Holy Spirit*.

that the difference of opinion could in fact be overcome. Thus Duns Scotus (c. 1265–1308), following other scholastic thinkers of the thirteenth century, answered negatively the question of whether the procession from the Father alone would abolish the distinction between the second and third persons of the Trinity.

On the other hand, through the recitation of the creed, the dispute did have a direct impact on the pious practice of the Christian faithful. The "Nicene" Creed, promulgated at the Council of Constantinople (381) stated: "And I believe in the Holy Spirit, the Lord, the giver of life, who proceeds from the Father . . . ," and the recitation of this text remained the same throughout Christendom for centuries. The *filioque* clause ("who proceeds from the Father *and the Son*") was first added at the Council of Toledo in 589, probably out of a desire to distinguish Christian orthodoxy from Arianism (it is to be remembered that this is the same council that saw the conversion of King Recared): the point was to show the Word's eminence. This slight nod of veneration was of no tremendous doctrinal import since in patristic theology there coexisted formulations suggesting both a procession of the Spirit from the Father through the Son and a procession from both the Father and the Son. However, the liturgical stakes were high: in Byzantium and in Spain the creed was recited during the mass – something unknown in the contemporary Frankish church. Together with other uses, this liturgical practice gradually spread in Gaul and in England, and the creed was recited with the *filioque* in the Palatine chapel at Aachen, perhaps from the arrival of Alcuin at court in 786. The relative antiquity of these practices and liturgical formulae roused from time to time mutual and occasionally genuine accusations of textual falsification. For example, in 1054 Humbert of Silva-Candida (d. 1061) accused the Greeks of having suppressed the *filioque* of the ancient textual sources. It was, however, political circumstances, namely the tension between the Carolingian and the Byzantine empires, that drove Charlemagne to ask his theologians, and notably Alcuin, to examine the question. The acts of the Second Council of Nicaea (787) included a profession of the patriarch Tarasius (d. 806) which proclaimed the procession from the Father through the Son. Pope Hadrian rejected any modification of the creed. The Frankish church nonetheless went ahead with its attack, rejecting Nicaea II at Frankfurt in 794, and at the Council of Cividale (Friuli) in 796, it condemned the Byzantine church on the question of the *filioque*. A few years later, Charlemagne charged his theologians to put together doctrinal dossiers in preparation for a Council at Aachen (809). Despite this pressure, Pope Leo III (d. 816) refused to include the new formula, and suggested that the creed cease to be sung in the mass. Indeed, the

Latin interpolation was only introduced into the mass at Rome in 1014 under Benedict VIII on the occasion of the coronation of Henry II, and at his request.

The question remains, however, as to whether the liturgical variants and mutual accusations of textual falsification had any significant repercussions with respect to the general understanding of the triune God, and of the third person of the Trinity. This is difficult to gauge. It is, however, the case that the earliest discursive (Rupert of Deutz) and iconic representations of the Spirit as a person with a human appearance date from the beginning of the twelfth century.[5] Indeed, throughout the twelfth century, the importance was recognized of a theology of history linked with the expectation of an age of the Spirit or, more generally, of a special manifestation of the third person of the Trinity (e.g., Rupert of Deutz, Anselm of Havelberg, Joachim of Fiore).

From the visible to the intelligible: new thoughts

These doctrinal and liturgical deliberations had, as indicated, increased the number of images of the Godhead: the incarnate Word, in the course of the Christological debates, drew closer to man. Thus, the divide that had opened in connection with the miaphysite tendencies had an immediate impact on the pictorial representation of the Godhead. The Quinisext Council "in Trullo," held in 691–92, ten years after the Third Council of Constantinople (the same council that condemned monothelitism) ordered in its eighty-second canon the abandonment of symbolic representations of Christ (in the form of a lamb) in favor of human features: "The painting must lead us, as by hand, to the remembrance of Jesus living in the flesh, suffering and dying for our salvation, and thereby winning the redemption of the world."[6] In the years that followed, the Emperor Justinian II had gold coins struck on the obverse of which was represented the bust of the human Christ replacing the imperial bust which was relegated to the reverse side in place of the cross potencé.

The long battle surrounding the worship of images, which saw the rise and domination of the "iconoclasts" (or "image smashers") [7] and their leanings in the Byzantine East from around 725 to 842 (the echoes of which resounded throughout Christendom), must be understood as they relate to these developments in the Chalcedonian Christology discussed above. It ought not to

5 Boespflug, *Dieu dans l'art*.
6 Nedungatt and Featherstone, *Council in Trullo*, 162–64.
7 See *Histoire du Christianisme* 4, Pt. 1: "Le christianisme du VIIe au milieu du XIe siècle," 7–371.

be forgotten, however, that iconoclasm spread at the Byzantine emperors' initiative and entailed important stakes for the church. The influence of the monks, who defended the adoration of icons, was consequently lessened in favor of the episcopate under the authority of the patriarchs and the emperors. The concern to defend monotheism in competition with Islam and Judaism also, no doubt, played an important role, even if accusations of collusion between the iconoclasts and miaphysites, Judaizers, and other heterodox parties owed more to the extremist polemics of the period, than to substantial evidence.

It was not representation as such that proponents of iconoclasm were attacking, but worship of representation, which they judged to be unwarranted and unseemly. The numbers of sacred images had multiplied in the sixth and seventh centuries of the Byzantine era and had engendered a whole series of rituals attached to the image: images were lit, censed, kissed, worshippers prostrated themselves before them (*proskunesis*), prayers were addressed to them, and miracles expected of them. Dust scratched from the paintings themselves was even mingled with the Eucharist, and icons could be used as altar tables.

It is difficult precisely to ascertain the iconoclasts' line of argument: most of their writings were destroyed by their opponents. However, a clear Christological argument does arise from the documents of the Council of Hiereia (754) and from the edition of the *Interrogations* (*Peuseis*) of the emperor Constantine V (741–75; son and successor of Leo III, 717–41) who began the imperial condemnation of images. According to this Christology, an image of Christ is only able to represent his human nature and is, therefore, false either because of the impossibility of presenting to sight the divine nature, or by reason of the error that would deny the existence of this same nature. An authentic image, worthy of veneration, can only be one that is consubstantial with its model; hence, the only representation of Christ is the Eucharist. This criticism can, in fact, be taken as a perfectly Chalcedonian objection. Images of Christ claim to represent one person, but only admit the adoration of just one of the two natures of which Christ's person is formed.

The final defeat of the iconoclasts established the veneration of icons in Byzantine Christendom on a lasting basis, while at the same time it profoundly altered the structures of the church and its relationship to the empire. A practice of adoration which had formerly been tolerated, or at best looked upon with benevolence, had, in the course of the debates, been made the object of a veritable theorization. While the contribution of John Damascene (d. c. 749) or of the debates at Nicaea II (787; the council which, for the time being, restored "iconodulism" – the veneration of images) were still somewhat summary in nature and defensive in tone,[8] Theodore the Studite (d. 826) and Nicephorus I Patriarch of Constantinople (d. c. 829) deepened the theology of images by demonstrating that the adoration of icons was not in the least idolatrous since the image was a symbol through which the faithful worshiper addressed the person represented, the "prototype." Even as they drew on the vocabulary of the veneration of the images of the emperors of antiquity, theologians of the image developed their own doctrine of symbolic analogy, largely founded on Neoplatonic exemplarism, according to which all creation reflects the divine forms. On the other hand, the iconoclasts, adhering to the strict distinction between theology (in the Greek sense), and the economy of revelation, would only accord the possibility of sacrality to *signs* intentionally used by the Godhead, of which the primary models were sacraments, and principally the sacrament of the Eucharist.[9]

The conflict surrounding iconoclasm had important repercussions in the Latin West. Charlemagne and the Frankish church defined their doctrinal position in the *Opus Caroli Regis* (probably composed under the direction of Theodulf of Orleans), the tenor of which was confirmed by the Council of Frankfurt in 794, and refused to accept the canons of Nicaea II – canons which had been ratified by the pope. Leaving aside the institutional dimension of this refusal (the ecumenicity of the Nicaean council was rejected and the council judged "Byzantine"), it was the Byzantine *theology* of images that was rejected: images only had worth as decoration, or as a pastoral instrument, with no possible connection between the object itself and the prototype. This standpoint is explained by a profound difference in doctrine to which we shall return, but also by the interference of Christological debates which were also raised at Frankfurt, where Adoptionism was condemned. It is possible that the interpretation of the Spanish heresy as "Nestorian" did influence the Carolingian teaching regarding images. The connection between the two questions did emerge later in the 820s in the case of Bishop Claudius of Turin (d. after 827).[10] Though Claudius was denounced by Abbot Theutmir of Psalmody for his iconoclast practices, Claudius's actual position is only known through the summary of his response to Theutmir prepared by order of Louis the Pious (814–40) for the benefit of Jonas of Orleans (c. 760–c. 841) and Dungal of Pavia (fl. c. 800–c. 840) (who was charged with the task of refuting Claudius's iconoclasm). Claudius was rather severe in his rejection of religious mediations, refusing to allow images, relics, pilgrimages, and even images of the cross.

8 von Schönborn, *L'icône du Christ*.
9 Mondzain, *Image, Icon, Economy*.
10 Boureau, "Les théologiens carolingiens."

He was not, however, alone in his extreme position. For one thing, rather more nuanced but nonetheless strongly rigorist viewpoints were defended in the *Liber de imaginibus*, written in 825–26 and attributed to Agobard of Lyons (c. 769–840) or to his disciple Florus (d. c. 860). It was to Lyons that Felix of Urgel was exiled, and at which he arrived escorted by Claudius, who was also Spanish. Agobard became bishop of Lyons around 815, shortly before the appointment of Claudius to Turin and the death of Felix. Claudius's extreme iconoclasm assured the Frankish church of the middle ground. This standpoint was defined at the Council of Paris in 825 and solidified the West's mistrust of images, with lasting consequences. To make matters yet more complicated, the opponent of Elipandus of Toledo, Beatus of Liebana, composed a celebrated commentary on the Apocalypse which was illustrated with pictures no less famous in the tenth century than now. Christ was represented there as Judge, in a pose formally very close to that of the Christ Pantocrator of the Byzantines.

The doctrinal resolution of the iconoclast controversy and, to a lesser degree, the response to the Adoptionist heresy, allowed the proposition of a fundamental distinction between two modes of representation of the incarnate Godhead: the symbol and the sign. Claudius of Turin decried the elision of metaphor into mimetic analogy, writing:

> They would venerate rocks because, when the Lord was taken down from the cross, he was placed in a tomb hewn of rock, and because the Apostle says: "But the rock was Christ." But Christ is called rock, lamb and lion metaphorically (*tropice*) not properly speaking, according to the meaning of these things, not their substance.[11]

This is one of the earliest iconoclast arguments regarding the absence of any consubstantiality between the image and its model. The iconodules' symbol remained ontologically distinct from reality: it was useful for instruction or meditation alone. This was the argument that prevailed in the West, too, at least since the debate between Gregory the Great (590–604) and Serenus of Marseilles at the end of the sixth century. In contrast, the idea of a sign, since it introduced the notion of a real relationship, and of a connection that is relational without being substantial, surmounted this representational *aporia*. This was not a direction taken up in the Byzantine world, won over as it was to the cause of the symbol and to the veneration of images. The Latin West, on the other hand, ever reticent with respect to images, transferred this promotion of signs as sacred mediations to the sacraments.

11 Claudius of Turin, *Apologeticum atque rescriptum*, 462C.

Reflection on the sacraments as mediations between the Godhead and human beings was, in fact, peculiar to the West, and prepared the way for the great syntheses of the twelfth and thirteenth centuries on the history, structure, and causality of the sacraments. The relative moderation exhibited in the Christological debates in the Latin West after 600 was, perhaps, one of the reasons for the privileged place accorded in the West to the divine economy, and the works of the incarnate Word. Another was the considerable influence of St. Augustine and notably his teaching regarding the transmission of original sin. The particular importance of the theme of Christ the redeemer issued from this, as did the development of a sacramental doctrine of penance strengthened by Irish and Anglo-Saxon influences, while baptism ceased to hold pride of place in western treatments of the sacraments.

It was, however, the Eucharist, more than penance, that raised a number of complex problems. As we have seen, the Byzantine iconoclasts admitted the Eucharist alone as being a mode of Christ's presence in the world precisely because of the intentional and causal relationship which Christ had established between the bread and his body. It is exactly this nexus of questions surrounding the Eucharist which occupied the Frankish church for several centuries. Paschasius Radbertus (c. 790–c. 860), abbot of Corbie, composed in 831 a treatise entitled *De corpore et sanguine domini* on the request of his pupil Placidus Varinus, abbot of Corbie's daughter house of Corvey in Germany. A revised copy of the text was sent to Charles the Bald in 844, who in turn submitted the text to Ratramnus of Corbie (d. c. 870), and later Hrabanus Maurus (c. 780–856) joined in the debate. Paschasius had affirmed that the Eucharistic flesh (*caro*) was "in no way distinct from that which was born of Mary, and suffered on the cross and knew the resurrection from the grave." Ratramnus retorted that the Eucharistic body, despite its essential identity with the historical body of Jesus, had only a spiritual mode of existence, as an "invisible substance." In the same period, at Hincmar of Rheims's (806–82) request John Scottus Eriugena wrote a treatise on the Eucharist, the text of which (judged to be of dubious worth by Hincmar) has not survived, but of which we may gain some idea from the reaction of Hincmar and from other writings of Eriugena. The latter writes in his *Commentary on the Celestial Hierarchy*,

> once this visible Eucharist, which priests confect each day from the sensible matter of bread and wine and which they receive corporeally, has been made and has been blessed, it is the symbolic similitude of spiritual participation (*typicam esse similitudinem spiritualis participationem*).[12]

12 John Scottus Eriugena, *Expositiones in hierarchiam coelestem*, I.3, 16–17.

Paschasius had treated the Eucharistic species as *figura* offered to the senses. This approach, presented in historiography as "realist," corresponds, in fact, to the symbolist tendencies in iconodule thought. It was taken up again, two centuries later, by Lanfranc of Bec (1010–89), following many others (Odo of Cluny, Rather of Verona, Gezo of Tortona).

This time the attack came from an opponent of the real presence, Berengar of Tours, who, from 1050 and during a period of roughly forty years, was condemned fourteen times in synods and councils punctuated by later fiercely disputed recantations. The length of these debates is a measure of what was at stake. The doctrine of transubstantiation itself was coming to fruition, even if the origins of the word itself remain obscure, sometimes being attributed to Peter Damian (1007–72), sometimes to Hubert of Lavardin, and occasionally to Roland Bandinelli, the future Pope Alexander III (d. 1181).

The precise origin of the term is of little import: the word was in the air at the time, and in a certain sense its creation paradoxically suggests a Berengarian triumph, since it transposes into theology precisely the Aristotelian ontological vocabulary which he was able to impose on the discussion. Taking semiological and linguistic arguments as his point of departure, Berengar proposed considering the Eucharistic sacrament not as the *signified* symbolizing a transcendent reality (namely, the redemption of humanity by the suffering Christ), but as a *sign*: the bread was the signified of the body of Christ.[13] This is why, for Berengar, the concrete reality of the bread could not disappear any more than the signified of any sign could annihilate that which represented it. Following an Augustinian tradition, Berengar insisted on the voluntary and contractual nature of the sign: Christ had used the bread of the Last Supper and continued to use the bread of the Eucharistic sacrifice as a means of expressing the gift of his redeeming grace. The presence of the body of Christ is certainly real, but its reality is treated as one that implies the instituting will of the Godhead: real, but relational rather than material. Berengar's defeat did not consign his theory of the sacred sign to oblivion. On the contrary, the fact that his conclusions were rejected did not preclude the success of his means of demonstration – the development of a doctrine of the sacramental sign which was so intensively worked upon in the West in the twelfth and thirteenth centuries. It is possible that the western form of the unleavened Eucharistic host (the use of which had been forcibly condemned by the Byzantine church) contributed to this abstraction of the Eucharistic sign, by being radically different from the visual

13 See Rosier-Catach, *La parole efficace*.

reality of everyday bread. Moreover, the centrality of the Eucharist, whether as material symbol or as sign of the relation between God and humankind, opened up the way both to theoretical speculation and to a very concrete devotion to the host that was to become characteristic of the later Middle Ages.[14]

For half a millennium, the human perception of the God of the Christians was then constructed according to new mediations, both visual and discursive. In the East, with the passing of the iconoclast crisis, the abiding legitimacy of the representation of the divine and of meditation on the incarnate God was established. In the West, it was rather the cult of the Eucharist which had assured this mediation. Throughout Christendom, crosses, images, and buildings transformed the human landscape. From the ninth century in the Byzantine East, the proliferation of churches built in the shape of a Greek cross around a domed apse provided ideal canvasses for huge Christological decorative programs. Further, around the year 1000, the famous white mantle of churches evoked by Rodulfus Glaber (d. 1047) – a sign of both tremendous economic growth and the invention in the West of the parish-village – was studded with crucifixes and religious images. Nineteenth-century art historians styled this sudden rise in artistic activity "Romanesque Art," but, regardless of contemporary debates about the precise chronology and origins of this artistic movement, a prodigious supply of sacred images did certainly begin to take shape in the eleventh century. The Christianization of Europe and western Asia was accompanied by the appropriation of time itself which took place in this period, from the invention of the Christian era by Dionysius Exiguus (in the sixth century) to its adoption in the papal chancellery (in the tenth century). In some ways, it is still the mediated vision of God that was at stake in this institution of a Christian demarcation of time, especially in the West. The Last Coming of Christ as savior was no longer thought of as being close at hand. St. Augustine had made the definitive declaration on this matter; thereafter, the idea of this delay found its way into representations of the long duration of time, even if cognizance of a lengthy chronology affected only a small minority of scholars, and if the rather notorious "terrors of the year 1000" have been greatly exaggerated by nineteenth-century historians.[15] On the other hand, the long preparation for the Second or Last Coming of Christ, was visibly included in the worship of the savior as seen in the monumental

14 Rubin, *Corpus Christi*.

15 For a contrary perspective, see the works of Richard Landes, and in particular his "Sur les traces du Millennium."

architecture of the Carolingians,[16] centered on the evocation of the site of Christ's passion. At the end of the period under consideration, the capture of Jerusalem (1099) was as much a culmination (of Christocentrism, and of the early Middle Ages) as a beginning (the crusades).

Devising systems of divine logic

The last form of mediation between God and humanity in our treatment, that founded upon the logic proper to human discourse, seems to have been more specifically a western and Latin phenomenon. Like the doctrine of the holy sign, it too appears to stem from the writings of St. Augustine, who had established, especially in his *De Trinitate*, that the human spirit presents an image, a mirror of the divine Trinity. St. Paul's mirror takes on a positive meaning here: the human spirit is no longer considered the mere reflection or symbol of the divine creative activity among all things created, but as the very means chosen by God to bring about a likeness, a sign of his choice. Memory, intelligence, and the will (or love) in the human spirit reflect the three persons of the Trinity. Corresponding to the second person of the Trinity – the Word – human intellection produces a *human* word capable of linking together incommensurable things.

This Augustinian approach is readily discernible in the works of St. Anselm (1033–1109). In the *Monologion*, Anselm demonstrates that divine intelligence – the creating Word who contains all being – gives himself as the guiding principle of all creation. The model of the creature thus implies a certain form in the spirit of the Creator. Anselm strove as a logician to encounter the divine Word by beginning with a human word which expresses necessary things and acts. Thus he argues that, before they were made, things had been spoken in God. Accordingly, it is the task of human beings to attain knowledge of things from universal concepts, or *verba naturalia* – indeed, by speaking soundly, the rational creature could imitate the Word. However, since access to universal ideas is hampered by the constraints of the flesh, the utterance of correct words entails an ascesis of reason achieved by the practice of dialectic – that is, by the practice of logic. Faith is thereby set in quest of reason (*fides quaerens intellectum*). For Anselm, it is not reason's task to prove things; rather, reason allows for a gradual transition from the truth of things said to ontological truth, and next to the truth of "significations" (i.e., of universal concepts or ideas) in order that the ultimate point of reference, God himself, might at last be held in view. This

16 Cf. Centula (Saint-Riquier) and Aachen, among others.

is the frame within which the famous argument (which since Kant has been described as the "ontological" argument and which is also found in Anselm's *Proslogion*) must be situated: the argument deduces the existence of God from the possibility of human beings to formulate a proposition including the idea of a being "than which we cannot conceive anything greater" (*id quo maius cogitari nequit*).

The use of dialectic in theological discourse, based on the small corpus of the *Logica vetus* (Aristotle, Boethius, Pseudo-Augustinian texts, etc.) and which greatly increased in the eleventh century,[17] had begun already in the ninth. One of its chief proponents was, paradoxically, John Scottus Eriugena,[18] who had taught the liberal arts before he translated and commented upon the Greek fathers, and notably on Pseudo-Dionysius. His central and guiding question concerned the relationship between ontology and theology: could divine realities be evoked by means of Aristotle's ten ontological categories? Eriugena's answer in the end consisted in rejecting this possibility, all the while proposing a "super category," namely, *ousia* – a sort of substance of substances – which made it possible to transcend the limits of the human description of nature. Eriugena has long been considered as something of an exception among contemporary authors, as the only true Neoplatonist of the Latin Middle Ages, and as a writer whose influence was still further hampered by the condemnation of his work at the Council of Paris in 1210, which was confirmed by Pope Honorius III in 1225. Recent research, however, has revealed the scope of the influence of Eriugena's methods, especially at the monastic school of Auxerre.[19] It is one of the paradoxes of western theology that its direction was guided intellectually by authors whom the church censured institutionally (John Scottus Eriugena, Berengar of Tours).

Supplied with the feared and revered tools of logic, Latin Christian thought could now return to theology in the Greek sense of the term as it attempted to define the divine attributes. Anselm's works exhibit a concern to understand the divine essence from its evident attributes: infinitude, immutability, omnipotence, and the triune nature. Even in his treatise *Cur deus homo?* Anselm chose to leave aside those teachings revealed in the economy of the incarnation and to think "as if nothing were known of Christ." Reflections on divine knowledge and the divine will actually nursed the theological controversies which shook the West, especially that surrounding the teaching of Godescalc of Orbais

17 Holopainen, *Dialectic and Theology*.
18 Moran, *Philosophy of John Scottus Eriugena*.
19 Marenbon, *From the Circle of Alcuin*. See also Jolivet, *Godescalc d'Orbais*, and Iogna-Prat, Jeudy, and Lobrichon, *L'école carolingienne*.

(d. c. 868), who maintained the double predestination of the elect to salvation, and of the damned to hell.[20] The reactions against Godescalc's teaching were lively, from John Scottus Eriugena to Anselm: double predestination bound God, it was argued, to time and to a fixed order. Peter Damian developed a treatment of the power of God: his *Letter on Divine Omnipotence*[21] paved the way for a distinction between absolute power and ordered power which, in fact, located divine revelations on the side of God's infinite power. The theme of divine omnipotence, so omnipresent in the writings of the beginning of the second millennium, was no doubt aimed at freeing God from the web of restrictive determinations which dialectic discourse was in danger of casting over the works of God. At the same time it upheld the theocratic pretensions of the papacy at the time of the Gregorian reforms.

These aims, which were quite new in their totalizing scope and in their logicist methods, led to the birth in the eleventh century of a new discourse named "theology," *theologia* in Latin, without any direct reference to patristic use of the term. In the West, from around 1100, the term began to be used to designate a science of divine realities including in one and the same discipline both the question of God's essence and that of the divine economy. The ancient preeminence of revealed theology did, however, continue in the West, as the alternating use of *theologia* and *sacra pagina* for either "theology" (in today's sense of the word) or the biblical text clearly shows. Whilst the word *theologia* is generally thought to have been a novelty peculiar to the writings of Peter Abelard (c. 1120) and although it certainly does not appear in Anselm precisely where the famous formula *fides quaerens intellectum* seems to call for it, a letter of Master Gozechinus,[22] written around 1070, does bear witness to the emergence of a new way of conceiving the Godhead. The Liègeois master, exiled to Cologne, writes to his disciple Walcherus that he considers himself too old to follow his colleagues Hermann of Rheims, Drogo of Paris, Rudiger of Speyer, and Meinhard of Bavaria in the pursuit of a new science – "theology."

This was an intellectual novelty, as we have seen; but it was also a cultural one. The dialectic approach entailed systematic instruction, and the learning of a complicated technique; it gave rise to lively debates as it was constantly brushing up against error. The quick succession of monastic controversies from the ninth century on paved the way for the urban schools and, later, the university. It would be wrong to see an inevitable and unique process in this

20 See Jolivet, *Godescalc d'Orbais*.
21 Peter Damian, *Lettre sur la toute-puissance divine*.
22 Published in Gozechinus, *Epistola ad Walcherum*, 35.

development of western theological systems of logic. In Byzantium at this time, a "cultural renaissance" led to the dissemination of a number of antique texts. Greek patristic writers always retained an important place in the West: they remained a resource especially, though not exclusively, through the successive translations of and commentaries on Pseudo-Dionysius. Moreover, the West maintained a theology tied to Scripture and to the symbolic decoding of nature which reached full maturity in the writings of St. Bernard. Nothing was put into play; nonetheless, we may posit that the dialectical approach of this new Latin theology was sparked by the scarcity of sacred mediations admitted by the West – the consequence of Augustinian criticisms of the symbol and of the institutional rejection of the Greek theology of an analogical presence of the Godhead. God could indeed allow himself to be seen in the mirror of reason, for the mystery to be resolved or at least circumscribed.

25

Orthodoxy and deviance

E. ANN MATTER

The period covered by this volume, c. 600–c. 1100, stands alone in Christian history as an age in which there were very few major struggles over definitions of orthodoxy. This is not to say that there were no disputes among learned churchmen about points of doctrine; indeed, there were some very interesting controversies revolving around familiar problems of theology and practice. Yet none of these disputes ended in a new doctrinal definition that was passed on to future centuries as authoritative, like the great theological syntheses created in the patristic and scholastic ages. Nor could one say that there were no early medieval movements of popular piety, or lay people who followed charismatic religious leaders. This period provides several examples of this sort of challenge to the ecclesiastical orthodoxy, but none, at least until the eleventh century, ended up changing the shape of the church of the time like the great movements of lay piety in the later Middle Ages. Nor did early medieval conflicts over theological issues have the geographical and chronological scope of later disputes; many, indeed, were quite localized and fleeting. Nevertheless, the theological issues that came to the fore in the early Middle Ages are important as windows on the development of theology in an especially fluid period that mediated between the age of the fathers and the towering syntheses of later medieval theology. This chapter, consequently, has a double task: to summarize the disputes that did arise among Christians from approximately 600 to 1100, and to suggest some reasons for why the dynamic of early medieval heresy and orthodoxy is so strikingly different from the periods that came before and after.

Learned disputes about Christian theology and practice, I: the Latin West

Starting with the disputes among the theologically educated, it is important to reflect a bit on how official theology is set. The development of Christian orthodoxy is a complicated process, one that takes place at the interstices of theological truth and cultural relativity. Of course debates about whether theological positions are deemed orthodox, deviant, heterodox, or even heretical are fought on a battleground of eternal truth; but they always tell us something important also about the transient, time-bound protagonists in the dispute. The Nicene formulation of Trinitarian orthodoxy is a good example of this. Why was it so important to state that Jesus Christ, the only begotten Son of the Father, was *homoousios*, of the same substance or essence as the Father? Here is a doctrine of faith that makes excellent sense in the context of the social and political turmoil of the first period of Christian empire, and in a world infused with Neoplatonic thought, but has been a source of confusion for much of Christian history.[1]

Like the definitions of Nicaea, the dogmatic disputes of Christianity's first five centuries cast a long shadow over the early Middle Ages, setting important parameters for the very definition of orthodoxy. The relationship of early medieval theologians to "remembered" heresy differs from the relationship between the original protagonists of the dispute. This is because heresy and orthodoxy are defined in a dialectical exchange; in the original context, the position that later comes to be called heretical could actually help shape the orthodox consensus, just by suggesting an alternative, for example. But that sense of exchange, even the sense that these debates, in important ways, were disputes between equals, is lost to subsequent generations who do not know the protagonists firsthand, and who have only the dogmatic proclamations of orthodoxy – sometimes mere lists.[2] This was the case in the early Middle Ages, when a theological world far removed from the philosophical schools of Hellenism still found itself armed with such documents as the canons of the ecumenical councils and dogmatic summaries like Augustine's (354–430) *De haeresibus* or the *Book of the Dogmas of the Church* attributed to Gennadius of Marseilles (fl. 470–80).[3] For early medieval theologians, the decisions about heresy and orthodoxy of earlier centuries provided a standard against which questions about orthodoxy were to be judged, even if the questions were very different.

Consider, for example, the controversy over the nature of Christ that erupted among Frankish churchmen at the turn of the ninth century. The debates over "Adoptionism," the first major dogmatic dispute in this period, are interesting

1 Chadwick, *Early Church*, gives an excellent discussion of the political and philosophical ramifications of the theological positions of the Council of Nicaea I.
2 For an interesting exploration of this problem, see Cameron, "How to Read Heresiology."
3 Augustine, *De haeresibus*; Turner, "*Liber ecclesiasticorum dogmatum*."

on many levels, including the way they show the propensity of early medieval theologians to interpret novel or unusual theological ideas by means of a traditional list of "heresies." The Adoptionists were condemned for claiming (as they were understood to say by their opponents) that, even though the divine Christ is co-eternal with the Father, the man Jesus was not the Son of God until he was "adopted" into that position at his baptism.[4] This movement, if it was a "movement" rather than a colossal misunderstanding among ecclesiastical leaders, was led by Elipandus, the bishop of Toledo (783–808), and Felix (d. 818), the bishop of Urgel, a town in the Pyrenees. Adoptionism has been explained as a revival of a heresy dating from the second and third centuries, and connected to some forms of Arianism;[5] in this, Spanish Adoptionism seems an old-fashioned and backwards-looking theological position, attributable to the isolation of Christianity on the Iberian peninsula for several centuries. Spain was isolated first because the Visigoths were Arians until the conversion to Catholicism of King Recared (d. 601) around 589, and again after 712 because of the Muslim domination of much of the peninsula.[6]

The opponents of Adoptionism included most of the notable church leaders of Carolingian Francia, and some important Spanish and Italian theologians, too. The Northumbrian Alcuin (d. 804), one of the leaders of Charlemagne's school at Aachen and later abbot of the monastery of St. Martin at Tours, led the charge. Alcuin's obsession with the errant theology of Felix occupied the last twelve years of his life, from 792 to 804.[7] A number of Alcuin's letters to Charlemagne (768–814) deal specifically with the Adoptionist problem, showing the emperor's concern about possible political ramifications of the controversy.[8] Charlemagne's concern that a dissident theology was attracting followers in the Spanish March was certainly part of the reason that Felix, Elipandus, and their "Adoptionism" were condemned by Frankish synods in 792, 794, and 799.[9]

Over and over, Alcuin accused Felix and Elipandus of heresy, or rather, of heresies; and here we see again how much early medieval theologians relied on earlier definitions of orthodoxy and heresy. The Adoptionists, Alcuin said, were Arians, who did not believe the Son was equal to the Father; or perhaps

4 For the traditional take on the Adoptionist controversy, see Russell, *Dissent and Reform*, 11–14; Lambert, *Medieval Heresy*, 26.

5 Russell, *Dissent and Reform*, 155 and 294, note 5, for bibliography on the survival of Arianism.

6 For an interpretation of Adoptionism that depends on Spain's isolation, see Cabaniss, "Heresiarch Felix".

7 Heil, *Alcuinstudien I*, see especially the timeline, 66–72.

8 Alcuin, *Epistolae* 23, 41, 137, 138, 139, 146, 148, 160, 166, 194, 201, 205, 208.

9 Regensburg (792), Frankfurt (794), Aachen (799); cf. Zeddies, "Bonifatius," 225 and note 23; Heil, *Alcuinstudien I*; Cavadini, "Elipandus."

they were more like Eutychians, who disputed the two natures of Christ by making him one with the Father in his adoption; or possibly they held the opposite theological position, that of the Nestorians, who were thought to downplay the divinity of Christ, claiming that Mary was not the Mother of God.[10] Other critics, Beatus of Liebana (c. 730–98) and Paulinus of Aquileia (730/740–802), echoed especially the charge of Arianism, but Beatus also hinted that Elipandus may have been some sort of dualist, like a Manichee.[11] When Felix was an elderly man living in house arrest in Lyons, his last opponent, the implacable Archbishop Agobard (d. 840), showed even more theological and historical imagination by comparing Felix to the fourth-century Semi-Arian bishop Photinus (d. 376), an accusation found also in an anonymous juridical text against Adoptionism from the late eighth or early ninth century.[12]

It may be true that the teachings of Photinus, as far as we can reconstruct them, came exceedingly close to Adoptionist doctrines,[13] but it is also, nonetheless, clear that the Frankish opponents of the Spanish theology expounded by Felix and Elipandus were reaching into a bag of definitions, theological trots left over from a different period of the formulation of Christian doctrine, rather than trying to understand the Christology of Felix and Elipandus on its own terms. It is hard to fathom exactly what Felix and Elipandus did say about the nature of Christ, since we have so little testimony in their own words.[14] In fact, Adoptionism has also been described as a perfectly legitimate, native western, Christian theological position, but the theological traditions (perhaps we could say the theological disposition) of the leaders of the church of Charlemagne made it impossible for them to understand the teachings of Elipandus and Felix this way.[15]

Was Adoptionism really a theological movement, or was it only an obscure doctrinal dispute among a theological elite? This question could be answered in part by determining whether it was ever a movement that attracted followers

10 Alcuin, *Liber contra haeresin Felicis, Contra Felicem*, and *Adversus Elipandum*. Alcuin also suggests that the Adoptionists followed the teachings of the anti-predestinarian Pelagians, but that is somewhat harder to understand.

11 Beatus of Liebana, *Ad Elipandum*; Paulinus of Aquileia, *Contra Felicem*; another churchman who entered the dispute was Benedict of Aniane, *Disputatio adversus Felicianam*, and *Liber sacrosyllabus*.

12 Agobard of Lyons, *Adversus dogma Felicis Urgellensis*. For the anonymous juridical text, see Firey, "Carolingian Ecclesiology and Heresy," 294–99.

13 Firey, "Carolingian Ecclesiology and Heresy," 294.

14 Letters of Elipandus are published in *PL* 96 and quoted by some of these sources; Felix is also quoted by Alcuin and Agobard, and his *Confessio fidei* is published in Alcuin's letters, *Epistola* 199.

15 The idea that Adoptionism was a perfectly orthodox western Christology is the thesis of Cavadini, *Last Christology*.

and developed something like an "Adoptionist church." Alcuin says that it did, claiming in two of his letters that there were twenty thousand of the faithful in the Spanish Marches in the Adoptionist camp.[16] Our difficulty in assessing this claim is that we have no other information about these "Adoptionist" Christians, unless Alcuin was simply referring to the faithful of the dioceses of Toledo and Urgel, and claiming that the followers were the faithful Christians under the ecclesiastical rule of Bishops Felix and Elipandus. The ongoing tendency of Carolingian theologians to portray "heretics" in the language of the patristic age makes this an attractive solution to the question.

It is also possible that Adoptionist Christology was in some way an Iberian Christian accommodation to Islamic theology. Scholars of Adoptionism have debated this question: one side points out that all of the theological elements of the Adoptionist Christology were native to Christian theology before the rise of Islam, while the other marshals evidence for Christian apologetic in the face of Islamic rule in most of the Iberian peninsula.[17] After all, the Toledo of Bishop Elipandus was deep in the territory of the Umayyad Caliphate of Cordoba, and therefore the Christians of Toledo were subject to certain constraints. According to Islamic law, both Christians and Jews bore the special designation *dhimmī*; they were allowed to practice their religions, but only under conditions that would not offend Muslim religious sensibilities.[18] For example, Christians were not allowed to ring bells to announce their services, nor to hold public processions with religious objects. In spite of these strictures, or perhaps because of them, it has been suggested that the Christian majority in Spain saw an increasing number of the faithful assimilate to Islamic customs in order to gain the favor of the Muslim rulers and gain places at court. Some have also suggested that there were many conversions to Islam in the first half of the ninth century.[19] From the 820s to the 850s, according to two Spanish authors, Paul Albar (d. c. 861) and Eulogius (d. 859), Christians began to resist the Islamicization of Iberian life; as a result, many were martyred for their faith.[20] The phenomenon known as the "Martyrs of Cordoba" took place a generation after the Adoptionists were defeated by the Frankish ecclesiastical leaders. Eulogius and Paul Albar are enthusiastic in their descriptions of this

16 Alcuin, *Epistolae* 200, 208.

17 Cavadini, *Last Christology*, 2–3, 132 note 14, 39–40, and 159 notes 112, 113 for a discussion of the positions. While Cavadini, *Last Christology*, 39, believes that Adoptionism was a thoroughly Christian theological phenomenon, he allows that the Islamic context may have had some effect on Elipandus.

18 Ye'or, *Dhimmi*; Lewis, *Jews of Islam*; Coope, *Martyrs of Córdoba*.

19 Bulliet, *Conversion to Islam*.

20 Eulogius, *Documentum martyriale*, *Epistulae*, *Liber apologeticus*, *Memoriale sanctorum*; Paul Albar, *Epistulae*, *Indiculus luminosus*, *Vita Eulogii*; discussed in Coope, *Martyrs of Córdoba*.

resistance as a rejection of Christian assimilation to Islam, even to the point of stirring up Christian antagonism to any concessions to Islamic rule. Perhaps the Adoptionism of the previous generation was also, at least in part, an attempt to moderate Christian theology, an accommodation of Christology to the strict monotheism of Islam. If so, Adoptionism was bound for rejection by those who understood it as a threat to Christian orthodoxy, whether or not Islam was ever specifically mentioned in the controversy, and whether or not Adoptionism was ever widely practiced.

Other official theologians of the Carolingian age also thought about heresy in categories inherited from another time and place. Haimo of Auxerre (d. c. 855), one of the most prolific expositors of the Bible whose works date from the middle of the ninth century, actually seems somewhat obsessed with naming heretics. Haimo warns the readers of his biblical commentaries against a long list: Donatists, Novatianists, Apollinarians, Arians, Adoptionists, Sabellians, Photians, Marcionites, Ebionites, Cerinthians, Nicolaitans, Pricillianists, Tatianites, Jovinians, Pelagians, and Eutycians.[21] It is an interesting list, especially if we wonder about the reality of the threats represented by these names. Some are easier to understand than others; for example, Adoptionists were obviously still a fresh memory, and Arians and Pelagians had been known in western Europe up to the sixth century at least, so maybe Haimo had some realistic idea of who they were. Nicolaitan could mean any priest living with a woman, and there may well have been some of those around Auxerre in Haimo's time.[22] But other names on the list are less understandable: Haimo had a very slim chance of ever meeting an early Christian heretic like a Marcionite or a Eutycian, for instance. So why did he specifically mention them? Do Haimo's many references to Manicheans suggest there may have been some dualistic preaching in northern Francia in the late ninth century?[23] The answer may be simply that he tended to look at his contemporary theological scene through the lens of the ancient heresies in his reference works, and that this lens colored his view of the issues related to orthodoxy in his own century.

Nor was Haimo the only ninth-century theologian to think this way. One of his reference works may have been the *Instruction to the Clergy* of Hrabanus

21 These references are found especially in Haimo's commentaries on the New Testament Epistles. See Contreni, "Haimo of Auxerre," 309 note 1, building on Riggenbach, *Die älteste lateinischen Kommentare*, and Quadri, "Aimone di Auxerre."

22 Not all priests of the ninth century were monastics like Haimo, see Russell, *Dissent and Reform*, 126.

23 Russell, *Dissent and Reform*, 193–94 thinks these may be references to the earlier dualistic sects in Thuringia reported by the missionary Boniface; but a comprehensive study of Boniface and his opponents does not find any evidence for dualism, cf. Zeddies, "Bonifatius," 221–26.

Maurus (c. 776–856) which also gives a list of ancient heretical groups.[24] This was written about 819, but in the mid 840s, when Hrabanus returned to the topic of heresy in his work *On the Universe*, he gave much more attention to the theological disputes in his immediate environment.[25] For example, Hrabanus defends the addition of the word *filioque* ("and the Son") to describe the descent of the Holy Spirit in the Nicene Creed, an innovation of the western church that was bitterly contested by Greek Christians. He is also careful to assert that Christ is the Son of God "not by adoption," a clear reference to the Adoptionist controversy. Perhaps this shows Hrabanus's increasing awareness of contemporary theological disputes.

In fact, starting in the 840s it is easy to find explicit theological debates among the major figures of Carolingian monastic schools, but these are most often limited to a small circle of theologians, and rarely end in theological condemnations. The disputes between two monks of the important Frankish monastery of Corbie, Paschasius Radbertus (c. 790–c. 860) and Ratramnus (d. c. 870), show this well. The writings of Radbertus and Ratramnus are probably rooted in the necessity to explain the mysteries of the Eucharist to newly converted Christians in Saxon lands on the edge of the Carolingian Empire.[26] The debate concerns what is necessary to believe about the Eucharist, and what is absurd. Radbertus and Ratramnus argue different points of view about the nature of the Real Presence of Christ in the Eucharist and the virginity of Mary *in partu*, at the moment of the birth of Jesus, but scholars have pointed out that the real theological debate here is about the nature of the historical body of Christ.[27] The dispute may have led to unrest in the monastery of Corbie, and it certainly had some repercussions in the theological debates of the Protestant Reformation, but in the context of early medieval theology, it shows more about the search for satisfactory philosophical language in theology than anything else, and cannot really be counted as a struggle over orthodoxy.[28]

24 Hrabanus Maurus, *De institutione clericorum*.

25 Hrabanus Maurus, *De universo*, IV.8–10; this shift is pointed out by Russell, *Dissent and Reform*, 176.

26 The first version of the Eucharistic treatise of Paschasius Radbertus was intended for the novices at Corbie's daughter-house, Corvey, in Saxony. For an excellent discussion of the importance of the conversion of the Saxons, see Fulton, *From Judgment to Passion*, 11–27.

27 Paschasius Radbertus, *De corpore et sanguine Domini*, *De partu Virginis*; Ratramnus of Corbie, *De corpore et sanguine Domini*, *De eo quod Christus ex Virgine natus est*. See Bouhot, *Ratramne de Corbie*, 50–57, 77–111; Chazelle, "Figure, Character and the Glorified Body," and *Crucified God*, 215–38.

28 For the way Ratramnus's text has been misunderstood by Protestant scholars who have erroneously understood it as arguing against the Real Presence of Christ in the Eucharist,

Likewise, the possible allegorical excesses of Amalarius of Metz (c. 780–c. 850), who explained the entire liturgy on various levels of interpretation, and the hierarchical Neoplatonism of John Scottus Eriugena (800/817-after 866), while certainly unusual and out of step with the development of Carolingian thought (and even offensive to some contemporaries), are also not really debates about orthodoxy.[29]

The theology of the "unfortunate monk," Godescalc of Orbais (d. c. 868), on the other hand, resonated with some classic questions of orthodoxy. In or about 829, Godescalc insisted on leaving the monastic community of Fulda, where Hrabanus Maurus was abbot, before taking his final vows. Godescalc became a wandering preacher in northern Italy. Around 840, word reached Hrabanus that he was preaching a dangerous doctrine of double or "twinned" predestination. In fact, Godescalc had rediscovered an issue that had been a potential time bomb in western Christianity since the fifth century, and so the perennial and unanswerable issue of free will and predestination came back into the spotlight. Predestination had been the major doctrinal dispute of the last years of the life of Augustine of Hippo, when he had argued bitterly against the British monk Pelagius (c. 354–418) and his followers that not just salvation, but also damnation were in God's hands alone, and could not be effected by any human effort.[30] Modern scholars have pointed out that much of the later view of "Pelagianism" as an actual heretical movement seems to have been created by Augustine's zeal, but there is no doubt that Augustine, especially late in his life, was very concerned to emphasize the power of God, and therefore to argue a predestinarian over a free-will position.[31] Godescalc came to his radical predestinarian position by reading Augustine and taking him seriously; he was the first theologian in his century to do so.[32]

This position aroused the opposition of a number of ecclesiastical leaders, who were alarmed mostly by the potential for pastoral chaos and were determined to stop the spread of a teaching that humans have no responsibility for their salvation. Godescalc's teaching was formally condemned at the Council of Quierzy in 849, where he was obliged to burn his codex of accumulated

see Bouhot, *Ratramne de Corbie*, 77–162; for examples of this, see the translations of McCracken and Cabaniss, and McGrath.

29 Amalarius of Metz, *Liber officialis*; John Scottus Eriugena, *Periphyseon*.

30 Augustine became concerned with Pelagian teachings about predestination when he met the wealthy refugees from Rome, many of whom were followers of Pelagius, after the sack of Rome in 410; see Brown, *Augustine of Hippo*, especially chs. 32 and 33.

31 See Markus, *End of Ancient Christianity*, 45–83; and O'Donnell, *Augustine*, 161–86.

32 For Godescalc and the predestinarian quarrels, see Bouhot, *Ratramne de Corbie*, 35–41, and Chazelle, *Crucified God*, 165–81.

patristic texts on the subject,[33] but not everyone agreed that Godescalc's ideas were so dangerous. Eventually, the sides were drawn between the supporters of Godescalc (Ratramnus of Corbie, Prudentius of Troyes (d. 861), and Lupus of Ferrières (c. 805–62)) and the eventually victorious ecclesiastical heavyweights (Hrabanus Maurus, Hincmar of Rheims (806–82), and John Scottus Eriugena). Their determination to stop Godescalc's teaching may have been unnecessary, since Godescalc's writings were especially dense and difficult to follow, especially by the theologically uneducated. But Godescalc's enemies took no chances, and so, like the Adoptionist leader Felix of Urgel a generation earlier, Godescalc was imprisoned for the rest of his life.

Godescalc was also involved in a dispute over speculation about the world-soul, a philosophical issue with a pedigree that extended back to Plato (427–347 BCE).[34] This question seems to have obsessed the Carolingian courts: in the age of Charlemagne, someone at court spurred Alcuin to write a treatise on the subject; a generation later, Emperor Lothar I (840–55) asked for an answer to this question from Hrabanus Maurus. Finally, around 850, Charles the Bald (840–77) asked his churchmen specifically whether the soul had a materiality to it and whether it took up space or time. This query was answered by an anonymous author who has been copied under the name of Hincmar.[35] We also have an outline of a treatise on this subject attributed to Godescalc, which is so close to the Pseudo-Hincmar text that they may actually be by the same author.[36] There are also extant two treatises of Ratramnus on the nature of the soul – both discovered and edited in the twentieth century – both representing essentially Augustinian positions and using Boethian categories to deny the materiality and consubstantiality of the soul.[37]

Overall, the theological disputes of the Carolingian age did not give rise to the sort of ecclesiological wrath that becomes common in later centuries; most telling is the fact that no one in the eighth or ninth centuries was executed for theological error. Yet, Godescalc's story shows the rise of a sort of theological

33 Quierzy (Frühjahr 849). For a supporting position, but one that also gives some latitude for human effort in responding to divine predestination, see Ratramnus, *De predestinatione Dei* and Bouhot, *Ratramne de Corbie*, 41.

34 For a brief survey of the early history of this question, see Delhaye, *Une controverse*, 7–18.

35 Alcuin, *De animae ratione*; Hrabanus Maurus, *De anima*; Pseudo-Hincmar, *De diversa animae ratione*.

36 Godescalc, *Responsa de diversis*. For the suggestion that "Pseudo-Hincmar" may actually be Godescalc, see Bouhot, *Ratramne de Corbie*, 44–47.

37 Ratramnus, *De anima* and *Liber de anima*; Bouhot, *Ratramne de Corbie*, 41–50, 57–60. The second treatise was inspired by differing readings of Augustine's *De quantitate animae*, 32.69, 1073 and shows the influence of Pseudo-Augustine, *Categoriae* and Boethius, *Commentaria in Porphyrium*.

intolerance that was more intransigent and more harshly punishing than that directed against Felix of Urgel half a century earlier. This gradual rise of harsh intolerance for dissenting theological views is also apparent in the Eucharistic controversy between Berengar of Tours (c. 1010–88) and Lanfranc of Bec (c. 1010–89) at the end of the period covered by this volume.

Berengar was a well-known figure in the cathedral schools who was enjoying a rising ecclesiastical career when, in 1050, he criticized Lanfranc, the powerful abbot of Bec and later archbishop of Canterbury, for his support of the theology of Paschasius Radbertus on the Eucharist. Berengar had come across a copy of the Eucharistic treatise of Ratramnus (circulating under the name of John Scottus Eriugena), and he found it a particularly intelligent understanding of the Real Presence in the Eucharist.[38] Lanfranc was alarmed at what he understood as the low Christology of Berengar's position, and he pursued him relentlessly.[39] Berengar was dragged before numerous councils. He was condemned and made some admission of error at synods in Vercelli (1050), Tours (1054), Rome (1059 and 1078), and Bordeaux (1080). He was imprisoned by King Henry I of France (c. 1031–60) early in the controversy, and died on the Island of Cosme, near Tours, in 1088. As in the Adoptionist controversy, the learned ecclesiastics who pursued Berengar were joined by secular authorities; but this time the dissident figure also had the support of Count Geoffrey Martel of Anjou (1006–60), who was not afraid to shelter him, even at the risk of displeasing the king. Berengar's story shows us that, by the eleventh century, the stakes of theological dissidence in western Europe had grown much higher. As the twin edifices of western medieval theology and secular authority became more imposing, more centralized, and more in conflict with one another, the concern about heresy grew more common and the response to it more severe.

Learned disputes about Christian theology and practice, II: the eastern churches

In the Orthodox world of eastern Christianity, the question of theological deviance in the eighth and ninth centuries has a very different profile. For one

38 We have Berengar's own words only from the later part of the controversy in his *Rescriptum contra Lanfrancum*; see also MacDonald, *Berengar*, for the life of the protagonist.

39 Lanfranc of Bec, *De corpore et sanguine Dominii*; see de Montclos, *Lanfranc et Bérengar*, and more recently, Radding and Newton, *Theology, Rhetoric, and Politics*, for analysis of the controversy. On Lanfranc, see Gibson, *Lanfranc of Bec*, and most recently, Cowdrey, *Lanfranc*, who gives an excellent summary of the dispute with Berengar, 59–74.

thing, the Byzantine Christians understood many of the theological developments of western Christianity (for instance, the addition of the *filioque* to the Nicene Creed, prohibition of clerical marriage, and improper Lenten fasting) as heretical.[40] Furthermore, Christians of the eastern and southern Mediterranean included the confessional groups that were destined to become the minority traditions of Christianity. In the East, the very theological positions that were declared heretical at the ecumenical councils of the fourth and fifth centuries continued in live Christian communities, not just as names on heretic lists. These included Nestorian Christians on the steppes of Asia, and the miaphysite churches of Armenia and Egypt.[41] The Christians who did not accept the dogmatic formulations of the Council of Chalcedon in 451 are an especially interesting case.[42] Their opponents called them "monophysites," because it was thought they taught that Christ had only one *physis* (one spirit, a composite of human and divine), rather than a fully human and a fully divine nature. Whether this designation was accurate has been debated by modern scholars, as well as by modern churchmen East and West, but what is indisputable is the fact that by the sixth century, non-Chalcedonian Christians were the majority in Syria, Armenia, Mesopotamia, and Egypt.[43]

In the Byzantine world, then, looking east to the great Persian Empire, home to many diverse Christian communities, it was impossible not to be aware that some of the ancient heresies did indeed live on, and the people your church deemed heretical were fully empowered to return the compliment. This is a notable contrast to western Europe where, by the seventh century, the Arian Lombards, Ostrogoths, and Visigoths had converted to Catholicism. The religious horizons of Byzantine Christians were therefore, perhaps, more complicated than those of early medieval western Christians. Also, because of the continued strong presence of an imperial state strongly involved in the legislation of orthodoxy, Byzantine theological definitions were less tenuous than those of their brethren in western Europe, at least until the rise of Islam.

Eastern Christians, especially those in Palestine and Syria, were the first to encounter the Islamic faith. Not only did they encounter it, but they were soon subsumed into Islamic political entities as, over the course of the seventh

40 For a good summary of how western theology offended Byzantine Christians, see Kolbaba, *Byzantine Lists*, 32–87.

41 For the history of these churches, see the chapter by Dorfmann-Lazarev in this volume.

42 The chapter by Louth in this volume describes the struggle between the anti-Chalcedonians and the emperors and patriarchs in Constantinople; the chapter by Kolbaba describes the political ramifications of these theological differences between eastern and western Christians from c. 600 to c. 1100.

43 For a history of the miaphysite churches, see Frend, *Rise*, and the chapters by Louth and Dorfmann-Lazarev in this volume.

century, an Islamic political hegemony was established all the way from North Africa to Syria. As *dhimmī*, Christians and Jews were protected under Islamic law and allowed to live in their own communities, although with some notable restrictions on public practice of their religions and a prohibition against proselytizing. Quite a scholarly battle has been waged about the extent to which Christians living under Islam were religiously disadvantaged;[44] but that is not as important for this chapter as is the fact that some Christians understood Islam as another heresy. John of Damascus (c. 676–749), writing in the eighth century, added Islam to his recapitulation of an earlier list of heresies.[45] When western Christians truly understood Islam to be a lasting alternative faith (something that did not happen until the twelfth century), they took the same point of view.[46]

Islamic theology, likewise, found a number of points of Christian theology potentially blasphemous. The very concept that God has a Son who was born on earth as a human being is problematic for the strict monotheism of Islam; as we have seen, this may have been a factor in the Christology of Adoptionism. Another point of strict Islamic law that ran into conflict with Christian belief and practice was the disallowing of any form of art that made representations of the divinity, and, in some constructions, holy persons or even any human beings. In the Umayyad Caliphate of Damascus, where Christians and Muslims lived side by side, the question of images sometimes became controversial, as happened in 721, when Caliph Yazīd II (687–724) promulgated an edict against images in both Muslim and Christian public spaces.[47] A striking destruction of Christian images in churches of Muslim Asia Minor can be documented in the years around 721, suggesting that this edict was most likely not the beginning point of Islamic iconoclasm, but rather, a culmination of increasing Islamic intolerance of images over several decades and encompassing a broad geographical expanse.[48] Did this Islamic intolerance of images influence the major theological dispute of eighth- and ninth-century Byzantium: the iconoclastic controversy?

The struggle over iconoclasm in the Byzantine church began officially with the edict against icons promulgated by Emperor Leo III (717–41) in 726. Contemporary Byzantine historians explain this as a pious action inspired

44 For this debate, see Griffith's "Review of *Decline of Eastern Christianity*."
45 See John of Damascus, "'Hérésie 100.'"
46 Kritzeck, *Peter the Venerable*; Southern, *Western Views*.
47 For a discussion of this edict and a consideration of its effect on Byzantine Christians, see Brubaker and Haldon, *Byzantium*, 36 and note 173.
48 See the studies of Gero, *Byzantine Iconoclasm – Leo III* and *Constantine V*.

by a major earthquake that year.[49] A tradition of iconodule historians blame Leo's "boon companion," Bashir or Beser, a Syrian Christian convert to Islam, for influencing the emperor. This story (with a much more positive view of Bashir) is also found in Islamic histories.[50] Modern historians have focused on the influence of the Paulicians, a Christian group that came out of Armenia in the mid-sixth century.[51] The Paulicians perhaps are so called because they were followers of Paul of Samosata, bishop of Antioch (fl. 260). Another explanation for their name is that they were adherents of the earliest form of Christianity, that of the Apostle Paul. The Byzantines understood them as survivors of the Manichees. Their beliefs included a type of dualism that contrasted good and evil, a rejection of secular authority, and a hatred of monastic practice and all forms of worship that looked superstitious, such as the veneration of images. The Paulicians, much like other outlying groups of Christians, were tolerated by Byzantine emperors through the reign of Nicephorus I (802–11). For the next forty years, they were persecuted by the Byzantine state, reaching a peak in 843, in the reign of Empress Theodora (d. 867). The persecution of the Paulicians was fierce; many were massacred, but they did not go away. Another explanation of the iconoclasm controversy, then, is the existence of an anti-image strand within Byzantine Christianity, seen both in the Paulicians and among others who were not part of their group, but who shared their antipathy towards images.

Most scholars see the long history of Byzantine iconoclasm (from Leo III's first edict in 726 to the accession of the Empress Irene (d. 803) as regent in 780) as a combination of factors including the desire of the emperors to keep control of the religious climate, the growing power of the monks (who tended to be image-venerators), native Christian iconoclasm, and the influence of the Paulicians and the Muslims outside of the Orthodox consensus.[52] Whatever the causes of iconoclasm, it was certainly the most bitter dispute in the eastern church of the eighth century. Even though it is probable that the hysteria of the iconodules may have been out of proportion to the actual damage done, nevertheless, the accusations of destruction of images of Christ, the Virgin Mary, the saints, and even the Holy Cross had consequences far beyond the theological elite. Indeed, this theological conflict could hardly fail to be noticed by common Christians, who suddenly found their church walls painted over,

49 This is discussed in the essay by Louth in this volume.
50 See Griffith, "Bashir/Beser," for a fascinating description of this legend.
51 For the Paulicians, see Loos, *Dualist Heresies*, 32–40; Obolensky, *Bogomils*, 29–58; Hamilton and Hamilton, *Christian Dualist Heresies*, 5–25, and their translations of texts, 57–114.
52 Griffith, "Theodore Abu Qurrah's Arabic Tract"; Barnard, "Sources."

their mosaic floors pulled up, and their icons smashed. In this way, iconoclasm was more significant for all levels of Christian society than any comparable theological dispute in the West.

Iconoclasm also had repercussions in western Europe. Nicaea II, the council called by the Empress Irene in 787 to reinstate the cult of images, motivated a reaction from the Frankish church and king that was as official as their response to any native western theological controversies. A treatise against the errors of Nicaea II, attributed to Charlemagne and thus called the *Books of Charles* (*Libri Carolini*) was put together by Theodulf (c. 760–821), a Visigoth from the Spanish Marches who served as a master at Charlemagne's Palatine School.[53] This text equated image veneration with idolatry. In 794, in Frankfurt, Charlemagne called a council to respond to the Greeks and a number of home-grown issues, including Adoptionism.[54] Frankfurt rejected Nicaea II as an ecumenical council, and took a mediating position on images: they could be made and displayed, but not as the center of a cult. It has even been suggested that the specific condemnation of Adoptionism at the 794 Council of Frankfort is related to the Frankish campaign against iconoclasm.[55] The anti-image campaign of Bishop Claudius of Turin (d. after 827) in the 820s may also have been directly related to this Frankish concern about image veneration.[56] The controversy over images seems to have touched a deep chord for Christians in both the East and the West. Even as the ninth century was the beginning of the formal declaration of errors between the churches of the East and the West,[57] there were many concerns about orthodoxy and deviance that were shared at opposite ends of the Christian world.

Byzantine Christians also shared with Latin Christians a missionary zeal, since both groups in this period were actively involved in expanding the borders of Christian faith to the north. As we have seen, the original controversy over the Eucharist in Frankland began in a missionizing context. The Byzantines had similar catechetical efforts among the tribes of the Rus (a missionary activity that had begun in the late antique period) and in the Balkans, where, in the ninth century, the Bulgarians were converted to Christianity. Popular

53 Theodulf of Orleans, *Opus Caroli regis*; Freeman, "Scripture and Images"; Gero, "*Libri Carolini*"; Chazelle, "Matter, Spirit, and Image," and "Not in Painting."

54 For the Frankfurt council of 794, see Berndt, *Das Frankfurter Konzil*; Auzépy, "Francfort et Nicée II," deals specifically with the relationship between Nicaea II and Frankfurt 794.

55 Cavadini, "Elipandus," 805.

56 van Banning, "Claudius von Turin."

57 An answer to the Byzantine list of errors of the West (Kolbaba, *Byzantine Lists*) is Ratramnus's *Contra Graecorum*, which also mentions the *filioque*, clerical marriage, and Lenten fasting. After the tenth century, this polemical literature between East and West increases dramatically.

superstition, newly converted peoples, and the charges of credulity among the theologically naïve raise the question of a very different idea of theological deviance, what is generally called "popular" heresy.

"Popular" heresies: dualist movements, charismatic preachers, and visionaries East and West

In the early Middle Ages, the churches of the East appear to have greater popular responses to theological differences than the western church. For one thing, there was already more diversity in the eastern Christian realm, and perhaps because of this, there was more of a tendency for people to follow religious leaders who contested the hegemony of the emperors and bishops. The Paulicians are an interesting example of this. Although they were understood in their own time as a continuation of the ancient Manichees, and thus elicited a response at the level of learned theological dispute, they had a following among the common Christians as well, and so constituted a well-defined alternative Christian community, a "heretical church." This is not a phenomenon we see in the West until nearly the end of our period; not even the Adoptionists were a popular movement in the same way as the Paulicians.

But another group in the Byzantine lands, the dualist sect known as the Bogomils, attracted an even more popular following, and was a greater challenge to the established state religion. The Bogomils may have had their origin when Paulician missionaries reached the newly converted lands of the Bulgars; at least that is what the earliest Byzantine account of dualists in Bulgaria suggests.[58] The Bulgarian popular movement reminded Byzantine ecclesiastics of a heresy condemned at the Council of Ephesus in 431, the Messalians. It is not clear whether Messalians were actually preaching in the Balkans in the ninth century, or whether mention of the Messalians was another example of how heresies were understood in the categories of the past.[59] Paulicians, Messalians, and Bogomils all had in common a disdain for the power of the official ecclesiastical structures, a rejection of sacraments, and a belief in the indwelling of the Holy Spirit that is associated with a type of radical dualism. This message had great popular appeal. That it constituted a serious threat to the Byzantine church is obvious from the fact that Bogomil leaders associated the established church with the powers of evil.

58 Theophylact Lecapenus, patriarch of Constantinople (933–56), *Letter to Peter*; on sources for the Bogomils, see Hamilton and Hamilton, *Christian Dualist Heresies*, 25–55.

59 Obolensky, *Bogomils*, 94–95; Loos, *Dualist Heresies*, 72; Hamilton and Hamilton, *Christian Dualist Heresies*, 136 note 6.

The high-point of Bogomil activity is associated with the reign of Tsar Peter I of the Bulgars (927–70). This was also a period of growth in Bulgarian monasticism; the simultaneous flourishing of ascetics and dualists shows the spiritual fervor of tenth-century Bulgaria. The *Sermon against the Heretics* written by the Presbyter Cosmas (fl. c. 970) shortly after 972 claims that dualism and rejection of the material world were well established in Bulgaria, and had even impacted the monastics.[60] Cosmas does not call this group Bogomils, but that name appears in the eleventh century, when a letter from Euthymius (fl. c. 1045), a monk in Constantinople, attests to the spread of dualism to the center of the Byzantine Empire.[61] Euthymius is the first to say that these heretics are called Bogomils ("God-lovers"), but he says they are also known in some places as Phundagiagitae.[62] The account of Euthymius shows that this dualist movement had spread both east and west from the land of the Bulgars. Anna Comnena (1083–c. 1148) relates that in the early twelfth century (perhaps in 1110), during the reign of her father, the Emperor Alexius (1048–1118), Bogomils were subjected to a public trial, and one of their leaders, Basil, was burned at the stake.[63]

One of the most interesting aspects of the history of the Bogomils is the way that they relate to similar groups both earlier and later. The Byzantines called them Manichees, Paulicians, and Messalians. Perhaps this was because of the same dynamic seen in western accounts of contemporary heresies, that the teachings of a contemporary group seemed similar to some heresy from the age of the councils. Dualist theologies are part of the apocalyptic background of Christianity, and may be independently rediscovered from generation to generation, especially by those who feel they should stand up to an established church allied with a secular state. But some scholars have suggested that dualism may have never died out after Christian antiquity; that there were actually Manichees who preached to Paulicians, Messalians who spread the word to Bogomils, and Bogomil preachers who inspired the dualist theology of the Albigensians or Cathars in southern France in the twelfth century.[64]

60 Cosmas the Presbyter's work against the Bogomils was written in Slavonic and obviously intended for the monks of Bulgaria; see also Loos, *Dualist Heresies*, 50–60; Obolensky, *Bogomils*, 104–106.

61 Euthymius, *Against the Phoundagiagites and Bogomils*; Obolensky, *Bogomils*, 174–84; Loos, *Dualist Heresies*, 66–77.

62 This may mean something like "those who beg using a small bag," but Ficker disputes this, *Die Phundagiagiten*, 193–94; see Obolensky, *Bogomils*, 177–78, and Hamilton and Hamilton, *Christian Dualist Heresies*, 32 for the problems with this name.

63 Anna Comnena, *Alexiad* (trans. Dawes), XV.8–10; Obolensky, *Bogomils*, 197–205; Loos, *Dualist Heresies*, 189–205.

64 The most famous exposition of this is found in Runciman, *Medieval Manichee*. The fortunes of this book, which has gone in and out of print for the past five decades, have been related to how seriously this thesis of the survival of dualism is taken at any given time.

Although there is nothing quite like the popular fervor of the Bogomil movement in the West before 1100, there were always popular preachers and spiritual leaders who inspired followings in the Latin church of the early Middle Ages. Boniface (c. 675–754), whose English name was Winfrid,[65] was a missionary to the German tribes in the eighth century. He wrote to Pope Zachary (741–52) about two false priests, Clemens (fl. c. 740), who called himself a bishop and promulgated Jewish marriage customs, and Aldebert (fl. c. 740), who affected an apostolic calling, and claimed such holiness for himself that he gave bits of his hair and fingernails to his followers as relics.[66] Aldebert, who preached in the region of Soissons, attracted many followers, enough to alarm Boniface, and even Pope Zachary in Rome. Aldebert was condemned at synods in 744 in Soissons and in 745 in Rome. He was briefly imprisoned in 744, but managed to escape and continue preaching. When he was forbidden to preach in villages, he set up crosses and small chapels in the countryside as gathering places for his followers. In 746, Boniface collected his writings and asked Pope Zachary for permission to burn them; the pope instead suggested keeping them in the papal archives for further study. Outside of the fragments included in the letters of Boniface, we do not know what happened to these writings. Nor, indeed, do we know what happened to Aldebert, who vanishes after 746; but his activities clearly show that there were popular preachers in the West.

A female prophet named Thiota, who preached in the area of Mainz in 847 or 848, shows the continuing power of apocalypticism in the Latin West.[67] Thiota attracted a following (including, it was said, some clergy) because she claimed to know the date of the end of the world. She was called before a synod in Mainz, flogged, and forbidden to continue preaching, after which she vanishes from the historical record. Although the chiliastic tradition of numbering the years until the end of the world had been condemned in the fifth century by authors like Augustine and Jerome (c. 340–420), the western church (which, unlike the eastern tradition, counted the Apocalypse of John as fully canonical and used it in liturgies) continued to have a semi-official tradition of apocalypticism.[68] This has repeatedly been a vehicle for popular religious movements in western Christianity, up to the modern period. There

65 See Noble's introduction in Boniface, *Letters*, viii–xxvii, for the life of Boniface.

66 These details are in a letter of 745 from Boniface to Zachary. Boniface, *Letters*, 76–89; see also Russell, "Saint Boniface," 235–47. For the wandering preacher Aldebert, see Lambert, *Medieval Heresy*, 25. Clemens (a "Scot," or Irishman) is a minor figure compared to Aldebert, but the accusation of Judaizing is interesting.

67 *Annales Fuldenses*. Her name is also given as Theuda, see Russell, *Dissent and Reform*, 107–108.

68 See the preface by McGinn, *Apocalyptic Spirituality* for a discussion of this phenomenon.

were doubtless other apocalyptic figures like Thiota in our period, even though the major apocalyptic movements of the West did not catch fire until the twelfth century.

Nevertheless, the eleventh century does show a marked increase of popular movements led by charismatic preachers in the West. In the first years of the century, a peasant named Leutard (fl. c. 1000), from the area of Châlons-sur-Marne, felt himself possessed by a swarm of bees, and began to preach. Leutard showed a strange mixture of the religious forces that had been active in eastern Christendom in the past two centuries: he left his wife, claimed marriage was immoral, broke religious images, and denied the holiness of parts of the Old Testament.[69] Leutard was called before Gebuin II, the bishop of Châlons, where he was thoroughly bested in a theological argument. In 1004, he committed suicide by throwing himself into a well, but his followers continued to spread his puritanical doctrine for another decade. Finally, in 1015, the new bishop, Roger I, held a synod that declared war against the remnants of the sect, after which nothing more is heard from or about them.

Even more dramatic is the story of the heretics of Orleans, a group that probably flourished from about 1015 until they were stamped out in 1022. In the summer of 1022, Heribert, a priest in the household of a pious knight named Arefast, journeyed to Orleans, where he discovered the teachings of two priests, Stephen and Lisois, who had attracted a group of followers. This band included canons and nuns of the city, including some noted church leaders. Stephen had been the confessor of Queen Constance (973–1032) wife of King Robert II (Robert the Pious) of France (996–1031). The teachings of Stephen and Lisois seem to have been rather esoteric, since Heribert returned to Arefast with tales of their "resplendent wisdom."[70] Arefast, alarmed at the unorthodoxy of what he heard, infiltrated the group in the guise of a possible follower. The sources differ on what the group actually believed, but it was certainly some type of secret doctrine that involved rejection of various sacramental teachings of the church, and a special faith in the working of the Holy Spirit. When they had revealed their secrets and initiated Arefast into their group, word was sent to King Robert and the heretics were arrested, Arefast among them. On Christmas Day of 1022, they were brought before the king and the ecclesiastical authorities of Orleans for questioning. Arefast was

69 The primary source for this figure is Rodulfus Glaber, *Historiarum*, II.xi.22; see also Lambert, *Medieval Heresy*, 29–30; Russell, *Dissent and Reform*, 111–14.

70 The sources for the heretics of Orleans are many and complex, including Rodulfus Glaber, *Historiarum*, III.viii.26–31; see Russell, *Dissent and Reform*, 276–77 note 24. For the heresy in general, see Russell, *Dissent and Reform*, 27–35.

let go, and many followers recanted, but Stephen, Lisois, and another dozen of the group refused to deny their creed, and were sentenced to death. The heretics of Orleans were burned alive on 28 December 1022. This is the first official execution of heretics in the western church.

Several things about the heretics of Orleans show how the world of religious dissent was changing during the eleventh century. For one thing, their beliefs were more complex and theologically learned than those of preachers such as Leutard; if they were not influenced by the teachings of the Bogomils, it is easy to see that they could lay the groundwork for the arrival of full-fledged dualism in the West in the twelfth century. Also, it is hard to ignore the political ramifications of this story, the assertion of authority by King Robert at a particularly troubled time of his reign. Finally, the severity of the sentence was shocking, especially considering the relatively mild punishments given to earlier dissidents like Felix, Godescalc, and Thiota. The monastic authors of the eleventh century give us a long list of theological dissidents and their followers, almost a group every decade, most of them in France and northern Italy.[71] We know about dissident groups with charismatic leaders in Liège (1010–24), the Midi (1018), Monteforte, Italy (c. 1028), Hungary (1045), northern France (1046–54), Cambrai (1077, where the reformist preacher Ramihrd was put to death by an angry mob), and Milan (the clerical reform group known as the "Patarini," at the end of the century). Recently, students of these documents have begun to analyze their rhetoric to show that they tell us as much or more about the authors than about the purported heretics. It has even been suggested that one process, at Arras in 1025, was essentially a made-up polemic against heretics (who in this case were all said to have fallen to their knees and recanted) for the sake of the ecclesiastical authorities.[72] This rather suggests that the fervor of ecclesiastical reformers had at least as much to do with the concern of the hierarchy to guard against heresy as it did with the actual existence of heretical groups. Perhaps this dynamic even helped set the stage for the huge battles with groups like the Cathars and the Heresy of the Free Spirit in the twelfth and thirteenth centuries.

Even if this is true, that is, if the perceived increase in heresy may have been a result of increased activity from the top of the ecclesiastical world as

71 Russell briefly discusses many of these groups, *Dissent and Reform*, 35–47; Lobrichon, "Arras, 1025" gives a list, 75–76. Contemporary sources for these groups include Rodulfus Glaber, Adémar of Chabannes, Ecbert of Liège, and others.

72 See Lobrichon, "Arras, 1025." The argument is based in part on the fact that this trial record (which is not mentioned in the chronicle of the city) was copied into a manuscript of antiheretical polemic put together by Cistercians at the end of the twelfth century. On this, see also Lobrichon, "Chiaroscuro," and Moore, "Literacy," 20–22.

well as from the bottom, the question remains: why did the situation change so drastically in the eleventh century? Such a growth in heretical movements over the course of five or six decades probably cannot have just one cause, but must be related to complex social and ecclesiastical changes on various levels. For instance, it is striking how many of these religious leaders spoke out against abuses of ecclesiastical leaders, against simony and sexual laxity, which were also abuses that were targeted by the Gregorian Reforms. Julia Barrow's chapter in this volume suggests that the idea of an "age of reform" has been overstated in this period, at least outside of a monastic context. It is worth noting, though, that the monasticization of the western church was one of the goals associated with Pope Gregory VII (1073–1085), and a sign of the power of the Cluniac Order, which did tend to pit religious leaders against aristocratic rulers. At Canossa in 1077, a humbled Henry IV (1056–1106) did penance in front of Gregory VII; but in Orleans in 1022, it was King Robert who won the dispute with the religious reformers. Likewise, it is the "heretical" Patarini who upheld the ideal of a celibate clergy in the diocese of Milan. In other words, the very fact that this was the age of religious reform in the West could have been an inspiration to popular religious movements. The increased literacy and theological education of cathedral canons would be an important part of this story.[73]

It has also been suggested that the conciliar movement known as the "Pax Dei" or "Peace of God" in the late tenth and early eleventh centuries had an impact on the growth of popular heresy in the West.[74] The movement was marked by large public meetings called to declare a peace between different sectors of society. Knights, swearing oaths on relics, promised to withhold violence from civilians, churches, and other sacred spaces and objects. Following the decline of the centralized authority of the Carolingians, and the shaky control of the Capetian dynasty, such a movement was received by enthusiastic crowds who gathered and shouted "Peace! Peace!" It has been noted that this is one of the first times there were large public gatherings in western Europe, and that such a movement was intricately connected to the apocalyptic expectations of the millennium of the birth of Jesus (the year 1000) and the millennium of the Crucifixion (the year 1033),[75] and thus could well have been a catalyst for popular religious movements.

73 See Moore, "Literacy" for a fuller development of this idea.

74 See Head and Landes, *Peace of God*, for various approaches to this movement and its impact.

75 Landes, "Birth of Heresy" develops this idea in relation to millennial thought, relying primarily on Glaber's *Historiarum*.

An even broader viewpoint would suggest that the eleventh century is a turning point in western Christianity because this is the period in which the struggle for outward expansion of the faith, classically seen in the forced subjugation of the Saxons and the missions to the pagans of Frisia and Scandinavia, comes to an end. As Europe is Christianized, it also becomes a world of more formalized theology and a more towering ecclesiastical institution. The western church becomes more of a "church of the town," and a militant evangelical movement finds a resonance both among those in control, and among the clergy and laity (now more literate, more worldly, and more self-assertive) who do not always agree with the decisions made by the hierarchy.[76] Perhaps the relative sophistication and cosmopolitan nature of the Byzantine church made such popular religious movements possible in the late ninth century; but in the West, they begin just where we leave the story of orthodoxy and deviance at the end of our period, just before 1100.

76 See Lobrichon, "Chiaroscuro," for an interesting development of this idea.

26

Making sense of the Bible

GUY LOBRICHON

In his capacity as adviser to Charlemagne, Alcuin (d. 804) thought that he could introduce his master to all the subtleties of rhetoric and moral philosophy. In the famous *Dialogue on Rhetoric and the Virtues*, Alcuin cast himself in conversation with the future emperor of the Franks. He prudently made sure to show his patron in a good light by having him pose apposite questions to which he, as teacher, replied by playing with all the resources of the classical Latin art of rhetoric that he taught, the better to persuade his royal audience. Where rhetoricians had drawn the examples necessary for their demonstration from pagan antiquity, Alcuin brandished biblical examples.[1] The lesson is clear. The courtier of the *Dialogus de rhetorica* was not content only to cajole a king who aspired to be a man of letters, but thus proclaimed with gusto the enduring value of classical learning in the Frankish realms, the triumph of Christian letters, and the absolute primacy of the Bible over all other masterpieces of literary history.

Of course, this is only propaganda. It matters little, however, whether this *Dialogue* was really written for the benefit of Charlemagne or whether it was a fiction created for use exclusively in schools. In just a few lines it upsets commonly accepted notions of an edition of the Bible by Alcuin (our teacher "forgets" to cite his own version of the Book of Genesis!) and of widespread ignorance of the Scriptures outside clerical circles (the mere mention of the

1 Alcuin, *Dialogus de rhetorica et de virtutibus*, ch. 5: "Ars rhetorica in tribus versatur generibus, id est demonstrativo, deliberativo et iudicali. Demonstrativum genus, quod tribuitur in alicuius certae personae laudem vel vituperationem, ut in Genesi de Abel et Cain legitur: *Respexit dominus ad Abel et ad munera eius, ad Cain autem et munera eius non respexit* (Gen. 4.4–5). Deliberativus est in suasione et dissuasione, ut in Regum legitur, quomodo Achitophel suasit David perdere, et quomodo Chusai dissuasit consilium eius ut regem salvaret (2 Sam. 15–17). Iudiciale est, in quo accusatio et defensio, ut in Actibus legimus apostolorum, quomodo Iudaei cum Tertullo quodam oratore Paulum accusabant apud Felicem praesidem et quomodo Paulus se defendebat apud eundem praesidem."

characters of Cain and Abel, Achitophel, Chusai, Tertullus, and Felix, although elaborated orally by the teacher, suffices for the audience of the stories). But Alcuin did not stop there. In addition, he confirmed the status of the Bible as a work of literature, to which the traditional techniques of the "liberal arts" might ordinarily be applied, and also perhaps invited his listener to recognize in the Bible a resource for higher learning. In short, he forces the modern reader to reevaluate the coherence of knowledge in Charlemagne's time. On the strength of three examples drawn from Genesis, 2 Samuel, and from the Acts of the Apostles, Alcuin aligned the analytical classification of the three kinds of rhetoric with the historical succession of the three ages: before the Law, under the Law, and under Grace. In other words, he constructs an evolutionary schema of secular sciences and of biblical wisdom which led directly to the Christian fulfillment of history.

If we accept this reading of Alcuin, the Bible and its exegesis can no longer be confined to the world of ideas and the lofty controversies of theology. We know that the Bible has a history, and that its exegesis shifts and changes with the ebb and flow of this history; for this reason it merits renewed attention from historians, some of whom have recently undertaken to reestablish its historical status.[2] In the Christian early Middle Ages, finding meaning in the Bible meant not only teaching and explicating it to whomever would listen from schoolroom to the church nave or in spiritual conversations, but it also entailed making the Bible into a point of reference for the identity of a group, a whole society – in effect establishing it as the book of the foundations and norms of life itself. To interpret Sacred Writ was to use, as it were, the spectacles of the Bible to bring into proper focus the history of humankind. The following is a brief overview of what is a complex history, that of a text and of its transmission, that of its readers and its hearers, and also that of an acculturation to the Sacred Book which remains one of the most striking features of western history. In sum, this chapter demonstrates how Christian societies fertilized the already loamy soil of biblical use and interpretation to their own benefit during the early Middle Ages and how the societies of western Europe, once Christianized, cut themselves free from the Byzantine hermeneutical tradition and created – somewhat laboriously it must be said – a consensus regarding an art of interpretation which contributed in its own way to the fragmentation of Europe from the year 1000.

2 See the bibliography for this chapter.

The patrimony of Jews and Christians

The Bible brings together the sacred books of both Jews and Christians in one enormous corpus, which from the earliest centuries was denoted by the words *bibliotheca, scriptura sacra, scriptura divina*. Lactantius (d. c. 320) and Zeno of Verona (d. c. 375) were among the earliest to write of a *historia sacra*;[3] they exhibit an appreciation of the Bible as a historical sequence of the same kind as that to which their contemporary, Eusebius of Caesarea (d. c. 340), provided the key characteristics by creating the literary genre of universal world history. From the sixth century, the Bible was recognized as a work belonging to the common patrimony of the eastern empire and of the Christian kingdoms in the European West. Copies of it circulated in ever increasing numbers, in tandem with the ever widening bounds of Christendom. Its dissemination supplied several needs: those of churches (Constantine I had ordered Eusebius of Caesarea to have around fifty copies of the Bible made to furnish the churches of Constantinople[4]); of Christian teachers, for Cassiodorus (d. 580) had introduced the study of the Bible into literary studies; and, finally, of those wealthy aristocrats possessing both spiritual concerns and a conspicuous taste for luxury. St. Jerome's remonstrations against the excesses of bibliophiles attests to the Roman elite's attraction to these precious books. From the fifth century the elite were acquiring copies of the books of Kings (e.g., the *Itala* of Quedlinburg[5]), or more frequently, of Gospels such as the *Codex Vindobonensis* containing the Gospels of Luke and Mark.[6] From the fourth and fifth centuries the Bible began to find its way into the homes of the powerful, and readily became diffused into the possession of ever broader social groups among both Christians and Jews. The sacred book had many roles: as an object of liturgical veneration and display; sometimes as a talisman believed to be endowed with apotropaic powers (such as the Cathach of Columba, a seventh-century Psalter); as a cultural tool (the Psalter gradually became the reading primer for the aristocratic classes); as an aid for private devotion (often then being reduced to the four Gospels – a *tetraevangelion* or Gospel book – or to the Passion narratives such as the Book of Nunnaminster, which appears to have belonged to the wife of King Alfred[7]); and as a mirror of good government

3 Duchet-Suchaux and Lefèvre, "Les noms de la Bible," 12–23; Lactantius, *Divinae institutiones*, I.13, 17; Zeno of Verona, *Tractatus*, I.4.
4 Eusebius of Caesarea, *Life of Constantine*, 4.34–36.
5 Degering and Bockler, *Die Quedlinburger Itala Fragmente*.
6 *Codex Vindobonensis*; cf. d'Aiuto, Morello, and Piazzoni, *I Vangeli dei popoli*, 140–41.
7 *Book of Nunnaminster*.

(of which emperors, kings, and princes from Justinian I to the end of the Middle Ages were obliged to make assiduous use[8]). The Bible was in reality the fount from which all the leaders of the Christian communities of Jerusalem, Rome, Constantinople, and all other churches drew the founding principles of their teachings. All those responsible for the missions, consequently, used the same source. As a result, the Bible was destined to nourish the most fervent aspirations for reform, for change, and for the building up of the common weal. Until a local ruling in 1229, no one dared to restrict access to it.[9]

Agent of unity?

One might think that this common use of the Bible as a reference point would suggest that the sacred book functioned as an agent of social unity. This is far from the case. The history of Bibles, whether Greek or Latin, is marked by textual diversity. The canon of Scriptures was not easily settled upon, neither in the Greek East (cf. Athanasius of Alexandria, *Festal Letter* 39, of 367) nor in the Latin West (cf. the *Decretum Gelasii* composed by a cleric of Southern Gaul at the beginning of the sixth century).[10] On the threshold of the seventh century, the Bible was circulating in multiple languages and for each language in several different but concurrent versions and various forms. It is worth noting that the eastern and western canons are not strictly speaking identical: with the exception of its appearance in the writings of a very few commentators, such as Arethas of Caesarea (d. c. 940), the Apocalypse (Revelation) figured neither in the liturgical nor in the biblical canon of the Byzantine church before the fourteenth century. The order of the "sacred books" was slow to become fixed in the West, varying considerably from one corner of the Mediterranean to another. The history of their use followed different routes in the former Roman Empire, in the Byzantine Empire, and in Christian societies of Coptic Egypt, Syria, Armenia, and the Rus. What is more, westerners renounced the three languages (Greek, Aramaic, and Hebrew) of the earliest Judeo-Christians once they had a sufficient supply of Bibles translated into Latin. The triumphal progress of the "Vulgate," the Latin version of the Bible which gradually superseded earlier versions in Italy between the fifth and seventh centuries, furnishes proof not only that Christians in the West rapidly judged recourse to the Hebrew text to be obsolete, but they similarly discarded the Greek of the

8 Cf. the will of the Eberhard, Margrave of Friuli (d. 866) in *Cartulaire de l'abbaye de Cysoing*, 1–5.
9 Synod of Toulouse (1229), canon 14 (Mansi 23, 197).
10 Amphoux and Elliott, *New Testament Text*; Kottje, *Studien*.

Septuagint and of the New Testament. A few western copies of the Psalter – the most widely circulated and best-known and most studied of the books of the Bible – contain a transliterated Greek text, but it is always accompanied by two or even three Latin versions.[11] This phenomenon is all the more remarkable since the subjects of the Greek Empire never reflected upon the usefulness of the Latin language or the Latin fathers in their copies (whether partial or otherwise) of the Bible nor in their collection of patristic quotations. In the church of Rome, however, though bilingualism did persist for some time, the language of the Romans forged a new path among the established sacred languages. When Isidore of Seville (d. 636) ranked Latin on the same level as Hebrew and Greek, he was in effect recognizing its actual dominance in the West.

From the seventh century the cause of the languages of the eastern Mediterranean within those churches obedient to Rome was lost. From then on, words and names of the Bible would no longer signify the same realities and would no longer carry the same meanings for Greeks and Latins. While it is true that, through the centuries, a few scholars did attempt to master the Greek language (for example, in order to understand the conflict brewing between the Roman church and the Greeks, Pope Leo IX (d. 1054) at the age of fifty or thereabouts resolved to learn Greek[12]), and others, such as perhaps Hrabanus Maurus in the ninth century, and more assuredly Stephen Harding and Nicholas Maniacoria in the twelfth century, did consult contemporary Hebrew and Greek speakers, the import of these activities is less clear. The fact remains nonetheless that, up until the fifteenth century, ignorance of Greek troubled neither masters nor dissidents any more than did ignorance of Hebrew. In neither the East nor the West did anyone call for a return to the original languages of the Bible. It was an exceptional circumstance that allowed Bede to correct an early version of his commentary on the Acts of the Apostles thanks to the presence at Iona or Wearmouth-Jarrow of a bilingual copy of Acts in Greek and Latin. Together with the Greeks at Canterbury in the seventh century, he was one of the few scholars to recognize the use of returning to the most brilliant of Christendom's mother tongues.[13] Christian translators of Aristotle may have

11 *Psalter*, Bamberg, Staatsbibliothek Bibl. 44 (copied in 909), and *Psalter*, Bamberg, Staatsarchiv A 246 (c. 1100). Cf. Berschin, "Salomons III." Other quadruple Psalters mentioned in Gryson, *Altlateinische Handschriften*, include: Admont, Stiftsbibliothek 42 (XII; no. 461); Graz, Universitätsbibliothek 86 ($XII^{1/2}$; no. 462); and the triple Psalter in Brussels, BR II.1639 (c. 1100; no. 463).

12 Parisse, *Vie du pape Léon IX*, 116–17.

13 Oxford, Bodleian Library Laud. gr. 35, Sardinia, s.VI-VII (*Chartae Latinae Antiquiores* II, 251). Bischoff and Hofmann, *Libri Sancti Kyliani*, 90–91; Mango, "La culture grecque," 689–90 and plates 1–3.

played an important role in scholarly centers of the ancient western empire as well as in the East, but we know as little about how these works were received as we do about how widely available they were. The works translated, for example, by the convert Johannes Philiponus (c. 490–c. 570) seem only to have been of interest to "Latins" from the sixteenth century. Why did the popes of Syrian roots who occupied the Roman see in the eighth century not call upon their Near Eastern friends (Theophilus of Edessa, Yaḥya ibn al-Biṭrīq) who had undertaken new translations of the Greek writings of Aristotle into Syriac? Was not Greek still being used at this time in the offices of the pontifical chancellery? Had not Gerbert of Aurillac, the future Pope Sylvester II (d. 1003), profited from the Arabic resources gathered together at Cordoba, and which would have been accessible to him during his sojourn in Catalonia? And why, in the ninth century, was John of Damascus the last of the Greek writers to receive the benefit of a Latin translation before the great scholarly movements of the twelfth century? Doubtless because westerners considered that they had no further need of these scholarly contributions to the art and technique of interpretation whether in law or in biblical exegesis. They no longer looked to the Greeks for anything.

A book of law?

The Bible, the Law of the Jews (Torah), is in no wise a law for all Christians. However, when the western kingdoms were won over by Christians obedient to Rome (c. 600) from Hadrian's Wall to the Rhine and from there to the Mediterranean and to the Atlantic coasts of the Mozarabic kingdoms, many of the converted peoples saw in the Bible the foundational book defining Christian identity. It remained, let us not forget, the primordial code for Jews and Christians, containing the Law of God himself, and it took on this role above all for those peoples converted by missionaries from Rome. "To conform is fitting, to violate is harmful" as Eugenius II of Toledo (d. 657) wrote with respect to Sacred Scripture.[14] The rules decreed were supposed then to exercise the same obligations on those who read them as a law collection. As its title suggests, the New Testament took pride of place in the Bible: whereas Eugenius names each of its authors, he shrouds those of the Old Testament in silence.[15] Christianity's triumph itself furnished the justification for such a prioritization. But why then canonize the entire Bible, and not simply the New Testament?

14 Eugenius of Toledo, *Carmen* VIII, lines 27–28 (ed. Vollmer, 239): "Haec sunt sacra dei, iuris haec mystica divi,/Haec servare decet, haec temerare nocet."

15 Stella, *La poesia carolingia latina*, 32.

Because the entire Bible both describes the norms of Christian living and propounds general moral instruction.

The jurists of the Roman Empire had never succumbed to the temptation to associate Sacred Scriptures with law books. Only rather vaguely did Constantine put forward the "most holy Law."[16] His political savvy inclined him to read the Bible less as a norm than as a way of strengthening a Christian reading of his victory over his enemies.[17] In effect, the allegorical interpretation of his vision at the Milvian Bridge in 313 founded the Christian construction of history. Theodosius, in contrast, made explicit mention in 394 (?) of "the apostolic teaching and the doctrine of the Gospel" as the rule of life for all the citizens of the Empire.[18] The change from Constantine's use of the Bible to that of Theodosius appears to have been radical: apologetic justifications gave way to normative prescriptions. It is worth noting, however, that Theodosius simply evoked Christian doctrine and evaded any reference to specific Old Testament laws. During the iconoclast crisis, some Byzantine jurists attempted to slip laws of biblical derivation into Roman law. The most revealing document in this regard, the *Mosaic Law* (a work compiled between the seventh and ninth centuries), drew together a collection of quotations from the books of Exodus, Leviticus, Numbers, and Deuteronomy.[19] The work had only limited success, except in certain monastic circles of the eleventh and twelfth centuries. In the West, the Irish churches of the seventh and eighth centuries alone dared to circulate rulings which made reference to the Bible.[20] None of the codes in use in the continental kingdoms, whether Ostrogothic, or Visigothic, Burgundian, Frankish, or Lombard, whether early or late, ceded to this inclination which, in actual fact, would accord precedence to the Mosaic Law over the Law of Christ, since the latter remains irreducible to any juridical code. This Law, as the entire Christian tradition since Paul (1 Cor. 12.6–11) has maintained, is, in effect, about wisdom and discipline of living as much as it is about *scientia*.[21]

A controlled text?

Being considered of divine inspiration, the Bible has always enjoyed a peculiar status. In the Middle Ages, this had the effect of depriving the episcopate of any

16 Eusebius of Caesarea, *Church History*, 381.
17 Eusebius of Caesarea, *Life of Constantine*, I.33; cf. also II.17.
18 *Codex Theodosianus*, XVI.1.2 in *Documents of the Christian Church*, 31.
19 Biondi, *Il diritto cristiano*.
20 Meens, "Uses of the Old Testament," 75.
21 Berndt, "Scientia et disciplina."

particular authority over the Bible: no institution – council, synod, court of any kind – was indispensable for correcting its text and, therefore, for defining correct interpretation. The latter was the province of two groups, one dead but with formidable authority (the church fathers), the other alive and exercising considerable personal spiritual influence but minimal institutional authority (the masters of the monastic and cathedral schools, the guardians of exegetical memory and counselors of theological orthodoxy).

The writings of the early church fathers distilled a discernible biblical doctrine, much like the interior decoration of churches that we can envisage with the help of the descriptions of Paulinus of Nola (d. 431) and Prudentius (d. c. 410)[22] or those of Emperor Leo VI (d. 902) concerning the Constantinopolitan monastery of Tou Kaleos.[23] Nothing, however, suggests an institutional control over exegetical writing or image production. When Constantine I ordered Eusebius of Caesarea to have copies of the Bible made, his primary concern was to equip Christian places of worship, rather than to produce an edition bearing his name.[24] The sheer number of different texts does, nonetheless, raise some questions. The modern scholar is confronted with a critical choice, even before approaching the subject at hand: what biblical text, which Bible are we talking about? A Vulgate to be sure, and therefore a Latin text. As far as medieval commentators were concerned, the only textual variants that mattered were those in the Latin tradition. However, it should be noted that the Carolingian reform of the Bible did not reach the Iberian Peninsula, and hardly touched the libraries of the British Isles and Italy. It has not been proven that it had any lasting influence outside the Frankish kingdom, and even there it was unable to change liturgical uses in which pre-Vulgate or Visigothic versions coexisted. When a master cited the Septuagint, Symmachus, "alia editio," or "quidam codices," or when he evoked the "translatio Theodotionis" or "alia translatio,"[25] he faithfully reproduced Jerome whose authority was such that it was considered unnecessary to hunt down the sources themselves. For all that, an anonymous Irish writer of the ninth century made no bones about the need to revise the current Latin versions on the basis of the Greek; there

22 Davis-Weyer, *Early Medieval Art*, 17–33, 59–66, 75.

23 Janin, *La géographie ecclésiastique*, 39–41; Frolow, "Deux églises byzantines."

24 Eusebius of Caesarea, *Life of Constantine*, II.34 and II.36.

25 Septuagint: Munich, Bayerische Staatsbibliothek Clm 6221, f. 21r; Symmachus, Clm 6221, f. 73r; alia editio: Rabanus Clm 6221, f. 7v. ("quidam codices habent eden, ad ortum"); translatio Theodotionis: Clm 6221, f. 18r; cf. also Clm 6221, f. 24v – Alia translatio habet: "non iudicabit spiritus meus homines in aeternum quia caro sunt" (restoring a phrase omitted by the copyist, but which is not a variant from the Vulgate).

is, however, no evidence that he lifted a finger to do so himself.[26] Since there was no "reference Bible," the question was where to find a complete Bible containing a high-quality text. At Fulda, Hrabanus Maurus followed the new editions inspired by Alcuin; his disciple Ercanbert distanced himself from the text of John's Gospel as revised by Alcuin's team, though he was aware of its variants.[27] Thus, each had recourse to a different version of the biblical text. Haimo of Auxerre seems to follow an "Alcuinian" text when commenting upon the Apocalypse, but did not hesitate frequently to deviate from this version; his successor, Remigius of Auxerre, had no qualms about commenting upon a non-Alcuinian text of the book of Genesis.[28] Around 1109/12, Stephen Harding set about obtaining the best possible text, indicating thereby his knowledge that Roman attempts to do the same in the mid-eleventh century had not been entirely successful. The Parisian glossators of the Bible in the second decade of the twelfth century were rather more pragmatic and were content to use whatever text was at hand; copyists no longer took the trouble to indicate divergences between the main text and that of the glossator.

The interpretation of the Bible

Let us turn now to the moment of interpretation itself.[29] Early medieval usage continued to distinguish between two types of interpretation: Alexandrian and Antiochene. The guiding principles of Alexandrian exegesis took shape as early as Clement of Alexandria (d. 215) and were formulated into a system by Origen (d. c. 253–54) and exploited by Athanasius (d. 373), Cyril of Alexandria (d. 444), and Didymus the Blind (d. 398). Origen distinguished three "senses" conforming to a threefold division in human nature: body, soul, and spirit, matching closely the triad of literal, allegorical, and tropological senses of which Latin writers would later write. Antiochene exegesis, illustrated by

26 Munich, Bayerische Staatsbibliothek Clm 343 (Milan, s.IX), f. 1v-9v: *MGH Epistolae* 6, 201–205; McNamara, "Psalter Text and Psalter Study," 235–37.

27 John 1.16: "omnes accepimus et gratiam pro gratia" (*Bible*, Fischer and Weber ed. Latin Vulgate); "gratiam omnes acceptimus pro gratia" (Clm 6269, f. 3v). Later Ercanbert notes that "Quidam codices habent 'et gratiam pro gratia' huic interpositae coniunctioni. Iste sensus aptatur. De plenitudine accepimus, subaudias remissionem peccatorum, et pro illa perpetuae uitae coronam" (f. 4v).

28 Gen. 1.4 – "divisit lucem a tenebris" (Clm 6221, ff. 2r, 3r), "lucem *ac* tenebras" (*Bible*, Fischer and Weber ed. Latin Vulgate); Gen. 1.14 – "et diuidant" (Clm 6221, f. 2v), "ut diuidant" (Fischer and Weber ed.); Gen. 3.7 – "oculi eorum" (Clm 6221, f. 13v; Amiatensis), "oculi amborum" (Fischer and Weber ed.).

29 de Lubac, *Exégèse médiévale*.

the writings of Lucian of Samosata (d. 312), John Chrysostom (d. 407), and Theodoret of Cyrrhus (d. c. 466), esteemed the "literal" (i.e., etymological, grammatical, and stylistic) and historical explication of the text. The reality was, however, rather more complex. The base principle of exegesis surfaced as early as the first generation of the disciples of Christ, who, in competition with the Jewish tradition from which they sought to differentiate themselves, were called upon to define their precise position with respect to Mosaic Law: like all radicals, they said that they were this Law's fulfillment. The words, deeds, and actions of Christ were collected together in what they styled the *New* Testament, which was understood to fulfill the promises of the Old Law of the Jews (e.g., the Burning Bush of Exod. 3.1–6 became a figure or *typos* of the Virgin Mary). This principle of Christian fulfillment, common to both East and West, was strengthened, especially in the West, by the principle of prophetic concordance. There was, it was believed, a formal parallelism (both literary and historical) not only between the Old and New Testaments, but also at the very heart of world history. Thus, the history of ancient pagan religions and of Judaism was understood as a prelude to the history of Christianity. The Christian genre of the world chronicle was first formulated by Eusebius of Caesarea; St. Jerome's re-reading of him allowed Christians to combine elements of history and of pagan culture with the Judeo-Christian account of redemption by Christ.[30] Pictorial narrative cycles of the Old and New Testaments appear frequently in churches (Rome: S. Maria Maggiore; Ravenna: S. Apollinare Nuovo[31]) and on carved caskets from the fourth century (the Lipsanoteca at Brescia). Their coherence was reinforced by the division of world history into three periods (before the Law, under the Law, and under Grace), seven ages (Adam–Noah; Noah–Abraham; Abraham–David; David–Babylonian Captivity or the prophets; the prophets–Christ; Christ–the end of time) and into four empires (generally: Babylon, Persia, Greece, Rome) in accordance with the vision of the prophet Daniel (Dan. 2).[32] It was thought that, from the beginning of the world, there had been a long line of pioneering figures each of whom had revealed either one more step toward the realization of God's plan for creation, or a novel and fruitless attempt on the part of humans to build their own history. Thus, Moses was the *primus legislator* of a series that reached its fulfillment in Christ and was then prolonged by his vicars, the Roman pontiffs. Certainty of this fact never faltered. In the

30 Momigliano, "L'historique païenne et chrétienne."
31 von Schlosser, *Quellenbuch*, 1–36; Davis-Weyer, *Early Medieval Art*.
32 Augustine, *De civitate Dei*, XXII.30. Cf. Schmid, "Aetates mundi"; Tristram, *Sex aetates mundi*.

very thick of the Investiture Controversy, which set the pope and the emperor in direct opposition in their claims to world rule, Bernold of Constance (d. 1100) reminded the imperial party that pontifical supremacy drew its founding sources and its legitimacy straight from the Bible itself.[33]

Control of biblical interpretation?

Was the text of the Bible in the strictly "literal sense" understood in the same way in Syriac, Coptic, or Latin cultures, which knew the Bible only with the aid of its translators, as it was in a Greek culture conserving the heritage of the earliest Christian communities in a direct line? Jerome had opened the doors to literal interpretation and had demonstrated a Christian aptitude for it that rivaled pagan rhetoricians, but no sooner had he put together the indispensable dictionary for this purpose (of which he published the summary in his *Interpretationes nominum hebraicorum*), than Latin writers found it unnecessary to follow further in his footsteps: they took into account the results already gained and made do without the Greeks. The historical defeat of a Rome that had been deprived of the imperial seat of power and devastated by the barbarians underlined, moreover, the need for some detachment from burdensome contemporary realities. Augustine and his followers pointed the way to survival in advocating the quest for the invisible and the inexpressible in order to compensate for the evil of this world. Why then persist in hunting down the literal sense as Jerome had done?

And so another fracture opened up in the community of interpreters, this time between north and south, on the primordial question of the Judeo-Christian world: how far is the Bible to be followed? What is to be done, concretely speaking, with the Old Testament, that is, with the oldest part of the texts received by Christians?[34] This was a critical problem in the early centuries as much because of the Jewish origins of Christianity as because of the fact that so many of its followers belonged to a world utterly ignorant of Judaism, particularly in the British Isles, Frisia, and Germany. Pope Gregory the Great, a faithful follower of Augustinian thought, counseled his emissary Augustine, the first archbishop of Canterbury (d. c. 604) to avoid the literal sense and to stress rather the spiritual sense.[35] He had no difficulty convincing

33 Bernold of Constance, *Chronica*, ad annum 1095, in Berthold of Reichenau and Bernold of Constance, *Die Chroniken*, 518.

34 The question is posed by de Jong, "Old Law and New-Found Power."

35 Gregory the Great, *Libellus responsionum*, addressed to Augustine of Canterbury in Bede, *HE*, i.27. Cf. Meyvaert, "Les 'Responsiones'"; his *Benedict, Gregory, Bede*; his "Le *Libellus responsionum*"; and de Dreuille, *L'Église et la mission au VIe siècle*.

continental churchmen of this, for they were long accustomed to it; in contrast, this approach ran contrary to insular practice, and Irish monks could hardly abide it. The two peculiar questions of the calendar (treated at the Synod of Whitby in 664) and of Irish preaching (forbidden by Anglo-Saxon bishops at the Council of Chelsea in 816) reveal the huge scale of the problem. Beneath the appearances of political contest another equally serious debate is discernible, namely the question of literal observance of the prescribed law. The Irish beat a retreat, but nonetheless continued to admonish each other to put the precepts of their Christianity according to the Old Testament into practice to the letter and without compromise.[36] Overall, if not totally disallowed, recourse to the linguistic and historical sources of the Bible was decisively devalued; in contrast, the spiritual sense, which was but a watered-down development of ancient allegory, became the established norm.

Theodore of Tarsus, the Greek archbishop of Canterbury (668–90), introduced into Britain teachings based on writings of Antiochene inspiration. He did not regard Origen favorably: the leader of the competing school of Alexandria was not mentioned in works composed under Theodore's influence. Thus, if we examine, for example, what Theodore had to say about John 10.3, "Et vocem meam audient" ("And they shall hear my voice"), we find that he explains quite concretely that "It is the custom of Eastern shepherds to walk in front of their flock singing." The mysterious *chyrogrillius* (*hyrax*, *choerogryllus*) of Lev. 11.5 is explicated in the most literal sense: the animal is said to resemble a pig, but is smaller and roams the steeps of Mt. Sinai. The *pepones* mentioned in Num. 11.5 are described as enormous melons found at Edessa of such proportions that a camel can carry two only with great difficulty.[37] To be sure, insular writers did not await the arrival of Gregory the Great's emissaries to practice literal interpretation on a wide scale. It may well be, however, that Theodore and his companions were forced to cede some ground to a resurgence of continental influence in a mode of biblical interpretation largely dominated by an allegorical and moral model: the canons of the Synod of Hatfield (679 or 680) evince in effect a rallying to Alexandrian approaches.[38] Nonetheless, the West only developed belatedly the techniques of realism and proximity between view and image which, thanks to their assiduous practice of the rhetorical genre of *ekphrasis*, was so championed by the Byzantine

36 Herren, "'Judaizing Tendencies.'"

37 Bischoff, *Mittelalterliche Studien*, 208.

38 "We acknowledge . . . the fifth council which met in Constantinople in the time of Justinian the second to condemn Theodore [of Mopsuestia, d. 428] and the letters of Theodoret [of Cyrrhus, d. 457] and Ibas [of Edessa, d. 457] and their teachings in opposition to Cyril [of Alexandria, d. 444]": Bede, *HE*, 4.17 [15], 387.

iconodules.[39] The "Vienna Genesis," copied and decorated probably in Constantinople in the sixth century either for a member of the imperial family or as an offering on the part of such a person,[40] shows that text and literal images could be used to support each other without the intervention of accompanying commentary. This simple use of biblical books was long maintained in Constantinople, through to the famous "friezed Gospels" of the eleventh and twelfth centuries.[41]

The rupture between East and West

To understand the Latin exegesis of Christian antiquity and the early Middle Ages, there is no need to have recourse to eastern formulae. Literary genres and modes of interpretation differed from one end of the Mediterranean to the other and from the Mediterranean to the north Atlantic coasts. Consider the example of florilegia. Since its development in the sixth century by Procopius of Gaza (c. 465–529), the genre of "collections of exegetical fragments" (comparable to *centuria* or "chapters" of spiritual literature) dominated Byzantine centers of learning. Of numerous original exemplars, there survive the eighth-century *Sacra Parallela* attributed to John of Damascus and the ninth-/tenth-century *Melissa* sequence, which added the secular *gnomai* of Nicetas of Herakleia (d. 1100) to a biblical and patristic florilegium. Like the collection that brought together scriptural and patristic quotations that the patriarch of Constantinople John VII the Grammarian (837–43) had compiled for the purposes of justifying renewed iconoclasm, these florilegia served various purposes – didactic, spiritual, and political.[42] As the lively mistrust of the rulers of the Byzantine Empire with regard to innovation was exacerbated, the dominance of tradition channeled interpreters into the genre of the exegetical florilegia and ossified the work of the masters.[43] In 692, the Council in Trullo, held in Justinian II's palace in Constantinople, put lasting limits on exegetical creativity. After a brief outburst at the beginning of the tenth century (Arethas of Caesarea), this creativity would take refuge in the realms of the Tsar of Bulgaria, and would not regain its vitality in Constantinople until the Comnenian era of the late-eleventh and twelfth centuries.

39 Cf. Kazhdan and Jeffreys, "Ekphrasis."
40 For the Vienna Genesis, see Mazal, *Wiener Genesis*.
41 Velmans, *Le Tétraévangile*.
42 Cf. Talbot and Cutler, "John VII Grammatikos." See also Talbot, "Antony I Kassymatas."
43 Jeffreys and Kazhdan, "Florilegium."

Western writers long accepted the limitations of the florilegium. In his *Liber scintillarum*, written between 632 and c. 750, the French monk Defensor of Ligugé explained that his master Ursinus (who has been identified with the author of the *Vita S. Leodegarii* of Autun) enjoined him to write his work and taught him how to do so. He drew on the resources of a good library since he was able to cite appropriate passages of Ambrose of Milan, Augustine, Jerome, Pseudo-Clement, a Pseudo-Cyprian, Caesarius of Arles, and Hilary of Poitiers, together with Greek writers known to Latin authors such as Origen, Basil of Caesarea, and Eusebius of Caesarea, and as rarely cited an author as Ephraim. Defensor identified his sources out of a concern, he claimed, to avoid the confusion of authentic and apocryphal writings.[44] From the eighth century, however, Latin writers began to free themselves from the constraints of the florilegium genre, the clearest indicator of their disaffection being their focus on just one or two of the church fathers: Bede set to work on the Augustinian corpus, and when Florus undertook a collection of exegetical writings on the Pauline epistles, he deliberately turned to Saint Jerome.[45] They also privileged the commentary and the homily (Carolingian commentators valued the sermon genre, recognizable by its closing doxology), and adapted the methods used in the interpretation of the Latin classics to the reading of the Bible, producing biblical "glosses" (influenced, perhaps, by the Byzantine *catenae*).

From the sixth to the eighth century another split opened up in the West. The widely used and available works of those authors who were already being called the fathers of the church, starting with those of Ambrose (d. 397), Jerome (d. 420), and Augustine (d. 430) and followed much later by those of Gregory the Great (d. 604), delimited the field of a peculiarly western mode of interpretation that was both insensible to the pleas of the "Judaizers" and likewise indifferent to the various eastern schools, being neither Alexandrian, nor Antiochene, but Roman. The Roman Empire, which was divided in 395 and vanished from the West in 476, might collapse ineluctably, and the city of Rome, devastated in 410, might kneel before barbarians, but what did it matter? For Saint Augustine, the City of the Devil and the City of God were henceforth joined in a combat whose favorable outcome for Christians living according to the Law was assured, albeit unobtainable as long as this world endured. For those who knew how to look and see beyond mere appearances,

44 "Sed ne opus, quasi sine auctore, putetur apocrifum, unicuique sententiae per singula proprium scripsi auctorem." Cf. Ganz, "Knowledge"; Kirchmeyer and Hemmerdinger-Iliadou, "S. Ephrem."

45 Fransen, "Description." Cf. Rochais, "Florilèges."

there was absolutely no cause to doubt the victory of the church. Thus from the sixth century, two fault-lines demarcated the two great interpretive realms. Western Christians were conscious of one fault-line (at once both linguistic and doctrinal) which rapidly separated them from the East where the original languages of the Bible continued to be understood. Far from moving to bridge the divide, they disparaged the insalubrious ideas continually being debated in the cities of the Byzantine Empire, catalogued the dangers of heresies using Greek names, and finally, applauded when the emperor of Constantinople relieved them of their Ostrogothic masters in Italy, who had made the error of being hardened heretics, heirs of Arius (d. c. 336). Encouraged by this example, the Franks (around 550) and the Visigoths (after 587) hastened to rid themselves of the last of the Arians and arranged the triumph of Augustinian interpretation as relayed by the senator Cassiodorus.

Henceforth, what amounted to virtually two separate Europes of the Bible, two separate hermeneutical Europes, were set in opposition: the Europe of the North and the Isles, and that of the South. The one followed the lead of St. Jerome, the hermit who withdrew to Bethlehem, the other saw itself in the line of Augustine, the bishop governing the community of Hippo in North Africa. One devoted itself to private or collective meditation (through the liturgy); being of literalist or even fundamentalist inspiration and nourished on symbolism (preferring to introduce the Evangelists using their standard animal symbols drawn from Ezechiel's vision – man-Matthew; lion-Mark; ox-Luke; eagle-John – rather than their "portraits"). It advocated a statutory moral code, professed indifference to temporal pressures, and tended to restrict, or at least circumscribe, the forces of social change. The other saw itself as directive, voluntaristic, and organizational: it used the Bible more as a lever of societal transformation. The one may be identified as monastic, the other as episcopal.

This bipartite division allows us to describe two modes of interpreting the Bible. Interpreters from the North, especially those from the northwest and their followers on the Continent, from Columbanus to Pirmin, accorded literal interpretation primacy. They drew inspiration and authority from St. Jerome – indeed, some even borrowed his name[46] – and from the eastern writers who had come to England with Theodore of Tarsus.[47] When moving on to allegorical interpretation, they always privileged the Christological sense. These writers seem not to have been concerned with transforming the world, but with saving it by engineering its escape from temporality. This

46 For the "Pseudo-Jeromes," see Albert in this volume.
47 Bischoff and Lapidge, *Biblical Commentaries*; Lapidge, "Career of Theodore."

privileging of literal exegesis had weighty consequences: it induced certain forms of fundamentalism. Probably the most volatile ferment of the literal mode of interpretation in the early Middle Ages was iconoclasm in both East and West. This was accompanied by liturgical and especially Eucharistic symbolism (we know that the iconoclasts in Constantinople argued that there was no true icon of Christ other than the consecrated bread and wine).[48] The more perspicacious commentators were well aware of the danger. Bede, influenced by Ceolfrith of Wearmouth-Jarrow, resolved to employ a rather more supple exegetical method, wedding the two aspects of the *littera*, philological and historical. For him, the letter provided an entrée to pedagogy by leading the reader to re-read the history of the present age and of humanity through the lens of biblical history from creation to the end of time. Bede was not the only insular author to use this approach. According to his own account, the enigmatic Caedmon, inspired by Augustine's *De catechizandis rudibus*, outlined the same catechetical course.[49] In effect, Bede sided with the Roman sphere of influence: he took exception to insular radicalism, laboring rather for the advancement of a form of monasticism rather more reconciled with the values of contemporary society. We must not delude ourselves, however; Bede remained exceptional, albeit sufficiently renowned for numerous ninth-century anonymous authors to shelter under the authority of his name.

Other commentators, primarily from the South, were unable entirely to avoid dealing with the literal sense, but did leave it to one side as soon as possible in order to take up the tropological or moral sense, a mode of interpretation that found expression in preaching and was intended to be the moral instruction of communities. Following Gregory the Great, these continental ecclesiastical interpreters accompanied, supported, and occasionally directed and guided movements in European societies which recognized themselves in the patrimony of the Bible. Let us now turn to the split provoked by insular activism, dominated by a small group of radical monks, and by the domination of the old episcopal institutions on the Continent.

Monastic influence in the West

Between the mid-eighth and the mid-ninth centuries, under pressure from Benedictine-inspired monks and in reaction against certain irregularities which the Franks considered intolerable – in particular, the avatars of Arianism and

48 Taft, "Eucharist," 737.
49 Bede, *HE*, 4.24 [22], 419; see Bede, *Histoire ecclésiastique* in the translation by Szerwiniack et al., vol. 2, 178 note 196.

the excesses of eastern iconoclasm and of its iconodule opponents – there occurred an important reversal in the Frankish kingdom. Doctrinal Arianism, according to which the Son of God was created by the Father, had disappeared in the West, but nonetheless continued to preoccupy missionaries to central Europe, many of whose peoples had in the past subscribed to Arius's ideas. Indeed, some of these evangelists carried with them anti-Arian treatises such as those contained in the famous *Codex Ragyndrudis*.[50] Adoptionism, which emphasized the distance between transcendence of God and the humanity of Christ by teaching that Christ was a man elected and adopted by God, very likely flowed from an Antiochene mode of interpretation, and led some to read the story of Jesus as a kind of human adventure. The slide toward Adoptionism exhibited in the writings of some eastern exegetes of the Antiochene school, such as Paul of Samosata, supports this connection. This teaching, circulated by a group at Toledo in the second half of the eighth century, sufficiently perturbed the Franks for the court of Charlemagne to attack it with considerable ferocity. These two cases of Arianism and its Adoptionist variant illustrated the perils of literal interpretation; the same held for iconoclasm. Biblical interdictions were the staple of the instigators of the iconoclast crisis, and the emperor, Leo III, readily appealed to the Bible in order to justify his policies against images.[51] The arguments were poorly understood in the West, and the Franks decided it best for the time being to reserve judgment.

The acculturation of monasticism into western society and the intimate connection of monks such as Boniface, Virgil of Salzburg, and Hrabanus Maurus with the control of churches blurred the divide between monastic and episcopal traditions.[52] Continental monastic centers adopted the Augustinian line (e.g., Ambrosius Aupertus, Alcuin) and brought about a fusion of the two biblical hermeneutical approaches. Well-versed in the works of Bede, they enriched the literal sense (*littera*) by henceforth systematically having recourse to *historia* which compared, contrasted, and reunited the past of ancient Rome with that of the new empire. The Bible became once more a history book, intended to prove the triumph of Frankish Christianity. The great art of typology blossomed at this time to the benefit of Charlemagne and his sons, the administrators of this new world. The painted murals of Ingelheim depict the fulfillment of the Old Testament in the New and showed how Christian history itself, from Constantine through to Charlemagne, had reached sublime

50 Fulda, Bibliothek des bischöflichen Priesterseminar, Bonifatianus 2; Luxeuil script, second quarter of s.VIII. Cf. Hussey, "Franco-Saxon *Synonyma*."

51 Cf. Gero, *Byzantine Iconoclasm*.

52 See the chapter by Helvétius and Kaplan in this volume.

perfection.[53] At Louis the Pious's court, there was a show of practicing the four "senses," that is the four levels of interpretation of biblical texts: the literal, the spiritual, the moral, and the anagogical.[54] But whether anyone thought of actually governing in accordance with the Bible is another matter. As a rule, learned doctrine ceded to perfunctory practice. When Theutmir of Psalmody sent a list of questions on the books of Kings to his friend Claudius of Turin (c. 820–30), he invited the bishop to reply by tracing the allegorical or moral meanings as well as paying attention to the letter.[55]

The influence of Irish exegesis in the ninth century

The masters of what has been called "Irish exegesis" had as their goal the formation of a monastic elite. They drew much more than has usually been acknowledged from the Visigoths of the seventh century, particularly the method of the *quaestio*, pushing it into new directions. In the course of the ninth century, the Irish were little by little reduced by the continentals to shadows of their former selves. Carolingian scholars expected from Irish exegetical traditions what they also sought from the Visigothic: handbooks, the "Bible Reference Books," which they sometimes recopied. In fact, they absorbed and digested the insular hermeneutical method: Alcuin, Walafrid Strabo, and Haimo and Heiric of Auxerre mastered Irish exegesis, following its usual formulae (*persona–tempus–locus*), groups of seven (e.g., seven heavens), and mannerisms (such as the phrases *et reliqua, aliter, alii dicunt*, etc.) with aplomb. They also definitively emptied it of its spiritual potential, reckoning that it could not be assimilated into the empire they served, which was organized by immense willpower, so utterly unlike the context where the Irish masters worked. They searched the Bible to draw from it on the one hand tropological figures, especially those that would serve as examples to the elite of the empire (this was, for example, Hrabanus Maurus's approach in his reading of the books of Kings) and, on the other hand, the rites and customs that had for so long been of benefit to the chosen people of God and to the people of the kingdom of Israel of which they considered themselves the successors (notably, the obligatory levies for churches – oblations and tithes – and the rites hallowing the cultic space and objects – dedication and blessing). As Remigius observed regarding

53 Ermold the Black, *Poem to Louis the Pious*, translated in Davis-Weyer, *Early Medieval Art*, 84–88 (no. 12).

54 "Sensum vero in omnibus scripturis spiritalem et moralem necnon et anogogen optime noverat [imperator]" in Thegan, *Gesta Hludowici imperatoris*, ch. 19, 200.

55 "Secundum historiam, sed etiam secundum allegoriam vel tropologiam" in Claudius of Turin, *Questiones*, 624A.

the Deuteronomic laws, "all this taken literally is of enormous value in human law" (*in iure humano*). However, there were, it was acknowledged, some rather formidable precepts which could not be observed *iuxta historiam*;[56] it was recommended to observe some but not all precepts to the letter. Thus, Remigius comments,

> *A woman shall not be clothed with man's apparel* [Deut. 22.5], that is she shall not usurp the office of preacher. . . . The bird sitting on her nest signifies the *historia* at the heart of which the spiritual or allegorical sense is to be found, that is, the newly hatched young. . . . *But thou shalt let her go, keeping the young which thou hast caught* [Deut. 22.7]: this signifies that the letter must be abandoned in order to follow allegory, especially if the expression is difficult or vulgar.[57]

With the use of principles of common sense, the avoidance of simplism, and the preference for the *solutio difficilior*, spiritual exegesis was soon making a backdoor reappearance. Indeed, in the writings of Haimo of Auxerre and Ercanbert of Fulda, this mode of interpretation intervened as a cautionary principle, correcting the hermeneutical obsessions of the day.

Exegesis as applied by western scholars met with triumphal success, comparable to that of the widespread circulation of the great patristic commentaries. Benefiting from a renewal of diplomatic relations with Constantinople, the Franks were able to free themselves from insular tutelage in the second quarter of the ninth century. John Scottus Eriugena attempted to import the teachings of the Greek fathers, translating notably Maximus the Confessor (d. 662) and Pseudo-Dionysius (second half of the fifth century), as others had John Chrysostom. This opening up toward the East was, however, short-lived[58] and was not reciprocated, because Constantinopolitan scholarly circles continued to mistrust westerners. Augustine, whom Maximus the Confessor seems to have read, was by the ninth century known in Constantinople only through

56 Remigius, *Expositio in Deuteronomium*: "Neque enim aliquis in agendis rebus uel negociis, motum animi sui, id est uel amorem, uel odium sequi non debet, sed natura. *SS. Si genuerit filium contumacem*. Minale est hoc preceptum . . . Hoc tantum distat, quia quod tunc agebatur lapidibus, nunc agitur duris increpationibus" in Munich, Bayerische Staatsbibliothek, Clm 6227, f. 77r.

57 Ibid., f. 77v: "*Non induetur mulier ueste uirili*, id est officium predicandi non usurpet, quod et apostolus prohibit. *Nec uir utetur ueste feminea*, id est fluxa, et dissoluta opera non imitetur . . . Auis pullis incubans significat historiam, in qua spiritalis uel allegoricus sensus manifestatus est, sicut pulli iam ex ouo egressi. Quis uero auis incubat, cum non aperte, sed ex parte spiritalis sensus in historia est. Tunc ergo dimittenda est . . . hoc est reliquenda est hystoria et allegoria sequenda, maxime si res difficilis et turpis fuerit, ut illud apostoli, hoc enim faciens carbones ignis congeres super caput eius, hic enim ad hystoriam et allegoriam confugiendum est."

58 See the chapter by Boureau in this volume.

florilegia. As for Jerome, he had long since sunk into oblivion, and his successors, the Irish and Frankish masters of the eighth and ninth centuries, no longer warranted even the condescension of explicit quotation in the writings of Byzantine authors.

A Bible for everyone?

Exegetical method does seem to have been determined by the religious allegiance of its practitioner. Was it, however, as stable for the New Testament as for the Old? Moreover, was it accessible to all, or did it remain the prerogative of specialists? In response to the Capetian king Robert the Pious's anxiety at the sight of blood rain falling in Aquitaine around 1015, Bishop Fulbert of Chartres replied that the techniques for interpreting the natural world were exactly the same as those for the heavenly spheres. The solution lay in finding an analogical model. In a universe replete with dormant mysteries, which nonetheless ought to be recognized as being endowed with significance, the question was how to decipher what lay hidden on first examination. Exegesis proposed reflecting upon language, and upon the need for techniques of interpretation, as the interpreter had to effect the metamorphosis of the *vox*, the physical utterance, into a meaningful *sermo*. This ninth-century question persisted: it was still being raised at the turn of the eleventh and twelfth centuries.[59]

One could, of course, be content with the letter alone. For Ercanbert of Fulda, the letter provided simple (moral) instruction which it was necessary, occasionally, to imitate. Confronted with a choice between Abel, the just man, and Cain, the fratricide, a good man would not hesitate to follow the example of the former.[60] The monks' vocation led them to more elevated considerations, to be sure, but herein lay a risk, since did not searching for the deeper meaning betray, in fact, an obscene *curiositas*, precisely the kind which St. Paul denounced?[61] It was a question of fundamental importance, and one repeatedly evoked. The Carolingian nuns Gisla and Rotruda appealed to Alcuin to bestow on them his knowledge of the Scriptures, holding nothing back; Alcuin gave his consent, since he saw it as a matter of formation in the religious life.[62] What was to be done, however, when, at the beginning of the eleventh century in Flanders, the Île-de-France, Champagne, and in the south

59 Munich, Staatsbibliothek Clm 6268, f. 17r drawing on Hrabanus Maurus, *Commentaria in Mattheum*, 806. On this theme, see Luscombe, " 'Scientia' and 'Disciplina.' "

60 "In huiusce modi facto qui nuda est historia contentus, horrescit praui cain factum, et exemplum imitator abel iusti" in Munich, Staatsbibliothek Clm 6269, f.9v.

61 Rom. 11.20: "Noli saltum sapere"; cf. Ginzburg, "High and Low."

62 Alcuin, *Epistola*, 739–40.

of France, small textual communities wrenched the Bible from the control of the established authorities both celestial (the church fathers) and terrestrial (the bishops and abbots)? A resurgence of biblical fundamentalism spread. Based on enacting the revealed discourse and on insisting on a *vita vere apostolica*, it upset and destabilized traditional interpretations. In 1025 the dissident "heretics" of Arras had only asked to read, or at the very least to hear the reading of the Scriptures, but they were suspected of wanting to dispense with the church's control and drink straight, and without intermediary, from the living waters of the Gospels themselves.[63] The clerics condemned at Orleans in 1022 seem, in contrast, to have been partisans of a sort of esotericism which disgusted their contemporaries.[64] These new interpretations provoked varied scholarly and political responses, except on one ancient principle which withstood every test: prudence and wisdom were not the same as *curiositas*. Knowledge entailed conscience. The same distinction was, of course, revived by the controversy between Abelard and Bernard of Clairvaux in the second quarter of the twelfth century.

Renewal

In the second half of the eleventh century, a reaction developed in two regions, Latium and northern France, inspired by two different groups. In central Italy, it was led by ecclesiastics associated with the college of cardinals, but in northern France by the masters in urban schools associated with the new elites who were driving the expansion of western Europe. In conformity with the hopes of early eleventh-century "textual communities,"[65] the Bible's future was henceforth intimately connected with the idea of reform.[66] This evolution, which burgeoned very rapidly, exploded with the intense production of biblical glosses and commentaries during the period between 1060 and 1115. Masters Lambert of Paris, Bruno of Segni, Bruno of Rheims, Lanfranc of Canterbury, Anselm of Laon, Berengaudus, and Lambert of Saint-Omer attempted to forge new paths tackling the same themes that the Roman reformers of the second half of the eleventh century had propounded. Like them, they re-read the sacred texts and drew from them some important guiding principles. The first prescribed the distinction between the sacred and the profane. This radical

63 Lobrichon, "Arras."

64 Rodulfus Glaber, *Historiae*, III.8, §§ 26–27 in his *Opera*, 138–42; Andrew of Fleury, *Vie de Gauzlin*, 96ff., 180–82; Bautier, "L'hérésie d'Orléans."

65 Stock, *Implications of Literacy*.

66 See the chapter by Barrow in this volume.

separation, invoked in Ezek. 22.26 with which all their predecessors were very familiar, was the undergirding principle of their actions, as Berthold of Reichenau recalled around 1080, bemoaning the actions of the emperor.[67] The second principle recalled the need for circumspection in the quest for *altiora* and *superiora*, and called for a return to the use of allegory in the best sense of that word. Lanfranc used this to his advantage when he attacked the arguments of Berengar of Tours and the new logicians.[68] The third principle invoked the Second Coming and the end of time to rouse a reaction.[69] This drastically widened the gap between secular masters on the one hand, who, cognizant of the increasing inadequacy of traditional biblical teaching in the face of new experiences of pilgrimage and of the crusades in Spain and the Holy Land, increasingly hunted down the literal and historical sense, and monks on the other, who, in accordance with the principle of typology, strove to build their city in heaven. The interest of commentators in the three books of the Bible central to the reform (and perhaps of every reform thereafter) – the Pauline epistles, the Apocalypse, and the Song of Songs – their taste for grand schemas of world history, and the restoration of a historical vision of the church thanks to the Venerable Bede, were signs of the transformations occurring around 1100. Scholars deployed new techniques of biblical interpretation. They found new uses for the genre of glosses, with which the insular masters had experimented at the end of the eighth century.[70] They perfected the technique of the introduction (*introitus*) by clarifying literary genres and forms of discourse. They adjusted the hierarchy of the sciences to include the biblical books, which were subject to the same analyses as works of ethics, logic, and physics, and were re-read in the same spirit with which the chronicles of the period were being rewritten.[71]

Epilogue

The generation that witnessed the departure for and the return from the First Crusade had a new awareness of history: all masters were required to

67 "Nulla inter sacrum et non sacrum differentia, nulla in tot miseries miseratio fuerat" in Berthold of Reichenau, *Die Chroniken*, 33 (anno 1078), 337.

68 See Lanfranc of Canterbury, *Opera omnia*, 144B, on Rom. 12.30 against Berengar of Tours and ibid., 344A, on 1 Cor. 2.1 against the new logicians.

69 See Lanfranc of Canterbury, *Opera omnia*, 344A, on 2 Thess. 2.13–14 regarding the Roman emperor during the time of St. Paul and referring to Emperor Henry IV (1056–1106).

70 Lobrichon, "Une nouveauté," and his "Conserver"; Gorman, "La plus ancienne édition commentée."

71 Cf. Bruno (probably the Carthusian), *Expositio in psalmos*, 638B, and *Expositio in epistolas Pauli*, 11ff.

reconsider the Bible through the lens of world history. It was in this period that the typological way of thinking reached its apogee. Based on the principle of the identity and constant reiteration which engendered an immobilizing determinism, this approach was further enriched by embracing the idea of fulfillment, which turned accounts of the past into prefigurations of the present, and propelled history forward. Figural or typological modes of thought were no more Germanic than they were French or English; they were of benefit to all the peoples who practiced them. For societies around 1100, the Bible became once again a history book, a source of the inspiration for and occasionally the motivating incitement to change. The administrators of this renewal were no longer the rulers of the empire, neither kings nor princes, but the rulers of the reformed church, connected with the new holders of ecclesiastical power, the bishops. It was then that the designation *historiae divinae* returned to vigorous currency and spread, just as the term *biblia* became the standard word used to describe the complete corpus of the Scriptures.[72] It was then, too, that the western secular elites discovered their unprecedented power, and that they strove to justify and purify their drive toward world domination through the notion of a "holy war." Happily, the new intelligentsia knew enough not to join in. They were already beginning to appropriate the spoils of Greek antiquity and Byzantium.

72 Cf. Duchet-Suchaux and Lefèvre, "Les noms de la Bible," 18.

27

The Christian book in medieval Byzantium

LESLIE BRUBAKER AND MARY B. CUNNINGHAM

Of all the artisanal productions preserved from the time since Constantine I (the Great) began calling Byzantium, the capital of the old eastern Roman empire, by a new name (Constantinople – Constantine's *polis*, or city), probably the most familiar today are icons and buildings such as Hagia Sophia. But it is arguable that Byzantine books should share pride of place.

Across the imperial centuries, Greek manuscripts – usually deluxe copies of the Gospels or service books, but also theological treatises such as the copy of Dionysius the Areopagite sent to Louis the Pious in 827 – served as valuable diplomatic gifts.[1] After the fall of Constantinople to the Ottoman Turks in 1453 they were collected by humanist scholars, particularly, though not exclusively, for the ancient Greek authors whose texts they preserved; and by the French kings who saw themselves as the successors to the Byzantine emperors and surrounded themselves with the trappings of their purported ancestors.[2] Beyond the role of Greek manuscripts in cultural history, their contents – and decoration – are important as testimony to the ways medieval Byzantines ordered and arranged their thoughts, and for the ways that images were used to reinforce and shape the world of the largely urban elite who had access to, and could actively read, books.

The Byzantine book: a brief history of its origins and development

Early manuscript production was broadly similar in Latin-speaking western Christendom and the Greek-speaking Orthodox East. The development of

1 See, e.g., Lowden, "Luxury Book." For the Dionysius manuscript (Paris. gr. 437), see Omont, "Manuscrit"; Brubaker and Haldon, *Byzantium in the Iconoclast Era*, 41–42, with earlier literature; and note 77 below.

2 See Nelson, "Italian Appreciation"; Auzépy and Grélois, *Byzance retrouvée*.

the Christian book traced here is therefore largely applicable to both unless otherwise specified. Before books (codices), written records were normally kept on scrolls (*rotuli*, rolls) made of papyrus, though waxed wooden tablets were bound together and already used as notebooks for commercial records during the Roman period. The earliest evidence for books as we know them now – cut pages bound together between covers – dates from the first century, but preserved examples only begin to become statistically significant in the third. At the same time, parchment (animal skin treated to remove hair and fat so that it will accept ink) became an increasingly frequent replacement for sheets cut from papyrus, originally prepared for use in making scrolls.[3]

The advantages of codices over rotuli were many. Most significant were increased ease of storage and reference, and decreased expense. Scrolls had normally been stored in a round container that looked like a modern hatbox, called a *capsa*. Codices were stored flat, on shelves, and could be piled one on top of another. The text on rolls was usually written parallel to the long side, in columns so that the reader unfurled the scroll enough to read a column then rolled the left side back up whilst simultaneously unrolling the right side to make the next column of text visible. To find a particular passage entailed considerable effort – one cannot "flip through" a scroll as one can through a book – and it made indexing through marginal tabs awkward. The reading process also meant that it was normally only practicable to write on one side of a scroll, whereas in codices both sides of the page were used, thereby allowing considerable economy of space and material.[4] These advantages resulted in the almost complete replacement of the roll by the codex during the fourth century, though scrolls, now with script parallel to the short side, continued to be used in Byzantium and Byzantine areas of Italy for certain high status documents such as imperial documents (chrysobulls) and liturgical rolls, where the expense and inconvenience of the format enhanced the prestige of the text.[5]

3 For good overviews, see Gamillscheg and McCormick, "Codex"; Turner, *Terms Recto and Verso*; Devreesse, *Introduction*; Weitzmann, *Late Antique*; Irigoin, "Les cahiers." We primarily deal with Greek books in this chapter. For other eastern Christian manuscripts, see, e.g., Der Nersessian, *Miniature Painting in the Armenian Kingdom*; Leroy, *Les manuscrits syriaques*.

4 Roberts and Skeat, *Birth of the Codex*; Weitzmann, *Illustrations*.

5 See Nelson, Gamillscheg, and Talbot, "Rolls, Liturgical." Another example is Biblioteca apostolica vaticana, cod. palat. gr. 431, a tenth-century luxury scroll illustrating the Old Testament book of Joshua; see Weitzmann, *Joshua Roll*.

The shift was apparently also helped along by an increased need for texts with the emergence of Christianity as a major force in the fourth century. Christianity depended upon access to the Gospels, the story of Christ's life, and Eusebius tells us that Constantine ordered "fifty volumes with ornamental leather bindings, easily legible and convenient for portable use . . . of the Divine Scriptures, the provision and use of which you well know to be necessary for reading in church."[6]

The benefits of parchment over papyrus were less blatant. Papyrus, made from the pith of a reed that grows abundantly along the Nile, was relatively inexpensive and reasonably durable, though it survives better in dry climates than in wet ones, for which reason most surviving papyri have been found in Egypt. It was made in bulk in Egypt, and distributed along well-developed trade routes until at least the ninth century.[7] In contrast, parchment was always expensive, and no production and distribution system seems to have been developed. Even a large animal skin yielded no more than eight pages, and the preparation – which involved a lime bath, stretching, and scraping – was time-consuming and required specialized equipment.[8] Depending upon details of the process followed, parchment color ranged from nearly white to pale yellow, a distinction that is sometimes used to pinpoint a manuscript's place of origin.[9] Against the expense of production, however, parchment had several advantages over papyrus. It could be produced anywhere with available animals (normally goats or sheep), was longer-lasting and more flexible than papyrus, and provided a smoother surface on which to write. It was thus also better suited to decoration; and, in addition, paint and gold leaf adhere better and longer to parchment than to papyrus.

To make a book, the prepared parchment was cut to size, ruled, and written on. Usually each sheet was cut large enough to fold in the middle, thereby creating four sides on which to write.[10] These double sheets – called *bifolia* – were then pricked along the margins and lines were incised horizontally and vertically between the prickings to indicate where the text was to be written. The ruling patterns thus provided varied considerably, and are sometimes

6 Eusebius, *Life of Constantine*, 166–67. See further Roberts and Skeat, *Birth of the Codex*; McCormick, "Birth of the Codex"; and, for an indication of the various debates surrounding this issue, Bagnall, "Jesus Reads a Book."

7 Lewis, *Papyrus*, 64–94; McCormick, *Origins*, 704–708.

8 Wilson, "Books and Readers," especially 1–3; Gamillscheg and Talbot, "Parchment," with further bibliography.

9 E.g., yellow parchment is sometimes seen as evidence for an Italian origin, see Leroy, "Les manuscrits grecs d'Italie."

10 There was no standard size, except, occasionally, within individual workshops. See, e.g., Anderson, "Twelfth-Century Instance."

(problematically) used to identify particular writing workshops (scriptoria) or country of origin.[11] The text was then written, after which the *bifolia* were nested together, in Byzantium usually in groups of four to form a *quaternion* of eight leaves, each of which is called a *folio*. For visual unity, Greek bookmakers always arranged the *bifolia* so that what had once been the hair side of the parchment faced another hair side, while flesh sides – often slightly yellower than the hair sides – faced each other as well: this is known as Gregory's law, after the scholar who first noted it.[12] Each segment, called a gathering or quire, was numbered so that it could easily be arranged in its proper order after the writing had been completed. Often these numbers, called quire signatures, still survive; they are usually in the outer top margin of the first folio of the quire.[13] Once the text was complete, the gatherings were sewn together, and encased within a cover. The outer edges were often decorated, though this has frequently been lost as a result of later trimming. Much later, individual folia were numbered, almost always in Arabic numerals rather than in Greek. Usually, only one side of each leaf received a number, and to distinguish front and back they are designated as recto (always the page on the right, as the book is open) and verso (on the left); folio 4 recto (or 4r) is thus faced by folio 3 verso (3v), and so forth.

Paper, much cheaper than parchment but far less durable, was perhaps introduced in Byzantium around the year 800, but was not widely used until the eleventh century. Even after paper became widely available, however, parchment continued to be used for luxury manuscripts.[14] As with the rolls used (archaically) for chrysobulls and some versions of the liturgy, the expense and rarity value of parchment prompted its use for important documents long after paper had superseded it as the common writing surface.

Writing and copying

The study of book production, called codicology, also embraces the study of scripts (paleography).[15] Most generally, early Greek manuscripts were written

11 Leroy, *Les types de réglure*.
12 Gregory, "Les cahiers"; further discussion in Hoffmann, *Recherches*.
13 Mondrain, "Les signatures."
14 Gamillscheg, Talbot, and Ševčenko, "Paper."
15 The bibliography on Byzantine paleography is vast. The classic studies are Gardthausen, *Griechische Palaeographie*; Thompson, *Handbook*; and Dain, *Les manuscrits*. Good English surveys include Wilson, *Mediaeval Greek Bookhands*; Barbour, *Greek Literary Hands*. An excellent collection of articles pertaining to many aspects of Byzantine codicology and paleography is *La paléographie grecque et byzantine*, and more recently, Prato, *I manoscritti greci*.

in what we would now call capital letters (majuscule or uncial), with neither punctuation nor accents. Around 800 – clearly an important watershed for book production – majuscule began to be replaced by minuscule, most closely approximated in modern terms by script: minuscule letters are in "lower case" (e.g., Α becomes α, Β becomes β, Γ becomes γ, etc.), are often joined together (forming "ligatures"), and in addition, often sport abbreviations (such as κ/ for καί = and) and start to be augmented by both accents and punctuation. This process is associated with the Studios Monastery in Constantinople, a fifth-century complex which received a new family of monks in the late seventh century and came to prominence in the 780s. As we shall discuss in more detail shortly, its leader at the turn of the century, Theodore, wrote a set of rules that privileged book reading and writing, and the Studios scriptorium (writing studio) is one of the few that has been at least tentatively reconstructed. The invention of minuscule made books considerably cheaper to produce: it was faster to write than majuscule, and smaller, so that more letters could be written on a page.[16] It soon supplanted majuscule for all but deluxe manuscripts and presentation scripts (e.g., inscriptions on icons). The archaic was, obviously, recognized as a marker of status – and scholars who insist that the Byzantines did not recognize the past as "different" should acknowledge this – to the extent that, by the tenth century, a scroll made of parchment and written in majuscule would have to have been an extremely important text indeed.

Ornament in manuscripts began mostly as a scribal form of indexing and codifying. From at least the fourth century, enlarged initials, in the ink of the text, introduced new text sections. Decorative borders and endpieces (also in scribal ink) marked the colophon at the end of large text sections, where the title was restated and the word length was sometimes noted (and occasionally the scribe's name was recorded). Marginal signs indicated passages of particular importance or quotations.[17] In Latin manuscripts, these initials and text breaks soon became much more elaborately ornamented, but in Byzantium this process waited until the ninth century and manuscript illumination was never so exuberant as it was in the West. As we shall see, literacy was probably always higher in the eastern Roman Empire than in what remained of the western Roman world. Perhaps for this reason illumination never – at least in

16 The variant on this same process occurred almost simultaneously in the Frankish kingdoms of the West, though here the first step was the development of "capital" letters (Caroline majuscule), followed shortly thereafter by Caroline minuscule. The relationship between eastern and western writing systems has been noted for some time, but whether the developments were independent of one another or whether one system influenced the other is not clear. See, e.g., Mango, "L'origine."

17 Nordenfalk, *Die spätantike Zierbuchstaben*; Astruc, "Remarques."

books – acquired the highly symbolic role that allowed letters to function kinetically as they do in, for example, seventh- and eighth-century Northumbria.[18] But by the ninth century a fairly stable hierarchy of book ornamentation had been established for Greek books, and this continued throughout the remainder of the Byzantine period.[19] The text remained largely inviolate, and decoration was subservient to the written word. Whole pages of painted and embellished letters, which continued to appear in Latin books and soon developed in the Arabic world, simply did not occur in Greek manuscripts. But by the ninth century, enlarged initials were increasingly painted and gilded, perhaps under the influence of western motifs which appear to have been transmitted to Byzantium through manuscripts written in the Greek monasteries of Rome. By the eleventh century these letters were increasingly elaborated into anthropomorphic and zoomorphic forms – rarely, however, did they infringe on the blocks of text.[20] Headpieces also became increasingly elaborate from the ninth century onward, and, in deluxe manuscripts of the eleventh and twelfth centuries, sometimes incorporated narrative scenes.[21]

The scribes who wrote the text and the illuminators who decorated it were occasionally the same people, especially in the period before around 900, though the miniaturists responsible for figurative scenes were normally a different group of artisans.[22] The organization of the teams that put together Byzantine books is elusive, and seems to have been far more *ad hoc* than was the case in the West. Only rarely can we find traces of the same group or groups working together, and documentary evidence for any coherent scriptoria is virtually nonexistent.[23] Names of scribes appear occasionally, and, far more rarely, those of miniaturists.[24] But these mostly occur in isolation, and it has been suggested that scriptoria, as are recorded in the monasteries of Europe, simply did not appear in Byzantium. Instead, people desiring books may have

18 See, e.g., Nordenfalk, *Celtic and Anglo-Saxon Painting*.

19 Hutter, "Decorative Systems."

20 Again, the bibliography is large. Weitzmann, *Die byzantinische Buchmalerei* is the classic study; an appendix – Weitzmann, *Die Byzantinische Buchmalerei, Addenda und Appendix* – should be used with caution. On the introduction of initials, see Brubaker, "Introduction." Other important studies appear in Prato, *I manoscritti greci*, along with extensive reference to earlier literature.

21 E.g., in the "liturgical" homilies of Gregory of Nazianzus. See Galavaris, *Illustrations of the Liturgical Homilies*.

22 See, e.g., Brubaker, "Introduction"; Hutter, "*Le copiste du Métaphraste*"; Anderson, "Illustration of cod. Sinai. gr. 339."

23 For some of the rare examples, see Hutter, "*Le copiste du Métaphraste*"; Anderson, "Cod. Vat. gr. 463"; Buchthal and Belting, *Patronage*, with Nelson and Lowden, "Palaeologina Group."

24 See, e.g., I. Ševčenko, "Illuminators"; Nelson, *Theodore Hagiopetrites*.

gone to one place to order the text, another to decorate it, and still another to provide miniatures.[25] Pricing is equally problematic, and even the terms that the Byzantines used for various aspects of book production have only recently begun to be understood.[26]

Miniatures

Illustrations had already appeared in papyrus scrolls, and continued in books, where they are normally called miniatures. From the beginning, several formats were favored, with images either sharing a page with text or not. In the sixth-century Vienna Genesis, half of the page contains an image, and the other half the relevant Old Testament text, abbreviated so that the pattern of text and image remained coherent. Here, in a deluxe manuscript with parchment stained purple and with silver script, the images were as important as the words.[27] In the Rossano Gospels, also of the sixth century and with some purple-stained pages, narrative images of Christ's passion are clustered at the beginning of the manuscript. Most share a page with four prophets carrying Old Testament passages suggested by the Orthodox liturgy, where they were recited as prefigurations of the New Testament episodes portrayed above them.[28] Here, too, the images were obviously important, and created a commentary visualizing liturgical practice and showing how the Old Testament supported the New. The Rabbula Gospels (dated by colophon to 586) contains full-page illustrations along with marginal scenes flanking the Canon Tables (introductory lists, in columns framed by architectural motifs, that provide a concordance of the four Gospels).[29] The badly-damaged Cotton Genesis, another sixth-century book, was dominated by images inserted in the columns of text.[30] The Vienna Dioskourides (c. 512) – the most important non-religious manuscript of the early period, with pictures of the plants and animals discussed – included full-page miniatures, column pictures, and occasionally small botanical images inserted within the running text.[31] This

25 See Nelson and Lowden, "Palaeologina Group."

26 See Wilson, "Books and Readers," 3–4, 14; Kravari, "Note"; Atsalos, "Termes byzantins," all with earlier bibliography.

27 Vienna, National Library, cod. theol. gr. 31, see Gerstinger, *Wiener Genesis*; Lowden, "Concerning the Cotton Genesis."

28 Rossano, Cathedral Treasury, see Loerke, *I vangeli*.

29 Florence, Laur. Plut. I, 56, see Cecchelli, Furlani, and Salmi, *Rabbula Gospels*; Mundell Mango, "Where was Beth Zagba?"

30 London, British Library, cod. Cotton Otho B. VI, see Weitzmann and Kessler, *Cotton Genesis*.

31 Vienna, National Library, cod. med. gr. 1, see Gerstinger, *Dioscorides*; Brubaker, "Vienna Dioskorides."

variety of formats continued throughout the Byzantine period, though some formats predominated at different times. In the ninth century, for example, marginal formats were favored, perhaps, as we shall discuss in more detail shortly, because they allowed images to be placed in close correspondence to the words they illustrated.[32] In the eleventh and twelfth centuries, an upsurge of huge volumes, copiously illustrated, apparently revived the interest in column pictures, which allowed hundreds of small images to provide a running visual narrative to accompany the four Gospels, the first eight books of the Old Testament (Octateuch), and the four books of Kings.[33] Mostly, however, illustrated Greek books of the tenth through to the fifteenth century contained full-page miniatures, relatively few in number. These were most commonly Gospelbooks with a portrait of the relevant evangelist inserted before each of the four Gospels,[34] or psalters with images at the first, seventy-seventh, and final psalm (in Byzantium, the one-hundred and fifty-first), and sometimes author portraits with each of the odes at the end.[35] Increasingly, full-page miniatures were painted on unruled, single sheets of parchment that were "tipped in" – that is, they did not form part of the regular quire structure but were additional to it.

Christian books: a hierarchy

Most preserved Byzantine books have Christian content, though there are a not-insignificant number of other works such as military treatises, medical and scientific manuals, literary texts, and so forth.[36] The range of material available to the Byzantines is evident from one unusual but extremely important source: the *Bibliotheke*, a list of 280 works, each accompanied by a "book report," compiled by the future patriarch Photius (c. 810–c. 895, patriarch 858–67, 877–86) sometime in the mid-ninth century for his brother.[37] Photius ignores the standard range of Christian works, which he assumed his audience would know already, and thus provides summaries of a range of unusual texts, many

32 See Corrigan, *Visual Polemics*.

33 Omont, *Évangiles*; Velmans, *Le Tétraévangile*; Weitzmann and Bernabò, *Byzantine Octateuchs*, which should be read with the reviews by Brubaker and Hutter; Lassus, *L'illustration byzantine*.

34 Galavaris, *Illustrations of the Prefaces*; Nelson, *Iconography*.

35 Cutler, "Aristocratic Psalter" and *Aristocratic Psalters in Byzantium*.

36 Krumbacher, *Geschichte der byzantinischen Literatur*; Kazhdan (with Sherry and Angelidi), *History*; Beck, *Kirche und theologische Literatur*; Quasten, *Patrologie*; Rahlfs, *Verzeichnis der griechischen Handschriften*; Hunger, *Die hochsprachliche profane Literatur der Byzantiner*.

37 Photius, *Bibliotheke*; Treadgold, *Nature*; and for the date, Maas, "Photius' Treatment of Josephus."

no longer preserved. The great bulk of the books included, about two-thirds of the total, are religious – apologetics, lives of famous Christians, devotional and dogmatic texts, histories, sermons, letters, and so forth – but there is also a range of pre-Christian authors and texts about secular themes such as mathematics, medicine, and mythology, along with novels and poetry.[38]

In Byzantium, as noted earlier, by far the most numerous Christian books preserved are copies of the Gospels, which, as they told the story of Christ's life, were of critical importance to Orthodoxy. Psalters come second, in large part because they were crucial to the Byzantine liturgy, had to be recited at least annually (and often more frequently) by monks in many monastic houses, and were the prime text used to teach children to read.[39] One of the most popular works after that was a collection of the Homilies of Gregory of Nazianzus, mostly in the so-called liturgical edition: a selection of (usually) sixteen of the church father's forty-odd preserved fourth-century sermons that were read in various ecclesiastical contexts.[40]

Texts connected in one way or another with the Orthodox liturgy were collected in a variety of formats such as, from the ninth century onward, the lectionary (liturgical readings – lections – from the Bible and a few other sources, arranged in calendar order, usually with the feasts, movable and stationary, also listed),[41] various texts concerning the saints commemorated in daily services across the year (*menologia* – a collection of saints' lives; *synaxaria* – short notes about each saint; *menaia* – poems and prayers for the celebration of each saint),[42] and so forth. The Bible was normally broken into its constituent parts – such as the Pentateuch (the first five books of the Old Testament), the Octateuch (the first eight), or the psalter – but occasionally the whole Old Testament, New Testament, or even both were joined together in huge volumes.[43] Works of the church fathers – especially John Chrysostom, Basil of Caesarea, and, as noted earlier, Gregory of Nazianzus – appear regularly, and so do selections of quotations from a variety of patristic (and other) texts. Called florilegia, these were particularly common in the seventh, eighth, and ninth centuries when they were used to confirm the validity of patristic quotations to church councils.[44] Though the vast majority of Byzantine books remained

38 See the handy index of codices by subject matter in Treadgold, *Nature*, 173–76.

39 See Moffat, "Schooling," and Mullett, "Writing."

40 Galavaris, *Illustrations of the Liturgical Homilies*.

41 *Evangelia* contain only the Gospel passages; *praxapostoloi* contain the passages from the rest of the New Testament, see Taft, "Lectionary." Liturgical calendars (*typika*) add instructions for daily services, see Mateos, *Le typicon*.

42 See Taft, "Menaion"; N. P. Ševčenko, "Menologion"; Taft and Ševčenko, "Synaxarion."

43 See the references in note 36 above.

44 See Brubaker, *Vision and Meaning*, 51–57.

unillustrated, examples of all of the types of books just noted have survived with pictures. These miniatures enhanced the material value of the books, but they also played other roles.

Text and image: the roles of miniatures in Byzantine books

Miniatures, more than any other visual medium, presuppose and interact with text. In Byzantium, they did this in a variety of ways.

On the most basic level, miniatures can illustrate – by visualizing the action described in the textual narrative, by portraying the author writing the text or in the case of sermons, the priest delivering the sermon – the text they accompany. Even in cases of what appear to be straightforward illustrations of a text, however, a process of selection went on: which of the various moments in the story to show and what extratextual details would be included were not necessarily spontaneous decisions. Sometimes the story pattern and its particulars were determined by tradition (though that tradition had, of course, been started by someone, somewhere, making a conscious decision that was subsequently agreed upon by consensus and reinforced by repetition). For example, though Christ's attire is nowhere described in the Bible, he usually wears purple, an expensive color associated with the imperial house in Byzantium.[45] Adam's head-in-hand pose during his lament after the Fall – often used as well for Joseph at the nativity – appears with equal consistency across the Byzantine period, though, again, the position is never specified in the relevant biblical texts. Choice, rather than convention, often conditions the images selected in longer narrative sequences, and the episodes chosen can provide a sort of commentary-by-selection on the text. Gregory of Nazianzus's sermon, "To Julian the Tax Collector," has sacrifice and offering as its main theme, and uses a great many biblical parallels to reinforce them. From among them, the unknown illustrator of a copy of the sermons produced in Constantinople around the year 880 selected two, the adoration of the Magi and the massacre of the innocents (fig. 3), because these were most relevant to this theme.

On the same page, he added another scene that reinforced the same point but was not mentioned in the sermon: the Presentation of Christ in the Temple.[46] Here the miniature supplies a visual parallel to the text that augments the sense of the sermon but is in important respects independent of it: though the

45 James, *Light and Colour*.
46 Brubaker, *Vision and Meaning*, 62–71.

picture responds to the words, it moves the argument beyond them and recasts the theme in a new way. In this example, there are no explanatory captions to help us, but in other manuscripts the legends associated with the pictures help the modern (and the original) viewer understand their intent. In the Leo Bible (c. 940), for example, framing verses explain the commentary visualized by the miniatures that preface each book.[47]

Sometimes the images alone validate the truth, and true meaning, of the words. In a ninth-century florilegium now in Paris (Bibliothèque nationale de France, cod. gr. 923), for example, marginal images of the authors quoted sometimes point to their texts, or hold open a book as if discharging their words onto the page, or even hold a pen to the actual text itself (fig. 4) to show that they had truly written the words ascribed to them.

The portraits here guarantee the accuracy of the citation, an important issue in the eighth and ninth centuries, when accusations of deliberate forgery were customarily hurled at the opposing side during the iconoclast debates over the legitimacy of religious representations.[48] This is not the only manuscript from this period to favor marginal illustrations. The great majority of all Greek manuscripts following this format date from the ninth century, apparently because the margins were where commentaries that explained the meaning of the text (the *catena*) were written at the time, and pictures took on the same roles in the wake of iconoclasm. In a famous example, the Khludov Psalter of, probably, 843–47, portraits of David accompany captions that explain what the psalm meant.[49] For example, Psalm 53 begins "For with thee is the fountain of life," and the psalter miniaturist accompanied this passage with a picture (fig. 5) of Christ speaking to the Samaritan woman at the well (John 4.5–26).

To the left, a smaller figure of David gestures toward the scene, accompanied by the inscription "David says, Christ is the source of life." Here, and frequently throughout the manuscript, word and image join forces to comment on the psalm text, and it is significant that neither the words alone, nor the images alone, were considered sufficient: instead, the two media worked together to authorize a particular interpretation of the psalms.

While this – and especially the florilegium example – may seem to modern viewers to over-privilege the image, it is first worth remembering that, to the Byzantines, texts could be falsified and forged but images could not;[50] and

47 Biblioteca apostolica vaticana, cod. Reg. gr. 1, see Mango, "Date of cod. Vat. Regin. Gr. 1"; Mathews, "Epigrams."
48 Brubaker, *Vision and Meaning*, 52–57.
49 Corrigan, *Visual Polemics*, first made this point.
50 Brubaker, *Vision and Meaning*, 49.

Figure 3. Adoration of the Magi; Massacre of the Innocents; Presentation of Christ in the Temple: Paris, Bibliothèque nationale de France, ms. Gr. 510, fol. 137r. Reproduced by permission of the Bibliothèque nationale de France.

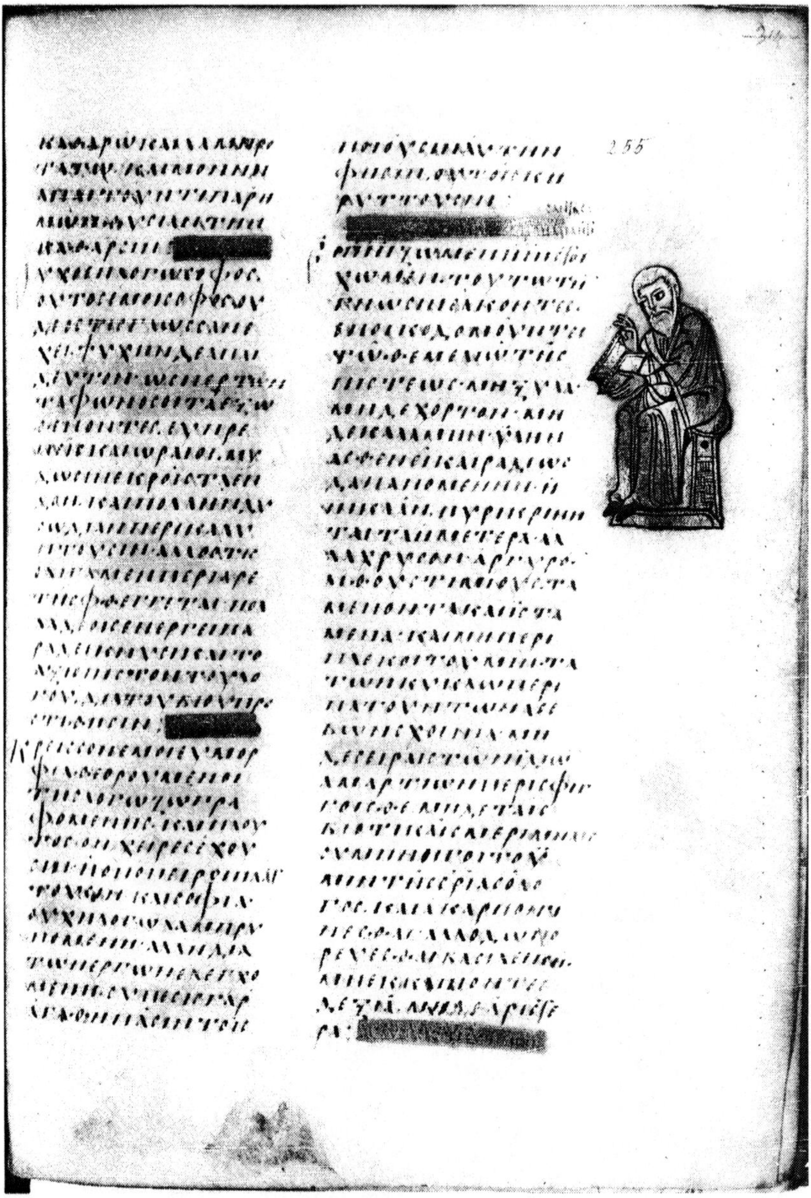

Figure 4. Gregory of Nazianzus holds his pen and opens his book to the text: Paris, Bibliothèque nationale de France, ms. Gr. 923, fol. 255r. Reproduced by permission of the Bibliothèque nationale de France.

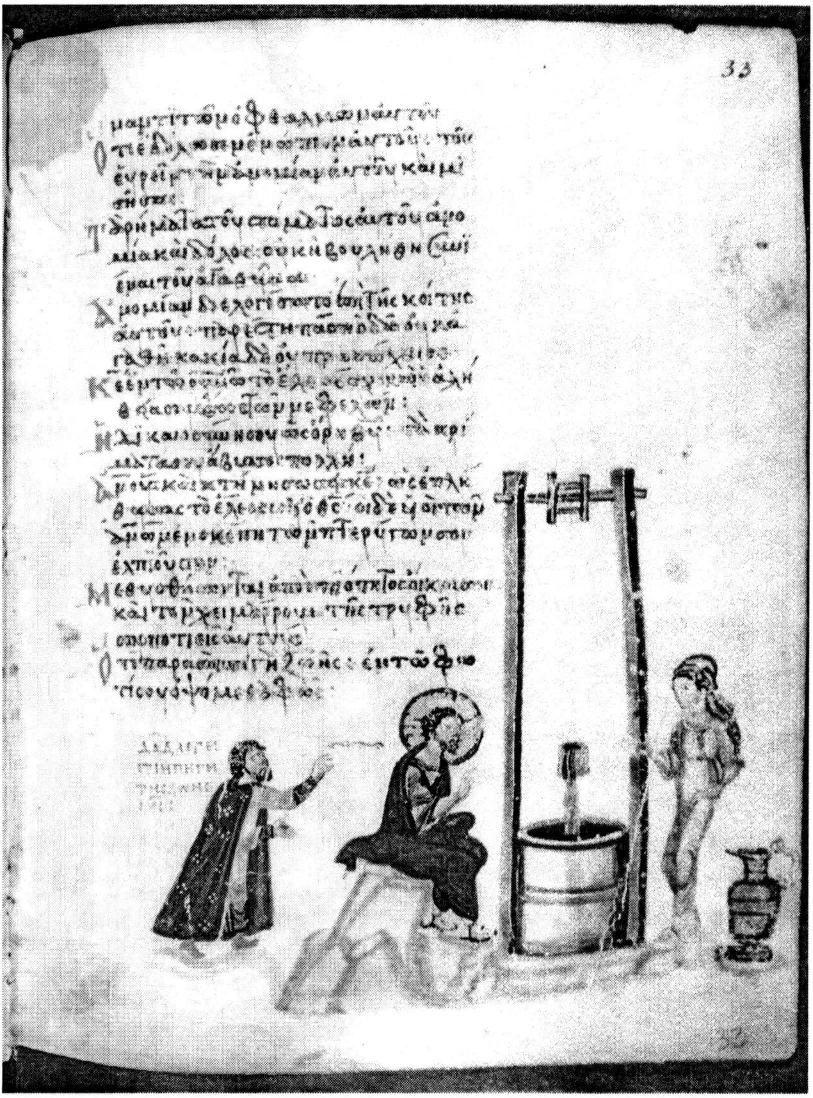

Figure 5. David, Christ, and the Samaritan woman at the well: Moscow, Historical Museum, cod. 129, fol. 33r.

second, that the audience with ready access to Byzantine manuscripts – and especially deluxe books with elaborate miniatures – was severely limited and largely confined to that literate strata of elite males who wrote most of the exegetical and commentary texts on which our modern understanding of Byzantium rests.[51]

In short, when miniatures are present, they virtually always supplement the text in some more or less important fashion. At the very least, miniatures frame the text that they accompany in a particular way, and prompt the viewer to remember and interpret the words in the manner that the image shows.[52]

Ownership and libraries

Much of the evidence concerning the ownership of books and the existence of libraries in the medieval period survives in monastic sources. Since monasteries apparently housed most of the scriptoria in both East and West, it is not surprising that their libraries flourished. Ownership of books, even by solitary monks in the Egyptian desert, is attested in hagiography and *apophthegmata* ("sayings") from as early as the fourth century, when Abba Serapion, a companion of St. Antony who became bishop of Thmuis in the Nile delta from c. 339, reprimanded a visiting monk for possessing too many books which might have been converted into money for feeding orphans and widows.[53] Serapion's criticism notwithstanding, knowledge of the Scriptures, which represented an essential skill for monks and nuns, required constant access to the holy books. The fifth-century bishop, Epiphanius of Cyprus, is recorded in the same collection of *apophthegmata* as saying that "the acquisition of Christian books is necessary for those who can use them" since "reading the scriptures is a great safeguard against sin."[54]

Cenobitic monasteries, judging by hagiographical and administrative evidence such as early foundation documents or rules (*typika*), began to establish collections of books at an early period. In the fourth century, for example, Pachomian communities in Upper Egypt possessed libraries, guarded by the *praepositus* of each house, from which monks could borrow books on a weekly

51 Ibid., 23–24.

52 Ibid., 24, 411.

53 *Apophthegmata patrum*, 416, C (trans. Ward, 227). This "saying" is also included in the eleventh-century florilegium, the *Synagoge*, of the Evergetis Monastery in Constantinople, as an example of the need for "unpossessiveness" in monastic life. See the *Evergetinos*, 33.

54 *Apophthegmata patrum*, 165, B (trans. Ward, 58).

basis.[55] Basil of Caesarea, like Pachomius, emphasized the importance of reading Scripture; in addition to forming the spiritual outlook of monks, this would enable them to provide a religious education for lay children.[56] Documents associated with the Studios Monastery in Constantinople, led by the reforming abbot Theodore between 798–99 and c. 815, provide more detailed information not only about the library, but also about its scriptorium, than any other monastic source in the middle or late Byzantine periods. According to the Studite Rule, which circulated in two versions and was extremely influential in later monasteries,[57] monks were expected on certain days of the year to assemble at a "book station" where they would choose a book and read it until the evening. Before the final office of the day, the librarian would sound the *semantron* (wooden clapper) as a signal for the books to be returned to the library.[58] A collection of "penances" (*epitimia*) attributed to Theodore himself states that monks who mistreat books, touch volumes on loan to another monk, or attempt to exchange one book for another, are banned from reading for the rest of the day. If a monk is found to have hidden a book in his cell instead of returning it to the librarian at the appointed time, he will be punished by having to stand in the refectory.[59]

The ownership of books in a monastic context was thus indisputably a *desideratum* from Late Antiquity through the medieval period, since Scripture and other instructive volumes could advance the spiritual development of monks and nuns. The occasional negative reference with regard to solitaries in the early period relates more to the issue of personal possessions than it does to the inherent nature of book ownership. In the West, Benedict of Nursia addressed this question directly when, in his influential Rule, he forbade private ownership of books, tablets, or pens,[60] but prescribed private reading on a daily basis, especially during Lent.[61] Monastic libraries also provided the necessary volumes for communal reading in the offices, especially matins, and in the refectory. The liturgical collections described earlier in this chapter offered

55 Rousseau, *Pachomius*, 81; Pachomius, *Vita Prima*, ch. 59; Pachomius, *Praecepta*, ch. 25.

56 Basil of Caesarea, *Regulae brevius tractatae*.

57 *The Rule of the Monastery of St. John Stoudios in Constantinople*; both versions cited appear in side-by-side English translation in *BMFD*.

58 *Rule of the Monastery of St. John Stoudios in Constantinople*, ch. 26, in *BMFD* 1, 108. See also Leroy, "La vie quotidienne," 47.

59 Featherstone and Holland, "Note on Penances," 259; Theodore the Studite, *Poenae monasteriales*, 1740, C. On the authenticity of this text, see Beck, *Kirche und theologische Literatur*, 494, and Leroy, "La réforme Studite," 210.

60 *Rule of St. Benedict*, ch. 33, 84–87.

61 *Rule of St. Benedict*, ch. 48, 110–13.

appropriate texts for the entire liturgical year; monastic typika frequently assigned the precise texts to be chosen in individual houses.

The largest collection of religious books in Constantinople was probably to be found in the patriarchal library, located close to the Great Church, Hagia Sophia. It is possible that this library was founded, or at least greatly refurbished and amplified, by the patriarch Sergius in the early seventh century.[62] At the time of the seventh ecumenical council of Nicaea (787), patristic texts to support the iconophile position were brought "from the stores of the glorious patriarchate."[63] The same council provides us with the interesting information that heretical books (in this case the writings of the iconoclasts) were stored in a special chest in the patriarchal library.[64] The purpose of saving banned books, albeit in a separate space from those deemed orthodox, must have been to provide the church with records of heresies which might be informative for bishops in future controversies. This conflicts, however, with the desire to burn offensive material which is attested in other canons,[65] and other religious texts.[66] The same sources suggest that, in addition to their reverence for the patristic wisdom contained in ancient books, Byzantine bishops possessed a healthy scepticism concerning the possibility of later alterations or other defacements of these sources. Those officiating at the seventh ecumenical council took special care that complete volumes rather than loose folios or extracts were produced as evidence. In the preparations for Leo V's second iconoclastic council in 815, a study group led by the future patriarch, John the Grammarian, searched for "old books everywhere, namely those that are deposited in monasteries and churches . . ."[67]

Whether or not a public library associated with a "university," or state institution of higher learning, existed throughout the Byzantine period remains unclear. The evidence, including statements that a library containing 120,000 volumes was burnt down during the reign of Basiliscus (475–76), cannot be substantiated; it is unknown, for example, exactly where this library was located and how many books it actually contained.[68] The library was probably rebuilt in 491, but, along with the university, declined from the sixth century

62 Lemerle, *Byzantine Humanism*, 107, note 81.
63 Mansi 12, 1019. Hereafter references will be to the English translation in *Select Library of Nicene and Post-Nicene Fathers* (= *NPNF*).
64 Canon 9, *NPNF*, 561. See also Lemerle, *Byzantine Humanism*, 107, note 81.
65 Canon 63, *NPNF*, 394.
66 For example, the *Life of St. Theodora*, 75 and 362, accuses iconoclasts of altering or burning books that advocated images. See also Reynolds and Wilson, *Scribes and Scholars*, 44–45.
67 Mango, "Availability of Books," 35. On problems of forgery in Byzantium, see Bardy, "Faux et fraudes littéraires."
68 Wilson, "Libraries"; Lemerle, *Byzantine Humanism*, 68–73.

onward owing to a lack of imperial support for what were viewed as essentially secular institutions. During the middle and later centuries of the Byzantine empire, private individuals, as well as monasteries, are known to have collected books. The prohibitive price of manuscripts, however, suggests that private libraries remained very small.[69] Scholars continue to puzzle over the manner in which the patriarch Photius gained access to the 280 books that he reviewed in his *Bibliotheke*, discussed earlier.[70] It is possible that he had access to a state, or imperial, library in Constantinople whose existence is simply not attested in contemporary historical sources.

The book as holy presence

In addition to transmitting texts, medieval books were sometimes viewed as holy presences in themselves; like saints, relics, or icons, they symbolically represented a meeting place of the divine and created worlds. The nature of the book of course has much to do with this: the holiest book of all is the Bible, especially the four Gospels that contain revelation about the incarnate God, Jesus Christ. Various eastern commentators on the Divine Liturgy, including Germanus, patriarch of Constantinople in the early eighth century, express this concept in symbolic terms. In his explanation of the Eucharistic synaxis, Germanus describes the first entrance, when the Gospel is brought into the nave of the church, as signifying "the coming of the Son of God and his entrance into this world."[71] As in the case of icons, the Gospel book was censed, kissed, and venerated in church.[72] It was treated with reverence since it contained the evangelists' accounts of Christ's incarnation, death, and resurrection, which together represented the culmination of God's saving dispensation for humankind.

Miracle stories involving holy books, especially the Gospels, do not appear frequently in medieval hagiography; more often cures or exorcisms occur as a result of contact with living saints or their relics after death, holy oil, or the sign of the cross. Sometimes, however, the reading of the Gospels mediates a healing miracle, as in the eleventh-century Life of St. Lazarus of Mt. Galesion, when a monk becomes possessed by demons after spending time on his own in a cave. Lazarus, who fulfilled his role as abbot of the monastery from the top

69 Wilson, "Books and Readers," and our note 26 above.
70 References in our note 37 above.
71 Germanus of Constantinople, *Commentary*, ch. 24, in trans. Meyendorff, 73, or Greek ed. Borgio, *Il commentario*.
72 See, for example, *BMFD* 1, 99.

of the pillar on which he stood for approximately forty years, recommended that the holy Gospel be read to the possessed monk. When this had been done "in accordance with the father's order, the monk was seen to be sober again and sound in mind as before."[73] Lazarus carried out similar cures on other occasions, always with respect to monks who were possessed by demons.[74] It is possible that this form of miracle reflects a belief that the Gospels, as the Word of God, conveyed, miraculously or otherwise, intellectual reason, as opposed to the irrational mania caused by demons.[75]

In addition to the power of the written words that they contain, holy books occasionally function as objects that can mediate divine power. The eleventh-century chronicler Skylitzes provides an account of the Byzantine mission to Vladimir, pagan ruler of the Rus, in the course of which a codex of the Gospels was thrown into a furnace and miraculously survived. This, says the chronicler, dumbfounded the "barbarians"; without any more hesitation they sought Christian baptism.[76] Another instance of a miraculous book involves not the Gospels, but the volume of the purported works of Dionysius the Areopagite, presented – as noted earlier – by the Byzantine emperor Michael II to the Carolingian ruler Louis the Pious in 827. We are told that the book was placed immediately in the abbey of St. Denis on the eve of the saint's feast day, 8 October 827, and that same night, the codex brought about nineteen miraculous cures in the church.[77] Quite apart from the recorded miracles, this case is particularly interesting because it demonstrates the importance of a book written in Greek as a diplomatic gift from the Byzantine to the Carolingian court in this period. But it could not, of course, have been read by many Franks, and scholars have traced the precise methods used for translating the texts contained in the manuscript (which still survives in the Bibliothèque nationale in Paris) from Greek to Latin by Carolingian translators and scribes.[78] It is perhaps significant that in both cases noted here, the object itself – the physical book rather than the text it contained – was the active agent: the words inside could not have been read by most of the audience, few if any of whom knew Greek. For those who understood the contents, books could also contain evil powers, however, reflecting the heretical or otherwise blasphemous texts that they contained. The seventh-century traveler and hagiographer John Moschus tells the

73 *Life of St. Lazaros*, 130.
74 *Life of St. Lazaros*, 134, 156–57, 161.
75 See also Greenfield, *Traditions of Belief*, 135–48, 264–65, 270–71.
76 John Skylitzes, *Synopsis historiarum*, 165–66.
77 Loenertz, "La légende Parisienne," 217–37.
78 Lemerle, *Byzantine Humanism*, 6–8; and, more generally, Wickham, "Ninth-Century Byzantium," 245–56.

story of Abba Cyriacus, a priest at the Lavra of Kalamon in Palestine. This man dreamt that the Virgin Mary, John the Baptist, and John the Evangelist came to visit him but refused to enter his cell on the grounds that it contained an enemy of theirs. Puzzled because the cell was empty except for himself, the priest eventually remembered that he had borrowed a scroll containing the writings of the heretical bishop Nestorius.[79]

As we saw above, the practice of burning heretical books, so well-established from the earliest centuries of Christianity onward, was eventually replaced in Byzantium at least partially by the practice of preserving these texts in a special cupboard in the Constantinopolitan patriarchate. It is possible that popular spiritual views concerning holy versus subversive books was eventually recognized as inhibiting the successful refutation of new heretical threats. In any case, it is clear that stories such as these reveal more about contemporary attitudes toward the written word and the volumes that contain it than they do about real events. Manuscripts or scrolls, each of which represents a unique exemplar, acted as precious objects, transmitters of divine revelation to posterity, talismans against evil demons, and much more. The ability of a book to stand in the place of a person, as in the story of Moschus's priest Kyriakos, reflects the significance that is attached to the written word in early medieval society.

Literacy and orality

Literacy was confined to a small elite in both East and West in the early Middle Ages. Probably more people, especially monks and clerics, could read in the Byzantine Empire, but most of these would have been capable only of reading the Scriptures or simple, "low-style" narratives.[80] From Pachomius onward, monastic leaders emphasized the importance of reading the Bible, especially the psalter and the New Testament. Most monasteries maintained schools that taught lay children and novices, usually separately, an elementary course of letters and Scripture reading.[81] Monks were expected to learn the psalter by

79 John Moschus, *Pratum spirituale*, ch. 46, in trans. Wortley, 37–38.

80 Kazhdan, "Literacy."

81 See Magdalino, *Constantinople médiévale*, 37–40, 48. Moffatt concludes, on the basis of contemporary saints' lives, that at least during the period of iconoclasm, elementary education took place not only in domestic settings but also in schools. However, the information provided in hagiography about these schools is vague. See her "Schooling," 90. The eleventh-century *Typikon* of Gregory Pakourianos, for the Monastery of the Mother of God in Bačkovo, mentions a school at the dependency of St. Nicholas where an old priest trained six boys intended for the priesthood in the reading of Scripture. See *BMFD* 2, 550–51.

heart, for recitation both in solitude and in communal worship. The fourth-century bishop of Cyprus, Epiphanius, who lived for part of his life as a monk in Palestine, remarked that "the true monk should have prayer and psalmody continually in his heart."[82] This view is echoed in monastic writings from Ireland to Egypt from Late Antiquity onward.

That levels of literacy, in the narrowest sense of the word, were low even among the higher clergy in the early Byzantine period, however, is indicated by scattered laws and canons of the ecumenical councils. Justinian I found it necessary to legislate against illiterate monks or clerics becoming bishops in the middle of the sixth century.[83] The second canon of the seventh ecumenical council (787) decrees that all bishops should know the psalter by heart and, further, that they should "read diligently, and not merely now and then, the sacred canons, the holy gospel, and the book of the divine apostle [Paul], and all other divine scripture."[84] The symbolic importance of being able to access the holy written word is clear from hagiography, where saints are usually either taught (often by their mothers) to read at an early age or miraculously find themselves able to recite sections of the Bible, especially the psalms, without the benefit of education.[85] It has been rather controversially argued, with respect to the West before the so-called revival of learning in the eleventh and twelfth centuries, that societies that communicate primarily by oral methods develop different attitudes toward books and the written word than do predominantly literate ones.[86] Though the strict divide between written and oral culture is overstated – and it is perhaps more useful to speculate about hierarchies of knowledge – the point that technologies of literacy shape culture informs our understanding of how books containing holy texts, as we saw above, acquired importance as physical links between contemporary users and the divine truth that they contained.

When assessing levels of literacy in the early Middle Ages, it is important to remember that, even if the majority of people were unable to read, they were accustomed to listening to texts being read aloud and to public speeches or sermons. It is likely that regular churchgoers in the Byzantine Empire would therefore have understood the language of the Old and New Testaments in Greek, even though this was already somewhat removed from the colloquial

82 *Apophthegmata patrum*, 164, C (trans. Ward, 57).
83 Beck, *Ideen und Realitäten in Byzanz*, ch. 3, 72.
84 Canon 2, *NPNF*, 556.
85 Patlagean, "Ancienne hagiographie," 109–10. Parenthetically, this topos indicates that female literacy was not unthinkable in the Byzantine world, and nor was home schooling.
86 Clanchy, *From Memory to Written Record*.

language of late antique or medieval society. Low-style hagiography, apocryphal texts, exegetical homilies, and collections of miracle stories would also have been easily comprehensible since their literary style was similar to the *koine* of the Scriptures.[87] It has been much debated, however, whether high-style orations, such as the festal sermons delivered in the middle Byzantine period mainly in vigils, would have been comprehensible to any but a few, educated members of the congregation.[88] In fact, on closer study it is apparent that even the most complicated and archaizing sermons contain elements that would aid audience comprehension, including repetition, quotation of Scripture, devices such as anaphora, rhetorical questions, and exclamation.[89] Rhythm, often strengthened by parallelism and antithesis, formulaic phrases, repetition, and additive clauses also reflect the origin of texts in oral tradition.[90] In the medieval period, this tradition did not simply evolve out of informal story telling; it was also shaped by the rules of late antique rhetoric or the art of public speaking.

The progression from a spoken, informal text to a more literary one may be illustrated again by the example of the liturgical homily.[91] We know that from a very early date most Christian preachers delivered their exegetical or panegyrical sermons extempore. Indeed, given the conventions of late antique rhetoric, it is likely that they would have been ridiculed or even expelled from the church if they had been seen to employ notes or a prepared text when preaching. Contemporaries recorded that the homilies of preachers such as Origen (c. 185–c. 254), John Chrysostom (c. 345–407), and others were recorded by stenographers in the audience. The survival of both edited and unedited versions of their homilies suggests that the preachers, or perhaps their assistants, prepared these texts later for publication.[92] Even as late as the ninth century in Constantinople, the patriarch Tarasius's sermons were recorded in this way, although similar evidence is lacking for his contemporaries.[93]

While oral elements clearly survive in sermons, as we noted above, the life of these texts after their first delivery in church becomes more literary

87 On the various levels of style in Byzantine texts, see I. Ševčenko, "Levels of Style."

88 Maguire, *Art and Eloquence*, 6.

89 Cunningham, "Preaching and Community," 45–47.

90 Ong, *Orality and Literacy*, 34–41.

91 A good introduction to the development of the Byzantine homily between the fourth and tenth centuries may be found in Antonopoulou, *Homilies of Emperor Leo VI*, 95–115.

92 Goodall, *Homilies of St. John Chrysostom*, 65–73.

93 See Mango, *Homilies of Photius*, 8.

and liturgical. Most high-style sermons appear to have been carefully edited and polished; festal homilies and encomia especially follow the conventions of each genre, employ unusual vocabulary, and, generally speaking, display their authors' erudition to full advantage. Copied into mixed collections of readings arranged around the liturgical year, they appear to have been intended either for private, devotional study or for liturgical reading in the monastic offices, especially *orthros* (matins).[94] The versions of these texts, which survive in numerous manuscripts scattered through western and Middle Eastern libraries, reveal all of the stages of textual development, from the spoken, sometimes extempore, oration to the devotional or liturgical reading, edited thoroughly but without complete eradication of the oral roots of the text.

One other aspect of the Byzantine approach to texts and books should be mentioned here. In this outwardly unified, orthodox society, tremendous efforts were made to harmonize texts, from the canonical Scriptures to theological treatises or sermons. One way of demonstrating the continuity of divine revelation through all of these genres was to create florilegia or collections of writings, mentioned earlier in connection with church councils. It is likely that instruction in schools or institutions of higher learning was largely carried out by means of such digests. Sermons or treatises in some cases resemble florilegia more than original compositions as they present a series of carefully selected passages from earlier authors in order to prove a point. In such a cultural milieu, it is not surprising that we find saints' lives occasionally borrowing large sections of earlier works. Plagiarism was not a crime: it was a sign of homage and reverence toward an earlier author. Another aspect of medieval writing which deserves much closer study is intertextuality, that is, the weaving together of a text out of words, citations, and even long quotations from other sources, especially Scripture.[95] This reflects not only clerics' recollection of whole sections of the Bible; it also represents a deliberate theological and literary aim, that of demonstrating the unity of divine revelation from the moment of creation to the present day.

The writing of hagiography, or the lives of saints, was much more than a simple literary endeavor in the early Christian and Byzantine periods.[96] Such composition in fact represented an act of worship, or an ascetic practice, on the part of the writer. The relationship between divine revelation and the written word represented one more way in which the gulf between a

94 For descriptions of such collections, see Ehrhard, *Überlieferung und Bestand*.

95 Young, *Biblical Exegesis*, 87–89, 103, 109, 130, 133, 235, 254.

96 Krueger, *Writing and Holiness*.

transcendent God and his creation was bridged. The author was conscious of his (or, rarely, her) role not only as a tool, but also as an interpreter, of divine truth. This idea is expressed symbolically in such stories as that in which the sixth-century hymnographer, Romanus the Melodist, was instructed by the Virgin Mary in a vision to swallow a sacred scroll: after this, he was able to compose his *kontakia*.[97] Romanus used imagery in some of his hymns that vividly expounded the relationship between Christ's incarnation and the writing of a text.[98] Both acts symbolized the manifestation of divinity in creation; whereas texts were inevitably bound by the limitations of human language and earthly metaphors, they might also be infused with divine inspiration from God.

It is clear that books were much more than simple purveyors of the written word in the medieval period. The relationship between divine truth, human interpretation, and textual and visual transmission was not static in our period; there is not space here to explore possible changes in this dynamic, but it is likely that it was being reassessed, along with saints, relics, and icons, in the period of iconoclasm. John of Damascus argued in his orations in defense of images in the early eighth century that books served as reminders of divine things, but that they also reflected the holiness that they recorded:

> Since [Christ] is no longer present, we hear his words read from books; and by hearing, our souls are sanctified and filled with blessing, and so we worship, honouring the books from which we hear his words.[99]

Modern concepts of authorship clearly have no place in the medieval understanding of literary composition. As we have already mentioned, the borrowing of scriptural, patristic, or secular passages was not viewed as plagiarism; instead, such citations lent authority to a text. We must imagine a society in which, as John reminds us elsewhere in the same treatise, oral tradition jostles and overlaps with the written word in peoples' minds.[100] Books had

97 The story is told in two eleventh-century synaxaria, or liturgical calendars: that of Constantinople, published in Delehaye, *Propylaeum*, 97, and in Basil II's *Menologion*, *PG* 117, 81, B–C.

98 Krueger, *Writing and Holiness*, esp. 159–88.

99 John of Damascus, *On the Divine Images*, in Kotter, *Die Schriften* 3, 123 (trans. Anderson, 72).

100 "The tradition of the Church is not only passed on in written documents, but has also been given in an unwritten form . . ." John of Damascus, *On the Divine Images*, I.23, see Kotter, *Die Schriften* 3, 111 (trans. Anderson, 31); cf. Basil of Caesarea, *De Spiritu sancto*, 27.66, in Pruche, *Basile de Cesarée*, 478.15–480.9.

great authority, but divine revelation could be channeled through a variety of media. Discerning audiences learned to recognize the authentic, or orthodox, message by means of remembered scriptural texts, doctrinal formulations, and canons of the church.

Books that survive and books as luxury objects

While texts, and hence manuscripts, in themselves had very significant roles in Byzantium, there was a distinct hierarchy of books. This is, however, only partly reflected in surviving examples, where basic service texts and luxury manuscripts are the two dominant categories. The first group is not surprising: books without special scribal attention that were important to the Byzantines in their daily routine were, one may assume, the most commonly produced. That deluxe tomes survive in such numbers might suggest that the cultural capital of the well-presented volume was especially important in the Byzantine world. It is more likely, however, that luxury books survive because they were kept in treasuries of some sort and hence were available to be collected by bibliophiles after the fall of the empire in the fifteenth century. The survival rate of a significant proportion of deluxe books was also raised because they were less often consulted: they were valuable, and hence sequestered, thus avoiding the wear and tear of daily use that eventually leads to replacement.

The main characteristics of luxury books are size (dimensions and, correspondingly, heft – major books like the Vienna Dioscourides and the Paris Gregory can weigh up to fourteen pounds), archaizing elements (for example, rolls when codices had become dominant, majuscule when minuscule ruled, parchment after paper appeared), and the quality of ornament, including miniatures, applied. Pages dyed with rare colors (purple from murex, blue from lapis lazuli); scripts written in expensive inks (gold and silver); elaborate book covers, precious bindings, and painted or gilded exterior margins – all were visible indicators of wealth and status that were presumably recognized as both due acknowledgment of the sacrality of content and of the patron's financial ability to be able to make that acknowledgment concrete/material.

When books or scrolls are represented in the Byzantine world, however, they rarely show these deluxe attributes. Prophets nearly always carry simple, unadorned scrolls in neutral tones; and books shown open rarely picture decoration on the page displayed. Representations of text, in other words, follow the general tendency to privilege word over decoration that we have already observed in the format of the manuscript page itself. It is only representations of closed books that display the attributes of luxury books, normally by depicting a gold and jewelled cover.[101] Even here, however, pictures of books present plain and undecorated casings (fig. 4) as often as they do elaborate ones.

Conclusion

Books played a critical role in orthodox Christianity, and were clearly desirable objects for those who could read. Yet they were far from commonplace: even though service books may have been mass-produced, they were never, it seems, readily available;[102] and most manuscripts seem to have been made to commission, not for random sale. The choices this entailed would seem to make manuscripts a good focus for a study of Byzantine self-representation. On one level, this has proven at least partially successful, particularly in studies of individual manuscripts or groups of manuscripts, as studies of the ninth-century marginal psalters, the twelfth-century Kokkinobaphos manuscripts, and the late thirteenth-century "Palaiologina" group have shown.[103] But any attempt to reconstruct the Byzantine world through its self-representation in and through books has two main problems, both of which we have already noted. First, any understanding of the Byzantine world through books can never be representative, because the books we have left are not. And, secondly, books were seen, used, owned, commented upon, represented, and commissioned by only a very small and relatively elite segment of the Greek-speaking world. This, however, has certain advantages, for the same group also produced most of our written evidence about the Byzantine world, so that text and image can be interpreted together to form a richly nuanced picture of the thought-world of at least one demographic. What is particularly interesting about a comparative approach to written and visual communication is that the messages considered appropriate to each medium were often different, so that miniatures supplement the text not only by supplying details that the

101 E.g., at San Vitale, on which see Mathews, *Early Churches*, 146–47, and, for other examples of gold and jeweled Gospel books, see the *Menologion* of Basil II (ibid., fig. 90) or the miniature of Pentecost in the Paris Gregory (Brubaker, *Vision and Meaning*, fig. 30).

102 Mango, "Availability of Books," 29–45.

103 Corrigan, *Visual Polemics*; Linardou, "Couch of Solomon," and references in note 23 above.

Byzantines never committed to parchment, and not only by augmenting the written examples with visual ones, but also by carrying different types of messages altogether.[104] Beyond providing us with the raw data of orthodoxy, the Christian book provides microcosmic insight into the structure of communication in the Byzantine world.[105]

104 See Brubaker, "Pictures Are Good."

105 Leslie Brubaker would like to express gratitude to the staffs at the Historical Museum and Conservation Laboratories in Moscow for access to the Khludov Psalter, and to the Bibliothèque nationale de France for access to the *Sacra Parallela* and Paris Gregory.

28

Saints and their cults

JULIA M. H. SMITH

In 628, the Persians executed a Christian monk at Kirkuk. The death of Anastasius was a minor episode in decades of conflict between the Byzantine and Sasanian empires, but his was no ordinary fate.[1] A Persian soldier who converted from Zoroastrianism to Christianity and became a monk near Jerusalem, Anastasius had strengthened his new identity by contemplating wall-paintings of early Christian martyrs, and then set out to seek death at the hands of his former comrades. Three years after his decapitation, his fellow monks managed to retrieve his head, and as they carried it back to their Palestinian monastery, it started working miracles. Anastasius had become a potent symbol of Christian triumph in desperate times, and when his monastic community fled to Rome after the fall of Jerusalem to the Arabs in 638, they took his head with them. There, accounts of his martyrdom and miracles were soon rendered from Greek into Latin. Taken to England in the later seventh century, the stories of Anastasius took new form in Old English by the late ninth century, in testimony to his popularity throughout early medieval Christendom.[2]

"My heart trembles and my insides are loosened whenever I remember [the] miracles which our Lord Jesus Christ accomplished through his blessed martyr Anastasius," announced the cleric who recorded a dramatic event which had occurred in Rome in 713. It concerned a young woman confined to a nunnery, whom the devil was believed to have possessed at the instigation of a jilted suitor. Her father, Theopentus, a Syrian bishop from Osrhoene, had turned for help to the renowned saint from his eastern homeland and had taken his daughter into a church on whose altar the martyr's head lay. One of his teeth was hung around her neck but failed to dislodge the demon, and for a month she flailed around with the devil inside her yelling abuse at Christ, his saints, and the Christian clergy. Finally, when Theopentus and the

1 See Brown in this volume.

2 Franklin, *Latin Dossier*; Flusin, *Saint Anastase*; *Das altenglische Martyrologium* 2, 24; Biggs et al., *Sources*, 77–79.

entire monastic congregation were gathered in penitential prayer, the martyr made his presence felt. A candle in front of his relics had blown out and miraculously rekindled: at this signal, the liturgical intercession intensified. Demonic howling alternated with monastic chanting as the girl writhed and hurled herself in the air until the devil acknowledged that Anastasius had defeated him, and departed. Then, "At the third hour of the night, the girl bent her knees before the icon of the Lord Jesus Christ for almost half an hour; and she got up with her mind and body cured, and stood before the holy altar, and received the body and blood of our Lord Jesus Christ and she was healed from that hour."[3]

This tale of cosmic drama introduces us to the deeds and reputations of holy personalities in the early Middle Ages. By c. 600 Christian notions of holiness already had a long history.[4] By that date, the primary, but never unique, use of the terms *hagios* (Greek) and *sanctus* (Latin) was to designate those individuals whom Christians deemed to partake, in some way, of the divinity and whose status commonly received liturgical recognition – saints. This chapter pursues that evolution through to c. 1100. In situating saints and their cults at the intersection of the temporal past and the eschatological future, it demonstrates their exquisite sensitivity to the ever-shifting political and cultural parameters of the early medieval present. It also emphasizes their capacity to provide direct experience of the holy amid the cares of the world for believers of any class, age, or gender. By drawing attention to ways in which saints and their cults supplemented the sacramental and priestly functions of ecclesiastical institutions, it explains saintly thaumaturgy (miracle-working) as the lightning conductor of divine energy between the heavenly and the mundane. After some contextualizing remarks, the analysis starts with living holy persons; then a steadily lengthening chronological focus takes us to the deceased, then to the very distant time of Christian origins and, finally, to Jerusalem, the place where the story began.

Background

Few medieval theologians paused to elaborate on saints and their cults. Their lack of sustained reflection signals not dismissal but an almost unanimous agreement that they were a normal part of Christian practice. Since about

3 "The Roman Miracle," in Franklin, *Latin Dossier*, 44–52, 347–61, quotations at 51–52.

4 Delehaye, *Sanctus*, and for places, Iogna-Prat in this volume.

1965, saints – living holy men and women as well as cults of the deceased – have attracted much attention from scholars of medieval history, art, literature, and liturgy alike. Other disciplines have contributed, too, including epigraphy, onomastics, and numismatics.[5] The reader must approach the huge bibliography with two cautions in mind. First, attention should not be confined to narrative texts of the lives and deeds (lifetime and posthumous) of saints, for they give a distorted impression of the place of saints in early medieval Christianity.[6] On the one hand, they ignore the hundreds, indeed thousands, of saints never commemorated by anything more than very brief liturgical notices. Most saints were never the subject of narrative commemoration, relic cults, or any non-liturgical expressions of devotion.[7] On the other hand, literary commemoration did not guarantee liturgical cult, let alone devotional popularity. Second, it is misplaced to think in terms of the *cult* of saints. Cults took plural forms, even for an individual saint: a falsely homogenized, static account of this multifaceted phenomenon is unhelpful. This chapter outlines some of these varieties.

Long before 600, notions, locations, and expressions of Christian sainthood had already gelled into the forms which were to remain normative until the thirteenth century. In the century or so following the Peace of the Church (following Constantine's Edict of Milan in 313), Christian communities had gradually and painfully come to terms with the shift from persecuted minority to dominant majority. In a world where martyrdom in the arena was no longer the ultimate expression of Christian identity, additional categories for the holy few had emerged. Sanctity had became closely associated with asceticism and the subjugation of torments and demons (both internalized and exterior), and occasionally also with success in converting pagans to Christianity (missionaries) or the formulation of doctrine (the so-called "fathers" of the church). Reflecting this decisive shift in the dominant register of holiness, most saints were henceforth hermits, monks, or monastic founders, for they embodied the religion's refashioned aspirations and performed them most completely during their own lives. Pressing issues of origins, identities, and links to the past had also been rethought and renegotiated. New forms of cohesion had developed – ones that knitted local communities together but nevertheless

5 Aigrain, *L'hagiographie*, for an overview.

6 Surveyed by Philippart, *Hagiographies*; Ehrhard, *Überlieferung und Bestand*.

7 The relics of approximately 12.5 per cent of Orthodox saints were the object of cults, see Cotsonis, "Contribution of Byzantine Lead Seals," 392. The western proportion would be similarly low.

gave them a place in what had already become an imperial history of salvation. Whether miracles had any role in this had been controversial. Saints' cults had emerged as not only crucial markers of identity and legitimacy but also as triggers for conflict about manifestations of the holy in a rapidly changing world.[8]

By c. 600, these disputes had, for the time being, lost some of their passion – although Pope Gregory I, the Great (590–604), remained ambivalent about the place of miracles in his own times.[9] Wherever the Christian religion had taken hold, expressions of holiness shared common characteristics, modulated by local particularities. As manifested in humans, living or dead, it signaled those whom, it was agreed, enjoyed exceptional closeness to Christ. There was a consensus that such persons were conduits between the heavenly and the mundane in two principal ways. They acted as advocates in the heavenly court where they interceded for their clients. By performing miracles, they brought relief from the grievous afflictions which beset suffering individuals (the cure of illness, disfigurement, or deformity; release from captivity, possession, childlessness, and the like) or entire communities (overcoming fire, famine, flood, and other disasters). Secondly, they voiced the words of the Christians' God with prophetic foresight or spiritual insight, speaking face to face or through dreams and visions. Their utterances predicted momentous future events, cautioned the powerful or negligent with fearless frankness, and discerned the hidden truths of a troubled conscience, a concealed crime, or an unacknowledged saint.

The living had achieved this closeness through the hard discipline of asceticism and a literal-minded emulation of a Christ-like life. Theirs was the white martyrdom of living renunciation, rather than the red martyrdom of gruesome torture and death.[10] The deceased, whether or not martyrs, were those whose souls had immediately joined Christ in paradise, yet their graves (if known) nevertheless held their presence, too, a hotspot of holiness that was often mediatized through tangible objects – bones, locks of hair, threads of fabric, personal possessions – and liquids or quasi-liquids (oil, washing water, dust) – that derived from the shrine, had been in contact with the holy body, or had even oozed out of it, like blood or *myron* (an aromatic unguent characteristic of Byzantine saints). Commonly, those renowned in their own lifetime died with a blaze of publicity that marked the immediate commencement of

8 Markus, *End of Ancient Christianity*, 70–71, 92–95, 142–49; Grig, *Making Martyrs*; Van Uytfanghe, "La controverse."

9 Markus, *Gregory the Great*, 51–67; McCready, *Signs of Sanctity*.

10 Stancliffe, "Red, White and Blue."

posthumous veneration. Throughout our period, however, such high-profile, publicly sponsored cults of the dead, replete with literary and liturgical documentation, vied with informal devotions. These are only recalled for us now in the occasional inscription, place name, or graffito, constituting in some places a palimpsest of an early culture of intensely local affiliations later overwritten by politically charged national cults, and, elsewhere, the remnants of a Christianity that subsequently collapsed.[11] And so powerful was the allure of saintly intercession that not only was burial *ad sanctos* – as near as possible to the holy shrine – a much sought-after privilege, but also individual saints were easily replicated in multiple places, whether by moving body parts, instituting liturgical feast days, or copying texts.

In brief, by c. 600 there was an inherited repertoire of manifestations of "personalized" holiness, with associated textual discourses and rituals to enhance – or constrain – it. Despite the impact of changing circumstances, that repertoire remained a powerful script for enacting and representing sainthood throughout the five centuries under discussion here.

Holy men

Late Antiquity was the age of the living holy man.[12] From Ireland and Wales to Syria and Persia in c. 600, the holy man's charismatic presence, manifested in miracle-working, frank speaking, and notable proficiency in defusing community tensions, was widely discussed, written about, and critically debated.[13] His career, however, continued to flourish beyond the end of antiquity, and in c. 1100 we will find him alive and well in contexts that no late antique Christian could have envisaged. His evolution had three principal aspects. In the first place, early medieval norms and practices of Christian living were as strongly gendered as ancient ones, and the holy man was no exception. Secondly, the inherited repertoire of textual exempla remained cogent. Thirdly, the weight of those ancient precedents was often in acute tension with current political and institutional imperatives.

The gendered dimension requires initial, brief mention. In Late Antiquity, holy women had been few in number and rarely attracted much biographical interest. Some were ornaments of aristocratic familial virtue; others humble

11 Thacker and Sharpe, *Local Saints and Local Churches*; Papaconstantinou, *Le culte des saints*.
12 The work of Brown is seminal: "Rise and Function"; "Saint as Exemplar"; *Authority and the Sacred*, 55–78; "Rise and Function, 1971–1997"; "Holy Men." Main critiques: Elm, "Introduction"; Cameron, "Defining the Holy Man"; Rousseau, "Ascetics as Mediators."
13 Rapp, "Hagiography and Monastic Literature."

intercessors for local communities. A handful sought to emulate the rigors of desert asceticism or to repent a life of prostitution: they changed their gender by cross-dressing, enabling them to live undetected in Egyptian or Syrian monasteries, miracle enough to prove their holiness.[14] These ambiguous characters did excite attention, and the rollicking narratives of their achievements spread from Greek and Syriac into Latin, Arabic, Armenian, Slavic, and Old English. Nevertheless, despite their textual popularity, these gender-defying women served more as a stimulus to meditation and imagination rather than as realistic models for early medieval feminine piety.[15] In contrast to the widespread posthumous renown of these "women disguised as monks," very few holy women after c. 600 were exemplary enough to merit textual representation. Between c. 600 and c. 1100, scarcely 10 per cent of Greek saints' lives had female subjects, although in the Latin West, the figure is significantly greater, approximately 15 per cent.[16] Despite the rhetorical commonplace that "God the prize-giver generously grants the rewards and victory crowns to both sexes equally," women remained a small minority of those deemed to manifest holiness.[17]

There were, nevertheless, significant developments which confirmed that the re-gendered female asceticism of Late Antiquity was firmly confined to the written page. In Byzantium, by the ninth and tenth centuries, the tiny number of holy women comprised either nuns in cenobitic communities, devout married laywomen, or widows living out their days in quiet piety and good works in or near Constantinople – women whose domestic humility was recognized as holiness. Elsewhere, notably in Wales, Brittany, and Italy (both Latin- and Greek-speaking parts) there was an absence of recorded holy women of any sort – confirmation, if any be needed, of the gendered nature of holiness. In other parts of the Latin West, holy women were almost always to be found in the convent not the home, clustering in the Frankish lands and Germany, Anglo-Saxon England, and Ireland. They were most commonly dedicated virgins of aristocratic or royal birth, women whose careers as abbesses of their families' monastic foundations ensured a context that was dynastic without being domestic.[18]

14 Patlagean, "L'histoire"; Harvey, "Women."

15 For example, Mary of Egypt and Pelagia of Antioch. See Coon, *Sacred Fictions*, 71–94; Petitmengin, *Pélagie la pénitente*; Poppe and Ross, *Legend of Mary the Egyptian*.

16 Percentages calculated from Nesbitt, "Geographical and Chronological Guide," and Schulenberg, "Sexism." The percentages conceal wide chronological fluctuations.

17 *Life of St. Mary the Younger*, 254.

18 Heene, "Female Saints"; Wittern, *Frauen*; Smith, "Problem"; Helvétius, "*Virgo et virago*"; Stafford, "Queens, Nunneries and Reforming Churchmen"; Yorke, '"Carriers of the Truth"'.

The only deviation from this predominant western pattern came from the tenth century onward, at the most elevated social level. When pressed into assisting the dynastic stability of insecure rulers, female holiness necessarily included motherhood as well as matrimony. But fecundity alone did not make Matilda (d. 968), Adalheid (d. 999), or Margaret of Scotland (d. 1093) into holy women. Each coupled motherhood with personal piety modeled on that of the episcopal ideal of the era – assiduous personal devotions, generous almsgiving, church foundations, intercession for mercy, and the release of prisoners.[19]

If holy women were more commonly a literary construct derived from an earlier age than a social reality, one reason was the absence of authoritative and practicable role models inherited from the heroic era of ascetic origins. Another was women's subordinated position in the early medieval gender order. It was quite otherwise with early medieval holy men. Inasmuch as biographies of the holy few upheld norms and stimulated aspirations, early medieval masculine holiness remained deeply indebted to inherited ideals of closeness to God achieved through individual ascetic endeavor.[20] And it remained intimately associated – sometimes in apposition, sometimes in opposition – with dominant political formations and ideologies of power.

The enduring influence of the hagiographical "classics" of Late Antiquity was not confined to quotations from works such as Athanasius's *Life of Antony* (d. 356), Sulpicius Severus's *Life of Martin*, monk-bishop of Tours (d. 397), Gregory the Great's account of Benedict of Nursia (founder of the monastery at Monte Cassino, d. c. 480), or Cyril of Scythopolis's *Life* of the great Palestinian ascetic Sabas (d. 532), much cited though they were. The use that monks and hermits made of such texts as guides to their own search for the Christian life was especially notable. In 774, the Visigothic nobleman Witiza (d. 821) underwent a dramatic religious conversion at Charlemagne's court and, having experimented with various modes of ascetic life, settled on the Rule of Benedict as his preferred option. In changing his own name to Benedict, he not only embraced the spirit of Benedictine monasticism, he assimilated himself into the role of its founding father. Two centuries later, the monks of Monte Cassino gave shelter to the renowned, if temperamental, Greek hermit Nilus of Rossano (c. 941–1004), whom Saracen raids on the southernmost, Byzantine, provinces of Italy had driven northwards. Lacking a firmly established local monastic tradition in his native Calabria, Nilus had learned his asceticism largely from books, applying what he read to his own situation

19 Corbet, *Les saints ottoniens*; Huneycutt, "Idea"; Wall, "Queen Margaret."

20 See Helvétius and Kaplan in this volume on inherited norms of the ascetic life; Flusin, "L'hagiographie monastique"; Poulin, *L'idéal de sainteté*.

with a literalness that smacks of fundamentalism. And the monks of Monte Cassino were quick to frame their guest within familiar narratives of past holy men and to assimilate him into their own Benedictine tradition: "they seemed to hear and see the great Antony come from Alexandria, or better, the great Benedict, their holy law-giver and master, risen from the dead."[21]

Not only his long years in a hermitage made Nilus remarkable; his biographer expressed wonderment at the many miracles he worked. Although the holy men of Late Antiquity had commonly undertaken dramatic acts of thaumaturgy – healings, exorcisms, and more – by the turn of the millennium, holy men (western or eastern) seldom worked miracles on that grand scale. In addition to inherited doubts about the propriety of miracles, there remained alternative cosmologies with their own compelling logic, especially in Byzantium.[22] The twin traumas of the Muslim conquest of large parts of the Byzantine Empire and the iconoclast disputes had posed in unavoidably acute form the question of what manifestations of holiness might be theologically and politically permissible. As Byzantine Christianity was gradually formed anew in the ninth and tenth centuries, it took on profoundly different characteristics, disrupting any easy continuity with the pre-iconoclast past but presenting an opportunity for persecuted iconophiles to be refashioned as saints, beacons of continuity in an age of change. The ascetic life was also deeply affected, becoming conditioned by greater institutional regulation and an emphasis on interiorized spiritual direction. The ability to perform miracles – or the readiness to ascribe them to others – now waned.[23] In this environment, holy men were far less likely than earlier to ignore or disrupt other bearers of power and authority (bishops, secular rulers); they turned as readily into counselors as critics and were as likely to be the organizers of monastic communities as lone hermits or pillar-dwelling stylites. By the end of the tenth century, miracle-working, Byzantine holy men were as often fictional constructs as flesh-and-blood realities; by the twelfth century, they had become figures of derision.[24]

The trajectory of the living Latin miracle worker differed. There are several, overlapping reasons for this. In the first place, whereas the distinction between asceticism and high ecclesiastical office had been largely maintained

21 *Vita S. Nili*, ch. 73, 124–25; Howe, "Neilos"; Déroche, "L'obsession."

22 Dagron, "L'ombre d'un doute."

23 Auzépy, "L'évolution"; Patlagean, "Sainteté et pouvoir"; Kazhdan, "Hermitic, Coenobitic, and Secular Ideals."

24 Magdalino, "'What We Have Heard'" and "Byzantine Holy Man."

in the East, it became blurred in the West.[25] And, as Christianity gradually extended far beyond the former Roman provinces, into Germanic, Celtic, and Slavic regions, the miracle-working monk often made a strong impression as a missionary bishop, since thaumaturgy was a useful supplement to preaching.[26] Whereas the Byzantine holy man stood in counterpoint to the local bishop, the western bishop often was the local holy man. In view of the huge weight of authority vested in bishops in the mosaic of "micro-Christendoms" which constituted early medieval western Christianity, other holy men became marginalized.[27] Furthermore, with the active assistance of the priestly caste, the Carolingian dynasty asserted itself as the primary channel through which divine grace flowed to the Frankish people. Carolingian kings and their bishops together built an empire which spanned the entirety of continental Latin Christianity; together they appropriated all forms of holiness so thoroughly that they stifled the holy man. His charisma was antithetical to theocratic kingship. Carolingian asceticism remained firmly constrained by state-sponsored monasticism, never able to manifest itself in miracle working or prophecy.[28]

By the late tenth century, the political and religious landscape of western Europe had changed so dramatically that the holy man was able to stage a comeback. We find him in the mountainous hinterland of the western Mediterranean, where many besides Nilus of Rossano were finding direct inspiration for an eremitic life in the lives of sixth-century holy men and ignoring the grand Benedictine tradition as reinvented in the ninth century. The high valleys of the southern Pyrenees and the Apennines were also where imperial rule had crumbled into a mosaic of small, competing princedoms whose rulers were unable to lay effective claim to the theocratic ideologies which had supported the Carolingian emperors and their Ottonian successors. To counter their deficit of sacrality, these princes made allies of their local holy men, presenting themselves as patrons and supporters. Dominic of Silos (d. 1073) was one such. After a spell as a hermit in the mountains of the Rioja, he became the reforming abbot of San Millán de la Cogolla, until he fell out with Garcia, king of Navarre. Fleeing into exile, he was courted by Ferdinand I of Castile, who in 1041 gave him the derelict monastery of Silos to restore, right on the highly

25 See Helvétius and Kaplan in this volume.
26 See Abrams, Charles-Edwards, and Shepard in this volume; also Wood, *Missionary Life*.
27 Brown, *Rise of Western Christendom*, 355–79.
28 Fouracre, "Origins."

insecure Christian–Muslim frontier.[29] As abbot, Dominic modeled himself on Martin, Antony, and Benedict, working miracles to protect his monastery's property or to cure the local folk, to great renown.[30]

The western, miracle-working holy man had been reinvented under the aegis of lay patronage. By the early twelfth century, the scope of his activities had been further extended and often smacked of firm lordship: we find him founding a new monastic order, becoming a bishop or, in the person of Bernard of Clairvaux (d. 1153), working numerous miracles as a means of countering heretics and preaching a crusade. In Bernard, thaumaturgical prowess reached a new apogee of institutional expression.[31]

It is mistaken, because it is ahistorical, to present the history of medieval Christianity in terms of a supposed antithesis between charisma and authority. Although the holy man could, and often did, recalibrate political relationships, his very presence constituted a notable form of power, and his representation as textual subject another equally significant one. In short, he was bound up with, not separated from, the world in which he lived, or in which he was commemorated. As a person who had achieved a special connection to the divinity that was manifested in prophetic and miracle-working abilities, the early medieval holy man (and the occasional holy woman) was the product of a complex, finely balanced nexus of individual ascetic preparation, textual exemplars, political opportunity, and social need. He was also, fundamentally, the product of a predisposition to believe that divine action might erupt in the actions of living persons, that an individual could be the bearer of heaven-sent powers. Although these preconditions were only intermittently realized in the centuries between 600 and 1100, the holy man remained textually potent even when socially latent.

Making saints

When Dominic of Silos died in 1073, the monks buried him within their cloister but in a tomb accessible to the laity. The locals visited it in some numbers and a handful of miracles occurred. By 1076, enough attention had been paid to the grave to prompt the local bishop to move the holy man's body into the abbey church, a translation which prompted a spate of cures at his new shrine. Nevertheless, the monks paid little attention to his rapidly growing posthumous power, and when they consecrated a new church in 1088, they

29 See Kennedy in this volume.
30 Lappin, *Medieval Cult*, ch. 1. See also Howe, *Church Reform and Social Change*.
31 Moore, "Between Sanctity and Superstition"; Sigal, *L'homme et le miracle*, 17–35.

named him merely as codedicatee of a subsidiary altar. But the ceremony was interrupted by the arrival of a man who burst in, carrying fetters, to give thanks to the saint: he had been imprisoned by the Muslims some 200 km away, and Dominic had freed him. From that moment, the postmortem cult grew rapidly. Pilgrims traveled ever greater distances to reach Dominic's tomb. They passed a night or more in vigil at the shrine and then, as the monks said mass, were healed of their ailments or released from the demons who possessed them. Far away from Silos, some received help in escaping from Muslim ambushes and prisons; others were cured in their own locale, and then made the journey to the shrine in thanksgiving. Then, around 1100, Dominic's friend Grimald faced down the monks' ambivalence about the saint in their midst and wrote an account of his life and posthumous miracles.[32]

Dominic's posthumous career reminds us that the transition from holy man to culted saint might be fraught with ambiguity, and that postmortem veneration as a "saint" was multi-faceted. Some generalizations are nevertheless possible. In the first place, cults were about the ideals, aspirations, and politics of the living, not the departed. However much political, social, and cultural imperatives might constrain the acknowledgment of lifetime holiness, they did so far more when it came to the matter of recognizing that select individuals could manifest exceptional closeness to God from the tomb. Secondly, only a very small proportion of saints ever manifested themselves in posthumous miracles. Those that did rarely maintained the cosmic energy in more than short spurts: like volcanoes, more miracle-working cults were quiescent or extinct than active at any given time. Often, they only flared into dramatic activity decades, even centuries, after the saint's death. Thirdly, the use of the written word to promulgate postmortem thaumaturgical prowess was itself a power play that reshaped the holy landscape. The cluster of lengthy miracle books from sixth- and seventh-century Byzantium was a head-on challenge to disbelievers of various sorts; similar books from the ninth-century Carolingian heartland became an integral part of the institutional canalization of holiness; and those from eleventh- and twelfth-century France were the product of intershrine rivalry in an environment beset by competing secular potentates.[33] All responded to specific anxieties about the nature and location of the holy.

On occasion, a dying person might take positive steps to foster the transition to sainted status. Aware of the importance of grave cults for the success of an insecure new monastery, the missionary Amandus (d. c. 675) bequeathed

32 Lappin, *Medieval Cult*, chs. 2–5.
33 Déroche, "Pourquoi écrivait-on"; Smith, "Oral and Written"; Sigal, *L'homme et le miracle*.

his body to his foundation at Elnone, hurling excommunication and eternal damnation on anyone who dared to try to remove it.[34] In all probability, Æthelwold (d. 984), reforming monk-bishop of Winchester and high-minded scholar rather than simple holy man, had briefed the student who, a decade or so later, wrote his master's *vita* and launched his cult.[35] His contemporary, Oswald of Worcester (d. 992), another bishop with monastic affiliations, constructed a shrine for his church, but left it empty, declaring that "he had built it for the honour of God and that it was most surely known to him whose remains would be buried in it": years later, his own bones were placed there.[36] Stage managing one's own funeral might also help. At the end of his controversial career as a populist preacher urging repentance in the Peloponnese, Nikon "Ho Metanoeite" ("Repent ye!") summoned all the citizens and monks of Sparta to attend his deathbed in c. 1000, ensuring that he died in a blaze of publicity. As the news spread, everyone rushed up:

> One hastened to carry away something from the squalid locks on the blessed man's head, another something from the hairs in his beard, still another a patch from his old cloak and from his goatskin outer garment. And so it was a great and illustrious thing for all to carry away some one of the things touching the skin of the holy remains, for relief from sufferings and every sort of disease.[37]

The bishop of Sparta, whom Nikon had run out of town, promptly stepped in, ensuring a funeral fit for a saint – and thereby reasserted his own authority.

On other occasions, friends and associates might take a key role in aiding the cult's emergence. A companion of Anastasius fed an eyewitness account of his execution directly back to his hagiographer. Those gathered round a more peaceful deathbed knew to look out for precious exudations, sweet-smelling "odors of sanctity," failure to decompose, and other physiological signs of holiness. When Queen Balthild (herself later to be regarded as a saint) paid her final respects to Eligius of Noyon (d. 660) as he lay on the bier, she noticed blood flowing from his nose. "Seeing this, the bishops and the most Christian queen quickly placed a linen napkin there. Diligently, they collected the blood wherever it ran and, the better to conserve the gift, separated it into three pieces."[38] In 831, Euthymius of Sardis had died in the arms of Methodius

34 Amandus, *Testamentum*.
35 Wulfstan of Winchester, *Life of St. Æthelwold*, xcix-ci.
36 Eadmer of Canterbury, *Lives and Miracles*, 272 for *Vita Sancti Oswaldi*, ch. 28.
37 Kazhdan, Talbot, and Ševčenko, "Nikon 'Ho Metanoeite'"; *Life of Saint Nikon*, ch. 47, 162–65. Cf. Kaplan, "L'ensevelissement des saints."
38 *Vita Eligii*, II.37, 721 or trans. McNamara, 163.

(d. 847), future patriarch of Constantinople, who later testified that the holy man's body remained undecayed:

> to this day the saint is bonny. His cheeks are ruddy, his eyebrows in good shape, his brow unfurrowed, his limbs supple to the touch. He remains as if death has not stiffened him; neither icy nor dissolving away, his flesh is shining. His rosy skin is damp like that of a living person: beads of sweat gather on his brow as on one in pain, making clear, even after death, the sufferings he endured for Christ and whose marks he bore."[39]

If the general public were admitted to the funeral, the saintly identity of the deceased might be announced in more dramatic ways. When Radegund, Frankish queen turned ascetic, was buried in 587, "possessed people shouted, acknowledged this saint of God, and said she was tormenting them."[40] The early tenth-century holy housewife Thomaïs of Lesbos had prophesied that miracles would occur at her grave. Forty days after her death, a man possessed by a "violent demon" was cured there, the signal to the nuns of the convent in whose forecourt she was buried to transfer her body into the church, where more miracles were soon reported.[41]

The inauguration of a cult need not follow immediately upon death, however. In the case of Theodore the Studite, (d. 826), there was an interval of eighteen years; in the case of Æthelwold of Winchester, twelve years. To enhance his cathedral, Æthelwold had turned one of his distant episcopal predecessors, Swithun (d. 863) into a miracle-working saint in 971, complete with elaborate shrine, special prayers and mass sets, two feast days, several versions of his *vita* (Latin, prose and verse; Old English), and a carefully composed miracle collection.[42] The interval could easily be even longer than in Swithun's case. Abbot Richard (d. 1046) transformed his impoverished monastery of Saint-Vanne at Verdun into a rich and powerful center, and subsequently became bishop of the city. Long ago, Saint-Vanne had been the episcopal seat: Richard "discovered" the graves of former bishops including Vanne, who had died c. 500, and who emerged from Richard's pen as a powerful posthumous miracle worker.[43]

Richard of Saint-Vanne was heir to a western tradition stretching back to c. 800 which entrusted the formal recognition of sainthood to bishops.

39 Methodius, "La vie d'Euthyme", ch. 27, 58–59. Cf. Angenendt, "*Corpus incorruptum.*"

40 Gregory of Tours, *Liber in gloria confessorum*, ch. 104, 815 or trans. Van Dam, 107.

41 *Vita S. Thomaidis*, chs. 16–17, 239–40 or trans. Halsall, 315–17. Kaplan, "De la dépouille à la relique" on the significance of the forty-day interval.

42 Lapidge et al., *Cult of St. Swithun*.

43 Richard of Saint-Vanne, *Vita et miracula Vitoni*; Geary, *Furta Sacra*, 65–74.

Carolingian attempts to prohibit the veneration of figures about whom nothing certain was known vested in the bishop the right to authorize cults within his diocese.[44] While this regulatory effort was of limited overall success, it nevertheless gave vigorous bishops, such as Æthelwold of Winchester or Richard of Saint-Vanne, an opportunity to control cults or to strengthen their own position by asserting the sanctity of their predecessors.[45] Gerard of Toul (d. 994) had been a widely respected prelate who was hailed as a miracle worker after his death. In 1049, the then bishop of Toul, Bruno, was elected pope, taking the name Leo IX; the following year, he received a petition from the clergy of his former cathedral requesting that he confirm Gerard's sainthood. Having listened to the evidence of his life and miracles, and consulted the Roman synod, he declared that Gerard deserved to be "numbered, named and venerated among the saints" and specified a date for his annual commemoration.[46] Leo IX was not quite the first pope to involve himself with saint making – in 1032, Benedict VIII had given the monks of Camaldoli permission to build an altar over the tomb of their founder, the uncompromisingly ascetic hermit, moral reformer, and monastic founder Romuald (d. 1027)[47] – but he was not the last.[48] Formalized saint-making conventionally either involved a widespread readiness to seek miracles at the tomb of an individual, coupled with a varying level of episcopal encouragement and liturgical commemoration, or, for those saints who were not miracle workers, reflected an episcopal reform agenda. Papal participation was thus a novel, prestigious adjunct to established practice, not a replacement for it. Heavily politicized, it remained so long after 1100.

In Byzantium, episcopal and patriarchal involvement continued to be erratic. Although Constantine VII Porphyrogenitus (945–59) commissioned the *synaxarion* of Hagia Sophia – an authoritative list of all saints to whom liturgical veneration was due – and thereby made possible the textual standardization of cults, no formalized patriarchal procedure for declaring sainthood emerged before the late thirteenth century.[49] This did not necessarily mean that cults were consensual, however, as the case of Symeon Eulabes indicates. Symeon the New Theologian (d. 1022) had been determined to get his former

44 Herrmann-Mascard, *Les reliques des saints*.

45 Cf. Picard, *Le souvenir des évêques*.

46 Widric, *Vita S. Gerardi*, 506–507.

47 Peter Damian, *Vita beata Romualdi*, ch. 72, 114–15.

48 Kemp, *Canonization and Authority*; Vauchez, *Sainthood*. The involvement of the papacy in saint-making does not extend back to 993, as generally claimed: Schimmelpfennig, "Afra und Ulrich"; Wolf, "Die Kanonisationsbulle von 993."

49 Talbot, "Canonization."

spiritual father, the Studite monk Symeon Eulabes (d. c. 986), accepted as a saint. He wrote a life and hymns in his honor, marked his annual feast "like that of all other saints," had an icon painted of him, and drew popular attention to this new saint; the patriarch of Constantinople agreed to send candles and incense on the annual feast day. Others, however, deemed the public veneration excessive, denying the holiness of Eulabes. Between 1003 and 1008, the case for and against this cult was argued in the patriarchal synod on three occasions. Despite being sent into exile, Symeon the New Theologian clung to his determination, praying to Eulabes thus: "You bear Christ within yourself, whom you have loved, and who loved you so very much. You, whose holiness, which equals that of the apostles, was revealed to me by a voice from on high, come now to my defence." But Symeon's main opponent simply stepped up to the icon, and scratched out the words "the holy" from in front of the name "Symeon," thus demoting the icon to a mere portrait and immediately canceling Eulabes's sainthood. Little wonder, then, that among Symeon the New Theologian's copious writings, those in honor of Eulabes have not survived.[50]

So saint-making was a delicate business. Varied in its impetus, unpredictable in its outcome, and potentially controversial, it constituted one of the ways in which early medieval Christianity blurred the distinction between life and death, between time and eternity. A successful cult brought heavenly power down to earth; an unsuccessful one vanished, leaving minimal trace. Whereas long-dead saints could be "revived" to provide buoyancy to their institutional successors' claims to authority, the death of a holy man could be a moment of acute insecurity for his community. The ubiquity of saints' cults belies the contingency of their creation.

The very special dead

Those who turned to the deceased for succor, penned commemorative texts, or organized liturgical veneration added their heavenly patrons to a centuries-old company of saints shared by Byzantium and the West. That multitude grew by accretion, expanding a core which had been formed many centuries previously.[51] Despite the high-profile cults of miracle-working saints, the bedrock of early medieval sainthood remained the "very special dead," the martyrs and

50 Nicetas Stethatos, *Vie de Syméon*, chs. 72–93, 98–128, quotations at 98, 124, 126. Kazhdan, "Symeon"; Barber, "Icon and Portrait."

51 Attempts to purge saints from the calendar were exceptional, although Norman skepticism toward some indigenous Anglo-Saxon cults in the wake of the Norman Conquest of England is notable: Yarrow, *Saints*, 4–7.

apostles whose heavenly afterlife had been assured in the very earliest days of Christianity.[52]

Martyr shrines were scattered very unevenly throughout the late Roman Empire. Though they served as the focal points for Christian civic identity, lay religious enthusiasm, and ongoing efforts to inculcate higher standards of Christian conduct, their location only partly reflected the varying zealousness of third- and early fourth-century persecutors.[53] Quite apart from the toll taken by failures of local memory, the geographical distribution of martyr cults was modified by "discoveries" of bodily remains, their "translation" from one place to another from the middle years of the fourth century onward, and the activities of relic collectors.[54]

Textual dissemination brought additional dislocations. Ever since the later fourth century, churches had been sharing their own local martyrs with other communities, forming ever longer lists of names to be commemorated. In textual and commemorative form, many martyr cults had a liturgical distribution by c. 600 which bore little connection with the geographical distribution of their corporeal remains or the original site of martyrdom. This disjuncture grew during the early Middle Ages. As martyrs multiplied, the calendar of religious feast days became increasingly crowded. Martyrs hitherto only known as names on a list acquired their own life stories. Collections of texts of martyr lives (however fictitious) were formed, becoming ever fuller.[55] More recent saints and their "rediscovered" predecessors joined the martyrs, swelling the size of Latin martyrologies (calendrical lists of feast days), passionaries (collections of martyrial *acta*), and legendaries (collections of saints' lives of all sorts, usually in calendar order), and Greek *synaxaria*, *menologia* (calendrical collections of *vitae*), and *menaia* (calendrical collections of liturgical poems and prayers for saints' days).

Gathering information about saints and martyrs sometimes went hand-in-hand with collecting their relics. As texts and relics multiplied, so multiple claims and conflicting narratives developed, all believed by those who upheld them, if not by competitors or skeptical, post-medieval critics. This hoarding of textual and physical tokens of deceased holy persons fulfilled many needs – for multiple intercessors and secure heavenly patronage, for political prestige

52 Brown, *Cult of Saints*, 70.

53 Grabar, *Martyrium*; Brown, "Enjoying the Saints"; Limberis, "Cult of the Martyrs."

54 Heinzelmann, *Translationsberichte*; McCormick, *Origins*, 283–318, for the contents of relic collections.

55 Dubois, *Les martyrologes*; Philippart, *Les légendiers latins*; Ševčenko, "Menologion"; Taft and Ševčenko, "Synaxarion."

and pious display, for comfort and healing. But it also responded to changing ideas about the relevance of holiness in the present, and to shifting perceptions of the past. Both were especially in the forefront in the ninth century. In Byzantium, one outcome of the iconoclast crisis was a reconnection with the early Christian past (now so distant as to be uncontroversial) which manifested itself in renewed attention to the martyrs and saints of old, the tokens of an authentic, shared heritage. In the West, Carolingian hostility to living holy men put a premium on dead sanctity, stimulating the "updating" of the prose style and contents of many older texts and also the compilation of large "historical martyrologies," potted biographies of hundreds of saints and martyrs, in calendrical order.[56]

Although new members constantly swelled the company of saints, Roman-era martyrs remained at the heart of early medieval saintly devotion. In late tenth-century Constantinople, the imperial official Symeon Metaphrastes (d. c. 1000) compiled a ten-volume collection of Greek texts (copied, revised, or new) following the order of the liturgical year, made up of lives of saints, accounts of notable relic translations, and texts for major feasts associated with both Christ and Mary. Of these texts, 55 per cent (81 out of 148) dealt with martyrs.[57] Meanwhile, his West Saxon contemporary, Ælfric of Eynsham (d. c. 1010) was at work producing homilies and hagiographical texts in Old English for comparable occasions: 41 per cent of his choices (22 out of 54) comprised martyr narratives.[58] Both Symeon Metaphrastes and Ælfric naturally included many saints from their own locality, but the shared martyr inheritance of East and West is nevertheless evident in the overlap between the collections.[59]

The significance of martyr cults emerges with particular clarity in regions where Christianity was either receding or expanding in the early Middle Ages. At the very least, ancient martyrial shrines helped local Christian communities assert their identity in a changing world. This was the context for the persistance of cults such as those of Menas at Abu Mina (in the western desert of Egypt) and Sergius at Rusafa (in the Roman–Persian borderlands) long after the Muslim conquest of Egypt and Syria.[60] Where Christians felt threatened, martyr cults also provided symbols of resistance to oppression, as the story

56 Rapp, "Byzantine Hagiographers"; Høgel, *Metaphrasis*; cf. Goullet, *Écriture et réécriture hagiographiques*.
57 Kazhdan and Ševčenko, "Symeon Metaphrastes"; Høgel, *Symeon Metaphrastes*.
58 Lapidge, "Ælfric's *Sanctorale*."
59 This comprises: Forty martyrs of Sebaste (9 March), George (23 April), Peter and Paul (29 June), Maccabees (1 August), Beheading of John the Baptist (29 August), Andrew (30 November), Eugenia (24/25 December).
60 Papaconstantinou, *Le culte des saints*, 146–54; Fowden, *Barbarian Plain*.

of Anastasius indicates. Although his cult disappeared from Palestine after the Arab invasions, the Church of the East continued to venerate a considerable number of other Christians martyred at Persian hands.[61] In its turn, Muslim rule reinvigorated the martyr tradition as a template for contemporary action and text. In ninth-century Palestine and Spain, as conversion to Islam and assimilation into Arabic cultural norms gathered pace, dwindling Christian communities turned the ideology of martyrdom to powerful effect, energetically mobilizing the early Christian past to reinforce their identity and venerating as martyrs those of their number recently killed by their Muslim rulers.[62] Whether in Latin, Greek, Arabic, or Georgian, these neomartyr narratives shared a common frame of reference that harked back to antiquity in order to promise future salvation to their beleaguered audience.

Where Christianity was expanding in the early Middle Ages, martyrs took on very different resonances, evoking an authoritative past and offering a link to distant places and persons. Missionary activity was an important vector in disseminating the cults of Roman martyrs in seventh-century Canterbury (southeast England) and eleventh-century Trondheim (Norway) alike.[63] In addition, popes drew on Rome's many martyr shrines to issue tokens of the city's early Christian heritage to anchor cult centers elsewhere. Although at first only prepared to release secondary relics (cloths which had been in contact with the tomb, filings from the chains of St. Peter, and the like), ninth-century popes more readily conferred gifts of bodily remains.[64] These relics indicated Roman affiliation – by no means jurisdictional before c. 1100, but certainly cultural – and a respect for Rome as the source of authentic Christianity.

In areas where conversion was in progress, the martyr template could be invoked in other ways. In many places, the violent death of convert kings rapidly resulted in their being regarded as martyrs, and often energetic miracle workers, thereby rooting new Christianities in indigenous martyr traditions. The Northumbrian king Oswald (634–42), the Norwegian Olaf Haraldsson (d. 1030), the Bohemian Wenceslas (d. 929/935), and the Rus princes Boris and Gleb (d. 1015) all were widely celebrated as symbols of their respective emerging national Christianities.[65] As Latin and Orthodox Christianities spread, martyr cults were reinvigorated and reconfigured to meet new political circumstances.

61 Brock, "Christians"; Brock and Harvey, *Holy Women*, 63–99.
62 See Griffith in this volume.
63 Brooks, "Canterbury, Rome"; Thacker, "In Search of Saints"; Crawford, "Churches Dedicated to St. Clement."
64 McCulloh, "From Antiquity to the Middle Ages"; Smith, "Old Saints, New Cults."
65 See Abrams and Shepard in this volume.

Only the Irish stood somewhat aloof. Their conversion, relatively peaceful, had not generated any local martyrs, and they remained more interested in their own local saints (numbering 750, according to an eighth-century catalogue) than imported ones.[66] The full complement of martyr cults only arrived in Ireland with papal Christianity in the twelfth century. Noting the omission of "the multitude of the saints of the rest of the world" from earlier Irish martyrologies, the Martyrology of Gorman (compiled 1166–74) produced a huge compendium of saints – biblical, Roman, British, English, and Irish – totaling 3,450 names.[67]

Part of the significance of martyr cults derives from the almost total absence of historical information about these persons. Indeed, some of the most famous of all – Catherine, Cosmas and Damian, George, Margaret – cannot be proven ever to have existed as historical persons, nor can many of the extremely obscure. But for that very reason, martyr cults were exceptionally flexible, capable of endless relocation and reinvention. Renowned for the miracles he wrought to protect the citizens of seventh-century Thessaloniki from the attacks of Slavs and Avars, Demetrius may or may not have been a local martyr, and it remains uncertain whether the city actually possessed his body at all. That the physician saints Cosmas and Damian may have been the conflated identity of three different pairs of saints was no impediment to the growth of their healing cult in Constantinople, from where it spread widely throughout the Mediterranean and beyond.

The malleability of martyrs was exceeded by that of apostles and evangelists, men whose post-biblical careers were the stuff of fanciful legends masquerading as historical fact. For that reason, they were exceptionally useful. Assertions of apostolic origins trumped efforts at control by churches who relied on more recent claims to jurisdiction: thus it was convenient for the Armenians (whose historical evangelizer, Gregory the Illuminator, lived in the fourth century) to rebut Byzantine Chalcedonianism by insisting, from the mid-fifth century onward, that the apostle Thaddeus had first preached to them. When faced c. 1100 with the jurisdictional claims of the English archbishopric of York, a see of known seventh-century origins, the Scots emphasized their claim to relics of the apostle Andrew and encouraged a major pilgrimage center at his shrine at St. Andrews. The "discovery" of the relics of the apostle James at Compostela in the ninth century likewise transformed the holy topography

66 *Catalogus Sanctorum Hiberniae* in Haddan and Stubbs 2, 292–94.
67 *Félire húi Gormáin*, 4–5.

and ecclesiastical hierarchy of Spain.[68] Equally notable consequences attended the Venetian theft of the evangelist Mark's relics from Alexandria in 827, for their acquisition enabled the nascent city-state to reject the jurisdiction of Rome and Constantinople alike, and to deploy the lion, symbol of Mark, as the trademark of its unique mercantile identity.[69]

Of all biblical characters, Mary was the most elaborated in legend and myth. Unlike apostles and evangelists, her cult was slow to develop. Richly endowed with doctrinal meaning she remained for long a subsidiary of Christological doctrines and a potent political cipher. Moreover, she lacked tomb, body, or any of the other usual characteristics of a saint's cult. The void was filled by a scramble to "find" equivalent corporeal tokens – phials of her milk, her milk teeth, her girdle and robe – and by doctrines (developing differently in eastern and western versions) that she had ascended bodily into heaven. (In this she was unlike saints, whose souls, but not yet bodies, were believed to have reached paradise.)

Her reputation as a protector and trusty guardian was especially slow to develop, although it emerged much earlier in Byzantium than in the West. Miracle stories about her gradually seeped westward, translated or retold in Latin versions from the sixth century on. The Latin liturgical and exegetic elaboration of her maternal role only began in the ninth century and gathered pace from the eleventh, again building on Byzantine precedents. In much of this, Rome enjoyed a medial position between East and West, but developed a political iconography of Mary earlier than did Constantinople. Byzantine Christians had been convinced of her miracle-working abilities ever since she was deemed to have rescued the Great City from the Avar siege of 626, but not until the late eleventh century did miraculous intercession become a feature of western veneration. Thus, only right at the end of our period did her cult finally become ubiquitous in its devotional and personal, as well as doctrinal and public, aspects. Supercharged with symbolism, so universal that she could be localized anywhere, Mary's attributes of motherhood and mediation set her at the apex of the hierarchy of saints in West and East alike. The most popular saint's cult of the central Middle Ages had taken fully a millennium to gestate.[70]

68 Maksoudian, "Armenian Saints"; Ash and Broun, "Adoption of St. Andrew"; Fletcher, *St. James's Catapult*. See Rousseau and Dorfmann-Lazarev in this volume on the theology and politics of Chalcedonianism.

69 Osborne, "Politics, Diplomacy and the Cult of Relics"; Dale, "Inventing a Sacred Past."

70 Warner, *Alone of all her Sex*; Pelikan, *Mary through the Centuries*; Pentcheva, *Icons and Power*; Vassilaki, *Images* and *Mother of God*; Iogna-Prat, Palazzo, and Russo, *Marie*; Clayton, *Cult of the Virgin Mary*.

The heavy theological freighting of the cult of Mary is the exception that proves the general rule that saints' cults were so integral to early medieval Christian cosmologies that their raison d'être needed no explicit articulation. But we should not let that distract us from the ways in which the cults of the dead of the remote past provided a source of identity, authority, and community and thus offered a way of coping with the massive changes experienced by all early medieval communities. Their symbolism was part of a cultural inheritance frequently rewritten in the service of the present, and so was the frequent subject of discursive reevaluation and political revisionism. Besides providing devotional assurance and thaumaturgical assistance, the "very special dead" fixed the past in the present in a form that offered reassurance about the future. The more chronologically distant the saint, the more authoritative, the more open to remaking his – or her – cult proved to be.

Jerusalem, old and new

In about 1090, Joseph, a monk from Canterbury, went to pray in the holy places in Jerusalem. As a form of spiritual refreshment, pilgrimage to local and distant shrines had been the natural concomitant of saints' cults since Late Antiquity, and despite the political, and often financial, challenges, Jerusalem always retained its central place in holy topographies.[71] Yet the city Joseph visited bore only limited resemblance to the Herodean city, or even its Hadrianic refoundation in 135. Eleventh-century pilgrims made their way round the massive basilicas built by Constantine (306–37) and Justinian (527–65), but now semi-ruinous in a city which had been under Muslim control for many centuries. Nevertheless, they were already familiar, in idealized form, with the landscape they would experience on arrival. It was not simply that pilgrim descriptions of the routes and its shrines had been in circulation since the fourth century: the cycle of the Christian liturgical year mapped out that itinerary in symbolic form transposed to the major churches of West and East alike.[72] The multiplication of churches modeled on the distinctive rotunda of the church of the Holy Sepulcher meant that many pilgrims had already been there, in anticipation, before they set foot on the road. And, since the Holy Land, like holy persons, was easily represented by tangible, portable fragments, others again had encountered it in reliquaries full of pilgrim "souvenirs" – handfuls

71 Talbot, "Pilgrimage"; Kaplan, *Le sacré*; Albert, *Le pèlerinage*.

72 Holum and Vikan, "Jerusalem"; Wilkinson, *Jerusalem Pilgrims*; Morris, *Sepulchre of Christ*; Kuelzer, "Byzantine and Early Post-Byzantine Pilgrimage"; Baldovin, *Urban Character*; Wilken, *Land Called Holy*.

of soil, collections of stones, and flasks of oil from the shrines at the sites of Christ's life and death – such as the neatly labeled collection of pebbles assembled by a sixth-century pilgrim and kept in the Holy of Holies in the private papal chapel in Rome.[73]

But, for all the emotions stirred by Jerusalem, Joseph, like other westerners, realized that his pilgrimage would be incomplete without a visit to Constantinople. By the closing decades of the eleventh century, westerners had become only too aware of the "incomparable treasure-hoard of relics" housed in the imperial city.[74] Whereas Rome distributed relics, Constantinople hoarded them. Although martyr-poor at the time of its fourth-century foundation, Constantinople was relic-rich by 600, and would become even more so in following centuries. Acquiring over 3,600 items representing 476 saints, the city became "a royal and unshakably safe home" for Christian treasures after the Muslim conquest of the Middle East.[75]

> This city is more amazing than all other cities of the world for its gold and silver, marble and lead, tapestries and silks, and is far more glorious than all other glories of the world because of the bodies of the saints which it possesses, and especially on account of the most precious relics of our Lord Jesus Christ which are believed to be greater there than in all the other parts of the world.

Thus began a detailed Latin listing of the contents of the city's relic treasuries composed shortly before the First Crusade.[76] Constantinople's accumulation of the relics of martyrs and apostles amazed; the relics of Christ and his crucifixion and of Mary underwrote imperial authority and guaranteed imperial orthodoxy in the most cogent possible terms. They set the Great City apart, qualitatively and quantitatively, from everywhere else, lending tangible content to its rhetorical, if apocalyptic, sobriquet "New Jerusalem" and giving the Byzantine emperors a trump card for diplomatic bargaining.[77] Westerners gawped enviously at what they saw: and Joseph did his best to use his remaining travel allowance to purchase a relic of the apostle Andrew as a memento.

Western fascination with the Byzantine relic collections reflected a preoccupation with body parts and associated relics which ignored the symbols of holiness which were at least as important to the Byzantines themselves: icons. By c. 1100, sacred images had become firmly established in Byzantine

73 Kessler and Zacharias, *Rome 1300*, 38–64; Thunø, *Image and Relic*.
74 Haskins, "Canterbury Monk," 294.
75 Robert of Rheims, *Historia Iherosolimitana*, II.20, 750 or trans. Sweetenham, 102.
76 Ciggar, "Une description de Constantinople," 120.
77 Maraval, *Lieux saints*, 49, 92–101, 401–10; James, "Bearing Gifts"; Kalavrezou, "Helping Hands"; Magdalino, "L'église du Phare"; Lerou, "L'usage des reliques."

theology as appropriate signifiers of divinity and hence conduits of intercession (prayer, miracles, protection), but they had not always been so. They had become prominent in the late seventh century. As the Byzantine Empire fought for survival in the face of Muslim onslaught, icons became so controversial that, from 720, strife erupted over what representations of Christ (other than the Eucharist) were theologically permissible and what role, if any, might be assigned to visual mediators of the veneration of saints. The definitive rehabilitation of images in 843 affirmed that icons were, in essence, holy, and opened the way for the development of their authoritative role in cult as well as theology. Operating in a dialectical relationship with texts and relics, icons brought the cults of saints out of churches and into the home or onto battlefields, giving each saint a precise visual identity that was lacking in the West, even for the same saints. In the post-iconoclast era icons made and unmade saints, as Symeon the New Theologian's controversial attempt to launch a cult of Symeon Eulabes indicates.[78]

Central to redefining Byzantine cults of saints, the iconoclast dispute had much more modest repercussions in the Latin world. The problem of the visual representation of holiness certainly hit a nerve with some western thinkers in the years around 800, although translation difficulties between Greek and Latin made it hard to engage in the debate on equal terms. And despite the intensification of commercial and political contacts between East and West, it was symptomatic of diverging religious identities that icons never became established in western devotions. For the Byzantines, iconoclasm was a convulsive redefinition of the relationship between society and the holy at the deepest possible level; for the West, it appeared as surface ripples on a cultural reservoir no longer filled from the same wellsprings.[79]

Icons and relics alike mediated the heavenly presence of saints in tangible form. They were thus in an inevitable, if oblique, relationship with the eucharist in its role as a symbolic bridge between humanity and divinity. When, in due course, that relationship came under discussion in the West, the debate turned not on icons but on relics. Relics had much in common with Eucharistic bread: in both cases, any number of representative tokens stood for the complete whole. Moreover, the custom of depositing consecrated bread in an altar whenever saints' relics were unavailable hinted at their comparability. It is thus

78 See Louth, in this volume, for more detail on iconoclasm; for general background, see the subject entries on "Iconoclasm," "Iconography," "Iconophiles," and "Icons," by various authors in *ODB* 2, 975–81; Brubaker, "Icons before Iconoclasm?"; Maguire, *Icons of their Bodies*; Ousterhout and Brubaker, *Sacred Image*.

79 Herrin, *Formation*, 307–476; Appleby, "Holy Relics and Holy Image"; Noble, "Tradition and Learning."

unsurprising that, when deviant practices or intellectual speculation turned the spotlight toward the Eucharist on either side of the year 1100, the role of relics came under unprecedented scrutiny.[80] Nevertheless, reasoned definitions of the mediatory, miracle-working role of body-part relics vis-à-vis the central Christian sacrament failed to cut through the wealth of traditional practice and unvoiced assumptions which underpinned the cults of saints.

Guibert of Nogent had especially strong views on the subject. Writing around 1120, his arguments about the wholeness of Christ's body in the Eucharist drew his attention to – and excoriation of – the unrestricted multiplication of implausible body-part relics of Christ and the saints. He sought to return saints' cults to the criteria of early canonical legislation. He failed – but the premise of his analysis nevertheless deserves emphasis. He predicated his argument upon a clear distinction between "those matters which are practiced and taught by the Church . . . such as baptism and the sacrament of the Lord's host" and "certain other matters which are practiced but not taught, such as the customs of fasting and the singing of psalms." The former, he commented "are by authority always practiced without difference and everywhere without change . . . the doctrine which informs them and which is learned from them being identical," a statement broad-minded Christians – East and West – could have accepted.[81] The "other matters" did not constitute "the very highest necessities for our salvation" and were those characterized by "diversity." In categorizing saints' cults among the matters which were "practiced but not taught," Guibert identified their essential characteristics: the veneration of saints supplemented the sacramental relationship of Christians to their God but was not defined by formal doctrine or adumbrated in scriptural exegesis. Instead, authorized by long practice, variety was the hallmark. Although Guibert echoed centuries-old concerns about authenticating individual saints' credentials, he stood firm on the general principle: "the saints are people worthy of our reverence and honor in exchange for their example and protection."[82]

In encapsulating the place of saints and their cults in Christian tradition, Guibert pinpointed enduring characteristics which had remained unchanged since Late Antiquity. Nevertheless, the saints and their cults in 1100 were not the same as they had been in 600, whether in discourse, image, liturgy, or

80 Lobrichon, "Le culte des saints"; Platelle, "Guibert de Nogent"; Ferrari, "*Lemmata sanctorum*."

81 But see Kolbaba in this volume for eleventh-century polemics about whether the "sacrament of the Lord's host" should use leavened or unleavened bread.

82 Guibert of Nogent, *De sanctis et eorum pigneribus*, 85–87 or trans. Head, 405–406.

action. The changing geopolitics of Christianity combined with the passing of centuries had encouraged a greatly enhanced diversity of perception and practice. So, too, had evolving remedies for sin, and the ever-volatile relationship of lived, ascetic holiness to institutional authority, ecclesiastical and secular. Convenience and criticism alike had affected the uses of texts and tangible objects to mediate, relocate, and represent saintly power. "Practiced but not taught," saints and their cults remained capable of endless reinvention: the attribution of sanctity remained rooted in the needs of living communities to find holiness in their midst in ways which made sense of the world.

29

Last Things

JANE BAUN

Bound to Colum, while I speak,
may the bright one guard me in the seven heavens.
When I go to the road of fear,
I'm not lordless: I have strength.

Early medieval Christians faced the Last Things – death and judgment; heaven, hell, and the places in between; the Second Coming and the Last Judgment – with mingled hope and dread. These verses by a seventh-century Irish monk capture both.[1] Like countless Christians after him, Beccán derived particular consolation from trust in a powerful heavenly patron – in his case, St. Columba. His expectations regarding the Last Things, while expressed personally, drew on a stock of otherworld images and ideas which circulated throughout Christendom, transmitted by texts of universal appeal such as the *Apocalypse of Paul* and the *Dialogues* of Gregory the Great (d. 604). Christians worldwide began the early medieval period bound together in a common eschatological culture (from Greek *eschatos*, "last"). But Gregory the Great would be the last universal Christian author, read and respected throughout Christendom. By 1100, definite divergences in eschatological expectation had emerged among the European, Near Eastern, and Asian Christendoms. Attitudes toward the afterlife, the nature of the otherworld, the final destiny of human kingdoms at the end of time, and the coming Kingdom of God, were shaped profoundly by lived experience of earthly authority. The post-Roman societies of the early medieval West, the continuing eastern Roman Empire in Byzantium, and Christians living in the non-Christian kingdoms of the Near and Far East, began to perceive the otherworld, constructed largely in the image of *this* world, very differently. This parting of the eschatological ways was, however, a long, gradual process. And throughout the early medieval period, the critical

1 Clancy and Márkus, *Iona*, 137.

mass of beliefs regarding the Last Things that all Christians continued to hold in common outweighed the points of detail which began to divide them.

Streams

Much of the common discourse of early medieval eschatology originates in the Bible, but the biblical witness on otherworld matters was patchy and often cryptic, and a voluminous literature was generated to fill in the gaps. Since meditation on the Last Things and visionary experience were open to all, otherworld literature was surprisingly democratic. We find recorded not only the opinions of eminent bishops, but also the visionary experience of humbler lay people and monastics, both male and female. Anonymous visions jostled for influence in the eschatological "marketplace" with authoritative treatises by named church figures – and often won. Officially sanctioned bishops, monastics, and theologians had a clear advantage, but unofficial and visionary writers were copied and disseminated with equal vigor, and exercised a widespread, enduring influence on the early medieval "otherworld-view."

On fundamentals, official and unofficial thinkers were not often so far apart. Everyone knew certain things about the Last Things. Otherworld beings, whether angels or demons, attended the actual hour of death, assisting with the parting of soul from body. If the departed's moral or penitential status was ambiguous, angels and demons might argue over whose the soul should be. The soul then underwent its own particular judgment, often passing through a multistage ordeal or examination. Its sins and good deeds were reviewed, sometimes read out of books, sometimes weighed, sometimes tested by fire. Each soul then entered one of four possible places or states to await the Last Judgment. True saints might go straight into the presence of God, in the city of Christ. More normal mortals, if virtuous and completely confessed, might enjoy an interim paradise outside the gates of heaven proper. A minority of hardened, unrepentant sinners guilty of unspeakable crimes were thought by many (though not all) to go straight to eternal punishment. Most sinners entered various interim punishments, where their unconfessed or unatoned sins were purged away gradually by the cleansing, refining fire. Sorted into appropriate domains of punishment or reward, all awaited the General Judgment – the dread Last Day – when Christ would come again on earth to judge the living and the dead, sealing their eternal fate, and ushering in his eternal kingdom.

Most writers, visionaries, and preachers agreed on such eschatological basics. But the embryonic state of doctrinal definition fostered speculation and elaboration. Early medieval eschatology was a greatly variegated landscape, watered by two great streams of inspiration, which this study will call the apocryphal (literally, "hidden away") and the patristic. In the apocryphal stream flowed ideas of anonymous, ambiguous, or idiosyncratic provenance, not necessarily embraced by the official church; in the patristic, flowed those ideas which originated among, or were taken up by, recognized ecclesiastical authorities. The wellspring of both streams was biblical, mingling canonical Scripture with venerable extra-canonical works. Both apocryphal and patristic authors consulted the Old Testament pseudepigrapha and New Testament apocrypha as primary sources of revelation on the Last Things.

The apocryphal stream

The most influential apocrypha for the otherworld were the early Christian *Descent* narratives (*Descensus Christi ad Inferos*), and the third-century *Apocalypse of Paul*. Numerous early apocrypha explore the legend of Jesus's descent to the underworld, or "harrowing of hell" – the tale of how Christ broke down the doors of Hades, bound Satan, freed Adam and Eve from the ancient curse, and conquered death and sin.[2] Enjoying a wide circulation in diverse languages, *Descensus* tales enlivened Eastertide homilies throughout medieval Christendom, from Anglo-Saxon England to Egypt. They found visual expression in the developing iconography of the *Anastasis* ("resurrection") composition, in which Christ tramples down the underworld gates and a personified Hades, while pulling Adam and Eve up from their tombs. The earliest known *Anastasis* images date from early eighth-century Rome, whence the motif traveled east to become the archetypal Byzantine paschal icon, ubiquitous in monumental painting and mosaic, manuscript illumination, portable icons, devotional objects, and even jewellery.[3]

Even more influential worldwide was the *Apocalypse of Paul*, which originated in the monastic culture of late-antique Egypt, but spread rapidly throughout medieval Christendom.[4] Paul's apocalypse ("revelation") set the pattern of a visionary progression through an otherworld in which the wicked are punished in various fiery rivers, furnaces, and lakes, with gruesome "made-to-measure" punishments, and dazzling glimpses, too, of the blessed places. Extant in hundreds of manuscripts, and translated into every major medieval language, *Paul* shaped the otherworld-view of diverse peoples far beyond its early Mediterranean milieu. From Augustine of Hippo in fifth-century North

2 MacCulloch, *Harrowing*, 131–73; *Apocryphal New Testament*, 164–204, 652–58.
3 Kartsonis, *Anastasis*; numerous examples in Evans and Wixom, *Glory*.
4 *Apocryphal New Testament*, 616–44.

Africa, to Aldhelm of Sherborne (d. 709) in England, to the Patriarch Nicephorus of Constantinople (d. 828) and Ælfric, abbot of Eynsham in England (d. c. 1020), eminent churchmen warned their flocks – to little apparent avail – that *Paul* was a wolf in saint's clothing.[5] *Paul* was used by numerous homilists in Anglo-Saxon England, including the early eleventh-century archbishop of York, Wulfstan (d. 1023), as if canonical scripture.[6] Visionary authors in Ireland and Byzantium broadly contemporary with Wulfstan used it as a compositional base. And as far afield as Iceland, elements of a monumental woodcarving of the Last Judgment in a late eleventh-century hall follow *Paul*'s otherworld descriptions.[7]

Alongside *Paul*, Christians in the early medieval West were also reading a rich corpus of contemporary visionary journeys to the otherworld. The visions, revelations, and "near-death" experiences of named individuals such as Fursey and Dryhthelm, recorded by Bede (d. 735), and of Barontus, the monk of Wenlock, Wetti of Reichenau, and the Frankish emperor Charles the Fat (880–87), among others, provide further witness to otherworld *mentalités*. While such visions loom large in the discussions of modern scholars, generalizations from their very concrete, individual accounts to wider religious attitudes in Europe must be made with caution. These are highly idiosyncratic narratives, often written for internal monastic or court consumption. Many advance a particular political cause, such as monastic reform or dynastic succession. They were certainly less widely disseminated than *Paul*, and some betray *Paul*'s influence.

The patristic stream

Not everyone was pleased with the Pauline otherworld. As already noted, prominent churchmen in both East and West swam purposefully against the apocryphal tide. The Anglo-Saxon abbot Ælfric warned his early eleventh-century monks to shun apocrypha, especially *Paul*, and to read only the fathers, most notably Augustine, Jerome, Gregory the Great, and Bede.[8] Patristic authors were accessible especially through florilegia, compilations of excerpts arranged by topic. The *Prognosticon futuri saeculi* ("Forecast of the Future Age"), an eschatological florilegium compiled in Visigothic Spain by Julian of Toledo

5 *Visio Sancti Pauli*, 3–5; Healey, *Old English Vision*, 41; Nicephorus, *Canones*, 852.
6 Healey, *Old English Vision*, 41–57; Wright, *Irish Tradition*, 106–74.
7 Jónsdóttir, *11th-Century Byzantine Last Judgement*.
8 Kabir, *Paradise, Death and Doomsday*, 14–15; Gatch, *Preaching and Theology*, 70–76.

(d. 690), was widely read throughout the Latin West.[9] It offered a complete guide regarding death and the afterlife, gleaned from a half dozen patristic authors, but especially Augustine. Augustine dominated the learned theological tradition in the West, but his writings were less influential in early medieval Christendom as a whole. Augustinian views on original sin, and on predestination to damnation or salvation, were never accepted in the East, and could be controversial even in the West, as evidenced by heated Carolingian debates over predestination, culminating in the condemnation of the strict predestinarian views of the Saxon theologian Godescalc (d. c. 869).[10]

Rather than Augustine, the true father of medieval European eschatology was Pope Gregory the Great, the second most-quoted author in Julian's *Prognosticon*. Gregory set the eschatological tone for the entire period, through his *Dialogues*, homilies, and biblical exegesis. Presented in an accessible question-and-answer format, enriched with homely anecdotes, his *Dialogues* were especially popular. They were translated into Greek in the eighth century and Old English in the late ninth century, with a personal preface written by King Alfred himself.[11] Book 4 of the *Dialogues*, which provided a *summa* on the afterlife and the end times, was particularly influential.[12] Its imagery and doctrine permeate the Merovingian *Vision of Barontus*.[13] When Wetti, a monk at Reichenau in the early ninth century, sensed the approach of death, he asked his fellow monks to read to him from the *Dialogues*.[14] Gregory also guided Byzantine contemplation of the Last Things, especially as the seventh most frequently cited author in the *Synagoge* of Paul of Evergetis (d. 1054), a widely-influential florilegium on the ascetic life which has shaped the consciousness of many generations of Orthodox Christians.[15]

Part of the appeal of Gregory's *Dialogues* lay in its transmission of "tales useful for the soul." Such edifying tales originated in ascetic circles, but circulated broadly, and tales in early medieval collections began to reflect the everyday concerns of lay Christians living in the world, as well as those of monastic men and women. The stories run the gamut of eschatological anxieties, including the efficacy of almsgiving and prayers for the dead, resuscitation of the dead, the particular judgment of the soul, the struggle for the soul between angels

9 See Hillgarth's introduction to Julian of Toledo, *Opera*, xix–xxi; Gatch, *Preaching and Theology*, 129–46.
10 Ganz, "Theology," 767–73.
11 Asser, *Alfred the Great*, 123.
12 Gregory the Great, *Dialogues* 3, IV, 18–207 (trans. Zimmerman, 189–275).
13 Contreni, "Building Mansions."
14 Heito, *Visio Wettini*, IV, 269.
15 Wortley, "Genre and Sources," 314–17.

and demons, interim afterlife zones, and the particulars of otherworld punishment and reward.[16] Written in simple language, they impressed their teachings on sin, repentance, judgment, and the afterlife on the minds of hearers in concrete, unforgettable terms. Like the monk Wetti on his deathbed, Christians throughout the ages have derived both compunction and consolation from these short, homely tales of the death and afterlife fate of both ordinary and extraordinary people.

Landscapes

What was the early medieval otherworld, watered by the two streams, apocryphal and patristic, actually like? Where was it located, and how did one get there? Two points are essential for orientation in otherworld geography. Firstly, the sheer *multifariousness* of the landscape: the early medieval otherworld was truly a "house of many mansions" (John 14.2) with ample space for theological and mystical creativity – the dreaming of many different types of otherworld. Secondly, otherworld geography was above all an *allegorical* geography, meant to be understood on multiple levels. The primary purpose of otherworld narratives was not the transmission of factual information. As Gregory the Great explained,

> the pyre of wood which Repartus saw does not mean that wood is burned in hell. It was meant, rather, to give him a vivid picture of the fires of hell, so that, in describing them to the people, they might learn to fear the eternal fire through their experience with natural fire.[17]

The early medieval otherworld narratives seek above all to teach truths about God and the soul, using images by turns familiar and strange, but always memorable. The visionary's progress through an external otherworld landscape traces simultaneously an internal, soul's journey, and maps an inner spiritual landscape – of compunction, repentance, purgation, and illumination.

Outer landscapes

Locations for early medieval otherworlds varied considerably. Pre-Christian conceptions of an underworld, entered from openings in the earth or sea, persisted in many parts of Europe. In the Welsh *Mabinogion* legends, as in much of Celtic and Germanic Europe, belief in Hades as a magical, parallel kingdom in close contact with this world coexisted with normative Christian

16 Wortley, "Death, Judgment, Heaven, and Hell."
17 Gregory the Great, *Dialogues* 3, IV.32.5, 109 (trans. Zimmerman, 229–30).

teachings. Gregory the Great recorded popular belief in southern Italy that the lava pits in the islands around Sicily were entrances into the infernal fire:

> And these are becoming larger every day, as well-informed people tell us, for, with the end of the world approaching, it seems that the openings to hell are enlarged in order to receive the great number of lost souls who will be gathered there to be cast into eternal punishment. God made these fires appear on the surface of the earth in order to correct the minds of men. Unbelievers who had heard of the torments of hell and still refused to believe were to see these realms of torture with their own eyes.[18]

Irish Christians venerated a cave on an island in a large lake (Lough Derg) in County Donegal as their very own entrance to the infernal regions. Legend takes the association back to the time of St. Patrick (d. c. 460). Whatever its origins, by the twelfth century, "St. Patrick's Purgatory" had become a renowned destination for arduous, life-changing pilgrimage. Irish Christians also experienced the otherworld as a seascape: in the Irish *imrama* visions (literally, "rowings"), the hero endures a penitential voyage across perilous seas, punctuated by island halts. An oft-copied and retold eighth-century penitential tale, the *Voyage of St. Brendan*, recounted how the Abbot Brendan (d. 578) and his companions rowed the seas for seven years. Contending with sea monsters and consorting with hermits along the way, they saw natural and supernatural wonders, grew in wisdom and virtue, and encountered many colorful figures, most notably Judas Iscariot enjoying a brief respite from torment. Brendan's voyage culminated on a paradisical island – the Land of Promise of the Saints. Legendary material in both East and West frequently sought a terrestrial Paradise, equated with the lost Garden of Eden, and situated to the furthest east of the known world.

Such older traditions of associating the otherworld with particular landscapes endured, and belief in an underground hell was propagated by authors such as Julian of Toledo, but early medieval Christians increasingly tended to understand the entire otherworld as being somewhere "up," above this world. Beyond that, however, the otherworld was envisioned in as many ways as there were visionaries. Numbers of heavens vary widely, from one to seven or more. Some schemes stack the multiple levels of the journey vertically; others experience them as ranged across a plain. Some describe a linear progression through an integrated landscape, divided by valleys and rivers and connected by bridges; others read as collections of discrete scenes or zones, giving no clear sense of connection. Some texts envision an entirely natural world, of

18 Ibid., IV.36.12, 122–23 (trans. Zimmerman, 235–36).

pleasant flowery meadows for the blessed, and fiery rivers and lakes and jagged cliffs for the damned. Others use built metaphors: reservoirs, wells, furnaces, gates, walls, arches, enclosures, and mansions. Paradise is often a walled garden of marvelous fruit trees, inhabited by the Virgin Mary, the Good Thief, and Abraham (bearing innocent souls in his bosom), located outside heaven proper – a reception zone in which blessed souls awaited the Last Judgment. The nerve center of heaven, the heavenly Jerusalem, is typically visualized as a gorgeous city surrounded by golden, bejeweled walls. Description of the otherworld torments is stereotypical in most visions, featuring "made-to-measure" punishments, in which the penalty symbolizes the crime, and various fiery features (rivers, pits, lakes), in the manner of *Paul*. But some of the medieval near-death narratives also surprise, with haunting images of poetic originality. The late seventh-century Northumbrian layman Dryhthelm was granted a startling vision of the damned:

> I saw, as the globes of fire now shot up and now fell back again ceaselessly into the bottom of the pit, that the tips of the flames as they ascended were full of human souls which, like sparks flying upward with the smoke, were now tossed on high and now, as the vaporous flames fell back, were sucked down into the depths.[19]

Another Englishman, the anonymous monk of Wenlock (early eighth century), saw human souls in the form of birds, which

> flew through the flames lamenting, with human cries, their deserts and their present punishment. They rested, hanging for a little time on the edges of the pits, and then, screaming, fell into the depths.[20]

In another striking image, the Frankish emperor Charles the Fat was guided on his visionary ordeal by a glistening white being who held

> a ball of flaxen thread that shone with a very bright radiance as comets commonly do when they appear; and he began to unroll the ball, and said to me, "Take the thread from this shining ball, and tie it firmly in a knot on your right thumb, for by this you shall be led in the labyrinth of infernal punishment."[21]

The radiant thread, unprecedented in otherworld literature, protected the emperor from demonic attack, and provided a glowing lifeline through the trackless otherworld gloom. All three visionaries were terrified and chastened by their soul's ordeal. The emperor Charles, in a neat after-the-fact prophecy,

19 Bede, *HE*, V.12, 491.
20 Boniface, *Epistola* 10, 254 (trans. Kylie, 82).
21 *Visio Karoli*, in William of Malmesbury, *Gesta regum Anglorum*, II.111.1, 162–65.

learned in his vision that he would lose his empire, and was instructed to abdicate in favor of his nephew. The two English visionaries, Dryhthelm and the Wenlock monk, are said to have returned home to bear witness and lead lives of repentance.

Inner landscapes

The early medieval otherworld was thus more a process than a place. The descriptions of otherworld realities were not simple tourist guides, but morality tales, and systems of signs conveying meaning on multiple levels. Gregory the Great castigated naive literalism in the *Dialogues*:

> *Peter*: But how is it that the house in the beautiful meadow was constructed with bricks of gold? It seems rather ridiculous that in eternity we should still need metals of this kind.
> *Gregory*: Surely, no one with common sense will take the phrase literally.[22]

Gregory emphasized instead the inner, spiritual meaning:

> We arrive at a true understanding through images. For example, the just were seen passing over a bridge to a beautiful meadow, because the road that leads to eternal life is narrow. The soldier saw a river of polluted water because the noisome stream of carnal vices continues daily to flow on toward the abyss.[23]

Near-death experiences and otherworld journeys describe simultaneously both a journey through an external landscape and an inward journey of increasing self-awareness. Progression through the otherworld topography changes the visionary, as each new feature demands a response, of wonder or compunction, and the visionary becomes acutely sensitive to the state of his or her soul. The ordeal itself is purgative, but further repentance is still required in the body once back on earth. In the Irish voyaging tales, the sea itself is an instrument of penance, from which the voyager emerges cleansed of sin.[24]

"Repent, *now*, before it is too late!" – is the urgent message of all otherworld tales. Among otherworld visions are numerous tales of sinners who are granted precautionary pre-death visions, followed by the mercy of a fixed time for repentance. A tenth-century Byzantine edifying tale tells the story of a woman named Anna, a Constantinopolitan housewife, who died and was taken to the terrible, dark "lower regions," where she was confined with the sinners in torment.[25] In despair, she called upon the Mother of God, at whose intercession

22 Gregory the Great, *Dialogues* 3, IV.37.15–16, 134–35 (trans. Zimmerman, 241).
23 Ibid., IV.38.3, 136–37 (trans. Zimmerman, 242).
24 Clancy, "Subversion at Sea," 194.
25 Paul of Monemvasia, *Spiritually Beneficial Tales*, 108–11.

she was granted two more months of life on earth for repentance and bearing witness. Sinners in the elite punishment zone of the *Apocalypse of Anastasia*, a Byzantine vision of the turn of the tenth century, ask Anastasia to go and plead with their relatives to reform their lives, lest they enter the same torments, and also to pray and give alms on their behalf. Peter the *protospatharios*, a former imperial official, lamenting his many sins while in office, concludes:

> I left behind wealth and much treasure. Report these things to my wife and to my children: Be vigilant, lest you enter these fearsome places of punishment! Be zealous through almsgiving, and supplicate God, and give these things on my behalf, so that I might have rest from this bitter torment!"[26]

The punishments seen by most early medieval visionaries are clearly envisioned as temporary states, holding zones until the Last Judgment. In the meantime, visions, tracts, and homilies all affirm that almsgiving and good works, prayers, vigils, and psalm-chanting can improve both one's own afterlife fate and also that of the souls already in the punishments. The emperor Charles the Fat was shocked to encounter his father, Louis the German (d. 876), being tormented in the otherworld, but Louis was confident that his trials were transient:

> But if you will help me quickly, you and the bishops and abbots who were loyal to me and the whole estate of the clergy, with masses and offerings and psalm-singing and vigils and alms, I shall swiftly be set free from this tun of boiling water; for my brother Lothar and his son Louis have been freed from these penalties by the prayer of St. Peter and St. Remigius, and have already entered into the joy of the Paradise of God.[27]

The visions and homilies thus rarely describe Heaven – the final place of eternal blessedness – or Hell – the final place of eternal punishment. These would be realized in full form only after the Last Judgment, when souls and bodies would be reunited to meet their eternal fate. Early medieval discussions most often describe less definitely located, interim zones, with fluid, permeable boundaries, zones of both punishment and blessedness. Whether these zones are conceived as actual places, or more as states of mind, varies from text to text, and how such texts were received changed with each new reader or hearer. But those who preached the absolute certainty of eternal punishment for the damned, following church fathers such as Tertullian and Augustine, constituted a minority. In the Greek and Syriac East, prominent early fathers

26 *Apocalypsis Anastasiae*, VI, 29–30.
27 *Visio Karoli*, in William of Malmesbury, *Gesta regum Anglorum*, II.111.7, 166–67.

of the second to fourth centuries, such as Clement of Alexandria, Origen, Evagrius, and Gregory of Nyssa, had preferred to leave open the possibility that God's ultimate eschatological intent was the complete restoration of the cosmos, including all of fallen humanity. Strict Latin and Byzantine orthodoxy condemned such talk of a complete *apokatastasis* ("restoration"), but the hope was kept alive in modified form by figures such as Maximus the Confessor in Byzantium (d. 662), John Scottus Eriugena in Carolingian Francia (d. c. 877), and Isaac the Syrian in the church of the East (d. c. 700).[28] Isaac expressed a particularly radiant hope:

> I am of the opinion that He is going to manifest some wonderful outcome, a matter of immense and ineffable compassion on the part of the glorious Creator, with respect to the ordering of this difficult matter of gehenna's torment: out of it the wealth of his love and power and wisdom will become known all the more – and so will the insistent might of the waves of his goodness.[29]

The early medieval otherworld, if not entirely uncharted territory, was still open to discovery. It was *terra nova*, explored by mystics, monastics, penitents, and ordinary people caught up into near-death experiences and visions, as well as by saints, bishops, and theologians. The emergence of a fixed, tripartitite otherworld, with eternal heaven above, eternal hell and temporary purgatory somewhere below, was still in the future for the Latin West, and never took complete hold among Eastern Christians.

Structures

Authority

The landscape of the otherworld was punctuated by a great variety of imaginative constructions. Especially prominent are structures of authority – palaces, judgment seats, tribunals, halls – cast in the mould of the built and political environment with which the author was most familiar. Here, divergences between West and East are most marked. In the Byzantine East, administrative expectations were still Roman: Byzantine Christians knew centralized government under an emperor, and Roman law. The Latin, Germanic, and Celtic West comprehended diverse social and political arrangements, from post-Roman or sub-Roman to "never-Roman." Rather than acknowledging one universal monarch, western Christians were governed by a multiplicity of

28 Ludlow, "Universalism," 195–96.
29 Alfeyev, *Spiritual World*, 283–92; quotation at 287.

local kings, lords, and chieftains, and as many local law codes. Kin groups or clans shaped political and social organization in many areas of Celtic and Germanic Europe. Christians living under the Muslim, Buddhist, and Confucian rulers of Asia also learned to survive within diverse social and political configurations. These Far Eastern Christians, unconstrained by political authority interested in enforcing Christian orthodoxy, had perhaps the greatest theological freedom, which may help account for the originality and optimism of the otherworld vision of Isaac the Syrian. Given such radical divergence in their experience of earthly kingdoms, it is no wonder that Christians in the West, East, and Far East began to conceptualize the heavenly realm in radically divergent ways.

It has been observed that early medieval East and West increasingly differed broadly in their understanding of personal eschatology according to one of two models: "amnesty" or "penance."[30] In societies which retained memories of Rome, sin, judgment, forgiveness, and condemnation tended to be comprehended more according to an "amnesty" model, of God as the serene universal emperor, granting impartial pardons to sinners. In societies which had never known Rome, the tendency was towards a "penance" model, in which a jealous God demanded the due individual satisfaction for each infraction, according to intricate penitential codes. Such broad tendencies are undeniable. Yet, amnesty did not entirely die in the West: translations of the *Apocalypse of Paul* circulating throughout western Europe promoted late Roman concepts of universal pardon, balancing the emphasis in the named otherworld visions on satisfaction for individual sins. Preachers in Ireland and England took up with alacrity *Paul*'s impartial, universal amnesty from punishment for sinners on the Lord's Day.[31] And the East was not unconcerned with penance: an individual's penitential status could haunt him or her in the passage to the otherworld, with demonic toll collectors demanding payment for sins, or at the Judgment, in the form of enormous ledgers of sins and good deeds kept by scrupulous angelic scribes.[32] Both solutions to the problem of sin – amnesty and penance – were current in varying degrees in both the post-Roman West and the still-Roman East. And as we shall see, adherence to the "amnesty" model of God as emperor could generate as much personal anxiety for the sinner as the "penance" model – if not more.

Medieval adaptations of the *Apocalypse of Paul* composed toward the end of our period reveal further, fundamental divergence between East and West in

30 Brown, "Decline."
31 Healey, *Old English Vision*, 48–50; Seymour, "Irish Versions," 55.
32 Every, "Toll Gates"; *Apocalypsis Anastasiae*, V, 24.

their understanding of God and his otherworld kingdom. Written at opposite ends of Europe, one in Ireland and two in Byzantium, all three anonymous visions used *Paul* as a point of departure, but made him into very different otherworlds. The *Apocalypse of the Theotokos*, composed in Greek sometime between the ninth and eleventh centuries, relates an otherworld tour undertaken on behalf of sinners by the Virgin Mary.[33] Hundreds of surviving manuscripts in diverse languages and versions testify to its popularity, and to its influence on the eastern Christian otherworld-view, not only in Byzantium, but as far as the Caucasus, Slav lands, the Near East, and Ethiopia. The *Apocalypse of Anastasia*, a more modest text, composed in Greek around the turn of the tenth century, recounts the near-death experience of a pious nun named Anastasia.[34] The *Fís Adomnán*, composed in Irish during the tenth or eleventh century, describes an afterlife journey ascribed to Adomnán, a seventh-century abbot of the Iona monastery.[35] Divergence between the Byzantine and Irish visions are especially striking on three basic points of comparison: God, punishments, and intercession.

A contrast between God as clan chieftain and God as emperor presents itself immediately. *Adomnán* describes a wonderfully warm image of the household of heaven, in its brightly-lit hall, pulsating with lovely music.[36] Over it rules the High King, surrounded by his heavily armed angel hosts, his women (the Virgin Mary and ranks of virgins), and his loyal retainers, the saints. Outside, all is dark, cold, and desolate – the howling winds of an Irish winter. For *Anastasia* and other Byzantine visions, heaven is an imperial palace, a strange, alienating place, with no direct access to the throne or the emperor, and God is a faceless abstraction.[37] There is no lovely music, there are no beautiful birds, fragrant blossoms, luminous crystal walls, jeweled furniture, or glowing light in either medieval Byzantine vision, but only the grim throne of judgment.

The generally positive attitude towards the heavenly authorities in the medieval Irish vision echoes the late antique otherworld-view of the *Apocalypse of Paul*. The center of heaven for *Paul* is the city of Christ, a warm, golden, glowing city of beauty, worship, music, and praise.[38] Within it all the guardian angels gather every day at vespers to take part in the celestial praises before the throne, and to deliver reports on their charges, directly to the

33 *Apocryphal New Testament*, 686–87; *Apocalypsis Mariae Virginis*, 115–26, trans. Baun, *Tales*, 391–400.

34 *Apocalypsis Anastasiae*, trans. Baun, *Tales*, 401–24.

35 Herbert and McNamara, *Irish Biblical Apocrypha*, 137–48.

36 *Fís Adomnán*, chs. 5–16, 138–41.

37 *Apocalypsis Anastasiae*, I, 5–6.

38 See *Apocalypse of Paul*, 29 in *Apocryphal New Testament*, 631–32.

divine presence.[39] Seven centuries or so later, in *Anastasia*, the guardian angels also come to report, but to angel-scribes who staff a celestial records bureau, ceaselessly updating the big books of sins and good deeds.[40] God appears as a disembodied voice over the office loudspeaker. There is no direct access to authority in this Byzantine bureaucratic heaven. Even the Virgin Mary, in her apocalypse, must use extraordinary means to reach the throne.[41]

The Irish vision presents an unequivocally personal God, with whom both visionary and heavenly hosts enjoy a face-to-face relationship.[42] God's actual appearance is not described, but one can see and feel his glory, and be attracted by his power and beauty – this God is no abstraction. There is none of the sense of alienation from the centers of power – terrestrial and celestial – which pervades the Byzantine visions. The Irish otherworld proclaims God as a personal Lord, with heaven his warm, inviting hall. Damnation is to be deprived of such a lord, thrown into the marshy outer bog of the punishments, or further into the stormy, rocky wasteland of hell. The Byzantine otherworld experiences God as a distant emperor, heaven as a multichambered palace, difficult of access. The punishments are overseen by angelic functionaries carrying out orders, as each sinner makes satisfaction to the state, often through symbolic mutilations in the spirit of the Byzantine penal code.[43] Divergent political and social experience in this world has clearly shaped the construction of each author's otherworld.

Following from their different attitudes towards central authority, the Irish and Byzantine visions diverge notably in their attitude toward otherworld punishments. In *Adomnán*, those who do not repent, but grieve and dishonor so great a lord as the High King of Heaven, richly deserve their punishments and the more horrific the torture, the better.[44] Punishments match the particular sins in creative and gruesome ways, and there is no sense that the Irish visionary thinks these might be disproportionate. Sin in a clan and chieftain society is conceived of personally – as an offense against a particular person whose honor you have taken away.[45] A payment or symbolic act is required to restore the other's face, whether it is one's neighbor or one's God, and until honor is restored, no punishment is too horrible.

39 See *Apocalypse of Paul*, 7–10 in *Apocryphal New Testament*, 622–23.
40 *Apocalypsis Anastasiae*, V, 24–25.
41 *Apocalypsis Mariae Virginis*, ch. 26, 124.
42 *Fís Adomnán*, ch. 10, 139.
43 See, for example, *Apocalypsis Mariae Virginis*, ch. 4, 116–17; Baun, *Tales*, ch. 7.
44 *Fís Adomnán*, chs. 30–40, 143–46.
45 Brown, *Rise of Western Christendom*, 241–46; "Decline," 52.

Sin and punishment in the imperial society of Byzantium were perceived less personally. One offended not the honor of one's lord or neighbor, but impersonal imperial law, issuing from a centralized power, and administered by indifferent, corrupt officials, of the type which abound in *Anastasia*'s punishment zones. Both Byzantine visions project ambivalence toward central authority and its powers of punishment. Their otherworld torments are markedly less horrific than those found in the earlier *Paul* or their Irish contemporary, *Adomnán*. The *Theotokos* apocalypse retains the idea of made-to-measure punishments found in earlier visions (and elaborated in *Adomnán*), but removes the iron torture implements and malevolent demons. The sinners whom Mary sees are tormented more by beasts which come from within themselves – the serpent-like creatures of their own remorse – than by external forces. *Anastasia* goes even further in the process of editing out torture and turning down the heat, especially for lay people guilty of minor sins. Neither Byzantine vision revels in the terrible stenches and pitiful shrieks of sinners which enliven many such visions in the Latin West. Mary's tour is rather one long lament for hapless sinners, almost an otherworld protest march on their behalf. At one point, she cries:

> "Have mercy, O Master, on the Christian sinners, for I have seen them being punished and I cannot bear their lamentation. May I go forth, and may I myself be punished with the Christian sinners!"[46]

Mary's plea highlights a final aspect of the very different relationship to authority which underlies the Irish and Byzantine otherworld visions: intercession, and in particular, the cult of Mary's intercession. *Adomnán* describes a direct, personal relationship with one's lord, with little need for intermediaries. The *Theotokos* apocalypse and *Anastasia* assert that an individual can get nowhere with God without powerful intercessors, such as archangel Michael or Mary, the Mother of God. In the late antique *Paul*, Mary appears as a gracious hostess, attended by angels, who welcomes the souls of the righteous.[47] She has no intercessory role. Similarly, in *Adomnán*, Mary's place in the household of heaven is purely decorative.[48]

Nothing could be further from the dynamic Mother of God who dominates the religious consciousness of early medieval Byzantium. Byzantine religious culture was saturated with images of Mary as humanity's paramount

46 *Apocalypsis Mariae Virginis*, ch. 26, 124.
47 See *Apocalypse of Paul*, 46, in *Apocryphal New Testament*, 640.
48 *Fís Adomnán*, ch. 6, 138.

intercessor. The *Apocalypse of the Theotokos* and *Anastasia* both promote Mary's intercession unequivocally, and a tense scene which pits Mary against the grim men on thrones marks the dramatic climax of both visions. In the *Theotokos* apocalypse, after protracted dialogue with a reluctant Christ, Mary achieves two concessions: firstly, that any sinner who calls upon her name as soul is parted from body will be saved; secondly, that the sinners will receive respite from punishment for the fifty days of Eastertide (Paul in his apocalypse had already secured a Sabbath rest for sinners).[49] For Byzantine Christians from early on, intercession was the only hope of surviving divine judgment, and Mary was the mother of unfailing compassion and intercessory persistence. No wonder that the *Apocalypse of Anastasia* hails her as:

> the hope of the Christians and the champion of those who have been wronged, the warmest champion of sinners, the harbour of the tempest-tossed and the physician of the ill, the bread of the hungry and surety of sinners, she who alone has boldness (*parresia*) before God![50]

But as Mary's passivity in *Adomnán* suggests, the cult of her intercession was developing at different rates across Europe. Mary does not appear as intercessor in any of the early western otherworld visions; in fact, she barely impinges on the consciousness of Irish, English, Frankish, or German otherworld visionaries before the late twelfth century.[51] Highlighting the dangers of generalizing from visionary literature, however, other types of evidence attest a firm belief in Mary's intercession in western Europe. She appears as interceding for sinners, and for the departed, in private devotion as early as the seventh century, in liturgical texts by the ninth, and by the eleventh century her intercession was an established homiletic and artistic theme from Ireland to Italy.[52] Some homilists in Anglo-Saxon England even preached that at the Last Day, the Virgin Mary, the archangel Michael, and the apostle Peter would each plead for, and achieve the salvation of, a third of humanity – a folk belief condemned, as ever, by Ælfric.[53] While impressive, this was not quite the final redemption of all, since the homilists assert that "the rest" will go off to eternal punishment. The *apokatastasis* proper was a dream kept alive mostly in the smaller, ancient churches east of Byzantium. In one of the medieval Armenian versions of *Paul*, the combined intercessory efforts of Mary, Paul, and all the angels and saints

49 *Apocalypsis Mariae Virginis*, chs. 26–30, 125–26.
50 *Apocalypsis Anastasiae*, II, 14–15; see also Baun, *Tales*, ch. 8.
51 See texts in Ciccarese, *Visioni*.
52 Clayton, *Cult*, 53, 91–93.
53 Clayton, *Cult*, 253–55.

achieve the complete and total redemption of all the sinners, and the emptying of hell![54]

The end of this world

The ultimate imaginative structure is the cosmos itself. Medieval Christians were sure that the present order was passing away, to be replaced at the end of time by a new heaven and a new earth, purged of all imperfection and evil. The apocalyptic expectations of western Christendom were based largely on the Apocalypse of John, the biblical Revelation. John's Apocalypse needed careful interpretation, but its status as the set text for eschatology was unchallenged in the West. For eastern Christendom – Greek, Syriac, Caucasian, Slavic – apocalyptic was more complicated, and more intimately bound up with secular power structures, with the Roman (i.e., Byzantine) emperor and empire playing a special role in the End. The seventh-century *Apocalypse of Pseudo-Methodios* and the eighth and ninth-century *Vision of Daniel* texts transmitted a belief which persisted to the end of the Byzantine Empire: that the Second Coming would be triggered by the emperor placing his diadem on the Holy Cross at Golgotha in Jerusalem, thereby yielding the scepter of earthly dominion back to God the Father.

When would the End come? Some bishops and theologians in the West, following Augustine, labored to place the End safely in the indefinite future, but the early medieval consensus was much less cautious. Again following Gregory the Great, the majority of Irish, Anglo-Saxon, Frankish, and Byzantine preachers, bishops, and monastic moralists sensed the days ripening and the End coming soon.[55] Like Gregory, reporting premonitions experienced by his friend and fellow bishop Redemptus, they read the birthpangs of the new creation in their own experience:

> It was not long after this vision that wild hordes of Lombards unleashed from their own native land descended on us. The population of Italy, which had grown vast, like a rich harvest of grain, was cut down to wither away. . . . I do not know what is happening elsewhere, but in this land of ours, the world is not merely announcing its end, it is pointing directly to it. . . . The things of earth are quickly slipping from our grasp.[56]

Just as Gregory suspected the Lombards in the sixth century as harbingers of the End, so Irish, Anglo-Saxon, and Frankish Christians identified the savage

54 *Apocrypha Apostolorum Armeniaca*, I, 171–72.
55 Daley, *Hope*, 211–14; Gatch, *Preaching and Theology*, 60–116.
56 Gregory the Great, *Dialogues* 3, III.38, 428–31 (trans. Zimmerman, 186–87).

Viking raids of the ninth century with the tribulations which presaged the End Times. They formed an appreciative audience for a lively literature which sprang up enumerating and describing the signs of the Doom. And despite Jesus's express warnings (Matt. 24.36; Acts 1.7), there was always the temptation to try to predict exactly when the End would come, through reading the signs of the times and in the heavens. The millennial year *anno Domini* 1000 seems to have been a time of heightened expectation for some in the West, and also in Byzantium – but as *anno mundi* ("from the creation of the world") 6500, the midpoint of the seventh age.

What would trigger the apocalypse? A persistent strain of thought in both East and West held human sin to be a major factor. Western moralists such as Alcuin and Wulfstan joined Byzantine apocryphal writers in warning that the cosmos suffered unbearable pressure from the weight of human sin, and that the accumulated defilement would eventually force God to wipe out humanity and cleanse his creation. Another apocalyptic tendency was to search for the machinations of Antichrist in current events, and to look to the appearance of a Messiah figure, a political savior, who would rescue the Christians from their infidel enemies. Whether one's taste in apocalyptic tended toward the moral or the political, the one early medieval certainty was that the End was near, and coming when least expected.

Consolations

> Christ is the morning star, who, when the night of this world is past, brings to his saints the promise of the light of life and opens everlasting day.[57]

Why was apocalyptic and otherworld literature so popular? This famous pericope from the Apocalypse commentary of Bede, the northern English monk and scholar, provides a clue. Early medieval Christians responded to talk of sin, fire, punishment, judgment, the End Times, and the final conflagration because it offered comfort. This may seem counter-intuitive. Meditation on the Last Things – death, heaven, hell, and the Doom – was meant to unsettle the soul, the better to inspire repentance. But although the Last Things first inspire salutary fear and holy dread, their ultimate function is to console. Meditation on both hell and the Doom affirms supremely that humanity lives in a moral universe, in which justice will prevail, transgressions will be punished, and virtue rewarded. Much hell literature is a literature of the reversal of this-world realities. Following the New Testament lead, in *Anastasia* and

57 Bede, *Expositio Apocalypseos*, II.28, 265.

countless other visions, evildoers who prospered in this world are shown in the next world crying out for mercy, while the Lazaruses of this world, who had no earthly reward, are elevated to the bosom of Abraham (Luke 16.19–31). This belief in the ultimate triumph of God's perfect justice, coupled with the promise of the resurrection, was each Christian's personal bulwark against existential anxiety.

Apocalyptic was also comforting on a broader level. For Christians in Ireland, Britain, and Francia, savaged by Vikings; in Italy, overrun successively by Ostrogoths, Byzantine troops, and Lombards; in Byzantium, traumatized by Muslim Arab military success, literature on the end of the world provided strength and solace. It gave meaning to what otherwise was senseless, intolerable violence, and it tied their sufferings into some larger plan, some destiny which would eventually work out for the good. As early medieval Christians throughout Europe and the Near East adjusted to the loss of old certainties and the eruption of terrible new insecurities, affirming that God was still in control, working his purpose out, was key to sustaining morale. Hell and the Doom were embraced with such fervor, not because of their negative aspects, on which modern criticism tends to dwell, but because of their positive proclamation that God's perfect justice would prevail, and that the universe was drawing nearer and nearer to its perfect consummation, according to God's providential plan. The Last Things helped early medieval Christians to make sense of their existence in this world of sorrows. They formed the bedrock of Christian hope.

Conclusion: Christendom, c. 1100

JOHN H. VAN ENGEN

On the cusp of the twelfth century: Latin Christendom and the kingdoms of the christened

In January 1076, as the confrontation between German king and Roman pope spun out of control, King Henry IV, together with most of the assembled German bishops, called upon Hildebrand ("no pope but false monk") to step down.[1] Word of this action reached Rome about the time its Lenten synod (February 14–20) went into session. Pope Gregory resolved to depose and excommunicate the king, in that order, but he first delivered a lengthy sermon, at least as Paul of Bernried told it fifty years later (1128). The "precursor to Antichrist" had arisen in the church, Gregory announced, and the assembled churchmen were entering upon a new age:

> It's enough that we have lived up until now in the peace of the church. Now, indeed, the harvest, long dried-out, should again be watered, fittingly, with the blood of the saints, so that Christ's fruit, weakened over length of years by old age, might return, moistened afresh, to its original beauty. We shall see the devil's war . . . break out in open field. Now is the time for Christ's recruits to fight back.[2]

The words, whether or not they retain an echo of Gregory's sermon, are Paul's, their combative tone informed by the beleaguered situation of the Gregorian party around Regensburg. But they captured sentiments that drove Gregory and his partisans. In January 1075 Pope Gregory had called upon Duke Rudolf of Swabia and Duke Bertolf of Carinthia openly to resist simoniac office holders and unchaste clerics in the face of recalcitrant bishops.

1 *Die Briefe Heinrichs IV*, nn. 11 and 12, 13–17.
2 Paul of Bernried, *Vita Gregorii*, 71, 513.

> We know that your prudence has weighed with a clear mind the pitiable desolation of the Christian religion, which for our sins is placed in such extremity now that no one living has seen more unhappy times, nor can anyone find such in any writings inherited since the time of our father the blessed Sylvester.[3]

Pope Sylvester I, legend held, had healed and baptized Constantine, ending the persecution of the early church. In ecclesiastical mythology, reinforced by liturgy and commentaries on the Apocalypse, the age of persecutors and martyrs had given way to heretics and confessors, then finally to an extended era of "peace," troubled only by "false brothers." But now, as Gregory and the reformers saw it, seven hundred years of "peace" had finally run out. "Truth" would face down inherited "custom" (another of Pope Gregory's formulations) in an epoch-making battle for the church's autonomy (*libertas*).[4] Short of such a decisive confrontation, the reformers feared, religion itself might wither away: the "Christian era" could end.

The time subsumed under the rubric post-Constantinian "peace" corresponded, at least in Pope Gregory's version of it, to what we call early medieval Christianity. Twentieth-century historians, too, posited a major break in European history at the turn of the twelfth century (meaning in practice the mid-eleventh century, or even the turn of the millennium). Invoking a variety of markers, they pointed initially to population growth, economic expansion, and the crusades as agents of change, together with resurgent monarchy and new learning (Haskins's "Renaissance"). After World War II, historians emphasized the role of religion, primarily as a force for good, an impulse for renewal, even marking the beginning of Europe as such.[5] These "religious movements" (with a new and large place for women) represented a first "reformation," a transformation of monastic life across Europe, born perhaps of a post-millennial exuberance breaking out in revivals and heresies, alternatively a "Gregorian Reform" of the church propelled and steered by a centralizing papacy – themes that have now mostly entered our textbooks. Over the last generation, historians have drawn insistent attention instead to a darker side, also religious in character, Europe's first pogroms in 1096, a state-like church extending a new persecuting apparatus into local communities, an inclination

3 *Register Gregorii VII*, II.45, 183.

4 Gratian, *Decretum* d.8 c.3, ed. Friedberg 1, 14.

5 Rosenstock-Huessy, *Out of Revolution*, argued already earlier that Europe was born of revolutions, the first being the Gregorian Reform and the last the Russian in 1917; his book first appeared in German in 1931. When he rewrote it in English in 1938, he reversed the chronology, moving from the Russian to the Gregorian Revolution. The religious dimension was taken up immediately after World War II by Heer, see *Aufgang Europas*.

to marginalize "others" in order to justify new powers assumed by clerics or first-born noblemen or nascent universities.[6]

Twelfth-century contemporaries, in fact, spoke of their times in all differing moods. Until recently we have mostly lifted out their vibrant sense of optimism and novelty, of change and choice, even progress, "moderns" (= present-day) against "antiques" (= a dusky past). But there were other voices. Hildegard of Bingen, for instance, looking back in her sixties to the time of her birth "at the eleven-hundredth year after Christ's," saw the preceding epoch (our early medieval Christianity) as a time when true teaching and animated righteousness (*doctrina apostolorum et ardens justicia*) still informed Christian lives, especially the "spiritual" among them. About the time of her birth (1098), she said, those markers began to fade and turn doubtful (*tardare cepit et in hesitationem uertebatur*).[7] Her lifetime, our twelfth century, she berated as "childish" and "womanish," not virile with uprightness (*iustitia*) and bold teaching – hence the need for a startling reversal, a "mere" woman called to teach and prophesy in a senescent and corrupt church.

We look back now from a millennium's distance, and as citizens of a global world. However much local events intrigue us, and rightly so, we as historians must also increasingly position Europe's history in the broad stream of humanity. The same holds for positioning its religion, whether as a presence or an agent, and this holds *par excellence* for Christianity, a religion that has traditionally anchored itself in historical claims, even European historical claims. In that story the era of post-Constantinian *pax*, the centuries of early medieval Christianity, emerge as pivotal. Did early European culture and society then become inextricably interwoven with, even unimaginable or unintelligible apart from, the Christian religion? If so, how, and in what senses? The questions are broad, disputed now at the highest levels across Europe, and admit of no simple answer; no more so than questions, equally legitimate in my view, about Confucian and Hindu traditions in the long-term making of China or India's peoples. We come to these questions now, moreover, and look back historically, at a moment when the Christian religion seems more likely to have a future, or at least an expansive one, ironically, in Africa, or Asia, or the Americas. This has itself provoked historical rethinking, including efforts to circumscribe religion's role as a formative agent in earlier European

6 The bibliography offers a short sampling of books on twelfth-century Europe. Here I allude to Haskins, *Renaissance of the Twelfth Century*; Grundmann, *Religious Movements*; Constable, *Reformation of the Twelfth Century*; Fried, "Endzeiterwartung"; Moore, *First European Revolution* and *Formation of a Persecuting Society*; Cohen, *Sanctifying the Name of God*; Chazan, *Fashioning Jewish Identity*.

7 *Vita S. Hildegardis*, II.2, 22.

history. But it also elicits creative and more inclusive approaches to religion in history, even broadening the scope of Christian communities in the story. This volume invites readers to recover the worlds of early medieval Christianities in all their multiplicity and varying dynamics. But how should we frame those centuries? Under what rubrics? Conversion? Multiple Christendoms? This epilogue asks whether we may look back still too much through a lens ground in a post-twelfth-century European world. I might liken the interpretive dilemma to a frustration some history teachers face trying to convey the character of "Old" or "traditional" Europe to students who now live unselfconsciously in post-Revolutionary societies and a largely post-Christian milieu.

Peter Brown opened with a grand tour of Christian communities in the year 600. That is hard to do in the year 1100. About 600, whether or not they identified as Romans, Christians could claim the Mediterranean, with communities stretched around and beyond it, reaching to the Irish Isle in the northwest, nearly to inner Asia in the northeast, to Nubia in the southeast. These christened peoples differed increasingly among themselves in language, liturgy, organization, key teachings, and routine practices. But for all their multiplicity ("Christendoms") they also retained at the turn of the seventh century vague memories of origins and interconnection, how one got founded out of another or split from another, on what point of doctrine, practice, or organization. Alongside open hostility, a vague sense of connectedness survived, sometimes to exacerbate hostilities. At the same time communities steadily put down local roots and cultivated their own Christian ways – with pride in origins or connection still to origins (tradition) – their own qualities of worship or teaching, each with an expanding sense of what had shaped their community over time into a distinct cultural and social entity with a distinctive history.

Arguments for epoch-making change in the twelfth century hinge finally upon our angle of vision, the markers by which we measure. A good case could be made, for instance, for the Carolingian era as engendering real shifts in religious and ecclesiastical culture, at least for the part of the world that emerged as Europe. Alternatively, in contradistinction to all this emphasis upon twelfth-century renewal by late-twentieth century historians (and the still earlier historiography on the fifteenth-century renaissance), recent historians have envisioned an "Old Europe" stretching from about 1200 to 1750, a period when, among other things, Christianization is projected to have reached deepest into the soil of Europe's peoples and cultures. This would presuppose more epoch-making transformations around the year 1200 than in any other period since Late Antiquity or before the French Revolution. Whatever we make of that, speculation about how to periodize European history forces us back to our original query: how do we come at the world of early medieval Christianities and under what rubric? A common approach has represented these centuries as the complex working-out of dis-locations and re-locations springing ultimately from the gradual disappearance of late antique, Christian Roman structures of government. That Roman world, after all, was what Charlemagne sought to emulate in 800 and Otto III in 1000. This approach, whatever its truths, frames the historical dynamic too simplistically, derives it too unilaterally from the imperial inheritance, and allows too little room for formative creativities at work regionally, some indeed arising from the Christian religion itself. That is what interests us. This epilogue accordingly directs attention to those features of the Christian religion that marked the early medieval period, and sets them in contrast to what emerged during the twelfth century.

The world of Christians in the year 1100 did not spin out from the Mediterranean; nor indeed did it orient around any single point, even if Rome or Constantinople or Jerusalem might have disputed that. In 1095–96 crusaders undertook to cross the sea in force to conquer Palestine as their "Holy Land" (its peoples by then subject to Muslim regimes for nearly five hundred years), in an undertaking highly dubious to Byzantine Christians for its means, as much as for its accompanying claims. Final contact with Christian remnants in North Africa was registered in a letter of Pope Gregory VII dated May 1076.[8] Roman Iberia, lost to Christian rule for four hundred years, boasted a flourishing Muslim culture, with only the first stirrings in the Christian north of "reconquest," and memories still of martyrs in Cordoba in the 850s. Three of the five patriarchates (Jerusalem, Antioch, and Alexandria) headed Christian communities whose peoples were shrinking decisively into minority status, more and more out of contact with other Christians, originally by choice (due to matters of doctrine, ethnicity, and language), later by isolation. When Jacques de Vitry, university man, preacher, and cardinal, arrived at Acre in the early thirteenth century, he could only fulminate at the odd sorts of peoples he encountered there, hardly recognizable to him as "Christians."[9] After 1071 Asia Minor, the heartland of Greek Christianity, began to give way to Turkish Islam, the beginnings of that land's "de-Hellenization." The two free-standing patriarchates, in Rome and Constantinople, after years of thinning relations and mutual name-calling, read one another out of the true church in 1054,

8 *Register Gregorii VII*, III.20–21, 286–88.
9 *Lettres de Jacques de Vitry*, *Epistola* II, 79–97.

a break exacerbated subsequently by crusade, conquest, and their setting up rival hierarchies, capped in 1204 by Rome conquering New Rome and installing its own Latin prelates.

The early medieval world was a world of bishops, with certain of them (as metropolitans or primates or patriarchs) claiming broader and higher regional powers. In this world a bishop was usually a *sacerdos* and the *parochia* his diocese, with various other priestly figures – high to low – answering to the term *papa*. Churches had formed primarily in Roman cities, and bishops presided there, often over the cities as well, at least in the West. To move the church beyond Roman limits into comparable centers of local power, like Irish clan configurations, for instance, or into settlements in Germanic and Slavic lands, required creativity. All this changed in the world of Latin Christendom after the year 1100 or so, with a singular claim now made on the term *papa*, while "priests" and "parishes" emerged across the landscape in their thousands ("curates" being named as such only in the thirteenth and fourteenth centuries). In this new world, religious leadership and community bifurcated, in effect, with bishops (despite their elevated political and social status) often lost in the middle. This diminution was mirrored theologically by a new contention over whether episcopal consecration represented a sacrament distinct from priestly ordination, with the matter decided in the negative.

Juridically, too, bishops lost ordinary power to plenary papal jurisdiction above, and local power to cathedral chapters, archdeacons, and rural deans below. The Roman court now increasingly initiated policy, its decretals functioning as imperial rescripts, and its courts extending jurisdiction into every diocese. Potentially this jurisdiction could extend into the lowliest parish by way of papally appointed judges delegate, through whom the bishop of Rome acted as a "universal ordinary," his rulings overshadowing local ordinaries (bishops).

Beginning with Pope Innocent III (1198–1216), more and more bishops were appointed to their sees in Rome, a scene unthinkable in the early medieval world outside the province of central Italy. So, too, Rome's liturgical rite was to supersede all others as the proper way to intercede with the Godhead, supplanting more regionally colored observances (such as the Ambrosian rite in Milan), though in practice, local usages persisted until the Council of Trent (1545) and the printing press. All this is well known, but its momentum advanced straight through the Avignon papacy (1309–77), broken only by the Great Schism (1378–1417) and a host of political compromises struck in its aftermath.

At the other end of the social scale, less studied until recently, mother churches came fully into their own legally and ritually from the twelfth century, each possessing a font and offering a sacred canopy for community, for christening, marrying, reconciling, and burying. The groundwork was laid by Carolingian legislation on tithing, a move which coincidentally rendered local churches desirable objects for income. But a full network of parishes emerged only in the course of the twelfth and thirteenth centuries, coming fully into their own in the fourteenth and fifteenth centuries. Writing before 1140, Gratian notably included almost nothing on parishes as such in his *Concord of*[4000] *Discordant Canons*, the textbook after 1160 for teaching church law.

The mark of a parish was its font, the birthing place of the christened. That object and rite set it off from chapels (altars) and shrines (saints' relics) scattered all about. The twelfth century put stone fonts in place massively across the landscape (this still little studied), also wooden ones in some areas, anchoring a mother church. Communities now also cordoned off their own churchyard, where bodies waited in sacred ground for the day of resurrection. The church porch, serving as a meeting point for everything from civic assemblies to village markets, likewise the site of sacred rites like churching women after childbirth, set the scene for the other key life-marker, marriage. There a couple met for priestly blessing and public recognition, their hands entwined, wrapped in a priestly stole, the rite itself now first lifted to sacramental status. Three sites, then, the font, the churchyard, and the porch, served together to locate a Christian community and to frame the life-span of the christened. The cultural change this engendered was real, if not easy to measure religiously. Only in this era did people forget that they had once traipsed some distance at least once a year to the bishop's church to acknowledge the source of their Christian name or to a baptismal church to christen their children, with marriage and burial still handled in a variety of local ways.

But we must return to the bishop: whether it was policy and judgments coming from afar and above (Rome and its courts), or the comforts of religion lived between font and churchyard in a mother parish, after the year 1100 bishops ceased to play the shaping role in Latin Christendom they had regularly exercised in early medieval Christian societies. This book has evoked a world largely without papacy or parish. It has required historical imagination to grasp how christening and marrying and burying, not to say preaching and absolving, may have worked for all those bearing the Christian name, how bishops – or priests with female partners – acted to shape communities on the ground.

An even more pervasive figure in early medieval Christian societies was the monk. Holiness was measured in good part, going back to Late Antiquity, by ascetic withdrawal, from family life, property and power, self-rule, towns.

The ideal persisted even as monasteries grew into great property-holding complexes as well as social and administrative and pastoral care centers, and monks (originally lay) became priests and bishops. Prevailing notions of perfection and community interacted in a creative tension never resolved. The "holy" meant ordinarily "persons of God" (*vir dei*), exalted ascetic elites removed to the "desert," yet without excluding entirely the whole "people of God" (*populus dei*), all those christened and hoping to enter the heavenly kingdom. Monks and nuns in this era might withdraw into cloisters for intercessory prayer. But many monks also served as advisers to kings and princes, as schoolmasters, missionaries, bishops, preachers, or spiritual guides. In twelfth-century Latin Christendom this tension broke fully into the open, swinging radically one direction and then the other. Most of the figures and groups associated with the "twelfth-century reformation" demanded withdrawal, pulling back from towns and parishes and property management and schools to pursue in retreat a life of contemplative prayer. There they discovered the interior life, which issued in a harvest of spiritual writing of lasting influence in the West. But they too got drawn back in (Bernard of Clairvaux, Norbert of Xanten). The predominant impulse, nonetheless, was to separate, and to admit into their number only those who made a mature decision for conversion, no more children channeled in by family.

Then in thirteenth-century towns mendicants ("beggars") moved dramatically and deliberately in the reverse direction, back into the world. They challenged nearly a thousand years of monastic history, justifying life in the world as apt, even necessary, for the pursuit of perfection. They aimed to live hand-to-mouth on alms in urban centers, not on landed endowments in the countryside. They openly defended a "mixed" life (preaching and teaching and hearing confessions in the world) as perfect – a higher calling since it returned the fruits of contemplation to others, an act of charity. The twelfth century had anticipated the creation of mixed forms in its own way when lay brothers were allowed to combine peasant labor with a monk's cowl and military orders united warrior skill with monastic consecration. The thirteenth century opened holiness both to the lay penitent (Francis) and to the clerical teacher and preacher (Dominic). Their new paradigm soon predominated, along with bottom-up forms of organization: their ministers or priors, however authoritative, were not abbots obeyed as Christ himself.

This world of the twelfth and thirteenth centuries could never quite make up its mind, however, about the proper behavior of women dedicated for religion's sake to active labor or charity. Even though women streamed to these newer forms of religious life in unprecedented numbers, some – the beguines, for instance – often lived under a hint of suspicion. A critical element in all this was a paradigm shift in theory as well as practice. Though monks and nuns had operated actively in early medieval Christianities and proved crucial to evangelizing and teaching, it was the friars and beguines who first redefined the ideal itself, and then also reorganized practice, in order to move the "holy" into the "world."

Equally pervasive in the world of early medieval Christianities was the saint, recognized as a living person or by way of icons, shrines, relics, miracles, or storied lives. Here it is harder to identify a true paradigm shift. We can point to variations and new emphases, but we see the same adjustments in early medieval Christianities as well. From the later twelfth century, Rome claimed a monopoly right to name saints – a matter earlier settled locally by consensus and results (which in fact persisted in local practice). From the thirteenth century, biblical and saints' names multiplied exponentially in families across Europe, perhaps along with greater emphasis upon imitating or internalizing the saints' virtues. In the fourteenth century, there came an arithmetic heaping up of relics or indulgences, an eager or anxious "reckoning-up" of sacred chits in all available forms. What also emerged were Christ-centered and Marian devotions (the rosary) with a long future centered on the consecrated host (the Corpus Christi feast, reserved hosts, miraculously bloody hosts, etc.) as well as the stations of the cross. Whether all this added up to a paradigm shift seems less clear. But that, too, would beg for explanation – even as it is noteworthy that early medieval historians, for the most part, first opened up our eyes to seeing all this.

Were these dimensions of Christian practice closer to the ground, thus less susceptible to dramatic paradigm shifts from outside or on-high? Yet, parishes were newly built ground-up, people often actively campaigning to secure their own font. Or is it a perspectival issue, the cult of saints looming large in early medieval Christianities in the relative absence of other forms of expression or divine intercession and of the full-fledged parish?

Two other matters, complexly interrelated, certainly represented paradigm shifts. They are well known, if still inadequately interpreted, in part because their reach was so all-pervasive: a move from, to use broad terms, conversion to reform in both persons and society, and from baptism to the Eucharist as the paradigmatic sacrament. Over the centuries early medieval kingdoms and peoples moved steadily beyond their initial conversionary moment, while always taking for granted still their social and cultural worlds (Roman, Irish, Armenian, Germanic, Slavic). Churchmen might ban some practices outright and early, but most people operated routinely and fully inside those inherited worlds, with infant christening now a part of the inheritance. This proved all the more confusing as there were increasingly no non-christened populations against whom to measure, except the occasional Jew or the largely unknown infidels. As for those communities now inside a larger Muslim world, members were steadily peeling off to join what was slowly becoming the majority. Meanwhile, in the christened world, ever more practices or objects were themselves christened, from houses and bells to cemeteries and coronations. Conversion, nonetheless, remained the foundational point of collective self-definition – what peoples perceived as having set them apart. It lived on as a moment in time and as a historical momentum, always being fallen away from or improved upon. Even the Carolingian reforms, crucial as they were for European history, advanced in a spirit of "correction," going back to basics and setting things straight (which, like all such moves, if successful, turn innovative).

From the mid-eleventh century, reform came to serve as the signal historical marker in the western imagination, the conversionary moment now relegated mostly to a storied past. Reform, like conversion, may be grasped as individual or collective. Grounded in the principle of humans renewing their image-likeness to God, in this new era it took on a decidedly collective or institutional dimension. Conversion, if ultimately personal in Christian understanding, was socially collective, and also largely remembered as such – Augustine's *Confessions*, in this regard, for all its rhetorical power, historically misleading. Reform likewise aimed now not only at remaking persons but recasting the papacy, monastic orders, even kingdoms, reordering them to divine norms. This might involve looking back to authentic exemplars (the early church, early papal law, and so on) but with an eye to a better future (*in melius*). Thus papal decretals ultimately became the key instrument, brazenly issuing "new law" according to the "needs of the times," a right first claimed in Pope Gregory VII's *Dictatus pape* of March 1075.[10]

But how should we imagine this broad shift from conversion to reform? Conversion turned in new directions after the year 1000, broadly to institutions or penetratingly to the human interior, because, scholars often intimate, its earlier social or communitarian task was long since finished. But that seems superficial. After all, early medieval kingdoms had lived contentedly with their christening for a long time. Reform required, among other things, a new orientation toward time, an urgency to make things better in incarnate time, in "years of the Lord," as the calendar now increasingly read, even if (or, because) people also lived with the sense of a final reckoning not all that far off. When

10 *Register Gregorii VII*, II.55a, 203.

reform itself seemed to languish in the later twelfth century (as Hildegard held), Joachim of Fiore (d. 1202) projected it into a new and third age, an age of the Spirit about to dawn. The epoch of perfect peace and contemplation he envisioned would extend – proceed from – time elapsed under the aegis of the Father and the Son, roughly that of the first covenant and the incarnate church – a consciously apocalyptic stance after reform itself had disappointed. Most medieval Europeans were oriented to incarnate time. And there it was no longer good enough that people were baptized, or recalled to their baptismal duties (a point commonly invoked in early medieval texts and one largely absent from the new reformers). After so many centuries, all that could be taken for granted, the stuff of infants. A fuller realization was sought: twelfth- and thirteenth-century reformers, papal or Cistercian or Franciscan, aimed to put the kingdom of Christ in order here and now by re-forming christened society itself, its very laws and institutions and practices.

This was not to neglect the human interior which, at least conceptually, had always represented the heart of Christian notions of reform. Scholars point as well to a radical turn inward of spirit and thought from the twelfth century onward – Bernard's insistence on "experience" and "love," Abelard's on "intention," Francis's on the human Jesus, and more broadly the new monks' "adult converts" rather than "child conscripts," the church opting for mutual consent rather than parental will or sexual consummation in making a marriage. Some of these views, to be fair, were not wholly without early medieval (or at least late antique) precedent. Central to it all, a recent study holds, is the transition from a victorious to a suffering Christ, and the compassion of his mother.[11] At issue is which came first, the remaking of the human interior in all its passion and pity or the remaking of the Savior and his mother – or both at the same time?

At the level of more routine practice, reform supplanting conversion finds its expression in individual private penance. Confession, required annually of each parishioner to his or her "own priest" after 1215, now complemented the font in defining parochial spiritual jurisdiction, the "curate" charged with care of souls. Medieval historians have been tempted of late to rest strong claims on this annual face-to-face encounter in some corner of the church on Shrove Tuesday (no confessional boxes, no real privacy). It was often routine, a kind of checking in, or rather checking-off, initially against the vices and virtues, latterly against the ten commandments. But it created a platform for expectations, and the more devout, especially increasing numbers of women,

11 See now Fulton, *From Judgment to Passion*.

took those expectations upon themselves, the more spiritually inclined seeking out someone on their own (often a friar) to act as a guide in earnest (sometimes, too, a spiritual tyrant). The paradigm had shifted, and was now shifting for everyone, not just for dedicated monks or nuns. A penitential model of constant reforming, completed only by a personal confession at last rites, introduced an entirely different dynamic and prospect than a return to the original purity of conversion and christening.

Sacramental rites enacted the church's presence in the exchange between humans and the deity, the material and the divine, a position no lay power or person could replicate or assume. In early medieval Christianities baptism remained paradigmatic in practice and theory. Disputes about any sacramental form of divine presence and its invisible brand (*character*) all took baptism as their point of departure, be it ordaining clerics, blessing monks, sacring kings, or consecrating the Eucharist. That changed after the mid-eleventh century in Latin Christendom. By forces that cannot be put down to conscious policy, the Eucharist came to replace baptism as paradigmatic, even as reform preempted conversion, whether collective or personal. The Eucharist assumed its place as the central and defining rite, for liturgy as for theology. The church's spiritual presence in the world was made real not so much in its power to make Christians as to make the Body of Christ. Even lay women (midwives) might baptize, but only priests could confect the Eucharist. Gregorian reformers said nothing about baptism but warned partisan adherents to stay away from masses said by priests whose anointed hands were polluted by intimacy with women – their Eucharist illicit, perhaps invalid. The defining power of a priest, defined as the culmination of holy orders, thereby surpassed in some real sense a bishop's unique power to confirm or ordain. From the twelfth century, reverence for this sacrament only grew in medieval Christendom: the reserving and elevating of the host, the withholding of the cup from the laity, a feast day devoted to the "corpus Christi" itself hymned and processed through the city, that feast day in turn gathering the whole community in procession as well as for instruction and entertainment (plays). Society was confronted with an incarnate presence of a visible but increasingly untouchable kind, reverenced far more by communing with the eyes than taking into the mouth, and offering an intriguing juxtaposition with the ever more human and bloodied Christ. So fundamental were the accompanying transformations in concept and practice across society that we may rightly ask how accurately we can see the inner shape of early medieval Christianities, if we peer back too unselfconsciously through the framing of this subsequent order. That challenge is part of what this volume has taken up.

Two other developments, amounting to paradigm shifts in my view, deserve notice. The ever sharper insistence upon celibacy for western deacons and priests after 1049 (whatever the slowness in effecting it) and the enforcement of separate juridical status for churchmen and their properties (reinforced by Becket's fight with Henry II and culminating in his murder at Canterbury in 1170) helped create a separate clerical caste more distinctly set apart in Latin Christendom than any found in most early medieval Christianities. The late antique world, to be sure, had first established a privileged clergy, and in early medieval kingdoms they assumed an ever more expanded role, ambivalently supportive of and distinct from princely power. But the sharpening of caste lines in the West after 1100 changed how the christened saw themselves and their clergy. Anticlericalism quickly emerged as a cultural staple, and the laity were recast as the butt of a comparable "anti-laicism," with depictions of them as coarse, violent, ignorant, and bursting with uncontained lusts, whence their lower standing in the church and their need for regulation and penance. It was as if, with the attempted desacralizing of kingship, the lay state itself was also actively being desacralized. At the same time a literature of "contempt for the world" thrived from the mid-eleventh century onward, with especially lurid sections devoted to the woes of marriage, women, child-rearing, and family – nearly always written from a male standpoint. Meanwhile chapters and clerical confraternities tended over time to foster all-male atmospheres of camaraderie and privilege, even if clerics on occasion availed themselves of the sexual services of companions or prostitutes. One might object, justly, that courts of knights also emerged in this era and were no less male-oriented. But there women's influence and presence remained – or, to hear the literature of Romance, even was exalted.

Separating out clergy and laity, fostering a cult of sublime chastity, the Virgin Mary elevated ever more prominently as the exemplar of holiness and emblem of the church – all this rippled out paradoxically for the married and for women in particular. In daily practice women's lives hinged as much upon local customs and expectations as upon anything the church said or wanted. At the same time ascetic literature proclaimed the dangerous allure of women and elevated the Virgin Mary to the paradigm of purity, while Romance literature, a fair amount of it written by clerics and featuring women, now set a style at noble courts that turned on flirtation if not illicit love. Yet women, too, sought participation in this new religious life, indeed in unprecedented numbers, and were not easily put off by male reluctance to receive them or offer spiritual care. Again, even as the church deepened the divide between celibate clergy and married people, it insisted that marriages henceforth be formed by mutual consent, like entrance into religious life, and thus an adult decision taken equally by a woman and a man. In church law women could protest violations of their bodies or marriages as fully and rightfully as men, at least in principle. On the other hand, this celibate clerical caste now staked full claim to oversight of the law over marriage and raised it to a sacrament, its grace understood as removing the stain of concupiscence that accompanied sexual union. All this taken together created a world unlike that in which most early medieval Christians had lived, both in their relation to clergy and in inherited notions about marriage and how it fit into local societies.

Christendom in the twelfth century introduced another new figure, the learned master, exclusively male, and clerical everywhere but in Italy. The guild of masters, that is, the university and its products, soon came to stand notionally (also to a remarkable degree practically) as the third column upholding Christian society, alongside clerics and princes. From the twelfth century, the term "clergy" came to mean "book-man" as well as "church-man," thus "literate," the word on occasion transferred to a literate woman as well (Christine de Pizan). In the late antique world of the fourth and fifth centuries learned rhetors transitioned from performing in a civil world of schools and courts to an ecclesiastical world of worship, preaching, adjudication, and theology, as manifested in Ambrose, Augustine, and John Chrysostom. These bishops and leaders presumed still a vast civil and profane world of learning and career. They sought self-consciously to appropriate the skills of teaching, orating, and commentary for the sacred world – focusing their skills especially on the biblical books – exemplarily in Augustine's *On Christian Learning* (*De doctrina christiana*). But in the early medieval world, absent in the West now that civil world of learning, the church's endeavor came to stand largely alone, with Augustine's book and model singularly influential. Latin churchmen cultivated as well a language that was sacred, set apart for worship and God-talk (theology), yet one that could reach into people's lives directly. In most early medieval societies this generated exceedingly varied and complex experiments, with profane learning and local languages still persisting alongside – or even in rivalry with – this new church learning.

As overseers of a Bible-based book religion, churchmen needed books and mastered them; they also feared them, since the prestige books available for teaching and as literary paradigms were mostly non-Christian. This paradox held to the end of the Middle Ages. Profane books, significantly, were absorbed into the heart of the church's educational and cultural profile, and thus also into Europe's. This was less true, importantly, where schools (or bards) and learning persisted outside the church, as in Byzantium or Ireland. Out of all this emerged in the twelfth century something new in western Christendom: "church-men" organized into a free-standing guild as "book-men," coming out of the heart of the church, yet standing apart from it, claiming authority to speak on the basis now of expertise in reason and reading (not of faith or rank, or at least not exclusively on those). Out of this volatile mix arose, strikingly, theology and church law as formal disciplines taught, debated, applied, and practiced in "disputed questions" and even heady academic free-for-alls ("quodlibets"). In 1208 Pope Innocent III first prepared a selection of decretals (rescripts, edicts, and advisory responses) from his first ten years in office for use as binding precedents in court, and sent them on to the masters at Bologna for teaching as well. At the risk of becoming repetitious, let me say again: When we take up matters of theology or law in early medieval Christianities, it requires real effort and imagination not to read divine teaching or sacred law through these later disciplinary prisms.

These paradigm shifts were not all of a piece, though they intersected. The constantly repeated Eucharistic sacrifice, along with a requirement of at least annual confession, invited attention to reform in a way that infant baptism did not. A more autonomous clergy and a new guild of masters served local societies as much as they did an international church, yet depended ultimately on Rome to guarantee their leveraged position in society. Professed religion could now be conceived of as people withdrawn for prayer and contemplation while also called to preach and teach and confess. They projected holiness into the world, supplying ready manpower for the transformations in society that a Christian order seemed now to demand. Internationally networked, based in every town worthy of the name, friars could reach the laity directly both pastorally and intellectually, disrupting the all too comfortable routines of local parishes. All these patterns, disclosed only in retrospect and in combinations that functioned more like multiple permutations, hardly sprang from any single vision – indeed the vision was itself rife with rivalry and difference, but that is another story. As these ways settled in to become everyday realities across European Christendom an older way of being a Christian community slipped out of practice and memory.

We may conclude by pondering the larger significance of these shifting paradigms. What was their import for a people's sense of polity or place, that which informs, as we now say, identity? In the early Middle Ages policy making took place primarily in bishop's assemblies (councils or synods), ordinarily summoned by kings or princes acting as heirs to the emperor. Church law itself consisted primarily of "canons" issued in those assemblies, often kept in law books chronologically. A mischievous invention, the

Pseudo-Isidorean forgeries of ninth-century Frankland aimed at subverting metropolitan power on behalf of bishops, by way of elevating a distant papal power. But to make papal pronouncements themselves central to defining church law arose in the twelfth century as an innovative response to "new needs and times."

In the mid-eleventh century Roman reformers had launched (or relaunched) more exclusive claims for their *papa*, invoking texts especially from the late imperial papacy (Leo I) as well as these Frankish forgeries. They raised their episcopal/patriarchal see to an order apart (with a new term: *papatus*, papacy), even as they claimed for it insignia once reserved for the Roman emperor, the kissing of papal feet, a singular name (*unicum*), a right to depose emperors, and a quality of *sanctus* inherent in the office (its meaning here ambivalently "holy" (as in the Christian order) or "sacred" (as in the Roman)).[12] They also invented a new election procedure, setting up a closed constitutional circle – popes appointing cardinals and cardinals electing popes – the disruptive role of local clergy and people thus reduced in principle to a formality. Not quite a generation later, in 1095, this papacy called out an army, not the regional militias and feudatories many bishops could command, but warriors from any land or obedience prepared to march on the Holy Land in armed pilgrimage in return for the Vicar of St. Peter's promise of "remission of sins" (a plenary indulgence, whatever the term preached, however heard or understood). The new popes, taking fresh names from the list of early bishops of Rome, now also claimed for themselves an exclusive right to call general councils, and added their own (Lateran I–IV, 1123–1215) to the number of those accounted "universal," creating a further divide with the patriarch of New Rome – even as Charlemagne had once protested the addition of a second Nicene council there (on icons). This new papacy met with resistance and some failure in the twelfth century, the crusading enterprise retreating into defensive positions after early success, the new election system throwing up double candidates as well as schisms and Roman exiles during a majority of the years between 1059 and 1177. But the claim to preemptive plenary power in matters ecclesiastical finally won through. If there was after the twelfth century a regnant general "peace" in the religious fabric of medieval Europe, albeit troubled still by "false" or dissident souls and threatened in imagination or fact by infidel Islam and unyielding Judaism, that overarching peace was defined now by the papal court in Rome.

12 *Register Gregorii VII*, II.55a, 204 and 207.

The term for that "pax" was Christendom. It referred – a sweeping gesture and extravagant claim, but also a reality – to a sense of comprehensive order, a "common" law (as church law was called, not local like regional customs, or varied like "national" ordinances), with an international organization, a single language, a recognizable set of rites, and a coherent body of teachings. When Innocent III (1198–1216), pope of the Fourth Lateran Council and the Fourth Crusade, sought to characterize the society he led and over which he projected himself as arbiter, he spoke simply of Christendom ("christianitas"), meaning all those christened and subject to the rites and jurisdiction of the Roman church. The word itself had arisen in Late Antiquity, a slang term actually, largely avoided by the rhetorically self-conscious. First an everyday word for the baptized, it gained usage colloquially to identify all those who had taken upon themselves the name and mark of Christ their God. The term then acquired multiple meanings over time, from "the christened" and "christening" to "Christianity" and "Christendom." From the later twelfth century, however, its primary usage was to signify collectively the peoples and cultures that acknowledged the religion of Rome, its laws, institutions, and worship – what we call "Latin Christendom." This conceptual unit, though becoming ever fuzzier around the edges and more layered in definition, held broadly into the eighteenth century, even if humanists introduced the classicizing term "Europe" with its redirected nuances, and sixteenth-century reformers ardently disputed any link between their religious culture (still "Christendom") and the papal court.

When historians describe the world of the early Middle Ages as made up of "Christendoms," we project that term into an earlier world, usefully jolting us into awareness of prior histories and multiple communities – a striking instance of deploying a rubric to help bring past societies to life. At issue, however, is whether in so doing we subconsciously import meanings and expectations derived from post-twelfth-century Latin Christendom, and thus perceive early medieval Christianities too much through its lens, its definitional prism. Yet, if we acknowledge the historical reality of European Christendom after c. 1100, we confront another historical dilemma: how to conceive of the earlier communities in their ongoing reality – Byzantium and the Orthodox world most crucially, others, too – an issue surviving into our day (and actually, another unacknowledged vestige of medieval Christendom). For the twelfth century, from the standpoint of papal Christendom, the communities of eastern Christianity needed both rescuing from the infidel and assimilation into Rome, dual aims that made those "Christendoms" at once important causes and contemptible deviants – an ambivalence that tragically informed Innocent III's reaction to the Fourth Crusade. Pope Gregory VII had already declared that no one could be called "catholicus," truly "Christian," unless they were in harmony with Rome.[13]

In the fifth century the Roman Empire began to expect christening of everyone inside their jurisdiction or "pax," Jews excepted. Roman law, compiled in Constantinople in 533–34, dealt at the opening of its Code (the newer imperial contribution to the *Corpus Iuris Civilis*) with churches and what came with them (including baptizing and laws against rebaptizing). But Rome remained Rome, and religion was fit under its laws and institutions, even if it now appeared first in importance among imperial edicts. Seven centuries later Rome had ceased to operate in most of Europe, in much of Asia Minor, and all of Africa; in 1204 the pope's crusaders conquered what remained of it in Constantinople. In 1234, exactly seven centuries later, Pope Gregory IX issued a body of law consisting almost entirely of papal decretals (edicts / rescripts), a text which would end up serving as the authoritative law of the Roman church until 1917. His authorizing letter self-consciously echoed Justianian's, as did many rubrics ("customs," "constitutions," "rescripts," and so on). The "pax" comprehended by this common papal law reached deep into society: marriage, wills, property attached to churches, force exercised on behalf of religion (crusade, inquisition), even the status of Jews and Muslims. But it dealt first of all with the church, its personnel, structure, procedures, properties, and rites, understood as an autonomous legal entity looming over and reaching into the rights and practices of local communities and kingdoms across Latin Christendom. This is not so different, intriguingly, from how we imagine the Roman pax extended into subject territories, interacting with and sometimes overruling indigenous practices and customs. And yet it is not at all the same, for in Latin Christendom local communities and kingdoms persisted in all their fullness and powers, pursuing their own interests and agendas, sometimes resisting the church's pax, sometimes cooperating with it, sometimes getting the better of it. To summarize all the resultant complexities under the rubrics "church and state" or "dualism" will never capture all the intricate overlapping, since the church's interests were often decidedly material (properties, powers, laws) and the kingdoms' surprisingly spiritual (in certain of their ends, claims, and warrants).

But we return finally to the world of early medieval Christianities, the work of this volume. What terms might suitably articulate the kind of community that thrived in the centuries between a christened Roman Empire and an

13 Ibid., 207.

emergent Latin Christendom c. 1100? The early Middle Ages brought forth something new, creative, never specially named, not limited to the borders of the earlier Roman pax. Here we find forms of society and notions of power that blended attributes from Rome, the Christian church, and local culture into units which increasingly claimed, or employed, Christianity as the ultimate justification for their way of doing things, sanction for their powers, norms for their ethical order, rites by which they interceded with the divine. The Frankish kingdom and the Irish and the Armenian, indeed the "Romaioi" of Constantinople, all worked out differing forms of what we have taken to calling multiple Christendoms. These were historical units – religious, political, and social – imbued with the working assumptions and institutions of neither imperial Rome (Byzantium partly excepted) nor papal Christendom, though with elements like each, especially the former, including a strong inclination to vest leadership, including in matters of religion, in emperors or kings (sometimes called a "theocratic" orientation). These leaders, whatever their political powers or human ambitions, grasped such leadership as part of their charge. These units – their formation and evolution over time – comprise the heart of this volume, and laid the foundations for Christian cultures in many parts of the world. They were, quite simply, "kingdoms of the christened." Whether Irish, Anglo-Saxon, Frankish, Byzantine, or Armenian, they acted as relatively autonomous units, and took pride in, even self-definition from (e.g., the Frankish "new Israel"), the social reality that their people were first of all christened (or supposed to be). Each existed in its own world, if tied in principle or practice to some distant patriarch or prince; each with its own balance of powers shared between princes and churchmen; each with its own liturgy, saints, icons, monks, even its own form of the cross; in some real sense (visually, even doctrinally) its own Christ. This last remains a historical dimension still entirely underexplored and lost when these kingdoms get subsumed under a broader history of the church or Christian religion. Recognizable commonalities existed among them, to be sure, those too explored in the foregoing chapters. All that said, real paradigm shifts came with the emergence of Latin Christendom in the twelfth century. From it emerged a new and different pax, an overarching churchly presence in the religious imagination and social reality of medieval Europe. Latin Christendom represented a new way of being a Christian community, so new that it requires a volume such as this to help us think our way back into a world shaped by kingdoms of the christened.

Bibliography

Introduction: Christendom, c. 600
Peter Brown

Primary sources

Book of the Himyarites. Ed. A. Moberg. Lund: C. W. K. Gleerup, 1924.

Cosmas Indicopleustes. *Topographie chrétienne*. Ed. W. Wolska-Conus. *SC* 141. Paris: Éditions du Cerf, 1968.

Gregory the Great. *Epistolae*. In his *Registrum epistularum*. *CCSL* 140–140A. Ed. D. Norberg. Turnhout: Brepols, 1982.

Gregory of Tours. *Passio sanctorum martyrum septem dormientium apud Ephysum*. In his *Miracula et opera minora*. Ed. B. Krusch. *MGH SRM* 1, pt. 2. Hanover: Hahn, 1885.

John of Biclaro. *Chronicon*. In *Conquerors and Chroniclers of Early Medieval Spain*. Trans. K. B. Wolf. Liverpool: Liverpool University Press, 1990.

John of Ephesus. *Lives of the Eastern Saints*. Ed. and trans. E. W. Brooks. 1st of 3 vols. *PO* 17. Paris: Firmin-Didot, 1923.

Julian of Toledo. *De comprobatione sextae aetatis*. Ed. J. N. Hillgarth. *CCSL* 115. Turnhout: Brepols, 1976.

Procopius. *Wars*. Ed. H. B. Dewing. Loeb Classical Library, Cambridge, MA: Harvard University Press 1954.

Sebeos. *The Armenian History Ascribed to Sebeos*. Trans. R. W. Thomson. Liverpool: Liverpool University Press, 1999.

Severus of Antioch. *The Sixth Book of the Select Letters of Severus, Patriarch of Antioch, in the Syriac Version of Athanasius of Nisibis*. Ed. and trans. E. W. Brooks. Text and Translation Society. London: Williams and Norgate, 1902.

Synodicon orientale. Ed. J. B. Chabot. Paris: Imprimerie nationale, 1902.

Theophylact Simocatta. *The History of Theophylact Simocatta*. Trans. M. Whitby and M. Whitby. Oxford: Clarendon Press, 1986.

Secondary sources

Beaucamp, J., F. Briquel-Chatonnet, and C. J. Robin. "La persécution des chrétiens de Nagrân et la chronologie Himyarite." *Aram* 11–12 (1999–2000): 15–83.

Bowersock, G. W. *The Hadramawt between Persia and Byzantium*. In *Convegno internazionale: La Persia e Bisanzio (Roma, 14–18 ottobre 2002)*. Rome: Accademia nazionale dei Lincei, 2004, 263–73.

Brakmann, H. *Die Einwürzelung der Kirche im spätantiken Reich von Aksum*. Bonn: Borengässer, 1994.

Brock, S. "Christians in the Sasanian Empire: A Case of Divided Loyalties." In Mews, *Religion and National Identity*, 1–19.

Brown, P. *The Rise of Western Christendom: Triumph and Diversity, A.D. 200–1000*. 2nd ed. Oxford: Blackwell, 2003.

Camps, G. "Rex gentium Maurorum et Romanorum: Recherches sur les royaumes de Maurétanie du VIe et VIIe siècles." *Antiquités Africaines* 20 (1984): 183–218.

Charles-Edwards, T. M. *Early Christian Ireland*. Cambridge: Cambridge University Press, 2000.

Crum, W. E., and H. G. Evelyn-White. *The Monastery of Epiphanius at Thebes*. 2 vols. New York: Metropolitan Museum of Art, 1926.

Curtis, J., ed. *Mesopotamia and Iran in the Parthian and Sasanian Periods: Rejection and Revival, c. 238 BC–AD 642*. London: British Museum Press, 2000.

Delogu, P. "Solium imperii-urbs ecclesiae. Roma fra tarda antichità e l'alto medio evo." In Ripoll and Gurt Esparraguera, *Sedes Regiae*, 83–108.

Feissel, D., and I. Kaygusuz. "Un mandement impérial du VIème siècle sur une inscription d'Hadrianoupolis de l'Honoriade." *Travaux et mémoires* 9 (1985): 397–419.

Fiey, J. M. *Communautés syriaques en Iran et Irak des origines à 1552*. London: Variorum Reprints, 1979.

Finster, B., and J. Schmidt. *Die Kirche des Abraha in San'â*. In Richter and Nebes, *Arabia Felix*, 67–86.

Fowden, E. Key *The Barbarian Plain: Saint Sergius between Rome and Iran*. Berkeley, CA: University of California Press, 1999.

Fowden, G. *Empire to Commonwealth: The Consequences of Monotheism in Late Antiquity*. Princeton, NJ: Princeton University Press, 1993.

Gameson, R., ed. *St. Augustine and the Conversion of England*. Stroud: Sutton, 1999.

Gatier, P. L. "Nouvelles inscriptions de Gérasa: le prison de l'évêque Paul." *Syria* 62 (1982): 297–305.

Godlewski, W. "A New Approach to the Christianization of Makuri: An Archaeological Note." In *Hommages à Jean Leclant*. Ed. C. Berger, G. Clerc, and N.-C. Grimal. 4 vols. Cairo: Institut français d'archéologie orientale, 1994, 169–76.

Hermann, G., et al. "The International Merv Project: Preliminary Report on the Second Season." *Iran* 32 (1993): 53–75.

Herren, M., and S. A. Brown. *Christ in Celtic Christianity: Britain and Ireland from the Fifth to the Tenth Century*. Woodbridge: Boydell & Brewer, 2002.

Holum, K. "Inscription in the Imperial Revenue Office of Byzantine Caesarea Palestina." *Journal of Roman Archaeology: Supplement* 14 (1995): 333–45.

Ivanov, S. A. *Vizantiiskoe missionerstvo: Mozhno li sdelat' iz "varvara" khristianina [Byzantine Missionary Activity: Can a "Barbarian" Be Turned into a Christian?]*. Moscow: Iazyki Slavianskoi Kul'tury, 2003.

Kazanski, M., and V. Soupault. *Les sites archéologiques en Crimée et au Caucase durant l'Antiquité tardive et le Haut Moyen Âge*. Leiden: Brill, 2000.

Kirwan, L. *Studies in the History of Late Antique and Christian Nubia*. Aldershot: Ashgate Variorum, 2002.

Liebeschuetz, J. H. W. G. *Decline and Fall of the Roman City*. Oxford: Oxford University Press, 2001.

Maas, M. "'Delivered from their Ancient Customs': Christianity and the Question of Cultural Change in Early Byzantine Ethnography." In Mills and Grafton, *Conversion in Late Antiquity*, 127–51.

Markus, R. A. *Gregory the Great and his World*. Cambridge: Cambridge University Press, 1997.

Mathisen, R. W. "Barbarian Bishops and Churches 'in barbaricis gentibus' during Late Antiquity." *Speculum* 72 (1997): 664–97.

Mews, S., ed. *Religion and National Identity*. *SCH* 18. Oxford: Basil Blackwell, 1982.

Mikawaya, H., and A. Kollautz. "Ein Dokument zum Fernhandel zwischen Byzanz und China." *Byzantinische Zeitschrift* 77 (1984): 6–19.

Mills, K., and A. Grafton, eds. *Conversion in Late Antiquity and the Early Middle Ages: Seeing and Believing*. Rochester, NY: University of Rochester Press, 2003.

Mitchell, K. "Marking the Bounds: The Distant Past in Gregory of Tours." In Mitchell and Wood, *World of Gregory of Tours*, 295–306.

—, and I. Wood, eds. *The World of Gregory of Tours*. Leiden: Brill, 2003.

Monneret de Villard, U. *Le leggende orientali sui Magi evangelici*. Studi e testi 163. Vatican City: Biblioteca apostolica vaticana, 1952.

Munro-Hay, S. *Aksum: An African Civilization of Late Antiquity*. Edinburgh: Edinburgh University Press, 1991.

Nebe, G. W., and A. Sima. "Die aramäisch/hebräisch-sabäische Grabinschrift der Lea." *Arabian Archaeology and Epigraphy* 15 (2004): 76–83.

Pelliot, P., and A. Forte. *L'inscription nestorienne de Si-ngan-fou*. Kyoto: Scuola di studi sull'Asia orientale/Paris: Collège de France, Institut des Hautes Études Chinoises, 1996.

Richter, R., and N. Nebes, eds. *Arabia Felix: Beiträge zur Sprache und Kultur des vorislamischen Arabien: Festschrift Walter W. Müller zum 60*. Wiesbaden: Harrassowitz 1994.

Ripoll, G., and J. M. Gurt Esparraguera. *Sedes Regiae (ann. 400–800)*. Barcelona: Reial Acadèmia de Bones Lletres, 2000.

Robin, C. *L'Arabie antique de Karibîl à Mahomet: nouvelles données sur l'histoire des arabes grâce aux inscriptions*. Aix-en-Provence: Édisud, 1991.

Sharpe, R. "Martyrs and Local Saints in Late Antique Britain." In Thacker and Sharpe, *Local Saints and Local Churches*, 75–154.

Simpson, St. J. "Mesopotamia in the Sasanian Period: Settlement Patterns, Arts and Crafts." In Curtis, *Mesopotamia and Iran*, 57–66.

Stancliffe, C. "The British Church and the Mission of Augustine." In Gameson, *St. Augustine and the Conversion of England*, 107–51.

Thacker, A. T., and R. Sharpe. *Local Saints and Local Churches in the Early Medieval West*. Oxford: Oxford University Press, 2002.

Walker, J. "The Limits of Late Antiquity: Philosophy between Rome and Iran." *The Ancient World* 33 (2002): 45–69.

Ward-Perkins, B. "Constantinople: Imperial Capital of the Fifth and Sixth Centuries." In Ripoll and Gurt Esparraguera, *Sedes Regiae*, 63–82.

Wolska-Conus, W. *La topographie chrétienne de Cosmas Indicopleustés: théologie et science au VIe siècle*. Paris: Presses universitaires de France, 1962.

1 Late Roman Christianities
Philip Rousseau

Primary sources

Acta conciliorum oecumenicorum. Ed. E. Schwartz. 4 vols. in 15. Berlin: de Gruyter, 1914–84.

Al-Balâdhuri, Al-Imâm abu-l Abbâs Ahmad ibn-Jâbir. *Kitâb fitûh al-buldân*. Trans. P. K. Hitti. *The Origins of the Islamic State*. New York: Columbia University Press, 1916.

Anonymus Valesianus, "pars posterior," in *Ammianus Marcellinus* 3. Trans. (with Latin text) J. C. Rolfe. Loeb Classical Library. Cambridge, MA: Harvard University Press, 1952.

Avitus of Vienne. *Homilia de rogationibus. PL* 59, 289–94.

Blockley, R. C. *The Fragmentary Classicizing Historians of the Later Roman Empire*. 2 vols. Liverpool: Francis Cairns, 1981–83.

Caesarius of Arles. *Caesarius of Arles: Life, Testament, Letters*. Trans. W. E. Klingshirn. Translated Texts for Historians 19. Liverpool: Liverpool University Press, 1994.

—. *Sermones*. Ed. G. Morin. *CCSL* 103, 104. Turnhout: Brepols, 1953; Eng. trans. M. M. Mueller. *Caesarius of Arles: Sermons*. 3 vols. Fathers of the Church 31, 47, 66. New York: Fathers of the Church, 1956; Washington, DC: Catholic University of America Press, 1963, 1973.

Cassiodorus. *Institutiones*. Ed. R. A. B. Mynors. Oxford: Clarendon Press, 1937.

Codex Theodosianus. Ed. P. Krueger. Berlin: Weidmann, 1923–26; Eng. trans. C. Pharr. *The Theodosian Code and Novels, and the Sirmondian Constitutions*. In collaboration with T. Sherrer Davidson and M. Brown Pharr, and with an introduction by C. Dickerman Williams. Princeton, NJ: Princeton University Press, 1952.

Collectio Avellana. Ed. O. Günther. *CSEL* 35. Vienna: Tempsky, 1895, 1898.

Concilia Galliae, 511–695. Ed. C. de Clercq. *CCSL* 148A. Turnhout: Brepols, 1963.

Corippus. *Flavius Cresconius Corippus: In laudem Iustini Augusti minoris*. Ed. and trans. A(veril) Cameron. London: Athlone Press, 1976.

—. *Flavii Cresconii Corippi: Iohannidos libri VIII*. Ed. J. Diggle and F. R. D. Goodyear. Cambridge: Cambridge University Press, 1970.

Corpus iuris civilis. Vol. 1: *Institutiones*. Ed. P. Krueger; *Digesta*. Ed. T. Mommsen and P. Krueger. Vol. 2: *Codex Justinianus*. Ed. P. Krueger. Vol. 3: *Novellae*. Ed. R. Schoell and W. Kroll. Berlin: Weidmann, 1928–29.

Cyril of Alexandria. *Cyril of Alexandria: Select Letters*. Ed. and trans. L. R. Wickham. Oxford: Clarendon Press, 1983.

Drei dogmatische Schriften Iustinians. Ed. E. Schwartz, Abhandlungen der Bayerischen Akademie der Wissenschaften, phil.-hist. Abteilung, neue Folge 18. Munich: Beck, 1939.

Ephraim. *The Harp of the Spirit: Eighteen Poems of Saint Ephrem*. Trans. S. Brock. 2nd ed. London: Fellowship of St. Alban and St. Sergius, 1983.

—. *Hymns on Paradise*. Trans. S. Brock. Crestwood, NY: St. Vladimir's Seminary Press, 1990.

Eugippius. *Vita Severini*. Ed. P. Knöll. *CSEL* 9, part 2. Vienna: C. Geroldi, 1886; Eng. trans. L. Bieler. *The Life of Saint Severin*. With the collaboration of L. Krestan.

Fathers of the Church 55. Washington, DC: Catholic University of America Press, 1965.

Evagrius Scholasticus. *The Ecclesiastical History of Evagrius with the Scholia*. Ed. J. Bidez and L. Parmentier. London: Methuen, 1898; reprinted New York: AMS Press, 1979; Eng. trans. M. Whitby. *The Ecclesiastical History of Evagrius Scholasticus*. Liverpool: Liverpool University Press, 2000.

Facundus of Hermiane. *Pro defensione trium capitularum, libri XII*. Ed. J.-M. Clément and R. Vander Plaetse. *CCSL* 90A. Turnhout: Brepols, 1974, 3–398; French trans. A. Fräisse-Bétoulières. *Facundus d'Hermiane: Défense des trois chapîtres. SC* 471, 478–79. Paris: Éditions du Cerf, 2002–2003.

Gregory the Great. *Cura pastoralis [Pastoral Care]*. Ed. F. Rommel. Introduction and notes B. Judic. French trans. C. Morel. *Grégoire le Grand: Règle pastorale. SC* 381–82. Paris: Éditions du Cerf, 1992; English trans. H. Davis. Ancient Christian Writers 11. New York: Newman Press, 1950.

—. *Dialogues*. Ed. and French trans. A. de Vogüé. *Grégoire le Grand: Dialogues. SC* 251, 260, 265. Paris: Éditions du Cerf, 1978–80; English trans. O. J. Zimmerman. Fathers of the Church 39. New York: Fathers of the Church, 1959.

—. *Sancti Gregorii Magni Registrum epistularum*. Ed. D. Norberg. *CCSL* 140. Turnhout: Brepols, 1982.

Gregory of Tours. *Gregorii Episcopi Turonensis Libri historiarum X*. Ed. B. Krusch and W. Levison. *MGH SRM* 1.1. Hanover: Hahn, 1951, 1993; English trans. L. Thorpe. *Gregory of Tours: The History of the Franks*. Harmondsworth: Penguin Books, 1974.

Honoratus. *Life of Hilary of Arles*. Ed. S. Cavallin. Introduction, French trans., and notes P.-A. Jacob. *Honorat de Marseille: La vie d'Hilaire d'Arles. SC* 404. Paris: Éditions du Cerf, 1995.

John Chrysostom. *De sacerdotio*. Ed. with introduction, French trans., and notes by A.-M. Malingrey. *Jean Chrysostome: Sur le sacerdoce. SC* 272. Paris: Éditions du Cerf, 1980.

John of Ephesus. *Historiae ecclesiasticae pars tertia*. Ed. E. W. Brooks. 2 vols. *CSCO* 105–106, Scriptores syri 54–55. Reprinted Louvain: Durbecq, 1952.

—. *Lives of the Eastern Saints*. Ed. and trans. E. W. Brooks. *PO* 17, fasc. 1 (chapters 1–23); *PO* 18, fasc. 4 (chapters 24–49); *PO* 19, fasc. 2 (chapters 50–58). Paris: Firmin-Didot, 1923–26.

Jonas of Susa. *Vita Columbani*. Ed. B. Krusch, *MGH SRM* 4. Hanover: Hahn, 1902.

Junillus. *De partibus divinae legis. PL* 68, 15–42.

Leontius. *Leontius, Presbyter of Constantinople: Fourteen Homilies*. Trans. with introduction and notes P. Allen and C. Datema. *Byzantina Australiensia* 9. Brisbane: Australian Association for Byzantine Studies, 1991.

Menander Protector. *The History of Menander the Guardsman*. Introductory essay, text, trans., and historiographical notes R. C. Blockley. Liverpool: Francis Cairns, 1985.

Priscus. *Fragmentum Historicorum Graecorum* 4. Ed. C. Müller. Paris: Firmin-Didot, 1885.

Procopius. *Wars*, *Secret History*, and *Buildings*. English trans., introduction, and notes H. B. Dewing. 7 vols. Loeb Classical Library. Cambridge, MA: Harvard University Press, 1914–40.

Publizistische Sammlungen zum acacianischen Schisma. Ed. E. Schwartz, Abhandlungen der Bayerischen Akademie der Wissenschaften, phil.-hist. Abteilung, n. F., Heft 10. Munich: Beck, 1934.

Romanos. *Romanos le Mélode: hymnes*. Ed. with introduction, French trans., and notes J. Grosdidier de Matons. *SC* 99, 110, 114, 128, 283. Paris: Éditions du Cerf, 1964–81.

Severus of Antioch. *Sévère d'Antioche: la polémique antijulianiste*. Ed. with French trans. R. Hespel. *CSCO* 244–45, 295–96, 301–302, 318–19, Scriptores syri 104–105, 124–25, 126–27, 136–37. Louvain: Secrétariat du CSCO, 1964–71.

Sidonius. *Sidonius: Poems and Letters*. English trans., introduction, and notes W. B. Anderson. 2 vols. Loeb Classical Library. Cambridge, MA: Harvard University Press, 1936–65.

Sulpicius Severus. *Sulpice Sévère: vie de saint Martin*. Ed. with introduction, French trans., and notes J. Fontaine. *SC* 133–35. Paris: Éditions du Cerf, 1967–69.

Tírechán. *Life of St. Patrick*. In L. Bieler. *Patrician Texts in the Book of Armagh*. Dublin: Dublin Institute for Advanced Studies, 1979.

van der Wal, N., and B. H. Stolte. *Collectio Tripartita: Justinian on Religious and Ecclesiastical Affairs*. Groningen: Forsten, 1994.

Van Roey, A., and P. Allen, eds. *Monophysite Texts of the Sixth Century*. Louvain: Peeters, 1994.

Vies des pères du Jura. Ed. with introduction, French trans., and notes F. Martine. *SC* 142. Paris: Éditions du Cerf. 1968; English trans. T. Vivian, K. Vivian, and J. B. Russell. *The Lives of the Jura Fathers*. Cistercian Series 178. Kalamazoo, MI: Cistercian Publications, 1999.

Vigiliusbriefe: zur Kirchenpolitik Iustinians. Ed. E. Schwartz, rev. ed. A. Rehm. Sitzungsberichte der Bayerischen Akademie der Wissenschaften, phil.-hist. Abteilung, 1940, 2. Munich: Beck, 1940.

Secondary sources

Allen, P. *Evagrius Scholasticus the Church Historian*. Louvain: Spicilegium Sacrum Lovaniense, 1981.

—, and C. T. R. Hayward. *Severus of Antioch*. London: Routledge, 2004.

—, and E. Jeffreys, eds. *The Sixth Century: End or Beginning?* Brisbane: Australian Association for Byzantine Studies, 1996.

Atiya, A. S. *A History of Eastern Christianity*. 2nd ed. Millwood, NY: Kraus Reprint, 1980.

Bailey, L. "Building Urban Christian Communities: Sermons on Local Saints in the Eusebius Gallicanus Collection." *EME* 12 (2003): 1–24.

Baum, W., and D. W. Winkler. *Die apostolische Kirche des Ostens: Geschichte der sogenannten Nestorianer*. Klagenfurt: Kitab, 2000; English trans.: *The Church of the East: A Concise History*. London: Routledge / Curzon, 2003.

Baynes, N. H. "Alexandria and Constantinople: A Study in Ecclesiastical Diplomacy" (first published 1926), reprinted in his *Byzantine Studies and Other Essays*. London: University of London Athlone Press, 1955, 97–115.

Bowersock, G. W. *Hellenism in Late Antiquity*. Ann Arbor, MI: University of Michigan Press, 1990.

Brock, S. *The Luminous Eye: The Spiritual World Vision of St. Ephrem*. Rev. ed. Kalamazoo, MI: Cistercian Publications, 1992.

—. *Studies in Syriac Christianity: History, Literature and Theology*. Aldershot: Variorum, 1992.

—. *Syriac Perspectives on Late Antiquity*. London: Variorum, 1984.

Brogiolo, G. P., N. Gauthier, and N. Christie, eds. *Towns and their Territories between Late Antiquity and the Early Middle Ages*. Leiden: Brill, 2000.

—, and B. Ward-Perkins, eds. *The Idea and Ideal of the Town between Late Antiquity and the Early Middle Ages*. Leiden: Brill, 1999.

Brown, P. *The Cult of the Saints: Its Rise and Function in Latin Christianity*. Chicago: University of Chicago Press, 1981.

—. *Poverty and Leadership in the Later Roman Empire*. Hanover, MA: University of New England Press, 2001.

—. *Power and Persuasion in Late Antiquity: Towards a Christian Empire*. Madison, WI: University of Wisconsin Press, 1992.

—, L. Cracco Ruggini, and M. Mazza, eds. *Governanti e intellettuali, popolo di Roma e popolo di dio (I–VI secolo)*. Turin: Giappichelli, 1982.

Brown, T. S. *Gentlemen and Officers: Imperial Administration and Aristocratic Power in Byzantine Italy, A.D. 554–800*. London: British School at Rome, 1984.

Browning, R. *Justinian and Theodora*. Rev. ed. London: Thames and Hudson, 1987.

Burns, T. S. *A History of the Ostrogoths*. Bloomington, IN: Indiana University Press, 1984.

—, and J. W. Edie, eds. *Urban Centers and Rural Contexts in Late Antiquity*. East Lansing, MI: Michigan State University Press, 2001.

Cameron, A(veril). *Agathias*. Oxford: Clarendon Press, 1970.

—. *Procopius and the Sixth Century*. Berkeley, CA: University of California Press, 1985.

—, B. Ward-Perkins, and M. Whitby, eds. *Cambridge Ancient History*. Vol. 14. Cambridge: Cambridge University Press, 2000.

Canivet, P., and J. P. Rey-Coquais, eds. *La Syrie de Byzance à l'Islam VIIe–VIIIe siècles*. Damascus: Institut français d'études Arabes de Damas, 1992.

Chesnut, R. C. *Three Monophysite Christologies: Severus of Antioch, Philoxenus of Mabbug, and Jacob of Sarug*. Oxford: Oxford University Press, 1976.

Christie, N. *The Lombards: The Ancient Longobards*. Oxford: Blackwell, 1995.

—, and S. T. Loseby, eds. *Towns in Transition: Urban Evolution in Late Antiquity and the Early Middle Ages*. Aldershot: Scolar Press, 1996.

Clarke, H. B., and M. Brennan, eds. *Columbanus and Merovingian Monasticism*. British Archaeological Reports, International Series 113. Oxford: British Archaeological Reports, 1981.

Coakley, J. F., and K. Parry, eds. *The Church of the East: Life and Thought*. *Bulletin of the John Rylands University Library* 78/3 (1996).

Cormack, R. *The Byzantine Eye: Studies in Art and Patronage*. London: Variorum Reprints, 1989.

Dagron, G. *Empereur et prêtre: étude sur le "césaropapisme" byzantin*. Paris: Gallimard, 1995; English trans. J. Birrell. *Emperor and Priest: The Imperial Office in Byzantium*. Cambridge: Cambridge University Press, 2003.

—. *Naissance d'une capitale: Constantinople et ses institutions de 330 à 451*. Paris: Presses universitaires de France, 1974.

—. "L'ombre d'un doute: l'hagiographie en question, VIe–XIe siècle." *DOP* 46 (1992): 59–68.

—. *La romanité chrétienne en Orient: héritages et mutations*. London: Variorum, 1984.

De Clercq, C. *La législation religieuse franque de Clovis à Charlemagne: étude sur les actes des conciles et des capitulaires, les statuts diocésains et les règles monastiques, 507–814*. Louvain: Bureaux du Receuil, Bibliothèque de l'Université, 1936–58.

De Halleux, A. *Philoxène de Mabbog: sa vie, ses écrits, sa théologie*. Louvain: Imprimerie orientaliste, 1963.

De Jong, M., and F. Theuws, with C. van Rhijn, eds. *Topographies of Power in the Early Middle Ages*. Leiden: Brill, 2001.

De Nie, G. *Views from a Many-Windowed Tower: Studies of Imagination in the Works of Gregory of Tours*. Amsterdam: Rodopi, 1987.

—. *Word, Image and Experience: Dynamics of Miracle and Self-Perception in Sixth-Century Gaul*. Collected Studies 771. Aldershot: Ashgate, 2003.

De Paor, M. B. *Patrick, the Pilgrim Apostle of Ireland* (including the *Confessio* and *Epistola*). Ed. and trans. with analysis and commentary. Dublin: Veritas, 1998.

Draguet, R. *Julien d'Halicarnasse et sa controverse avec Sévère d'Antioche sur l'incorruptibilité du corps du Christ: étude d'histoire littéraire et doctrinale suivie des fragments dogmatiques de Julien (texte syriaque et traduction grecque)*. Louvain: Smeesters, 1924.

Drijvers, H. J. W. *History and Religion in Late Antique Syria*. Aldershot: Variorum, 1994.

Elm, E. *Die Macht der Weisheit: Das Bild des Bischofs in der Vita Augustini des Possidius und anderen spätantiken und frühmittelalterlichen Bischofsviten*. Leiden: Brill, 2003.

Elsner, J. *Art and the Roman Viewer: The Transformation of Art from the Pagan World to Christianity*. Cambridge: Cambridge University Press, 1995.

Flint, V. I. J. *The Rise of Magic in Early Medieval Europe*. Princeton, NJ: Princeton University Press, 1991.

Frankfurter, D., ed. *Pilgrimage and Holy Space in Late Antique Egypt*. Leiden: Brill, 1998.

Frend, W. H. C. *The Rise of the Monophysite Movement: Chapters in the History of the Church in the Fifth and Sixth Centuries*. London: Cambridge University Press, 1972.

Gero, S. *Barsauma of Nisibis and Persian Christianity in the Fifth Century*, *CSCO* 426, Subsidia 63. Louvain: Peeters, 1981.

Gillman, I., and H.-J. Klimkeit. *Christians in Asia before 1500*. Ann Arbor, MI: University of Michigan Press, 1999.

Goetz, H.-W., J. Jarnut, and W. Pohl, eds. *Regna et gentes: The Relationship between Late Antique and Early Medieval Peoples and Kingdoms in the Transformation of the Roman World*. Leiden: Brill, 2003.

Grabar, A. *Martyrium: recherches sur le culte des reliques et l'art chrétien antique*. 3 vols. Paris: Collège de France, 1946.

Gray, P. T. R. *The Defense of Chalcedon in the East (451–553)*. Leiden: Brill, 1979.

Gregory, T. E. *Vox populi: Popular Opinion and Violence in the Religious Controversies of the Fifth Century A.D.* Columbus, OH: Ohio State University Press, 1979.

Griffith, S. H. "Ephraem, the Deacon of Edessa, and the Church of the Empire." In *Diakonia: Studies in Honor of Robert T. Meyer*. Ed. T. Halton and J. P. Williman. Washington, DC: Catholic University of America Press, 1986, 22–52.

—. "Images of Ephraem: The Syrian Holy Man and his Church," *Traditio* 45 (1989–90): 7–33.

Grillmeier, A. *Jesus der Christus im Glauben der Kirche*. Freiburg im Breisgau: Herder, 1979; English trans. J. Bowden. *Christ in Christian Tradition*. Atlanta, GA: John Knox Press, 1975.

—, and H. Bacht, eds. *Das Konzil von Chalkedon: Geschichte und Gegenwart*. Würzburg: Echter-Verlag, 1951–54.

Grosdidier de Matons, J. *Romanos le Mélode et les origines de la poésie religieuse à Byzance*. With a preface by P. Lemerle. Paris: Beauchesne, 1977.

Haas, C. *Alexandria in Late Antiquity: Topography and Social Conflict*. Baltimore, MA: Johns Hopkins University Press, 1997.

Hayward, P. A., and J. Howard-Johnston, eds. *The Cult of Saints in Late Antiquity and the Early Middle Ages: Essays on the Contribution of Peter Brown*. Oxford: Oxford University Press, 1999.

Heinzelmann, M. *Bischofsherrschaft in Gallien: zur Kontinuität römischer Führungsschichten vom 4. bis zum 7. Jahrhundert: soziale, prosopographische und bildungsgeschichtliche Aspekte*. Beihefte der Francia 5. Munich: Artemis, 1976.

—. *Gregor von Tours (538–594), "zehn Bücher Geschichte": Historiographie und Gesellschaftskonzept im 6. Jahrhundert*. Darmstadt: Wissenschaftliche Buchgesellschaft, 1994; English trans. C. Carroll. *Gregory of Tours: History and Society in the Sixth Century*. Cambridge: Cambridge University Press, 2001.

—. *Translationsberichte und andere Quellen des Reliquienkultes*. Turnhout: Brepols, 1979.

Hen, Y. *Culture and Religion in Merovingian Gaul, AD 481–751*. Leiden: Brill, 1995.

—, and R. Meens, eds. *The Bobbio Missal: Liturgy and Religious Culture in Merovingian Gaul*. Cambridge: Cambridge University Press, 2004.

Herrin, J. *The Formation of Christendom*. Princeton, NJ: Princeton University Press, 1987.

Hevelone-Harper, J. L. *Disciples of the Desert: Monks, Laity, and Spiritual Authority in Sixth-Century Gaza*. Baltimore: Johns Hopkins University Press, 2005.

Hunt, E. D. *Holy Land Pilgrimage in the Later Roman Empire, AD 312–460*. Oxford: Clarendon Press, 1982.

Jones, A. H. M. "Were Ancient Heresies National or Social Movements in Disguise?" *Journal of Theological Studies* 10 (1959): 280–98. Reprinted in his *The Roman Economy*. Ed. P. A. Brunt. Oxford: Blackwell, 1974, 308–29.

—, J. R. Martindale, and J. Morris. *The Prosopography of the Later Roman Empire*. 3 vols. Cambridge: Cambridge University Press, 1971–92.

Kaldellis, A. *Procopius of Caesarea: Tyranny, History, and Philosophy at the End of Antiquity*. Philadelphia, PA: University of Pennsylvania Press, 2004.

Klingshirn, W. E. *Caesarius of Arles: The Making of a Christian Community in Late Antique Gaul*. Cambridge: Cambridge University Press, 1994.

Krautheimer, R. *Early Christian and Byzantine Architecture*. Baltimore, MD: Penguin Books, 1965. 4th ed. rev. R. Krautheimer and S. Ćurčić. New York: Penguin Books, 1986.

Krumbacher, K. *Geschichte der byzantinischen Litteratur*. 2nd ed. Ed. A. Ehrhard and H. Gelzer. Munich: Beck, 1897.

Laga, C., J. A. Munitiz, and L. Van Rompay, eds. *After Chalcedon: Studies in Theology and Church History Offered to Professor Albert Van Roey for his Seventieth Birthday*. Orientalia Lovaniensia Analecta 18. Louvain: Peeters, 1985.

Lang, U. M. *John Philoponus and the Controversies over Chalcedon in the Sixth Century: A Study and Translation of the Arbiter*. Louvain: Peeters, 2001.

Lapidge, M., ed. *Columbanus: Studies on the Latin Writings*. Woodbridge: Boydell Press, 1997.

Le Coz, R. *L'église d'Orient: chrétiens d'Irak, d'Iran et de Turquie*. Paris: Éditions du Cerf, 1995.

Lee, A. D. *Information and Frontiers: Roman Foreign Relations in Late Antiquity*. Cambridge: Cambridge University Press, 1993.

Leyser, C. *Authority and Asceticism from Augustine to Gregory the Great*. Oxford: Oxford University Press, 2001.

MacCormack, S. G. *Art and Ceremony in Late Antiquity*. Berkeley, CA: University of California Press, 1981.

MacDonald, A. A., M. W. Twomey, and G. J. Reinink, eds. *Learned Antiquity: Scholarship and Society in the Near East, the Greco-Roman World and the Early Medieval West*. Louvain: Peeters, 2003.

MacMullen, R. *Christianity and Paganism in the Fourth to Eighth Centuries*. New Haven, CT: Yale University Press, 1997.

Magdalino, P., ed. *New Constantines: The Rhythm of Imperial Renewal in Byzantium, 4th–13th Centuries*. Aldershot: Variorum, 1994.

Mainstone, R. J. *Hagia Sophia: Architecture, Structure, and Liturgy of Justinian's Great Church*. New York: Thames and Hudson, 1988.

Mango, C. *Byzantine Architecture*. New York: Abrams, 1974.

—. *Studies on Constantinople*. Aldershot: Variorum, 1993.

Markus, R. A. *The End of Ancient Christianity*. Cambridge: Cambridge University Press, 1990.

—. *Gregory the Great and his World*. Cambridge: Cambridge University Press, 1997.

Mathews, T. F. *Art and Architecture in Byzantium and Armenia: Liturgical and Exegetical Approaches*. Aldershot: Variorum, 1995.

—. *The Clash of Gods: A Reinterpretation of Early Christian Art*. Rev. ed. Princeton, NJ: Princeton University Press, 1999.

—. *The Early Churches of Constantinople: Architecture and Liturgy*. University Park, PA: Pennsylvania State University Press, 1971.

Mathisen, R. W. *Ecclesiastical Factionalism and Religious Controversy in Fifth-Century Gaul*. Washington, DC: Catholic University of America Press, 1989.

—, and D. Shanzer, eds. *Society and Culture in Late Antique Gaul: Revisiting the Sources*. Aldershot: Ashgate, 2001.

Mayr-Harting, H. *The Coming of Christianity to Anglo-Saxon England*. London: Batsford, 1972.

Meier, J. L. *L'épiscopat de l'Afrique romaine, vandale, et byzantine*. Rome: Institut suisse de Rome, 1973.

Meyendorff, J. *Imperial Unity and Christian Divisions: The Church, 450–680 AD*. Crestwood, NY: St. Vladimir's Seminary Press, 1989.

Miles, R., ed. *Constructing Identities in Late Antiquity*. London: Routledge, 1999.

Miller, P. Cox. *Dreams in Late Antiquity: Studies in the Imagination of a Culture*. Princeton, NJ: Princeton University Press, 1994.

Mills, K., and A. Grafton, eds. *Conversion in Late Antiquity and the Early Middle Ages: Seeing and Believing*. Rochester, NY: University of Rochester Press, 2003.

Mitchell, S., and G. Greatrex, eds. *Ethnicity and Culture in Late Antiquity*. London: Duckworth, 2000.

Moreira, I. *Dreams, Visions and Spiritual Authority in Merovingian Gaul*. Ithaca, NY: Cornell University Press, 2000.

O'Donnell, J. J. *Cassiodorus*. Berkeley, CA: University of California Press, 1979.

Palmer, A. *Monk and Mason on the Tigris Frontier: The Early History of Tur 'Abdin*. Cambridge: Cambridge University Press, 1990.

Patlagean, E. "Ancienne hagiographie byzantine et histoire sociale." *Annales* 23 (1968): 106–26. English trans. J. Hodgkin in S. Wilson, ed. *Saints and their Cults: Studies in Religious Sociology, Folklore, and History*. Cambridge: Cambridge University Press, 1983.

—. *Pauvreté économique et pauvreté sociale à Byzance, 4e–7e siècles*. Paris: Mouton, 1977.

Petersen, W. L. *The Diatessaron and Ephrem Syrus as Sources of Romanos the Melodist. CSCO* 475, subsidia 74. Louvain: Peeters, 1985.

Pohl, W., ed. *Kingdoms of the Empire: The Integration of Barbarians in Late Antiquity*. Leiden: Brill, 1997.

Rapp, Claudia. *Holy Bishops in Late Antiquity: The Nature of Christian Leadership in an Age of Transition*. Berkeley, CA: University of California Press, 2005.

Réal, I. *Vies de saints, vie de famille: représentation et système de la parenté dans le royaume mérovingien (481–751) d'après les sources hagiographiques*. Turnhout: Brepols, 2001.

Reinink, G. J., and A. C. Klugkist, eds. *After Bardaisan: Studies on Continuity and Change in Syriac Christianity in Honour of Professor Han J. W. Drijvers*. Louvain: Peeters, 1999.

Richards, J. *Consul of God: The Life and Times of Gregory the Great*. London: Routledge & Kegan Paul, 1980.

Riché, P. *Éducation et culture dans l'occident barbare*. Paris: Éditions du Seuil, 1962; English trans. J. J. Contreni. *Education and Culture in the Barbarian West, Sixth through Eighth Centuries*. Columbia, SC: University of South Carolina Press, 1976.

Rousselle, A. *Croire et guérir: la foi en Gaule dans l'antiquité tardive*. Paris: Fayard, 1990.

Sako, L. R. M. *Le rôle de la hiérarchie syriaque orientale dans les rapports diplomatiques entre la Perse et Byzance aux Ve–VIIe siècles*. Paris: n.p., 1986.

Schork, R. J. *Sacred Song from the Byzantine Pulpit: Romanos the Melodist*. Gainesville, FL: University Press of Florida, 1995.

Schwartz, S. *Imperialism and Jewish Society, 200 B.C.E. to 640 C.E.* Princeton, NJ: Princeton University Press, 2004.

Segal, J. B. *Edessa "The Blessed City."* Oxford: Clarendon Press, 1970.

Stancliffe, C. *Saint Martin and his Hagiographer: History and Miracle in Sulpicius Severus*. Oxford: Clarendon Press, 1983.

Steppa, J.-E. *John Rufus and the World Vision of Anti-Chalcedonian Culture*. Piscataway, NJ: Gorgias Press, 2002.

Sterk, A. *Renouncing the World yet Leading the Church: The Monk-Bishop in Late Antiquity*. Cambridge, MA: Harvard University Press, 2004.

Straw, C. *Gregory the Great: Perfection in Imperfection*. Berkeley, CA: University of California Press, 1988.

Taft, R. F. *Liturgy in Byzantium and Beyond*. Aldershot: Variorum, 1995.

Thompson, E. A. *Who Was Saint Patrick?* New York: St. Martin's Press, 1985.

Torrance, I. R. *Christology after Chalcedon: Severus of Antioch and Sergius the Monophysite*. Eugene, OR: Wipf and Stock, 1998.

Vööbus, A. *History of the School of Nisibis. CSCO* 266, Subsidia 26. Louvain: Secrétariat du CSCO, 1965.

Walker, P. W. *Holy City, Holy Places: Christian Attitudes to Jerusalem and the Holy Land in the Fourth Century*. Oxford: Clarendon Press, 1990.

Ward-Perkins, B. *From Classical Antiquity to the Middle Ages: Urban Public Building in Northern and Central Italy, AD 300–850*. Oxford: Oxford University Press, 1984.
Wessel, S. *Cyril of Alexandria and the Nestorian Controversy*. Oxford: Oxford University Press, 2004.
Whittaker, C. R. *Frontiers of the Roman Empire: A Social and Economic Study*. Baltimore, MD: Johns Hopkins University Press, 1994.
Wickham, C. *Early Medieval Italy: Central Power and Local Society, 400–1000*. London: Macmillan, 1981.
Wilken, R. L. *The Land Called Holy: Palestine in Christian History and Thought*. New Haven, CT: Yale University Press, 1992.
Wood, I., ed. *Franks and Alamanni in the Merovingian Period: An Ethnographic Perspective*. Woodbridge: Boydell Press, 1998.
—. *The Merovingian Kingdoms, 450–751*. London: Longman, 1994.
—. *The Missionary Life: Saints and the Evangelisation of Europe, 400–1050*. Harlow: Longman, 2001.

2 The emergence of Byzantine Orthodoxy, 600–1095
Andrew Louth

Primary sources

Byzantine Defenders of Images. Ed. A.-M. Talbot. Byzantine Saints' Lives in Translation 2. Washington, DC: Dumbarton Oaks, 1998.
Christian Dualist Heresies in the Byzantine World, c. 650–c. 1405. Trans. J. Hamilton and B. Hamilton. Manchester: Manchester University Press, 1998.
The Chronicle of Theophanes the Confessor: Byzantine and Near Eastern History AD 284–813. Ed. C. Mango and R. Scott with the assistance of G. Greatrex. Oxford: Clarendon Press, 1997.
Germanus of Constantinople. *On the Divine Liturgy*. Ed. and trans. P. Meyendorff. Crestwood, NY: St. Vladimir's Seminary Press, 1984.
Icon and Logos: Sources in Eighth-Century Iconoclasm. Ed. and trans. D. J. Sahas. Toronto Medieval Texts and Translations 4. Toronto: University of Toronto Press, 1986.
Die ikonoklastische Synode von Hiereia 754. Ed. and trans. T. Krannich, C. Schubert, and C. Sode. Studien und Texte zu Antike und Christentum 15. Tübingen: Mohr Siebeck, 2002.
John of Damascus. *Three Treatises on the Divine Images*. Trans. A. Louth. Crestwood, NY: St. Vladimir's Seminary Press, 2003.
The Life of Lazaros of Mt. Galesion, an Eleventh-Century Pillar Saint. Trans. R. P. H. Greenfield. Byzantine Saints' Lives in Translation 3. Washington, DC: Dumbarton Oaks, 1999.
The Life of Maximus the Confessor: Recension 3. Ed. and trans. B. Neil and P. Allen. Early Christian Studies 6. Strathfield, Australia: St. Paul's Publications, 2003.
Life of Michael the Synkellos. Ed. and trans. M. B. Cunningham. Belfast Byzantine Texts and Translations 1. Belfast: Belfast Byzantine Enterprises, 1991.
The Life of Patriarch Tarasios by Ignatios the Deacon. Ed. and trans. S. Efthymiadis. Birmingham Byzantine and Ottoman Monographs 4. Aldershot: Variorum, 1998.

The Life of Saint Nikon. Ed. and trans. D. F. Sullivan. Brookline, MA: Hellenic College Press, 1987.

Maximus the Confessor. *Maximus Confessor: Selected Writings*. Trans. G. C. Berthold. London: SPCK, 1985.

——. *Maximus the Confessor and his Companions: Documents from Exile*. Ed. and trans. P. Allen and B. Neil. Oxford: Oxford University Press, 2002.

I Mystagogia tou Agiou Maximou tou Omologitou. Ed. C. Sotiropoulos. Athens, 1993.

Nikephoros Patriarch of Constantinople, Short History. Trans. C. Mango, Dumbarton Oaks Texts 10. Washington, DC: Dumbarton Oaks, 1990.

Photius. *The Homilies of Photius, Patriarch of Constantinople*. English trans. C. Mango. Dumbarton Oaks Studies 3. Cambridge, MA: Harvard University Press, 1958.

Le Synodikon d'Orthodoxie. Ed. and trans. J. Gouillard. Travaux et mémoires 2. Paris: Édition de Bocard, 1967, 1–270.

Theodore the Studite. *On the Holy Icons*. Trans. C. P. Roth. Crestwood, NY: St. Vladimir's Seminary Press, 1981.

La vie d'Étienne le Jeune par Étienne le Diacre. Ed. and trans. M.-F. Auzépy. Birmingham Byzantine and Ottoman Monographs 3. Aldershot: Variorum, 1997.

Secondary sources

Afinogenov, D. E. "Κωνσταντινούπολις ἐπίσκοπον ἔχει: The Rise of the Patriarchal Power in Byzantium from Nicaenum II to Epanagoga." *Erytheia* 15 (1994): 45–65; 17(1996): 43–71.

Alexander, P. *The Patriarch Nicephorus of Constantinople: Ecclesiastical Policy and Image Worship in the Byzantine Empire*. Oxford: Clarendon Press, 1958.

Auzépy, M.-F. *L'hagiographie et l'iconoclasme byzantin: le cas de la vie d'Étienne le Jeune*. Birmingham Byzantine and Ottoman Monographs 5. Aldershot: Variorum, 1999.

Barber, C. *Figure and Likeness: On the Limits of Representation in Byzantine Iconoclasm*. Princeton, NJ: Princeton University Press, 2002.

Belting, H. *Likeness and Presence: A History of the Image before the Era of Art*. Trans. E. Jephcott. Chicago: University of Chicago Press, 1994.

Brubaker, L., and J. Haldon. *Byzantium in the Iconoclast Era (c. 680–850): The Sources, an Annotated Survey*. Birmingham Byzantine and Ottoman Monographs 7. Aldershot: Ashgate, 2001.

Bryer, A., and J. Herrin, eds. *Iconoclasm*. Birmingham: Centre for Byzantine Studies, 1977.

Cameron, A(veril). "The Language of Images: The Rise of Icons and Christian Representation." In D. Woods, ed. *The Church and the Arts*. *SCH* 28. Oxford: Blackwell, 1992, 1–42.

Chadwick, H. *East and West: the Making of a Rift in the Church*. Oxford: Oxford University Press, 2003.

Cormack, R. *Painting the Soul: Icons, Death Masks and Shrouds*. London: Reaktion Books, 1997.

——. *Writing in Gold: Byzantine Society and its Icons*. London: George Philip, 1985.

Corrigan, K. *Visual Polemics in the Ninth-Century Byzantine Psalters*. Cambridge: Cambridge University Press, 1992.

Dagron, G. *Empereur et prêtre: étude sur le "césaropapisme" byzantin*. Paris: Gallimard, 1995; English trans. J. Birrell. *Emperor and Priest: The Imperial Office in Byzantium*. Cambridge: Cambridge University Press, 2003.

Gero, S. *Byzantine Iconoclasm during the Reign of Constantine V. CSCO* Subsidia 52. Louvain: Secrétariat du CSCO, 1973.

—. *Byzantine Iconoclasm during the Reign of Leo III. CSCO* Subsidia 41. Louvain: Secrétariat du CSCO, 1973.

Grabar, A. *L'iconoclasme byzantin: dossier archéologique*. Rev. ed. Paris: Flammarion, 1984.

Haldon, J. F. *Byzantium in the Seventh Century: The Transformation of a Culture*. Cambridge: Cambridge University Press, 1990; rev. ed. 1997.

Hussey, J. M. *The Orthodox Church in the Byzantine Empire*. Oxford: Clarendon Press, 1986.

Lemerle, P. *Le premier humanisme byzantin*. Bibliothèque Byzantine, Études 6. Paris: Presses universitaires de France, 1971.

Leroy, J. "Le monachisme studite." In Théodore Studite, *Les grandes catecheses (Livre I), Les Épigrammes (I à XXIX)*. Spiritualité orientale 79. Bégrolles en Mauge: Abbaye de Bellefontaine, 2002, 39–116.

Louth, A. "The Literature of the Monastic Movement." In *The Cambridge History of Early Christian Literature*. Ed. F. Young, L. Ayres, and A. Louth. Cambridge: Cambridge University Press, 2004.

—. *St. John Damascene: Tradition and Originality in Byzantine Theology*. Oxford: Oxford University Press, 2002.

Mango, C. *The Art of the Byzantine Empire, 312–1453*. Englewood Cliffs, NJ: 1972; repr. Medieval Academy Reprints for Teaching 16. Toronto: University of Toronto Press, 1986.

Mathew, G. *Byzantine Aesthetics*. London: John Murray, 1963.

Mathews, T. F. *The Clash of Gods: A Reinterpretation of Early Christian Art*. Princeton, NJ: Princeton University Press, 1993.

Meyendorff, J. *Imperial Unity and Christian Divisions: The Church, 450–680 AD*. Crestwood, NY: St. Vladimir's Seminary Press, 1989.

Morris, R. *Monks and Laymen in Byzantium, 843–1118*. Cambridge: Cambridge University Press, 1995.

Obolensky, D. *The Byzantine Commonwealth: Eastern Europe, 500–1453*. London: Weidenfeld and Nicolson, 1971.

Pelikan, J. *Imago Dei: The Byzantine Apologia for Icons*. New Haven, CT: Yale University Press, 1990.

—. *The Spirit of Eastern Christendom (600–1700)*. Vol. 2 in *The Christian Tradition: A History of the Development of Doctrine*. Chicago: University of Chicago Press, 1974.

Pratsch, T. *Theodoros Studites (759–826) – zwischen Dogma und Pragma*. Berliner Byzantinische Studien 4. Frankfurt am Main: Peter Lang, 1998.

Sode, C. *Jerusalem–Konstantinopel–Rom: Die Viten des Michael Synkellos und der Brüder Theodoros und Theophanes Graptoi*. Altertumswissenschaftliches Kolloquium 4. Stuttgart: Franz Steiner Verlag, 2001.

Treadgold, W. *The Byzantine Revival, 780–842*. Stanford, CA: Stanford University Press, 1988.

—, ed. *Renaissances before the Renaissance*. Stanford, CA: Stanford University Press, 1984.

Von Harnack, A. *History of Dogma*. 7 vols. London: Williams & Norgate, 1894–99.
Whittow, M. *The Making of Orthodox Byzantium, 600–1025*. London: Macmillan, 1996.

3 Beyond empire I: Eastern Christianities from the Persian to the Turkish conquest, 604–1071
Igor Dorfmann-Lazarev

Primary sources

Cyril of Alexandria. *Commentarii in Iohannem*. In *S. P. N. Cyrilli archiepiscopi Alexandrini in D. Ioannis evangelium*. Ed. P. E. Pusey. 3 vols. Oxford 1872; Brussels 1965. Cf. *Clavis Patrum Graecorum* (hereafter *CPG*). Ed. M. Geerard. Turnhout: Brepols, 1974–87, 5208.
—. *Contra Nestorium, liber II, proemium*. In *Acta conciliorum oecumenicorum* I, I, 6, pp. 32–34 (hereafter *ACO*). Ed. E. Schwartz. 4 vols. in 15. Berlin: de Gruyter, 1914–84. Cf. *CPG* 5217.
—. *Epistula 40: ad Acacium Melitenum*. In *ACO* I, I, 4, pp. 20–31. Cf. *CPG* 5340.
—. *Epistula 45: ad Successum episc. Dioocaesareae (prima)*. In *ACO* I, I, 6, pp. 151–57. Cf. *CPG* 5345.
—. *Epistula 46: ad Successum episc. Dioocaesareae (secunda)*. In *ACO* I, I, 6, pp. 157–62. Cf. *CPG* 5346.
—. *Scholia de incarnatione Unigeniti*. In *ACO* I, 5, 1, pp. 219–231. Cf. *CPG* 5225.
John of Ōjun. *Sermon against the Phantasiasts* (in Armenian). In *Yovhannu Ōjnec'uoy matenagrut'iwnk'*. Ed. J. Aucher. Venice: San Lazzaro, 1833, 48–80.
Pseudo-Dionysius Areopagita. *Epistola 4: ad Gaium*. In *Corpus dionysiacum* 2. Ed. G. Heil and A. M. Ritter. Berlin: de Gruyter, 1991, 160–61. Cf. *CPG* 6607.
Stephen of Siwnik'. *Response to Patriarch Germanus of Constantinople* (in Armenian). In *Girk' T'łt'oc'*. [= *The Book of Letters*]. Ed. N. Bogharian. Jerusalem: St. James Patriarchate, 1994, 435–66.
Timothy I (patriarch). *Epistula de incarnatione* (34) (in Syriac). In *Timothei Patriarchae I Epistulae*. Ed. O. Braun. *CSCO*, Scriptores syri II, 67. Paris: E Typographeo Reipublicae, 1914, 156–205.
Xosrovik T'argmanič'. Chapter I (in Armenian). In *Xosrovik T'argmanič' ew erkasirut'iwnk' norin* [= *Xosrovik the Translator and his Works*]. Ed. G. Yovsepean. Ejmiacin: Catholicossate of Ejmiacin, 1903, 3–75.

Secondary sources

Albert, M., R. Beylot, R.-G. Coquin, B. Outtier, and C. Renoux, eds. *Christianismes orientaux: introduction à l'étude des langues at des littératures*. Paris: Éditions du Cerf, 1993.
Allen, W. E. D. *A History of the Georgian People*. London: Routledge & Kegan Paul, 1971.
Asmussen, J. P. "The Sogdian and Uighur-Turkish Christian Literature in Central Asia before the Real Rise of Islam: A Survey." In *Indological and Buddhist Studies: Volume in Honour of Professor J. W. de Jong on his Sixtieth Birthday*. Ed. L. A. Hercus et al. Canberra: Australian National University, Faculty of Asian Studies, 1982, 11–29.
Atiya, A. S. *A History of Eastern Christianity*. London: Methuen, 1968.
Bakhayt, M. A., and I. Abbas, eds. *Proceedings of the Second Symposium on the History of Bilad-al-Sham*. Amman: Al-Jami'ah al-Urduniyah, 1987.

Baum, W. "Zeitalter der Araber. 650–1258)." In W. Baum and D. W. Winkler, *Die apostolische Kirche des Ostens. Geschichte der sogenannten Nestorianer*. Klagenfurt: Kitab, 2000, 43–76. English trans. *The Church of the East: A Concise History*. London: Routledge / Curzon, 2003.

Beaucamp, J., and C. Robin. "Le christianisme dans la péninsule arabique d'après l'épigraphie et l'archéologie." *Travaux et mémoires* 8 (1981): 45–61.

Béridzé, V. "L'architecture géorgienne à coupole de la seconde moitié du Xe à la fin du XIIIe siècle." *Bedi Kartlisa* 33 (1975): 233–60.

—. "Architecture géorgienne de la période transitoire (milieu VIIe–deuxième moitié du Xe siècle)." *Bedi Kartlisa* 42 (1984): 91–103.

—. "L'architecture religieuse géorgienne des IVe–VIIe siècles." *Bedi Kartlisa* 36 (1978): 25–42.

Berkey, J. P. *The Formation of Islam: Religion and Society in the Near East, 600–1800*. Cambridge: Cambridge University Press, 2003.

Bettiolo, P. "Lineamenti di patrologia siriaca." In *Complementi interdisciplinari di patrologia*. Ed. A. Quacquarelli. Rome: Città Nuova, 1989, 503–603.

Beurdeley, C. *Sur les routes de la soie: le grand voyage des objets d'art*. Fribourg: Office du Livre, 1985.

Bondi, S. F. *Studi in onore di Edda Bresciani*. Pisa: Giardini, 1985.

Brock, S. "Christ the 'Hostage': A Theme in the East Syriac Liturgical Tradition and its Origin." In *Logos: Festschrift für Luise Abramowski*. Ed. H. C. Brennecke, E. L. Grasmuck, and C. Markschies. Berlin: De Gruyter, 1993, 472–85.

—. "Christians in the Sasanian Empire: A Case of Divided Loyalties." In *Religion and National Identity*. Ed. S. Mews. *SCH* 18. Oxford: Basil Blackwell, 1982, 1–19.

—. "The Christology of the Church of the East in the Synods of the Fifth to Early Seventh Centuries." Chapter 12 of his *Studies in Syriac Christianity*. Aldershot: Variorum, 1992.

—. "The Christology of the Church of the East." In *Traditions and Heritage of the Christian East*. Ed. D. Afinogenov and A. Muraviev. Moscow: Izdatelstvo "Indrik," 1996, 159–79.

Bulliet, R. W. *Conversion to Islam in the Medieval Period: An Essay in Quantitative History*. Cambridge, MA: Harvard University Press, 1979.

Cahen, C. "Note sur l'accueil des chrétiens d'Orient à l'Islam." *Revue de l'Histoire des Religions* 166 (1964): 51–58.

Canivet, P., and J.-P. Rey-Coquais, eds. *La Syrie de Byzance à l'Islam: VIIe–VIIIe siècles*. Damascus: Institut français d'études Arabes de Damas, 1992.

Charbonnier, J. *Histoire des chrétiens de Chine*. Paris: Desclée, 1992.

Chauleur, S. *Histoire des Coptes d'Égypte*. Paris: La Colombe, 1960.

Chiu, P. C.-H. "An Historical Study of Nestorian Christianity in the T'ang Dynasty between A.D. 636–845". Ph.D. dissertation, Southwestern Baptist Theological Seminary, Fort Worth, TX, 1987.

Courbage, Y., and P. Fargues. *Chrétiens et Juifs dans l'Islam arabe et turc*. Paris: Librairie Arthème Fayard, 1992.

Cragg, K. *The Arab Christian: A History in the Middle East*. London: Mowbray, 1992.

Crone, P. *Slaves on Horses: The Evolution of the Islamic Polity*. Cambridge: Cambridge University Press, 1980.

Cuoq, J. *Islamisation de la Nubie chrétienne: VIIe–XVIe siècle*. Paris: Librairie orientaliste P. Geuthner, 1986.

Dagron, G. "L'église et la chrétienté byzantine entre les invasions et l'iconoclasme (VIIe–début VIIIe siècle)." In *Histoire du christianisme* 4, 9–92.

Dauvillier, J. *Histoire et institutions des églises orientales au Moyen Âge*. London: Variorum Reprints, 1983.

—. "Archéologie des anciennes églises de rite chaldéen." In *Mélanges offerts au R. P. François Graffin, S. J.* Parole de l'Orient (Melto) 6–7. Kaslik, Lebanon: Université Saint-Esprit, 1978, 357–86.

Décobert, C. "Sur l'arabisation et l'islamisation de l'Égypte médiévale." In *Itinéraires d'Égypte: Mélanges offerts au père Maurice M. Martin, S. J.* Ed. C. Décobert. Cairo: Institut français d'archéologie orientale, 1992, 273–300.

Dédéyan, G., ed. *Histoire des arméniens*. Toulouse: Privat, 1982.

Déroche, V. *Entre Rome et l'Islam: les chrétientés d'Orient, 610–1054*. Paris: SEDES, 1996.

Donner, F. M. *The Early Islamic Conquests*. Princeton, NJ: Princeton University Press, 1981.

Dorfmann-Lazarev, I. *Arméniens et Byzantins à l'époque de Photius: deux débats théologiques après le triomphe de l'orthodoxie. CSCO* 609, Subsidia 117. Louvain: Peeters, 2004.

Du Bourguet, P. *Les Coptes*. Paris: Presses universitaires de France, 1988.

Ducellier, A. *Chrétiens d'Orient et Islam au Moyen Âge: VIIe–XVe siècle*. Paris: A. Colin, 1996.

—. *Le miroir de l'Islam: musulmans et chrétiens d'Orient au Moyen Âge, VIIe–XIe siècle*. Paris: Julliard, 1971.

Dupuy, B. "Comment le Christ fut annoncé à la Chine: l'accueil fait en 638 en Chine à la doctrine chrétienne." *Istina* 47 (2002): 350–69.

—. "L'expansion de l'église de l'Orient en Chine: la christologie de la stèle de Si-ngan-fou' (781)." *Istina* 40 (1995): 205–209.

Eskildsen, S. "Christology and Soteriology in the Chinese Nestorian Texts," *B.C. Asian Review* 5 (1991): 41–97.

Evetts, B. T. A. *The Churches and Monasteries of Egypt and Some Neighbouring Countries*. Oxford: Clarendon Press, 1895.

Fattal, A. *Le statut légal des non-musulmans en pays d'Islam*. Beirut: Institut de lettres orientales, 1958.

Fedalto, G. *Le chiese d'Oriente: da Giustiniano alla caduta di Costantinopoli*. Milan: Jaca Book, 1984.

Ferré, A. "Chrétiens de Syrie et de Mésopotamie aux deux premiers siècles de l'Islam." *Islamochristiana* 14 (1988): 71–106.

Fiaccadori, G., and R. Farioli Campanati. *Teofilo Indiano*. Ravenna: M. Lapucci, Edizioni del girasole, 1992.

Fiey, J.-M. *Assyrie chrétienne: contribution à l'étude de l'histoire, de l'archéologie et de la géographie ecclésiastiques et monastiques du Nord de l'Iraq*. 3 vols. Beirut: Imprimerie Catholique, 1965–68.

—. *Chrétiens syriaques sous les Abbasides surtout à Baghdad, 749–1258. CSCO* 420 Subsidia 59. Louvain: Peeters, 1980.

—. *Communautés syriaques en Iran et en Irak des origines à 1952*. London: Variorum Reprints, 1979.

—. "Conversion à l'Islam de juifs et de chrétiens sous les Abbassides d'après les sources arabes et syriaques." In *17e Congrès International des Sciences Historiques. II: section chronologique. méthodologie: la biographie historique*. Madrid: Comité International des Sciences Historiques, 1992, 585–94.

—. "Coptes et Syriaques, contacts et échanges." *Studia Orientalia Christiana Collectanea* 15 (1972–73): 295–366.

—. "L'expansion de l'église de Perse." *Istina* 40 (1995): 149–57.

—. *Jalons pour une histoire de l'église en Iraq. CSCO* Subsidia 36. Louvain: Peeters, 1970.

Flusin, B. "Église monophysite et église chalcédonienne en Syrie à l'arrivée des Arabes." In *Cristianità d'Occidente e cristianità d'Oriente (secoli VI–IX)*. Settimane di studio 51. Spoleto: Centro italiano di studi sull'alto medioevo, 2004, 667–705.

Fowden, G. *Empire to Commonwealth: Consequences of Monotheism in Late Antiquity*. Princeton, NJ: Princeton University Press, 1993.

Frend, W. H. C. *The Rise of the Monophysite Movement: Chapters in the History of the Church in the Fifth and Sixth Centuries*. Cambridge: Cambridge University Press, 1972.

Friedmann, Y. "Islam is Superior . . ." *Jerusalem Studies in Arabic and Islam* 11 (1979): 36–42.

Fritsch, E. *Islam und Christentum im Mittelalter: Beiträge zur Geschichte der muslimischen Polemik gegen das Christentum in arabischer Sprache*. Breslau: Müller & Seifert, 1930.

Gerhards, A., and H. Brakmann, eds. *Die koptische Kirche: Eine Einführung in das ägyptische Christentum*. Stuttgart: W. Kohlhammer, 1994.

Gervers, M., and R. J. Bikhazi, eds. *Conversion and Continuity: Indigenous Christian Communities in Islamic Lands, Eighth to Eighteenth Centuries*. Toronto: Pontifical Institute of Mediaeval Studies, 1990.

Graf, G. *Geschichte der christlichen arabischen Literatur*. 5 vols. Studi e testi 118, 133, 146–47, 172. Vatican City: Biblioteca apostolica vaticana, 1944–53.

Griffith, S. H. "Jews and Muslims in Christian Arabic Texts of the Ninth Century." *Jewish History* 3 (1988): 65–94.

Grillmeier, A. *Jesus der Christus im Glauben der Kirche: Die Kirche von Alexandrien mit Nubien und Äthiopien nach 451*. Vol. 2, pt. 4. Freiburg: Herder, 1990.

Hage, W. "Christentum und Schamanismus: Zur Krise des Nestorianertums in Zentralasien." In *Traditio-Krisis-Renovatio aus theologischer Sicht: Festschrift Winfried Zeller zum 65. Geburtstag*. Marburg: Elwert, 1976, 114–24.

—. "Der Weg nach Asien: Die ostsyrische Missionskirche." In *Die Kirche des früheren Mittelalters*. Ed. K. Schäferdiek. Kirchengeschichte als Missionsgeschichte 2/1. Munich: Kaiser, 1978, 360–93.

—. *Die syrisch-jacobitische Kirche in frühislamischer Zeit: Nach orientalischen Quellen*. Wiesbaden: O. Harrassowitz, 1966.

—. "Kulturelle Kontakte des ostsyrischen Christentums in Zentralasien." In *III Symposium Syriacum 1980: les contacts du monde syriaque avec les autres cultures*. Ed. R. Lavenant. Rome: Pontificium Institutum Studiorum Orientalium, 1983, 143–59.

—. *Syriac Christianity in the East*. Kottayam (Kerala): St. Ephrem, 1986.

Hagemann, L. *Christentum contra Islam: Eine Geschichte gescheiterter Beziehungen*. Darmstadt: Primus, 1999.

Haldon, J. *Byzantium in the Seventh Century: The Transformation of a Culture*. Cambridge: Cambridge University Press, 1990.

Havenith, A. *Les Arabes chrétiens nomades au temps de Mohammed*. Collection Cerfaux-Lefort 7. Louvain-la-Neuve: Centre d'histoire des religions, 1988.

Hewsen, R. *Armenia: A Historical Atlas*. Chicago: University of Chicago Press, 2001.

Heyer, F. *Die Kirche Äthiopiens: Eine Bestandsaufnahme*. Berlin: de Gruyter, 1971.

Hovannisian, R., ed. *The Armenian People from Ancient to Modern Times.* Vol. 1: *The Dynastic Periods: From Antiquity to the Fourteenth Century.* New York: St. Martin's Press, 1997.

Hoyland, R., ed. *Muslims and Others in Early Islamic Society.* Aldershot: Ashgate, 2004.

Hsü, C. H. "Nestorianism and the Nestorian Movement in China." *Asian Culture Quarterly* 14 (1986): 41–81.

Irmscher, J., ed. *Rapports entre juifs, chrétiens et musulmans: eine Sammlung von Forschungsbeiträgen.* Amsterdam: A. M. Hakkert, 1995.

Kaegi, W. E. *Byzantium and the Early Islamic Conquests.* Cambridge: Cambridge University Press, 1995.

—. *Heraclius: Emperor of Byzantium.* Cambridge: Cambridge University Press, 2003.

Kallfelz, W. *Nichtmuslimische Untertanen im Islam: Grundlage, Ideologie und Praxis der Politik frühislamischer Herrscher gegenüber ihren nichtmuslimischen Untertanen mit besonderem Blick auf die Dynastie der Abbasiden, 749–1248.* Wiesbaden: Harrassowitz, 1995.

Karmiris, J. N. "The Problem of the Unification of the Non-Chalcedonian Churches of the East with the Orthodox on the Basis of Cyril's Formula *mia physis tou Theou Logou Sesarkomene.*" *Greek Theological Review* 10 (1964–65): 61–81.

Kawerau, P. *Das Christentum des Ostens.* Stuttgart: W. Kohlhammer, 1972.

—. *Die jakobitische Kirche im Zeitalter der syrischen Rennaissance.* Berlin: Akademie-Verlag, 1955.

Lamoreaux, J. C. "Early Eastern Christian Responses to Islam." In *Medieval Christian Perceptions of Islam.* Ed. J. V. Tolan. New York: Garland, 1996, 3–31.

Landron, B. *Chrétiens et musulmans en Irak: attitudes nestoriennes vis-à-vis de l'Islam.* Paris: Cariscript, 1994.

Li, T. *A Study of the History of Nestorian Christianity in China and its Literature in Chinese. Together with a New English Translation of the Dunhuang Nestorian Documents.* Frankfurt: Peter Lang, 2002.

Mahé, J.-P. "L'église arménienne de 611 à 1066." In *Histoire du christianisme* 4, 457–547.

Maraval, P. "L'échec en Orient: le développement des églises dissidentes dans l'Empire." In *Histoire du christianisme* 3, 457–81.

—. *Lieux saints et pèlerinages d'Orient: Histoire et géographie des origines à la conquête arabe.* Paris: Éditions du Cerf, 1985.

Martin-Hisard, B. "Christianisme et église dans le monde géorgien." In *Histoire du christianisme* 4, 549–603.

McAuliffe, J. D. *Qur'ānic Christians: An Analysis of Classical and Modern Exegesis.* Cambridge: Cambridge University Press, 1991.

Mécérian, J. *Histoire et institutions de l'église arménienne: évolution nationale et doctrinale, spiritualité, monachisme.* Beirut: Imprimerie Catholique, 1965.

Meynardus, O. F. A. *Christian Egypt, Ancient and Modern.* 2nd rev. ed. Cairo: American University in Cairo Press, 1977.

Moeller, C. "Le chalcédonisme et le néo-chalcédonisme en Orient de 451 à la fin du IV siècle." In *Das Konzil von Chalkedon: Geschichte und Gegenwart* 1. Ed. A. Grillmeier and H. Bacht. Würzburg: Echter-Verlag, 1951, 637–720.

Moffett, S. H. *A History of Christianity in Asia.* Vol. 1: *Beginnings to 1500.* San Francisco: HarperSanFrancisco, 1992.

Moorhead, J. "The Monophysite Response to the Arab Invasions." *Byzantion* 51 (1981): 579–91.
Morony, M. G. "The Age of Conversions: A Reassessment." In Gervers and Bikhazi, *Conversion and Continuity*, 135–50.
Müller, C. D. G. "Georgien und der christliche Orient." *Ostkirchliche Studien* 35 (1986): 168–75.
—. *Geschichte der orientalischen Nationalkirchen*. Göttingen: Vandenhoeck & Ruprecht, 1981.
—. "La position de l'egypte chrétien dans l'Orient ancien: influences et communications avec les pays voisins d'Afrique et d'Asie." *Le Muséon* 92 (1979): 105–25.
Nasrallah, J. "Abdallah Ibn al-Fadl." *Proche-Orient Chrétien* 33 (1983): 143–59.
—. *Histoire du mouvement littéraire dans l'église melchite du cinquième au vingtième siècle*. Vol. 2, pt. 1: *634–750*. Damascus: Editions de l'institut français d'études Arabes de Damas, 1996; Vol. 2, pt. 2: *750-Xe s*. Louvain: Peeters, 1988; Vol. 3, pt. 1: *969–1250*. Louvain: Peeters, 1983.
Nevo, Y. D., and J. Koren. *Crossroads to Islam: The Origins of the Arab Religion and the Arab State*. Amherst, NY: Prometheus Books, 2003.
Nyssen, W., H.-J. Schulz, P. Wiertz, et al., eds. *Handbuch der Ostkirchenkunde*. 2 vols. Düsseldorf: Patmos, 1984, 1989.
Orlandi, T. "La patrologia copta." In *Complementi interdisciplinari di patrologia*. Ed. A. Quacqarelli. Rome: Città Nuova, 1989, 457–502.
Palmer, A. *Monk and Mason on the Tigris Frontier: The Early History of Tur 'Abdin*. Cambridge: Cambridge University Press, 1990.
Panaino, A. "La chiesa di Persia e l'impero sasanide: conflitto e integrazione." In *Cristianità d'Occidente e cristianità d'Oriente, secoli VI–IX*. Settimane di studio 51. Spoleto: Centro italiano di studi sull'alto medioevo, 2004, 765–863.
Parry, K. M. "Images in the Church of the East: The Evidence from Central Asia and China." *Bulletin of the John Rylands University Library of Manchester* 8/3 (1996): 143–62.
Pelliot, P. *L'inscription nestorienne de Si-ngan-fou*. Ed. with supplements A. Forte. Kyoto: Scuola di studi sull'Asia orientale, 1996.
—. *Recherches sur les chrétiens d'Asie Centrale et d'Extrême Orient*. Paris: Imprimerie nationale, 1973.
Pines, S. "Notes on Islam and on Arabic Christianity and Judaeo-Christianity." *Jerusalem Studies in Arabic and Islam* 4 (1984): 135–52.
Putman, H. *Communautés syriaques en Iran et en Irak des origines à 1552*. London: Variorum Reprints, 1979.
—. *Chrétiens syriaques sous les Abbassides surtout à Baghdad, 749–1258*. *CSCO* 420 Subsidia 59. Louvain: Peeters, 1980.
—. *L'église et l'Islam sous Timothée Ier, 780–823*. Beirut: Librairie orientale, 1975.
Rabbat, I. *L'Orient chrétien à la veille de l'Islam*. Beirut, Université libanaise / Librairie orientale, 1980.
Reinink, G. J., and B. H. Stolte, eds. *The Reign of Heraclius (610–641): Crisis and Confrontation*. Louvain: Peeters, 2002.
Riboud, P. "Tang." In *Handbook of Christianity in China*. Vol. 1: *635–1800*. Ed. N. Standaert. Leiden: Brill, 2001, 1–42.
Ridgeon, L. V. J., ed. *Islamic Interpretations of Christianity*. Richmond: Curzon, 2001.

Rissanen, S. *Theological Encounter of Oriental Christians with Islam during Early Abbasid Rule*. Åbo: Åbo Akademis Förlag, 1993.

Roncaglia, M. P. *Histoire de l'église copte*. 4 vols. Beirut: Librairie St. Paul, 1985.

Rubin, U., and D. Wasserstein, eds. *Dhimmis and Others: Jews and Christians and the World of Classical Islam*. Israel Oriental Studies 17. Winona Lake, IN: Eisenbrauns, 1997.

Schick, R. *The Christian Communities of Palestine from Byzantine to Islamic Rule*. Princeton, NJ: Darwin Press, 1995.

Scott, D. "Christian Responses to Buddhism in pre-Mediaeval Times." *Numen* 32/1 (1985): 88–100.

Segal, J. B. *Edessa "The Blessed City."* Oxford: Clarendon Press, 1970.

Selb, W. *Orientalisches Kirchenrecht*. Vol. 2: *Die Geschichte des Kirchenrechts des Westsyrer, von den Anfängen bis zur Mongolenzeit*. Vienna: Österreichische Akademie der Wissenschaften, 1989.

Shahid, I. *Byzantium and the Arabs in the Sixth Century*. Vol. 1, pt. 2. Washington: Dumbarton Oaks, 1995.

Sims-Williams, N. "Sogdian and Turkish Christians in the Turfan and Tun-huang Manuscripts." In *Turfan and Tun-huang: The Texts. Encounter of Civilisations on the Silk Route*. Ed. A. Cadonna. Florence: Leo S. Olschki Editore, 1992.

Spuler, B. "Die west-syrische (monophysitische) Kirche unter dem Islam." *Saeculum* 9 (1958): 322–44.

Tajadod, N. *À l'est du Christ: Vie et mort des chrétiens dans la Chine des Tang (VIIe–IXe siècles)*. Paris: Plon, 2000.

Tarchnishvili, M. *Geschichte der kirchlichen georgischen Literatur, auf Grund des ersten Bandes der georgischen Literaturgeschichte von K. Kekelidze*. Studi e testi 185. Vatican City: Biblioteca apostolica vaticana, 1955.

Ter-Ghewondyan, A. N. *The Arab Emirates in Bagratid Armenia*. Lisbon: Livraria Bertrand, 1976.

Ter-Minassiantz, E. *Die armenische Kirche in ihren Beziehungen zu den syrischen Kirchen bis zum Ende des 13. Jahrhunderts*. Leipzig: J. C. Hinrichs, 1904.

Thomas, D., ed. *Christians at the Heart of Islamic Rule: Church Life and Scholarship in 'Abbasid Iraq*. Leiden: Brill, 2003.

—. "Early Muslim Responses to Christianity." In his *Christians at the Heart*, 231–54.

Toepel, A. "Traces of Nestorianism in Manchuria and Korea." *Oriens Christianus* 89 (2005): 77–85.

Toumanoff, C. *Studies in Christian Caucasian History*. Washington, DC: Georgetown University Press, 1963.

Tritton, A. S. *The Caliphs and their non-Muslim Subjects: A Critical Study of the Covenant of 'Umar*. London: Frank Cass, 1970.

Troupeau, G. "Églises et chrétiens dans l'Orient musulman." In *Histoire du christianisme* 4, 375–456.

—. *Études sur le christianisme arabe au Moyen Âge*. Aldershot: Variorum, 1995.

—. "La littérature arabe chrétienne du Xe au XIIe siècle." *Cahiers de Civilisation Médiévale* 14 (1971): 1–20.

Tubach, J. "Die Heimat des China-Missionars Alopen." *Oriens Christianus* 76 (1992): 95–100.

Van Dieten, J. L. *Geschichte der Patriarchen von Sergios I. bis Johannes VI., 610–715*. Amsterdam: A. M. Hakkert, 1972.

Van Esbroeck, M. "Les églises orientales non syriennes." *Le Muséon* 106 (1993): 97–117.

—. "Perspectives pour l'étude des églises du Caucase." In *The Christian East, its Institutions and its Thought: A Critical Reflection*. Ed. R. F. Taft. Rome: Pontificio istituto orientale, 1996, 129–44.

Van Rompay, L. "Development of Biblical Interpretation in the Syrian Churches of the Middle Ages." In *Hebrew Bible/Old Testament: The History of Its Interpretation*. Vol. 1, pt. 2: *The Middle Ages*. Ed. M. Saebo. Göttingen: Vandenhoeck & Ruprecht, 2000.

Verghese, P., ed. *Koptisches Christentum: Die orthodoxen Kirchen Ägyptens und Äthiopiens*. Stuttgart: Evangelisches Verlagswerk, 1973.

Voicu, S. J. "La patristica nella letteratura armena (V–X sec.)." In *Complementi interdisciplinari di patrologia*. Ed. A. Quacqarelli. Rome: Città Nuova, 1989, 657–96.

Vööbus, A. *History of Asceticism in the Syrian Orient: A Contribution to the History of Culture in the Near East*. 3 vols. *CSCO 184, 197, 500* Subsidia 14, 17, 81. Louvain: Peeters, 1958, 1960, 1988.

Waardenburg, J. J., ed. *Muslims and Others: Relations in Context*. Religion and Reason 41. Berlin: de Gruyter, 2003.

—. *Muslim Perceptions of Other Religions: A Historical Survey*. Oxford: Oxford University Press, 1999.

Watt, W. M. "The Christianity Criticised in the Qur'ān." *The Muslim World* 57 No. 3 (1967): 197–201.

Winkelmann, F. "Die Quellen zur Erforschung des monoenergetisch-monotheletischen Streites." *Klio* 69 (1987): 515–69.

Winkler, D. W. *Koptische Kirche und Reichskirche: Altes Schisma und neuer Dialog*. Innsbrucker theologische Studien 48. Innsbruck: Tyrolia-Verlag, 1997.

—. "Zeitalter der Sassaniden bis 653." In W. Baum and D. W. Winkler. *Die apostolische Kirche des Ostens: Geschichte der sogenannten Nestorianer*. Klagenfurt: Verlag Kitab, 2000, 13–42.

Ye'or, B. *Les chrétientés d'Orient entre Jihâd et Dhimmitude: VIIe–XXe siècle*. Paris: Éditions du Cerf, 1991.

Zanetti, U. "Les chrétiens du Nil: Basse et Haute Égypte, Nubie, Étiopie." In *The Christian East, its Institutions and its Thought: A Critical Reflection*. Ed. R. F. Taft. Rome: Pontificio istituto orientale, 1996, 181–216.

4 Beyond empire II: Christianities of the Celtic peoples
Thomas M. Charles-Edwards

Primary sources

Adomnán. *Vita Sancti Columbae*. Ed. and trans. A. O. and M. O. Anderson. *Adomnan's Life of Columba*. London, 1961; rev. ed.: Oxford Medieval Texts. Oxford: Oxford University Press, 1991; Trans. R. Sharpe. *Adomnán of Iona: Life of St. Columba*. Harmondsworth: Penguin Classics, 1995.

Aldhelm. *Letter IV*. Ed. R. Ehwald. *Aldhelmi Opera Omnia*. *MGH Auctores antiquissimi* 15. Berlin: Weidmann, 1919, 480–86; Trans. M. Lapidge and M. Herren. *Aldhelm: The Prose Works*. Ipswich: D. S. Brewer, 1979, 155–60.

Annales Cambriae, A Version. Ed. E. Phillimore. "The *Annales Cambriae* and the Old Welsh Genealogies from Harleian MS. 3859." *Y Cymmrodor* 9 (1888): 141–83.

The Annals of Ulster (to A.D. 1131). Ed. S. Mac Airt and G. Mac Niocaill. Part I: *Text and Translation*. Dublin: Dublin Institute for Advanced Studies, 1983.

Anonymous Life of St. Cuthbert. Ed. and trans. B. Colgrave. *Two Lives of Saint Cuthbert*. Cambridge: Cambridge University Press, 1940, 60–139.

Asser. *Asser's Life of King Alfred*. Ed. W. H. Stevenson. Oxford: Clarendon Press, 1904.

Bonedd y Saint. Ed. P. Bartrum. *Early Welsh Genealogical Tracts*. Cardiff: University of Wales, 1966.

Cáin Adamnáin. Ed. and trans. K. Meyer. Anecdota Oxoniensia 12. Oxford: Oxford University Press, 1905; Trans. M. Ní Dhonnchadha. "The Law of Adomnán: A Translation." In *Adomnán at Birr, AD 697*. Ed. T. O'Loughlin. Dublin: Four Courts Press, 2001, 53–68.

Cath Maige Tuired. Ed. and trans. E. Gray. Irish Texts Society 52. Naas: Irish Texts Society, 1982.

The Chronicle of Ireland. Trans. with intro. and notes T. Charles-Edwards. Translated Texts for Historians. Liverpool: Liverpool University Press, 2006.

Chronicum Scotorum. Ed. and trans. W. M. Hennessy. London: Longmans, Green, Reader, and Dyer, 1866.

Cogitosus. *Vita S. Brigidae. AASS* Feb. 1, 135–41. Trans. S. Connolly and J.-M. Picard. *Journal of the Royal Society of Antiquaries of Ireland* 117 (1987): 11–27.

Columbanus. *Sancti Columbani Opera*. Ed. and trans. G. S. M. Walker. Scriptores Latini Hiberniae 2. Dublin: Dublin Institute for Advanced Studies, 1957.

Corpus Iuris Hibernici. Ed. D. A. Binchy. 6 vols. Dublin: Dublin Institute for Advanced Studies, 1978.

Críth Gablach. Ed. D. A. Binchy. Mediaeval and Modern Irish Series 11. Dublin: Stationery Office, 1941.

Cummian. *De Controversia Paschali*. Ed. and trans. M. Walsh and D. Ó Cróinín. *Cummian's Letter De Controversia Paschali and the De Ratione Computandi*. Toronto: University of Toronto Press, 1988.

Dicuili Liber de Mensura Orbis Terrae. Ed. and trans. J. J. Tierney with L. Bieler. Scriptores Latini Hiberniae 6. Dublin: Dublin Institute for Advanced Studies, 1967.

Echrys ynys. Ed. and trans. R. G. Gruffydd. "A Welsh 'Dark-Age' Poem." In *Ildánach Ildírech: A Festschrift for Proinsias Mac Cana*. Ed. J. Carey, J. T. Koch, and P.-Y. Lambert. Andover: Celtic Studies Publications, 1999, 39–48.

Epistolae Austrasicae. Ed. W. Gundlach. In *MGH Epistolae Merowingici et Karolini Aevi* 1 (= *MGH Epistolarum* 3). Ed. E. Dümmler. Berlin: Weidmann, 1892, 110–53.

Fingal Rónáin. Ed. D. Greene. In *Fingal Ronáin and Other Stories*. Dublin: Dublin Institute for Advanced Studies, 1955, 3–11. Trans. M. Ní Dhonnchadha. In J. T. Koch and J. Carey, eds., *The Celtic Heroic Age: Literary Sources for Ancient Celtic Europe and Early Ireland and Wales*. 4th ed. Aberystwyth: Celtic Studies Publications, 2003, 274–82.

"The First Third of *Bretha Nemed Toísech*." Ed. and trans. L. Breatnach. *Ériu* 40 (1989): 1–40.

Fredegar. *Chronica*. Ed. B. Krusch. *MGH SRM* 2. Hanover: Hahn, 1888, 1–193. Partially edited by A. Kusternig and H. Haupt. *Quellen zur Geschichte des 7. und 8. Jahrhunderts*. Darmstadt: Wissenschaftliche Buchgesellschaft, 1982, 1–325; Partially edited by J. M.

Wallace-Hadrill. *The Fourth Book of the Chronicle of Fredegar with its Continuations*. Nelson Medieval Classics. London: Thomas Nelson, 1960.

Gildas. *The Ruin of Britain and Other Works*. Ed. and trans. M. Winterbottom. Chichester: Phillimore, 1978.

Gregory of Tours. *Libri historiarum X*. Ed. B. Krusch and W. Levison. *MGH SRM* 1.1. Hanover: Hahn, 1951.

Immram Curaig Maíle Dúin. Ed. and trans. H. Oskamp. *The Voyage of Máel Dúin*. Groningen: Wolters-Noordhoff, 1970.

The Irish Penitentials. Ed. and trans. L. Bieler. Dublin: Dublin Institute for Advanced Studies, 1963.

Jonas. *Vita S. Columbani*. Ed. B. Krusch. *Ionae Vitae Sanctorum Columbani, Vedastis, Iohannis*. *MGH SRG*. Hanover: Hahn, 1905.

The Martyrology of Óengus the Culdee: Félire Óengusso Céli Dé. Ed. and trans. W. Stokes. Henry Bradshaw Society 29. London: Harrison and Sons, 1905; reprint, Dublin: Dublin Institute for Advanced Studies, 1984.

The Monastery of Tallaght. Ed. and trans. E. J. Gwynn and W. J. Purton. *Proceedings of the Royal Irish Academy* 29 C (1911) No. 5: 115–79.

Pactus Legis Salicae. Ed. K. A. Eckhardt. *MGH Legum* I.iv.1. Hanover: Hahn, 1962; Trans. T. J. Rivers. *Laws of the Salian and Ripuarian Franks*. New York: AMS Press, 1986.

The Poems of Blathmac son of Cú Brettan together with the Irish Gospel of Thomas and a Poem on the Virgin Mary. Ed. and trans. J. Carney. Irish Texts Society 47. Dublin: Educational Co. of Ireland, 1964.

Rhigyfarch. *Vita S. Dauid*. Ed. A. W. Wade-Evans. *Vitae sanctorum Britanniae et genealogiae*. Cardiff: University of Wales Press Board, 1944, 150–70.

Stephen. *Vita S. Wilfridi*. Ed. and trans. B. Colgrave. *The Life of Bishop Wilfrid by Eddius Stephanus*. Cambridge: Cambridge University Press, 1927.

The Text of the Book of Llan Dâv. Ed. J. Gwenogvryn Evans with J. Rhys. Oxford: privately published, 1893; reprint, Aberystwyth: National Library of Wales, 1979.

Theodore. *Penitential* (in the version compiled by the *discipulus Umbrensium*). Ed. P. W. Finsterwalder. *Die Canones Theodori und ihrer Überlieferungsformen*. Weimar: H. Böhlaus, 1929, 285–334; Trans. J. T. McNeill and H. Gamer. *Medieval Handbooks of Penance*. New York: Columbia University Press, 1938, 182–215.

Tírechán. *Collectanea*. Ed. and trans. L. Bieler. *The Patrician Texts in the Book of Armagh*. Scriptores Latini Hiberniae 10. Dublin: Dublin Institute for Advanced Studies, 1979, 122–62.

Uraicecht na Ríar. Ed. and trans. L. Breatnach. Early Irish Law Series 2. Dublin: Dublin Institute for Advanced Studies, 1987.

Venantius Fortunatus. *Opera Poetica*. Ed. F. Leo. *MGH Auctores antiquissimi* 4.1. Berlin: Weidmann, 1881.

Secondary sources

Ahronson, K. "Further Evidence for a Columban Iceland: Preliminary Results of Recent Work." *Norwegian Archaeological Review* 33 (2000): 117–24.

Brooks, N. "Canterbury, Rome and the Construction of English Identity." In *Early Medieval Rome and the Christian West: Essays in Honour of Donald A. Bullough*. Ed. J. M. H. Smith. Leiden: Brill, 2000, 221–47.

Carey, J. "A British Myth of Origins?" *Journal of the History of Religions* 31 (1991): 24–37.

Charles-Edwards, T. M. "The Context and Uses of Literacy in Early Christian Ireland." In *Literacy in Medieval Celtic Societies*. Ed. H. Pryce. Cambridge: Cambridge University Press, 1998, 62–82.

—. *Early Christian Ireland*. Cambridge: Cambridge University Press, 2000.

—. "Language and Society among the Insular Celts, 400–1000." In *The Celtic World*. Ed. M. J. Aldhouse-Green. London: Routledge, 1995, 703–36.

—. "The Seven Bishop Houses of Dyfed." *Bulletin of the Board of Celtic Studes* 24 (1970–72): 247–62.

—. "The Social Background to Irish *Peregrinatio*." *Celtica* 11 (1976): 43–59.

Chédeville, A., and H. Guillotel. *La Bretagne des saints et des rois, Ve–Xe siècle*. Rennes: Ouest France, 1984.

Davies, J. R. "Church, Property, and Conflict in Wales, AD 600–1100." *Welsh History Review* 18 (1996–97): 387–406.

Davies, W. *An Early Welsh Microcosm: Studies in the Llandaff Charters*. London: Royal Historical Society, 1978.

—. "The Myth of the Celtic Church." In *The Early Church in Wales and the West*. Ed. A. Lane and N. Edwards. Oxford: Oxford University Press, 1992, 12–21.

—. "Priests and Rural Communities in East Brittany in the Ninth Century." *Études Celtiques* 20 (1983): 177–97.

—. *Small Worlds: The Village Community in Early Medieval Brittany*. London: Duckworth, 1988.

Doherty, C. "The Cult of St. Patrick and the Politics of Armagh in the Seventh Century." In *Ireland and Northern France AD 600–850*. Ed. J.-M. Picard. Dublin: Four Courts Press, 1991, 53–94.

Edwards, N. "Early Medieval Inscribed Stones and Stone Sculpture in Wales: Context and Function." *Medieval Archaeology* 45 (2001): 15–39.

—, and A. Lane, eds., *The Early Church in Wales and the West*. Oxford: Oxford University Press, 1991.

Etchingham, C. *Church Organization in Ireland, AD 650 to 1000*. Maynooth: Laigin Publications, 1999.

—. *Viking Raids on Irish Church Settlements in the Ninth Century*. Maynooth Monographs, Series Minor 1. Maynooth: Department of Old and Middle Irish, St. Patrick's College, 1996.

Fisher, I. *Early Medieval Sculpture in the West Highlands and Islands*. Royal Commission on the Ancient and Historical Monuments of Scotland, Monograph Ser. 1. Edinburgh: Society of Antiquaries of Scotland, 2001.

Graham-Campbell, J. "The Early Viking Age in the Irish Sea Area." In *Ireland and Scandinavia in the Early Viking Age*. Ed. H. B. Clarke, M. Ní Mhaonaigh, and R. Ó Floinn. Dublin: Four Courts Press, 1998, 104–30.

Grosjean, P. "Sur quelques exégètes irlandais du VIIe siècle." *Sacris Erudiri* 7 (1955): 67–98.

Higgitt, J. "The Dedication Inscription at Jarrow and its Context." *Antiquaries Journal* 59/2 (1979): 343–74.

Hughes, K. W. "The Celtic Church: Is this a Valid Concept?" *Cambridge Medieval Celtic Studies* 1 (Summer 1981): 1–20.

—. *The Church in Early Irish Society*. London: Methuen, 1966.

—. "The Church in Irish Society, 400–800" and "The Irish Church, 800–c. 1050." In Ó Cróinín, *New History of Ireland*, 301–30 and 635–55.

Kelly, F. *A Guide to Early Irish Law*. Early Irish Law Series 3. Dublin: Dublin Institute for Advanced Studies, 1988.

Kenney, J. *Sources for the Early History of Ireland: Ecclesiastical*. New York: Octagon Books, 1929.

Lapidge, M. "The Welsh-Latin Poetry of Sulien's Family." *Studia Celtica* 8–9 (1973–74): 68–106.

Mac Cana, P. "The Influence of the Vikings on Celtic Literature." In *The Impact of the Scandinavian Invasions on the Celtic-Speaking Peoples, c. 800–1100 AD*. Ed. B. Ó Cuív. Dublin: Dublin Institute for Advanced Studies, 1962, 78–118.

Mac Shamhráin, A. *Church and Polity in Pre-Norman Ireland: The Case of Glendalough*. Maynooth: An Sagart, 1996.

Meek, D. E. *The Quest for Celtic Christianity*. Edinburgh: Handsel Press, 2000.

O'Brien, E. "Churches of South-East County Dublin, Seventh to Twelfth Century." In *Keimelia: Studies in Medieval Archaeology and History in Memory of Tom Delaney*. Ed. G. Mac Niocaill and P. F. Wallace. Galway: Galway University Press, 1988, 506–24.

—. *Post-Roman Britain to Anglo-Saxon England: Burial Practices Reviewed*. British Archeological Reports, Brit. Ser. 289. Oxford: British Archeological Reports, 1999.

Ó Corráin, D. "The Early Irish Churches: Some Aspects of Organization." In his *Irish Antiquity*, 327–41.

—, ed. *Irish Antiquity: Essays and Studies Presented to M. J. O'Kelly*. Cork: Tower Books, 1981.

Ó Cróinín, D. *Early Medieval Ireland, 400–1200*. London: Longman, 1995.

—, ed. *A New History of Ireland*. Vol.1: *Prehistoric and Early Ireland*. Oxford: Oxford University Press, 2005.

O'Dwyer, P. *Céli Dé: Spiritual Reform in Ireland, 750–900*. 2nd ed. Dublin: Editions Tailliura, 1981.

Ó Fiaich, T. "The Church of Armagh under Lay Control." *Seanchas Ard Mhacha* 3, pt. 1 (1969): 75–127.

Olson, [B.] L. *Early Monasteries in Cornwall*. Studies in Celtic History 11. Woodbridge: Boydell Press, 1989.

—, and O. J. Padel. "A Tenth-Century List of Cornish Parochial Saints." *Cambridge Medieval Celtic Studies* 12 (Winter 1986): 33–71.

Pryce, H. "Ecclesiastical Wealth in Early Medieval Wales." In Edwards and Lane, *Early Church in Wales*, 22–32.

—, ed. *Literacy in Medieval Celtic Societies*. Cambridge: Cambridge University Press, 1998.

—. "Pastoral Care in Early Medieval Wales." In *Pastoral Care before the Parish*. Ed. J. Blair and R. Sharpe. London: Leicester University Press, 1992, 48–61.

Reeves, W. *The Culdees of the British Islands*. Dublin: M. H. Gill, 1864.

Sharpe, R. "Hiberno-Latin *Laicus*, Irish *Láech* and the Devil's Men." *Ériu* 30 (1979): 75–92.

—. "Martyrs and Local Saints in Late Antique Britain." In *Local Saints and Local Churches in the Early Medieval West*. Ed. A. Thacker and R. Sharpe. Oxford: Oxford University Press, 2002, 75–154.

—. "Some Problems Concerning the Organization of the Church in Early Medieval Ireland." *Peritia* 3 (1984): 230–70.

Sims-Williams, P. *Religion and Literature in Western England, 600–800*. Cambridge: Cambridge University Press, 1990.

Smith, J. M. H. *Province and Empire: Brittany and the Carolingians*. Cambridge: Cambridge University Press, 1992.

Stancliffe, C. "The British Church and the Mission of Augustine." In *St. Augustine and the Conversion of England*. Ed. R. Gameson. Stroud: Sutton, 1999, 107–51.

Toner, G. "The Ulster Cycle: Historiography or Fiction?" *Cambrian Medieval Celtic Studies* 40 (2000): 1–20.

5 Germanic Christianities
Lesley Abrams

Primary sources

Adam of Bremen. *Gesta*. In *Hamburgische Kirchengeschichte*. Ed. B. Schmeidler. *MGH SRG*. Hanover and Leipzig: Hahn, 1917; Trans. F. J. Tschan and rev. ed. T. Reuter, *History of the Archbishops of Hamburg-Bremen*. New York: Columbia University Press, 2002.

Ælfric. *Ælfric's Prefaces*. Ed. J. Wilcox. Durham Medieval Texts 9. Durham: Department of English Studies, 1994.

Alcuin. *Alcuin of York*. Trans. S. Allott. York: William Sessions, 1974.

Aldhelm. *Aldhelmi opera omnia*. Ed. R. Ehwald. *MGH Auctores antiquissimi* 15. Berlin: Weidmann, 1919.

—. *Aldhelm, The Prose Works*. Trans. M. Lapidge and M. Herren. Ipswich: D. S. Brewer, 1979.

Anglo-Saxon Missionaries in Germany. Ed. and trans. C. H. Talbot. London: Sheed and Ward, 1954.

Anglo-Saxon Poetry. Ed. and trans. S. A. J. Bradley. London: Everyman, 1982.

Anglo-Saxon Wills. Ed. and trans. D. Whitelock. Cambridge: Cambridge University Press, 1930.

Asser. *Alfred the Great. Asser's Life of King Alfred and Other Contemporary Sources*. Trans. S. Keynes and M. Lapidge. Harmondsworth: Penguin Books, 1983; *Asser's Life of King Alfred*. Ed. W. H. Stevenson. Oxford: Clarendon Press, 1959.

Bede. *Bedae opera didascalia*. Ed. C. W. Jones. 3 vols. *CCSL* 123. Turnhout: Brepols, 1975–80.

—. *Bede: The Reckoning of Time*. Trans. F. Wallis. Liverpool: Liverpool University Press, 1999.

Early English Christian Poetry. Trans. C. M. Kennedy. New York: Galaxy, 1963.

Einhard. *Charlemagne's Courtier: The Complete Einhard*. Trans. P. Dutton. Peterborough, Canada: Broadview Press, 1998.

—. *Einhardi vita Karoli magni*. Ed. G. Waitz. *MGH SRG*. Hanover: Hahn, 1911.

English Historical Documents, c. 500–1042. Trans. D. Whitelock. 2nd ed. London: Eyre Methuen, 1979.

English Historical Documents, 1042–1189. Trans. D. C. Douglas and G. W. Greenway. 2nd ed. London: Routledge, 1996.

Epistolae karolini aevi, 2. Ed. E. Dümmler. *MGH Epistolae* 4. Berlin: Weidmann, 1895.

Fredegar. *Fredegarii et aliorum chronica*. Ed. B. Krusch. *MGH SRM* 2. Hanover: Hahn, 1888.

Hrabanus Maurus. *De institutione clericorum libri tres*. Ed. D. Zimpel. Frankfurt: Peter Lang, 1996.

Íslendingabók. Landnámabók. Ed. J. Benediktsson 2 vols. in 1. Reykjavík: Íslensk fornrit, 1968. Ed. and English trans. H. Hermannsson. *The Book of the Icelanders (Íslendingabók)*. London: Humphrey Milford / Oxford University Press, 1930.

The Laws of the Kings of England from Edmund to Henry I. Ed. and trans. A. J. Robertson. Cambridge: Cambridge University Press, 1925.

Medieval Handbooks of Penance. Trans. J. T. McNeill and H. M. Gamer. New York: Columbia University Press, 1990.

The Old English Version of the Heptateuch. Ed. S. J. Crawford; rev. ed. N. R. Ker. Early English Text Society os 160. London: Oxford University Press for the Early English Text Society, 1922/1969.

Saxo Grammaticus. *History of the Danes*. 2 vols. Trans. P. Fisher and ed. H. E. Davidson. Cambridge: D. S. Brewer, 1979.

Snorri Sturluson. *Snorri Sturluson: Edda*. Trans. and ed. A. Faulkes. London: J. M. Dent, 1987.

Thietmar of Merseburg. *Thietmari Merseburgensis episcopi chronicon*. Ed. R. Holtzmann. *MGH SRG* ns 9. Berlin: Weidmann, 1935; *Ottonian Germany: The Chronicon of Thietmar of Merseburg*. Trans. D. A. Warner. Manchester: Manchester University Press, 2001.

Widukind. *Die Sachsengeschichte des Widukind von Korvei*. Ed. H.-E. Lohmann and P. Hirsch. 5th ed. *MGH SRG*. Hanover: Hahn, 1935.

Secondary sources

Aðalsteinsson, J. N. *A Piece of Horse Liver: Myth, Ritual and Folklore in Old Icelandic Society*. Trans. T. Gunnell and J. Turville-Petre. Reykjavík: Háskólaútgáfan, 1998.

Behr, C. "The Origins of Kingship in Early Medieval Kent." *EME* 9 (2000): 25–52.

Blair, J. *The Anglo-Saxon Church*. Oxford: Oxford University Press, 2005.

Bostock, J. K., ed. *A Handbook on Old High German Literature*. Rev. ed. K. C. King and D. R. McLintock. Oxford: Clarendon Press, 1976.

Brink, S. "Mythologizing Landscape: Place and Space of Cult and Myth." In *Kontinuitäten und Brüche in der Religionsgeschichte: Festchrift für Anders Hultgård*. Ed. M. Stausberg. Berlin: de Gruyter, 2001, 76–112.

Brooke, C. N. L., and G. Keir. *London 800–1216: The Shaping of a City*. London: Secker and Warburg, 1975.

Brown, G. "Introduction: The Carolingian Renaissance." In *Carolingian Culture: Emulation and Innovation*. Ed. R. McKitterick. Cambridge: Cambridge University Press, 1994, 1–51.

Campbell, J. "Observations on English Government from the Tenth to the Twelfth Century." In *Essays in Anglo-Saxon History*. London: Hambledon Press, 1986, 155–70.

Chaney, W. A. *The Cult of Kingship in Anglo-Saxon England: The Transition from Paganism to Christianity*. Manchester: Manchester University Press, 1970.

Chase, C., ed. *The Dating of Beowulf*. Toronto: University of Toronto Press, 1981.

Clunies Ross, M., ed. *Old Icelandic Literature and Society*. Cambridge: Cambridge University Press, 2000.

—. *Prolonged Echoes: Old Norse Myths in Medieval Society*. 2 vols. Odense: Odense University Press, 1994.

Cormack, M. "Murder and Martyrs in Anglo-Saxon England." In *Sacrificing the Self: Perspectives on Martyrdom and Religion*. Ed. M. Cormack. Oxford: Oxford University Press, 2002, 58–77.

Cramer, P. *Baptism and Change in the Early Middle Ages, c. 200–c. 1150*. Cambridge: Cambridge University Press, 1993.

Cusack, C. M. *Conversion among the Germanic Peoples*. London and New York: Cassell, 1998.

Davidson, H. R. E. *Gods and Myths of Northern Europe*. Harmondsworth: Penguin Books, 1994.

de Jong, M. and F. Theuws, eds. *Topographies of Power in the Early Middle Ages*. Leiden: Brill, 2001.

Dumville, D. N. "Kingship, Genealogies and Regnal Lists." In *Early Medieval Kingship*. Ed. P. H. Sawyer and I. N. Wood. Leeds: University of Leeds, 1977, 72–104. Reprinted in D. N. Dumville, *Histories and Pseudo-Histories of the Insular Middle Ages*. Aldershot: Variorum, 1990.

Edwards, C. "German Vernacular Literature." In *Carolingian Culture: Emulation and Innovation*. Ed. R. McKitterick. Cambridge: Cambridge University Press, 1994, 141–70.

Edwards, D. "Christian and Pagan References in Eleventh-Century Norse Poetry: The Case of Arnórr Jarlaskáld." *Saga-Book of the Viking Society* 21 (1982–83): 34–53.

Effros, B. "Monuments and Memory: Repossessing Ancient Remains in Early Medieval Gaul." In de Jong and Theuws, *Topographies of Power in the Early Middle Ages*, 93–118.

Faulkes, A. "Descent from the Gods." *Mediaeval Scandinavia* 11 (1978–79): 92–125.

Fletcher, R. *The Conversion of Europe: From Paganism to Christianity 371–1386 AD*. London: HarperCollins, 1997.

Flint, V. I. J. *The Rise of Magic in Early Medieval Europe*. Oxford: Clarendon Press, 1991.

Foot, S. *Veiled Women, I: The Disappearance of Nuns from Anglo-Saxon England*. Aldershot: Ashgate, 2000.

Foote, P. "Observations on 'Syncretism' in Early Icelandic Christianity." In *Aurvandilstá*. Ed. M. Barnes et al. Odense: Odense University Press, 1984, 84–100.

Frank, R. "Germanic Legend in Old English Literature." In *The Cambridge Companion to Old English Literature*. Ed. M. Godden and M. Lapidge. Cambridge: Cambridge University Press, 1991, 88–106.

—. "King Cnut in the Verse of his Skalds." In *The Reign of Cnut: King of England, Denmark and Norway*. Ed. A. R. Rumble. London: Leicester University Press, 1994, 106–24.

Gameson, R., ed. *St. Augustine and the Conversion of England*. Stroud: Sutton, 1999.

Green, D. H. *Language and History in the Early Germanic World*. Cambridge: Cambridge University Press, 1998.

Harris, J. "Saga as Historical Novel." In *Structure and Meaning in Old Norse Literature: New Approaches to Textual Analysis and Literary Criticism*. Ed. J. Lindow, L. Lonroth, and G. W. Weber. Odense: Odense University Press, 1986, 187–219.

Hedeager, L. "Myth and Art: A Passport to Political Authority in Scandinavia during the Migration Period." In *The Making of Kingdoms: Papers from the 47th Sachsensymposium, York, September 1996*. Ed. T. M. Dickinson and D. Griffiths. Anglo-Saxon Studies in Archaeology and History 10. Oxford: Oxford University Committee for Archaeology, 1999, 151–60.

Hen, Y. *Culture and Religion in Merovingian Gaul, AD 481–751*. Leiden: Brill, 1995.

Higham, N. J. *The Convert Kings: Power and Religious Affiliation in Early Anglo-Saxon England*. Manchester: Manchester University Press, 1997.

Hillgarth, J. N., ed. *Christianity and Paganism, 350–750: The Conversion of Western Europe*. Rev. ed. Philadelphia: University of Pennsylvania Press, 1986.

Hofstra, T., et al., eds. *Pagans and Christians: The Interplay between Christian Latin and Traditional Germanic Cultures in Early Medieval Europe*. Groningen: Egbert Forsten, 1995.

Innes, M. "Teutons or Trojans? The Carolingians and the Teutonic Past." In *The Uses of the Past in the Early Middle Ages*. Ed. Y. Hen and M. Innes. Cambridge: Cambridge University Press, 2000, 227–49.

Jesch, J. "Scandinavians and 'Cultural Paganism' in Late Anglo-Saxon England." In *The Christian Tradition in Anglo-Saxon England: Approaches to Current Scholarship and Teaching*. Ed. P. Cavill. Woodbridge: D. S. Brewer, 2004, 55–68.

Jochens, J. "Late and Peaceful: Iceland's Conversion through Arbitration in 1000." *Speculum* 74 (1999): 621–55.

Jolly, K. L. *Popular Religion in Late Saxon England: Elf Charms in Context*. Chapel Hill, NC: University of North Carolina Press, 1996.

Keynes, S. "The Vikings in England, c. 790–1016." In *The Oxford Illustrated History of the Vikings*. Ed. P. Sawyer. Oxford: Oxford University Press, 1997, 48–82.

Kissan, B. W. "An Early List of London Properties." *Transactions of the London and Middlesex Archaeological Society* ns 8 (1940): 57–69.

Leyser, K. J. *Rule and Conflict in an Early Medieval Society*. Oxford: Blackwell, 1979.

Lönnroth, L. "The Noble Heathen: A Theme in the Sagas." *Scandinavian Studies* 41 (1969): 1–29.

Lynch, J. H. *Christianizing Kinship: Ritual Sponsorship in Anglo-Saxon England*. Ithaca, NY: Cornell University Press, 1988.

Markus, R. A. *The End of Ancient Christianity*. Cambridge: Cambridge University Press, 1990.

—. "From Rome to the Barbarian Kingdoms." In *The Oxford Illustrated History of Christianity*. Ed. J. McManners. Oxford: Oxford University Press, 1990, 62–91.

Mayr-Harting, H. *The Coming of Christianity to Anglo-Saxon England*. 3rd ed. London: B. T. Batsford, 1991.

McKitterick, R., ed. *The Uses of Literacy in Early Medieval Europe*. Cambridge: Cambridge University Press, 1990.

Meaney, A. L. "Anglo-Saxon Idolators and Ecclesiasts from Theodore to Alcuin: A Source Study." *Anglo-Saxon Studies in Archaeology and History* 5 (1992): 103–25.

Murphy, G. R. *The Saxon Saviour: The Transformation of the Gospel in the Ninth-Century Heliand*. Oxford: Oxford University Press, 1989.

Nelson, J. L. "Kingship and Empire." In *The Cambridge History of Medieval Political Thought*. Ed. J. H. Burns. Cambridge: Cambridge University Press, 1988, 211–51. Reprinted in *Carolingian Culture: Emulation and Innovation*. Ed. R. McKitterick. Cambridge: Cambridge University Press, 1993, 52–87.

—. "Royal Saints and Early Medieval Kingship." *Studies in Church History* 20 (1983): 15–30. Reprinted in her *Politics and Ritual in Early Modern Europe*. London: Hambledon Press, 1986, 69–74.

—. "The Wary Widow." In *Property and Power in the Early Middle Ages*. Ed. W. Davies and P. Fouracre. Cambridge: Cambridge University Press, 1995, 82–113.

North, R. *Pagan Words and Christian Meanings*. Amsterdam: Rodopi, 1991.

Page, R. I. *Chronicles of the Vikings: Records, Memorials and Myths*. London: British Museum Press, 1995.

——. *Runes*. London: British Museum Publications, 1987.

Poole, R. "The 'Conversion Verses' of Hallfreðr vandræðaskáld." *Maal og mine* 1 (2002): 15–37.

Quinn, J. "From Orality to Literacy in Medieval Iceland." In *Old Icelandic Literature and Society*. Ed. M. Clunies Ross. Cambridge: Cambridge University Press, 2000, 30–60.

Reynolds, S. *Fiefs and Vassals: The Medieval Evidence Reinterpreted*. Oxford: Oxford University Press, 1994.

Ridyard, S. J. *The Royal Saints of Anglo-Saxon England: A Study of West Saxon and East Anglian Cults*. Cambridge: Cambridge University Press, 1988.

Rollason, D. *Saints and Relics in Anglo-Saxon England*. Oxford: Blackwell, 1989.

Russell, J. C. *The Germanization of Christianity: A Sociohistorical Approach to Religious Transformation*. Oxford: Oxford University Press, 1994.

Sawyer, P. H., et al., eds. *The Christianization of Scandinavia*. Alingsås: Viktoria Bokförlag, 1987.

Sims-Williams, P. *Religion and Literature in Western England, 600–800*. Cambridge: Cambridge University Press, 1990.

Sisam, K. "Anglo-Saxon Royal Genealogies." In *British Academy Papers on Anglo-Saxon England*. Ed. E. G. Stanley. Oxford: Oxford University Press, 1990, 145–204.

Smith, J. M. H. "Old Saints, New Cults: Roman Relics in Carolingian Francia." In *Early Medieval Rome and the Christian West: Essays in Honour of Donald A. Bullough*. Ed. J. M. H. Smith. Leiden: Brill, 2000, 317–39.

——. "Religion and Lay Society." *NCMH* 2, 654–78.

Thacker, A. "*Membra disjecta*: The Division of the Body and the Diffusion of the Cult." In *Oswald: Northumbrian King to European Saint*. Ed. C. Stancliffe and E. Cambridge. Stamford: Paul Watkins, 1995, 97–127.

Theuws, F., and J. L. Nelson, eds. *Rituals of Power from Late Antiquity to the Early Middle Ages*. Leiden: Brill, 2000.

Thompson, E. A. *The Visigoths in the Time of Ulfila*. Oxford: Clarendon Press, 1966.

Treharne, E. M., and M. Swan, eds. *Rewriting Old English in the Twelfth Century*. Cambridge: Cambridge University Press, 2000.

Tulinius, T. *The Matter of the North: The Rise of Literary Fiction in Thirteenth-Century Iceland*. Odense: Odense University Press, 2002.

Van Engen, J. "The Christian Middle Ages as an Historiographical Problem." *American Historical Review* 91 (1986): 519–52.

Vésteinsson, O. *The Christianization of Iceland: Priests, Power, and Social Change, 1000–1300*. Oxford: Oxford University Press, 2000.

Wallace-Hadrill, J. M. *The Frankish Church*. Oxford: Clarendon Press, 1983.

Ward-Perkins, B. "Reconfiguring Sacred Space: From Pagan Shrines to Christian Churches." In *Die spätantike Stadt und ihre Christianisierung*. Ed. G. Brands and H.-G. Severin. Wiesbaden: Reichert Verlag, 2003, 285–90.

Wood, I. *The Missionary Life: Saints and the Evangelisation of Europe, 400–1050*. Harlow: Longman, 2001.

—. "Pagan Religions and Superstitions East of the Rhine from the Fifth to the Ninth Century." In *After Empire: Towards an Ethnology of Europe's Barbarians*. Ed. G. Ausenda. Woodbridge: Boydell and Brewer, 1995, 253–79.
Wormald, P. "Anglo-Saxon Society and its Literature." In *The Cambridge Companion to Old English Literature*. Ed. M. Godden and M. Lapidge. Cambridge: Cambridge University Press, 1991, 1–22.
—. "Bede, 'Beowulf' and the Conversion of the Anglo-Saxon Aristocracy." In *Bede and Anglo-Saxon England*. Ed. R. T. Farrell. *British Archeological Reports* 46 (1978): 32–95.
Yorke, B. "The Adaptation of the Anglo-Saxon Royal Courts to Christianity." In *The Cross Goes North: Processes of Conversion in Northern Europe, AD 300–1300*. Ed. M. Carver. York: York Medieval Press, 2003, 243–57.
—. *Nunneries and the Anglo-Saxon Royal Houses*. London: Continuum, 2003.

6 Slav Christianities, 800–1100
Jonathan Shepard

Primary sources

Adalbert. *Continuatio Reginonis*. Ed. and German trans. A. Bauer et al. Ausgewählte Quellen zur deutschen Geschichte des Mittelalters 8. Darmstadt: Wissenschaftliche Buchgesellschaft, repr. 2002.
Angelov, B. S. *Iz starata b'lgarska, ruska i sr'bska literatura*. Vol. 3. Sofia: Bulgarian Academy of Sciences Publishing House, 1978.
Artsikhovsky, A. V., and V. I. Borkovsky. *Novgorodskie gramoty na bereste (iz raskopok 1956–1957 gg.)*. Vol. 5. Moscow: Publishing House of the Academy of Sciences of the USSR, 1963.
Christian Dualist Heresies in the Byzantine World, c. 650–c. 1405. Trans. B. Hamilton and J. Hamilton. Manchester: Manchester University Press, 1998.
Constantine VII. *De administrando imperio*. Ed. and trans. G. Moravcsik and R. J. H. Jenkins. Corpus Fontium Historiae Byzantinae 1. 2nd ed. Washington, DC: Dumbarton Oaks, 1967.
— *De cerimoniis aulae byzantinae*. Ed. I. I. Reiske. Vol. 1. Corpus Scriptorum Historiae Byzantinae. Bonn: Weber, 1829.
Cosmas the Priest. *Kozma presviter v slavianskikh literaturakh*. Ed. I. K. Begunov. Sofia: Bulgarian Academy of Sciences Publishing House, 1973, 297–392.
—. *Le traité contre les Bogomiles de Cosmas le Prêtre*. Trans. H.-C. Puech and A. Vaillant. Paris: Imprimerie nationale, 1945.
Diplomata Ottonis. MGH Diplomata regum et imperatorum Germaniae 1, pt. 2. Ed. T. Sickel. Hanover: Hahn, 1879–84.
Ebo. *Vita S. Ottonis*. Ed. J. Wikarjak. *Monumenta Poloniae historica (Pomniki dzeijowe polski)*, n. s. (= series 2) 7, pt. 2. Warsaw: Państwowe Wydawnictwo Naukowe, 1969.
Gallus Anonymus. *Cronicae et gesta ducum sive principum Polonorum*. Ed. K. Maleczyński. *Monumenta Poloniae historica (Pomniki dzeijowe polski)*, n. s. (= series 2) 2. Cracow: Nakładen Polskiej Akademii Umiejętności, 1952.

Ibn Khurradadhbih. *Kitab al-Masalik wa'l Mamalik*. Ed. T. Lewicki. *Żródla arabskie do dziejów slowiańszczyzny*. Wrocław-Cracow: Zakład narodowy im. Ossolinskich, 1956; Trans. M. Hadj-Sadok. *Ibn Khurradadhbih, Ibn al-Faqih al-Hamadhani et Ibn Rustih*. Algiers: Carbonel, 1949.

Ilarion. *Sermon on Law and Grace*. In *Biblioteka literatury drevnei Rusi*. Vol. 1. Ed. and Russian trans. D. S. Likhachev et al. St. Petersburg: Nauka, 1997, 26–61.

Iliev, I. G. "The Long Life of Clement of Ohrid: A Critical Edition." *Byzantinobulgarica* 9 (1995): 62–120.

Ivanov, I. *Zhitiia na sv. Ivana Rilski, Annuaire de l'Université de Sofia. Faculté historico-philologique* 32.13 (1936): 1–109.

[John II, metropolitan]. "Otvety mitropolita Ioanna II (1080–89)." *Sbornik pamiatnikov po istorii tserkovnogo prava*. Ed. V. N. Beneshevich. Petrograd: Izdaniia tovarishchestva "Kul'tura i Znanie," 1915, 108–20.

John Scylitzes. *Synopsis Istoriōn*. Ed. H. Thurn. Corpus Fontium Historiae Byzantinae 5. Berlin: de Gruyter, 1973.

Kodeks Matyldy. Księga obrzędów z kartami dedykacyjnymi. Ed. and commentary B. Kürbis. Monumenta Sacra Polonorum 1. Cracow: Polska Akademia Umiejętności, 2000.

Leo VI. *Tactica*. *PG* 107, 671–1094.

Life of Constantine-Cyril. In *Kliment Okhridski. S'brani s'chineniia*. Vol. 3. Ed. B. S. Angelov and K. Kodov. Sofia: Bulgarian Academy of Sciences Publishing House, 1973, 89–109.

Life of Methodius. In *Kliment Okhridski. S'brani s'chineniia*. Vol. 3. Ed. B. S. Angelov and K. Kodov. Sofia: Bulgarian Academy of Sciences Publishing House, 1973, 185–92.

Life of Theodosius. In *Biblioteka literatury drevnei Rusi*. Vol. 1. Ed. and Russian trans. D. S. Likhachev et al. St. Petersburg: Nauka, 1997, 352–433. Trans. M. Heppell. *The Paterik of the Kievan Caves Monastery*. Cambridge, MA: Ukrainian Research Institute of Harvard University, 1989, 24–88.

Nicholas I [patriarch of Constantinople]. *Letters*. Ed. R. J. H. Jenkins and L. G. Westerink. Corpus Fontium Historiae Byzantinae 6. Washington, DC: Dumbarton Oaks, 1973.

Nicholas I [pope]. *Epistolae*. Ed. E. Perels. *MGH Epistolae* 6 (= *Epistolae Karolini Aevi* 4). Berlin: Weidmann, 1925, 257–690.

Les plus anciens recueils des miracles de Saint Démétrius. Vol. 1. Ed. and trans. P. Lemerle. Paris: Éditions du Centre national de la recherche scientifique, 1979.

Povest' Vremennykh Let. Ed. V. P. Adrianova-Peretts and D. S. Likhachev. Rev. ed. M. B. Sverdlov. St. Petersburg: Nauka, 1996.

Prosopographie der mittelbyzantinischen Zeit. Ed. F. Winkelmann and R.-J. Lilie et al. 6 vols. Berlin: de Gruyter, 1998–2002.

Registrum Gregorii VII. Ed. E. Caspar. *MGH Epistolae selectae* 2, pt. 1. Berlin: Weidmann, 1920.

Rimbert. *Vita Anskarii*. Ed. and German trans. W. Trillmich and R. Buchner. Ausgewählte Quellen zur deutschen Geschichte des Mittelalters 11. Darmstadt: Wissenschaftliche Buchgesellschaft, repr. 2000.

S. Ottonis episcopi Bambergensis Vita Prieflingensis. Ed. J. Wikarjak. *Monumenta Poloniae Historica (Pomniki dzeijowe polski)*, n. s. (= series 2) 7, pt. 1. Warsaw: Państwowe Wydawnictwo Naukowe, 1966.

Sermons and Rhetoric of Kievan Rus'. Trans. S. Franklin. Cambridge, MA: Ukrainian Research Institute of Harvard University, 1991.

Sharaf al-Zamān Tahār Marvāzi. *Sharaf al-Zamān Tahār Marvāzi on China, the Turks and India*. Trans. and commentary V. Minorsky. London: The Royal Asiatic Society, 1942.

Simeonov Sbornik (po Svetoslavoviia prepis ot 1073 g.). Ed. P. Dinekov et al. Vol. 1. Sofia: Izdatelstvo na Bulgarskata Akademiia na Naukite, 1991.

Tale of the Passion of Boris and Gleb (Skazanie o sviatykh muchenikakh Borise i Glebe). In *Zhitiia sviatykh muchenikakh Borisa i Gleba i sluzhby im*. Ed. D. I. Abramovich. Petrograd: Izdatel'stvo otdeleniia russkogo iazyka i slovesnosti Imperatorskoi Akademii Nauk, 1916; partial reproduction with introduction by L. Müller. *Die altrussischen hagiographischen Erzählungen und liturgischen Dichtungen über die Heiligen Boris und Gleb*. Slavische Propyläen 14. Munich: Wilhelm Fink, 1967. Trans. P. Hollingsworth. *The Hagiography of Kievan Rus'*. Cambridge, MA: Ukrainian Research Institute of Harvard University, 1992.

Theophanes. *Chronographia*. Ed. C. de Boor. Vol. 1. Leipzig: B. G. Teubnerei, 1883. Trans. C. Mango and R. Scott. *Chronicle of Theophanes Confessor*. Oxford: Oxford University Press, 1997.

Theophanes Continuatus. *Chronographia*. Ed. I. Bekker. Corpus Scriptorum Historiae Byzantinae. Bonn: Weber, 1838.

Thietmar of Merseburg. *Chronicon*. Ed. and German trans. R. Holtzmann and W. Trillmich. Ausgewählte Quellen zur deutschen Geschichte des Mittelalters 9. Darmstadt: Wissenschaftliche Buchgesellschaft, repr. 2002.

Yahyah of Antioch. *Histoire*. Ed. and trans. A. Vasiliev and J. Kratchkovsky. Patrologia Orientalis 23.3. Paris: Firmin-Didot, 1932.

Secondary sources

Akimova, O. A. "Khristianstvo v dalmatinskikh, khorvatskikh i serbskikh zemliakh v X–XI vv." In *Khristianstvo v stranakh vostochnoi, iugo-vostochnoi i tsentral'noi Evropy na poroge vtorogo tysiacheletiia*. Ed. B. N. Floria. Moscow: Iazyki Slavianskoi Kul'tury, 2002, 267–339.

Antonsson, H. "The Cult of St. Ólafr in the Eleventh Century and Kievan Rus'." *Middelalderforum*, nos. 1–2 (2003): 143–60.

Beshevliev, V. *P'rvob'lgarski nadpisi*. 2nd ed. Sofia: Bulgarian Academy of Sciences Publishing House, 1992.

Curta, F. "The Cave and the Dyke: A Rock Monastery on the Tenth-Century Frontier of Bulgaria." *Studia Monastica* 41 (1999): 129–49.

—, ed. *East Central and Eastern Europe in the Early Middle Ages*. Ann Arbor, MI: University of Michigan Press, 2005.

—. *The Making of the Slavs: History and Archaeology of the Lower Danube Region c. 500–700*. Cambridge: Cambridge University Press, 2001.

Dewey, H. C., and A. E. Kleimola. "Russian Collective Consciousness: The Kievan Roots." *Slavonic and East European Review* 62 (1984): 180–91.

Ditten, H. "Prominente Slawen und Bulgaren in byzantinischen Diensten." In *Studien zum 8. und 9. Jahrhundert in Byzanz*. Ed. H. Köpstein and F. Winkelmann. Berlin: Akademie-Verlag, 1983, 95–119.

Duczko, W. *Viking Rus: Studies on the Presence of Scandinavians in Eastern Europe*. Leiden: Brill, 2004.

Fine, J. V. A. *The Early Medieval Balkans*. Ann Arbor, MI : University of Michigan Press, 1983.
Floria, B. N., ed. *Khristianstvo v stranakh vostochnoi, iugo-vostochnoi i tsentral'noi Evropy na poroge vtorogo tysiacheletiia*. Moscow: Iazyki Slavianskoi Kul'tury, 2002.
— et al. *Sud'by Kirillo-Mefodievskoi traditsii posle Kirilla i Mefodiia*. St. Petersburg: Aleteiia, 2000.
Franklin, S. *Byzantium-Rus-Russia: Studies in the Translation of Christian Culture*. Aldershot: Variorum, 2002.
—. *Writing, Society and Culture in Early Rus, c. 950–1300*. Cambridge: Cambridge University Press, 2002.
—, and J. Shepard. *The Emergence of Rus, 750–1200*. London: Longman, 1996.
Gieysztor, A. et al., eds. *History of Poland*. 2nd ed. Warsaw: Polish Scientific Publishers, 1979.
Gräslund, A.-S. *Ideologi och Mentalitet: om religionsskiftet i Skandinavien från en arkeologisk horisont*. Occasional Papers in Archaeology 29. Uppsala: Uppsala Universitet, 2002.
Halecki, O. *A History of Poland*. London: Kegan Paul, 1983.
Hannick, C. "Les nouvelles chrétientés du monde byzantin: Russes, Bulgares et Serbes." In *Histoire du christianisme* 4, 909–39.
Ingham, N. W. "The Martyrdom of Saint John Vladimir of Dioclea." *International Journal of Slavic Linguistics and Poetics* 35–36 (1987): 119–216.
Iurukova, I., and V. Penchev. *B'lgarski srednovekovni pechati i moneti*. Sofia: Izdatelstvo Bulgarski khudozhnik, 1990.
Ivanov, S. A. "Religious Missions." In *The Cambridge History of the Byzantine Empire, c. 500–1492*. Ed. J. Shepard. Cambridge: Cambridge University Press, forthcoming.
—. *Vizantiiskoe missionerstvo. Mozhno li sdelat' iz "varvara" khristianina?* Moscow: Iazyki Slavianskoi Kul'tury, 2003.
Kloczowski, J. *A History of Polish Christianity*. Cambridge: Cambridge University Press, 2000.
Kostova, R. "Monasite v b'lgarskoto srednovekovno obshchestvo prez IX–X v.: opit za portret po pismeni i arkheologicheski danni." In *L'image et la parole. Eikona kai logos. Recueil à l'occasion du 60ᵉ anniversaire du Prof. Axinia Džurova*. Studia Slavico-Byzantina et Mediaevalia Europensia 8. Sofia: Éditions Universitaires "St. Clément d'Ohrid," 2004, 133–44.
Kürbis, B. "Dagome iudex – studium krytyczne." In *Początki państwa polskiego. Księga tysiąclecia*. Vol. 1. Ed. K. Tymienecki. Poznań: P.T.P.N., 1962, 363–424.
Kurnatowska, Z. "Elementy sacrum w topografii tworzonej przez pierwszych Piastów domeny i jej głównych ośrodków." In *Człowiek, sacrum, środowisko. Miejsca kultu we wczesnym średniowieczu*. Ed. S. Moździoch. Warsaw: Institute of Archaeology and Ethnology, 2000, 111–26.
—. "Ostrów Lednicki in the Early Middle Ages." In *Polish Lands at the Turn of the First and the Second Millennium*. Ed. P. Urbańczyk. Warsaw: Institute of Archaeology and Ethnology, 2004, 167–84.
—. "The Stronghold in Giecz in the Light of New and Old Research." In *Polish Lands at the Turn of the First and the Second Millennium*. Ed. P. Urbańczyk. Warsaw: Institute of Archaeology and Ethnology, 2004, 207–22.
—, and S. Kurnatowski. "Parę uwag o odmiennościach kultorowych Małopolski. (Widzianych od północy)." In *Polonia Minor medii aevi. Studia ofiarowane . . . Andrzejowi Żakiemu*. Ed. Z. Wózniak and J. Gancarski. Cracow-Krosno: Polska Akademia Umiejętności Muzeum Podkarpackie, 2003, 166–80.

Makarov, N. A. "Far Northern Parts of Ancient Russia on their Way to Christianity." In *Rom und Byzanz im Norden: Mission und Glaubenswechsel im Ostseeraum während des 8.-14. Jahrhunderts*. Ed. M. Müller-Wille. Vol. 2. Stuttgart: F. Steiner, 1998, 259–73.

—. "Kresty-tel'niki iz raskopok srednevekovykh selishch i problema khristianizatsii severnorusskoi derevni." *Istoricheskie Zapiski* 7: 125 (2004): 251–74 .

—. "On the Christianization of the Rural Areas of Russia in the 11th–13th Centuries: Burials with Crosses and Small Icons in Beloserie Cemeteries." *Suomen Museo* 96 (1989): 49–59.

Mango, C. *Byzantine Architecture*. London: Faber and Faber / Electa, 1986.

—, ed. *Oxford History of Byzantium*. Oxford: Oxford University Press, 2002.

Mikhailov, K. "Drevnerusskie kamernye pogrebeniia i Gnezdovo." *Arkheologicheskii sbornik. Trudy Gosudarstvennogo Istoricheskogo Muzeia* 124 (2001): 159–75.

Moździoch, S. "Archeologiczne ślady kultu pogańskiego na Śląsku." In *Człowiek, sacrum, środowisko. Miejsca kultu we wczesnym średniowieczu*. Ed. S. Moździoch. Warsaw: Institute of Archaeology and Ethnology 2000, 155–93.

—. "Wrocław-Ostrów Tumski in the Early Middle Ages." In *Polish Lands at the Turn of the First and the Second Millennium*. Ed. P. Urbańczyk. Warsaw: Institute of Archaeology and Ethnology, 2004, 319–38.

Nikolov, A. "Tsariat–bogopodrazhatel: Edin prenebregnat aspekt ot politicheskata kontseptsiia na Simeon I." *Annuaire de l'Université de Sofia "St. Kliment Ohridski"* 91:10 (2001 [2002]): 109–22.

Nystazopoulou-Pelekidou, M. "Sceaux byzantins, improprement appelés protobulgares." *Byzantiaka* 11 (1991): 13–22.

Obolensky, D. *The Bogomils*. Cambridge: Cambridge University Press, 1948.

—. *The Byzantine Commonwealth: Eastern Europe, 500–1453*. London: Weidenfeld and Nicolson, 1971.

—. *The Byzantine Inheritance of Eastern Europe*. London: Variorum Reprints, 1982.

—. *Byzantium and the Slavs*. New York: St. Vladimir's Seminary Press, 1994.

—. *Six Byzantine Portraits*. Oxford: Oxford University Press, 1988.

Pavlova, R. *Pet'r chernorizets, starob'lgarski pisatel ot X vek*. Kirilo-Metodievski Studii 9. Sofia: Izdatelstvo na Bulgarskata Akademiia na Naukite, 1994.

Petrukhin, V. I. "Khristianstvo na Rusi vo vtoroi polovine X-pervoi polovine XIv." In *Khristianstvo v stranakh vostochnoi, iugo-vostochnoi i tsentral'noi Evropy na poroge vtorogo tysiacheletiia*. Ed. B. N. Floria. Moscow: Iazyki Slavianskoi Kul'tury, 2002, 60–132.

Podskalsky, G. *Khristianstvo i bogoslovskaia literatura v kievskoi Rusi (988–1237 gg.)*. St. Petersburg: Vizantinorossica, 1996.

—. *Theologische Literatur des Mittelalters in Bulgarien und Serbien 865–1459*. Munich: C. H. Beck, 2000.

Poppe, A. "The Christianization and Ecclesiastical Structure of Kyivan Rus' to 1300." *Harvard Ukrainian Studies* 21 (1997): 311–92.

—. "Losers on Earth, Winners from Heaven: The Assassinations of Boris and Gleb and the Making of Eleventh-Century Rus." *Quaestiones Medii Aevi Novae* 8 (2003): 133–68.

—. *The Rise of Christian Russia*. London: Variorum Reprints, 1982.

Primov, B. "Spread and Influence of Bogomilism in Europe." *Byzantinobulgarica* 6 (1980): 317–37.

Rappoport, P. A. *Building the Churches of Kievan Russia*. Aldershot: Variorum, 1995.

Rosik, S. *Interpretacja chrześcijańska religii pogańskich Słowian w świetle kronik niemieckich XI–XII wieku (Thietmar, Adam z Bremy, Helmold)*. Wrocław: Wydawnictwo Uniwersytetu Wrocławskiego, 2000.

Runciman, S. *History of the First Bulgarian Empire*. London: G. Bell and Sons, 1930.

Savova, A. "A Newly Discovered Hymnographic Work of St. Clement of Oxrid." *Scripta & e-scripta* 1 (2003): 121–32.

Seibt, W. "Siegel als Quelle für Slawenarchonten in Griechenland." *Studies in Byzantine Sigillography* 6 (1999): 27–36.

—. "Weitere Beobachtungen zu Siegeln früher Slawenarchonten in Griechenland." In *Byzantium: State and Society. In Memory of Nikos Oikonomides*. Eds. A. Avramea, A. Laiou, and E. Chrysos. Athens: Institouto Vyzantinon Ereunon, Ethniko Hidryma Ereunon, 2003, 459–66.

Shchapov, I. N. *State and Church in Early Russia, 10th–13th centuries*. Trans. V. Schneierson. New Rochelle, NY: Aristide D. Caratzas, 1993.

Ševčenko, I. "Religious Missions Seen from Byzantium." *Harvard Ukrainian Studies* 12/13 (1988/89): 7–27.

—. "Re-reading Constantine Porphyrogenitus." In *Byzantine Diplomacy*. Ed. J. Shepard and S. Franklin. Aldershot: Ashgate, 1992, 167–95.

—. "Three Paradoxes of the Cyrillo-Methodian Mission." *Slavic Review* 23 (1964): 220–36. Reprinted in his *Ideology, Letters and Culture in the Byzantine World*. No. 4. London: Variorum Reprints, 1982.

Shepard, J. "The Coming of Christianity to Rus: Authorized and Unauthorized Versions." In *The Conversion Process: From Late Antiquity to the Early Modern Period*. Ed. W. Philipps et al. Minneapolis, MN: University of Minneapolis Press, forthcoming.

—. "Conversions Compared: Vladimir of Rus and Boleslaw of the Poles." In Curta, *East Central and Eastern Europe*, 254–82.

—. "Otto III, Boleslaw Chrobry and the 'Happening' at Gniezno, AD 1000 . . ." In *Byzantium and East-Central Europe*. Ed. G. Prinzing et al. Byzantina et Slavica Cracoviensia 3. Cracow: Historia Iagellonica, Jagiellonian University, 2001, 27–48.

—. "Slavs and Bulgars." In *NCMH* 2, 228–48.

—. "Spreading the Word: Byzantine Missions." In Mango, *Oxford History of Byzantium*, 230–47.

Skwierczyński, K. "Custodia civitatis: sakralny system ochrony miasta w Polsce wczesniejszego średniowiecza na przykładzie siedzib biskupich." *Kwartalnik Historyczny* 103.3 (1996): 1–51.

Staecker, J. "The Cross Goes North: Christian Symbols and Scandinavian Women." In *The Cross Goes North: Processes of Conversion in Northern Europe, AD 300–1300*. Ed. M. Carver. Woodbridge: York Medieval Press, 2003, 463–82.

—. *Rex regum et dominus dominorum: Die wikingerzeitlichen Kreuz- und Kruzifixanhänger als Ausdruck der Mission in Altdänemark und Schweden*. Stockholm: Ethnographisch-Archäologische Zeitschrift, 1999.

Stanchev, S. "Nadgrobniiat nadpis na edin preslavski boliarin ot X v." *Istoricheski Pregled* 11.4 (1955): 61–76.

Stepanov, T. "The Bulgar Title *Kanasybigi*: Reconstructing the Notions of Divine Kingship in Bulgaria, AD 822–836." *EME* 10 (2001): 1–19.

Stephenson, P. "Balkan Borderlands, 1018–1204." In *The Cambridge History of the Byzantine Empire*, c. 500–1492. Ed. J. Shepard. Cambridge: Cambridge University Press, forthcoming.

—. *Byzantium's Balkan Frontier: A Political Study of the Northern Balkans, 900–1204*. Cambridge: Cambridge University Press, 2000.

—. *The Legend of Basil the Bulgar-Slayer*. Cambridge: Cambridge University Press, 2003.

Tachiaos, A.-E. N. *Cyril and Methodius of Thessalonica*. Crestwood, NY: St. Vladimir's Seminary Press, 2001.

Thomson, F. J. *The Reception of Byzantine Culture in Russia*. Aldershot: Ashgate, 1999.

Turilov, A. A. "Vizantiiskii i slavianskii plasty v 'Skazanii inoka Khristodula.'" *Slaviane i ikh sosedi* 6 (1996) = *Grecheskii i slavianskii mir v srednie veka i rannee novoe vremia. Sbornik statei k 70-letiiu . . . G. G. Litavrina*. Ed. B. N. Floria. Moscow: Indrik, 1996, 81–99.

—, and B. N. Floria. "Khristianskaia literatura u slavian v seredine X-seredine XI v. i mezhslavianskie kul'turnye sviazi." In *Khristianstvo v stranakh vostochnoi, iugo-vostochnoi i tsentral'noi Evropy na poroge vtorogo tysiacheletiia*. Ed. B. N. Floria. Moscow: Iazyki Slavianskoi Kul'tury, 2002, 398–458.

Turlej, S. *The Chronicle of Monemvasia: The Migration of the Slavs and Church Conflicts in the Byzantine Sources from the Beginning of the 9th Century*. Byzantina et Slavica Cracoviensia 4. Cracow: Historia Iagellonica, Jagiellonian University, 2001.

—. "The Legendary Motif in the Tradition of Patras. . . ." *Byzantinoslavica* 60 (1999): 374–99.

Urbańczyk, P., ed. *The Neighbours of Poland in the 10th Century*. Warsaw: Institute of Archaeology and Ethnology, Polish Academy of Sciences, 2000.

—, ed. *The Neighbours of Poland in the 11th Century*. Warsaw: Institute of Archaeology and Ethnology, Polish Academy of Sciences, 2002.

—, ed. *Polish Lands at the Turn of the First and the Second Millennium*. Warsaw: Institute of Archaeology and Ethnology (forthcoming).

—., and S. Rosile "Poland." In *Christianization and the Rise of Christian Monarchy: Scandinavia, Central Europe and Rus' c. 900–1200*. Ed. N. Berend. Cambridge: Cambridge University Press 2007, 263–318.

Vavřínek, V. "The Introduction of the Slavonic Liturgy and the Byzantine Missionary Policy." In *Beiträge zur byzantinischen Geschichte im 9.–11. Jahrhundert*. Ed. V. Vavřínek. Prague: Kabinet pro studia řecká, římská a latinská, 1978, 255–81.

Vlasto, A. P. *The Entry of the Slavs into Christendom*. Cambridge: Cambridge University Press, 1970.

Wamers, E. "Hammer und Kreuz: Typologische Aspekte einer nordeuropäischen Amulettsitte aus der Zeit des Glaubenwechsels." *Akademie der Wissenschaften Mainz: Abhandlungen der Geistes- und Sozialwissenschaftlichen Klasse* 3.1 (1997): 83–107.

Zaimov, I., and V. Zaimova. *Bitolski nadpis na Ivan Vladislav*. Sofia: Izdatelstvo na Bulgarskata Akademiia na Naukite, 1970.

Zaroff, R. "The Origins of Sventovit of Rügen." *Studia Mythologica Slavica* 5 (2002): 9–18.

—. "Perception of Christianity by the Pagan Polabian Slavs." *Studia Mythologica Slavica* 4 (2001): 81–96.

Zoll-Adamikowa, H. "Postępy chrystianizacji Słowian przed rokiem 1000 (na podstawie źródeł nekropolicznych)." In *Święty Wojciech i jego czasy*. Ed. A. Żaki. Cracow: Polska Akademia Umiejętności, 2000, 103–09.

Żydok, P. "Wczesnośredniowieczne pochówki antywampiryczne." In *Hereditatem cognoscere. Studia i szkice dedykowane Profesor Marii Miśkiewicz*. Ed. Z. Kobyliński. Warsaw: Państwowe Muzeum Archeologiczne, 2004, 38–66.

7 Christians and Jews
Bat-Sheva Albert

Primary sources

Agobard of Lyons. *Contra praeceptum impium de baptismo iudaicorum mancipiorum*. In *Agobardi Lugdunensis opera omnia*. Ed. L. van Acker. *CCCM* 52. Turnhout: Brepols, 1981, 183–88.

—. *De iudaicis superstitionibus et erroribus*. In *Agobardi Lugdunensis opera omnia*. Ed. L. van Acker. *CCCM* 52. Turnhout: Brepols, 1981, 197–221.

Ahimaaz of Oria. *Megillat Ahimaaz: The Chronicle of Ahimaaz (with a Collection of Poems from Southern Italy and Additions)*. Ed. and annotated B. Klar. 1944; Jerusalem: Tarshish, 1974.

Amolo of Lyons. *Epistola seu liber contra Judaeos ad Carolum regem*. *PL* 116, 141–84.

Angelomus of Luxeuil. *Enarrationes in Libros Regum*. *PL* 115, 245–627.

Claudius of Turin. *Quaestiones XXX super Libros Regum*. *PL* 104, 640–722.

Concilios visigóticos e hispano-romanos. Ed. J. Vives, with the collaboration of T. Marín Martínez and G. Martínez Díez. España Cristiana textos 1. Barcelona–Madrid: Consejo Superior de Investigaciones Científicas, 1963.

Hrabanus Maurus. *Commentaria in Libros IV Regum*. *PL* 109, 1–280.

—. *Expositio super Jeremiam*. *PL* 111, 793–1271.

Isidore of Seville. *Allegoriae quaedam Scripturae*. *PL* 83, 97–129.

—. *De fide catholica ex veteri et novo testamento contra Judaeos ad Florentinam sororem suam*. *PL* 83, 449–538.

—. *Quaestiones in vetus testamentum sive Mysticorum expositiones sacramentorum*. *PL* 83, 207–434.

The Jews in the Legal Sources of the Early Middle Ages. Ed. and trans. A. Linder. Detroit: Wayne State University Press, 1997.

Julian of Toledo. *De comprobatione sextae aetatis*. Ed. J. N. Hillgarth. *CCSL* 115. Turnhout: Brepols, 1976.

The Polemic of Nestor the Priest. Intro., trans., and commentary D. Y. Lasker and S. Stroumsa; appendix J. Niehoff-Panagiotides. 2 vols. Jerusalem: Ben-Zvi Institute for the Study of Jewish Communities in the East, 1996.

Secondary sources

Albert, B.-S. "*Adversus Iudaeos* in the Carolingian Empire." In *Contra Iudaeos. Ancient and Medieval Polemics between Christians and Jews*. Ed. O. Limor and G. G. Stroumsa. Tübingen: J. C. B. Mohr (Paul Siebeck), 1996, 119–42.

—. "Isidore of Seville: His Attitude towards Judaism and his Impact on Early Medieval Canon Law." *The Jewish Quarterly Review* 80 (1990): 207–20.

—. "Un nouvel examen de la politique anti-juive wisigotique. À propos d'un article récent." *Revue des études juives* 141 (1982): 289–316.

Alexander, P. J. *Byzantine Apocalyptic Tradition*. Berkeley, CA: University of California Press, 1985.

Bachrach, B. S. *Early Medieval Jewish Policy in Western Europe*. Minneapolis, MN: University of Minnesota Press, 1977.

—. "A Reassessment of Visigothic Jewish Policy, 589–711." *American Historical Review* 78 (1973): 11–34.

Baron, S. W. *A Social and Religious History of the Jews*. 2nd ed. Vol. 3. New York: Columbia University Press, 1952–1980.

Blumenkranz, B. "Anti-Jewish Polemics and Legislation in the Middle Ages: Literary Fiction or Reality?" *Journal of Jewish Studies* 15 (1964): 125–40.

—. *Les auteurs chrétiens latins du moyen âge sur les juifs et le judaïsme*. Paris: Mouton, 1963.

—. *Juifs et chrétiens dans le monde occidental, 430–1096*. Paris: Mouton, 1960.

Cazier, P. "De la coercition à la persuasion: L'attitude d'Isidore de Séville face à la politique anti-juive des souverains visigothiques." In *De l'antijudaïsme antique à l'antisémitisme contemporain*. Ed. V. Nikiprowetzky. Lille: Presses universitaires de Lille, 1979, 125–46.

Cohen, J. "Introduction." In *Essential Papers on Judaism and Christianity in Conflict from Late Antiquity to the Reformation*. Ed. J. Cohen. New York: New York University Press, 1991, 1–36.

—. "The Jews as the Killers of Christ in the Latin Tradition from Augustine to the Friars." *Traditio* 39 (1983): 1–27.

Cohen, M. R. *Under Crescent and Cross: The Jews in the Middle Ages*. Princeton, NJ: Princeton University Press, 1994.

—, and S. Somekh. "Interreligious *Majaālis* in Early Fatimid Egypt." In *The Majlis: Interreligious Encounters in Medieval Islam*. Studies in Arabic Language and Literature 4. Ed. H. Lazarus-Yafeh et al. Wiesbaden: Otto Harrassowitz, 1999, 128–36.

Colorni, V. "Gli ebrei nei territori italiani a norte di Roma dal 568 agli inizi del secolo XIII." In *Gli ebrei nell Alto Medioevo: 30 marzo–5 aprile 1978*. Settimane di studio 26. Spoleto: Centro italiano di studi sull'alto medioevo, 1980, 241–312.

Dahan, G. *La polémique chrétienne contre le judaïsme au Moyen Âge*. Paris: Albin Michel, 1991.

De Lange, N. R. M. "Jews and Christians in the Byzantine Empire: Problems and Prospects." In *Christianity and Judaism: Papers Read at the 1991 Summer Meeting and the 1992 Winter Meeting of the Ecclesiastical Society*. Ed. D. Wood. Studies in Church History 29. Oxford: Oxford University Press, 1992.

Drews, W. *Juden und Judentum bei Isidor von Sevilla: Studien zum Traktat De fide catholica contra Iudaeos*. Berlin: Duncker & Humblot, 2001.

Eggers, H. *Der althochdeutsche Isidor: Nach der Pariser Handschrift und der Monseer Fragmenten*. Altdeutsche Textbibliothek 63. Tübingen: Max Niemeyer Verlag, 1964.

Geisel, C. *Die Juden im Frankenreich: Von den Merowingern bis zum Tode Ludwigs des Frommen*. Freiburger Beiträge zum mittelaterlichen Geschichte 10. Frankfurt: Peter Lang, 1998.

Gorman, M. "Theodulf of Orléans and the Exegetical Miscellany in Paris lat. 15679." *Revue bénédictine* 109 (1999): 278–323.

Griffith, S. H. "Jews and Muslims in Christian Syriac and Arabic Texts in the Ninth Century." *Jewish History* 3 (1988): 65–94.

—. "The Monk in the Emir's *Majlis*: Reflections on a Popular Genre of Christian Apologetics in Arabic in the Early Islamic Period." In *The Majlis: Interreligious Encounters in Medieval Islam*. Studies in Arabic Language and Literature 4. Ed. H. Lazarus-Yafeh, et al. Wiesbaden: Otto Harrassowitz, 1999, 13–65.

Grossman, A. "The Migration of the Kalonymos Family from Italy to Germany." *Zion* 40 (1975): 154–85.

Heil, J. "Agobard, Amolo, das Kirchengut und die Juden von Lyon." *Francia: Forschungen zur westeuropäischen Geschichte* 25 (1998): 39–76.

—. *Kompilation oder Konstruktion? Die Juden in den Pauluskommentaren des 9. Jahrhunderts.* Forschungen zur Geschichte der Juden A.6. Hanover: Hahn, 1998.

Kaegi, W. E. *Heraclius: Emperor of Byzantium.* Cambridge: Cambridge University Press, 2003.

Külzer, A. *Disputationes Graecae contra Iudaeos: Untersuchungen zur byzantinischen antijüdischen Dialogliteratur und ihrem Judenbild.* Stuttgart: B. G. Teubner, 1999.

Langmuir, G. "Anti-Judaism as the Necessary Preparation for Anti-Semitism." *Viator* 2 (1971): 383–89.

Lotter, F. "The Scope and Effectiveness of Imperial Jewry Law in the High Middle Ages." *Jewish History* 4 (1989): 31–58.

—. "Die Vertreibung des Juden aus Metz um 1012 und der anti-judische Traktat des Hofgeistlichen Heinrich." In *Judenvertreibungen in Mittelalter und früher Neuzeit.* Ed. F. Burgard, A. Haverkamp, and G. Mentgen. Hanover: Hahn, 1999, 37–74.

Luzatti, M. "Zwischen Akzeptanz und Ablehnung: Lucca und die Juden vom 9 bis zum 16. Jarhundert," In *Judenvertreibungen in Mittelalter und früher Neuzeit.* Ed. F. Burgard, A. Haverkamp, and G. Mentgen. Hanover: Hahn, 1999, 3–26.

Olster, D. M. *Roman Defeat, Christian Response and the Literary Construction of the Jew.* Philadelphia, PA: University of Pennsylvania Press, 1994.

Orlandis, J. "Hacia una mejor comprensión del problema judío en el reino visigodo católico de España." In *Gli ebrei nell Alto Medioevo: 30 marzo–5 aprile 1978.* Settimane di studio 26. Spoleto: Centro italiano di studi sull'alto medioevo, 1980, 149–78.

Ostberg, K. "Aspects of the Old High German Isidore Translation." In *Germanic Studies in Honor of Edward Henry Sehrt.* Ed. F. A. Raven, W. K. Legner, and J. C. King. Miami Linguistics Series 1. Coral Gables, FL: University of Miami Press, 1968, 123–31.

Parente, Fausto. "La controversia tra Ebrei e Cristiani in Francia e in Spagna dal VI al IX secolo." In *Gli ebrei nell Alto Medioevo: 30 marzo–5 aprile 1978.* Settimane di studio 26. Spoleto: Centro italiano di studi sull'alto medioevo, 1980, 529–39.

Parkes, J. W. *The Conflict of the Church and the Synagogue: A Study in the Origins of Antisemitism.* London: Soncino Press, 1934.

Rabello, A. M. *Visigothic Spain in the Light of the Legislation.* Jerusalem: Merkaz Shazar, 1983.

Saitta, B. *L'antisemitismo nella Spagna visigotica.* Rome: Erma di Bretschneider, 1995.

Saltman, A., ed. *Pseudo-Jerome: Quaestiones on the Book of Samuel.* Leiden: Brill, 1975.

—. "Rabanus Maurus and the Pseudo-Hieronymian *Quaestiones Hebraecae in Libros Regum et Paralipomenon.*" *Harvard Theological Review* 66 (1973): 43–75.

Sapir Abulafia, A. "An Eleventh-Century Exchange between a Christian and a Jew." In her *Christians and Jews in Dispute: Disputational Literature and the Rise of Anti-Judaism in the West (c. 1000–1150).* Variorum Collected Studies Series. Aldershot: Ashgate Publishing, 1998.

Schreckenberg, H. *Die christlichen Adversus-Judaeos Texte und ihre literarisches und historisches Umfeld (1.–11. Jh).* 3rd ed. Frankfurt: Peter Lang, 1995.

Schwarzfuchs, S. *Les juifs au temps des Croisades en Occident et en Terre Sainte.* Paris: Albin Michel, 2005.

Sharf, A. *Byzantine Jewry from Justinian to the Fourth Crusade*. New York: Schocken Books, 1971.
—. "Jews in Byzantium." In his *Jews and Other Minorities in Byzantium*. Ramat-Gan: Bar-Ilan University Press, 1995.
Stow, K. R. *Alienated Minority: The Jews of Medieval Latin Europe*. Cambridge, MA: Harvard University Press, 1992.
Trachtenberg, J. *The Devil and the Jews: The Medieval Conception of the Jews and its Relation to Modern Antisemitism*. New Haven, CT: Yale University Press, 1943.
Weinhold, K. *Die altdeutschen Bruchstücke des Tractats des Bischof Isidorus von Sevilla: De fide catholica contra Judaeos*. Paderborn: F. Schöningh, 1874.
Williams, A. L. *Adversus Judaeos: A Bird's View of Christian Apologiae until the Renaissance*. London: Cambridge University Press, 1935.
Yuval, I. J. *Two Nations in your Womb: Perceptions of Jews and Christians*. Tel-Aviv: 'Alma / 'Am 'oved, 2000.

8 The Mediterranean frontier: Christianity face to face with Islam, 600–1050
Hugh Kennedy

Primary sources

Itinerarium Bernardi Monachi Franci. In *Itinerera Hierosolymitana et descriptiones Terrae Sanctae*. Ed. T. Tobler and A. Molinier. Paris: Société de l'orient latin, 1879. Reprint, Osnabrück: Zeller, 1966, 309–20. Trans. J. Wilkinson. *Jerusalem Pilgrims before the Crusades*. Warminster: Aris and Phillips, 2002, 260–69.
Miskawayh, Abu Ali. *The Eclipse of the Abbasid Caliphate*. 3 vols. Trans. D. S. Margoliouth. London: Luzac, 1921.
Nasir-i Khusraw. *Book of Travels*. Ed. and trans. W. Thackston. Costa Mesa, CA: Mazda, 2001.
Vita Sancti Willibaldi. In *Itinerera Hierosolymitana et descriptiones Terrae Sanctae*. Ed. T. Tobler and A. Molinier. Paris: Société de l'orient latin, 1879. Reprint, Osnabrück: Zeller, 1966, 243–81. Trans. J. Wilkinson. *Jerusalem Pilgrims before the Crusades*. Warminster: Aris and Phillips, 2002, 233–51.

Secondary sources

Bishko, C. J. "Salvus of Albelda and Frontier Monasticism in Tenth-Century Navarre." *Speculum* 23 (1948): 559–90.
Bonner, M. *Aristocratic Violence and Holy War: Studies in Jihad and the Arab–Byzantine Frontier*. New Haven, CT: American Oriental Society, 1996.
Collins, R. *The Arab Conquest of Spain, 710–797*. Oxford: Blackwell, 1989.
Constable, O. R. *Housing the Stranger in the Mediterranean World: Lodging, Trade and Travel in Late Antiquity and the Middle Ages*. Cambridge: Cambridge University Press, 2003.
—. *Trade and Traders in Muslim Spain*. Cambridge: Cambridge University Press, 1994.
Couasnon, C. *The Church of the Holy Sepulchre in Jerusalem*. London: British Academy, 1975.
Creswell, K. A. C. *Early Muslim Architecture*. 2 vols. Oxford: Oxford University Press, 1938–40.

Dagron, G. "Minorités ethniques et religieuses; l'immigration syrienne." *Travaux et mémoires* 6 (1976): 177–222.

De Palol, P., and M. Hirmer. *Early Medieval Art in Spain*. London: Thames and Hudson, 1967.

Donner, F. M. *The Early Islamic Conquests*. Princeton, NJ: Princeton University Press, 1981.

Eickhoff, E. *Seekrieg und Seepolitik zwischen Islam und Abendland: das Mittelmeer unter byzantinischer und arabischer Hegemonie (650–1040)*. Berlin: de Gruyter, 1966.

El Cheikh, N. M. *Byzantium Viewed by the Arabs*. Cambridge, MA: Harvard University Press, 2004.

El-Hajji, A. *Andalusian Diplomatic Relations with Western Europe During the Umayyad Period*. Beirut: Dar Al-Irshad, 1970.

Fahmy, A. M. *Muslim Naval Organisation in the Eastern Mediterranean from the Seventh to the Tenth Century AD*. Cairo: National Publication and Printing House, 1966.

Firestone, R. *Jihad: The Origin of Holy War in Islam*. Oxford: Oxford University Press, 1999.

Gibb, H. A. R. "Arab–Byzantine Relations under the Umayyad Caliphate." *DOP* 12 (1958): 219–33.

Goitein, S. D. *A Mediterranean Society: The Jewish Communities of the Arab World as Portrayed in the Documents of the Cairo Geniza*. 6 vols. Berkeley, CA: University of California Press, 1967–93.

Haldon, J., and H. Kennedy. "The Arab–Byzantine Frontier in the Eighth and Ninth Centuries: Military Organization and Society in the Borderlands." *Zbornik Radova Visantoloskog Instituta* (Belgrade) 19 (1980): 79–116.

Halm, H. *The Empire of the Mahdi: The Rise of the Fatimids*. Leiden: Brill, 1996.

Honigmann, E. *Die Ostgrenze des byzantinischen Reiches von 363 bis 1071*. Vol. 3 in Vasiliev, *Byzance et les arabes*.

Hordern, P., and N. Purcell. *The Corrupting Sea: A Study of Mediterranean History*. Oxford: Blackwell, 2000.

Kaegi, W. E. *Byzantium and the Early Islamic Conquests*. Cambridge: Cambridge University Press, 1992.

Kennedy, H. "Byzantine–Arab Diplomacy." In Shepard and Franklin, *Byzantine Diplomacy*, 133–44.

——. *Muslim Spain and Portugal: A Political History of al-Andalus*. London: Longman, 1996.

——. *The Prophet and the Age of the Caliphates*. 2nd ed. London: Longman, 2004.

Manzano Moreno, E. *La frontera de al-Andalus en epoca de los Omeyas*. Madrid: CSIC, 1991.

McCormick, M. *The Origins of the European Economy: Communications and Commerce, AD 300–900*. Cambridge: Cambridge University Press, 2001.

Sanchez-Albornoz, C. *Despoblacion y Repoblacion del valle del Duero*. Buenos Aires: Instituto de Historia de España, 1966.

Shepard, J., and S. Franklin. *Byzantine Diplomacy*. Aldershot: Variorum, 1992.

Taha, A. *The Muslim Conquest and Settlement of North Africa and Spain*. London: Routledge, 1989.

Vasiliev, A. A. *Byzance et les arabes*. 3 vols. Brussels: Éditions de l'Institut de Philologie et d'Histoire Orientales, 1935–1968.

Walker, P. *Exploring an Islamic Empire: Fatimid History and its Sources*. London: I. B. Tauris, 2002.
Wilkinson, J. *Jerusalem Pilgrims before the Crusades*. Warminster: Aris and Phillips, 2002.

9 Christians under Muslim rule
Sidney H. Griffith

Primary sources

Abū 'Abd Allāh al-Ḥumaydī. *Jadhwat al-Muqtabis*. Ed. M. ibn Tāwīt al-Ṭanjī. Cairo: n.p., 1953.
Fiey, J. M. *Chrétiens syriaques sous les Abbasides surtout à Bagdad (749–1258)*. *CSCO* 420. Louvain: Secrétariat du CSCO, 1980.
Graf, G. *Geschichte der christlichen arabischen Literatur*. Studi e testi 118, 133, 146, 147, 172. Vatican City: Biblioteca apostolica vaticana, 1944–53.
Khoury, P. *Matériaux pour servir à l'étude de la controverse théologique islamo-chrétienne de langue arabe du VIIIe au XIIe siècle*. Religionswissenschaftliche Studien 11:1–4. 4 vols. Würzburg and Altenberge: Echter and Oros Verlag, 1989–99.
Le Coz, R. *Jean Damascène: écrits sur l'Islam*. *SC* 383. Paris: Éditions du Cerf, 1992.
Michel, T. F. *A Muslim Theologian's Response to Christianity: Ibn Taymiyya's al-Jawāb al-Ṣaḥīḥ*. Delmar, NY: Caravan Books, 1984.
Newman, N. A. *The Early Christian–Muslim Dialogue: A Collection of Documents from the First Three Islamic Centuries (632–900 A.D.), Translations with Commentary*. Hatfield, PA: Interdisciplinary Biblical Research Institute, 1993.
Reinink, G. J. *Die syrische Apokalypse des Pseudo-Methodios*. *CSCO* 540, 541. Louvain: Peeters, 1993.
Samir, S. K. "Un traité du cheikh Abū 'Alī Na īf Ibn Yumnsur l'accord des chrétiens entre eux malgré leur disaccord dans l'expression." *Mélanges de l'Université Saint-Joseph* 51 (1990): 329–43.
Thomas, D. *Anti-Christian Polemic in Early Islam: Abū 'Īsā al-Warrāq's "Against the Trinity."* University of Cambridge Oriental Publications 45. Cambridge: Cambridge University Press, 1992.
—. *Early Muslim Polemic against Christianity: Abū 'Īsā al-Warrāq's "Against the Incarnation."* University of Cambridge Oriental Publications 59. Cambridge: Cambridge University Press, 2002.
Yaḥyā Ibn-'Adī. *The Reformation of Morals*. Ed. S. K. Samir. Trans. S. H. Griffith. Eastern Christian Texts 1. Provo, UT: Brigham Young University Press, 2002.
Zaborowski, J. R. *The Neo-Martyr John of Phanijoit: A Late Coptic Text Describing a Public Conversion from Islam to Christianity in Ayyūbid Cairo*. Leiden: Brill, 2004.

Secondary sources

Allard, M. "Les chrétiens à Baghdad." *Arabica* 9 (1962): 375–88.
Bosworth, C. E. "The Concept of *Dhimma* in Early Islam." In *Christians and Jews in the Ottoman Empire: The Functioning of a Plural Society*. Ed. B. Braude and B. Lewis. Vol. 1. New York: Holmes & Meier, 1982, 37–51.

—. "The 'Protected Peoples' (Christians and Jews) in Medieval Egypt and Syria." *Bulletin of the John Rylands University Library of Manchester* 62 (1979): 11–36.

Bouamama, A. *La littérature polémique musulmane contre le christianisme depuis ses origines jusqu'au XIIIe siècle*. Alger: Entreprise nationale du livre, 1988.

Bulliet, R. W. *Conversion to Islam in the Medieval Period: An Essay in Quantitative History*. Cambridge, MA: Harvard University Press, 1979.

Burman, T. E. *Religious Polemic and the Intellectual History of the Mozarabs, c. 1050–1200*. Leiden: Brill, 1994.

Butterworth, C. E. et al. *The Introduction of Arabic Philosophy into Europe*. Studien und Texte zur Geistesgeschichte des Mittelalters 39. Leiden: Brill, 1997.

Coope, J. A. *The Martyrs of Córdoba: Community and Family Conflict in an Age of Mass Conversion*. Lincoln, NE: University of Nebraska Press, 1995.

Courbage, Y., and P. Fargues. *Christians and Jews under Islam*. Trans. J. Mabro. London: I. B. Tauris, 1997.

Daniel, N. *Islam and the West: The Making of an Image*. Edinburgh: Edinburgh University Press, 1960.

De Blois, F. "*Nasrānī* (Ναζωραιος) and *Ḥanīf* (εθνικος): Studies on the Religious Vocabulary of Christianity and Islam." *Bulletin of the School of Oriental and African Studies* 65 (2002): 1–30.

Dennett, D. C. *Conversion and the Poll Tax in Early Islam*. Cambridge, MA: Harvard University Press, 1950.

Ducellier, A. *Chrétiens d'Orient et Islam au Moyen Âge: VIIe-XVe siècle*. Paris: Armand Colin / Masson, 1996.

Fattal, A. *Le statut légal des non-musulmans en pays d'Islam*. Beyrouth: Imprimerie Catholique, 1958.

Feldtkeller, A. *Die "Mutter der Kirchen" im "Haus des Islam": gegenseitige Wahrnehmung von arabischen Christen und Muslimen im West- und Ostjordanland*. Erlangen: Erlanger Verlag für Mission und Ökumene, 1998.

Fowden, G. *Empire to Commonwealth: Consequences of Monotheism in Late Antiquity*. Princeton, NJ: Princeton University Press, 1993.

Friedman, Y. *Tolerance and Coercion in Islam: Interfaith Relations in the Muslim Tradition*. Cambridge: Cambridge University Press, 2003.

Gaudeul, J.-M. *Encounters and Clashes: Islam and Christianity in History*. 2 vols. Rome: Pontificio Istituto di Studi Arabi e Islamistica, 1984.

Griffith, S. H. *Arabic Christianity in the Monasteries of Ninth-Century Palestine*. Collected Studies Series 380. Aldershot: Variorum, 1992.

—. *The Beginnings of Christian Theology in Arabic: Muslim–Christian Encounters in the Early Islamic Period*. Collected Studies Series 746. Aldershot: Variorum, 2002.

—. "Christians, Muslims and Neo-martyrs: Saints' Lives and Holy Land History." In *Sharing the Sacred: Religious Contacts and Conflicts in the Holy Land: First–Fifteenth Centuries CE*. Ed. A. Kofsky and G. G. Stroumsa. Jerusalem: Yad Izhak Ben Zvi, 1998, 163–207.

—. "From Aramaic to Arabic: The Languages of the Monasteries of Palestine in the Byzantine and Early Islamic Periods." *DOP* 51 (1997): 11–31.

—. "Images, Islam and Christian Icons: A Moment in the Christian / Muslim Encounter in Early Islamic Times." In *La Syrie de Byzance à l'Islam VIIe-VIIIe siècles: Actes du Colloque*

International Lyon-Maison de l'Orient Mediterranéen, Paris–Institut du Monde Arabe, 11–15 Septembre 1990. Ed. P. Canivet and J.-P. Rey-Coquais. Damascus: Institut français d'études Arabes de Damas, 1992, 121–38.

—. "The *Kitāb misbāh al-'aql* of Severus ibn al-Muqaffa': A Profile of the Christian Creed in Arabic in Tenth Century Egypt." *Medieval Encounters* 2 (1996): 15–42.

—. "Melkites, Jacobites and the Christological Controversies in Arabic in Third/Ninth-Century Syria." In Thomas, *Syrian Christians under Islam*, 9–55.

—. "The Monk in the Emir's *Majlis*: Reflections on a Popular Genre of Christian Literary Apologetics in Arabic in the Early Islamic Period." In *The Majlis: Interreligious Encounters in Medieval Islam*. Studies in Arabic Language and Literature 4. Ed. H. Lazarus-Yafeh et al. Wiesbaden: Otto Harrassowitz, 1999, 13–65.

Gutas, D. *Greek Thought, Arabic Culture: The Graeco-Arabic Translation Movement in Baghdad and Early 'Abbāsid Society (2nd–4th/8th–10th Centuries)*. London: Routledge, 1998.

Haddad, R. *La trinité divine chez les théologiens arabes (750–1050)*. Paris: Beauchesne, 1985.

Hourani, A. *A History of the Arab Peoples*. New York: Warner Books, 1992.

Hoyland, R. G. *Seeing Islam as Others Saw it: A Survey and Evaluation of Christian, Jewish and Zoroastrian Writings on Early Islam*. Studies in Late Antiquity and Early Islam 13. Princeton, NJ: The Darwin Press, 1997.

Khoury, A.-T. "Apologétique byzantine contre l'Islam." *Proche Orient Chrétien* 29 (1979): 242–300; 30 (1980): 132–74; 32 (1982): 14–49.

—. *Polémique byzantine contre l'Islam*. Leiden: Brill, 1972.

—. *Les théologiens byzantins et l'Islam: Textes et auteurs, VIIIe-XIIIe s*. Louvain: Nauwelaerts, 1969.

Kraemer, J. L. *Humanism in the Renaissance of Islam: The Cultural Revival during the Buyid Age*. Leiden: Brill, 1986.

Landron, B. *Chrétiens et musulmans en Irak: attitudes Nestoriennes vis-à-vis de l'Islam*. Paris: Cariscript, 1994.

Makdisi, G. *The Rise of Humanism in Classical Islam and the Christian West: With Special Reference to Scholasticism*. Edinburgh: Edinburgh University Press, 1990.

Martínez, J. "La literatura apocalíptica y las primeras reacciones cristianas a la conquista islámica en Oriente." In *Europa y el Islam*. Ed. G. Anes y Álvarez de Castrillón. Madrid: Real Academia de la Historia, 2003, 143–222.

Massignon, L. "La politique islamo-chrétienne des scribes nestoriens de Deir Qunna à la cour de Bagdad au IXe siècle de notre ère." *Vivre et penser* 2 (1942): 7–14.

McAuliffe, J. D. *Qur'ānic Christians: An Analysis of Classical and Modern Exegesis*. Cambridge: Cambridge University Press, 1991.

Millet-Gérard, D. *Chrétiens mozarabes et culture islamique dans l'Espagne des VIIIe-IXe siècles*. Paris: Études augustiniennes, 1984.

Peeters, F. E. *Aristotle and the Arabs: The Aristotelian Tradition in Islam*. New York: New York University Press, 1968.

Peri, O. *Christianity under Islam in Jerusalem: The Question of the Holy Sites in Early Ottoman Times*. Leiden: Brill, 2001.

Piccirillo, M. *L'Arabia Cristiana: Dalla provincia imperiale al primo periodo islamico*. Milan: Jaca Book, 2002.

Reynolds, G. S. *A Muslim Theologian in the Sectarian Milieu: 'Abd al-Jabbār (415/1025) and the "Critique of Christian Origins."* Leiden: Brill, 2004.

Rissanen, S. *Theological Encounter of Oriental Christians with Islam during Early Abbasid Rule.* Åbo: Åbo Akademis Förlag-Åbo Akademi University Press, 1993.

Roisse, P. "La circulation du savoir des Arabes chrétiens en Méditerranée médiévale: approche des sources manuscrites." *Collectanea Christiana Orientalia* 1 (2004): 185–231.

Rubenson, S. "Translating the Tradition: Some Remarks on the Arabicization of the Patristic Heritage in Egypt." *Medieval Encounters* 2 (1996): 4–14.

Sahas, D. J. *John of Damascus on Islam: The "Heresy of the Ishmaelites."* Leiden: Brill, 1972.

Samir, S. K. *Foi et culture en Irak au XIe siècle: Elie de Nisibe et l'Islam*, Collected Studies Series, 544. Aldershot: Variorum, 1996.

—. "The Prophet Muḥammad as Seen by Timothy I and Some Other Arab Christian Authors." In Thomas, *Syrian Christians under Islam*, 75–106.

—, and J. S. Nielsen, eds. *Christian Arabic Apologetics during the Abbasid Period (750–1258).* Studies in the History of Religions 63. Leiden: Brill, 1994.

Shedd, W. A. *Islam and the Oriental Churches: Their Historical Relations.* Philadelphia: Presbyterian Board of Publication and Sabbath-School Work, 1904. Reprint, Piscataway, NJ: Gorgias Press, 2004.

Thomas, D., ed. *Christians at the Heart of Islamic Rule: Church Life and Scholarship in 'Abbasid Iraq.* The History of Christian–Muslim Relations 1. Leiden: Brill, 2003.

—, ed. *Syrian Christians under Islam: The First Thousand Years.* Leiden: Brill, 2001.

Trimingham, J. S. *Christianity among the Arabs in Pre-Islamic Times.* London: Longman, 1979.

Tritton, A. S. *The Caliphs and their Non-Muslim Subjects: A Critical Study of the Covenant of 'Umar.* London: Oxford University Press, 1930.

Troupeau, G. *Études sur le christianisme arabe au Moyen Âge.* Collected Studies Series 515. Aldershot: Variorum, 1995.

Ursinus, M. O. H. "Millet." In *The Encyclopaedia of Islam: New Edition.* Ed. C. E. Bosworth et al. Vol. 7. Leiden: Brill, 1993, 61–64.

Waardenburg, J. *Muslim Perceptions of Other Religions.* New York and Oxford: Oxford University Press, 1999.

Wolf, K. B. *Christian Martyrs in Muslim Spain.* Cambridge: Cambridge University Press, 1988.

Ye'or, B. *The Decline of Eastern Christianity under Islam: From Jihad to Dhimmitude: Seventh–Twentieth Century.* Teaneck, NJ: Fairleigh Dickinson University Press, 1996.

—. *The Dhimmī: Jews and Christians under Islam.* Teaneck, NJ: Fairleigh Dickinson University Press, 1985.

—. *Islam and Dhimmitude: Where Civilizations Collide.* Teaneck, NJ: Fairleigh Dickinson University Press, 2002.

10 Latin and Greek Christians

Tia M. Kolbaba

Primary sources

Bios kai politeia tou osiou patros emon Neilou tou Neou. Ed. G. Giovanelli. Grottaferrata, 1972; Italian trans. G. Giovanelli. *Vita di S. Nilo, fondatore e patrono di Grottaferrata.* Grottaferrata: Badia di Grottaferrata, 1966.

Brubaker, L., and J. F. Haldon. *Byzantium in the Iconoclast Era (c. 680–850): The Sources, An Annotated Survey*. Aldershot: Ashgate, 2000.

Gregory I (Pope). *Registrum epistolarum*. Ed. P. Ewald and L. M. Hartmann. *MGH Epistolae* 2 vols. Berlin: Weidmann, 1957.

Humbert of Silva Candida. *Adversus graecorum calumnias. PL* 143, 929–74.

—. *Brevis et succincta commemoratio. PL* 143, 1001–1004.

Leo I (pope). *Epistola XXVIII ad Flavianum ep. constantinopolitanum. PL* 54, 756–82.

Leo IX (pope) [written by Humbert of Silva Candida]. *Epistola ad Michaelem constantinopolitanum ptr. PL* 143, 744–69.

— [written by Humbert of Silva Candida]. *Epistola ad Michaelem constantinopolitanum ptr. PL* 143, 773–77.

Leo of Ohrid. *Epistola ad Ioannem episcopum tranensem [de azymis]. PG* 120, 835–44.

Liutprand of Cremona. *The Works of Liudprand of Cremona: Antapodosis, Liber de rebus gestis Ottonis, Relatio de legatione constantopolitana*. Eng. trans. F. A. Wright. London: George Routledge and Sons, 1930.

Michael Cerularius. *Edictum synodale. PG* 120, 736–47.

—. *Epistola ad Petrum sanctissimum ptr. Antiochiae. PG* 120, 781–96.

—. *Epistola ad Petrum sanctissimum ptr. Antiochiae. PG* 120, 816–20.

Monumenta graeca ad Photium eiusque historiam pertinentia. Ed. J. Hergenroether. Regensburg: George Joseph Manz, 1869. Reprint, Farnborough: Gregg International Publishers, 1969.

Nicholas I (patriarch of Constantinople). "Tract on the Tetragamy." In *Miscellaneous Writings*. Ed. and trans. L. G. Westerink. *Corpus fontium historiae byzantinae* 20. Washington, DC: Dumbarton Oaks, 1981, 36–55.

Opus Caroli Regis contra synodum (Libri carolini). Ed. A. Freeman. *MGH Concilia* 2, supp. 1. Hanover: Hahn, 1998.

Pelagius II (pope). *Epistola VI ad Ioannem ep. constantinopolitanum. PL* 72, 738–44.

Peter III (patriarch of Antioch). *Dissertatio [ad Michaelem Cerularium] eo tempore scripta quo advenit Italus Argyrus. PG* 120, 795–816.

Photius (patriarch of Constantinople). "Encyclica ad sedes orientales." In *Photius: Epistulae et amphilochia*. Ed. B. Laourdas and L. B. Westerink. Vol. 1, ep. 2. Leipzig: Teubner, 1988.

Rhalles, G. A., and M. Potles. *Suntagma ton theion kai ieron kanonon*. 6 vols. Athens: G. Chartophylax, 1852–59.

The Synodikon Vetus. Ed., trans., and notes J. Duffy and J. Parker. *Corpus fontium historiae byzantinae* 15. Washington, DC: Dumbarton Oaks, 1979.

Theophylact of Ohrid. *Proslalia tini ton autou omileton peri on egkalountai Latinoi*. Ed. P. Gautier. In *Théophylacte d'Achrida, discours, traités, poesies. Corpus fontium historiae byzantinae* 16.1. Thessaloniki: Association de recherches byzantines, 1980, 246–85.

Secondary sources

Anastos, M. V. "Constantinople and Rome: A Survey of Relations between the Byzantine and Roman Churches." Chapter 8 in his *Aspects of the Mind of Byzantium*. Aldershot: Ashgate, 2001.

—. "The Transfer of Illyricum, Calabria and Sicily to the Jurisdiction of the Patriarchate of Constantinople in 732–33." *Studi bizantini e neoellenici* 9 (1957): 14–31.

Balard, M. "Amalfi et Byzance (Xe-XIIe siècles)." *Travaux et mémoires* 6 (1976): 85–95.

Beck, H.-G. *Geschichte der orthodoxen Kirche im byzantinischen Reich*. Göttingen: Vanderhoeck & Ruprecht, 1980.

—. *Kirche und theologische Literatur im byzantinischen Reich*. Munich: C. H. Beck, 1959.

Bréhier, L. "Avant la séparation du XIe siècle: les relations normales entre Rome et les églises d'orient." *Istina* 3 (1959): 352–72.

Brown, P. "Eastern and Western Christendom in Late Antiquity: A Parting of the Ways." In *The Orthodox Churches and the West*. Ed. D. Baker. Oxford: Basil Blackwell, 1976, 1–24. Reprinted in P. Brown. *Society and the Holy in Late Antiquity*. Berkeley, CA: University of California Press, 1982, 166–95.

—. "*Mohammed and Charlemagne* by Henri Pirenne." *Daedalus* 103 (1974): 25–33. Reprinted in P. Brown. *Society and the Holy in Late Antiquity*. Berkeley, CA: University of California Press, 1982, 63–79.

Callahan, D. "The Problem of the 'Filioque' and the Letter from the Pilgrim Monks of the Mount of Olives to Pope Leo III and Charlemagne: Is the Letter Another Forgery by Adémar of Chabannes?" *Revue bénédictine* 102 (1992): 75–134.

Chazelle, C. "Matter, Spirit, and Image in the *Libri Carolini*." *Recherches augustiniennes* 21 (1986): 163–84.

—. Review of *Opus Caroli Regis*. Ed. A. Freeman. *The Medieval Review* (an on-line publication of the Medieval Institute and the Department of History at Western Michigan University, and of the Scholarly Publishing Office at the University Library, University of Michigan, Ann Arbor). 1999: http://name.umdl.umich.edu/baj9928.9912.004.

La chiesa greca in Italia dall'VIII al XVI secolo. 3 vols. *Italia sacra* 20–22. Padua: Editrice Antenore, 1973.

de Vries, W. *Orient et Occident: les structures ecclésiales vues dans l'histoire des sept premiers conciles œcuméniques*. Paris: Éditions du Cerf, 1974.

Dumeige, G. *Nicée II*. Histoire des conciles œcuméniques 4. Paris: Éditions de l'Orante, 1978.

Dvornik, F. *Byzantine Missions among the Slavs: SS. Constantine-Cyril and Methodius*. New Brunswick, NJ: Rutgers University Press, 1970.

—. *Byzantium and the Roman Primacy*. New York: Fordham University Press, 1966.

—. *The Photian Schism: History and Legend*. Cambridge: Cambridge University Press, 1948.

—. "The Significance of the Missions of Cyril and Methodius." *The Slavic Review* 23 (1964): 195–211.

—. *Les slaves, Byzance et Rome au IXe siècle*. Paris, 1926. Reprint, Hattiesburg, MS: Academic International, 1970.

Fine, J. V. A., Jr. *The Early Medieval Balkans*. Ann Arbor, MI: University of Michigan Press, 1983.

Freeman, A. "Carolingian Orthodoxy and the Fate of the *Libri Carolini*." *Viator* 16 (1985): 65–108.

—. "Further Studies in the *Libri Carolini* I–II." *Speculum* 40 (1965): 203–89.

—. "Further Studies in the *Libri Carolini* III: The Marginal Notes in *Vaticanus Latinus 7207*." *Speculum* 46 (1971): 597–612.

—. "Theodulf of Orléans and the *Libri Carolini*." *Speculum* 32 (1957): 663–705.

Gay, J. *L'Italie méridionale et l'empire byzantin depuis l'avènement de Basil Ier jusqu'à la prise de Bari par les Normands*. Bibliothèque des écoles françaises d'Athènes et de Rome 90. Paris: A. Fontemoing, 1904.

Gero, S. "The *Libri Carolini* and the Image Controversy." *Greek Orthodox Theological Review* 18 (1973): 7–34.

Gilchrist, J. "Cardinal Humbert of Silva-Candida (d. 1061)." *Annuale mediaevale* 3 (1962): 29–42. Reprinted as Chapter 1 in his *Canon Law in the Age of Reform, 11th-12th Centuries*. London: Variorum, 1993.

Grumel, V. "Photius et l'addition du Filioque au symbole de Nicée-CP." *Revue des études byzantines* 5 (1947): 218–34.

Guillou, A. "Grecs d'Italie du sud et de Sicile au Moyen Âge: les moines." *Mélanges d'archéologie et d'histoire* 75 (1963): 79–110. Reprinted as Chapter 12 in his *Studies on Byzantine Italy*. London: Variorum Reprints, 1970.

—. "Italie méridionale byzantine ou Byzantins en Italie méridionale?" *Byzantion* 44 (1974): 152–190. Reprinted as Chapter 15 in his *Culture et société en Italie byzantine (VIe-XIe s.)*. London: Variorum Reprints, 1978.

Haldon, J. *Byzantium in the Seventh Century: The Transformation of a Culture*. Cambridge: Cambridge University Press, 1990.

Hamilton, B. "The City of Rome and the Eastern Churches in the Tenth Century." *Orientalia Christiana Periodica* 27 (1961): 5–26.

—. "The Monastery of S. Alessio and the Religious and Intellectual Renaissance in Tenth-Century Rome." *Studies in Medieval and Renaissance History* 2 (1965): 265–310.

Haugh, R. *Photius and the Carolingians: The Trinitarian Controversy*. Belmont, MA: Nordland Publishing Co., 1975.

Herrin, J. *The Formation of Christendom*. Princeton, NJ: Princeton University Press, 1987.

Hussey, J. *The Orthodox Church in the Byzantine Empire*. Oxford: Clarendon Press, 1986.

Kaegi, W. E. *Byzantium and the Early Islamic Conquests*. Cambridge: Cambridge University Press, 1992.

Kolbaba, T. M. *The Byzantine Lists: Errors of the Latins*. Urbana, IL: University of Illinois Press, 2000.

—. "The Legacy of Humbert and Cerularius: The Tradition of 'the Schism of 1054' in Byzantine Texts and Manuscripts of the Twelfth and Thirteenth Centuries." In *Porphyrogenita: Essays in Honour of Julian Chrysostomides*. Aldershot: Ashgate, 2003, 47–61.

Laurent, V. "L'église de l'Italie méridionale entre Rome et Byzance à la veille de la conquête normande." In *La chiesa greca in Italia dall'VIII al XVI secolo*. Vol. 1. *Italia sacra* 20. Padua: Editrice Antenore, 1973, 5–24.

—. "L'œuvre canonique du concile in Trullo (691–92), source primaire du droit de l'église orientale." *Revue des études byzantines* 23 (1965): 7–41.

—. "Le titre de patriarche œcuménique et la signature patriarcale." *Revue des études byzantines* 6 (1948): 5–26.

Leib, B. *Rome, Kiev et Byzance à la fin du XIe siècle; rapports religieux des Latins et des gréco-russes sous le pontificat d'Urbain II*. Paris: Picard, 1924. Reprint, New York: B. Franklin, 1968.

Lemerle, P. "Les archives du monastère des Amalfitains au Mont Athos." *Epeteris Etaireias Byzantinon Spoudon* 23 (1953): 548–66.

Leroy, J. "S. Athanase l'Athonite et la Règle de S. Benoit." *Revue d'ascétique et de mystique* 29 (1953): 108–122.

Markus, R. *The End of Ancient Christianity*. Cambridge: Cambridge University Press, 1990.

McNulty, P. M., and B. Hamilton. "Orientale Lumen et Magistra Latinitas: Greek Influences on Western Monasticism (900–1100)." In *Le millénaire du Mont Athos, 963–1963*. Études et mélanges 1. Chevetogne: Éditions de Chevetogne, 1963, 181–216.

Meyvaert, P. J. "The Authorship of the 'Libri Carolini': Observations Prompted by a Recent Book." *Revue bénédictine* 89 (1979): 29–57.

Michel, A. *Humbert und Kerullarios: Studien*. 2 vols. Paderborn: F. Schöningh, 1924, 1930.

Morris, R. *Monks and Laymen in Byzantium, 843–1118*. Cambridge: Cambridge University Press, 1995.

Murphy, F. X., and P. Sherwood. *Constantinople II et Constantinople III*. Histoire des conciles œcuméniques 3. Paris: Éditions de l'Orante, 1974.

Nedungatt, G., and M. Featherstone. *The Council in Trullo Revisited*. Kanonika 6. Rome: Pontificio istituto orientale, 1995.

Noble, T. F. X. *The Republic of St. Peter: The Birth of the Papal State, 680–825*. Philadelphia, PA: University of Pennsylvania Press, 1984.

—. "Tradition and Learning in Search of Ideology: The *Libri Carolini*." In *"The Gentle Voices of Teachers:" Aspects of Learning in the Carolingian Age*. Ed. R. E. Sullivan. Columbus, OH: Ohio State University Press, 1995, 227–60.

Ohme, H. *Das Concilium Quinisextum und seine Bischofsliste: Studien zum Konstantinopeler Konzil von 692*. Berlin: de Gruyter, 1990.

Olster, D. *Roman Defeat, Christian Response, and the Literary Construction of the Jew*. Philadelphia, PA: University of Pennsylvania Press, 1994.

Papadakis, A., and J. Meyendorff. *The Christian East and the Rise of the Papacy: The Church, 1071–1453 A.D.* Crestwood, NY: St. Vladimir's Seminary Press, 1994.

Patlagean, E. "Recherches récentes et perspectives sur l'histoire du monachisme italo-grec." *Rivista di storia della chiesa in Italia* 22 (1968): 146–66.

Pertusi, A. "Monasteri e monaci italiani all'Athos nell'alto medioevo." In *Le millénaire du Mont Athos 963–1963*. Études et mélanges 1. Chevetogne: Éditions de Chevetogne, 1963, 217–51.

—. "Nuovi documenti sui Benedettini Amalfitani dell'Athos." *Aevum* 27 (1953): 400–29.

Rousseau, O. "L'ancien monastère bénédictin du Mont-Athos." *Revue liturgique et monastique* 14 (1929): 530–47.

—. "La visite de Nil de Rossano au Mont-Cassin." In *La chiesa greca in Italia dall'VIII al XVI secolo*. Vol. 3. *Italia sacra* 22. Padua: Editrice Antenore, 1973, 1111–37.

Runciman, S. *The Eastern Schism: A Study of the Papacy and the Eastern Churches during the Eleventh and Twelfth Centuries*. Oxford: Clarendon Press, 1955.

Sansterre, J.-M. "Les coryphées des apôtres, Rome et la papauté dans les *Vies* des Saints Nil et Barthélemy de Grottaferrata." *Byzantion* 55 (1985): 516–43.

—. "Les missionnaires latins, grecs et orientaux en Bulgarie dans la seconde moitié du IXe siècle." *Byzantion* 52 (1982): 375–88.

—. *Les moines grecs et orientaux à Rome aux époques byzantine et carolingienne (milieu du VIe s.–fin du IXe s.)*. 2 vols. Brussels: Palais des Académies, 1983.

Ševčenko, I. "Three Paradoxes of the Cyrillo-Methodian Mission." *Slavic Review* 23 (1964): 220–36.

Smith, M. H., III. *And Taking Bread . . . Cerularius and the Azyme Controversy of 1054*. Paris: Éditions Beauchesne, 1978.

Sode, C. *Jerusalem–Konstantinopel–Rom: Die Viten des Michael Synkellos und der Brüder Theodoros und Theophanes Graptoi*. Altertumswissenschaftliches Kolloquium 4. Stuttgart: Franz Steiner, 2001.

Talbot, A.-M., and A. Kazhdan. "Athos, Mount." *ODB* 1, 224–26.

von Falkenhausen, V., and D. Kinney. "Amalfi." *ODB* 1, 73–74.

11 The northern frontier: Christianity face to face with paganism
Ian N. Wood

Primary sources

Adam of Bremen. *Gesta Hammaburgensis ecclesiae pontificum*. Ed. W. Trillmich. Quellen des 9. und 11. Jahrhunderts zur Geschichte der hamburgischen Kirche und des Reiches. Darmstadt: Wissenschaftliche Buchgesellschaft, 1961. Trans. F. J. Tschan and rev. ed. T. Reuter. *History of the Archbishops of Hamburg-Bremen*. New York: Columbia University Press, 2002.

Alcuin. *Epistolae*. Ed. E. Dümmler. *MGH Epistolae* 4 (= *Karolini Aevi* 2). Berlin: Weidmann, 1895.

Altfrid. *Vita Liudgeri*. In *Die Vitae sancti Liudgeri*. Ed. W. Diekamp. Münster: Theissing'schen Buchhandlung, 1881.

Boniface. *Epistolae*. Ed. M. Tangl. *MGH Epistolae Selectae* 1. Berlin: Weidmann, 1916. Trans. E. Emerton. *The Letters of Saint Boniface*. New York: Columbia University Press, 2000.

Helmold of Bosau. *Cronica Slavorum*. Ed. B. Schmeidler. *MGH SRG*. Hanover and Leipzig: Hahn, 1909. Trans. F. J. Tschan. *The Chronicle of the Slavs*. New York: Columbia University Press, 1935.

Ratramnus. *Epistolae*. Ed E. Dümmler. *Epistolae variorum* 12. *MGH Epistolae* 6 (= *Karolini Aevi* 4). Berlin: Weidmann, 1925. Trans. P. Dutton. *Carolingian Civilization: A Reader*. 2nd ed. Peterborough, Ontario: Broadview, 2004, 452–55.

The Reign of Charlemagne: Documents on Carolingian Government and Administration. Ed. H. R. Loyn and J. Percival. Documents of Medieval History 2. London and New York: Edward Arnold, 1975.

Rimbert. *Vita Anskarii*. Ed. W. Trillmich. Quellen des 9. und 11. Jahrhunderts zur Geschichte der hamburgischen Kirche und des Reiches. Darmstadt: Wissenschaftliche Buchgesellschaft, 1961. Trans. P. Dutton. *Carolingian Civilization: A Reader*. 2nd ed. Peterborough, Ontario: Broadview, 2004, 400–51.

Saxo Grammaticus. *Gesta Danorum: Danorum regum heroumque historia, Books X–XVI*. Ed. and trans. E. Christiansen. 3 vols. *British Archaeological Reports* international series 84 (1980), 118i (1981), 118ii, (1981).

Thietmar of Merseburg. *Chronicon*. Ed. W. Trillmich. Darmstadt: Wissenschaftliche Buchgesellschaft, 1957. Trans. D. A. Warner. *Ottonian Germany: The Chronicle of Thietmar of Merseburg*. Manchester: Manchester University Press, 2001.

Vita Lebuini antiqua. Ed. A. Hofmeister. *MGH Scriptorum* 30.2. Leipzig: Hiersemann, 1934. Trans. C. H. Talbot. *The Anglo-Saxon Missionaries in Germany*. London: Sheed and Ward, 1954.

Secondary sources

Abrams, L. J. "The Anglo-Saxons and the Christianization of Scandinavia." *Anglo-Saxon England* 24 (1995): 213–49.

Boudriot, W. *Die altgermanische Religion*. Bonn: Rohrscheid, 1928.

Büttner, H. "Mission und Kirchenorganisation des Frankenreichs bis zum Tode Karls des Großen." In *Karl der Große 1: Persönlichkeit und Geschichte*. Ed. H. Beumann. Düsseldorf: Schwann, 1965, 454–87.

Campbell, J. "The First Century of Christianity in England." In his *Essays in Anglo-Saxon History*. London: Hambledon Press, 1986, 49–67.

—. "Observations on the Conversion of England." In his *Essays in Anglo-Saxon History*. London: Hambledon Press, 1986, 69–84.

Dierkens, A. "Superstitions, christianisme et paganisme à la fin de l'époque mérovingienne: à propos de l'Indiculus superstitionum et paganiarum." In *Magie, sorcellerie, parapsychologie*. Ed. H. Hasquin. Brussels: Éditions de l'Université de Bruxelles, 1984.

Dutton, P. *Carolingian Civilization: A Reader*. 2nd ed. Peterborough, Ontario: Broadview, 2004.

Green, D. H. *Language and History in the Early Germanic World*. Cambridge: Cambridge University Press, 1998.

Helm, K. *Altgermanische Religionsgeschichte 2. (Die nachrömische Zeit: 2, Die Westgermanen.)* Heidelberg: Carl Winter, 1953.

Lebecq, S. "Religiosa femina nomine Frideburg: la communité chrétienne de Birka au milieu du IXe siècle d'après de chapitre 20 de la *Vita Anskarii*." In *Recueil d'études en hommage à Lucien Musset*. Cahiers des Annales de Normandie 23. Caen: Musée de Normandie, 1990, 127–37.

—. "Vulfran, Willibrord et la mission de Frise: pour une relecture de la Vita Vulframni." In *L'évangélisation des régions entre Meuse et Moselle et la fondation de l'abbaye d'Echternach: Ve–IXe siècle*. Ed. M. Polfer. Publications de la Section Historique de l'Institut Grand-Ducal CXVII-Publications du CLUDEM 16. Luxemburg: Institut Grand-Ducal de Luxembourg, 2000, 431–51.

Mayr-Harting, H. *The Coming of Christianity to Anglo-Saxon England*. 3rd ed. London: Batsford, 1991.

Nelson, J. L. "Les femmes et l'évangélisation au IXe siècle." *Revue du Nord* 68. No. 269 (1986): 471–85.

Nilsson, B. "Early Christian Burials in Sweden." In *Christianizing Peoples and Converting Individuals*. Ed. G. Armstrong and I. N. Wood. International Medieval Research 7. Turnhout: Brepols, 2000, 73–82.

Palmer, J. T. "Rimbert's *Vita Anskarii* and Scandinavian Mission in the Ninth Century." *Journal of Ecclesiastical History* 55 (2004): 235–56.

Rabe, S. A. *Faith, Art and Politics at Saint-Riquier: The Symbolic Vision of Angilbert*. Philadelphia, PA: University of Pennsylvania Press, 1995.
Sawyer, P. "The Process of Scandinavian Christianization in the Tenth and Eleventh Centuries." In *The Christianization of Scandinavia*. Ed. B. Sawyer, P. Sawyer, and I. Wood. Alingsås: Viktoria Bokförlag, 1987, 68–87.
Sims-Williams, P. *Religion and Literature in Western England, 600–800*. Cambridge: Cambridge University Press, 1990.
Slupecki, L. P. *Slavonic Pagan Sanctuaries*. Warsaw: Institute of Archaeology and Ethnology, Polish Academy of Sciences, 1994.
Strömbäck, D. *The Conversion of Iceland: A Survey*. Trans. P. Foote. London: Viking Society for Northern Research, 1975.
Wolfram, H. *Conversio Bagoariorum et Carantanorum: das Weißbuch der Salzburger Kirche über die erfolgreiche Mission in Karantanien und Pannonien*. Vienna: Böhlau, 1979.
Wood, I. N. "Augustine and Aidan: Bureaucrat and Charismatic?" In *L'église et la mission au VIe siècle*. Ed. C. de Dreuille. Paris: Éditions du Cerf, 2000, 148–79.
—. *The Missionary Life: Saints and the Evangelisation of Europe*. London: Longman, 2001.
—. "Pagan Religion and Superstitions East of the Rhine from the Fifth to the Ninth Century." In *After Empire*. Ed. G. Ausenda. Woodbridge: Boydell Press, 1995, 253–68.
—. "Pagans and Holy Men, 600–800." In *Irland und die Christenheit*. Ed. P. Ni Chatháin and M. Richter. Stuttgart: Klett-Cotta, 1987, 347–61.
—. "Some Historical Re-identifications and the Christianization of Kent." In *Christianizing Peoples and Converting Individuals*. Ed. G. Armstrong and I. N. Wood. International Medieval Research 7. Turnhout: Brepols, 2000, 27–35.

12 The Christian church as an institution
Thomas F. X. Noble

Primary sources

Adam of Bremen. *Storia degli arcivescovi della chiesa di Amburgo*. Ed. I. Pagni. Turin, 1996. Eng. trans. F. J. Tschan. *History of the Archbishops of Hamburg-Bremen*. Records of Civilization 53. New York: Columbia University Press, 1959.
Agnellus of Ravenna. *Liber Pontificalis ecclesiae Ravennatis*. Ed. D. Deliyannis. *CCCM* 199. Turnhout: Brepols, 2006. Eng. trans. D. M. Deliyannis. *The Book of Pontiffs of the Church of Ravenna*. Washington, DC: Catholic University of America Press, 2004.
Amalarius of Metz. *Liber Officialis*. In his *Opera liturgica omnia*. 3 vols. Ed. J. M. Hanssens. Studi e testi 139. Vatican City: Biblioteca apostolica vaticana, 1948.
Annales Bertiniani. Ed. F. Grat. Paris: Klincksieck, 1964.
Capitula episcoporum. Ed. P. Brommer, R. Pokorny, et al. 4 vols. *MGH*. Hanover: Hahn, 1994–2005.
Concilia aevi Karolini. Ed. A. Werminghoff. *MGH Concilia* 2. Hanover: Hahn, 1906–1908.
Flodoard of Rheims. *Annales: les annales de Flodoard*. Ed. P. Lauer. Paris: Alphonse Picard et Fils, 1905. Eng. trans. S. Fanning and B. S. Bachrach. *The Annals of Flodoard of Reims, 919–966*. Readings in Medieval Civilizations and Cultures 9. Peterborough, Ontario: Broadview, 2004.

Gesta episcoporum Neapolitanorum. Ed. Waitz. *MGH Scriptores rerum Langobardicarum et Italicarum*. Hanover: Hahn, 1878, 398–436.

Gregory VII. *The Correspondence of Pope Gregory VII*. Trans. E. Emerton. New York: Columbia University Press, 1932.

Hincmar. *Capitula quibus de rebus magistri et decani per singulas ecclesias inquirere, et episcopo renuntiare debeant*. In his *Opera omnia*. *PL* 125, 716–30.

——. *Collectio de ecclesiis et capellis*. Ed. M. Stratmann. *MGH Fontes iuris Germanici antiqui in usum scholarum separatim editi* 14. Hanover: Hahn, 1990.

Hrabanus Maurus. *De institutione clericorum libri tres*. Ed. D. Zimpel. Freiburger Beiträge zur mittelalterlichen Geschichte 7. Frankfurt: Peter Lang, 1996.

Isidore of Seville. *De ecclesiasticis officiis*. *CCSL* 113. Ed. C. M. Lawson. Turnholt: Brepols, 1989.

Jaffé, P. *Regesta Pontificum Romanorum*. 2nd ed. Leipzig: Veit, 1885.

John of Avranches. *Ordo servicii de l'insigne cathédrale d'Évreux: édition du ms. 95 de la bibliothèque d'Évreux (XIV siècle) avec les variantes des mss L. 64 et L. 76 (XV siècle)*. Ed. R. Delamare. Paris: Picard, 1925.

Die Konzilien der karolingischen Teilreiche 843–859. Ed. W. Hartmann. *MGH Concilia* 3. Hanover: Hahn, 1984.

Die Konzilien Deutschlands und Reichsitaliens, 916–1001. Ed. E.-D. Hehl. *MGH Concilia* 6. Hanover: Hahn, 1987.

Liber Pontificalis. Ed. L. M. O. Duchesne. 3 vols. 2nd ed. Paris: Éditions de Boccard, 1955–57.

Nicholas I. *Epistola* 88. *MGH Epistolarum* 6 (= *Epistolae Karolini Aevi* 4). Berlin: Wiedmann, 1974, 454–87.

Papsturkunden, 896–1046. Ed. H. Zimmermann. Vol. 1. Vienna: Österreichishcen Akademie der Wissenschaften, 1984.

Rather of Verona. *Praeloquiorum Libri VI*. Ed. F. Dolbeau. *CCCM* 46A. Turnhout: Brepols, 1984. Eng. trans. P. L. D. Reid. *The Complete Works of Rather of Verona*. Medieval and Renaissance Texts and Studies 76. Binghamton, NY: Medieval and Renaissance Texts and Studies, 1991.

Regino of Prüm. *Chronicon*. Ed. R. Rau. Quellen zur karolingischen Reischgeschichte 3. Darmstadt: Wissenschaftliche Buchgesellschaft, 1966.

——. *Libri duo de synodalibus causis et disciplinis ecclesiasticis*. In *Das Sendbuch des Regino von Prüm*. Ed. and trans. W. Hartmann (based on the earlier edition of F. W. H. Wasserschleben, Leipzig, 1840.). Ausgewählte Quellen zur deutschen Geschichte des Mittelalters 42. Darmstadt: Wissenschaftliche Buchgesellschaft, 2004.

Walafrid Strabo. *Libellus de exordiis et incrementis quarundam in observationibus ecclesiasticis rerum*. Ed. and trans. A. Harting-Correa. Mittellateinsiche Studien und Texte 19. Leiden: Brill, 1996.

Secondary sources

Addleshaw, G. W. O. *The Development of the Parochial System from Charlemagne to Urban II*. St. Anthony's Hall Publication 3. 3rd ed. York: St. Anthony's Press, 1970.

Angenendt, A. *Das Frühmittelalter: die abendländische Christenheit von 400 bis 900*. Stuttgart: Kohlhammer, 1990.

Anton, H. H. *Studien zu den Klosterpriviligien der Päpste im frühen Mittelalter*. Beiträge zur Geschichte und Quellenkunde des Mittelalters 4. Berlin: de Gruyter, 1975.

Atiya, A. S. *A History of Eastern Christianity*. Rev. ed. Milwood, NY: Kraus Reprint, 1980.

Aubrun, M. *La paroisse en France des origines au XVe siècle*. Paris: Picard, 1986.

Baldovin, J. *The Urban Character of Christian Worship: The Origins, Development, and Meaning of Stational Liturgy*. Orientalia Christiana Analecta 228. Rome: Pontificium institutum studiorum orientalium, 1987.

Barford, P. *The Early Slavs: Culture and Society in Early Medieval Eastern Europe*. Ithaca, NY: Cornell University Press, 2001.

Baumgartner, F. J. *Behind Locked Doors: A History of Papal Elections*. New York: Palgrave Macmillan, 2003.

Baus, K. "North African Christianity from the Beginnings of Vandal Rule to the Muslim Invasion." In Baus, *Imperial Church*, 602–14.

—. et al., eds. *The Imperial Church from Constantine to the Early Middle Ages*. Vol. 2 in *Handbook of Church History*. Ed. H. Jedin and J. Dolan. Trans. A. Biggs. New York: Herder and Herder, 1980.

Birch, D. J. *Pilgrimage to Rome in the Middle Ages*. Studies in the History of Medieval Religion 13. Woodbridge: Boydell Press, 1998.

Blair, J. *The Church in Anglo-Saxon Society*. Oxford: Oxford University Press, 2005.

—, and R. Sharpe, eds. *Pastoral Care before the Parish*. London: Leicester University Press, 1992.

Blumenthal, U.-R. *The Investiture Controversy: Church and Monarchy from the Ninth to the Twelfth Century*. Philadelphia, PA: University of Pennsylvania Press, 1988.

Boyd, C. E. *Tithes and Parishes in Medieval Italy: The Historical Roots of a Modern Problem*. Ithaca, NY: Cornell University Press, 1952.

Brink, S. "The Formation of the Scandinavian Parish: With Some Remarks Regarding the English Impact on the Process." In *The Community, the Family and the Saint: Patterns of Power in Early Medieval Europe*. Ed. J. Hill and M. Swan. Turnhout: Brepols, 1998, 19–44.

Čaplovič, D. "Archaeology and the Beginnings of Christianity in Slovakia." In Urbańczyk, *Early Christianity*, 95–100.

Charles-Edwards, T. M. *Early Christian Ireland*. Cambridge: Cambridge University Press, 2000.

Claussen, M. A. *The Reform of the Frankish Church: Chrodegang of Metz and the* Regula canonicorum *in the Eighth Century*. Cambridge: Cambridge University Press, 2004.

Constable, G. "Monasteries, Rural Churches, and the *cura animarum* in the Early Middle Ages." In *Cristianizzazione ed organizzazione ecclesiastica delle campagne nell'Alto Medioevo: espansione e resistenze*. Settimane di studio 28. Spoleto: Centro italiano di studi sull'alto medioevo, 1982, 349–89.

Cubitt, C. *Anglo-Saxon Church Councils, c. 650–c. 850*. London: Leicester University Press, 1995.

Dagron, G. "L'église et la chrétienté byzantines entre les invasions et l'iconoclasme." In *Histoire du christianisme* 4, 9–91.

Darrouzès, J. *Recherches sur les offikia de l'église Byzantine*. Archives de l'Orient chrétien 11. Paris: Institut français d'études byzantines, 1970.

Dell'arche, M. *Scomparsa del cristianesimo ed espansione dell'Islam nell'Africa settentrionale*. Rome: Fiamma Nova, 1967.

Dvornik, F. *Byzantium and the Roman Primacy*. New York: Fordham University Press, 1966.

Etchingham, C. *Church Organisation in Ireland, A.D. 650 to 1000*. Naas: Laigin Publications, 2002.

Fennell, J. L. I. *A History of the Russian Church to 1448*. London: Longman, 1995.

Gams, P. B. *Series episcoporum Ecclesiae Catholicae*. Repr. Graz: Akademische Druck- und Verlagsanstalt, 1957.

Giesztor. A. "L'Europe chrétienne autour de l'an mille." In Urbanczyk, *Early Christianity*, 13–19.

Gil, M. *A History of Palestine, 634–1099*. Cambridge: Cambridge University Press, 1992.

Giuzelev, V., and R. Pillinger, eds. *Das Christentum in Bulgarien und auf der übrigen Balkanhalbinsel*. Vienna: Verein "Freunde des Hauses Wittgenstein," 1987.

Gottlob, T. *Der abendländlischen Chorepiskopat*. Kanonistische Studien und Texte 1. Repr. Amsterdam: P. Schippers, 1963.

Gresser, G. *Die Synoden und Konzilien in der Zeit des Reformpapsttums in Deutschland und Italien von Leo IX. bis Calixt II: 1049–1123*. Paderborn: Ferdinand Schöningh, 2006.

Hartmann, W. *Die Synoden der Karolingerzeit im Frankreich und in Italien*. Paderborn: Ferdinand Schöningh, 1989.

Hauck, A. *Kirchengeschichte Deutschlands*. 5 vols. in 6. Repr. Berlin: Akademie Verlag, 1952–53.

Hughes, K. *The Church in Early Irish Society*. London: Methuen, 1966.

Hussey, J. M. *The Orthodox Church in the Byzantine Empire*. Oxford: Oxford University Press, 1986.

Imbart de la Tour, P. *Les élections épiscopales dans l'Église de France: étude sur la décadence du principe électif*. Repr. Geneva: Slatkine, 1974.

—. *Les paroisses rurales du IVe au Xie siècle*. Paris: A. Picard, 1900.

Imbert, J. *Les temps carolingiens (741–891): l'église: les institutions*. Paris: Cujas, 1994.

Kaufhold, M. *Europas Norden im Mittelalter: Die Integration Skandinaviens in das christliche Europa (9.–13. Jahrhundert)*. Darmstadt: Wissenschaftliche Buchgesellschaft, 2001.

Kazhdan, A. "Constantinople, Patriarchate." *ODB* 1, 520–23.

Kemp, E. W. *Canonization and Authority in the Western Church*. London: Oxford University Press, 1948.

Kempf, F. et al. *The Church in the Age of Feudalism*. Vol. 3 in *Handbook of Church History*. Ed. H. Jedin and J. Dolan. Trans. A. Biggs. New York: Herder and Herder, 1969.

—. "Diocesan Organization." In Kempf et al., *Church*, 258–69.

—. "The Evangelization of the Slavs and Magyars in the Tenth and Eleventh Centuries." In Kempf et al., *Church*, 235–47.

—. "Metropolitans, Primates, and Papacy." In Kempf et al., *Church*, 285–300.

—. "The Spread of Christianity among the Scandinavians in the Tenth and Eleventh Centuries." In Kempf et al., *Church*, 230–34.

Kéry, L. *Canonical Collections of the Early Middle Ages (c. 400–1140): A Bibliographical Guide to the Manuscripts and Literature*. Washington, DC: Catholic University of America Press, 1998.

Kłoczowski, J. "La nouvelle chrétienté du monde occidentale: la christianisation des Slaves, des Scandinaves et des Hongrois." In *Histoire du christianisme* 4, 869–908.

Lot, F., and R. Fawtier, eds. *Histoire des institutions françaises au moyen âge*. Vol. 3: *Les institutions écclésiastiques*. Paris: Presses universitaires de France, 1957.

Mahé, J.-P. "L'église arménienne de 611 à 1066." In *Histoire du christianisme* 4, 457–547.

Martin, J.-M., and M. Parisse. "La chrétienté occidentale." In *Histoire du christianisme* 4, 767–866.

Morrison, K. F. *Tradition and Authority in the Western Church, 300–1140*. Princeton, NJ: Princeton University Press, 1969.

—. *The Two Kingdoms: Ecclesiology in Carolingian Political Thought*. Princeton, NJ: Princeton University Press, 1964.

Nicholas, D. *The Growth of the Medieval City: From Late Antiquity to the Early Fourteenth Century*. London: Longman, 1997.

Noble, T. F. X. "The Papacy in the Eighth and Ninth Centuries." In *NCMH* 2, 563–86.

—. *The Republic of St. Peter: The Birth of the Papal State, 680–825*. Philadelphia, PA: University of Pennsylvania Press, 1984.

Obolensky, D. *The Byzantine Commonwealth: Eastern Europe, 500–1453*. Crestwood, NY: St. Vladimir's Seminary Press, 1971.

Oxford Dictionary of the Christian Church. Ed. F. L. Cross. 3rd ed. Rev. E. A. Livingstone. Oxford: Oxford University Press, 2005.

Papadakis, A. "Deaconesses." In *ODB* 1, 592–93.

—. "Synkellos." In *ODB* 3, 1993–94.

Peri, V. "La pentarchia: instituzione ecclesiale (IV–VII sec.) e teoria canonico-teologica." In *Bisanzio, Roma e l'Italia nell'Alto Medioevo*. Settimane di studio 34. Spoleto: Centro italiano di studi sull'alto medioevo, 1988, 209–311.

Picker, H.-C. *Pastor Doctus: Klerikerbild und karolingische Reformen bei Hrabanus Maurus*. Mainz: von Zabern, 2001.

Polek, K. "The Great Moravian State." In Urbańczyk, *Early Christianity*, 75–85.

Potz, R. *Patriarch und Synode in Konstantinopel: Das Verfassungsrecht des ökumenischen Patriarchates*. Vienna: Herder, 1971.

Price, H. "The Christianization of Society." In *From the Vikings to the Normans*. Ed. W. Davies. *Short Oxford History of the British Isles*. Oxford: Oxford University Press, 2003, 139–67.

Reuter, T. "The 'Imperial Church System' of the Ottonian and Salian Rulers: A Reconsideration." *Journal of Ecclesiastical History* 32 (1982): 347–74.

Reynolds, R. "Marginalia on a Tenth-Century Text of the Ecclesiastical Offices." In *Law, Church, and Society: Essays in Honor of Stephan Kuttner*. Ed. K. Pennington and R. Somerville. Philadelphia, PA: University of Pennsylvania Press, 1977, 115–30.

—. "The Organisation, Law, and Liturgy of the Western Church, 700–900." In *NCMH* 2, 587–621.

Riché, P. "Le christianisme dans l'Occident carolingien." In *Histoire du christianisme* 4, 683–765.

—. "De Grégoire le Grand à Pépin le Bref." In *Histoire du christianisme* 4, 605–866.

Sághy, M. "Aspects de la christianisation des hongrois." In Urbańczyk, *Early Christianity*, 53–65.

Santifaller, L. *Zur Geschichte des ottonisch-salischen Reichskirchensystems*. 2nd ed. Österreichische Akademie der Wissenschaften, Phil.-Hist. Klasse, Sitzungsberichte 229. Vienna: Bohlau, 1964.

Sawyer, B., and P. Sawyer. *Medieval Scandinavia*. Minneapolis, MN: University of Minnesota Press, 1993.

—. "Scandinavia Enters Christian Europe." In *The Cambridge History of Scandinavia*. Ed. K. Helle. Cambridge: Cambridge University Press, 2003, 147–59.

—, and I. Wood, eds. *The Christianization of Scandinavia*. Alingsås: Viktoria Bokförlag, 1987.

Schieffer, T. "Der Ottonische Reichsepiskopat zwischen Königtum und Adel." *Frühmittelalterliche Studien* 23 (1989): 291–300.

Somerville, R., and B. Brasington. *Prefaces to Canon Law Books in Latin Christianity: Selected Translations, 500–1245*. New Haven, CT: Yale University Press, 1998.

Stancliffe, C. "From Town to Country: The Christianization of the Touraine." *SCH* 16 (1979): 43–59.

Steinhübel, J. "Kirchliche Organisation in Großmahren." In Urbańczyk, *Early Christianity*, 87–94.

Stutz, U. *Geschichte des kirchlichen Benefizialwesen von seinen Anfängen bis auf die Zeit Alexanders III*. Repr. Aalen: Scientia, 1972.

Sullivan, R. E. "The Papacy and Missionary Activity." *Mediaeval Studies* 17 (1955): 46–106.

Tomljenović, I. "Wann begegneten die Kroaten dem Christentum?" In Urbańczyk, *Early Christianity*, 43–46.

Troupeau, G. "Églises et chrétiens dans l'Orient musulman." In *Histoire du christianisme* 4, 375–603.

Ullmann, W. *The Carolingian Renaissance and the Idea of Kingship*. London: Methuen, 1969.

—. *The Growth of Papal Government in the Middle Ages*. 2nd ed. London: Methuen, 1962.

Urbańczyk, P., ed. *Early Christianity in Central and Eastern Europe*. Warsaw: Wydawnictwo Naukowe Semper, 1997.

Van Engen, J. "The Christian Middle Ages as an Historiographical Problem." *American Historical Review* 91 (1986): 519–52.

—. "The Future of Medieval Church History." *Church History* 71 (2002): 492–522.

Vlasto, A. P. *The Entry of the Slavs into Christendom*. Cambridge: Cambridge University Press, 1970.

Vodola, E. *Excommunication in the Middle Ages*. Berkeley, CA: University of California Press, 1986.

Vogel, C. "Les échanges liturgiques entre Rome et les pays franques jusqu'à l'époque de Charlemagne." In *Le chiese nei regni dell'Europa occidentale e i loro rapporti con Roma sino all'800*. Settimane di studio 7. Spoleto: Centro italiano di studi sull'alto medioevo, 1960, 185–295.

Vollrath, H. *Die Synoden Englands bis 1066*. Paderborn: Ferdinand Schöningh, 1985.

Waldmüller, L. *Die Synoden in Dalmatien, Kroatien und Ungarn: Von der Völkerwanderung bis zum Ende der Arpaden (1311)*. Paderborn: Ferdinand Schöningh, 1987.

Wallace-Hadrill, J. M. *The Frankish Church*. Oxford: Oxford University Press, 1983.

Wasilewski, T. "L'église de la Bulgarie danubienne." In Urbańczyk, *Early Christianity*, 47–52.

Wood, I. *The Merovingian Kingdoms, 450–751*. London: Longman, 1994.

Wood, S. *The Proprietary Church in the Medieval West*. Oxford: Oxford University Press, 2006.

13 Asceticism and its institutions
Anne-Marie Helvétius and Michel Kaplan

Primary sources

Actes d'Iviron. Ed. J. Lefort, N. Oikonomidès, D. Papachryssanthou, and H. Metrevelli. Vol. 1. Archives de l'Athos 14. Paris: Lethielleux, 1985.

Actes de Lavra. Ed. P. Lemerle, A. Guillou, N. Svoronos, and D. Papachryssanthou. Vol 1. Archives de l'Athos 5. Paris: Lethielleux, 1970.

Actes du Prôtaton. Ed. D. Papachryssanthou. Archives de l'Athos 7. Paris: Lethielleux, 1975.

"The Acts of Thomas." Trans. H. J. W. Drijvers. In *New Testament Apocrypha*. Vol. 2. Ed. E. Hennecke, W. Schneemelcher, and R. McL.. Wilson. 2nd ed. Westminster: John Knox Press, 1992, 322–38.

Athanasius of Alexandria. *Vie d'Antoine*. Ed. G. J. M. Bartelink. *SC* 400. Paris: Éditions du Cerf, 1994. Eng. trans. C. White. *Early Christian Lives*. London: Penguin, 1998, 1–70.

Athanasius the Athonite. *Typikon du monastère de Lavra*. In *Die Haupturkunden für die Geschichte der Athosklöster*. Ed. P. Meyer. 1894. Reprinted Amsterdam: Hakkert, 1965, 130–40. Eng. trans. G. Dennis, *BMFD* 1, 221–28.

Benedict of Aniane. *Concordia regularum*. In *Benedictus Anianensis, Concordia regularum: praefatio, concordantiae, indices*. Ed. P. Bonnerue. *CCCM* 168–168A. 2 vols. Turnhout: Brepols, 1999.

Capitulare Haristallense. *MGH capitularia regum francorum* 1, no. 20, 47–52.

Capitularia monastica concilii Aquisgranensis. Ed. J. Semmler. In *Corpus Consuetudinum Monasticarum*. Ed. K. Hallinger. Vol. 1. Siegburg: F. Schmitt, 1963, 453–68 (anno 816) and 471–82 (anno 817).

Capitularia regum francorum. Ed. A. Boretius. 2 vols. *MGH Legum Sectio* 2. Hanover: Hahn, 1883–87.

Council in Trullo. In *Discipline générale antique*, 98–241.

Council of Chalcedon. In *Discipline générale antique*, 66–97.

Council of Nicaea II. In *Discipline générale antique*, 241–84.

Cyril of Scythopolis. *Vita Euthymii*. In *Kyrillos von Skythopolis*. Ed. E. Schwartz. Texte und Untersuchungen zur Geschichte der altchristlichen Literatur 49.2. Leipzig: Hinrichs, 1934, 3–85. English trans. R. M. Price. *Cyril of Scythopolis: Lives of the Monks of Palestine*. Cistercian Studies 114. Kalamazoo, MI: Cistercian Publications, 1991.

—. *Vita Sabae*. In *Kyrillos von Skythopolis*, 85–200. Eng. trans. Price, *Cyril of Scythopolis*.

Discipline générale antique (IIe–XIe s.). Ed. P.-P. Joannou. Vol. 1.1: *Les canons des conciles œcuméniques*. Rome: Tipografia Italo-Orientale "S. Nilo," 1962.

Gregory of Tours. *Libri historiarum* X. Ed. B. Krusch. *MGH SRM* 1.1. Hanover: Hahn, 1885.

—. *Liber Vitae patrum*. Ed. B. Krusch. *MGH SRM* 1.2. Hanover: Hahn, 1885; repr. 1969, 661–744. Eng. trans. E. James. *Gregory of Tours: Life of the Fathers*. 2nd. ed. Translated Texts for Historians 1. Liverpool: Liverpool University Press, 1991.

Gregory the Great. *Dialogues*. Ed. A. de Vogüé. 3 vols. *SC* 251, 260, and 265. Paris: Éditions du Cerf, 1978–80.

Institutio canonicorum concilii Aquisgranensis (816). In *The Rules for the Common Life of the Secular Clergy from the Eighth and Ninth Centuries: Critical Texts with Translations and Commentary*. Ed. J. Bertram. Aldershot: Ashgate, 2005, 96–131.

Institutio sanctimonialium concilii Aquisgranensis (816–817). Ed. A. Werminghoff. *MGH Leges: Concilia* 2 (= *Concilia aevi Karolini* 1.1). Hanover: Hahn, 1906–1908, 421–56.

John of Antioch. *Treatise against Charistikè*. In P. Gautier, ed. "Diatribes de Jean l'Oxite contre Alexis Ier Comnène." *Revues des études byzantines* 28 (1970): 5–35.

Jonas of Bobbio. *Vita Columbani abbatis discipulorumque eius*. Ed. B. Krusch. *MGH SRM* 4. Hanover: Hahn, 1902, 1–152.

John Climacus. *Ladder of Divine Ascent*. In *Scala paradisii*. Vol. 1: *Gradini, 1–15*. Vol. 2: *Gradini 16–30, Testo con introduzione, versione e note*. Ed. P. Trevisan. Turin: Società editirice nazionale, 1951. Eng. trans. C. Luibheid and N. Russell. *John Climacus: The Ladder of Divine Ascent*. New York: Paulist Press, 1982.

Justinian. *Corpus Juris Civilis*. Vol. 2: *Codex Justinianus*. Ed. P. Krueger and W. Kunkel. 11th ed. Hildesheim: Weidmann, 1997.

——. *Corpus Juris Civilis*. Vol. 3: *Novellae*. Ed. R. Schoell and W. Kroll. 13th ed. Hildesheim: Weidmann, 1993.

The Lives of Simeon Stylites. Trans. R. Doran. Kalamazoo, MI: Cistercian Publications, 1992.

Michael Attaleiates. *Diataxis*. In "La diataxis de Michel Attaliate." Ed. P. Gautier. *Revues des études byzantines* 39 (1981): 17–130. Eng. trans. A.-M. Talbot, *BMFD* 1, 333–70.

Possidius. *Vita Augustini*. In *Vita di Cipriani, Vita di Ambrogio, Vita di Agostino*. Ed. A. A. R. Bastiaensen. Vite dei santi 3. Milan: Mondadori, 1975, 127–241.

La règle du Maître. Ed. A. de Vogüé. 3 vols. *SC* 105–107. Paris: Éditions du Cerf, 1964–65.

La règle de saint Benoît. Ed. A. de Vogüé. 6 vols. *SC* 181–86. Paris: Éditions du Cerf, 1971–72.

Les règles des saints Pères. Ed. A. de Vogüé. 2 vols. *SC* 297–98. Paris: Éditions du Cerf, 1982.

Sancti Athanasii Athonitae vita prima, auctore Athanasio monacho. Ed. J. Noret. In *Vitae duae antiquae sancti Athanasii athonitae*. *CCSG* 9. Turnhout: Brepols, 1982, 3–124.

Theodore the Studite. *Jamben auf verschiedende Gegenstande, Einleitung, kritischer Text, Übersetzung und Kommentar*. Ed. P. Speck. Supplementa Byzantina 1. Berlin: de Gruyter, 1968.

Typikon of Gregory Pakourianos. In "Le typikon du sébaste Grégoire Pakourianos." Ed. P. Gautier. *Revues des études byzantines* 42 (1984): 19–133. Eng. trans. R. Jordan, *BMFD* 2, 519–57.

Typikon of Theotokos Evergetis. In "Le typikon de la Théotokos Évergétis." Ed. P. Gautier. *Revues des études byzantines* 40 (1982): 15–95. Eng. trans. R. Jordan, *BMFD* 2, 472–500.

Vita Fursei abbatis Latiniacensis. In Carozzi, C. *Le voyage de l'âme dans l'Au-delà d'après la littérature latine (Ve–XIIIe siècle)*. Bibliothèque de l'école française de Rome 189. Rome: École française de Rome, 1994.

Vita S. Lazari auctore Gregorio monacho. *AASS* Nov. 3, 508–88. Trans. R. P. H. Greenfield. *The Life of St. Lazaros of Mt. Galesion: An Eleventh-Century Pillar Saint, Introduction, Translation, and Notes*. Byzantine Saints' Lives in Translation 3. Washington, DC: Dumbarton Oaks, 2000.

Secondary sources

Angenendt, A. *Geschichte der Religiosität im Mittelalter*. Darmstadt: Primus Verlag, 1997.

—. *Monachi peregrini: Studien zu Pirmin und den monastischen Vorstellungen des frühen Mittelalters*. Münstersche Mittelalter-Schriften 6. Munich: Wilhelm Fink Verlag, 1972.

Angold, M., ed. *The Byzantine Aristocracy: IX–XIII Centuries. British Archaelogical Reports* 221. Oxford: British Archaeological Reports International Series, 1984.

Atsma, H., ed. *La Neustrie: les pays au Nord de la Loire de 650 à 850. Colloque historique international*. 2 vols. Beihefte der Francia 16. Sigmaringen: Jan Thorbecke Verlag, 1989.

Auzépy, M.-F. "La place des moines à Nicée II (787)." *Byzantion* 58 (1988): 5–21.

Berlière, U. "L'exercice du ministère paroissial par les moines. Pt. 1: dans le Haut Moyen Âge. Pt. 2: du XIIe au XVIIIe siècle." *Revue bénédictine* 39 (1927): 227–50, 340–64.

Bertram, J. *The Chrodegang Rules: The Rules for the Common Life of the Secular Clergy from the Eighth and Ninth Centuries, Critical Texts with Translations and Commentary*. Aldershot: Ashgate, 2005.

Bishko, C. J. *Spanish and Portuguese Monastic History 600–1300*. London: Variorum Reprints, 1984.

Blair, J. "Debate: Ecclesiastical Organization and Pastoral Care in Anglo-Saxon England." *EME* 4.2 (1995): 193–212.

Borgolte, M. "*Memoria*: Bilan intermédiaire d'un projet de recherche sur le Moyen Âge." In Schmitt and Oexle, *Les tendances actuelles*, 53–69.

Bouet, P., G. Otranto, and A. Vauchez, eds. *Culte et pèlerinages à saint Michel en Occident: Les trois monts dédiés à l'archange*. Collection de l'école française de Rome 316. Rome: École française de Rome, 2003.

Bozóky, E., and A.-M. Helvétius, eds. *Les reliques: objets, cultes, symboles. Actes du colloque international de l'Université du Littoral-Côte d'Opale (Boulogne-sur-Mer)*. Hagiologia 1. Turnhout: Brepols, 1999.

Brown, P. *The Making of Late Antiquity*. Cambridge, MA: Harvard University Press, 1978.

Caby, C. "*Finis eremitarum?* Les formes régulières et communautaires de l'érémitisme médiéval." In Vauchez, *Ermites de France et d'Italie*, 47–80.

Cambridge, E., and D. Rollason. "Debate: The Pastoral Organization of the Anglo-Saxon Church: A Review of the 'Minster Hypothesis.'" *EME* 4.1 (1995): 87–104.

Caner, D. *Wandering, Begging Monks: Spiritual Authority and the Promotion of Monasticism in Late Antiquity*. Berkeley, CA: University of California Press, 2002.

Carrias, M. "Vie monastique et règle à Lérins au temps d'Honorat." *Revue d'histoire de l'église de France* 74 (1988): 191–211.

Chadwick, H. "Gregory the Great and the Mission to the Anglo-Saxons." In *Gregorio Magno e il suo tempo: XIX incontro di studiosi dell'antichità cristiana*. Vol. 1. Rome: Institutum Patristicum Augustianum, 1991, 199–212.

Chadwick, O. *John Cassian: A Study in Primitive Monasticism*. 2nd ed. Cambridge: Cambridge University Press, 1968.

Charles-Edwards, T. M. *Early Christian Ireland*. Cambridge: Cambridge University Press, 2000.

Chitty, D. J. *The Desert a City: An Introduction to the Study of Egyptian and Palestinian Monasticism under the Christian Empire*. Oxford: Blackwell, 1966.

Constable, G. *Cluniac Studies*. London: Variorum Reprints, 1980.

—. *Religious Life and Thought (11th–12th centuries)*. London: Variorum Reprints, 1979.

Contreni, J. J. "The Carolingian Renaissance: Education and Literary Culture." In *NCMH* 2, 709–57.
Cubitt, C. "Review Article: The Tenth-Century Benedictine Reform in England." *EME* 6.1 (1997): 77–94.
Dagron, G. "Économie et société chrétiennes (VIIIe–Xe siècles)." In *Histoire du Christianisme* 4, 241–96.
—. "Les moines et la ville: le monachisme à Constantinople jusqu'au concile de Chalcédoine." *Travaux et mémoires* 4 (1970): 229–76; reprinted as ch. 8 in his *La romanité chrétienne en Orient*. London: Variorum Reprints, 1984.
Darrouzés, J. "Le patriarche Méthode contre les Iconoclastes et les Stoudites." *Revues des études byzantines* 45 (1987): 15–57.
de Jong, M. "Carolingian Monasticism: The Power of Prayer." In *NCMH* 2, 622–53.
—. *In Samuel's Image: Child Oblation in the Early Medieval West*. Leiden: Brill, 1996.
—. "Monastic Prisoners or Opting Out? Political Coercion and Honour in the Frankish Kingdoms." In de Jong and Theuws, *Topographies of Power*, 291–328.
—, and F. Theuws, with C. van Rhijn, eds. *Topographies of Power in the Early Middle Ages*. The Transformation of the Roman World 6. Leiden: Brill, 2001.
de Vogüé, A. "Les débuts de la vie monastique à Lérins: remarques sur un ouvrage récent." *Revue d'Histoire Ecclésiastique* 88 (1993): 5–53. Reprinted in his *Regards sur le monachisme des premiers siècles: recueil d'articles*. Studia Anselmiana 130. Rome: Centro studi S. Anselmo, 2000, 207–57.
—. *Histoire littéraire du mouvement monastique dans l'Antiquité*. Vol. 1: *Le monachisme latin de la mort d'Antoine à la fin du séjour de Jérôme à Rome*. Paris: Éditions du Cerf, 1991.
Devroey, J.-P. *Économie rurale et société dans l'Europe franque (VIe–IXe siècles)*. Vol. 1: *fondements, matériels, échanges et lien social*. Paris: Édition Belin, 2003.
Díaz, P. C. *Formas económicas y sociales en el monacato visigodo*. Salamanca: Universidad de Salamanca, 1987.
—. "El monacato y la cristianizacíon del NO hispano: un progreso de aculturación." In *Cristianismo y aculturación en tiempos del Impero romano*. Ed. A. Gonzalez Blanco and J. M. Blasquez Martínez. Murcia: Universidad de Murcia, 1990, 531–39.
—. "Monasticism and Liturgy in Visigothic Spain." In *The Visigoths: Studies in Culture and Society*. Ed. A. Ferreiro. Leiden: Brill, 1999, 169–99.
Diem, A. *Das monastische Experiment: die Rolle der Keuschheit bei der Entstehung des westlichen Klosterwesens*. Münster: LIT Verlag, 2005.
—. "Was bedeutet *regula Columbani*?" In *Integration und Herrschaft: Ethnische Identitäten und soziale Organisation im Frühmittelalter*. Ed. W. Pohl and M. Diesenberger. Denkschriften der Österreichischen Akademie der Wissenschaften: Philosophisch-Historische Klasse 301; Forschungen zur Geschichte des Mittelalters 3. Vienna: Österreichische Akademie der Wissenschaften, 2002, 63–89.
Dierkens, A. *Abbayes et chapitres entre Sambre et Meuse (VIIe–XIe siècles): contribution à l'histoire religieuse des campagnes du Haut Moyen Âge*. Beihefte der Francia 14. Sigmaringen: Jan Thorbecke Verlag, 1985.
—. "Prolégomènes à une histoire des relations culturelles entre les îles britanniques et le continent pendant le Haut Moyen Âge: la diffusion du monachisme dit colombanien ou iro-franc dans quelques monastères de la région parisienne au VIIe siècle et la politique religieuse de la reine Bathilde." In Atsma, *La Neustrie* 2, 371–94.

—, D. Misonne, and J.-M. Sansterre, eds. *Le monachisme à Byzance et en Occident du VIIIe au Xe siècle: aspects internes et relations avec la société. Actes du colloque international de Bruxelles/Maredsous, 14–16 mai 1992. Revue bénédictine* 103, pt. 1/2 (1993).

Dumville, D. N. "The Origins and Early History of Insular Monasticism: Aspects of Literature, Christianity, and Society in Britain and Ireland, A.D. 400–600." *Bulletin of the Institute of Oriental and Occidental Studies, Kansai University* 30 (1997): 85–107.

Ewig, E. *Spätantikes und fränkisches Gallien: Gesammelte Schriften (1952–1973)*. Ed. H. Atsma. 2 vols. Zürich: Jan Thorbecke Verlag, 1976–79.

Falkenstein, L. "Monachisme et pouvoir hiérarchique à travers les textes pontificaux (Xe–XIIe siècles)." In Lemaître, Dmitriev, and Gonneau, *Moines et monastères*, 389–418.

Felten, F. J. *Äbte und Laienäbte im Frankenreich: Studie zum Verhältnis von Staat und Kirche im früheren Mittelalter*. Stuttgart: Anton Hiersemann, 1980.

Flusin, B. "L'essor du monachisme oriental." In *Histoire du christianisme* 3, 555–608.

—. *Miracle et histoire dans l'œuvre de Cyrille de Scythopolis*. Paris: Études Augustiennes, 1984.

Fonseca, C. D. "Constat . . . monasterium esse tam canonicorum quam et monachorum: le influenze monastiche sulle strutture instituzionali delle Canoniche e delle Congregazioni canonicali." In Keller and Neiske, *Vom Kloster zum Klosterverband*, 239–51.

Frank, H. *Die Klosterbischöfe des Frankenreichs*. Beiträge zur Geschichte des alten Mönchtums und Benediktinertums 17. Münster: Aschendorff, 1932.

Fried, J. "Le passé à la merci de l'oralité et du souvenir: le baptême de Clovis et la vie de Benoît de Nursie." In Schmitt and Oexle, *Les tendances actuelles*, 71–104.

Ganz, D. "Book Production in the Carolingian Empire and the Spread of Caroline Minuscule." In *NCMH* 2, 786–808.

—. "The Ideology of Sharing: Apostolic Community and Ecclesiastical Property in the Early Middle Ages." In *Property and Power in the Early Middle Ages*. Ed. W. Davies and P. Fouracre. Cambridge: Cambridge University Press, 1995, 17–30.

Gribomont, J. *Saint Basile, évangile et église: mélanges*. 2 vols. Spiritualité Orientale 36–37. Bégrolles-en-Mauges: Abbaye de Bellefontaine, 1984.

Guillaumont, A. "Le dépaysement comme forme d'ascèse dans le monachisme ancien." *Annuaire de l'École pratique des Hautes Études, Ve section: Sciences religieuses* 76 (1968–69): 31–58.

Häussling, A. A. *Mönchskonvent und Eucharistiefeier: eine Studie über die Messe in der abendländischen Klosterliturgie des frühen Mittelalters und zur Geschichte der Messhäufigkeit*. Liturgiewissenschaftliche Quellen und Forschungen 58. Münster: Aschendorff, 1973.

Helvétius, A.-M. *Abbayes, évêques et laïques: une politique du pouvoir en Hainaut au Moyen Âge (VIIe–XIe siècle)*. Collection Histoire in-8° 92. Brussels: Crédit Communal, 1994.

—. "Comment écrire une nouvelle histoire du monachisme?" In *Mediävistik im 21. Jahrhundert: Stand und Perspektiven der internationalen und interdisziplinären Mittelalterforschung*. Ed. H.-W. Goetz and J. Jarnut. Munich: Wilhelm Fink Verlag, 2003, 443–55.

—. "Ermites ou moines: solitude et cénobitisme du Ve au Xe siècle (principalement en Gaule du nord)." In Vauchez, *Ermites de France et d'Italie*, 1–27.

—. "Du monastère double au chapitre noble: moniales et chanoinesses en Basse-Lotharingie." In *Les chapitres de dames nobles entre France et Empire*. Ed. M. Parisse and P. Heili. Paris: Messene, 1998, 31–45.

–, and M. Gaillard. "Production de textes et réforme d'un monastère double: l'exemple de Remiremont du VIIe au IXe siècle." In *Frauen–Kloster–Kunst–Neue Forschungen zur Kulturgeschichte des Mittelalters*. Ed. J. Hamburger, C. Jäggi, S. Marti, and H. Röckelein. Turnhout: Brepols, 2007, 455–67.

Herity, M. "The Layout of Irish Early Christian Monasteries." In *Irland und Europa: Die Kirche im Frühmittelalter*. Ed. P. Ní Chatháin and M. Richter. Stuttgart: Klett-Cotta, 1984, 105–16.

Hirschfeld, Y. *The Judean Desert Monasteries in the Byzantine Period*. New Haven, CT: Yale University Press, 1992.

Hughes, K. *The Church in Early Irish Society*. London: Methuen, 1966.

—. *Early Christian Ireland: Introduction to the Sources*. London: Hodder and Stoughton, 1972; reprint, Ithaca, NY: Cornell University Press, 1972.

Iogna-Prat, D. *Agni immaculati: recherches sur les sources hagiographiques relatives à saint Maieul de Cluny (954–994)*. Paris: Éditions du Cerf, 1988.

—. *Ordonner et exclure: Cluny et la société chrétienne face à l'hérésie, au judaïsme et à l'islam 1000–1150*. 2nd ed. Paris: Aubier, 2000. Eng. trans. G. Edwards. *Order and Exclusion: Cluny and Christendom Face Heresy, Judaism, and Islam (1000–1150)*. Ithaca, NY: Cornell University Press, 2003.

Kaplan, M. *Byzance, villes et campagnes*, Les medievistes français 7. Paris: Picard, 2006.

—. "L'évêque à l'époque du second iconoclasme." In *Monastères, images, pouvoirs et société à Byzance*. Ed. M. Kaplan. Byzantina Sorbonensia, 23. Paris: Publications de la Sorbonne, 2006, 183–206.

—. "Evergetis *Typikon* and the Management of Monastic Estates in the XIth Century." In Mullet and Kirby, *Theotokos Evergetis*, 103–23. Reprinted in French in *Byzance, villes et campagnes*, 228–39.

—. "Forme di ascesi tra originalità e contestazione." In *Oriente Cristiano e Santità, figure e storie di santi tra Bisanzio et l'Occidente*. Ed. S. Gentile. Rome: Centro Tibaldi, 1998, 53–60.

—. *Les hommes et la terre à Byzance du VIe au XIe siècle: propriété et exploitation du sol*. Byzantina Sorbonensia 10. Paris: Publications de la Sorbonne, 1992.

—. "Maisons impériales et fondations pieuses: réorganisation de la fortune impériale et assistance publique de la fin du VIIIe à la fin du Xe siècle." *Byzantion* 61 (1991): 441–64. Reprinted in *Byzance, villes et campagnes*, 167–83.

—. "Les moines et leurs biens fonciers à Byzance du VIIIe au Xe siècle: acquisition, conservation et mise en valeur." In Dierkens, Misonne, and Sansterre, *Le monachisme à Byzance*, 209–23. Reprinted in *Byzance, villes et campagnes*, 216–27.

—. "Les monastères et le siècle à Byzance: les investissements des laïcs au XIe siècle." *Cahiers de Civilisation Médiévale* 27 (1984): 71–83. Reprinted in *Byzance, villes et campagnes*, 123–37.

—. *Les propriétés de la couronne et de l'église dans l'empire byzantin (Ve–VIIe siècles)*. Byzantina Sorbonensia 2. Paris: Publications de la Sorbonne, 1976.

Kasper, C. M. *Theologie und Askese: die Spiritualität des Inselmönchtums von Lérins*. Beiträge zur Geschichte des alten Mönchtums und des Benediktinertums 40. Münster: Aschendorff, 1991.

Keller, H., and F. Neiske, eds. *Vom Kloster zum Klosterverband: das Werkzeug der Schriftlichkeit*. Münstersche Mittelalter-Schriften 74. Munich: Wilhelm Fink Verlag, 1997.

Klingshirn, W. E. *Caesarius of Arles: The Making of a Christian Community in Late Antique Gaul.* Cambridge: Cambridge University Press, 1994.

Kottje, R., and H. Maurer, eds. *Monastische Reformen im 9. und 10. Jahrhundert*. Vorträge und Forschungen 38. Sigmaringen: Jan Thorbecke Verlag, 1989.

Le Jan, R. "Convents, Violence, and Competition for Power in Seventh-Century Gaul." In de Jong and Theuws, *Topographies of Power*, 243–69.

Lebecq, S. "La Neustrie et la mer." In Atsma, *La Neustrie* 1, 405–40.

—. "The Role of Monasteries in the Frankish World." In *The Long Eighth Century: Production, Distribution and Demand.* Ed. I. L. Hansen and C. Wickham. The Transformation of the Roman World 11. Leiden: Brill, 2000, 121–48.

Lemaître, J.-L., M. Dmitriev, and P. Gonneau, eds. *Moines et monastères dans les sociétés de rite grec et latin*. École Pratique des Hautes Études IVe section V: Hautes Études Médiévales et Modernes 76. Geneva: Droz, 1996.

Lemerle, P. *Cinq études sur le XIe siècle byzantin*. Paris: Centre national de la recherche scientifique, 1977.

—. *Le premier humanisme byzantin: notes et remarques sur enseignement et culture à Byzance des origines au Xe siècle*. Bibliothèque byzantine 6. Paris: Presses universitaires de France, 1971.

—. "La vie ancienne d'Athanase l'Athonite composée au début du XIe siècle par Athanase de Lavra." In *Le millénaire du Mont Athos, 963–1963: études et mélanges*. Vol. 1. Chevetogne: Chevetogne, 1963, 59–100. Reprinted in his *Le monde de Byzance: histoire et institutions*. London: Variorum Reprints, 1978.

Leroy, J. "L'influence de S. Basile sur la réforme studite d'après les catéchèses." *Irènikon* 52 (1979): 491–506.

—. "La réforme studite." In *Il monachesimo orientale*. Orientalia Christiana Analecta 153. Rome: Pontificio istituto orientale, 1958, 181–214.

Leyser, C. *Authority and Asceticism from Augustine to Gregory the Great*. Oxford: Oxford University Press, 2000.

—. "This Sainted Isle: Panegyric, Nostalgia, and the Invention of Lerinian Monasticism." In *The Limits of Ancient Christianity: Essays on Late Antique Thought and Culture in Honor of R. A. Markus*. Ed. W. E. Klingshirn and M. Vessey. Ann Arbor, MI: University of Michigan Press, 1999, 188–206.

Leyser, H. *Hermits and the New Monasticism: A Study of Religious Communities in Western Europe, 1000–1150*. London: Macmillan, 1984.

Magdalino, P. "The Byzantine Aristocratic *Oikos*." In Angold, *Byzantine Aristocracy*, 92–111. Reprinted as ch. 2 in his *Tradition and Transformation in Medieval Byzantium*. Aldershot: Variorum, 1991.

Markus, R. A. *The End of Ancient Christianity*. Cambridge: Cambridge University Press, 1990.

McKitterick, R. *The Carolingians and the Written Word*. Cambridge: Cambridge University Press, 1989.

—. "Le rôle culturel des monastères dans les royaumes carolingiens du VIIIe au Xe siècle." In Dierkens, Misonne, and Sansterre, *Le monachisme à Byzance*, 117–30.

Méhu, D. *Paix et communautés autour de l'abbaye de Cluny (Xe–XVe siècle)*. Lyons: Presses universitaires de Lyon, 2001.

Milis, L. *Angelic Monks and Earthly Men: Monasticism and its Meaning to Medieval Society*. Woodbridge: Boydell Press, 1992.

Misonne, D. "La restauration monastique de Gérard de Brogne." In *Naissance et fonctionnement des réseaux monastiques et canoniaux*. Saint-Étienne: Centre européen de recherches sur les congrégations et ordres religieux, 1991, 117–23; reprinted in *Revue bénédictine* 111 (2001): 62–67.

Il monachesimo nell'Alto Medioevo e la formazione della civiltà occidentale. Settimane di studio 4. Spoleto: Centro italiano di studi sull'alto medioevo, 1957.

Morris, R. "The Byzantine Aristocracy and the Monasteries." In Angold, *Byzantine Aristocracy*, 112–37.

—. "Monasteries and their Patrons in the Tenth and Eleventh Centuries." *Byzantinische Forschungen* 10 (1985): 185–231.

—. *Monks and Laymen in Byzantium: 843–1118*. Cambridge: Cambridge University Press, 1995.

Mostert, M. "Les moines à Utrecht au temps de Willibrord." In *Les moines dans la ville: actes du colloque de Lille*. Lille: Université catholique de Lille, 1996.

Moyse, G. "Les origines du monachisme dans le diocèse de Besançon (Ve–Xe siècles)." *Bibliothèque de l'École des Chartes* 131 (1973): 21–104, 369–485.

Mullet, M., and A. Kirby, eds. *The Theotokos Evergetis and Eleventh-Century Monasticism*. Belfast Byzantine Texts and Translations 6.1. Belfast: Belfast Byzantine Enterprises, 1994.

Mundò, A. "Il monachesimo nella penisola iberica fino al sec. VII." In *Il monachesimo nell'alto medioevo*, 73–108.

Muschiol, G. *Famula Dei: zur liturgie in merowingischen Frauenklöstern*. Beiträge zur Geschichte des alten Mönchtums und des Benediktinertums 41. Münster: Aschendorff, 1994.

Neiske, F. "Papsttum und Klosterverband." In Keller and Neiske, *Vom Kloster zum Klosterverband*, 252–76.

Oexle, O. G. "Les moines d'Occident et la vie politique et sociale dans le haut Moyen Âge." In Dierkens, Misonne, and Sansterre, *Le monachisme à Byzance*, 255–72.

Orlandis, J. *Estudios sobre institutiones monásticas medievales*. Pamplona: Ediciones Universidad de Navarra, 1971.

Papachryssanthou, D. "La vie monastique dans les campagnes byzantines du VIIIe au XIe siècle: ermitages, groupes, communautés." *Byzantion* 43 (1973): 159–80.

Patrich, J. *Sabas: Leader of Palestinian Monasticism, Fourth to Seventh Centuries*. Dumbarton Oaks Studies 32. Washington, DC: Dumbarton Oaks, 1995.

Picard, J.-M. "Pour une réévaluation du rôle et du statut de l'évêque dans l'Irlande du Haut Moyen Âge." *Médiévales* 42 (2002): 131–52.

Poeck, D. W. *Cluniacensis ecclesia: der cluniacensische Klosterverband (10.-12. Jahrhundert)*. Münstersche Mittelalter-Schriften 71. Münster: Wilhelm Fink Verlag, 1997.

Pratsch, T. *Theodoros Studites (759–826) – zwischen Dogma und Pragma: der Abt des Studiosklosters in Konstantinopel im Spannungsfeld von Patriarch, Kaiser und eigenem Anspruch*. Berliner Byzantinische Studien 4. Frankfurt: Peter Lang, 1998.

Pricoco, S. *L'isola dei Santi: il cenobio di Lerino e le origine del monachesimo gallico*. Roma: Ateneo e Bizzarri, 1978.

Prinz, F. *Frühes Mönchtum im Frankenreich: Kultur und Gesellschaft in Gallien, den Rheinlanden und Bayern am Beispiel der monastischen Entwicklung (4. bis 8. Jahrhundert)*. Munich: R. Oldenbourg Verlag, 1965; 2nd ed. Darmstadt: Wissenschaftliche Buchgesellschaft, 1988.

Rebenich, S. *Hieronymus und sein Kreis: Prosopographische und sozialgeschichtliche Untersuchungen*. Historia: Einzelschriften 72. Stuttgart: Franz Steiner, 1992.

Röckelein, H. *Reliquientranslationen nach Sachsen im 9. Jahrhundert: über Kommunikation, Möbilität und Öffentlichkeit im Frühmittelalter*. Beihefte der Francia 48. Stuttgart: Jan Thorbecke Verlag, 2002.

Rosenwein, B. H. *Negotiating Space: Power, Restraint, and Privileges of Immunity in Early Medieval Europe*. Ithaca, NY: Cornell University Press, 1999.

—. "One Site, Many Meanings: Saint-Maurice d'Agaune as a Place of Power in the Early Middle Ages." In de Jong and Theuws, *Topographies of Power*, 271–90.

—. "Perennial Prayer at Agaune." In *Monks and Nuns, Saints and Outcasts: Religion in Medieval Society. Essays in Honor of Lester K. Little*. Ed. S. Farmer and B. H. Rosenwein. Ithaca, NY: Cornell University Press, 2000, 37–56.

Ryan, J. *Irish Monasticism: Origins and Early Development*. London: Longman, 1931; 2nd ed. Dublin: Irish Academy Press, 1986.

Sansterre, J.-M. "Attitudes à l'égard de l'errance monastique en Occident du VIe au XIe siècle." In *Voyages et voyageurs à Byzance et en Occident du VIe au XIe siècle*. Ed. A. Dierkens and J.-M. Sansterre, with J.-L. Kupper. Bibliothèque de la Faculté de Philosophie et Lettres de l'Université de Liège 278. Geneva: Droz, 2000, 215–34.

—. "Les saints stylites du Ve au XIe siècle, permanence et évolution d'un type de sainteté." In *Sainteté et martyre dans les religions du Livre*. Ed. J. Marx. Problèmes d'histoire du christianisme 19. Brussels: Université libre de Bruxelles, 1989, 33–45.

Schilp, T. *Norm und Wirklichkeit religiöser Frauengemeinschaften in Frühmittelalter: die "institutio sanctimonialium Aquisgranensis" des Jahres 816 und die Problematik der Verfassung von Frauenkommunitäten*. Göttingen: Vandenhoeck and Ruprecht, 1998.

Schmitt, J.-C., and O. G. Oexle, eds. *Les tendances actuelles de l'histoire du Moyen Âge en France et en Allemagne*. Paris: Publications de la Sorbonne, 2002.

Semmler, J. "Benediktinische Reform und kaiserliches Privileg: zur Frage des institutionellen *Zusammenschlusses* der Klöster um Benedikt von Aniane." In *Institutionen und Geschichte: Theoretische Aspekte und Mittelalterliche Befunde*. Ed. G. Melville. Cologne: Böhlau, 1992, 259–93.

—. "Benedictus II: una regula – una consuetudo." In *Benedictine Culture, 750–1050*. Ed. W. Lourdaux and D. Verhelst. Mediaevalia Lovaniensia 1.11. Louvain: Louvain University Press, 1983, 1–49.

—. "Das Erbe der Karolingische Klosterreform im 10. Jahrhundert." In Kottje and Maurer, *Monastische Reformen*, 29–77.

—. "Die Kanoniker und ihre Regel im 9. Jahrhundert." *Studien zum weltlichen Kollegiatstift in Deutschland*. Ed. I. Crusius. Göttingen: Vandenhoeck and Ruprecht, 1995, 62–109.

—. "Karl der Grosse und das fränkische Mönchtum." In *Karl der Grosse: Lebenswerk und Nachleben*. Ed. W. Braunfels. Vol. 2: *Das geistige Leben*. Ed. B. Bischoff. Düsseldorf: Schwann, 1966, 255–89.

—. "Le monachisme occidental du VIIIe au Xe siècle: formation et réformation." In Dierkens, Misonne, and Sansterre, *Le monachisme à Byzance*, 68–89.

—. "Mönche und Kanoniker im Frankenreiche Pippins III. und Karls des Grossen." In *Untersuchungen zu Kloster und Stift*. Veröffentlichungen des Max-Planck-Instituts für Geschichte 68. Göttingen: Vandenhoeck and Ruprecht, 1980, 78–111.

—. "Pippin III und die fränkischen Klöster." *Francia* 3 (1975): 88–146.

—. "Saint-Denis: von der bischöflichen Coemeterialbasilika zur königlichen Benediktinerabtei." In Atsma, *La Neustrie* 2, 75–123.

—. "Zehngebot und Pfarrtermination in karolinger Zeit." In *Aus Kirche und Reich: Studien zur Theologie, Politik und Recht im Mittelalter, Festschrift für Friedrich Kempf*. Ed. H. Mordek. Sigmaringen: Jan Thorbecke Verlag, 1983, 33–44.

Sharpe, R. "Some Problems Concerning the Organization of the Church in Early Medieval Ireland." *Peritia* 3 (1984): 230–70.

Svoronos, N. *Les novelles des empereurs macédoniens concernant la terre et les stratiotes: introduction, édition, commentaires*. Athens: Centre de recherche byzantines, F.N.R.S./Fondation culturelle de la Banque Nationale, 1994.

Talbot, A.-M. "A Comparison of Monastic Experience of Byzantine Men and Women." *Greek Orthodox Theological Review* 30 (1985): 1–20. Reprinted as ch. 12 in her *Women and Religious Life in Byzantium*. Aldershot: Ashgate, 2001.

—. "Les saintes montagnes à Byzance." In *Le sacré et son inscription dans l'espace à Byzance et en Occident: études comparées*. Ed. M. Kaplan. Byzantina Sorbonensia 18. Paris: Publications de la Sorbonne, 2001, 263–76.

Theurillat, J.-M. *L'abbaye de Saint-Maurice d'Agaune des origines à la réforme canoniale, 515–830*. *Vallesia* 9 (1954): 1–128.

Van Dam, R. *Saints and their Miracles in Late Antique Gaul*. Princeton, NJ: Princeton University Press, 1993.

Van Rossem, M. "De poort in de muur: vrouwenkloosters onder de Regel van Caesarius." *Jaarboek voor vrouwengeschiedenis* 4 (1983): 41–91.

Vauchez, A., ed. *Ermites de France et d'Italie (XIe–XVe siècle)*. Collection de l'école française de Rome 313. Rome: École française de Rome, 2003.

von Campenhausen, H. F. "The Ascetic Ideal of Exile in Ancient and Early Medieval Monasticism." In his *Tradition and Life in the Church*. London: Collins, 1968, 231–51.

Wollasch, J. *Cluny, Licht der Welt: Aufstieg und Niedergang der klösterlichen Gemeinschaft*. Zürich: Artemis and Winkler, 1996.

—. *Mönchtum des Mittelalters zwischen Kirche und Welt*. Münstersche Mittelalter-Schriften 7. Munich: Wilhelm Fink Verlag, 1973.

Wood, I. "The Mission of Augustine of Canterbury to the English." *Speculum* 69 (1994): 1–17.

—. *The Missionary Life: Saints and the Evangelisation of Europe, 400–1050*. Harlow: Pearson Education, 2001.

—. "A Prelude to Columbanus: The Monastic Achievement in the Burgundian Territories." In *Columbanus and Merovingian Monasticism*. Ed. H. B. Clarke and M. Brennan. *British Archaeological Reports* 113. Oxford: British Archaeological Reports International Series, 1981, 3–32.

14 Law and its applications
Janet L. Nelson

Primary sources

Agobard of Lyons. *Adversus legem Gundobadi*. In *Agobardi Lugdunensis opera omnia*. Ed. L. van Acker. *CCCM* 52. Turnhout: Brepols, 1981, 17–28.

Annales Bertiniani: Annales de Saint-Bertin. Ed. F. Grat, J. Vielliard, and S. Clémencet. Paris: Librairie C. Klincksieck, Librairie de la Société de l'histoire de France, 1964. Trans. J. L. Nelson. *The Annals of St-Bertin: Ninth-Century Histories I*. Manchester: Manchester University Press, 1991.

Annales regni Francorum. Ed. F. Kurze. *MGH SRG*. Hanover: Hahn, 1895.

Ansegis. *Collectio capitularium: Die Kapitulariensammlung des Ansegis*. Ed. G. Schmitz. *MGH Capitularia regum Francorum, nova series* 1. Hanover: Hahn, 1996.

Burchard of Worms. *Decretorum libri XX*. *PL* 140, 537–1058.

Les canons des conciles mérovingiens (VIe–VIIe siècles). Ed. J. Gaudemet and B. Basdevant. *SC* 353, 354. Paris: Éditions du Cerf, 1989.

Canterbury Professions. Ed. M. Richter. Canterbury and York Society 67. Torquay: Devonshire Press, 1973.

Capitula episcoporum. Ed. P. Brommer, R. Pokorny, and M. Stratmann. *MGH Capitula episcoporum* 1–3. Hanover: Hahn, 1984–95.

Capitularia regum Francorum. Ed. A. Boretius and V. Krause. *MGH Legum sectio* II. 2 vols. Reprint of 1883, 1897 eds. Hanover: Hahn, 1984.

Carmen de Timone Comite. Ed. E. Dümmler. *MGH Poetae latinae* 1.2. Berlin: Weidmann, 1881, 120–24.

Caroli Magni Diplomata. Ed. E. Mühlbacher, A. Dopsch, J. Lechner, and M. Tangl. *MGH Diplomata regum Karolinorum*. Hanover, Hahn, 1906, 81–478.

Codex Theodosianus. Ed. T. Mommsen and P. M. Meyer. Berlin: Weidmann, 1905. Trans. C. Pharr et al. *The Theodosian Code and the Sirmondian Constitutions*. New York: Princeton University Press, 1952.

La colección canónica Hispana. Ed. G. Martínez Díez and F. Rodriguez. Vols. 1, 4, 5, and 6. Monumenta Hispaniae Sacra, serie canónica 1, 4, 5, and 6. Madrid: Consejo Superior de Investigaciones Científicas, 1966, 1984, 1992, 2002.

Concilia aevi Karolini, 742–842. Vol. 1, pt. 1 (742–842). Ed. A. Werminghoff. *MGH Concilia* 2, pt. 1 (= *MGH Leges* 3). Reprint of 1906 ed. Hanover: Hahn, 1997.

Concilia aevi Karolini, 860–874. Ed. W. Hartmann. *Die Konzilien der Karolingischen Teilreiche, 860–874*. *MGH Concilia* 4 (= *MGH Leges* 4). Hanover: Hahn, 1998.

Conciliorum oecumenicorum decreta: Decrees of the Ecumenical Councils. Ed. and trans. N. P. Tanner. London: Sheed and Ward, 1990; alternate translation at website: http: // www.piar.hu / councils

Council in Trullo decrees. In Nedungatt and Featherstone, *Council in Trullo*, 45–186.

Cresconius. *Concordia canonum*. In *Die Concordia canonum des Cresconius: Studien und Edition*. Ed. K. Zechiel-Eckes. 2 vols. Freiburger Beiträge zur mittelalterliche Geschichte 5. Freiburg: Peter Lang, 1992, 419–798.

Diversorum patrum sententiae sive Collectio in LXXIV titulos digesta. Ed. J. T. Gilchrist. *Monumenta Iuris Canonici*. Vatican City: Biblioteca apostolica vaticana, 1973. Trans. J. T. Gilchrist. *The Collection in Seventy-Four Titles: A Canon Law Manual of the Gregorian Reform*. Toronto: Pontifical Institute of Medieval Studies, 1980.

Flodoard. *Historia remensis ecclesiae: Die Geschichte der Reimser Kirche*. Ed. M. Stratmann. *MGH Scriptores* 36. Hanover: Hahn, 1998.

Formulae Andegavenses. Ed. K. Zeumer. *MGH Formulae Merowingici et Karolini Aevi* (= *MGH Legum* 5). Hanover: Hahn, 1886, 91–95.

Hadrian I. *Domino excell. filio carulo magno regi. MGH Poetae latinae* 1, 90–91.
Hadrian II. *Epistolae*. Ed. E. Perels. *MGH Epistolae* 6. Berlin: Weidmann, 1925.
Hincmar of Rheims. *Collectio de ecclesiis et capellis*. Ed. M. Stratmann. *MGH Fontes iuris germanici antiqui* 14. Hanover: Hahn, 1990.
—. *De coercendo et exstirpando raptu viduarum, puellarum et sanctimonialium. PL* 125, 1017–36.
—. *De divortio Lotharii*. Ed. L. Böhringer. *MGH Concilia* 4, *Supplementum* 1. Hanover: Hahn, 1992.
—. *De ordine palatii*. Ed. T. Gross and R. Schieffer. *MGH Fontes* 145. Hanover: Hahn, 1990.
—. *De presbiteris criminosis: Ein Memorandum Erzbischof Hinkmars von Reims über straffällige Kleriker*. Ed. G. Schmitz. *MGH Studien und Texte* 34. Hanover, Hahn, 2004.
—. *De villa Noviliaco et capitula*. In Mordek, *Studien zur fränkischen Herrschergesetzgebung*, 293–305.
—. *Epistolae. PL* 126, 1–280.
—. *Epistolae* [845–68]. Ed. E. Perels. *MGH Epistolae* 7 (i). Berlin: Weidmann, 1939.
—. *Opuscula et Epistolae. PL* 126, 279–648.
Die Konzilsordines des Früh- und Hochmittelalters. Ed. H. Schneider. *MGH Ordines de celebrando concilio*. Hanover: Hahn, 1996.
Liber Pontificalis, texte, introduction et commentaire. Ed. L. Duchesne. 2 vols. Paris: E. de Boccard, 1886–92. Reprinted with additional material and indices in a third volume. Ed. C. Vogel. Paris: E. de Boccard, 1955–57. Trans. R. Davis. Vol. 1: *The Book of the Pontiffs (Liber Pontificalis)*. Liverpool: Liverpool University Press, 1989; Vol. 2: *The Eighth-Century Popes*. Liverpool: Liverpool University Press, 1992; Vol. 3: *The Ninth-Century Popes*. Liverpool: Liverpool University Press, 1995.
Martin of Braga. *Capitula. PL* 84, 575–87.
Nicholas I. *Epistolae*. Ed. E. Perels. *MGH Epistolae* 6. Berlin: Weidmann, 1925.
Pontificale Romano-Germanicum. Ed. C. Vogel and R. Elze. *Le pontifical romano-germanique du Xe siècle*. Studi e Testi 206, 207, 269. Vatican City: Biblioteca apostolica vaticana, 1966, 1972.
Regino of Prüm. *Libri duo de synodalibus causis et disciplinis ecclesiasticis*. In *Das Sendbuch des Regino von Prüm*. Ed. and trans. W. Hartmann (based on the earlier edition of F. W. H. Wasserschleben, Leipzig, 1840.). Ausgewählte Quellen zur deutschen Geschichte des Mittelalters 42. Darmstadt: Wissenschaftliche Buchgesellschaft, 2004.
Schieffer, R., ed. *Die Streitschriften Hinkmars von Reims und Hinkmars von Laon (869–871). MGH Concilia* 4, *Supplementum* 2. Hanover: Hahn, 2003.
Thegan. *Gesta Hludowici imperatoris*. Ed. E. Tremp. *MGH SRG* 64. Hanover: Hahn, 1995.
Theodulf. *Contra iudices* (Carmen xxviii). Ed. E. Dümmler. *MGH Poetae latinae* 1, 493–517.
Weidemann, M., ed. *Geschichte des Bistums Le Mans von der Spätantike bis zur Karolingerzeit: Actus Pontificum Cenomannis in urbe degentium und Gesta Aldrici*. 3 vols. Mainz: Verlag des Römisch-Germanischen Zentralmuseums, 2002.

Electronic sources

21st International Congress of Byzantine Studies: http://www.byzantinecongress.org.uk/plenary/VI/VI_Magdalino.pdf

Decrees of the Ecumenical Councils, in English translation: http://www.fordham.edu/halsall/sbook-law.html#ROMAN%20LAW (Internet Medieval Source Book) http://www.piar.hu/councils/

Projekt Pseudoisidor website: http://www.pseudoisidor.mgh.de/html contains Pseudo-Isidore *Decretals* with introduction and explanatory material. Ed. K.-G. Schon and K. Zechiel-Eckes.

Secondary sources

Airlie, S. "Private Bodies and the Body Politic in the Divorce Case of Lothar II." *Past and Present* 161 (199): 3–38.

Anderson, P. *Passages from Antiquity to Feudalism*. London: Verso, 1974.

Austin, G. "Jurisprudence in the Service of Pastoral Care: The *Decretum* of Burchard of Worms." *Speculum* 79 (2004): 929–59.

Becher, M., and J. Jarnut, eds. *Der Dynastiewechsel von 751: Vorgeschichte, Legitimationsstrategien und Erinnerung*. Münster: Scriptorium, 2004.

Blair, J. *The Church in Anglo-Saxon Society*. Oxford: Oxford University Press, 2005.

Brown, W. *Unjust Seizure: Conflict, Interest and Authority in an Early Medieval Society*. Ithaca, NY: Cornell University Press, 2001.

Brubaker, L., ed. *Byzantium in the Ninth Century: Dead or Alive?* Aldershot: Ashgate, 1998.

Brundage, J. A. *Medieval Canon Law*. London: Longman, 1995.

Chadwick, H. *East and West: The Making of a Rift in the Church from Apostolic Times until the Council of Florence*. Oxford: Oxford University Press, 2003.

Claussen, M. A. *The Reform of the Frankish Church: Chrodegang of Metz and the Regula canonicorum in the Eighth Century*. Cambridge: Cambridge University Press, 2004.

Constable, G. *Monastic Tithes from their Origins to the Twelfth Century*. Cambridge: Cambridge University Press, 1964.

Cubitt, C. *Anglo-Saxon Church Councils c. 650–c. 850*. London: Leicester University Press, 1995.

Cushing, K. *Papacy and Law in the Gregorian Revolution: The Canonistic Work of Anselm of Lucca*. Oxford: Oxford University Press, 1998.

Dagron, G. *Emperor and Priest: The Imperial Office in Byzantium*. Cambridge: Cambridge University Press, 2003.

Davies, R. "The Medieval State: The Tyranny of a Concept?" *Journal of the History of Sociology* 16 (2003): 280–300.

Davies, W. "Clerics as Rulers: Some Implications of the Terminology of Ecclesiastical Authority in Early Medieval Ireland." In *Latin and the Vernacular Languages in Early Medieval Britain*. Ed. N. P. Brooks. Leicester: Leicester University Press, 1982, 81–97.

—, and P. Fouracre, eds. *Property and Power in the Early Middle Ages*. Cambridge: Cambridge University Press, 1995.

Dură, N. "The Ecumenicity of the Council in Trullo: Witnesses of the Canonical Tradition in East and West." In Nedungatt and Featherstone, *Council in Trullo*, 229–62.

Epp, V. "499–799: von Theoderich dem Großen zu Karl dem Großen." In *Am Vorabend der Kaiserkrönung: das Epos "Karolus magnus et Leo papa" und der Papstbesuch in Paderborn 799*. Ed. P. Godman, J. Jarnut, and P. Johanek. Berlin: Akademie Verlag, 2002, 219–30.

Esders, S., and H. J. Mierau. *Der althochdeutsche Klerikereid: bischöfliche Diözenangewalt, kirchliches Benefizialwesen und volkssprachliche Rechtspraxis im frühmittelalterlichen Baiern.* Hanover: Hahn, 2000.

Fälschungen im Mittelalter: Internationaler Kongreß der MGH, München, 16.–19. September 1986. 6 vols. *MGH Schriften* 33. Hanover: Hahn, 1988.

Fichtenau, H. *Heretics and Scholars in the High Middle Ages, 1000–1200.* University Park, PA: Pennsylvania State University Press, 1998.

Fletcher, R. *The Conversion of Europe: From Paganism to Christianity, 371–1386.* London: HarperCollins, 1997.

Fögen, M. T. "Reanimation of Roman Law in the Ninth Century: Remarks on Reasons and Results." In Brubaker, *Byzantium*, 11–22.

Fournier, P. "Le *Liber ex Lege Moysi* et les tendances bibliques du droit canonique irlandais." *Revue Celtique* 30 (1909): 221–34.

Fransen, G. *Les collections canoniques: typologie des sources du Moyen Âge occidental.* Turnhout: Brepols, 1973.

Fuhrmann, H. *Einfluß und Verbreitung der pseudoisidorischen Fälschungen.* 3 vols. *MGH Schriften* 24. Stuttgart: Hiersemann, 1972–74.

—. "Fälscher unter sich." In Gibson and Nelson, *Charles the Bald*, 224–34.

—. "Papst Gregor VII. und das Kirchenrecht: zum Problem des *Dictatus Papae*." *Studi Gregoriani* 13 (1989): 123–49.

Ganz, D. "The Ideology of Sharing: Apostolic Community and Ecclesiastical Property in the Early Middle Ages." In Davies and Fouracre, *Property and Power*, 17–30.

Gibson, M. T., and J. L. Nelson, eds. *Charles the Bald: Court and Kingdom.* 2nd ed. Aldershot: Variorum, 1991.

Gierke, O. *Political Theories of the Middle Ages.* Trans. with an introduction by F. W. Maitland. Cambridge: Cambridge University Press, 1900.

Gilchrist, J. T. "Canon Law Aspects of the Eleventh-Century Gregorian Reform Programme." *Journal of Ecclesiastical History* 13 (1962): 21–38; reprint in Gilchrist, *Canon Law*, ch. 3.

—. *Canon Law in the Age of Reform, 11th–12th Centuries.* Aldershot: Variorum, 1993.

—. "Gregory VII and the Juristic Sources of his Ideology." *Studia Gratiana* 12 (1967): 3–37; reprint in Gilchrist, *Canon Law*, ch. 5.

Goffart, W. *The Le Mans Forgeries: A Chapter from the History of Church Property in the Ninth Century.* Cambridge, MA: Harvard University Press, 1966.

Haldon, J. "The Byzantine State in the Ninth Century: An Introduction." In Brubaker, *Byzantium*, 3–10.

Hamilton, S. *The Practice of Penance, 900–1050.* Woodbridge: Boydell Press, 2001.

Harries, J., and I. Wood, eds. *The Theodosian Code: Studies in the Imperial Law of Late Antiquity.* London: Duckworth, 1993.

Harrington, C. *Women in a Celtic Church: Ireland 450–1150.* Oxford: Oxford University Press, 2002.

Hartmann, W. "Der Bischof als Richter. Zum geistlichen Gericht über kriminelle Vergehen von Laien im früheren Mittelalter (6–11 Jahrhundert)." *Römische Historische Mitteilungen* 28 (1986): 103–24.

—, ed. *Bischof Burchard von Worms, 1000–1025.* Mainz: Gesellschaft für mittelrheinische Kirchengeschichte, 2000.

—. "Probleme des geistlichen Gerichts im 10. und 11. Jahrhundert: Bischöfe und Synoden als Richter im ostfränkisch-deutschen Reich." In *La guistizia nell-alto medioevo (secoli IX-XI), 11–17 aprile 1996*. Vol. 2. Settimane di studio 44. Spoleto, Centro italiano di studi sull'alto medioevo, 1997, 631–74.

—, and G. Schmitz, eds. *Fortschritt durch Fälschungen? Ursprung, Gestalt und Wirkungen der pseudoisidorischen Fälschungen. MGH Studien und Texte* 31. Hanover: Hahn, 2002.

Hen, Y. *The Royal Patronage of Liturgy in Frankish Gaul to the Death of Charles the Bald (877)*. Henry Bradshaw Society Subsidia 3. London: Boydell, 2001.

—, and M. Innes, eds. *The Uses of the Past in the Early Middle Ages*. Cambridge: Cambridge University Press, 2000.

Herrin, J. *The Formation of Christendom*. London: Weidenfeld and Nicolson, 1986.

—. "The Pentarchy: Theory and Reality in the Ninth Century." In *Cristianità d'Occidente et Cristianità d'Oriente (secoli VI–XI)*. Vol 1. Settimane di studio 51. Spoleto: Centro italiano di studi sull'alto medioevo, 2004, 591–628.

Hoffmann, H., and R. Pokorny. *Das Dekret des Bischofs Burchard von Worms: Textstufen, Frühe Verbreitung, Vorlagen. MGH Hilfsmittel* 12. Munich: MGH, 1991.

Innes, M. "Danelaw Identities: Ethnicity, Regionalism, and Political Allegiance." In *Cultures in Contact: Scandinavian Settlement in England in the Ninth and Tenth Centuries*. Ed. D. M. Hadley and J. D. Richards. Turnhout: Brepols, 2000, 65–88.

Kéry, L. *Canonical Collections of the Early Middle Ages (c. 400–1140): A Bibliographical Guide to the Manuscripts and Literature*. Washington, DC: Catholic University of America, 1999.

Körntgen, L. "Canon Law and the Practice of Penance: Burchard of Worms' Penitential." *EME* 14 (2006): 103–17.

Kottje, R. "Einheit und Vielfalt des kirchlichen Lebens in der Karolingerzeit." *Zeitschrift für Kirchengeschichte* 76 (1965): 323–42.

—. *Studien zum Einfluß des Alten Testament auf Recht und Liturgie des früheren Mittelalters (6.–8. Jahrhunderts)*. Bonn: L. Röhrscheid, 1964.

Landau, P. "Gefälschte Recht in den Rechtssammlungen bis Gratian." In *Fälschungen im Mittelalter* 2, 11–49.

—. "Überlieferung und Bedeutung der Kanones des Trullanischen Konzils im westlichen kanonischen Recht." In Nedungatt and Featherstone, *Council in Trullo*, 215–28.

Leyser, K. "The Polemics of the Papal Revolution." In *Trends in Medieval Political Thought*. Ed. B. Smalley. Oxford: Blackwell, 1965, 42–64; reprinted in his *Medieval Germany and its Neighbours, 900–1250*. London: Hambledon, 1982, 138–60.

Löwe, H., ed. *Die Iren und Europa*. 2 vols. Stuttgart: Klett-Cotta, 1982.

Magdalino, P. "The Making of Byzantine Orthodoxy: Definition and Display, Inclusion and Exclusion." 21st International Congress of Byzantine Studies website (see Electronic Sources above).

Markus, R. *The End of Ancient Christianity*. Cambridge: Cambridge University Press, 1990.

McKitterick, R. "Knowledge of Canon Law in the Frankish Kingdoms before 789: The Manuscript Evidence." *Journal of Theological Studies n.s.* 36 (1985): 97–117; reprinted in her *Books, Scribes and Learning in the Frankish Kingdoms, 6th–9th Centuries*. Aldershot: Variorum, 1994, ch. 2.

Meens, R. "Penitential Questions: Sin, Satisfaction and Reconciliation in the Tenth and Eleventh Centuries." *EME* 14 (2006): 1–6.

—. "Penitentials and the Practice of Penance in the Tenth and Eleventh Centuries." *EME* 14 (2006): 7–21.

—. "The Uses of the Old Testament in Early Medieval Canon Law: The *Collectio Vetus Gallica* and the *Collectio Hibernensis*." In Hen and Innes, *Uses of the Past*, 67–77.

Mordek, H. "Aachen, Frankfurt, Reims. Beobachtungen zu Genese und Tradition des 'Capitulare Franconofurtense' (794)." In *Das Frankfurter Konzil von 794*. Ed. R. Berndt. 2 vols. Mainz: Selbstverlag der Gesellschaft für mittelrheinische Kirchengeschichte, 1997, 125–48.

—. "Dionysio-Hadriana und Vetus Gallica – historisches geordnetes und systematisches Kirchenrecht." *Zeitschrift für Rechtsgeschichte* (Kanonistische Abteilung) 55 (1969): 39–63.

—. "Ein exemplarischer Rechtsstreit: Hinkmar von Reims und das Landgut Neuilly-Saint-Front." *Zeitschrift für Rechtsgeschichte* (Kanonistische Abteilung) 83 (1997): 86–112; reprinted in Mordek, *Studien*, 279–305.

—. *Kirchenrecht und Reform im Frankenreich: die Collectio Vetus Gallica, die älteste systematische Kanonessammlung des fränkischen Gallien: Studien und Edition*. Berlin: de Gruyter, 1975.

—. "Zur Kirchenrechtsreform am Beispiel des Frankfurter Kapitulars." In *794–Karl der Große in Frankfurt am Main: ein König bei der Arbeit*. Ed. J. Fried. Sigmaringen: Thorbecke, 1994, 133–36.

—. *Studien zur fränkischen Herrschergesetzgebung: Aufsätze über Kapitulariensammlung ausgewählt zum 60. Geburtstag*. Frankfurt: Peter Lang, 2000.

Müller, J. "Die Kirchenrechtssammlung des Bischofs Burchard I. von Worms." In Hartmann, *Bischof Burchard*, 162–81.

Nedungatt, G., and M. Featherstone, eds. and trans. *The Council in Trullo Revisited*. Rome: Pontificio istituto orientale, 1995.

Nees, L. *A Tainted Mantle: Hercules and the Classical Tradition at the Carolingian Court*. Philadelphia, PA: Pennsylvania University Press, 1991.

Nelson, J. L. "England and the Continent in the Ninth Century, IV: Bodies and Minds." *Transactions of the Royal Historical Society* 15 (2005): 1–27.

—. *The Frankish World, 750–900*. London: Hambledon, 1996.

—. "Making Ends Meet: Wealth and Poverty in the Carolingian Church." *SCH* 24 (1987): 25–36; reprinted in her *Frankish World*, 145–54.

—. "'Not Bishops' Bailiffs but Lords of the Earth': Charles the Bald and the Problem of Sovereignty." In *The Church and Sovereignty: Essays in Honour of Michael Wilks*. Ed. D. Wood. *SCH*, Subsidia 9. Oxford: Blackwell, 1991, 23–34; reprinted in her *Frankish World*, 133–44.

—. *Politics and Ritual in Early Medieval Europe*. London: Hambledon, 1986.

—. "The Wary Widow." In Davies and Fouracre, *Property and Power*, 82–113.

Ní Chathaín, P., and M. Richter, eds. *Ireland and Christendom: The Bible and Missions*. Stuttgart: Klett-Cotta, 1987.

Pitsakis, C. "Clergé marié et célibat dans la legislation du Concile in Trullo: le point de vue oriental." In Nedungatt and Featherstone, *Council in Trullo*, 263–306.

Prinz, F. *Klerus und Krieg im früheren Mittelalter*. Stuttgart: Hiersemann, 1971.

Reuter, T. "Ein Europa der Bischöfe: das Zeitalter Burchards von Worms." In Hartmann, *Bischof Burchard*, 1–28.

Reynolds, R. E. "Rites and Signs of Conciliar Decisions in the Early Middle Ages." *Segni e riti nella chiesa altomedioevale occidentale*. Vol 1. Settimane di studio 33. Spoleto: Centro italiano di studi sull'alto medioevo, 1987, 207–49.

—. "Unity and Diversity in Carolingian Canon Law Collections: The Case of the *Collectio hibernensis* and its Derivatives." In *Carolingian Essays*. Ed. U.-R. Blumenthal. Washington, DC: Catholic University of America Press, 1984, 99–135.

Rio, A. "Early Medieval Frankish Formularies." Ph.D. diss., University of London, 2006.

Robinson, I. S. "Church and Papacy." In *The Cambridge History of Medieval Political Thought, c. 350–c. 1450*. Ed. J. H. Burns. Cambridge: Cambridge University Press, 1988, 252–305.

—. "Gregory VII and the Soldiers of Christ." *History* 58 (1973): 169–92.

Rouche, M. *L'Aquitaine des Wisigoths aux Arabes, 418–781: naissance d'une région*. Paris: Éditions de l'école des hautes études en sciences sociales, 1979.

Schmitz, G. "Ansegis und Regino." *Zeitschrift für Rechtsgeschichte* (Kanonistische Abteilung) 74 (1988): 95–132.

Schröder, I. *Die westfränkische Synoden von 888 bis 987 und ihre Überlieferung. MGH Hilfsmittel* 3. Hanover: Hahn, 1980.

Schulz, K. "Das Wormser Hofrecht Bischof Burchards." In Hartmann, *Bischof Burchard*, 251–78.

Semmler, J. *Der Dynastiewechsel von 751 und die fränkische Königssalbung*. Düsseldorf: Droste Verlag, 2003.

Sheehy, M. P. "The Bible and the *Collectio Canonum Hibernensis*." In Ni Chatháin and Richter, *Ireland and Christendom*, 277–83.

—. "The *Collectio Canonum Hibernensis*–A Celtic Phenomenon." In Löwe, *Die Iren und Europa* 1, 525–35.

Smith, J. M. H. *Europe after Rome*. Oxford: Oxford University Press, 2005.

Somerville, R., and B. C. Brasington. *Prefaces to Canon Law Books in Latin Christianity: Selected Translations*. Yale, CT: Yale University Press, 1998.

Southern, R. W. *Western Society and the Church in the Middle Ages*. Harmondsworth: Penguin, 1970.

Stone, R. "The Invention of a Theology of Abduction: Hincmar of Rheims on *raptus*." *Journal of Ecclesiastical History* 60 (2009), forthcoming.

Stratmann, M. *Hinkmar von Reims als Verwalter von Bistum und Kirchenprovinz*. Quellen und Forschungen zum Recht im Mittelalter, Band 6. Sigmaringen: Thorbecke, 1991.

Tellenbach, G. *The Church in Western Europe from the Tenth to the Early Twelfth Century*. [*Die westliche Kirche vom 10. bis zum frühen 12. Jahrhundert*. (1988)] Trans. T. Reuter. Cambridge: Cambridge University Press, 1993.

Tinti, F. "The 'Costs' of Pastoral Care: Church Dues in Late Anglo-Saxon England." In *Pastoral Care in Late Anglo-Saxon England*. Ed. F. Tinti. Woodbridge: Boydell Press, 2005, 27–51.

Ullmann, W. *The Growth of Papal Government in the Middle Ages*. London: Methuen, 1955.

—. *Law and Politics in the Middle Ages*. London: Hodder and Stoughton, 1975.

van der Wal, N., and J. H. A. Lokin. *Historiae iuris graeco-romani delineatio: les sources du droit byzantin de 300 à 1453*. Groningen: Egbert Forsten, 1985.

van Rhijn, C. *Shepherds of the Lord: Priests and Episcopal Statutes in the Carolingian Period.* Cultural Encounters in Late Antiquity and the Middle Ages 6. Turnhout: Brepols, 2007.

Wemple, S. Fonay. *Women in Frankish Society: Marriage and the Cloister*. Philadelphia, PA: University of Pennsylvania Press, 1981.

Wolfram, H. *Die Geburt Mitteleuropas*. Vienna: Siedler Verlag, 1987.

Wood, I. "The Code in Merovingian Gaul." In Harries and Wood, *Theodosian Code*, 161–77.

Wood, S. *The Proprietary Church in the Medieval West*. Oxford: Oxford University Press, 2006.

Wormald, P. *The Making of English Law: King Alfred to the Twelfth Century.* Vol. 1: *Legislation and its Limits*. Oxford: Blackwell, 1999.

Zechiel-Eckes, K. "Auf Pseudoisidors Spur. Oder: Versuch, einen dichten Schleier zu lüften." In Hartmann and Schmitz, *Fortschritt durch Fälschungen?* 1–28.

—. "Der 'unbeugsame' Exterminator? Isidorus Mercator und der Kampf gegen der Chorepiskopat." In *Scientia Veritatis: Festschrift für Hubert Mordek zum 65. Geburtstag.* Ed. O. Münsch and T. Zotz. Sigmaringen: Thorbecke, 2004, 173–90.

15 The problems of property
Rosemary Morris

Primary sources

Basil II. *Novel* (996). In Svoronos and Gounarides, *Les novelles*. Document 14, 190–217. Eng. trans. McGeer, *Land Legislation*, Document O, 111–13.

Bede. *Epistola ad Ecgbertum*. In *Venerabilis Baedae Opera Historica*. Ed. C. Plummer. Vol. 1. Oxford: Clarendon Press, 1896, 405–23. Eng. trans. in *English Historical Documents*. Ed. D. C. Douglas. Vol. 1, no. 170. London: Eyre and Spottiswoode, 1955, 735–45.

Chartae Latinae Antiquiores. Ed. A. Bruckner. Vols. 1–2. Olten: URS Garf-Verlag, 1954.

Chronicon Farfense di Gregorio di Catino. Ed. U. Balzani. 2 vols. Fonti per la storia d'Italia 33–34. Rome: Istituto storico Italiano, 1903.

Chronicon Vulturnense. Ed. V. Federici. 3 vols. Fonti per la storia d'Italia 58–60. Rome: Istituto storico Italiano, 1925 (58, 59) 1938 (60).

Constantinus Porphyrogenitus. *De administrando imperio*. Vol. 1: *Text*. Ed. G. Moravcsik, trans. R. J. H. Jenkins. Rev. ed. Washington, DC: Dumbarton Oaks, 1967. Vol. 2: *Commentary*. Ed. R. J. H. Jenkins. London: Athlone Press, 1962.

Eddius Stephanus. *The Life of Bishop Wilfrid*. Ed. and trans. B. Colgrave. Cambridge: Cambridge University Press, 1985.

Gregory Pakourianos. *Typikon*. In P. Gautier, ed. "Le typikon du sébaste Grégoire Pakourianos." *Revue des études byzantines* 42 (1964): 5–145. Eng. trans. R. Jordan, *BMFD* 2, document 23, 507–63.

Life of St. Nikon. Ed. and trans. D. Sullivan. Brookline, MA: St. Vladimir's Seminary Press, 1987.

McGeer, E. *The Land Legislation of the Macedonian Emperors*. Toronto: Pontifical Institute of Medieval Studies, 2000.

Nicephorus II Phocas. *Novel* (963/4). In Svoronos and Gounarides, *Les novelles*. Document 8, 151–61. Eng. trans. McGeer, *Land Legislation*, Document J, 90–96.

Noailles, P., and A. Dain, eds. *Les novelles de Léon VI le Sage: texte et traduction*. Paris: Les Belles Lettres, 1944.

Svoronos, N., and P. Gounarides, eds. *Les novelles des empereurs macédoniens concernant la terre et les stratiotes*. Athens: Centre de recherches byzantins/Fondation culturelle de la Banque nationale, 1994.

Syntagma canonum. *PG* 104, 441–976.

Vita S. Lazari auctore Gregorio monacho. *AASS* Nov. 3, 508–88. Trans. R. P. H. Greenfield. *The Life of St. Lazaros of Mt. Galesion: An Eleventh-Century Pillar Saint, Introduction, Translation, and Notes*. Byzantine Saints' Lives in Translation 3. Washington, DC: Dumbarton Oaks Research Library and Collection, 2000.

Secondary sources

Abrams, L. *Anglo-Saxon Glastonbury: Church and Endowment*. Woodbridge: Boydell Press, 1996.

—. "Conversion and Assimilation." In Hadley and Richards, *Cultures in Contact*, 135–53.

Anton, H. H. *Studien zu den Klosterprivilegien der Päpste im frühen Mittelalter*. Berlin: de Gruyter, 1975.

Barrow, J. "Survival and Mutation: Ecclesiastical Institutions in the Danelaw in the Ninth and Tenth Centuries." In Hadley and Richards, *Cultures in Contact*, 155–176.

Berlière, U. "Le nombre des moines dans les anciens monastères." *Revue bénédictine* 41 (1929): 231–61; 42 (1930): 19–42.

Bernhardt, J. W. *Itinerant Kingship and Royal Monasteries in Early Medieval Germany, c. 936–1075*. Cambridge: Cambridge University Press, 1993.

Blair, J., and R. Sharpe, eds. *Pastoral Care before the Parish*. London: Leicester University Press, 1992.

Bloch, H. *Monte Cassino in the Middle Ages*. 3 vols. Cambridge, MA: Harvard University Press, 1983.

Bouchard, C. B. *Sword, Miter and Cloister: Nobility and the Church in Burgundy, 980–1198*. Ithaca, NY: Cornell University Press, 1987.

Boyd, C. E. *Tithes and Parishes in Medieval Italy: The Historical Roots of a Modern Problem*. Ithaca, NY: Cornell University Press, 1952.

Charles-Edwards, T. M. "The Pastoral Role of the Church in the Early Irish Laws." In Blair and Sharpe, *Pastoral Care*, 63–80.

Clanchy, M. J. *From Memory to Written Record: England, 1066–1307*. London: Edward Arnold, 1979.

Constable, G. "Forgery and Plagiarism in the Middle Ages." *Archiv für Diplomatik* 29 (1983): 1–41.

—. *Monastic Tithes: From their Origins to the Twelfth Century*. Cambridge: Cambridge University Press, 1964.

Cowdrey, H. E. J. *The Age of Abbot Desiderius*. Oxford: Clarendon Press, 1983.

Crawford, B. E. "The Vikings." In Davies, *From the Vikings*, ch. 2.

Cubitt, C. R. E. *Anglo-Saxon Church Councils, c. 650–c. 850*. London: Leicester University Press, 1995.

Davies, W., ed. *From the Vikings to the Normans*. Oxford: Oxford University Press, 2003.

—. *Small Worlds: The Village Community in Early Medieval Brittany*. London: Duckworth, 1988.

——, and P. Fouracre, eds. *Property and Power in the Early Middle Ages*. Cambridge: Cambridge University Press, 1995.

——, and P. Fouracre, eds. *The Settlement of Disputes in Early Medieval Europe*. Cambridge: Cambridge University Press, 1986.

Dembinska, M. "Diet: A Comparison of Food Consumption between Some Eastern and Western Monasteries in the 4th–12th Centuries." *Byzantion* 55 (1985): 431–62.

Devroey, J.-P. *Études sur le grand domaine carolingien*. Aldershot: Variorum, 1993.

Dyer, C. *Lords and Peasants in a Changing Society: The Estates of the Bishopric of Worcester, 680–1540*. Cambridge: Cambridge University Press, 1980.

Feine, H. E. *Kirchliche Rechtesgeschichte: die katholische Kirche*. 4th ed. Cologne: Böhlau, 1964.

Fleckenstein, J. *Early Medieval Germany*. Trans. B. S. Smith. Amsterdam: North-Holland Publishing, 1978.

Fouracre, P. *The Age of Charles Martel*. Harlow: Longman, 2000.

Gautier, P. "Réquisitoire du patriarche Jean d'Antioche contre le charisticariat." *Revue des études byzantines* 33 (1975): 77–132.

Geary, P. J. *Living with the Dead in the Middle Ages*. Ithaca, NY: Cornell University Press, 1994.

Goffart, W. *The Le Mans Forgeries: A Chapter from the History of Church Property in the Ninth Century*. Cambridge, MA: Harvard University Press, 1966.

Hackel, S., ed. *The Byzantine Saint*. Studies Subordinate to *Sobornost* 5. London: Fellowship of St. Alban and St. Sergius, 1981.

Hadley, D. M. "Conquest, Colonization and the Church: Ecclesiastical Organization in the Danelaw." *Historical Research* 69 (1996): 109–208.

——, and J. D. Richards, eds. *Cultures in Contact: Scandinavian Settlement in England in the Ninth and Tenth Centuries*. Turnhout: Brepols, 2000.

Hansen, I. L., and C. Wickham, eds. *The Long Eighth Century*. The Transformation of the Roman World 11. Leiden: Brill, 2000.

Hartung, W. "Adel, Erbrecht, Schenkung: die strukturellen Ursachen der frühmittelalterlichen Besitzübertragungen an die Kirche." In *Gesellschaftsgeschichte: Festschrift für Karl Bosl zum 80. Geburtstag*. Ed. F. Siebt. Munich: Oldenbourg, 1988, 417–38.

Hirschfeld, Y. *The Judean Desert Monasteries in the Byzantine Period*. New Haven, CT: Yale University Press, 1992.

Hodges, R. *Light in the Dark Ages: The Rise and Fall of San Vincenzo al Volturno*. London: Duckworth, 1997.

——, ed. *San Vincenzo al Volturno 2: The 1980–86 Excavations, Pt. II*. Archaeological Monographs of the British School at Rome, no. 9. London: British School, 1995.

Howe, J. *Church Reform and Social Change in Eleventh-Century Italy: Dominic of Sora and his Patrons*. Philadelphia, PA: University of Pennsylvania Press, 1997.

Hughes, K. *The Church in Early Irish Society*. London: Methuen, 1966.

Innes, M. *State and Society in the Early Middle Ages: The Middle Rhine Valley, 400–1000*. Cambridge: Cambridge University Press, 2000.

Kaplan, M. *Les hommes et la terre à Byzance de VIe au XIe siècle: propriété et exploitation du sol*. Paris: Publications de la Sorbonne, 1992.

Lebecq, S. "The Role of Monasteries in the Systems of Production and Exchange in the Frankish World between the Seventh and the Ninth Centuries." In Hansen and Wickham, *Long Eighth Century*, 123–39.

Lesne, E. *Histoire de la propriété ecclésiastique en France*. 6 vols. Lille: Facultés catholiques, 1910–43; repr. New York: Johnson Reprint Corp., 1964.
—. "Les origins de la prébende." *Revue historique de droit français et étranger*. 4th ser. 8 (1929): 242–90.
Leyser, H. *Hermits and the New Monasticism*. London: Macmillan, 1984.
Leyser, K. "The German Aristocracy from the Ninth to the Early Twelfth Century: A Historical and Cultural Sketch." *Past and Present* 41 (1968): 25–53; reprinted in his *Medieval Germany*, 161–89.
—. *Medieval Germany and its Neighbours*. London: Hambledon, 1982.
—. "Ottonian Government." *English Historical Review* 96 (1981): 721–53; reprinted in his *Medieval Germany*, 69–101.
—. *Rule and Conflict in an Early Medieval Society: Ottonian Saxony*. London: Edward Arnold, 1979.
Lifshitz, F. "The Migration of Neustrian Relics in the Viking Age: The Myth of Voluntary Exodus, the Reality of Coercion and Theft." *EME* 4/2 (1995): 175–92.
Linehan, P., and J. L. Nelson, eds. *The Medieval World*. London: Routledge, 2001.
Little, L. K. *Religious Poverty and the Profit Economy in Medieval Europe*. London: Paul Elek, 1978.
Magdalino, P. "The Byzantine Holy Man in the Twelfth Century." In Hackel, *Byzantine Saint*, 51–66.
McKitterick, R. *The Frankish Kingdoms under the Carolingians, 751–987*. London: Longman, 1983.
Miller, E. *The Abbey and Bishopric of Ely*. Cambridge: Cambridge University Press, 1951.
Morris, R. "Dispute Settlement in the Byzantine Provinces in the Tenth Century." In Davies and Fouracre, *Settlement of Disputes*, 125–47.
—. "Monastic Exemptions in Tenth- and Eleventh-Century Byzantium." In Davies and Fouracre, *Property and Power*, 200–20.
—. *Monks and Laymen in Byzantium, 843–1118*. Cambridge: Cambridge University Press, 1995.
—. "Mount Athos." In *Oxford Handbook of Byzantine Studies*. Eds. E. Jeffreys et al. Oxford: Oxford University Press, forthcoming.
Mullett, M. E. "Byzantium: A Friendly Society?" *Past and Present* 118 (1988): 3–24.
Nelson, J. L. "England and the Continent in the Ninth Century, I: Ends and Beginnings." *Transactions of the Royal Historical Society* 12 (2002): 1–21.
—. "England and the Continent in the Ninth Century, II: The Vikings and Others." *Transactions of the Royal Historical Society* 13 (2003): 1–28.
—. "Making Ends Meet: Wealth and Poverty in the Carolingian Church." In Sheils and Wood, *Church and Wealth*, 25–35.
—. "Medieval Monasticism." In Linehan and Nelson, *Medieval World*, 576–604.
Nightingale, J. *Monasteries and Patrons in the Gorze Reform: Lotharingia, 850–1000*. Oxford: Clarendon Press, 2001.
Oikonomidès, N. *Fiscalité et exemption fiscale à Byzance (IXe–XIe s.)*. Athens: Fondation nationale de la recherche scientifique, 1996.
Papadakis, A. "Kaniskion." *ODB* 2, 1101.
Pryce, H. "The Christianization of Society." In Davies, *From the Vikings*, ch. 5.

—. "Pastoral Care in Early Medieval Wales." In Blair and Sharpe, *Pastoral Care*, 41–62.

Raftis, J. A. *The Estates of Ramsey Abbey: A Study in Economic Growth and Organization*. Toronto: Pontifical Institute of Medieval Studies, 1957.

Redgate, A. E. *The Armenians*. Oxford: Blackwell, 1998.

Renard, E. "La gestion des domains de l'abbaye au VIIIe–Xe siècles." *De la Meuse à l'Ardenne* 29 (1999): 117–50.

Rosenwein, B. H. *Negotiating Space: Power, Restraint and Privileges of Immunity in Early Medieval Europe*. Manchester: Manchester University Press, 1999.

—. *Rhinoceros Bound: Cluny in the Tenth Century*. Philadelphia, PA: University of Pennsylvania Press, 1982.

—. *To Be the Neighbor of St. Peter: The Social Meaning of Cluny's Property, 909–1049*. Ithaca, NY: Cornell University Press, 1989.

—, T. Head, and S. Farmer. "Monks and their Enemies: A Comparative Approach." *Speculum* 66 (1991): 764–96.

Sheils, W. J., and D. Wood, eds. *The Church and Wealth*. *SCH* 24. Oxford: Blackwell, 1987.

Stroll, M. *The Medieval Abbey of Farfa: Target of Papal and Imperial Ambitions*. Leiden: Brill, 1997.

Stutz, U. *Geschichte des kirchlichen Benefizialwesens von seinen Anfängen bis auf Alexander III*. Berlin: Müller, 1895. 2nd ed. with foreword by H. E. Feine. Aalen: Scientia, 1961.

—. "The Proprietary Church as an Element of Mediaeval Germanic Ecclesiastical Law." In *Mediaeval Germany, 911–1250: Essays by German Historians*. Ed. and trans. G. Barraclough. 1938 ed. reprinted Oxford: Basil Blackwell, 1967, 35–70.

Talbot, A.-M. "The Byzantine Family and the Monastery." *DOP* 44 (1990): 119–29.

—. "Typikon, Monastic." *ODB* 3, 2132.

Tellenbach, G. *The Church in Western Europe from the Tenth to the Early Twelfth Century*. [*Die westliche Kirche vom 10. bis zum frühen 12. Jahrhundert*. (1988)] Trans. T. Reuter. Cambridge: Cambridge University Press, 1993.

Thacker, A. "Æthelwold and Abingdon." In Yorke, *Bishop Æthelwold*, 43–64.

Thomas, J. P. *Private Religious Foundations in the Byzantine Empire*. Washington, DC: Dumbarton Oaks, 1987.

Toubert, P. *Les structures du Latium medieval: le Latium méridionale et la Sabine du IXe siècle à la fin du XIIe siècle*. 2 vols. Bibliothèque des Écoles françaises d'Athènes et de Rome 221. Rome: École française de Rome, 1973.

van der Wal, N., and J. H. A. Lokin. *Historiae iuris graeco-romani delineatio: les sources du droit byzantin de 300 à 1453*. French trans. H. Boon. Groningen: Egbert Forsten, 1985.

Verhulst, A. *Carolingian Economy*. Cambridge: Cambridge University Press, 2002.

Wallace-Hadrill, J. M. *The Frankish Church*. Oxford: Clarendon Press, 1983.

White, S. D. *Custom, Kinship and Gifts to Saints: The* laudatio parentum *in Western France, 1050–1100*. Chapel Hill, NC: University of North Carolina Press, 1988.

—. "Inheritances and Legal Arguments in Western France, 1050–1150." *Traditio* 43 (1987): 55–103.

Wickham, C. J. "Monastic Lands and Monastic Patrons." In Hodges, *San Vincenzo al Volturno* 2, 138–52.

—. *The Mountains and the City: The Tuscan Appennines in the Early Middle Ages*. Oxford: Clarendon Press, 1988.

Wood, I. N. *The Merovingian Kingdoms, 450–751*. London: Longman, 1994.

—. "Teutsind, Witlaic and the History of Merovingian *Precaria*." In Davies and Fouracre, *Property and Power*, 31–52.

Wormald, P. *Bede and the Conversion of England: The Charter Evidence*. Jarrow: Parish of Jarrow, 1984.

Yorke, B., ed. *Bishop Æthelwold: His Career and Influence*. 2nd ed. Woodbridge: Boydell Press, 1977.

16 Ideas and applications of reform
Julia Barrow

Primary sources

Ardo. *Vita S. Benedicti Anianensis auctore Ardone seu Smaragdo eius discipulo*. Ed. J. Mabillon. *PL* 103, 351–84.

Atto of Vercelli. *Capitulare. PL* 134, 27–52

—. *De pressuris ecclesiasticis. PL* 134, 51–96.

Bede. *Ad Ecgbertum episcopum*. In his *Venerabilis Baedae Opera Historica*. Ed. C. Plummer. 2 vols. Oxford: Clarendon Press, 1896: vol. 1, 405–23. Eng. trans. in *HE*, 343–57.

Capitularia regum francorum. Ed. A. Boretius. *MGH Legum Sectio* II. 2 vols. Hanover: Hahn, 1883–87.

Chrodegang of Metz. *S. Chrodegangi Metensis Episcopi (742–766) Regula Canonicorum aus dem Leidener Codex Vossianus latinus 94 mit Umschrift der tironischen Noten*. Ed. W. Schmitz. Hanover: Hahn, 1889.

Concilia aevi karolini. Ed. A. Werminghoff. 2 vols. *MGH Legum Sectio* III. *Concilia* 2. Hanover and Leipzig: Hahn, 1906–1908.

Councils and Synods with Other Documents Relating to the English Church. Vol. 1: *A.D. 871–1204*. Ed. D. Whitelock, M. Brett, and C. N. L. Brooke. 2 parts. Oxford: Clarendon Press, 1981.

Epistola ad Arnulfum comitem. In *Memorials of Saint Dunstan*. Ed. W. Stubbs. Rolls Series 63. London, 1874, 361–62.

Germanus. *Epistolae dogmaticae. PG* 98, 147–222.

Gregory I. *Gregorii I Papae Registrum Epistolarum*. Ed. P. Ewald and L. M. Hartmann. 2 vols. *MGH Epistolae* 1. Berlin: Weidmann, 1887–99.

Gregory VII. *The Epistolae Vagantes of Pope Gregory VII*. Ed. and trans. H. E. J. Cowdrey. Oxford: Clarendon Press, 1972.

—. *Das Register Gregors VII*. Ed. E. Caspar. *MGH Epistolae Selectae in usum scholarum* 2. Berlin: Weidmann, 1920–23.

Humbert of Silva Candida. *Libri III adversus simoniacos*. Ed. F. Thaner. In *Libelli de lite* 1, 95–253.

Jacques de Vitry. *The Historia Occidentalis of Jacques de Vitry*. Ed. J. F. Hinnebusch. Fribourg: Fribourg University, 1972.

Jean Mabillon, *Elogium S. Odonis. PL* 133, 20.

John, Abbot of St. Arnulf. *Vita Iohannis abbatis Gorziensis*. Ed. G. H. Pertz. *MGH Scriptores* 4. Hanover: Hahn, 1841, 335–77.

Libelli de lite imperatorum et pontificum saeculis XI. et XII. conscripti. MGH. 3 vols. Hanover: Hahn, 1891–97.

Michael the Monk. *Vita et conversatio Theodori praepositi Studitarum. PG* 99, 113–328.

Odo of Cluny. *Secundi Collationum libri tres*. Ed. D. Marrier. *PL* 133, 517–638.

Paul the Deacon. *Liber de episcopis Mettensibus*. Ed. G. H. Pertz. *MGH Scriptores* 2. Hanover: Hahn, 1829, 260–70.

Peter Damian. *Contra intemperantes clericos. PL* 145, 387–424.

—. *Contra philargyriam. PL* 145, 529–42.

—. *Liber gratissimus*. Ed. L. de Heinemann. In *Libelli de lite* 1, 15–75.

Property and Piety in Early Medieval Winchester: Documents Relating to the Topography of the Anglo-Saxon and Norman City and its Minsters. Ed. A. R. Rumble. Winchester Studies 4.iii. Oxford: Clarendon Press, 2002.

Rather of Verona. *Synodica ad presbyteros. PL* 136, 553–68.

Rodulfus Glaber. *Opera*. Ed. J. France and N. Bulst. Oxford: Clarendon Press, 1989.

Theodore the Studite. *Adversus iconomachos capita septem. PG* 99, 485–98.

Theophanes Confessor. *The Chronicle of Theophanes Confessor: Byzantine and Near Eastern History, A.D. 284–813*. Trans. C. Mango and R. Scott, with G. Greatrex. Oxford: Clarendon Press, 1997.

Die Urkunden Friedrichs I. Ed. H. Appelt. 5 vols. *MGH Diplomata regum et imperatorum Germaniae* 10. Hanover: Hahn, 1975–90.

Die Urkunden Konrads III und seines Sohnes Heinrich. Ed. F. Hausmann. *MGH Diplomata regum et imperatorum Germaniae* 9. Vienna: Hermann Böhlaus Nachfolger, 1969.

Vita Gerardi abbatis Broniensis. Ed. L. de Heinemann. *MGH Scriptores* 15.2. Hanover: Hahn, 1888, 654–73.

Widric. *Vita S. Gerardi episcopi Tullensis*. Ed. D. G. Waitz. *MGH Scriptores* 4. Hanover: Hahn, 1841, 485–505.

Widukind of Corvey. *Rerum Gestarum Saxonicarum Libri Tres*. Ed. P. Hirsch. *MGH Scriptores rerum Germanicarum in usum scholarum ex Monumentis Germaniae historicis recusi* 60. Hanover: Hahn, 1935.

Wulfstan of Winchester. *The Life of St. Æthelwold*. Ed. M. Lapidge and M. Winterbottom. Oxford: Clarendon Press, 1991.

Secondary sources

Anastos, M. V. "The Argument for Iconoclasm as Presented by the Iconoclastic Council of 754." In *Late Classical and Medieval Studies in Honor of Albert Mathias Friend, Jr*. Ed. K. Weitzmann. Princeton, NJ: Princeton University Press, 1955, 177–88.

Baronius (Baronio, Cesare). *Annales Ecclesiastici auctore Caesare Baronio*. 12 vols. Mainz: Balthasar Lippius, 1601–1608.

Barrow, J. "English Cathedral Communities and Reform in the Late Tenth and the Eleventh Centuries." In *Anglo-Norman Durham, 1093–1193*. Ed. D. Rollason, M. Harvey, and M. Prestwich. Woodbridge: Boydell Press, 1994, 25–39.

Benson, R. L., and G. Constable, eds., with C. D. Lanham. *Renaissance and Renewal in the Twelfth Century*. Oxford: Clarendon Press, 1982.

Benson, R. L., G. Constable, and J. Van Engen. "Gerhart Burian Ladner." *Speculum* 71 (1996): 802–804.

Blumenthal, U.-R. *Gregor VII.: Papst zwischen Canossa und Kirchenreform*. Darmstadt: Wissenschaftliche Buchgesellschaft, 2001.

Bullough, D. *Alcuin: Achievement and Reputation*. Leiden: Brill, 2004.

Burdach, K. "Sinn und Ursprung der Worte Renaissance und Reformation." Reprinted in his *Reformation, Renaissance, Humanismus: Zwei Abhändlungen über die Grundlage moderner Bildung und Sprachkunst*. 2nd ed. Berlin: Gebrüder Paetel, 1926, 1–84.

Calmette, J-L. *Charlemagne, sa vie et son œuvre*. Paris: A. Michel, 1945.

Cholij, R. *Theodore the Stoudite: The Ordering of Holiness*. Oxford: Oxford University Press, 2002.

Claussen, M. A. *The Reform of the Frankish Church: Chrodegang of Metz and the* Regula Canonicorum *in the Eighth Century*. Cambridge: Cambridge University Press, 2004.

Constable, G. "Renewal and Reform in Religious Life: Concepts and Realities." In Benson et al., *Renaissance and Renewal in the Twelfth Century*, 37–67.

Cowdrey, H. E. J. *The Cluniacs and the Gregorian Reform*. Oxford: Clarendon Press, 1970.

—. *Pope Gregory VII, 1073–1085*. Oxford: Oxford University Press, 1998.

Cristiani, L. "Réforme." In *Dictionnaire de théologie catholique*. Ed. A. Vacaut, E. Mangenot, and E. Amann. 15 vols. in 33. Paris: Letouzey, 1925–72.

Cubitt, C. *Anglo-Saxon Church Councils, c. 650–c. 850*. London: Leicester University Press, 1995.

Dawson, C. *The Making of Europe: An Introduction to the History of European Unity*. London: Sheed and Ward, 1932.

De Smet, J. M. "Recherches critiques sur la *Vita Gerardi Abbatis Broniensis*." *Revue bénédictine* 70 (1960): 5–61.

Dickinson, J. C. *The Origins of the Austin Canons and their Introduction into England*. London: Society for Promoting Christian Knowledge, 1950.

Dierkens, A. "La christianisation des campagnes de l'Empire de Louis le Pieux: l'exemple du diocèse de Liège sous l'épiscopat de Walcaud (c. 809–c. 931)." In *Charlemagne's Heir: New Perspectives on the Reign of Louis the Pious*. Ed. P. Godman and R. Collins. Oxford: Clarendon Press, 1990, 309–29.

Fleckenstein, J. *Die Bildungsreform Karls des Grossen als Verwirklichung der Norma Rectitudinis*. Bigge-Ruhr: Josefs-Druckerei, 1953.

Fliche, A. *La réforme grégorienne*. Vol. 1: *La formation des idées grégoriennes*. Louvain: Spicilegium Sacrum Lovaniense Bureaux and E. Champion, 1924.

Fuhrmann, H. "Papstgeschichtsschreibung." In *Geschichte und Geschichtswissenschaft in der Kultur Italiens und Deutschlands*. Ed. A. Esch and J. Petersen. Tübingen: Niemeyer, 1989, 141–91.

Guizot, F. *Histoire générale de la civilisation en Europe*. Paris, 1828. Eng. trans. W. Hazlitt. *The History of Civilization in Europe* (1846). Ed. L. Siedentop. Harmondsworth: Penguin, 1997.

Hallinger, K. *Gorze-Kluny: Studien zu den monastischen Lebensformen und Gegensatzen im Hochmittelalter*. 2 vols. Studia Anselmiana 22/3 and 24/5. Rome: Herder 1950–51.

Halphen, L. *Charlemagne et l'empire carolingien*. Paris: A. Michel, 1947.

Herrin, J. *The Formation of Christendom*. Oxford: Blackwell, 1987.

Hiestand, R. "100 Jahre Papsturkundenwerk." In *Hundert Jahre Papsturkundenforschung: Bilanz–Methoden–Perspektiven*. Ed. R. Hiestand. Göttingen: Vandenhoeck und Ruprecht, 2003, 11–44.

Innes, J. "'Reform' in English Public Life: The Fortunes of a Word." In *Rethinking the Age of Reform: Britain, 1780–1850*. Ed. A. Burns and J. Innes. Cambridge: Cambridge University Press, 2003, 71–97.

Kottje, R., and H. Maurer, eds. *Monastische Reformen im 9. und 10. Jahrhundert*. Vorträge und Forschungen 38. Sigmaringen: Thorbecke, 1989.

Ladner, G. B. "Gregory the Great and Gregory VII: A Comparison of their Concepts of Renewal" (with "A Note on the Computer Methods Used" by D. W. Packard). *Viator* 4 (1973): 1–31.

—. *The Idea of Reform: Its Impact on Christian Thought and Action in the Age of the Fathers*. Cambridge, MA: Harvard University Press, 1959.

—. "Die mittelalterliche Reform-Idee und ihr Verhältnis zur Idee der Renaissance." *Mitteilungen des Instituts für Österreichische Geschichtsforschung* 60 (1952): 31–59.

—. "Two Gregorian Letters: On the Sources and Nature of Gregory VII's Reform Ideology." In *Studi Gregoriani*. Vol. 2. Ed. G. B. Borino. Rome: Abbazia di San Paolo, 1956, 221–42.

Lapidge, M. "Æthelwold as Scholar and Teacher." In his *Anglo-Latin Literature, 900–1066*. London: Hambledon, 1993, 183–211, with additional notes on p. 482. Originally published in *Bishop Æthelwold: His Career and Influence*. Ed. B. Yorke. Woodbridge: Boydell Press, 1988, 89–117.

Lawrence, C. H. *Medieval Monasticism: Forms of Religious Life in Western Europe in the Middle Ages*. 2nd ed. London: Longman, 1989.

Le Barbier, E. *Saint-Christodule et la réforme des couvents grecs au XIe siècle*. Paris: Firmin Didot Frères and L. Hachette, 1863.

Leroy, J. "La réforme studite." In *Il monachesimo orientale*. Orientalia Christiana Analecta 153. Rome: Pontificium institutum orientalium studiorum, 1958, 181–214.

Levison, W. *England and the Continent in the Eighth Century*. Oxford: Clarendon Press, 1946.

Lohmeyer, H. K. "Voigt, Johannes." In *Allgemeine deutsche Biographie*. Vol. 40. Ed. R. von Lilienkron, et al. 56 vols. Leipzig: Duncker und Humblot, 1875–1912, 205–10.

Magdalino, P. *The Empire of Manuel I Komnenos, 1143–1180*. Cambridge: Cambridge University Press, 1993.

—. "The Reform Edict of 1107." In *Alexios I Komnenos*. Vol. 1: *Papers*. Ed. M. Mullett and D. Smythe. Belfast Byzantine Texts and Translations 4, vol. 1. Belfast: Belfast Byzantine Enterprises, 1996, 199–218.

Matthias Flacius Illyricus, see Vlachich, Matthias.

McKitterick, R. *The Frankish Church and the Carolingian Reforms, 789–895*. London: Royal Historical Society, 1977.

Miethke, J. "Reform, Reformation." In *Lexikon des Mittelalters*. 9 vols. Munich: Artemis Verlag, 1977–98, vii and 543–50.

Morris, R. *Monks and Laymen in Byzantium, 843–1118*. Cambridge: Cambridge University Press, 1995.

Morrison, K. *Tradition and Authority in the Western Church, 300–1140*. Princeton, NJ: Princeton University Press, 1969.

Nedungatt, G., and M. Featherstone, eds. *The Council in Trullo Revisited.* Kanonika 6. Rome: Pontificio istituto orientale, 1995.

Nightingale, J. *Monasteries and Patrons in the Gorze Reform: Lotharingia c. 850–1000.* Oxford: Clarendon Press, 2000.

Orlandis J., and D. Ramos-Lisson. *Historia de los concilios de la España romana y visigoda.* Pamplona: Ediciones Universidad de Navarra, S.A., 1986.

Patzelt, E. *Die karolingische Renaissance: Beiträge zur Geschichte des frühen Mittelalters.* Vienna: Österreichischer Schulbuchverlag, 1924.

Pontal, O. *Histoire des conciles mérovingiens.* Paris: Éditions du Cerf, 1989.

Reuter. T. "'Kirchenreform' und 'Kirchenpolitik' im Zeitalter Karl Martells: Begriffe und Wirklichkeit." In *Karl Martell in seiner Zeit.* Ed. J. Jarnut, U. Nonn, and M. Richter. Sigmaringen: Thorbecke, 1994, 35–59.

Robinson, I. S., trans. *The Papal Reform of the Eleventh Century: Lives of Pope Leo IX and Pope Gregory VII.* Manchester: Manchester University Press, 2004.

—. "Reform and the Church, 1073–1122," In *The New Cambridge Medieval History.* Vol. 4: *c. 1024–c. 1198.* Ed. D. Luscombe and J. Riley-Smith, part 1. Cambridge: Cambridge University Press, 2004, 268–334.

Rosenwein, B. *To Be the Neighbor of St. Peter: The Social Meaning of Cluny's Property, 909–1049.* Ithaca, NY: Cornell University Press, 1989.

Schieffer, R. *Die Entstehung des päpstlichen Investiturverbots für den deutschen König. Schriften der MGH* 28. Stuttgart: Hiersemann, 1981.

Schramm, P. E. "Karl der Grosse: Denkart und Grundauffassung: Die von ihm bewirkte 'Correctio' (nicht 'Renaissance')." *Historische Zeitschrift* 198 (1964): 306–45. Reprinted in Vol. 1 of his *Kaiser, Könige und Päpste: Gesammelte Aufsätze zur Geschichte des Mittelalters.* 4 vols. in 5. Stuttgart: Hiersemann, 1968, 302–41.

Smith, J. M. H. "'Emending Evil Ways and Praising God's Omnipotence': Einhard and the Uses of Roman Martyrs." In *Conversion in Late Antiquity and the Early Middle Ages: Seeing and Believing.* Ed. K. Mills and A. Grafton. Rochester, NY: University of Rochester Press, 2003, 189–223.

Sotinel, C. "The Church in the Roman Empire: Changes without Reform and Reforms without Change." In *Reforming the Church before Modernity: Patterns, Problems, and Approaches.* Ed. C. M. Bellitto and L. I. Hamilton. Burlington, VT: Ashgate, 2005, 155–72.

Staubach, N. "Cultus divinus und karolingische Reform." *Frühmittelalterliche Studien* 18 (1984): 546–81.

Stratmann, M. *Hinkmar von Reims als Verwalter von Bistum und Kirchenprovinz.* Sigmaringen: Thorbecke, 1991.

Tellenbach, G. *The Church in Western Europe from the Tenth to the Early Twelfth Century.* [*Die westliche Kirche vom 10. bis zum frühen 12. Jahrhundert.* (1988)]. Eng. trans. T. Reuter. Cambridge: Cambridge University Press, 1993.

—. *Libertas: Kirche und Weltordnung im Zeitalter des Investiturstreites.* Stuttgart: W. Kohlhammer, 1936.

Thacker, A. "Bede's Ideal of Reform." In *Ideal and Reality in Frankish and Anglo-Saxon Society: Studies Presented to J. M. Wallace-Hadrill.* Ed. P. Wormald, with D. Bullough and R. Collins. Oxford: Basil Blackwell, 1983, 130–53.

Tupper, F., Jr. "History and Texts of the Benedictine Reform of the Tenth Century." *Modern Language Notes* 8 (1893): 344–67.

Van Engen, J. "Images and Ideas: The Achievements of Gerhart Burian Ladner, with a Bibliography of his Published Works." *Viator* 20 (1989): 85–115.

Vlachich, M. [Matthias Flacius Illyricus] et al. *Ecclesiastica Historia.* 13 vols. Basle: Johannes Oporinus, 1561–74.

Voigt, J. *Hildebrand, als Papst Gregorius der Siebente und sein Zeitalter, aus den Quellen dargestellt.* Weimar: Verlag des G. H. S. priviligierten Landes-Industrie-Comptoirs, 1825. French trans. M. L'Abbé (J.-N.) Jager. *Histoire du Pape Grégoire VII et de son siècle.* 2 vols. Paris: A. Vaton, 1838.

Vollrath, H. *Die Synoden Englands bis 1066.* Paderborn: Schöningh, 1985.

Wallace-Hadrill, J. M. *The Frankish Church.* Oxford: Oxford University Press, 1983.

Wolgast, E. "Reform, Reformation." In Vol. 5 of *Geschichtliche Grundbegriffe: Historisches Lexikon zur politisch-sozialen Sprache in Deutschland.* Ed. O. Brunner, W. Conze, and R. Koselleck. 8 vols. in 9. Stuttgart: Klett-Cotta, 1972–97, 313–60.

Wormald, P. "Æthelwold and his Continental Counterparts: Contact, Comparison, Contrast." In *Bishop Æthelwold: His Career and Influence.* Ed. B. Yorke. Woodbridge: Boydell Press, 1988, 13–42.

17 Churches in the landscape
Dominique Iogna-Prat

Primary sources

Acta synodi Atrebatensis, III–IV. PL 142, 1284B–1288B.

Ambrose of Milan. *Epistola 22 dominae sorori. PL* 16, 119–26.

Andrew of Fleury. *Vita Gauzlini.* Ed. R.-H. Bautier and G. Labory. Paris: Éditions du Centre national de la recherche scientifique, 1969.

Angilbert. *De perfectione Centulensis ecclesiae libellus.* In Hariulf, *Chronique.*

Augustine of Hippo. *De civitate Dei.* Ed. B. Dombart and A. Kalb. *CCSL* 47, 48. Turnhout: Brepols, 1955.

Deed of the Endowment of Sainte-Marie in the Territory of Saint-Maximin (1062). Archives départmentales des Bouches-du-Rhône, 13–1 H 42 n.197.

Hariulf. *Chronique de l'abbaye de Saint-Riquier.* Ed. F. Lot. Paris: Picard, 1894.

Hincmar of Rheims. *De ecclesiis et capellis.* Ed. M. Stratmann. *MGH Fontes iuris germanici antiqui* 14. Hanover: Hahn, 1990.

Isidore of Seville. *De ortu et obitu patrum.* Ed. C. Chaparro Gómez. Paris: Les Belles Lettres, 1985.

Ivo of Chartres. *Sermo IV de sacramentis dedicationis. PL* 162, 527B–535C.

Liber miraculorum sancte Fidis. Ed. L. Robertini. Biblioteca di Medioevo latino 3. Spoleto: Centro italiano di studi sull'alto medioevo, 1994.

Odo of Cambrai. *Expositio in canonem missae. PL* 160, 1053–70.

Pontifical romano-germanique du dixième siècle. Ed. C. Vogel and R. Elze. Vatican City: Biblioteca apostolica vaticana, 1963.

Rodulfus Glaber. *Historiarum libri quinque.* In his *Opera.* Ed. J. France. Oxford: Oxford University Press, 1989.

The Theodosian Code and Novels and the Sirmondian Constitutions. Trans. C. Pharr. Princeton, NJ: Princeton University Press, 1952.

Walafrid Strabo. *Libellus de exordiis et incrementis quarumdam observationibus ecclesiasticis rerum: A Translation and Liturgical Commentary*. Trans. and notes A. L. Harting Correa. Leiden: Brill, 1996.

Secondary sources

Andrieu, M. *Les* ordines romani *du haut Moyen Âge*. Vol. 4. Louvain: Université catholique, 1956.

Cebrià Baraut, P. "Les actes de consagracions d'esglésies del bisbat d'Urgell (segles IX–XII)." *Urgellia* 1 (1978): 11–182.

Constable, G. *Three Studies in Medieval Religious and Social Thought*. Cambridge: Cambridge University Press, 1995.

Crook, J. *The Architectural Setting of the Cult of Saints in the Early Christian West, c. 300–c. 1200*. Oxford: Clarendon Press, 2000.

Farias Zurita, V. "La sagrera catalana (c. 1025–c. 1200): características y desarollo de un tipo de asentameniento eclesial." *Studia historica-Historia medieval* 11 (1993): 81–121.

Fossier, R. *Enfance de l'Europe, Xe–XIIe siècles: aspects économiques et sociaux*. 2 vols. Paris: Presses universitaires de France, 1982.

Guerreau, A. "Il significato dei luoghi nell'Occidente medievale: struttura e dinamica di uno 'spazio' specifico." In *Arti e storia nel Medioevo*. Vol. 1: *Tempo, spazi, istituzioni*. Ed. E. Castelnuovo and G. Sergi. Turin: Einaudi, 2002.

Iogna-Prat, D. *La Maison Dieu: une histoire monumentale de L'Église au Moyen Âge*. Paris: Seuil, 2006.

Kohlschein, F., and P. Wünsche. *Heiliger Raum: Architektur, Kunst und Liturgie im mittelalterlichen Kathedralen und Stiftskirchen*. Münster: Aschendorff, 1998.

Lauwers, M. *Naissance du cimetière: lieux sacrés et terres des morts dans l'Occident médiéval*. Paris: Aubier, 2005.

—. and L. Ripart "Représentation et gestion de l'espace dans l'Occident médiéval (Ve–XIIIe siècle)". In *Rome et l'état moderne européen*. Ed. J.-P. Genet. Rome: École française de Rome, 2007, 115–71.

Linder, A. "The Liturgy of the Liberation of Jerusalem." *Medieval Studies* 52 (1990): 110–31.

Méhu, D. *Paix et communauté autour de l'abbaye de Cluny, Xe–XVe siècle*. Lyons: Presses universitaires de Lyon, 2001.

Moore, R. I. *The Formation of a Persecuting Society: Power and Deviance in Western Europe, 950–1250*. Oxford: Blackwell, 1987.

Morris, R. "Baptismal Places: 600–800." In *People and Places in Northern Europe, 500–1600: Essays in Honour of P. H. Sawyer*. Ed. I. Wood and N. Lund. Woodbridge: Boydell Press, 1991, 15–24.

—. *Churches in the Landscape*. London: Dent, 1989.

Noble, T. F. X. *The Republic of St. Peter: The Birth of the Papal State, 680–825*. Philadelphia, PA: University of Pennsylvania Press, 1984.

Rebillard, É. *Religion et sepulture: l'église, les vivants et les morts dans l'Antiquité tardive*. Paris: École des hautes études en sciences sociales, 2004.

Respher, B. V. *The Rite of Church Dedication in the Early Medieval Era*. Lewiston, NY: E. Mellen Press, 1998.

Rosenwein, B. H. *Negotiating Space: Power, Restraint, and Privileges of Immunity in Early Medieval Europe*. Ithaca, NY: Cornell University Press, 1999.

Toubert, P. *Les structures du Latium médiéval: le Latium méridonial et la Sabine du IXe siècle à la fin du XIIe siècle*. Rome: École française de Rome, 1973.

Treffort, C. "Consécration de cimetière et contrôle épiscopal des lieux d'inhumation au IXe siècle." In *Le sacré et son inscription dans l'espace à Byzance et en Occident: études comparées*. Ed. M. Kaplan. Paris: Presses de la Sorbonne, 2001, 286–99.

Violante, C. "Le strutture organizzative della cura d'anime nelle campagne dell'Italia centrosettentionale (secoli V–X)." In *Cristianizzione ed organizzazione ecclesiastica delle campagne nell'Alto Medioevo*. Settimane di studio 28. Spoleto: Centro italiano di studio sull'alto medioevo, 1982, 963–1162.

Zadora-Rio, É. "Lieux d'inhumation et espaces consacrés: le voyage d'Urbain II en France (août 1095–août 1096)." In *Lieux sacrés, lieux de culte, sanctuaires: approches terminologiques, méthologiques, historiques et morphologiques*. Ed. A. Vauchez. Rome: École française de Rome, 2000, 197–213.

—. "The Making of Churchyards and Parish Territories in the Early-Medieval Landscape of France and England in the 7th–12th Centuries: A Reconsideration." *Medieval Archaeology* 47 (2003): 1–19.

—. "Le village des historiens et le village des archéologues." In *Campagnes médiévales: l'homme et son espace. Études offertes à R. Fossier*. Ed. É. Mornet. Paris: Presses de la Sorbonne, 1994, 145–53.

18 Birth and death
Frederick S. Paxton

Primary sources

Keefe, S. A. *Water and the Word: Baptism and the Education of the Clergy in the Carolingian Empire*. 2 vols. Notre Dame, IN: University of Notre Dame Press, 2002.

Peters, E. *Heresy and Authority in Medieval Europe*. Philadelphia: University of Pennsylvania Press, 1980.

Temkin, O., trans. *Soranus' Gynecology*. Baltimore, MD: Johns Hopkins University Press, 1956.

Wakefield, W. L., and A. P. Evans. *Heresies of the High Middle Ages*. New York: Columbia University Press, 1969.

Secondary sources

Abrahamse, D. "Rituals of Death in the Middle Byzantine Period." *The Greek Orthodox Theological Review* 29 (1984): 125–34.

Agapitos, P. "La mort à Byzance: images fragmentaires d'un monde inconnu." *Europe* 75, No. 822 (October 1997): 47–59.

Alexiou, M. *The Ritual Lament in Greek Tradition*. 2nd ed. Rev. D. Yatromanolakis and P. Roilos. Lanham, MD: Rowman & Littlefield, 2002.

Althoff, G. "Gandersheim und Quedlinburg: Ottonische Frauenklöster als Herrschafts- und Überlieferungszentren." *Frühmittelalterliche Studien* 25 (1991): 123–44.

Angenendt, A. "*Missa specialis*: Zugleich ein Beitrag zur Entstehung der Privat-Messen." *Frühmittelalterliche Studien* 17 (1983): 153–221.

Baun, J. "The Fate of Babies Dying before Baptism in Byzantium." In *The Church and Childhood*. Ed. D. Wood. *SCH* 31. Oxford: Blackwell, 1994, 115–25.

Biraben, J.-N., and J. Le Goff. "The Plague in the Early Middle Ages." In *Biology of Man and History*. Ed. R. Forster and O. Ranum. Trans. E. Forster and P. M. Ranum. Baltimore, MD: Johns Hopkins University Press, 1975, 48–80.

Blumenfeld-Kosinski, R. *Not of Woman Born: Representations of Caesarean Birth in Medieval and Renaissance Culture*. Ithaca, NY: Cornell University Press, 1990.

Boswell, J. *The Kindness of Strangers: The Abandonment of Children in Western Europe from Late Antiquity to the Renaissance*. New York: Pantheon, 1988.

Brown, P. *The Cult of the Saints: Its Rise and Function in Late Antiquity*. Chicago: University of Chicago Press, 1981.

—. "Vers la naissance de la Purgatoire: amnistie et pénitence dans le christianisme occidental de l'Antiquité tardive au Haut Moyen Âge." *Annales* 52 (1997): 1247–61.

Bullough, D. "Burial, Community and Belief in the Early Medieval West." In *Ideal and Reality in Frankish and Anglo-Saxon Society: Studies Presented to J. M. Wallace-Hadrill*. Ed. P. Wormald, with D. Bullough and R. Collins. Oxford: Basil Blackwell, 1983, 175–201.

Bynum, C. Walker. *The Resurrection of the Body in Western Christendom, 200–1336*. New York: Columbia University Press, 1995.

Carver, R. O. "Cemetery and Society at Sutton Hoo: Five Awkward Questions and Four Contradictory Answers." In Karkov et al. *Spaces of the Living and the Dead*, 1–14.

Congourdeau, M.-H., and M. Melhaoui. "La perception de la peste en pays chrétien byzantin et musulman." *Revue des études byzantines* 59 (2001): 95–124.

Cramer, P. *Baptism and Change in the Early Middle Ages, c. 200–c. 1150*, Cambridge Studies in Medieval Life and Thought. Cambridge: Cambridge University Press, 1993.

Crawford, S. "Children, Death and the Afterlife in Anglo-Saxon England." In *Archaeology of Anglo-Saxon England: Basic Readings*. Ed. C. E. Karkov. New York: Garland, 1999, 339–58.

—. *Childhood in Anglo-Saxon England*. Stroud: Sutton, 1999.

Dagron, G. "Le christianisme dans la ville byzantine." *DOP* 31 (1977): 1–25.

Daniell, C., and V. Thompson. "Pagans and Christians: 400–1150." In *Death in England: An Illustrated History*. Ed. P. C. Jupp and C. Gittings. New Brunswick, NJ: Rutgers University Press, 2000, 65–89.

de Jong, M. *In Samuel's Image: Child Oblation in the Early Medieval West*. Leiden: Brill, 1996.

Dierkens, A. "Autour de la tombe de Charlemagne: considérations sur les sépultures et les funérailles des souverains carolingiens et des membres de leur famille." *Byzantion: Revue internationale des études byzantines* 61 (1991): 156–80.

Effros, B. *Caring for Body and Soul: Burial and the Afterlife in the Merovingian World*. University Park, PA: Pennsylvania State University, 2002.

Fedwick, P. J. "Death and Dying in Byzantine Liturgical Traditions." *Eastern Churches Review* 8 (1976): 152–71.

Freistedt, E. *Altchristliche Totengedächtnistage und ihre Beziehung zum Jenseitsglauben und Totenkultus der Antike*. Liturgiegeschichtliche Quellen und Forschungen 24. Münster: Aschendorff, 1928.

Galinié, H. "Tours from an Archaeological Standpoint." In Karkov et al. *Spaces of the Living and the Dead*, 87–105.

Geary, P. J. "Exchange and Interaction between the Living and the Dead in Early Medieval Society." In Geary, *Living with the Dead in the Middle Ages*. Ithaca, NY: Cornell University Press, 1994, 77–92.

—. *Phantoms of Remembrance: Memory and Oblivion at the End of the First Millennium*. Princeton, NJ: Princeton University Press, 1994.

Heene, K. *The Legacy of Paradise: Marriage, Motherhood and Women in Carolingian Edifying Literature*. Frankfurt: Peter Lang, 1997.

Huyghebaert, N., and J. L. Lemaître. *Les documents necrologiques*. Typologie des sources du moyen âge occidental 4. Turnhout: Brepols, 1972.

Innes, M. "Keeping it in the Family: Women and Aristocratic Memory, 700–1200." In *Medieval Memories: Men, Women and the Past, 700–1300*. Ed. E. van Houts. Harlow: Longman, 2001, 17–35.

Iogna-Prat, Dominique. "Les morts dans la comptabilité des Clunisiens de l'an Mil." In *Religion et culture autour de l'an mil: royaume capétien et Lotharingie*. Ed. D. Iogna-Prat and J.-C. Picard. Paris: Picard, 1990, 55–69.

—. "Des morts très spéciaux aux morts ordinaires: la pastorale funéraire clunisienne (XIe–XIIe siècles)." *Médiévales* 31 (1996): 79–91.

—. *Ordonner et exclure: Cluny et la société chrétienne face à l'hérésie, au judaïsme et à l'islam 1000–1150*. Paris: Aubier, 2000.

Ivison, E. A. "Burial and Urbanism in Late Antique and Early Byzantine Corinth (*c*. AD 400–700)." In *Towns in Transition: Urban Evolution in Late Antiquity and the Early Middle Ages*. Ed. N. Christie and S. T. Loseby. Aldershot: Scolar Press, 1996, 99–125.

Karkov, C. "Whitby, Jarrow and the Commemoration of Death in Northumbria." In *Northumbria's Golden Age*. Ed. J. Hawkes and S. Mills. Stroud: Sutton Publishing, 1999, 126–35.

—, K. Wickham-Crowley, and B. Young, eds. *Spaces of the Living and the Dead: An Archaeological Dialogue*. American Early Medieval Studies 3. Oxford: Oxbow, 1999.

Kelly, H. Ansgar. *The Devil at Baptism: Ritual, Theology, and Drama*. Ithaca, NY: Cornell University Press, 1985.

Kyriakakis, J. "Byzantine Burial Customs: Care of the Deceased from Death to the Prothesis." *Greek Orthodox Theological Review* 19 (1974): 37–72.

Le Goff, J. *The Birth of Purgatory*. Trans. A. Goldhammer. Chicago: University of Chicago Press, 1984.

Little, L. K. *Religious Poverty and the Profit Economy in Medieval Europe*. Ithaca, NY: Cornell University Press, 1978.

Lynch, J. H. *Christianizing Kinship*. Ithaca, NY: Cornell University Press, 1998.

—. *Godparents and Kinship in Early Medieval Europe*. Princeton, NJ: Princeton University Press, 1986.

McLaughlin, M. *Consorting with Saints: Prayer for the Dead in Early Medieval France*. Ithaca, NY: Cornell University Press, 1994.

Nelson, J. L. "Gender and Genre in Women Historians of the Early Middle Ages." In her *The Frankish World, 750–900*. London: Hambledon, 1996, 183–97.

—. "Parents, Children, and the Church in the Earlier Middle Ages." In *The Church and Childhood*. Ed. D. Wood. *SCH* 31. Oxford: Blackwell, 1994, 81–114.

—. "Women and the Word in the Earlier Middle Ages." In her *The Frankish World, 750–900*. London: Hambledon, 1996, 199–221.

Orme, N. *Medieval Children*. New Haven, CT: Yale University Press, 2001.

Paxton, F. S. *Christianizing Death: The Creation of a Ritual Process in Early Medieval Europe*. Ithaca, NY: Cornell University Press, 1990.

—. "Communities of the Living and the Dead in Late Antiquity and the Early Medieval West." In *The Making of Christian Communities in Late Antiquity and the Middle Ages*. Ed. M. Williams. London: Hambledon, 2005, 49–62.

—. "Death by Customary at Eleventh-Century Cluny." In *From Dead of Night to End of Day: The Medieval Customs of Cluny*: Ed. S. Boynton and I. Cochelin. Turnhout: Brepols, 2005, 297–318.

—. "*Oblationes defunctorum*: The Poor and the Dead in Late Antiquity and the Early Medieval West." In *Proceedings of the Tenth International Congress of Medieval Canon Law*. Ed. K. Pennington, S. Chodorow, and K. H. Kendall. Monumenta Iuris Canonici, Series C: Subsidia 11. Vatican City: Biblioteca apostolica vaticana, 2001, 245–67.

—. "Remembering the Dead at Cluniac Funerals" In *Erinnerungskultur im Bestattungsritual*. Ed. J. Jarnut and M. Wemhoff. Mittelalterstudien des Instituts zur Interdisziplinären Erforschung des Mittelalters und seines Nachwirkens, Paderborn 3. Munich: Wilhelm Fink Verlag, 2003, 177–90.

—. "*Signa mortifera*: Death and Prognostication in Early Medieval Monastic Medicine." *Bulletin of the History of Medicine* 67 (1993): 631–50.

Picard, J.-C. *Les souvenirs des évêques: sépultures, listes épiscopales, et cultes des évêques en Italie du Nord des origines au Xe siècle*. Bibliothèque des Écoles françaises d'Athenes et de Rome 268. Rome: Écoles françaises de Rome, 1988.

Poeck, D. "Laienbegräbnisse in Cluny." *Frühmittelalterliche Studien* 14 (1980): 68–179.

Rebillard, É. *In hora mortis: évolution de la pastorale chrétienne de la mort aux IVe et Ve siècles dans l'occident Latin*. Rome: École française de Rome, 1994.

Reynolds, A. "The Definition and Ideology of Anglo-Saxon Execution Sites and Cemeteries." In *Death and Burial in Medieval Europe: Papers of the "Medieval Europe Brugge 1997" Conference*. Vol. 2. Ed. G. de Boe and F. Verhaeghe. Zellik: Instituut voor het Archeologisch Patrimonium, 1997, 33–41.

Riddle, J. *Contraception and Abortion from the Ancient World to the Renaissance*. Cambridge, MA: Harvard University Press, 1992.

Sapin, C. "Architecture and Funerary Space in the Early Middle Ages." In Karkov et al. *Spaces of the Living and the Dead*, 39–60.

Schmid, K., and J. Wollasch, eds. *Memoria: der geschichtliche Zeugniswert des liturgischen Gedenkens im Mittelalter*. Münstersche Mittelalter-Schriften 48. Munich: Wilhelm Fink Verlag, 1984.

Schmitt, J.-C. *Ghosts in the Middle Ages: The Living and the Dead in Medieval Society*. Trans. T. L. Fagan. Chicago: University of Chicago Press, 1998.

Shahar, S. *Childhood in the Middle Ages*. London: Routledge, 1990.
Smith, J. M. H. "Religion and Lay Society." In *NCMH* 2, 654–78.
Stathakopoulos, D. "The Justinianic Plague Revisited." *Byzantine and Modern Greek Studies* 24 (2000): 256–76.
Thompson, V. *Dying and Death in Later Anglo-Saxon England*. Anglo-Saxon Studies 4. Woodbridge: Boydell, 2004.
Treffort, C. *L'église carolingienne et la mort: christianisme, rites funéraires et pratiques commémoratives*. Collection d'histoire et d'archéologie médiévales 3. Lyons: Centre interuniversitaire d'histoire et d'archéologie médiévales, 1996.
Walter, C. "Death in Byzantine Iconography." *Eastern Churches Review* 8 (1976): 113–27.
Williams, H. "Death, Memory and Time: A Consideration of the Mortuary Practices at Sutton Hoo." In *Time in the Medieval World*. Ed. C. Humphrey and W. M. Ormrod. Woodbridge: Boydell & Brewer, 2001, 35–71.

19 Remedies for sins
Rob Meens

Primary sources

Alcuin. *Epistolae. MGH Epistolae* 6 (= *Karolini Aevi* 4). Ed. E. Dümmler. Berlin: Weidmann, 1895, 1–481.
Basil the Great. *Letters*. Ed. Yves Courtonne. 3 vols. Paris: Les Belles Lettres, 1957–66.
Boniface. *Briefe des Bonifatius: Willibalds Leben des Bonifatius. Nebst einigen zeitgenössischen Dokumenten. AQ* IVb. Darmstadt: Wissenschaftliche Buchgesellschaft, 1968.
Burchard of Worms. *Decretum. PL* 140, 537–1065.
Die Bussbücher und das kanonische Bussverfahren: Nach handschriflichen Quellen dargestellt. Ed. H. J. Schmitz. Düsseldorf: Verlag L. Schwann, 1898; reprint, Graz: Akademische Druck- und Verlagsanstalt, 1958.
Die Bussbücher und die Bussdisciplin der Kirche. Ed. H. J. Schmitz. Mainz: Verlag Franz Kirchheim, 1883; reprint, Graz: Akademische Druck- und Verlagsanstalt, 1958.
Die Bussordnungen der abendländischen Kirche. Ed. H. Wasserschleben. Halle: Ch. Graeger, 1851; reprint, Graz: Akademische Druck- und Verlagsanstalt, 1958.
Caesarius of Arles. *Sermones*. In *Sancti Caesarii episcopi Arelatensis opera omnia nunc primum in unum collecta*. Ed. G. Morin. *CCSL* 103–104. Turnhout: Brepols, 1953.
Capitula Episcoporum. MGH Capitula Episcoporum 1. Ed. Peter Brommer. Hanover: Hahn, 1984.
Capitula Episcoporum. MGH Capitula Episcoporum 2. Ed. R. Pokorny, M. Stratmann, with the assistance of W.-D. Runge. Hanover: Hahn, 1995.
Capitula Episcoporum. MGH Capitula Episcoporum 3. Ed. R. Pokorny. Hanover: Hahn 1995.
Collectio Hibernensis. In *Die irische Kanonensammlung*. Ed. H. Wasserschleben. 2nd ed. Leipzig: Bernard Tauchnitz, 1885; reprint, Aalen: Scientia Verlag, 1966.
Columbanus. *Regula Coenobialis. Sancti Columbani Opera. Scriptores latini Hiberniae* 2. Ed. G. Walker. Dublin: Dublin Institue for Advanced Studies, 1957. 2nd ed. 1970, 142–69.

Council of Clichy (626/27). *Concilia Galliae A.511–A.695*. *CCSL* 148A. Ed. C. De Clercq. Turnhout: Brepols, 1963, 290–97.
Council of Mainz (852). *Die Konzilien der karolingischen Teilreiche, 843–859*. *MGH Concilia* 3. Ed. W. Hartmann. Hanover: Hahn, 1984, 235–52.
Einhard. *Epistolae*. *MGH Epistolae* 5 (= *Karolini Aevi* 3). Ed. K. Hampe. Berlin: Weidmann, 1899, 105–45.
—. *Translatio SS. Marcellini et Petri*. *MGH Scriptores* 15.1. Ed. G. Waitz. Hanover: Hahn, 1887, 238–64.
Gregory the Great. *Dialogi*. *SC* 251, 260, 265. Ed. A. de Vogüé. Paris: Éditions du Cerf, 1978–80.
Gregory of Tours. *Historiae Libri X*. *MGH SRM* 1. Ed. B. Krusch and W. Levison. Hanover: Hahn, 1937–51.
Heito. *Visio Wettini*. *MGH Poetae Latini* 2. Ed. E. Dümmler. Berlin: Weidmann, 1884, 479–87.
The Irish Penitentials. *Scriptores latini Hiberniae* 5. Ed. L. Bieler with an appendix by D. A. Binchy. Dublin: Dublin Institute for Advanced Studies, 1963.
John Cassian. *Collationes XXIIII*. *CSEL* 13. Ed. M. Petschenig. Vienna: Verlag der Österreichischen Akademie der Wissenschaften, 2004.
Jonas of Orleans. *De Institutione Laicali*. *PL* 106, 121–278.
Lex Baiuvariorum. *MGH Leges Nationum Germanicarum* 5.2. Ed. E. von Schwind. Hanover: Hahn, 1929, 197–473.
Origen. *Homélies sur le Lévitique*. *SC* 286–87. Ed. M. Borret. 2 vols. Paris: Éditions du Cerf, 1981.
Paenitentialia Hispaniae. *CCSL* 156A. Ed. F. Bezler. Turnhout: Brepols, 1998.
Paenitentialia minora Franciae et Italiae saeculi VIII–IX. *CCSL* 156. Ed. R. Kottje. Turnhout: Brepols, 1994.
Paulinus of Aquilea. *Epistola* 16. *MGH Epistolae* 6 (= *Karolini Aevi* 4). Ed. E. Dümmler. Berlin: Weidmann 1895, 520–22.
I penitenziali Bizantini. Il Protokanonarion o Kanonarion Primitivo di Giovanni Monaco e Diacono e il Deuterokanonarion o "Secondo Kanonarion" di Basilio Monaco. Kanonika 3. Ed. M. Arranz. Rome: Pontificio istituto orientale, 1993.
Peri Exagoreuseos (Περὶ Ἐξαγορεύσεως). (attributed to Theodore the Studite) *PG* 99, 1721–30.
Pontificale Romano-Germanicum. In *Le Pontifical Romano-Germanique du dixième siècle*. Ed. C. Vogel and R. Elze. 3 vols. Studi e Testi 226, 227, and 269. Vatican City: Biblioteca apostolica vaticana, 1963–72.
Pseudo-Bonifatius. *Sermones*. *PL* 89, 843–72.
Regino of Prüm. *Libri duo de synodalibus causis et disciplinis ecclesiasticis*. Ed. H. Wasserschleben. Leipzig: Engelmann, 1840; reprint, Graz: Akademische Druck- und Verlagsanstalt, 1964.
Robert Grosseteste. *Deus est*. Ed. S. Wenzel in his "Robert Grosseteste's Treatise on Confession, 'Deus est.'" *Franciscan Studies* 30 (1970): 218–93.
Sacramentary of Fulda. In *Sacramentarium Fuldense saeculi X: Cod. Theol 231 der k. Universitätsbibliothek zu Göttingen. Text und Bilderkreis (43 Tafeln)*. Ed. G. Richter and A. Schönfelder. Quellen und Abhandlungen zur Geschichte der Abtei und der Diözese Fulda IX. Fulda: Fuldaer Actiendruckerei, 1912.
Sancta synodus octava generalis: Constantinopolitana quarta. Mansi 16, 1–550.

Symeon the New Theologian. *Letter on Confession*. In *Enthusiasmus und Bussgewalt beim Mönchtum: Eine Studie zu Symeon dem neuen Theologen*. Ed. K. Holl. Leipzig: J. C. Hinrichs'sche Buchhandlung, 1898, 110–27.

Theodore of Canterbury. *Penitential*. In *Die Canones Theodori Cantuariensis und ihre Überlieferungsformen*. Ed. P. W. Finsterwalder. Untersuchungen zu den Bußbüchern des 7., 8., und 9. Jahrhunderts 1. Weimar: Hermann Böhlaus Nachfolger, 1929.

Theodulf of Orleans. In *Capitula Episcoporum* 1, 73–184.

Willibald. *Vita Bonifatii*. Ed. W. Levison. In Boniface, *Briefe*.

Wulfstan of York. *Sermo Lupi ad Anglos*. Ed. D. Whitelock. 3rd ed. London: Methuen, 1963.

Zachary. *Letter. MGH Epistolae* 3.2. Ed. W. Gundlach. Berlin: Weidmann, 1892, 479–87.

Secondary sources

Alfeyev, H. *St. Symeon the New Theologian and Orthodox Tradition*. Oxford Early Christian Studies. Oxford: Oxford University Press, 2000.

Althoff, G. *Die Macht der Rituale: Symbolik und Herrschaft im Mittelalter*. Darmstadt: Wissenschaftliche Buchgesellschaft, 2003.

Andrade, J. M. "Textos penitenciales y penitencia en el Nordeste de la peninsula ibérica." In *Latin Culture in the Eleventh Century: Proceedings of the Third International Conference on Medieval Latin Studies, Cambridge, 9–12 September 1998*. Ed. C. J. McDonough, M. W. Herren, and R. G. Arthur. Turnhout: Brepols, 2002, 29–38.

Angenendt, A. "Deus, qui nullum peccatum impunitum dimittit: Ein 'Grundsatz' der mittelalterlichen Bußgeschichte." In *Und dennoch ist von Gott zu reden: Festschrift für Herbert Vorgrimler*. Ed. M. Lutz-Bachmann. Freiburg: Herder, 1994, 142–56.

—. *Geschichte der Religiosität im Mittelalter*. Darmstadt: Wissenschaftliche Buchgesellschaft, 1997.

—. "Der Taufritus im frühen Mittelalter." In *Segni e riti nella chiesa altomedievale occidentale*. Settimane di studio 33. Spoleto: Centro italiano di studi sull'alto medioevo, 1987, 275–336.

—, T. Braucks, R. Busch, T. Lentes, and H. Lutterbach. "Gezählte Frömmigkeit." *Frühmittelalterliche Studien* 29 (1995): 1–71.

Aronstam, R. A. "The Blickling Homilies: A Reflection of Popular Anglo-Saxon Belief." In *Law, Church and Society: Essays in Honor of Stephan Kuttner*. Ed. K. Pennington and R. Somerville. Philadelphia, PA: University of Philadelphia Press, 1977, 271–80.

Asbach, F.-B. "Das Poenitentiale Remense und der sogen. Excarpsus Cummeani: Überlieferung, Quellen und Entwicklung zweier kontinentaler Bußbücher aus der 1. Hälfte des 8. Jahrhunderts." Unpublished Inaugural Dissertation. University of Regensburg, 1975.

Bachrach, D. S. "Confession in the Regnum Francorum (742–900)." *Journal of Ecclesiastical History* 54 (2003): 3–22.

Barringer, R. "The Pseudo-Amphilochian Life of Basil: Ecclesiastical Penance and Byzantine Hagiography." *Theologia* 51 (1980): 49–61.

Bezler, F. *Les pénitentiels espagnols: contribution à l'étude de la civilisation de l'Espagne chrétienne du haut Moyen Âge*. Münster: Aschendorff, 1994.

Blair, J., and R. Sharpe, eds. *Pastoral Care before the Parish*. London: Leicester University Press, 1992.

Brommer, P. "Die bischöfliche Gesetzgebung Theodulfs von Orléans," *Zeitschrift der Savigny-Stiftung für Rechtsgeschichte, kan. Abt.* 60 (1974): 1–120.

—. "Capitula episcoporum: Bemerkungen zu den bischöflichen Kapitularien," *Zeitschrift für Kirchengeschichte* 91 (1980): 207–36.

—. *"Capitula Episcoporum." Die bischöflichen Kapitularien des 9. und 10. Jahrhunderts*. Typologie des sources 43. Turnhout: Brepols, 1985.

Brown, P. *The Cult of Saints: Its Rise and Function in Latin Chistianity*. Chicago: University of Chicago Press, 1981.

—. "Eastern and Western Christendom in Late Antiquity: A Parting of the Ways." In his *Society and the Holy in Late Antiquity*. Berkeley, CA: University of California Press, 1982, 166–95.

—. "The Rise and Function of the Holy Man in Late Antiquity." In his *Society and the Holy in Late Antiquity*. Berkeley, CA: University of California Press, 1982, 103–52.

—. *The Rise of Western Christendom: Triumph and Diversity, AD 200–1000*. 2nd ed. Oxford: Blackwell, 2003.

—. "Vers la naissance du purgatoire: amnistie et pénitence dans le christianisme occidental de l'Antiquité tardive au Haut Moyen Âge." *Annales-Histoire, Sciences Sociales* 52 (1997): 1247–61.

Brundage, J. *Law, Sex, and Christian Society in Medieval Europe*. Chicago: University of Chicago Press, 1987.

Buc, P. *The Dangers of Ritual: Between Early Medieval Texts and Social Scientific Theory*. Princeton, NJ: Princeton University Press, 2001.

Bullough, D. "The Carolingian Liturgical Experience." In *Continuity and Change in Christian Worship*. Ed. R. Swanson. *SCH* 35. Woodbridge: Boydell Press, 1999, 29–64.

Caie, G. D. *The Old English Poem Judgment Day II: A Critical Edition with Editions of* De die iudicii *and the Hatton 113 homily* Be domes daege. Anglo-Saxon Texts 2. Cambridge: D. S. Brewer, 2000.

Carozzi, C. *Le voyage de l'âme dans l'au-delà d'après la littérature latine (Ve–XIIIe siècle)*. Collection de l'École française de Rome 189. Rome: École française de Rome, 1994.

Carr, E. "Penance among the Armenians: Notes on the History of its Practice and its Theology." *Studia Liturgica* 11 (1976): 65–100.

Charles-Edwards, T. *Early Christian Ireland*. Cambridge: Cambridge University Press, 2000.

—. "The Pastoral Role of the Church in the Early Irish Laws." In Blair and Sharpe, *Pastoral Care*, 63–80.

—. "The Penitential of Columbanus." In *Columbanus: Studies on the Latin Writings*. Ed. M. Lapidge. Studies in Celtic History 17. Woodbridge: Boydell Press, 1997, 217–39.

—. "The Penitential of Theodore and the *Iudicia Theodori*." In *Archbishop Theodore: Commemorative Studies on his Life and Influence*. Ed. M. Lapidge. Cambridge Studies in Anglo-Saxon England 11. Cambridge: Cambridge University Press, 1995, 141–74.

Cholij, R. *Theodore the Stoudite: The Ordering of Holiness*. Oxford Theological Monographs. Oxford: Oxford University Press, 2002.

Cowdrey, H. E. J. "The Spirituality of Pope Gregory VII." In his *Popes and Church Reform in the Eleventh Century*. Vol. 2. Aldershot: Variorum, 2000. Originally pub. in *The Mystical Tradition and the Carthusians*. Ed. J. Hogg. Analecta Cartusiana 130. Salzburg: Institut für Anglistik und Amerikanistik, Universität Salzburg, 1995, 1–22.

Cramer, P. *Baptism and Change in the Early Middle Ages, c. 200–c. 1150*. Cambridge: Cambridge University Press, 1993.

Davies, W., and P. Fouracre, eds. *The Settlement of Disputes in Early Medieval Europe*. Cambridge: Cambridge University Press, 1986.

de Jong, M. B. "Carolingian Monasticism: The Power of Prayer." In *NCMH* 2, 622–53.

—. "Pollution, Penance and Sanctity: Ekkehard's Life of Iso." In *The Community, the Family, and the Saint: Patterns of Power in Early Medieval Europe*. Ed. J. Hill and M. Swan. Turnhout: Brepols, 1998, 145–58.

—. "Power and Humility in Carolingian Society: The Public Penance of Louis the Pious." *EME* 1 (March 1992): 29–52.

—. "Transformations of Penance." In *Rituals of Power: From Late Antiquity to the Early Middle Ages*. Ed. F. Theuws and J. L. Nelson. Leiden: Brill, 2000, 185–224.

—. "What Was Public about Public Penance? *Paenitentia publica* and Justice in the Carolingian World." In *La giustizia nell'alto medioevo II (secoli IX–XI)*. Settimane di studio 44. Spoleto: Centro italiano di studi sull'alto medioevo, 1997, 863–904.

Delen, K. M., A. H. Gaastra, M. D. Saan, and B. Schaap. "The *Paenitentiale Cantabrigiense*: A Witness of the Carolingian Contribution to the Tenth-Century Reforms in England." *Sacris Erudiri: A Journal on the Inheritance of Early and Medieval Christianity* 41 (2002): 341–73.

Devailly, G. "La pastorale en Gaule au IXe siècle." *Revue d'histoire de l'église de France* 59 (1973): 23–54.

Diem, A. *Das monastische Experiment: die Rolle der Keuschheit bei der Entstehung des westlichen Mönchtums*. Münster: LIT Verlag, 2005.

Dierkens, A. "Prolégomènes à une histoire des relations culturelles entre les îles britanniques et le continent pendant le Haut Moyen Âge: la diffusion du monachisme dit colombanien ou iro-franc dans quelques monastères de la région parisienne au VIIe siècle et la politique religieuse de la reine Bathilde." In *La Neustrie: les pays au nord de la Loire de 650 à 850*. Ed. H. Atsma. Vol. 2. Beihefte der Francia 16. Sigmaringen: Thorbecke Verlag, 1989, 371–94.

Driscoll, M. S. *Alcuin et la pénitence à l'époque carolingienne*. Münster: Aschendorff Verlag, 1999.

—. "Penance in Transition: Popular Piety and Practice." In *Medieval Liturgy: A Book of Essays*. Ed. L. Larson-Miller. New York: Garland, 1997, 121–63.

Dutton, P. E. *The Politics of Dreaming in the Carolingian Empire*. Lincoln, NE: University of Nebraska Press, 1994.

Erickson, J. H. "Penitential Discipline in the Orthodox Canonical Tradition." In his *The Challenge of Our Past: Studies in Orthodox Canon Law and Church History*. Crestwood, NY: St. Vladimir's Seminary Press, 1991, 23–38.

Flandrin, J.-L. *Un temps pour embrasser: aux origines de la morale sexuelle occidentale (VI–XI siècle)*. Paris: Éditions du Seuil, 1983.

Flint, V. *The Rise of Magic in Early Medieval Europe*. Oxford: Clarendon Press, 1991.

Fournier, P. "Études sur les pénitentiels." *Revue d'histoire et de littérature religieuses* 6 (1901): 289–317; 7 (1902): 59–70 and 121–127; 8 (1903): 528–53; and 9 (1904): 97–103.

Fransen, G. "Le décret de Burchard de Worms: valeur du texte de l'édition. Essai de classement des manuscrits." *Zeitschrift der Savigny-Stiftung für Rechtsgeschichte* (Kanonistische Abteilung) 63 (1977): 1–19.

Frantzen, A. J. "Between the Lines: Queer Theory, the History of Homosexuality, and Anglo-Saxon Penitentials." *Journal of Medieval and Early Modern Studies* 26 (1996): 255–96.

—. *The Literature of Penance in Anglo-Saxon England*. New Brunswick, NJ: Rutgers University Press, 1983.

—. "The Penitentials Attributed to Bede." *Speculum* 58 (1983): 573–97.

—. "The Significance of the Frankish Penitentials." *Journal of Ecclesiastical History* 30 (1979): 409–21.

—. "The Tradition of Penitentials in Anglo-Saxon England." *Anglo-Saxon England* 11 (1982): 23–56.

—. "Where the Boys Are: Children and Sex in the Anglo-Saxon Penitentials." In *Becoming Male in the Middle Ages*. Ed. J. J. Cohen and B. Wheeler. New York: Garland, 1997, 43–66.

Goering, J. "The Internal Forum and the Literature of Penance and Confession." *Traditio* 59 (2004): 175–227.

—, and F. A. C. Mantello. "The Early Penitental Writings of Robert Grosseteste." *Recherches de théologie ancienne et médiévale* 54 (1987): 52–112.

—. "The 'Perambulavit Iudas . . . (Speculum confessionis)' Attributed to Robert Grosseteste." *Revue bénédictine* 96 (1986): 125–68.

Goez, W. "Canossa als *deditio*?" In *Studien zur Geschichte des Mittelalters: Jürgen Petersohn zum 65. Geburtstag*. Ed. M. Thumser, A. Wenz-Haubfleisch, and P. Wiegand. Stuttgart: Theiss, 2000, 92–99.

Gurevich, A. J. *Medieval Popular Culture: Problems of Belief and Perception*. Cambridge: Cambridge University Press, 1988.

Hägele, G. *Das Paenitentiale Vallicellianum I. Ein oberitalienischer Zweig der frühmittelalterlichen kontinentalen Bußbücher. Überlieferung, Verbreitung und Quellen*. Quellen und Forschungen zum Recht im Mittelalter 3. Sigmaringen: Thorbecke Verlag, 1984.

Haggenmüller, R. "Frühmittelalterliche Bußbücher-Paenitentialien-und das Kloster Lorsch." *Geschichtsblätter Kreis Bergstraße* 25 (1992): 125–54.

—. *Die Überlieferung der Beda und Egbert zugeschriebenen Bußbücher*. Frankfurt: Peter Lang, 1991.

—. "Zur Rezeption der Beda und Egbert zugeschriebenen Bußbücher." In *Aus Archiven und Bibliotheken: Festschrift für Raymund Kottje zum 65. Geburtstag*. Ed. H. Mordek. Frankfurt: Peter Lang, 1992, 149–59.

Hamilton, S. "A New Model for Royal Penance? Helgaud of Fleury's *Life of Robert the Pious*." *EME* 6 (1997): 189–200.

—. "Otto III's Penance: A Case Study of Unity and Diversity in the Eleventh-Century Church." In *Unity and Diversity in the Church*. Ed. R. Swanson. *SCH* 32. Oxford: Blackwell, 1995, 83–94.

—. "Penance in the Age of the Gregorian Reform." In *Retribution, Repentance, and Reconciliation*. Ed. K. Cooper and J. Gregory. *SCH* 40. Woodbridge: Boydell Press, 2004, 47–73.

—. *The Practice of Penance, 900–1050*. Woodbridge: Boydell Press, 2001.

—. "The Unique Favour of Penance: The Church and the People c. 800–c. 1100." In *The Medieval World*. Ed. P. Linehan and J. L. Nelson. London: Routledge, 2001, 229–45.

Harmening, D. *Superstitio: Ueberlieferungs- und theoriegeschichtliche Untersuchungen zur kirchlich-theologischen Aberglaubensliteratur des Mittelalters*. Berlin: E. Schmidt, 1979.

Hartmann, W. "Neue Texte zur bischöflichen Reformgesetzgebung aus den Jahren 829–31: Vier Diözesansynoden Halitgars von Cambrai." *Deutsches Archiv* 35 (1979): 368–94.

Hausherr, I. *Spiritual Direction in the Early Christian East*. Cistercian Studies Series 116. Kalamazoo: Cistercian Publications 1990. Originally pub. as *Direction spirituelle en orient autrefois*. Orientalia Christiana Analecta 144. Rome: Pontificium institutum orientalium studiorum, 1955.

Hen, Y. *Culture and Religion in Merovingian Gaul, A.D. 481–751*. Leiden: Brill, 1995.

—. "Knowledge of Canon Law among Rural Priests: The Evidence of Two Carolingian Manuscripts from around 800." *Journal of Theological Studies* N.S. 50 (1999): 117–34.

—. "The Structure and Aims of the *Visio Baronti*." *Journal of Theological Studies* N.S. 47 (1996): 477–97.

Hermann, E. "Il più antico penitenziale greco." *Orientalia Christiana Periodica* 19 (1953): 71–127.

Hoffmann, H., and R. Pokorny. *Das Dekret des Bisschofs Burchard von Worms: Textstufen-Frühe Verbreitung-Vorlagen. MGH Hilfsmittel* 12. Munich: MGH, 1991.

Holl, K. *Enthusiasmus und Bußgewalt beim Mönchtum: Eine Studie zu Symeon dem neuen Theologen*. Leipzig: J. C. Hinrichs'sche Buchhandlung, 1898.

Ireland, C. "Penance and Prayer in Water: An Irish Practice in Northumbrian Hagiography." *Cambrian Medieval Celtic Studies* 34 (1997): 51–66.

Jehl, R. "Die Geschichte des Lasterschemas und seiner Funktion: von der Väterzeit bis zur karolingischen Erneuerung." *Franziskanische Studien* 64 (1982): 261–359.

Jungmann, J. A. *Die lateinischen Bussriten in ihrer geschichtlichen Entwicklung*. Innsbruck: Rauch, 1932.

Keefe, S. A. *Water and the Word: Baptism and the Education of the Clergy in the Carolingian Empire*. 2 vols. Notre Dame, IN: University of Notre Dame Press, 2002.

Kerff, F. "Libri paenitentiales und kirchliche Strafgerichtsbarkeit bis zum Decretum Gratiani: Ein Diskussionsvorschlag." *Zeitschrift der Savigny-Stiftung für Rechtsgeschichte* (Kanonistische Abteilung) 75 (1989): 23–57.

—. "Mittelalterliche Quellen und mittelalterliche Wirklichkeit: zu den Konsequenzen einer jüngst erschienenen Edition für unser Bild kirchlicher Reformbemühungen." *Rheinische Vierteljahrsblätter* 51 (1987): 275–86.

—. "Das Paenitentiale Pseudo-Gregorii: eine kritische Edition." In *Aus Archiven und Bibliotheken: Festschrift für Raymund Kottje zum 65. Geburtstag*. Ed. H. Mordek. Frankfurt: Peter Lang, 1992, 161–88.

—. "Das Paenitentiale Pseudo-Gregorii III: ein Zeugnis karolingischer Reformbestrebungen." *Zeitschrift der Savigny-Stiftung für Rechtsgeschichte* (Kanonistische Abteilung) 69 (1983): 46–63.

—. *Der Quadripartitus: ein Handbuch der karolingischen Kirchenreform. Überlieferung, Quellen und Rezeption*. Quellen und Forschungen zum Recht im Mittelalter 1. Sigmaringen: Thorbecke, 1982.

—. "Das sogenannte Paenitentiale Fulberti: Überlieferung, Verfasserfrage, Edition." *Zeitschrift der Savigny-Stiftung für Rechtsgeschichte* (Kanonistische Abteilung) 73 (1987): 1–40.

Klingshirn, W. E. *Caesarius of Arles: The Making of a Christian Community in Late Antique Gaul*. Cambridge: Cambridge University Press, 1994.

Körntgen, L. "Der *Excarpsus Cummeani*, ein Bußbuch aus Corbie." In *Scientia veritatis: Festschrift für Hubert Mordek zum 65. Geburtstag*. Ed. O. Münsch and T. Zotz. Ostfildern: Jan Thorbecke Verlag, 2004, 59–75.

—. "Fortschreibung frühmittelalterlicher Bußpraxis: Burchards 'Liber corrector' und seine Quellen." In *Bischof Burchard von Worms, 1000–1025*. Ed. W. Hartmann. Mainz: Gesellschaft für mittelrheinische Kirchengeschichte, 2000, 199–226.

—. "Ein italienisches Bußbuch und seine fränkische Quellen: das anonyme Paenitentiale der Handschrift Vatikan, Arch. S. Pietro H 58." In *Aus Archiven und Bibliotheken: Festschrift für Raymund Kottje zum 65. Geburtstag*. Ed. H. Mordek. Frankfurt: Peter Lang, 1992, 189–205.

—. "Kirchenbuße." *Reallexikon der Germanischen Altertumskunde* 16, 561–64.

—. *Studien zu den Quellen der frühmittelalterlichen Bußbücher*. Quellen und Forschungen zum Recht im Mittelalter 7. Sigmaringen: Thorbecke, 1993.

Kottje, R. "Bußbücher." *Lexikon des Mittelalters* 2. Munich: Artemis Verlag, 1983, 1118–22.

—. *Die Bussbücher Halitgars von Cambrai und des Hrabanus Maurus: Ihre Überlieferung und ihre Quellen*. Beiträge zur Geschichte und Quellenkunde des Mittelalters 8. Berlin: de Gruyter, 1980.

—. "Buße oder Strafe? Zur 'Iustitia' in den 'Libri Paenitentiales.'" In *La giustizia nell'Alto Medioevo (secoli V–VIII)*. Settimane di studio 42. Spoleto: Centro italiano di studi sull'alto medioevo 1995, 443–74.

—. "Busspraxis und Bussritus." In *Segni e riti nella chiesa altomedievale occidentale*. Settimane di studio 33. Spoleto: Centro italiano di studi sull'alto medioevo, 1987, 369–95.

—. "Ehe und Eheverständnis in den vorgratianischen Bussbüchern." In *Love and Marriage in the Twelfth Century*. Ed. W. van Hoecke and A. Welkenhuysen. Leuven: Leuven University Press, 1981, 18–40.

—. "Einheit und Vielfalt des kirchlichen Lebens in der Karolingerzeit." *Zeitschrift für Kirchengeschichte* 60 (1965): 323–42.

—. "Paenitentiale Theodori." In *Handwörterbuch zur deutschen Rechtsgeschichte*. Vol. 3. Berlin: Schmidt, 1984, 1413–16.

—. "Überlieferung und Rezeption der irischen Bußbücher auf dem Kontinent." In *Die Iren und Europa im früheren Mittelalter*. Ed. H. Löwe. Vol. 1. Stuttgart: Klett-Cotta, 1982, 511–24.

Lapidge, M., ed. *Archbishop Theodore: Commemorative Studies on his Life and Influence*. Cambridge Studies in Anglo-Saxon England 11. Cambridge: Cambridge University Press, 1995.

—, ed. *Columbanus: Studies on the Latin Writings*. Studies in Celtic History 17. Woodbridge: Boydell Press, 1997.

Le Goff, J. *La naissance du purgatoire*. Paris: Éditions Gallimard, 1981.

Leyser, K. "Early Medieval Canon Law and the Beginnings of Knighthood." In *Institutionen, Kultur und Gesellschaft im Mittelalter: Festschrift für Josef Fleckenstein zu seinem 65. Geburtstag*. Ed. L. Fenske, W. Rösener, and T. Zotz. Sigmaringen: Thorbecke, 1984, 549–66; reprinted in *Communication and Power in Medieval Europe: The Carolingian and Ottonian Centuries*. Ed. T. Reuter. London: Hambledon Press, 1994, 51–71.

Lutterbach, H. "Intentions- oder Tathaftung? Zum Bußverständnis in den frühmittelalterlichen Bußbüchern." *Frühmittelalterliche Studien* 29 (1995): 120–43.

—. "Die mittelalterlichen Bußbücher-Trägermedien von Einfachreligiosität?" *Zeitschrift für Kirchengeschichte* 114 (2003): 227–44.
—. *Sexualität im Mittelalter: eine Kulturstudie anhand von Bußbüchern des 6. bis 12. Jahrhundert.* Beihefte zum Archiv für Kulturgeschichte 43. Cologne: Böhlau Verlag, 1999.
—. "Die Speisegesetzgebung in den mittelalterlichen Bußbüchern (600–1200): Religionsgeschichtliche Perspektiven." *Archiv für Kulturgeschichte* 80 (1998): 1–37.
Lynch, J. H. *Christianizing Kinship: Ritual Sponsorship in Anglo-Saxon England.* Ithaca, NY: Cornell University Press, 1998.
—. *Godparents and Kinship in Early Medieval Europe.* Princeton, NJ: Princeton University Press, 1986.
Mahadevan, L. "Überlieferung und Verbreitung des Bussbuchs 'Capitula Iudiciorum.'" *Zeitschrift der Savigny-Stiftung für Rechtsgeschichte* (Kanonistische Abteilung) 72 (1986): 17–75.
Manselli, R. "Vie familiale et éthique sexuelle dans les pénitentiels." In *Famille et parenté dans l'occident mediéval.* Ed. G. Duby and J. Le Goff. Rome: École française de Rome, 1977, 363–78.
Mansfield, M. C. *The Humiliation of Sinners: Public Penance in Thirteenth-Century France.* Ithaca, NY: Cornell University Press, 1995.
Markus, R. A. *The End of Ancient Christianity.* Cambridge: Cambridge University Press, 1990.
—. "From Caesarius to Boniface: Christianity and Paganism in Gaul." In *Le septième siècle: changements et continuités (The Seventh Century: Change and Continuity).* Ed. J. Fontaine and J. Hillgarth. London: Warburg Institute, 1992, 154–72.
McKitterick, R. "Anglo-Saxon Missionaries in Germany: Reflections on the Manuscript Evidence." *Transactions of the Cambridge Bibliographical Society* 9 (1989): 291–329.
—. *The Carolingians and the Written Word.* Cambridge: Cambridge University Press, 1989.
—. "Unity and Diversity in the Carolingian Church." In *Unity and Diversity in the Church.* Ed. R. Swanson. *SCH* 32. Oxford: Blackwell, 1995, 59–82.
McNeill, J. T., and H. Gamer. *Medieval Handbooks of Penance.* 2nd ed. New York: Columbia University Press, 1990.
Meens, R. "'Aliud benitenciale': The Ninth-Century *Paenitentiale Vindobonense C.*" *Mediaeval Studies* 66 (2004): 1–26.
—. "Children and Confession in the Early Middle Ages." In *The Church and Childhood.* Ed. D. Wood. *SCH* 31. Oxford: Blackwell, 1994, 53–65.
—. "Christentum und Heidentum aus der Sicht Willibrords? Überlegungen zum *Paenitentiale Oxoniense II.*" In *L'évangélisation des régions entre Meuse et Moselle et la fondation de l'abbaye d'Echternach (Ve–IXe siècle).* Ed. M. Polfer. Publications de CLUDEM 16. Luxemburg: Imprimerie Linden, 2000, 415–28.
—. "The Frequency and Nature of Early Medieval Penance." In *Handling Sin: Confession in the Middle Ages.* Ed. P. Biller and A. J. Minnis. York Studies in Medieval Theology 2. Woodbridge: York Medieval Press, 1998, 35–61.
—. "Kanonisches Recht in Salzburg am Ende des 8. Jahrhunderts: das Zeugnis des *Paenitentiale Vindobonense B.*" *Zeitschrift der Savigny-Stiftung für Rechtsgeschichte* (Kanonistische Abteilung) 82 (1996): 13–34.
—. "*Paenitentia publica* en *paenitentia privata.* Aantekeningen bij de oorsprong van de zogeheten Karolingische dichotomie." In *Die Fonteyn der ewiger wijsheit: opstellen aangeboden*

aan prof. dr. A. G. Weiler ter gelegenheid van zijn 25-jarig jubileum als hoogleraar. Eds. P. Bange and P. de Kort. Nijmegen: Centrum voor Middeleeuwse Studies, 1989, 65–74.

—. "The Penitential of Finnian and the Textual Witness of the *Paenitentiale Vindobonense B*." *Mediaeval Studies* 55 (1993): 243–55.

—. "Pollution in the Early Middle Ages: The Case of the Food Regulations in Penitentials." *EME* 4 (1995): 3–19.

—. "Reforming the Clergy: A Context for the Use of the Bobbio Penitential." In *The Bobbio Missal: Liturgy and Religious Culture in Merovingian Gaul*. Ed. Y. Hen and R. Meens. Cambridge Studies in Palaeography and Codicology 11. Cambridge: Cambridge University Press, 2004, 154–67.

—. *Het tripartite boeteboek: overlevering en betekenis van vroegmiddeleeuwse biechtvoorschriften (met editie en vertaling van vier tripartita)*. Hilversum: Verloren, 1994.

—. "Willibrords boeteboek?" *Tijdschrift voor Geschiedenis* 106 (1993): 163–78.

Michaud-Quantin, P. "Un manuel de confession archaïque dans le manuscrit Avranches 136." *Sacris Erudiri* 17 (1966): 5–54.

Mordek, H. *Kirchenrecht und Reform im Frankenreich: die Collectio Vetus Gallica, die älteste systematische Kanonessammlung des fränkischen Gallien. Studien und Edition*. Beiträge zur Geschichte und Quellenkunde des Mittelalters, 1. New York: de Gruyter, 1975.

Morris, R. *Monks and Laymen in Byzantium, 843–1118*. Cambridge: Cambridge University Press, 1995.

Murray, A. "Confession before 1215." *Transactions of the Royal Historical Society*, 6th ser., 3 (1993): 51–81.

Muschiol, G. "Men, Women and Liturgical Practice in the Early Medieval West." In *Gender in the Early Medieval World: East and West, 300–900*. Ed. L. Brubaker and J. M. H. Smith. Cambridge: Cambridge University Press, 2004, 98–216.

Muzzarelli, M. G., ed. *Una componente della mentalità occidentale: i penitenziali nell'alto medioevo*. Il mondo medievale: Studi di storia e storiografia 9. Bologna: Patron Editore, 1980.

—. "Le donne e i bambini nei libri penitenziali: regole di condotta per una società in formazione." In *Profili di donne: Mito, immagine, realtà fra medioevo ed età contemporanea*. Galatino: Congedo Editore, 1986, 145–92.

—. "Norme di comportamento alimentare nei libri penitenziali." *Quaderni Medievali* 13 (1982): 45–80.

—. *Penitenze nel Medioevo: uomini e modelli a confronto*. Il mondo medievale: Studi di storia e storiografia 22. Bologna: Patron Editore, 1994.

—. "Il valore della vita nell'Alto Medioevo: la testimonianza dei libri penitenziali." *Aevum* 62 (1988): 171–85.

Nelson, J. L. "Literacy in Carolingian Government." In *The Uses of Literacy in Early Medieval Europe*. Ed. R. McKitterick. Cambridge: Cambridge University Press, 1990, 258–96.

Newhauser, R. N. "Towards *modus in habendo*: Transformations in the Idea of Avarice: The Early Penitentials through the Carolingian Reforms." *Zeitschrift der Savigny-Stiftung für Rechtsgeschichte* (Kanonistische Abteilung) 75 (1989): 1–22.

O'Loughlin, T. "Penitentials and Pastoral Care." In *A History of Pastoral Care*. Ed. G. R. Evans. London: Cassell, 2000, 93–111.

Paxton, F. S. "*Bonus liber*: A Late Carolingian Clerical Manual from Lorsch (Biblioteca Vaticana MS Pal. lat. 485)." In *The Two Laws: Studies in Medieval Legal History Dedicated to Stephan Kuttner*. Ed. L. Mayali and S. Tibbets. Studies in Medieval and Early Modern Canon Law 1. Washington, DC: Catholic University of America Press, 1991, 1–30.

———. *Christianizing Death: The Creation of a Ritual Process in Early Medieval Europe*. Ithaca, NY: Cornell University Press, 1990.

Payer, P. J. "Early Medieval Regulations Concerning Marital Sexual Relations." *Journal of Medieval History* 6 (1980): 353–76.

———. "The Humanism of the Penitentials and the Continuity of the Penitential Tradition." *Mediaeval Studies* 46 (1984): 340–54.

———. *Sex and the Penitentials: The Development of a Sexual Code, 550–1150*. Toronto: University of Toronto Press, 1984.

Platelle, H. "La violence et ses remèdes en Flandre au IXe siècle." *Sacris Erudiri* 20 (1971): 101–73.

Poschmann, B. *Die abendländische Kirchenbusse im frühen Mittelalter*. Breslauer Studien zur historischen Theologie 16. Breslau: Müller & Seiffert, 1930.

———. *Penance and the Anointing of the Sick*. New York: Herder and Herder, 1964.

Price, R. "Informal Penance in Early Medieval Christendom." In *Retribution, Repentance, and Reconciliation*. Ed. K. Cooper and J. Gregory. *SCH* 40. Woodbridge: Boydell Press for the Ecclesiastical History Society, 2004, 29–39.

Rafnsson, S. "The Penitential of St. Thorlakur in Its Icelandic Context." *Bulletin of Medieval Canon Law* 15 (1985): 19–30.

Rosenwein, B. H. *Negotiating Space: Power, Restraint, and Privileges of Immunity in Early Medieval Europe*. Ithaca, NY: Cornell University Press, 1999.

Sauer, H. *Theodulfi Capitula in England*. Texte und Untersuchungen zur Englischen Philologie 8. Munich: Wilhelm Fink Verlag, 1978.

———. "Zur Überlieferung und Anlage von Erzbischof Wulfstans 'Handbuch.'" *Deutsches Archiv* 36 (1980): 341–84.

Schwaibold, M. "Mittelalterliche Bussbücher und sexuelle Normalität." *Ius Commune: Zeitschrift für Europäische Rechtsgeschichte* 15 (1988): 107–33.

Smith, J. M. H. "Einhard: The Sinner and the Saints." *Transactions of the Royal Historical Society* 13 (2003): 55–77.

———. "Religion and Lay Society." In *NCMH* 2, 654–78.

Spindler, R. *Das altenglische Bussbuch (sog. Confessionale Pseudo-Egberti)*. Leipzig: Bernhard Tauchnitz, 1934.

Stancliffe, C, "Jonas' Life of Columbanus and his Disciples." In *Studies in Irish Hagiography*. Ed. J. Carey, M. Herbert, and P. Ó Riain. Dublin: Four Courts Press, 1999, 189–220.

Stewart, C. "The Desert Fathers on Radical Self-Honesty." *Vox Benedictina* 8 (1991): 7–53.

Thacker, A. "Bede's Ideal of Reform." In *Ideal and Reality in Frankish and Anglo-Saxon Society: Studies Presented to J. M. Wallace-Hadrill*. Ed. P. Wormald and R. Collins. Oxford: Blackwell, 130–53.

———. "Monks, Preaching, and Pastoral Care in Early Anglo-Saxon England." In Blair and Sharpe, *Pastoral Care*, 137–70.

Turner, H. *St. Symeon the New Theologian and Spiritual Fatherhood*. Leiden: Brill, 1990.
van Dam, R. *Saints and their Miracles in Late Antique Gaul*. Princeton, NJ: Princeton University Press, 1993.
van Rhijn, C. *Shepherds of the Lord: Priests and Episcopal Statutes in the Carolingian Period*. Cultural Encounters in Late Antiquity and the Middle Ages 6. Turnhout: Brepols, 2007.
Vogel, C. "Composition légale et commutations dans le système de la pénitence tarifée." *Revue de Droit Canonique* 8 (1958): 289–318 and 9 (1959): 1–38 and 341–59.
—. "La discipline pénitentielle en Gaule des origines à la fin du IXe siècle: le dossier hagiographique." *Revue des Sciences Religieuses* 30 (1956): 1–26 and 157–86.
—. *La discipline pénitentielle en Gaule des origines à la fin du VIIe siècle*. Paris: Letouzey, 1952.
—. *Les "Libri Paenitentiales."* Typologie des sources du Moyen Âge occidental 27. Turnhout: Brepols, 1978. Updated by A. J. Frantzen. Turnhout: Brepols, 1985.
—. *Le pécheur et la pénitence au Moyen Âge: textes choisis, traduits et présentés par Cyrille Vogel*. Paris: Éditions du Cerf, 1969.
—. "Pratiques superstitieuses au début du XIe siècle d'après le Corrector sive Medicus du Burchard, évèque de Worms (965–1025)." *Mélanges E. R. Labande*. Poitiers: CÉSCM, 1974, 751–61.
Wagner, G. "Bussdisziplin in der Tradition des Ostens." In *Liturgie et remission des péchés: Conférences Saint-Serge XXe Semaine d'Études Liturgiques*. Rome: Edizioni Liturgiche, 1975, 251–64.

20 Sickness and healing

Peregrine Horden

Primary sources

Alexander von Tralles: Original-text und Übersetzung. Ed. T. Puschmann. 2 vols.; reprint, Amsterdam: M. Hakkert, 1963.
Anastasius Sinaita. *Interrogationes et responsiones*. *PG* 89, 311–823.
Anglo-Saxon Remedies, Charms, and Prayers from British Library MS Harley 585: The Lacnunga. Ed. E. Pettit. 2 vols. Mellen Critical Editions and Translations 6a. Lewiston, NY: Edwin Mellen Press, 2001.
Anskar. *Miracula Sancti Willehadi*. *AASS* Nov. 3, 8.847–51.
The Book of St. Gilbert. Ed. R. Foreville and G. Keir. Oxford: Oxford University Press, 1987.
Brock, S. P. "A Syriac Life of John of Dailam." *Parole de l'Orient* 10 (1981–82): 123–89.
Burchard of Worms. *Corrector et medicus* (*Decretum* book 19). *PL* 140, 943–1018.
Constantine Porphyrogenitus. *Le livre des cérémonies*. Ed. A. Vogt. 4 vols. Paris: Les Belles Lettres, 1935–40.
Ekkehard IV. *Casus Sancti Galli*. Ed. and trans. H. F. Haefele. Ausgewählte Quellen zur deutschen Geschichte des Mittelalters 10. Darmstadt: Wissenschaftliche Buchgesellschaft, 1980.
Gregory the Great. *Regula pastoralis*. Ed. and trans. B. Judic, F. Rommel, and C. Morel. *Règle pastorale*. 2 vols. *SC* 381–82. Paris: Éditions du Cerf, 1992.
Guillaume de Saint-Pathus. *Les miracles de Saint Louis*. Ed. P. B. Fay. Paris: J. Champion, 1931.

Haddan, A. W., and W. Stubbs. *Councils and Ecclesiastical Documents Relating to Great Britain and Ireland*. 3 vols. Oxford: Clarendon Press, 1869–78.

[Hippocratic author]. *On Breaths*. Ed. I. L. Heiberg. Corpus Medicorum Graecorum 1.1. Leipzig: Teubner, 1927.

Jeanselme, E. "Sur un aide-mémoire de thérapeutique byzantin contenu dans un manuscrit de la Bibliothèque nationale de Paris (Supplément grec 764): traduction, notes et commentaires." In Vol. 1 of *Mélanges Charles Diehl*. 2 vols. Études sur l'histoire et sur l'art de Byzance. Paris: E. Leroux, 1930, 147–70.

Kaiser, D. H., ed. and trans. *The Laws of Rus', Tenth to Fifteenth Centuries*. Salt Lake City, UT: Charles Schlacks, Jr., 1992.

Das "Lorscher Arzneibuch": ein medizinisches Kompendium des 8. Jahrhunderts. Codex Bambergensis medicinalis 1. Text, Übersetzung und Fachglossar. Ed. U. Stoll. Sudhoffs Archiv Beiheft 28. Stuttgart: Franz Steiner, 1992.

MacKinney, L. C. "An Unpublished Treatise from the Age of Charlemagne." *Speculum* 18 (1943): 494–96.

McNeill, J. T., and H. M. Gamer. *Medieval Handbooks of Penance*. New York: Columbia University Press, 1938; repr., New York: Octagon Books, 1979.

Michael Italicus. *Michel Italikus: lettres et discours*. Ed. P. Gautier. Paris: Institut française d'études byzantines, 1972.

Maxwell-Stuart, P. G., ed. and trans. *The Occult in Mediaeval Europe*. Basingstoke: Palgrave Macmillan, 2005.

Regula Benedicti, de codice 914 in bibliotheca monasterii S. Galli servato. Ed. B. Probst. St. Ottilien: EOS, 1983.

Tanner, N., ed. *Decrees of the Ecumenical Councils*. 2 vols. Washington, DC: Georgetown University Press, 1990.

Theophanes Chrysobalantes. *Theophanis Nonni epitome de curatione morborum Graece ac Latine*. Ed. J. St. Bernard. 2 vols. Amsterdam: Gotha, 1794–95.

"Le typikon du Christ Sauveur Pantokrator." Ed. P. Gautier. *Revue des études byzantines* 32 (1974): 1–145.

Vie de Théodore de Sykéôn. Ed. A.-J. Festugière. 2 vols. Subsidia hagiographica 48. Brussels: Société des Bollandistes, 1970. Trans. E. Dawes and N. Baynes. *Three Byzantine Saints*. Oxford: Mowbray, 1977, 87–192.

Vitas sanctorum patrum Emeretensium. Ed. A. Maya Sánchez. *CCSL* 116. Turnhout: Brepols, 1992. Trans. A. T. Fear. *Lives of the Visigothic Fathers*. Liverpool: Liverpool University Press, 1997.

Secondary sources

Agrimi, J., and C. Crisciani. "Medicina del corpo e medicina dell'anima: note sul sapere del medico fino all'inizio del sec. XIII." *Episteme* 10 (1976): 5–102.

Amundsen, D. W. *Medicine, Society, and Faith in the Ancient and Early Medieval Worlds*. Baltimore, MD: Johns Hopkins University Press, 1996.

Arbesmann, R. "The Concept of *Christus medicus* in St. Augustine." *Traditio* 10 (1954): 1–28.

Bennett, D. "Medical Practice and Manuscripts in Byzantium." In *Social History of Medicine* 13, pt. 2 (2000), special issue: *The Year 1000*. Ed. P. Horden and E. Savage-Smith, 279–91.

—. "Xenonika: Medical Texts Associated with *xenones* in the Late Byzantine Period." Unpublished Ph.D. dissertation, University of London, 2003.

Biller, P., and J. Ziegler, eds. *Religion and Medicine in the Middle Ages*. Woodbridge: Boydell Press, 2001.

Burnett, C., and D. Jacquart, eds. *Constantine the African and 'Alī ibn al-'Abbās al-Maǧūsī: The Pantegni and Related Texts*. Leiden: Brill, 1994.

Campbell, S., B. Hall, and D. Klausner, eds. *Health, Disease and Healing in Medieval Culture*. Basingstoke: Macmillan, 1992.

Conrad, L. I., M. Neve, V. Nutton, R. Porter, and A. Wear. *The Western Medical Tradition, 800 BC to AD 1800*. Cambridge: Cambridge University Press, 1995.

Constantelos, D. J. *Byzantine Philanthropy and Social Welfare*. 2nd ed. New Rochelle, NY: Aristide D. Caratzas, 1991.

Cunningham, G. *Religion and Magic: Approaches and Theories*. Edinburgh: Edinburgh University Press, 1999.

Davies, W. "The Place of Healing in Early Irish Society." In *Sages, Saints and Storytellers: Celtic Studies in Honour of Professor James Carney*. Ed. D. Ó Corráin, L. Breatnach, and K. McCone. Maynooth: An Sagart, 1989, 43–55.

Dawtry, A. F. "The *modus medendi* and the Benedictine Order in Anglo-Norman England." *SCH* 19 (1982): 25–38.

Déroche, V. "Pourquoi écrivait-on des recueils de miracles? L'exemple des miracles de Saint Artémios." In *Les saints et leurs sanctuaires à Byzance: textes, images, et monuments*. Ed. C. Jolivet-Lévy, M. Kaplan, and J.-P. Sodini. Byzantina Sorbonensia 11. Paris: Sorbonne, 1993, 95–116.

Dickinson, T. M. "An Anglo-Saxon 'Cunning Woman' from Bidford-on-Avon." In *In Search of Cult: Archaeological Investigations in Honour of Philip Rahtz*. Ed. M. Carver. Woodbridge: Boydell Press, 1993, 45–54.

Duffy, J. "Byzantine Medicine in the Sixth and Seventh Centuries: Aspects of Teaching and Practice." *DOP* 38 (1984): 21–27.

—. "Reactions of Two Byzantine Intellectuals to the Theory and Practice of Magic." In *Byzantine Magic*. Ed. H. Maguire. Washington, DC: Dumbarton Oaks, 1995, 83–97.

Farmer, S. *Surviving Poverty in Medieval Paris: Gender, Ideology and the Daily Lives of the Poor*. Ithaca, NY: Cornell University Press, 2002.

Ferngren, G. B. "Early Christianity as a Religion of Healing." *Bulletin of the History of Medicine* 66 (1992): 1–15.

Finucane, R. C. *Miracles and Pilgrims: Popular Beliefs in Medieval England*. London: J. M. Dent, 1977.

Flint, V. I. J. "The Early Medieval *medicus*, the Saint – and the Enchanter." *Social History of Medicine* 2 (1989): 127–45.

—. *The Rise of Magic in Early Medieval Europe*. Oxford: Oxford University Press, 1991.

Franklin, S., and J. Shepard. *The Emergence of Rus 750–1200*. London: Longman, 1996.

Gil-Sotres, P. "The Regimens of Health." In *Western Medical Thought from Antiquity to the Middle Ages*. Ed. M. D. Grmek. Cambridge, MA: Harvard University Press, 1998, 291–318.

Glaze, F. E. "The Perforated Wall: The Ownership and Circulation of Medical Books in Medieval Europe, c. 800–1200." Unpublished Ph.D. dissertation, Duke University, 1999.

Green, M. H., ed. and trans. *The Trotula: A Medieval Compendium of Women's Medicine*. Philadelphia, PA: University of Pennsylvania Press, 2001.

—. *Women's Healthcare in the Medieval West: Texts and Contexts*. Aldershot: Ashgate, 2000.

Grmek, M. D., ed. *Western Medical Thought from Antiquity to the Middle Ages*. Cambridge, MA: Harvard University Press, 1998.

Grumel, V. "La profession médicale à Byzance à l'époque des Comnènes." *Revue des études byzantines* 7 (1949): 42–46.

Haldon, J. "The Works of Anastasius of Sinai: A Key Source for the History of Seventh-Century East Mediterranean Society and Belief." In *The Byzantine and Early Islamic Near East*. Vol. 1: *Problems in the Literary Source Material*. Ed. A. Cameron and L. I. Conrad. Princeton, NJ: Darwin Press, 1992, 107–47.

Horden, P. "The Christian Hospital in Late Antiquity – Break or Bridge?" In *Gesundheit–Krankheit: Kulturtransfer medizinischen Wissens von der Spätantike bis in die Frühe Neuzeit*. Ed. F. Steger and K. P. Jankrift. Beiheft zum Archiv für Kulturgeschichte 55. Cologne: Böhlau Verlag, 2004, 77–99.

—. "The Earliest Hospitals in Byzantium, Western Europe, and Islam." *Journal of Interdisciplinary History* 35 (2005): 361–89.

—. "Family History and Hospital History in the Middle Ages." In *Living in the City*. Ed. E Sonnino. Rome: Università La Sapienza, 2004, 255–82.

—. "Household Care and Informal Networks: Comparisons and Continuities from Antiquity to the Present." In *The Locus of Care: Families, Communities, Institutions and the Provision of Welfare since Antiquity*. Ed. P. Horden and R. Smith. London: Routledge, 1998, 21–67.

—. "Ritual and Public Health in the Early Medieval City." In *Body and City: Histories of Urban Public Health*. Ed. S. Sheard and H. Power. London: Ashgate, 2000, 17–40.

—. "Saints and Doctors in the Early Byzantine Empire: The Case of Theodore of Sykeon." *SCH* 19 (1982): 1–13.

Horn, W., and E. Born, *The Plan of St. Gall: A Study of the Architecture and Economy of and Life in a Paradigmatic Carolingian Monastery*. 3 vols. Berkeley, CA: University of California Press, 1979.

Jacquart, D. *Le milieu médical en France du XII au XVe siècle, en annexe 2e supplément au 'Dictionnaire' d'Ernest Wickersheimer*. Geneva: Droz and Champion, 1981.

Jolly, K. [L.] "Medieval Magic: Definitions, Beliefs, Practices." In *The Athlone History of Witchcraft and Magic in Europe*. Vol. 3: *The Middle Ages*. Ed. K. Jolly, C. Raudvere, and E. Peters. London: Athlone Press, 2002, 1–71.

—. *Popular Religion in Late Saxon England: Elf Charms in Context*. Chapel Hill, NC: University of North Carolina Press, 1996.

Knipp, D. "The Chapel of Physicians at Santa Maria Antiqua" [eighth-century Rome]. *DOP* 56 (2002): 1–23.

Kroll, J., and B. Bachrach. "Sin and the Etiology of Disease in Pre-Crusade Europe." *Journal of the History of Medicine and Allied Sciences* 41 (1986): 395–414.

Leven, K.-H. "Attitudes towards Physical Health in Late Antiquity." In *Coping with Sickness: Perspectives on Health Care, Past and Present*. Ed. J. Woodward and R. Jütte. Sheffield: European Association for the History of Medicine and Health, 1996, 73–89.

MacKinney, L. C. *Early Medieval Medicine with Special Reference to France and Chartres*. Baltimore, MD: Johns Hopkins University Press, 1937.

MacMullen, R. *Christianity and Paganism in the Fourth to Eighth Centuries*. New Haven, CT: Yale University Press, 1997.

Magoulias, H. J. "The Lives of the Saints as Sources of Data for the History of Byzantine Medicine in the Sixth and Seventh Centuries." *Byzantinische Zeitschrift* 57 (1964): 127–50.

Maguire, H. "Introduction." In *Byzantine Magic*. Ed. H. Maguire. Washington, DC: Dumbarton Oaks, 1995, 1–7.

McVaugh, M. R. "Bedside Manners in the Middle Ages." *Bulletin of the History of Medicine* 71 (1997): 201–23.

—. *Medicine before the Plague: Practitioners and their Patients in the Crown of Aragon, 1285–1345*. Cambridge: Cambridge University Press, 1994.

Meaney, A. L. *Anglo-Saxon Amulets and Curing Stones*. *British Archaeological Reports*, British Series 96. Oxford: British Archaeological Reports, 1981.

—. "The Anglo-Saxon View of the Causes of Illness." In Campbell, Hall, and Klausner, *Health, Disease and Healing*, 12–33.

—. "The Practice of Medicine in England about the Year 1000." In *Social History of Medicine* 13, pt. 2 (2000), special issue: *The Year 1000*. Ed. P. Horden and E. Savage-Smith, 224–27.

—. "Women, Witchcraft and Magic in Anglo-Saxon England." In *Superstition and Popular Medicine in Anglo-Saxon England*. Ed. D. G. Scragg. Manchester: University of Manchester Centre for Anglo-Saxon Studies, 1989, 9–40.

Meens, R. "Magic and the Early Medieval World View." In *The Community, the Family and the Saint: Patterns of Power in Early Medieval Europe*. Ed. J. Hill and M. Swan. Turnhout: Brepols, 1998, 285–95.

Miller, T. S. *The Birth of the Hospital in the Byzantine Empire*. 2nd ed. Baltimore, MD: Johns Hopkins University Press, 1997.

Möhler, R. *"Epistula de vulture": Untersuchungen zu einer organotherapeutischen Drogenmonographie des Frühmittelalters*. Pattensen/ Hanover: Horst Wellm, 1990.

Murray, A. "Missionaries and Magic in Dark-Age Europe." *Past and Present* 136 (1992): 186–205.

Nutton, V. *Ancient Medicine*. London: Routledge, 2004.

—. "Archiatri and the Medical Profession in Antiquity." *Papers of the British School at Rome* 45 (1977): 191–226; reprinted in his *From Democedes to Harvey: Studies in the Social History of Medicine*. London: Variorum, 1988.

—. "From Galen to Alexander: Aspects of Medicine and Medical Practice in Late Antiquity." *DOP* 38 (1984): 1–14.

—. "Healers in the Medical Market Place: Towards a Social History of Graeco-Roman Medicine." In *Medicine in Society*. Ed. A. Wear. Cambridge: Cambridge University Press, 1992, 15–58.

Park, K. "Medicine and Society in Medieval Europe 500–1500." In *Medicine in Society*. Ed. A. Wear. Cambridge: Cambridge University Press, 1992, 59–90.

Paxton, F. S. "Anointing the Sick and the Dying in Christian Antiquity and the Early Medieval West." In Campbell, Hall, and Klausner, *Health, Disease and Healing*, 93–102.

—. "*Bonus liber*: A Late Carolingian Clerical Manual from Lorsch (Bibliotheca Vaticana MS Pal. lat. 485)." In *The Two Laws: Studies in Medieval Legal History Dedicated to Stephan*

Kuttner. Ed. L. Mayali and S. A. J. Tibbetts. Washington, DC: Catholic University of America Press, 1990, 1–30.

———. "Curing Bodies–Curing Souls: Hrabanus Maurus, Medical Education, and the Clergy in Ninth-Century Francia." *Journal of the History of Medicine* 50 (1995): 230–52.

———. "Liturgy and Healing in an Early Medieval Saint's Cult: The Mass *in honore sancti Sigismundi* for the Cure of Fevers." *Traditio* 49 (1994): 23–43.

Pollock, L. *With Faith and Physic: The Life of a Tudor Gentlewoman, Lady Grace Mildmay, 1552–1620*. London: Collins and Brown, 1993.

Richards, J. *Consul of God: The Life and Times of Gregory the Great*. London: Routledge and Kegan Paul, 1980.

Riché, P. *Education et culture dans l'occident barbare 6e–8e siècle*. Paris: Seuil, 1962. Trans. J. J. Contreni from 3rd French ed. *Education and Culture in the Barbarian West: Sixth Through Eighth Centuries*. Columbia, SC: University of South Carolina Press, 1976.

Riddle, J. M. "Theory and Practice in Early Medieval Medicine." *Viator* 5 (1974): 158–84.

Sigal, P.-A. *L'homme et le miracle dans la France médiévale XIe–XIIe siècle*. Paris: Éditions du Cerf, 1985.

Siraisi, N. G. *Medieval and Early Renaissance Medicine: An Introduction to Knowledge and Practice*. Chicago: University of Chicago Press, 1990.

Skinner, P. *Health and Medicine in Early Medieval Southern Italy*. Leiden: Brill, 1997.

———. *Women in Medieval Italian Society, 500–1200*. Harlow: Longman 2001.

Sonderkamp, J. A. "Theophanes Nonnus: Medicine in the Circle of Constantine Porphyrogenitus." *DOP* 38 (1984): 29–41.

Sternberg, T. *Orientalium more secutus: Räume und Institutionen der Caritas des 5. bis 7. Jahrhunderts in Gallien*. Münster: Aschendorff, 1991.

Stolte, B. H. "Magic and Byzantine Law in the Seventh Century." In *The Metamorphosis of Magic from Late Antiquity to the Early Modern Period*. Ed. J. N. Bremmer and J. R. Veenstra. Louvain: Peeters, 2002, 105–15.

Sumption, J. *Pilgrimage: An Image of Mediaeval Religion*. London: Faber, 1975.

Talbot, A.-M. "Pilgrimage to Healing Shrines: The Evidence of Miracle Accounts" [Byzantine]. *DOP* 56 (2002): 153–73.

Temkin, O. *Hippocrates in a World of Pagans and Christians*. Baltimore, MD: Johns Hopkins University Press, 1991.

Vikan, G. "Art, Medicine and Magic in Early Byzantium." *DOP* 38 (1984): 65–86.

Voigts, L. "Anglo-Saxon Plant Remedies and the Anglo-Saxons." *Isis* 70 (1979): 250–68.

Wallis, F. "The Experience of the Book: Manuscripts, Texts, and the Role of Epistemology in Early Medieval Medicine." In *Knowledge and the Scholarly Medical Traditions*. Ed. D. Bates. Cambridge: Cambridge University Press, 1995, 101–26.

———. "Signs and Senses: Diagnosis and Prognosis in Early Medieval Pulse and Urine Texts." In *Social History of Medicine* 13, pt. 2 (2000), special issue: *The Year 1000*. Ed. P. Horden and E. Savage-Smith, 265–78.

Ziegler, J. *Medicine and Religion, c. 1300: The Case of Arnau de Vilanova*. Oxford: Clarendon Press, 1998.

21 Gender and the body
Lynda L. Coon

Primary sources

Alcuin. *Liber de virtutibus et vitiis*. *PL* 101, 613–38.

Bede. *Commentarii in Pentateuchum*. *PL* 91, 189–394.

Benedict of Aniane. *Concordia regularum*. In *Benedicti Anianensis Concordia Regularum*. Ed. P. Bonnerue. *CCCM* 168, 168A. Turnhout: Brepols, 1999.

Benedict of Nursia. *Regula*. Ed. A. de Vogüé and trans. J. Neufville. *SC* 181–86. Paris: Éditions du Cerf, 1971–72. Eng. trans. T. Fry. *RB 1980*. Collegeville, MN: Liturgical Press, 1981.

Cicero. *Epistulae ad familiares*. Ed. D. R. Shackleton Bailey. 2 vols. Cambridge: Cambridge University Press, 1977.

Concilium Parisiense. Ed. A. Weminghoff. *MGH Leges* 3: *Concilia* 2, pt. 2 (= *Concilia aevi Karolini* 1, pt. 2). Hanover: Hahn, 1908.

Fructuosus of Braga. *Regula monachorum complutensis*. *PL* 87, 1099–1127.

Gregory the Great. *Expositio in canticis canticorum*. In *Grégoire le Grand Commentaire sur le cantique des cantiques*. Ed. and trans. R. Bélanger. *SC* 314. Paris: Éditions du Cerf, 1984.

—. *Moralia in Iob*. Ed. M. Adriaen. *CCSL* 143, 143A, 143B. Turnhout: Brepols, 1979–85.

—. *Regula pastoralis*. In *Grégoire le Grand Règle Pastorale*. Ed. B. Judic. *SC* 381–82. Paris: Éditions du Cerf, 1992. Trans. H. Davis. *St. Gregory the Great: Pastoral Care*. Ancient Christian Writers 11. New York: Newman Press, 1950.

Hildemar of Corbie / Civate. *Expositio regulae S. Benedicti*. In *Expositio regulae ab Hildemaro tradita et nunc primum typis mandata*. Ed. Rupert Mittermüller. Regensburg: Frederick Pustet, 1880.

Hincmar of Rheims. *De divortio Lotharii Regis et Theutbergae Reginae*. In *Hinkmar von Reims, De Divortio Lotharii Regis et Theutbergae Reginae*. Ed. L. Böhringer. *MGH Concilia* 4, *Supplement* 1. Hanover: Hahn, 1992.

Hrabanus Maurus. *De institutione clericorum*. In *Hrabanus Maurus: De institutione clericorum libri tres*. Ed. D. Zimpel. Freiburger Beiträge zur mittelalterlichen Geschichte: Studien und Text 7. Frankfurt: Peter Lang, 1996.

—. *De universo*. *PL* 111, 9–614.

—. *Expositio in proverbia Salomonis*. *PL* 111, 679–792.

—. *In honorem S. Crucis*. In *Rabani Mauri in honorem sanctae crucis*. Ed. M. Perrin. *CCCM* 100. Turnhout: Brepols, 1997.

Isidore of Seville. *De ecclesiasticis officiis*. In *Sancti Isidori Episcopi Hispalensis, de ecclesiasticis officiis*. Ed. C. M. Lawson. *CCSL* 113. Turnhout: Brepols, 1989.

—. *De natura rerum*. In *Traité de la nature*. Ed. Jacques Fontaine. Série moyen âge et temps modernes 39. Paris: Institut d'études augustiniennes, 2002.

—. *Etymologies*. In *Isidori Hispalensis episcopi etymologiarum sive originum libri XX*. Ed. W. M. Lindsay. 2 vols. Oxford Classical Texts. Oxford: Oxford University Press, 1911. Eng. trans. of Book XI in W. D. Sharpe. "Isidore of Seville: The Medical Writings: An English Translation with an Introduction and Commentary." *Transactions of the American Philosophical Society*, 54.2 (1964): 5–75.

—. *Liber differentiarum*. *PL* 83, 9–98.

Jerome. *De exodo, in vigilia paschae*. In *S. Hieronymi Presbyteri tractatus sive homiliae in Psalmos, in Marci Evangelium aliaque varia argumenta*. Ed. G. Morin. *CCSL* 78. Turnhout: Brepols, 1958, 536–41.

Lex Thuringorum. In *Leges Saxonum und Lex Thuringorum*. Ed. C. von Schwerin. *MGH Fontes iuris Germanici antiqui in usum scholarum* 4. Hanover: Hahn, 1918.

Peter Damian. *Liber Gomorrhianus*. In *Die Briefe des Petrus Damiani*. Ed. K. Reindel. 4 vols. *MGH Die Briefe der deutschen Kaiserzeit* 4. Munich: Monumenta Germaniae Historica, 1983, vol. 1: 284–330 (*Epistle* 31). Eng. trans. P. J. Payer. *Book of Gomorrah: An Eleventh-Century Treatise against Clerical Homosexual Practice*. Waterloo, Ontario: Wilfrid Laurier University Press, 1982.

Pliny the Elder. *Historia naturalis*. Trans. H. Rackham, W. H. S. Jones, and D. E. Eicholz. 10 vols. Loeb Classical Library. Cambridge, MA: Harvard University Press, 1938–63.

Poenitentiale Baedae. In Haddan and Stubbs 3, 326–34.

Poenitentiale Theodori. In Haddan and Stubbs 3, 173–204.

Quintilian. *Institutio Oratoria*. In *M. Fabi Quintiliani Institutionis Oratoriae Libri Duodecim*. Ed. M. Winterbottom. 2 vols. Oxford Classical Texts. Oxford: Oxford University Press, 1970. Eng. trans. H. E. Butler. *The Institutio Oratoria of Quintilian*. 4 vols. Loeb Classical Library. Cambridge, MA: Harvard University Press, 1929.

Smaragdus of Saint-Mihiel. *Expositio in regulam S. Benedicti*. Ed. A. Spannagel and P. Engelbert. Corpus Consuetudinum Monasticarum 8. Siegburg: F. Schmitt, 1974.

Theodulf of Orleans. *Capitulare ad eosdem*. Ed. P. Brommer. In *MGH Capitula episcoporum*. Hanover: Hahn, 1984. Eng. trans. of *Capitula* 1: G. E. McCracken with A. Cabaniss. *Early Medieval Theology*. The Library of Christian Classics 9. Philadelphia: Westminster Press, 1957, 382–99.

Vita S. Glodesindae. *AASS* July 6, 25.198–224. Eng. trans. J. A. McNamara, J. E. Halborg, and E. G. Whatley. *Sainted Women of the Dark Ages*. Durham, NC: Duke University Press, 1992, 141–54.

Secondary sources

Adams, J. N. *The Latin Sexual Vocabulary*. Baltimore, MD: Johns Hopkins University Press, 1982.

Airlie, S. "The Anxiety of Sanctity: St. Gerald of Aurillac and his Maker." *Journal of Ecclesiastical History* 43 (1992): 372–95.

—. "Private Bodies and the Body Politic in the Divorce Case of Lothar II." *Past & Present* 161 (1998): 3–38.

Angenendt, A. "Mit reinen Händen: Das Motiv der kultischen Reinheit in der abendländischen Askese." In *Herrschaft, Kirche, Kultur: Beiträge zur Geschichte des Mittelalters: Festschrift für Friedrich Prinz zu seinem 65. Geburtstag*. Ed. G. Jenal and S. Haarländer. Monographien zur Geschichte des Mittelalters 37. Stuttgart: Hiersemann, 1993.

—, T. Braucks, R. Busch, and H. Lutterbach. "Counting Piety in the Early and High Middle Ages." In *Ordering Medieval Society: Perspectives on Intellectual and Practical Modes of Shaping Social Relations*. Ed. B. Jussen. Philadelphia, PA: University of Pennsylvania Press, 2001, 15–54.

Bailey, D. S. *Homosexuality and the Western Christian Tradition*. Hamden, CT: Archon, 1975.

Bakhtin, M. *Rabelais and his World*. Trans. H. Iswolski. Cambridge, MA: MIT Press, 1968.

Bartsch, Shadi. *The Mirror of the Self: Sexuality, Self-Knowledge, and the Gaze in the Early Roman Empire*. Chicago: University of Chicago Press, 2006.

Beckwith, S. *Christ's Body: Identity, Culture, and Society in Late Medieval Writings*. New York: Routledge, 1993.

Bennett, J. "Feminism and History." *Gender and History* 1 (1989): 251–72.

Bitel, L. *Land of Women: Tales of Sex and Gender from Early Ireland*. Ithaca, NY: Cornell University Press, 1998.

—. *Women in Early Medieval Europe, 400–1100*. Cambridge: Cambridge University Press, 2002.

Blackmore, J., and G. S. Hutcheson, eds. *Queer Iberia: Sexualities, Cultures, and Crossings from the Middle Ages to the Renaissance*. Durham, NC: Duke University Press, 1999.

Boswell, J. *Christianity, Social Tolerance, and Homosexuality: Gay People in Western Europe from the Beginning of the Christian Era to the Fourteenth Century*. Chicago: University of Chicago Press, 1980.

Bourdieu, P. *Outline of a Theory of Practice*. Trans. R. Nice. Cambridge: Cambridge University Press, 1977.

Boyarin, D. *Carnal Israel: Reading Sex in Talmudic Culture*. Berkeley, CA: University of California Press, 1993.

—. *Dying for God: Martyrdom and the Making of Christianity and Judaism*. Stanford, CA: Stanford University Press, 1999.

—. "On the History of the Early Phallus." In *Gender and Difference in the Middle Ages*. Ed. S. Farmer and C. Braun Pasternack. Minneapolis, MN: University of Minnesota Press, 2003, 3–44.

Brock, S., and S. Harvey. *Holy Women of the Syrian Orient*. Berkeley, CA: University of California Press, 1987.

Brooten, B. *Love between Women: Early Christian Responses to Female Homoeroticism*. Chicago: Chicago University Press, 1996.

Brown, P. *Body and Society: Men, Women, and Sexual Renunciation in Early Christianity*. New York: Columbia University Press, 1988.

Brubaker, L., and J. M. H. Smith, eds. *Gender in the Early Medieval World: East and West, 300–900*. Cambridge: Cambridge University Press, 2004.

Bruce, S. G. "Lurking with Spiritual Intent: A Note on the Origin and Functions of the Monastic Roundsman (*Circator*)." *Revue Bénédictine* 109 (1999): 75–89.

Brundage, J. A. *Law, Sex and Christian Society in Medieval Europe*. Chicago: University of Chicago Press, 1987.

Bullough, V. L., and J. A. Brundage, eds. *Medieval Sexuality: A Handbook*. New York: Garland, 1996.

Burger, G., and S. Kruger, eds. *Queering the Middle Ages*. Minneapolis, MN: University of Minnesota Press, 2001.

Burgwinkle, W. *Sodomy, Masculinity, and Law in Medieval Literature*. Cambridge: Cambridge University Press, 2004.

Burrus, V. *Begotten, not Made: Conceiving Manhood in Late Antiquity*. Stanford, CA: Stanford University Press, 2000.

Butler, J. *Bodies that Matter: On the Discursive Limits of "Sex."* New York: Routledge, 1993.

—. *Gender Trouble: Feminism and the Subversion of Identity*. New York: Routledge, 1999.

Bynum, C. Walker. *Fragmentation and Redemption: Essays on Gender and the Human Body in Medieval Religion*. New York: Zone, 1991.

—. *Holy Feast and Holy Fast: The Religious Significance of Food to Medieval Women*. Berkeley, CA: University of California Press, 1987.

Cadden, J. *Meanings of Sex Difference in the Middle Ages: Medicine, Science, and Culture*. Cambridge: Cambridge University Press, 1993.

Cameron, A. "Sacred and Profane Love: Thoughts on Byzantine Gender." In James, *Women, Men and Eunuchs*, 1–23.

—. "Virginity as Metaphor." In her *History as Text*. London: Duckworth, 1989, 184–205.

—, and A. Kuhrt, eds. *Images of Women in Antiquity*. Detroit, MI: Wayne State University Press, 1983.

Camille, M. "Mouths and Meanings: Towards an Anti-Iconography of Medieval Art." In *Iconography at the Crossroads*. Ed. B. Cassidy. Princeton, NJ: Index of Christian Art, 1993, 43–54.

Carr, A. Weyl. "Women and Monasticism in Byzantium." *Byzantinische Forschungen* 9 (1985): 1–15.

Carruthers, M. "Reading with Attitude: Remembering the Book." In Frese and O'Brien O'Keeffe, *Book and the Body*, 1–33.

Carson, A. "Putting Her in Her Place: Woman, Dirt, and Desire." In Halperin, Winkler, and Zeitlin, *Before Sexuality*, 135–69.

Chazelle, C. *The Crucified God in the Carolingian Era: Theology and Art of Christ's Passion*. Cambridge: Cambridge University Press, 2001.

Clark, E. *Ascetic Piety and Women's Faith: Essays on Late Ancient Christianity*. Studies in Women and Religion 1. Lewiston, NY: Edward Mellen Press, 1986.

—. *History–Theory–Text: Historians and the Linguistic Turn*. Cambridge, MA: Harvard University Press, 2004.

—. "The Lady Vanishes: Dilemmas of a Feminist Historian after the 'Linguistic Turn.'" *Church History* 67 (1998): 1–31.

—. *Reading Renunciation: Asceticism and Scripture in Early Christianity*. Princeton, NJ: Princeton University Press, 1999.

Clark, G. *Women in Late Antiquity: Pagan and Christian Lifestyles*. Oxford: Oxford University Press, 1994.

Clarke, J. R. "The Décor of the House of Jupiter and Ganymede at Ostia Antica: Private Residence Turned Gay Hotel." In E. K. Gazda, ed. *Roman Art in the Private Sphere: New Perspectives on the Architecture and Décor of the Domus, Villa, and Insula*. Ann Arbor, MI: University of Michigan Press, 1991, 89–104.

—. "Hypersexual Black Men in Augustan Baths: Ideal Somatotypes and Apotropaic Magic." In Kampen, *Sexuality in Ancient Art*, 184–98.

—. "Look Who's Laughing at Sex: Men and Women Viewers in the *Apodyterium* of the Suburban Baths at Pompeii." In Fredrick, *Roman Gaze*, 149–81.

Cloke, G. *This Female Man of God: Women and Spiritual Power in the Patristic Age, 350–450*. London: Routledge, 1995.

Clover, C. J. "Regardless of Sex: Men, Women, and Power in Early Northern Europe." In *Studying Medieval Women*. Ed. N. F. Partner. Cambridge, MA: Medieval Academy of America, 1993, 61–85.

Cohen, J. J., and B. Wheeler, eds. *Becoming Male in the Middle Ages*. New York: Garland, 1997.

Coletti, T. *Mary Magdalene and the Drama of Saints: Theatre, Gender, and Religion in Late Medieval England*. Philadelphia, PA: University of Pennsylvania Press, 2004.

Connor, C. L. *Women of Byzantium*. New Haven, CT: Yale University Press, 2004.

Coon, L. "'What is the Word if not Semen'? Priestly Bodies in Carolingian Exegesis." In Brubaker and Smith, *Gender in the Early Medieval World*, 278–300.

Cooper, K. "Insinuations of Womanly Influence: An Aspect of the Christianization of the Roman Aristocracy." *Journal of Roman Studies* 82 (1992): 150–64.

—. *The Virgin and the Bride: Idealized Womanhood in Late Antiquity*. Cambridge, MA: Harvard University Press, 1996.

—, and C. Leyser. "The Gender of Grace: Impotence, Servitude, and Manliness in the Fifth-Century West." *Gender & History* 12/3 (2000): 536–51.

Corbeill, A. *Controlling Laughter: Political Humor in the Late Roman Republic*. Princeton, NJ: Princeton University Press, 1996.

—. "Dining Deviants in Roman Political Invective." In Hallett and Skinner, *Roman Sexualities*, 99–128.

—. *Nature Embodied: Gesture in Ancient Rome*. Princeton, NJ: Princeton University Press, 2004.

—. "Political Movement: Walking and Ideology in Republican Rome." In Fredrick, *Roman Gaze*, 182–215.

Daston, L., and K. Park. *Wonders and the Order of Nature, 1150–1750*. New York: Zone, 2001.

De Certeau, M. *The Practice of Everyday Life*. Trans. S. Rendall. Berkeley, CA: University of California Press, 1984.

de Jong, M. "Exegesis for an Empress." In *Medieval Transformations: Texts, Power, and Gifts*. Ed. E. Cohen and M. De Jong. Leiden: Brill, 2001, 69–100.

—. "*Imitatio Morum*: The Cloister and Clerical Purity in the Carolingian World." In *Medieval Purity and Piety: Essays on Medieval Clerical Celibacy and Religious Reform*. Ed. M. Frassetto. New York: Garland, 1998, 49–80.

Dean-Jones, L. "The Politics of Pleasure: Female Sexual Appetite in the Hippocratic Corpus." *Helios* 19 (1992): 72–91.

—. *Women's Bodies in Classical Greek Science*. Oxford: Oxford University Press, 1994.

Detienne, M. *The Gardens of Adonis*. Trans. J. Lloyd. Princeton, NJ: Princeton University Press, 1994.

Diem, A. *Das monastische Experiment: die Rolle der Keuschheit bei der Entstehung des westlichen Klosterwesens*. Münster: LIT Verlag, 2005.

Dinshaw, C. *Getting Medieval: Sexualities and Communities, Pre- and Postmodern*. Durham, NC: Duke University Press, 1999.

Douglas, M. *Purity and Danger: An Analysis of the Concept of Pollution and Taboo*. New York: Routledge, 2002.

Drijvers, J. W. *Helena Augusta: The Mother of Constantine the Great and the Legend of her Finding of the True Cross*. Leiden: Brill, 1992.

Dunbabin, K. M. D., and M. W. Dickie. "Invidia Rumpantur Pectora: The Iconography of Phthonos/Invidia in Graeco-Roman Art." *Jahrbuch für Antike und Christentum* 26 (1983): 7–37.

Edwards, C. *The Politics of Immorality in Ancient Rome*. Cambridge: Cambridge University Press, 1993.

Effros, B. *Creating Community with Food and Drink in Merovingian Gaul*. The New Middle Ages Series. New York: Palgrave MacMillan, 2002.

Eilberg-Schwartz, H., and W. Doniger, eds. *Off with her Head! The Denial of Women's Identity in Myth, Religion, and Culture*. Berkeley, CA: University of California Press, 1995.

Elliott, D. *Fallen Bodies: Pollution, Sexuality, and Demonology in the Middle Ages*. Philadelphia, PA: University of Pennsylvania Press, 1999.

—. *Proving Woman: Female Spirituality and Inquisitional Culture in the Later Middle Ages*. Princeton, NJ: Princeton University Press, 2004.

—. *Spiritual Marriage: Sexual Abstinence in Medieval Wedlock*. Princeton, NJ: Princeton University Press, 1993.

Elm, S. *Virgins of God: The Making of Asceticism in Late Antiquity*. Oxford: Clarendon Press, 1994.

Farmer, S., and C. Braun Pasternack, eds. *Gender and Difference in the Middle Ages*. Minneapolis, MN: University of Minnesota Press, 2003.

Fell, C. *Women in Anglo-Saxon England*. Oxford: Blackwell, 1987.

Flint, V. J. "Space and Discipline in Early Medieval Europe." In *Medieval Practices of Space*. Ed. B. A. Hanawalt and M. Kobialka. Minneapolis, MN: University of Minnesota Press, 2000, 149–66.

Foucault, M. *Discipline and Punishment: The Birth of the Prison*. Trans. A. Sheridan. New York: Vintage, 1977.

—. *History of Sexuality*. Vol. 1: *An Introduction*. Trans. R. Hurley. New York: Vintage, 1978.

—. *History of Sexuality*. Vol. 3: *The Care of the Self*. Trans. R. Hurley. New York: Vintage, 1988.

Frantzen, A. J. *Before the Closet: Same-Sex Love from Beowulf to Angels in America*. Chicago: University of Chicago Press, 1998.

—. "When Women Aren't Enough." *Speculum* 68 (1993): 445–71.

—. "Where the Boys Are: Children and Sex in the Anglo-Saxon Penitentials." In *Becoming Male in the Middle Ages*. Ed. J. J. Cohen and B. Wheeler. New York: Garland, 1997, 43–66.

Frassetto, M., ed. *Medieval Purity and Piety: Essays on Medieval Clerical Celibacy and Religious Reform*. New York: Garland, 1998.

Fredrick, D. "Invisible Rome." In his *Roman Gaze*, 1–30.

—. "Mapping Penetrability in Late Republican and Early Imperial Rome." In his *Roman Gaze*, 236–64.

—. "Reading Broken Skin: Violence in Roman Elegy." In Hallett and Skinner, *Roman Sexualities*, 172–93.

—, ed. *The Roman Gaze: Vision, Power, and the Body*. Baltimore, MD: Johns Hopkins University Press, 2002.

Frese, D. Warwick, and K. O'Brien O'Keeffe, eds. *The Body and the Book*. Notre Dame, IN: University of Notre Dame Press, 1997.

Garland, L., ed. *Byzantine Empresses: Women and Power in Byzantium, AD 527–1204*. London: Routledge, 1999.

Gilchrist, R. *Gender and Material Culture: The Archaeology of Religious Women*. London: Routledge, 1994.

Glancy, J. A. "Boasting of Beatings (2 Corinthians 11:23–25)." *Journal of Biblical Literature* 123/1 (2004): 99–135.

Gleason, M. W. *Making Men: Sophists and Self-Presentation in Ancient Rome*. Princeton, NJ: Princeton University Press, 1995.

Golden, M., and P. Toohey, eds. *Inventing Ancient Culture: Historicism, Periodization, and the Ancient World*. London: Routledge, 1997.

Gowers, E. "The Anatomy of Rome from Capital to Cloaca." *Journal of Roman Studies* 85 (1995): 23–32.

Green, M. H. *The Trotula: A Medieval Compendium of Women's Medicine*. Philadelphia, PA: University of Pennsylvania Press, 2001.

Gunderson, E. *Staging Masculinity: The Rhetoric of Performance in the Roman World*. Ann Arbor, MI: University of Michigan Press, 2000.

Hadley, D., ed. *Masculinity in Medieval Europe*. London: Longman, 1999.

Hallett, J. "Female Homoeroticism and the Denial of Roman Reality in Latin Literature." *Yale Journal of Criticism* 3 (1989): 209–27.

—, and M. Skinner, eds. *Roman Sexualities*. Princeton, NJ: Princeton University Press, 1997.

Halperin, D. *One Hundred Years of Homosexuality; and Other Essays on Greek Love*. New York: Routledge, 1990.

—, J. Winkler, and F. Zeitlin, eds. *Before Sexuality: The Construction of Erotic Experience in the Ancient Greek World*. Princeton, NJ: Princeton University Press, 1990.

Halsall, G. "Gender and the End of Empire." *Journal of Medieval and Early Modern Studies* 34/1 (2004): 17–39.

Hamburger, J. *The Visual and the Visionary: Art and Female Spirituality in Late Medieval Germany*. New York: Zone, 1998.

Hanawalt, B. A., and M. Kobialka, eds. *Medieval Practices of Space*. Minneapolis, MN: University of Minnesota Press, 2000.

Harrison, V. E. F. "The Allegorization of Gender." In Wimbush and Valantasis, *Asceticism*, 520–34.

Harvey, S. "Sacred Bonding: Mothers and Daughters in Early Syriac Hagiography." *Journal of Early Christian Studies* 4 (1996): 27–56.

—. "Some Implications: The Case of Women." In her *Asceticism and Society in Crisis: John of Ephesus and the Lives of the Eastern Saints*. Berkeley, CA: University of California Press, 1990, 108–33.

—. "Women in Early Byzantine Hagiography: Reversing the Story." In *That Gentle Strength: Historical Perspectives on Women in Christianity*. Ed. L. L. Coon, K. J. Haldane, and E. W. Sommer. Charlottesville, VA: University of Virginia Press, 1990, 36–59.

Heffernan, T. J. *Sacred Biography: Saints and their Biographers in the Middle Ages*. New York: Oxford University Press, 1988.

Herdt, G. H., ed. *Third Sex, Third Gender: Beyond Sexual Dimorphism in Culture and History*. New York: Zone, 1994.

Herrin, J. "In Search of Byzantine Women: Three Avenues of Approach." In Cameron and Kuhrt, *Images of Women in Antiquity*, 167–89.

—. *Women in Purple: Rulers of Medieval Byzantium*. Princeton, NJ: Princeton University Press, 2001.

—, A. Kazhdan, and A. Cutler. "Women." In *ODB* 3, 2201–04.

Hill, B. *Imperial Women in Byzantium, 1025–1204: Power, Patronage, and Ideology*. New York: Longman, 1999.

Hillman, D., and C. Mazzio, eds. *The Body in Parts: Fantasies of Corporeality in Early Modern Europe*. New York: Routledge, 1997.

Holsinger, B. W. *Music, Body, and Desire in Medieval Culture: Hildegard of Bingen to Chaucer*. Stanford, CA: Stanford University Press, 2001.

Holum, K. G. *Theodosian Empresses: Women and Imperial Domination in Late Antiquity*. Berkeley, CA: University of California Press, 1982.

Hunt, L. *The Invention of Pornography: Obscenity and the Origins of Modernity, 1500–1800*. New York: Zone, 1993.

Jacquart, D., and C. Thomasset. *Sexuality and Medicine in the Middle Ages*. Trans. Matthew Adamson. Princeton, NJ: Princeton University Press, 1988.

Jaeger, S. *Ennobling Love: In Search of a Lost Sensibility*. Philadelphia, PA: University of Pennsylvania Press, 1999.

James, L. *Empresses and Power in Early Byzantium*. London: Leicester University Press, 2001.

—, ed. *Women, Men and Eunuchs: Gender in Byzantium*. London: Routledge, 1997.

Jochens, J. *Old Norse Images of Women*. Philadelphia, PA: University of Pennsylvania Press, 1996.

Johnson, P. *Equal in Monastic Profession: Religious Women in Medieval France*. Chicago: University of Chicago Press, 1991.

Jordan, M. D. *The Invention of Sodomy in Christian Theology*. Chicago: University of Chicago Press, 1997.

Kalavrezou, I., and A. E. Laiou, eds. *Byzantine Women and their World*. Cambridge, MA: Harvard University Art Museums / New Haven, CT: Yale University Press, 2003.

Kampen, N. B., ed. *Sexuality in Ancient Art*. Cambridge: Cambridge University Press, 1996.

Karras, R. Mazo. "Active / Passive, Acts / Passions: Greek and Roman Sexualities." *American Historical Review* 105 / 4 (2000): 1250–65.

—. *Common Women: Prostitution and Sexuality in Medieval England*. New York: Oxford University Press, 1996.

—. *From Boys to Men: Formations of Masculinity in Late Medieval Europe*. Philadelphia, PA: University of Pennsylvania Press, 2003.

—. "Sex and the Middle Ages." In her *Sexuality in Medieval Europe: Doing unto Others*. London: Routledge, 2005, 1–27.

—. *Sexuality in Medieval Europe: Doing unto Others*. London: Routledge, 2005.

—. "Sexuality in the Middle Ages." In *The Medieval World*. Ed. P. Linehan and J. Nelson. London: Routledge, 2001, 279–93.

Kay, S., and M. Rubin, eds. *Framing Medieval Bodies*. Manchester: Manchester University Press, 1994.

Kellum, B. "The Phallus as Signifier: The Forum of Augustus and Rituals of Masculinity." In Kampen, *Sexuality in Ancient Art*, 170–83.

Kraemer, R., and M. D'Angelo, eds. *Women and Christian Origins*. Oxford: Oxford University Press, 1999.
Krenkel, W. "Fellatio et Irrumatio." *Wissenschaftliche Zeitschrift der Wilhelm Pieck-Universität Rostock* 29 (1980): 77–88.
Kuefler, M. *The Manly Eunuch: Masculinity, Gender Ambiguity, and Christian Ideology in Late Antiquity*. Chicago: University of Chicago Press, 2001.
Laiou, A. E. *Gender, Society, and Economic Life in Byzantium*. Brookfield, VT: Variorum, 1992.
—. "The Role of Women in Byzantine Society." *Jahrbuch der Österreichische Byzantinistik* 31 (1981): 233–60.
Laqueur, T. W. *Making Sex: Body and Gender from the Greeks to Freud*. Cambridge: Cambridge University Press, 1990.
—. *Solitary Sex: A Cultural History of Masturbation*. New York: Zone, 2002.
Larson, J. "Paul's Masculinity." *Journal of Biblical Literature* 123/1 (2004): 85–97.
Lebecq, S., ed. *Femmes et pouvoirs des femmes à Byzance et en Occident: Vie–Xie siècles*. Centre de recherche sur l'histoire de l'Europe du Nord-Ouest 19. Villeneuve d'Ascq: Centre de recherche sur l'histoire de l'Europe du Nord-Ouest, Université Charles de Gaulle-Lille 3, 1999.
Lees, C. A., ed. *Medieval Masculinities: Regarding Men in the Middle Ages*. Minneapolis, MN: University of Minnesota Press, 1994.
Lefebvre, H. *The Production of Space*. Trans. D. Nicholson-Smith. Oxford: Blackwell, 1991.
Leyser, C. *Authority and Asceticism from Augustine to Gregory the Great*. Oxford: Oxford University Press, 2000.
—. "Masculinity in Flux: Nocturnal Emissions and the Limits of Celibacy." In *Masculinity in Medieval Europe*. Ed. D. Hadley. London: Longman, 1999, 103–20.
Lloyd, G. E. R. *Science, Folklore and Ideology*. Cambridge: Cambridge University Press, 1983.
Lomperis, L., and S. Stanbury, eds. *Feminist Approaches to the Body in Medieval Literature*. Philadelphia, PA: University of Pennsylvania Press, 1993.
Martin, D. B. *The Corinthian Body*. New Haven, CT: Yale University Press, 1995.
Mathews, T. F. *The Clash of Gods: A Reinterpretation of Early Christian Art*. Princeton, NJ: Princeton University Press, 1993.
Matter, A. "My Sister, my Spouse: Woman-Identified Women in Medieval Christianity." *Journal of Feminist Studies in Religion* 2/2 (1986): 88–93.
—. *The Voice of my Beloved: The Song of Songs in Western Medieval Christianity*. Philadelphia, PA: University of Pennsylvania Press, 1990.
McNamara, J. A. *Sisters in Arms: Catholic Nuns through Two Millennia*. Cambridge, MA: Harvard University Press, 1996.
Meens, R. "Politics, Mirrors of Princes and the Bible: Sins, Kings, and the Well-Being of the Realm." *EME* 7 (1998): 345–57.
—. "Pollution in the Early Middle Ages: The Case of the Food Regulations in the Penitentials." *EME* 4 (1995): 3–19.
Miller, P. Cox. "Dreaming the Body: An Aesthetics of Asceticism." In Wimbush and Valantasis, *Asceticism*, 281–300.
—. "Is there a Harlot in this Text? Hagiography and the Grotesque." *Journal of Medieval and Early Modern Studies* 33 (2003): 419–35.

Mooney, C. M., ed. *Gendered Voices: Medieval Saints and their Interpreters*. Philadelphia, PA: University of Pennsylvania Press, 1999.

Moore, S. D. *God's Beauty Parlor and Other Queer Spaces in and around the Bible*. Stanford, CA: Stanford University Press, 2001.

Muschiol, G. *Famula Dei: zur Liturgie in merowingischen Frauenklöstern*, Beiträge zur Geschichte des alten Mönchtums und des Benediktinertums 41. Münster: Aschendorff, 1994.

Myerowitz, M. "The Gendered Grammar of Ancient Mediterranean Hair." In Eilberg-Schwartz and Doniger, *Off with her Head!* 76–130.

Nelson, J. "Monks, Secular Men and Masculinity, c. 900." In Hadley, *Masculinity in Medieval Europe*, 121–42.

—. "Queens as Jezebels: The Careers of Brunhild and Balthild in Merovingian History." In *Medieval Women*. Ed. D. Baker and R. Hill. Oxford: Blackwell, 31–77.

Newman, B. *From Virile Woman to WomanChrist: Studies in Medieval Religion and Literature*. Philadelphia, PA: University of Pennsylvania Press, 1995.

Noble, T. F. X. "The Transformation of the Roman World: Reflections on Five Years of Work." In *East and West: Modes of Communication*. Ed. E. Chrysos and I. Wood. Transformation of the Roman World 5. Leiden: Brill, 1999, 259–77.

O'Keeffe, K. O'Brien. "Body and Law in Late Anglo-Saxon England." *Anglo-Saxon England* 27 (1998): 209–32.

Parker, H. N. "The Teratogenic Grid." In Hallet and Skinner, *Roman Sexualities*, 47–65.

Partner, N., ed. *Studying Medieval Women: Sex, Gender, Feminism*. Cambridge, MA: Medieval Academy of America, 1993.

Patlagean, E. "L'histoire de la femme déguisée en moine et l'évolution de la sainteté feminine à Byzance." *Studi Medievali*, ser. 3, 17 (1976): 597–623.

Paxton, F. *Christianizing Death: The Creation of a Ritual Process in Early Medieval Europe*. Ithaca, NY: Cornell University Press, 1990.

Payer, P. J. *Sex and the Penitentials: The Development of a Social Code, 550–1150*. Toronto: University of Toronto Press, 1984.

Peers, G. *Subtle Bodies: Representing Angels in Byzantium*. Berkeley, CA: University of California Press, 2001.

Pouchelle, M.-C. *The Body and Surgery in the Middle Ages*. Trans. R. Morris. New Brunswick, NJ: Rutgers University Press, 1990.

Rapp, C. "Figures of Female Sanctity: Byzantine Edifying Manuscripts and their Audience." *DOP* 50 (1996): 313–32.

Réal, I. *Vies de saints, vie de famille: représentation et système de la parenté dans le Royaume mérovingien (481–751) d'après les sources hagiographiques*. Hagiologia: Études sur la Sainteté en Occident – Studies on Western Sainthood 2. Turnhout: Brepols, 2001.

Riches, S., and S. Salih, eds. *Gender and Holiness: Men, Women, and Saints in Late Medieval Europe*. London: Routledge, 2002.

Richlin, A. *The Garden of Priapus*. New Haven, CT: Yale University Press, 1983.

—. "Towards a History of Body History." In Golden and Toohey, *Inventing Ancient Culture*, 16–35.

Ringrose, K. M. *The Perfect Servant: Eunuchs and the Social Construction of Gender in Byzantium*. Chicago: University of Chicago Press, 2003.

Rousselle, A. *Porneia: On Desire and the Body in Antiquity*. Trans. F. Pheasant. New York: Blackwell, 1988.

Rubin, G. "The Traffic in Women: Notes on the Political Economy of Sex." In R. R. Reiter, ed. *Toward an Anthropology of Women*. New York: Monthly Review Press, 1975, 157–210.

Salisbury, J. *Blood of Martyrs: Unintended Consequences of Ancient Violence*. New York: Routledge, 2004.

—. *Perpetua's Passion: The Death and Memory of a Young Roman Woman*. New York: Routledge, 1997.

Scarry, E. *The Body in Pain: The Making and Unmaking of the World*. New York: Oxford University Press, 1987.

Schroeder, C. T. "A Suitable Abode for Christ: The Church Building as Symbol of Ascetic Renunciation in Early Monasticism." *Church History* 73 (2004): 472–521.

Schulenburg, J. Tibbetts. *Forgetful of their Sex: Female Sanctity and Society, c. 500–1000*. Chicago: University of Chicago Press, 1998.

Scott, J. Wallach. "Gender: A Useful Category of Historical Analysis." *American Historical Review* 91/5 (1986): 1053–75.

Sedgwick, E. Kosofsky. *Epistemology of the Closet*. Berkeley, CA: University of California Press, 1990.

Skinner, M. "Zeus and Leda: The Sexuality Wars in Contemporary Classical Scholarship." *Thamyrus* 3 (1996): 103–23.

Smith, J. M. H. "Did Women Have a Transformation of the Roman World"? *Gender & History* 12/3 (2000): 552–71.

—. "Gender and Ideology." In *Gender and Christian Religion*. Ed. R. N. Swanson. *SCH* 35. Woodbridge: Boydell Press, 1998, 51–73.

—. "The Problem of Female Sanctity in Carolingian Europe *c.* 780–921." *Past and Present* 146 (1995): 3–37.

Stafford, P. *Queens, Concubines, and Dowagers: The King's Wife in the Early Middle Ages*. Athens, GA: University of Georgia Press, 1983.

Stewart, S. "The Imaginary Body." In her *On Longing: Narratives of the Miniature, the Gigantic, the Souvenir, the Collection*. Baltimore, MD: Johns Hopkins University Press, 1984, 104–31.

Talbot, A.-M. *Holy Women of Byzanium: Ten Saints' Lives in English Translation*. Washington, DC: Dumbarton Oaks, 1996.

—. *Women and Religious Life in Byzantium*. Aldershot : Ashgate, 2001.

Tougher, S., ed. *Eunuchs in Antiquity and Beyond*. Swansea: The Classical Press of Wales, 2002.

Townsend, D., and A. Taylor, eds. *The Tongue of the Fathers: Gender and Ideology in Twelfth-Century Latin*. Philadelphia, PA: University of Pennsylvania Press, 1998.

Van Houts, E. *Memory and Gender in Medieval Europe 900–1200*. Toronto: University of Toronto Press, 1999.

Venarde, B. *Women's Monasticism and Medieval Society: Nunneries in France and England, 890–1215*. Ithaca, NY: Cornell University Press, 1997.

Walters, J. "Invading the Roman Body: Manliness and Impenetrability in Roman Thought." In Hallett and Skinner, *Roman Sexualities*, 29–43.

Ward, B. *Harlots of the Desert: A Study of Repentance in Early Monastic Sources*. Kalamazoo, MI: Cistercian Press, 1987.

Warnke, G. "Intersexuality and the Categories of Sex." *Hypatia: A Journal of Feminist Philosophy* 16/3 (2001): 126–37.

Wathen, A. G. *Silence: The Meaning of Silence in the Rule of St. Benedict*. Cistercian Studies Series 22. Washington, DC: Cistercian Publications, 1973.

Wemple, S. F. *Women in Frankish Society: Marriage and the Cloister*. Philadelphia, PA: University of Pennsylvania Press, 1981.

Williams, C. A. *Roman Homosexuality: Ideologies of Masculinity in Classical Antiquity*. Oxford: Oxford University Press, 1999.

Wimbush, V. L., and R. Valantasis, eds. *Asceticism*. Oxford: Oxford University Press, 1996.

Winkler, J. *The Constraints of Desire: The Anthropology of Sex and Gender in Ancient Greece*. New York: Routledge, 1990.

Winstead, K. A. *Virgin Martyrs: Legends of Sainthood in Late Medieval England*. Ithaca, NY: Cornell University Press, 1997.

Wogan-Browne, J. *Saints' Lives and Women's Literary Culture: Virginity and its Authorizations*. Oxford: Oxford University Press, 2001.

22 Sacrifice, gifts, and prayers in Latin Christianity
Arnold Angenendt

Primary sources

Admonitio generalis. Ed. A. Boretius. *MGH Leges: Capitularia Regum Francorum* 1. Hanover: Hahn, 1883.

Annales Regni Francorum. Ed. G. H. Pertz. *MGH SRM*. Hanover: Hahn, 1895.

The Bobbio-Missal: A Gallican Mass-Book. Ed. E. A. Lowe. Henry Bradshaw Society 58. London: Harrison and Sons, 1920.

Capitulatio de partibus Saxoniae. Ed. A. Boretius. *MGH Leges: Capitularia Regum Francorum* 1. Hanover: Hahn, 1883.

Codex Carolinus. Ed. E. Dümmler. *MGH Epistolae* 3. Berlin: Weidmann, 1892.

Concilium Aquisgranense. Ed. A. Werminghoff. *MGH Leges: Concilia* 2 (= *Concilia aevi Karolini* 1, pt. 1). Hanover: Hahn, 1906.

Concilium Aurelianense (a. 511). Ed. C. de Clercq. *CCSL* 148A. Turnhout: Brepols, 1963.

Concilium Parisiense. Ed. A. Werminghoff. *MGH Leges 3: Concilia* 2, pt. 2 (= *Concilia aevi Karolini* 1, pt. 2). Hanover: Hahn, 1908.

Constitutum Constantini. Ed. H. Fuhrmann. *MGH Leges: Fontes iuris germanici antiqui* 10. Hanover: Hahn, 1968.

Einmütig in der Liebe: die frühesten Quellentexte von Cîteaux. Ed. H. Brem and A. M. Altermatt. Quellen und Studien zur Zisterzienserliteratur 1. 2nd ed. Langwaden: Bernardus, 1998.

Epistulorum Fuldensium fragmenta. Ed. E. Dümmler. *MGH Epistolae* 5. Berlin: Weidmann, 1892.

Gesta abbatum Trudonensium. Ed. G. H. Pertz. *MGH Scriptores* (folio) 10. Hanover: Hahn, 1852.

John Beleth. *Summa de ecclesiasticis officii*. Ed. H. Douteil. *CCCM* 41A. Turnhout: Brepols, 1976.

Liber Pontificalis. In *Le Liber Pontificalis: texte, introduction et commentaire*. Ed. L. Duchesne. 3 vols. Paris: de Boccard, 1981.

Paenitentiale Merseburgense a. Ed. R. Kottje. *CCSL* 156. Turnhout: Brepols, 1994.
Regino of Prüm. *De synodalibus causis et disciplinis ecclesiasticis*. Ed. F. G. A. Wasserschleben. Leipzig: Engelmann, 1840.
Regula Stephani Muretensis. Ed. J. Becquet. *CCCM* 8. Turnhout: Brepols, 1968.
Sacramentarium Rhenaugiense. Ed. A. Hänggi and A. Schönherr. Spicilegium Friburgense 15. Fribourg: Universitätsverlag, 1970.
Widukind of Corvey. *Res gestae Saxonicae*. Ed. A. Bauer and R. Rau. Quellen zur Geschichte der sächsischen Kaiserzeit: Ausgewählte Quellen zur deutschen Geschichte des Mittelalters 8. Darmstadt: Wissenschaftliche Buchgesellschaft 1971.

Secondary sources

Althoff, G. *Adels- und Königsfamilien im Spiegel ihrer Memorialüberlieferung: Studien zum Totengedenken der Billunger und Ottonen*. Munich: Wilhelm Fink Verlag, 1984.
Angenendt, A. "Cartam offerre super altare: zur Liturgisierung von Rechtsvorgängen." *Frühmittelalterliche Studien* 36 (2002): 1–26.
—. "Missa specialis: zugleich ein Beitrag zur Entstehung der Privatmessen." In his *Liturgie im Mittelalter: Ausgewählte Aufsätze zum 70. Geburtstag*. Ed. T. Flammer and D. Meyer. Ästhetik–Theologie–Liturgik 35. Münster: LIT Verlag, 2004.
—. "'Mit reinen Händen': Das Motiv der kultischen Reinheit in der abendländischen Askese." In his *Liturgie im Mittelalter: Ausgewählte Aufsätze zum 70. Geburtstag*. Ed. T. Flammer and D. Meyer. Ästhetik–Theologie–Liturgik 35. Münster: LIT Verlag, 2004.
Bischoff, B., ed. *Mittelalterliche Schatzverzeichnisse*. Vol. 1: *Von der Zeit Karls des Großen bis zur Mitte des 13. Jahrhunderts*. Veröffentlichung des Zentralinstituts für Kunstgeschichte in München 4. Munich: Prestel-Verlag, 1967.
de Jong, M. B. *In Samuel's Image: Child Oblation in the Early Medieval West*. Brill's Studies in Intellectual History 12. Leiden: Brill, 1996.
Gross, K. *Menschenhand und Gotteshand in Antike und Christentum*. Ed. W. Speyer. Stuttgart: Hiersemann, 1985.
Hallam, E. M. "Monasteries as War Memorials: Battle Abbey and La Victoire." In *The Church and War*. Ed. W. J. Sheils. *SCH* 20. London: Eccesiastical History Society, 1983, 47–59.
Häussling, A. A. *Mönchskonvent und Eucharistiefeier: eine Studie über die Messe in der abendländischen Klosterliturgie des frühen Mittelalters und zur Geschichte der Meßhäufigkeit*. Liturgiewissenschaftliche Quellen und Forschungen 58. Münster: Aschendorff, 1973.
Homann, H. "Indiculus superstitionum et paganiarum, §1: Kulturgeschichtliches." *Reallexikon der germanischen Altertumskunde* 15 (2000): 369–79.
Iserloh, E. "Der Wert der Messe in der Diskussion der Theologen vom Mittelalter bis zum 16. Jahrhundert." In his *Kirche–Ereignis und Institution: Aufsätze und Vorträge*. 2 vols. Reformationsgeschichtliche Studien und Texte, Supplement vol. 3, pts. 1–2. 2 vols. Münster: Aschendorff, 1985, vol. 2, 375–413.
Jungmann, J. A. "Von der 'Eucharistie' zur 'Messe,'" *Zeitschrift für katholische Theologie* 89, no. 1 (1967): 29–40.
Lutterbach, H. *Sexualität im Mittelalter: eine Kulturstudie anhand von Bußbüchern des 6. bis 12. Jahrhunderts*. Beihefte zum Archiv zur Kulturgeschichte 43. Cologne: Böhlau, 1999.

Macy, G. *The Theologies of the Eucharist in the Early Scholastic Period: A Study of the Salvific Function of the Sacrament According to the Theologians, c. 1080–c. 1220*. Oxford: Clarendon Press, 1984.

McCormick, M. *Eternal Victory: Triumphal Rulership in Late Antiquity, Byzantium and the Early Medieval West*. Cambridge: Cambridge University Press, 1990.

Nelson, J. L. "Violence in the Carolingian World and the Ritualization of Ninth-Century Warfare." In *Violence and Society in the Early Medieval West*. Ed. G. Halsall. Woodbridge: Boydell Press, 1998, 90–107.

Nussbaum, O. *Klöster, Priestermönch und Privatmesse: ihr Verhältnis im Westen von den Anfängen bis zum hohen Mittelalter*. Theophaneia 14. Bonn: Hanstein, 1961.

Schmid, K. "Salische Gedenkstiftungen für fideles, servientes und milites." In *Institutionen, Kultur und Gesellschaft im Mittelalter*. Ed. L. Fenske, W. Rösener, and T. Zotz. Sigmaringen: Thorbecke, 1984, 245–64.

Schmitz, P. "La liturgie de Cluny." In *Convegni del Centro di Studi sulla Spiritualità Medievale*. Vol. 2. Todi: Presso l'Accademia Tudertina, 1959–85, 85–99.

Staubach, N. *Rex Christianus: Hofkultur und Herrschaftspropaganda im Reich Karls des Kahlen*. Vol. 2: *Die Grundlegung der 'religion royale,' Pictura et Poesis*. Cologne: Böhlau 1993.

Van Engen, J. "The Crisis of Coenobitism." *Speculum* 61 (1986): 269–304.

23 Performing the liturgy
Éric Palazzo

Primary sources

Amalarius of Metz. *Liber officialis*. In *Amalarii episcopi opera liturgica omnia*. Ed. J.-M. Hanssens. Studi e testi 139. Vatican City: Biblioteca apostolica vaticana, 1948.

Ardo. *Vie de Benoît d'Aniane*. Trans. F. Baumes. Revised A. de Vogüé. Intro., notes P. Bonnerue. Vie Monastique 39. Bégrolles en Mauges, France: Abbaye de Bellefontaine, 2001.

Hrabanus Maurus. *Homiliae*. *PL* 110, 1–468.

Theodulf of Orleans. *Erstes Kapitular*. Ed. P. Brommer. *MGH Capitula episcoporum* I. Hanover: Hahn, 1984.

Walafrid Strabo. *Libellus de exordiis et incrementis quarundam in observationibus ecclesiasticis rerum*. In *Walahfrid Strabo's Libellus de exordiis et incrementis quarundam in observationibus ecclesiasticis rerum: A Translation and Liturgical Commentary*. Ed. and trans. A. L. Harting-Correa. Leiden: Brill, 1996.

William Durandus. *Rationale divinorum officiorum*. Ed. A. Davril and T. M. Thibodeau. *CCCM* 140, 140A, 140B. Turnhout: Brepols, 1995–2000.

Secondary sources

Althoff, G. "The Variability of Rituals in the Middle Ages." In *Medieval Concepts of the Past: Ritual, Memory, Historiography*. Ed. G. Althoff, J. Fried, and P. J. Geary. Cambridge: Cambridge University Press, 2003, 71–87.

Avant-nefs et espaces d'accueil dans l'église: entre le IVe et le XIIe siècle. Paris: CTHS, 2002.

Baschet, J. *Lieu sacré, lieu d'images: les fresques de Bominaco (Abruzzes, vers 1263), thèmes, parcours, fonctions*. Paris: Découverte, 1991.

Bock, N., ed. *Art, cérémonial et liturgie au Moyen Âge: actes du colloque de 3e cycle romand de Lettres Lausanne-Fribourg, 24–25 mars, 14–15 avril, 12–13 mai 2000*. Rome: Viella, 2002.

—, S. de Blaauw, C.L. Frommel, and H. Kessler, eds. *Kunst und Liturgie im Mittelalter: Akten des internationalen Kongresses der Bibliotheca Hertziana und des Nederlands Instituut te Rome, Rom, 28–30 September 1997. 2 vols.* Munich: Hirmer, 2000.

Bonne, J.-C. "Rituel de la couleur: fonctionnement et usage des images dans le sacramentaire de Saint-Étienne de Limoges." In *Image et signification, février 1983*. Rencontres de l'école du Louvre. Paris: Documentation française, 1983, 129–39.

Collomb, P. "Vox clamantis in ecclesia: contribution des sources liturgiques médiévales occidentales à une histoire du cri." In *Haro! Noël! Oyé! Practiques du cri au Moyen Âge*. Ed. D. Left and N. Offenstadt. Paris: Publications de la Sorbonne, 2003, 117–30.

Cullin, O. *Laborintus: essais sur la musique au Moyen Âge*. Paris: Fayard, 2004.

de Blaauw, S. "Architecture and Liturgy in Late Antiquity and the Middle Ages: Traditions and Trends in Modern Scholarship." *Archiv für Liturgiewissenschaft* 33 (1991): 1–34.

Le drame liturgique médiéval: sens et représentations (Colloque co-organisé par la SFM et l'École pratique des hautes études, Centre culturel de l'Ouest, Abbaye de Fontevraud, avril 1996). Published in *Revue de Musicologie* 86/1 (2000): 5–142.

Durliat, M. "L'architecture du XIe siécle à Saint-Michel de Cuxa." In *Études d'art medieval offertes à Louis Grodecki*. Ed. S. M. Crosby. Paris: Ophrys, 1982, 49–62.

Fritz, J.-M. *Paysages sonores du Moyen Âge: le versant épistémologique*. Paris: H. Champion, 2000.

Gy, P.-M. *La liturgie dans l'histoire*. Paris: Éditions Saint Paul, 1990.

Kohlschein, F., and P. Wünsche, eds. Heiliger Raum: Architektur, Kunst und Liturgie in mittelalterlichen Kathedralen und Stiftskirchen. Liturgiewissenschaftliche Quellen und Forschungen 82. Münster: Aschendorff, 1998.

Hiscock, N., ed. *The White Mantle of Churches: Architecture, Liturgy and Art Around the Millennium*. Turnhout: Brepols, 2003.

Kelly, T. Forrest. *The Exultet in Southern Italy*. Oxford: Oxford University Press, 1996.

Klein, P., ed. *Der mittelalterliche Kreuzgang: Architektur, Funktion und Programm*. Regensburg: Schnell & Steiner, 2004.

Le Goff, J., J.-C. Bonne, M.-N. Colette, and É. Palazzo. *Le sacre royal à l'époque de Saint-Louis*. Paris: Gallimard, 2001.

Lowden, J. "Illuminated Books and the Liturgy: Some Observations." In *Objects, Images and the Word*. Ed. C. Hourihane. Index of Christian Art Occasional Papers 6. Princeton, NJ: Princeton University Press, 2003, 17–55.

Palazzo, É. "L'espace et le sacré dans l'Antiquité et au haut Moyen Âge: les autels portatifs." In *Cristianità d'Occidente e cristianità d'Oriente (secoli VI-XI), Spoleto 24–30 aprile 2003*. Settimane di studio 51. Spoleto: Centro italiano di studi sull'alto medioevo, 2004, 1117–60.

—. *L'espace rituel et le sacré dans le christianisme. La liturgie de l'autel portatif dans l'Antiquité et an Moyen Âge*. Turnhout: Brepols, 2008.

—. *L'évêque et son image: l'illustration du pontifical au Moyen Âge*. Turnhout: Brepols, 1999.

—. *Histoire des livres liturgiques: le Moyen Âge, des origins au XIIIe siècle*. Paris: Beauchesne, 1993.

—. "Jalons pour une histoire de la liturgie (Ve-XIIIe siècles)." In *Divina official*. Catalogue of the Exhibition of the Herzog August Bibliothek, Wolfenbüttel (in press).

—. *Liturgie et société au Moyen Âge*. Paris: Aubier, 2000.
—. "Liturgia e Medioevo." In *Il Medioevo europeo di Jacques Le Goff*. Ed. D. Romagnoli. Milan: Silvana, 2003, 247–53.
—. "La lumière et la liturgie au Moyen Âge." *PRIS-MA: Bulletin de liaison de l'Équipe de recherche sur la littérature d'imagination du Moyen Âge* 27 (2001): 91–104.
Post, P. "Ritual Studies." *Archiv für Liturgiewissenschaft* 45 (2003): 21–45.
Reynolds, R. E. "Image and Text: A Carolingian Modification in the Early Roman Eucharistic Ordines." *Viator* 14 (1983): 59–82.
—. "Liturgy, Treatises on." In *Dictionary of the Middle Ages*. Ed. J. R. Strayer. Vol. 7. New York: Charles Scribner, 1986, 624–33.
—. "The Portrait of Ecclesiastical Officers in the Raganaldus Sacramentary and its Liturgico-Canonical Significance." *Speculum* 46 (1971): 432–42.
Schmitt, J.-C. *Le corps, les rites, les rêves, le temps: essais d'anthropologie médiévale*. Paris: Gallimard, 2001.
—. "Rites." In *Dictionnaire raisonné de l'Occident médiéval*. Ed. J. Le Goff and J.-C. Schmitt. Paris: Fayard, 1999, 969–84.
Steenbock, F. *Der kirchliche Prachteinband im Mittelalter von dem Angfängen bis zum Beginn der Gotik*. Berlin: Verlag für Kunstwissenschaft, 1965.
Taft, R. "L'apport des liturgies d'Orient à l'intelligence du culte Chrétien." In *La liturgie: lieu théologique*. Ed. P. de Clerck. Paris: Beauchesne, 1999, 97–122.
—. *Le rite byzantin: bref historique*. Trans. J. Laporte. Paris: Cerf, 1996.
Werckmeister, O. K. "The Lintel Fragment Representing Eve from S. Lazare in Autun." *The Journal of the Warburg and Courtauld Institutes* 35 (1972): 1–30.
Young, K. *The Drama of the Medieval Church*. 2 vols. Oxford: Clarendon Press, 1962.
Zumthor, P. *La lettre et la voix de la "littérature" médiévale*. Paris: Éditions du Seuil, 1987.

24 Visions of God
Alain Boureau

Primary sources

Claudius of Turin. *Apologeticum atque rescriptum Claudii episcopi adversus Theutmirum abbatem*. *PL* 105, 459–464.
Dúngal. *Responsa contra Claudium*. Ed. P. Zanna. Per verba 17. Florence: SISMEL Edizioni del Galluzzo, 2002.
Gozechinus. *Epistola ad Walcherum*. In *Apologiae Duae*. Ed. R. B. C. Huygens. *CCCM* 62. Turnhout: Brepols, 1985, 11–43.
John Scottus Eriugena. *Expositiones in hierarchiam coelestem*. Ed. J. Barbet. *CCCM* 31. Turnhout: Brepols, 1975, 1–215.
Jonas of Orleans. *De cultu imaginum*. *PL* 106, 305–88.
Peter Damian. *Lettre sur la toute-puissance divine*. Ed. and trans. A. Cantin. *SC* 191. Paris: Éditions du Cerf, 1972.

Secondary sources

Armstrong, A. H. *The Cambridge History of Later Greek and Early Medieval Philosophy*. Cambridge: Cambridge University Press, 1970.

Boespflug, F. *Dieu dans l'art: Sollicitudini Nostrae de Benoît XIV (1745) et l'affaire Cresence de Kaufbeuren*. Paris: Éditions du Cerf, 1984.

Boureau, A. "Les théologiens carolingiens devant les images religieuses: la conjuncture de 825." In *Nicée II, 787–1987: douze siècles d'images religieuses*. Ed. F. Boespflug and N. Lossky. Paris: Éditions du Cerf, 1987, 247–62.

Chadwick, H. *Boethius: The Consolations of Music, Logic and Theology, and Philosophy*. Oxford: Oxford University Press, 1981.

Congar, Y. M. J. *I Believe in the Holy Spirit*. Trans. D. Smith. 3 vols. New York: Seabury Press, 1983.

D'Onofrio, G., ed. *Storia della teologia*. 3 vols. Casale Monferrato: PIEMME, 1995.

de Libera, A. *La philosophie médiévale*. Paris: P.U.F., 1993.

De Rijk, L. M. *La philosophie au Moyen Âge*. Leiden: Brill, 1985.

Eco, U., and Marmo, C., eds. *On the Medieval Theory of Signs*. Amsterdam: John Benjamins, 1989.

Flasch, K. *Das philosophische Denken im Mittelalter: von Augustin zu Machiavelli*. Stuttgart: P. Reclam, 1986.

Gersh, S. *From Iamblicus to Eriugena*. Leiden: Brill, 1978.

Gilson, E. *History of Christian Philosophy in the Middle Ages*. New York: Random House, 1955.

Heil, W. "Der Adoptianismus, Alkuin und Spanien." In *Karl der Große: Lebenswerk und Nachleben*. Ed. B. Bischoff. Vol. 2: *Das geistige Leben*. Düsseldorf: L. Schwann, 1965, 95–155.

Holopainen, T. J. *Dialectic and Theology in the Eleventh Century*. Leiden: Brill, 1996.

Iogna-Prat, D., C. Jeudy, and G. Lobrichon, eds. *L'école carolingienne d'Auxerre, de Muretach à Remi, 830–908: entretiens d'Auxerre 1989*. Paris: Beauchesne, 1991.

Jolivet, J. *Godescalc d'Orbais et la Trinité: la méthode de la théologie à l'époque carolingienne*. Paris: Vrin, 1958.

Landes, R. "Sur les traces du Millennium: la via negativa." *Le Moyen Âge* 99 (1993): 5–26.

Marenbon, J. *Early Medieval Philosophy (480–1150): An Introduction*. London: Routledge and Kegan Paul, 1983.

—. *From the Circle of Alcuin to the School of Auxerre: Logic, Theology and Philosophy in the Early Middle Ages*. Cambridge: Cambridge University Press, 1981.

Mondzain, M. J. *Image, Icon, Economy: The Byzantine Origins of the Contemporary Imaginary*. Trans. R. Franses. Stanford, CA: Stanford University Press, 2004.

Moran, D. *The Philosophy of John Scottus Eriugena: A Study of Realism in the Middle Ages*. Cambridge: Cambridge University Press, 1989.

Nedungatt, G., and M. Featherstone, eds. *The Council in Trullo Revisited*. Kanonika 6. Rome: Pontificio istituto orientale, 1995.

Pelikan, J. *The Christian Tradition: A History of the Development of Doctrine*. Vol. 2: *The Spirit of Eastern Christendom (600–1700)*; Vol. 3: *The Growth of Medieval Theology (600–1300)*. Chicago: University of Chicago Press, 1974.

Rivera Recio, J. F. *El adopcionismo en España, siglo VIII: historia y doctrina*. Toledo: Estudio Teológico de San Ildefonso, Seminario Conciliar, 1980.

Rosier-Catach, I. *La parole efficace: signe ritual, sacré*. Paris: Seuil, 2004.

Rubin, M. *Corpus Christi: The Eucharist in Late Medieval Culture*. Cambridge: Cambridge University Press, 1991.

Schulthess, P., and R. Imbach. *Die Philosophie im lateinischen Mittelalter: ein Handbuch mit einem bio-bibliographischen Repertorium*. Zürich: Artemis and Winkler, 1996.
Southern, R. W. *Saint Anselm: A Portrait in a Landscape*. Cambridge: Cambridge University Press, 1990.
Vignaux, P. *Philosophy in the Middle Ages: An Introduction*. Trans. E. C. Hall. New York: Meridian Books, 1959.
von Schönborn, C. *L'icône du Christ: fondements théologiques élaborés entre le 1er et le 2e Concile de Nicée (325–787)*. Fribourg: Éditions universitaires, 1976.
Winkelmann, F. "Die Quellen zur Erforschung des monoenergetisch-monothelischen reiten." *Klio* 69 (1987): 515–59.

25 Orthodoxy and deviance
E. Ann Matter

Primary sources

Agobard of Lyons. *Adversus dogma Felicis Urgellensis*. *PL* 104, 29–70.
Alcuin. *Adversus Elipandum Toletanum libri IV*. *PL* 101, 243–300.
—. *Contra Felicem Urgellitanum episcopum libri VII*. *PL* 101, 128–230.
—. *De animae ratione liber ad Eulalium virginem*. *PL* 101, 639–47.
—. *Epistolae*. Ed. E. Dümmler. *MGH Epistolae Karolini Aevi* 4.
—. *Liber contra haeresin Felicis*. *PL* 101, 87–120.
Amalarius of Metz. *Liber officialis*. In *Opera liturgica omnia*. Ed. J. M. Hanssens. Studi e testi 139. Vatican City: Biblioteca apostolica vaticana, 1949.
Anna Comnena. *Alexias*. Ed. Diether Roderich Reinsch. Berlin: de Gruyter, 2001. Trans. E. A. S. Dawes. *The Alexiad of the Princess Anna Comnena: Being the History of the Reign of her Father, Alexius I, Emperor of the Romans, 1081–1118 A.D.* New York: AMS Press, 1978.
Annales Fuldenses. Ed. G. H. Pertz. *MGH SRG* 7. Hanover: Hahn, 1891.
Augustine of Hippo. *De haeresibus*. Ed. R. van der Plaetse and C. Beukers. *CCSL* 46. Turnhout: Brepols, 1969, 263–345. Trans. L. G. Müller. *The* De Haeresibus *of Saint Augustine: A Translation with an Introduction and Commentary*. Catholic University of America Patristic Studies 90. Washington, DC: Catholic University of America Press, 1956.
—. *De quantitate animae*. *PL* 32, 1035–80.
Beatus of Liebana. *Ad Elipandum libri II*. *PL* 96, 893–1030.
Benedict of Aniane. *Disputatio adversus Felicianam impietatem*. *PL* 103, 1399–1411.
—. *Liber sacrosyllabus contra Elipandum*. *PL* 99, 151–166.
Berengar of Tours. *Rescriptum contra Lanfrancum (De sacra coena)*. Ed. R. B. C. Huygens. *CCCM* 84, 84A. Turnhout: Brepols, 1988.
Boethius. *Commentaria in Porphyrium a se translatum*. *PL* 64, 71–158.
Boniface (Winfrid). *Epistolae*. Ed. M. Tangl. *MGH Epistolae Selectae*. Berlin, 1916. Trans. E. Emerton. *The Letters of Saint Boniface*. Ed. T. F. X. Noble. New York: Columbia University Press, 2000.
Cosmas the Presbyter. *Le traité contre les bogomiles de Cosmas le prêtre*. Ed. A. Vaillant and H.-C. Puech. Paris: Imprimerie nationale, 1945; trans. in Hamilton and Hamilton, *Christian Dualist Heresies*, 114–34.
Elipandus of Toledo. *Epistolae*. *PL* 96, 859–82.

Eulogius. *Documentum martyriale*. In *Corpus scriptorum muzarabicorum* 2. Ed. J. Gil. Madrid: Instituto Antonio de Nebrija, 1971, 459–75.

—. *Epistulae*. In *Corpus scriptorum muzarabicorum* 2. Ed. J. Gil. Madrid: Instituto Antonio de Nebrija, 1971, 495–503.

—. *Liber apologeticus martyrum*. In *Corpus scriptorum muzarabicorum* 2. Ed. J. Gil. Madrid: Instituto Antonio de Nebrija, 1971, 475–95.

—. *Memoriale sanctorum*. In *Corpus scriptorum muzarabicorum* 2. Ed. J. Gil. Madrid: Instituto Antonio de Nebrija, 1971, 363–459.

Euthymius. *Against the Phoundagiagites and Bogomils*. In *Die Phundagiagiten: ein Beitrag zur Ketzergeschichte des byzantinischen Mittelalters*. Ed. G. Ficker. Leipzig: J. A. Barth, 1908; selections in Eng. trans. Hamilton and Hamilton, *Christian Dualist Heresies*, 142–64.

Felix of Urguel. *Confessio fidei*. See Alcuin. *Epistola* 199. Ed. E. Dümmler. *MGH Epistolae Karolini Aevi* 4.

Godescalc. *Responsa de diversis ab ipsomet alicui censori transmissa*. In *Œuvres théologiques et grammaticales de Godescalc d'Orbais. Textes en majeure parte inédits*. Ed. C. Lambot. Spicilegium sacrum lovaniense 20. Louvain: Université Catholique de Louvain, 1945.

Hrabanus Maurus. *De anima*. *PL* 110, 1110–20.

—. *De institutione clericorum libri tres*. Ed. D. Zimpel. Freiburger Beiträge zur mittelalterlichen Geschichte 7. Frankfurt: Peter Lang, 1996.

—. *De universo*. *PL* 111, 9–614.

John of Damascus. "'Hérésie 100': l'Islam." In *Jean Damascène: écrits sur l'Islam*. Ed. L. Le Coz. SC 383. Paris: Éditions du Cerf, 1992.

John Scottus Eriugena. *De predestinatione*. Ed. G. Madec. *CCCM* 50. Turnhout: Brepols, 1958.

—. *Periphyseon (De divisione naturae)*. Ed. E. Jeauneau. *CCCM* 161–65. Turnhout: Brepols, 1996–2003. Eng. trans. I. P. Sheldon-Williams. Revised J. J. O'Meara. *Periphyseon (The Division of Nature)*. Montreal: Éditions Bellarmin, 1987.

Lanfranc of Bec (Lanfranc of Canterbury). *De corpore et sanguine Domini adversus Berengarium Turonensem Liber*. *PL* 150, 407–42.

Paschasius Radbertus. *De corpore et sanguine Domini*. Ed. B. Paulus. *CCCM* 16. Turnhout: Brepols, 1969.

—. *De partu Virginis*. Ed. E. A. Matter. *CCCM* 56C. Turnhout: Brepols, 1985, 1–96; J. M. Canal, ed. "La virginidad de Maria segun Ratramno y Radberto monjes de Corbie. Nueva edición de los textos." *Marianum* (1968): 61–108.

Paul Albar. *Epistulae*. In *Corpus scriptorum muzarabicorum* 1. Ed. J. Gil. Madrid, Instituto Antonio de Nebrija, 1971, 144–270.

—. *Indiculus luminosus*. In *Corpus scriptorum muzarabicorum* 1. Ed. J. Gil. Madrid, Instituto Antonio de Nebrija, 1971, 270–315.

—. *Vita Eulogii*. In *Corpus scriptorum muzarabicorum* 1. Ed. J. Gil. Madrid, Instituto Antonio de Nebrija, 1971, 330–43.

Paulinus of Aquileia. *Contra Felicem Urgellitanum episcopum libri III*. *PL* 99, 349–468.

Pseudo-Augustine. *Categoriae decem ex Aristotele decerptae*. *PL* 32, 1419–40.

Pseudo-Hincmar. *De diversa animae ratione*. *PL* 125, 929–52.

Quierzy (Frühjahr 849). *MGH Concilia* 3. Ed. W. Hartmann. Hanover: Hahn, 1984, 194–99.

Ratramnus of Corbie. *Contra Graecorum opposita*. *PL* 121, 225–346.

—. *De anima*. In A. Wilmart, ed. "L'opuscule inédit de Ratramne sur la nature de l'âme." *Revue bénédictine* 43 (1931): 207–23.

—. *De corpore et sanguine Domini*. Ed. J. N. Bakhuizen van den Brink. Amsterdam: North-Holland Publishing Company, 1954. Trans. G. E. McCracken and A. Cabaniss. *Early Medieval Theology*. The Library of Christian Classics 9. Philadelphia: The Westminster Press, 1958, 109–47. Trans. A. McGrath. *The Christian Theology Reader*. Oxford: Blackwell, 1995, 269–97.

—. *De eo quod Christus ex Virgine natus est*. *PL* 121, 81–102; in J. M. Canal, ed. "La virginidad de Maria segun Ratramno y Radberto monjes de Corbie. Nueva edición de los textos." *Marianum* (1968): 32–60.

—. *De predestinatione Dei I, II*. *PL* 121, 11–80.

—. *Liber de anima ad Odonem Bellovacensem*. Ed. C. Lambot. Analecta Medievalia Namurcensia 2. Namur: Éditions Godenne, 1951.

Rodulfus Glaber. *Historiarum libri quinque*. Ed. and trans. J. France. Oxford: Clarendon Press, 1989.

Theodulf of Orleans. *Opus Caroli regis adversus synodum (Libri Carolini)*. Ed. A. Freeman. *MGH Legum III, Concilia 2, suppl. 1*. Hanover: Hahn, 1998.

Theophylact Lecapenus. *Letter to Peter, King of Bulgaria*. See "L'epistola sui Bogomili del patriarcha constantinopolitano Teofilatto." Ed. I. Dujcev. In *Mélanges E. Tisserant*. Vol. 2. Studi e Testi 232. Vatican City: Biblioteca apostolica vaticana 1964, 88–91; trans. Hamilton and Hamilton, *Christian Dualist Heresies*, 98–102.

Secondary sources

Auzépy, M.-F. "Francfort et Nicée II." In Berndt, *Das Frankfurter Konzil* 1, 279–300.

Barnard, L. W. "The Sources of the Byzantine Iconoclastic Controversy: Leo III and Yazid II – A Reconsideration." In *Überlieferungsgeschichte In Untersuchungen*. Ed. F. Paschke, J. Dummer, J. Irmscher, and K. Treu. Berlin: Akademie-Verlag, 1981, 29–37.

Berndt, R., ed. *Das Frankfurter Konzil von 794: Kristillisationspunkt karolingischer Kultur*. 2 vols. Mainz: Selbstverlag der Gellschaft für Mittelrheinische Kirchengeschichte, 1977.

Biller, P., and A. Hudson, eds. *Heresy and Literacy, 1000–1530*. Cambridge: Cambridge University Press, 1994.

Bouhot, J.-P. *Ratramne de Corbie: histoire littéraire et controverses doctrinales*. Paris: Études augustiniennes, 1976.

Brandes, W. "*Tempora periculosa sunt*: Eschatologisches im Vorfeld der Kaiserkrönung Karls des Grossens." In Berndt, *Das Frankfurter Konzil* 1, 49–79.

Brown, P. *Augustine of Hippo: A Biography, New Edition with an Epilogue*. Berkeley, CA: University of California Press, 2000.

Brubaker, L., and J. Haldon. *Byzantium in the Iconoclast Era (c. 680–850): The Sources: An Annotated Survey (with a section on the architecture of iconoclasm: the buildings by Robert Ousterhout)*. Aldershot: Ashgate, 2001.

Bulliet, R. W. *Conversion to Islam in the Medieval Period*. Cambridge, MA: Harvard University Press, 1979.

Cabaniss, A. *Amalarius of Metz*. Amsterdam: North Holland Publishing Co., 1954.

—. "The Heresiarch Felix." *Catholic Historical Review* 39 (1953): 130–31.

Cameron, A. "How to Read Heresiology." *Journal of Medieval and Early Modern Studies* 33 (2003): 471–92.

Cavadini, J. C. "Elipandus and his Critics at the Council of Frankfort." In Berndt, *Das Frankfurter Konzil* 2, 788–807.

—. *The Last Christology of the West: Adoptionism in Spain and Gaul, 785–820*. Philadelphia, PA: University of Pennsylvania Press, 1992.

Chadwick, H. *The Early Church*. Harmondsworth: Penguin Press, 1967.

Chazelle, C. *The Crucified God in the Carolingian Era: Theology and Art of Christ's Passion*. Cambridge: Cambridge University Press, 2001.

—. "Exegesis in the Ninth-Century Eucharistic Controversy." In *The Study of the Bible in the Carolingian Era*. Ed. C. Chazele and B. Van Name Edwards. Turnholt: Brepols, 2003, 167–87.

—. "Figure, Character and the Glorified Body in the Carolingian Eucharistic Controversy." *Traditio* 47 (1992): 1–36.

—. "Matter, Spirit, and Image in the *Libri Carolini*." *Recherches augustiniennes* 21 (1986): 163–84.

—. "Not in Painting but in Writing: Augustine and the Supremacy of the Word in the *Libri Carolini*." In *Reading and Wisdom: The* De doctrina Christiana *of Augustine in the Middle Ages*. Ed. E. D. English. Notre Dame, IN: University of Notre Dame Press, 1994, 1–22.

Contreni, J. J. "Haimo of Auxerre, Abbot of *Sasceium* (Cessy-Les-Bois) and a New Sermon on 1 John V, 4–10." *Revue bénédictine* 85 (1975): 303–20.

Coope, J. A. *The Martyrs of Córdoba: Community and Family Conflict in an Age of Mass Conversion*. Lincoln, NE: University of Nebraska Press, 1995.

Cowdrey, H. E. J. *Lanfranc: Scholar, Monk, and Archbishop*. Oxford: Oxford University Press, 2003.

de Monclos, J. *Lanfranc et Bérenger: la controverse eucharistique du XIe siècle*. Spicilegium sacrum Lovaniense: Études et documents 37. Louvain, 1971.

Delhaye, P. *Une controverse sur l'âme universelle au IXe siècle*. Analecta Medievalia Namurcensia 1. Namur: Éditions Godenne, 1950.

Ficker, G. *Die Phundagiagiten: ein Beitrag zur Ketzergeschichte des byzantinischen Mittelalters*. Leipzig: J. A. Barth, 1908.

Firey, A. "Carolingian Ecclesiology and Heresy: A Southern Gallic Judicial Tract against Adoptionism." *Sacris erudiri* 39 (2000): 253–316.

Freeman, A. "Scripture and Images in the *Libri Carolini*." *Testo e immagine nell'Alto Medioevo* 1. Spoleto: Centro Italiano di Studi sull'alto medioevo, 1994, 163–95.

Frend, W. H. C. *The Rise of the Monophysite Movement: Chapters in the History of the Church in the Fifth and Sixth Centuries*. Cambridge: Cambridge University Press, 1972.

Fulton, R. *From Judgment to Passion: Devotion to Christ and the Virgin Mary, 800–1200*. New York: Columbia University Press, 2002.

Gero, S. *Byzantine Iconoclasm during the Reign of Constantine V with Particular Attention to the Oriental Sources. CSCO* 384, Subsidia 52. Louvain: Secrétariat du CSCO, 1977.

—. *Byzantine Iconoclasm during the Reign of Leo III with Particular Attention to the Oriental Sources. CSCO* 346, Subsidia 41. Louvain: Secrétariat du CSCO, 1973.

—. "*Libri Carolini* and the Image Controversy." *Greek Orthodox Theological Review* 18, no 1–2 (1973): 7–34.

Gibson, M. T. *Lanfranc of Bec*. Oxford: Clarendon Press, 1978.

Griffith, S. "Bashir/Beser: Boon Companion of the Byzantine Emperor Leo III: The Islamic Recension of his Story in Leiden Oriental MS 951 (2)." *Le Museon* 103 (1990): 293–327.

—. Review of *The Decline of Eastern Christianity under Islam: From Jihad to Dhimmitude, Seventh–Twentieth Centuries*, by Bat Ye'Or, trans. M. Kochan and D. Littman, Madison, NJ; Fairleigh Dickinson University Press, 1996, in *International Journal of Middle East Studies* 30 (1998): 619–21.

—. "Theodore Abu Qurrah's Arabic Tract on the Christian Practice of Venerating Images." *Journal of the American Oriental Society* 105 (1985): 53–73.

Hamilton, J., and B. Hamilton. *Christian Dualist Heresies in the Byzantine World, c. 650–c. 1450*. Manchester: Manchester University Press, 1998.

Head, T., and R. Landes, eds. *The Peace of God: Social Violence and Religious Response in France around 1000*. Ithaca, NY: Cornell University Press, 1995.

Heil, W. *Alcuinstudien I: Zur Chronologie und Bedeutung des Adoptianismusstreites*. Düsseldorf: Verlag L. Schwann, 1970.

Iogna-Prat, D. "L'argumentation défensive: de la polémique grégorienne au *Contra Petrobrusianos* de Pierre le Vénérable, 1140." In Zerner, *Inventer l'hérésie?*, 87–118.

Kolbaba, T. *The Byzantine Lists: Errors of the Latins*. Urbana, IL: University of Illinois Press, 2000.

Kritzeck, J. *Peter the Venerable and Islam*. Princeton, NJ: Princeton University Press, 1964.

Lambert, M. *Medieval Heresy: Popular Movements from the Gregorian Reform to the Reformation*. 2nd ed. Oxford: Blackwell, 1992.

Landes, R. "The Birth of Heresy: A Millennial Phenomenon." *Journal of Religious History* 24 (2000): 26–43.

Lauwers, M. "Un écho des polémiques antiques? À Saint-Victor de Marseille à la fin du Xie siècle." In Zerner, *Inventer l'hérésie?* 37–66.

Lewis, B. *The Jews of Islam*. Princeton, NJ: Princeton University Press, 1984.

Lobrichon, G. "Arras, 1025, ou le vrai procés d'une fausse accusation." In Zerner, *Inventer l'hérésie?*, 67–86.

—. "The Chiaroscuro of Heresy in Early Eleventh-Century Aquitaine: A Letter from Auxerre." In Head and Landes, *Peace of God*, 80–103.

Loos, M. *Dualist Heresies in the Middle Ages*. Prague: Academia Publishing House, 1974.

MacDonald, A. J. *Berengar and the Reform of Sacramental Doctrine*. London: Longmans, Green, 1930.

Markus, R. A. *The End of Ancient Christianity*. Cambridge: Cambridge University Press, 1990.

McGinn, B., ed. and trans. *Apocalyptic Spirituality: Treatises and Letters of Lactantius, Adso of Montier-en-Der, Joachim of Fiore, the Franciscan Spirituals, Savonarola*. New York: Paulist Press, 1979.

Moore, R. I. "Heresy, Repression, and Social Change in the Age of Gregorian Reform." In Waugh and Diehl, *Christendom and its Discontents*, 19–46.

—. "Literacy and the Making of Heresy, c. 1000–c. 1150." In Biller and Hudson, *Heresy and Literacy*, 19–37.

Obolensky, D. *The Bogomils: A Study in Balkan Neo-Manichaeism*. Cambridge: Cambridge University Press, 1948.

O'Donnell, J. J. *Augustine: A New Biography*. New York: Ecco, 2005.

Quadri, R. "Aimone di Auxerre alla luce dei Collectanea di Heiric di Auxerre". *Italia medioevale e umanistica* 6 (1963): 1–48.

Radding, C., and F. Newton. *Theology, Rhetoric, and Politics in the Eucharistic Controversy, 1078–1079: Alberic of Monte Cassino against Berengar of Tours*. New York: Columbia University Press, 2003.

Riggenbach, E. *Die älteste lateinischen Kommentare zum Hebräerbrief*. Leipzig: Georg Böhme, 1907.

Runciman, S. *The Medieval Manichee: A Study of the Christian Dualist Heresy*. New York: Viking Press, 1961.

Russell, J. B. *Dissent and Reform in the Early Middle Ages*. Berkley, CA: University of California Press, 1968.

—. "Saint Boniface and the Eccentrics." *Church History* 33 (1964): 235–47.

Southern, R. W. *Western Views of Islam in the Middle Ages*. Cambridge, MA: Harvard University Press, 1962.

Turner, C. H. "The *Liber ecclesiasticorum dogmatum* Attributed to Gennadius." *Journal of Theological Studies* 7 (1905): 78–96.

van Banning, J. "Claudius von Turin als eine extreme Konsequenz des Konzils von Frankfurt." In Berndt, *Das Frankfurter Konzil* 2, 731–49.

Waugh, S. L., and P. Diehl, eds. *Christendom and its Discontents: Exclusion, Persecution, and Rebellion, 1000–1500*. Cambridge: Cambridge University Press, 1996.

Ye'or, Bat. *The Dhimmi*. Trans. D. Maisel, P. Fenton, and D. Littman. Rutherford, NJ: Farleigh Dickinson University Press, 1985.

Zeddies, N. "Bonifatius und zwei nützliche Rebellen: die Häretiker Aldebert und Clemens." In M. T. Fögen, ed. *Ordnung und Aufruhr im Mittelalter: historische und jurustische Studien zur Rebellion*. Frankfurt: Vittorio Klostermann, 1995, 217–63.

Zerner, M. *Inventer l'hérésie? Discours polémiques et pouvoirs avant l'inquisition*. Nice: Centre d'études médiévales, 1998.

26 Making sense of the Bible
Guy Lobrichon

Primary sources–manuscripts

Book of Nunnaminster. London, BL Harley 2965, s. $IX^{2/2}$, Ireland.

Codex Vindobonensis. Naples, Biblioteca Nazionale 3, s. V, 143 ff.

Munich, Bayerische Staatsbibliothek. Clm 343.

Munich, Staatsbibliothek. Clm 6261.

Munich, Staatsbibliothek. Clm 6268.

Munich, Staatsbibliothek. Clm 6269.

Psalter. Bamberg, Staatsarchiv. A 246.

Psalter. Bamberg, Staatsbibliothek. Bibl. 44.

Remigius (Autissiodorensis), *Expositio in Deuteronomium*. Munich, Bayerische Staatsbibliothek. Clm 6227.

Septuagint. Munich, Bayerische Staatsbibliothek. Clm 6221.

Primary sources–printed

Alcuin. *Dialogus de rhetorica et de virtutibus*. *PL* 101, 919–46.

—. *Epistola*. *PL* 100, 738–40.

Andrew of Fleury. *Vie de Gauzlin, abbé de Fleury*. Ed. R.-H. Bautier and G. Labory. Sources d'histoire médiévale 2. Paris: CNRS, 1998.

Augustine of Hippo. *De civitate Dei*. Ed. B. Dombart and A. Kalb. *CCSL* 47, 48. Turnhout: Brepols, 1955.

—. *In Iohannis evangelium tractatus CXXIV*. Ed. R. Willems. *CCSL* 36, 38. Turnhout: Brepols, 1954.

Bede. *Histoire ecclésiastique du peuple anglais*. Ed. O. Szerwiniack et al. 2 vols. Paris: Les Belles Lettres, 2004.

—. *Histoire ecclésiastique du peuple anglais. Historia ecclesiastica gentis Anglorum. Vol. 1: Livres I–II*. Notes A. Crépin. Ed. M. Lapidge. Trans. P. Monat and P. Robin. *SC* 489. Paris: Éditions du Cerf, 2005.

—. *Opera*. Pars II: *Opera exegetica*. 2B: *In Tobiam, In Proverbia, In Cantica Canticorum*. Ed. D. Hurst. *In Habacuc*. Ed. J. E. Hudson. *CCSL* 119B. Turnhout: Brepols, 1983.

Berthold of Reichenau and Bernold of Constance. *Die Chroniken Bertholds von Reichenau und Bernolds von Konstanz, 1054–1100*. Ed. I. S. Robinson. *MGH SRG, NS* 14. Hanover: Hahn, 2003.

Bible. (Latin Vulgate) Ed. B. Fischer and R. Weber. Stuttgart: Deutsch Bibelgesellschaft, 1994.

Bruno [the Carthusian?]. *Expositio in epistolas Pauli*. *PL* 153, 11–566.

—. *Expositio in psalmos*. *PL* 152, 637–1420.

Cartulaire de l'abbaye de Cysoing et de ses dépendances. Ed. I. de Coussemaker. Lille: Imprimerie St.-Augustin, 1883, 1–5.

Claudius of Turin. *Questiones super libros regum*. *PL* 104, 623–834.

Documents of the Christian Church. Ed. and trans. H. Bettenson. London: Oxford University Press, 1943.

Eugenius of Toledo. *Carmen* VIII. Ed. F. Vollmer. *MGH Auctorum antiquissimorum* 14. Berlin: Weidmann, 1905, 238–39.

Eusebius of Caesarea. *Church History*. Trans. A. C. McGiffert. In *A Select Library of Nicene and Post-Nicene Fathers of the Christian Church: A New Series*. Vol. 1. Ed. P. Schaaf. Grand Rapids: Christian Classics Ethereal Library, 1890.

—. *Life of Constantine*. Intro., trans., and commentary by A. Cameron and S. G. Hall. Oxford: Clarendon Press, 1999.

Expositiones Pauli epistolarum ad Romanos, Galathas et Ephesios e codice Sancti Michaelis in periculo Maris (Avranches, Bibl. Mun. 79). Ed. G. de Martel. *CCCM* 151. Turnhout: Brepols, 1995.

Hrabanus Maurus. *Commentaria in Mattheum*. *PL* 107, 730–1156.

Jerome. *Epistula 22 (Ad Eustochium)*. In *Sancti Eusebii Hieronymi Epistulae*. Pt. 1. Ed. I. Hilberg. 2nd ed. *CSEL* 54. Vienna: Verlag der Österreichischen Akademie der Wissenschaften, 1996, 143–211.

—. *Epistula* 107 *(Ad Laetam de institutione filiae)*. In *Sancti Eusebii Hieronymi Epistulae*. Pt. 2. Ed. I. Hilberg, 2nd ed. *CSEL* 55. Vienna: Verlag der Österreichischen Akademie der Wissenschaften, 1996, 290–305.

Lactantius. *Divinae institutiones*. In *L. Caeli Firmiani Lactanti Opera omnia*. Pt 1. Ed. S. Brandt. *CSEL* 19. Vienna: F. Tempsky, 1890.

Lanfranc of Canterbury. *Opera omnia*. *PL* 150.

Paschasius Radbertus. *Paschasii Radberti Expositio in psalmum XLIV*. Ed. B. Paulus. *CCCM* 94. Turnhout: Brepols, 1991.

Remigius of Auxerre. *Expositio super Genesim*. Ed. B. Van Name Edwards. *CCCM* 136. Turnhout: Brepols, 2000. Eng. trans. B. Van Name Edwards. "The Two Commentaries on Genesis Attributed to Remigius of Auxerre with a Critical Edition of Stegmüller 7195". Ph.D. dissertation, University of Pennsylvania. Ann Arbor: University Microfilms International, 1990.

Rodulfus Glaber. *Opera*. Ed. J. France, N. Bulst, and P. Reynolds. Oxford: Oxford University Press, 1989.

Thegan. *Gesta Hludowici imperatoris/Astronomus. Vita Hludowici imperatoris*. Ed. E. Tremp. *MGH SRG in usum scholarum separatim editi* 64. Hanover: Hahn, 1995.

Thietland of Einsiedeln. *In Epistolam II ad Thessalonicenses*. In *Second Thessalonians: Two Early Medieval Apocalyptic Commentaries; Haimo of Auxerre, Expositio in Epistolam II ad Thessalonicenses. Thietland of Einsiedeln, In Epistolam II ad Thessalonicenses*. Intro. and trans. S. R. Cartwright and K. L. Hughes. Kalamazoo, MI: Medieval Institute Publications, 2001.

Zeno of Verona. *Tractatus*. Ed. B. Löfstedt. *CCSL* 22. Turnhout: Brepols, 1971.

Secondary sources

Amphoux, C. B., and J. K. Elliott, eds. *The New Testament Text in Early Christianity: Proceedings of the Lille Colloquium, July 2000*. Lausanne: Éditions du Zèbre, 2003.

Bautier, R.-H. "L'hérésie d'Orléans et le mouvement intellectual au début du XIe siècle: documents et hypothèses." In *Actes du 95e Congrès National des Sociétés Savantes, Reims, 1970, Section de philologie et d'histoire jusqu'à 1610. Vol.1: Enseignement et vie intellectuelle (IXe-XVIe siècle)*. Paris: Comité des Travaux historiques et scientifiques, 1975, 63–88.

Berndt, R. "Scientia et disciplina in der lateinischen Bible und in der Exegese des hohen Mittelalters." In Berndt, Lutz-Bahmann, and Stammberger, *"Scientia" and "Disciplina,"* 9–36.

—, M. Lutz-Bachmann, and R. M. W. Stammberger, eds. *"Scientia" und "Disciplina": Wissenstheorie und Wissenschaftspraxis im 12. und 13. Jahrhundert*. Berlin: Akademie Verlag, 2002.

Berschin, W. "Salomons III: Psalterium quadrupartitum in Köln und Heidelberg. Mit Anhang, Die Bamberg/Coburg/Freiburger Fragmente eines Psalterium quadrupartitum." In Vol. 1 of *Kaiserin Theophanu: Begegnung des Ostens und Westens um die Ende des ersten Jahrtausends*. 2 vols. Ed. A. von Euw and P. Schreiner. Cologne: Schnütgen-Museum, 1991, 327–34.

Biondi, B. *Il diritto cristiano*. 3 vols. Milan: Giuffrè, 1952.

Bischoff, B. *Mittelalterliche Studien*. Vol. 1. Stuttgart: Hiersemann, 1966–81.

—, and J. Hofmann, *Libri Sancti Kyliani: die Würzburger Schreibschule und die Dombibliothek im VIII. und IX. Jahrhundert*. Würzburg: Schöningh, 1952.

—, and M. Lapidge, eds. *Biblical Commentaries from the Canterbury School of Theodore and Hadrian*. Cambridge Studies in Anglo-Saxon England 10. Cambridge: Cambridge University Press, 1994.

Buc, P. *L'ambiguité du livre: prince, pouvoir et peuple dans les commentaires de la Bible au Moyen Âge*. Paris: Beauchesne, 1994.

Cahn, W. *La Bible romane: chefs-d'œuvre de l'enluminure*. Fribourg-Paris: Office du Livre-Vilo, 1982.

Caspary, G. *Politics and Exegesis: Origen and the Two Swords*. Berkeley, CA: University of California Press, 1979.

Chazelle, C., and B. Van Name Edwards, eds. *The Study of the Bible in the Carolingian Era*. Medieval Church Studies 3. Turnhout: Brepols, 2003.

Chiesa, P. "Tradizioni e traduttori dal greco nel XI secolo." *Giovanni Scoto nel suo tempo*. Spoleto: Centro italiano di studi sull'alto medioevo, 1989, 171–200.

Contreni, J. J. *Carolingian Learning, Masters and Manuscripts*. Brookfield, VT: Ashgate, 1992.

Cremascoli, G., and C. Leonardi, eds. *La Bibbia nel Medioevo*. Bologna: Edizioni Dehoniane, 1996.

Cristianità d'Occidente e cristianità d'Oriente (secoli VI–XI). Settimane di studio 51. Spoleto: Centro italiano di studi sull'alto medioevo, 2004.

Crombie, A. C. *Styles of Scientific Thinking in the European Tradition: The History of Argument and Explanation Especially in the Mathematical and Biomedical Sciences and Arts*. Vol. 2. London: Duckworth, 1994.

Curti, C., and B. M. Antonietta. "Catene esegetiche greche." In *Patrologia*. Ed. A. di Berardino. Genova: Marietti, 2000, vol. 5: 609–55. English ed. *Patrology: From Chalcedon to John of Damascus*. Ed. A. Di Berardino. Trans. A. Walford. Cambridge: James Clarke, 2006.

d'Aiuto, F., G. Morello, and A. M. Piazzoni, eds. *I Vangeli dei popoli: la parola e l'immagine del Cristo nelle culture e nella storia. Città del Vaticano, Palazzo della Cancelleria, 21 giugno–10 dicenbre 2000*. No. 6. Vatican City: Biblioteca apostolica vaticana, 2000.

Davis-Weyer, C. *Early Medieval Art, 300–1150*. Toronto: University of Toronto Press, 1986.

de Dreuille, C., ed. *L'Église et la mission au VIe siècle: la mission d'Augustin de Cantorbéry et les églises de Gaule sous l'impulsion de Grégoire le Grand. Actes du Colloque d'Arles de 1998*. Paris: Éditions du Cerf, 2000.

De Hamel, C. *The Book: A History of the Bible*. London: Phaidon Press, 2001.

de Jong, M. "Old Law and New-Found Power: Hrabanus Maurus and the Old Testament." In *Centres of Learning: Learning and Location in Pre-Modern Europe and the Near-East*. Ed. J.-W. Drijvers and A. MacDonald. Leiden: Brill, 1995, 161–74.

de Lubac, H. *Exégèse médiévale*. 4 vols. Paris: Aubier, 1959–63.

Degering, H., and A. Bockler. *Die Quedlinburger Itala Fragmente*. Berlin: Cassiodor Gesellschaft, 1932.

Depreux, P., and B. Judic, eds. *Alcuin, de York à Tours: écriture, pouvoir et réseaux dans l'Europe du haut Moyen Âge*. Rennes: Presses universitaires de Rennes, 2004.

Dorival, G. *Les chaînes exégétiques grecques sur les psaumes: contribution à l'étude d'une forme littéraire*. 4 vols. Spicilegium Sacrum Lovaniense études et documents 43–46. Louvain: Spicilegium Sacrum Lovaniense, 1986–95.

Duchet-Suchaux, M., and Y. Lefèvre. "Les noms de la Bible." In Riché and Lobrichon, *Le Moyen Âge et la Bible*, 13–23.

Flynt, W. T. *Medieval Music as Medieval Exegesis*. Lanham, MD: Scarecrow Press, 1999.

Fransen, I. "Description de la collection hiéronymienne de Florus de Lyon sur l'Apôtre." *Revue bénédictine* 94 (1984): 195–228.

Frolow, A. "Deux églises byzantines." *Études Byzantines* 3 (1945): 43–63.

Gameson, R., ed. *The Early Medieval Bible: Its Production, Decoration and Use*. Cambridge: Cambridge University Press, 1994.

Ganz, D. "Knowledge of Ephraim's Writings in the Merovingian and Carolingian Age." *Hugoye: Journal of Syriac Studies* 2 (1999) at http://syrcom.cua.edu/Hugoye/Vol2No1/HV2N1Ganz.html

Gero, S. *Byzantine Iconoclasm during the Reign of Leo III. CSCO* 346, Subsidia 41. Louvain: Secrétariat du CSCO, 1973.

Gibson, M. *"Artes" and Bible in the Medieval West*. Aldershot: Variorum Reprints, 1993.

Ginzburg, C. "High and Low: The Theme of Forbidden Knowledge in the Sixteenth and Seventeenth Centuries." *Past and Present* 73 (1976): 28–41.

Gneuss, H. *Handlist of Anglo-Saxon Manuscripts: A List of Manuscripts and Manuscript Fragments Written or Owned in England Up to 1100*. Medieval and Renaissance Texts and Studies 241. Tempe, AZ: Arizona Center for Medieval and Renaissance Studies, 2001.

Gorman, M. M. *Biblical Commentaries from the Early Middle Ages*. Florence: SISMEL, 2002.

—. "La plus ancienne édition commentée: The Ezechiel Fragment in Irish Minuscule, now in Zürich (CLA 7.1008)." *Revue bénédictine* 114 (2004): 276–88.

Grant, E. *The Foundations of Modern Science in the Middle Ages: Their Religious, Institutional and Intellectual Contexts*. Cambridge: Cambridge University Press, 1996.

Gryson, R. *Altlateinische Handschriften: manuscrits vieux latins, répertoire descriptif. Deuxième partie: Mss. 300–485 (Manuscrits du Psautier). Vetus Latina* 2, pt. 2B. Freiburg: Herder, 2004.

Herren, M. "The 'Judaizing Tendencies' of the Early Irish Church." *Filologia mediolatina* 3 (1996): 73–80.

Hussey, M. T. "The Franco-Saxon *Synonyma* in the Ragyndrudis Codex: Anglo-Saxon Design in a Luxeuil-Scripted Booklet." *Scriptorium* 58 (2004): 227–38.

Janin, R. *La géographie ecclésiastique de l'empire byzantin: Pt. 1, "Le siège de Constantinople et le patriarcat cuménique."* Vol. 3: *Les églises et les monastères*. Paris: Institut français des études byzantines, 1969.

Jeffreys, E. M., and A. Kazhdan. "Florilegium." *ODB* 2, 793–94.

Kazhdan, A., and E. M. Jeffreys. "Ekphrasis." *ODB* 1, 683.

Kirchmeyer, J., and D. Hemmerdinger-Iliadou. "S. Ephrem et le *Liber Scintillarum*." *Revue des sciences religieuses* 46 (1958): 545–50.

Kottje, R. *Studien zum Einfluss des Alten Testaments auf Recht und Liturgie des früheren Mittelalters (6.–8. Jahrhundert)*. Bonner Historische Forschungen 23. Bonn: Röhrscheid, 1970.

Lampe, G. W., ed. *The Cambridge History of the Bible*. Vol. 2: *The West from the Fathers to the Reformation*. Cambridge: Cambridge University Press, 1969.

Lapidge, M. "The Career of Theodore." In *Archbishop Theodore: Commemorative Studies on his Life and Influence*. Ed. M. Lapidge. Cambridge Studies in Anglo-Saxon England 11. Cambridge: Cambridge University Press, 1995, 1–29.

—, and R. Sharpe. *A Bibliography of Celtic-Latin Literature, 400–1200*. Dublin: Royal Irish Academy, 1985.

Leanza, S. "La letteratura esegetica in frammenti: la tradizione catenaria." *Augustinianum* 37 (1997): 25–36.

Lobrichon, G. "Arras, 1025, ou le vrai procès d'une fausse accusation." In *Inventer l'hérésie? Discours polémiques et pouvoirs avant l'Inquisition*. Ed. M. Zerner. Nice: Centre d'études médiévales, 1998, 67–85.

—. *La Bible au Moyen Âge*. Les Médiévistes français. Paris: Picard, 2003.

—. "Conserver, réformer, transformer le monde? Les manipulations de l'Apocalypse au Moyen Âge central." In *The Role of the Book in Medieval Culture: Proceedings of the Oxford International Symposium (26 September–1 October, 1982)*. Ed. P. Ganz. Turnhout: Brepols, 1986, 75–94; reprinted in Lobrichon, *La Bible au Moyen Âge*, 109–28.

—. "Une nouveauté: les gloses de la Bible," in Riché and Lobrichon, *Le Moyen Âge et la Bible*, 95–114; reprinted in Lobrichon, *La Bible au Moyen Âge*, 158–72.

—. "La relecture des Pères chez les commentateurs de la Bible dans l'Occident latin (IXe-XIIe siècles)." In *Ideologie e pratiche del reimpiego nell'Alto Medioevo*. Settimane di studio 46. Spoleto: Centro italiano di studi sull'alto medioevo, 1999, 253–82.

Lourdaux, W., and D. Verhelst, eds. *The Bible and Medieval Culture*. Louvain: Louvain University Press, 1979.

Luscombe, D. "'Scientia' and 'Disciplina' in the Correspondence of Peter Abelard and Heloise." In Berndt, Lutz-Bahmann, and Stammberger, *"Scientia" and "Disciplina,"* 79–89.

Maas, M. *Exegesis and Empire in the Early Byzantine Mediterranean: Junilius Africanus and the "Instituta Regularia Divinae Legis."* Studien und Texte zur Antike und Christentum 17. Tübingen: Mohr Siebeck, 2003.

Mango, C. "La culture grecque et l'occident au VIIIe siècle." In *I problemi dell'occidente nel secolo VIII*. Settimane di studio 20, vol. 2. Spoleto: Centro italiano di studi sull'alto medioevo, 1973, 683–721.

Matter, E. A. *The Voice of my Beloved: The "Song of Songs" in Western Medieval Christianity*. Philadelphia, PA: University of Philadelphia Press, 1990.

Mazal, O., ed. *Wiener Genesis*. 2 vols. Frankfurt: Insel Verlag, 1980.

McNamara, M. "Psalter Text and Psalter Study in the Early Irish Church (A.D. 600–1200)." *Proceedings of the Royal Irish Academy* 73C (1973): 201–98.

Meens, R. "The Uses of the Old Testament in Early Medieval Canon Law: The *Collectio Vetus Gallica* and the *Collectio Hibernensis*." In *The Uses of the Past in the Early Middle Ages*. Ed. Y. Hen and M. Innes. Cambridge: Cambridge University Press, 2000, 69–77.

Meyvaert, P. *Benedict, Gregory, Bede and Others*. London: Variorum Reprints, 1983.

—. "Le *Libellus responsionum* à Augustin de Canterbury: une œuvre authentique de saint Grégoire le Grand." In *Grégoire le Grand: Chantillly, Centre Culturel Les Fontaines, 15–19 septembre 1982. Colloque international du Centre national de la recherche scientifique*. Ed. J. Fontaine, R. Gillet, and S. Pellistrandi. Paris: Centre national de la recherche scientifique, 1986, 543–50.

—. "Les 'Responsiones' de S. Grégoire le Grand à S. Augustin de Canterbury: À propos d'un article récent." *Revue d'histoire ecclésiastique* 54 (1959): 879–94.

Momigliano, A. "L'historique païenne et chrétienne au IVe siècle après Jésus-Christ." In his *Problèmes d'historiographie ancienne et moderne*. Paris: Gallimard, 1983, 145–68.

Mondésert, C., ed. *Le monde grec ancien et la Bible*. Bible de tous les temps 1. Paris: Beauchesne, 1984.

Norton, D., ed. *A History of the Bible as Literature*. Vol. 1: *From Antiquity to 1700*. Cambridge: Cambridge University Press, 2004.

O'Loughlin, T., ed. *The Scriptures and Early Medieval Ireland*. Turnhout: Brepols, 1999.

Parisse, M., ed. *Vie du pape Léon IX: Brunon, évêque de Toul*. Trans. M. Goullet. Paris: Les Belles Lettres, 2002.

Reinhardt, K., and I. Santiago-Otero. *Biblioteca bíblica ibérica medieval*. Madrid: Consejo Superior de Investigaciones Científicas, 1986.

Reynolds, S. *Medieval Reading: Grammar, Rhetoric and the Classical Text*. Cambridge: Cambridge University Press, 1996.

Riché, P., and G. Lobrichon, eds. *Le Moyen Âge et la Bible*. Bible de tous les temps 4. Paris: Beauchesne, 1983.

Rochais, H. "Florilèges spirituels. Florilèges latins." In *Dictionnaire de spiritualité ascétique et mystique, doctrine et histoire*. Vol. 5. Paris: G. Beauchesne, 1962, 435–60.

Rogerson, J., ed. *The Oxford Illustrated History of the Bible*. Oxford: Oxford University Press, 2001.

Santiago-Otero, H., and K. Reinhardt. *La Biblia en la península ibérica durante la edad media (siglos XII-XV): el texto y su interpretación*. Coimbra: Arquivo da Universidade de Coimbra, 2001.

Schmid, R. "Aetates mundi: Die Weltalter als Gliederungsprinzip der Geschichte." *Zeitschrift für Kirchengeschichte* 67 (1955/56): 288–317.

Serres, M., ed. *Eléments d'histoire des sciences*. Paris: Bordas, 1989. Eng. trans. *A History of Scientific Thought: Elements of a History of Science*. Ed. M. Serres. Oxford: Blackwell, 1995.

Smalley, B. *The Gospels in the Schools, c. 1100–c. 1280*. London: Hambledon, 1985.

—. *Medieval Exegesis of Wisdom Literature: Essays*. Ed. R. E. Murphy. Atlanta: Scholars Press, 1986.

—. *The Study of the Bible in the Middle Ages*. 3rd ed. Oxford: Blackwell, 1983.

Smith, L., trans. *Medieval Exegesis in Translation: Commentaries on the Book of Ruth*. Kalamazoo, MI: Medieval Institute Publications, 1996.

Stella, F. *La poesia carolingia Latina a tema biblico*. Biblioteca di "Medioevo Latino." Società Internazionale per lo Studio del Medioevo Latino 9. Spoleto: Centro italiano di studi sull'alto medioevo, 1993.

Stock, B. *The Implications of Literacy: Written Language and Models of Interpretation in the Eleventh and Twelfth Centuries*. Princeton, NJ: Princeton University Press, 1983.

Suckale-Redlefsen, G., and B. Schemmel, eds. *Das Buch mit 7 Siegeln: die Bamberger Apokalypse, eine Ausstellung der Staatsbibliothek Bamberg in Zusammenarbeit mit dem Haus der Bayerischen Geschichte*. Lucerne: Faksimile Verlag, 2000.

Taft, R. F. "Eucharist." *ODB* 2, 737–38.

Talbot, A.-M. "Antony I Kassymatas." *ODB* 1, 124–25.

—, and A. Cutler. "John VII Grammatikos." *ODB* 2, 1052.

Tristram, H. L. C. *Sex aetates mundi: die Weltzeitalter bei den Angelsachsen und den Iren*. Anglistische Forschungen 165. Heidelberg: C. Winter, 1985.

Velmans, T. *Le Tétraévangile de la Laurentienne*. Paris: Klincksieck, 1971.

Verkerk, D. *Early Medieval Illumination and the Ashburnham Pentateuch*. Cambridge: Cambridge University Press, 2004.

von Schlosser, J. *Quellenbuch: repertorio di fonti per la Storia dell'Arte del Medioevo occidentale*. Florence: Le Lettere, 1992.

Ward, J. D. *Ciceronian Rhetoric in Treatise, Scholion and Commentary*. Typologie des sources du Moyen Âge occidental 58. Turnhout: Brepols, 1995.

Young, F. M. *Biblical Exegesis and the Formation of Christian Culture*. Cambridge: Cambridge University Press, 1997.

27 The Christian book in medieval Byzantium
Leslie Brubaker and Mary B. Cunningham

Primary sources

Apophthegmata patrum. *PG* 65, 71–440. Eng. trans. *The Sayings of the Desert Fathers: The Alphabetical Collection*. Trans. B. Ward. Kalamazoo, MI: Cistercian Publications, 1975; rev. ed. 1984.

Basil II. *Menologion*. *PG* 117, 19–614.

Basil of Caesarea. *De Spiritu sanctu*. In *Basile de Césarée: sur le Saint-Esprit*. Ed. B. Pruche. *SC* 17bis. Paris: Éditions du Cerf, 1968.

—. *Regulae brevius tractatae*. *PG* 31, 1080–1306.

Delehaye, H., ed. *Propylaeum ad Acta Sanctorum Novembris*. *AASS*. Brussels: Société des Bollandistes, 1902.

Eusebius. *Life of Constantine*. Ed. and trans. A. Cameron and S. Hall. Oxford: Oxford University Press, 1999.

Evergetinos or Synagoge IV. Ed. Makarios of Corinth and Nikodemos Hagiorites. Athens: Matthaios Lange, 1980.

Germanus of Constantinople. *Commentary on the Divine Liturgy*. Trans. P. Meyendorff. *St. Germanus of Constantinople: On the Divine Liturgy*. Crestwood, NY: St. Vladimir's Seminary Press, 1984. Greek edition in N. Borgia. *Il commentario liturgico di S. Germano patriarca Constantinopolitano e versiona Latina di Anastasio Bibliotecario*. Studi Liturgici 1. Grottaferrata: n.p., 1912.

John Moschus. *Pratum spirituale*. *PG* 87:3, 2851–3112. Trans. J. Wortley. *The Spiritual Meadow of John Moschos*. Kalamazoo, MI: Cistercian Publications, 1992.

John of Damascus. *On the Divine Images*. In *Die Schriften des Johannes von Damaskos*. Ed. B. Kotter. Vol. 3. Berlin: de Gruyter, 1975. Trans. D. Anderson. *St. John of Damascus: On the Divine Images*. Crestwood, NY: St. Vladimir's Seminary Press, 1980.

John Skylitzes. *Synopsis historiarum*. Ed. I. Thurn. *Corpus fontium historiae byzantinae* 5. Berlin: de Gruyter, 1973.

The Life of St. Lazaros Galesiotes of Mt. Galesion: An Eleventh-Century Pillar Saint. Trans. R. P. H. Greenfield. Washington, DC: Dumbarton Oaks, 2000.

The Life of St. Theodora. In *Holy Women of Byzantium: Ten Saints' Lives in English Translation*. Trans. A.-M. Talbot. Washington, DC: Dumbarton Oaks, 1996, 159–237.

Pachomius. *Praecepta*. In *Œuvres de S. Pachôme et de ses disciples*. Ed. and trans. L.-T. Lefort. *CSCO* 159, 30–36 and 160, 30–37. Louvain: L. Durbecq, 1953.

—. *Vita Prima*. In *Sancti Pachomii vitae graecae*. Ed. F. Halkin. Subsidia hagiographica 19. Brussels: Société des Bollandistes, 1932.

Photius. *Bibliotheke*. In *Photius: Bibliothèque*. Ed. and trans. R. Henry. 9 vols. Paris: Les Belles Lettres, 1959–91.

The Rule of St. Benedict in Latin and English. Ed. and trans. J. McCann. London: Burns Oates, 1952.

The Rule of the Monastery of St. John Stoudios in Constantinople. First recension published in *Opisanie liturgicheskikh rykopisei*. Vol. 1. Ed. A. Dmitrievsky. Kiev, 1895, 224–38; second recension in *PG* 99, 1704–20. Both versions trans. T. Miller, *BMFD* 1, 97–119.

A Select Library of Nicene and Post-Nicene Fathers of the Christian Church. 2nd series. Vol. 14: *The Seven Ecumenical Councils*. Ed. P. Schaff and H. Wace. Repr. Peabody, MA: Hendrickson Publishers, 1995.

Theodore the Studite. *Poenae monasteriales*. *PG* 99, 1733–58.

Secondary sources

Alexiou, M. *After Antiquity: Greek Language, Myth, and Metaphor*. Ithaca, NY: Cornell University Press, 2002.

Anderson, J. "Cod. Vat. gr. 463 and an Eleventh-Century Byzantine Painting Center." *DOP* 32 (1978): 177–96.

—. "The Illustration of cod. Sinai. gr. 339." *Art Bulletin* 61 (1979): 167–85.

—. "A Twelfth-Century Instance of Reused Parchment: Christ Church College, Wake gr. 32." *Scriptorium* 44 (1990): 207–16.

Antonopoulou, T. *The Homilies of the Emperor Leo VI*. Leiden: Brill, 1997.

Astruc, C. "Remarques sur les signes marginaux de certains manuscrits de S. Grégoire de Nazianze." *Analecta bollandiana* 92 (1974): 289–95.

Atsalos, B. "Termes byzantins relatifs à la décoration des manuscrits grecs." In Prato, *I manoscritti greci* 2, 445–511.

Auzépy, M.-F., and J.-P. Grélois, eds. *Byzance retrouvée, érudits et voyageurs français (XVIe–XVIIIe siècles)*. Paris: Centre d'études byzantines, 2001.

Bagnall, R. "Jesus Reads a Book." *Journal of Theological Studies* 51 (2000): 577–88.

Barbour, R. *Greek Literary Hands, AD 400–1600*. Oxford: Clarendon Press, 1981.

Bardy, G. "Faux et fraudes littéraires dans l'antiquité chrétienne." *Revue d'histoire ecclésiastique* 32 (1936): 5–23, 275–302.

Beck, H.-G. *Ideen und Realitäten in Byzanz: gesammelte Aufsätze*. London: Variorum Reprints, 1972.

—. *Kirche und theologische Literatur im byzantinischen Reich*. Munich: C. H. Beck, 1959.

Browning, R. "Literacy in the Byzantine World." *Byzantine and Modern Greek Studies* 4 (1978): 39–54.

Brubaker, L. "The Introduction of Painted Initials in Byzantium." *Scriptorium* 45 (1991): 22–46.

—. "Pictures Are Good to Think with: Looking at Byzantium." In *L'écriture de la mémoire: la littérarité de l'historiographie*. Ed. P. Odorico, P. Agapitos, and M. Hinterberger. Paris: Centre d'études byzantines, néo-helléniques, et sud-est européennes, 2006, 221–40.

—. Review of *The Byzantine Octateuchs* by K. Weitzmann and M. Bernabò. *Speculum* 76, No. 4. (Oct. 2001): 1121–24.

—. "The Vienna Dioskorides and Anicia Juliana." In *Byzantine Garden Culture*. Ed. A. Littlewood, H. Maguire, and J. Wolschke-Bulmahn. Washington, DC: Dumbarton Oaks, 2002, 189–214.

—. *Vision and Meaning in Ninth-Century Byzantium: Image as Exegesis in the Homilies of Gregory of Nazianzus*. Cambridge Studies in Palaeography and Codicology 6. Cambridge: Cambridge University Press, 1999.

—, and J. Haldon. *Byzantium in the Iconoclast Era (c. 680–850): The Sources*. Birmingham Byzantine and Ottoman Monographs 7. Aldershot: Ashgate, 2001.

Buchthal, H., and H. Belting. *Patronage in Thirteenth-Century Constantinople: An Atelier of Late Byzantine Book Illumination and Calligraphy*. Dumbarton Oaks Studies 16. Washington, DC: Dumbarton Oaks, 1978.

Burton-Christie, D. *The Word in the Desert: Scripture and the Quest for Holiness in Early Christian Monasticism*. Oxford: Oxford University Press, 1993.

Byzantine Books and Bookmen. Washington, DC: Dumbarton Oaks, 1975.

Cameron, A. *Christianity and the Rhetoric of Empire: The Development of Christian Discourse*. Berkeley, CA: University of California Press, 1991.

Cecchelli, C., G. Furlani, and M. Salmi. *The Rabbula Gospels*. Olten: Urs Graf, 1959.

Clanchy, M. T. *From Memory to Written Record, England 1066–1307*. London: Edward Arnold, 1979.

Corrigan, K. *Visual Polemics in the Ninth-Century Byzantine Psalters*. Cambridge: Cambridge University Press, 1992.

Cunningham, M. B. "Preaching and the Community." In *Church and People in Byzantium: 20th Spring Symposium of Byzantine Studies, Manchester 1986*. Ed. R. Morris. Birmingham: Centre for Byzantine, Ottoman and Modern Greek Studies, 1990, 29–47.

—, and P. Allen. *Preacher and Audience: Early Christian and Byzantine Homiletics*. Leiden: Brill, 1998.

Cutler, A. "The Aristocratic Psalter: The State of Research." *Rapports et co-rapports, XVe Congrès international d'études byzantines III: art et archéologie*. Athens: Association Internationales des Études Byzantines, 1976, 229–57.

—. *The Aristocratic Psalters in Byzantium*. Bibliothèque des Cahiers archéologiques 13. Paris: Picard, 1984.

Dain, A. *Les manuscrits*. 3rd ed. Paris: Les Belles Lettres, 1975.

Daniélou, J. *The Bible and the Liturgy*. Liturgical Studies 3. Notre Dame, IN: University of Notre Dame Press, 1956.

—. *From Shadows to Reality: Studies in the Biblical Typology of the Fathers*. Trans. W. Hibberd. London: Burns and Oates, 1960.

Der Nersessian, S. *Miniature Painting in the Armenian Kingdom of Cilicia from the Twelfth to the Fourteenth Century*. 2 vols. Dumbarton Oaks Studies 31. Washington, DC: Dumbarton Oaks, 1993.

Devreesse, R. *Introduction à l'étude des manuscrits grecs*. Paris: C. Klincksieck, 1954.

Ehrhard, A. *Überlieferung und Bestand der hagiographischen und homiletischen Literatur*. 3 vols. Leipzig: J. C. Hinrichs Verlag, 1937–39.

Featherstone, M., and M. Holland. "A Note on Penances Prescribed for Negligent Scribes and Librarians in the Monastery of Studios." *Scriptorium* 36.2 (1982): 258–60.

Fox, R. L. "Literacy and Power in Early Christianity." In *Literacy and Power in the Ancient World*. Ed. A. K. Bowman and G. Woolf. Cambridge: Cambridge University Press, 1994, 126–48.

Galavaris, G. *The Illustrations of the Liturgical Homilies of Gregory Nazianzenus*. Studies in Manuscript Illumination 6. Princeton, NJ: Princeton University Press, 1969.

—. *The Illustrations of the Prefaces in Byzantine Gospels*. Byzantina vindobonensia 11. Vienna: Österreichischen Akademie der Wissenschaften, 1979.

Gamble, H. Y. *Books and Readers in the Early Church: A History of Early Christian Texts*. New Haven, CT: Yale University Press, 1995.

Gamillscheg, E., and M. McCormick. "Codex." *ODB* 1, 473.

—, and A.-M. Talbot. "Parchment." *ODB* 3, 1587.

—, A.-M. Talbot, and I. Ševčenko. "Paper." *ODB* 3, 1579.

Gardthausen, V. *Griechische Palaeographie*. 2nd ed. 2 vols. Leipzig: Zentralantiquariat der DDR, 1978.

Gerstinger, H. *Dioscorides. Codex Vindobonensis med.gr.1 der Österreichischen Nationalbibliothek*. 2 vols. with *Kommentarband zu der Faksimileausgabe*. Graz: Akademische Druk und Verlagsanstalt, 1970.

—. *Die Wiener Genesis*. Vienna: Filser, 1931.

Gilliard, F. D. "More Silent Reading in Antiquity: *non omne verbum sonabat*." *Journal of Biblical Literature* 112 (1993): 689–94.

Goodall, B. *The Homilies of St. John Chrysostom on the Letters of St. Paul to Titus and Philemon: Prolegomena to an Edition*. University of California Publications in Classical Studies 20. Berkeley, CA: University of California Press, 1979.

Greenfield, R. P. H. *Traditions of Belief in Late Byzantine Demonology*. Amsterdam: Hakkert, 1988.

Gregory, C. "Les cahiers des manuscrits grecs." *Comptes rendus de l'Académie des Inscriptions et Belles-Lettres* (Paris, 1885): 261–68.

Harrison, V. "Word as Icon in Greek Patristic Theology." *Sobornost* 10 (1988): 38–49.

Hoffmann, P., ed. *Recherches de codicologie comparée: la composition du codex au Moyen Âge, en orient et en occident*. Paris: Presses de l'École normale supérieure, 1998.

Hunger, H. "The Classical Tradition in Byzantine Literature: The Importance of Rhetoric." In *Byzantium and the Classical Tradition: University of Birmingham 13th Spring Symposium of Byzantine Studies, 1979*. Ed. M. Mullett and R. Scott. Birmingham: Centre for Byzantine Studies, 1981, 35–47.

—. *Die hochsprachliche profane Literatur der Byzantiner*. 2 vols. Munich: Beck, 1978.

Hutter, I. "*Le copiste du Métaphraste*: On a Center for Manuscript Production in Eleventh-Century Constantinople." In Prato, *I manoscritti greci* 2, 535–86.

—. "Decorative Systems in Byzantine Manuscripts, and the Scribe as Artist: Evidence from Manuscripts in Oxford." *Word and Image* 12/1 (1996): 4–22.

—. Review of *The Byzantine Octateuchs* by K. Weitzmann and M. Bernabò. *Byzantinische Zeitschrift* 94 (2001): 359–65.

Irigoin, J. "Les cahiers des manuscrits grecs." In Hoffmann, *Recherches*, 1–19.

—. "Centres de copie et bibliothèques." In *Byzantine Books*, 17–27.

James, L. *Light and Colour in Byzantine Art*. Oxford: Oxford University Press, 1996.

Jeffreys, E., ed. *Rhetoric in Byzantium: Papers from the 35th Spring Symposium of Byzantine Studies, Exeter College, University of Oxford, March 2001*. Aldershot: Ashgate, 2003.

Kazhdan, A. "Literacy." *ODB* 2, 1234.

—, with L. F. Sherry and C. Angelidi. *A History of Byzantine Literature (650–850)*. Athens: The National Hellenic Research Foundation, Institute for Byzantine Research, 1999.

Kravari, V. "Note sur le prix des manuscrits (IXe–XVe siècle)." In *Hommes et richesses dan l'Empire byzantin*. Vol. 2: *VIIIe–XVe siècle*. Ed. V. Kravari, J. Lefort, and C. Morrisson. Réalités byzantines 3. Paris: P. Lethielleux, 1991, 375–84.

Krueger, D. *Writing and Holiness: The Practice of Authorship in the Early Christian East*. Philadelphia, PA: University of Pennsylvania Press, 2004.

Krumbacher, K., A. Ehrhard, and H. Gelzer. *Geschichte der byzantinischen Literatur von Justinian bis zum Ende des oströmischen Reiches (527–1453)*. 2nd ed. Munich: Beck, 1897.

Lassus, J. *L'illustration byzantine du Livre des Rois*. Bibliothèque des Cahiers archéologiques 9. Paris: Klincksieck, 1973.

Lemerle, P. *Byzantine Humanism*. Trans. H. Lindsay and A. Moffatt. Canberra: Australian Association for Byzantine Studies, 1986.

Leroy, J. "Les manuscrits grecs d'Italie." *Codicologica* 2 (1978): 52–71.

—. *Les manuscrits syriaques à peintures conservés dans les bibliothèques d'europe et d'orient*. 2 vols. Institut français d'archéologie de Beyrouth. Bibliothèque archéologique et historique 77. Paris: P. Geuthner, 1964.

—. "La réforme Studite." *Orientalia christiana analecta* 153 (1958): 181–214.

—. *Les types de réglure des manuscrits grecs*. Paris: Éditions du Centre national de la recherche scientifique, 1976.

—. "La vie quotidienne du moine studite." *Irénikon* 27 (1954): 21–50.

Lewis, N. *Papyrus in Classical Antiquity*. Oxford: Clarendon Press, 1974.

Linardou, K. "The Couch of Solomon, a Monk, a Byzantine Lady, and the Song of Songs." In *The Church and Mary*. Ed. R. Swanson. *SCH* 39. Woodbridge: Boydell Press, 2004, 73–85.

Loenertz, R. J. "La légende Parisienne de saint Denys l'Aréopagite, sa genèse et son premier témoin." *Analecta bollandiana* 69 (1951): 217–37.

Loerke, W. *I vangeli di Rossano: le miniature/The Rossano Gospels: The Miniatures*. Rome: Salerno editrice, 1987.

Lowden, J. "Concerning the Cotton Genesis and Other Illustrated Manuscripts of Genesis." *Gesta* 31 (1992): 40–53.

—. "The Luxury Book as Diplomatic Gift." In *Byzantine Diplomacy*. Ed. J. Shepard and S. Franklin. Aldershot: Ashgate, 1992, 249–60.

Maas, M. "Photius' Treatment of Josephus and the High Priesthood." *Byzantion* 40 (1990): 183–94.

Magdalino, P. *Constantinople médiévale: études sur l'évolution des structures urbaines*. Paris: De Boccard, 1996.

Maguire, H. *Art and Eloquence in Byzantium*. Princeton, NJ: Princeton University Press, 1981.

Mango, C. "The Availability of Books in the Byzantine Empire, A.D. 750–850." In *Byzantine Books*, 29–45.
—. "The Date of cod. Vat. Regin. Gr. 1 and the 'Macedonian Renaissance.'" *Acta ad archaeologiam et artium historiam pertinentia* 4 (1969): 121–26.
—. *The Homilies of Photius, Patriarch of Constantinople*. Cambridge, MA: Harvard University Press, 1958.
—. "L'origine de la minuscule." In *La paléographie grecque et byzantine*, 175–80.
Markus, R. *Signs and Meanings: World and Text in Ancient Christianity*. Liverpool: Liverpool University Press, 1996.
Mateos, J. *Le typicon de la Grande Église: Ms. Sainte-Croix no. 40, Xe siècle*. 2 vols. Orientalia christiana analecta 165–66. Rome: Pontificium institutum orientalium studiorum, 1963.
Mathews, T. *The Early Churches of Constantinople: Architecture and Liturgy*. University Park, PA: Pennsylvania State University Press, 1971.
—. "The Epigrams of Leo Sacellarios and an Exegetical Approach to the Miniatures of Vat. Reg. gr. 1." *Orientalia christiana periodica* 43 (1977): 94–133.
McCormick, M. "The Birth of the Codex and the Apostolic Life-Style." *Scriptorium* 39 (1985): 150–58.
—. *Origins of the European Economy: Communications and Commerce, AD 300–900*. Cambridge: Cambridge University Press, 2001.
McKitterick, R., ed. *The Uses of Literacy in Early Medieval Europe*. Cambridge: Cambridge University Press, 1990.
Moffat, A. "Schooling in the Iconoclast Centuries." In *Iconoclasm*. Ed. A. A. M. Bryer and J. Herrin. Birmingham: Centre for Byzantine and Modern Greek Studies, 1977, 85–92.
Mondrain, B. "Les signatures des cahiers dans les manuscrits grecs." In Hoffmann, *Recherches*, 21–48.
Mullett, M. "Writing in Early Mediaeval Byzantium." In McKitterick, *Uses of Literacy*, 156–85.
Mundell Mango, M. "Where Was Beth Zagba?" In *Okeanos: Essays Presented to Ihor Ševčenko*. Ed. C. Mango and O. Pritsak. Harvard Ukrainian Studies 7. Cambridge, MA: Ukrainian Research Institute, Harvard University, 405–30.
Nelson, R. *The Iconography of Preface and Miniature in the Byzantine Gospel Book*. New York: New York University Press, 1980.
—. "The Italian Appreciation and Appropriation of Illuminated Byzantine Manuscripts, c. 1200–1450." *DOP* 49 (1995): 209–35.
—. *Theodore Hagiopetrites, a Late Byzantine Scribe and Illuminator*. 2 vols. Österreichische Akademie der Wissenschaften, philosophisch-historische Klasse, Denkschriften 217. Vienna: Verlag der Österreichischen Akademie der Wissenschaften, 1991.
—, and J. Lowden. "The Palaeologina Group: Additional Manuscripts and New Questions." *DOP* 45 (1991): 58–68.
—, E. Gamillscheg, and A.-M. Talbot. "Rolls, Liturgical." *ODB* 3, 1803–1804.
Nordenfalk, C. *Celtic and Anglo-Saxon Painting: Book Illumination in the British Isles, 600–800*. New York: Braziller, 1977.
—. *Die spätantike Zierbuchstaben*. 2 vols. Stockholm: Egnellska boktr., 1970.
Omont, H. *Évangiles avec peintures byzantines du XIe siècle*. 2 vols. Paris: Imprimerie Berthaud Frères, 1908.

———. "Manuscrit des œuvres de S. Denys l'Aréopagite envoyé de Constantinople à Louis le Débonnaire en 827." *Revue des études grecques* 17 (1904): 230–36.

Ong, W. *Orality and Literacy: The Technologizing of the Word*. 2nd ed. London: Routledge, 2002.

La paléographie grecque et byzantine. Colloques internationaux du Centre national de la recherche scientifique 559. Paris: CNRS, 1977.

Patlagean, E. "Ancienne hagiographie byzantine et histoire sociale." *Annales* 1 (1968): 106–26. Eng. trans. "Ancient Byzantine Hagiography and Social History." In *Saints and Their Cults: Studies in Religious Sociology, Folklore, and History*. Ed. S. Wilson. Cambridge: Cambridge University Press, 1983, 101–21.

Prato, G., ed. *I manoscritti greci tra riflessione e dibattito: Atti del V Colloquio Internazionale di Paleografia Greca, Cremona, 4–10 ottobre 1998*. 3 vols. Florence: Gonnelli, 2000.

Quasten, J. *Patrologie*. 3 vols. Utrecht: Spectrum, 1950–60.

Rahlfs, A. *Verzeichnis der griechischen Handschriften des Alten Testaments*. Berlin: Weidmann, 1914.

Rapp, C. "Byzantine Hagiographers as Antiquarians, Seventh to Tenth Centuries." *Byzantinische Forschungen* 21 (1995): 31–44.

Reynolds, L. D., and N. G. Wilson. *Scribes and Scholars: A Guide to the Transmission of Greek and Latin Literature*. 2nd ed. Oxford: Clarendon Press, 1974.

Roberts, D., and T. Skeat. *The Birth of the Codex*. London: Oxford University Press for the British Academy, 1983.

Rousseau, P. *Pachomius: The Making of a Community in Fourth-Century Egypt*. Berkeley, CA: University of California Press, 1985.

Sainger, P. *Space between Words: The Origins of Silent Reading*. Stanford, CA: Stanford University Press, 1997.

Ševčenko, I. "The Illuminators of the Menologion of Basil II." *DOP* 16 (1962): 245–76.

———. "Levels of Style in Byzantine Prose." *Jahrbuch der Österreichischen Byzantinistik* 31 (1981): 289–312.

Ševčenko, N. Patterson. "Menologion." *ODB* 2, 1341.

Stock, B. *The Implications of Literacy: Written Language and Models of Interpretation*. Princeton, NJ: Princeton University Press, 1983.

Taft, R. F. "Lectionary." *ODB* 2, 1201.

———. "Menaion." *ODB* 2, 1338.

———, and N. Patterson Ševčenko. "Synaxarion." *ODB* 3, 1991.

Thompson, E. *Handbook of Greek and Latin Palaeography*. 2nd ed. London: Kegan Paul, Trench, Trübner, and Co., 1894.

Treadgold, W. *The Nature of the Bibliotheca of Photius*. Dumbarton Oaks Studies 18. Washington, DC: Dumbarton Oaks, 1980.

Turner, E. G. *The Terms Recto and Verso: The Anatomy of the Papyrus Roll*. Actes du XVe Congrès international de papyrologie 1. Brussels: Fondation égyptologique Reine Élisabeth, 1978.

Velmans, T. *Le Tétraévangile de la Laurentienne*. Bibliothèque des Cahiers archéologiques 6. Paris: Klincksieck, 1971.

Weitzmann, K. *Die byzantinische Buchmalerei des 9. und 10. Jahrhunderts*. Österreichische Akademie der Wissenschaften, philosophisch-historische Klasse Denkschriften 243.

Veröffentlichungen der Kommission für Schrift- und Buchwesen des Mittelalters IV.2.1. Reprint of Berlin 1935 ed. Vienna: Verlag der Österreichischen Akademie der Wissenschaften, 1996.

— . *Die byzantinische Buchmalerei des 9. und 10. Jahrhunderts: Addenda und Appendix* . Österreichische Akademie der Wissenschaften, philosophisch-historische Klasse Denkschriften 244. Veröffentlichungen der Kommission für Schrift- und Buchwesen des Mittelalters IV.2.2. Vienna: Verlag der Österreichischen Akademie der Wissenschaften, 1996.

—. *Illustrations in Roll and Codex: A Study in the Origin and Method of Text Illustration*. Studies in Manuscript Illumination 2. Princeton, NJ: Princeton University Press, 1947; rev. ed., 1970.

—. *The Joshua Roll: A Work of the Macedonian Renaissance*. Studies in Manuscript Illumination 3. Princeton, NJ: Princeton University Press, 1948.

—. *Late Antique and Early Christian Book Illumination*. New York: Braziller, 1977.

—, and M. Bernabò, with R. Tarasconi. *The Byzantine Octateuchs*. 2 vols. The Illustrations in the Manuscripts of the Septuagint 2. Princeton, NJ: Princeton University Press, 1999.

—, and H. Kessler. *The Cotton Genesis: British Library, Codex Otho B.VI*. The Illustrations in the Manuscripts of the Septuagint 1. Princeton, NJ: Princeton University Press, 1986.

Wickham, C. "Ninth-Century Byzantium through Western Eyes." In *Byzantium in the Ninth Century: Dead or Alive?* Ed. L. Brubaker. Aldershot: Ashgate, 1998, 245–56.

Wilson, N. "Books and Readers in Byzantium." In *Byzantine Books*, 1–15.

—. "Libraries of the Byzantine World." *Greek, Roman, and Byzantine Studies* 8 (1968): 53–80.

—. *Mediaeval Greek Bookhands: Examples Selected from Greek Manuscripts in Oxford Libraries*. 2 vols. Mediaeval Academy of America Publications 81. Cambridge, MA: Mediaeval Academy of America, 1973.

—. *Scholars of Byzantium*. London: Duckworth, 1983.

Young, F. M. P. *Biblical Exegesis and the Formation of Christian Culture*. Cambridge: Cambridge University Press, 1997.

Saints and their cults
Julia M. H. Smith

Primary sources

Das altenglische Martyrologium. Ed. G. Kotzor. 2 vols. Abhandlungen der Bayerische Akademie der Wissenschaften, philosophisch-historische Klasse, neue Folge 88/1–2. Munich: Bayerische Akademie der Wissenschaften, 1981.

Amandus. *Testamentum*. Ed. B. Krusch. *MGH SRM* 5. Hanover, 1910, 483–85. Trans. J. N. Hillgarth. In *Christianity and Paganism, 350–750: The Conversion of Western Europe*. Philadelphia, PA: University of Pennsylvania Press, 1969, 149.

Brock, S., and S. Ashbrook Harvey. *Holy Women of the Syrian Orient*. Berkeley, CA: University of California Press, 1987.

Ciggar, K. N. "Une description de Constantinople dans le Tarragonensis 55." *Revue des études byzantines* 53 (1995): 117–40.

Eadmer of Canterbury. *Lives and Miracles of Saints Oda, Dunstan and Oswald*. Ed. and trans. A. J. Turner and B. J. Muir. Oxford Medieval Texts. Oxford: Oxford University Press, 2006.

Félire hui Gormáin. The Martyrology of Gorman. Ed. W. Stokes. Henry Bradshaw Society 9. London: Harrison and Sons, 1895.

Flusin, B. *Saint Anastase le Perse et l'histoire de la Palestine au début du VIIe siècle*. Vol. 1: *Les Textes*. Vol. 2: *Commentaire: Les moines de Jérusalem et l'invasion perse*. Le monde byzantin. Paris: Éditions du Centre national de la recherche scientifique, 1992.

Franklin, C. Vircillo. *The Latin Dossier of Anastasius the Persian: Hagiographic Translations and Transformations*. Studies and Texts 147. Toronto: Pontifical Institute of Mediaeval Studies, 2004.

Gregory of Tours. *Liber in gloria confessorum*. Ed. B. Krusch, *MGH SRM* 1, pt. ii. Hanover: Hahn, 1885, 294–370. Trans. R. Van Dam. *Gregory of Tours: Glory of the Confessors*. Liverpoool: Liverpool University Press, 1988.

Guibert of Nogent. *De sanctis et eorum pigneribus*. Ed. R. B. C. Huygens. *CCCM* 127. Turnhout: Brepols, 1993, 79–175. Trans. T. Head. In *Medieval Hagiography: An Anthology*. Ed. T. Head. New York: Garland, 2000, 399–427.

Haskins, C. H. "A Canterbury Monk at Constantinople, c. 1090." *English Historical Review* 25 (1910): 293–95.

Life of St. Mary the Younger. Trans. A. Laiou. In *Holy Women of Byzantium: Ten Saints' Lives in English Translation*. Ed. A.-M. Talbot. Washington, DC: Dumbarton Oaks, 1996, 254–89.

The Life of Saint Nikon: Text, Translation and Commentary. Ed. D. F. Sullivan. Brookline, MA: Hellenic College Press, 1987.

Methodius. "La vie d'Euthyme de Sardes (d. 831)." Ed. J. Gouillard. *Travaux et mémoires* 10 (1987): 1–101.

Nicetas Stethatos. *Vie de Syméon le nouveau théologien (949–1022) par Nicétas Stethatos*. Ed. I. Hausherr and G. Horn. Orientalia Christiana 12. Rome: Pontificium institutum orientalium studiorum, 1928.

Peter Damian. *Vita beati Romualdi*. Ed. G. Tabacco. Fonti per la storia d'Italia 94. Rome: Istituto storico italiano per il medio evo, 1957. Trans. H. Leyser in *Medieval Hagiography: An Anthology*. Ed. T. Head. New York: Garland, 2000, 295–316.

Richard of Saint-Vanne. *Vita et miracula Vitoni*. Ed. L. d'Achery and J. Mabillon. *Acta Sanctorum Ordinis S. Benedicti*. Paris: L. Billaine, 1668–1701, Vol. VI, pt. ii, 565–69.

Robert of Rheims. *Historia Iherosolimitana*. In *Recueil des historiens des croisades, historiens occidentaux* 3. Paris: Académie des Inscriptions et Belles-Lettres, 1866, 721–882. Trans. C. Sweetenham. *Robert the Monk's History of the First Crusade*. Aldershot: Ashgate, 2005.

Vita Eligii. Ed. B. Krusch. *MGH SRM* 4. Hanover: Hahn, 1902, 663–741. Trans. J. A. McNamara. In *Medieval Hagiography: An Anthology*. Ed. T. Head. New York: Garland, 2000, 137–67.

Vita S. Nili. *PG* 120, 15–165.

Vita S. Thomaidis. *AASS Nov*. IV.234–42. Trans. P. Halsall. In *Holy Women of Byzantium: Ten Saints' Lives in English Translation*. Ed. A.-M. Talbot. Washington, DC: Dumbarton Oaks, 1996, 297–322.

Widric. *Vita S. Gerardi episcopi Tullensis*. Ed. G. Waitz. *MGH Scriptores* 4. Hanover: Hahn, 1841, 485–520.

Wilkinson. J., ed. *Jerusalem Pilgrims before the Crusades*. Warminster: Aris and Phillips, 2002.

Wulfstan of Winchester. *Life of St. Æthelwold*. Ed. and trans. M. Lapidge and M. Winterbottom. Oxford Medieval Texts. Oxford: Oxford University Press, 1991.

Secondary sources

Aigrain, R. *L'hagiographie: ses sources – ses méthodes – son histoire*. 2nd ed. Ed. R. Godding. Subsidia Hagiographica 80. Brussels: Société des Bollandistes, 2000.

Albert, B.-S. *Le pèlerinage à l'époque carolingienne*. Bibliothèque de la Revue d'histoire ecclésiastique 82. Brussels: Éditions Nauwelaerts, 1999.

Angenendt, A. "*Corpus incorruptum*: eine Leitidee der mittelalterlichen Reliquienverehrung." *Saeculum: Jahrbuch für Universalgeschichte* 42 (1991): 320–48.

Appleby, D. F. "Holy Relics and Holy Image: Saints' Relics in the Western Controversy over Images in the Eighth and Ninth Centuries." *Word and Image* 8 (1992): 333–50.

Ash, M., and D. Broun. "The Adoption of St. Andrew as Patron Saint of Scotland." In *Medieval Art and Architecture in the Diocese of St. Andrews*. Ed. J. Higgitt. Tring: British Archaeological Association, 1994, 16–24.

Auzépy, M.-F. "L'évolution de l'attitude face au miracle à Byzance (VIIe–IXe siècle)." In *Miracles, prodiges et merveilles au Moyen Âge: XXVe congrès de la SHMES (Orléans, juin 1994)*. Paris: Publications de la Sorbonne, 1994, 31–46.

Baldovin, J. F. *The Urban Character of Christian Worship: The Origins, Development, and Meaning of Stational Liturgy*. Rome: Pontificium institutum studiorum orientalium, 1987.

Barber, C. "Icon and Portrait in the Trial of Symeon the New Theologian." In *Icon and Word: The Power of Images in Byzantium, Studies Presented to Robin Cormack*. Ed. A. Eastmond and L. James. Aldershot: Ashgate, 2003, 25–33.

Biggs, F. M., T. D. Hill, P. E. Szarmach, and E. G. Whatley. *Sources of Anglo-Saxon Literary Culture, I: Abbo of Fleury, Abbo of Saint-Germain-des-Prés, and Acta Sanctorum*. Kalamazoo, MI: Medieval Institute Publications, 2001.

Bozóky, E., and A.-M. Helvétius, eds. *Les reliques: objets, cultes, symboles*. Hagiologia 1. Turnhout: Brepols, 1999.

Brock, S. P. "Christians in the Sasanian Empire: A Case of Divided Loyalties." In *Religion and National Identity*. Ed. S. Mews. *SCH* 18. Oxford: Blackwell, 1982, 1–19.

Brooks, N. "Canterbury, Rome and the Construction of English Identity." In Smith, *Early Medieval Rome*, 221–47.

Brown, P. *Authority and the Sacred: Aspects of the Christianisation of the Roman World*. Cambridge: Cambridge University Press, 1995.

—. *The Cult of Saints: Its Rise and Function in Latin Christianity*. London: SCM Press, 1981.

—. "Enjoying the Saints." *EME* 9 (2000): 1–24.

—. "Holy Men." In *The Cambridge Ancient History*. Vol. 14: *Late Antiquity: Empire and Successors, A.D. 425–600*. Ed. A. Cameron, B. Ward-Perkins, and M. Whitby. Cambridge: Cambridge University Press, 2000, 781–810.

—. "The Rise and Function of the Holy Man in Late Antiquity." *Journal of Roman Studies* 61 (1971): 80–101.

—. "The Rise and Function of the Holy Man in Late Antiquity, 1971–1997." *Journal of Early Christian Studies* 6 (1998): 353–76.

—. *The Rise of Western Christendom: Triumph and Diversity, A.D. 200–1000*. 2nd ed. Oxford: Blackwell, 2003.

—. "The Saint as Exemplar." *Representations* 1 (1983): 1–25.

Brubaker, L. "Icons before Iconoclasm?" In *Morfologie sociali e culturali in Europa tra tarda antichità e Alto Medioevo*. Settimane di studio 45. Spoleto: Centro italiano di studi sull'alto medioevo, 1998, II.1215–54.

Cameron, A. "On Defining the Holy Man." In Howard-Johnston and Hayward, *Cult of Saints*, 27–43.

Carr, A. Weyl. "Icons: Painted, Bilateral, Metal, Mosaic." In *ODB* 2, 978–81.

Clayton, M. *The Cult of the Virgin Mary in Anglo-Saxon England*. Cambridge Studies in Anglo-Saxon England 2. Cambridge: Cambridge University Press, 1990.

Coon, L. L. *Sacred Fictions: Holy Women and Hagiography in Late Antiquity*. Philadelphia, PA: University of Pennsylvania Press, 1997.

Corbet, P. *Les saints ottoniens: sainteté dynastique, sainteté royale et sainteté féminine autour de l'an mil*. Sigmaringen: Thorbecke, 1986.

Cotsonis, J. "The Contribution of Byzantine Lead Seals to the Study of the Cult of Saints (Sixth-Twelfth Century)." *Byzantion* 75 (2005): 383–497.

Crawford, B. E. "The Churches Dedicated to St. Clement in Norway: A Discussion of their Origin and Function." *Collegium Medievale* 17 (2004): 100–31.

Cutler, A. "Iconography." In *ODB* 2, 977.

Dagron, G. "L'ombre d'un doute: l'hagiographie en question, VI-VIIe siècle." *DOP* 46 (1992): 59–68.

Dale, T. E. A. "Inventing a Sacred Past: Pictorial Narratives of St. Mark the Evangelist in Aquileia and Venice, c. 1000–1300." *DOP* 48 (1994): 53–104.

Delehaye, H. *Sanctus: essai sur le culte des saints dans l'antiquité*. Subsidia hagiographica 17. Brussels: Société des Bollandistes, 1927.

Déroche, V. "L'obsession de la continuité: Nil de Rossano face au monachisme ancien." In *L'autorité du passé dans les sociétés médiévales*. Ed. J.-M. Sansterre. Rome: École française de Rome, 2004.

—. "Pourquoi écrivait-on des recueils de miracles? L'exemple des miracles de Saint Artémios." In *Les saints et leurs sanctuaires à Byzance: textes, images et monuments*. Ed. C. Jolivet-Lévy, M. Kaplan, and J.-P. Sodini. Byzantina Sorbonensia 11. Paris: Publications de la Sorbonne, 1993.

Dubois, J. *Les martyrologes du Moyen Âge latin*. Typologie des sources du moyen âge occidental 26. Turnhout: Brepols, 1978.

Ehrhard, A. *Überlieferung und Bestand der hagiographischen und homiletischen Literatur der griechischen Kirche von den Anfängen bis zum Ende des 16. Jahrhunderts*. Texte und Untersuchungen zur Geschichte der altchristlichen Literatur 50–52. Leipzig: J. C. Hinrichs Verlag, 1937–52.

Elm, S. "Introduction." *Journal of Early Christian Studies* 6 (1998): 343–51.

Ferrari, M. C. "*Lemmata sanctorum*: Thiofrid d'Echternach et le discours sur les reliques au XIIe siècle." *Cahiers de civilisation médiévale* 38 (1995): 215–25.

Fletcher, R. A. *St. James's Catapult: The Life and Times of Diego Gelmírez of Santiago de Compostela*. Oxford: Clarendon Press, 1984.

Flusin, B. "L'hagiographie monastique à Byzance au IX et au Xe siècle: modèles anciens et tendances contemporaines." *Revue Bénédictine* 103 (1993): 31–50.

Fouracre, P. "The Origins of the Carolingian Attempt to Regulate the Cult of Saints." In Howard-Johnston and Hayward, *Cult of Saints*, 143–65.

Fowden, E. Key. *The Barbarian Plain: Saint Sergius between Rome and Iran*. Berkeley, CA: University of California Press, 1999.

Geary, P. J. *Furta Sacra: Thefts of Relics in the Central Middle Ages*. 2nd ed. Princeton, NJ: Princeton University Press, 1990.

Goullet, M. *Écriture et réécriture hagiographiques: essai sur les réécritures de vies de saints dans l'Occident latin médiéval (VIIIe–XIIe s.)*. Hagiologia 4. Turnhout: Brepols, 2005.

Grabar, A. *Martyrium: recherches sur le culte des reliques et l'art chrétien antique*. 3 vols. Paris: Collège de France, 1943.

Grig, L. *Making Martyrs in Late Antiquity*. London: Duckworth, 2004.

Harvey, S. Ashbrook. "Women in Early Byzantine Hagiography: Reversing the Story." In *"That Gentle Strength": Historical Perspectives on Women in Christianity*. Ed. L. L. Coon, K. J. Haldane, and E. W. Sommer. Charlottesville, VA: University of Virginia Press, 1990, 36–59.

Heene, K. "Female Saints and their Lives: The Geographical Distribution of the Carolingian *vitae feminarum*." In *Aevum inter utrumque: mélanges offerts à Gabriel Sanders*. Ed. M. van Uytfanghe and R. Demeulenaere. Instrumenta Patristica 23. Steenbrugge: In abbatia S. Petri, 1991, 205–26.

Heinzelmann, M. *Translationsberichte und andere Quellen des Reliquienkultes*. Typologie des sources du moyen âge occidental 33. Turnhout: Brepols, 1979.

Helvétius, A.-M. "*Virgo et virago*: réflexions sur le pouvoir du voile consacré d'après les sources hagiographiques de la Gaule du Nord." In *Femmes et pouvoirs des femmes à Byzance et en Occident (VIe–XIe siècles)*. Ed. S. Lebecq, A. Dierkens, R. Le Jan, and J.-M. Sansterre. Villeneuve d'Ascq: Centre de recherche sur l'histoire de l'Europe du nord-ouest, 1999, 189–203.

Herrin, J. *The Formation of Christendom*. Oxford: Blackwell, 1987.

Herrmann-Mascard, N. *Les reliques des saints: formation coutumière d'un droit*. Paris: Éditions Klincksieck, 1975.

Høgel, C., ed. *Metaphrasis: Redactions and Audiences in Middle Byzantine Hagiography*. Oslo: Research Council of Norway, 1996.

—. *Symeon Metaphrastes: Rewriting and Canonization*. Copenhagen: Museum Tusculanum Press, University of Copenhagen, 2002.

Hollingsworth, P. A. "Iconophiles." *ODB* 2, 977.

—, and A. Cutler. "Iconoclasm." *ODB* 2, 975–77.

Holum, K. G., and G. Vikan. "Jerusalem." *ODB* 2, 1033–36.

Howard-Johnston, J., and P. A. Hayward, eds. *The Cult of Saints in Late Antiquity and the Early Middle Ages*. Oxford: Oxford University Press, 1999.

Howe, J. *Church Reform and Social Change in Eleventh-Century Italy: Dominic of Sora and his Patrons*. Philadelphia, PA: University of Pennsylvania Press, 1997.

—. "Neilos of Rossano." *ODB* 2, 1450–51.

Huneycutt, L. L. "The Idea of the Perfect Princess: The *Life of St. Margaret* in the Reign of Matilda II (1100–1118)." *Anglo-Norman Studies* 12 (1990): 81–97.

Iogna-Prat, D., É. Palazzo, and D. Russo, eds. *Marie: le culte de la Vierge dans la société médiévale*. Paris: Beauchesne, 1996.

James, L. "Bearing Gifts from the East: Imperial Relic Hunters Abroad." In *Eastern Approaches to Byzantium: Papers from the Thirty-Third Spring Symposium of Byzantine Studies, University of Warwick, Coventry 1999*. Ed. A. Eastmond. Aldershot: Ashgate, 2001, 119–31.

Kalavrezou, I. "Helping Hands for the Empire: Imperial Ceremonies and the Cult of Relics at the Byzantine Court." In *Byzantine Court Culture from 829 to 1204*. Ed. H. Maguire. Washington, DC: Dumbarton Oaks, 1997.

Kaplan, M. "De la dépouille à la relique: formation du culte des saints à Byzance du Ve au XIIe siècle." In Bozóky and Helvétius, *Les reliques*, 19–38.

—. "L'ensevelissement des saints: rituel de création des reliques et sanctification à Byzance (Ve–XIIe siècles)." In *Mélanges Gilbert Dagron*, published as *Travaux et mémoires* 14 (2002): 319–32.

—, ed. *Le sacré et son inscription dans l'espace à Byzance et en Occident: études comparées*. Byzantina Sorbonensia 18. Paris: Publications de la Sorbonne, 2001.

Kazhdan, A. "Hermitic, Cenobitic, and Secular Ideals in Byzantine Hagiography of the Ninth Centuries [sic]." *Greek Orthodox Theological Review* 30 (1985): 473–87.

—. "Symeon the Theologian." *ODB* 3, 1987.

—, and N. Patterson Ševčenko. "Symeon Metaphrastes." *ODB* 3, 1983–84.

—, A.-M. Talbot, and N. Patterson Ševčenko. "Nikon 'Ho Metanoeite.'" *ODB* 3, 1484.

Kemp, E. W. *Canonization and Authority in the Western Church*. London: Oxford University Press, 1948.

Kessler, H. L., and J. Zacharias. *Rome 1300: On the Path of the Pilgrim*. New Haven, CT: Yale University Press, 2000.

Kuelzer, A. "Byzantine and Early Post-Byzantine Pilgrimage to the Holy Land and Mount Sinai." In *Travel in the Byzantine World*. Ed. R. Macrides. Aldershot: Ashgate, 2002, 149–61.

Lapidge, M. "Ælfric's *Sanctorale*." In *Holy Men and Holy Women: Old English Prose Saints' Lives and their Contexts*. Ed. P. E. Szarmach. Albany, NY: State University of New York Press, 1996, 115–29.

—, J. Crook, R. Deshman, and S. Rankin. *The Cult of St. Swithun*. Oxford: Clarendon Press, 2003.

Lappin, A. *The Medieval Cult of Saint Dominic of Silos*. Modern Humanities Research Association Texts and Dissertations 56. Leeds: Maney, 2002.

Lerou, S. "L'usage des reliques du Christ par les empereurs aux XIe et XIIe siècles: le saint bois et les saintes pierres." In *Byzance et les reliques du Christ*. Ed. J. Durand and B. Flusin. Paris: Association des amis du Centre d'histoire et civilisation de Byzance, 2004, 159–82.

Limberis, V. "The Cult of the Martyrs and the Cappadocian Fathers." In *Byzantine Christianity*. Ed. D. Krueger. Vol. 3 of *A People's History of Christianity*. Minneapolis, MN: Fortress Press, 2006, 39–58.

Lobrichon, G. "Le culte des saints, le rire des hérétiques, le triomphe des savants." In Bozóky and Helvétius, *Les reliques*, 95–108.

Magdalino, P. "The Byzantine Holy Man in the Twelfth Century." In *The Byzantine Saint*. Ed. S. Hackel. London: Fellowship of St. Alban and St. Sergius, 1981, 51–66.

—. "L'église du Phare et les reliques de la Passion à Constantinople (VIIe/VIIIe–XIIIe siècles)." In *Byzance et les reliques du Christ*. Ed. J. Durand and B. Flusin. Paris: Association des amis du Centre d'histoire et civilisation de Byzance, 2004, 15–30.

—. "'What We Have Heard in the Lives of the Saints We Have Seen with Our Own Eyes': The Holy Man as Literary Text in Tenth-Century Constantinople." In Howard-Johnston and Hayward, *Cult of Saints*, 83–112.

Maguire, H. *The Icons of their Bodies: Saints and their Images in Byzantium*. Princeton, NJ: Princeton University Press, 1996.

Maksoudian, K. "Armenian Saints." In *Dictionary of the Middle Ages*. Vol. 1. Ed. J. R. Strayer. New York: Scribner, 1982, 517–21.

Maraval, P. *Lieux saints et pèlerinages d'Orient: histoire et géographie des origines à la conquête arabe*. Paris: Éditions du Cerf, 1985.

Markus, R. A. *The End of Ancient Christianity*. Cambridge: Cambridge University Press, 1990.

—. *Gregory the Great and his World*. Cambridge: Cambridge University Press, 1997.

McCormick, M. *Origins of the European Economy: Communications and Commerce, AD 300–900*. Cambridge: Cambridge University Press, 2001.

McCready, W. *Signs of Sanctity: Miracles in the Thought of Gregory of the Great*. Toronto: Pontifical Institute of Medieval Studies, 1989.

McCulloh, J. M. "From Antiquity to the Middle Ages: Continuity and Change in Papal Relic Policy." In *Pietas: Festschrift für Bernhard Kötting*. Ed. E. Dassmann and K. Frank. Münster: Aschendorff, 1980, 313–24.

Moore, R. I. "Between Sanctity and Superstition: Saints and their Miracles in the Age of Revolution." In *The Work of Jacques Le Goff and the Challenges of Medieval History*. Ed. M. Rubin. Woodbridge: Boydell & Brewer, 1997, 55–67.

Morris, C. *The Sepulchre of Christ and the Medieval West: From the Beginning to 1600*. Oxford: Oxford University Press, 2005.

Nesbitt, J. W. "A Geographical and Chronological Guide to Greek Saints' Lives." *Orientalia Christiana Periodica* 39 (1969): 443–89.

Noble, T. F. X. "Tradition and Learning in Search of Ideology: The *Libri Carolini*." In *"The Gentle Voices of Teachers": Aspects of Learning in the Carolingian Age*. Ed. R. E. Sullivan. Columbus, OH: Ohio State University Press, 1995, 227–60.

Osborne, J. "Politics, Diplomacy and the Cult of Relics in Venice and the Northern Adriatic in the First Half of the Ninth Century." *EME* 8 (1999): 369–86.

Ousterhout, R., and L. Brubaker, eds. *The Sacred Image East and West*. Urbana, IL: University of Illinois Press, 1994.

Papaconstantinou, A. *Le culte des saints en Égypte des Byzantines aux Abbasides: l'apport des inscriptions et des papyrus grecs et coptes*. Le monde byzantin. Paris: Éditions du Centre national de la recherche scientifique, 2001.

Patlagean, E. "L'histoire de la femme déguisée en moine et l'évolution de la sainteté féminine à Byzance." *Studi Medievali* 3rd ser. 17 (1976): 597–623.

—. "Sainteté et pouvoir." In *The Byzantine Saint*. Ed. S. Hackel. London: Fellowship of St. Alban and St. Sergius, 1981, 88–105.

Pelikan, J. *Mary through the Centuries: Her Place in the History of Culture*. New Haven, CT: Yale University Press, 1996.

Pentcheva, B. V. *Icons and Power: The Mother of God in Byzantium*. University Park, PA: Pennsylvania State University Press, 2006.

Petitmengin, P. *Pélagie la pénitente: métamorphoses d'une légende*. Paris: Études augustiniennes, 1981.

Philippart, G. *Hagiographies: histoire internationale de la littérature hagiographique latine et vernaculaire en Occident des origines à 1550*. 4 vols. Corpus Christianorum, Hagiographies. Turnhout: Brepols, 1994–2006.

—. *Les légendiers latins et autres manuscrits hagiographiques*. Typologie des sources du moyen âge occidental 24–25. Turnhout: Brepols, 1977.

Picard, J. *Le souvenir des évêques: sépultures, listes épiscopales et culte des évêques en Italie du Nord des origines au Xe siècle*. Bibliothèque des Écoles françaises d'Athènes et de Rome 268. Rome: École française de Rome, 1988.

Platelle, H. "Guibert de Nogent et le *De pignoribus sanctorum*: richesses et limites d'une critique médiévale des reliques." In Bozóky and Helvétius, *Les reliques*, 109–21.

Podskalsky, G., and Stichel, R. "Icons." *ODB* 2, 977–78.

Poppe, E., and B. Ross. *The Legend of Mary the Egyptian in Medieval Insular Hagiography*. Blackrock: Four Courts Press, 1996.

Poulin, J.-C. *L'idéal de sainteté dans l'Aquitaine carolingienne, d'après les sources hagiographiques, 750–950*. Travaux du Laboratoire d'histoire religieuse de l'Université Laval 1. Quebec: Presses de l'Université Laval, 1975.

Rapp, C. "Byzantine Hagiographers as Antiquarians, Seventh to Tenth Centuries." *Byzantinische Forschungen* 21 (1995): 31–44.

—. "Hagiography and Monastic Literature between Greek East and Latin West in Late Antiquity." In *Cristianità d'Occidente e Cristianità d'Oriente (secoli VI-XI)*. Settimane di studio 51. Spoleto: Centro italiano di studi sull'alto medioevo, 2004, II.1221–81.

Rousseau, P. "Ascetics as Mediators and as Teachers." In Howard-Johnston and Hayward, *Cult of Saints*, 45–59.

Schimmelpfenning, B. "Afra und Ulrich. Oder: wie wird man heilig?" *Zeitschrift der historischen Vereins für Schwaben* 86 (1993): 23–44.

Schulenberg, J. Tibbetts. "Sexism and the Celestial Gynaeceum." *Journal of Medieval History* 4 (1978): 117–33.

Ševčenko, N. Patterson. "Menologion." *ODB* 2, 1341.

Sigal, P.-A. *L'homme et le miracle dans la France médiévale, XIe–XIIe siècle*. Histoire. Paris: Éditions du Cerf, 1985.

Smith, J. M. H., ed. *Early Medieval Rome and the Christian West: Essays in Honour of Donald A. Bullough*. Leiden: Brill, 2000.

—. "Old Saints, New Cults: Roman Relics in Carolingian Francia." In her *Early Medieval Rome*, 317–39.

—. "Oral and Written: Saints, Miracles and Relics in Brittany, c. 850–1250." *Speculum* 65 (1990): 309–43.

—. "The Problem of Female Sanctity in Carolingian Europe, c. 780–920." *Past & Present* 146 (1995): 3–37.

Stafford, P. "Queens, Nunneries and Reforming Churchmen: Gender, Religious Status and Reform in Tenth- and Eleventh-Century England." *Past & Present* 163 (1999): 3–35.

Stancliffe, C. "Red, White and Blue Martyrdom." In *Ireland in Early Mediaeval Europe: Studies in Memory of Kathleen Hughes*. Ed. D. Whitelock, R. McKitterick, and D. Dumville. Cambridge: Cambridge University Press, 1982, 21–46.

Taft, R. F., and N. Patterson Ševčenko. "Synaxarion." *ODB* 3, 1991.

Talbot, A.-M. "Canonization." *ODB* 1, 372–73.

—, ed. "Pilgrimage in the Byzantine Empire: 7th–15th Centuries." *DOP* 56 (2002): 57–241.

Thacker, A. T. "In Search of Saints: The English Church and the Cult of Roman Apostles and Martyrs in the Seventh and Eighth Centuries." In Smith, *Early Medieval Rome*, 247–77.

—, and R. Sharpe. *Local Saints and Local Churches in the Early Medieval West*. Oxford: Oxford University Press, 2002.

Thunø, E. *Image and Relic: Mediating the Sacred in Early Medieval Rome*. Analecta Romana Instituti Danici, supplementum 32. Rome: Erma di Bretschneider, 2002.

Van Uytfanghe, M. "La controverse biblique et patristique autour du miracle, et ses répercussions sur l'hagiographie dans l'Antiquité tardive et le haut Moyen Âge latin." In *Hagiographies, cultures, sociétés IVe –XIIe siècles: actes du colloque organisé à Nanterre et à Paris (2–5 mai 1979)*. Paris: Études augustiniennes, 1981, 205–31.

Vassilaki, M., ed. *Images of the Mother of God: Perceptions of the Theotokos in Byzantium*. Aldershot: Ashgate, 2005.

—, ed. *Mother of God: Representations of the Virgin in Byzantine Art*. Milan: Skira, 2000.

Vauchez, A., trans. J. Birrell. *Sainthood in the Later Middle Ages*. Cambridge: Cambridge University Press, 1997.

Wall, V. "Queen Margaret of Scotland (1070–93): Burying the Past, Enshrining the Future." In *Queens and Queenship in Medieval Europe: Proceedings of a Conference Held at King's College London, April 1995*. Ed. A. J. Duggan. Woodbridge: Boydell & Brewer, 1997, 27–38.

Warner, M. *Alone of All her Sex: The Myth and the Cult of the Virgin Mary*. London: Weidenfeld & Nicholson, 1976.

Wilken, R. L. *The Land Called Holy: Palestine in Christian History and Thought*. New Haven, CT: Yale University Press, 1992.

Wittern, S. *Frauen, Heiligkeit und Macht: lateinische Frauenviten aus dem 4. bis 7. Jahrhundert*. Ergebnisse der Frauenforschung 33. Stuttgart: J. B. Metzler, 1994.

Wolf, G. "Die Kanonisationsbulle von 993 für den Hl. Oudalrich von Augsburg und Vergleichbares." *Zeitschrift der Savigny-Stiftung für Rechtsgeschichte* (Kanonistische Abteilung) 122 (2005): 742–57.

Wood, I. *The Missionary Life: Saints and the Evangelisation of Europe 400–1050*. Harlow: Longman, 2001.

Yarrow, S. *Saints and their Communities: Miracle Stories in Twelfth-Century England*. Oxford: Clarendon Press, 2006.

Yorke, B. "'Carriers of the Truth': Writing the Biographies of Anglo-Saxon Female Saints." In *Writing Medieval Biography 750–1250: Studies in Honour of Professor Frank Barlow*. Ed. D. Bates, J. Crick, and S. Hamilton. Woodbridge: Boydell, 2006, 49–60.

29 Last Things
Jane Baun

Primary sources

Apocalypsis Anastasiae, ad trium codicum auctoritatem Panormitani Ambrosiani Parisini. Ed. R. Homburg. Leipzig: Teubner, 1903. Eng. trans. J. Baun, *Tales from Another Byzantium*.

Apocalypsis Mariae Virginis (Apocalypse of the Theotokos). In *Apocrypha anecdota*. Ed. M. R. James. Texts and Studies 2.3. Cambridge: Cambridge University Press, 1893, 115–26.

Apocrypha Apostolorum Armeniaca. Ed. and trans. L. Leloir. CC Series Apocryphorum 3. Turnhout: Brepols, 1986.

The Apocryphal New Testament. Ed. J. K. Elliott. Oxford: Clarendon Press, 1993.

Asser. *Alfred the Great (Asser's Life of King Alfred and Other Contemporary Sources)*. Trans. S. Keynes and M. Lapidge. London: Penguin Books, 1983.

Bede. *Expositio Apocalypseos*. In *Bedae presbyteri expositio Apocalypseos*. Ed. R. Gryson. *CCSL* 121A. Turnhout: Brepols, 2001.

Boniface. *Epistolae*. Ed. E. Dümmler. *MGH Epistolae* 3 (= *Merovingici et Karolini Aevi* 1). Berlin: Weidmann, 1892, 215–433. Eng. trans. E. Kylie. *The English Correspondence of St. Boniface*. London: Chatto and Windus, 1911.

Carey, J., trans. *King of Mysteries: Early Irish Religious Writings*. Dublin: Four Courts Press, 1998.

Ciccarese, M. P. *Visioni dell'aldilà in occidente: fonti, modelli, testi*. Florence: Nardini Editore, 1987.

Clancy, T. O., and G. Márkus, eds. *Iona: The Earliest Poetry of a Celtic Monastery*. Edinburgh: Edinburgh University Press, 1995.

Fís Adomnán. In Herbert and McNamara, *Irish Biblical Apocrypha*, 137–48.

Gregory the Great. *Dialogues*. Ed. A. de Vogüé. *SC* 251 = Vol. 1.; *SC* 260 = Vol. 2; *SC* 265 = Vol. 3. Paris: Éditions du Cerf, 1978–80. Eng. trans. O. J. Zimmerman. *Saint Gregory the Great: Dialogues*. Fathers of the Church 39. Washington, DC: Catholic University of America Press, 1959.

Heito. *Visio Wettini*. Ed. E. Dümmler. *MGH Poetae Latini Aevi Carolini* 2. Berlin: Weidmann, 1884, 267–75.

Herbert, M., and M. McNamara, trans. *Irish Biblical Apocrypha: Selected Texts in Translation*. Edinburgh: T&T Clark, 1989.

Julian of Toledo. *Prognosticum futuri saeculi: libri tres*. In *Sancti Juliani Toletanae sedis episcopi opera*. Vol. 1. Ed. J. N. Hillgarth. *CCSL* 115. Turnhout: Brepols, 1966, 10–126.

The Mabinogion. Trans. G. Jones and T. Jones. London: Everyman, 1949; rev. ed. 1993.

Navigatio Sancti Brendani abbatis. Ed. C. Selmer. Notre Dame, IN: University of Notre Dame Press, 1959. Eng. trans. J. O'Meara and J. Wooding. In *The Voyage of Saint Brendan: Representative Versions of the Legend in English Translation*. Ed. W. R. J. Barron and G. S. Burgess. Exeter: University of Exeter Press, 2005.

Nicephorus. *Canones*. In Nicephorus. *Opera*. *PG* 100, 851–54.

Paul of Monemvasia. *The Spiritually Beneficial Tales of Paul, Bishop of Monembasia*. Trans. J. Wortley. Cistercian Studies Series 159. Kalamazoo, MI: Cistercian Publications, 1996.

Visio Sancti Pauli: The History of the Apocalypse in Latin Together with Nine Texts. Ed. T. Silverstein. London: Christophers, 1935. *Apocalypse of Paul: A New Critical Edition of*

Three Long Latin Versions. Ed. T. Silverstein and A. Hilhorst. Geneva: P. Cramer, 1997.

William of Malmesbury. *Gesta regum Anglorum*. Ed. and trans. R. A. B. Mynors. *The History of the English Kings*. Oxford: Oxford University Press, 1998.

Secondary sources

Alexander, P. *The Byzantine Apocalyptic Tradition*. Berkeley, CA: University of California Press, 1985.

Alfeyev, H. *The Spiritual World of Isaac the Syrian*. Cistercian Studies Series 175. Kalamazoo, MI: Cistercian Publications, 2000.

Bauckham, R. 1998. "The Four Apocalypses of the Virgin Mary." In his *The Fate of the Dead: Studies on the Jewish and Christian Apocalypses*. Leiden: Brill, 1998, 332–62.

Baun, J. "Middle Byzantine 'Tours of Hell': Outsider Theodicy?" In *Strangers to Themselves*. Ed. D. Smythe. Aldershot: Ashgate, 2000, 47–60.

—. *Tales from Another Byzantium: Celestial Journey and Local Community in the Medieval Greek Apocrypha*. Cambridge: Cambridge University Press, 2007.

Boswell, C. S. *An Irish Precursor of Dante: A Study on the Vision of Heaven and Hell Ascribed to the Eight-Century Irish Saint Adamnán*. London: D. Nutt, 1908.

Brenk, B. "Die Anfänge der Byzantinischen Weltgerichtsdarstellung." *Byzantinische Zeitschrift* 57 (1964): 106–26.

—. *Tradition und Neuerung in der christlichen Kunst des ersten Jahrtausends*. Vienna: Österreichische Akademie der Wissenschaften, 1966.

Brown, P. "The Decline of the Empire of God: Amnesty, Penance and the Afterlife from Late Antiquity to the Middle Ages." In Bynum and Freedman, *Last Things*, 41–59.

—. *The Rise of Western Christendom: Triumph and Diversity, AD 200–1000*. 2nd ed. Oxford: Blackwell, 2003.

Bynum, C. Walker, and P. Freedman, eds. *Last Things: Death and the Apocalypse in the Middle Ages*. Philadelphia, PA: University of Pennsylvania Press, 2000.

Carozzi, C. "Les Carolingiens dans l'au-delà." In *Haut Moyen-Âge: culture, éducation et société*. Ed. C. Lepelley et al. La Garenne-Colombes: Éditions Publidix, [1990], 367–76.

—. "La géographie de l'au-delà et sa signification pendant le haut Moyen-Âge." In *Populi e paesi nella cultura altomedievale*. Vol. 2. Spoleto: Centro italiano di studi sull'alto medioevo, 1983, 423–81.

—. *Le voyage de l'âme dans l'au-delà, d'après la littérature latine, Ve–XIIIe siècle*. Rome: École française de Rome, 1994.

—., and H. Taviani-Carozzi, eds. *Année mille, an mil*. Aix-en-Provence: Publications de l'université de Provence, 2002.

Casey, R. P. "The Apocalypse of Paul." *Journal of Theological Studies* 34 (1933): 1–32.

Clancy, T. O. "Subversion at Sea: Structure, Style and Intent in the *Immrama*." In Wooding, *Otherworld Voyage*, 194–225.

Clayton, M. *The Cult of the Virgin Mary in Anglo-Saxon England*. Cambridge: Cambridge University Press, 1990.

Contreni, J. J. "'Building Mansions in Heaven': The *Visio Baronti*, Archangel Raphael, and a Carolingian King." *Speculum* 78 (2003): 673–706.

Daley, B. *The Hope of the Early Church: A Handbook of Patristic Eschatology*. Cambridge: Cambridge University Press, 1991.

Dinzelbacher, P. *Revelationes*. Typologie des Sources du Moyen Âge Occidental 57. Turnhout: Brepols, 1991.

—. *Vision und Visionsliteratur im Mittelalters*. Stuttgart: Hiersemann, 1981.

Dumville, D. "Biblical Apocrypha and the Early Irish: A Preliminary Investigation." *Proceedings of the Royal Irish Academy* 73 (1973): 299–338.

—. "Towards an Interpretation of *Fís Adamnán*." *Studia Celtica* 12/13 (1977/8): 62–77.

Dutton, P. E. *The Politics of Dreaming in the Carolingian Empire*. Lincoln, NE: University of Nebraska Press, 1994.

Emmerson, R. K., and B. McGinn, eds. *The Apocalypse in the Middle Ages*. Ithaca, NY: Cornell University Press, 1992.

Evans, H. C., and W. D. Wixom, eds. *The Glory of Byzantium: Art and Culture of the Middle Byzantine Era, A.D. 843–1261*. New York: Metropolitan Museum of Art, 1997.

Every, G. "Toll Gates on the Air Way." *Eastern Churches Review* 8 (1976): 139–50.

Ganz, D. "Theology and the Organisation of Thought." *NCMH* 2, 758–85.

Gardiner, E. *Medieval Visions of Heaven and Hell: A Sourcebook*. London: Garland, 1993.

—, ed. and trans. *Visions of Heaven and Hell Before Dante*. New York: Italica Press, 1989.

Gatch, M. McC. "The Harrowing of Hell: A Liberation Motif in Medieval Theology and Devotional Literature." Ch. 3 in his *Eschatology and Christian Nurture*. Aldershot: Ashgate, 2000.

—. *Preaching and Theology in Anglo-Saxon England: Ælfric and Wulfstan*. Toronto: University of Toronto Press, 1977.

Healey, A. Di Paolo. *The Old English Vision of St. Paul*. Cambridge, MA: Mediaeval Academy of America, 1978.

Himmelfarb, M. *Ascent to Heaven in Jewish and Christian Apocalypses*. Oxford: Oxford University Press, 1993.

—. *Tours of Hell: An Apocalyptic Form in Jewish and Christian Literature*. Philadelphia, PA: Fortress Press, 1983.

Hudson, B. "Time Is Short: The Eschatology of the Early Gaelic Church." In Bynum and Freedman, *Last Things*, 101–23.

Jarman, A. O. H., and G. R. Hughes. *A Guide to Welsh Literature*. Vol. 1. Cardiff: University of Wales Press, 1992.

Jónsdóttir, S. *An 11th-Century Byzantine Last Judgement in Iceland*. Reykjavik: Almenna Bókafélagid, 1959.

Kabir, A. Jahanara. *Paradise, Death and Doomsday in Anglo-Saxon Literature*. Cambridge: Cambridge University Press, 2001.

Kartsonis, A. *Anastasis: The Making of an Image*. Princeton, NJ: Princeton University Press, 1986.

Le Goff, J. *The Birth of Purgatory*. Aldershot: Scolar Press, 1984.

Lucey-Roper, M. "Uniting the Community of the Living with the Dead: The Use of Other-World Visions in the Early Middle Ages." In *Authority and Community in the Middle Ages*. Ed. D. Mowbray et al. Stroud: Sutton Publishing, 1999, 19–41.

Ludlow, M. "Universalism in the History of Christianity." In *Universal Salvation?* Ed. R. A. Parry and C. H. Partridge. Carlisle: Paternoster, 2003, 191–215.

MacCulloch, J. A. *The Harrowing of Hell: A Comparative Study of an Early Christian Doctrine*. Edinburgh: T&T Clark, 1930.

Magdalino, P. "The History of the Future and its Uses: Prophecy, Policy and Propaganda." In *The Making of Byzantine History: Studies Dedicated to Donald M. Nicol*. Ed. R. Beaton and C. Roueché. Aldershot: Variorum, 1993, 3–34.

—. "The Year 1000 in Byzantium." In *Byzantium in the Year 1000*. Ed. P. Magdalino. Leiden: Brill, 2003, 233–70.

McGinn, B. *Visions of the End: Apocalyptic Traditions in the Middle Ages*. New York: Columbia University Press, 1979.

Moreira, I. *Dreams, Visions and Spiritual Authority in Merovingian Gaul*. Ithaca, NY: Cornell University Press, 2000.

O'Connor, D. *St. Patrick's Purgatory, Lough Derg: Its History, Traditions, Legends*. Dublin, 1895.

Podskalsky, G. "Paradise." *ODB*, 1582–83.

Seymour, St. J. D. "Irish Versions of the *Vision of St. Paul*." *Journal of Theological Studies* 24 (1923): 54–59.

Sim-Williams, P. "The Unseen World: The Monk of Wenlock's Vision." In his *Religion and Literature in Western England, 600–800*. Cambridge: Cambridge University Press, 1990, 243–72.

Vassilaki, M., ed. *Images of the Mother of God: Perceptions of the Theotokos in Byzantium*. Aldershot: Ashgate, 2005.

—, ed. *Mother of God: Representations of the Virgin in Byzantine Art*. Athens: Benaki Museum, 2000.

Ware, K. "Dare we Hope for the Salvation of All? Origen, St. Gregory of Nyssa and St. Isaac the Syrian." In his *The Inner Kingdom*. Crestwood, NY: St. Vladimir's Seminary Press, 2001, 193–215.

Wooding, J., ed. *The Otherworld Voyage in Early Irish Literature*. Dublin: Four Courts Press, 2000.

Wortley, J. "Death, Judgment, Heaven, and Hell in Byzantine 'Beneficial Tales.'" *DOP* 55 (2001): 53–69.

—. "The Genre and Sources of the *Synagoge*." In *The Theotokos Evergetis and Eleventh-Century Monasticism*. Ed. M. Mullet and A. Kirby. Belfast: Belfast Byzantine Enterprises, 1994, 306–24.

Wright, C. D. *The Irish Tradition in Old English Literature*. Cambridge: Cambridge University Press, 1993.

Zaleski, C. *Otherworld Journeys: Accounts of Near-Death Experience in Medieval and Modern Times*. Oxford: Oxford University Press, 1987.

Conclusion: Christendom, c. 1100
John H. Van Engen

Primary sources

Die Briefe Heinrichs IV. Ed. C. Erdmann. *MGH Briefe* 1. Leipzig: K. W. Hiersemann, 1937.

Gratian. *Decretum*. Ed. E. Friedberg. *Corpus iuris canonici*. Leipzig, 1879.

Lettres de Jacques de Vitry (1160/70–1240). Ed. R. B. C. Huygens. Leiden: Brill, 1960.

Paul of Bernried. *Vita Gregorii*. Ed. J. M. Watterich. *Pontificum romanorum Vitae*. Leipzig, 1862.

Register Gregorii VII. Ed. E. Caspar. *MGH Epistolae selectae* 2. Berlin: Weidmann, 1920.

Vita S. Hildegardis. Ed. M. Klaes. *CCCM* 126. Turnhout: Brepols, 1993.

Secondary sources

Benson, R., and G. Constable. *Renaissance and Renewal in the Twelfth Century*. Cambridge, MA: Harvard University Press, 1982.

Chazan, R. *Fashioning Jewish Identity in Medieval Western Christendom*. Cambridge: Cambridge University Press, 2004.

Cohen, J. *Living Letters of the Law: Ideas of the Jew in Medieval Christianity*. Berkeley, CA: University of California Press, 1999.

—. *Sanctifying the Name of God: Jewish Martyrs and Jewish Memories of the First Crusade*. Philadelphia, PA: University of Pennsylvania Press, 2004.

Constable, G. *The Reformation of the Twelfth Century*. Cambridge: Cambridge University Press, 1996.

Fried, J. "Endzeiterwartung um die Jahrtausendwende." *Deutsches Archiv* 45 (1989): 381–473.

Fulton, R. *From Judgment to Passion: Devotion to Christ and the Virgin Mary, 800–1200*. New York: Columbia University Press, 2002.

Grundmann, H. *Religious Movements in the Middle Ages: The Historical Links between Heresy, the Mendicant Orders, and the Women's Religious Movement in the Twelfth and Thirteenth Century*. Notre Dame, IN: University of Notre Dame Press, 1995 (first published in German in 1935).

Haskins, C. H. *The Renaissance of the Twelfth Century*. Cambridge, MA: Harvard University Press, 1927.

Heer, F. *Aufgang Europas: eine Studie zu den Zusammenhängen zwischen politischer Religiosität, Frömmigkeitsstil und dem Werden Europas im 12. Jahrhundert*. Vienna: Europa Verlag, 1949.

Kedar, B. *Crusade and Mission: European Approaches Toward the Muslims*. Princeton, NJ: Princeton University Press, 1984.

Ladner, G. B. *Images and Ideas in the Middle Ages: Selected Studies in History and Art*. 2 vols. Rome: Edizioni de storia e letteratura, 1983.

Leclercq, J. *The Love of Learning and the Desire for God: A Study of Monastic Culture*. New York: Fordham University Press, 1982 (first published in French in 1957).

Moore, R. I. *The First European Revolution, c. 970–1215*. Oxford: Blackwell, 2000.

—. *The Formation of a Persecuting Society: Power and Deviance in Western Europe, 950–1250*. New York: B. Blackwell, 1987.

Murray, A. *Reason and Society in the Middle Ages*. Oxford: Clarendon Press, 1978.

Rosenstock-Huessy, E. *Die europäischen Revolutionen und der Charakter der Nationen*. Stuttgart: W. Kohlhammer, 1951 (reprint of 1931 edition).

—. *Out of Revolution: Autobiography of Western Man*. Norwich, VT: Argo Books, 1969 (reprint of 1938 edition).

Rubin, M. *Corpus Christi: The Eucharist in Late Medieval Culture*. Cambridge: Cambridge University Press, 1991.

Southern, R. W. *The Making of the Middle Ages*. New Haven, CT: Yale University Press, 1953.

—. *Scholastic Humanism and the Unification of Europe*. 2 vols. Oxford: Blackwell, 1995, 2001.

Stock, B. *The Implications of Literacy*. Princeton, NJ: Princeton University Press, 1983.

Van Engen, J. *Religion in the History of the Medieval West*. Aldershot: Ashgate, 2004.

Index

CPSIA information can be obtained at www.ICGtesting.com
Printed in the USA
LVOW11s2326250714

395532LV00005B/21/P